— BICENTENNIAL EDITION —

SHULCHAN ARUCH

OF RABBI SHNEUR ZALMAN OF LIADI

שלחן ערוך

מכבוד קדושת אדונינו מורינו ורבינו הגדול הגאון האלקי
החסיד המפורסם אור עולם מופת הדור
נזר ישראל ותפארתו קדוש ה'

מרנא ורבנא

מוה' **שניאור זלמן** נבג"מ

❖

Vocalized and Punctuated Hebrew Text

Translated and Annotated by
Rabbi Eliyahu Touger and Uri Kaploun

ROSH HASHANAH, YOM KIPPUR, SUKKAH & LULAV

Orach Chayim • Sections 582—651

אורח חיים, סימנים תקפב-תרנא

Kehot Publication Society
770 Eastern Parkway • Brooklyn, New York 11213
5775 • 2015

THE SHULCHAN ARUCH OF RABBI SHNEUR ZALMAN OF LIADI
WITH ENGLISH TRANSLATION
ROSH HASHANAH, YOM KIPPUR, SUKKAH & LULAV

KEHOT PUBLICATION SOCIETY
770 Eastern Parkway, Brooklyn, New York 11213
718-774-4000 / Fax 718-774-2718

Order Department:
291 Kingston Avenue, Brooklyn, New York 11213
718-778-0226 / Fax 718-778-4148
www.kehotonline.com

Library of Congress Cataloging-in-Publication Data

Shneur Zalman, of Lyady, 1745-1812

[Shulhan 'arukh. English & Hebrew]

The Shulchan Aruch of Rabbi Shneur Zalman of Liadi = [Shulhan 'arukh] / vocalized and punctuated Hebrew text translated and annotated by Eliyahu Touger and Uri Kaploun.—Bilingual ed.

v. cm.

Includes bibliographical references.

Contents:—Orach Chayim, sec. 582-651.

ISBN 978-0-8266-0870-3, 978-0-8266-0860-4 (set)

1. Judaism—Customs and practices. 2. Jewish law. 3. Hasidism. 4. Shneur Zalman, of Lyady, 1745-1812. I. Title: Shulchan aruch. II. Title: Shulhan 'arukh. III. Touger, Eliyahu. IV. Kaploun, Uri. V. Title

BM700 .S45413 2002
296.1'8—dc21

20022040651

Typography, template and cover design by Spotlight Design
Printed in China

לזכרון עולם בהיכל ה'

הנגיד החסידי הנודע לשם ולתהילה

מקושר בלו"נ לכ"ק אדמו"ר זי"ע, מחשובי ונכבדי חסידי חב"ד ושמו מפארים בכל החוגים

איש החסד והצדקה אשר פיזר נתן לאביונים, מגדולי תמכין דאורייתא

בר אוריין ומוקיר רבנן, קבע עיתים לתורה בכל עת ובכל זמן, טוב לשמים וטוב לבריות

הרה"ח הנעלה

ר' **ישכר דוב**

ב"ר יונה ע"ה

נפטר ז"ך אייר, ה'תשע"א

ולעילוי נשמת אשת חבר

האשה החשובה הצנועה והחסודה

שעמדה לימין בעלה במעשה הצדקה

מרת **מרים**

בת ר' אלטער מרדכי ע"ה

נפטרה ר"ח שבט, ה'תשע"א

ווייס

ת. נ. צ. ב. ה.

In Memory of

R. **Yisochor Dov** and **Miriam Weiss**

Dedicated by

R. **Yonah Mordechai** and **Hadassah Weiss** and family

and

R. **Moshe Aaron Tzvi** and **Ruty Weiss** and family

וצדקתם עומדת לעד

זה הכותב ספרים ומשאילם לאחרים (ע"פ כתובות דף נ.)

מהדורה חדשה של שו"ע רבינו נדפס ביוזמת וע"י

הרה"ת **ר' יונה מרדכי** בן מרים

וזוגתו מרת **הדסה עלקא** בת צפורה פייגא

והרה"ת ר' **משה אהרן צבי** בן מרים

וזוגתו מרת **העניא רבקה רות** בת צפורה

שיחיו

וויים

שלוחי כ"ק אדמו"ר זי"ע

בשערמאן אוקס, קאליפורניא

ימלא השי"ת כל משאלותיהם לטובה ולברכה, מתוך בריאות
הנכונה והשלימה, אריכת ימים ושנים טובות, והצלחה רבה ומופלגה
בכל אשר יפנו בגשמיות וברוחניות ומתוך הרחבה

ולזכות

בנם **מנחם מאניש** בן הדסה עלקא וזוג' **רבקה** בת חי' מאשא
ובניהם **לאה** בת רבקה, **בן ציון ישראל מאיר** בן רבקה, **ישכר דוב** בן רבקה **וויים**

בתם **שרה ביילא** בת הדסה עלקא ובעלה **חיים ברוך הכהן** בן אסתר שיינדל
ובניהם **חנה חי' מושקא** בת שרה ביילא, **רבקה** בת שרה ביילא, **ישראל יעקב הכהן** בן שרה ביילא,
ישכר דוב הכהן בן שרה ביילא **פרידמן**

בנם **שמואל** בן הדסה עלקא וזוג' **ראשא** בת בריינדל העניא
ובניהם **צבי הירש** בן ראשא, **מרים** בת ראשא **וויים**

בתם **מנוחה רחל** בת הדסה עלקא ובעלה **מרדכי דובער** בן אסתר
ובניהם **רפאל משה** בן מנוחה רחל, **בן ציון ישראל מאיר** בן מנוחה רחל, **מרים** בת מנוחה רחל **ווילהלם**

בתם **חנה חי' מושקא** בת הדסה עלקא ובעלה **אהרן יעקב** בן ליבא ציפורה
ובנם **ישכר דוב** בן חנה חי' מושקא **מאצקין**

בנם **בן ציון ישראל מאיר** בן הדסה עלקא

שלום אליעזר בן העניא רבקה רות, **מנחם מענדל** בן העניא רבקה רות,
יונה מרדכי בן העניא רבקה רות, **חנה פערל** בת העניא רבקה רות

שיחיו

שיגדלו להיות חסידים יראי שמים ולומדים מקושרים לכ"ק אדמו"ר זי"ע
והולכים בדרכיו אשר הורנו נס"ו

CONTENTS

LAWS REGARDING THE SUKKAH

Sec.

LAWS REGARDING THE LULAV

Sec.

PUBLISHER'S FOREWORD

To study the laws as the Alter Rebbe[1] presents them in this work is more than to master hundreds of static bottom lines. To work one's way through the laws as presented here is to participate in the dynamic age-old process whereby Scriptural verses and Rabbinic teachings fuse and crystallize into the *Halachah.*[2]

But that is not all. Like everything else in this world, a law, too, comprises a body and a soul. Accordingly, the Alter Rebbe is often not content with merely delineating the body of a law: he momentarily lifts the veil that hides its soul. In this way, rulings that might otherwise have been perceived as technical minutiae spring to life: If a person has already fulfilled his obligation to hear the *shofar* on Rosh HaShanah, why is he permitted to recite a seemingly superfluous blessing afresh on behalf of an unlettered stranger who has not yet fulfilled his obligation?[3] If the verse beginning *VaAni Tefilasi* appears in the *Minchah* service of every *Shabbos* throughout the year, why do we omit it whenever Yom Kippur falls on *Shabbos?*[4] The answers to these questions – and to many others, perhaps unasked – provide a reader with food for thought. They become catalysts for his private labors of spiritual maturation.

Because of its timely subject, this volume on the Days of Awe and the Days of Rejoicing of Sukkos has been allowed to jump the line and appear ahead of its turn. Like its predecessors, it is the product of lively electronic interaction between: R. Eliyahu Touger and Uri Kaploun, who translated and annotated the text; R. Levi Yitzchok Raskin, *Dayan* (rabbinic judge) of the Lubavitch community of North London and *Moreh Horaah* (halachic authority) for London's Union of Orthodox Hebrew Congregations, who meticulously scrutinized the entire volume and enhanced and amplified the footnotes; R. Sholom Ber Levin, Head Librarian of the Central Chabad-Lubavitch Library in New York, whose corrected and annotated Hebrew edition of the original text served as a valuable resource and whose guidance was used to advantage;[5] Spotlight Design of

---

1. Familiar chassidic name for R. Shneur Zalman of Liadi (5505-5573/1745-1812), halachist and philosopher, founder of *Chabad Chassidus* and progenitor of the dynasty of Lubavitcher Rebbes. He is widely known as *Baal HaTanya* and *Baal HaShulchan Aruch* – for his authorship of, respectively, *Sefer HaTanya* and the *Shulchan Aruch* (Code of Jewish Law).

For a documented account of his unique place in the development of the Oral Law, and in particular the relationship between his Code (commonly called *Shulchan Aruch HaRav,* which first appeared in 1814) and the parent *Shulchan Aruch* of R. Yosef Caro (published in 1565), see the Overview to Vol. 1 of the present Bilingual Edition.

2. This does not mean that mastery of this (or any other) halachic text renders every reader an expert. In the realm of actual practice, there is no substitute for ready consultation with an accessible *moreh horaah,* an authoritative *posek* who can clearly state how the law applies in any of life's situations.

3. See sec. 585:5.

4. See sec. 622:3.

5. Another rich resource was *Otzar Minhagei Chabad: Elul-Tishrei* by R. Yehoshua Mondshine (Kehot/ Heichal Menachem, Jerusalem, 5755/1995).

Brooklyn, NY, who designed the layout; Yosef Yitzchok Turner, who has endowed this series with typographical excellence; and R. Yonah Avtzon, Director of Sichos In English, who nurtured this volume, too, from its germination to its present flowering.

A wealth of information that will enhance the reader's encounter with the present volume appears in the Publisher's Foreword and in the Overview that introduced the first volume of this Bilingual Edition. Their manifold subjects include: the interaction between the legal and mystical dimensions of the Torah; a comprehensive history that documents the unfolding of the Oral Tradition; and the goals and translation policy of the present series.

The Hebrew text presented here retains the entire gamut of ancient and modern sources and crossreferences. Only the more basic ones are translated in the English footnotes, leaving space for hundreds of definitions and explanations, as well as updates that state the *halachah* and its associated customs as practiced in *Chabad*-Lubavitch today.

The page references of the various prayers discussed in this volume are geared to three bilingual prayer books recently produced by Kehot Publication Society: *Siddur Tehillat HaShem,* Annotated Edition; *Machzor for Rosh HaShanah,* Annotated Edition; *Machzor for Yom Kippur,* Annotated Edition. The Hebrew and English texts of all three volumes are reset, and the sources and directions appear in English.

For some halachic subjects, graphic illustrations are dispensable frills. Not so when the subjects described verbally are the structural specifications of a kosher *sukkah* or the botanical identification of the Four Species. Accordingly, this edition owes a debt of warm gratitude to R. Chaim Porush of Jerusalem, who kindly allowed us to reproduce a number of the attractive and instructive drawings that appear in his *Peirush Chai al Maseches Sukkah* (Regensburg Institute, 5746/1986). Those used in the present volume, some with very minor adjustments, are figs. 7-12, 14-17, and 23-28. For the use of figs. 13, 19 and 20, reproduced from the bilingual *Mishneh Torah* translated by R. Eliyahu Touger, the undersigned wish to thank Moznaim Publishing Corporation. All the remaining illustrations were created for the present edition by the in-house graphic staff of Sichos In English.

Because of the unique nature of the material concerning the laws pertaining to a *sukkah*, summaries for selected sections have been appended. Needless to say, these summaries do not pretend to embrace all the practical directives that must be mastered if one is to rest assured that his *sukkah* is in fact kosher.

A word in the Holy Tongue is no arbitrary conglomeration of letters.[6] Accordingly, if the letters that spell one word coincide with the letters that spell another, there is good reason to try to crack their common code, to seek out the semantic symmetry that underlies two seemingly mismatched words. This theme is developed by the Rebbe[7] – on a mystical and cosmic level – in a number of contexts, including the recurring cycle of the New Year.[8]

In the name of the New Year, Rosh HaShanah, the root of the word *shanah* ("year") means "to repeat," but it also means "to change." As each Rosh HaShanah duly arrives, one's first thought – on a practical, temporal level – might be a weary sensation of *déjà vu.* The same root, however, also calls for change and personal renewal – but to break free of stale mindsets and oft-repeated behaviors requires an energetic burst of escape velocity. What can trigger it? It is the hope of the publishers and of the editorial team that a study of the present translation will help its readers generate that velocity. And the Alter Rebbe assures us[9] that when living a life of change and renewal becomes the occupation of our people at large, the ultimate Redemption will be at hand, and[10] "the glory of G-d will fill the entire world."

Sichos In English
12 Sivan, 5775 (2015)

---

6. The Alter Rebbe's *Shaar HaYichud VehaEmunah,* ch.1. See *Lessons In Tanya* (Kehot, N.Y., 1982), Vol. 3, p. 836ff., with its sources and footnotes.

7. Throughout the present work, "the Rebbe" signifies the Lubavitcher Rebbe, Rabbi Menachem M. Schneerson זי"ע.

8. See *Likkutei Sichos* (Kehot, N.Y.), Vol. 17, p. 150.

9. *Tanya,* ch. 37.

10. *Bamidbar* 14:21.

הִלְכוֹת רֹאשׁ הַשָּׁנָה
THE LAWS OF ROSH HASHANAH

סִימָן תקפב סֵדֶר תְּפִלּוֹת עֲשֶׂרֶת יְמֵי תְּשׁוּבָה וְרֹאשׁ הַשָּׁנָה וּבוֹ י"ז סְעִיפִים:

א כָּל הַשָּׁנָה אָדָם מִתְפַּלֵּל "הָאֵל הַקָּדוֹשׁ" בִּבְרָכָה ג' וּ"מֶלֶךְ אוֹהֵב צְדָקָה וּמִשְׁפָּט"[1] בִּבְרָכָה י"א, חוּץ מֵעֲשָׂרָה יָמִים שֶׁבֵּין רֹאשׁ הַשָּׁנָה לְיוֹם הַכִּפּוּרִים[2] שֶׁבָּהֶן צָרִיךְ לוֹמַר "הַמֶּלֶךְ הַקָּדוֹשׁ" "הַמֶּלֶךְ הַמִּשְׁפָּט",[א] לְפִי שֶׁבְּיָמִים הַלָּלוּ הַקָּדוֹשׁ בָּרוּךְ הוּא מַרְאֶה מַלְכוּתוֹ לִשְׁפֹּט אֶת הָעוֹלָם.[ב]

וְאִם טָעָה[ג] וְאָמַר "הָאֵל הַקָּדוֹשׁ", אוֹ שֶׁהוּא מְסֻפָּק[ד] אִם אָמַר "הַמֶּלֶךְ הַקָּדוֹשׁ", אִם נִזְכַּר לְאַחַר שֶׁשָּׁהָה[ה] כְּדֵי שְׁאִילַת שָׁלוֹם תַּלְמִיד לְרַבּוֹ[ו,3] אַחַר גְּמַר הַבְּרָכָה, וְאֵין צָרִיךְ לוֹמַר אִם נִזְכַּר לְאַחַר שֶׁהִתְחִיל בְּרָכָה רְבִיעִית[ז] — צָרִיךְ לַחֲזֹר לְרֹאשׁ הַתְּפִלָּה, מִפְּנֵי שֶׁשָּׁלֹשׁ בְּרָכוֹת רִאשׁוֹנוֹת חֲשׁוּבוֹת כְּאַחַת:[ח,4]

SECTION 582 The Order of Prayers During the Ten Days of Repentance and Rosh HaShanah. (1–17)

1 Throughout the year, one [concludes] the third blessing of *Shemoneh Esreh* [with the words] *HaE-l hakadosh* ("the holy G-d"), and the eleventh blessing [with the words] *Melech ohev tzedakah u'mishpat* ("the King who loves charity and justice").[1] During the ten days from Rosh HaShanah through Yom Kippur,[2] however, one must say *HaMelech hakadosh* ("the holy King") and *HaMelech hamishpat* ("the King of judgment"), for on these days the Holy One, blessed be He, reveals His Sovereignty [by] standing in judgment over the [entire] world.

[The following principles apply] if one errs and says *HaE-l hakadosh* or is uncertain if he said *[HaE-l hakadosh* or*] HaMelech hakadosh:* If he became aware [of his error] only after he ended [the third] blessing — and needless to say, if he already began the fourth blessing — and the time it takes for a student to greet his teacher[3] had already elapsed, he must recommence *Shemoneh Esreh.* [He cannot simply repeat the third blessing,] because the first three blessings [of *Shemoneh Esreh*] are considered as one unit.[4]

1. *Berachos* 12b.

2. I.e., the days (lit., "between Rosh HaShanah and Yom Kippur") known as *Aseres Yemei Teshuvah* — "the Ten Days of Repentance."

3. I.e., the time it takes to say the three words, *Shalom alecha rabi* — "Greetings to you, my teacher" (sec. 206:3; see *Makkos* 6a). In the original, this timespan is called *kdei she'eilas shalom.*

4. See sec. 114:8.

א גמרא ברכות יב, ב. טור ושו"ע ס"א. וראה לעיל סי' קיד ס"ח. סי' קיח ס"א. **ב** רש"י שם ד"ה המלך הקדוש. והטעם להמלך המשפט יתבאר לקמן ס"ב. ופירושו נתבאר לעיל סי' קיח ס"א. **ג** רב שם, כפירוש הרי"ף שם (ז, א) דהיינו אפילו בדיעבד. רמב"ם הל' תפלה פ"י הי"ג. תוס' שם ד"ה הלכתא. רא"ש שם פ"א סי' טז. טור ושו"ע שם. **ד** תוס' שם. רא"ש שם. שו"ע שם. וכדלעיל סי' קיד ס"י (לענין הזכרת הגשם). **ה** שו"ת הרשב"א ח"א סי' לה (כדי דיבור). שו"ע ס"ב. וכ"ה לעיל סי' קיד ס"ח. וראה גם לעיל סי' תפז ס"א. סי' תפט ס"ג. **ו** ב"ק עג, ב (שלושת התיבות: שלום עליך רבי, שהוא שיעור כדי דיבור). וכדלעיל סי' רו ס"ג. **ז** ראה גם לעיל סי' קיד ס"ז (שכשהתחיל ברכה שלאחריה נקרא סיום ברכה זו לגמרי). סי' קפח ס"ט (אין לו תקנה בהזכרה כאן שהיא שלא במקומה). וראה מ"מ וציונים. **ח** טור. לבוש ס"ב. וכדלעיל סי' קיד ס"ח. **ט** רשב"א שם. שו"ע ס"ב. **י** שו"ע שם. **יא** רבנו יונה ברכות (ז, א) ד"ה ומיהו. ב"י

2 If one became aware [of his error immediately,] before this timespan passes, he should [correct himself and] say *HaMelech hakadosh*; there is no need to recommence *[Shemoneh Esreh]*.

Similar laws apply with regard to [correcting oneself if one said *Melech ohev tzedakah u'mishpat* instead of] *HaMelech hamishpat*. However, if one became aware [of his error] after this timespan, he need not return to the beginning of *Shemoneh Esreh*, because [by saying the former phrase, he also] mentioned G-d's Kingship.

Some authorities, however, maintain that if one became aware [of his error] before completing *Shemoneh Esreh*, he should return to [the eleventh] blessing, *Hashivah [shofteinu*, and repeat it and all the following blessings*]*. If he became aware [of his error] after completing *Shemoneh Esreh*, he should recommence *Shemoneh Esreh*, according to the principle explained in sec. 117[:3-5].[5]

[Their rationale is] that there is a [significant] difference between the phrases *Melech ohev tzedakah u'mishpat* and *HaMelech hamishpat*. Throughout the year, *tzedakah* ("charity") is the dominant theme, and that is why [the Sages] gave it precedence over the theme of judgment. On these days, by contrast, *mishpat* ("judgment") is the dominant theme, so charity is not mentioned at all. [Thus the conclusion recited throughout the year is not appropriate during these days.]

With regard to the actual ruling, [we follow the principle that] whenever there is a doubt [as to whether or not] a blessing [should be recited], we rule leniently;[6] [i.e., the blessing should not be recited].[7] Therefore, if one became aware of his error before completing *Shemoneh Esreh*, he is not required to return

ב וְאִם נִזְכַּר קֹדֶם שֶׁשָּׁהָה כְּדֵי שִׁעוּר הַזֶּה – אוֹמֵר "הַמֶּלֶךְ הַקָּדוֹשׁ", וְאֵינוֹ צָרִיךְ לַחֲזֹר לָרֹאשׁ.[ט]

וְכֵן הַדִּין בְּ"הַמֶּלֶךְ הַמִּשְׁפָּט".[י] וְאִם נִזְכַּר לְאַחַר שֶׁשָּׁהָה כְּדֵי שִׁעוּר הַזֶּה שֶׁאָמַר "מֶלֶךְ אוֹהֵב צְדָקָה וּמִשְׁפָּט" – אֵינוֹ צָרִיךְ לַחֲזֹר לָרֹאשׁ,[יא] כֵּיוָן שֶׁהִזְכִּיר לְשׁוֹן מַלְכוּת.[יב]

וְיֵשׁ אוֹמְרִים[יג] דְּאִם נִזְכַּר קֹדֶם שֶׁסִּיֵּם תְּפִלָּתוֹ חוֹזֵר לְרֹאשׁ בִּרְכַּת הָשִׁיבָה, וְאִם נִזְכַּר לְאַחַר שֶׁסִּיֵּם תְּפִלָּתוֹ חוֹזֵר לְרֹאשׁ הַתְּפִלָּה, וְעַל דֶּרֶךְ שֶׁנִּתְבָּאֵר בְּסִימָן קי"ז,[יד,5] מִשּׁוּם דְּיֵשׁ הֶפְרֵשׁ בֵּין "מֶלֶךְ אוֹהֵב צְדָקָה וּמִשְׁפָּט" לְ"הַמֶּלֶךְ הַמִּשְׁפָּט", דִּבְכָל הַשָּׁנָה הַצְּדָקָה עִקָּר וּלְכָךְ הִקְדִּימוּהָ לְמִשְׁפָּט, אֲבָל בַּיָּמִים הַלָּלוּ הַמִּשְׁפָּט עִקָּר וּלְכָךְ אֵין מַזְכִּירִין צְדָקָה כְּלָל.[טו]

וּלְעִנְיַן הֲלָכָה סְפֵק בְּרָכוֹת[6] לְהָקֵל,[טז,7] וּלְפִיכָךְ אִם נִזְכַּר קֹדֶם שֶׁסִּיֵּם תְּפִלָּתוֹ – אֵין צָרִיךְ לַחֲזֹר

---

5. That section speaks about a parallel error in the ninth blessing — requesting rain when it is inappropriate to do so, or failing to make such a request when it is required.

6. In the original, *safek berachos — lehakel.*

7. For fear of reciting a blessing in vain. A blessing that is not required is in fact not permitted.

ד"ה כתבו תלמידי. דרכי משה ס"ק ג. רמ"א סי' קיח ס"א. **יב** רבנו יונה שם. ראה טור סי' קיח בשם אחיו ה"ר יחיאל. **יג** רמב"ם הל' תפלה פ"י הי"ג. ב"י בשם ארחות חיים הל' תפלה אות קד, בשם הראב"ד, ושכן משמעות הפוסקים. **יד** סוף ס"ה. **טו** ט"ז סי' קיח סק"ב. **טז** ב"ח ס"ב ד"ה כתב ב"י בשם הרשב"א.

לְבִרְכַּת הָשִׁיבָה, כְּדֵי שֶׁלֹּא יְבָרֵךְ סְפֵק בְּרָכָה לְבַטָּלָה,[יז] אֲבָל לְאַחַר שֶׁעָקַר רַגְלָיו[8] — טוֹב שֶׁיִּתְפַּלֵּל עוֹד פַּעַם בְּתוֹרַת נְדָבָה,[יח,9] וְאֵינוֹ צָרִיךְ לְחַדֵּשׁ בָּהּ דָּבָר כֵּיוָן שֶׁמִּתְפַּלֵּל אוֹתָהּ מֵחֲמַת הַסָּפֵק כְּמוֹ שֶׁנִּתְבָּאֵר בְּסִימָן ק״ז:[יט]

to the blessing *Hashivah,* in order that he should not recite a blessing that is possibly unwarranted. After completing *Shemoneh Esreh,*[8] however, it is advisable to repeat *Shemoneh Esreh* as a freewill [prayer],[9] [and this time recite the appropriate wording in the eleventh blessing]. One is not obligated to make a personal addition [to justify the repetition, as is usually required if *Shemoneh Esreh* is recited as a freewill prayer], because its present recitation is due to the doubt [as to whether or not he had previously fulfilled his obligation], as stated in sec. 107[:1].

ג אִם אָמַר צ׳ פְּעָמִים[10] ״בָּרוּךְ אַתָּה ה׳ הַמֶּלֶךְ הַקָּדוֹשׁ״ אוֹ ״בָּרוּךְ אַתָּה ה׳ הַמֶּלֶךְ הַמִּשְׁפָּט״ וְאַחַר כָּךְ נִסְתַּפֵּק לוֹ בַּתְּפִלָּה אִם אָמַר ״הַמֶּלֶךְ הַקָּדוֹשׁ״ — אַף עַל פִּי כֵן צָרִיךְ לַחֲזֹר לָרֹאשׁ לְדִבְרֵי הַכֹּל. וְאֵינוֹ דוֹמֶה לְמַה שֶׁנִּתְבָּאֵר בְּסִימָן קי״ד,[כ,11] דְּכָאן כֵּיוָן שֶׁאֵינוֹ רַשַּׁאי לוֹמַר הַשֵּׁם כִּקְרִיאָתוֹ מִשּׁוּם בְּרָכָה לְבַטָּלָה, וְאִם כֵּן בַּתְּפִלָּה כְּשֶׁאוֹמֵר אֶת הַשֵּׁם כִּקְרִיאָתוֹ — הוּא חוֹזֵר לְלִמּוּדוֹ לוֹמַר ״הָאֵל הַקָּדוֹשׁ״:[כא]

3 [The fact that] one has said *Baruch Atah HaShem HaMelech hakadosh* ("Blessed are You, *HaShem,* the holy King") or *Baruch Atah HaShem HaMelech hamishpat* ("Blessed are You, *HaShem,* the King of judgment") 90 times[10] [is of no avail in removing the above doubt]. If one is [nevertheless] unsure as to whether he said *HaMelech hakadosh* in *Shemoneh Esreh,* all authorities agree that he must repeat *Shemoneh Esreh.* This situation does not resemble [the case] explained in sec. 114[:11, with regard to adding the words *morid hageshem*].[11] In this situation, he is not permitted to pronounce G-d's name as it should be pronounced, because doing so would constitute the recitation of a blessing in vain. [This repetition will thus not serve to change his habit, and] therefore, when he pronounces G-d's name properly in the course of *Shemoneh Esreh,* he will [presumably] revert to his established pattern and say *HaE-l hakadosh.*

---

8. Lit., "after he has moved his feet" — because one stands at attention while reciting *Shemoneh Esreh.*

9. In the original, *[tefillas] nedavah;* i.e., a voluntary repetition of *Shemoneh Esreh* (see sec. 107:1 of the present work). However, since this repetition requires uninterrupted concentration from beginning to end, it is rarely practiced (see that source, subsection 5), other than in some cases of doubt.

10. The three daily prayers of the Ten Days of Repentance obviously do not provide this number of opportunities to habituate oneself to any change in wording. The Alter Rebbe is thus considering an individual who endeavors to alter his habit by repeating the new phrase to himself over and over, at a time other than prayer.

11. There it is explained that when the change in the seasons mandates a change in the wording of the second blessing of *Shemoneh Esreh,* once 30 days (each with three daily prayers) have elapsed it can be assumed that one has become habituated to the new version. By extension, the same

יז כדלעיל סי׳ קסז סי״ב וש״נ. וראה תהלה לדוד סי׳ קח ס״ק טז. ארץ צבי ח״א סוס״י כד. יח ט״ז שם וכאן סק״א. יט סעיף א. כ סעיף יא (ב׳ דעות, אם זה מועיל במוריד הטל). כא מ״א ס״ק א. כב ה״ר מנוח הל׳ תפלה פ״י. שו״ע ס״ג (ראה גם לקמן סי׳ תקצז ס״א: שבת תשובה. ולעיל סי׳ רפד סוף ס״ח וסי׳

ד בְּשַׁבַּת תְּשׁוּבָה,[כב,12] וְכֵן אִם חָל רֹאשׁ הַשָּׁנָה אוֹ יוֹם הַכִּפּוּרִים בְּשַׁבָּת,[כג] אוֹמֵר הַשְּׁלִיחַ צִבּוּר בִּבְרָכָה מֵעֵין שֶׁבַע שֶׁבְּלֵיל שַׁבָּת "הַמֶּלֶךְ הַקָּדוֹשׁ", וְחוֹתֵם בְּשֶׁל שַׁבָּת לְבַד,[כד] וְאֵינוֹ מַזְכִּיר לֹא רֹאשׁ הַשָּׁנָה וְלֹא יוֹם הַכִּפּוּרִים מִטַּעַם שֶׁנִּתְבָּאֵר בְּסִימָן רס"ח:[כה,13]

4 On *Shabbos Teshuvah,*[12] and similarly when either Rosh HaShanah or Yom Kippur falls on *Shabbos,* when the *sheliach tzibbur* recites the blessing *[Meiein Sheva]* that summarizes the seven blessings of [the *Shemoneh Esreh* of] Friday evening, he should say *HaMelech hakadosh* [instead of *HaE-l hakadosh*]. When concluding the blessing, however, he should mention only *Shabbos* and not Rosh HaShanah or Yom Kippur, for the reason explained in sec. 268[:14].[13]

ה יֵשׁ נוֹהֲגִין לְהִתְפַּלֵּל בְּרֹאשׁ הַשָּׁנָה וּבְיוֹם הַכִּפּוּרִים בִּכְרִיעָה,[כו,14] וּצְרִיכִים הֵם לִזְקֹף בִּתְחִלַּת כָּל בְּרָכָה[כז] וּבְסוֹף כָּל בְּרָכָה[כח] קֹדֶם שֶׁיֹּאמַר "בָּרוּךְ אַתָּה",[כט] כְּדֵי שֶׁלֹּא יְהֵא נִרְאֶה כְּמוֹסִיף עַל תַּקָּנַת חֲכָמִים[ל] שֶׁתִּקְּנוּ לִשְׁחוֹת בִּתְחִלַּת בִּרְכַּת אָבוֹת וּבְסוֹפָהּ וּבִתְחִלַּת בִּרְכַּת הוֹדָאָה וּבְסוֹפָהּ עַיֵּן בְּסִימָן קי"ג,[לא] וּבְבִרְכַּת אָבוֹת וּבְבִרְכַּת הוֹדָאָה צָרִיךְ לִזְקֹף כְּשֶׁיַּגִּיעַ לְאֵיזֶה תֵּבוֹת קֹדֶם הַחֲתִימָה, וְאַחַר כָּךְ כְּשֶׁיַּגִּיעַ לַהֲחֲתִימָה יִשְׁחֶה כְּתַקָּנַת חֲכָמִים[לב] מִטַּעַם שֶׁנִּתְבָּאֵר שָׁם:[לג]

5 There are people whose custom is to stoop somewhat while reciting *Shemoneh Esreh* on Rosh HaShanah and Yom Kippur.[14] They must, however, stand erect at the beginning of every blessing and its conclusion, before saying *Baruch Atah,* so that they will not appear to be adding to the directive of our Sages who ordained that we bow [four times in *Shemoneh Esreh*]: at the beginning and end of the first blessing, and at the beginning and end of the blessing [that begins with the word *Modim*]; see sec. 113[:1].

In the first blessing [called *Avos*] and in the latter blessing [called *Hodaah*], [a person who prays while stooped] must stand upright when he comes to the last few words before the conclusion of the blessing, and then bow again when he reaches its conclusion as ordained by the Sages, for the reason explained in [the above-mentioned section].

---

is assumed if one repeats the beginning of the second blessing with — or without — this addition 90 times.

12. The *Shabbos* between Rosh HaShanah and Yom Kippur, which frame the Ten Days of Repentance, is sometimes referred to as *Shabbos Teshuvah* ("the *Shabbos* of Repentance"). It is also referred to as *Shabbos Shuvah,* because the *Haftorah* recited on that day begins with the words *Shuvah Yisrael* ("Return, O Israel"). See *Likkutei Sichos,* Vol. 14, p. 143-144.

13. There the Alter Rebbe writes that the recitation of this blessing was instituted only for *Shabbos* and not for the festivals. Hence, even when a festival falls on *Shabbos,* it is not mentioned.

14. As an expression of submissiveness.

תכט ס"ב: שבת שובה). **כג** מהרי"ל הל' עשי"ת (ע' דש). רמ"א ס"ג. **כד** גמרא שבת כד, ב (לענין יום טוב). דרכי משה ס"ק ג. רמ"א שם. וכ"ה בסידור. **כה** סי"ד. וראה גם לקמן סי' תריט ס"י. מ"מ וציונים. **כו** תוס' ברכות יב, ב ד"ה כרע. סמ"ק סי' יא (ע' טו). טור ושו"ע ס"ד. וראה גם לעיל סי' קיג סוף ס"ב. **כז** ב"ח ד"ה אבל, ממשמעות סמ"ק שם. ט"ז סי' קיג ס"ק ג. וכ"ה לעיל שם. **כח** תוס' שם. סמ"ק שם. טור ושו"ע שם. **כט** מ"א סק"ג. ט"ז ס"ק ב. **ל** ראה ט"ז שם, ובסימן קיג ס"ק א. לעיל סי' קיג סוף ס"ב. **לא** סעי' א־ב. **לב** ט"ז שם, ובסימן קיג ס"ק ג. **לג** סעיף ב.

ו הַגְּאוֹנִים[לד,15] תִּקְּנוּ לוֹמַר בַּעֲשֶׂרֶת יְמֵי תְּשׁוּבָה בְּבִרְכַּת אָבוֹת "זָכְרֵנוּ", וּבִגְבוּרוֹת "מִי כָמוֹךָ", וּבְהוֹדָאָה "וּכְתֹב", וּבְ"שִׂים שָׁלוֹם" "בְּסֵפֶר".[לה,16] וְאִם שָׁכַח לְאָמְרָם וְנִזְכַּר קֹדֶם שֶׁסִּיֵּם הַבְּרָכָה שֶׁשָּׁכַח בָּהּ – אוֹמְרָם בְּמָקוֹם שֶׁנִּזְכַּר.[לו] וְאִם נִזְכַּר לְאַחַר שֶׁהִזְכִּיר אֶת הַשֵּׁם שֶׁבַּחֲתִימַת הַבְּרָכָה[לז] – לֹא יֹאמַר בְּמָקוֹם שֶׁנִּזְכַּר, וְגַם לֹא יַחֲזֹר לְרֹאשׁ הַבְּרָכָה, מִשּׁוּם אִסּוּר בְּרָכָה לְבַטָּלָה,[לח] כֵּיוָן דְּאֵינָן אֶלָּא תִּקּוּן הַגְּאוֹנִים:[לט,17]

6 The *Geonim*[15] ordained that [several additions be made to *Shemoneh Esreh*] during the Ten Days of Repentance. In the first blessing, [one should add the phrase beginning] *Zochreinu* ("Remember us..."); in the second blessing, [the phrase beginning] *Mi Chamocha* ("Who is like You..."); in the blessing *Modim*, [the phrase beginning] *U'Chsov* ("Inscribe..."), and in the blessing *Sim Shalom*, [the phrase beginning] *BeSefer*[16] ("In the book...").

If one forgot to recite [any of] these phrases and remembered before he finished the blessing in which they should be recited, he should recite them when he remembers. If, however, one forgot to recite [any of] these phrases and [did not] remember [until] after he mentioned G-d's name in the conclusion of the blessing, he should not recite them when he remembers. Nor should he repeat the blessing, for it is forbidden to [recite] a blessing in vain. [This ruling is given,] because [these] additions were ordained only by the *Geonim*.[17]

15. The Sages of the post-Talmudic period. See the Overview in Vol. 1 of the present work, pp. xv-xvi.

16. Here, as is his practice throughout his *Shulchan Aruch*, the Alter Rebbe cites the wording that appears in the Ashkenazic order of prayer *(Nussach Ashkenaz)*. In his *Siddur*, by contrast, he follows the Sephardic order *(Nussach Sepharad*, popularly pronounced *Nussach Sephard)*, and writes *U'veSefer*.

To briefly clarify the terms: Sephardim are Jews originating from Spain ("Sepharad") or the Orient, as distinct from Ashkenazim ("Ashkenaz" being the classical Hebrew name for Germany), who originate from other European countries. However, the prayer rites known as *Nussach Sephard* and *Nussach Ashkenaz* do not coincide with these "ethnic" categories. True, *Nussach Ashkenaz* is the prayer rite that developed in German-speaking and other European lands. But many of the worshipers whose *Siddurim* follow *Nussach Sephard* are not of Spanish or Oriental origin; they include many chassidim and non-chassidim of Ashkenazic background, both in *Eretz Yisrael* and the Diaspora. And the prayer rite followed by the Sephardim proper, basically of North African origin, is different again.

The prayer rite sometimes referred to in these footnotes as "the Lubavitch custom" is the version laid down by the *AriZal* — a variant of *Nussach Sephard* — as defined by the Alter Rebbe in his *Siddur*.

"The Alter Rebbe's Siddur" is the popular name for *Seder Tefillos MiKol HaShanah al pi Nussach HaAriZal*. It first appeared in Shklov in 1803, during the lifetime of the compiler, who personally corrected its earliest editions. Ever since the Kopust edition of 1816, when the Alter Rebbe's extensive mystical commentaries were first appended to each of its component liturgies, it has also been known as the *Siddur Im Dach*, i.e., "the *Siddur* with chassidic discourses." Its basic text, without the commentaries, is reproduced in the numerous editions of *Siddur Tehillat HaShem*, first published in Rostov in 1918.

The halachic decisions

לד רא"ש ברכות סוף פ"א (שהיא תקנת הגאונים). וראה גם תוס' שם לד, א ד"ה אל, וטור, בשם רב האי גאון. לה תוס' שם יב, ב ד"ה והלכתא. רא"ש שם. רמב"ם הל' תפלה פ"ב הי"ט. טור ולבוש ס"ה. וכ"ה בסידור (ובספר). לו כדלעיל סי' קיד ס"ז (לענין הזכרת גשם וטל). סי' רצד סוף ס"ז (לענין הבדלה בחונן הדעת). וראה סי' רפא ס"ב. קובץ אור ישראל ח"ט ע' ריז. לז תרומת הדשן סי' קמד (אפילו לא עקר רגליו). רמ"א ס"ה (שסיים אותה ברכה). וראה שו"ע סי' תרפב ס"א. לעיל סי' רצד ס"ז. סי' תעז ס"ט. לח תרומת הדשן שם. לט רא"ש שם. טור. תרומת הדשן שם. לבוש שם. מ בנוסח זכרנו לחיים. מא וכ"ה

7 [The word] *lechayim* ("for life") [in the phrase *Zochreinu lechayim*] should be vocalized with a *sheva* under the *lamed* and not a *patach,* so that the word would not be sounded as *"lachayim,"* which could be misunderstood as *lo chayim* ("not life").[18] [The rationale is that] these days are days of judgment, and therefore one must be precise and articulate carefully when reciting one's prayers. During the other days of the year, we say *vehaamideinu malkeinu lachayim,* with a *patach.*[19] We are not concerned [there with the possibility of misinterpretation], for the words are understood according to the intent[20] of one's heart.

ז "לְחַיִּים"[מ] יֹאמַר בִּשְׁבָ"א תַּחַת הַלָּמֶ"ד,[מא] וְלֹא יֹאמַר בְּפַתָּ"ח דְּלָא לִשְׁתַּמַע "לאחַיִּים", כְּלוֹמַר לֹא חַיִּים,[מב,18] וּבַיָּמִים הָאֵלּוּ שֶׁהֵן יְמֵי דִּין צָרִיךְ לְדַקְדֵּק וּלְפָרֵט הֵיטֵב תְּפִלָּתוֹ.[מג] אֲבָל בִּשְׁאָר יְמוֹת הַשָּׁנָה אָנוּ אוֹמְרִים "וְהַעֲמִידֵנוּ מַלְכֵּנוּ לַחַיִּים" בְּפַתָּ"ח,[מד,19] וְאֵין אָנוּ חוֹשְׁשִׁין, לְפִי שֶׁאַחַר כַּוָּנַת הַלֵּב[20] הֵן הֵן הַדְּבָרִים:[מה]

8 [In the phrase *Zochreinu,*] one should simply say *lechayim* ("for life") and not *lechayim tovim* ("for good life"); only later, in the phrase *U'Chsov lechayim,* should one say *lechayim tovim.* [The rationale is that] a request should first be modest and only later should be expanded.

ח וְלֹא יֹאמַר "לְחַיִּים טוֹבִים" רַק "לְחַיִּים", עַד שֶׁיַּגִּיעַ לְ"וּכְתֹב לְחַיִּים כו'" אָז יֹאמַר "לְחַיִּים טוֹבִים", כִּי הַמְבַקֵּשׁ צָרִיךְ לְבַקֵּשׁ תְּחִלָּה דָּבָר מוּעָט וְאַחַר כָּךְ מוֹסִיף וְהוֹלֵךְ:[מו]

9 On *Rosh HaShanah,* [during *Shemoneh Esreh,*] one should say *Vatiten lanu es Yom HaZikaron hazeh* ("You have granted us this Day of Remembrance"). There is no need to mention Rosh Chodesh[21] by adding the words *ve'es yom Rosh HaChodesh hazeh* ("and this day of Rosh Chodesh"),

ט בְּרֹאשׁ הַשָּׁנָה[מז] אוֹמֵר "וַתִּתֶּן לָנוּ אֶת יוֹם הַזִּכָּרוֹן הַזֶּה", וְאֵין צָרִיךְ לְהַזְכִּיר רֹאשׁ חֹדֶשׁ[מח,21] וְלוֹמַר וְאֶת יוֹם רֹאשׁ חֹדֶשׁ הַזֶּה,[מט]

---

interspersed in the Alter Rebbe's *Siddur* (and known as *Piskei HaSiddur*) were written later than his *Shulchan Aruch.* They thus represent his final stance — and not only for *Chabad* chassidim.

On the *machzor* of *Chabad,* see sec. 619, footnote 9 below.

17. And thus are not of the same degree of authority as are directives ordained by the Sages of the *Talmud.* (See the historical Overview in Vol. 1 of this work, pp. xiv-xv.)

18. Cf. *Nedarim* 1:3; see Bartenura there, and *Ran* there, 10b. The misunderstanding described in the text is more readily conceivable when the accent is mistakenly placed on the first syllable.

19. This phrase is found in the blessing *Hashkiveinu,* which is recited before *Shemoneh Esreh* in the Evening Service and before the recitation of the *Shema* before retiring at night *(Siddur Tehillat HaShem* Annotated Edition, pp. 122, 141, *et al.).* Significantly, in his *Siddur,* the Alter Rebbe chooses the pronunciation *lechayim* for the term in that blessing as well.

20. Lit., "the words follow the intent."

21. I.e., even though Rosh HaShanah is also Rosh Chodesh, the beginning of the month of Tishrei *(Eruvin* 9a).

בסידור. **מב** מהר"ם מרוטנברג בתשב"ץ סי' קיט. הובא בטור. לבוש ס"ה. מ"א סק"ד. **מג** ראה גם לקמן סי' תקצא סוף סי"ב. **מד** בברכת השכיבנו בערבית. מטה משה סי' תקצו. ב"ח ס"ו ד"ה והר"מ. ט"ז סק"ב. מ"א סק"ד (ובסידור הוא בשב"א). **מה** ראה מ"א סי' תרז סק"ה. **מו** מהר"ם מרוטנבורג בתשב"ץ סי' קיט. הובא בטור. לבוש ס"ה. ט"ז סוף ס"ק ב. מ"א סק"ד. וראה גם לקמן סי' תקפד ס"ג. סי' תרז ס"ו. סי' תרכא סי"ג. **מז** בתפילה ובקידוש. **מח** גמרא עירובין מ, א. לפירוש רש"י שם ד"ה זכרון. טור ושו"ע ס"ו. וכ"ה בסידור. **מט** רש"י עירובין שם ד"ה אמרינן. טור ולבוש ס"ו.

דִּכְשֶׁאוֹמֵר "יוֹם הַזִּכָּרוֹן" גַּם רֹאשׁ חֹדֶשׁ בִּכְלָל, שֶׁנִּקְרָא זִכָּרוֹן,[נ] שֶׁנֶּאֱמַר[נא, 22] "וּבְיוֹם שִׂמְחַתְכֶם וּבְמוֹעֲדֵיכֶם וּבְרָאשֵׁי חָדְשֵׁיכֶם וגו' וְנִזְכַּרְתֶּם".[נב]

אִם חָל בְּחֹל[נג] אוֹמְרִים בַּתְּפִלָּה וּבַקִּדּוּשׁ[נד] "יוֹם תְּרוּעָה מִקְרָא קֹדֶשׁ",[22] וְאִם חָל בְּשַׁבָּת[24] אוֹמְרִים "זִכְרוֹן תְּרוּעָה":[25]

י בְּרֹאשׁ הַשָּׁנָה וְיוֹם כִּפּוּר אֵין אוֹמְרִים "מוֹעֲדִים לְשִׂמְחָה חַגִּים וּזְמַנִּים לְשָׂשׂוֹן",[נה, 26] מִפְּנֵי שֶׁיָּמִים אֵלּוּ לֹא נִתְּנוּ לְשִׂמְחָה וּלְשָׂשׂוֹן.[נו, 27] וְכֵן אֵין אוֹמְרִים "וְהַשִּׂיאֵנוּ אֶת בִּרְכַּת מוֹעֲדֶיךָ כו'",[נז] לְפִי שֶׁדָּבָר זֶה לֹא נֶאֱמַר אֶלָּא בְּשָׁלֹשׁ רְגָלִים שֶׁנֶּאֱמַר[נח, 28] "שָׁלֹשׁ פְּעָמִים בַּשָּׁנָה וגו' כְּבִרְכַּת ה' אֱלֹהֶיךָ וגו'".[נט] וּבְמוּסָף אֵין אוֹמְרִים "וְאֵין אֲנוּ יְכוֹלִים לַעֲלוֹת וְלֵרָאוֹת לְפָנֶיךָ",[29] אֶלָּא "וְאֵין אֲנוּ יְכוֹלִין[30] לַעֲשׂוֹת חוֹבוֹתֵינוּ",[ס] לְפִי שֶׁמִּצְוַת רְאִיָּה אֵינָהּ אֶלָּא בְּשָׁלֹשׁ רְגָלִים:[סא]

because the phrase *Yom HaZikaron* includes Rosh Chodesh, which is referred to by the term *zikaron*, as it is written,[22] "On your days of rejoicing, on your festivals, and on your Rosh Chodesh days…, they shall be a remembrance for you."

If [Rosh HaShanah] falls during the week, in *Shemoneh Esreh* and in *Kiddush*, we say *yom teruah mikra kodesh*[23] ("a day for sounding [the *shofar*], a holy convocation"). If it falls on *Shabbos*,[24] we say *zichron teruah*[25] ("a remembrance of sounding [the *shofar*]").

10 On Rosh HaShanah and on Yom Kippur, we do not say *moadim lesimchah, chagim u'zmanim lesason*[26] ("festivals for rejoicing, holidays and seasons for gladness"), because these days were not given [to us] for rejoicing and gladness.[27] Similarly, we do not say *Vehasieinu… es birkas moadecha* ("Grant us… the blessing of Your festivals"), because this phrase relates only to the three Pilgrim Festivals, as it is written,[28] "Three times a year [all your males shall appear]… according to the blessing which G-d your L-rd [has granted you]." Likewise, in the *Mussaf* prayers [on Rosh HaShanah], we do not say *ve'ein anu yecholim la'alos veleiraos… lefanecha*[29] ("and we are not able to go up and appear… before You"). Instead, we say: *ve'ein anu yecholim*[30] *la'asos chovoseinu…*("and we are not able to fulfill our obligations") — for the *mitzvah* of *re'iyah* [i.e., appearing before G-d in the *Beis HaMikdash*] applies only to the three Pilgrim Festivals.

22. *Bamidbar* 10:10.

23. *Ibid.* 29:1.

24. When the *shofar* is not sounded.

25. *Vayikra* 23:24.

26. As we say in every *Shemoneh Esreh* of the three Pilgrim Festivals.

27. See *Likkutei Sichos*, Vol. 24, p. 304, footnote 22.

28. *Devarim* 16:16-17.

29. As we say in *Shemoneh Esreh* for the *Mussaf* of the three Pilgrim Festivals.

30. In the original, *yecholin*, which means the same, but with an Aramaic suffix.

נ גמרא ורש"י ותוס' שם ד"ה זכרון. טור ולבוש שם. מ"א סק"ה. וראה גם לקמן סי' תקצא ס"ו. נא במדבר י, י. נב שם י, ט. רא"ש ר"ה פ"ד סי' יד (מ, א). לבוש שם. אבל במלבושי יום טוב שם, ובאליה זוטא ס"ק ז, כתבו שצריך להיות: והיו לכם לזכרון (כברש"י ותוס' שם). וכן תוקן בשוע"ר דפוס תרס"ה ואילך. נג מסכת סופרים פי"ט ה"ח. רא"ש שם (מ, ב) בשם רבי שמואל בר רבי חפני. טור ושו"ע ס"ז. וראה גם לקמן סט"ו. נד תרומת הדשן סי' קמה בשם הג"ה על גליון הרמב"ם. ב"י ד"ה ומ"ש שאם חל. מ"א סק"ו. נה רא"ש ר"ה פ"ד סי' יד (מ, ב), בשם רב האי גאון. טור ושו"ע ס"ח. נו ב"ח סוף הסי'. וראה לעיל סי' קפח ריש סי"א. סי' תקכט ס"ו. לקמן סי' תקצט ס"א. סי' תקצז ס"א. מ"מ וציונים. נז רא"ש שם (מ, א), בשם כמה גאונים. טור ושו"ע שם. נח דברים טז, טז-יז.

11 At the conclusion of the blessing — in *Shemoneh Esreh,* after the *haftorah,* and in *Kiddush* — one says *udvarcha emes* ("And Your word is true..."); one should not say *udvarcha Malkeinu emes* ("And Your word, our King, is true...").[31]

יא בַּחֲתִימַת הַבְּרָכָה אוֹמְרִים "וּדְבָרְךָ אֱמֶת וכו'",[סב] בֵּין בַּתְּפִלָּה בֵּין בַּהַפְטָרָה בֵּין בַּקִּדּוּשׁ,[סג] וְלֹא יֹאמַר "וּדְבָרְךָ מַלְכֵּנוּ"[31] אֶלָּא "וּדְבָרְךָ אֱמֶת":[סד]

12 The word *shehashaltan* should be pronounced with a *kamatz* under the second *shin,* so that the word will mean "sovereignty." That letter should not be pronounced with a *chirik,* because then the meaning would be "the ruler."

יב "שֶׁהַשָּׁלְטָן"[סה] בְּקָמַ"ץ תַּחַת הַשִּׁי"ן שְׁנִיָּה[סו] שֶׁפֵּרוּשׁוֹ הַמֶּמְשָׁלָה, וְלֹא יֹאמַר בְּחִירִי"ק שֶׁפֵּרוּשׁוֹ אָדָם הַשַּׁלִּיט:[סז]

13 The word *veharish'ah* should be pronounced with a *chirik* under the *resh.*

יג "וְהָרִשְׁעָה"[סח] בְּחִירִי"ק תַּחַת (הַשִּׁי"ן) [הָרֵי"שׁ]:[סט]

14 One does not say *Ve'az tzaddikim* ("And then the righteous"), but *U'vechein tzaddikim* ("And accordingly, the righteous").[32]

יד אֵין אוֹמְרִים "וְאָז צַדִּיקִים" אֶלָּא "וּבְכֵן צַדִּיקִים":[ע, 32]

15 We do not say *be'ahavah mikra kodesh* ("with love, a holy convocation"),[33] but rather *yom teruah mikra kodesh* ("a day of sounding [the *shofar*], a holy convocation). On *Shabbos,* [one should say] *zichron teruah*

טו אֵין אוֹמְרִים "בְּאַהֲבָה מִקְרָא קֹדֶשׁ"[עא, 33] אֶלָּא "יוֹם תְּרוּעָה מִקְרָא קֹדֶשׁ", וּבְשַׁבָּת "זִכְרוֹן תְּרוּעָה[עב]

---

31. This is the ruling of the *Tur* and *Rama (Orach Chayim,* sec. 582:8*). Machtzis HaShekel* explains that the term *Malkeinu* ("our King") is not included because the blessing echoes *Tehillim* 119:89: "Your word, O G-d, is always standing" — and there G-d's Kingship is not mentioned.

In his *Siddur* (see *Machzor for Rosh Hashanah* Annotated Edition, pp. 37, 46, *et al.*), the Alter Rebbe includes the term *Malkeinu,* because the theme of Rosh HaShanah is the acceptance of G-d's Kingship. In this way, the concluding blessing *(chasimah)* of the paragraph (i.e., *Baruch atah HaShem, Melech al kol haaretz...*) echoes the immediately preceding words (i.e., *udvarcha Malkeinu emes...*). See *Shaar HaKollel* 42:11. See also *Likkutei Sichos,* Vol. 19, pp. 293, 617.

32. *Shaar HaKollel* 42:4 cites the *Zohar,* Vol. II, p. 52a, which explains the differences in Kabbalistic terms.

33. The term *be'ahavah* ("with love") is associated specifically with *Shabbos,* which the Jewish people accepted "with love," i.e., on their own volition, for this *mitzvah* was given at Marah, before Sinai. The people were not commanded concerning the other holy days until the Giving of the Torah, when G-d "poised the mountain over them like a barrel" *(Shabbos* 88a*)*. Hence those days are not considered to have been granted "with love." *(Levush,* sec. 487, quoted in the commentary of the Rebbe to the *Haggadah shel Pesach, s.v. Kadesh.)*

נט רא"ש שם, בשם רבנו יצחק הלוי. טור ולבוש ס"ח. **ס** רא"ש שם. טור ושו"ע שם. וכ"ה בסידור. **סא** רא"ש וטור ולבוש שם. **סב** טור. רמ"א ס"ח. וראה גם לקמן סי' תרכא ס"ב. **סג** ב"י ד"ה ודברך. מ"א סק"ז. **סד** מנהגים (טירנא) ר"ה (ע' צב). דרכי משה ס"ק ז. מ"א סק"ד. ובסידור הנוסח בין בתפלה בין בהפטרה בין בקידוש: ודברך מלכנו אמת. וראה שער הכולל פמ"ב אות יא. **סה** בנוסח ובכן תן פחדך. **סו** מנהגים (טירנא) ר"ה (ע' צב). לבוש ס"ה. ט"ז סוף סק"ב. מ"א סק"ד. וכ"ה בסידור. **סז** ט"ז שם. וראה יגדיל תורה (נ.י.) א ע' נד. **סח** בנוסח ובכן צדיקים. **סט** ט"ז שם. וכ"ה בסידור. **ע** מ"א סק"ו, בשם הזהר ח"ג ריט, ב. וכ"ה בסידור. **עא** בתפלה ובקידוש בשבת בר"ה (אף שאומרים בשבת יום טוב, כדלעיל סי' תפז ס"ו). וראה גם לקמן סי' תריט סי"ב (ביוהכ"פ). **עב** כדלעיל סוף ס"ט.

מִקְרָא קֹדֶשׁ":[עג,34]

טז בְּכָל הַקַּדִּישִׁים[35] מֵרֹאשׁ הַשָּׁנָה עַד יוֹם הַכִּפּוּרִים אוֹמְרִים "לְעֵלָּא [וּ]לְעֵלָּא מִכָּל בִּרְכָתָא":[עד,36]

יז וְנוֹהֲגִין שֶׁכָּל אֶחָד וְאֶחָד אוֹמֵר לַחֲבֵרוֹ "לְשָׁנָה טוֹבָה תִּכָּתֵב",[עה,37] וְאֵין לוֹמַר דָּבָר זֶה בְּיוֹם שֵׁנִי שֶׁל רֹאשׁ הַשָּׁנָה[עו] אַחַר חֲצוֹת הַיּוֹם,[עז] לְפִי שֶׁכְּבָר נִגְמְרָה הַכְּתִיבָה שֶׁל רֹאשׁ הַשָּׁנָה:

mikra kodesh ("a remembrance of sounding [the *shofar*], a holy convocation").[34]

16 In all the *Kaddeishim*[35] that are recited from Rosh HaShanah through Yom Kippur, [instead of *le'eila min kol birchasa* — "beyond all the blessings...,"] one says *le'eila ule'eila mikol birchasa* — "sublimely beyond all the blessings."[36]

17 It is customary for people to wish each other *LeShanah Tovah Tikaseiv*[37] ("May you be inscribed for a good year"). This blessing should not be given after midday on the second day, for the inscription of Rosh HaShanah has already been completed.

---

34. Here the Alter Rebbe appears to imply that the word *be'ahavah* should not be included even when Rosh HaShanah falls on *Shabbos,* perhaps because the theme of its Divine service is awe. Nevertheless, in his *Siddur* (see *Machzor for Rosh HaShanah* Annotated Edition, pp. 36, 46, *et al.*), his text for *Shabbos* reads: *zichron teruah be'ahavah mikra kodesh.*

35. Here transliterated according to the popular usage of Ashkenazic pronunciation; strictly speaking, *Kaddishim.*

36. According to *Sefer Minhagim: The Book of Chabad-Lubavitch Customs,* pp. 118 and 136, this change should be made only in the *Ne'ilah* service. See also: the *Hagahos* of the *Tzemach Tzedek* — R. Menachem Mendel (1789-1866), the third Rebbe of Lubavitch — to his *Siddur; Otzar Minhagei Chabad: Elul-Tishrei,* p. 237ff., and references there.

The number of words in the *Kaddish* is monitored precisely, on Kabbalistic grounds. Hence, when the word *ule'eila* is added, the two words *min kol* are contracted into the single word *mikol.*

37. In his *Siddur,* the Alter Rebbe writes that after the evening prayers "on the first night" people customarily exchange the following blessing: *Leshanah tovah tikaseiv veseichaseim* ("May you be inscribed and may [that inscription] be sealed for a good year"). See *Kaf HaChayim* 582:63. As explained in *Sefer HaSichos 5751,* Vol. 1, p. 37, note 76, the inscription is sealed to some degree even before the *shofar* is sounded the next morning.

Sefer HaMinhagim, p. 188, states that when expressing this wish one should make a point of using the singular form of the Hebrew verb (as transliterated above). See *Likkutei Dibburim* (in English translation; Kehot, N.Y., 1987), Vol. 1, p. 102.

עג לבוש ס"ז. מ"א סק"ד. ובסידור (בשבת): זכרון תרועה באהבה מקרא קדש. **עד** לבוש ס"ח. מ"א סק"ד. וראה שער הכולל פ"ד אות ט. ומנהג חב"ד לכפול רק בקדישים של תפילת נעילה (ספר המנהגים – חב"ד ע' 56). **עה** טור סוף הסי' (תכתב בשנת טובה). רמ"א ס"ט (לשנה טובה תכתב). ובסידור: נוהגין בליל הראשון של ר"ה לומר לחבירו לשנה טובה תכתב ותחתם (ראה מ"א ס"ק ח, בשם מעגלי צדק). וראה בספר המנהגים – חב"ד ע' 56 (בלשון יחיד דוקא). התוועדויות תנש"א ח"א ע' 66 הערה 76. **עו** ט"ז סק"ד. **עז** מ"א סק"ח.

SECTION 583 Foods which are Customarily Eaten on Rosh HaShanah. (1–8)

1 On [the eve of] Rosh HaShanah, one should observe the custom[1] of eating leek, beets, dates, squash, fenugreek,[2] and any other foods whose name implies increase in the language spoken locally.[3] The people of each country should eat the foods whose name [leads to such associations] in their language.

Before one eats fenugreek or the like, he should say,[4] "May it be Your will that our merits increase."[5] Before he eats leek, he should say: "May it be Your will that those who hate us be cut off."[6] Before he eats beets, he should say: "May it be Your will that our foes be removed."[7] Before he eats dates, he should say: "May it be Your will that those who hate us perish."[8] And before he eats squash, he should say: "May it be Your will that the verdict rendered against us be torn, and our merits be read in Your presence."[9]

Some people[10] are accustomed to partake

סימן תקפג דברים שנוהגים לאכל בראש השנה ובו ח' סעיפים:

א יהא אדם רגיל[1] לאכל בראש השנה כרתי, סילקא[א] דהינו תרדין,[ב] תמרי, קרא, רוביא דהינו תלתן,[ג,2] והוא הדין מה שנקרא בלשונות אחרים לשון רבוי יאכלו כל אנשי מדינה ומדינה כלשונם.[ד,3] וכשאוכל רוביא וכיוצא בו יאמר[ה,4] "יהי רצון[ו] מלפניך[ז] שירבו זכיותינו",[5] וכשיאכל כרתי יאמר "יהי רצון מלפניך שיכרתו שונאינו",[6] וכשיאכל סילקא יאמר "יהי רצון מלפניך שיסתלקו אויבינו",[7] וכשיאכל תמרי יאמר "יהי רצון מלפניך שיתמו[ח] שונאינו",[ט,8] וכשיאכל קרא יאמר "יהי רצון מלפניך שיקרע גזר דיננו[י] ויקראו לפניך זכיותינו",[יא,9]

ויש נוהגים[יב,10] לאכל תפוח מתוק

---

1. *Kerisos* 6a.

2. A leguminous Asiatic herb (chilbe).

3. For example, in Yiddish-speaking countries it is customary to eat carrots, because the Yiddish equivalent of that name, *merrn*, also means "to increase." This is Lubavitch custom. (The vernacular in Talmudic times was Aramaic, hence the examples cited below.) With the exception of the apple dipped in honey, it is not Lubavitch custom to make a point of eating any of the other foods mentioned in this paragraph.

4. It is not Lubavitch custom to say *Yehi ratzon...* ("May it be Your will...") before eating any of the foods other than the apple (*Sefer HaMinhagim*, p. 119).

5. The Aramaic name for fenugreek (רוביא) recalls the Hebrew word (רבוי) that means "increase."

6. The Aramaic name for leek (כרתי) recalls the Hebrew root (כרת) that means "cut off."

7. The Aramaic name for beets (סילקא) recalls the Hebrew root (סלק) that means "remove."

8. The Aramaic name for dates (תמרי) recalls the Hebrew root (תמם) that means "perish."

9. The Aramaic name for squash (קרא) recalls both the Hebrew root (קרע) that means "rend" and the Hebrew root (קרא) that means "read."

10. This custom is in fact virtually universal.

א גמרא כריתות ו, רע"א. הוריות יב, א. טור ושו"ע ס"א. ב רש"י שבת עג, ב ד"ה דקניב. ג רש"י שם ושם. טור ושו"ע שם. ד מ"א ריש הסי'. ה ר"ן סוף ר"ה (יב, ב) ד"ה גרסינן בשם רב האי גאון. שו"ע שם. ו כל בו ר"ה (כט, א). אבודרהם סדר תפלת ר"ה (ע' רסו) ד"ה גרסינן. שו"ע שם. ז אבודרהם וכל בו שם. לבוש ס"א. ח ר"ן שם. טור ושו"ע שם. ט טור ושו"ע שם. י ר"ן וכל בו ואבודרהם שם. שו"ע שם. יא כל בו שם. שו"ע שם. וראה פעמי יעקב מא ע' קטו. יב טור. רמ"א ס"א. וכ"ה בסידור.

מְטֻבָּל בִּדְבַשׁ וְאוֹמְרִים "תִּתְחַדֵּשׁ עָלֵינוּ[12] שָׁנָה מְתוּקָה",[11] וִיבָרֵךְ עַל הַתַּפּוּחַ[13] וְלֹא עַל הַדְּבַשׁ, לְפִי שֶׁהַדְּבַשׁ הוּא טָפֵל לַתַּפּוּחַ:[יג]

of a sweet apple dipped in honey, and to say: "May the renewed year be sweet[11] for us."[12] A blessing should be recited over the apple,[13] and not over the honey, since the honey is ancillary to the apple.

ב וְיֵשׁ אוֹכְלִים דָּגִים לִפְרוֹת וְלִרְבּוֹת כְּדָגִים,[14] וְאֵין מְבַשְּׁלִים בְּחֹמֶץ:[יד,15]

2 There are people who follow the custom of eating fish [thereby expressing the hope that] they will be fruitful and multiply like fish.[14] [The fish] should not be cooked in vinegar.[15]

ג כָּל הַמִּינִים שֶׁצָּרִיךְ לְבָרֵךְ כְּשֶׁאוֹכְלָם בְּתוֹךְ הַסְּעוּדָה כְּגוֹן תַּפּוּחִים וּתְמָרִים יֹאמַר הַבַּקָּשָׁה[16] אַחַר הַתְחָלַת הָאֲכִילָה, מִפְּנֵי שֶׁאָסוּר לְהַפְסִיק בֵּין הַבְּרָכָה לָאֲכִילָה:[טו,17]

3 When partaking of foods, such as apples or dates, for which a blessing is required when they are eaten in the course of a meal, the [accompanying] request[16] should be made after one begins to eat, because it is forbidden to make an interruption between the recitation of the blessing and partaking [of the food].[17]

---

11. The Alter Rebbe's *Siddur* follows the wording in the *Siddur* of the *AriZal* and begins the request differently: *Yehi ratzon milfanecha shetechadesh aleinu...* — "May it be Your will to renew for us...." Also, the Alter Rebbe closes this request with the words, *shanah tovah u'mesukah* — "a *good* and sweet year."

12. The intentional omission of the Divine name from this request is discussed in *Shaar HaKollel* 42:2. Moreover, since — according to *Chabad* custom — the request is made directly after the blessing over the apple (see footnote 17 below), the mention of the Divine name in that blessing extends and relates also to this request.

13. Although, according to *Chabad* custom, the apple is eaten *after* reciting the blessing *HaMotzi* and partaking of the bread (see subsection 3), a blessing must be recited before partaking of it, since it is not part of the main body of the meal.

The sequence of events on the second night is different. On that night, when there is a doubt as to whether the blessing *Shehecheyanu* should be recited, a new fruit — which in any case would call for the recitation of that blessing — is eaten immediately *after* the recitation of *Kiddush*, and *before* the hands are washed for the meal. The *Shehecheyanu* thus covers both the festival *and* the new fruit that follows that blessing immediately. (See sec. 600:6 below.)

14. See also subsection 7.

15. Because the emphasis on Rosh HaShanah should be on sweetness.

16. As in subsection 1 above.

17. However, speaking of the apple dipped in honey, *Sefer HaMinhagim* states that the request should be made *after* reciting the blessing and *before* partaking of the apple. In an elaborate explanation of this practice — halachic, Kabbalistic, historical — the Rebbe points to the link between the beginning of the blessing ("Blessed are You...") and the subsequent request, and explains that the request does not constitute an interruption between the blessing and the eating, since it relates to the purpose of eating the apple. (The entire letter, with all its documentation, appears in English translation in *Sefer Minhagim: The Book of Chabad-Lubavitch Customs*, pp. 203-9.)

יג מ"א ס"ק א. **יד** אבודרהם שם. מ"א ריש הסי'. **טו** מ"א סק"ב. ובסידור: בר"ה בלילה ראשונה נוהגין לאכול תפוח מתוק בדבש בתחילת הסעודה וצריך לברך בתחילה ברוך אתה כו' בורא פרי העץ, ואחר כך יאמר יהי רצון מלפניך שתחדש עלינו שנה טובה ומתוקה. וכ"ה מנהג חב"ד לומר יהי רצון על התפוח אחר הברכה קודם אכילה (ספר המנהגים – חב"ד ע' 56), וכמובא במ"א שם ממעגלי צדק. וראה אג"ק ח"ג ע' קמ־קמד (הטעם דלא הוי הפסק). שלחן המלך ח"ב ע' קפז־קצא. ס' המנהגים שם (שאכילת התפוח בליל ראשון צ בתחלת הסעודה, והפרי חדש בליל שני – קודם נטילת ידים לסעודה). אג"ק ח"ג ע' רט־רי (טעם החילוק). יגדיל תורה (נ.י.) ב ע' לו. **טז** מ"א סק"א. וכ"ה מנהג חב"ד, ונוהגין כן עד לאחר הושענה רבה. ראה אוצר מנהגי חב"ד ר"ה ע'

4 There are those whose custom is to dip the piece of bread [eaten after reciting] the blessing *HaMotzi* in honey.[18] Some people eat pomegranates[19] and say: "May our merits be as numerous as [the seeds of] a pomegranate."[4]

It is customary to eat succulent meat, drink honey, and [partake of] other sweet foods as a sign that the year should be one of sweetness and plenty, as it is written in the Book of *Ezra*,[20] "Eat succulent foods and drink sweet beverages...."[21]

ד וְיֵשׁ נוֹהֲגִים לִטְבֹּל פְּרוּסַת הַמּוֹצִיא בִּדְבַשׁ.[טז, 18] וְיֵשׁ אוֹכְלִין רִמּוֹנִים וְאוֹמְרִים[19] "נִרְבֶּה זְכֻיּוֹת כָּרִמּוֹן".[יז, 4] וְנוֹהֲגִין לֶאֱכֹל בָּשָׂר שָׁמֵן וְלִשְׁתּוֹת דְּבַשׁ וְכָל מִינֵי מְתִיקָה כְּדֵי שֶׁתְּהֵא הַשָּׁנָה הַזֹּאת מְתוּקָה וּשְׁמֵנָה, וְכֵן כָּתוּב בְּעֶזְרָא[20] "אִכְלוּ מַשְׁמַנִּים וּשְׁתוּ מַמְתַקִּים":[יח, 21]

5 One should partake of the head of a ram[22] to commemorate the ram [sacrificed instead] of Yitzchak.[23] If a head of a ram is not available, one should partake of the head of a lamb, and if [that] is not available, one should partake of the head of another animal — so as to say, "May we be a head and not a tail."

ה יֵשׁ לֶאֱכֹל רֹאשׁ אַיִל זָכָר[22] לְאֵילוֹ שֶׁל יִצְחָק,[יט, 23] וְאִם אֵין רֹאשׁ אַיִל – יֹאכַל רֹאשׁ כֶּבֶשׂ;[כ] וְאִם אֵין רֹאשׁ כֶּבֶשׂ – יֹאכַל רֹאשׁ אַחֵר,[כא] לוֹמַר נִהְיֶה לְרֹאשׁ וְלֹא לְזָנָב:[כב]

6 There are people who make a point of not eating walnuts and hazelnuts because they generate phlegm and mucus and thus disturb one while he is praying.[24]

ו יֵשׁ מְדַקְדְּקִים שֶׁלֹּא לֶאֱכֹל אֱגוֹזִים וְלוּזִים (פֵּרוּשׁ אֱגוֹזִים קְטַנִּים[כג]), מִפְּנֵי שֶׁהֵם מַרְבִּים כִּיחָה וְנִיעָה[כד] וּמְבַטְּלִים הַתְּפִלָּה:[כה, 24]

---

18. Rather than in salt, as is done throughout the year, again because of the theme of sweetness. This custom, too, is virtually universal.

Otzar Minhagei Chabad: Elul-Tishrei, p. 75, mentions that the Rebbe would (a) dip the *challah* in the honey three times (as also with the apple; *ibid.*, p. 78), and would (b) dip a further piece of *challah* three times in salt.

19. This custom is practiced in Lubavitch *(Sefer HaMinhagim)*, as also in many other circles.

20. *Nechemiah* 8:10. These adjoining Books are counted as one, like *I Kings* and *II Kings.*

21. The verse continues: "...and send portions to those who have nothing prepared, for today is sacred to our G-d." The "day" referred to is Rosh HaShanah (see v. 2).

The Rebbe *(Likkutei Sichos,* Vol. 14, p. 369ff.*)* cited this verse as a source when urging his listeners to enable needy families to celebrate the holiday appropriately.

22. *Sefer HaMinhagim* states that this is Lubavitch custom. The Rebbe Rayatz — R. Yosef Yitzchak Schneersohn (1880-1950), the sixth Rebbe of Lubavitch — and the Rebbe were known to partake of the head of a fish, but not the head of a ram.

23. For the Binding of Yitzchak (the *Akeidah*) is one of the eternal merits that confer Divine favor upon his descendants.

24. See sec. 53:15.

עה״ע. **יז** אבודרהם שם. רמ״א ס״א. ומנהג חב״ד לאכול רימון אבל לא אומרים יהי רצון כי אם על התפוח (ספר המנהגים – חב״ד ע׳ 56). **יח** נחמיה ח, י.
מרדכי יומא רמז תשכג בשם תשובת הגאונים. רמ״א ס״א. וראה לקמן סי׳ תקצז ס״א. **יט** טור בשם מהר״ם מרוטנבורג, בתשב״ץ סי׳ קיח. וראה שו״ע ס״ב.
כ מרדכי שם בשם הגאונים. טור ושו״ע ס״ב. **כא** מ״א סק״ג. **כב** מרדכי בשם הגאונים שם. טור ושו״ע שם. וראה ס׳ המנהגים – חב״ד (ע׳ 56): אוכלים
רימון וראש איל, אבל אין אומרים יה״ר כי אם על התפוח. **כג** מ״א סק״ד. **כד** מהרי״ל הל׳ שופר (ע׳ רפז). רמ״א ס״ב. וראה לקמן סי׳ תקצב ס״ח. **כה** דרכי
משה ס״ק א, בשם המהרי״ל. רמ״א שם.

ז וְנוֹהֲגִים לֵילֵךְ אֶל הַנָּהָר[כו, 25] שֶׁיֵּשׁ בּוֹ דָּגִים חַיִּים[כז] לְסִימָן שֶׁלֹּא תִּשְׁלֹט בָּנוּ עַיִן הָרָע וְנִפְרֶה וְנִרְבֶּה כְּדָגִים,[כח, 26] וְאוֹמְרִים שָׁם פָּסוּק[27] "יָשׁוּב יְרַחֲמֵנוּ וגו' וְתַשְׁלִיךְ וגו'".[כט, 28] וְטוֹב שֶׁיִּהְיֶה מִחוּץ לָעִיר. וְיֵשׁ לֵילֵךְ בְּיוֹם רִאשׁוֹן שֶׁל רֹאשׁ הַשָּׁנָה[ל, 29] אַחַר מִנְחָה קֹדֶם שְׁקִיעַת הַחַמָּה, וְלוֹמַר פָּסוּק "מִי אֵל כָּמוֹךָ וגו'":[לא, 30]

7 It is customary to go to a river[25] with live fish, which serve as a sign that the Evil Eye should have no power over us and that we be fruitful and multiply like fish.[26] [At the riverbank,] we recite the verse,[27] "He will again show mercy to us.... You will cast [all their sins into the depths of the sea]."[28] It is preferable that this be done outside the city. [This custom is practiced] on the first day of Rosh HaShanah[29] after the *Minchah* service, before sunset. One should [also] recite the verse [that precedes the above, viz.], "Who is a G-d like You...."[30]

ח וְנוֹהֲגִין שֶׁלֹּא לִישַׁן בְּיוֹם רֹאשׁ הַשָּׁנָה, כְּדֵי שֶׁלֹּא יִישַׁן מַזָּלוֹ.[לב, 31] וְהַיּוֹשֵׁב וּבָטֵל – הֲרֵי זֶה כְּיָשֵׁן.[לג, 32] וְיֵשׁ נוֹהֲגִים לִישַׁן אַחַר חֲצוֹת הַיּוֹם:[לד]

8 It is customary not to sleep by day on Rosh HaShanah so that one's *mazal*[31] will not sleep. One who sits idly is considered as if asleep.[32] There are those who [maintain that one may] sleep after midday.

---

25. The river is reminiscent of the *Akedah* (see footnote 23 above), on the way to which Avraham was obstructed by Satan in the guise of a river *(Midrash Tanchuma, Parshas Vayeira).* In the *Siddur* the Alter Rebbe writes of a well or a spring, and mentions that water also symbolizes *Chessed,* the Divine attribute of kindness.

26. In his *Siddur,* the Alter Rebbe adds that the lidless eyes of fish remind one of the ever-open eye of G-d's Providence.

27. *Michah* 7:19.

28. This is an additional reason for which these verses are recited at the edge of water. Indeed, the very name of this custom *(Tashlich)* is the Hebrew word for "You will cast."

29. If the first day of Rosh HaShanah falls on *Shabbos, Tashlich* is deferred to the second day. This postponement developed in recent generations, evidently because of the possibility that *Siddurim* might be carried on *Shabbos* beyond the bounds of the town's *eruv.* (See the *sichah* of the Rebbe on 6 Tishrei, 5730, and *Otzar Minhagei Chabad: Elul-Tishrei,* p. 146.)

30. *Michah* 7:18. It is *Chabad* custom to recite the three verses of *Michah* 7:18-20 in order. The *Kabbalah* teaches how the words of these verses parallel the Thirteen Attributes of Mercy that appear in *Shmos* 34:6-7 (see *Zohar,* Vol. III, p. 131b). These are followed by the verses from *Tehillim* 118:5-9 that correspond to the nine attributes of mercy enumerated in *Bamidbar* 14:18 (see *Zohar, loc. cit.,* p. 134b). The concluding verses and supplications (see *Machzor for Rosh Hashanah* Annotated Edition, p. 291-2) include Psalm 33, which comprises 22 verses, alluding to the sum (13 and 9) of both sets of merciful attributes *(Siddur HaArizal).*

31. The term *mazal* usually means "fortune"; in the context of *Kabbalah* and *Chassidus* it signifies an individual's soul-root.

32. The Rebbeim of *Chabad* earnestly urged that every available moment of Rosh HaShanah be utilized for prayer and the recitation of *Tehillim.* See: *Igros Kodesh* (Letters) of the Rebbe Rayatz, Vol. 4, p. 132; *Sefer HaMinhagim,*

כו מנהגים (טירנא) ר"ה (ע' ק). מהרי"ל הל' ר"ה (ע' רעז). רמ"א שם. ובסידור: אל באר המים או מעין (פרי עץ חיים שער השופר פ"ה ד"ה נכון). כז מנהגים שם. דרכי משה ס"ק ב. מ"א סק"ה. כח דרכי משה שם. ובסידור: רומזים על עינא פקיחא. כט מיכה ז, יט. מנהגים שם (תשוב תרחמנו). דרכי משה שם בשם מהרי"ל. רמ"א שם. ל ואם חל בשבת הולכים ביום ב' (רשימות חוברת ד ע' 9. אוצר מנהגי חב"ד ע' קמו). לא מיכה שם יח. מ"א שם בשם כתבים (פרי עץ חיים שם). וכ"ה בסידור, וראה עוד שם. ומנהג חב"ד לנער שולי הטלית קטן אחר סדר תשליך (ראה פרי עץ חיים שם. סידור האריז"ל וסידור השל"ה. הגהת אדמו"ר הרש"ב בתורה אור. ספר המנהגים – חב"ד ע' 57). לב דרכי משה ס"ק ב, בשם הירושלמי. רמ"א ס"ב. לג מ"א סק"ו. לד מ"א שם בשם אר"י (פרי עץ חיים שער השופר פ"ה ד"ה בענין השינה).

SECTION 584 The Order of the Torah Reading on Rosh HaShanah. (1–9)

1 *Hallel*[1] is not recited on Rosh HaShanah and Yom Kippur,[2] because [on these days] the Holy One, blessed be He, sits on the Throne of Judgment and the Books of Life and Death are open before Him. How could one recite [joyous] songs of praise [at such a time]?

Nevertheless, if it happens that people whose daily reading of *Tehillim* includes [the psalms of] *Hallel* on Rosh HaShanah or Yom Kippur, they may read them as part of their daily routine,[3] because they are reciting them not as joyous songs, but as prayers and supplications.

2 The prayer *Avinu Malkeinu* is recited in its [traditional] order, though some people omit the phrase, "Our Father our King, we have sinned before You."[4] [The rationale is that] one does not recite confessional prayers on Rosh HaShanah so as not to give the Accuser [in the Heavenly Court] an opportunity for expression. There is, however, no need to be concerned about reciting verses [from the *Tanach*[5]] that mention sin, since they are not being recited as confessional prayers.

Moreover, one need not refrain even from actual confession while the *shofar* is being sounded, because [at that time] Satan is confounded. Indeed, it is proper to confess silently between the sets of *shofar* blasts,

סימן תקפד סֵדֶר קְרִיאַת הַתּוֹרָה בְּרֹאשׁ הַשָּׁנָה וּבוֹ ט' סְעִיפִים:

א אֵין אוֹמְרִים הַלֵּל[1] בְּרֹאשׁ הַשָּׁנָה וְיוֹם הַכִּפּוּרִים,[א,2] לְפִי שֶׁהַקָּדוֹשׁ בָּרוּךְ הוּא יוֹשֵׁב עַל כִּסֵּא דִּין וְסִפְרֵי חַיִּים וְסִפְרֵי מֵתִים פְּתוּחִים לְפָנָיו וְאֵיךְ יֹאמְרוּ שִׁירָה.[ב] וְאוֹתָם הָאוֹמְרִים תְּהִלִּים בְּכָל יוֹם וְאֵרַע לָהֶם בְּרֹאשׁ הַשָּׁנָה וְיוֹם הַכִּפּוּרִים אֲמִירַת הַלֵּל – מֻתָּרִים לוֹמַר כְּדַרְכָּן,[3] כֵּיוָן שֶׁאֵין אוֹמְרִים אוֹתָן דֶּרֶךְ שִׁירָה רַק דֶּרֶךְ תְּחִנָּה וּבַקָּשָׁה:[ג]

ב וְנוֹהֲגִים לוֹמַר "אָבִינוּ מַלְכֵּנוּ" עַל הַסֵּדֶר.[ד] וְיֵשׁ שֶׁמְּדַלְּגִין בְּרֹאשׁ הַשָּׁנָה "אָבִינוּ מַלְכֵּנוּ חָטָאנוּ לְפָנֶיךָ",[4] לְפִי שֶׁאֵין אוֹמְרִים וִדּוּי בְּרֹאשׁ הַשָּׁנָה[ה] שֶׁלֹּא לִתֵּן פִּתְחוֹן פֶּה לַמְקַטְרֵג,[ו] אֲבָל לוֹמַר פְּסוּקִים[5] שֶׁיֵּשׁ בָּהֶן הַזְכָּרַת חֵטְא – אֵין קְפֵידָא, כֵּיוָן שֶׁאֵינוֹ דֶּרֶךְ וִדּוּי.[ז] וַאֲפִלּוּ וִדּוּי מַמָּשׁ אֵין לִמְנֹעַ בִּשְׁעַת הַתְּקִיעוֹת שֶׁהַשָּׂטָן הוּא מְעֻרְבָּב. וְנָכוֹן הַדָּבָר לְהִתְוַדּוֹת בְּלַחַשׁ בֵּין הַתְּקִיעוֹת[ח]

---

pp. 117-8; *Otzar Minhagei Chabad: Elul-Tishrei,* pp. 48-53.

SECTION 584

1. This section also deals with matters that precede and follow the Torah Reading.

2. *Arachin* 10b; *Rosh HaShanah* 32b.

3. Similarly, those who recite the entire Book of *Tehillim* on Rosh HaShanah (as is Lubavitch custom; see sec. 583, footnote 32 above) may recite the psalms of *Hallel.*

4. In his *Siddur,* unlike the present text, the Alter Rebbe follows this opinion, and other phrases that mention sin and the need for atonement are likewise omitted there on Rosh HaShanah.

5. Acronym for Torah (the Five Books of Moses), *Nevi'im* (the Prophetic Books), and *Kesuvim* (the Writings).

א ערכין י, ב. ר"ה לב, ב. טור ושו"ע ס"א. **ב** ערכין שם. ר"ה שם. טור. ט"ז סק"א. **ג** מ"א סק"א. **ד** כלבו סי' סד (כח, ד). רמ"א ס"א. **ה** ב"י ד"ה נוהגין. מ"א סק"ב. ובסידור: אין לומר בר"ה אבינו מלכנו שיש בו הזכרת חטא או עון כגון אבינו מלכנו חטאנו לפניך או סלח ומחול וכו' וכיוצא בזה. **ו** תולעת יעקב ר"ה ד"ה שנינו בפרק בתרא. הובא בשל"ה מסכת ר"ה עמוד הדין (ריד, א) ד"ה להיות. **ז** כנסת הגדולה סי' רלז הגב"י. מ"א שם. **ח** פרי עץ חיים שער השופר פ"ה ד"ה

בְּשָׁעָה שֶׁהַצִּבּוּר אוֹמְרִים "יְהִי רָצוֹן מִלְּפָנֶיךָ וכו'".[ט]

while the congregation is reciting the prayer *Yehi ratzon.*

ג צָרִיךְ לוֹמַר[י] "סְלַח וּמְחַל[יא] מְחֵה וְהַעֲבֵר חַטֹּאתֵינוּ[6] וּפְשָׁעֵינוּ",[יב] כִּי מְחִילָה גְּדוֹלָה מִסְּלִיחָה[יג] וּפֶשַׁע גָּדוֹל מֵחַטָּאת,[יד] וְצָרִיךְ לְבַקֵּשׁ תְּחִלָּה עַל הַמּוּעָט וְאַחַר כָּךְ מוֹסִיף וְהוֹלֵךְ:[טו]

3 [In the *Avinu Malkeinu* prayer,] the words within each of the phrases, "pardon and forgive" and "blot out and remove our sins[6] and transgressions," should appear [in that order. The rationale is] that forgiveness *(mechilah)* is greater than pardon *(selichah),* and a transgression *(pesha)* is more serious than a sin *(chatas).* [The rationale is that] a request should first be modest and only later should be expanded.

ד צָרִיךְ לוֹמַר "רֹעַ גְּזַר" בִּנְשִׁימָה אַחַת, דְּהַיְנוּ שֶׁיִּקְרַע הוּא יִתְבָּרַךְ הָרֹעַ שֶׁבַּגְּזֵרָה, וּמַה שֶּׁנִּשְׁאַר בַּגְּזֵרָה יִהְיֶה לְרַחֲמִים:[טז]

4 [In this prayer,] the words *ro'a gzar* ("the evil [aspect] of the verdict") should be recited in a single breath. [The implication is that] G-d should cut out "the evil aspect" from the verdict and thus the remainder of the decree will be merciful.

ה אֵין אוֹמְרִים "אָבִינוּ מַלְכֵּנוּ" בְּשַׁבָּת,[יז] מִפְּנֵי שֶׁאָסוּר לִתְבֹּעַ צְרָכָיו בְּשַׁבָּת,[יח] וַאֲפִלּוּ בְּעֶרֶב שַׁבָּת בְּמִנְחָה אֵין אוֹמְרִים אוֹתוֹ:[יט]

5 The *Avinu Malkeinu* prayer is not recited on *Shabbos,* because it is forbidden to ask for one's [material] needs on *Shabbos.* Indeed, it is not even said at *Minchah* on Friday afternoon.

ו בְּרֹאשׁ הַשָּׁנָה מַאֲרִיכִין בְּפִיּוּטִים[7] וּבִתְפִלּוֹת עַד חֲצוֹת הַיּוֹם[כ] לְכָל הַפָּחוֹת,[כא] וְאִם חָל בְּשַׁבָּת אֵין לְהַאֲרִיךְ יוֹתֵר מֵחֲצוֹת,[8] אֲבָל בְּחֹל יָכוֹל לְהַאֲרִיךְ יוֹתֵר.[כב] בַּמֶּה דְּבָרִים אֲמוּרִים? בְּפִיּוּטִים וּבִתְפִלּוֹת, אֲבָל בְּנִגּוּנִים אֵין לְהַאֲרִיךְ יוֹתֵר מֵחֲצוֹת,[כג] כֵּיוָן שֶׁהוּא יוֹם טוֹב:[כד, 9]

6 On Rosh HaShanah, [the prayer service] is extended by the addition of liturgical hymns[7] and prayers [of supplication] until at least midday, but if Rosh HaShanah falls on *Shabbos,* it should not be extended past midday.[8] On a weekday it may be extended beyond that time, but only for liturgical hymns and supplications. The service should not be extended for melodies alone, for the day is a festival.[9]

---

6. The word for "our sins" *(chatoseinu)* does not appear at this point in the Alter Rebbe's *Siddur,* even when *Avinu Malkeinu* is recited on days other than Rosh HaShanah.

7. In the original, *piyyutim.*

8. Because one should not eat before praying, and even a half-day fast is forbidden on *Shabbos.*

9. And should be honored with food and drink — like all the

בענין הווידוי. הובא בשל"ה שם (ריד, ב) ד"ה אחר כך. מ"א שם. וכ"ה בסידור. **ט** בסידור אמירת יהי רצון הוא לאחר התקיעות. וראה מ"מ וציונים. **י** בנוסח אבינו מלכנו. **יא** מ"א סק"ג. ובסידור כתב רבנו שלא לאמרו בר"ה, ושם: ומחול. **יב** מ"א סוף סק"ג. ובסידור כתב רבנו שלא לאמרו, ושם: מחה והעבר פשעינו. **יג** מ"א שם. **יד** ראה יומא לו, ב: פשעים אלו המרדים . . . חטאתם אלו השגגות. **טו** מ"א סי' תרז סק"ג. וכדלעיל סי' תקפב ס"ח וש"נ. **טז** ט"ז סי' תרכב סק"ו. **יז** ר"ן ר"ה (ט, א) ד"ה גמ'. שו"ת הריב"ש סי' תקיב. רמ"א ס"א. **יח** ר"ן שם. ריב"ש שם. מ"א סק"ג. וכדלעיל סי' קפח ס"ד וש"נ. וראה שער הכולל פל"ו אות ב. **יט** מעגלי צדק (אחרי מוסף יום ב' דר"ה). מהרי"ל הל' ר"ה (ע' רפא). מ"א שם. וראה גם לקמן סי' תרב ס"ב (עשי"ת) וש"נ. **כ** מהרי"ל

ז מוֹצִיאִין שְׁנֵי סִפְרֵי תוֹרָה,[כה] בָּרִאשׁוֹן קוֹרִין חֲמִשָּׁה[כו,10] מִן "וַה' פָּקַד אֶת שָׂרָה"[כז] עַד פָּרָשַׁת הָעֲקֵדָה,[כח,11] לְפִי שֶׁבְּרֹאשׁ הַשָּׁנָה נִפְקְדָה שָׂרָה,[כט,12] וְאִם הוּא שַׁבָּת קוֹרִין בּוֹ שִׁבְעָה,[ל] וּמַפְטִיר[13] קוֹרֵא[14] בְּסֵפֶר תוֹרָה שֵׁנִי בְּפָרָשַׁת פִּינְחָס[15] "וּבַחֹדֶשׁ הַשְּׁבִיעִי",[לא] וּמַפְטִיר בִּתְחִלַּת סֵפֶר שְׁמוּאֵל[לב,16] עַד "וְיָרֵם קֶרֶן מְשִׁיחוֹ",[לג,17] לְפִי שֶׁגַּם חַנָּה נִפְקְדָה בְּרֹאשׁ הַשָּׁנָה:[לד]

ח וְיֵשׁ מְקוֹמוֹת שֶׁנּוֹהֲגִים לִקְרוֹת הַתּוֹקֵעַ מִמִּנְיַן חֲמִשָּׁה הָעוֹלִים לְסֵפֶר תוֹרָה.[לה] וְיֵשׁ מְקוֹמוֹת נוֹהֲגִים לִקְרוֹת גַּם הַמִּתְפַּלֵּל מוּסָף, וְכֵן בְּיוֹם הַכִּפּוּרִים:[לו]

7 Two Torah scrolls are taken out [of the Ark for the reading]. From the first scroll, [on the first day,] we read five *[aliyos*[10]*]* from "And G-d remembered Sarah..." until the passage concerning the Binding of Yitzchak.[11] [This reading was chosen,] because Sarah conceived on Rosh HaShanah.[12] If [Rosh HaShanah] falls on *Shabbos,* [the reading is divided into] seven *aliyos.*

[For the *aliyah* for] the *Maftir,*[13] [one] reads[14] the passage from *Parshas Pinchas* [beginning][15] "And in the seventh month" from the second Torah scroll. For the *Haftorah,* one reads from the beginning of the Book of *Shmuel*[16] until "May He raise high the standard of His anointed one."[17] [This reading was chosen,] because Chanah also conceived on Rosh HaShanah.

8 There are places where the person who sounds the *shofar* is given one of the five *aliyos* on Rosh HaShanah. In other places, an *aliyah* is also given to the *sheliach tzibbur* who recites the *Mussaf* prayers. The [latter] practice is also followed on Yom Kippur.

---

festivals, "half of which should be for G-d and half for yourselves." (See sec. 529:10.)

10. Plural of *aliyah,* which refers to both the honor of being called to the Reading of the Torah and, as here, the passage read for each such individual.

Mateh Ephraim advises that one should endeavor to receive an *aliyah* in the course of the High Holidays (in the original, *Yamim Nora'im* — lit., "Days of Awe").

11. *Bereishis,* ch. 21. On the second day we read of the Binding of Yitzchak *(Bereishis,* ch. 22*),* to recall the merit of the devotion of Avraham and Yitzchak (see sec. 601).

12. *Rosh HaShanah* 11a.

13. I.e., the person who recites the *Haftorah,* the reading from the Prophets.

14. The original is worded as if the person called to the reading from the Prophets first read from the Torah personally. This wording reflects the practice in earlier eras, when each congregant honored with an *aliyah* to the Torah would read his passage from the scroll himself — which is still the case today in many Yemenite and some Sephardic congregations. According to the prevalent Ashkenazic custom, the passages are read for everyone by a designated reader, popularly known as a *baal koreh* (or, more grammatically, *baal keriah*). The congregant honored with the *aliyah* should read along with him in an undertone. (See the *Shulchan Aruch* of R. Yosef Caro, sec. 141:2.)

15. *Bamidbar* 29:1-6.

16. *I Shmuel* 1:1 — 2:10.

17. For the *Haftorah* of the second day, we read the prophecy of redemption from *Yirmeyahu* 31:1-19 (see sec. 601).

סדר מוסף של ר"ה (ע' ש). רמ"א ס"א. **כא** מהרי"ל שם. מ"א סק"ד. **כב** יש"ש ביצה פ"ב סי' ד. מ"א שם. וראה לעיל סי' תקכט ס"ח. לקמן סי' תקצז ס"א וס"ז. **כג** מ"א שם. וראה לעיל סי' תקכט סוף ס"י. **כד** ראה לקמן סי' תקצז ס"ג. **כה** טור ושו"ע ס"ב. וראה גם לעיל סי' תפח סוף ס"ו. **כו** טור ושו"ע שם. וראה גם לעיל סי' תפח ס"ה וס"ו. **כז** מגילה לא, א. טור ושו"ע שם. **כח** טור ושו"ע שם. **כט** ר"ן שם (י, ב) ד"ה גמ'. לבוש ס"ב. מ"א סק"ה. והוא בגמרא ר"ה י, סוע"ב. **ל** טור ושו"ע שם. וראה גם לעיל סי' רפב ס"א וס"ב. **לא** משנה מגילה פ"ד ל, ב. טור ושו"ע שם. **לב** מגילה לא, א. טור ושו"ע שם. **לג** טור ושו"ע שם. **לד** רש"י שם ד"ה מפטירין. לבוש שם. מ"א שם. והוא בגמרא ר"ה יא, א. **לה** כלבו סי' סד (כט, סוע"א). רמ"א ס"ב. **לו** לבוש ס"ב. מ"א סק"ו.

ט אִם יֵשׁ תִּינוֹק לָמוּל בְּרֹאשׁ הַשָּׁנָה — אֵין מַמְתִּינִים לְמוּלוֹ עַד אַחַר גְּמַר הַתְּפִלָּה,[לז,18] מִשּׁוּם[19] דִּזְרִיזִין מַקְדִּימִין לְמִצְוָה,[לח] אֶלָּא מָלִין אוֹתוֹ אַחַר קְרִיאַת הַתּוֹרָה קֹדֶם תְּקִיעַת שׁוֹפָר,[לט] לְפִי שֶׁעַל יְדֵי תְּקִיעַת שׁוֹפָר הַקָּדוֹשׁ בָּרוּךְ הוּא זוֹכֵר עֲקֵדַת יִצְחָק[מ] טוֹב לִסְמֹךְ הַמִּילָה בְּרִית אַבְרָהָם וַעֲקֵדַת יִצְחָק.[מא]

בַּמֶּה דְּבָרִים אֲמוּרִים? בְּמָקוֹם שֶׁמָּלִין בְּבֵית הַכְּנֶסֶת, אֲבָל בְּמָקוֹם שֶׁנּוֹהֲגִים לָמוּל כָּל אֶחָד בְּבֵיתוֹ — מָלִין אוֹתוֹ אַחַר יְצִיאָה מִבֵּית הַכְּנֶסֶת:[מב]

9 If there is an infant who is due to be circumcised on Rosh HaShanah, one does not wait until after the prayers[18] to circumcise him, because[19] "those who are eager perform the *mitzvos* early." Instead, the circumcision should take place after the Reading of the Torah, before the sounding of the *shofar*. [The rationale is] that by the sounding of the *shofar*, [a ram's horn,] G-d recalls the Binding of Yitzchak, [because a ram was sacrificed in his stead]. It is therefore appropriate to link the circumcision, which is the covenant of Avraham, to the Binding of Yitzchak.

The above applies in places where it is customary to circumcise children in the synagogue. Wherever circumcisions customarily take place at home, the child should be circumcised after the congregation leaves the synagogue.

סימן תקפה סֵדֶר הַתְּקִיעוֹת מְיֻשָּׁב וּבוֹ י"א סְעִיפִים:

SECTION 585 The Series of *Shofar* Blasts during which One may Sit. (1–11)

א צָרִיךְ לִתְקֹעַ מְעֻמָּד,[א,1] שֶׁנֶּאֱמַר[ב,2] "יוֹם תְּרוּעָה יִהְיֶה לָכֶם", וּלְהַלָּן הוּא אוֹמֵר[ג,3] "וּסְפַרְתֶּם לָכֶם", מַה "לָּכֶם" הָאָמוּר שָׁם מְעֻמָּד כְּמוֹ שֶׁנִּתְבָּאֵר בְּסִימָן תפ"ט[ד] אַף כָּאן

1 The *shofar* must be sounded while standing. [This concept is derived[1] as follows:] It is written,[2] "It shall be a day of sounding [the *shofar*] for you (לכם)," and [with regard to the counting of the *Omer*] it is written,[3] "And you shall count for yourselves (לכם)." Just as לכם in the latter verse [signifies that the counting of the *Omer* must be performed] while standing, as clarified in sec. 489[:4], so, too,

---

18. Which will end late in the day.

19. *Pesachim* 4a.

SECTION 585

1. The obligation to stand while fulfilling certain *mitzvos* originated in the Talmudic era (see end of this subsection), but is not stated in the *Talmud*. A few centuries thereafter, the *Rishonim* sought to buttress this obligation by a Scriptural underpinning (an *asmachta*). The Scriptural allusion described in the above text follows the Talmudic interpretative technique called *gezeirah shavah*, i.e., an analogy between two laws which was handed down by the Oral Tradition, and which is established on the basis of identical expressions in the Biblical text.

2. *Bamidbar* 29:1.

3. *Vayikra* 23:15.

לז לבוש ס"ד. לח פסחים ד, א. לבוש שם. לט הגהות אשרי ר"ה פ"א סי' ה. שו"ע ס"ד. מ ר"ה טז, א. הובא לקמן סי' תקפו ס"ב. מא ראה תרומת הדשן סי' רסו. לבוש שם. עי' ט"ז סק"ב. מב כנסת הגדולה הגב"י. הובא במ"א סק"ז. וראה לקמן סי' תרכא ס"ג.

סימן תקפה: א הגהת סמ"ק סי' צב אות ה. טור ושו"ע ס"א. וראה ארחות חיים הל' ציצית סי' כז, בשם הירושלמי (לעמוד לשרת כו' בעשותנו המצות). ב במדבר כט, א. ג ויקרא כג, טו. ד סעיף ד. ה הגהת סמ"ק שם. טור ולבוש ס"א. ט"ז סק"א. ו מהרי"ל הל' שופר (ע' רפח). דרכי משה ס"ק א. מ"א סק"א.

in the former verse [does it signify that the *shofar* must be sounded] while standing.

Accordingly, [while sounding the *shofar*, one] should not lean on any object in such a way that he would fall if it were to be removed. [Such a stance] is called leaning, not standing. Nevertheless, if one transgressed and sounded the *shofar* even while sitting, he has fulfilled his obligation and need not sound the *shofar* again while standing. For [the obligation to] stand [at this point] is merely Talmudic in origin, as explained in sec. 8[:4,] and sec. 489[:4]; see that source.

מְעֻמָּד.[ה] וּלְפִיכָךְ לֹא יִסְמֹךְ עַל שׁוּם דָּבָר בְּעִנְיָן שֶׁאִם יִנָּטֵל אוֹתוֹ דָּבָר שֶׁסָּמַךְ עָלָיו הָיָה נוֹפֵל,[ו] שֶׁאֵין זוֹ עֲמִידָה אֶלָּא סְמִיכָה.[ז] וּמִכָּל מָקוֹם אִם עָבַר וְתָקַע אֲפִלּוּ מְיֻשָּׁב – יָצָא,[ח] וְאֵין צָרִיךְ לַחֲזֹר וְלִתְקֹעַ מְעֻמָּד, לְפִי שֶׁעֲמִידָה זוֹ אֵינָהּ אֶלָּא מִדִּבְרֵי סוֹפְרִים כְּמוֹ שֶׁנִּתְבָּאֵר בְּסִימָן ח'[ט] וּבְסִימָן תפ"ט[י] עַיֵּן שָׁם:

2 Those who listen to the *shofar* blasts need not stand, even if they have not yet fulfilled their obligation.[4]

ב הַשּׁוֹמְעִין הַתְּקִיעוֹת אַף עַל פִּי שֶׁעֲדַיִן לֹא יָצְאוּ יְדֵי חוֹבָתָן[יא,4] – אַף עַל פִּי כֵן אֵינָן צְרִיכִים לַעֲמֹד:[יב]

3 It is customary to sound the *shofar* on the reader's platform from which the Torah is read.[5] It is appropriate to appoint a person who is righteous and honorable [to sound the *shofar*. The choice should be made, however,] in a manner that will avert contention.

ג נוֹהֲגִים לִתְקֹעַ עַל הַבִּימָה[יג] בְּמָקוֹם שֶׁקּוֹרִין.[יד,5] וְרָאוּי לִתֵּן לִתְקֹעַ לְצַדִּיק וְהָגוּן, וּבִלְבַד שֶׁלֹּא יְהֵא מַחֲלֹקֶת בַּדָּבָר:[טו]

4 Before sounding the *shofar*, while standing, [the person sounding the *shofar*] should recite the blessing [aloud]:[6] "[Blessed are You…] Who has sanctified us with His commandments and has commanded us to

ד קֹדֶם שֶׁיִּתְקַע יְבָרֵךְ[טז,6] מְעֻמָּד[יז] "אֲשֶׁר קִדְּשָׁנוּ בְּמִצְוֹתָיו וְצִוָּנוּ

---

4. And are intending to do so with the present *shofar* blasts.

It is not imperative to stand when listening to these *shofar* blasts, but it has become universal custom to do so. Nevertheless, these blasts are still called *tekios meyushav* — "the *shofar* blasts [during which] one may sit," because of the leniency originally granted.

In contrast, all are obligated to stand while the *shofar* is sounded during the *Shemoneh Esreh* of *Mussaf* (sec. 592:2); hence the name, *tekios me'umad* — "the *shofar* blasts [during which] one stands."

5. I.e., the *bimah*.

Citing the statement of Rav Saadiah Gaon, that the sounding of the *shofar* recalls the sound of the *shofar* at Mount Sinai, *Likkutei Sichos* explains (Vol. 39, p. 43) that we allude to this link by sounding the *shofar* immediately after the Torah Reading. See sec. 592:9 below.

6. The listeners should intend to fulfill their obligation to recite this blessing (and the blessing *Shehecheyanu* spoken of in the next subsection) by listening to the person sounding the *shofar* and responding *Amen*.

וראה גם לעיל סי' צד סוף ס"ח. לקמן סי' תרז ס"ז. **ז** ראה מ"א סי' קמא סק"ב. רמ"א חו"מ סי' יז סוף ס"א ובנו"כ שם. **ח** מ"א סק"א. **ט** סעיף ד. **י** סעיף ד. **יא** היינו כשלא שמע בתפלת מעומד ועתה בא לשמוע. ראה לבוש ס"א. כנסת הגדולה הגה"ט. מ"א סוף סק"א. **יב** רי"ף ר"ה פ"ד (י, ב). רמב"ם הל' שופר פ"ג ה"י. הגהת סמ"ק שם. **יג** דרכי משה ס"ק א. רמ"א ס"א. וראה לקמן סי' תקצב ס"ט (שהוא מפני כבוד הצבור). העו"ב תרלט ע' 14. **יד** רמ"א שם. וראה לקו"ש חל"ט ע' 43 הערה 1. **טו** עטרת זקנים בשם ספר חסידים סי' תשסא. **טז** סדר רב עמרם גאון. רי"ף ורמב"ם שם. ראבי"ה סי' תקלד בשם הירושלמי. טור ושו"ע ס"ב. **יז** רמב"ם הל' שופר פ"ג ה"י. וראה גם לעיל סי' ח ס"ג, וש"נ.

לִשְׁמֹעַ קוֹל שׁוֹפָר", וְלֹא יֹאמַר "בְּקוֹל שׁוֹפָר" דְּמַשְׁמַע לְצַיֵּת לְקוֹל הַשּׁוֹפָר.[יח] וְלָמָּה אֵין מְבָרְכִין "לִתְקֹעַ בְּשׁוֹפָר", לְפִי שֶׁהַתְּקִיעָה אֵינָהּ עִקַּר הַמִּצְוָה אֶלָּא שְׁמִיעַת קוֹל שׁוֹפָר הוּא עִקַּר הַמִּצְוָה,[יט] שֶׁהֲרֵי הַתּוֹקֵעַ וְלֹא שָׁמַע קוֹל שׁוֹפָר לֹא יָצָא[כ] כְּמוֹ שֶׁ[יִּ]תְבָּאֵר בְּסִימָן תקפ"ז[כא] עַיֵּן שָׁם. וּמִכָּל מָקוֹם אִם עָבַר אוֹ טָעָה וּבֵרַךְ "לִתְקֹעַ בְּשׁוֹפָר"[כב] אוֹ "עַל תְּקִיעַת שׁוֹפָר"[כג] — יָצָא:

hear the sound of the *shofar*" לשמוע קול שופר. He should not say לשמוע בקול שופר, for that would imply "to heed the sound of the *shofar*."

Why do we not say, "to sound the *shofar*"? Because the essence of the *mitzvah* is not to sound the *shofar* but to hear it. [This principle is exemplified by the ruling in] sec. 587[:2], that a person who sounded the *shofar* but did not hear its blasts has not fulfilled his obligation. Nevertheless, if one transgressed or erred and [concluded] the blessing [with the words] "to sound the *shofar*" or "concerning the sounding of the *shofar*," he has fulfilled his obligation.

ה וְאַחַר בְּרָכָה זוֹ יְבָרֵךְ שֶׁהֶחֱיָנוּ,[כד,7] לְפִי שֶׁהִיא מִצְוָה הַבָּאָ[ה] מִזְּמַן לִזְמַן.[כה] וְאֶחָד הַתּוֹקֵעַ לְעַצְמוֹ וְאֶחָד מִי שֶׁיָּצָא יְדֵי חוֹבָתוֹ וְתוֹקֵעַ לְהוֹצִיא אֲחֵרִים יְדֵי חוֹבָתָן — מְבָרֵךְ שְׁתֵּי בְּרָכוֹת אֵלּוּ.[כו] בַּמֶּה דְּבָרִים אֲמוּרִים? כְּשֶׁאֵין הַשּׁוֹמֵעַ יוֹדֵעַ לְבָרֵךְ, אֲבָל אִם הוּא יוֹדֵעַ לְבָרֵךְ — יְבָרֵךְ בְּעַצְמוֹ,[כז] וְלֹא יִשְׁמַע מִמִּי שֶׁכְּבָר יָצָא יְדֵי חוֹבָתוֹ[8] כְּמוֹ שֶׁנִּתְבָּאֵר בְּסִימָן רע"ג,[כח] עַיֵּן שָׁם:[9]

5 After reciting this blessing, [the person sounding the *shofar*] should recite the blessing *Shehecheyanu*,[7] because the *mitzvah* [of sounding the *shofar*] comes only from time to time. These two blessings should be recited both by one who is sounding the *shofar* to fulfill his own obligation, and by one who has fulfilled his own obligation and is sounding the *shofar* to enable others to fulfill their obligations.

When does the [latter case] apply? When the listener does not know how to recite the blessings. If, however, he knows how to recite the blessings, he should recite them himself instead of hearing them from someone who has already fulfilled his obligation,[8] as clarified in sec. 273[:6]; see that source.[9]

---

7. The blessing that thanks G-d for preserving us in life until the present time.

8. If the person sounding the *shofar* has not yet fulfilled his obligation, he should recite the blessings on behalf of all the listeners. Different rules apply when a man sounds the *shofar* for women; see sec. 589:2.

9. There the Alter Rebbe writes that one may recite *Kiddush* on behalf of others, even though he is not fulfilling his own obligation for *Kiddush* at that time. Why? The Jewish people share bonds of mutual responsibility (*areivus* — lit., "guarantorship"). Hence, when one individual has not fulfilled a *mitzvah*, every other Jew — even one who has already fulfilled the *mitzvah* — is responsible that this fellow Jew fulfill it. (Cf. *Rashi* on *Rosh HaShanah* 29a, *s.v. Af-al-pi.*) Accordingly, he may recite the blessing on his behalf. (See sec. 187:23 above.)

יח ב"ח ד"ה ומ"ש יברך. ט"ז סק"ב. מ"א סק"ב. יט ראב"ן סי' לה. ראבי"ה שם. רא"ש פ"ד סוס"י י. טור ולבוש ס"ב. עולת שבת סק"א. ט"ז סק"ב. וראה לקמן תקפו ס"ד. סי' תקפח ס"ו (במוסגר) וס"ז. קובץ כינוס תורה ח"ג ע' סז. פעמי יעקב מא ע' קיד. כ ראב"ן וראבי"ה ורא"ש שם. טור ולבוש שם. כא סעי' ב־ג. כב ב"ח שם. מ"א שם. כג ראה רא"ש שם בשם ר"ת. לעיל סי' תלב ס"ד. כד סדר רב עמרם גאון. ראבי"ה שם בשם הירושלמי. רמב"ם הל' שופר פ"ג ה"י. טור ושו"ע ס"ב. כה עירובין מ, ב. רמב"ם הל' ברכות פי"א ה"ט. וכדלעיל סי' תלב ס"ג וש"נ. כו רמ"א ס"ב. ב"י ד"ה כתב הרמב"ם. כז מ"א סק"ג. כח סעיף ו. כט רמב"ם הל'

6 After reciting these two blessings, *tekiah-shevarim-teruah-tekiah* should be sounded three times, *tekiah-shevarim-tekiah* three times, and *tekiah-teruah-tekiah* three times, as will be explained in sec. 590[:1-2]; see that source.

If one is in doubt whether he heard the sounding of the *shofar* [properly] on the first day of Rosh HaShanah, when the requirement to hear it is of Scriptural origin, he must [hear the] sounding [of the *shofar* again]. He should not recite a blessing, however, because whenever there is a doubt [as to whether or not] a blessing [should be recited], we rule leniently; [i.e., the blessing should not be recited].[10] On the second day of Rosh HaShanah, [when the requirement to hear the sounding of the *shofar*] is merely Rabbinic in origin, there is no need to [hear the] sounding [of the *shofar* a second time], because whenever there is a doubt with regard to a Rabbinic obligation, we rule leniently.

It is preferable to sound the *shofar* from the right side of the mouth if that is possible,[11] for it is written,[12] "Satan was standing at his right side" — and Satan is confounded by the blasts of the *shofar*.[13]

ו וְאַחַר שֶׁבֵּרַךְ שְׁתֵּי בְּרָכוֹת אֵלּוּ יִתְקַע תשר"ת ג' פְּעָמִים וְתש"ת ג' פְּעָמִים וְתר"ת ג' פְּעָמִים,[כט] כְּמוֹ שֶׁיִּתְבָּאֵר בְּסִימָן תק"צ,[ל] עַיֵּן שָׁם.

מִי שֶׁנִּסְתַּפֵּק לוֹ אִם שָׁמַע קוֹל שׁוֹפָר בְּיוֹם רִאשׁוֹן שֶׁל רֹאשׁ הַשָּׁנָה שֶׁהוּא מִן הַתּוֹרָה — צָרִיךְ לִתְקֹעַ, אֲבָל לֹא יְבָרֵךְ שֶׁסְּפֵק בְּרָכוֹת לְהָקֵל,[10] וְאִם הוּא בְּיוֹם שֵׁנִי שֶׁאֵינוֹ אֶלָּא מִדִּבְרֵי סוֹפְרִים — אֵין צָרִיךְ לִתְקֹעַ,[לא] דִּסְפֵק דִּבְרֵי סוֹפְרִים לְהָקֵל.

טוֹב[לב] לִתְקֹעַ בְּצַד יָמִין[לג] שֶׁל פִּיו[לד] אִם אֶפְשָׁר לוֹ בְּכָךְ,[לה,11] מִשּׁוּם שֶׁנֶּאֱמַר[לו,12] "וְהַשָּׂטָן עוֹמֵד עַל יְמִינוֹ", וְהַתְּקִיעָה מְעַרְבֶּבֶת הַשָּׂטָן:[לז,13]

7 It is desirable that the mouth of the *shofar* be pointed upward rather than to the side, in the spirit of the phrase,[14] "G-d ascends through the sounding [of the *shofar*]."

ז וְטוֹב שֶׁיַּעֲמִיד פֶּה הַשּׁוֹפָר לְמַעְלָה[לח] וְלֹא יַטֶּנּוּ לִצְדָדִים,[לט] שֶׁנֶּאֱמַר[מ,14] "עָלָה אֱלֹהִים בִּתְרוּעָה וגו'":

8 If one began sounding the *shofar* and was unable to complete all 30 *shofar* blasts,[15]

ח אִם הִתְחִיל לִתְקֹעַ וְלֹא יָכוֹל לְהַשְׁלִים כָּל הַשְּׁלֹשִׁים תְּקִיעוֹת[15]

Nevertheless, as stated in the present work (in the above-cited sources and in sec. 8:11), with regard to *Kiddush* and other blessings, this leniency is granted only when the person for whom the blessing is being recited does not know how to recite the blessing himself.

10. For fear of reciting a blessing in vain. A blessing that is not required is in fact not permitted.

11. This applies even to a left-handed person *(Shaar HaTziyun* 585:18*)*.

12. *Zechariah* 3:1; see also *Tehillim* 109:6.

13. *Rosh HaShanah* 16b.

14. *Tehillim* 47:6.

15. Sec. 590:1-2 explains why 30 blasts are required.

שופר פ"ג ה"ג. טור ושו"ע ס"ב. **ל** סעי' א־ב. **לא** כנסת הגדולה הגה"ט. מ"א סוף סק"ג. **לב** בקונטרס השלחן כתב שכאן מתחיל ס"ז. **לג** מנהגים (טירנא) ר"ה (ע' צו). רמ"א ס"ב. **לד** מ"א סק"ד. **לה** רמ"א שם. **לו** זכריה ג, א. מנהגים שם. מ"א שם. **לז** ראה ר"ה טז, רע"ב. לקמן סי' תקצב ס"ז (במוסגר). משנה ברורה שעה"צ אות יח. לקו"ש חכ"ד ע' 223 והערה 18. שלחן המלך ח"ב ע' קצג־קצד. **לח** רוקח סוס"י רא. מהרי"ל הל' שופר (ע' רפח). רמ"א ס"ב. **לט** מ"א סק"ה. **מ** תהלים מז, ו.

– יִתְקַע אַחֵר תַּחְתָּיו, וְאִם גַּם הַשֵּׁנִי אֵינוֹ יָכוֹל לְהַשְׁלִים – יַשְׁלִים אַחֵר תַּחְתָּיו, וְכֵן לְעוֹלָם. וְכֻלָּם אֵינָם צְרִיכִים לְבָרֵךְ,[16] לְפִי שֶׁכְּבָר נִפְטְרוּ כֻּלָּם בְּבִרְכַּת הָרִאשׁוֹן.[מא] וַאֲפִלּוּ אִם הָרִאשׁוֹן לֹא הָיָה יָכוֹל לִתְקֹעַ אֲפִלּוּ תְּקִיעָה אַחַת[מב] – אַף עַל פִּי כֵן לֹא הָיְתָה בִּרְכָתוֹ לְבַטָּלָה,[מג] כֵּיוָן שֶׁכַּוָּנָתוֹ הָיְתָה בְּבִרְכָתוֹ לְהוֹצִיא כָּל הַשּׁוֹמְעִין,[17] וְאִם כֵּן הַתּוֹקְעִין אַחֲרוֹנִים וְכָל הַקָּהָל שֶׁשָּׁמְעוּ בִּרְכָתוֹ אֵינָם צְרִיכִים עוֹד לְבָרֵךְ.[מד]

אֲבָל אִם בָּא לִתְקֹעַ תַּחְתָּיו מִי שֶׁלֹּא שָׁמַע בִּרְכָתוֹ – צָרִיךְ לְבָרֵךְ קֹדֶם שֶׁיִּתְקַע,[מה] שֶׁהֲרֵי הוּא לֹא יָצָא בְּבִרְכַּת הָרִאשׁוֹן:[18]

ט בַּמֶּה דְּבָרִים אֲמוּרִים? כְּשֶׁתּוֹקֵעַ זֶה לֹא יָצָא עֲדַיִן יְדֵי חוֹבָתוֹ שֶׁלֹּא שָׁמַע עֲדַיִן כָּל הַתְּקִיעוֹת, אֲבָל אִם כְּבָר יָצָא יְדֵי חוֹבָתוֹ שֶׁשָּׁמַע כְּבָר כָּל הַתְּקִיעוֹת בְּבֵית הַכְּנֶסֶת אַחֶרֶת – אֵינוֹ צָרִיךְ לְבָרֵךְ קֹדֶם שֶׁיִּתְקַע, שֶׁהֲרֵי הַצִּבּוּר שָׁמְעוּ כְּבָר הַבְּרָכָה מִן הַתּוֹקֵעַ הָרִאשׁוֹן:[מו,19]

another person should replace him. If he, too, cannot complete [the *mitzvah*], he should be replaced by still another person, and so on [until the *mitzvah* is completed].

None of these [replacements] are required to recite the blessing,[16] because they all fulfilled their obligation with the blessing recited by the first individual. [Moreover,] even if that individual was unable to sound even one note, his blessing was not recited in vain, because his intent in reciting it was that all the listeners should discharge their obligation.[17] This is why those who sound the *shofar* after him and the congregation who heard his blessing do not have to recite a blessing again.

If, by contrast, he is replaced by a person who did not hear his blessing, that person must recite a blessing before he sounds the *shofar,* because he did not fulfill his obligation with the blessing recited by the first individual.[18]

9 When does this apply? When the person sounding the *shofar* has not fulfilled his own obligation, for he has not heard the sounding of the *shofar* at all. If, however, he heard the sounding of all the *shofar* blasts in another synagogue, he is not required to recite a blessing before he sounds the *shofar,* because the congregation already heard the blessings from the first person who [attempted to] sound the *shofar*.[19]

16. And hence, they should not do so.

17. To hear the blasts of the *shofar,* not that he should sound the *shofar.*

18. Moreover, in order to fulfill his own obligation, he must begin the sequence of *shofar* blasts from the beginning.

19. This issue is discussed in detail in *Kuntreis Acharon,* gloss #5 to sec. 263 and gloss #2 to sec. 432.

מא מ"מ פ"ג הי"א בשם רבנו האי. ראבי"ה סי' תקנב (ע' 263) בשם כמה פוסקים. רא"ש פ"ד סוס"י יא. טור בשם ר"י. שו"ע ס"ג. **מב** רא"ש שם. טור ושו"ע שם. **מג** טור ושו"ע שם. **מד** ראה ב"י ד"ה ומ"ש רבנו וברכה. לבוש ס"ג. **מה** ב"י סוד"ה ואם. וראה לעיל סי' רסג קו"א סק"ה סוד"ה ומיהו. **מו** עולת שבת ס"ב. אליה זוטא סק"ד. וכ"ה לעיל תלב ס"ט וקו"א שם ס"ק ב (שמוכיח מכאן גם לענין בדיקת חמץ), ודעה הא' דלעיל סי' רסג סט"ו וקו"א ס"ק ה. וראה דעה הב' שם, שגם המחויב לתקוע להם מדין ערבות חייב בברכה (אף שהם כבר בירכו). ומסיק שלא למחות ביד המברכות בהדלקת הנרות, משא"כ בשופר ובדיקת חמץ שאין שם מנהג יש לנהוג שאין לברך. ועוד אופן מבואר לעיל סי' תלב בקו"א שם בהג"ה, שמה שהתוקע כבר שמע התקיעות עם הברכה מועיל

10 It is customary for the *[sheliach tzibbur]* who led the Morning Service to read out the order of the *shofar* blasts word by word for the person sounding the *shofar,* so that he will not err. This is a desirable custom.[20] See also sec. 590.[21]

י נוֹהֲגִין שֶׁהַמִּתְפַּלֵּל שַׁחֲרִית מַקְרִיא סֵדֶר הַתְּקִיעוֹת לִפְנֵי הַתּוֹקֵעַ מִלָּה בְּמִלָּה כְּדֵי שֶׁלֹּא יִטְעֶה בִּתְקִיעוֹתָיו, וּמִנְהָג יָפֶה הוּא.[מז, 20] וְעַיֵּן בְּסִימָן תק״צ:[מח, 21]

11 (It is forbidden to receive payment for sounding the *shofar* on Rosh HaShanah, even if one was hired before the festival began.[22] [The rationale is that] he would be receiving wages for [working on] the festival, and this is forbidden for the reasons explained in sec. 306[:11]; see that source.[23] If one receives payment [for sounding the *shofar*], he will never realize any blessing from that payment.)[24]

יא (אָסוּר לִטֹּל שָׂכָר לִתְקֹעַ שׁוֹפָר בְּרֹאשׁ הַשָּׁנָה אֲפִלּוּ שְׂכָרוּהוּ מֵעֶרֶב יוֹם טוֹב,[22] לְפִי שֶׁהוּא נוֹטֵל שְׂכַר יוֹם טוֹב[מט] וְאָסוּר מִטַּעַם שֶׁנִּתְבָּאֵר בְּסִימָן ש״ו[נ] עַיֵּן שָׁם.[23] וְאִם נָטַל — אֵינוֹ רוֹאֶה סִימַן בְּרָכָה[נא] מֵאוֹתוֹ שָׂכָר[נב] לְעוֹלָם):[24]

20. This is not the custom in Lubavitch *(Otzar Minhagei Chabad: Elul-Tishrei,* p. 120). Moreover, *Sefer HaMinhagim* states that according to Lubavitch custom, the person (called the *makri*) who guides the individual sounding the *shofar* (the *tokeia*) does not actually voice the names of the required *shofar* blasts, but simply points to them in the *Siddur,* one by one.

21. That section deals with the required length of the *shofar* blasts and the order in which they must be sounded.

22. And thus no transaction was conducted on that day.

23. There the Alter Rebbe states that it is forbidden to receive payment specifically for an activity performed on *Shabbos* or a festival. He adds that many authorities — and indeed, this is common practice — take a lenient approach and permit hiring a person for such activities, because a *mitzvah* is involved and the prohibition is merely a safeguard for a Rabbinic ordinance. Furthermore, there is an option of hiring the person to provide ongoing services for the community including some that are performed on weekdays. In such an instance, the sounding of the *shofar* is not being paid for separately as a distinct task. A global payment of this kind — which is also common in the case of *chazzanim,* for example — is permitted by all authorities.

24. Cf. *Pesachim* 50b. The Alter Rebbe adds that whatever this individual gains by this means he will lose by some other means (sec. 468:3).

In the original, the whole of subsection 11 is enclosed by parentheses. In a letter appearing in *Igros Kodesh,* Vol. 2, p. 140, the Rebbe writes that parentheses in this work possibly indicate a matter which the Alter Rebbe desired to reconsider at a later date. (See *She'eris Yehudah,* Responsum 363, and *Shaar HaKollel* 1:2.) The doubt in this case possibly involved the diverse views as to whether payment may be made for an activity performed on *Shabbos* because it is required for the fulfillment of a *mitzvah.*

גם לתקיעות אלו. וראה קובץ יגדיל תורה (נ.י.) ב ע׳ לח. ו ע׳ נו. **מז** דרכי משה ס״ק ב. רמ״א ס״ד. מ״א סקי״א. ומנהג חב״ד שאינו מקריא בדיבור אלא מורה באצבעו בסידור (ספר המנהגים – חב״ד ע׳ 56). **מח** סעי׳ טו־יט (אם טעה בסדר התקיעות). **מט** טור בשם אחיו ה״ר יחיאל (ד״ח). מרדכי כתובות רמז קפט בשם ה״ר ברוך. **נ** סעיף יא. ושם הביא שיש אומרים שבמקום מצוה לא גזרו (כדעת המרדכי כתובות רמז קפט בשם ה״ר שמואל) ושכן המנהג להקל. וראה גם לעיל סי׳ תקכו סי״ד. וראה חקרי הלכות ח״א לב, ב. **נא** פסחים נ, ב (שכר המתורגמנין). ב״י ד״ה ולא ידעתי (לדעת המתירים). שו״ע ס״ה. מ״א ס״ק יב (לדעת המתירים). וכ״ה לעיל סי׳ שו (לדעת המתירים). **נב** ראה לעיל סי׳ רנא ס״א. סי׳ תסח ס״ג וש״נ.

סימן תקפו דִּינֵי שׁוֹפָר שֶׁל רֹאשׁ הַשָּׁנָה וּבוֹ כ"ז סְעִיפִים:

א שׁוֹפָר שֶׁל רֹאשׁ הַשָּׁנָה מִצְוָתוֹ שֶׁיִּהְיֶה כָּפוּף,[א,1] כְּדֵי שֶׁיִּכְפְּפוּ אֶת לִבָּם לְהַקָּדוֹשׁ בָּרוּךְ הוּא בַּתְּפִלָּה.[ב]

וְכָל הַשּׁוֹפָרוֹת הַכְּפוּפִין[2] כְּשֵׁרִים[3] חוּץ מִשֶּׁל פָּרָה[ג] וְשֶׁל שׁוֹר,[ד] מִפְּנֵי שֶׁאֵינוֹ נִקְרָא שׁוֹפָר אֶלָּא קֶרֶן,[ה] שֶׁנֶּאֱמַר[ו,4] "בְּכוֹר שׁוֹרוֹ וגו' וְקַרְנֵי רְאֵם קַרְנָיו",[5] וְהוּא הַדִּין קַרְנֵי רֹב הַחַיּוֹת שֶׁהֵם עֶצֶם אֶחָד[ז] וְאֵין שְׁמָם שׁוֹפָר, שֶׁאֵין נִקְרָא שׁוֹפָר אֶלָּא קַרְנַיִם הַחֲלוּלִים שֶׁיֵּשׁ לָהֶם זַכְרוּת בִּפְנִים וְנִקְלָף[7] גִּידָן[ח] מִן הַזַּכְרוּת,[ט,6] כְּגוֹן שֶׁל כְּבָשִׂים וְאֵילִים וְעִזִּים,[י] כִּי שׁוֹפָר הוּא מִלְּשׁוֹן שְׁפוֹפֶרֶת,[יא,8] אֲבָל קַרְנֵי רֹב הַחַיּוֹת[9] הֵם עֶצֶם אֶחָד וּפְסוּלִין אֲפִלּוּ בְּדִיעֲבַד כְּמוֹ שֶׁל פָּרָה וְשֶׁל שׁוֹר:[10]

ב וּמִצְוָה מִן הַמֻּבְחָר לִתְקֹעַ בְּשׁוֹפָר שֶׁל אַיִל[יב] כְּדֵי שֶׁיִּזָּכֵר לָנוּ עֲקֵדַת

SECTION 586 Laws Relating to the Shofar Used on Rosh HaShanah. (1–27)

1 [For optimal fulfillment of] the *mitzvah,* the *shofar* [sounded] on Rosh HaShanah should be curved,[1] [as a reminder that people] should bend their hearts [in submission] to the Holy One, blessed be He, in prayer.

All curved *Shofaros*[2] are valid[3] except those of a cow and an ox, for their [outgrowth] is not called a *shofar* but a *keren* ("horn"), as implied by the verse,[4] "Like a firstborn ox..., his horns are like the horns of a wild ox."[5] Similarly [excluded] is the horn of most beasts, which is bone[-like] and monolithic. This is not called a *shofar,* for that term refers only to a hollow horn, inside which there is a solid protrusion whose outer layer[6] can be peeled off.[7] This is the case with sheep, rams, and goats. For the word *shofar* derives from *shfoferes* [meaning "tube"].[8] In contrast, the horns of most beasts[9] are bone[-like] and monolithic, and are unacceptable, even after the fact, like those of a cow or an ox.[10]

2 The choicest [way to perform] the *mitzvah* is to sound a ram's horn, so that G-d

---

1. *Rosh HaShanah* 26b.

2. Plural of *shofar.* In popular Ashkenazic pronunciation, the middle syllable of *shofaros* is commonly elided *("shofros").*

3. *Rosh HaShanah* 26a.

4. *Devarim* 33:17.

5. In the original, *re'em,* also translated as antelope, aurochs, bison, rhinoceros, unicorn, *et al.* The ox *(shor)* and the wild ox *(re'em)* are similar species; one of their differences is that the horns of the wild ox are more imposing. The inference here is that in both species the horn is not called a *shofar* but a *keren.*

6. In the original, *gidan* ("their sinew") should read *gildan* ("their outer layer"); see *Kuntreis HaShulchan.*

7. The rough filling of woodlike texture is separated from the tough outer shell of a ram's horn by a thin jelly-like layer. After heating, the inner protrusion can be pulled out, and the remaining outer shell constitutes the *shofar* proper.

8. See subsection 15.

9. E.g., deer.

10. According to Scriptural Law, they may never be used to fulfill the *mitzvah (Mishnah Berurah* 586:7).

א רבי לוי בגמרא כו, ב. טור ושו"ע ס"א. ב ירושלמי ר"ה פ"ג ה"ד. טור ולבוש ס"א. ג משנה כו, א. טור ושו"ע שם. ד מ"א סק"ב. ה גמרא שם. מ"א שם. ו דברים לג, יז. גמרא שם. לבוש שם. ז תוס' שם ד"ה חוץ. רמב"ן שם ד"ה ולי נראה. טור ושו"ע שם. ח בקונטרס השלחן הגיה: גילדן. ט רמב"ן שם. וראה גם לקמן סט"ו. י טור. יא ר"ן (ו, א) ד"ה וכתבו. לבוש שם. יב רבי אבהו בגמרא טז, א. רא"ש פ"ג סי' א. טור (מצוה מן המובחר) ושו"ע ס"א (מצותו).

יִצְחָק,[יג] אֲבָל אִם אֵין לוֹ שׁוֹפָר שֶׁל אַיִל – יוֹצֵא בִּשְׁאָר מִינִים,[יד,11] חוּץ מִשֶּׁל פָּרָה וְכַיּוֹצֵא בוֹ,[טו] וַאֲפִלּוּ בְּפָשׁוּט[12] אִם אֵין לוֹ כָּפוּף,[טז] שֶׁלֹּא אָמְרוּ כָּפוּף אֶלָּא לְכַתְּחִלָּה,[13] אֲבָל בְּדִיעֲבַד[יז,14] אִם תָּקַע בְּפָשׁוּט – יָצָא, וְזֶה שֶׁאֵין לוֹ כָּפוּף – הֲרֵי זֶה כְּדִיעֲבַד:[יח]

should recall the Binding of Yitzchak for our merit. If one does not have a ram's horn,[11] he may fulfill his obligation with the horns of other animals, except those of a cow or the like.

[Moreover,] if he does not have a curved horn, he may use even a straight horn.[12] For a curved horn is recommended only as the initial, preferred option;[13] after the fact,[14] one who sounds a straight horn fulfills his obligation. When one does not have a curved *[shofar]*, this is considered as after the fact.

ג שׁוֹפָר מִבְּהֵמָה טְמֵאָה[15] יֵשׁ לְפָסְלוֹ[יט,16] אֲפִלּוּ בְּדִיעֲבַד,[כ] לְפִי שֶׁלֹּא הֻכְשְׁרוּ לִמְלֶאכֶת שָׁמַיִם[17] אֶלָּא טְהוֹרִים בִּלְבַד:[כא]

3 A *shofar* from a non-kosher species[15] should be considered invalid,[16] even after the fact, for only kosher species of animals are fit to be used for our Divine service.[17]

ד הַגּוֹזֵל[18] שׁוֹפָר וְתָקַע בּוֹ – יָצָא,[כב] אֲפִלּוּ לֹא נִתְיָאֲשׁוּ הַבְּעָלִים מִמֶּנּוּ,[כג,19] וְאֵינוֹ דּוֹמֶה לְלוּלָב[כד,20] וּמַצָּה[כה,21] וְצִיצִית[כו,22] הַגְּזוּלִים, לְפִי שֶׁמִּצְוַת הַשּׁוֹפָר[כז] אֵינוֹ אֶלָּא הַשְּׁמִיעָה בִּלְבַד,

4 If one stole[18] a *shofar* and sounded it, he has fulfilled his obligation, even if the owner has not despaired of its recovery.[19] [Its status] differs from that of a stolen *lulav*,[20] *matzah*,[21] or *tzitzis*,[22] because the *mitzvah* of the *shofar* involves hearing alone. No concept

---

11. A gloss of *Turei Zahav* (586:1) observes that a ewe's horn also recalls the Binding of Yitzchak, because it is of the same species. If a ram's horn is not available, it should be used rather than a *shofar* from a goat or other species.

12. *Turei Zahav (op. cit.)* states that a curved horn from another species is preferable to a straight ram's horn.

13. In the original Hebrew, *lechat'chilah*.

14. In the original Aramaic, *bedia-vad* (popularly mispronounced *bedieved*).

15. By contrast, the horn of an animal of a kosher species that died or was not slaughtered according to the laws of *kashrus* may be used *(Mishnah Berurah* 586:8*)*.

16. Just as *tefillin* may be made of the hide of a kosher animal only (Rabbeinu Nissim).

17. Lit., "for the work of Heaven." See *Shabbos* 28b.

18. Strictly speaking, the root *g-z-l* used here is reserved for taking an object from its owner overtly and by force *(Rambam, Hilchos Geneivah* 1:3*)*, whereas the term *geneivah* is used when the object is taken in stealth. In our context, the distinction is immaterial.

19. Since a stolen object remains the property of its owner so long as he has not despaired of recovering it, one might assume that it could not be used for a *mitzvah* without his permission.

20. See sec. 649:4-7.

21. See sec. 454:9-11.

22. See sec. 11:11-12.

ב"י ד"ה ומ"ש רבנו נמצא. ט"ז סק"א (מצוה מן המובחר). **יג** גמרא שם. רא"ש וטור וט"ז שם. מ"א ס"ק א. **יד** רא"ש שם. טור וב"י ד"ה והשתא. **טו** כדלעיל ס"א. **טז** טור. **יז** רא"ש שם. טור ושו"ע שם. **יח** ב"י שם. **יט** ר"ן (ו, א) ד"ה ומיהו (שמסתפק). דרכי משה ס"ק א (טוב להחמיר). רמ"א ס"א (פסול). **כ** אליה זוטא סק"ב. **כא** שבת כח, ב. ר"ן שם. לבוש סוף ס"א. מ"א ס"ק ג. וראה גם לעיל סי' לב סי"ד וש"נ. **כב** גמרא כח, א (שלא אסרו אלא בכתותי מיכתת שיעוריה, וכדלקמן ס"ה). ירושלמי סוכה פ"ג ה"א, כרבי אלעזר ורבי חייא ורבי יוסה (ראה ב"י ד"ה כתבו הגהות אשירי). רמב"ם פ"א ה"ג. רא"ש פ"ג סי' ט. טור ושו"ע ס"ב. **כג** טור ושו"ע שם. **כד** כדלקמן סי' תרמט ס"ד. **כה** כדלעיל סי' תנד ס"ט. **כו** כדלעיל סי' יא סי"א. **כז** ראה לעיל סי' תקפה ס"ד.

וְאֵין בִּשְׁמִיעַת קוֹל דִּין גָּזֵל, שֶׁהֲרֵי בִּשְׁמִיעָתוֹ אֵינוֹ נוֹגֵעַ בַּשּׁוֹפָר כְּלָל, וּלְפִיכָךְ אַף עַל פִּי שֶׁתָּקַע בּוֹ בְּאִסּוּר גָּזֵל, כֵּיוָן שֶׁבְּעִקַּר הַמִּצְוָה דְּהַיְנוּ הַשְּׁמִיעָה אֵין בָּהּ אִסּוּר גָּזֵל — יָצָא יְדֵי חוֹבָתוֹ.[כח]

וּמִכָּל מָקוֹם, כֵּיוָן שֶׁעַל יְדֵי גָּזֵל בָּאָה הַמִּצְוָה אֵלָיו — לֹא יְבָרֵךְ עָלֶיהָ, כְּדִין מִצְוָה הַבָּאָה בַּעֲבֵרָה[כט] שֶׁנִּתְבָּאֵר בְּסִימָן י"א[ל] וּבְסִימָן תרמ"ט[לא,23] עַיֵּן שָׁם:

of theft is involved here, for when hearing the sound one does not touch the *shofar* at all. Therefore, even though sounding such a *shofar* involves the prohibition against theft, since the essence of the *mitzvah* — hearing [the *shofar* blast] — does not contravene a prohibition against theft, the person fulfills his obligation.

Nevertheless, since the fulfillment of the *mitzvah* came about through theft, one should not recite a blessing over it, as is the law with regard to [any] *mitzvah* that is made possible by a sin, as explained in sec. 11[:11,] and sec. 649[:5].[23]

ה מֻתָּר לִטֹּל שׁוֹפָר שֶׁל חֲבֵרוֹ שֶׁלֹּא מִדַּעְתּוֹ לִתְקֹעַ בּוֹ תְּקִיעָה שֶׁל מִצְוָה וּמְבָרֵךְ עָלָיו,[לב] דִּמִן הַסְּתָם נוֹחַ לוֹ לְאָדָם שֶׁיֵּעָשׂוּ מִצְוָה בְּמָמוֹנוֹ בְּדָבָר שֶׁאֵין בּוֹ חֶסְרוֹן כִּיס כְּמוֹ שֶׁנִּתְבָּאֵר בְּסִימָן י"ד[לג,24] עַיֵּן שָׁם:

5 It is permitted to take a *shofar* belonging to another without his knowledge in order to sound it as required by the *mitzvah,* and the blessing may be recited. [The rationale is] that it is assumed that a person is willing to allow a *mitzvah* to be performed with his property provided he does not suffer a loss, as stated in sec. 14[:9-13].[24]

ו הַתּוֹקֵעַ בְּשׁוֹפָר שֶׁל עֲבוֹדָה זָרָה שֶׁל יִשְׂרָאֵל,[לד] כְּגוֹן שֶׁהִשְׁתַּחֲוָה לְהַשּׁוֹפָר[לה,25] — לֹא יָצָא,[26] מִשּׁוּם דְּשׁוֹפָר צָרִיךְ שֶׁיְּהֵא בּוֹ טֶפַח כְּמוֹ שֶׁיִּתְבָּאֵר,[לו,27]

6 If one sounded a *shofar* owned by a Jew who worships it as a false deity by prostrating himself before it, for example,[25] he has not fulfilled his obligation.[26] [The rationale is that] the *shofar* must be at least a handbreadth long, as will be explained.[27] Since this *shofar*

---

23. Despite his ongoing financial liability to the original owner, a thief may become the legal owner of wool for *tzitzis* or a *lulav* by causing it to undergo a major change. It may therefore be used for the fulfillment of its *mitzvah,* but the theft that made this possible renders a blessing inappropriate. Regarding such situations, *Bava Kama* 94a interprets *Tehillim* 10:3 as, "A robber who recites a blessing blasphemes G-d."

24. From those laws it is apparent that the *shofar* should not be removed from the building in which it is kept, it should be returned to its original spot after use, and of course should be handled with care.

25. The same laws apply if the *shofar* had been sounded in the service of a false deity *(Mishnah Berurah* 586:10).

26. *Chullin* 89a. In contrast, if such a *shofar* belonged to a non-Jew, the *Shulchan Aruch (Orach Chayim* 586:3) rules that one should not sound it to fulfill the *mitzvah,* but if one did so, he has fulfilled his obligation. The *Rama* maintains that this is possible only if the non-Jew nullified the association of the *shofar* with idol worship before the festival began.

27. See subsection 13 below.

כח רבי אלעזר בירושלמי שם. רמב"ם ומגיד משנה שם. מ"א ס"ק ד. **כט** מ"א שם. וראה שדי חמד אס"ד מערכת ר"ה סי' ב אות ל. יגדיל תורה (נ.י.) נה ע' שנז. **ל** סעיף יב. **לא** ס"ה. וכן בסימן תנד ס"י. **לב** מ"א סק"ד. **לג** ס"ט, וש"נ. **לד** גמרא חולין פט, סוע"א. רא"ש פ"ג סי' ט. טור ושו"ע ס"ג. **לה** ראה לעיל סי' יא סי"ג (כשהשתחווה במחובר לבעלי חיים). לקמן סי' תרמט סי"א (שקנה אותה מיד עובדיה). **לו** סעיף יג. **לז** סימן זה בשוע"ר לא הגיע לידינו, וראה

וְזֶה שֶׁהוּא עוֹמֵד לִשָּׂרֵף,[28] שֶׁהֲרֵי עֲבוֹדָה זָרָה שֶׁל יִשְׂרָאֵל אֲפִלּוּ אִם יְבַטְּלֶנָּה גּוֹי אֵינָהּ מְבֻטֶּלֶת כְּמוֹ שֶׁיִּתְבָּאֵר בְּיוֹרֶה דֵעָה סִימָן קל״ט,[לז, 29] וְצָרִיךְ לִשְׂרֵפָה, וְכָל הָעוֹמֵד לִשָּׂרֵף הֲרֵי הוּא כִּכְבָר נִשְׂרָף, וְאִם כֵּן אֵין בּוֹ שִׁעוּר[לח] טֶפַח:[30]

is a false deity belonging to a Jew, it is due to be destroyed by fire[28] — for a false deity belonging to a Jew can never be nullified even if a non-Jew [seeks to] nullify it, as stated in [the *Shulchan Aruch,*] *Yoreh Deah,* sec. 139.[29] Instead it must be destroyed by fire. And since it is due to be destroyed by fire, it is considered as if it had already been destroyed. Thus it does not possess the required measure of one handbreadth.[30]

חָסֵר[לט, 31]

Part of the text is missing.[31]

ז וְכֵן הַדִּין[מ, 32] אִם הַסֶּדֶק הוּא רָחָב וּכְשֶׁמְּדַבְּקוֹ בְּדֶבֶק נִכָּר הַדֶּבֶק בֵּין הַסְּדָקִים, מִפְּנֵי שֶׁהוּא סוֹתֵם אֶת הֶחָלָל שֶׁבֵּינֵיהֶם דִּינוֹ כְּסוֹתֵם נֶקֶב בְּדָבָר שֶׁאֵינוֹ מִמִּין הַשּׁוֹפָר[מא] שֶׁנִּתְבָּאֵר לְמַעְלָה:[מב, 33]

7 The same law applies[32] if a crack is wide and when it was glued closed, the glue is noticeable between the cracks because it fills the empty space between them. This is considered as closing a hole with a substance alien to the *shofar,* as explained above.[33]

---

28. I.e., destroyed in a manner that makes its substance unfit for use.

29. When a false deity belonging to a non-Jew has been nullified by a non-Jew as an object of worship, it can be used by a Jew for other purposes. When, however, a false deity belongs to a Jew, even after he nullifies it as an object of worship, it remains forbidden and must be destroyed.

30. I.e., the required measure is meaningless if the object itself has no ongoing existence.

31. It appears from the subsequent subsections that the Alter Rebbe also wrote the text for the part that was lost or destroyed. (It also appears that the numbers of the subsections that follow subsection 6 were added later by printers; i.e., subsection 7 would not have been #7 in the Alter Rebbe's original manuscript.)

In the *Shulchan Aruch* of R. Yosef Caro *(Orach Chayim,* 586:3-7*),* the corresponding issues are: (a) a *shofar* belonging to a non-Jew that was worshiped as a false deity (see footnote 137); (b) a *shofar* from an animal sacrificed to a false deity (which may not be used, even if the animal belonged to a non-Jew); (c) a *shofar* remains valid, regardless of the sounds it produces; and (d) a *shofar* with a hole. The *Shulchan Aruch* rules that such a *shofar* is valid even if the sound of the *shofar* changes, unless the hole was closed with an alien substance. If the hole was closed with fragments of a *shofar,* it is acceptable only if the majority of the *shofar* is intact and the *shofar* sounds like it did before the hole was made. In certain instances, the above principles are relaxed when no other *shofar* is available.

After the missing passage, the text of the Alter Rebbe's *Shulchan Aruch* resumes by dealing with subjects that appear in subsection 8 of the *Shulchan Aruch* of R. Yosef Caro, the laws that govern a cracked *shofar.* It appears that here, too, part of the Alter Rebbe's text — the laws governing a situation where the crack is closed — is also missing.

32. I.e., the law mentioned in the above note with regard to filling a hole with another substance, in which case the *shofar* is invalidated. Nevertheless, in an extreme situation, if the majority of the *shofar* remains intact and the sound of the *shofar* does not change, the *shofar* may be used.

33. I.e., in the part of the text that is missing. The law is that this disqualifies a *shofar.*

טור ושו״ע שם ס״ב. **לח** חולין שם פט, רע״ב ורש״י שם ד״ה שיעורא. ר״ה כח, א (בשל עיר הנידחת) ורש״י שם ד״ה כתותי. וראה גם לעיל סי׳ שסג סי״ח. לקמן סי׳ תרמט סי״א. וראה קובץ דברי תורה ג ע׳ מז. **לט** דיני שופר של ע״ז של נכרי (ראה לקמן סי׳ תרמט סי״א־ד בד׳ מינים. ומציין לכאן, שנתבאר כ״ז), ושאר הדינים שבשו״ע סעיפים ד־ז ותחלת ס״ח. **מ** כמו בנסדק לארכו ודבקו בחתיכה אחרת שאינו מינו, שפסול, כמבואר ברא״ש פ״ג סי׳ ב ובטור, כן הדין כו׳. **מא** משמעות רא״ש שם, וטור ומ״א סקי״ד. **מב** סעיף זה בשוע״ר לא הגיע לידינו, וראה טור שו״ע ס״ז.

ח נִסְדַּק[34] מִעוּט אֹרֶךְ הַשּׁוֹפָר וְנִשְׁאַר רֹב אָרְכּוֹ שָׁלֵם[מג] וְלֹא דִּבְּקוֹ בְּדֶבֶק וְלֹא חִבְּרָם בָּאוּר,[מד] יֵשׁ אוֹמְרִים שֶׁדִּינָם כְּנִקַּב, שֶׁאֲפִלּוּ לֹא נִשְׁתַּיֵּר מִסִּיּוּם הַסֶּדֶק עַד מְקוֹם הַנָּחַת הַפֶּה[35] כְּדֵי שִׁעוּר שׁוֹפָר[מה, 36] כָּשֵׁר כְּמוֹ שֶׁנִּתְבָּאֵר,[מו, 37] וְיֵשׁ אוֹמְרִים[מז] שֶׁאֵינוֹ דּוֹמֶה לְנִקַּב נֶקֶב שֶׁיֵּשׁ בּוֹ חֶסְרוֹן מִגּוּף הַשּׁוֹפָר שֶׁיֵּשׁ מָקוֹם לְהָרוּחַ שֶׁמֵּחֲמַת הַתְּקִיעָה לְהִכָּנֵס שָׁם דֶּרֶךְ הַחֶסְרוֹן וְיוֹצֵא הַחוּצָה וְאֵינוֹ מִתְחַזֵּק לְהַסְדִּיק הַשּׁוֹפָר, מַה שֶּׁאֵין כֵּן בְּסֶדֶק שֶׁאֵין בּוֹ חֶסְרוֹן מִגּוּף הַשּׁוֹפָר וְאֵין מָקוֹם לְהָרוּחַ לָצֵאת שָׁם וְעַל כֵּן הוּא מִתְחַזֵּק וּמַסְדִּיק הַסֶּדֶק יוֹתֵר[מח] וְסוֹפוֹ לְהַסְדִּיק כָּל אֹרֶךְ הַשּׁוֹפָר,[מט] וּלְפִיכָךְ אֲפִלּוּ אִם לֹא נִסְדַּק אֶלָּא כָּל שֶׁהוּא — פָּסוּל, לְפִי שֶׁאֵין שֵׁם שׁוֹפָר עָלָיו[נ, 38] כֵּיוָן שֶׁסּוֹפוֹ לְהַסְדִּיק כֻּלּוֹ,[נא] וְאִם הִדְּקוֹ הַרְבֵּה בְּחוּט אוֹ בִּמְשִׁיחָה — כָּשֵׁר, שֶׁהֲרֵי הַחוּט מַעֲמִידוֹ שֶׁלֹּא יִתְבַּקַּע יוֹתֵר.[נב]

וּלְעִנְיַן הֲלָכָה, יֵשׁ לְהַחְמִיר

8 [Opinions differ if] less than half of the length of the *shofar* became cracked,[34] leaving the majority of the length intact, and [the cracked part] was not glued together or fused with fire. Some [authorities] maintain that [this situation] is governed by the same laws that apply to a perforated *[shofar]*. Thus, even if the length that remains — from the end of the crack until the mouthpiece[35] — is less than the minimum length of a *shofar*,[36] the *shofar* remains valid, as was explained.[37]

Other authorities maintain that a crack cannot be likened to a hole, where the absence of material from the body of the *shofar* allows the current of air caused by the *shofar*-blast to enter and then frees it, without pressure that might extend the crack. In the case of a crack, in contrast, nothing is missing from the substance of the *shofar*. Since the current of air has no way out, the resulting pressure may cause the crack to extend further, and eventually split the entire length of the *shofar*. [These authorities argue,] therefore, that any crack — even of the slightest size — disqualifies the *shofar*. It cannot be called a *shofar*, because ultimately[38] it will become cracked from end to end. However, if it is held together tightly with string or a cord, it is acceptable, because the string will prevent it from splitting further.

With regard to the *halachah*, one should be

---

34. The laws that follow apply to a crack that penetrates the entire thickness of the *shofar*.

35. Throughout this discussion, "mouthpiece" does not signify any appendage to the *shofar*; it simply means the narrow end of the *shofar* that is held against the lips.

36. I.e., a handbreadth, as stated in subsection 13.

37. The explanation was in the missing part of the Alter Rebbe's text. Based on the *Shulchan Aruch* of R. Yosef Caro, *Orach Chayim* 586:6-7, it appears that the rationale is that even if the sound will change, any sound produced by a *shofar* is acceptable.

38. It cannot truly be called a *shofar* if it will not continue to exist as such.

מג מ"מ פ"א ה"ה בשם הרבה מן המפרשים. דעה הב' בשו"ע ס"ח. מד ראה שו"ע ס"ח ב' דעות, אי כשר בדבק, או דוקא כשדבקו בעצמו באור עד שנפשר וחבר קצותיו זה עם זה (ונתבאר לעיל, בסעיפים החסרים). מה תוס' כח, ב ד"ה נסדק לארכו. ב"י ד"ה נסדק בשם רא"ם בביאורו לסמ"ג הל' שופר (יג, ג) ד"ה נסדק (אפילו לא נשתייר שיעור שופר). מ"א סקי"ב. מו סעיף זה בשוע"ר (שמבאר דין נקב) לא הגיע לידינו, וראה שו"ע ס"ז (שנשתייר רובו), וט"ז סק"ז (אף שלא נשתייר שיעור שופר). מז רא"ש פ"ג סי' ו בשם יש מפרשים. ר"ן (ו, ב) ד"ה מתניתין, בשם רבנו יונתן. טור. דעה א' בשו"ע שם. מח ט"ז סקי"א. מט רא"ש שם. לבוש ס"ח. ט"ז שם. נ ראה תוס' כז, א ד"ה שופר. נא לבוש שם. נב ר"ן שם, בשם דרשת הראב"ד לר"ה (לונדון) ע' לה. הובא בכל בו סי'

כסברא האחרונה, אבל בשעת הדחק שאין שופר אחר מצוי יש לסמוך על סברא הראשונה:

ט נסדק השופר לרחבו[נג] דהינו סביב הקפו,[נד,39] אם הסדק הוא מיעוט[נה] הקף השופר ונשתייר רב הקפו באותו מקום שלם – כשר, אפילו אם נשתנה קולו מכמות שהיה קודם שנסדק,[נו] שכל הקולות כשרים בשופר,[נז] ואפילו אין בסדק חסרון מגוף השופר שאין שם מקום לרוח לצאת, לפי שאין הרוח מסדיק יותר אלא אם כן נסדק לארכו.[נח]

אבל אם לא נשתייר רב הקפו שלם, אם אין מהסדק עד מקום הנחת הפה כדי שיעור שופר[36] – פסול,[נט] דכיון שנסדק רבו הרי הוא כאלו נחתך כלו באותו מקום[ס] ואם כן הרי נחסר השופר משיעורו, ולפיכך אף על פי שלא נשתנה קולו מכמות שהיה קודם שנסדק – פסול.

אבל אם יש מהסדק עד מקום הנחת הפה כדי שיעור שופר,[סא] אף על פי שנשתנה קולו מכמות שהיה קודם שנסדק – כשר. ואף על פי שהקול יוצא דרך החלק שלמעלה מהסדק[סב]

stringent and follow the latter opinion. In a pressing situation, when there is no other *shofar* available, one may rely on the first opinion.

9 [The following laws apply] if the *shofar* becomes cracked around its circumference.[39] If the crack encompasses the minority of the circumference and the majority of the circumference remains intact at that point, the *shofar* is valid. [This applies] even if the sound of the *shofar* changed from what it was originally, before it was cracked, for all sounds [produced by] a *shofar* are acceptable. The *shofar* [is valid] even if nothing is missing from its substance at the point of the crack and thus the current of air has no way out, for an air current will not extend a crack unless the *shofar* is cracked along its length.

[Different rules apply, however,] if the majority of the circumference of the *shofar* does not remain intact. If the length that remains — from [the end of] the crack until the mouthpiece — is less than the minimum length of a *shofar*,[36] the *shofar* is invalid. Since the majority is cracked, it is considered as if the *shofar* has been entirely cut off at that point, and thus [the length of] the *shofar* is less than its required minimum measure. Therefore, even if its sound did not change from what it was originally, before it was cracked, the *shofar* is invalid.

If, by contrast, the length that remains — from [the end of] the crack until the mouthpiece — is [at least] equal to the minimum length of a *shofar*, [the *shofar*] is valid, even if its sound changed from what it was originally, before it was cracked. Even if the sound emerges from the part [of the *shofar*] which is above the crack, it is not disqualified on the grounds

---

39. *Rosh HaShanah* 27b.

סד (כז, ג). שו"ע שם. **נג** גמרא [ברייתא] כז, ב. טור ושו"ע ס"ט. **נד** רש"י שם ד"ה נסדק. ט"ז סקי"ג. **נה** רא"ש פ"ג סי' ו. טור ושו"ע שם. **נו** ט"ז ס"ק ח (אפילו להאוסרים בנקוב). **נז** ברייתא שם. טור ושו"ע ס"ו. וראה גם לקמן סי"ח. **נח** ט"ז סקי"א. **נט** גמרא [ברייתא] שם ורש"י ד"ה אם נשתייר. טור ושו"ע שם. **ס** רש"י שם. רא"ש שם. ר"ן (ז, א) ד"ה אם. לבוש ס"ט. ט"ז סקי"ד. מ"א ס"ק יז. **סא** ברייתא שם, כפירוש רש"י ור"ן שם. טור ושו"ע שם. **סב** ט"ז סקי"ד.

— אֵין פּוֹסְלִין אוֹתוֹ מִשּׁוּם קוֹל שׁוֹפָר וְדָבָר אַחֵר,[סג,40] אוֹ מִשּׁוּם קוֹל שְׁנֵי שׁוֹפָרוֹת,[סד,41] דְּכֵיוָן שֶׁבִּשְׁעַת עֲשִׂיַּת הַשּׁוֹפָר הָיָה זֶה הַחֵלֶק מְחֻבָּר לְעִקַּר הַשּׁוֹפָר וְלֹא נִפְרַד מִמֶּנּוּ לְעוֹלָם,[סה] לָכֵן הֵן נֶחְשָׁבִין כְּשׁוֹפָר אֶחָד לְעִנְיָן זֶה שֶׁלֹּא לְפָסְלָן מִשּׁוּם שְׁנֵי שׁוֹפָרוֹת, אֲבָל מִכָּל מָקוֹם אֵינָן נֶחְשָׁבִין כְּשׁוֹפָר אֶחָד לְגַמְרֵי כְּדֵי לְהַשְׁלִים לְשִׁעוּר שׁוֹפָר,[42] כֵּיוָן שֶׁנִּסְדְּקוּ וְנִפְרְדוּ זֶה מִזֶּה בְּרֹב הֶקֵּף:

י דִּבֵּק שִׁבְרֵי שׁוֹפָר זֶה עִם זֶה[43] וְעָשָׂה מֵהֶם שׁוֹפָר אֶחָד שָׁלֵם — פָּסוּל,[סו,44] לְפִי שֶׁאֵין זֶה קָרוּי שׁוֹפָר,[סז] וַאֲפִלּוּ יֵשׁ בַּשֶּׁבֶר שֶׁכְּנֶגֶד פִּיו שִׁעוּר שׁוֹפָר[סח] שָׁלֵם מִכָּל צְדָדָיו[סט] — אַף עַל פִּי כֵן הוּא נִפְסַל מֵחֲמַת הַשְּׁבָרִים הַנּוֹסָפִים עַל שֶׁבֶר זֶה שֶׁהַקּוֹל יוֹצֵא דֶּרֶךְ שָׁם,[ע] וְהַתּוֹרָה אָמְרָה[עא] קוֹל הַיּוֹצֵא מִשּׁוֹפָר אֶחָד וְלֹא הַיּוֹצֵא מִשְּׁנֵי שׁוֹפָרוֹת:[עב,45]

יא וְכֵן מִטַּעַם זֶה[עג] אִם הוֹסִיף כָּל שֶׁהוּא[עד] עַל אֹרֶךְ הַשּׁוֹפָר שָׁלֵם[עה] בְּעִנְיָן שֶׁהַקּוֹל יוֹצֵא דֶּרֶךְ הַתּוֹסֶפֶת הַהִיא,[עו] בֵּין שֶׁהַתּוֹסֶפֶת מִמִּין

that the sound of the *shofar* is [now] combined with the sound coming from another source[40] or on the grounds that the sound [now emerges from] two *shofaros.*[41] [The rationale is that] at the time the *shofar* was made, this part was connected to the main body of the *shofar* and was never [actually] separated from it. [The two parts] are therefore considered as one *shofar* in this respect, and [the *shofar*] is not disqualified on the grounds that the sound [now emerges from] two *shofaros.* [The two parts] are not, however, entirely considered as one *shofar* [to the extent that their joint length can be held to constitute] the minimum required length of the *shofar,*[42] because [the *shofar*] is cracked and [the two parts] are separated from each other over the majority of its circumference.

10 If broken pieces of a *shofar* were fused together[43] to produce a single complete *shofar,* it is invalid,[44] because this is not called a *shofar.*

Moreover, even if the part of the *shofar* near the mouthpiece has the minimum measure of a complete *shofar* on all sides, it is nevertheless invalid, because of the broken pieces of the *shofar* which were added to this piece, and from [those pieces] the sound emerges — for the Torah requires a sound that emerges from one *shofar,* not from two *shofaros.*[45]

11 Following the same rationale, if even a minimal addition is made to the length of a complete *shofar* in a manner that causes the sound to emerge from that addition, [the *shofar*] is disqualified.[46] [This applies] whether

40. See subsection 16 below.

41. See subsection 10 below.

42. Hence, if the part near the mouthpiece is shorter than a handbreadth, the *shofar* is invalid.

43. Either with glue or by heating the pieces.

44. *Rosh HaShanah* 27a.

45. *Ibid.* 26a.

46. *Ibid.* 27b.

סג ראה ב"י ד"ה ניקב וסתמו. לקמן סוף סט"ז. **סד** ט"ז שם. וכדלקמן ס"י־יא. **סה** ט"ז שם. **סו** משנה כז, סוע"א. טור ושו"ע ס"י. **סז** תוס' שם ד"ה שופר. **סח** טור ושו"ע שם. **סט** מ"א סקי"ט. **ע** רא"ש פ"ג סי' ב. **עא** ראה גמרא כו, א. **עב** רש"י כז, סוע"א ד"ה פסול. רא"ש שם. לבוש ס"י. ט"ז ס"ק טו. וראה גם לקמן ס"כ. **עג** רא"ש שם סי' ד בסופו. ר"ן (ו, ב) ד"ה הוסיף. לבוש סי"א. **עד** גמרא [ברייתא] כז, ב. טור ושו"ע סי"א. **עה** רא"ש שם. טור ושו"ע שם.

הַשּׁוֹפָר, בֵּין שֶׁאֵינוֹ מִמִּין הַשּׁוֹפָר,[עז] בֵּין שֶׁהוֹסִיף בְּצַד הַקָּצָר,[47] בֵּין שֶׁהוֹסִיף בְּצַד הָרָחָב[48] — פָּסוּל,[46] מִטַּעַם שֶׁנִּתְבָּאֵר:[עח]

the addition is made of the material of which the *shofar* is made or from a different substance, and whether the addition is made to the narrow end[47] of the *shofar* or to the wider end,[48] for the reason explained [above].

יב הֲפָכוֹ[46] וְתָקַע בּוֹ — לֹא יָצָא,[עט] בֵּין שֶׁהֲפָכוֹ כְּדֶרֶךְ שֶׁהוֹפְכִין חָלוּק שֶׁהֶחֱזִיר פְּנִימִיּוּת הַשּׁוֹפָר לִהְיוֹת חִיצוֹנִיּוּתוֹ וְחִיצוֹנִיּוּתוֹ לִהְיוֹת פְּנִימִיּוּתוֹ,[פ] בֵּין שֶׁהִנִּיחוֹ כְּמוֹת שֶׁהָיָה אֶלָּא שֶׁהִרְחִיב אֶת צַד הַקָּצָר שֶׁלּוֹ וְקִצֵּר אֶת הָרָחָב[פא] בְּרוֹתְחִין[פב] וְתָקַע בֵּין בְּצַד הַקָּצָר בֵּין בְּצַד הָרָחָב[פג] שֶׁהָיָה קָצָר מִתְּחִלָּה — לֹא יָצָא, שֶׁנֶּאֱמַר[פד, 49] "וְהַעֲבַרְתָּ שׁוֹפָר וגו'", כְּדֶרֶךְ הַעֲבָרָתוֹ[פה, 50] שֶׁהָאַיִל מַעֲבִירוֹ בְּרֹאשׁוֹ מֵחַיִּים,[פו] פְּרָט לְהֵפֶךְ.[פז] וְעַיֵּן בְּסִימָן תק"צ:[פח, 51]

12 One does not fulfill his obligation by sounding [a *shofar*] if he first reversed [its shape],[47] whether by turning it inside out as one does a cloak, so that its interior is on the outside and [vice versa], or by leaving that aspect [of the *shofar*] as it was, but widening its narrow end and narrowing its wider end by means of boiling water. [In the latter case] one does not fulfill his obligation, whether he sounds [it from] the end which is [now] narrow, or from the end that was originally narrow and is now wide.

[This concept is derived from] the verse,[49] והעברת שופר [תרועה] — "You shall cause the sounds of the *shofar* to pass… [throughout your land]." [Implied is that the *shofar*] should be sounded in the same manner in which the ram carries it[50] on its head while alive. This excludes [a *shofar*] that has been reversed. See also sec. 590[:20].[51]

יג הָיָה אָרֹךְ וְקִצְּרוֹ,[פט, 46] אִם נִשְׁאַר בּוֹ שִׁעוּר שׁוֹפָר[צ] — כָּשֵׁר.

וְכַמָּה שִׁעוּר שׁוֹפָר — טֶפַח,[צא, 52] כְּדֵי שֶׁיֹּאחֲזֶנּוּ[צב] הַתּוֹקֵעַ[צג] בְּיָדוֹ,[53] דְּהַיְנוּ

13 If a *shofar* was long and was shortened,[47] but the minimum required measure remained, it is valid.

What is the minimum measure of a *shofar?* A handbreadth,[52] so that [when] the person sounding the *shofar* holds it in his hand,[53] i.e.,

---

47. I.e., the mouthpiece.

48. I.e., the opening from which the sound emerges.

49. *Vayikra* 25:9.

50. Lit., "passes it along." In the Hebrew original, the verb here (מעבירו) shares a root with the verb in the verse quoted.

51. That subsection states that a *shofar* may not be sounded at its wide end.

52. In the original, a *tefach;* 8 cm. (a little over three inches), according to *Shiurei Torah* 3:25.

53. *Rosh HaShanah* 27b; *Niddah* 26a.

עו כדלעיל ס"י. **עז** ברייתא שם. טור ושו"ע שם. **עח** סעיף י, מטעם שופר אחד ולא שני שופרות (במינו. ובאינו מינו, ראה לקמן סי"ז – מטעם קול שופר ודבר אחר). **עט** גמרא [ברייתא] כז, ב. טור ושו"ע סי"ב. **פ** רב פפא שם, וכפירוש הא' בראשׁ פ"ג סי' ד, ור"ן (ו, ב) ד"ה גמרא, בשם הירושלמי ר"ה פ"ג ה"ז. טור ושו"ע שם. **פא** רב פפא שם. טור ושו"ע שם. **פב** רש"י שם ד"ה שקיצר. **פג** ראה רמ"א סי"ב, ור"ן שם. **פד** ויקרא כה, ט. **פה** רב מתנה בגמרא שם. **פו** רש"י שם ד"ה והעברת. לבוש סי"ב. ט"ז סקט"ז. **פז** רש"י לד, א ד"ה דרך (למעוטי הפכו). בקונטרס השלחן הגיה: להפוך. **פח** סעיף כ. וראה שדי חמד אס"ד מערכת ר"ה סי' ב אות לד. **פט** גמרא [ברייתא] כז, ב. טור ושו"ע סי"ג. **צ** ר"ן (ו, ב) ד"ה היה ארוך. טור ושו"ע שם. **צא** נדה כו, א. רא"ש פ"ג סי' ו. טור ושו"ע ס"ט. וראה תניא אגה"ק סי' י. **צב** רשב"ג ר"ה כו, ב. נדה שם. רמב"ם פ"א ה"ה. רא"ש שם. טור. **צג** רא"ש שם. לבוש ס"ט.

כְּד' אֶצְבְּעוֹתָיו בֵּינוֹנִים,צד,54 וְיֵרָאֶה הַשּׁוֹפָר מִכָּאן וּמִכָּאן,צה שֶׁהַטֶּפַח הוּא ד' אֶצְבָּעוֹת גּוּדָלִין,צו כְּדֵי שֶׁלֹּא יֹאמְרוּ לְתוֹךְ יָדוֹ הוּא תּוֹקֵעַ.צז וַאֲפִלּוּ אִם הַתּוֹקֵעַ הוּא אָדָם גָּדוֹל וְאֵין הַשּׁוֹפָר נִרְאֶה מִתּוֹךְ יָדוֹ – אַף עַל פִּי כֵן אֵין צָרִיךְ יוֹתֵר מִטֶּפַח שֶׁל אָדָם בֵּינוֹנִיצח דְּהַיְנוּ ד' גּוּדָלִין. וּמוֹדְדִין בִּמְקוֹם הָרָחָב שֶׁל הַגּוּדָלצט כְּמוֹ שֶׁיִּתְבָּאֵר בְּסִימָן י"א.ק וְכֵן הַדִּין בְּכָל אֶצְבָּעוֹת שֶׁבַּתּוֹרָה:קא

יד גְּרָדוֹ בֵּין מִבִּפְנִים בֵּין מִבַּחוּץ עַד שֶׁעֲשָׂאוֹ דַּק מְאֹד כְּמוֹ גֶּלֶד – כָּשֵׁר,קב,46 וְאַף עַל פִּי שֶׁאֵינוֹ כְּדֶרֶךְ שֶׁהָאַיִל מַעֲבִירוֹ בְּרֹאשׁוֹ מַמָּשׁ,55 מִכָּל מָקוֹם כֵּיוָן שֶׁהוּא כְּדֶרֶךְ צְמִיחָתוֹ בְּרֹאשׁ הָאַיִל נִקְרָא כְּדֶרֶךְ הַעֲבָרָתוֹ, וְלֹא מִעֵטוֹ אֶלָּא אִם הֲפָכוֹ שֶׁשִּׁנָּה אוֹתוֹ מִדֶּרֶךְ צְמִיחָתוֹ בְּרֹאשׁ הָאַיִל:קג

טו אִם הוֹצִיא הַזַּכְרוּת מִן הַקֶּרֶן וְעָשָׂה מִמֶּנּוּ שׁוֹפָר כְּגוֹן שֶׁנִּקֵּב בּוֹ – פָּסוּל,קד,46 לְפִי שֶׁאֵין נִקְרָא שׁוֹפָר אֶלָּא דָּבָר שֶׁהוּא חָלוּל בְּטִבְעוֹ, שֶׁשּׁוֹפָר הוּא לְשׁוֹן שְׁפוֹפֶרֶת, וְהַזַּכְרוּת כֵּיוָן שֶׁאֵינוֹ חָלוּל בְּטִבְעוֹ – אֵינוֹ נִקְרָא שׁוֹפָר.קה אֲבָל אִם לֹא הוֹצִיא הַזַּכְרוּת

[covering the width of] four medium-sized fingers, the *shofar* will [still] be visible from either side of his hand, for a handbreadth is equal to four thumbbreadths.[54] [This minimum length is required] so that no one will say [that the person sounding the *shofar*] is blowing into his hand.

Even if the person sounding the *shofar* is very large and the *shofar* cannot be seen outside his hand, [the *shofar*] does not have to be larger than the handbreadth of an ordinary person, i.e., four thumbbreadths. One measures at the wide part of the thumb, as mentioned in sec. 11[:5]. This applies wherever the term "fingerbreadth" is mentioned in Torah [law].

14 If one files a *shofar,* whether from the inside or from the outside, until he makes it very thin like parchment, it is still valid.[47] Although this is not exactly the way a ram carries it on its head,[55] nevertheless, since this is the manner in which it grows on the ram's head, it is called "the way it carries it." [The verse] excludes only a situation where one reverses [the shape of the *shofar*], changing it from the way it grows on the ram's head.

15 If one extracted the solid protrusion from the horn [of the *shofar*] and turned it into a *shofar* — for example, by making a hole through it — it is not valid,[47] because the term *shofar,* from *shfoferes* [meaning "tube"], signifies only something that is hollow by nature. And since the protrusion [inside the *shofar*] is not naturally hollow, it is not called a *shofar.*

If, by contrast, one did not extract the

---

54. See *Bechoros* 59b; *Menachos* 41b. Since four thumbbreadths exceeds the width of four other fingers, the *shofar* will be visible from either side of the hand (Rabbeinu Nissim).

55. Since the *shofar* is now much thinner.

צד ר"ן (ז, א) ד"ה כדי. טור. לבוש שם. צה רשב"ג שם ושם. רמב"ם שם. רא"ש שם. טור. צו מנחות מא, ב. ר"ן שם. טור. צז רא"ש שם. לבוש סוף ס"ט. צח ר"ן שם. טור. מ"א סקי"ח. צט מ"א שם. ק סוף ס"ה. קא רמב"ם הל' שבת פי"ז הלכה לו. וכדלעיל סי' לב סס"ג וש"נ. קב גמרא [ברייתא] כז, ב. טור ושו"ע סי"ד. קג ב"י ד"ה ומ"ש אם נשאר, בשם הרא"ם בביאורו לסמ"ג הל' שופר (יג, ג). לבוש סי"ד. קד ר"ן (ו, א) ד"ה וכתבו. טור ושו"ע סט"ו. קה ר"ן

מִן הַקֶּרֶן אֶלָּא נָקַב בּוֹ נֶקֶב – כָּשֵׁר.[קו] וַאֲפִלּוּ לְכַתְּחִלָּה מֻתָּר לַעֲשׂוֹת כֵּן.[קז] וַאֲפִלּוּ הַזַּכְרוּת מַפְסִיק בֵּין הַקּוֹל לְהַדָּבָר הֶחָלוּל בְּטִבְעוֹ שֶׁנִּקְרָא שׁוֹפָר – אֵין בְּכָךְ כְּלוּם, דְּמִין בְּמִינוֹ אֵינוֹ חוֹצֵץ[קח,56] וַהֲרֵי הוּא כְּמוֹ שֶׁלֹּא הָיָה שָׁם זַכְרוּת כְּלָל:

protrusion from the horn [of the *shofar*], but [simply] made a hole through it, it is valid. Indeed, this may be done even as an initial option. Even though this [perforated] protrusion intervenes between [the current of air that produces] the sound and the entity that is naturally hollow and is therefore called a *shofar,* this is immaterial. An intervening [layer] is not considered as intercepting if it is made of the same type of substance.[56] Thus it is as if there was no protrusion there at all.

טז צָרִיךְ שֶׁלֹּא יְהֵא שׁוּם הֶפְסֵק[57] בֵּין פִּי הַתּוֹקֵעַ לְהַשּׁוֹפָר,[קט,58] לְפִיכָךְ אִם צִפָּהוּ זָהָב בִּמְקוֹם הַנָּחַת הַפֶּה[קי] כְּדֵי לְנָאוֹתוֹ,[קיא] אֲפִלּוּ אִם הַצִּפּוּי הוּא בְּאֹרֶךְ הַשּׁוֹפָר, אִם הוּא מִיָּד סָמוּךְ לְרֹאשׁוֹ בַּצַּד הַקָּצָר – פָּסוּל,[קיב,59] לְפִי שֶׁהַתּוֹקֵעַ מַכְנִיס קְצָתוֹ בְּפִיו וּשְׂפָתוֹ מְכַסָּה עָלָיו, וְנִמְצָא הַזָּהָב חוֹצֵץ בֵּין שְׂפָתוֹ לַשּׁוֹפָר.[קיג] אֲבָל אִם הַצִּפּוּי הוּא רָחוֹק מִפִּי הַתּוֹקֵעַ – כָּשֵׁר.[קיד]

בַּמֶּה דְּבָרִים אֲמוּרִים? כְּשֶׁלֹּא נִשְׁתַּנָּה קוֹלוֹ מֵחֲמַת הַצִּפּוּי,[קטו] אוֹ שֶׁאֵינוֹ יוֹדֵעַ אִם נִשְׁתַּנָּה,[46] דְּמִן הַסְּתָם לֹא נִשְׁתַּנָּה קוֹלוֹ בִּשְׁבִיל צִפּוּי כָּל שֶׁהוּא,[קטז] אֲבָל אִם יוֹדֵעַ שֶׁנִּשְׁתַּנָּה הַקּוֹל מֵחֲמַת הַצִּפּוּי, וְאַף עַל פִּי שֶׁהַשִּׁנּוּי הוּא מְעַט – פָּסוּל, לְפִי

16 Nothing may intervene[57] between the mouth of the person sounding [the *shofar*] and the *shofar*.[58] Therefore, the *shofar* is invalid[59] if the place that the mouth [touches] was coated with gold foil as an adornment, or even if the coating extended along the length of the *shofar* and reached [that] end — because the person sounding it will place its rim in his mouth and his lip will cover it. The gold will thus intervene between his lip and the *shofar*. If, however, the coating is distant from the mouth of the person sounding the *shofar,* the *shofar* is valid.

When does this apply? When the sound [of the *shofar*] was not changed by the coating, or [even] if one does not know whether it has changed,[47] for a thin coating will presumably not change the sound. If, however, one knows that the coating has caused even a minor change, [the *shofar*] is invalid, because

56. I.e., the perforated protrusion is not considered as intervening between the current of air and the outer shell that constitutes the actual *shofar,* for both the *shofar* and the protrusion that fills it are basically part of the same entity.

57. In this context, a substance and a space can equally constitute a *hefsek* ("intervention"). See subsection 19.

58. Thus one may not append an extraneous mouthpiece.

59. *Rosh HaShanah* 27b; see also *Sukkah* 37a.

שם. ב"י ד"ה ומ"ש רבנו אבל אם הוציא. לבוש סט"ו. ט"ז סקי"ז. וראה גם לעיל ס"א. **קו** גמרא כז, ב ורש"י שם ד"ה שקדחו. טור ושו"ע שם. **קז** ב"י ד"ה גרסינן בשם הירושלמי פ"ג סוף ה"ו. מ"א ס"ק כ. פר"ח סט"ו. **קח** רב אשי בגמרא שם. רמב"ם פ"א ה"ה. רא"ש פ"ג סי' ז. וראה גם לעיל סי' תעה סכ"ז. לקמן סי' תרנא ס"ה. **קט** מ"מ פ"א ה"ו, וטור, בשם הרמב"ן בדרשה לר"ה (כתבי הרמב"ן ח"א ע' רלו). הובא ב"י ד"ה ומ"ש ויש מפרשים. לבוש סי"ז. **קי** ברייתא כז, ב. רמב"ם שם. טור ושו"ע סט"ז. **קיא** ראה לקמן סי' תרנא ס"ד גבי נטילת לולב. וראה מ"מ וציונים. **קיב** רמב"ן שם. רא"ש פ"ג סי' ג. טור ודעה הב' בשו"ע שם. לבוש שם. **קיג** רמב"ן שם. טור ולבוש שם. **קיד** ברייתא שם, לפירוש הרא"ש שם. טור ושו"ע שם. **קטו** גמרא [ברייתא] שם. טור ושו"ע שם. **קטז** רא"ש פ"ג סי' ג. מ"א סקכ"א.

שֶׁאֵין קוֹל שׁוֹפָר לְבַד אֶלָּא קוֹל שׁוֹפָר וְקוֹל דָּבָר אַחֵר, דְּהַיְנוּ הַצִּפּוּי:[קיז]

[what is now heard] is not the sound of the *shofar* alone, but the sound of the *shofar* combined with a sound from another source, the coating.

יז בַּמֶּה דְּבָרִים אֲמוּרִים? כְּשֶׁהַצִּפּוּי הוּא הוֹסָפָה עַל עֳבִי הַשּׁוֹפָר אוֹ עַל רָחְבּוֹ, אֲבָל אִם הוּא הוֹסָפָה עַל אָרְכּוֹ, אֲפִלּוּ בַּצַּד הָרָחָב שֶׁלּוֹ, אִם נָתַן שָׁם זָהָב מַשֶּׁהוּ עַל עֳבִי הַשּׁוֹפָר בְּעִנְיַן שֶׁנִּתְאָרֵךְ הַשּׁוֹפָר מַשֶּׁהוּ – פָּסוּל,[קיח] אַף עַל פִּי שֶׁלֹּא נִשְׁתַּנָּה קוֹלוֹ[קיט] כְּלָל, מִטַּעַם שֶׁנִּתְבָּאֵר לְמַעְלָה:[קכ, 60]

17 When does the above apply? When the coating adds to the thickness of the *shofar* or its width. If it adds to the length of the *shofar* — even at its wider end — i.e., even a very small amount of gold was added to the circumference of the *shofar* and thereby lengthened it [even] slightly, [the *shofar*] is invalid for the reason stated above,[60] even if its sound did not change.

יח הַמְצַיְּרִים בַּשּׁוֹפָר צוּרוֹת כְּדֵי לְנָאוֹתוֹ[61] – לֹא יָפֶה הֵן עוֹשִׂין, אַף עַל פִּי שֶׁאֵין כֻּלּוֹ מְצֻפֶּה בְּמִינֵי הַצִּיּוּרִין, לִפְעָמִים הַקּוֹל מִשְׁתַּנֶּה.[קכא] אֲבָל מֻתָּר לַחְקֹק בַּשּׁוֹפָר עַצְמוֹ צוּרוֹת כְּדֵי לְנָאוֹתוֹ,[קכב] שֶׁאֲפִלּוּ אִם יִשְׁתַּנֶּה קוֹלוֹ עַל יְדֵי כֵן – אֵין בְּכָךְ כְּלוּם, שֶׁאֵין כָּאן קוֹל מִן דָּבָר אַחֵר אֶלָּא קוֹל הַשּׁוֹפָר לְבַד,[קכג] וְכָל הַקּוֹלוֹת כְּשֵׁרִים בַּשּׁוֹפָר:[קכד, 46]

18 Those who decorate a *shofar* with drawings[61] are not acting in a desirable manner, for even if [a *shofar*] is not covered entirely [with drawings], its sound sometimes changes.

It is, however, permitted to decorate a *shofar* with engravings. Even if this changes the sound of the *shofar,* that is not significant, because no sound from another source is heard, only the sound of the *shofar* alone. And all the sounds produced by a *shofar* are acceptable.[46]

יט הִרְחִיק אֶת הַשּׁוֹפָר מְעַט מִפִּיו וְנָפַח בּוֹ וְתָקַע – לֹא יָצָא יְדֵי חוֹבָתוֹ, כֵּיוָן שֶׁיֵּשׁ הֶפְסֵק מְעַט בֵּין פִּיו לַשּׁוֹפָר:[קכה]

19 If one holds a *shofar* at a small distance from his mouth, blows into it, and produces a sound, he has not fulfilled his obligation, because of the slight space that intervenes between his mouth and the *shofar*.

כ נָתַן שׁוֹפָר בְּתוֹךְ שׁוֹפָר,[46] אִם שָׁמַע

20 [The following laws apply if one] places one *shofar* inside another *shofar* [and blows].[46] If one hears only the

---

60. In subsections 10-11.

61. E.g., by adding dye or paint to its surface.

קיז רא"ש שם סי' ה (לענין ניקב וסתמו שלא במינו, שבשו"ע ס"ז). רבנו ירוחם נ"ו ח"ב (מח, ג. לענין ציפוי זהב). לבוש סי"ח. קיח תוס' כז, ב ד"ה ציפהו. רא"ש פ"ג סי' ג. טור ושו"ע סי"ח. וכדלעיל סי"א (בשאינו מינו). קיט טור ולבוש סי"ז. קכ סוף סט"ז, דהוי קול שופר ודבר אחר (לבוש שם). קכא רמב"ן בדרשה לר"ה (כתבי הרמב"ן ח"א ע' רלו). טור ושו"ע סי"ז. קכב ב"י ד"ה ומ"ש בשם הרמב"ן. רמ"א סי"ז. קכג לבוש סי"ט. קכד ברייתא כז, ב. טור ושו"ע

sound of the inner *shofar,* uncombined with any sound from the outer *shofar,* [he has fulfilled his obligation. This is possible if] the narrow end of the inner *shofar* protrudes beyond the outer *shofar* and [touches] the mouth of the person who sounds it, and if the wider end of the outer *shofar* does not extend more than the inner one: either the inner *shofar* protrudes more, or they are level. [In such a situation,] he has fulfilled his obligation, because only the sound of one *shofar* [is heard].

[The above applies,] provided the [inner] *shofar* does not change its sound by being placed inside the outer one. The obligation is not fulfilled if the sound [of the inner *shofar*] changes, or if the wide end of the outer *shofar* extends beyond that of the inner *[shofar],* or if the narrow end of [the outer *shofar*] is level with that of [the inner *shofar*] — for in any of these cases, it is impossible that one should not hear a sound from both *shofaros.* And the Torah requires a sound [that emerges] from one *shofar,* not one [that emerges] from two *shofaros.*[46]

קוֹל פְּנִימִי[קכו] לְבַד, כְּגוֹן שֶׁבְּצַד הַקָּצָר הוּא בּוֹלֵט יוֹתֵר מִן הַחִיצוֹן וְנָתַן הַפְּנִימִי בְּפִיו וְתָקַע[קכז] וּבְצַד הָרָחָב – אֵין הַחִיצוֹן בּוֹלֵט יוֹתֵר מִן הַפְּנִימִי, אֶלָּא הַפְּנִימִי בּוֹלֵט יוֹתֵר[קכח] אוֹ שֶׁשְּׁנֵיהֶם שָׁוִין,[קכט] דְּנִמְצָא שֶׁאֵין בִּתְקִיעָה זוֹ שׁוּם תַּעֲרוֹבוֹת קוֹל מִן הַחִיצוֹן אֶלָּא מִן הַפְּנִימִי לְבַד, לְפִיכָךְ יָצָא יְדֵי חוֹבָתוֹ, שֶׁאֵין כָּאן אֶלָּא קוֹל שׁוֹפָר אֶחָד.

וְהוּא שֶׁלֹּא נִשְׁתַּנָּה קוֹלוֹ מֵחֲמַת שֶׁהוּא נָתוּן בְּתוֹךְ הַחִיצוֹן, אֲבָל אִם נִשְׁתַּנָּה קוֹלוֹ,[קל] אוֹ שֶׁהַחִיצוֹן בְּצַד הָרָחָב שֶׁלּוֹ בּוֹלֵט יוֹתֵר מִן הַפְּנִימִי,[קלא] אוֹ שֶׁבְּצַד הַקָּצָר שֶׁלּוֹ הֵם שָׁוִים,[קלב] דְּאָז אִי אֶפְשָׁר שֶׁלֹּא שָׁמַע אֶלָּא קוֹל שְׁנֵיהֶם – לֹא יָצָא,[קלד] דְּקוֹל שׁוֹפָר אֶחָד אָמְרָה תּוֹרָה וְלֹא קוֹל שְׁנֵי שׁוֹפָרוֹת:[קלה,46]

21 Any factor that disqualifies a *shofar* on the first day [of Rosh HaShanah] disqualifies it on the second day, even though [the observance of] the second day is of Rabbinic authority.

כא כָּל דָּבָר הַפּוֹסֵל בְּיוֹם רִאשׁוֹן בְּשׁוֹפָר – פּוֹסֵל גַּם בְּיוֹם שֵׁנִי,[קלו] אַף עַל פִּי שֶׁאֵינוֹ אֶלָּא מִדִּבְרֵיהֶם:[קלז]

22 The festival may not be desecrated [by performing prohibited labor] in order [to obtain] a *shofar* for Rosh HaShanah.[62] [The rationale is] that the observance of a festival is mandated by both a positive and negative

כב שׁוֹפָר שֶׁל רֹאשׁ הַשָּׁנָה אֵין מְחַלְּלִין עָלָיו יוֹם טוֹב,[קלח,62] מִפְּנֵי שֶׁיּוֹם טוֹב הוּא עֲשֵׂה וְלֹא תַעֲשֶׂה

62. *Rosh HaShanah* 32b.

ס"ו. וראה גם לעיל ס"ט. קכה רמב"ן שם. טור ושו"ע סי"ט. קכו גמרא [ברייתא] כז, ב. טור ושו"ע ס"כ. קכז רא"ש פ"ג סי' ד. ר"ן (ו, ב) ד"ה אם קול. טור ושו"ע שם. קכח ב"י סוד"ה נתן שופר. שו"ע שם. קכט דרכי משה ס"ק ה. רמ"א ס"כ. ט"ז סקי"ט. קל רא"ש שם. טור ושו"ע שם. קלא דרכי משה שם. קלב טור. קלג רא"ש שם. טור. לבוש ס"כ. קלד ברייתא שם. רא"ש שם. טור. קלה רא"ש שם. טור ולבוש ס"כ. מ"א ס"ק כב. וכדלעיל ס"י. קלו שו"ת הרשב"א ח"א סי' כג וסי' תרל. דרכי משה ס"ק ג. מ"א סוף הסי'. וראה לעיל סי' תעה ס"ל (לענין מצה). לקמן סי' תרמט סכ"א (לענין ד' מינים). קלז ראה גם לקמן סי' תר סוף ס"ד. קלח משנה לב, סוע"ב. טור ושו"ע סכ"א.

כְּמוֹ שֶׁנִּתְבָּאֵר בְּסִימָן תצ"ח,[קלט, 63] וְאֵין עֲשֵׂה דְּשׁוֹפָר דּוֹחֶה אֶת לֹא תַעֲשֶׂה וַעֲשֵׂה.[קמ] וַאֲפִלּוּ בְּדָבָר שֶׁאִסּוּרוֹ אֵינוֹ אֶלָּא מִדְּרַבָּנָן אֵין מְחַלְּלִין עָלָיו,[קמא] לְפִי שֶׁחֲכָמִים הִשְׁווּ אֶת דִּבְרֵיהֶם לְשֶׁל תּוֹרָה,[קמב] וְהֶעֱמִידוּ דִּבְרֵיהֶם לְבַטֵּל דִּבְרֵי תוֹרָה בְּשֵׁב וְאַל תַּעֲשֶׂה:[קמג, 64]

כג כֵּיצַד? הָיָה הַשּׁוֹפָר בְּרֹאשׁ הָאִילָן אוֹ מֵעֵבֶר הַנָּהָר וְאֵין לוֹ שׁוֹפָר אַחֵר אֶלָּא הוּא[קמד] — אֵינוֹ עוֹלֶה בָּאִילָן וְאֵינוֹ שָׁט עַל פְּנֵי הַמַּיִם[קמה] כְּדֵי לַהֲבִיאוֹ.[קמו, 65] וְאִם נָפַל עָלָיו גַּל שֶׁל אֲבָנִים[קמז] — אָסוּר לְטַלְטֵל הָאֲבָנִים כְּדֵי לִטְּלוֹ.[קמח] וְאֵין לֵילֵךְ חוּץ לַתְּחוּם[קמט, 66] כְּדֵי לִשְׁמֹעַ קוֹל שׁוֹפָר.[קנ] וְאֵין צָרִיךְ לוֹמַר שֶׁאֵין מְבִיאִין אוֹתוֹ מִחוּץ לַתְּחוּם:[קנא]

כד בַּמֶּה דְּבָרִים אֲמוּרִים? עַל יְדֵי יִשְׂרָאֵל, אֲבָל עַל יְדֵי נָכְרִי מֻתָּר לַעֲשׂוֹת כָּל דָּבָר שֶׁאִסּוּרוֹ אֵינוֹ אֶלָּא מִדִּבְרֵי סוֹפְרִים,[קנב] כְּגוֹן לַעֲלוֹת בָּאִילָן[קנג]

commandment, as stated in sec. 495[:1].[63] And the positive commandment of [sounding] a *shofar* does not override both a negative and a positive commandment.

Moreover, the festival may not be desecrated [for this purpose] even by [the performance of] an activity forbidden only by the Sages. For the Sages equated their rulings with those [stemming] from Scriptural Law and buttressed the authority of their rulings even though they led to the negation of Scriptural Law, in cases in which one remains inactive and [simply] refrains from performing [an action required of him by the Torah].[64]

23 What is implied? If a *shofar* is at the top of a tree or across a river, [even though one] does not have another *shofar,* he may not climb the tree or swim across the water to bring it.[65] If a pile of stones fell on [the *shofar*], they may not be removed in order to take it. Nor may one walk beyond the *[Shabbos]* limits[66] to hear the sounding of the *shofar*. Needless to say, one may not bring a *shofar* from beyond the *[Shabbos]* limits.

24 When does the above apply? [When the forbidden activities are performed] by a Jew. It is, however, permitted to have any activity forbidden by Rabbinic Law performed by a non-

63. There it is explained that every festival involves both a positive commandment to rest, and a negative commandment that prohibits the performance of certain labors. ("Sec. 498" in some of the Hebrew editions is a typographical slip.)

64. In the situations soon to be described, Scriptural Law requires one to sound the *shofar,* yet he should refrain from doing so, because obtaining a *shofar* entails the violation of a Rabbinic prohibition (such as *muktzeh*).

This reflects a general principle. Generally, the Sages required that the safeguards they established to ensure that a negative commandment will not be violated should be upheld, even though this will prevent the fulfillment of a Scriptural commandment. This applies, provided one does not *act* in violation of the Scriptural commandment *(kum vaaseh),* but simply remains inactive *(shev ve'al taaseh).* See *Yevamos* 90a and *Rashi* there.

65. *Rosh HaShanah, loc. cit.* Nor may one cross a body of water by boat *(Mishnah Berurah* 586:85*).*

קלט סל"ד. ואוצ"ל: בסימן תצ"ה (ס"א). קמ גמרא שם. מ"א סקכ"ג. קמא משנה שם. טור ושו"ע שם. קמב מ"א סקכ"ג. קמג טור. לבוש סכ"א. וראה לעיל סי' תצח קו"א סק"ה. וראה גם לעיל סי' שלא ס"ז. סי' שמז סוף ס"ז. לקמן סי' תריג ס"י. סי' תרכח ס"ה. סי' תרמ ס"י. קמד שו"ע שם. וראה גם טור. קמה משנה שם. טור ושו"ע שם. קמו טור ושו"ע שם. קמז משנה שם. טור ושו"ע שם. קמח טור. מ"א סקכ"ג. וכל שכן לפקח במרא וקרדום שאסור מן התורה כדלעיל סי' שצד ס"ב. קמט משנה שם. קנ רש"י שם ד"ה שופר. ב"י ד"ה נפל. לבוש סכ"א. קנא טור. ב"י שם. לבוש שם. קנב טור בשם ה"ר יונה,

וְלַהֲבִיאוֹ מִחוּץ לַתְּחוּם[קנד, 67] וְכָל כַּיּוֹצֵא בָּזֶה.[68] אֲבָל אָסוּר לוֹמַר לַנָּכְרִי לַעֲשׂוֹת מְלָאכָה גְּמוּרָה[69] בִּשְׁבִילוֹ.[קנה]

וּמִכָּל מָקוֹם, אִם הַנָּכְרִי עָשָׂה מֵעַצְמוֹ מְלָאכָה גְּמוּרָה, כְּגוֹן שֶׁעָשָׂה שׁוֹפָר בְּיוֹם טוֹב — מֻתָּר לִתְקֹעַ בּוֹ,[קנו] וְאַף עַל פִּי שֶׁעָשָׂה בִּשְׁבִיל יִשְׂרָאֵל, וְאֵין חוֹשְׁשִׁין שֶׁמָּא יֹאמַר הַיִּשְׂרָאֵל לַנָּכְרִי לַעֲשׂוֹתוֹ,[קנז] אֵין חוֹשְׁשִׁין לָזֶה אֶלָּא בְּדָבָר שֶׁיֵּשׁ הֲנָאָה לְגוּף אָדָם, אֲבָל הַמִּצְוֹת שֶׁלֹּא נִתְּנוּ לַהֲנָאַת הַגּוּף[קנח, 70] — אֵין חוֹשְׁשִׁין שֶׁיַּעֲבֹר עֲבֵרָה כְּדֵי לְקַיֵּם הַמִּצְוָה:[קנט]

Jew [to make a *shofar* available], e.g., to have him climb a tree [to bring a *shofar*], or to have him bring it from beyond the [*Shabbos*] limits,[67] or the like.[68]

It is, however, forbidden to tell a non-Jew to perform labor [forbidden by Scriptural Law][69] for oneself [so that one will have a *shofar*]. Nevertheless, if a non-Jew performed an utterly forbidden labor on his own initiative, e.g., he made a *shofar* on the festival, a Jew is permitted to sound it. Even though the non-Jew made the *shofar* for the sake of the Jew, we are not concerned that the Jew may tell a non-Jew to make [a *shofar*] for him [on the festival]. This is a cause for concern only regarding matters that bring a person physical satisfaction. Since the *mitzvos*, by contrast, were not given for the sake of physical satisfaction,[70] there is no reason for concern that someone may transgress a prohibition in order to perform a *mitzvah*.

כה בַּמֶּה דְּבָרִים אֲמוּרִים? כְּשֶׁעָשָׂה הַנָּכְרִי הַשּׁוֹפָר מִקֶּרֶן שֶׁלּוֹ, דְּאֵין בּוֹ מִשּׁוּם אִסּוּר נוֹלַד בְּיוֹם טוֹב,[קס, 71] כֵּיוָן שֶׁבֵּין הַשְּׁמָשׁוֹת[72,73]

25 When does [the license to use a *shofar* made by a non-Jew on Rosh HaShanah] apply? When the non-Jew made the *shofar* from a horn that he owns, for then the prohibition against using *nolad* — something that came into existence on the festival[71] — does not apply. For during the period[72]

66. In the original, "the *techum*"; i.e., 2000 cubits from the place one spent the festival or from its external perimeters, as explained in sec. 396 and 397.

67. The permission granted in this subsection relates only to the more restrictive *Shabbos* limits imposed by Rabbinic law, i.e., 2000 cubits, which equal one *mil.* (R. Avraham Chayim Naeh defines a *mil* as approximately 1 km.) We are forbidden to tell a non-Jew to bring a *shofar* from beyond the wider *Shabbos* limits of twelve *mil* that are forbidden by Scriptural Law. See subsection 26.

68. For the prohibition against telling a non-Jew to perform an activity forbidden on *Shabbos* is itself a safeguard of Rabbinic origin. And in principle, the Rabbis do not institute a safeguard to protect a prohibition which is itself a safeguard of Rabbinic origin *(Rama, Orach Chayim* 586:21*)*.

69. In the original, *melachah gemurah* (lit., "a complete labor"); i.e., an outright forbidden labor.

70. *Rosh HaShanah* 28a.

71. On a festival, even for permitted activities, we are allowed to use only articles that we could have intended to use at the onset of the festival. Accordingly, it is forbidden to use an object that is *nolad* (lit., "born"), i.e., that first came into existence in its current state during the festival, for at the onset of the festival one could not have intended to use it. See sec. 495:13.

72. This period is called *bein hashmashos.*

כגירסת ב"י ד"ה וכתב ה"ר יונה. שו"ע סכ"א. וראה גם לעיל סי' שז סי"ב. **קנג** שו"ע שם. **קנד** הגהת הלבוש סכ"ב. מ"א סקכ"ד. וכ"ה לקמן סי' תקצה ס"ב (אפילו לצורך דרבנן). **קנה** ב"י שם. לבוש סכ"א. **קנו** מרדכי סוכה רמז תשמז. שו"ע סכ"ב. **קנז** כדלעיל סי' רמג ס"ב וש"נ. **קנח** ר"ה כח, א. וראה גם שו"ע ס"ה (שלא הגיע לידינו בשוע"ר). ט"ז ס"ק ד. לעיל סי' קכח ס"ס. סי' תמה ס"ח. לקמן סי' תקפט ס"ג. סי' תרמט סי"ב. הל' גזילה סי"ב. **קנט** לבוש סכ"ב. וכדלקמן סכ"ו לענין הביאו מחוץ לתחום, וש"נ. וראה זכרון יוסף אות עח. **קס** מ"א סקכ"ה.

הָיָה הַקֶּרֶן בְּיַד הַנָּכְרִי, וְהַנָּכְרִי לֹא הִקְצָה דַּעְתּוֹ מִלַּעֲשׂוֹת מִמֶּנּוּ שׁוֹפָר, שֶׁהֲרֵי בְּיָדוֹ וּבִרְשׁוּתוֹ הוּא לַעֲשׂוֹת מִמֶּנּוּ מַה שֶּׁיִּרְצֶה.[קסא]

אֲבָל אִם עָשָׂה נָכְרִי שׁוֹפָר בְּיוֹם טוֹב מִקֶּרֶן שֶׁל יִשְׂרָאֵל, כֵּיוָן שֶׁבֵּין הַשְּׁמָשׁוֹת לֹא הָיָה הַקֶּרֶן עוֹמֵד לַעֲשׂוֹת מִמֶּנּוּ שׁוֹפָר, שֶׁהֲרֵי לֹא הָיָה בִּרְשׁוּתוֹ שֶׁל נָכְרִי,[קסב] אִם כֵּן זֶה הַשּׁוֹפָר הוּא נוֹלַד בְּיוֹם טוֹב, וְאָסוּר הַיִּשְׂרָאֵל לְטַלְטְלוֹ כְּדֵי לִתְקֹעַ בּוֹ,[קסג] שֶׁאֵין דּוֹחִין שְׁבוּת מִפְּנֵי תְּקִיעַת שׁוֹפָר.[קסד]

וּמִכָּל מָקוֹם, אִם אֵין שָׁם שׁוֹפָר אַחֵר אֶלָּא הוּא — מֻתָּר לִתְקֹעַ בּוֹ, וְיֵשׁ לִסְמֹךְ עַל הַמַּתִּירִין[קסה] נוֹלַד בְּיוֹם טוֹב כְּדֵי שֶׁלֹּא לְבַטֵּל מִצְוַת עֲשֵׂה שֶׁל תּוֹרָה:[74]

כו אִם נָכְרִי הֵבִיא שׁוֹפָר בְּיוֹם טוֹב מִחוּץ לַתְּחוּם בִּשְׁבִיל יִשְׂרָאֵל,[קסו] אֲפִלּוּ הֱבִיאוֹ מִחוּץ לְי"ב מִיל[קסז, 75] — מֻתָּר לִתְקֹעַ בּוֹ אַף הַיִּשְׂרָאֵל שֶׁהוּבָא בִּשְׁבִילוֹ,[קסח] אֲפִלּוּ לְהָאוֹמְרִים[קסט] דְּחוּץ לְי"ב מִיל יֵשׁ אִסּוּר תְּחוּמִין מִן הַתּוֹרָה,[קע]

between sunset and the appearance of the stars,[73] the horn was in the possession of the non-Jew, and the non-Jew did not divert his attention from making it into a *shofar*. Since it was in his possession, it was his option to make it into whatever he desired.

[Different laws apply,] by contrast, if a non-Jew made a *shofar* on the festival from a horn that belongs to a Jew. At the time between sunset and the appearance of the stars, it was not [feasible] to make a *shofar* from this horn, for it was not in the non-Jew's domain at that time. This *shofar* is thus *nolad* on the festival. A Jew is therefore forbidden to move it in order to sound it, for [his obligation] does not override [even a Rabbinic prohibition in the category of] *shvus*.

Nevertheless, if no other *shofar* is available, it is permitted to sound it, relying on the [more lenient] authorities who permit the use of *nolad* on a festival so that the observance of a Scriptural commandment will not be negated.[74]

26 If during the festival a non-Jew brought a *shofar* for a Jew from beyond the *[Shabbos]* limits, even the Jew for whom it was brought is permitted to sound it. [This applies] even if [the non-Jew] brought it from beyond 12 *mil*.[75] Even those who maintain that the prohibition [against going beyond] twelve *mil* [from a town] is Scriptural in

73. At the commencement of the festival.

74. As explained in sec. 495, the Sages differ as to whether the prohibition against *nolad* must be observed. In ordinary matters, the more stringent view is followed. With regard to the observance of a *mitzvah,* since in this case there is no alternative, the more lenient view is followed, for the prohibition involved is only of Rabbinic origin.

75. As explained in sec. 396, some authorities maintain that according to Scriptural Law, one is forbidden to go beyond twelve *mil* (see footnote 67 above) from his "place" on the *Shabbos* and festivals. To safeguard this prohibition, the Sages restricted the radius to one *mil,* which is 2000 cubits. Some authorities, however, maintain that the entire prohibition is Rabbinic in origin.

קסא ראה גם לעיל סי' רנב סי"ב. סי' שכה ס"ו (ראה ב' הדעות שם). קסב ראה לעיל סי' שי סוף ס"ג. קסג מ"א שם. קסד כדלעיל סכ"ב. קסה לעיל סי' תצה סי"ג. סי' תקא ס"א. וראה ערוך השלחן סעיף לו. קסו הגהות אשרי פ"ד סי' ו. שו"ע סכ"ב. קסז שבפחות מותר אפילו לכתחלה, כדלעיל סכ"ד. קסח ראה העו"ב ר ע' יב. קסט לעיל סי' שצו ס"א. קע לבוש סכ"ב. מ"א סקכ"ד. קעא ראה לעיל סי' תקז קו"א סק"ד (ד"ה ואף שבהבא). קעב ס"א (בדעה

origin [would accept this ruling], for it is permitted to move an object that was brought from beyond the *[Shabbos]* limits. It is forbidden only to eat or derive benefit from it, i.e., to use it for one's own purposes, as stated in sec. 515[:13]. And one who sounds the *shofar* for the sake of the *mitzvah* is not at all considered as deriving personal satisfaction [i.e., pleasure] from this, as explained above.[76]

One must, however, be careful not to move the *shofar* four cubits [or more], as stated in sec. 515[:15].[77] See also the end [i.e., subsection 22] of that section.

27 Water or wine may be placed in [a *shofar*] to cleanse it;[78] this is not considered as repairing a utensil on the festival.[79] Urine, however, may not be used [for this purpose] even on weekdays, for this would be disrespectful.

SECTION 587 Laws Relating to One who Sounds the *Shofar* in a Cistern. (1–5)

1 The sound of the *shofar* must be heard without the admixture of any other sound at all. If one heard the sound [of the *shofar*] together with another sound, he has not fulfilled his obligation.[1] Therefore, [the following laws apply if] a person stands inside a large

שֶׁהֲרֵי דָּבָר הַבָּא מִחוּץ לַתְּחוּם מֻתָּר בְּטִלְטוּל, וְאֵינוֹ אָסוּר אֶלָּא בַּאֲכִילָה אוֹ בַּהֲנָאָה דְּהַיְנוּ לְהִשְׁתַּמֵּשׁ בּוֹ[קעא] כְּמוֹ שֶׁנִּתְבָּאֵר בְּסִימָן תקט"ו,[קעב] וְזֶה שֶׁתּוֹקֵעַ בּוֹ תְּקִיעָה שֶׁל מִצְוָה – אֵין זוֹ חֲשׁוּבָה הֲנָאָה כְּלָל[קעג] כְּמוֹ שֶׁנִּתְבָּאֵר לְמַעְלָה.[קעד,76]

וּמִכָּל מָקוֹם, צָרִיךְ לִזָּהֵר שֶׁלֹּא יְטַלְטְלֶנּוּ חוּץ לְד' אַמּוֹת,[קעה] וְעַל דֶּרֶךְ שֶׁנִּתְבָּאֵר בְּסִימָן תקט"ו,[קעו,77] וְעַיֵּן שָׁם בְּסוֹף הַסִּימָן:[קעז]

כז יָכוֹל לִתֵּן בְּתוֹכוֹ מַיִם אוֹ יַיִן[קעח] כְּדֵי לְצַחְצְחוֹ,[קעט,78] וְאֵין זֶה כִּמְתַקֵּן כְּלִי בְּיוֹם טוֹב.[קפ,79] אֲבָל מֵי רַגְלַיִם אַף בְּחֹל אָסוּר, מִפְּנֵי הַכָּבוֹד:[קפא]

סימן תקפז דִּין הַתּוֹקֵעַ לְתוֹךְ הַבּוֹר וּבוֹ ה' סְעִיפִים:

א שְׁמִיעַת קוֹל שׁוֹפָר צְרִיכָה לִהְיוֹת בְּלֹא עִרְבּוּב קוֹל אַחֵר כְּלָל, אֲבָל אִם שָׁמַע הַקּוֹל בְּעִרְבּוּבְיָא – לֹא יָצָא.[א,1] לְפִיכָךְ, הָעוֹמֵד בְּתוֹךְ חָבִית

---

76. Subsection 24. The rationale is the same. Benefiting from an object brought from beyond the *Shabbos* limits was prohibited, lest one tell a non-Jew to bring such an object, as explained in sec. 515:13.

77. An object that was brought from beyond its own *Shabbos* limits may be moved only within a radius of four cubits. Since it was taken beyond its original "place," the area it is granted is minimal.

78. *Rosh HaShanah* 32b.

79. For the *shofar* could have been used even if it had not been cleansed. *Mishnah Berurah* (#89) adds that because it is permitted to rinse dishes on *Yom-Tov,* cleansing as above does not appear to resemble repairing a vessel.

SECTION 587

1. As to listening to the *shofar* by means of a hearing aid, the Rebbe differentiates (in *Likkutei Sichos,* Vol. 21, p. 496) between an electronic device, and a mechanical device that operates like a simple trumpet. With the former — even

הב'). **קעג** שו"ת מהר"ם מרוטנבורג (פראג) סי' כב. שו"ת הרשב"א ח"א סי' תתמז (הובא בטור סי' תרנה). מרדכי עירובין רמז תקיד, בשם רבנו שמשון. הגהות אשרי שם. מ"א שם. **קעד** ראה סעיף כד וש"נ. **קעה** מ"א שם. **קעו** סעיף טו. **קעז** סעיף כב. **קעח** משנה לב, סוע"ב. טור ושו"ע סכ"ג. **קעט** ברייתא לג, א. טור ושו"ע שם. **קפ** רש"י במשנה שם ד"ה אם רצה. לבוש סכ"ג. **קפא** גמרא [ברייתא] שם. טור ושו"ע שם.
סימן תקפז: א טור. לבוש ס"א.

גְּדוֹלָה, אוֹ בְּבוֹר,[ב] אוֹ בְּדוּת[ג] דְּהַיְנוּ בִּנְיָן שֶׁרֻבּוֹ תַּחַת הַקַּרְקַע[ד,2] (אֲבָל אִם רֻבּוֹ לְמַעְלָה מִן הַקַּרְקַע אַף עַל פִּי שֶׁמִּקְצָתוֹ בְּתוֹךְ הַקַּרְקַע — דִּינוֹ כְּבַיִת[ה,6]), וְכֵן הָעוֹמֵד בְּתוֹךְ הַמְּעָרָה[ו] וְתוֹקֵעַ וְשָׁמְעוּ אֲחֵרִים מִבַּחוּץ,[3] אִם בָּרוּר לָהֶם שֶׁשָּׁמְעוּ קוֹל שׁוֹפָר — יָצְאוּ;[4] וְאִם לָאו — לֹא יָצְאוּ;[ז] לְפִי שֶׁהַקּוֹל מִתְבַּלְבֵּל בְּהֶבֶל הַבּוֹר וְהַדּוּת קֹדֶם שֶׁיֵּצֵא לַחוּץ וְאֶפְשָׁר שֶׁלֹּא שָׁמְעוּ אֶלָּא קוֹל הֲבָרָה.[ח] וְטוֹב לְהַחְמִיר שֶׁאַף שֶׁבָּרוּר לוֹ שֶׁקּוֹל שׁוֹפָר שָׁמַע — לֹא יִסְמֹךְ עַל בְּקִיאוּתוֹ, וְיַחֲזֹר וְיִשְׁמַע שֵׁנִית הַתְּקִיעוֹת שֶׁלֹּא מִן הַתּוֹקֵעַ בַּבּוֹר, אֲבָל לֹא יְבָרֵךְ שֵׁנִית, אֶלָּא אִם כֵּן בָּרוּר לוֹ שֶׁשָּׁמַע קוֹל הֲבָרָה,[ט] דִּסְפֵק בְּרָכוֹת לְהָקֵל:[5]

barrel, or in a cistern, or in a structure that is mainly underground,[2] or in a cave, and sounds the *shofar*, and others standing outside hear [the *shofar* blasts].[3] If they are certain that they heard the *shofar*, they have fulfilled their obligation.[4] If not, they have not fulfilled it, because the sound [of the *shofar*] is affected by the dank air of the cistern or the underground structure before it goes outside. Hence, it is possible that all they heard was an echo.

It is desirable to be stringent in such an instance. Even if one is certain that what he heard was the sound of a *shofar*, he should not rely on his certainty but should hear the [*shofar*] blasts again from someone who is sounding the *shofar* outside a cistern. He should not, however, recite the blessings again unless he is certain that what he heard was the sound of the echo. [The rationale is that when] there is a doubt whether [one should recite] a blessing, the lenient ruling should be followed.[5]

(If the majority of a structure is above ground, even though it is partly below ground, it is considered as [an ordinary] building.[6])

if its use does not entail labors forbidden on *Yom-Tov* — one does not fulfill his obligation, for what he hears is not the sound of the *shofar* itself, but the sound of the hearing aid. By contrast, a mechanical device presents no difficulty. (See also sec. 588, footnote 24 below.)

The above requirement — that one must hear the original sound, direct and unmediated — is what rules out the possibility of fulfilling one's obligation to hear the *Megillah* on Purim, via the telephone *(loc. cit.)* or the speakers of a microphone. (Needless to say, this question does not even arise in relation to hearing the *shofar* on Rosh HaShanah because, regardless of this consideration, neither telephone nor microphone may be used on *Yom-Tov*, just as on *Shabbos*.)

2. In the original, *dus;* i.e., a walled tank fixed in the ground. Some contemporary authorities apply this ruling to a basement as well.

3. *Rosh HaShanah* 27b. Noting that this law restates a *mishnah*, the *Mishnah Berurah* (sec. 587:1) quotes *Rishonim* — Rabbeinu Nissim and *Ritva* — who observe that this law dates from the era of Roman persecution, when Jews hid underground to fulfill the *mitzvah*. The same law became relevant again during the Spanish Inquisition and in other grim eras of Jewish history.

4. In addition (see sec. 589:7), both the person sounding the *shofar* and the person hearing the blasts must have the intent that the listener fulfill his obligation thereby.

5. And no blessing should be recited. For the recitation of almost all the blessings was instituted only by Rabbinic Law, and if the blessing one recites was not required, G-d's name was uttered in vain.

ב משנה כז, ב. טור ושו"ע ס"א. ג משנה שם. מ"א ס"ק א. ד רש"י עירובין קב, ב ד"ה של בור. מ"א שם. וראה לעיל סי' תנה סכ"ג. ה מ"א שם. ו רמב"ם פ"א ה"ח. שו"ע שם. ז משנה וגמרא שם, לפירוש רש"י שם ד"ה אותן, ורמב"ם שם , ושו"ע שם, שביאר הרא"ש פ"ג סי' ח, וב"י ד"ה ומ"ש הרא"ש, הובא בט"ז ס"ק א. לבוש שם. ח רא"ש שם. ט ט"ז שם. י גמרא שם. טור ושו"ע שם. יא רש"י שם. יב ר"ן (ז, א) ד"ה גמרא, בדעת הרמב"ם פ"א ה"ח. לבוש שם.

2 To whom does the above apply? To people standing outside[7] the cistern.[8] The person sounding the *shofar* and those standing with him in the cistern have fulfilled their obligation, for what they heard was certainly the sound of the *shofar*.

The above applies with regard to a cistern, or a structure that is mainly underground, or a cave. By contrast, since a large barrel echoes loudly, it is possible that what was heard by the person sounding the *shofar* and those standing with him was an echo. Accordingly, if they are certain that they heard the sound of the *shofar*, they have fulfilled their obligation; if [they are] not [certain], they have not fulfilled it.

ב בַּמֶּה דְּבָרִים אֲמוּרִים? בְּאוֹתָם הָעוֹמְדִים חוּץ[7] לַבּוֹר,[8] אֲבָל הַתּוֹקֵעַ עַצְמוֹ וְכֵן אוֹתָם הָעוֹמְדִים עִמּוֹ בַּבּוֹר – יָצְאוּ; שֶׁבְּוַדַּאי קוֹל שׁוֹפָר שָׁמְעוּ.[יא]

בַּמֶּה דְּבָרִים אֲמוּרִים? בְּבוֹר וְדוּת וּמְעָרָה, אֲבָל בְּחָבִית גְּדוֹלָה שֶׁהֲבָרָתָהּ גְּדוֹלָה, אַף הַתּוֹקֵעַ וְהָעוֹמְדִים עִמּוֹ בְּתוֹכָהּ אֶפְשָׁר שֶׁיִּשְׁמְעוּ קוֹל הֲבָרָה, לְפִיכָךְ אִם בָּרוּר לָהֶם שֶׁשָּׁמְעוּ קוֹל שׁוֹפָר – יָצְאוּ, וְאִם לָאו – לֹא יָצְאוּ:[יב]

3 If one began to sound the *shofar* in a cistern and [while doing so] ascended from the cistern and [outside it] completed the *tekiah* which he began while inside,[9] he has fulfilled his obligation.[10] For everything he heard, the part [in the cistern] and the part [outside it], was certainly the sound of the *shofar*. If, as he ascended, his ears were already above the edge of the cistern before he raised the *shofar* [to that height], he did not fulfill his obligation unless he is certain that what he heard at that moment was the sound of the *shofar*. Since it is not feasible that the ears of this individual and his *shofar* should both [reach that height] at exactly the same time, it is preferable that the *shofar* be raised above the edge of the cistern before his ears [reach that height], for then he will certainly hear the sound of the *shofar*, since [by that time] the *shofar* will be outside, in a place where there is no echo.

ג אִם הִתְחִיל לִתְקֹעַ בַּבּוֹר וְעָלָה חוּץ לַבּוֹר וְגָמַר אֶת הַתְּקִיעָה שֶׁהִתְחִיל בַּבּוֹר[9] – יָצָא יְדֵי חוֹבָתוֹ,[יג, 10] שֶׁכָּל מַה שֶּׁשָּׁמַע בֵּין כְּשֶׁהָיָה בִּפְנִים בֵּין כְּשֶׁהָיָה בַּחוּץ הָיָה בְּוַדַּאי קוֹל שׁוֹפָר.[יד] וְאִם כְּשֶׁעָלָה מֵהַבּוֹר הוֹצִיא אָזְנָיו חוּץ לַבּוֹר קֹדֶם שֶׁהוֹצִיא הַשּׁוֹפָר לַחוּץ – לֹא יָצָא,[טו] אֶלָּא אִם כֵּן בָּרוּר לוֹ שֶׁבָּרֶגַע הַהִיא שָׁמַע קוֹל שׁוֹפָר. וּלְפִי שֶׁאִי אֶפְשָׁר לְצַמְצֵם שֶׁיּוֹצִיא הָאָזְנַיִם וְהַשּׁוֹפָר כְּאֶחָד, לָכֵן טוֹב שֶׁיּוֹצִיא הַשּׁוֹפָר תְּחִלָּה קֹדֶם לָאָזְנַיִם,[טז] דְּאָז בְּוַדַּאי יִשְׁמַע קוֹל שׁוֹפָר, כֵּיוָן שֶׁהַשּׁוֹפָר הוּא בַּחוּץ בְּמָקוֹם שֶׁאֵין שָׁם קוֹל הֲבָרָה.

---

6. And one need not consider the possibility that he heard no more than an echo. (In the original, the above parenthetical statement appears earlier, in the middle of a long Hebrew sentence.)

7. As evident from subsection 3, what matters is not where a person is standing but whether his head is in the cistern or outside it.

8. *Rosh HaShanah, loc. cit.*

9. I.e., the same *shofar* blast.

10. *Ibid.* 28a.

(ד)מ"א סק"ב. **יג** גמרא כח, א. טור ושו"ע ס"ב. **יד** רש"י שם ד"ה בתוקע. טור ושו"ע שם. **טו** גמרא שם. מ"א סק"ג. **טז** מ"א שם.

וְאוֹתָם שֶׁהָיוּ עוֹמְדִים עִמּוֹ בַּבּוֹר בְּשָׁעָה שֶׁהִתְחִיל לִתְקֹעַ שָׁם,[יז] אַף עַל פִּי שֶׁלֹּא יָצְאוּ עִמּוֹ מֵהַבּוֹר, אַף עַל פִּי כֵן הֵם יוֹצְאִים בַּתְּקִיעוֹת, דִּכְשֶׁאָדָם בַּבּוֹר וְהַשּׁוֹפָר חוּץ לַבּוֹר בְּוַדַּאי שׁוֹמֵעַ קוֹל הַשּׁוֹפָר וְלֹא קוֹל הֲבָרָה כְּמוֹ שֶׁנִּתְבָּאֵר:[יח]

The people who were standing with him in the cistern while he began sounding the shofar fulfilled their obligation with his *shofar* blasts even though they did not ascend together with him. For when a person is in a cistern and the *shofar* is outside it, he certainly heard the sound of the *shofar* and not the sound of an echo, as explained above.

ד הַשּׁוֹמֵעַ מִקְצָת תְּקִיעַת קוֹל שׁוֹפָר וּמִקְצָת קוֹל הֲבָרָה, כְּגוֹן שֶׁהָיָה עוֹמֵד חוּץ לַבּוֹר וְהַתּוֹקֵעַ הִתְחִיל לִתְקֹעַ בַּבּוֹר וּבְאֶמְצַע הַתְּקִיעָה יָצָא חוּץ לַבּוֹר וּגְמָרָהּ שָׁם,[יט,10] וְכֵן הַשּׁוֹמֵעַ מִקְצָת תְּקִיעָה שֶׁלֹּא בְּחִיּוּב[כ] דְּהַיְנוּ קֹדֶם אוֹר הַיּוֹם וּמִקְצָתָהּ אַחַר אוֹר הַיּוֹם,[כא] וְכֵן הָאוֹמֵר לְמִי שֶׁמִּתְעַסֵּק בִּתְקִיעוֹת בְּלֹא כַּוָּנָה לְהוֹצִיא שׁוּם אָדָם בִּתְקִיעָתוֹ וּבְאֶמְצַע הַתְּקִיעָה אָמַר לוֹ כַּוֵּן לְהוֹצִיאֵנִי וְתָקַע[כב] וּמָשַׁךְ בָּהּ שִׁעוּר תְּקִיעָה, כָּל אֵלּוּ כֵּיוָן שֶׁמִּקְצָת הַתְּקִיעָה הוּא שֶׁלֹּא כְּתִקְנָהּ אַף עַל פִּי שֶׁבְּמִקְצָתָהּ שֶׁהִיא כְּתִקְנָהּ יֵשׁ בָּהּ שִׁעוּר תְּקִיעָה[כג] שֶׁיִּתְבָּאֵר בְּסִימָן תק"צ[כד] – לֹא יָצָא יְדֵי חוֹבָתוֹ, לְפִי שֶׁכָּל תְּקִיעָה צְרִיכָה שֶׁתְּהֵא בְּכַשְׁרוּת מִתְּחִלָּתָהּ וְעַד סוֹפָהּ אֲפִלּוּ הִיא אֲרֻכָּה הַרְבֵּה:

4 If one hears the sound of the *shofar* for part of a *tekiah* and hears an echo for part of it — e.g., he was standing outside the cistern, and the person sounding the *shofar* began sounding the *shofar* in the cistern and in the midst of the *tekiah* left it and completed [the *tekiah*] — [he has not fulfilled his obligation].[10]

[This same law applies] if one hears part of a *shofar* blast when he is not [yet] obligated, e.g., before daybreak, and part after daybreak. [It also applies] if one tells a person who is in the middle of casually sounding the *shofar* without the intent of having anyone fulfill his obligation: "Have the intent of enabling me to fulfill my obligation," and [the person sounding the *shofar*] thereupon extends the *tekiah* for the required length of time.

In all these instances, since the *tekiah* is partly invalid, even though the valid part is extended for the required measure as defined in sec. 590[:4-7], one has not fulfilled his obligation — because [a *tekiah*] must be valid from beginning to end, even if it is very extended.

ה הַתּוֹקֵעַ בְּבֵית הַכְּנֶסֶת וְיֵשׁ עוֹמְדִים בַּחוּץ רָחוֹק קְצָת מִבֵּית הַכְּנֶסֶת,

5 [The following laws apply if] a person sounds a *shofar* in a synagogue and there are people standing outside, at a slight

יז גמרא כז, סע"ב (כשכל התקיעה בפנים). רמ"א ס"ב (כשתחלת התקיעה בפנים). ב"י ד"ה ומ"ש אבל הוא (כשכל התקיעה בפנים). מ"א ס"ק ד (כשתחלת התקיעה בפנים). עיין מ"א סק"ג ודו"ק. **יח** שטוב שיוציא השופר תחלה קודם לאזניים. **יט** גמרא כח, א. טור ורמ"א ס"ג. **כ** רבנו ירוחם נתיב ו ח"ב (מח, ד). שו"ע ס"ג. **כא** רבה שם (קודם שיעלה עמוד השחר. וראה לקמן סי' תקפח ס"א). טור ושו"ע רס"י תקפח. ט"ז כאן ס"ק ב. **כב** רבנו ירוחם שם. שו"ע שם. **כג** טור בשם בעל העיטור הל' שופר (צט, א). רא"ש פ"ג סי' ח (מדסתם נראה דהיינו אפילו במשך שיעור תקיעה). רבנו ירוחם שם (שכן עיקר). דעה הא' בשו"ע שם. מ"א ס"ק ה (שכן עיקר). לבוש ס"ג. וראה גם לקמן סי' תקצב ס"ח. **כד** סעיף ז. **כה** ט"ז סק"א.

distance. If they are not certain that they heard the sound of a *shofar,* they must hear [the *shofar*][11] a second time, because they may [merely] have heard an echo. If, however, it is clear to them that what they heard was the sound of the *shofar,* they need not impose an [unnecessary] stringency upon themselves and [endeavor to] hear [the *shofar*] a second time.

אִם אֵין בָּרוּר לָהֶם שֶׁשָּׁמְעוּ קוֹל שׁוֹפָר – צְרִיכִים לִשְׁמֹעַ הַתְּקִיעוֹת[11] שֵׁנִית, לְפִי שֶׁאֶפְשָׁר שֶׁשָּׁמְעוּ קוֹל הֲבָרָה, אֲבָל אִם נִרְאֶה לָהֶם בָּרוּר שֶׁקּוֹל שׁוֹפָר שָׁמְעוּ – אֵינָם צְרִיכִים לְהַחְמִיר עַל עַצְמָן וְלִשְׁמֹעַ שֵׁנִית:[כה]

SECTION 588 The Time for the Sounding of the *Shofar.* (1-9)

1 The time for the sounding of the *shofar* is during the day,[1] as it is written,[2] "It shall be a day of sounding [the *shofar*]"; i.e., [the *shofar*] should be sounded by day and not at night. The entire day is acceptable for the sounding of the *shofar,* from dawn[3] until the appearance of the stars.[4]

Our Sages, nevertheless, required that we wait until sunrise, in order to remove any doubt as to whether it is [still] night, for not everyone is knowledgeable with regard to [the time of] dawn. However, if a person transgressed and sounded the *shofar* after dawn, before sunrise, he has fulfilled his obligation and is not obligated to sound it a second time.

סימן תקפח זְמַן תְּקִיעַת שׁוֹפָר ובו ט' סְעִיפִים:

א זְמַן תְּקִיעַת שׁוֹפָר בַּיּוֹם,[א,1] שֶׁנֶּאֱמַר[ב,2] "יוֹם תְּרוּעָה וגו'" – בַּיּוֹם וְלֹא בַּלַּיְלָה.[ג] וְכָל הַיּוֹם כָּשֵׁר לִתְקִיעַת שׁוֹפָר[ד] מֵעֲלוֹת הַשַּׁחַר[ה,3] עַד צֵאת הַכּוֹכָבִים,[ו,4] אֶלָּא שֶׁחֲכָמִים הִצְרִיכוּ לְהַמְתִּין עַד שֶׁתָּנֵץ הַחַמָּה[ז] שֶׁיֵּצֵא מִכְּלַל סְפֵק לַיְלָה,[ח] שֶׁאֵין הַכֹּל בְּקִיאִין בְּעַמּוּד הַשַּׁחַר.[ט] וּמִכָּל מָקוֹם אִם עָבַר וְתָקַע מִשֶּׁעָלָה עַמּוּד הַשַּׁחַר קֹדֶם הָנֵץ הַחַמָּה – יָצָא,[י] וְאֵין צָרִיךְ לִתְקֹעַ שֵׁנִית:

---

11. In the original, "the *tekios.*" In its plural form, as here, this word signifies not only the first of the three statutory sounds of the *shofar* (viz., *tekiah-shevarim-teruah;* see sec. 590:1), but also the *shofar* blasts collectively.

SECTION 588

1. *Megillah* 20b.

2. *Bamidbar* 29:1.

3. Dawn *(alos hashachar)* is defined as the first appearance of light on the eastern horizon before sunrise *(hanetz hachamah).* In sec. 89:1, the Alter Rebbe reckons the moment of dawn as preceding sunrise by the length of time that it takes to walk four *mil.* (A *mil* is defined by R. Avraham Chayim Naeh as approximately 1 km.) In sec. 459:10, the Alter Rebbe cites two figures for the time it takes to walk a *mil* — 18 minutes and 24 minutes, and recommends the latter figure. Thus, in this context, we are speaking of 96 minutes before sunrise as being the moment of dawn. The Alter Rebbe maintains that this figure must be translated into degrees. See Vol. 2 of the present work, sec. 58, footnote 7.

4. In the original, *tzeis hakochavim.*

סימן תקפח: א משנה מגילה כ, ב. טור ושו"ע ס"א. ב במדבר כט, א. גמרא שם. ג רש"י ר"ה כח, א ד"ה קודם. טור ושו"ע שם. ד משנה מגילה שם. טור. ה ר"ה כח, א. וראה משנה מגילה כ, א. טור ושו"ע שם. וראה גם לעיל סי' תפח ס"ג (לענין הלל). ו ראה גמרא שם כ, ב. טור. לעיל שם. ז משנה שם. טור ושו"ע שם. ח רש"י שם ד"ה עד הנץ. מ"א ס"ק א. ט רש"י שם ד"ה וכולן. וראה לעיל שם: לפי שהוא כלילה בעיני הבריות, וש"נ. י טור ושו"ע שם.

ב אִם שָׁמַע מִקְצָת תְּקִיעָה קֹדֶם עַמּוּד הַשַּׁחַר וּמִקְצָתָהּ אַחַר עַמּוּד הַשַּׁחַר – נִתְבָּאֵר בְּסִימָן תקפ״ז:[יא]

2 [The law governing a situation] in which one heard part of a *tekiah* before dawn and part after dawn is explained in sec. 587[:4].

ג שָׁמַע תֵּשַׁע תְּקִיעוֹת בְּתֵשַׁע שָׁעוֹת בַּיּוֹם אוֹ מִתֵּשַׁע בְּנֵי אָדָם שֶׁתָּקְעוּ כְּאֶחָד – נִתְבָּאֵר בְּסִימָן תק״צ:[יב,5]

3 [The law governing a situation] in which one heard nine *shofar* blasts over [the course of] nine hours during the day or from nine men who sounded [the *shofar*] simultaneously is explained in sec. 590[:13-14].[5]

ד יוֹם טוֹב שֶׁל רֹאשׁ הַשָּׁנָה שֶׁחָל לִהְיוֹת בְּשַׁבָּת – אֵין תּוֹקְעִין בַּשּׁוֹפָר,[יג,6] אַף עַל פִּי שֶׁהַתְּקִיעָה בַּשּׁוֹפָר אֵינָהּ מְלָאכָה[יד] וְאֵינָהּ אֲסוּרָה בְּשַׁבָּת וְיוֹם טוֹב אֶלָּא מִדִּבְרֵי סוֹפְרִים,[טו,7] מִשּׁוּם עוּבְדִין דְּחוֹל.[טז,8] וְלָמָּה אֵין דּוֹחִין אִסּוּר קַל כָּזֶה[יז] מִפְּנֵי מִצְוַת עֲשֵׂה שֶׁל תּוֹרָה[יח] כְּמוֹ שֶׁדּוֹחִין אוֹתוֹ בְּכָל יוֹם טוֹב שֶׁל רֹאשׁ הַשָּׁנָה[יט,9] הוֹאִיל וְאֵין בּוֹ שְׁבוּת[10] גָּמוּר,

4 When the festival of Rosh HaShanah falls on *Shabbos,* the *shofar* is not sounded.[6] Sounding the *shofar* does not involve a forbidden labor; it is forbidden on *Shabbos* and festivals only as a result of a Rabbinic decree,[7] [because] it is considered a mundane activity.[8] Why then does [the performance of] a Scriptural commandment not override such a light prohibition, as it does on every Rosh HaShanah?[9] It is not [even] designated as a *shvus*[10] in a complete sense.

---

5. In the first situation, one is considered — under certain conditions — to have fulfilled his obligation. The same applies to the second situation, under certain conditions; e.g., he heard all the *shofar* blasts in the proper sequence.

6. *Rosh HaShanah* 29b.

7. In the original, *midivrei sofrim.*

8. In the original, which appears in the plural, *uvdin dechol* (lit., "weekday activities").

In earlier Hebrew editions, the following two sentences appeared in the body of the text: "See: *Rashi,* Rabbeinu Yitzchak Alfasi and Rabbeinu Nissim, on *Shabbos* 3b; *Shabbos* 117b; *Beis Yosef, Orach Chayim* 254. In this respect, the sounding of the *shofar* is equivalent to removing a loaf of bread [attached to the wall of an oven]."

I.e., these two activities share the common denominator that each is defined as a skill *(chochmah),* not as a form of labor *(melachah).* Nonetheless, the Sages forbade both activities on *Shabbos.*

9. The Alter Rebbe's question is that the prohibition against sounding the *shofar* should apply on any festival — including Rosh HaShanah — as well as on *Shabbos.* Hence, just as the performance of the *mitzvah* overrides the prohibition on any Rosh HaShanah, should it not override it when Rosh HaShanah falls on *Shabbos?*

In a number of letters the Rebbe points out that the Alter Rebbe's argument here constitutes an innovative observation, a *chiddush,* namely: The reason that the *shofar* is not sounded on *Shabbos* is not simply the concern lest it be carried in a public thoroughfare; the Alter Rebbe writes here that the primary issue is the prohibition of mundane activity. And the other concern, about carrying,

יא סעיף ד. יב סי״ג־ד. יג משנה כט, ב. טור ושו״ע ס״ה. יד גמרא שם. לבוש ס״ה. טו רמב״ם פ״ב ה״ו. טז משמעות הגמרא ורש״י [עיין ברש״י שבת ג׳ ע״ב ד״ה הדביק (דרדיית הפת שבות היא), ובריי״ף ור״ן שם (א, ב) ד״ה אמר (לאו שבות היא אלא עובדין דחול), ובגמרא דף קי״ז ע״ב (כמה דאפשר לשנויי משנינן) ורש״י שם ד״ה מרדה (שהוא דרך חול), ובב״י סי׳ רנ״ד ד״ה ומ״ש ואם בשוגג, ולעיל שם ס״ט. ותקיעת שופר שוה לרדיית הפת כמבואר בר״ה שם ושבת שם]. וראה שלחן המלך ח״ב ע׳ קצה הערה 1. וראה גם לקמן סי׳ תקפט ס״ב. סי׳ תקצו ס״ב. סי׳ תרכג סי״א. יז ראה לעיל סי׳ רנד ס״ז וס״ט (שהתירו רדיה לצורך שבת). סי׳ שו סי״ח (שהתירו עובדין דחול מפני מצוה). יח רמב״ם שם. מ״א סק״ד. וראה רשימות חוברת ס. אג״ק ח״ב ע׳ רמג, רסה. ח״ט ע׳ רג. שלחן המלך שם ע׳ קצה־קצו. יט ראה לקו״ש ח״ג ע׳ 948 הערה 4. שלחן המלך שם ע׳ קצז״ח. כ רבה בגמרא ר״ה שם. רמב״ם

לְפִי שֶׁהַכֹּל חַיָּבִין בִּתְקִיעַת שׁוֹפָר וְאֵין הַכֹּל בְּקִיאִין בִּתְקִיעַת שׁוֹפָר גְּזֵרָה שֶׁמָּא יִטְּלֶנּוּ בְּיָדוֹ וְיֵלֵךְ אֵצֶל הַבָּקִי לִלְמֹד וְיַעֲבִירֶנּוּ ד׳ אַמּוֹת בִּרְשׁוּת הָרַבִּים:[כ,11]

[The prohibition was enacted, because] "everyone is obligated to hear the sounding of the *shofar* but not everyone knows how to sound the blasts [correctly. The Sages therefore] decreed [that the *shofar* should not be sounded], lest someone take the *shofar* in hand and go to an expert to learn [how to sound it], and thus carry it four cubits in the public domain."[11]

ה וְדִין טִלְטוּל[12] הַשּׁוֹפָר בְּשַׁבָּת זוֹ כְּדִין טִלְטוּלוֹ בְּכָל שַׁבְּתוֹת הַשָּׁנָה, שֶׁאֵין מְטַלְטְלִין אוֹתוֹ כִּי אִם לְצֹרֶךְ מְקוֹמוֹ אוֹ לְצֹרֶךְ גּוּפוֹ,[כא] דְּהַיְנוּ לִסְמֹךְ בּוֹ אֶת הַקְּעָרָה וְכַיּוֹצֵא בָּזֶה.[כב]

בַּמֶּה דְּבָרִים אֲמוּרִים? בְּשַׁבָּת, אֲבָל אִם חָל בְּחֹל אַף עַל פִּי שֶׁמֻּתָּר לְטַלְטְלוֹ[כג] אֲפִלּוּ שֶׁלֹּא לְצֹרֶךְ גּוּפוֹ וּמְקוֹמוֹ כֵּיוָן שֶׁתּוֹקְעִין בּוֹ בַּיּוֹם, וְדִינוֹ כִּכְלִי שֶׁמְּלַאכְתּוֹ לְהֶתֵּר

5 The laws pertaining to moving[12] the *shofar* on [Rosh HaShanah that falls on] a *Shabbos* are the same as those that apply on all other *Shabbosos* throughout the year; i.e., a *shofar* may be moved only because its place is needed or because it itself is needed for some purpose [which is not forbidden on *Shabbos*], e.g., to support a dish or the like.

When does the above apply? On *Shabbos*. If, however, [Rosh HaShanah] falls during the week, [different rules apply]. It is permitted to move the *shofar*, even if it is not needed for some purpose and even its place is not required. [The rationale is that] since it is sounded that day, it is governed by the laws applying to a utensil employed for a permitted

---

serves only to bolster the prohibition of mundane activity, so that it will not be overridden by the commandment to sound the *shofar*. See: *Igros Kodesh*, Vol. 2, p. 243, and Vol. 9, pp. 203, 223.

10. A Rabbinic prohibition enacted because an activity resembles — or may lead to the performance of — an activity forbidden by Scriptural Law *(Rambam, Hilchos Shabbos* 21:1*)*.

11. Thereby violating the Scriptural prohibition against doing so on *Shabbos (Rosh HaShanah* 29b*)*. Carrying the *shofar* four cubits in the public domain is a greater cause for concern than [the equal prohibition of] carrying it from a private to a public domain, because the latter two domains are clearly demarcated by fences and the like. (See *Tosafos* on *Beitzah* 18a, *s.v. Shema.*)

In their *maamarim,* the Rebbes of *Chabad* (beginning with the Alter Rebbe, in the *maamar* entitled *Yom-Tov shel Rosh HaShanah* in *Likkutei Torah*) raise the question: Why were Jews in general, including many men of stature, prevented from fulfilling this significant *mitzvah,* only because of the slender possibility that some simple people might transgress by carrying a *shofar* on *Shabbos?*

The *maamarim* explain that in fact the *Shabbos* day itself elicits spiritual influences similar to those elicited by the sounding of the *shofar.* Hence there is less spiritual imperative to sound the *shofar* on such a day. Accordingly, since there is a possibility that a Scriptural prohibition will be committed, the sounding of the *shofar* should be withheld.

12. The Hebrew word *tiltul* refers to moving an object within one domain, not transferring it from one domain to another. Since sounding the *shofar* is prohibited on *Shabbos,* the *shofar* is considered an object that is used for a forbidden purpose. The laws governing moving it are set out in sec. 308:2.

שם. טור ולבוש שם. מ״א שם. ט״ז ס״ק ה. **כא** אור זרוע הל׳ שבת סי׳ פו אות א. הגהות אשרי שבת פ״ב סי׳ כד. רמ״א ס״ה. וראה גם לעיל סי׳ שח ס״כ. **כב** ראה לעיל שם סי״ב. **כג** ראה ט״ז סי׳ תקצו בסופו.

שֶׁנִּתְבָּאֵר בְּסִימָן ש"ח,[כד,13] מִכָּל מָקוֹם אָסוּר לְהִשְׁתַּמֵּשׁ בּוֹ[כה] וְלֵהָנוֹת מִמֶּנּוּ[כו] בּוֹ בַּיּוֹם[כז] כְּגוֹן לִסְמֹךְ בּוֹ אֶת הַקְּעָרָה וְכַיּוֹצֵא בָּזֶה, שֶׁהֲרֵי הֻקְצָה לְמִצְוָתוֹ,[כח] וּכְמוֹ שֶׁיִּתְבָּאֵר בְּסִימָן תרס"ה,[כט] עַיֵּן שָׁם:[14]

purpose, which are described in sec. 308[:16].[13]

Nevertheless, on the day [of Rosh HaShanah] one may not use it or derive benefit from it, e.g., to use it to support a dish or the like, because it was set aside to be used only for its *mitzvah,* as will be clarified in sec. 665; see that source.[14]

ז קָטָן הַתּוֹקֵעַ בְּשַׁבָּת זוֹ – בֵּית דִּין[15] מְצֻוִּין לְהַפְרִישׁוֹ אַף עַל פִּי שֶׁלֹּא הִגִּיעַ לְחִנּוּךְ[ל,17] כְּמוֹ שֶׁנִּתְבָּאֵר בְּסִימָן שמ"ג,[לא] עַיֵּן שָׁם.[16]

(אַף[לב] עַל פִּי[18] שֶׁעִקַּר מִצְוַת שְׁמִיעַת שׁוֹפָר[לג] הִיא שְׁמִיעַת קוֹלוֹ בִּלְבַד,[לד,19] מִכָּל מָקוֹם) אִם הַתּוֹקֵעַ הוּא פָּטוּר מִמִּצְוָה זוֹ – אֵינוֹ מוֹצִיא אֲחֵרִים יְדֵי חוֹבָתָן בִּתְקִיעָתוֹ.[לה] וְאֵלּוּ הֵן הַפְּטוּרִים:

6 If a child sounded the *shofar* [on Rosh HaShanah that fell] on *Shabbos,* the rabbinic court[15] is required to restrain him from doing so, as clarified in sec. 343[:1]; see that source.[16] [This applies] even if he has not reached the age at which he should be trained [to observe the *mitzvos.*][17]

(Even[18] though the essence of the *mitzvah* of hearing the *shofar* is hearing its sound alone,)[19] if the person sounding the *shofar* is exempt from this *mitzvah,* his *shofar* blasts cannot enable others to discharge their obligation thereby.

The following individuals are exempt:

---

13. There it is written that a utensil that is used for a permitted purpose may be moved on *Shabbos* for any purpose, even for the sake of the utensil itself. It may not be moved for no purpose at all.

14. Sec. 665 of the Alter Rebbe's *Shulchan Aruch* is not extant. In the *Shulchan Aruch* of R. Yosef Caro, that section states that since an *esrog* is set aside for its *mitzvah,* it may not be eaten throughout the festival.

15. Not to mention his father (sec. 343: 2).

16. There the Alter Rebbe explains that if a child commits a transgression that affects only himself, the court is not required to restrain him. In the case of an act that becomes public knowledge, such as sounding the *shofar,* he must be restrained, to avert the impression that this act is permitted.

17. The last 16 English words in the above sentence translate the Hebrew term, *lo higiya lechinuch.*

18. *Kuntreis HaShulchan* points out that sec. 589 ("The Individuals who are Fit to Sound the *Shofar*") should begin at this point.

19. In a letter appearing in *Igros Kodesh,* Vol. 2, p. 140, the Rebbe writes that parentheses in this work possibly indicate a matter that the Alter Rebbe desired to reconsider at a later date. (Cf. *She'eris Yehudah,* Responsum 363, and *Shaar HaKollel* 1:2.) *Kuntreis HaShulchan* enumerates many other possible functions of parentheses in this work. In the present case, for example, a scribe may have indicated words that were added to bridge a gap in the manuscript before him.

כד סעיף טז. **כה** מ"א סק"ה. **כו** ראה לעיל סי' תקיד סכ"ד (בנר של יום טוב, שאסור להסתפק ולאכלו אבל מותר לטלטלו). לקמן סי' תרלח ס"ה (בסכך ודפנות סוכה, שאסור להסתפק לחצוץ בו שיניו אבל מותר להריח וכיו"ב). מ"מ וציונים. **כז** משא"כ לאחר זמנו. וראה לעיל סי' כא ס"א. סי' מב ס"ו. לקמן סי' תרלח סי"ט. **כח** מ"א שם. **כט** סימן זה בשוע"ר לא הגיע לידינו, וראה שו"ע שם ס"א־ב. לעיל סי' תקיד סכ"ד (לענין נר של יום טוב). לקמן סי' תרלח ס"א־ב (לענין סכך ודופני סוכה). קו"א לעיל סי' רסג ס"ק ז. סי' רסה ס"ק א. **ל** ר"ן (ט, ב) ד"ה והנ"מ. מ"מ פ"ב סוף ה"ז (ממשמעות הרמב"ם שם). ולענין יום טוב ראה לקמן סי' תקצו ס"ב. **לא** סוף ס"א, וש"נ. **לב** בקונטרס השלחן כתב שכאן מתחיל סי' תקפט. וכ"מ לקמן סי' תקצב סוף ס"ח. **לג** בקונטרס השלחן הגיה: תקיעת שופר. **לד** לבוש סי' תקפט ס"א. וכדלעיל סי' תקפה ס"ד. **לה** משנה כט, א. טור ושו"ע ס"א. **לו** גמרא ל, א ממשנה קידושין כט, א. טור ושו"ע ס"ג.

נָשִׁים[לו] וַעֲבָדִים[לז] מִפְּנֵי שֶׁהִיא מִצְוַת עֲשֵׂה שֶׁהַזְּמַן גְּרָמָא,[לח,20] וְחֵרֵשׁ וְשׁוֹטֶה[21] וְקָטָן[לט,22] אַף עַל פִּי שֶׁהִגִּיעַ לְחִנּוּךְ אֵינוֹ מוֹצִיא אֶת הַגְּדוֹלִים יְדֵי חוֹבָתָן שֶׁחַיָּבִים מִן הַתּוֹרָה:[מ,23]

women and bondmen, because this is a positive *mitzvah* whose observance is associated with a specific time;[20] and deaf-mutes, mentally and emotionally incompetent individuals,[21] and minors.[22]

[Hence, even if a minor] reaches an educable age, he cannot enable adults to discharge their obligation, for it is mandated by Scriptural Law.[23]

ז חֵרֵשׁ הַשּׁוֹמֵעַ וְאֵינוֹ מְדַבֵּר הֲרֵי הוּא כְּפִקֵּחַ[מא] וְחַיָּב בִּתְקִיעַת שׁוֹפָר,[24] וּלְפִיכָךְ הוּא מוֹצִיא אֲחֵרִים יְדֵי חוֹבָתָן,[מב] וְאֶחָד מֵהַשּׁוֹמְעִין מְבָרֵךְ וְהוּא תּוֹקֵעַ.[מג] אֲבָל הַמְדַבֵּר וְאֵינוֹ שׁוֹמֵעַ אֵינוֹ מוֹצִיא, דְּכֵיוָן דְּאֵינוֹ שׁוֹמֵעַ לָאו בַּר חִיּוּבָא הוּא,[מד] דְּאֵין הַמִּצְוָה בַּתְּקִיעָה אֶלָּא בַּשְּׁמִיעָה:[מה]

7 One who is mute who can hear but cannot speak is considered mentally competent and is obligated to hear the sounding of the *shofar.*[24] He can therefore fulfill the *mitzvah* on behalf of others; one of the listeners should recite the blessing and he should sound the *shofar.*

If a person can speak but cannot hear, he cannot fulfill the *mitzvah* on behalf of others, for since he cannot hear he is not obligated by the *mitzvah,* which is not to sound [the *shofar*], but to hear it.

ח סוּמָא חַיָּב בִּתְקִיעַת שׁוֹפָר. וְאִם הָיָה מֻחְזָק לִתְקֹעַ בְּכָל שָׁנָה וְסִלְּקוּהוּ מִפְּנֵי שֶׁחָשְׁשׁוּ לְדִבְרֵי הָאוֹמֵר[מו] דְּסוּמָא פָּטוּר מִכָּל הַמִּצְוֹת

8 A blind man is obligated to hear the *shofar* being sounded. If a blind man held the position of sounding the *shofar* every year and was then replaced because [the congregation] gave weight to the view that a blind person is exempt from all the

---

20. In the original, *mitzvas aseh shehazman grama (Rosh HaShanah 30a).* Sec. 589:2 states that it is customary, nevertheless, for women to observe this *mitzvah.*

21. The term *shoteh* in the Hebrew original relates to both mental and emotional incapacity.

22. *Rosh HaShanah* 29a. Being incompetent, and/or unable to take full responsibility for their conduct, individuals of the second category are exempt by Scriptural Law from the performance of *mitzvos.*

23. As to a boy who has passed the age of *bar-mitzvah,* the *Mishnah Berurah* 589:2 states that before he is allowed to sound the *shofar* on behalf of others, it must be certain that he has manifested signs of physical maturity (see sec. 55:12).

24. Responsa *Halachos Ketanos* (R. Yaakov Hagiz, Venice, 5464/1704, Vol. 2, sec. 45, cited in *Baer Heitev* 589:1 and in *Mishnah Berurah* 589:4) writes that if a person can hear by means of an instrument, such as a trumpet constructed for this purpose, he does not fall under the halachic definition of a *cheresh* and hence is obligated to hear the sounding of the *shofar.* Now, we see from sec. 587 that the *mitzvah* of hearing the *shofar* cannot be fulfilled by hearing its reverberations. (See sec. 587, footnote 1 there.) Evidently the authorities understand that the function of this trumpet is merely to focus the diffused soundwaves.

וראה גם לקמן סי׳ תקפט ס״ב. סי׳ תקצב ס״ח. **לז** רש״י כט, א ד״ה ועבדים. רמב״ם פ״ב ה״א. וראה גם לעיל סי׳ קפו סוף ס״א. **לח** גמרא ל, א. טור ושו״ע שם. **לט** משנה כט, א. טור ושו״ע ס״א. **מ** ראה לעיל סי׳ קפו ס״ג. סי׳ רעא ס״ז. **מא** חגיגה ב, ב. וכדלעיל סי׳ נה סי״א. סי׳ קצט ס״י. **מב** ב״י בשם התשב״ץ (ח״ג סי׳ קיג). רמ״א ס״ב. **מג** ב״ח סוד״ה אדם. מ״א סק״א. וראה לקמן יו״ד סי׳ א ס״ק מו. **מד** תשב״ץ שם. כלבו סי׳ סד. שו״ע ס״ב. **מה** תשב״ץ שם. וראה העו״ב ד ע׳ ז. ה ע׳ טז־יז. **מו** רב יהודה ב״ק פז, א. רבנו ירוחם נתיב ה ח״ד (מב, ד) ונתיב יג ח״א (קג, א).

הָאֲמוּרוֹת בַּתּוֹרָה,[25] אִם אֵין בָּקִי בִּתְקִיעָה כָּמוֹהוּ — יַחֲזִירוּהוּ לְמִנּוּיוֹ, אֲבָל לְכַתְּחִלָּה אֵין לְסַלְּקוֹ אַף עַל פִּי שֶׁנִּמְצָא בָּקִי כָּמוֹהוּ,[מז] לְפִי שֶׁהָעִקָּר אֶצְלֵנוּ דְּסוּמָא חַיָּב בְּכָל הַמִּצְוֹת הָאֲמוּרוֹת בַּתּוֹרָה:[מח]

mitzvos stated in the Torah,[25] he should be reinstated if no one else is equally capable. Initially, however, he should not have been displaced, even though there is someone equally capable, for we follow the principle that a blind person is obligated to observe all the *mitzvos* of the Torah.

ט טֻמְטוּם[26] וְאַנְדְּרוֹגִינוֹס[מט, 27] אֵין חַיָּבִין אֶלָּא מִסָּפֵק שֶׁמָּא הֵן זְכָרִים;[נ] לְפִיכָךְ אֵינָן מוֹצִיאִין אֶת אֲחֵרִים שֶׁחַיָּבִים בְּוַדַּאי,[נא] אֲבָל מוֹצִיא הוּא הָאַנְדְּרוֹגִינוֹס אֶת הָאַנְדְּרוֹגִינוֹס כְּמוֹתוֹ[נב] שֶׁאֵינוֹ חַיָּב אֶלָּא מִסָּפֵק, אֲבָל אֵינוֹ מוֹצִיא אֶת הַטֻּמְטוּם,[נג] וַאֲפִלּוּ טֻמְטוּם כְּמוֹתוֹ אֵינוֹ מוֹצִיא[נד] אַף עַל פִּי שֶׁשְּׁנֵיהֶם סָפֵק, דְּשֶׁמָּא לִכְשֶׁיִּקָּרַע טֻמְטוּם זֶה יִמָּצֵא זָכָר וְלִכְשֶׁתִּקָּרַע זוֹ תִּמָּצֵא נְקֵבָה:[נה, 28]

9 A *tumtum*[26] and a hermaphrodite[27] are obligated [to hear the *shofar*] only because of the doubt as to whether they are males. Therefore they cannot act on behalf of others whose obligation [in the performance of this *mitzvah*] is definite. One hermaphrodite may, however, fulfill the obligation on behalf of another hermaphrodite, who like himself is obligated only because of a doubt.

[A hermaphrodite] cannot fulfill the obligation on behalf of a *tumtum*. Indeed, even a *tumtum* cannot fulfill the obligation on behalf of a *tumtum* like himself, because though [both parties] are obligated by reason of a doubt, [the reasons for the doubt are different]: surgery may prove one *tumtum* to be a male and the other, a female. [28]

סימן תקפט מִי הֵם הָרְאוּיִים לִתְקִיעַת שׁוֹפָר וּבוֹ ט' סְעִיפִים:

SECTION 589 The Individuals who are Fit to Sound the *Shofar*. (1–9)

א מִי[1] שֶׁחֶצְיוֹ עֶבֶד וְחֶצְיוֹ בֶּן חוֹרִין[2] צָרִיךְ שֶׁיִּתְקַע לוֹ בֶּן חוֹרִין

1 If[1] a person is half bondman and half free,[2] it is necessary that a person who is [entirely] a free man sound the *shofar* to enable him to

---

25. See *Bava Kama* 87a.

26. A person of masked and indeterminate gender.

27. In the original, *androgynus*.

28. Whereas the doubt regarding the hermaphrodite is a theoretical question of halachic status, the doubt regarding the *tumtum* is a factual question — ignorance of the person's gender, which may prove to be either male or female.

SECTION 589

1. *Kuntreis HaShulchan* points out that sec. 589 ("The Individuals who are Fit to Sound the *Shofar*") actually begins earlier, see sec. 589, footnote 18.

2. This situation can occur if a bondman owned by two partners was freed by only one of them.

מז שו"ת רדב"ז ח"ד סי' נט (א'קלא). כנסת הגדולה הגה"ט. מ"א סק"א. **מח** רדב"ז שם. ב"י סי' תעג בסופו. וכדלעיל סי' נג סי"ח וש"נ. **מט** גמרא [ברייתא] כט, א. טומטום שהוא אטום לגמרי ולא נודע אם הוא זכר או נקבה, ואנדרוגינוס שיש לו זכרות ונקבות (לעיל סי' יז ס"ב). **נ** רש"י שם ד"ה וטומטום. דעה הב' בלבוש ס"ד. וראה ב"ח ד"ה אנדרוגינוס בשם רש"ל בביאורו לטור. אליה זוטא ס"ק א. וראה גם לעיל סי' יז ס"ב. לקמן סי' תרמ ס"ב. **נא** ברייתא שם. רמב"ם פ"ב ה"ב. מ"א סק"ב. **נב** ברייתא שם ורש"י ד"ה אנדרוגינוס. טור ושו"ע ס"ד. **נג** משמעות הברייתא שם (שאינו מוציא אלא מינו). **נד** ברייתא שם. טור ושו"ע שם. **נה** רש"י שם ד"ה טומטום. רמב"ם שם. טור ולבוש סוף ס"ד. וראה גם לעיל סי' קצט ס"ח.

לְהוֹצִיאוֹ,[א,3] אֲבָל אֵינוֹ יוֹצֵא בִּתְקִיעָתוֹ שֶׁל עַצְמוֹ,[ב] לְפִי שֶׁצַּד חֵרוּת שֶׁבּוֹ נִתְחַיֵּב[4] בְּתֵשַׁע תְּקִיעוֹת[5] שְׁלֵמוֹת בְּכַשְׁרוּתוֹ, וְאִם יִתְקַע בְּעַצְמוֹ תְּהֵא כָּל תְּקִיעָה וּתְקִיעָה שֶׁיּוֹצֵאת מִפִּיו חֶצְיָהּ פְּסוּלָה מֵחֲמַת צַד עַבְדוּת שֶׁבּוֹ:[ג,6]

fulfill his obligation.[3] He cannot fulfill it by sounding the *shofar* himself because, being partly free, he is required[4] to hear nine[5] complete and perfectly valid *shofar* blasts. And if he sounds the *shofar* himself, every blast that he emits is partially invalid, because in part he is a bondman.[6]

ב אַף עַל פִּי שֶׁהַנָּשִׁים פְּטוּרוֹת,[ד] מִכָּל מָקוֹם אִם רָצוּ לִתְקֹעַ בְּעַצְמָן הָרְשׁוּת בְּיָדָן.[ה,7] וְאַף עַל פִּי שֶׁהַתְּקִיעָה בְּיוֹם טוֹב בְּחִנָּם אֲסוּרָה מִדִּבְרֵי סוֹפְרִים,[ו] מִכָּל מָקוֹם כְּדֵי לַעֲשׂוֹת נַחַת רוּחַ לַנָּשִׁים הִתִּירוּ לָהֶן אִסּוּר קַל כָּזֶה[ז] שֶׁאֵין בּוֹ אֲפִלּוּ מִשּׁוּם שְׁבוּת גָּמוּר[8] אֶלָּא מִשּׁוּם עוּבְדִין דְּחֹל.[ח,9]

וְכֵן אָדָם אַחֵר שֶׁיָּצָא כְּבָר יְדֵי חוֹבָתוֹ מֻתָּר לִתְקֹעַ לָהֶן,[ט] וּמֻתָּר לְהוֹצִיא הַשּׁוֹפָר לִרְשׁוּת הָרַבִּים כְּדֵי לִתְקֹעַ לָהֶן:[י]

2 Women are not obligated [to hear the sounding of the *shofar*], yet if they desire to sound the *shofar* themselves, they may.[7] Although the Sages forbade the sounding of the *shofar* on *Yom-Tov* for no purpose, in order to generate satisfaction for the women they relaxed this lightweight prohibition. For this activity does not even fully entail a *shvus;*[8] it was forbidden merely because it resembles a mundane activity.[9]

Similarly, a person who has already fulfilled his obligation may sound the *shofar* for them and may take a *shofar* into the public domain to sound it for them.

---

3. *Rosh HaShanah* 29a.

4. Lit., "because his free dimension is required...."

5. In practice, 30 blasts, as explained in sec. 590.

6. Lit., "because of his bonded dimension."

7. *Rosh HaShanah* 33a.

8. A Rabbinic prohibition enacted because an activity resembles — or may lead to the performance of — an activity forbidden by Scriptural Law *(Rambam, Hilchos Shabbos* 21:1).

9. The Alter Rebbe's question is that the prohibition against sounding the *shofar* should apply on any festival — including Rosh HaShanah — as well as on *Shabbos*. Hence, just as the performance of the *mitzvah* overrides the prohibition on any Rosh HaShanah, should it not override it when Rosh HaShanah falls on *Shabbos?*

In a number of letters the Rebbe points out that the Alter Rebbe's argument here constitutes an innovative observation, a *chiddush,* namely: The reason that the *shofar* is not sounded on *Shabbos* is not simply the concern lest it be carried in a public thoroughfare; the Alter Rebbe writes here that the primary issue is the prohibition of mundane activity. And the other concern, about carrying, serves only to bolster the prohibition of mundane activity, so that it will not be overridden by the commandment to sound the *shofar.* See: *Igros Kodesh,* Vol. 2, p. 243, and Vol. 9, pp. 203, 223.

סימן תקפט: **א** רמב"ם פ"ב ה"ג. טור ושו"ע ס"ה. וראה גם לקמן סי' תרמ ס"א (לענין סוכה). **ב** ברייתא וגמרא כט, סוע"א. טור ושו"ע שם. **ג** רב נחמן שם. רמב"ם שם. לבוש ס"ה. ט"ז ס"ק ב. וראה שו"ת הר צבי ח"ב סי' פה. מקראי קודש (פורים) סי' יד. **ד** משנה קידושין כט, א. טור ושו"ע ס"ג. וכדלעיל סי' תקפח ס"ו וש"נ. **ה** ברייתא לג, א כאוקימתא דאביי דרבי יוסי ורבי שמעון היא, שכן פסקו רא"ש פ"ד סי' ז בשם ר"ת בתוס' שם ד"ה הא. טור. ראבי"ה סי' תקלד (ע' 215). ר"ן (ט, ב) ד"ה ולענין. ראב"ן ר"ה (קעז, ג). שו"ע ס"ו. **ו** רא"ש פ"ד סי"א, וטור, בשם ראב"ן סי' סא (שיש בזה שבות). מ"א סק"ג (שמכל מקום יכולות לתקוע). **ז** חגיגה טז, ב (לענין סמיכת נשים). הגהות מיימוניות פ"ב אות א (גם לענין שופר). **ח** משמעות הגמרא ורש"י, וכדלעיל סי' תקפח ס"ד וש"נ. **ט** ראבי"ה שם. רא"ש שם. טור ושו"ע שם. **י** ראבי"ה שם. רא"ש שם. טור וב"י ד"ה ומ"ש רבנו בשם ראבי"ה (שכדאי לסמוך עליהם).

וּכְבָר נִתְבָּאֵר בְּסִימָן י"[ז][יא] שֶׁנָּהֲגוּ הַנָּשִׁים לְבָרֵךְ עַל כָּל מִצְוֹת עֲשֵׂה שֶׁהַזְּמַן גְּרָמָא,[10] עַל כֵּן גַּם כָּאן יְבָרְכוּ הַנָּשִׁים לְעַצְמָן,[יב] אֲבָל אֲנָשִׁים לֹא יְבָרְכוּ לָהֶן אִם כְּבָר יָצְאוּ יְדֵי חוֹבָתָם וְאֵינָן תּוֹקְעִים רַק בִּשְׁבִיל הַנָּשִׁים,[יג] לְפִי שֶׁהִיא בְּרָכָה לְבַטָּלָה, שֶׁהֲרֵי הַנָּשִׁים בְּעַצְמָן אֵינָן חַיָּבוֹת בִּבְרָכָה זוֹ שֶׁיְּבָרֵךְ זֶה לְהוֹצִיאָן יְדֵי חוֹבָתָן בִּבְרָכָה זוֹ, אֶלָּא שֶׁלָּהֶן בְּעַצְמָן הָרְשׁוּת בְּיָדָן לְבָרֵךְ[יד] מִטַּעַם שֶׁנִּתְבָּאֵר שָׁם, אֲבָל אַחֵר לָמָּה יְבָרֵךְ בְּחִנָּם.

It was explained above, in sec. 17[:3], that it is the accepted custom for women to recite a blessing over all positive commandments whose observance is linked to a specific time.[10] Hence, in this instance as well, the women themselves should recite the blessing. A man who has fulfilled his own obligation and is now sounding the *shofar* only for sake of the women should not recite the blessing for them, for that would be reciting a blessing in vain. For the women are under no obligation that should warrant the recitation of this blessing by a man [for their sake alone]. It is only that they have permission to recite the blessing [themselves] for the reasons explained in the above source. Why should another person recite an unwarranted blessing?

וְהָרוֹצֶה לִתְקֹעַ לַנָּשִׁים וּלְבָרֵךְ לָהֶן – יִתְקַע לָהֶן קֹדֶם שֶׁיִּשְׁמַע הַתְּקִיעוֹת בְּבֵית הַכְּנֶסֶת,[טו,11] אוֹ שֶׁיְּכַוֵּן בְּלִבּוֹ שֶׁלֹּא לָצֵאת יְדֵי חוֹבָתוֹ בִּתְקִיעוֹת שֶׁל בֵּית הַכְּנֶסֶת, דְּאָז יָכוֹל לְבָרֵךְ בִּשְׁבִיל עַצְמוֹ שֶׁעֲדַיִן לֹא יָצָא יְדֵי חוֹבָתוֹ.[טז] וְאַף עַל פִּי שֶׁהוֹלֵךְ לָהֶן לִתְקֹעַ בְּבָתֵּיהֶן וְחוֹזֵר לְבֵית הַכְּנֶסֶת וְשׁוֹמֵעַ הַתְּקִיעוֹת דִּמְעֻמָּד[12] שֶׁעַל סֵדֶר הַבְּרָכוֹת – אֵינוֹ צָרִיךְ לַחֲזֹר וּלְבָרֵךְ

A person who desires to sound the *shofar* for women and recite a blessing for them should sound the *shofar* for them before he hears the sounding of the *shofar* in the synagogue.[11] Alternatively, he should intend not to fulfill his obligation [when hearing] the *shofar* blasts in the synagogue. He may then recite a blessing for himself, because he has not yet fulfilled his own obligation.

Even if he goes to sound the *shofar* for the women in their own homes, and then returns to the synagogue to hear the *tekios me'umad*[12] that are sounded in the course of the blessings [of *Mussaf*], he does not have to recite a blessing

---

10. There the Alter Rebbe explains that women "may [praise G-d for] 'commanding us to put on *tzitzis*,' even though they themselves are not commanded to do so, because men are so commanded."

11. The *Maharil* (cited by *Magen Avraham* 589:4) writes that an individual should not sound the *shofar* without a *minyan* during the first three hours of the day, for at that time the attribute of stern judgment prevails. Hence it is preferable to sound the *shofar* for the women after the prayer service, and one of them should recite the blessing. (See sec. 591:13-14 below.) Alternatively, if there is a break in the service, this could be done after *Shacharis*.

For a deeper understanding of the spiritual significance of these first three hours, see the Rebbe's *Sefer HaMaamarim — Melukat* (Kehot, N.Y., 5753/1993), Vol. 4, p. 386.

12. Lit., "the *shofar* blasts [during which] one stands." See sec. 592:2.

יא סעיף ג. **יב** ר"ת בתוס' שם. רא"ש שם. טור ורמ"א ס"ו. **יג** דרכי משה ס"ק ב. רמ"א שם. **יד** דרכי משה שם. **טו** רמ"א שם (שרק אם כבר יצאו לא יברכו). לבוש ס"ו. מ"א סק"ד. וראה לקמן סי' תקצא סוף סי"ד. **טז** מ"א שם. **יז** מ"א שם. וראה גם לעיל סי' ח קו"א סוף סק"ה. סי' קד ס"ב. סי' תלב ס"ז.

over them even though he made an interruption between the blessing and these [latter *shofar*] blasts by walking to the synagogue. For even if he made an interruption between the two by speaking, he would not be required to repeat the blessing, for the reason explained in sec. 592[:7].[13]

עֲלֵיהֶם, וְאַף עַל פִּי שֶׁהִפְסִיק בַּהֲלִיכָה לְבֵית הַכְּנֶסֶת בֵּין בִּרְכָתוֹ לִתְקִיעוֹת אֵלּוּ,[יז] שֶׁהֲרֵי אֲפִלּוּ אִם הִפְסִיק בְּשִׂיחָה בֵּינְתַיִם אֵינוֹ צָרִיךְ לַחֲזֹר וּלְבָרֵךְ מִטַּעַם שֶׁיִּתְבָּאֵר בְּסִימָן תקצ"ב:[יח, 13]

3 Even if a person has taken a vow not to derive benefit from a fellow Jew by saying, "It is banned for me to benefit from so-and-so," that fellow Jew may sound the *shofar* [to enable] him [to fulfill this] *mitzvah,*[14] because [in the context of vows, the fulfillment of a *mitzvah*] is not considered a [pleasurable] benefit, as explained in sec. 586[:24, 26].[15]

[The above applies] provided that fellow Jew sounds the *shofar* for him on his own volition. [He may not be asked to do so], for since [the person under ban] forbade himself from benefiting from him, he cannot designate him as an agent to sound the *shofar* for him.[16]

ג מִי שֶׁהוּא מֻדַּר הֲנָאָה מֵחֲבֵרוֹ שֶׁאָמַר קוֹנָם שֶׁאֲנִי נֶהֱנֶה מִפְּלוֹנִי – מֻתָּר חֲבֵרוֹ לִתְקֹעַ לוֹ תְּקִיעָה שֶׁל מִצְוָה,[יט, 14] שֶׁאֵין זוֹ חֲשׁוּבָה הֲנָאָה[כ] כְּמוֹ שֶׁנִּתְבָּאֵר בְּסִימָן תקפ"ו.[כא, 15] וְהוּא שֶׁיִּתְקַע לוֹ חֲבֵרוֹ מֵעַצְמוֹ, אֲבָל הוּא לֹא יֹאמַר לַחֲבֵרוֹ שֶׁיִּתְקַע לוֹ,[כב] דְּכֵיוָן שֶׁאָסַר חֲבֵרוֹ הֲנָאָתוֹ עָלָיו – אָסוּר לוֹ לַעֲשׂוֹת חֲבֵרוֹ שָׁלִיחַ לִתְקֹעַ לוֹ:[כג, 16]

4 When does the above apply? When he forbade himself from benefiting from this fellow Jew. If, however, he forbade himself from [listening to his] *shofar* blasts by saying, "I ban the *shofar* blasts of so-and-so upon myself," he is forbidden to hear even the *shofar* blasts his colleague sounds for the sake of a *mitzvah.*

ד בַּמֶּה דְּבָרִים אֲמוּרִים? כְּשֶׁאָסַר הֲנָאַת חֲבֵרוֹ עָלָיו, אֲבָל אִם אָסַר תְּקִיעַת חֲבֵרוֹ עָלָיו שֶׁאָמַר קוֹנָם תְּקִיעָתוֹ שֶׁל פְּלוֹנִי עָלָיו – אָסוּר לוֹ לִשְׁמֹעַ אֲפִלּוּ תְּקִיעָה שֶׁל מִצְוָה מֵחֲבֵרוֹ:[כד]

5 A person does not fulfill his obligation regarding any of the *mitzvos* unless he carries out the relevant activity with the intent

ה כָּל הַמִּצְוֹת אֵין אָדָם יוֹצֵא בָּהֶם יְדֵי חוֹבָתוֹ אֶלָּא אִם כֵּן נִתְכַּוֵּן[כה]

---

13. There the Alter Rebbe explains that the sounding of the *shofar* is considered as one continuous *mitzvah* activity.

14. *Rosh HaShanah* 28a.

15. As the *Gemara (loc. cit.)* expresses it, *mitzvos lav leihanos nitnu* — "The commandments were not given in order to enable people to derive pleasure from them." In his paraphrase of this, *Rashi* adds: "...but as a yoke on their necks." What is crucial is obedience to do G-d's bidding; any personal satisfaction is incidental.

16. Though he transgresses if he listens to the *shofar* blasts in such an instance, after the fact he has fulfilled his obligation *(Pri Chadash* 589:7*).*

יח סעיף ז. **יט** גמרא כח, א. טור ושו"ע ס"ז. **כ** רש"י שם ד"ה מותר לתקוע לו (דמצות לאו ליהנות ניתנו). טור. **כא** ראה ט"ז שם ס"ק ד (סעיף זה בשוע"ר לא הגיע לידינו). לעיל שם סעיף כד וש"נ. **כב** ר"ן (ז, ב) ד"ה אמר. שו"ע שם. **כג** ראה ר"ן שם. לבוש ס"ז. **כד** ר"ן שם בסופו. רמ"א ס"ז. וכדלעיל סי' תפה ס"ב (לענין אכילת מצה). **כה** גמרא כח, ב כרב זירא. שכן פסק הרי"ף (ז, ב), לפירוש הרא"ש פ"ג סי' יא. טור. ב"י ד"ה ולענין הלכה. ט"ז ס"ק ג.

of thereby performing a *mitzvah*, as stated in sec. 60[:5].[17] Therefore a person who sounds the *shofar* as a casual activity,[18] for practice, has not fulfilled his obligation. Similarly, a person who hears the *shofar* blasts from someone who sounded them as a casual activity has not fulfilled his obligation[19] even if he intended to [do so] — for since the person sounding the *shofar* did not have the [required] intent, the sounds [that were heard] were invalid.

6 Likewise, a person who sounded the *shofar* as a musical instrument without intending to fulfill the *mitzvah* thereby has not fulfilled his obligation, nor did a person who heard [those sounds] from him fulfill his obligation.[20]

7 If a person sounding the *shofar* had the intent of enabling a listener to fulfill his obligation, but the listener did not have the intent of fulfilling his obligation by listening, or if a listener had the intent of fulfilling his obligation, but the person sounding the *shofar* did not have the intent of enabling the listener to fulfill his obligation but [simply] sounded the *shofar* for himself, the listener did not fulfill his obligation.[21] Both the listener and the person sounding the *shofar* must [share the appropriate] intent.

If a person sounding the *shofar* has the intent that whoever hears his *shofar* blasts may fulfill his obligation thereby, and a listener hears those blasts and has the intent of fulfilling his obligation, the listener has fulfilled his obligation. [This applies] even though the person

בַּעֲשִׂיָּתָן שֶׁהוּא עוֹשֶׂה דָּבָר זֶה לְשֵׁם מִצְוָה[כו] כְּמוֹ שֶׁנִּתְבָּאֵר בְּסִימָן ס'.[כז,17] לְפִיכָךְ, הַמִּתְעַסֵּק בִּתְקִיעַת שׁוֹפָר כְּדֵי לְהִתְלַמֵּד[18] — לֹא יָצָא יְדֵי חוֹבָתוֹ.[19] וְכֵן הַשּׁוֹמֵעַ מִן הַמִּתְעַסֵּק — לֹא יָצָא,[כח] אַף עַל פִּי שֶׁנִּתְכַּוֵּן הַשּׁוֹמֵעַ לְשֵׁם מִצְוָה, כֵּיוָן שֶׁהַתּוֹקֵעַ לֹא נִתְכַּוֵּן אִם כֵּן תְּקִיעָה פְּסוּלָה שָׁמַע:

ו וְכֵן הַתּוֹקֵעַ לְשׁוֹרֵר וְלֹא נִתְכַּוֵּן לִתְקִיעַת מִצְוָה — לֹא יָצָא.[כט] וְכֵן הַשּׁוֹמֵעַ מִמֶּנּוּ — לֹא יָצָא:[20]

ז אִם נִתְכַּוֵּן הַתּוֹקֵעַ לְהוֹצִיא אֶת הַשּׁוֹמֵעַ יְדֵי חוֹבָתוֹ וְלֹא נִתְכַּוֵּן הַשּׁוֹמֵעַ לָצֵאת יְדֵי חוֹבָתוֹ בִּשְׁמִיעָה זוֹ, אוֹ שֶׁנִּתְכַּוֵּן הַשּׁוֹמֵעַ לָצֵאת יְדֵי חוֹבָתוֹ וְלֹא נִתְכַּוֵּן הַתּוֹקֵעַ לְהוֹצִיא אֶת הַשּׁוֹמֵעַ אֶלָּא תָּקַע לְעַצְמוֹ — לֹא יָצָא הַשּׁוֹמֵעַ יְדֵי חוֹבָתוֹ,[21] עַד שֶׁיִּתְכַּוְּנוּ שְׁנֵיהֶם שׁוֹמֵעַ וּמַשְׁמִיעַ.[ל]

מִי שֶׁתָּקַע וְנִתְכַּוֵּן לְהוֹצִיא כָּל מִי שֶׁיִּשְׁמַע תְּקִיעָתוֹ וְשָׁמַע הַשּׁוֹמֵעַ וְנִתְכַּוֵּן לָצֵאת יְדֵי חוֹבָתוֹ, אַף עַל פִּי שֶׁאֵין הַתּוֹקֵעַ מִתְכַּוֵּן לִפְלוֹנִי זֶה

17. As the Alter Rebbe explains in that source, some authorities maintain that a person who performs the deed required by a *mitzvah* — even without intending to fulfill G-d's will thereby — has fulfilled his obligation. Most authorities, however, subscribe to the view stated above. See *Pesachim* 114b and *Rosh HaShanah* 28b-29a and commentaries there.

18. In the original, *kemis'asek*.

19. *Rosh HaShanah* 32b.

20. *Ibid.* 33b.

21. *Ibid.* 29a; 33b.

כו מ"מ פ"ב ה"ד. וראה גם לקמן סי' תקצ סוף ס"ג. לעיל סי' תעה סכ"ח. כז דעה הא' שם ס"ה, ושכן הלכה. כח משנה לב, סוע"ב, וכמסקנת הגמרא לג, ב (בתוקע לשיר). רמב"ם פ"ב ה"ד (להתלמד). טור ושו"ע ס"ח. כט מסקנת הגמרא לג, ב (כרב זירא). טור ושו"ע ס"ח. ל שם כט, א וכמסקנת הגמרא לג ע"ב כרבי זירא שם. טור ושו"ע שם. לא רמב"ם פ"ב ה"ה. שו"ע ס"ט. לב משנה כז, ב. רמב"ם שם. שו"ע שם. לג גמרא כט, א. רמב"ם שם. שו"ע שם. לד ראה

שֶׁשָּׁמַע תְּקִיעָתוֹ וְאֵינוֹ יוֹדְעוֹ כְּלָל, אַף עַל פִּי כֵן יָצָא הַשּׁוֹמֵעַ יְדֵי חוֹבָתוֹ, שֶׁהֲרֵי הַתּוֹקֵעַ נִתְכַּוֵּן לְהוֹצִיא לְכָל מִי שֶׁיִּשְׁמָעֶנּוּ.[לא] לְפִיכָךְ מִי שֶׁהָיָה מְהַלֵּךְ בַּדֶּרֶךְ אוֹ יוֹשֵׁב בְּתוֹךְ בֵּיתוֹ וְשָׁמַע תְּקִיעוֹת מִשְּׁלִיחַ צִבּוּר – יָצָא אִם נִתְכַּוֵּן לָצֵאת בִּשְׁמִיעָה זוֹ,[לב] שֶׁהֲרֵי הַשְּׁלִיחַ צִבּוּר הוּא מִתְכַּוֵּן לְהוֹצִיא אֶת הָרַבִּים יְדֵי חוֹבָתָן בִּתְקִיעָתוֹ:[לג,22]

sounding the *shofar* did not have this intent for this particular individual who heard his *shofar* blasts and [indeed] knows nothing of him — for his intent was that anyone who heard him should thereby fulfill his obligation.

Accordingly, a person who was proceeding on his way or sitting at home, and heard the *shofar* blasts sounded by the *sheliach tzibbur,* has fulfilled his obligation, for a *sheliach tzibbur* has the intent of enabling the public to fulfill their obligation by hearing his *shofar* blasts.[22]

ח מִי שֶׁשָּׁמַע תְּקִיעַת מִצְוָה וְאַחַר כָּךְ נִסְתַּפֵּק לוֹ אִם נִתְכַּוֵּן לָצֵאת בִּשְׁמִיעָתוֹ – צָרִיךְ לִתְקֹעַ לוֹ שֵׁנִית מִסָּפֵק.[לד,23] אֲבָל מִי שֶׁהָיָה מְהַלֵּךְ וְעָמַד כְּדֵי לִשְׁמֹעַ הַתְּקִיעוֹת מִשְּׁלִיחַ צִבּוּר וְאַחַר כָּךְ נִסְתַּפֵּק לוֹ אִם נִתְכַּוֵּן לָצֵאת בִּשְׁמִיעָתוֹ – אֵין צָרִיךְ לִתְקֹעַ לוֹ שֵׁנִית, דְּכֵיוָן שֶׁעָמַד מֵהֲלִיכָתוֹ חֲזָקָה שֶׁנִּתְכַּוֵּן לָצֵאת יְדֵי חוֹבָתוֹ:[לה]

8 If a person heard the *shofar* blasts [sounded] for this *mitzvah,* but later became doubtful whether he had intended to fulfill his obligation by hearing them, the *shofar* should be sounded for him again because of the doubt.[23]

If, by contrast, a person was walking [on his way] and stopped to hear the *shofar* blasts from a *sheliach tzibbur,* but was later doubtful whether he had intended to fulfill his obligation by hearing them, there is no need to sound the *shofar* for him again. Since he stopped walking, it may be assumed that he intended to fulfill his obligation.

ט מִי שֶׁבָּא לְבֵית הַכְּנֶסֶת כְּדֵי לִשְׁמֹעַ הַתְּקִיעוֹת מִשְּׁלִיחַ צִבּוּר וְלָצֵאת יְדֵי חוֹבָתוֹ עִם הַצִּבּוּר, אַף עַל פִּי שֶׁבְּשָׁעָה שֶׁשָּׁמַע לֹא הָיָה לוֹ שׁוּם כַּוָּנָה אֶלָּא שָׁמַע סְתָם – יָצָא,[לו] לְפִי שֶׁהוּא נִגְרָר אַחַר מַחֲשַׁבְתּוֹ הָרִאשׁוֹנָה[לז] שֶׁבָּא לְבֵית הַכְּנֶסֶת כְּדֵי לָצֵאת יְדֵי חוֹבָתוֹ.

9 [The following rule applies when] a person goes to the synagogue with the intent of hearing [the *shofar*] sounded by the *sheliach tzibbur* and fulfilling his obligation with the congregation. Even if at the time he heard [the *shofar*] he had no intent in mind but simply heard [it], he has fulfilled his obligation, because he is considered to be acting in the wake of his initial intent — to go to the synagogue to fulfill his obligation.

---

22. *Ibid.* 29a.

23. *Talmud Yerushalmi, Rosh HaShanah* 3:7.

לעיל סי' ס רס"ה שהמתעסק אינו יוצא מהתורה (וא"כ הוי ספיקא דאורייתא ולחומרא). **לה** ירושלמי פ"ג ה"ז. ר"ן (ז, א) ד"ה ירושלמי. מ"א סק"ה. **לו** שו"ת רדב"ז ח"ב סי' תתט. מ"א סק"ד. **לז** ראה שבת צא, רע"א. **לח** מ"א שם בשם רדב"ז.

אֲבָל מִי שֶׁבָּא לְבֵית הַכְּנֶסֶת בִּסְתָם,[לח] שֶׁלֹּא נִתְכַּוֵּן בְּבִיאָתוֹ כְּדֵי לָצֵאת יְדֵי חוֹבָתוֹ בִּשְׁמִיעַת הַתְּקִיעוֹת מֵהַשְּׁלִיחַ צִבּוּר, וְאַחַר כָּךְ שָׁמַע בִּסְתָם בְּלֹא שׁוּם כַּוָּנָה – לֹא יָצָא, שֶׁמִּצְוֹת צְרִיכוֹת כַּוָּנָה כְּדֵי לָצֵאת בָּהֶן יְדֵי חוֹבָתָן:[24]

[Different rules apply when,] by contrast, a person went to the synagogue without any intent, i.e., he did not intend that by going there he would fulfill his obligation when hearing the *shofar* blasts sounded by the *sheliach tzibbur.* [If] he then heard [the *shofar*] without having any intent in mind, he has not fulfilled his obligation — because, [as stated above,] in order to fulfill one's obligation one must have the intent of performing a *mitzvah.*[24]

סימן תקצ סֵדֶר הָרָאוּי לִתְקִיעַת שׁוֹפָר וּבוֹ כ״א סְעִיפִים:

SECTION 590 The Order Appropriate for the Sounding of the *Shofar.* (1–21)

א כַּמָּה תְּקִיעוֹת[1] חַיָּב אָדָם לִשְׁמֹעַ בְּרֹאשׁ הַשָּׁנָה?[א] תֵּשַׁע – תר״ת תר״ת תר״ת, לְפִי[2] שֶׁשָּׁלֹשׁ פְּעָמִים

1 How many *shofar* blasts[1] is a person obligated to hear on Rosh HaShanah? Nine — *tekiah-teruah-tekiah,* three times. [This

---

24. In the original, *mitzvos tzrichos kavanah* — lit., "*mitzvos* require intent [as an indispensable condition]."

SECTION 590

1. In the original, *tekios* (pl. of *tekiah*). For the sake of clarity, this term and other key terms are defined at this point:

The *shofar* produces three kinds of statutory sounds, which are called *kolos:*

(a) *tekiah* is a long, simple blast;

(b) *shevarim* is a three-part groaning sound of undulating pitch;

(c) *teruah* is a quick succession of short staccato sobbing sounds, which are called *trumitin* or *kochos.*

In fact, the term *tekios* signifies not only, as in (a) above, *the first* of these three kinds of sounds. It can also signify, as in the opening Hebrew phrase of sec. 590:1 above, *any one* of those three kinds of sounds; i.e., it can serve as a synonym for *kolos.* Moreover, it can also signify *all the blasts* collectively (as in the phrase, "The *tekios* of this year's *baal tekiah* were faultless.")

Likewise, the term *teruah* signifies not only, as in (c) above, the third of these three kinds of sounds. Its original, Biblical meaning is discussed in subsections 1-2 above. (When the two meanings appear together and need to be distinguished, the former meaning is sometimes referred to in the present translation as "our *teruah.*")

On Rosh HaShanah, the three *kolos* are never sounded separately.

The series comprising *tekiah-shevarim-teruah-tekiah* is called by its Hebrew acronym תשר״ת, commonly pronounced *tashrat.*

The series comprising *tekiah-shevarim-tekiah* is called by its Hebrew acronym תש״ת, commonly pronounced *tashat.*

The series comprising *tekiah-teruah-tekiah* is called by its Hebrew acronym תר״ת, commonly pronounced *tarat.*

In this context, the word "series" in our text uniformly translates the Aramaic term *bava* (which is sometimes explicit and sometimes implied).

When any such series is repeated three times in succession (e.g., *tekiah-shevarim-teruah-tekiah, tekiah-shevarim-teruah-tekiah, tekiah-shevarim-teruah-tekiah*), this complete sequence is known by the Hebrew term *seder,* which in our text is uniformly translated as "set."

Occasionally, the term *seder* in the Hebrew original is also used in its broader meaning of "sequence," and thus also includes a "series."

2. *Rosh HaShanah* 34a.

סימן תקצ: א רמב״ם פ״ג ה״א. שו״ע ס״א. ב גמרא [ברייתא] לד, א. רמב״ם שם. טור ושו״ע שם. ג רש״י שם ד״ה ומנין. טור. בר״ה: זכרון תרועה (ויקרא

תְּרוּעָה נֶאֱמַר בַּתּוֹרָה,[ב] שְׁנַיִם בְּרֹאשׁ הַשָּׁנָה[3] וְאֶחָד בְּיוֹם הַכִּפּוּרִים שֶׁל יוֹבֵל,[ג,4] וּמִפִּי הַשְּׁמוּעָה לָמְדוּ שֶׁהֵן לְמֵדִין זֶה מִזֶּה,[ד,5] וּלְכָךְ הֲרֵי הוּא כְּאִלּוּ כָּל הַשָּׁלֹשׁ פְּעָמִים תְּרוּעָה נֶאֱמָרִים בְּכָל אַחַת מֵהֶן,[ה] וְכָל תְּרוּעָה צְרִיכָה לִהְיוֹת פְּשׁוּטָה לְפָנֶיהָ וּפְשׁוּטָה לְאַחֲרֶיהָ,[6] וְהֵן הַנִּקְרָאִים תְּקִיעוֹת[7] סְתָם, שֶׁנֶּאֱמַר[ו,8] "וְהַעֲבַרְתָּ שׁוֹפַר תְּרוּעָה", מַשְׁמַע שֶׁצָּרִיךְ לְהַעֲבִיר קוֹל פָּשׁוּט וְאַחַר כָּךְ תִּהְיֶה הַתְּרוּעָה,[ז] דִּלְשׁוֹן "וְהַעֲבַרְתָּ" מַשְׁמַע הַעֲבָרַת קוֹל פָּשׁוּט,[ח] וְאַחַר הַתְּרוּעָה נֶאֱמַר[ט] "תַּעֲבִירוּ שׁוֹפָר וגו'", מַשְׁמַע שֶׁאַחַר הַתְּרוּעָה צָרִיךְ גַּם כֵּן לְהַעֲבִיר קוֹל פָּשׁוּט, וְכֵן בְּכָל תְּרוּעָה וּתְרוּעָה בֵּין שֶׁל יוֹבֵל בֵּין שֶׁל רֹאשׁ הַשָּׁנָה שֶׁהֵן לְמֵדִין זֶה מִזֶּה:[יא]

concept is derived as follows:[2]] The term *teruah* is mentioned three times in the Torah [with regard to the month of Tishrei]: twice in connection with Rosh HaShanah[3] and once in connection with Yom Kippur of the Jubilee Year.[4] The Oral Tradition teaches that [the verses] are interrelated,[5] and thus it is as if all three mentions of the term *teruah* relate to each [occasion].

Whenever a *teruah* is sounded, it must be preceded by a [long,] plain [*shofar* blast], and followed by a [long,] plain [*shofar* blast].[6] These [long, plain blasts] are called *tekios,* without qualification.[6] [This pattern is derived from] the verse,[7] והעברת שופר תרועה — "You shall sound blasts on the *shofar*." [The initial verb] implies that a [long,] simple blast should be sounded; [the sequence of the Hebrew words] implies that this long, simple blast should be followed by a *teruah.* And after mentioning the *teruah,* [that verse] states, תעבירו שופר — "You shall sound the *shofar*." This implies that after the *teruah,* a [long,] simple blast should also be sounded.

[This sequence] applies to every *teruah,* whether of the Jubilee Year or of Rosh HaShanah, for lessons applying to one are also applied to the other.

ב תְּרוּעָה זוֹ הָאֲמוּרָה בַּתּוֹרָה[יב] מְתַרְגְּמִינַן "יַבָּבָא",[8] וּכְתִיב[יג,9] "בְּעַד הַחַלּוֹן נִשְׁקְפָה וַתְּיַבֵּב אֵם סִיסְרָא", מַשְׁמַע שֶׁהַיַּבָּבָא הִיא כְּקוֹל שֶׁאָדָם מַשְׁמִיעַ כְּשֶׁהוּא בּוֹכֶה וּמְיַלֵּל,[יד] וְיֵשׁ לְהִסְתַּפֵּק[טו] אִם יַבָּבָא זוֹ הִיא כְּמוֹ

2 The term *teruah* used in the Torah is rendered as יבבא in Aramaic.[8] [This verb appears in] the verse,[9] "And Sisrah's mother gazed through the window and wailed." This implies that יבבא resembles a sound that a person emits when he weeps and moans.

There is room to question whether the יבבא

3. *Vayikra* 23:24; *Bamidbar* 29:1.

4. In the original, *shnas hayovel* (*Vayikra* 25:9).

5. Lit., "learn from each other."

6. As in definition (a) in footnote 1 above.

7. *Vayikra, loc. cit.*

8. *Rosh HaShanah* 33b.

9. *Shoftim* 5:28.

כג, כד), יום תרועה יהיה לכם (במדבר כט, א), וביובל: שופר תרועה (ויקרא כה, ט). ד ברייתא שם. רמב"ם שם. שו"ע שם. ה רש"י שם. ו ויקרא כה, ט. ז ברייתא לג, סוע"ב. ח רש"י לד, א ד"ה והעברת. לבוש ס"א. ט ויקרא שם. י ברייתא שם. יא ברייתא שם. לבוש שם. רמב"ם שם. שו"ע שם. יב במדבר כט, א. יג שופטים ה, כח. גמרא לג, ב. יד טור. לבוש ס"ב. טו גמרא לד, סוע"א (מספקא ליה). רש"י סוכה נד, א ד"ה תשע. רמב"ם פ"ג ה"ב. שו"ע ס"ב. ב"י ד"ה וכתבו. וראה לקמן סי' תקצב ס"ד.

שֶׁדֶּרֶךְ הַחוֹלִים שֶׁמַּאֲרִיכִים בִּגְנִיחוֹתָם[טז] וּמַשְׁמִיעִים קוֹל אַחַר קוֹל וּמַאֲרִיכִים בָּהֶם קְצָת, וְזֶה נִקְרָא גָּנַח,[יז] אוֹ שֶׁהִיא כְּמוֹ אָדָם הַמְיַלֵּל וּמְקוֹנֵן שֶׁמַּשְׁמִיעַ קוֹלוֹת קְצָרִים מְאֹד תְּכוּפִים זֶה לָזֶה,[יח] וְזֶה נִקְרָא יְלִיל,[יט] אוֹ שֶׁהִיא כְּמוֹ שְׁנֵיהֶם בְּיַחַד זֶה אַחַר זֶה[10] הַיְלָלָה אַחַר הַגְּנִיחָה, שֶׁכֵּן דֶּרֶךְ הַבּוֹכֶה מְגַנֵּחַ וְאַחַר כָּךְ מְיַלֵּל:[כ]

וְתִקְּנוּ חֲכָמִים[כא] כְּדֵי לָצֵאת יְדֵי כָּל הַסְּפֵקוֹת[11] לִתְקֹעַ תשר"ת[12] ג' פְּעָמִים, שֶׁמָּא הַתְּרוּעָה הִיא גְּנִיחָה וִילָלָה בְּיַחַד, וְאַחַר כָּךְ תש"ת[13] ג' פְּעָמִים, שֶׁמָּא הַתְּרוּעָה הִיא גְּנִיחָה לְבַד, וְהָיוּ הַיְלָלוֹת הֶפְסֵק בֵּין הַתְּרוּעָה לְהַתְּקִיעָה שֶׁלְּאַחֲרֶיהָ,[כב] וְהַתּוֹרָה אָמְרָה פְּשׁוּטָה לְאַחֲרֶיהָ בְּלֹא הֶפְסֵק קוֹל שׁוֹפָר שֶׁאֵינוֹ פָּשׁוּט בֵּינְתַיִם,[כג] וְאַחַר כָּךְ תר"ת[14] ג' פְּעָמִים, שֶׁמָּא הַתְּרוּעָה הִיא הַיְלָלָה לְבַד, וְהָיוּ הַגְּנִיחָה שֶׁבְּסֵדֶר תשר"ת הֶפְסֵק בֵּין הַתְּרוּעָה לַתְּקִיעָה שֶׁלְּפָנֶיהָ:[כד]

ג אִם הִתְנָה בִּתְקִיעָה אַחֲרוֹנָה שֶׁל ג' סִדְרֵי תשר"ת שֶׁאִם סֵדֶר

spoken of here is the sound made by a sick person whose groans are extended, as he issues one groan after the other, prolonging them somewhat. The root that describes this is גנח. Or perhaps [יבבא] resembles the sound of a person who sobs and mourns, emitting very short sounds in quick succession. The word that describes this is יליל. Or perhaps it refers to both of them in turn,[10] with the sobbing following the groaning, for people who cry commonly groan and then sob.

[Accordingly,] our Sages ordained [the following practice] in order to accommodate all the possible explanations[11] of the term *[teruah]*. A series comprising *tekiah-shevarim-teruah-tekiah*[12] is sounded three times, for perhaps *teruah* means both groaning and sobbing. A series comprising *tekiah-shevarim-tekiah*[13] is then sounded three times, for perhaps *teruah* means groaning alone, and if so, the sobbing sounds [i.e., our *teruah*] would constitute an interruption between the *teruah* [required by the Torah] and the *tekiah* that follows it — whereas the Torah requires that a *teruah* be [immediately] followed by a [long,] simple blast without the interruption of any other *shofar* blast which is not [long and] simple. Finally, a series comprising *tekiah-teruah-tekiah*[14] is sounded three times, for perhaps *teruah* is [the staccato] sobbing alone, and the groans [i.e., our *shevarim*] in the series comprising *tekiah-shevarim-teruah-tekiah* would constitute an interruption between the *teruah* [required by the Torah] and the *tekiah* that precedes it.

3 [A person may] make a stipulation regarding the last *tekiah* in the set comprising [three series of] *tekiah-shevarim-teruah-tekiah:* "If the

10. *Rosh HaShanah* 34b.

11. Lit., "to fulfill the obligations resulting from all [these] doubts."

12. The Hebrew acronym is תשר"ת; see footnote 1 above.

13. The Hebrew acronym is תש"ת; see footnote 1 above.

14. The Hebrew acronym is תר"ת; see footnote 1 above.

טז רש"י לג, ב ד"ה מאן. יז טור. לבוש שם. ראה גמרא שם. יח רש"י שם ד"ה ילולי. יט טור. לבוש שם. ראה גמרא שם כ גמרא לד, סוע"א. רמב"ם שם. טור ושו"ע שם. כא גמרא לד, סוע"א אתקין רבי אבהו. רמב"ם פ"ג ה"ג. טור ושו"ע שם. כב גמרא שם. טור. לבוש ס"ב. מ"א סק"א. כג לבוש שם. כד גמרא שם. טור. לבוש שם. מ"א שם. כה ב"י סוד"ה ומ"ש רבנו דמסתפקא לן. רמ"א ס"ו. כו כדלעיל סי' תקפט ס"ה וש"נ. כז רא"מ בביאורו לסמ"ג הל' שופר

set comprising *tekiah-shevarim-teruah-tekiah* is the true [expression of] the *mitzvah,* this [final] *tekiah* should be considered as the last *tekiah* of that set. But if the [following] set comprising [three series of] *tekiah-shevarim-tekiah* is the true [expression of] the *mitzvah,* and it is through [these sounds that] one fulfills his obligation, this *tekiah* should be considered as the first *tekiah* of that set." [If one makes such a stipulation,] there is no need to sound another *tekiah* as the beginning of the [three-part] set that comprises *tekiah-shevarim-tekiah,* for from either perspective, he has fulfilled his obligation with the *tekiah* [concerning which he made the stipulation]. Similarly, if one made a stipulation that the final *tekiah* of the set comprising *tekiah-shevarim-tekiah* be counted conditionally as the first *tekiah* of the [following] set that comprises *tekiah-teruah-tekiah,* [he need not sound an extra *tekiah*].

If, however, he does not make such a stipulation, one *tekiah* cannot be counted both for the set comprising *tekiah-shevarim-teruah-tekiah* and the [following] set that comprises *tekiah-shevarim-tekiah,* nor for the set comprising *tekiah-shevarim-tekiah* and the [following] set that comprises *tekiah-teruah-tekiah.*

[The rationale is that] the *mitzvos* require intent. And if one intends that this *tekiah* complete the set comprising *tekiah-shevarim-teruah-tekiah,* it cannot [also] count as the beginning of the [following] set that comprises *tekiah-shevarim-tekiah.* For if the set comprising *tekiah-shevarim-tekiah* is the true [expression of] the *mitzvah,* then when the person intended that this *tekiah* would complete the set comprising *tekiah-shevarim-teruah-tekiah,* the *shofar* blast was not sounded with the intent of fulfilling the *mitzvah* at all. The same reasoning applies with regard to the *tekiah* between the set comprising *tekiah-shevarim-tekiah* and the [following] set that comprises *tekiah-teruah-tekiah.*

4 The [minimal] length of the *tekiah* required by the Torah is the same as the [total] length of the *teruah*

תשר"ת הֵן הֵן עִקַּר הַמִּצְוָה תַּעֲלֶה לוֹ תְּקִיעָה זוֹ לִתְקִיעָה אַחֲרוֹנָה שֶׁל תשר"ת וְאִם סִדְרֵי תש"ת הֵן עִקַּר הַמִּצְוָה וּבָהֶן הוּא יוֹצֵא יְדֵי חוֹבָה תַּעֲלֶה לוֹ תְּקִיעָה זוֹ לִתְקִיעָה רִאשׁוֹנָה שֶׁל תש"ת – אֵינוֹ צָרִיךְ לִתְקֹעַ שֵׁנִית לִפְנֵי תש"ת הָרִאשׁוֹן, שֶׁהֲרֵי מִמַּה נַּפְשָׁךְ הוּא יוֹצֵא בִּתְקִיעָה זוֹ. וְכֵן הַדִּין אִם הִתְנָה בִּתְקִיעָה אַחֲרוֹנָה שֶׁל תש"ת שֶׁתַּעֲלֶה לוֹ לִתְקִיעָה רִאשׁוֹנָה שֶׁל תר"ת.[כה]

אֲבָל אִם לֹא הִתְנָה כֵּן – אֵין תְּקִיעָה אַחַת עוֹלָה לִשְׁנֵי סְדָרִים תשר"ת וְתש"ת וְלֹא לְתש"ת וְתר"ת, לְפִי שֶׁמִּצְוֹת צְרִיכוֹת כַּוָּנָה.[כו] וְאִם נִתְכַּוֵּן בִּתְקִיעָה זוֹ לְהַשְׁלָמַת סֵדֶר תשר"ת – אֵינָהּ עוֹלָה לְהַתְחָלַת תש"ת,[כז] שֶׁאִם תש"ת עִקַּר הַמִּצְוָה אִם כֵּן כְּשֶׁנִּתְכַּוֵּן בִּתְקִיעָה זוֹ לְהַשְׁלָמַת תשר"ת לֹא תָּקַע לְשֵׁם מִצְוָה כְּלָל.[כח] וְכֵן בִּתְקִיעָה שֶׁבֵּין תש"ת לְתר"ת:

ד שִׁעוּר תְּקִיעָה הָאֲמוּרָה בַּתּוֹרָה כְּשִׁעוּר תְּרוּעָה

(יא, ד). ב"י שם. **כח** ראה העו"ב תתג ע' 66. תתה ע' 65.

הָאֲמוּרָה בַּתּוֹרָה,[6] וְשִׁעוּר תְּרוּעָה הָאֲמוּרָה בַּתּוֹרָה כְּג' יְבָבוֹת.[כט]

יֵשׁ אוֹמְרִים[ל] דְּהַיְנוּ ג' כֹּחוֹת בְּעָלְמָא,[15] וְהֵם נִקְרָאִים טְרוּמִיטִין,[לא] וְעַכְשָׁו שֶׁתִּקְּנוּ חֲכָמִים לִתְקֹעַ תשר"ת תש"ת תר"ת כְּדֵי לָצֵאת מִכָּל הַסְּפֵקוֹת שֶׁיֵּשׁ בַּתְּרוּעָה — צָרִיךְ לְהַאֲרִיךְ בִּתְקִיעָה שֶׁל תשר"ת כְּשִׁעוּר תְּרוּעָה שֶׁל סֵדֶר תשר"ת,[לב] דְּהַיְנוּ ג' שְׁבָרִים בֵּינוֹנִים שֶׁהֵם כְּג' גְּנִיחוֹת בֵּינוֹנִיּוֹת וּכְג' יְלָלוֹת קְטַנּוֹת, שֶׁהֲרֵי הַכֹּל בְּיַחַד הוּא תְּרוּעָה שֶׁל סֵדֶר תשר"ת, וּבְסֵדֶר תש"ת אֵינוֹ צָרִיךְ לְהַאֲרִיךְ בִּתְקִיעוֹתָיו אֶלָּא כְּדֵי שִׁעוּר ג' שְׁבָרִים בֵּינוֹנִים, שֶׁזֶּהוּ שִׁעוּר תְּרוּעָה שֶׁל סֵדֶר תש"ת, וּבִתְקִיעוֹת שֶׁל סֵדֶר תר"ת אֵינוֹ צָרִיךְ לְהַאֲרִיךְ אֶלָּא כְּדֵי שִׁעוּר ג' יְלָלוֹת קְטַנּוֹת, שֶׁזֶּהוּ שִׁעוּר תְּרוּעָה שֶׁל סֵדֶר תר"ת.[לג]

וְאִם רוֹצֶה לְהַאֲרִיךְ הַרְבֵּה בְּכָל תְּקִיעָה — הָרְשׁוּת בְּיָדוֹ לְהַאֲרִיךְ כַּמָּה שֶׁיִּרְצֶה, וְלֹא אָמְרוּ שִׁעוּר לַתְּקִיעוֹת אֶלָּא שֶׁלֹּא יִפְחֹת מֵהַשִּׁעוּר. וְכֵן בַּתְּרוּעָה יָכוֹל לְהַאֲרִיךְ בִּטְרוּמִיטִין כַּמָּה שֶׁיִּרְצֶה. וְכֵן בַּשְּׁבָרִים אִם מוֹסִיף עַל ג' שְׁבָרִים — אֵין בְּכָךְ כְּלוּם,[לד,16]

required by the Torah,[8] which is the length of three sobbing sounds. Some authorities interpret this as meaning merely three of the short staccato bursts[15] [which together constitute our *teruah,* and] which are called *trumitin.*

In the present age, now that the Sages have ordained that we should sound three diverse sets — *tekiah-shevarim-teruah-tekiah,* then *tekiah-shevarim-tekiah,* then *tekiah-teruah-tekiah* — in order to accommodate all the possible interpretations of the term *teruah,* [each] *tekiah* of the set comprising *tekiah-shevarim-teruah-tekiah* should be prolonged so that it is as long as the *teruah* of that set. Thus it must be the length of at least three average *shevarim,* i.e., three groaning sounds [i.e., *genichos*] of average length and three short sobbing sounds [i.e., *yelalos*] — for all these together constitute the required length of the [Biblical] *teruah* of the set that comprises *tekiah-shevarim-teruah-tekiah.*

For the set comprising *tekiah-shevarim-tekiah,* [each] *tekiah* need not be prolonged beyond the length of three average *shevarim,* for that is the required length of the *teruah* of that set. And for the set comprising *tekiah-teruah-tekiah,* [each] *tekiah* need not be prolonged beyond the length of three short sobbing sounds, for that is the required length of the *teruah* of that set.

A person who wishes to prolong any of the *tekios* extensively may prolong them as much as he desires, for the [above] length required [by the Sages] for each *tekiah* is only a minimum. Similarly, with regard to the *teruah,* one may add as many staccato blasts as he desires. And similarly, with regard to the *shevarim,* if one adds to the three *shevarim,* it is of no consequence.[16] This is

15. In the original, *kochos.*

16. Although one may add to the number of *shevarim* and to the number of *teruah* blasts, one may not prolong the actual blasts, as stated in subsection 5.

כט משנה לג, ב. טור ושו"ע ס"ג. ל רש"י שם ד"ה שלש יבבות. דעה הא' בטור ושו"ע שם (ודעה הב' תתבאר לקמן ס"ו). לא שו"ע שם. וראה ירושלמי פ"ד ה"א. לב תוס' שם ד"ה שיעור. רא"ש שם סי' י. טור ושו"ע שם. לג תוס' ורא"ש שם. טור ולבוש ס"ג. וראה מ"מ וציונים. לד תוס' ורא"ש שם. טור ושו"ע שם. לה ראה טור ושו"ע ס"ד. ר"ן (י, ב) ד"ה מתקיף, הובא ב"י ד"ה ונראה. לקמן ס"ח. מסגרת השלחן סי' קכט ס"ק י. לו שיירי כנסת הגדולה

וְאֵינוֹ כְּמַפְסִיק בֵּין הַתְּרוּעָה אוֹ הַשְּׁבָרִים לַתְּקִיעָה שֶׁלְּאַחֲרָיו, כֵּיוָן שֶׁעוֹשֶׂה כָּל הַשְּׁבָרִים אוֹ כָּל הַטְּרוּמִיטִין בִּנְשִׁימָה אַחַת.[לה]

וּמִכָּל מָקוֹם נָהֲגוּ שֶׁלֹּא לְהוֹסִיף עַל ג' שְׁבָרִים,[לו,17] אֲבָל טְרוּמִיטִין יָכוֹל לַעֲשׂוֹת כַּמָּה שֶׁיִּרְצֶה.[לז,18] וְיֵשׁ עוֹשִׂין בְּסוֹף הַג' שְׁבָרִים קוֹל פָּשׁוּט כְּעֵין תְּקִיעָה, וְכֵן עוֹשִׂין בְּסוֹף הַטְּרוּמִיטִין.[לח] אֲבָל אֵין הַמִּנְהָג לַעֲשׂוֹת כֵּן:[לט]

ה וְצָרִיךְ לִזָּהֵר בַּשְּׁבָרִים שֶׁל סֵדֶר תשר"ת שֶׁלֹּא יַאֲרִיךְ בְּשֶׁבֶר אֶחָד מֵהַג' שְׁבָרִים כְּדֵי שִׁעוּר ג' שְׁבָרִים בֵּינוֹנִים וְג' יְלָלוֹת דְּהַיְנוּ טְרוּמִיטִין, שֶׁזֶּהוּ שִׁעוּר תְּקִיעָה שֶׁל סֵדֶר תשר"ת, וְאִם מַאֲרִיךְ בְּשֶׁבֶר[19] אֶחָד כְּשִׁעוּר זֶה – יָצָא מִכְּלַל שֶׁבֶר וְיִקָּרֵא בְּשֵׁם תְּקִיעָה. וּבְסֵדֶר תש"ת שֶׁשִּׁעוּר תְּקִיעָה הוּא כְּג' שְׁבָרִים בֵּינוֹנִים – לֹא יַאֲרִיךְ בְּשֶׁבֶר אֶחָד כְּדֵי שִׁעוּר ג' שְׁבָרִים בֵּינוֹנִים, שֶׁלֹּא יֵצֵא מִכְּלַל שֶׁבֶר וְיִקָּרֵא בְּשֵׁם תְּקִיעָה.[מ] וְאִם לֹא נִזְהַר בְּכָךְ

not considered as interrupting between the *teruah* or the *shevarim* and the following *tekiah*, because all the *shevarim* — or all the staccato blasts [that constitute the *teruah*] — are sounded in one breath.

Nevertheless, it has become customary not to add to the three *shevarim*.[17] One may, however, sound as many staccato blasts [for the *teruah*] as one desires.[18] Some people sound a simple blast like a *tekiah* after the three *shevarim* and do the same at the conclusion of the *[teruah]* blasts. This, however, is not the [common] custom.

5 With regard to the *shevarim* of the set comprising *tekiah-shevarim-teruah-tekiah*, one should take care that none of the three *shevarim* should be as long as three average *shevarim* and three sobbing sounds, or *trumitin*, for this is the measure of a *tekiah* in this set. If a *shever*[19] were to be made as long as this, it would no longer be considered a *shever*, but would be called a *tekiah*.

[Similarly,] in the set comprising *tekiah-shevarim-tekiah*, where the length of a *tekiah* is three average *shevarim*, a *shever* should not be made longer than three average *shevarim*, so that it will not cease to be considered a *shever* and be called a *tekiah*.

If one is not careful with regard to this,

17. The Rebbe would follow the practice of the Rebbe Rashab — R. Shalom DovBer Schneersohn (1860-1920), the fifth Rebbe of Lubavitch — and sound three-and-a-half *shevarim*. Moreover, the Rebbe writes *(Igros Kodesh*, Vol. 20, p. 39*)* that since the Rebbe Rashab conducted himself this way in public, and would fulfill the *mitzvah* on behalf of others in this manner, this serves as a directive for chassidim.

18. It was the custom of the Rebbes to sound a *teruah* of very many blasts. The Rebbe Rayatz once related *(Sefer HaSichos 5701*, p. 28*)* that the *trumitin* sounded by the Rebbe Maharash — R. Shmuel Schneersohn (1834-1882), the fourth Rebbe of Lubavitch — numbered 42. This is a number of Kabbalistic significance.

19. I.e., one third of the three-part sound called *shevarim;* see footnote 1 above.

הגב"י אות ח, ומ"א סק"ב, בשם מהרי"ל הל' שופר (ע' רצא). ב"ח ד"ה ואם עשה. ומנהג חב"ד לתקוע שלשה שברים וחצי – ראה אג"ק ח"כ ע' לט. המלך במסיבו ח"א ע' נה־נז. לז מהרי"ל שם. וכ"ה מנהג חב"ד – ראה אוצר מנהגי חב"ד ר"ה ע' קכב־ג. לח ב"ח שם. לט מ"א שם. מ רמ"א ס"ג, כביאור מ"א סק"ב. הגהות אשרי פ"ד סי' י. מרדכי רמז תשכ.

– אֲפִלּוּ בְּדִיעֲבַד לֹא יָצָא (לְפִי סְבָרָא זוֹ).

וּלְכַתְּחִלָּה טוֹב לִזָּהֵר שֶׁאֲפִלּוּ בְּסֵדֶר תשר"ת לֹא יַאֲרִיךְ בְּשֶׁבֶר אֶחָד כְּדֵי שִׁעוּר [ג'] טְרוּמִיטִין, לְפִי שֶׁזֶּהוּ שִׁעוּר תְּקִיעָה שֶׁל סֵדֶר תר"ת, וְאִם יַאֲרִיךְ כְּשִׁעוּר הַזֶּה יְהֵא עָלָיו שֵׁם תְּקִיעַת תר"ת לֹא שֵׁם שֶׁבֶר,[מא] וּלְפִיכָךְ טוֹב לְקַצֵּר בְּכָל שֶׁבֶר וָשֶׁבֶר בְּכָל מַה דְּאֶפְשָׁר,[מב] רַק שֶׁלֹּא יְקַצֵּר יוֹתֵר מִדַּאי כְּדֵי שֶׁיְּהֵא עָלָיו שֵׁם גְּנִיחָה וְלֹא שֵׁם יְלָלָה[מג] דְּהַיְנוּ טְרוּמִיטִין:

ו וְיֵשׁ אוֹמְרִים[מד] שֶׁשִּׁעוּר יְבָבָא הִיא ג' טְרוּמִיטִין, וְשִׁעוּר תְּרוּעָה כְּג' יְבָבוֹת שֶׁהֵם ט' טְרוּמִיטִין, וְשִׁעוּר תְּקִיעָה כְּשִׁעוּר תְּרוּעָה גַּם כֵּן ט' טְרוּמִיטִין, וְשִׁעוּר שְׁבָרִים בְּוַדַּאי לֹא פָּחוֹת הוּא מִשִּׁעוּר תְּרוּעָה גַּם כֵּן ט' טְרוּמִיטִין[מה] לְכָל הַפָּחוֹת, וְאִם כֵּן צָרִיךְ לְהַאֲרִיךְ בְּכָל שֶׁבֶר לֹא פָּחוֹת מִג' טְרוּמִיטִין כְּדֵי שֶׁבְּג' שְׁבָרִים בְּיַחַד לֹא יְהֵא פָּחוֹת מִט' טְרוּמִיטִין כְּשִׁעוּר תְּרוּעָה.

וּלְפִי דִּבְרֵיהֶם צָרִיךְ לְהַאֲרִיךְ בִּתְקִיעוֹת שֶׁל תשר"ת[מו] לֹא פָּחוֹת מִן י"ח טְרוּמִיטִין,[מז] שֶׁזֶּהוּ שִׁעוּר תְּרוּעָה שֶׁל סֵדֶר תשר"ת, דְּהַיְנוּ ג' גְּנִיחוֹת וְג' יְבָבוֹת בְּיַחַד שֶׁהֵם לֹא פָּחוֹת מִי"ח טְרוּמִיטִין.[מח]

he has not fulfilled his obligation (according to this view) even after the fact. Moreover, as an initial and preferred option, it is desirable to be careful — even during the set comprising *tekiah-shevarim-teruah-tekiah* — not to prolong a *shever* more than three *trumitin,* for that is the length of a *tekiah* in the set comprising *tekiah-teruah-tekiah.* If [the *shofar* blast] were to be prolonged for this length, it would be called a *tekiah* of the series comprising *tekiah-teruah-tekiah,* and not a *shever.* Every *shever* should therefore be kept as short as possible — though not too short, so that it will [still] be called a groaning sound, or *genichah,* and not a sobbing sound, or *yelalah,* i.e., [one of the short] *trumitin.*

6 Some authorities, however, maintain that the length of a sobbing sound, or *yevava,* is three *trumitin,* and the length of a *teruah* equals three sobbing sounds, which is nine *trumitin.* Now, the length of a *tekiah* is the length of a *teruah;* thus it is also nine *trumitin.* And the [total] length of the *shevarim* is certainly no less than the length of a *teruah;* thus it is also at least nine *trumitin.* Accordingly, every *shever* should be extended to no less than the length of three *trumitin,* so that the three *shevarim* together will come to no less than the length of nine *trumitin,* which is the length of a *teruah.*

According to their view, the *tekios* of the set comprising *tekiah-shevarim-teruah-tekiah* must be extended to at least the length of eighteen *trumitin,* which is the [minimal] length of the *teruah* of that series, i.e., the total length of three groaning sounds and three sobbing sounds, which comes to no less than the length of eighteen *trumitin.* Every

---

מא תוס' לג, ב ד"ה שיעור. רא"ש פ"ד סי' י. טור ושו"ע ס"ג. מב ב"י ד"ה והמרדכי. מג מרדכי רמז שכ. הגהות אשרי שם. מד ריב"א וריב"ם בתוס' לג, ב ד"ה שיעור, ובר"ש פ"ד סי' י. מ"מ פ"ג ה"ד בדעת הרמב"ם. דעה הב' בשו"ע ס"ג. מה רמב"ם ומ"מ שם. ט"ז סק"ד. מו ריב"א וריב"ם שם. שו"ע שם. מז ב"ח סוד"ה ומ"ש וכן הוא דעת. ט"ז שם. מ"א סק"ג. וראה גם מ"מ שם בסופו בשם ויש מי שמחמיר. מח ט"ז שם. מט ריב"א וריב"ם שם. שו"ע שם.

shever may [thus] be extended to [a maximum of] a little less than the length of eighteen *trumitin,* because anything less than the length of eighteen *trumitin* is not called a *tekiah.*

Nevertheless, the initial and preferred option is that a *shever* should not be extended [even] for the length of nine *trumitin,* [for that] is the length of a *tekiah* in the set comprising *tekiah-teruah-tekiah,* and thus it would be called a *tekiah* of [that set]. After the fact, however, if a *shever* of the set comprising *tekiah-shevarim-teruah-tekiah* was extended, one's obligation has been fulfilled, as long as [this *shever*] was shorter than the length of eighteen *trumitin.* [The rationale is that] with regard to that set, it is not [long enough to be] called a *tekiah.*

In the set comprising *tekiah-shevarim-tekiah,* each *tekiah* must be as long as nine *trumitin,* for this is the required [minimum length] for this set. A *shever* may not be as long as nine *trumitin.* If the *shever* was this long, one's obligation has not been fulfilled even after the event, for such a blast is no longer considered a *shever;* for this series it is considered a *tekiah.*

7 With regard to [the actual application of the] *halachah,*[20] one should be stringent with regard to Scriptural [obligations] and follow the latter view; i.e., one should make each *tekiah* of the set comprising *tekiah-shevarim-teruah-tekiah* at least as long as eighteen *trumitin.* And each *tekiah* of the set comprising *tekiah-shevarim-tekiah* and *tekiah-teruah-tekiah* must be at least as long as nine *trumitin.* Every *shever* should be extended slightly, [at least] to the length of three *trumitin,* but not more than nine *trumitin,* even in the set comprising *tekiah-shevarim-teruah-tekiah.* And

וְיָכוֹל לְהַאֲרִיךְ בְּכָל שֶׁבֶר[מט] עַד פָּחוֹת מְעַט מִן י"ח טְרוּמִיטִין;[נ] לְפִי שֶׁעַד י"ח טְרוּמִיטִין אֵין שֵׁם תְּקִיעָה. וּמִכָּל מָקוֹם, לְכַתְּחִלָּה לֹא יַאֲרִיךְ בְּשֶׁבֶר אֶחָד כְּדֵי ט' טְרוּמִיטִין, שֶׁזֶּה שִׁעוּר תְּקִיעָה בְּסֵדֶר תר"ת,[נא] וְאִם כֵּן שֵׁם תְּקִיעַת תר"ת עָלָיו. אֲבָל בְּדִיעֲבַד יוֹצֵא אִם הֶאֱרִיךְ בְּשֶׁבֶר שֶׁל תשר"ת פָּחוֹת מִי"ח טְרוּמִיטִין,[נב] כֵּיוָן שֶׁבְּזֶה הַסֵּדֶר עֲדַיִן אֵין עָלָיו שֵׁם תְּקִיעָה.

וּבְסֵדֶר שֶׁל תש"ת צָרִיךְ לְהַאֲרִיךְ בַּתְּקִיעוֹת כְּשִׁעוּר ט' טְרוּמִיטִין, שֶׁזֶּהוּ שִׁעוּר [תְּרוּעָה[נג]] שֶׁל זֶה הַסֵּדֶר. וְלֹא יַאֲרִיךְ בְּשֶׁבֶר כְּשִׁעוּר ט' טְרוּמִיטִין, וְאִם הֶאֱרִיךְ – אֲפִלּוּ בְּדִיעֲבַד לֹא יָצָא, לְפִי שֶׁיָּצָא מִכְּלַל שֶׁבֶר וְנִכְנַס בִּכְלַל תְּקִיעוֹת שֶׁל זֶה הַסֵּדֶר:[נד]

ז וּלְעִנְיַן הֲלָכָה,[20] יֵשׁ לְהַחְמִיר בְּשֶׁל תּוֹרָה כִּסְבָרָא הָאַחֲרוֹנָה, דְּהַיְנוּ שֶׁיַּאֲרִיךְ בִּתְקִיעוֹת תשר"ת כְּשִׁעוּר י"ח טְרוּמִיטִין לְכָל הַפָּחוֹת, וּבִתְקִיעוֹת תש"ת תר"ת כְּשִׁעוּר ט' טְרוּמִיטִין לְכָל הַפָּחוֹת, וּבְכָל שֶׁבֶר יַאֲרִיךְ מְעַט כְּדֵי ג' טְרוּמִיטִין;[נה] וְלֹא יַאֲרִיךְ עַד ט' טְרוּמִיטִין אֲפִלּוּ בְּסֵדֶר תשר"ת,

20. In the original, *ule'inyan halachah.* This conclusive phrase typically appears after varying stances have been cited as hypotheses.

נ הגהות אשרי פ"ד סי' י. מרדכי רמז תשכ. ט"ז סק"ג. נא תוס' שם. רא"ש שם. ב"ח שם. ט"ז שם. מ"א סק"ב. נב ב"ח שם. נג כן הגיה בקונטרס השלחן. נד ב"ח שם. נה ראה חידושי צמח צדק עו, א.

וּבְכָל תְּרוּעָה צָרִיךְ לַעֲשׂוֹת ט' טְרוּמִיטִין כְּמוֹ שֶׁנִּתְבָּאֵר.[נו] אֲבָל בְּדִיעֲבַד שֶׁכְּבָר תָּקַע וְשִׁנָּה אֶחָד מִכָּל אֵלּוּ — אֵינוֹ צָרִיךְ לַחֲזֹר וְלִתְקֹעַ, מִפְּנֵי שֶׁיֵּשׁ לִסְמֹךְ עַל סְבָרָא הָרִאשׁוֹנָה.[נז]

אֲבָל אִם שִׁנָּה בִּשְׁנֵי דְבָרִים בְּעִנְיָן שֶׁלְּפִי שְׁתֵּי הַסְּבָרוֹת לֹא יָצָא, כְּגוֹן שֶׁלֹּא הֶאֱרִיךְ בִּתְקִיעוֹתָיו כְּשִׁעוּר שֶׁנִּתְבָּאֵר לְפִי סְבָרָא הָאַחֲרוֹנָה וְהֶאֱרִיךְ בְּשֶׁבֶר מִן הַשְּׁבָרִים יוֹתֵר מִשִּׁעוּר שֶׁנִּתְבָּאֵר לְפִי סְבָרָא הָרִאשׁוֹנָה,[נח] אוֹ שֶׁלֹּא הֶאֱרִיךְ בְּשֶׁבֶר אֶחָד מִן הַשְּׁבָרִים כְּשִׁעוּר שֶׁנִּתְבָּאֵר לְפִי סְבָרָא הָאַחֲרוֹנָה דְּהַיְנוּ ג' טְרוּמִיטִין וּבְשֶׁבֶר אֶחָד מִן הַשְּׁבָרִים הֶאֱרִיךְ יוֹתֵר מִשִּׁעוּר שֶׁנִּתְבָּאֵר לְפִי סְבָרָא הָרִאשׁוֹנָה — צָרִיךְ לַחֲזֹר וְלִתְקֹעַ (כְּדִין הַטּוֹעֶה בִּתְקִיעוֹתָיו וְעַל דֶּרֶךְ שֶׁיִּתְבָּאֵר[נט]), וְאֵינוֹ יָכוֹל לִתְפֹּס קוּלוֹת שֶׁל שְׁתֵּי הַסְּבָרוֹת כֵּיוָן שֶׁהֵן סוֹתְרוֹת זוֹ אֶת זוֹ:[ס]

ח הַיְבָבוֹת שֶׁל תְּרוּעוֹת וְכֵן הַג' שְׁבָרִים שֶׁהֵם בִּמְקוֹם תְּרוּעָה — צָרִיךְ לַעֲשׂוֹתָן בִּנְשִׁימָה אַחַת.[סא] וְאִם לֹא עֲשָׂאָן בִּנְשִׁימָה אַחַת — לֹא יָצָא,[סב] שֶׁתְּרוּעָה אַחַת אָמְרָה תּוֹרָה וְלֹא מְפֻסֶּקֶת לִשְׁתֵּי תְּרוּעוֹת.[סג]

אֲבָל הַשְּׁלֹשָׁה שְׁבָרִים וּתְרוּעָה דְּתשׁר"ת אַף עַל פִּי שֶׁשְּׁתֵּיהֶן בְּיַחַד הֵן

every *teruah* must comprise [at least] nine *trumitin,* as has been explained.

After the fact, however, i.e., after having sounded the *shofar,* if one deviated from one of these directives, there is no need to sound the *shofar* again, because one may rely on the former view.

However, if one deviated from two of these guidelines, in a manner that would not enable him to fulfill his obligation according to either approach, he has not fulfilled his obligation. For example, the *tekios* were not made as long as required by the second view, but one of the *shevarim* was made longer than the [maximum] length prescribed by the first view. Another example: one of the *shevarim* did not reach the [minimum] length required by the second view, i.e., three *trumitin,* but one of the *shevarim* exceeded the [maximum] length prescribed by the first view. [In such situations,] the *shofar* must be sounded again, (according to the laws that apply to a person who makes a mistake while sounding the *shofar,* as will be explained). One cannot grasp the leniencies of both approaches, because they contradict each other.

8 The sobbing sounds of the *teruos,* and similarly, the three *shevarim* that take the place of a *teruah,* must be sounded in one breath. If they were not sounded in one breath, one's obligation has not been fulfilled, for the Torah says "*teruah*" [in the singular, implying] one sequence of blasts and not a sequence divided in two.

[Different rules apply with regard to] the three *shevarim* and the *teruah* in the set comprising *tekiah-shevarim-teruah-tekiah,* where the two together take the place of the *teruah*

נו סעיף ו. נז ב"ח שם. מ"א שם. נח תוס' שם. רא"ש שם. שו"ע סוף ס"ג. נט סעי' טו־יז. ס תוס' ורא"ש שם. (טור ו)שו"ע שם. סא רמב"ן לד, א ד"ה ושוב מצאתי בתשובת ר"ת, ובדרשה לר"ה (כתבי רמב"ן ח"א ע' רמ). רא"ש פ"ד סי' י־יא. ר"ת בתשובה, הובא ברמב"ן שם ובטור. שו"ע ס"ד. סב שיירי כנסת הגדולה הגב"י אות ז. אליה זוטא סק"ז. לבוש ס"ד. סג רמב"ן שם (לענין שברים תרועה). סד כדלעיל ס"ב. סה ר"ת שם. מ"מ שם בדעת הרמב"ם. דעה הא'

בְּמְקוֹם תְּרוּעָה אַחַת הָאֲמוּרָה בַּתּוֹרָה, דְּשֶׁמָּא הִיא הַגְּנִיחָה וְהַיְלָלָה בְּיַחַד זוֹ אַחַר זוֹ,[סד, 21] אַף עַל פִּי כֵן אֵין צָרִיךְ לַעֲשׂוֹתָן בִּנְשִׁימָה אַחַת, לְפִי שֶׁאֵין דֶּרֶךְ הָאָדָם לִגְנֹחַ וּלְיַלֵּל בִּנְשִׁימָה אַחַת[סה] אֶלָּא מַפְסִיק בֵּינֵיהֶם כְּדֵי נְשִׁימָה, דְּהַיְנוּ שֶׁעוֹשֶׂה נְשִׁימָה בֵּינְתַיִם, וּלְפִיכָךְ גַּם הַתּוֹקֵעַ צָרִיךְ לַעֲשׂוֹת נְשִׁימָה בֵּינְתַיִם. וּמִכָּל מָקוֹם לֹא יַפְסִיק יוֹתֵר מִכְּדֵי לַעֲשׂוֹת נְשִׁימָה אַחַת בֵּינְתַיִם.[סו] וְלֹא יַמְתִּין מִלְּהָרִיעַ עַד שֶׁיִּקְרָא הַמַּקְרִיא לְפָנָיו מִלַּת תְּרוּעָה,[22] אֶלָּא יָרִיעַ מֵעַצְמוֹ אַחַר הַשְּׁבָרִים תֵּכֶף וּמִיָּד לְאַחַר שֶׁעָשָׂה נְשִׁימָה אַחַת:[סז]

required by the Torah — for this term may signify both groaning and sobbing, one after the other.[21] Nevertheless, they need not be sounded in one breath, for it is not usual for a person to groan and sob in the same breath. Usually, [his groans and sobs] are separated by the space of a breath; he takes a breath between them. Hence, the person sounding the *shofar* must also take a breath between them, though he should not separate them by more than the space of a single breath. He should not wait to sound the *teruah* until the person calling out the notes says *"teruah,"*[22] but should sound the *teruah* on his own initiative immediately after sounding the *shevarim* and taking a breath.

ט וְיֵשׁ אוֹמְרִים[סח] דְּאַף עַל פִּי שֶׁאֵין דֶּרֶךְ הָאָדָם לִגְנֹחַ וּלְיַלֵּל בִּנְשִׁימָה אַחַת, מִכָּל מָקוֹם כֵּיוָן דְּמַה שֶּׁאָנוּ תּוֹקְעִין שְׁבָרִים וּתְרוּעָה הוּא מֵחֲמַת סָפֵק דְּשֶׁמָּא זֶהוּ תְּרוּעָה הָאֲמוּרָה בַּתּוֹרָה,[סט] אִם כֵּן אֵין לָנוּ לְהַפְסִיק, שֶׁהֲרֵי תְּרוּעָה אַחַת אָמְרָה תּוֹרָה וְלֹא מְפֻסֶּקֶת לִשְׁתֵּי תְּרוּעוֹת.[ע] לְפִיכָךְ אִם עֲשָׂאָן בִּשְׁתֵּי נְשִׁימוֹת — לֹא יָצָא,[עא] אֶלָּא יַעֲשֶׂה אוֹתָן בִּנְשִׁימָה אַחַת.[עב] וּמִכָּל מָקוֹם יַפְסִיק מְעַט בֵּינֵיהֶם[עג] בְּעִנְיָן שֶׁיִּהְיוּ נֶחְלָקִין לִשְׁתֵּי קוֹלוֹת.

9 Other authorities, however, [differ,] even though it is not usual for a person to groan and sob in a single breath. [They maintain] that since the reason we sound the *shevarim* and the *teruah* together is that perhaps this [combination] is the *teruah* mandated by the Torah, the two should not be separated — for the Torah says *"teruah"* [in the singular, implying] one sequence of blasts, and not a sequence divided in two. Therefore, if a person sounded these notes in two breaths, he has not fulfilled his obligation. Rather, he should sound them in one breath, though with a slight pause between them, so that they will be [heard as] two distinct sounds.

---

21. See subsection 2 above.

22. For this reason, in many communities the person calling out the names of the sounds calls out *shevarim-teruah* together, as a single unit. As mentioned in sec. 587, footnote 20 above, the Lubavitch custom is not to call out any of these names, but to point to them in the *Machzor*.

בשו"ע שם. **סו** מרדכי רמז תשכ, והגהות אשרי פ"ד סי' י, כפרש"י סוכה נג, סוע"ב ד"ה ולא כלום. שו"ע שם. **סז** ט"ז סוף סק"ו. אליה רבה סק"ח. **סח** רמב"ן שם. רא"ש שם סי' י"א. טור בדעת הרי"ץ גיאת (ע' כו). דעה הב' בשו"ע שם. **סט** כדלעיל ס"ב. **ע** רמב"ן שם. **עא** ריב"ש בתשובה סי' לט. ב"י ד"ה ונראה. **עב** רא"ש שם סי' יא (שאם טעה יחזור ויעשה בנשימה אחת). **עג** תרומת הדשן סי' קמב. ב"י רד"ה ונראה דלדעת. ע"פ רש"י חולין כו, ב ד"ה בנשימה אחת.

וְהַמִּנְהָג בִּמְדִינוֹת אֵלּוּ[23] כַּסְּבָרָא הָרִאשׁוֹנָה,[עד] וְאֵין לְשַׁנּוֹת[עה] הַמִּנְהָג מִפְּנֵי הַמַּחֲלֹקֶת. אֲבָל בְּמָקוֹם שֶׁאֵין מִנְהָג קָבוּעַ יֵשׁ לְהַנְהִיג לַעֲשׂוֹת בִּתְקִיעוֹת מְיֻשָּׁב[24] בִּנְשִׁימָה אַחַת,[עו, 25] כְּדֵי שֶׁתִּהְיֶה הַבְּרָכָה שֶׁמְּבָרְכִין עֲלֵיהֶם כַּהֲלָכָה לְדִבְרֵי הַכֹּל, שֶׁאַף לַסְּבָרָא הָרִאשׁוֹנָה יֵשׁ אוֹמְרִים[עז] שֶׁאִם עֲשָׂאָן בִּנְשִׁימָה אַחַת יָצָא, כְּמוֹ הַתּוֹקֵעַ תר"ת אוֹ תש"ת בִּנְשִׁימָה אַחַת דְּיָצָא כְּמוֹ שֶׁיִּתְבָּאֵר. אֲבָל בִּתְקִיעוֹת מְעֻמָּד[26] שֶׁאֵין מְבָרְכִין עֲלֵיהֶם — יַעֲשֶׂה בִּשְׁתֵּי נְשִׁימוֹת,[עח] כְּדֵי לָחוּשׁ לִסְבָרַת מִי שֶׁאוֹמֵר[עט] דְּלַסְּבָרָא הָרִאשׁוֹנָה אִם עֲשָׂאָן בִּנְשִׁימָה אַחַת לֹא יָצָא.

הַתּוֹקֵעַ תר"ת אוֹ תש"ת בִּנְשִׁימָה אַחַת,[פ] אִם הִפְסִיק מְעַט בֵּינֵיהֶם בְּעִנְיָן שֶׁיִּהְיוּ נֶחֱלָקִין לְג' קוֹלוֹת[פא] — יָצָא. וְיֵשׁ אוֹמְרִים[פב] שֶׁלֹּא יָצָא, וְצָרִיךְ לַחֲזֹר וְלִתְקֹעַ כָּל הַג' קוֹלוֹת, שֶׁהַתְּקִיעָה הָרִאשׁוֹנָה

The custom in these lands[23] is to follow the first view. The custom should not be changed lest strife arise. In a place where there is no established custom, however, [the following] custom [should be adhered to]:

In the *tekios meyushav,*[24] [these two sounds] should be made in a single breath,[25] so that the blessing recited over these *[shofar* blasts*]* will accord with the *halachah* according to all authorities. For even according to the first opinion, some authorities hold that if these *shofar* blasts were sounded in a single breath, one has fulfilled his obligation, just as one who sounded the set comprising *tekiah-teruah-tekiah* or the set comprising *tekiah-shevarim-tekiah* in a single breath has fulfilled his obligation, as will be explained.

By contrast, the *tekios me'umad*[26] — for which a blessing is not recited — should be sounded in two breaths, out of deference to the view that according to the first approach, if [the *shevarim* and the *teruah*] were sounded in a single breath, one has not fulfilled his obligation.

If one sounded a series comprising *tekiah-teruah-tekiah* or a series comprising *tekiah-shevarim-tekiah* in a single breath, but paused slightly between the sounds so that they would be [heard as] three [distinct] sounds, he has fulfilled his obligation. Some authorities, however, maintain that in such a case one has not fulfilled his obligation, but must repeat all three sounds. [The rationale is that] the

23. I.e., in the European Ashkenazic community that follows the ruling of the *Rama (Orach Chayim* 590:4*)*.

24. Lit., "the *shofar* blasts [during which] one may sit"; i.e., the *shofar* blasts sounded before the *Mussaf* service. See sec. 585, footnote 4 above.

25. The Rebbe relates *(HaMelech BiMesibo,* Vol. 1, p. 236*)* that the Rebbe Rayatz once told him that the Rebbe Rashab would take a breath between the *shevarim* and the *teruah.* He did not inquire, however, whether he paused for reasons of health, or by choice. Cf. *Otzar Minhagei Chabad: Elul-Tishrei,* p. 122.

26. Lit., "the *shofar* blasts [during which] one stands"; i.e., the *shofar* blasts sounded during the *Mussaf* prayers. See sec. 592:2.

עד דרכי משה ס"ק ג. רמ"א ס"ד. עה רמ"א שם. וראה משמרת שלום סי' מא ס"ז. עו ב"י ד"ה ונראה דלדידן. שו"ע ס"ד. עז ב"י שם. ב"ח שם. ט"ז סק"ו. עח ב"י שם. שו"ע שם. עט תרומת הדשן סי' קמב. פ ירושלמי פ"ד ה"י. רא"ש פ"י ה"י. לפירוש הטור. דעה א' בשו"ע ס"ה. פא פרי מגדים א"א סק"ד. וכדלעיל ריש הסעיף. פב רבנו ירוחם נ"ו ח"ב (מט, ב), בדעת הרא"ש שם. ב"י ד"ה ומ"ש הרא"ש, בשם התוספתא פ"ב הי"ב. דעה הב' בשו"ע שם. אליה זוטא סק"ט, בדעת הלבוש ס"ה. פג רא"ש שם. טור. מ"א סק"ד. פד אליה זוטא שם בדעת השו"ע שם, שהביא דעה הא' בסתם. פה אליה זוטא

לֹא הָיָה לָהּ הֶפְסֵק וָסוֹף וְהַתְּקִיעָה הָאַחֲרוֹנָה לֹא הָיָה לָהּ רֹאשׁ וְהַתְחָלָה[פג] שֶׁעָשָׂה הַכֹּל בִּנְשִׁימָה אַחַת. וְאַף עַל פִּי שֶׁהָעִקָּר כַּסְּבָרָא הָרִאשׁוֹנָה,[פד] מִכָּל מָקוֹם יֵשׁ לָחוּשׁ לַסְּבָרָא הָאַחֲרוֹנָה וְיַחֲזֹר וְיִתְקַע כָּל הַג' קוֹלוֹת:[פה,27]

first *tekiah* had no conclusion nor end, nor did the final *tekiah* have a start or a beginning — for everything was included in a single breath.

Though the *halachah* follows the former view, one should show deference to the latter view and repeat all three sounds.[27]

י וְאִם מָשַׁךְ וְהֶאֱרִיךְ בַּתְּקִיעָה הָאַחֲרוֹנָה[פו] שֶׁל בָּבָא אַחַת[פז] (פֵּרוּשׁ סֵדֶר[28] תשר"ת אַחַת אוֹ תש"ת אַחַת אוֹ תר"ת אַחַת נִקְרֵאת בָּבָא אַחַת) מִבָּבוֹת תשר"ת אוֹ תש"ת אוֹ תר"ת כְּדֵי שִׁעוּר שְׁתֵּי תְּקִיעוֹת כְּדֵי שֶׁתַּעֲלֶה לוֹ תְּקִיעָה זוֹ לִשְׁתֵּי תְּקִיעוֹת, דְּהַיְנוּ לְשֵׁם תְּקִיעָה אַחֲרוֹנָה שֶׁל בָּבָא זוֹ וּלְשֵׁם תְּקִיעָה רִאשׁוֹנָה שֶׁל בָּבָא שֶׁלְּאַחֲרֶיהָ – לֹא עָלְתָה לוֹ אֶלָּא בִּשְׁבִיל תְּקִיעָה אַחַת,[פח] דְּהַיְנוּ תְּקִיעָה אַחֲרוֹנָה שֶׁל בָּבָא זוֹ,[פט,8] לְפִי שֶׁכָּל תְּקִיעָה צָרִיךְ לִהְיוֹת בּוֹ רֹאשׁ וָסוֹף, וְאִם נְחַלֵּק תְּקִיעָה זוֹ לִשְׁתֵּי תְּקִיעוֹת כְּמוֹ שֶׁחָשַׁב הַתּוֹקֵעַ אֵין כָּאן רֹאשׁ לַתְּקִיעָה הָאַחֲרוֹנָה וְלֹא סוֹף לַתְּקִיעָה רִאשׁוֹנָה,[צ] וּלְפִיכָךְ אֵין אָנוּ הוֹלְכִין אַחַר מַחֲשַׁבְתּוֹ בָּזֶה אֶלָּא אָנוּ חוֹשְׁבִין תְּקִיעָה זוֹ לִתְקִיעָה אַחַת אֲרֻכָּה, וְעוֹלָה לוֹ בִּשְׁבִיל תְּקִיעָה אַחֲרוֹנָה שֶׁל בָּבָא זוֹ:

10 (Each of the following is called a series:[28] *tekiah-shevarim-teruah-tekiah,* or *tekiah-shevarim-tekiah,* or *tekiah-teruah-tekiah.*) If the last *tekiah* of one of [these three] series was extended and prolonged to the length of two *tekios,* with the intent that it be considered as two *tekios* — i.e., the last of the current series and also the first of the following series — it counts as only one *tekiah,* the last *tekiah* of the current series.[8]

[The rationale is that] every *tekiah* must have a beginning and an end. If this [double] *tekiah* were to be divided as the person sounding the *shofar* desired, the second *tekiah* would have no beginning and the first *tekiah* would have no end. Therefore, we do not follow his intent. We consider this as one long *tekiah,* which is counted as the last *tekiah* of the current series.

יא וְיֵשׁ חוֹלְקִין[צא] וְאוֹמְרִים שֶׁהַכֹּל הוֹלֵךְ אַחַר מַחֲשַׁבְתּוֹ,[29] וְכֵיוָן שֶׁהוּא חָשַׁב

11 However, some authorities differ, maintaining that everything depends on the intent [of the person sounding the *shofar*].[29] And since he

---

27. This precaution is taken, because the question involves the observance of a Scriptural commandment.

28. In the original Aramaic, *bava.* See footnote 1 above.

29. *Talmud Yerushalmi, Rosh HaShanah* 4:11.

שם. **פו** משנה לג, ב. טור ושו"ע ס"ו. **פז** ב"ח ד"ה ומ"ש רבנו דין זה. מ"א סוף סק"ה. וראה לעיל ס"ג לענין תקיעה אחרונה של סדר תשר"ת או תש"ת. **פח** רמב"ם פ"ג ה"ד ומ"מ שם. רמב"ן כז, א ד"ה הא דתנן. רא"ש פ"ד סי' ח. טור שכן מוכח בגמרא דידן (כז, א). דעה הא' בשו"ע שם. **פט** ר"ן (יא, ב) ד"ה ולפיכך. **צ** גמרא כז, א. ט"ז סק"ז. **צא** ירושלמי פ"ד ה"י. רי"ץ גיאת (ע' מ). הובא ברמב"ן שם. רא"ש שם וטור. דעה הב' בשו"ע שם.

שֶׁתַּעֲלֶה לוֹ לִשְׁתֵּי תְקִיעוֹת[צב] אָנוּ חוֹשְׁבִין אוֹתָהּ כִּשְׁתֵּי תְקִיעוֹת וּשְׁתֵּיהֶן פְּסוּלוֹת מִטַּעַם שֶׁנִּתְבָּאֵר,[צג] וּלְכָךְ אֵינָהּ עוֹלָה לוֹ אֲפִלּוּ בִּשְׁבִיל תְּקִיעָה אַחַת, וְצָרִיךְ לַחֲזֹר וְלִתְקֹעַ תְּקִיעָה רִאשׁוֹנָה שֶׁל בָּבָא זוֹ[צד] וְיִגְמֹר מִשָּׁם וְאֵילָךְ עַל הַסֵּדֶר, כְּדִין מִי שֶׁטָּעָה בְּאֶמְצַע בָּבָא שֶׁחוֹזֵר לָרֹאשׁ כְּמוֹ שֶׁיִּתְבָּאֵר.[צה, 30]

וַהֲלָכָה כִּסְבָרָא הָרִאשׁוֹנָה,[צו] וּמִכָּל מָקוֹם טוֹב לָחוּשׁ לַסְּבָרָא הָאַחֲרוֹנָה:[צז, 27]

intended that this [long] *shofar* blast should count for two *tekios,* we also consider it as two *tekios,* both of which are invalid for the reason explained above. His [double] blast does not even count for a single *tekiah*. This person must therefore sound the first *tekiah* of this series again, and then complete all the remaining *shofar* blasts in the proper order. In this he is bound by the law that applies to a person who makes a mistake in the midst of a series of *shofar* blasts: he must return to the beginning, as will be explained.[30]

The *halachah* follows the first view. Nevertheless, it is advisable to show deference to the second view.[27]

יב אַף עַל פִּי שֶׁלְּכַתְּחִלָּה אָסוּר לְהָשִׂיחַ מִתְּחִלַּת תְּקִיעוֹת מְיֻשָּׁב עַד סוֹף הַתְּקִיעוֹת מְעֻמָּד כְּמוֹ שֶׁיִּתְבָּאֵר בְּסִימָן תקצ"[ב],[צח] מִכָּל מָקוֹם אִם עָבַר הַתּוֹקֵעַ וְשָׂח, אֲפִלּוּ הִפְסִיק כַּמָּה שָׁעוֹת בְּשִׂיחָה[צט] אֲפִלּוּ בֵּין תְּקִיעָה לִתְרוּעָה וּבֵין תְּרוּעָה לִתְקִיעָה וּבֵין בָּבָא לְבָבָא וּבֵין סֵדֶר לְסֵדֶר[ק] — אֵין צָרִיךְ לַחֲזֹר וְלִתְקֹעַ.[31]

אֲפִלּוּ הִפְסִיק בֵּין הַקּוֹלוֹת שֶׁבְּבָבָא אַחַת בְּקוֹלוֹת אֲחֵרִים, כְּגוֹן שֶׁלְּאַחַר שֶׁתָּקַע אוֹ לְאַחַר שֶׁהֵרִיעַ נִתְעַסֵּק בִּתְקִיעוֹת אוֹ בִּתְרוּעוֹת אֲחֵרוֹת וְהִפְסִיק בָּהֶם בֵּין הַתְּרוּעָה שֶׁל אוֹתָהּ הַבָּבָא לְהַתְּקִיעוֹת שֶׁלְּפָנֶיהָ וּלְאַחֲרֶיהָ — אֵין בְּכָךְ כְּלוּם, דְּכֵיוָן שֶׁלֹּא נִתְכַּוֵּן בְּקוֹלוֹת הָאֵלּוּ שֶׁנִּתְעַסֵּק בָּהֶם בְּאֶמְצַע

12 As the initial and preferred option, it is forbidden to talk from the beginning of the *tekios meyushav* until the conclusion of the *tekios me'umad,* as will be explained in sec. 592[:7]. Nevertheless, if the person sounding the *shofar* transgressed and spoke — even if he spent several hours in conversation, and even if he did so between a *tekiah* and a *teruah* or between one series and another, or between one set and another — he does not have to sound the *shofar* again.[31]

[Such an interruption] is not significant, even if the *shofar* blasts of one series were interrupted by other *shofar* blasts. For example, after one sounded a *tekiah* or a *teruah,* he casually sounded other *tekios* or *teruos,* which thus interrupt between the *teruah* of that series and the *tekios* that preceded or followed it. [The rationale is that] since he did not intend that these *shofar* blasts which he casually sounded in the middle of the series

30. In subsections 15-19 below. **31.** *Rosh HaShanah* 34a.

צב רא"ש שם (בביאור דעת הירושלמי). צג סעיף י. צד לבוש ס"ו. מ"א סק"ה. צה סט"ז־יז. צו מגיד משנה פ"ג ה"ד. ב"י ד"ה ואף על פי. דעה הא' בשו"ע בסתם. צז ב"י שם. צח סעיף ז. צט מ"א סק"י בפירוש דברי הגמרא לה, רע"ב. ק מ"א שם סי' תקצב סק"ד, בשם הרא"ש פ"ד סי' יב, בשם ראבי"ה ח"ב סי'

should count towards the fulfillment of the *mitzvah,* but viewed them as a casual act, they are not considered as an interruption between the *teruah* and the simple sound that preceded or followed it. For the Torah was insistent only that these two sounds should not be interrupted by a *shofar* blast which is not [long and] simple and which was sounded with the intent of fulfilling the *mitzvah.* In such an instance, there would not be a [long and] simple *shofar* blast preceding or following the *teruah;* it would be preceded or followed by a *shofar* blast that was not [long and] simple. If, however, the person sounding the *shofar* did not intend that these blasts fulfill the *mitzvah,* [the *teruah*] is not considered to be preceded or followed by a *shofar* blast that is not [long and] simple. Since the person did not intend to fulfill the *mitzvah* with [them, the other *shofar* blasts] are of no consequence at all; they are just like the sounds of an animal or a beast.

הַבָּבָא לְשֵׁם מִצְוָה אֶלָּא כְּמִתְעַסֵּק בְּעָלְמָא, לְפִיכָךְ אֵינָן חֲשׁוּבִין הֶפְסֵק בֵּין הַתְּרוּעָה לַפְּשׁוּטָה שֶׁלְּפָנֶיהָ וְשֶׁלְּאַחֲרֶיהָ, לְפִי שֶׁלֹּא הִקְפִּידָה תּוֹרָה אֶלָּא שֶׁלֹּא יַפְסִיק בֵּינֵיהֶם בְּקוֹל שׁוֹפָר שֶׁאֵינוֹ פָּשׁוּט שֶׁנִּתְכַּוֵּן בּוֹ הַתּוֹקֵעַ לְשֵׁם מִצְוָה,[קא] דְּאָז אֵין כָּאן פְּשׁוּטָה לְפָנֶיהָ אוֹ לְאַחֲרֶיהָ אֶלָּא קוֹל שׁוֹפָר שֶׁאֵינוֹ פָּשׁוּט לְפָנֶיהָ אוֹ לְאַחֲרֶיהָ, אֲבָל אִם לֹא נִתְכַּוֵּן בּוֹ הַתּוֹקֵעַ לְשֵׁם מִצְוָה אֵין כָּאן קוֹל שׁוֹפָר שֶׁאֵינוֹ פָּשׁוּט לְפָנֶיהָ אוֹ לְאַחֲרֶיהָ, לְפִי שֶׁאֵין קוֹלוֹ נֶחְשָׁב לִכְלוּם וְדוֹמֶה לְקוֹל בְּהֵמָה וְחַיָּה כֵּיוָן שֶׁלֹּא נִתְכַּוֵּן בּוֹ לְשֵׁם מִצְוָה:[קב]

13 Similar concepts [apply with regard to] a person hearing the *shofar* blasts. If one heard the *shofar* blasts in interludes, i.e., he interrupted extensively by talking, he has [nevertheless] fulfilled his obligation. [This applies] provided that in the midst of a series of *shofar* blasts he did not hear a *shofar* blast that is inappropriate at that point; i.e., provided that between the *teruah* of that series and the [long and] simple *shofar* blast that precedes or follows it, he did not hear a *shofar* blast which was not [long and] simple and which was sounded with the intent of fulfilling the *mitzvah* — as was explained above with regard to the person sounding the *shofar*.

יג וְכֵן הַשּׁוֹמֵעַ, אִם שָׁמַע הַתְּקִיעוֹת בְּסֵרוּגִין,[קג] דְּהַיְנוּ שֶׁהִפְסִיק בֵּינְתַיִם הַרְבֵּה בְּשִׂיחָה — יָצָא, וְהוּא שֶׁבְּאֶמְצַע הַבָּבָא לֹא שָׁמַע קוֹל שׁוֹפָר שֶׁאֵינוֹ רָאוּי בְּאוֹתוֹ מָקוֹם, דְּהַיְנוּ שֶׁבֵּין הַתְּרוּעָה שֶׁל הַבָּבָא לְהַפְּשׁוּטָה שֶׁלְּפָנֶיהָ וְשֶׁלְּאַחֲרֶיהָ לֹא שָׁמַע קוֹל שׁוֹפָר שֶׁאֵינוֹ פָּשׁוּט לְשֵׁם מִצְוָה,[קד] וְעַל דֶּרֶךְ שֶׁנִּתְבָּאֵר בְּתוֹקֵעַ:

14 Similarly, not all the *shofar* blasts must be heard from one person. Even if one hears them from several people — a *tekiah* from one, a *teruah* from another, and a [second] *tekiah*

יד וְכֵן אֵין צָרִיךְ שֶׁיִּשְׁמַע כָּל הַתְּקִיעוֹת מֵאָדָם אֶחָד, אֶלָּא אֲפִלּוּ אִם שָׁמַע אוֹתָן מִכַּמָּה בְּנֵי אָדָם תְּקִיעָה מִזֶּה וּתְרוּעָה מִזֶּה וּתְקִיעָה

תקלה. **קא** רמב"ן לד, א ד"ה הא דאקשינן (הואיל ותקע לשם מצוה תקיעות אחרות). הובא בר"ן (י, ב) ד"ה מתקיף. מ"א ס"ק י. **קב** מ"א שם. **קג** גמרא לד, רע"ב. טור ושו"ע סי' תקפח ס"ב. **קד** רמב"ן שם. ט"ז שם סק"ב, דלא כלבוש שם ס"ב. מ"א שם סוף סק"ג.

מִזֶּה[קה] וְכֵן עַד סוֹף כָּל הַקּוֹלוֹת – יָצָא.[32] אֲבָל אִם שָׁמַע תְּקִיעָה תְּרוּעָה תְּקִיעָה מִשְּׁלֹשָׁה בְּנֵי אָדָם שֶׁתָּקְעוּ כֻּלָּם כְּאֶחָד[קו] זֶה תְּקִיעָה וְזֶה תְּרוּעָה וְזֶה תְּקִיעָה – לֹא יָצָא, לְפִי שֶׁאֵין כָּאן פְּשׁוּטָה לְפָנֶיהָ וּפְשׁוּטָה לְאַחֲרֶיהָ כֵּיוָן שֶׁכֻּלָּם תָּקְעוּ בְּבַת אַחַת.[קז] וְאִם כָּל אֶחָד וְאֶחָד מִשְּׁלָשְׁתָּן תָּקְעוּ תְּקִיעָה תְּרוּעָה תְּקִיעָה,[קח] אַף עַל פִּי שֶׁכָּל הַקּוֹלוֹת יוֹצְאִין בְּבַת אַחַת[33] וּב' קוֹלוֹת הַיּוֹצְאִין בְּבַת אַחַת אֵין שׁוֹמְעִין אֲפִלּוּ אַחַת מֵהֶן כְּמוֹ שֶׁנִּתְבָּאֵר בְּסִימָן קמ"א,[קט,34] מִכָּל מָקוֹם בְּשׁוֹפָר כֵּיוָן דְּחָבִיב הוּא עַל הַשּׁוֹמֵעַ,[קי] לְפִי שֶׁאֵינוֹ אֶלָּא פַּעַם בְּשָׁנָה,[קיא,35] הוּא נוֹתֵן דַּעְתּוֹ וְשׁוֹמֵעַ אֲפִלּוּ כַּמָּה קוֹלוֹת.[קיב]

וּלְפִיכָךְ אֲפִלּוּ מִקְצָתָם תָּקְעוּ בַּחֲצוֹצְרוֹת[36] וּמִקְצָתָן תָּקְעוּ בְּשׁוֹפָר – יָצְאוּ,[קיג] דְּמֵחֲמַת חֲבִיבוּתוֹ נָתַן דַּעְתּוֹ עַל הַשּׁוֹפָר לִשְׁמֹעַ קוֹלוֹ:[קיד]

טו תּוֹקֵעַ הָעוֹמֵד בְּסֵדֶר תשר"ת וּלְאַחַר שֶׁתָּקַע שְׁנֵי שְׁבָרִים קֹדֶם שֶׁסִּיֵּם שֶׁבֶר הַשְּׁלִישִׁי טָעָה וְהִתְחִיל לְהָרִיעַ,[קטו] בֵּין שֶׁגָּמַר אֶת הַתְּרוּעָה

from still another person, following this pattern until [he has heard] all the *shofar* blasts — he has fulfilled his obligation.[32]

If, however, one hears a *tekiah* and a *teruah* and a *tekiah* sounded at the same time by three people respectively, he has not fulfilled his obligation. [The rationale is that the *teruah*] was neither preceded nor followed by a [long,] simple blast, because all [three] blasts were sounded at the same time.

Nevertheless, should each one of the three have sounded a series of *tekiah-teruah-tekiah,* then even though all the blasts were sounded at the same time, the listener has fulfilled his obligation.[33] [As a rule, we say that] when there are two simultaneous sounds, neither of them is heard [properly], as stated in sec. 141.[34] This case is exceptional. Since the *shofar* is cherished by a listener, because it is sounded only once a year,[35] he will listen attentively and [discern between even] several sounds. For the same reason, even if some people sounded trumpets,[36] and some sounded *shofaros,* [a listener] has fulfilled his obligation. Because he cherishes [the *mitzvah*], he pays attention to the *shofar* and hears its sound.

15 [The following laws apply if a person] sounding the *shofar* erred in the midst of the set comprising *tekiah-shevarim-teruah-tekiah,* and after sounding two *shevarim,* before completing the third *shever,* began the *teruah.* Whether he completed the *teruah*

---

32. *Ibid.* 34b.

33. *Ibid.* 27a.

34. Sec. 141 of the Alter Rebbe's *Shulchan Aruch* is not extant. The *Shulchan Aruch* of R. Yosef Caro states (in sec. 141:2) that two people should not read from the Torah at the same time.

35. I.e., as a *mitzvah*. The sounding of the *shofar* throughout the preceding month of Elul is merely a custom.

36. Which are unacceptable for the *mitzvah*.

קה ברייתא לד, ב. טור ושו"ע סי' תקפה ס"ב. קו גמרא [ברייתא] שם, לגירסת ופירוש תוס' שם ד"ה מתשעה. טור ושו"ע שם ס"ג. קז תוס' שם. רא"ש פ"ד סי' יג. לבוש שם ס"ד. קח רמ"א שם ס"ג. קט סימן זה בשוע"ר לא הגיע לידינו, וראה טור ושו"ע שם ס"ב ומ"א סק"ג. קי גמרא כז, א. וראה גם לעיל סי' תפח ס"ד. קיא משמעות רש"י שם ד"ה דחביבה. קיב גמרא שם. רמ"א שם. וראה לעיל שם. חקרי הלכות ח"א לג, ב. קיג הגהות אשרי פ"ג סי' א. ב"י שם ד"ה כתב הג"א. רמ"א שם. קיד גמרא שם. ב"י שם. קטו ראב"ן סי' סא (מעשה שהיה במגנצא בר"ה שנת תתק"ה). ראבי"ה סי' קעא. רא"ש פ"ד סי'

שֶׁהִתְחִיל בָּהּ בְּטָעוּת בֵּין שֶׁלֹּא גְמָרָהּ עֲדַיִן אֶלָּא נִזְכַּר בְּאֶמְצַע[קטז] — יַחֲזֹר וְיִתְקַע ג' שְׁבָרִים[37] וְיָרִיעַ וְיִגְמֹר מִשָּׁם וְאֵילָךְ עַל הַסֵּדֶר. אֲבָל אֵינוֹ צָרִיךְ לַחֲזֹר וְלִתְקֹעַ אֶת הַתְּקִיעָה הָרִאשׁוֹנָה שֶׁל בָּבָא זוֹ, שֶׁכְּבָר תָּקַע קֹדֶם שֶׁטָּעָה.[קיז] וְאַף עַל פִּי שֶׁהִפְסִיק בִּשְׁנֵי שְׁבָרִים וּתְרוּעָה שֶׁתָּקַע בְּטָעוּת בֵּין תְּקִיעָה רִאשׁוֹנָה שֶׁל בָּבָא זוֹ לִשְׁבָרִים וּתְרוּעָה שֶׁל בָּבָא זוֹ — אֵין בְּכָךְ כְּלוּם, דְּכֵיוָן שֶׁהַשְּׁבָרִים תְּרוּעָה שֶׁתָּקַע בְּטָעוּת הֵן מֵעֵין שְׁבָרִים תְּרוּעָה שֶׁיֵּשׁ לוֹ לִתְקֹעַ בְּבָבָא זוֹ — אֵין זֶה הֶפְסֵק, הָא לְמָה זֶה דּוֹמֶה לְתוֹקֵעַ שֶׁמַּתְחִיל לְהָרִיעַ וְאֵין הַקּוֹל עוֹלֶה יָפֶה וּפוֹסֵק וְחוֹזֵר וּמַתְחִיל לְהָרִיעַ, שֶׁאֵין הַקּוֹל הַקָּצָר שֶׁיִּשְׁמְעוּ בְּשׁוֹפָר חָשׁוּב הֶפְסֵק בֵּין תְּרוּעָה לִפְשׁוּטָה שֶׁלְּפָנֶיהָ, כֵּיוָן שֶׁהוּא מֵעֵין תְּרוּעָה שֶׁצָּרִיךְ לִתְקֹעַ:[קיח]

which he mistakenly began, or whether he did not complete it but [caught his mistake] while still in the midst of it, he must once again sound the three *shevarim*[37] and the *teruah.* He should then complete [the sounding of the *shofar*] in the proper order.

He does not have to repeat the first *tekiah* of the present series, which he sounded before he erred. [The fact that] the two *shevarim* and the mistimed *teruah* interrupt between the first *tekiah* of this series and the *shevarim-teruah* of this series is of no consequence. Since the mistaken *shevarim-teruah* are of the same type as the *shevarim-teruah* that were required [for] this series, this is not considered an interruption. To what can this be compared? To a person who began to sound a *teruah,* but since the notes did not come out well, he stopped and began another *teruah.* In such a case, the short blast[s] that people heard from the *shofar* are not considered as an interruption between the [valid] *teruah* and the [long,] simple blast that preceded it, because they are of the same type as the *teruah* that he was required to sound.

טז בַּמֶּה דְּבָרִים אֲמוּרִים?[38] בְּסֵדֶר תשר"ת, אֲבָל אִם עוֹמֵד בְּסֵדֶר תש"ת,[קיט] בֵּין שֶׁהִתְחִיל לְהָרִיעַ לְאַחַר שֶׁגָּמַר הַשְּׁבָרִים, בֵּין שֶׁהִתְחִיל לְהָרִיעַ קֹדֶם שֶׁגָּמַר הַשְּׁבָרִים אֲפִלּוּ לֹא עָשָׂה אֶלָּא שֶׁבֶר אֶחָד,[קכ] בֵּין שֶׁהִתְחִיל לְהָרִיעַ קֹדֶם שֶׁתָּקַע אֲפִלּוּ שֶׁבֶר אֶחָד — צָרִיךְ לַחֲזֹר וְלִתְקֹעַ גַּם תְּקִיעָה הָרִאשׁוֹנָה שֶׁל בָּבָא זוֹ, דְּכֵיוָן דִּתְרוּעָה זוֹ אֵינָהּ מֵעֵין

16 When does the above[38] apply? In the set comprising *tekiah-shevarim-teruah-tekiah.* In the set comprising *tekiah-shevarim-tekiah,* by contrast, [different rules apply]. Whether one began sounding the *teruah* after completing the *shevarim,* or before completing the *shevarim,* even if he only sounded one *shever,* or whether he sounded a *teruah* before he sounded even one *shever,* he must also repeat the first *tekiah* of this series. Since this *teruah* is not of the same type as the

37. I.e., not only the third *shever,* but all three.

38. I.e., The above statement that the superfluous *teruah* is not considered as an interruption.

יא. טור ושו"ע ס"ז. קטז ראבי"ה שם (ע' 187) בשם אביו רבנו יואל. הובא במרדכי השלם רמז תשכ (ע' מט). ב"ח ד"ה מעשה. ט"ז סק"ח. קיז רא"ש שם. טור ושו"ע שם. קיח רא"ש שם. טור. וראה משנה שכיר או"ח ח"ב סי' קנג. קיט משמעות הרא"ש שם. טור ושו"ע סוף ס"ז. קכ מ"א סק"ט.

הַשְּׁבָרִים שֶׁצָּרִיךְ לוֹ לִתְקֹעַ בְּבָבָא זוֹ, לְפִיכָךְ הִיא חֲשׁוּבָה הֶפְסֵק בֵּין הַשְּׁבָרִים לִפְשׁוּטָה שֶׁלְּפָנֶיהָ.[קכא]

וַאֲפִלּוּ בְּסֵדֶר תשר"ת לֹא אָמְרוּ שֶׁאֵין צָרִיךְ לַחֲזֹר וְלִתְקֹעַ תְּקִיעָה רִאשׁוֹנָה, אֶלָּא כְּשֶׁלֹּא הִפְסִיק בִּנְשִׁימָה בֵּין סִיּוּם הַשְּׁנֵי שְׁבָרִים לְהַתְחָלַת הַתְּרוּעָה שֶׁהֵרִיעַ בְּטָעוּת, אֲבָל אִם הִפְסִיק בֵּינֵיהֶם בִּנְשִׁימָה — צָרִיךְ לַחֲזֹר וְלִתְקֹעַ גַּם תְּקִיעָה הָרִאשׁוֹנָה שֶׁל בָּבָא זוֹ,[קכב,39] דְּכֵיוָן שֶׁהִפְסִיק בִּנְשִׁימָה בֵּין הַשְּׁבָרִים לְהַתְּרוּעָה — אֵין שְׁנֵיהֶם נֶחְשָׁבִים כִּתְקִיעָה הָא׳,[קכג] וְאֵין הַתְּרוּעָה מִצְטָרֶפֶת כְּלָל עִם הַשְּׁבָרִים, וַהֲרֵי זֶה דּוֹמֶה לְמִי שֶׁהֵרִיעַ תְּרוּעָה לְבַדּוֹ בְּלֹא שְׁבָרִים קֹדֶם שֶׁתָּקַע הַשְּׁלֹשָׁה שְׁבָרִים בְּסֵדֶר תשר"ת, דְּצָרִיךְ לַחֲזֹר וְלִתְקֹעַ תְּקִיעָה רִאשׁוֹנָה שֶׁל בָּבָא זוֹ,[קכד] לְפִי שֶׁהִפְסִיק בִּתְרוּעָה זוֹ בֵּין הַשְּׁבָרִים לִפְשׁוּטָה שֶׁלִּפְנֵיהֶם, שֶׁהֲרֵי תְּרוּעָה זוֹ אֵינָהּ מֵעֵין הַשְּׁבָרִים שֶׁצְּרִיכִים לוֹ לִתְקֹעַ בְּבָבָא זוֹ, וְאַף עַל פִּי שֶׁהוּא מֵעֵין הַתְּרוּעָה שֶׁצָּרִיךְ לוֹ לִתְקֹעַ בְּבָבָא זוֹ — אֵין זוֹ מוֹעִיל כְּלוּם, כֵּיוָן שֶׁלֹּא תָּקַע עֲדַיִן הַשְּׁבָרִים שֶׁל בָּבָא זוֹ:[קכה]

shevarim which must be sounded in this series, it is considered an interruption between the *shevarim* and the [long,] simple blast which preceded them.

Moreover, even in the set comprising *tekiah-shevarim-teruah-tekiah,* the statement that one is not required to repeat the first *tekiah* applies only if one did not interrupt and take a breath between the end of the two *shevarim* and the mistaken *teruah.* If one made an interruption by taking a breath, he must also repeat the first *tekiah* of this series.[39]

[The rationale is that] since he made an interruption by taking a breath between the *shevarim* and the *teruah,* the two are not considered as a single *shofar* blast, and the *teruah* is not connected with the *shevarim* at all. This is comparable to someone who sounded only a *teruah,* without any *shevarim,* before sounding the three *shevarim* in the set comprising *tekiah-shevarim-teruah-tekiah.* In such an instance, he must repeat the first *tekiah* of this series, because his *teruah* separated the *shevarim* from the [long,] simple blast that preceded them — for this *teruah* is not of the same type as the *shevarim* which it must accompany in this series. Although they are of the same type as the *teruah* that must be sounded in this series, this is of no consequence, since the *shevarim* of this set have not been sounded.

39. This would appear to accord only with the view stated in subsection 9, which recommends that the *shevarim-teruah* should be sounded in one breath. According to the view in subsection 8, which favors taking a breath at this point, surely this breath should not constitute an interruption. How our subsection nevertheless implies that it accords with both stances is a subject of debate. (See Hebrew footnote קכב.)

קכא רא"ש שם וטור. קכב ר"ן (י, ב) ד"ה סוד"ה מתקיף. ב"י ד"ה ומ"ש או לאחר (לדעה הב' דלעיל ס"ט. ומזה לומדים לדין הפסיק בנשימה אחר ב' השברים, דהוי כלא עשה שברים כלל והתחיל בתרועה). וראה בן הימין (ליקוטים או"ח) סי' ו. שו"ת קול יהודה (כ"ץ) סי' יג. מ"מ וציונים. קכג אוצ"ל: א' (כלומר תרועה אחת). קכד אבודרהם סדר תקיעות. ב"ח ד"ה י"א דלא. ט"ז סק"י. מ"א סוף סקי"א. קכה ב"ח שם. קכו טור בדעת הרמב"ן, ושו"ע ס"ח.

17 Similarly, whether in the set comprising *tekiah-shevarim-teruah-tekiah* or in the set *tekiah-shevarim-tekiah,* one must repeat the first *tekiah* of the series if he sounded three *shevarim,* then made an interruption by taking a breath,[40] and then sounded other *shevarim,* or even if he [added] only one other *shever,* [before sounding the following *teruah* or *tekiah*].

[The same laws apply if] after completing the *teruah,* i.e., [a minimum of] three staccato blasts according to the first opinion which we mentioned [in subsection 4], one made an interruption by taking a breath, and then sounded another *teruah.* Even if he did not complete this *teruah,* he must repeat the first *tekiah* of this series and then complete [all the remaining] blasts in order.

[The rationale is that there is a difficulty] since he made an interruption by sounding either additional *shevarim* or an additional *teruah* between the *shevarim* or the *teruah* and the [long,] simple blast that follows them. If he would [now] repeat [only] the *shevarim* or the *teruah*[41] and then continue in the proper order, the superfluous *shevarim* or *teruah* which he sounded previously would separate the acceptable *shevarim* or *teruah* of this series from the [long,] simple blast that preceded them. For [these superfluous blasts] are not precursors[42] of the *shevarim* or *teruah* which must be sounded in this series; nothing is lacking, since [the required blasts] were already sounded.

יז וְכֵן אִם לְאַחַר שֶׁתָּקַע שְׁלֹשָׁה שְׁבָרִים[קכו] בֵּין בְּסֵדֶר תשר"ת[קכז] בֵּין בְּסֵדֶר תש"ת הִפְסִיק בִּנְשִׁימָה[קכח, 40] וְחָזַר וְתָקַע שְׁבָרִים אֲחֵרִים, וַאֲפִלּוּ לֹא חָזַר וְתָקַע אֶלָּא שֶׁבֶר אֶחָד,[קכט] וְכֵן אִם לְאַחַר שֶׁגָּמַר אֶת הַתְּרוּעָה[קל] דְּהַיְנוּ שְׁלֹשָׁה טְרוּמִיטִין[קלא] לְפִי סְבָרָא הָרִאשׁוֹנָה שֶׁבֵּאַרְנוּ[קלב] הִפְסִיק בִּנְשִׁימָה[קלג] וְחָזַר וְהֵרִיעַ אֲפִלּוּ לֹא גָּמַר אֶת הַתְּרוּעָה — צָרִיךְ לַחֲזֹר וְלִתְקֹעַ גַּם תְּקִיעָה רִאשׁוֹנָה שֶׁל בָּבָא זוֹ וְגוֹמֵר מִשָּׁם וְאֵילָךְ עַל הַסֵּדֶר, דְּכֵיוָן שֶׁהִפְסִיק[קלד] בִּשְׁבָרִים יְתֵרִים אוֹ בִּתְרוּעָה יְתֵרָה בֵּין הַשְּׁבָרִים אוֹ בֵּין הַתְּרוּעָה לַפְּשׁוּטָה שֶׁלְּאַחֲרֵיהֶן, וְאִם יַחֲזֹר וְיִתְקַע הַשְּׁבָרִים אוֹ הַתְּרוּעָה[41] וְיִגְמֹר מִשָּׁם וְאֵילָךְ עַל הַסֵּדֶר — יִהְיוּ הַשְּׁבָרִים הַיְתֵרִים אוֹ הַתְּרוּעָה הַיְתֵרָה שֶׁתָּקַע כְּבָר הֶפְסֵק בֵּין הַשְּׁבָרִים אוֹ הַתְּרוּעָה הַכְּשֵׁרִים שֶׁל בָּבָא זוֹ לַפְּשׁוּטָה שֶׁלִּפְנֵיהֶן, לְפִי שֶׁאֵינָן מֵעֵין[42] שְׁבָרִים אוֹ תְּרוּעָה שֶׁצָּרִיךְ לוֹ לִתְקֹעַ בְּבָבָא זוֹ, שֶׁהֲרֵי אֵין צָרִיךְ לוֹ כְּלוּם כֵּיוָן שֶׁכְּבָר תָּקַע אוֹתָם:

40. If one did not make an interruption by taking a breath, this law does not apply. For although the Alter Rebbe states that one should not add to the number of *shevarim* (subsection 4), if one does, it is still acceptable.

41. Without sounding a new *tekiah* before them.

42. If they were preliminary sounds anticipating the actual blasts, they would not constitute an interruption (a *hefsek*).

קכז מ"א סקי"א ד"ה ודע (לענין ב' תרועות זה אחר זה). קכח ר"ן שם בדעת הרמב"ן. ב"י שם. קכט ר"ן שם. שו"ע שם. קל תוספתא פ"ב הי"ב, לגירסת הרמב"ן כז, א ד"ה וזה הפירוש. הובא בר"ן (י, ב) ד"ה מתקיף. טור ושו"ע שם. קלא מ"א ס"ק ח (לענין תרועה אחר ב' שברים). קלב סעיף ד. קלג ראה בן הימין (לקוטים או"ח) סי' ו. קלד ר"ן שם. טור ושו"ע שם.

יח כָּל מָקוֹם שֶׁנִּתְבָּאֵר שֶׁצָּרִיךְ לַחֲזֹר וְלִתְקֹעַ גַּם תְּקִיעָה רִאשׁוֹנָה שֶׁל הַבָּבָא, אִם לֹא נִזְכַּר מֵהַטָּעוּת עַד לְאַחַר שֶׁתָּקַע תְּקִיעָה אַחֲרוֹנָה שֶׁל הַבָּבָא – אוֹתָהּ תְּקִיעָה אַחֲרוֹנָה עוֹלָה לוֹ בִּמְקוֹם תְּקִיעָה רִאשׁוֹנָה וְגוֹמֵר מִשָּׁם וְאֵילָךְ עַל הַסֵּדֶר.[קלה]

וְאִם לֹא נִזְכַּר עַד שֶׁעוֹמֵד בְּבָבָא אַחֶרֶת, אוֹ אֲפִלּוּ בְּסֵדֶר אַחֵר, כְּגוֹן שֶׁטָּעָה מִסֵּדֶר תשר״ת וְלֹא נִזְכַּר עַד שֶׁעוֹמֵד בְּסֵדֶר תש״ת אוֹ תר״ת – גּוֹמֵר כָּל הַסֵּדֶר שֶׁנִּזְכַּר בּוֹ וְאַחַר כָּךְ תּוֹקֵעַ בָּבָא אַחַת תשר״ת. וְאַף עַל פִּי שֶׁהִפְסִיק בְּאֶמְצַע הַסֵּדֶר שֶׁל תשר״ת[43] בִּתְקִיעוֹת שֶׁל תש״ת – אֵין בְּכָךְ כְּלוּם, שֶׁלֹּא הִקְפִּידָה תּוֹרָה אֶלָּא שֶׁלֹּא לְהַפְסִיק בֵּין תְּרוּעָה לִפְשׁוּטָה שֶׁלְּפָנֶיהָ וְשֶׁלְּאַחֲרֶיהָ,[קלו] אֲבָל אִם מַפְסִיק בֵּין בָּבָא לְבָבָא אֲפִלּוּ בְּקוֹל שׁוֹפָר שֶׁאֵינוֹ רָאוּי לְאוֹתוֹ סֵדֶר – אֵין בְּכָךְ כְּלוּם:[קלז]

יט כָּל מָקוֹם שֶׁנִּתְבָּאֵר שֶׁאִם טָעָה צָרִיךְ לַחֲזֹר וְלִתְקֹעַ תְּקִיעָה רִאשׁוֹנָה שֶׁל בָּבָא זוֹ שֶׁטָּעָה בָּהּ – אֵין חִלּוּק בֵּין תְּקִיעוֹת מְעֻמָּד לִתְקִיעוֹת מְיֻשָּׁב בְּכָל אַחַת מֵהֶן צָרִיךְ לַחֲזֹר[קלח] וְעַל דֶּרֶךְ שֶׁנִּתְבָּאֵר. וַאֲפִלּוּ בְּמָקוֹם

18 Whenever it was stated that the person must go back and repeat the first *tekiah* of a [particular] series, if he did not catch his mistake until he had sounded the last *tekiah* of that series, that latter *tekiah* can be considered as the first *tekiah* of the series [now being repeated]. He should then proceed to complete all [the remaining blasts] in order.

If he did not catch his mistake until he had begun another series or even another set, [he should complete that series or set and then correct his mistake]. For example, if he erred while sounding the set comprising *tekiah-shevarim-teruah-tekiah,* and did not catch his mistake until he was in the midst of the set comprising *tekiah-shevarim-tekiah* or the set *tekiah-teruah-tekiah,* he should complete the entire set in the midst of which he realized that he had erred. He should then sound a series comprising *tekiah-shevarim-teruah-tekiah.* Although he interrupted the set comprising *tekiah-shevarim-teruah-tekiah*[43] by sounding the blasts of the set comprising *tekiah-shevarim-tekiah,* that is not significant. For the Torah was concerned only that no interruption be made between a *teruah* and the [long,] simple blast that precedes or follows it; if one separated one series from another by a *shofar* blast that is not appropriate for that set, this is of no consequence.

19 Whenever it was stated that [after a mistake] one must repeat even the first *tekiah* of the series in which he erred, there is no difference [whether the mistake was made in] the *tekios me'umad* or the *tekios meyushav.* In either instance the *shofar* must be sounded again, as explained. Even in places where all

43. For he did not complete that series until he sounded the set in which he made the error.

קלה מ״א סקי״ב. קלו כדלעיל ס״א־ב וסי״ב. קלז מ״א שם. וראה לעיל סי׳ רסג קו״א סק״ה קרוב לסופו למי שלא היה בתחילת התקיעות: יצטרך אחר כך לשמוע על הסדר. קלח מ״א שם. קלט כדלקמן סי׳ תקצב ס״ה. קמ מ״א שם. וראה העו״ב תתיא ע׳ 93. קמא מ״א שם. קמב ראה לקמן סי׳ תקצו ס״א.

30 blasts are sounded in the *tekios me'umad*,[44] if one erred in the *tekios meyushav* one may not rely on the [forthcoming] *tekios me'umad* and thereby be exempt from returning to correct the error. [The rationale is that] since a blessing was recited over these *shofar* blasts, they must be sounded in the proper manner so that the blessing will not be in vain.

If, by contrast, one erred in the blasts that follow the prayers,[45] this is not significant, for [sounding] these [blasts] is merely a custom.

20 If a person sounds the *shofar* by blowing into its wide end, he has not fulfilled his obligation. A hint of this may be found in the verse,[46] "From the straits[47] I called [to G-d]."

21 After sounding the *shofar*, the leader of the prayer service[48] should begin to recite [aloud] the verse,[49] *Ashrei haam yod'ei seruah* ("Happy are the people who know the sound of the *shofar*"). In some [communities] it is customary to continue until *tarum karneinu* ("...our glory be exalted").[50] He then begins *Ashrei yoshvei...*, and then the Torah scroll is returned to [the ark].[51]

שֶׁתּוֹקְעִין כָּל הַשְּׁלֹשִׁים קוֹלוֹת בִּתְקִיעוֹת מְעֻמָּד[קלט, 44] — אֵין אוֹמְרִים שֶׁאִם טָעָה הַתּוֹקֵעַ בִּתְקִיעוֹת מְיֻשָּׁב נִסְמֹךְ עַל תְּקִיעוֹת מְעֻמָּד וְלֹא יְהֵא צָרִיךְ לַחֲזֹר, דְּכֵיוָן שֶׁבֵּרַךְ עַל תְּקִיעוֹת אֵלּוּ צָרִיךְ לַעֲשׂוֹתָן כַּהֹגֶן[קמ] שֶׁלֹּא תְּהֵא בִּרְכָתוֹ לְבַטָּלָה.

אֲבָל אִם טָעָה בִּתְקִיעוֹת שֶׁאַחַר הַתְּפִלָּה[45] — אֵין בְּכָךְ כְּלוּם,[קמא] לְפִי שֶׁאֵינָן רַק מִנְהָג בְּעָלְמָא:[קמב]

כ אִם תָּקַע בְּצַד הָרָחָב שֶׁל שׁוֹפָר — לֹא יָצָא,[קמג] וְרֶמֶז לַדָּבָר[קמד, 46] "מִן הַמֵּצַר[47] קָרָאתִי וגו'":[קמה]

כא וְאַחַר שֶׁתָּקַע יַתְחִיל[49] הַשְּׁלִיחַ צִבּוּר[קמו, 48] "אַשְׁרֵי הָעָם יוֹדְעֵי תְרוּעָה וגו'",[קמז] וְיֵשׁ נוֹהֲגִין לוֹמַר עַד "תָּרוּם קַרְנֵנוּ",[קמח, 50] וְאַחַר כָּךְ יַתְחִיל "אַשְׁרֵי יוֹשְׁבֵי וכו'",[קמט] וְאַחַר כָּךְ מַחֲזִירִין הַסֵּפֶר תּוֹרָה לִמְקוֹמוֹ:[קנ, 51]

---

44. See sec. 592:4-5. Since these 30 *shofar* blasts are being sounded, the listeners will regardless fulfill their obligation as prescribed by Scriptural Law. Hence, one might think that there is no need to correct the error. This is not so, as the Alter Rebbe goes on to explain.

45. See sec. 596.

46. *Tehillim* 118:5.

47. In allusion to the narrow end.

48. In the original, "the *sheliach tzibbur*"; i.e., the person who sounded the *shofar*. In *Chabad* custom, these verses are intoned by the person who led the congregation in reciting the verses that preceded the sounding of the *shofar*. The congregation then begins *Ashrei* together *(Sefer HaMinhagim: The Book of Chabad-Lubavitch Customs*, p. 120*)*.

49. *Tehillim* 89:16.

50. I.e., verses 17 and 18 are also added, as in the version that the Alter Rebbe follows in his *Siddur*. In the last verse, the word *karneinu* ("our glory") literally means "our horn." Accordingly, *Eliyah Rabbah* (sec. 591:1) finds here an allusion to the horn that will be sounded at the time of the Resurrection.

51. It was the custom in past generations that after the *tekios meyushav*, the Rebbe of the time would return to his place and turn to face the congregants, who

קמג ירושלמי הובא בר״ן (ו, ב) סוד״ה גמ׳. שו״ע ס״ט. וראה לעיל סי׳ תקפו סי״ב. קמד ר״ן שם (סימנא). לבוש ס״י. ט״ז סקי״א. קמה תהלים קיח, ה. קמו טור ריש סי׳ תקצא. רמ״א ס״ט (אומר השליח צבור). קמז תהלים פט, טז. קמח תהלים שם טז־יח. טור שם. סדור האריז״ל (ר׳ שבתי). באה״ט סקי״ב. ומנהג חב״ד שהאומר את הפסוקים קודם התקיעות מנגן ג״כ לאחריהם את שלשת הפסוקים [והקהל אומר אחריו פסוק בפסוק] (ספר המנהגים – חב״ד ע׳ 56. וראה גם אוצר מנהגי חב״ד ר״ה ע׳ קכו). קמט ומנהג חב״ד שכל הקהל אומרים אותו יחדיו (ספר המנהגים – חב״ד שם. אוצר מנהגי חב״ד שם). קנ טור שם. רמ״א שם.

סימן תקצא סֵדֶר תְּפִלַּת מוּסָף בְּיָחִיד וּבוֹ ט"ו סְעִיפִים:

א אַף עַל פִּי שֶׁבְּשַׁבָּתוֹת וְיָמִים טוֹבִים אָדָם מִתְפַּלֵּל שֶׁבַע בְּרָכוֹת, דְּהַיְנוּ שָׁלֹשׁ רִאשׁוֹנוֹת וְשָׁלֹשׁ אַחֲרוֹנוֹת וּקְדֻשַּׁת הַיּוֹם בָּאֶמְצַע,[א] אֲבָל בְּרֹאשׁ הַשָּׁנָה תִּקְּנוּ חֲכָמִים[ב] לְהִתְפַּלֵּל בְּמוּסָף שֶׁל שְׁנֵי הַיָּמִים תֵּשַׁע בְּרָכוֹת,[ג,1] דְּהַיְנוּ שֶׁבְּבִרְכַּת קְדֻשַּׁת הַיּוֹם כּוֹלֵל פְּסוּקֵי מַלְכֻיּוֹת[ד,2] כְּדֵי לְקַבֵּל עָלֵינוּ עֹל מַלְכוּת שָׁמַיִם,[ה] וְאַחַר כָּךְ אוֹמְרִים בִּרְכַּת זִכְרוֹנוֹת,[3] וְאוֹמֵר בָּהּ פְּסוּקֵי זִכְרוֹנוֹת כְּדֵי שֶׁיַּעֲלֶה זִכְרוֹנֵנוּ לְפָנָיו לְטוֹבָה, וְעַל יְדֵי מָה עַל יְדֵי שׁוֹפָר,[ו,4] לְפִיכָךְ אוֹמֵר אַחַר כָּךְ בִּרְכַּת שׁוֹפָרוֹת וְאוֹמֵר פְּסוּקֵי שׁוֹפָרוֹת:

ב אַף עַל פִּי שֶׁבִּשְׁאָר יְמוֹת הַשָּׁנָה אֵין הַשְּׁלִיחַ צִבּוּר מוֹצִיא בִּתְפִלָּתוֹ אֶלָּא אֶת מִי שֶׁאֵינוֹ בָּקִי[5] אֲבָל הַבָּקִי אֵינוֹ יוֹצֵא בִּתְפִלַּת הַשְּׁלִיחַ

SECTION 591 The Order of the *Mussaf* Prayers [when Recited by a Person Praying] Alone. (1–15)

1 On *Shabbasos* and on festivals [throughout the year], seven blessings are recited [in *Shemoneh Esreh*]: the first three [standard blessings], the last three [standard blessings], and in the middle, [a blessing that speaks of] the holiness of the day. For Rosh HaShanah, however, our Sages ordained that nine blessings be recited in the *Mussaf* services of both days.[1] In the blessings that speak of the sanctity of the day we incorporate verses on the theme of *Malchiyos*,[2] in order to accept the yoke of the Kingdom of Heaven. We then recite the blessing on the theme of *Zichronos*,[3] that includes verses [recalling G-d's] remembrance [of us], so that a remembrance of us will ascend before Him and elicit Divine goodwill. How is this accomplished? By means of the *shofar*.[4] We therefore next recite the blessing on the theme of *Shofaros*, whose component verses [recall] the sounding of the *shofar*.

2 During the other days of the year, the *sheliach tzibbur* may, when he prays [aloud], fulfill the obligation [to recite *Shemoneh Esreh*] only for someone who is not proficient [in prayer].[5] A person who is proficient [and can recite the prayers himself] may not fulfill his

---

would gaze at him. The Rebbe once spoke of this revered Kabbalistic practice (*HaMelech BiMesibo*, Vol. 1, p. 113). See also *Otzar Minhagei Chabad: Elul-Tishrei*, p. 127.

SECTION 591

1. *Rosh HaShanah* 32a.

2. Lit., "sovereignty."

3. Lit., "remembrances."

4. The Alter Rebbe is restating a teaching of Rabbah (*Rosh HaShanah* 16a, 34b). Commenting on the former passage, *Ritva* offers two interpretations of this teaching: the goodwill is evoked either by the sound of the *shofar*, or by the recital of the related verses. The Rebbe links these two interpretations to classic parables of the Baal Shem Tov and of R. Levi Yitzchak of Berditchev. (See: *Likkutei Sichos*, Vol. 34, p. 181ff.; and in English, *The Chassidic Dimension: Festivals and Commemorative Days* (S.I.E., N.Y., 5762), Vol. 1, pp. 3-5.

5. *Rosh HaShanah* 33b, 34b.

א כדלעיל סי' רסח ס"ב (בתפלות שבת) וס"ג (מוסף). סי' תפז סעי' א־ב (תפלות יום טוב). ב רש"י שבת סא, ב ד"ה הברכות. ג משנה לב, א וכר"ע. רא"ש פ"ד סי' יד. שו"ע ס"א. ד ר"ע שם במשנה. ה גמרא טז, א. לד, ב. לבוש ס"ב. ו גמרא שם. לבוש שם. ז ס"א, ובסימן נט ס"ד. ח גמרא לה, א כר"ג במשנה

צִבּוּר כְּמוֹ שֶׁנִּתְבָּאֵר בְּסִימָן קכ"ד;[ז] אֲבָל בְּמוּסָף שֶׁל רֹאשׁ הַשָּׁנָה אַף הַבָּקִי יוֹצֵא בִּתְפִלַּת הַשְּׁלִיחַ צִבּוּר,[ח] לְפִי שֶׁהֵן בְּרָכוֹת אֲרֻכּוֹת,[ט] וְהוּא שֶׁיִּהְיֶה בְּבֵית הַכְּנֶסֶת עִם הַשְּׁלִיחַ צִבּוּר[י] וְיִשְׁמַע מִמֶּנּוּ הַתְּפִלָּה מֵרֹאשׁ וְעַד סוֹף.[יא] וּמִי שֶׁהוּא אָנוּס וְאֵינוֹ יָכוֹל לָבוֹא לְבֵית הַכְּנֶסֶת כְּגוֹן עַם שֶׁבַּשָּׂדוֹת[יב,6] וְזָקֵן וְחוֹלֶה[יג] — פּוֹטֵר הַשְּׁלִיחַ צִבּוּר אַף עַל פִּי שֶׁלֹּא שָׁמַע מִמֶּנּוּ הַתְּפִלָּה:[יד,7]

obligation [in this way], as stated in sec. 124[:1]. By contrast, even a person proficient [in prayer] can fulfill his obligation for the *Mussaf* service on Rosh HaShanah through the prayer of the *sheliach tzibbur,* because these are long blessings.

[Ordinarily, the above applies] provided the listener is in the synagogue together with the *sheliach tzibbur* and hears his recitation of *[Shemoneh Esreh]* from the beginning until the end. If, however, a person is prevented from coming to the synagogue by forces beyond his control — as is the case with people who are out in the open,[6] the elderly, and the sick — the *sheliach tzibbur* fulfills his obligation [on his behalf] even though he did not hear his recitation of *[Shemoneh Esreh]*.[7]

ג וְעַכְשָׁו שֶׁהַשְּׁלִיחַ צִבּוּר מַפְסִיק בְּפִיּוּטִים[8] בְּאֶמְצַע הַתְּפִלָּה — אֵין אָדָם יוֹצֵא בִּתְפִלַּת הַשְּׁלִיחַ צִבּוּר,[טו] אֲפִלּוּ אִם הוּא לֹא שָׁמַע הַפִּיּוּטִים, מִכָּל מָקוֹם הוּא שׁוֹהֶה כְּדֵי לִגְמֹר אֶת כָּל הַתְּפִלָּה וְצָרִיךְ לַחֲזֹר לָרֹאשׁ כְּמוֹ שֶׁנִּתְבָּאֵר בְּסִימָן ס"ה,[טז] וַאֲפִלּוּ אִם אֵינוֹ שׁוֹהֶה כָּל כָּךְ, מִכָּל מָקוֹם לְכַתְּחִלָּה אָסוּר לִפְסֹק אֲפִלּוּ מְעַט בַּתְּפִלָּה:

3 In the present age, when the *sheliach tzibbur* interrupts *[Shemoneh Esreh]* with liturgical hymns,[8] one cannot fulfill his obligation with the prayers of the *sheliach tzibbur,* even if he did not hear those hymns. [For even though he does not listen to this interruption,] he waits [while they are being recited] for a period of time long enough to have enabled him to complete the entire *[Shemoneh Esreh.* And in such an instance] he [does not fulfill his obligation and] is required to return to the beginning [of *Shemoneh Esreh*], as stated in sec. 65[:1]. Even if he does not wait this long, [such an arrangement is undesirable because,] as an initial and preferred option, it is forbidden to make even brief interruptions during *[Shemoneh Esreh]*.

ד וַאֲפִלּוּ בְּמָקוֹם שֶׁאֵין אוֹמְרִים פִּיּוּטִים בְּאֶמְצַע הַתְּפִלָּה — אַף עַל פִּי כֵן מוּטָב שֶׁיִּתְפַּלֵּל כָּל אֶחָד

4 Even in a community where it is not customary to recite liturgical hymns in the midst of *Shemoneh Esreh,* it is preferable that every person

---

6. Lit., "the people in the fields."

7. *Rosh HaShanah* 35a. This concept is discussed in the second-last essay of *Tanya — Kuntreis Acharon.*

8. In the original, *piyyutim.*

לג, ב ובברייתא לד, ב. רמב"ם הל' תפלה פ"ח ה"י. רא"ש פ"ד סי' יד. טור. מ"א בריש הסימן. **ט** גמרא לה, א ורש"י שם ד"ה אלא. רמב"ם שם. **י** ראה לעיל סי' נה סוף סכ"ב. **יא** רי"ף (יב, א). רא"ש שם. טור ומ"א שם. וראה גם לעיל סי' ריג ס"ד (בשאר ברכות). לעיל סי' קכד ס"א וס"ו (לענות אמן). לקמן סי' תקצד. תורת מנחם התוועדויות תשמ"ג ח"א ע' 67. שלחן המלך ח"ב ע' קצח־ט. **יב** גמרא שם. רי"ף שם. רא"ש שם. טור. וראה גם לעיל סי' קכח סל"ז (בברכת כהנים, שטרודין במלאכתן). **יג** טור. וראה לעיל סי' – ס"י. **יד** ראה תניא קו"א קסב, א: ויוצאים ידי חובת תפלת שמונה עשרה עצמה בחזרת השליח צבור כאלו שמעו ממש, וגם קדושה וברכו בכלל. **טו** מ"א ריש הסי'. **טז** ס"א. וראה סי' סח ס"ב.

וְאֶחָד בְּעַצְמוֹ, כִּי מִי שֶׁיִּרְצֶה לָצֵאת בִּתְפִלַּת הַשְּׁלִיחַ צִבּוּר צָרִיךְ שֶׁיְּכַוֵּן לְכָל מַה שֶּׁאוֹמֵר שְׁלִיחַ צִבּוּר,[יז] וְאִם חִסֵּר אֲפִלּוּ תֵּבָה אַחַת שֶׁלֹּא שָׁמַע אוֹתָהּ מֵהַשְּׁלִיחַ צִבּוּר – לֹא יָצָא, וְאֵין כָּל אָדָם יָכוֹל לַעֲמֹד בָּזֶה,[יח] לְפִיכָךְ נָהֲגוּ כָּל יִשְׂרָאֵל לְהִתְפַּלֵּל תְּפִלַּת מוּסָף תֵּשַׁע בְּרָכוֹת בְּלַחַשׁ תְּחִלָּה,[יט,9] וְגַם הַשְּׁלִיחַ צִבּוּר יִתְפַּלֵּל עִמָּהֶם כְּדֵי לְהַסְדִּיר תְּפִלָּתוֹ[כ] כְּמוֹ שֶׁנִּתְבָּאֵר בְּסִימָן קכ"ד:[כא,10]

pray individually. [The rationale is that] a person who desires to fulfill his obligation through the prayer [recited by] the *sheliach tzibbur* must concentrate on everything the *sheliach tzibbur* says. If he misses hearing even one word from the *sheliach tzibbur,* he has not fulfilled his obligation. Not everyone can meet this requirement. It has therefore become the universal Jewish custom [for every individual] to recite the nine blessings of the *Shemoneh Esreh* of *Mussaf* in a whisper before [the *sheliach tzibbur* recites the prayer aloud].[9] The *sheliach tzibbur* should also pray together with them in order to prepare his prayers, as stated in sec. 124.[10]

ה צָרִיךְ לְהַזְכִּיר פְּסוּקֵי קָרְבְּנוֹת הַמּוּסָפִים[11] בְּכָל תְּפִלּוֹת שֶׁל מוּסָף, בֵּין שֶׁל שַׁבָּת בֵּין שֶׁל רֹאשׁ חֹדֶשׁ בֵּין שֶׁל יוֹם טוֹב בֵּין שֶׁל רֹאשׁ הַשָּׁנָה וְיוֹם הַכִּפּוּרִים, כְּדֵי שֶׁתַּעֲלֶה לָנוּ הַזְכָּרָתָן בִּמְקוֹם הַקְרָבָתָם.[כב,12] וְאִם אָמַר "נַעֲשֶׂה וְנַקְרִיב לְפָנֶיךָ כְּמוֹ שֶׁכָּתַבְתָּ עָלֵינוּ בְּתוֹרָתֶךָ" – יָצָא, וְשׁוּב אֵין צָרִיךְ לוֹמַר מִקְרָאוֹת הַמּוּסָפִין.[כג] לְפִיכָךְ נוֹהֲגִין בִּסְפָרַד שֶׁאֵין אוֹמְרִים

5 The verses [from the Torah that prescribe] the additional festive sacrificial offerings[11] must be mentioned in all the *Mussaf* services, whether on *Shabbos,* on *Rosh Chodesh,* on festivals, on Rosh HaShanah, or on Yom Kippur, so that our remembrance [of these offerings] will be accepted in place of their actual sacrifice.[12]

If, [instead of reading the verses that describe the sacrifices,] a person says, "We will prepare and offer [the sacrifices] before You as You have prescribed for us in Your Torah," he has fulfilled his obligation, and there is no further need to read the verses concerning the *Mussaf* offerings. For this reason, it is customary in the Sephardic [community] to recite the

---

9. In the present age, there is another reason why a person should not endeavor to fulfill his obligation by listening to the prayers of the *sheliach tzibbur.* Today *siddurim* and *machzorim* are easily accessible and people have the option of reciting *Shemoneh Esreh* themselves in the Holy Tongue or in translation. Even the latter option is preferable to hearing *Shemoneh Esreh* from the *sheliach tzibbur.* See sec. 124:2.

10. The reference is to *Magen Avraham,* sec. 124:3, *s.v. U'vaGemara.* See also sec. 100:1 of the present work.

11. In the original, *korbenos hamussafim.*

12. In this vein, it is written *(Hoshea 14:3):* "We will render [the prayers of] our lips [in place of the sacrifice of] bulls."

יז ראה גם לעיל סי' קכד ס"ב. יח טור. לבוש ס"א. מ"א שם. יט טור ושו"ע ס"א. כ ברייתא לד, ב. שו"ת ריב"ש סי' לז. שו"ע ולבוש שם. כא ראה מ"א שם סק"ג ד"ה ובגמרא. לעיל סי' ק. כב רש"י לה, א ד"ה כיון וד"ה אין (שמעיקר הדין היה צריך לאומרם. וראה העו"ב תצג ע' 6). רמב"ם בסדר התפלות שבסוף ספר אהבה סוד"ה ברכה אמצעית. רא"ש פ"ד סי' יד. טור. וראה גם לעיל סי' תפח ס"ח. כג רש"י שם, בפירוש הגמרא שם. רא"ש שם. טור בשם שאר מפרשים. רמב"ם שם. וראה גם לעיל שם. כד רא"ש שם. טור ושו"ע ס"ב וט"ז סק"א. כה דרכי משה ס"ק ב. רמ"א ס"ב. וראה גם לעיל שם. וכ"ה

verses [prescribing] the *Mussaf* offerings only on *Shabbos* and *Rosh Chodesh*, because people are familiar with [these verses], and they will not come to err. On the other festivals, however, they do not recite the verses concerning the *Mussaf* offerings, lest the people err and their prayers thereby become confused.[13]

In these countries[14] this [possibility] does not arouse concern, and it is customary to recite the verses concerning the *Mussaf* offerings even on the festivals. On Rosh HaShanah, however, we do not recite the verses concerning the *Mussaf* offering of Rosh Chodesh,[15] because the phrase that we say — "in addition to the burnt-offering of [Rosh] Chodesh"[16] — suffices, since it includes all the *Mussaf* burnt-offerings of Rosh Chodesh. In order to mention the goat [offered on Rosh Chodesh] as a sin-offering, we say "and two goats for atonement."[17] Similarly, we say *es musfei Yom HaZikaron* — "the *Mussaf* offerings of the Day of Remembrance" — in the plural, in order to also include Rosh Chodesh, which is also called [a time of] "remembrance," as stated in sec. 582[:9].

Even on the second day [of Rosh HaShanah], which is not Rosh Chodesh, we nevertheless say [in the plural] *es musfei* — "the *Mussaf* offerings"[18] — "and two goats for atonement." [This was ordained so that] people should not demean

פְּסוּקֵי הַמּוּסָפִין אֶלָּא בְּשַׁבָּת וְרֹאשׁ חֹדֶשׁ שֶׁרְגִילִין בָּהֶם וְלֹא יָבוֹאוּ לִטְעוּת, אֲבָל בִּשְׁאָר הַמּוֹעֲדִים אֵין אוֹמְרִים פְּסוּקֵי הַמּוּסָפִין שֶׁמָּא יָבוֹאוּ לִטְעוּת עַל יְדֵי כָּךְ[כד] וְתִתְבַּלְבֵּל תְּפִלָּתָם.[13]

אֲבָל בִּמְדִינוֹת אֵלּוּ[14] אֵין חוֹשְׁשִׁין לְכָךְ וְנוֹהֲגִין לוֹמַר פְּסוּקֵי הַמּוּסָפִין אֲפִלּוּ בְּיוֹם טוֹב,[כה] אֶלָּא שֶׁאֵין אוֹמְרִים פְּסוּקֵי מוּסַף רֹאשׁ חֹדֶשׁ בְּרֹאשׁ הַשָּׁנָה,[15] לְפִי שֶׁדַּי בְּמַה שֶּׁאוֹמְרִים "מִלְּבַד עֹלַת הַחֹדֶשׁ וגו'",[16] שֶׁבָּזֶה נִכְלְלוּ כָּל הָעוֹלוֹת שֶׁל מוּסַף רֹאשׁ חֹדֶשׁ, וּכְדֵי לְהַזְכִּיר גַּם הַשָּׂעִיר שֶׁהוּא חַטָּאת אוֹמְרִים "וּשְׁנֵי שְׂעִירִים לְכַפֵּר",[כו,17] וְכֵן אוֹמְרִים "אֶת מוּסְפֵי יוֹם הַזִּכָּרוֹן" לְשׁוֹן רַבִּים, כְּדֵי לִכְלֹל גַּם מוּסָף שֶׁל רֹאשׁ חֹדֶשׁ[כז] שֶׁנִּקְרָא זִכָּרוֹן כְּמוֹ שֶׁנִּתְבָּאֵר בְּסִימָן תקפ"ב.[כח]

וְאַף בְּיוֹם שֵׁנִי שֶׁאֵינוֹ רֹאשׁ חֹדֶשׁ אַף עַל פִּי כֵן אוֹמְרִים "אֶת מוּסְפֵי וכו'[כט,18] וּשְׁנֵי שְׂעִירִים לְכַפֵּר",[ל] כְּדֵי

13. *Siddurim* and *machzorim* were so scarce in earlier times that worshipers often had to rely on their memories.

14. I.e., in the Ashkenazic community.

15. Since the first day of Rosh HaShanah coincides with Rosh Chodesh Tishrei, sacrifices were offered in the *Beis HaMikdash* to mark both of those dates.

16. *Machzor for Rosh HaShanah* Annotated Edition, p. 183, quoting *Bamidbar* 29:6.

17. *Machzor, loc. cit.* I.e., one of the goats was offered as part of the Rosh HaShanah offerings, and the other one was part of the Rosh Chodesh offerings.

18. The *Mishnah Berurah* 591:6 writes that if a person erred and said *es Mussaf Yom HaZikaron* ("the *Mussaf* offering [singular] of this Day of Remembrance") on the first day of Rosh HaShanah, he must repeat his prayers so that Rosh Chodesh will be included. If, however, he makes such an error on the second day, he is not required to repeat his prayers.

בסידור. כו ר"ת בתוס' לה, א ד"ה אילימא. טור בשמו (ושו"ע) ורמ"א ס"ב. וכ"ה בסידור. כז ר"ן (יב, ב) ד"ה מהו להזכיר. רבנו ירוחם נ"ו ח"א (מח, רע"א). רמ"א ס"ב ושו"ע ס"ג. וכ"ה בסידור. כח סעיף ט. כט ב"י ד"ה כתב הר"ן. שו"ע שם. ל לבוש ס"ג.

the second day [of Rosh HaShanah] once they realize that the second day is the second of the month, and [consequently] not Rosh HaShanah.[19]

שֶׁלֹּא יְזַלְזְלוּ בְּיוֹם שֵׁנִי[לא] מֵאַחַר שֶׁיֵּדְעוּ שֶׁיּוֹם שֵׁנִי הוּא שֵׁנִי בַּחֹדֶשׁ וְאֵינוֹ רֹאשׁ הַשָּׁנָה:[19]

6 Why is it customary not to mention Rosh Chodesh explicitly on Rosh HaShanah? So that people will not say that the second day of Rosh Chodesh is the principal day, as is the case with regard to other *Rashei Chadashim,* and then they would reckon the [dates of the coming] festivals from [the second day of Rosh Chodesh].[20] If Rosh Chodesh were to be mentioned on the second day [of Rosh HaShanah], for the reason stated above, they would say that there were two days of Rosh Chodesh.

[Rosh Chodesh is not mentioned explicitly for] an additional reason — to confuse Satan so that he will not know that this day is Rosh Chodesh Tishrei (and thus will not come to level accusations).[21] For the same reason, [in the preliminary morning prayers,] we do not say the passage beginning *U'VeRashei Chadsheichem* — "On your Rosh Chodesh days"[22] — before [the *Mishnayos* beginning] *Eizehu [Mekoman].*

ו וְלָמָּה אֵין נוֹהֲגִין לְהַזְכִּיר רֹאשׁ חֹדֶשׁ בְּפֵרוּשׁ בְּרֹאשׁ הַשָּׁנָה? כְּדֵי שֶׁלֹּא יֹאמְרוּ יוֹם שֵׁנִי שֶׁל רֹאשׁ חֹדֶשׁ עִקָּר כְּמוֹ בִּשְׁאָר רֹאשׁ חֹדֶשׁ וְיִמְנוּ מִמֶּנּוּ הַמּוֹעֲדוֹת,[לב,20] דְּכֵיוָן שֶׁיַּזְכִּירוּ רֹאשׁ חֹדֶשׁ גַּם בְּיוֹם שֵׁנִי[לג] מִטַּעַם שֶׁנִּתְבָּאֵר[לד] — יֹאמְרוּ שֶׁרֹאשׁ חֹדֶשׁ שְׁנֵי יָמִים, וְעוֹד לְעַרְבֵּב הַשָּׂטָן שֶׁלֹּא יֵדַע שֶׁהַיּוֹם הוּא רֹאשׁ חֹדֶשׁ תִּשְׁרֵי[לה] (וְלֹא יָבוֹא לְקַטְרֵג),[21] לְפִיכָךְ אֵין אוֹמְרִים פָּרָשַׁת "וּבְרָאשֵׁי חָדְשֵׁיכֶם"[22] קֹדֶם "אֵיזֶהוּ":[לו]

7 We should recite no fewer than three verses on the theme of *Malchiyos,* three verses on the

ז אֵין פּוֹחֲתִין מִשְּׁלֹשָׁה פְּסוּקֵי מַלְכֻיּוֹת וּמִשְּׁלֹשָׁה פְּסוּקֵי

19. I.e., people might think that because that day is not Rosh Chodesh, it is also not Rosh HaShanah *(Levushei Srad* on the Alter Rebbe's source — *Magen Avraham,* sec. 3*)*.

20. The Rosh Chodesh of other months is sometimes one day, sometimes two. In the latter case, the first day of Rosh Chodesh is counted as the thirtieth of the preceding month, and the second day is the first of the new month. Elul, the month preceding Rosh HaShanah, always has 29 days, and the first day of Rosh HaShanah is the first day of the month of Tishrei. Highlighting Rosh HaShanah as also being Rosh Chodesh would thus lead to confusion.

21. A mention of Rosh Chodesh would make our prayers even more acceptable. The fact that we willingly forego this powerful agent demonstrates our confidence that the verdict will be favorable — and this itself disarms Satan. (See *Likkutei Sichos,* Vol. 24, p. 222.)

22. I.e., the passage *(Bamidbar* 28:11-15*)* that prescribes the Rosh Chodesh offerings. According to Ashkenazic custom, it is usually recited on Rosh Chodesh together with the other *korbanos* in the course of the preliminary morning prayers. According to Lubavitch custom it is never recited at this point, neither on Rosh HaShanah nor on any Rosh Chodesh, nor are the *Shabbos* sacrifices mentioned there on any *Shabbos.*

לא מ"א סק"ג. לב טור ור"ן שם בשם הגאונים. ט"ז סק"ב. לג ב"י שם. לד סעיף ה. לה מנהגים (קלויזנר) סליחות סי' א הגהה א. מנהגים (טירנא) חדש אלול. לבוש סי' תקפא ס"א. סי' תקפב ס"ו. וראה לקו"ש חכ"ד ע' 222־7. שלחן המלך ח"ב ע' קצט־רב. לו במדבר כח, יא־טו. טור בשם הערוך ערך חדש. וראה לעיל סי' מח ס"ב. ובסידור לא הובאו (אף בר"ח שבכל השנה). לז שמואל לב, סוע"א כרבי יוחנן בן נורי במשנה שם. רמב"ם פ"ג ה"ח. טור. לח ברייתא

זִכְרוֹנוֹת וּמִשְׁלֹשָׁה פְּסוּקֵי שׁוֹפָרוֹת,[לז,23] פָּסוּק אֶחָד שֶׁל תּוֹרָה[24] וְהַשֵּׁנִי שֶׁל כְּתוּבִים וְהַשְּׁלִישִׁי שֶׁל נְבִיאִים,[לח,25] וְאִם פָּחַת – לֹא יָצָא. אֲבָל לְכַתְּחִלָּה צָרִיךְ שֶׁיֹּאמַר עֲשָׂרָה פְּסוּקִים שֶׁל מַלְכֻיּוֹת וַעֲשָׂרָה שֶׁל זִכְרוֹנוֹת וַעֲשָׂרָה שֶׁל שׁוֹפָרוֹת[לט] כְּנֶגֶד עֲשָׂרָה מַאֲמָרוֹת שֶׁבָּהֶן נִבְרָא הָעוֹלָם,[מ,26] שְׁלֹשָׁה פְּסוּקִים הָרִאשׁוֹנִים שֶׁל תּוֹרָה, וּשְׁלֹשָׁה פְּסוּקִים שֶׁל כְּתוּבִים, וּשְׁלֹשָׁה הָאַחֲרוֹנִים שֶׁל נְבִיאִים,[מא] וּמְסַיֵּם בְּפָסוּק אֶחָד שֶׁל תּוֹרָה,[מב] וְאִם סִיֵּם בְּנָבִיא שֶׁאָמַר אַרְבָּעָה פְּסוּקִים שֶׁל נְבִיאִים – יָצָא:[מג]

ח בַּמֶּה דְּבָרִים אֲמוּרִים? כְּשֶׁכְּבָר הִתְחִיל לוֹמַר פָּסוּק אֶחָד שֶׁל מַלְכֻיּוֹת אוֹ שֶׁל זִכְרוֹנוֹת אוֹ שֶׁל שׁוֹפָרוֹת, אָז צָרִיךְ לְהַזְכִּיר כָּל הָעֲשָׂרָה פְּסוּקִים, אֲבָל אִם לֹא הִתְחִיל עֲדַיִן בְּשׁוּם פָּסוּק, אִם הוּא רוֹצֶה אֵינוֹ צָרִיךְ לְהַזְכִּיר כְּלָל הַפְּסוּקִים, אֶלָּא אוֹמֵר "וּלְעוֹלְמֵי עַד תִּמְלֹךְ בְּכָבוֹד כַּכָּתוּב בְּתוֹרָתֶךָ,[מד] וְכֵן כָּתוּב בְּדִבְרֵי קָדְשֶׁךָ, וְכֵן נֶאֱמַר עַל יְדֵי

theme of *Zichronos*, and three verses on the theme of *Shofaros*.[23] One of the verses [in each bracket] should be from the Torah,[24] another from the Sacred Writings, and the third from the Prophets[25] — and if fewer verses were recited, one has not fulfilled his obligation. The initial and preferred option, however, is that a person recite ten verses of *Malchiyos*, ten verses of *Zichronos*, and ten verses of *Shofaros*, corresponding [in each case] to the Ten [Divine] Utterances with which the world was created.[26]

The first three verses [in each bracket of ten] should be from the Torah, the [next] three from the Sacred Writings, and the last three from the Prophets. One should then conclude with a verse from the Torah. If [instead] one concluded with a verse from the Prophets — i.e., he recited four verses from the Prophets — he has [nevertheless] fulfilled his obligation.

8 When does the above apply? When one has begun to recite at least one verse [of the bracket] of *Malchiyos*, of *Zichronos*, or of *Shofaros*. [In such an instance,] he should recite all ten verses. If, however, one had not begun to recite any verse, [different rules apply]. Should he so desire, he is not required to mention any of the verses at all. Instead, he could say: "And forever and ever reign in glory, as it is written in Your Torah, and so it is written in Your Sacred Writings, and so it was

---

23. *Rosh HaShanah* 32a.

24. I.e., the *Chumash*.

25. In the *Tanach*, the Books of the Prophets *(Nevi'im)* precede the Sacred Writings *(Kesuvim)*. Why is their sequence here reversed? Rabbeinu Nissim, commenting on *Rosh HaShanah* 32a, explains this in terms of the principle of *maalin bakodesh (Berachos* 28a*)*: "Matters of holiness should [only] be upgraded." The Sacred Writings were Divinely inspired; the words that the Prophets transmitted were Divinely dictated.

26. This preferred option has become the universal norm; see subsection 8 below.

שם. רמב"ם שם. טור. **לט** ב"י ד"ה ומ"ש רבנו ומכל מקום, ור"ן (ח, ב) ד"ה מתני' (שכ"ה גם לדעת ר' יוחנן בן נורי). רמב"ם שם. טור ושו"ע ס"ד. **מ** רבי יוחנן בגמרא שם. אבות פ"ה ה"א. **מא** משנה לב, סוע"א וגמרא שם ע"ב, ורש"י שם ד"ה ומתחיל. טור ושו"ע שם. **מב** כרבי יוסי במשנה, וכמסקנת הגמרא שם בדבריו. רי"ף (ט, א). רא"ש פ"ד סי' ג. טור ושו"ע שם. **מג** כרבי יוסי שם. טור. מ"א סק"ד. **מד** גמרא שם, כפירוש ר"ת בתוס' לה, א ד"ה אילימא. טור. רמ"א ס"ד. מ"א ס"ק ו.

עֲבָדֶיךָ הַנְּבִיאִים,[מה] אֱלֹקֵינוּ וֵאלֹקֵי אֲבוֹתֵינוּ מְלֹךְ עַל כָּל הָעוֹלָם כֻּלּוֹ[מו] וכו'",[27] וְכֵן בְּזִכְרוֹנוֹת וְכֵן בְּשׁוֹפָרוֹת.[מז]

בַּמֶּה דְּבָרִים אֲמוּרִים? בַּיָּמִים הָרִאשׁוֹנִים, אֲבָל בַּזְּמַן הַזֶּה אָסוּר לַעֲשׂוֹת כֵּן לְכַתְּחִלָּה, לְפִי שֶׁכְּבָר קִבְּלוּ כָּל יִשְׂרָאֵל עֲלֵיהֶם חוֹבָה לוֹמַר כָּל הָעֲשָׂרָה פְּסוּקִים וְאֵין לְשַׁנּוֹת:[מח]

stated by Your servants, the prophets. Our G-d, and G-d of our fathers, reign over the entire world…."[27] A similar pattern may be followed with regard to the blessings on the themes of *Zichronos* and *Shofaros.*

When did the above apply? In the earlier generations. In the present era it is forbidden to do this as an initial option, because the Jewish people have universally accepted it as an obligation to recite all ten verses. No deviation should be made.

ט אֵין אוֹמְרִים לֹא בְּמַלְכֻיּוֹת וְלֹא בְּזִכְרוֹנוֹת וְלֹא בְּשׁוֹפָרוֹת פְּסוּקִים שֶׁיֵּשׁ בָּהֶן פֻּרְעָנִיּוֹת שֶׁל יִשְׂרָאֵל,[מט] אֲבָל אוֹמְרִים פְּסוּקִים שֶׁיֵּשׁ בָּהֶם פֻּרְעָנֻיּוֹת שֶׁל נָכְרִים:[נ, 28]

9 In none of the blessings — whether on the themes of *Malchiyos, Zichronos* or *Shofaros* — do we include verses that speak of retribution to be visited upon the Jewish people. We may, however, include verses that mention retribution to be visited upon the non-Jew nations.[28]

י אֵין אוֹמְרִים פָּסוּק זִכְרוֹנוֹת שֶׁל יָחִיד,[נא] כְּגוֹן "זָכְרָה[נב] לִּי אֱלֹהַי לְטוֹבָה",[29] "זָכְרֵנִי[נג] ה' בִּרְצוֹן עַמֶּךָ":[נד, 30]

10 We do not say verses of remembrance that involve only individuals, e.g., "Remember me, O my G-d, for good,"[29] or "Remember me, O G-d, when Your people are favored."[30]

יא "שְׁמַע יִשְׂרָאֵל ה' אֱלֹהֵינוּ ה' אֶחָד"[נה] הוּא עוֹלֶה לְמִנְיַן הַמַּלְכֻיּוֹת,[נו] דְּמִלַּת אֶחָד הוּא עִנְיַן מַלְכוּת,[31] כְּלוֹמַר שֶׁהוּא יָחִיד וּמְיֻחָד וְאֵין דּוֹמֶה לוֹ וּמַלְכוּתוֹ בַּכֹּל מָשָׁלָה,[נז] וּלְפִיכָךְ אָנוּ מַשְׁלִימִין בּוֹ הַמַּלְכֻיּוֹת כְּדֵי לְסַיֵּם בְּשֶׁל תּוֹרָה:[נח]

11 The verse beginning *Shema Yisrael* — "Hear O Israel, G-d is our L-rd, G-d is One" — is considered as one of the verses of *Malchiyos,* for the word *echad* ("one") communicates the theme of sovereignty.[31] [The implication is that] He is unique and unified [with all existence]; there is none that can be likened to Him, and His Kingship reigns over all. For this reason we complete [the bracket of] *Malchiyos* with this verse, in order to conclude with a verse from the Torah.

---

27. I.e., he recites the text of the liturgy without the illustrative verses.

28. Thus the *Malchiyos* blessing includes the prophecy that "Deliverers will go up to Mount Zion to judge the mountain of Esav" *(Ovadiah* 1:21*).* So, too, the *Shofaros* blessing states: "His arrow will go forth like lightning…" *(Zechariah* 9:14-15*).*

29. *Nechemiah* 13:31.

30. *Tehillim* 106:4.

31. In place of an explicit mention of the concept of Kingship *(Rosh HaShanah* 32b*).* See sec. 61:6.

מה שלטי גבורים (ט, א) ד"ה ואם, בשם ריא"ז. כנה"ג הגה"ט. מ"א סק"ה. **מו** בסידור הנוסח: על העולם כולו – ראה שער הכולל פמ"ב אות י. **מז** שלטי גבורים וכנסת הגדולה שם. **מח** מ"א סק"ו. **מט** משנה לב, סוע"א. טור ושו"ע ס"ה. **נ** גמרא לב, ב. טור ולבוש ס"ה. **נא** גמרא שם. טור ושו"ע ס"ה. **נב** נחמיה ה, ט. **נג** תהלים קו, ד. **נד** גמרא שם. טור. **נה** דברים ו, ד. **נו** רבי יוסי בברייתא לב, ב. רמב"ם פ"ג ה"ט. טור. **נז** לבוש ס"ד. וראה לעיל סי' סא ס"ו. **נח** גמרא

יב תְּרוּעָה הֲרֵי הוּא כְּשׁוֹפָרוֹת, כְּגוֹן "יוֹם תְּרוּעָה יִהְיֶה לָכֶם"[נט,32] עוֹלֶה לְמִנְיַן הַשּׁוֹפָרוֹת.[ס,33] וְכֵן תְּקִיעָה הוּא כְּשׁוֹפָרוֹת, כְּגוֹן "וּתְקַעְתֶּם בַּחֲצוֹצְרוֹת וגו'",[סא,34] וְאַף עַל פִּי שֶׁכָּתוּב בּוֹ "חֲצוֹצְרוֹת" — אֵין בְּכָךְ כְּלוּם, כֵּיוָן שֶׁיֵּשׁ בּוֹ לְשׁוֹן תְּקִיעָה עוֹלֶה לְמִנְיַן שׁוֹפָרוֹת, וּלְפִיכָךְ אָנוּ מְסַיְּמִין בּוֹ הַשּׁוֹפָרוֹת כְּדֵי לְסַיֵּם בְּשֶׁל תּוֹרָה.[סב]

יֵשׁ מְדַקְדְּקִים[סג] לוֹמַר[סד] "וַעֲקֵדַת יִצְחָק לְזַרְעוֹ שֶׁל יַעֲקֹב הַיּוֹם תִּזְכֹּר", דְּאִם יֹאמַר "לְזַרְעוֹ תִּזְכֹּר" יִהְיֶה גַּם עֵשָׂו בִּכְלָל.[סה] וְיֵשׁ אוֹמְרִים[סו] שֶׁאֵין לְשַׁנּוֹת הַנֻּסְחָא הַיְשָׁנָה וְאַף עַל פִּי שֶׁאוֹמְרִים "לְזַרְעוֹ תִּזְכֹּר" אֵין עֵשָׂו בִּכְלָל זֶה, שֶׁהֲרֵי נֶאֱמַר[סז,35] "לְךָ וּלְזַרְעֲךָ אֶתֵּן אֶת כָּל הָאֲרָצוֹת הָאֵל", וּלְעֵשָׂו לֹא נִתַּן, מִכְּלָל שֶׁאֵינוֹ נֶחְשָׁב מִזַּרְעוֹ שֶׁל יִצְחָק כְּלָל.[סח] וּסְבָרָא הָרִאשׁוֹנָה הוּא עִקָּר,[סט,36] מִשּׁוּם דִּבְתְפִלַּת יָמִים נוֹרָאִים יֵשׁ

12 [Verses which include the term] *teruah,* e.g., "It shall be a day of sounding [the *shofar*] for you,"[32] are considered equivalent to those that include the term *shofar* and may be counted among the verses of the blessing on the theme of *Shofaros.*[33] Similarly, [verses that include the term] *tekiah,* e.g., "And you shall sound the trumpets,"[34] [are considered equivalent to those that include the term *shofar*]. Although that verse mentions "the trumpets" [and not the *shofar*], this is not significant. Since it uses the expression *tekiah,* it can be considered as one of the verses of the *Shofaros* blessing. Hence we complete [the bracket of] *Shofaros* with this verse in order to conclude with a verse from the Torah.

[In the conclusion of the *Zichronos* blessing,] some people make a point of saying, "And remember this day the Binding of Yitzchak for the descendants of Yaakov," for if one would say "for his [i.e., Yitzchak's] descendants," Esav's [descendants] would also be included.

Others maintain that the ancient wording [of the blessing] should not be changed. Even though we say "for his descendants," Esav is not included. This is reflected in [the verse],[35] "To you and to your descendants will I give all of these lands" — yet Esav was not given [a share of those lands]. This indicates that he is not at all considered a descendant of Yitzchak.

The first opinion is to be preferred,[36] because in the prayers of the Days of Awe we should be

32. In the original, *yom teruah yihyeh lachem (Bamidbar* 29:1).

33. *Rosh HaShanah, loc. cit.* Interestingly, the above-quoted verse is not included among those ten verses in the standard wording of *Mussaf* — possibly because it was already quoted earlier, in connection with the festive sacrifices.

34. In the original, *uskatem bachatzotzros (Bamidbar* 10:10).

35. *Bereishis* 26:3.

36. In his *Siddur* (see *Machzor for Rosh HaShanah* Annotated Edition, p. 188), however, the Alter Rebbe chooses the version, "And remember in mercy this day the Binding of Yitzchak for his descendants." (This wording is in keeping with the teachings of the *AriZal,* and of R. Menachem Azariah of Fano in *Asarah Maamaros,* Treatise *Em Kol Chai,* Part 2, sec. 12.)

שם. **נט** במדבר כט, א. **ס** גמרא שם, כרבי יוסי בברייתא שם. טור. **סא** במדבר י, י. **סב** רא"ש פ"ד סי' ג. ר"ן (ט, א) ד"ה ומיהו בשם הרא"ה. טור ושו"ע ס"ו. **סג** מהרי"ל הל' תפלת מנחה דיו"כ (ע' שנג). ט"ז סק"ג, בשם ספר זבחי שלמים להרמ"ק (ח"א לו, ד בהג"ה). מ"א סק"ח. **סד** בסוף ברכת זכרונות. **סה** ט"ז שם. **סו** ריב"ש סי' לח. שו"ע ס"ז. **סז** בראשית כו, ג. **סח** מ"א סק"ז. **סט** ט"ז שם. ובנוסח הסידור: לזרעו.

לָנוּ לְפָרֵשׁ בְּעִנְיָן שֶׁלֹּא יְהֵא שׁוּם סָפֵק בְּבַקָּשׁוֹתֵינוּ, כְּמוֹ שֶׁנִּתְבָּאֵר בְּסִימָן תקפ"ב[ע] עַיֵּן שָׁם:

explicit in their wording so that there will be no ambiguity in our requests, as stated in sec. 582[:7].

יג לֹא יִתְפַּלֵּל אָדָם בְּיָחִיד תְּפִלַּת מוּסָף בְּרֹאשׁ הַשָּׁנָה[עא] עַד אַחַר שָׁלֹשׁ שָׁעוֹת עַל הַיּוֹם,[עב,37] הוֹאִיל וְהוּא אוֹמֵר מַלְכֻיּוֹת זִכְרוֹנוֹת וְשׁוֹפָרוֹת[עג] יֵשׁ לוֹ לָחוּשׁ שֶׁמָּא יְעַיְּנוּ בְּמַעֲשָׂיו וְתִדָּחֶה תְּפִלָּתוֹ, שֶׁבְּשָׁעוֹת הַלָּלוּ אֵין הַקָּדוֹשׁ בָּרוּךְ הוּא עוֹשֶׂה לִפְנִים מִשּׁוּרַת הַדִּין, לְפִי שֶׁעוֹסֵק בַּתּוֹרָה שֶׁנִּקְרָא אֱמֶת,[38] אֲבָל אַחַר שָׁלֹשׁ שָׁעוֹת הוּא דָּן אֶת כָּל הָעוֹלָם כֻּלּוֹ, וְכֵיוָן שֶׁרוֹאֶה שֶׁאֵין הָעוֹלָם יָכוֹל לַעֲמֹד בַּדִּין נִכְנָס עִמָּהֶם לִפְנִים מִשּׁוּרַת הַדִּין וְלֹא תִדָּחֶה תְּפִלָּתוֹ:[עד]

13 A person praying alone should not recite the *Mussaf* service on Rosh HaShanah until three hours of the day have passed.[37] [The rationale is that] since he recites the blessings on the themes of *Malchiyos, Zichronos,* and *Shofaros,* he should be concerned that his conduct will be investigated and his prayer may be rejected. For the Holy One, blessed be He, does not extend consideration beyond the limits of the law during these hours, since He is then occupied with the Torah, which is called truth.[38]

After three hours have passed, He judges the entire world. When He sees that the world will not be able to survive [the rigidity of] judgment, He goes beyond the measure of the law. [At this time, therefore,] an individual's prayer will not be rejected.

יד אֲבָל מוּסָפִין שֶׁל כָּל הַשָּׁנָה,[עה] וְכֵן שַׁחֲרִית אֲפִלּוּ שֶׁל רֹאשׁ הַשָּׁנָה,[עו] הוֹאִיל וְאֵינָן אֶלָּא שִׁבְחוֹ שֶׁל הַקָּדוֹשׁ בָּרוּךְ הוּא וְסִפּוּרֵי מַעֲשֵׂה הַקָּרְבָּנוֹת – אַף אִם יִתְפַּלֵּל בְּיָחִיד לֹא יְעַיְּנוּ בְּמַעֲשָׂיו.

וְכֵן תְּפִלַּת שַׁחֲרִית שֶׁל חֹל אַף עַל פִּי שֶׁמְּבַקֵּשׁ בָּהּ צְרָכָיו וְיֵשׁ לָחוּשׁ שֶׁמָּא יְעַיְּנוּ בְּמַעֲשָׂיו,[עז] מִכָּל מָקוֹם

14 [This concept does not apply to] the *Mussaf* services recited throughout the year, nor to the *Shacharis* service even of Rosh HaShanah. Since [these services] involve merely the praise of the Holy One, blessed be He, or the description of the sacrificial offerings, then even if they are recited by an individual [praying without a *minyan*], his conduct will not be investigated.

Likewise with regard to a weekday *Shacharis* service: Though a person requests his needs and there is reason for concern that his conduct will be investigated, we can assume

37. *Avodah Zarah* 4b. See also sec. 589, footnote 11 above.

The "hours" referred to here are presumably "seasonal hours" (*shaos zemaniyos*), each lasting one twelfth of the day. Thus their length varies with the seasons. See sec. 58:3 in Vol. 2 of the present work.

38. As in *Mishlei* 23:23 — and a truthful reckoning conforms inflexibly to the letter of the law.

ע סעיף ז. **עא** רב יוסף ע"ז ד, ב. טור ושו"ע ס"ח. **עב** גמרא שם, לפירוש השו"ע שם. מ"א סק"ט. **עג** רש"י שם ד"ה דין. **עד** גמרא שם. **עה** רש"י שם. **עו** מ"א שם בדעת רש"י. **עז** מ"א שם. **עח** גמרא שם. לבוש שם. מ"א שם. וראה לעיל סי' – ס"יא. **עט** לבוש שם. וראה לעיל סי' – ס"י: ואין תפלתו נדחית אף

הוֹאִיל שֶׁמִּן הַסְּתָם יֵשׁ צִבּוּר אֶחָד שֶׁמִּתְפַּלְּלִים בְּשָׁעָה שֶׁהוּא מִתְפַּלֵּל[עח] שֶׁהֲרֵי זְמַנָּהּ בַּבֹּקֶר תִּתְקַבֵּל תְּפִלָּתוֹ עִם תְּפִלַּת הָרַבִּים,[עט] שֶׁאֵין הַקָּדוֹשׁ בָּרוּךְ הוּא מוֹאֵס בִּתְפִלַּת הָרַבִּים[פ] לְעוֹלָם[פא] שֶׁנֶּאֱמַר[פב] "הֵן אֵל כַּבִּיר לֹא יִמְאָס".[פג,39]

אֲבָל בִּתְפִלַּת הַמּוּסָף הוֹאִיל וּזְמַנָּהּ כָּל הַיּוֹם[40] וְיֵשׁ מַקְדִּימִין לְהִתְפַּלֵּל וְיֵשׁ מְאַחֲרִין[פד] — יֵשׁ לוֹ לָחוּשׁ שֶׁמָּא בְּשָׁעָה שֶׁהוּא מִתְפַּלֵּל אֵין מִתְפַּלְּלִים תְּפִלָּה זוֹ שׁוּם צִבּוּר בָּעוֹלָם וְתִדָּחֶה תְּפִלָּתוֹ.[פה]

וּלְפִיכָךְ יֵשׁ לִזָּהֵר בַּקַּיִץ שֶׁלֹּא לְהִתְפַּלֵּל שַׁחֲרִית שֶׁל חֹל בְּשָׁעָה רִאשׁוֹנָה, דִּבְוַדַּאי אֵין הַצִּבּוּר מִתְפַּלְּלִים בְּאוֹתָהּ שָׁעָה בַּזְּמַן הַזֶּה,[פו] וְכֵן בַּחֹרֶף לֹא יְאַחֵר לְאַחַר שְׁתֵּי שָׁעוֹת עַל הַיּוֹם, דִּבְוַדַּאי כְּבָר הִתְפַּלְּלוּ כָּל הַמְּקוֹמוֹת,[פז] וְצָרִיךְ הַיָּחִיד לִזָּהֵר שֶׁלֹּא לְהִתְפַּלֵּל בַּשָּׁעָה הַשְּׁלִישִׁית.[פח]

וְכֵן יִזָּהֵר הַיָּחִיד שֶׁלֹּא יִתְקַע תְּקִיעַת מִצְוָה עַד אַחַר שָׁלֹשׁ שָׁעוֹת עַל הַיּוֹם,[פט] מִטַּעַם שֶׁנִּתְבָּאֵר:[צ,41]

that there is a congregation [elsewhere] that is praying at [this] time, for this is the time of the morning prayer. His prayer will therefore be accepted together with the prayers of the multitude, "for the Holy One, blessed be He, will never spurn the prayers of the multitude, as it is written, 'G-d is mighty and will not spurn.' "[39]

By contrast, the *Mussaf* service [of Rosh HaShanah] can be recited throughout the day,[40] so that some [congregations] recite it earlier and others recite it later. It is thus possible that at the time that a particular individual is praying, no other congregation in the world will be praying, and hence his prayer may be rejected.

For the same reason, in the summer, one should make a point of not reciting the weekday Morning Service [alone] during the first hour of the day, for without a doubt no congregation in the present age is praying at that [early] hour. Similarly, in the winter, a person [praying alone] should not delay his prayers beyond the end of the second hour of the day, for [communal] prayer everywhere has certainly been completed by that time. A person praying without a *minyan* should [therefore] make a point of not praying during the third hour.

Likewise, for the reason explained above, a person sounding the *shofar* alone should not sound the blasts required for [the fulfillment of] the *mitzvah* until three hours of the day have passed.[41]

---

39. *Berachos* 8a, citing *Iyov* 36:5 — except that the prooftext appears to be unrelated to the teaching that the Sages derive from it.

To explain: The above translation of the verse renders its surface meaning, the *pshat,* in which the Hebrew word *kabir* is an adjective ("mighty") relating to G-d. Delving to the non-literal stratum of interpretation known as *derush,* however, the Sages view this word as a noun signifying a mighty multitude, which now serves as the object of the verb in the verse. The verse now implies that G-d will not spurn a mighty multitude.

40. This is acceptable only after the event *(bediavad).* Initially, the recitation of *Mussaf* should not be delayed beyond the end of the seventh seasonal hour (sec. 286:2). See also sec. 584:6 and 595:2.

41. See sec. 589:2 above, and sec. 598, footnote 11 there.

על פי שאינה מתקבלת ברצון כמו בבית הכנסת עם הצבור. **פ** ברייתא ברכות ח, א. **פא** ראה רמב"ם הל' תפלה פ"ח ה"א. לעיל סי' נב ס"א. **פב** איוב לו, ה (בפסוק "ולא ימאס"). **פג** ברייתא שם. רמב"ם שם. לבוש שם. **פד** רש"י ע"ז שם ד"ה צבורא. מ"א שם. **פה** לבוש שם. **פו** מ"א שם (ד"ה ובפרש"י). אבל ראה לעיל סי' — ס"י (אין לו להמתין . . . יתפלל מיד בנץ החמה). **פז** מ"א שם. **פח** תוס' שם ד"ה בתלת. מ"א שם. **פט** מ"א ריש ס"ק ט, ובסימן תקפט סק"ד, בשם מהרי"ל הל' שופר (ע' רצג). **צ** סעיף יג.

טו יֵשׁ[42] לוֹמַר "וְאֵין לְפָרֵשׁ עִלּוּם שְׁמֶךָ",[צא] אֲבָל לֹא יֹאמַר "וְאֵין פֵּרוּשׁ כו'", כִּי יֵשׁ פֵּרוּשׁ לְעִלּוּם שְׁמוֹ:[צב]

15 [In the repetition of the *Shemoneh Esreh* of *Mussaf*,[42] the *sheliach tzibbur*] should say *ein lefaresh eilum shmecha* — "One cannot explain the hidden [dimensions] of Your name." He should not say *ve'ein peirush...* — "There is no explanation...," for there *is* an explanation of the hidden dimensions of His name.

סימן תקצב תְּפִלַּת מוּסָף בְּקוֹל רָם וְסֵדֶר הַתְּקִיעוֹת וּבוֹ י"א סְעִיפִים:

SECTION 592 The *Mussaf* Prayers Recited Aloud and the Order of the *Shofar* Blasts [that are Sounded during *Mussaf*]. (1–11)

א כְּשֶׁמִּתְפַּלְלִים תְּפִלַּת מוּסָף בְּצִבּוּר[א] תִּקְנוּ חֲכָמִים[ב,1] לִתְקֹעַ תר"ת לְמַלְכֻיּוֹת תר"ת לְזִכְרוֹנוֹת ותר"ת לְשׁוֹפָרוֹת,[ג] וּלְפִי שֶׁבִּתְפִלַּת מוּסָף בְּלַחַשׁ כָּל אֶחָד וְאֶחָד מִתְפַּלֵּל לְעַצְמוֹ וְאֵין אֶחָד מְסַיֵּם בִּרְכוֹתָיו בְּשָׁעָה שֶׁחֲבֵרוֹ מְסַיֵּם, לְפִיכָךְ אֵין תּוֹקְעִין בִּתְפִלָּה זוֹ כְּמוֹ שֶׁאֵין תּוֹקְעִין בְּיָחִיד כְּמוֹ שֶׁיִּתְבָּאֵר,[ד,2] אֶלָּא מַמְתִּינִין מִלִּתְקֹעַ עַד שֶׁיַּחֲזֹר הַשְּׁלִיחַ צִבּוּר אֶת הַתְּפִלָּה.[ה]

וְיֵשׁ מְקוֹמוֹת שֶׁנּוֹהֲגִין לִתְקֹעַ ב' פְּעָמִים אַחַת בִּתְפִלַּת לַחַשׁ וְאַחַת בַּחֲזָרַת הַשְּׁלִיחַ צִבּוּר,[ו] אֲבָל בְּמָקוֹם שֶׁאֵין מִנְהָג אֵין לִנְהֹג כֵּן לְכַתְּחִלָּה:[ז,3]

1 Our Sages ordained[1] that when the congregation recites the *Mussaf* service, a series of *tekiah-teruah-tekiah* should be sounded for the *Malchiyos* blessings, and [repeated] for the blessings of *Zichronos* and *Shofaros*. When [the congregation recites] the whispered *Mussaf* prayer, every individual prays independently, and one does not conclude his blessings at the same time that another does. Accordingly, the *shofar* should not be sounded during this prayer, just as it is not sounded when this prayer is recited by an individual [without a congregation], as will be explained.[2] Instead, we wait [and do not] sound the *shofar* until the *sheliach tzibbur* repeats the *Shemoneh Esreh*.

There are places that follow the custom of sounding the *shofar* twice: once when [the congregation] prays in a whisper and once when the *sheliach tzibbur* repeats [the *Shemoneh Esreh*]. In a place where there is no [fixed] custom, however, this practice should not be initiated.[3]

---

42. *Machzor for Rosh HaShanah* Annotated Edition, p. 201.

SECTION 592

1. *Rosh HaShanah* 32b, 33b-34a.

2. Subsection 7.

3. In his *Siddur*, the Alter Rebbe writes that the *shofar* should be sounded both during the whispered *Shemoneh Esreh* and during its repetition by the *sheliach tzibbur*. To minimize the above-mentioned difficulty, when the person sounding the *shofar* is confident that most of the congregants have

צא בסוף פיוט ונתנה תוקף. צב מהר"ם מרוטנבורג בתשב"ץ סי' קיט. מ"א סוף סק"ט.

סימן תקצב: א משא"כ ביחיד, כדלקמן ס"ז וש"נ. ב ראה רמב"ן במלחמות (י, ב; יא, א). וראה לקמן שם. ג משנה לב, א כר"ע. לג, ב ורש"י ד"ה תוקע. רמב"ם פ"ג ה"ז. ד סעיף ז. ה שלטי גבורים י, סע"ב בשם ריא"ז. הובא בכנסת הגדולה הגה"ט. ט"ז. ו ערוך ערב הא', הובא בתוס' לג, ב ד"ה שיעור ובטור. פע"ח שער כו פ"ג. של"ה מסכת ר"ה (ריז, א) ד"ה אחר כך. וכ"ה בסידור. וראה אבני נזר סי' תמז. מנחת אלעזר ח"ד סי' לז. אוצר מנהגי חב"ד ר"ה

2 These *shofar* blasts are called *tekios me'umad*, "the *shofar* blasts [sounded] while standing,"[4] because [not only the person sounding the *shofar* but] also those listening must stand when hearing these *shofar* blasts. With regard to *tekios meyushav* ("the *shofar* blasts [during which one may] sit"), only the person sounding the *shofar* must stand, as stated in sec. 585[:1-2].

ב תְּקִיעוֹת אֵלּוּ נִקְרָאִים תְּקִיעוֹת מְעֻמָּד,[ח,4] לְפִי שֶׁאַף הַשּׁוֹמְעִין צְרִיכִין לַעֲמֹד בְּעֵת שְׁמִיעַת תְּקִיעוֹת הַלָּלוּ,[ט] מַה שֶּׁאֵין כֵּן בִּתְקִיעוֹת מְיֻשָּׁב שֶׁאֵין צָרִיךְ לַעֲמֹד אֶלָּא הַתּוֹקֵעַ בִּלְבַד כְּמוֹ שֶׁנִּתְבָּאֵר בְּסִימָן תקפ"ה:[י]

3 The Sages ordained that the *shofar* should be sounded in a manner that fulfills one's obligation according to all the different possible interpretations of the term *teruah;* see sec. 590[:2]. Now, therefore, it would be appropriate to sound a sequence of *tekiah-shevarim-teruah-tekiah* and *tekiah-shevarim-tekiah* and *tekiah-teruah-tekiah* for the *Malchiyos* blessings, and similarly for the blessings of *Zichronos* and *Shofaros,*[5] in order to fulfill all the possible interpretations of *teruah.*[6]

Nevertheless, since one may not overburden a congregation,[7] it is customary to sound only the series *tekiah-shevarim-teruah-tekiah* for the *Malchiyos* blessings, and similarly for the blessings of *Zichronos* and *Shofaros*. [The rationale is that] according to this approach, all the possible interpretations of *teruah* have been covered. The only difficulty is that perhaps (a *teruah* is only *shevarim* or only [our] *teruah,* and hence) one would be making an interruption between the

ג וְעַכְשָׁו שֶׁתִּקְּנוּ לָנוּ חֲכָמִים לָצֵאת מִידֵי כָל הַסְּפֵקוֹת שֶׁיֵּשׁ לְהִסְתַּפֵּק בִּתְרוּעָה כְּמוֹ שֶׁנִּתְבָּאֵר בְּסִימָן תק"צ[יא] עַיֵּן שָׁם, הָיָה מֵהָרָאוּי לִתְקֹעַ תשר"ת תש"ת תר"ת לְמַלְכֻיּוֹת וְכֵן לְזִכְרוֹנוֹת וְכֵן לְשׁוֹפָרוֹת[5] כְּדֵי לָצֵאת מִכָּל הַסְּפֵקוֹת שֶׁל תְּרוּעָה,[6] אֶלָּא לְפִי שֶׁאֵין מַטְרִיחִין עַל הַצִּבּוּר[יב,7] אֵין נוֹהֲגִין לִתְקֹעַ אֶלָּא תשר"ת לְמַלְכֻיּוֹת וְכֵן לְזִכְרוֹנוֹת וְכֵן לְשׁוֹפָרוֹת,[יג] שֶׁהֲרֵי בְּדֶרֶךְ זוֹ הוּא עוֹשֶׂה כָּל הַסְּפֵקוֹת שֶׁל תְּרוּעָה, וְאֵין כָּאן חֲשָׁשׁ אֶלָּא (שֶׁמָּא הַתְּרוּעָה אֵינָהּ אֶלָּא שְׁבָרִים לְבַד וּתְרוּעָה[יד] לְבַד וְנִמְצָא) שֶׁמָּא הוּא מַפְסִיק בֵּין

---

reached the end of the blessing, he should signal [by slapping the table or the like] and then sound the *shofar* (*Minchas Elazar,* Vol. 4, Responsum 37). *Mateh Ephraim* (591:13) writes that those who have completed each of the blessings of *Malchiyos, Zichronos,* and *Shofaros,* should wait until the *shofar* is sounded. Those who have not completed these blessings should pause while the *shofar* is being sounded and then resume their prayers at the point at which they left off.

4. See *Rosh HaShanah* 16b. After the fact, a person who heard these *shofar* blasts while seated has fulfilled his obligation (*Mateh Ephraim* 592:2).

5. This is the practice in Lubavitch communities today, following the Alter Rebbe's *Siddur.* See end of subsection 5 below.

6. See footnote 1 above.

7. In the original, *ein matrichin al hatzibbur.*

ע' קלג אות שכו. ז כנה"ג שם. מ"א ריש הסי'. ח ראה גמרא טז, רע"ב. ט לבוש סי' תקפה ס"א. מ"א כאן ריש הסי'. וראה לעיל סי' קכד ס"ז (במוסגר): ולכן נקראו התקיעות שבחזרת השליח צבור בראש השנה תקיעות מעומד לפי שכל העם עומדים בחזרת השליח צבור. י ס"א וס"ב. יא סעיף ב. יב רי"ף (יא, א). רמב"ם פ"ג הי"ב. רא"ש פ"ד סי' י. טור ולבוש ס"א. יג ר"ת בתוס' לג, ב ד"ה שיעור. הובא ברא"ש שם וטור. המנהגים (טירנא) ר"ה (ע' צט). רמ"א ס"א. יד בקונטרס השלחן הגיה: או תרועה.

תְּרוּעָה לִפְשׁוּטָה שֶׁלְּפָנֶיהָ אוֹ שֶׁלְּאַחֲרֶיהָ, וְאֵין אָנוּ חוֹשְׁשִׁין לָזֶה[טו] כֵּיוָן שֶׁכְּבָר יָצָאנוּ יְדֵי חוֹבָה מִן הַתּוֹרָה בִּתְקִיעוֹת מְיֻשָּׁב,[טז] שֶׁבַּתְּקִיעוֹת הָהֵם יָצָאנוּ מִכָּל הַסְּפֵקוֹת[יז] כְּמוֹ שֶׁנִּתְבָּאֵר בְּסִימָן תק"צ:[יח]

ד וְיֵשׁ נוֹהֲגִין[יט] לִתְקֹעַ לְמַלְכֻיּוֹת תשר"ת פַּעַם אַחַת וּלְזִכְרוֹנוֹת תש"ת וּלְשׁוֹפָרוֹת תר"ת, לְפִי שֶׁמִּן הַתּוֹרָה בֵּין שְׁבָרִים בֵּין תְּרוּעָה שֶׁלָּנוּ הַכֹּל נִקְרָא תְּרוּעָה, וְאֵיךְ שֶׁיַּעֲשֶׂה אָדָם בֵּין שְׁבָרִים לְבַד בֵּין תְּרוּעָה שֶׁלָּנוּ לְבַד הוּא יוֹצֵא יְדֵי חוֹבָתוֹ. וּבַדּוֹרוֹת הָרִאשׁוֹנִים הָיוּ מִקְצָת מְקוֹמוֹת נוֹהֲגִין לַעֲשׂוֹת שְׁבָרִים וּמִקְצָת נוֹהֲגִין לַעֲשׂוֹת תְּרוּעָה שֶׁלָּנוּ, וְאֵלּוּ וָאֵלּוּ יוֹצְאִין יְדֵי חוֹבָתָן מִן הַתּוֹרָה. אֶלָּא לְפִי שֶׁהָיָה הַדָּבָר נִרְאֶה כְּמַחֲלֹקֶת בְּעֵינֵי הֶהָמוֹן, לָכֵן רָאוּ חֲכָמִים לְתַקֵּן[8] שֶׁיִּהְיוּ כָּל יִשְׂרָאֵל עוֹשִׂין מַעֲשֶׂה אֶחָד וְלֹא יֵרָאֶה בֵּינֵיהֶם דָּבָר שֶׁנִּרְאֶה כְּמַחֲלֹקֶת בְּעֵינֵי הֶהָמוֹן, הִתְקִינוּ לִתְקֹעַ תשר"ת ג' פְּעָמִים תש"ת ג' פְּעָמִים וְתר"ת ג' פְּעָמִים כְּדֵי לָצֵאת מִסְּפֵיקוֹת הֶהָמוֹן מֵחֲמַת

teruah and the simple note that precedes it or that follows it. We are not concerned with this matter, since we already fulfilled the Scriptural obligation by hearing the *tekios meyushav*. By [hearing] these blasts we have steered clear of all the possible causes of doubt [regarding the term *teruah*], as was explained in sec. 590[:2].

4 There are those who follow the custom of sounding one series of *tekiah-shevarim-teruah-tekiah* for the *Malchiyos* blessings, one series of *tekiah-shevarim-tekiah* for the blessings of *Zichronos*, and one series of *tekiah-teruah-tekiah* for the *Shofaros* blessings.

[The rationale is that] according to Scriptural Law, both our *shevarim* and our *teruah* are referred to as *teruah*. No matter what one does, whether he sounds *shevarim* alone or our *teruah* alone, he has fulfilled his obligation. [Thus,] in the earlier generations, people in some places customarily sounded *shevarim*, and in others, people customarily sounded our *teruah*. Both these and those fulfilled their obligation according to Scriptural Law. Nevertheless, because this [diversity] was perceived as a conflict of opinion in the eyes of the common people, the Sages saw fit to ordain[8] that the entire Jewish people follow a single practice [for the *tekios meyushav*], so there would not be [any divergence] that would appear to people at large to be a conflict of opinion. [Hence] they ordained that there be sounded three series of *tekiah-shevarim-teruah-tekiah*, three series of *tekiah-shevarim-tekiah*, and three series of *tekiah-teruah-tekiah* so that there would be no doubt among people at large because of the

---

8. *Rosh HaShanah* 34b.

This view, advanced by Rav Hai Gaon, runs contrary to the opinion of others (e.g., *Rambam* as quoted in sec. 590:2), who maintain that the different definitions of *teruah* are in fact contradictory. This may be one of the reasons as to why in practice this approach is not followed today in some communities, including the Lubavitch community.

טו רא"ש שם. ט"ז סק"א. טז רמב"ן במלחמות (יא, א) סוד"ה אמר. יז רא"ש שם. ט"ז שם. יח סעיף ב. יט רי"ף (י, ב). רמב"ם פ"ג ה"י. טור ושו"ע ס"א. כ רב האי

different practices. For this reason,[9] [the Sages] did not require [congregations] to take [such] trouble when sounding the *tekios me'umad* as well.

Instead, [when sounding] the *tekios me'umad,* we show that all the [possible interpretations of] *teruah* are called *teruah,* and one fulfills his obligation by [hearing any of] them. Hence we sound one series of *tekiah-shevarim-teruah-tekiah,* one series of *tekiah-shevarim-tekiah,* and one series of *tekiah-teruah-tekiah* — to show that each one of these series is correct and acceptable.

חֲלֻקַּת מִנְהָגִים,[כ] לְפִיכָךְ[9] לֹא הִטְרִיחוּ עַל הַצִּבּוּר לִתְקֹעַ כְּדֶרֶךְ הַזֶּה גַּם בִּתְקִיעוֹת מְעֻמָּד,[כא] אֶלָּא מַרְאִין בִּתְקִיעוֹת מְעֻמָּד שֶׁכָּל סְפֵקוֹת הַתְּרוּעָה הֵן נִקְרָאִים תְּרוּעָה וְאָדָם יוֹצֵא בָּהֶם יְדֵי חוֹבָתוֹ, וּלְכָךְ תּוֹקְעִין פַּעַם אַחַת תשר״ת פַּעַם אַחַת תש״ת פַּעַם אַחַת תר״ת כְּדֵי לְהַרְאוֹת שֶׁכָּל אֶחָד וְאֶחָד מִסְדָּרִים הַלָּלוּ הֵן נְכוֹנִים וּכְשֵׁרִים:[כב]

5 There are some who follow the custom of sounding three series of *tekiah-shevarim-teruah-tekiah* for the *Malchiyos* blessings, three series of *tekiah-shevarim-tekiah* for the blessings of *Zichronos,* and three series of *tekiah-teruah-tekiah* for the *Shofaros* blessings. Others follow the custom of sounding a series of *tekiah-shevarim-teruah-tekiah,* then a series of *tekiah-shevarim-tekiah,* and then a series of *tekiah-teruah-tekiah* for the *Malchiyos* blessings. They then repeat this sequence for the blessings of *Zichronos* and *Shofaros.* This is the preferred custom.[5]

ה יֵשׁ נוֹהֲגִין[כג] לִתְקֹעַ ג׳ פְּעָמִים תשר״ת לְמַלְכֻיּוֹת ג׳ פְּעָמִים תש״ת לְזִכְרוֹנוֹת וְג׳ פְּעָמִים תר״ת לְשׁוֹפָרוֹת. וְיֵשׁ נוֹהֲגִין[כד] לִתְקֹעַ תשר״ת תש״ת תר״ת לְמַלְכֻיּוֹת וְכֵן לְזִכְרוֹנוֹת וְכֵן לְשׁוֹפָרוֹת. וּמִנְהָג זֶה הוּא הַמֻּבְחָר שֶׁבַּמִּנְהָגִים:[כה,5]

6 Whenever the *shofar* is sounded [in the repetition of the *Shemoneh Esreh* of *Mussaf*], it is customary to recite [thereafter] the passage beginning *Hayom haras olam*[10] and the passage beginning *Areshes sefaseinu.* Even on *Shabbos,* when the *shofar* is not sounded, we recite the passage *Hayom haras;* we do not, however, recite the passage *Areshes sefaseinu.*[11]

ו וְנוֹהֲגִים לוֹמַר בְּכָל פַּעַם שֶׁתּוֹקְעִין ״הַיּוֹם הֲרַת עוֹלָם וכו׳״,[כו,10] ״אֲרֶשֶׁת שְׂפָתֵינוּ וכו׳״. וַאֲפִלּוּ כְּשֶׁחָל בְּשַׁבָּת שֶׁאֵין תּוֹקְעִין אוֹמְרִים ״הַיּוֹם הֲרַת כו׳״,[כז] אֲבָל אֵין אוֹמְרִים ״אֲרֶשֶׁת כו׳״:[כח,11]

---

9. I.e., since this long sequence is not a Scriptural requirement, but was instituted merely to avert a misconception.

10. *Machzor for Rosh HaShanah* Annotated Edition, p. 210. The above phrase means, "Today the world was born," for Rosh HaShanah marks the anniversary of the creation of man, and thus is considered the birthday of the world. See *Timeless Patterns in Time* (Kehot, N.Y., 5753/1993), Vol. 1, p. 19ff.

11. Which speaks of G-d's listening to the sounds produced by our *shofar.*

גאון בתשובה, הובא ברא״ש פ״ד סי׳ י, ור״ן (י, סוע״א), ובב״י סי׳ תקצ ד״ה וכתבו הרא״ש והר״ן. וראה לעיל שם ס״ב. **כא** ר״ן (יא, רע״א). **כב** שו״ת ריטב״א סי׳ כט בסופו. הובא ב״י סי׳ תקצ שם. **כג** שו״ע ס״א. **כד** ערוך ערך ערב הא׳, הובא בתוס׳ לג, ב ד״ה שיעור ובטור. שלטי גבורים י, ב אות ב בשם ריא״ז. שו״ת רדב״ז ח״ד סי׳ כט. של״ה מסכת ר״ה (ריד, א) ד״ה בענין סדר התקיעות. וכ״ה בסידור. **כה** ראה לעיל סי׳ תקצ ס״ט שבתקיעות מעומד יעשה השברים ותרועה שתשר״ת בשתי נשימות. **כו** טור סי׳ תקצא. **כז** מהרי״ל סדר מוסף של ר״ה (ע׳ רחצ). רמ״א ס״א. **כח** מנהגים (טירנא) ר״ה (ע׳ צט). רמ״א שם.

ז הַמִּתְפַּלֵּל מוּסָף בְּיָחִיד – אֵין מַפְסִיק כְּדֵי לִתְקֹעַ סֵדֶר הַבְּרָכוֹת,[כט,12] וַאֲפִלּוּ יֵשׁ לוֹ מִי שֶׁתּוֹקֵעַ לוֹ[ל] אֵין מַפְסִיק[לא] לְשָׁמְעָם, שֶׁלֹּא תִּקְּנוּ אֶלָּא בְּצִבּוּר. וּמִכָּל מָקוֹם, הַתְּקִיעוֹת שֶׁחַיָּב לִשְׁמֹעַ מִן הַתּוֹרָה, דְּהַיְנוּ תשר"ת ג' פְּעָמִים תש"ת ג' פְּעָמִים תר"ת ג' פְּעָמִים,[לב] טוֹב שֶׁיִּשְׁמַע אוֹתָן קֹדֶם תְּפִלַּת מוּסָף.[לג,13]

אַף עַל פִּי שֶׁתְּקִיעוֹת מְעֻמָּד הֵן מִצְוָה מִדִּבְרֵי סוֹפְרִים[לד] אַף עַל פִּי כֵן אֵין מְבָרְכִין עֲלֵיהֶן[לה] כְּמוֹ שֶׁמְּבָרְכִין עַל כָּל מִצְוָה מִדִּבְרֵי סוֹפְרִים,[לו] לְפִי שֶׁנִּפְטָרִין בִּבְרָכָה שֶׁבֵּרְכוּ עַל תְּקִיעוֹת מְיֻשָּׁב.

וְכֵיוָן שֶׁהֵן נִפְטָרִין בִּבְרָכָה אַחַת לָכֵן יֵשׁ לִזָּהֵר שֶׁלֹּא לְהַפְסִיק בֵּינֵיהֶם בְּשִׂיחָה,[לז] וְלֹא הַתּוֹקֵעַ בִּלְבַד שֶׁבֵּרַךְ עַל הַשּׁוֹפָר, אֶלָּא אֲפִלּוּ הַצִּבּוּר שֶׁלֹּא בֵּרְכוּ לְעַצְמָן אֶלָּא שָׁמְעוּ בִּרְכַּת הַשּׁוֹפָר מֵהַתּוֹקֵעַ אַף הֵן לֹא יָשִׂיחוּ[לח] מִתְּחִלַּת תְּקִיעוֹת מְיֻשָּׁב עַד אַחַר תְּקִיעוֹת מְעֻמָּד.[לט]

וְאִם עָבַר וְשָׂח בֵּין הַתּוֹקֵעַ בֵּין

7 If one recites the *Mussaf* service alone, he should not make an interruption to sound the *shofar* in the midst of the blessings [of *Shemoneh Esreh*].[12] Even if he has someone to sound the *shofar* for him, he should not make an interruption to listen to [the *shofar* blasts], for this practice was instituted only for communal [prayer].

Nevertheless, it is preferable that [such a person, like others,] should hear the *shofar* blasts that he is obligated to hear according to Scriptural Law — i.e., three series of *tekiah-shevarim-teruah-tekiah*, three series of *tekiah-shevarim-tekiah,* and three series of *tekiah-teruah-tekiah* — [specifically] before the *Mussaf* prayers.[13]

Although the *tekios me'umad* are a *mitzvah* instituted by the Sages, no blessing is recited before [they are sounded] as is done before the observance of other Rabbinic *mitzvos,* because they are covered by the blessing that was recited over the *tekios meyushav.* Since [both these sets of *shofar* blasts] are included in one blessing, one should be careful not to make an interruption by speaking between them. [This applies] not only to the person who sounded the *shofar* and who recited its blessings, but even to the congregants who did not recite the blessings themselves, but [merely] heard them from [him]. They, too, should not speak from the beginning of the *tekios meyushav* until the end of the *tekios me'umad.*

[Nevertheless,] if either the person sounding the *shofar* or those listening did transgress

12. *Rosh HaShanah* 34b.

13. This is intended to "confuse Satan" and prevent him from disturbing the individual's prayer *(Levush* 592:3*)*. Regarding a congregation, see further in the present subsection.

כט ברייתא וגמרא לד, ב. טור ושו"ע ס"ב. ל ארחות חיים דין תקיעת שופר סט"ו. ט"ז. שו"ע שם. לא לבוש ס"ג. וראה שדי חמד אס"ד מערכת ר"ה סי' ב אות לו ד"ה ויש לי עד. לב כדלעיל סי' תקצ ס"ב. לג כלבו סי' סד (כח, ג). ארחות חיים שם. רמ"א ס"ב. וראה לקמן סי' תקצה ס"ב. לד כלומר, אף שיצאו רק חובת תקיעת שופר מהתורה, ותיקנו חכמים לתקוע במוסף כדלעיל ס"א, מ"מ אין מברכין על תקנת חכמים, שנפטרים בברכה שבירכו על החובה מהתורה. לה הרי"ץ גיאת (ע' מא), בשם רב האי גאון. הובא במ"מ פ"ג הי"א. טור. לו כדלעיל סי' תלב ס"א, וש"נ. לז הרי"ץ גיאת (ע' מב) בשם הגאונים. רי"ף (יא, א). רמב"ם פ"ג הי"א. רא"ש פ"ד סי' יב. טור ושו"ע ס"ג. לח רא"ש שם, בשם הרי"ץ גיאת שם. הגהות מיימוניות שם אות ט, בשם רבנו שמחה. טור ושו"ע שם. לט מרדכי רמז תשכא בהגהה בשם גדולים. מ הרי"ץ גיאת שם. רי"ף שם. רמב"ם שם. רא"ש שם. טור. ב"י ד"ה ואם שח. רמ"א ס"ג. ואפילו

הַשּׁוֹמְעִין — אֵין צָרִיךְ לְבָרֵךְ עַל תְּקִיעוֹת מְעֻמָּד.[מ,14] וְאַף שֶׁהַפּוֹטֵר שְׁתֵּי מִצְוֹת בִּבְרָכָה אַחַת וְשָׂח בֵּינֵיהֶם צָרִיךְ לַחֲזוֹר וּלְבָרֵךְ עַל מִצְוָה הַשֵּׁנִית כְּמוֹ שֶׁנִּתְבָּאֵר בְּסִימָן ח'[מא,15] וּבְסִימָן כ"ה,[מב,16] מִכָּל מָקוֹם כֵּיוָן שֶׁאֵלּוּ הַתְּקִיעוֹת מְעֻמָּד וּמְיֻשָּׁב הֵן כְּעֵין מִצְוָה אַחַת,[מג] שֶׁהַתּוֹרָה חִיְּבָה אוֹתָנוּ לִשְׁמֹעַ תֵּשַׁע תְּקִיעוֹת בְּרֹאשׁ הַשָּׁנָה,[מד] וְתִקְּנוּ חֲכָמִים לִשְׁמֹעַ אוֹתָן עַל סֵדֶר בִּרְכוֹת מַלְכֻיּוֹת זִכְרוֹנוֹת וְשׁוֹפָרוֹת,[מה] אֶלָּא כְּדֵי לְעַרְבֵּב אֶת הַשָּׂטָן[מו,17] (פֵּרוּשׁ כְּדֵי שֶׁיִּתְעַרְבֵּב מִיָּד בַּתְּקִיעוֹת שֶׁלִּפְנֵי הַתְּפִלָּה וְלֹא יְקַטְרֵג בַּתְּפִלָּה[מז]) עַל כֵּן נָהֲגוּ כָּל יִשְׂרָאֵל לְחַלֵּק אֶת הַתְּקִיעוֹת שֶׁל תּוֹרָה וְשֶׁל דִּבְרֵי סוֹפְרִים לִשְׁתֵּי פְּעָמִים, וְתוֹקְעִין מְיֻשָּׁב כְּדֵי לְקַיֵּם מִצְוָה מִן הַתּוֹרָה וּמְבָרְכִין עֲלֵיהֶן, וְגוֹמְרִין אֶת הַמִּצְוָה שֶׁל דִּבְרֵי סוֹפְרִים בִּתְקִיעוֹת מְעֻמָּד שֶׁעַל סֵדֶר הַבְּרָכוֹת כְּמוֹ שֶׁתִּקְּנוּ חֲכָמִים.

and speak, there is no need to recite a blessing over the *tekios me'umad.*[14] [This would appear to contradict a ruling stated elsewhere, for] when one includes [the observance of] two *mitzvos* in a single blessing, and speaks [before observing the second *mitzvah*], he is obligated to recite a blessing over the second *mitzvah,* as stated in sec. 8[:21][15] and sec. 25[:18].[16] Nevertheless, [a different rationale applies here, for] the *shofar* blasts that are sounded while we are standing, and those during which we may sit, are like a single *mitzvah:* the Torah obligated us to hear nine *shofar* blasts on Rosh HaShanah and the Sages ordained that they be heard in the course of the blessings *Malchiyos, Zichronos,* and *Shofaros.* However, in order to confuse Satan[17] (i.e., in order that he be confused immediately during the *shofar* blasts that precede the prayers and thus will not level any accusations during prayer), Jews everywhere have adopted the custom of separating the *shofar* blasts required by Scriptural Law and those ordained by the Sages, sounding them at two different times. [First,] the *shofar* is sounded when [the congregation has license] to sit, in order to fulfill the *mitzvah* required by Scriptural Law. The blessings are recited over these *shofar* blasts. The *mitzvah* as ordained by the Sages is then completed by the *tekios me'umad,* which are sounded during the recitation of the blessings [of *Shemoneh Esreh*], as they ordained.

---

14. This ruling applies when one spoke between one *shofar* blast and another. Needless to say, one may not speak when the *shofar* itself is being sounded, for then he will not be able to concentrate on hearing the *shofar* blasts.

15. This law states that when putting on several garments to which *tzitzis* have been attached, only one blessing is required, unless one makes an interruption by speaking between one garment and another.

16. That law states that if one speaks between putting on the arm-*tefillin* and putting on the head-*tefillin,* he must recite a second blessing.

17. *Rosh HaShanah* 16b.

באמצע תקיעות מיושב, כדלעיל סי' תקצ סי"ב־ג וש"נ. **מא** סעיף כא. **מב** סעיף יח. **מג** הרי"ץ גיאת שם (מצוה אחת). רי"ף ורא"ש שם. מ"א סק"ד. וראה לקמן בהמשך הסעיף (מצוה אחת ונראין כשתי מצות), וש"נ. **מד** כדלעיל סי' תקצ ס"א. **מה** כדלעיל ס"א. **מו** גמרא טז, רע"ב. **מז** טור סי' תקפה. ט"ז כאן סק"ב. וראה לעיל סי' תקפה ס"ו. שלחן המלך ח"ב ע' קצד הערה 5.

וְכֵיוָן שֶׁהֵן מִצְוָה אַחַת וְנִרְאִין כִּשְׁתֵּי מִצְוֹת,[מח] לְפִיכָךְ אֵין לְהָשִׂיחַ בֵּינֵיהֶם דְּבָרִים בְּטֵלִים, אֲבָל מֻתָּר לְהָשִׂיחַ בֵּינֵיהֶם מֵעִנְיְנֵי הַתְּפִלָּה[מט] וְהַתְּקִיעוֹת,[נ] כֵּיוָן שֶׁהֵן בֶּאֱמֶת מִצְוָה אַחַת. וְכֵן אִם עָבַר וְשָׂח אֲפִלּוּ דְּבָרִים בְּטֵלִים — אֵין צָרִיךְ לַחֲזֹר וּלְבָרֵךְ, דְּאֵין שַׁיָּךְ הֶפְסֵק בְּאֶמְצַע מִצְוָה אַחַת,[נא] כְּמוֹ שֶׁהַיּוֹשֵׁב בַּסֻּכָּה[נב] וְהַלָּבוּשׁ תְּפִלִּין מֻתָּר לָשׂוּחַ אַף עַל פִּי שֶׁכָּל רֶגַע וָרֶגַע שֶׁהוּא יוֹשֵׁב בַּסֻּכָּה[נג] וְלָבוּשׁ בַּתְּפִלִּין[נד] הוּא מְקַיֵּם מִצְוַת הַקָּדוֹשׁ בָּרוּךְ הוּא.[18]

Since [the two soundings of the *shofar*] are one *mitzvah* that appears to be two *mitzvos*, one should not indulge in idle conversation between [the first and second sounding. At that time,] however, it is permitted to speak about the prayer service or about the sounding of the *shofar*, since [both requirements] in fact constitute one *mitzvah*. Similarly, if one transgressed and spoke, even about idle matters, there is no need to repeat the blessing, because there is no concept of making an interruption in the midst of an [ongoing] *mitzvah*. This resembles the case of a person who is sitting in a *sukkah* or wearing *tefillin:* he is permitted to speak, even though every moment that he sits in the *sukkah* or wears the *tefillin* he is fulfilling a *mitzvah* prescribed by the Holy One, blessed be He.[18]

אֲבָל אִם שָׂח בֵּין בְּרָכָה לִתְקִיעוֹת מְיֻשָּׁב, אֲפִלּוּ שָׂח מֵעִנְיְנֵי הַתְּפִלּוֹת — צָרִיךְ לַחֲזֹר וּלְבָרֵךְ, כֵּיוָן שֶׁהִפְסִיק בֵּין הַבְּרָכָה לְהַדָּבָר שֶׁמְּבָרֵךְ עָלָיו. אֲבָל אִם שָׂח מֵעִנְיְנֵי הַתְּקִיעוֹת — אֵינוֹ צָרִיךְ לַחֲזֹר וּלְבָרֵךְ.[נה,19] אֲבָל לְכַתְּחִלָּה אָסוּר לָשׂוּחַ בֵּין הַבְּרָכָה לַתְּקִיעָה אֲפִלּוּ מֵעִנְיְנֵי הַתְּקִיעוֹת, אֶלָּא אִם כֵּן אִי אֶפְשָׁר לוֹ לְקַיֵּם הַמִּצְוָה אִם לֹא יָשִׂיחַ, כְּגוֹן שֶׁאוֹמֵר תְּנוּ לִי הַשּׁוֹפָר וְכַיּוֹצֵא בָּזֶה:[נו]

If, however, one spoke between [the recitation of] the blessing and the *tekios meyushav* — even if he spoke about the prayers — he is required to recite the blessing again, because he made an interruption between the blessing and [the *mitzvah*] over which it was recited. If, however, he spoke about the sounding of the *shofar*, he does not have to repeat the blessing.[19] Initially, however, it is forbidden to speak — even about the sounding of the *shofar* — between reciting the blessing and sounding the *shofar*, unless the *mitzvah* cannot be fulfilled without [first] speaking, by saying "Give me the *shofar*," or the like.

18. By contrast to the ongoing *mitzvah* of wearing *tefillin*, or the two complementary stages in the sounding of the *shofar*, putting on the head-*tefillin* and the arm-*tefillin* are two distinct *mitzvos*, each of which warrants its own blessing. Hence, if one spoke between one and the other, a second blessing would be required. (See *Magen Avraham* 592:4.) The same applies to several garments with *tzitzis;* see footnote 15 above.

19. Because such words are not considered as an interruption.

מח ראה לעיל סי' תלב ס"ז, שאף במצוה אחת ממש יש אומרים שהוי הפסק, כשהוא מוכרח לגמור אותה, כמו בדיקת חמץ. וכאן אפשר דומה למצות סוכה ותפילין דלקמן. ומ"מ אין להשיח כיון שנראין כשתי מצות, הא' מהתורה והב' מד"ס. וראה מ"מ וציונים. רשימת שיעורים פסחים ח"ב סי' כז אות יב, וסי' כט אות ג והערה 2. מט מהרי"ל הל' שופר (ע' רפח). רמ"א ס"ג. נ ראבי"ה סי' תקלה. הובא במרדכי רמז תשכא בהגהה. מהרי"ל שם. רמ"א שם. וראה פרדס חב"ד גליון 8 ע' 96־95. נא ראה פרדס חב"ד 10 ע' 176. נב רא"ש פסחים פ"א סי' י. נג ראה לקמן סי' תרלט ס"ד וסט"ז. נד ראה לעיל סי' לח ס"ז. לקו"ש חל"ט ע' 22 ואילך. שלחן המלך ח"א ע' ס־סב ובהערה 17. נה מ"א סק"ה. נו מ"א שם. וראה גם לעיל סי' קסז ס"ט. סי' תלב ס"ו. נז מהרי"ל הל' שופר (ע' רפז). דרכי משה סי' תקפט סק"ג. מ"א סק"ב. וראה לעיל סי' תקפג ס"ו. נח מהרי"ל שם. דרכי משה שם. נט ראה שם ס"י. וראה גם סי' תקפז ס"ד.

ח וּבִשְׁעַת הַתְּקִיעוֹת עַצְמָן, בֵּין תְּקִיעוֹת מְיֻשָּׁב בֵּין תְּקִיעוֹת מְעֻמָּד, אָסוּר לָרֹק,[נז,20] לְפִי שֶׁצָּרִיךְ לִשְׁמֹעַ כָּל הַתְּקִיעָה מֵרֹאשָׁהּ עַד סוֹפָהּ[נח] אֲפִלּוּ הִיא אֲרֻכָּה הַרְבֵּה כְּמוֹ שֶׁנִּתְבָּאֵר בְּסִימָן תק"צ.[נט] וּלְפִיכָךְ אֵין לְהָבִיא קְטַנִּים שֶׁלֹּא הִגִּיעוּ לְחִנּוּךְ לְבֵית הַכְּנֶסֶת בְּעֵת הַתְּקִיעוֹת שֶׁלֹּא יְבַלְבְּלוּ דַּעַת הַשּׁוֹמְעִים, אַךְ הַנָּשִׁים יִקְחוּ אוֹתָן אֶצְלָן שֶׁהֵן פְּטוּרִין[ס] כְּמוֹ שֶׁנִּתְבָּאֵר בְּסִימָן תקפ"ט:[סא]

8 While the *shofar* is being sounded, whether the *tekios meyushav* or the *tekios me'umad,* it is forbidden to spit,[20] for each *shofar* blast must be heard in its entirety from beginning to end, even if it is very long, as stated in sec. 590[:10]. Accordingly, children who have not reached the age at which they can be trained in the observance of the *mitzvos* should not be brought to the synagogue during the sounding of the *shofar* lest they disturb the concentration of the listeners. The women should take them [into their section], because [the women] are not obligated to observe this *mitzvah,* as stated in sec. 589[:2].

ט נוֹהֲגִין שֶׁבִּתְקִיעוֹת מְיֻשָּׁב עוֹלֶה הַתּוֹקֵעַ עַל הַבִּימָה[סב] וְתוֹקֵעַ שָׁם מִפְּנֵי כְּבוֹד הַצִּבּוּר,[21] אֲבָל בִּתְקִיעוֹת מְעֻמָּד כֵּיוָן שֶׁהֵן בְּתוֹךְ הַתְּפִלָּה אֵין מַטְרִיחִין אוֹתוֹ לַעֲלוֹת אֶלָּא עוֹמֵד [בִּמְקוֹמוֹ[סג]] וְתוֹקֵעַ:[סד]

9 It is customary that the person sounding the *shofar* ascend the platform at which the Torah is read and sound the *tekios meyushav* there as an expression of deference to the congregation.[21] As to the *tekios me'umad,* since they are [sounded] in the midst of *Shemoneh Esreh* we do not trouble him to ascend; he may stand and sound the *shofar* [from his place].

י הַתְּקִיעוֹת שֶׁעַל סֵדֶר הַבְּרָכוֹת לֹא יִתְקַע אוֹתָן הַשְּׁלִיחַ צִבּוּר הַמִּתְפַּלֵּל מוּסָף, שֶׁמָּא יִתְבַּלְבֵּל וְלֹא יוּכַל לַחֲזֹר לִתְפִלָּתוֹ בְּלֹא טֵרוּף דַּעַת,[סה] אֲבָל אִם הוּא מֻבְטָח בְּעַצְמוֹ שֶׁחוֹזֵר לִתְפִלָּתוֹ בְּלֹא טֵרוּף דַּעַת,[סו] אוֹ שֶׁמִּתְפַּלֵּל מִתּוֹךְ הַסִּדּוּר שֶׁבְּוַדַּאי הוּא מֻבְטָח[סז] — יוּכַל לִתְקֹעַ אַף אִם יֵשׁ אָדָם אַחֵר שֶׁיּוֹדֵעַ

10 The *shofar* blasts [that are heard] in the course of the blessings should not be sounded by the *sheliach tzibbur* reciting the *Mussaf* prayers, lest he become confused and be unable to resume his prayers undistracted. If, however, [the *sheliach tzibbur*] is confident that he can resume his prayers without his concentration being diverted, or if he recites his prayers from a *Siddur,* in which instance he is assured of this, he may sound the *shofar.* [This applies] even if there is another person

---

20. *Levushei Srad* quotes the *Maharil* as explaining that even this would be considered as an interruption that would prevent one from hearing a *shofar* blast in its entirety. The *Mishnah Berurah* 592:10 adds that one should not cough or clear one's throat at this time.

21. See sec. 585:3 above, and sec. 585, footnote 5 there.

ס מהרי"ל שם. מ"א ריש סי' תקפט. **סא** ס"ב, וסי' תקפה ס"ו. **סב** ראה גם לעיל סי' תקפה ס"ג. **סג** כן הגיה בקונטרס השלחן. **סד** רמ"א בדרכי משה סי' תקפה אות א. מ"א סק"ו. **סה** רא"ש פ"ד סי' ד, ור"ן (ט, א) ד"ה וכתב (הב'), בשם רב האי גאון. טור ושו"ע סי' תקפה ס"ד. **סו** בעל העיטור הל' שופר (צט, ג). רא"ש ור"ן שם. טור ושו"ע שם. **סז** מ"א שם סק"ט. ראה גם לעיל סי' קכח סוף ס"ל, סל"ב וסוסל"ג.

לִתְקֹעַ כְּמוֹתוֹ,[סח] לְפִי שֶׁהַתְּקִיעָה אֵינָהּ הֶפְסֵק כְּלָל בַּתְּפִלָּה,[סט] כֵּיוָן שֶׁצָּרִיךְ לִתְקֹעַ עַל סֵדֶר הַבְּרָכוֹת אִם כֵּן הוּא צֹרֶךְ הַתְּפִלָּה.[ע,22]

וְלָכֵן[23] הַתּוֹקֵעַ תְּקִיעוֹת מְיֻשָּׁב רָאוּי שֶׁיִּתְקַע גַּם כֵּן תְּקִיעוֹת מְעֻמָּד,[עא] שֶׁהַמַּתְחִיל בְּמִצְוָה אוֹמְרִים לוֹ גְּמֹר,[עב,24] אֶלָּא אִם כֵּן שֶׁהוּא שְׁלִיחַ צִבּוּר הַמִּתְפַּלֵּל מוּסָף וְאֵינוֹ מֻבְטָח שֶׁחוֹזֵר לִתְפִלָּתוֹ בְּלֹא טֵרוּף דַּעַת:[עג]

present who can sound the *shofar* as well as he does, because sounding the *shofar* is not at all considered as an interruption in the midst of prayer. Since we are required to sound the *shofar* in the midst of the blessings, it is considered a necessary component of the prayers.[22]

[In view of the above-mentioned risk of distraction,[23]] it is appropriate for the person who sounded the *tekios meyushav* to sound the *tekios me'umad,* for "when someone has begun the performance of a *mitzvah,* we urge him to complete it."[24] [This does not apply to] a *sheliach tzibbur* reciting the *Mussaf* prayer who is unsure that he will be able to resume his prayers undistracted.

יא בַּמֶּה דְּבָרִים אֲמוּרִים?[25] בַּדּוֹרוֹת הָרִאשׁוֹנִים שֶׁהָיוּ נוֹהֲגִים לִתְקֹעַ בִּסְתָם, וְאִם כֵּן זָכָה מִיָּד בְּכָל הַתְּקִיעוֹת אֲפִלּוּ שֶׁל סֵדֶר הַבְּרָכוֹת מִטַּעַם שֶׁנִּתְבָּאֵר,[עד] וְאֵין לְהַעֲבִיר הַמִּצְוָה מִמֶּנּוּ.[עה] אֲבָל עַכְשָׁו שֶׁנּוֹהֲגִין בִּקְצָת מְקוֹמוֹת לִתֵּן הַתְּקִיעוֹת שֶׁמְּעֻמָּד לְאַחֵר אִם כֵּן מֵעוֹלָם לֹא זָכָה הָרִאשׁוֹן בִּתְקִיעוֹת מְעֻמָּד, וּמֻתָּר לִתֵּן אוֹתָן לְאָדָם אַחֵר בְּכָל מָקוֹם:[עו]

11 When did this apply?[25] In the early generations, when it was customary to [accord the honor of] sounding the *shofar* to one person, and no distinctions were drawn. Such a person thus acquired the right to all the *shofar* blasts, even those sounded during the blessings [of *Mussaf*], for the reason explained above. [Accordingly,] the *mitzvah* should not be taken from him.

In the present era, by contrast, it is customary in some places to grant [the honor of sounding] the *tekios me'umad* to a different person. Hence, the previous person is not considered to have [also] acquired the right to sound the *tekios me'umad,* and in any community [this second honor] may be given to another person.

22. The argument that a *sheliach tzibbur* should not sound the *shofar* is not that he would thereby be interrupting his prayers, but that he might lose the thread of his concentration.

23. In the original, "Therefore."

24. In the original, *Hamas'chil bemitzvah, omrim lo: "Gmor!"* (See *Talmud Yerushalmi, Rosh HaShanah* 1:8.)

25. I.e., that the person who began the *mitzvah* of sounding the *shofar* should complete it.

סח מ"א שם סק"י. וראה גם מ"א סי' קכח סקכ"ט וסקל"א. **סט** רא"ש שם. טור. מ"א שם. **ע** מ"א שם. **עא** רמב"ם פ"ג הי"א. כלבו סי' סד כט, רע"ד. שו"ע ס"ד וברמ"א. רמ"א סי' תקפה ס"ד. **עב** ירושלמי ר"ה פ"א ה"ח. כלבו שם. רמ"א שם. **עג** משמעות רמ"א שם. **עד** סוף ס"י. **עה** כלבו שם. מ"א סק"ז. **עו** רמ"א ס"ד, לפירוש המ"א שם.

SECTION 593 Whether the Blessings and the *Shofar* Blasts are Contingent on Each Other. (1–4)

1 The three [additional] blessings that are recited in the *Mussaf* prayers of Rosh HaShanah[1] — *Malchiyos, Zichronos,* and *Shofaros* — are contingent upon each other; i.e., if one does not know all three blessings, he should not recite even a blessing that he does know.[2] Throughout the year, by contrast, the blessings [of *Shemoneh Esreh*] are not contingent upon each other, and if one does not know all the blessings, he should recite those that he does know.[3]

2 The order of the blessings may not be changed. If one recited the *Zichronos* or the *Shofaros* blessing before the *Malchiyos* blessing, or the *Shofaros* blessing before the *Zichronos* blessing, he has not fulfilled his obligation.

3 Similarly, the *shofar* blasts are contingent upon each other;[4] i.e., if one knows how to sound a *tekiah* but not a *teruah,* he should not sound the *shofar* at all. For he does not fulfill a *mitzvah* unless he sounds — three

סימן תקצג אִם הַבְּרָכוֹת וְהַתְּקִיעוֹת מְעַכְּבוֹת זוֹ אֶת זוֹ וּבוֹ ד' סְעִיפִים:

א שָׁלֹשׁ בְּרָכוֹת שֶׁאוֹמְרִים בְּמוּסָף שֶׁל רֹאשׁ הַשָּׁנָה[1] שֶׁהֵן מַלְכֻיּוֹת זִכְרוֹנוֹת וְשׁוֹפָרוֹת מְעַכְּבוֹת זוֹ אֶת זוֹ,[א] שֶׁאִם אֵינוֹ יוֹדֵעַ כָּל הַשָּׁלֹשׁ בְּרָכוֹת – לֹא יֹאמַר כְּלוּם אֲפִלּוּ אוֹתָהּ בְּרָכָה שֶׁיּוֹדֵעַ,[ב,2] אֲבָל בְּרָכוֹת שֶׁל שְׁאָר יְמוֹת הַשָּׁנָה אֵין מְעַכְּבוֹת זוֹ אֶת זוֹ, אֶלָּא אִם אֵינוֹ יוֹדֵעַ כָּל הַבְּרָכוֹת – יֹאמַר הַמְּקֻצָּת שֶׁיּוֹדֵעַ:[ג,3]

ב סֵדֶר הַבְּרָכוֹת מְעַכֵּב, שֶׁאִם הִקְדִּים לוֹמַר זִכְרוֹנוֹת אוֹ שׁוֹפָרוֹת לְמַלְכֻיּוֹת אוֹ שׁוֹפָרוֹת לְזִכְרוֹנוֹת – לֹא יָצָא:[ד]

ג וְכֵן הַתְּקִיעוֹת מְעַכְּבוֹת זוֹ אֶת זוֹ,[4] שֶׁאִם יוֹדֵעַ לִתְקֹעַ וְאֵינוֹ יוֹדֵעַ לְהָרִיעַ – לֹא יִתְקַע כְּלוּם,[ה] לְפִי שֶׁאֵין כָּאן מִצְוָה כְּלָל, אֶלָּא אִם כֵּן תּוֹקֵעַ וּמֵרִיעַ וְתוֹקֵעַ ג'

---

1. This law applies also to the *Mussaf* prayers recited on Yom Kippur of the *Yovel,* the Jubilee Year.

2. *Rosh HaShanah* 34b. *Pri Megadim: Eshel Avraham* (sec. 593:1) suggests that in such an instance, if the congregants are familiar with the *Shemoneh Esreh* of *Mussaf* for the festivals, they should recite its seven blessings. *Biur Halachah* (sec. 593) maintains that if they do not know the proper *Shemoneh Esreh,* they should not recite the *Mussaf* service at all.

3. The Alter Rebbe's ruling is quoted from *Magen Avraham* 593:2. *Biur Halachah* (593) states that the words of *Magen Avraham* call for interpretation, for from the *Shulchan Aruch* 119:3 (corresponding to sec. 119:4 in the Alter Rebbe's *Shulchan Aruch*) it would appear that all the blessings of *Shemoneh Esreh* comprise a single entity and are contingent upon each other. The Alter Rebbe differs, and explains in sec. 104:4 that sec. 119 applies only to someone who knows all the blessings and must therefore recite them all. One who does not know them all may recite those blessings that he knows.

4. *Rosh HaShanah, loc. cit.*

א ברייתא וגמרא לד, ב. רמב"ם פ"ג ה"ח. רא"ש פ"ד ריש סי' יד. ר"ן (יא, ב) ד"ה תנו רבנו בפירוש הא'. טור ושו"ע ס"א. ב רא"ש שם. ר"ן שם. טור ושו"ע שם. ג מ"א סק"ב, ממשמעות הברייתא שם. וכ"ה לעיל סי' קד ס"ד (במוסגר). וראה סי' סט סוף ס"א וש"נ. ד ר"ן שם בפירוש הב'. מ"א סק"ד. ה גמרא [ברייתא] שם. רמב"ם שם ה"ו. רא"ש שם. ר"ן שם בפירוש הא'. טור ושו"ע ס"ב.

פְּעָמִים[ו] כְּמוֹ שֶׁנִּתְבָּאֵר בְּסִימָן תק"צ: אֲבָל אִם יוֹדֵעַ לְהָרִיעַ תְּרוּעָה שֶׁלָּנוּ וְאֵינוֹ יוֹדֵעַ לִתְקֹעַ הַשְּׁבָרִים – יִתְקַע תר"ת ג' פְּעָמִים, וְכֵן אִם יוֹדֵעַ לִתְקֹעַ שְׁבָרִים וְאֵינוֹ יוֹדֵעַ הַתְּרוּעָה שֶׁלָּנוּ – יִתְקַע תש"ת ג' פְּעָמִים, דְּשֶׁמָּא מַה שֶּׁהוּא יוֹדֵעַ זוֹ הִיא תְּרוּעָה הָאֲמוּרָה בַּתּוֹרָה וְנִמְצָא מְקַיֵּם הַמִּצְוָה כְּמַאֲמָרָהּ:[ח,5]

times — a *tekiah*, then a *teruah*, and then a *tekiah*, as stated in sec. 590[:1].

If, however, one knows how to sound [a *tekiah* and] what we call a *teruah*, but does not know how to sound *shevarim*, he should sound three series of *tekiah-teruah-tekiah*. Similarly, if he knows how to sound [a *tekiah* and] a *shevarim*, but does not know how to sound what we call a *teruah*, he should sound three series of *tekiah-shevarim-tekiah*. For perhaps the sound that he knows is the *teruah* required by the Torah, and thus he will be fulfilling the *mitzvah* as specified.[5]

ד הַתְּקִיעוֹת שֶׁעַל סֵדֶר הַבְּרָכוֹת אֵינָן מְעַכְּבוֹת אֶת הַבְּרָכוֹת,[6] שֶׁאִם אֵין בָּהֶם מִי שֶׁיּוֹדֵעַ לִתְקֹעַ אַף עַל פִּי כֵן יֹאמַר הַשְּׁלִיחַ צִבּוּר כָּל הַט' בְּרָכוֹת, וְכֵן הַבְּרָכוֹת אֵינָן מְעַכְּבוֹת אֶת הַתְּקִיעוֹת, שֶׁאִם אֵינָן יוֹדְעִים לְבָרֵךְ הַבְּרָכוֹת הָאֵלּוּ אַף עַל פִּי כֵן יִתְקְעוּ ג' סְדָרִים.[ט]

אִם הִתְפַּלְּלוּ בְּצִבּוּר הַט' בְּרָכוֹת וְלֹא תָקְעוּ עַד לְאַחַר שֶׁגָּמַר הַשְּׁלִיחַ צִבּוּר אֶת הַתְּפִלָּה – יָצְאוּ:[י,7]

4 The blessings [of the *Shemoneh Esreh* of *Mussaf*] are not contingent on the *shofar* blasts that are sounded during their recitation.[6] Thus if there is no one in [a congregation] who knows how to sound the *shofar*, the *sheliach tzibbur* should still recite all the nine blessings [of the *Shemoneh Esreh*].

Similarly, the sounding of the *shofar* is not contingent on the recitation of the blessings; i.e., if there is no one [in a congregation] who knows how to recite these blessings, the three series of *shofar* blasts should still be sounded.

If a congregation recited the nine blessings and did not sound the *shofar* until the *sheliach tzibbur* completed [the recitation of] the *Shemoneh Esreh*, they have [nevertheless] fulfilled their obligation.[7]

---

5. As explained in sec. 590:2, the Sages offer three different interpretations of the term *teruah*. To be certain that we fulfill our obligation, we follow all three views. If that is impossible, we should sound whichever series we can, for that may be the one that the Torah requires. In such an instance, however, a blessing should not be recited, for it is possible that the obligation is not being fulfilled in this way, and thus the blessing would have been recited in vain (*Mateh Ephraim* 593:3; *Biur Halachah* 593).

6. *Rosh HaShanah, loc. cit.*

7. I.e., after the fact, the obligation of such a congregation has been fulfilled, even if the blessings preceded the *tekios* (*Levush*).

ו רמב"ם שם. ראה העו"ב שי ע' ד. שטו ע' ג. תתח ע' 60. ז סעיף א. ח ר"ן שם ד"ה ודאמרינן. טור ושו"ע שם. מ"א סק"ג. וראה ט"ז סק"א. פרישה אות א ד"ה ואם. לעיל סי' תקצ ס"ב. סי' תקצב ס"ד. ט גמרא [ברייתא] שם (מצוה בתוקעין יותר מן המברכין), ומשנה לג, ב (מי שברך ואחר כך נתמנה לו שופר). ר"ן שם ד"ה תנו רבנן. טור. רמ"א ס"ב. י רמ"א שם. לבוש שם. מ"א סק"ד.

SECTION 594 A Person who has not Recited *Shemoneh Esreh* Cannot Fulfill his Obligation by [Listening to] his Fellow. (1)

1 With regard to the nine blessings of the *Mussaf* service of Rosh HaShanah, even a person who is knowledgeable in the prayers can fulfill his obligation by listening to the prayers of the *sheliach tzibbur,* as stated in sec. 591[:2]. Nevertheless, [this applies only to a *sheliach tzibbur* reciting a communal prayer]. If there are not nine people responding *Amen* to a person's blessings,[1] no other person — even someone who is not familiar with the prayers and who does not know how to pray on his own — can fulfill his obligation by [listening to] that person's prayers.

[This law applies] even in an instance when it is not necessary for [the person listening] to respond *Amen* [to the blessings being recited]; e.g., [the person praying] had not yet recited the whispered *Shemoneh Esreh* of *Mussaf,* and thus he is praying [to fulfill] his own [obligation to recite that prayer], but he is doing so aloud, in order to fulfill the obligation on behalf of the other person who is not familiar with the prayers. Hence, even if no one answered *Amen* to his blessings, there is no question of a blessing being recited in vain. Nevertheless, if there are not nine people responding *Amen* to his prayers, these are not considered as communal prayers. And one cannot fulfill his obligation by listening [to a prayer] other than a communal prayer.

[The rationale is that] this was the ordinance instituted [by our Sages] when they ordained

סימן תקצד יָחִיד שֶׁלֹּא הִתְפַּלֵּל אֵין חֲבֵרוֹ מוֹצִיאוֹ וּבוֹ סָעִיף אֶחָד:

א אַף עַל פִּי שֶׁבְּט' בְּרָכוֹת שֶׁל מוּסַף רֹאשׁ הַשָּׁנָה אַף הַבָּקִי יוֹצֵא בִּתְפִלַּת הַשְּׁלִיחַ צִבּוּר כְּמוֹ שֶׁנִּתְבָּאֵר בְּסִימָן תקצ"א,[א] מִכָּל מָקוֹם אִם אֵין שָׁם תִּשְׁעָה שֶׁעוֹנִין אָמֵן אַחַר בִּרְכוֹתָיו[ב,1] — אֵין אָדָם יוֹצֵא בִּתְפִלָּתוֹ, אֲפִלּוּ מִי שֶׁאֵינוֹ בָּקִי וְאֵינוֹ יוֹדֵעַ לְהִתְפַּלֵּל בְּעַצְמוֹ.[ג]

וַאֲפִלּוּ אִם הוּא בְּעִנְיָן שֶׁאֵין צָרִיךְ לַעֲנוֹת אָמֵן אַחַר בִּרְכוֹתָיו, כְּגוֹן שֶׁעֲדַיִן לֹא הִתְפַּלֵּל תְּפִלַּת מוּסָף בְּלַחַשׁ, וְנִמְצָא שֶׁהוּא צָרִיךְ לְהִתְפַּלֵּל בִּשְׁבִיל עַצְמוֹ בְּלַחַשׁ, אֶלָּא שֶׁהוּא מִתְפַּלֵּל בְּקוֹל כְּדֵי לְהוֹצִיא גַּם אֶת שֶׁאֵינוֹ בָּקִי,[ד] וְנִמְצָא דְּאַף אִם לֹא יַעֲנוּ אָמֵן אַחַר בִּרְכוֹתָיו אֵין כָּאן חֲשַׁשׁ בְּרָכָה לְבַטָּלָה,[ה] אַף עַל פִּי כֵן אִם אֵין תִּשְׁעָה שֶׁעוֹנִין אָמֵן — אֵין תְּפִלָּתוֹ נִקְרֵאת תְּפִלַּת הַצִּבּוּר, וְאֵין אָדָם יוֹצֵא יְדֵי חוֹבָתוֹ בִּשְׁמִיעָה אֶלָּא אִם כֵּן שׁוֹמֵעַ תְּפִלַּת הַצִּבּוּר, לְפִי שֶׁכָּךְ הָיְתָה הַתַּקָּנָה בַּתְּחִלָּה כְּשֶׁתִּקְּנוּ

---

1. At no time may *Shemoneh Esreh* be repeated unless there are nine men listening to the prayers of the *sheliach tzibbur* and responding *Amen,* as stated in sec. 124:6. Otherwise, his blessings "are close to being recited in vain."

א סעיף ב. ב הרב רבנו יונה ברכות (יג, ב) ד"ה ויש. ב"י ריש סי' סןה]. לבוש סי' [ז] ס"ד. וראה גם רמ"א סי' נט ס"ד. מ"א שם סק"ה. לעיל שם ס"ד. סי' קכד ס"א וס"ו. סי' נה ס"ז (במוסגר) וסי"א. ג רמב"ם הל' תפלה פ"ח ה"ד וה"ט, הובא במ"א סק"א. טור בשם הרי"ץ גיאת הל' ר"ה (ע' לא), בשם רב שרירא. ושו"ע ס"א. ד רבנו ירוחם נ"ג ח"ז (כז, ד). הובא במ"א ס"ק א, ובב"י ריש סי' קכד. ה ראה לעיל סי' נה ס"ז, וסי' קכד ס"ו.

תְּפִלַּת הַצִּבּוּר, שֶׁיַּחֲזִיר הַשְּׁלִיחַ צִבּוּר אֶת הַתְּפִלָּה בְּקוֹל רָם כְּדֵי לְהוֹצִיא מִי שֶׁאֵינוֹ בָּקִי;[ז] וְאִם אֵינוֹ מִתְפַּלֵּל תְּפִלַּת הַצִּבּוּר אֵינוֹ יָכוֹל לְהוֹצִיא אֲחֵרִים בִּתְפִלָּתוֹ;[ז] שֶׁהַתְּפִלָּה אֵינָהּ כִּשְׁאָר בְּרָכוֹת שֶׁאָדָם יוֹצֵא יְדֵי חוֹבָתוֹ בִּשְׁמִיעָה וַעֲנִיַּת אָמֵן;[ח] אֲבָל בִּתְפִלָּה צָרִיךְ כָּל אֶחָד וְאֶחָד לְבַקֵּשׁ רַחֲמִים;[ט] וְאֵין נָכוֹן לְבַקֵּשׁ עַל יְדֵי שָׁלִיחַ אֶלָּא אִם כֵּן הוּא שְׁלִיחַ צִבּוּר.

אֲבָל בַּתְּקִיעוֹת יָכוֹל אָדָם לָצֵאת בִּשְׁמִיעָה אֲפִלּוּ הוּא יוֹדֵעַ לִתְקֹעַ בְּעַצְמוֹ, וַאֲפִלּוּ אִם אֵין שָׁם צִבּוּר שֶׁיִּשְׁמְעוּ עִמּוֹ:[י,2]

communal prayer — that the *sheliach tzibbur* should repeat the *Shemoneh Esreh* aloud to fulfill the obligation of a person who is not familiar with the prayers. Thus if one is not reciting a communal prayer, he is unable to fulfill the obligation of another person with his prayer. For prayer is different from the other blessings, with regard to which one may fulfill his obligation by listening and responding *Amen*. With regard to prayer, by contrast, every individual must ask for mercy, and it is not proper to ask for mercy through an intermediary unless he is a *sheliach tzibbur* [who represents the congregation].

With regard to the sounding of the *shofar*, by contrast, one can fulfill his obligation by listening, even if he knows how to sound the *shofar* himself, and even if he is not in the presence of a congregation that is listening together with him.[2]

סימן תקצה מִי שֶׁאֵינוֹ בָּקִי בַּתְּקִיעוֹת וְלֹא בַּתְּפִלָּה וּבוֹ ב׳ סְעִיפִים:

א מִי שֶׁאֵינוֹ בָּקִי בְּסֵדֶר תְּפִלַּת מוּסָף[1] וְגַם אֵינוֹ יוֹדֵעַ לִתְקֹעַ[א] אוֹ שֶׁאֵין לוֹ שׁוֹפָר, וּלְפָנָיו שְׁתֵּי עֲיָרוֹת בְּאַחַת יוֹדְעִין לִתְקֹעַ אֲבָל אֵין בְּקִיאִין בִּתְפִלַּת מוּסָף וּבְאַחַת בְּקִיאִין בִּתְפִלַּת מוּסָף[ב] אֲבָל אֵין לָהֶם שׁוֹפָר[ג] אוֹ שֶׁאֵין יוֹדְעִין לִתְקֹעַ[ד] — יֵלֵךְ

SECTION 595 [The Laws that Apply to] one who Knows neither How to Sound the *Shofar* nor How to Recite the Blessings. (1–2)

1 [The following laws apply if one] does not know the order of the *Mussaf* prayer [of Rosh HaShanah],[1] nor does he know how to sound a *shofar* or there is no *shofar* available, and there are two towns in his region — in one they know how to sound the *shofar* but do not know how to recite the *Mussaf* prayers, and in the other, they know how to recite the *Mussaf* prayers, but do not possess a *shofar* or do not know how to sound it. [A person in this situation] should go

---

2. *Rosh HaShanah* 34b.

SECTION 595

1. I.e., he cannot recite *Shemoneh Esreh* alone, even with the aid of a *Machzor*.

ו ראה ברייתא לד, ב. לעיל סי׳ קכד ס״א וס״ד. מ״מ וציונים. ז ברייתא לד, ב. טור ושו״ע שם. ח ראה לעיל סי׳ ח סי״א. סי׳ קסז סי״ד. וראה סי׳ ריג ס״ד שבדיעבד יוצא גם אם לא ענה אמן. שלחן המלך ח״ב ע׳ קצח הערה 3. ט ירושלמי ברכות פ״ג ה״ג. הובא בר״ן (יא, ב) ד״ה יחיד, ובב״י. וראה גם לעיל סי׳ נט ריש ס״ד (לענין להוציא את הבקי בציבור), וש״נ. י גמרא [ברייתא] לד, ב. טור ושו״ע ס״א. וראה לעיל סי׳ תפט סוף ס״א (לענין ספירת העומר).

סימן תקצה: א שו״ע ס״א. ב גמרא [ברייתא] לד, ב. טור ושו״ע ס״א. ג טור ולבוש ס״א. ד שו״ע שם. ה גמרא שם. טור ושו״ע שם. ו גמרא שם. רמב״ם סופ״ג. ב״י. ט״ז ומ״א סק״א. ז ראה שו״ת צמח צדק יו״ד סי׳ רמז (ג, א), וסי׳ רפח אות ד, ואה״ע סי׳ רצה אות יג, ופס״ד קצה, ב (שלפעמים ספק דאורייתא קיל מודאי דרבנן). ח ירושלמי ר״ה פ״ד ה״י. הובא ב״י. רמ״א ס״א. ט מ״א סוף סק״ב. וכדלעיל סי׳ תקפ״ו סכ״ד, שמותר לעשות ע״י נכרי דבר שאסור מד״ס

לְמְקוֹם הַתְּקִיעוֹת,[2] אֲפִלּוּ אִם שֶׁל תְּקִיעוֹת הוּא בְּסָפֵק לוֹ וְשֶׁל מוּסָף בְּוַדַּאי,[ה] מִפְּנֵי שֶׁהַתְּקִיעוֹת הֵן מִן הַתּוֹרָה וּתְפִלַּת מוּסָף מִדִּבְרֵי סוֹפְרִים,[ו] וְסָפֵק שֶׁל תּוֹרָה קוֹדֵם לְוַדַּאי דִּבְרֵי סוֹפְרִים:[ז]

to the place where they will sound the *shofar*.[2]

The above applies even if he is uncertain that the *shofar* will be sounded [in that town], and the *Mussaf* prayers will certainly be recited [in the other town. The rationale is that hearing] the *shofar* blasts is a Scriptural obligation, while [reciting] the *Mussaf* prayers is a Rabbinic obligation, and the doubtful [opportunity for the] observance of a Scriptural obligation takes precedence over the certain observance of a Rabbinic obligation.

ב וְאִם יָכוֹל לֵילֵךְ לִמְקוֹם הַמִּתְפַּלְּלִים וְיֵשׁ שָׁהוּת בַּיּוֹם שֶׁיִּשְׁמַע אַחַר כָּךְ הַתְּקִיעוֹת בְּמָקוֹם שֶׁתּוֹקְעִין,[ח] כְּגוֹן שֶׁהוּא בְּתוֹךְ הַתְּחוּם אוֹ שֶׁיָּכוֹל לִשְׁלֹחַ נָכְרִי אַחַר הַשּׁוֹפָר לַהֲבִיאוֹ לְכָאן אֲפִלּוּ מִחוּץ לַתְּחוּם[ט] — יְקַיֵּם שְׁתֵּי הַמִּצְוֹת, שֶׁכָּל הַיּוֹם כָּשֵׁר לִתְקִיעַת שׁוֹפָר.[י] אֲבָל לֹא יֵלֵךְ תְּחִלָּה לַמָּקוֹם שֶׁתּוֹקְעִין וְאַחַר כָּךְ לַמָּקוֹם שֶׁמִּתְפַּלְּלִים, לְפִי שֶׁתְּפִלַּת מוּסָף זְמַנָּהּ קָצָר מִזְּמַן תְּקִיעַת שׁוֹפָר, שֶׁהֲרֵי לְכַתְּחִלָּה אֵין לְאַחֲרָהּ יוֹתֵר מִשֶּׁבַע שָׁעוֹת[3,יא] כְּמוֹ שֶׁנִּתְבָּאֵר בְּסִימָן רפ"ו:[יב]

2 However, if it is possible for [such a person] to go to the place where they pray and still have time to hear the *shofar* blasts that day in the place where they sound the *shofar* — either because [both places] are within his *[Shabbos]* limits, or because he could send a non-Jew to bring him the *shofar* in the place at which he is located, even from outside the *[Shabbos]* limits — he should [endeavor] to observe both *mitzvos*.

[He may delay hearing the *shofar*,] because the entire day is fit for the sounding of the *shofar*. He should not go first to the place where they sound the *shofar* and then to the place where they recite the prayers, because there is less time allowed for the *Mussaf* prayers than for the sounding of the *shofar*, since the initial and preferred option is not to delay [the *Mussaf* prayers] beyond the seventh hour of the day,[3] as stated in sec. 286[:2].

---

2. *Ibid.*

Even if he is physically able to walk to both places, his dilemma may be due to the holiday prohibitions. To explain: On *Shabbos* and on a festival, we are not permitted to proceed more than 2000 cubits beyond the town (or place) at which we are located at the commencement of the holy day and which thus serves as our base for that day. This limit is called *techum Shabbos.* (See sec. 397.) One may extend it by as much as an additional 2000 cubits by placing an *eruv techumin* at a given place within the original *Shabbos* limits before the onset of the holiday (see sec. 408). That place is then considered the person's place on *Shabbos* or the festival, and his radius of 2000 cubits begins from there.

In the situation described above, both towns are possibly beyond his *Shabbos* limits. If they are in opposite directions from his present location, he will not be able to walk to both of them, even by means of an *eruv techumin,* for one cannot extend his *Shabbos* limits in two opposite directions. Hence the question: Which of the two obligations — hearing the *shofar* or hearing the prayers — should be given priority? *(Meiri, Rosh HaShanah, loc. cit.)*

3. This refers to seasonal hours, i.e., one twelfth of the time between sunrise and sunset. The *shofar,* by contrast, may be sounded until sunset.

כדי לקיים מצוות שופר. **י** רמ"א שם. וכדלעיל סי' תקפה ס"א. **יא** מ"א סק"ב. **יב** סעיף ב.

סימן תקצו וּבוֹ ב' סְעִיפִים:

א יֵשׁ מְקוֹמוֹת נוֹהֲגִין שֶׁלְּאַחַר הַתְּפִלָּה מְרִיעִין תְּרוּעָה גְּדוֹלָה[1] בְּלֹא תְקִיעָה,[א] כְּדֵי לְעַרְבֵּב אֶת הַשָּׂטָן,[ב] שֶׁלֹּא יְקַטְרֵג אַחַר הַתְּפִלָּה שֶׁהוֹלְכִים וְאוֹכְלִים וְשׁוֹתִים וּשְׂמֵחִים לוֹמַר שֶׁאֵינָם יְרֵאִים מֵאֵימַת יוֹם הַדִּין;[ג] וְיֵשׁ מְקוֹמוֹת נוֹהֲגִים לַחֲזֹר וְלִתְקֹעַ שְׁלֹשִׁים קוֹלוֹת,[ד] לְפִי שֶׁחוֹשְׁשִׁין שֶׁמָּא מִקְצָת הַצִּבּוּר לֹא שָׁמְעוּ כָּל הַתְּקִיעוֹת כָּרָאוּי וְכַהֹגֶן וְיֵצְאוּ בִּשְׁמִיעַת תְּקִיעוֹת אֵלּוּ;[ה] וְיֵשׁ נוֹהֲגִין לִתְקֹעַ מֵאָה קוֹלוֹת,[ו,2] דְּהַיְנוּ שֶׁתּוֹקְעִין אַחַר הַתְּפִלָּה לְהַשְׁלִים מֵאָה קוֹלוֹת עִם הַתְּקִיעוֹת שֶׁל מְיֻשָּׁב וְשֶׁל מְעֻמָּד:[ז,3]

ב אֲבָל לְאַחַר שֶׁכְּבָר גָּמְרוּ כָּל מִנְיַן תְּקִיעוֹת אֵלּוּ – אֵין לִתְקֹעַ עוֹד

SECTION 596 [Sounding the *Shofar* at the Conclusion of the Prayers.] (1–2)

1 It is customary in some places to sound a long *teruah*[1] which is not [preceded by] a *tekiah* in order to confound Satan, so that after the prayer service, when [the people] go [to] eat, drink, and rejoice, he will not accuse them [in the Heavenly Court] of failing to stand in awe and dread of the Day of Judgment.

In other places it is customary to repeat the sounding of 30 *shofar*-blasts, lest some of the congregants did not hear all the blasts in an appropriate and acceptable manner. Thus they will fulfill their obligation with these blasts. It is the custom of some congregations to sound 100 blasts;[2] i.e., after the prayers are completed, they sound [many] blasts, so that together with [those sounded before *Mussaf* and those sounded during *Mussaf*], there will be 100 in all.[3]

2 However, once all these blasts have been sounded, the *shofar* should not be sounded

---

1. I.e., rather than a series of *tekiah-teruah-tekiah,* an extended series of staccato blasts is sounded.

2. The *Tur* (sec. 592), citing the *Aruch* (sec. 272a), connects this custom with the 100 wails of Sisrah's mother (see sec. 590:2 above).

On a mystical level, the early Kabbalists highlight the correspondence between (a) the customary total of 100 *shofar*-blasts and (b) the *s'chach.* Indeed, their thematic connection is reflected in their numerical equivalence (100). R. Levi Yitzchak Schneerson, father of the Rebbe, points out further that the *gematria* of each of the component letters of the Hebrew word סכך corresponds to the 60 sounds of *tekiah,* the 20 sounds of *shevarim,* and the 20 sounds of *teruah.* See *Days of Awe, Days of Joy* (Kehot, N.Y., 5757), p. 206.

3. According to the first-mentioned custom, 30 *shofar*-blasts are added. According to the second-mentioned custom, 40 *shofar*-blasts are added.

In most communities, 30 blasts *(tekios meyushav)* are sounded before *Mussaf,* 30 blasts *(tekios me'umad)* are sounded during *Mussaf,* 10 blasts are sounded in the midst of the *Kaddish* that follows *Mussaf,* and 30 at the end of the prayer service. (The last-mentioned 30 blasts are sounded — after the daily reading of *Tehillim* — according to Lubavitch custom, too, even though an additional 30 blasts were sounded during the recitation of the whispered *Shemoneh Esreh.* The total thus comes to 130.)

א סדר רב עמרם, הובא בתוס' לג, ב ד"ה שיעור, ובטור. שו"ע ס"א. ב רב עמרם שם. ט"ז ס"ק א. ג ט"ז שם. ד מנהגים (טירנא) מנהגי ר"ה (ע' ק). רמ"א ס"א. וכ"ה מנהג חב"ד (ספר המנהגים – חב"ד ע' 56), השברים והתרועה דתשר"ת בנשימה אחת כתקיעות מיושב (אוצר מנהגי חב"ד ר"ה ע' קלה אות שלט). ה ט"ז שם. ו ערוך ערך ערב הא', הובא בטור סי' תקצב. של"ה מסכת ר"ה (ריד, א) ד"ה בענין, (רכ, ב) ד"ה הרי לך. מ"א סק"א. ז ערוך שם. של"ה שם. ובסדור: בקדיש שלם קודם תתקבל תוקעין תשר"ת תש"ת תר"ת, וש"נ. ח תוס' ל, א ד"ה וביבנה (לענין ר"ה שחל בשבת). רמ"א ס"א. ט מ"א סק"ב.

בְּחִנָּם,[ח] שֶׁהֲרֵי הַתְּקִיעָה הִיא אֲסוּרָה בְּיוֹם טוֹב מִדִּבְרֵי סוֹפְרִים,[ט] וְלֹא הִתִּירוּהוּ אֶלָּא לְצֹרֶךְ כְּגוֹן כְּדֵי לַעֲשׂוֹת נַחַת רוּחַ לַנָּשִׁים לִתְקֹעַ לָהֶן,[י,4] וְכֵן הַנּוֹהֲגִין לִתְקֹעַ אַחַר הַתְּפִלָּה כֵּיוָן שֶׁהֵן צְרִיכִין לִתְקִיעָה זוֹ מִטַּעַם הַיָּדוּעַ לָהֶם[יא,5] הִתִּירוּ לָהֶם חֲכָמִים, לְפִי שֶׁאֵין בִּתְקִיעַת שׁוֹפָר שְׁבוּת גָּמוּר[6] אֶלָּא עוּבְדִין דְּחֹל,[יב] אֲבָל לִתְקֹעַ בְּחִנָּם הוּא זִלְזוּל יוֹם טוֹב.

וַאֲפִלּוּ מִי שֶׁיִּתְקַע בְּיוֹם שֵׁנִי — אָסוּר לוֹ לְהִתְלַמֵּד בַּיּוֹם הָרִאשׁוֹן, שֶׁהֲרֵי אָנוּ יוֹדְעִין וּבְקִיאִין[7] בִּקְבִיעַת הַחֹדֶשׁ, וְאָנוּ יוֹדְעִין שֶׁהָרִאשׁוֹן קֹדֶשׁ וְהַשֵּׁנִי חֹל, וְנִמְצָא תוֹקֵעַ תְּקִיעוֹת שֶׁאֵינָם צְרִיכִים לוֹ בְּיוֹם טוֹב אֶלָּא בְּחֹל.[יג]

וְאֵין צָרִיךְ לוֹמַר שֶׁאֵין לְהוֹצִיא אֶת הַשּׁוֹפָר לִרְשׁוּת הָרַבִּים לִתְקֹעַ תְּקִיעָה שֶׁאֵינוֹ צָרִיךְ לוֹ הַיּוֹם, שֶׁהֲרֵי הוּא מוֹצִיא מֵרְשׁוּת לִרְשׁוּת שֶׁלֹּא לְצֹרֶךְ יוֹם טוֹב.[יד]

אֲבָל מֻתָּר לוֹמַר לְקָטָן שֶׁיִּתְקַע כְּדֵי שֶׁיִּתְלַמֵּד, בֵּין שֶׁהִגִּיעַ לְחִנּוּךְ בֵּין שֶׁלֹּא הִגִּיעַ לְחִנּוּךְ,[טו] וּמֻתָּר לוֹ לִתְקֹעַ כָּל הַיּוֹם[טז] אֲפִלּוּ לְאַחַר שֶׁיִּשְׁמַע הַתְּקִיעוֹת בְּבֵית הַכְּנֶסֶת, לְפִי שֶׁמִּצְוָה עַל הַגְּדוֹלִים

without purpose, for sounding it on a festival is forbidden by Rabbinic decree. This prohibition was waived only for a purpose, e.g., to satisfy women by sounding the *shofar* for them.[4] Similarly, our Sages waived this prohibition for those who follow the custom of sounding the *shofar* after the prayer service, since they need [to hear] these *shofar* blasts for reasons known to them.[5] [The rationale is] that sounding the *shofar* is not [prohibited as] a complete *shvus,*[6] but merely as a mundane activity. Nevertheless, to sound the *shofar* for no reason is to treat the festival irreverently.

Even one who is designated to sound the *shofar* on the second day [of Rosh HaShanah] may not practice on the first, because we know well[7] on which day the month actually begins, and we know that the first day [of Rosh HaShanah] is holy and the second is not. Thus such a person would be sounding the *shofar* for blasts that he does not require for the festival, but for a weekday.

Needless to say, one should not take a *shofar* out to the public domain to sound a blast which he does not require that day, for he would be transferring an article from one domain to another for a purpose not associated with the festival. It is, however, permitted to tell a child to sound the *shofar* so that he becomes trained in sounding it. [This applies] whether or not he has reached the age at which he must be trained to observe the *mitzvos*. [The child] may sound the *shofar* the entire day, even after he heard the *shofar* blasts in the synagogue, because adults are commanded to

4. See sec. 589:2.

5. As in subsection 1 above.

6. A Rabbinic prohibition enacted because an activity resembles — or may lead to the performance of — an activity forbidden by Scriptural Law (*Rambam, Hilchos Shabbos* 21:1).

7. Now that we have a fixed calendar.

וכדלעיל סי' תקפה ס"ד (אף לענין יום טוב). י כדלעיל סי' תקפט ס"ב. יא כדלעיל ס"א. יב כדלעיל סי' תקפה ס"ד וש"נ. יג מ"א שם. יד מ"א שם, בשם הראב"ן (קעז, ג) ד"ה הכל. טו רמב"ם פ"ב ה"ז ומ"מ שם. רמ"א שם. ולענין שבת, ראה לעיל סי' תקפה ס"ו. טז רמ"א שם.

לְלַמֵּד אֶת הַקְּטַנִּים[יז] וּלְחַנְּכָם בְּמִצְוֹת:[יח,8]

teach children and train them in the observance of *mitzvos*.[8]

סימן תקצז אִם מֻתָּר לְהִתְעַנּוֹת בְּרֹאשׁ הַשָּׁנָה וּבוֹ ט' סְעִיפִים:

SECTION 597 Whether it is Permitted to Fast on Rosh HaShanah. (1–9)

א יֵשׁ אוֹמְרִים[א] שֶׁמִּצְוָה לְהִתְעַנּוֹת בְּרֹאשׁ הַשָּׁנָה וּבְשַׁבַּת תְּשׁוּבָה כְּמוֹ בְּכָל עֲשֶׂרֶת יְמֵי תְּשׁוּבָה, וְאֵין הֲלָכָה כְּדִבְרֵיהֶם, אֶלָּא אָסוּר לְהִתְעַנּוֹת בְּרֹאשׁ הַשָּׁנָה וְשַׁבַּת תְּשׁוּבָה[ב] כְּמוֹ שֶׁאָסוּר בִּשְׁאָר שַׁבָּת וְיוֹם טוֹב.[ג,1] וַאֲפִלּוּ רָאָה חֲלוֹם רַע וְסָפֵק לוֹ אִם הוּא מֵהַחֲלוֹמוֹת שֶׁמִּתְעַנִּין עֲלֵיהֶם בְּשַׁבָּת[2] — לֹא יִתְעַנֶּה.[ד]

וּמִצְוָה לֶאֱכֹל וְלִשְׁתּוֹת וְלִשְׂמֹחַ בְּרֹאשׁ הַשָּׁנָה[ה] כְּמוֹ שֶׁנִּתְבָּאֵר בְּסִימָן תקפ"א,[ו,3] אָמְנָם לֹא יֹאכְלוּ כָּל שָׂבְעָם לְמַעַן לֹא יָקֵלּוּ רֹאשָׁם וְתִהְיֶה יִרְאַת ה' עַל פְּנֵיהֶם:[ז]

1 Certain authorities maintain that it is a *mitzvah* to fast on Rosh HaShanah and on *Shabbos Shuvah* as on all of the Ten Days of Repentance. The *halachah,* however, does not follow their opinion; it is forbidden to fast on Rosh HaShanah and *Shabbos Shuvah,* just as it is forbidden to fast on any other *Shabbos* or festival.[1] Even if one has a disturbing dream, but is in doubt as to whether it is one of the dreams that would require him to fast on *Shabbos,*[2] he should not fast. On the contrary, it is a *mitzvah* for him to eat, drink, and rejoice on Rosh HaShanah, as stated in sec. 581.[3] Nevertheless, people should not eat to the point of satiety, so that they do not become frivolous, and so that the fear of G-d will be upon them.

ב יֵשׁ מְקוֹמוֹת שֶׁקַּבָּלָה בְּיָדָם שֶׁכָּל מִי שֶׁרָגִיל לְהִתְעַנּוֹת בְּרֹאשׁ הַשָּׁנָה וּמְשַׁנֶּה רְגִילוּתוֹ וְאֵינוֹ מִתְעַנֶּה — אֵינוֹ מַשְׁלִים שְׁנָתוֹ.[ח] וּמִכָּל מָקוֹם מִי שֶׁאֵינוֹ יָרֵא לְנַפְשׁוֹ — אֵין צָרִיךְ לְהִתְעַנּוֹת כָּל יָמָיו,[ט] רַק צָרִיךְ הַתָּרָה כִּשְׁאָר נֶדֶר:[י,4]

2 There is a tradition handed down in certain communities that whoever has established the custom of fasting on Rosh HaShanah, and then deviates from it and does not fast, will not live out that year. Nevertheless, one who is not anxious about his life need not fast throughout his life, though he must annul his commitment in the manner that other vows are annulled.[4]

---

8. In this case, by allowing them to practice — though not on *Shabbos* (sec. 588:6).

SECTION 597

1. However, see footnote 396 below.

2. See sec. 288:7.

3. This section is not in the Alter Rebbe's *Shulchan Aruch;* see sec. 583:4.

4. I.e., by a formal absolution of vows that must be performed by a court of at least three judges.

יז ראה הל' ת"ת לאדה"ז פ"א ה"ח (אף שאינו בנו). לעיל סי' קסז סוף סכ"ג. וראה סי' שמג ס"ב. **יח** ביאור הרא"ם לסמ"ג הל' שופר (יג, ג). מ"א סק"ג.

סימן תקצז: א מקצת הגאונים. הובא ברא"ש פ"ד סי' יד (מ, ג). הגהות מיימוניות פ"א אות א. טור. תרומת הדשן סי' רעח. רמ"א ס"ג בשם יש אומרים. **ב** רא"ש שם, והגהות מיימוניות שם, ומרדכי רמז תשח, בשם רב האי גאון וכמה גאונים. טור ושו"ע ס"א. וראה לקמן ס"ז. **ג** כדלעיל סי' רמב קו"א סק"א, וסי' רפח ס"ז (מן התורה). **ד** כנה"ג הגב"י בשם רבותיו. מ"א סק"ד. **ה** רא"ש שם ומרדכי שם וטור בשם הגאונים, ע"פ נחמיה ח, י־יב, וע"פ המדרש המובא בטור סוס"י תקפא. וראה לעיל סי' תקכט ס"ו. **ו** סימן זה בשוע"ר לא הגיע לידינו, ואוצ"ל: סי' תקפג (סעיף ד). **ז** אגודה ר"ה פ"ד סי' כא. כל בו סי' סה (ל, ב). שו"ע ס"א. דרכי משה ס"ק א בשם הכלבו סי' סה ל, ב. ולענין יום טוב ראה לעיל סי' תקכט ס"ב. **ח** אגור סי' תתקכ, בשם האגודה. שו"ע ס"ב. **ט** כלבו

3 If a person fasts on Rosh HaShanah, he must study or recite supplications throughout the day. For every festival must be divided, half "for G-d" and half "for yourselves,"[5] in order to fulfill [the charges] found in two verses, one[6] [which describes a festival as "an assembly] for G-d,"[7] and the other[8] [which refers to it as "an assembly] for yourselves."[9] This person who is fasting and who does not fulfill [the charge to celebrate the festival] "for yourselves" must dedicate the festival totally "for G-d," and in that way fulfill the commandment [to hold "an assembly] for G-d." [That verse does not mention] "for yourselves," indicating that [in such a case] the entire day should be [consecrated] to G-d alone.

ג הַמִּתְעַנֶּה בְּרֹאשׁ הַשָּׁנָה צָרִיךְ לִלְמֹד כָּל הַיּוֹם אוֹ לוֹמַר תְּחִנּוֹת,[יא] שֶׁהֲרֵי כָּל יוֹם טוֹב צָרִיךְ לְחַלֵּק חֶצְיוֹ לַה' וְחֶצְיוֹ לָכֶם,[יב,5] כְּדֵי לְקַיֵּם שְׁנֵי פְּסוּקִים שֶׁבְּאֶחָד כָּתוּב[6] "לַה'"[יג,7] וּבְאֶחָד כָּתוּב[8] "לָכֶם",[יד,9] וְזֶה שֶׁהוּא מִתְעַנֶּה וְאֵינוֹ מְקַיֵּם הַמִּקְרָא שֶׁנֶּאֱמַר בּוֹ "לָכֶם" – צָרִיךְ לַעֲשׂוֹת כֻּלּוֹ לַה',[טו] כְּדֵי לְקַיֵּם הַמִּקְרָא שֶׁנֶּאֱמַר בּוֹ "לַה'" וְלֹא נֶאֱמַר בּוֹ "לָכֶם", וּמַשְׁמָע שֶׁכָּל הַיּוֹם יִהְיֶה לַה' לְבַדּוֹ:

4 A person who fasts on Rosh HaShanah or on any other festival is forbidden to cook — or to perform any other labors necessary for the preparation of food — for the benefit of others, as stated in sec. 527[:30]. Note the reason explained there.

ד הַמִּתְעַנֶּה בְּרֹאשׁ הַשָּׁנָה אוֹ בִּשְׁאָר יוֹם טוֹב – אָסוּר לוֹ לְבַשֵּׁל אוֹ לַעֲשׂוֹת שְׁאָר מְלָאכוֹת אֹכֶל נֶפֶשׁ לְצֹרֶךְ אֲחֵרִים[טז] כְּמוֹ שֶׁנִּתְבָּאֵר בְּסִימָן תקכ"ז,[יז] עַיֵּן שָׁם הַטַּעַם:

5 Some people say that they have received the tradition that a person who fasted once on the first day of Rosh HaShanah because of a [disturbing] dream must fast on both days of Rosh HaShanah throughout his life, even if [one of them] falls on *Shabbos*. [The rationale:] Since he was once shown an unfavorable sign at the beginning of Rosh HaShanah, on the first night, this indicates that his fasting is cherished by the Holy One,

ה יֵשׁ אוֹמְרִים[יח] שֶׁקַּבָּלָה בְּיָדָם שֶׁהַמִּתְעַנֶּה פַּעַם אַחַת בְּרֹאשׁ הַשָּׁנָה תַּעֲנִית חֲלוֹם אִם הָיָה בְּיוֹם רִאשׁוֹן שֶׁל רֹאשׁ הַשָּׁנָה[יט] צָרִיךְ לְהִתְעַנּוֹת שְׁנֵי הַיָּמִים שֶׁל רֹאשׁ הַשָּׁנָה כָּל יָמָיו אֲפִלּוּ כְּשֶׁחָל בְּשַׁבָּת,[כ] הוֹאִיל וְהֶרְאוּ לוֹ סִימָן רַע פַּעַם אַחַת[כא] בְּהַתְחָלַת רֹאשׁ הַשָּׁנָה בַּלַּיְלָה הָרִאשׁוֹן רָמְזוּ לוֹ שֶׁתַּעֲנִיתוֹ חָבִיב לִפְנֵי

See the *Shulchan Aruch* of R. Yosef Caro, *Yoreh Deah* 228:1.

5. *Beitzah* 15b; *Pesachim* 68b. See also sec. 529:10 above.

6. *Devarim* 16:8.

7. I.e., centered on prayer and study.

8. *Bamidbar* 29:35.

9. I.e., including also eating, drinking, and material forms of celebration.

סי' סט (לד, סע"ד). מנהגים (טירנא) מנהגי ר"ה (ע' קב). רמ"א ס"ב. **י** ב"י ד"ה כתב הכלבו. רמ"א שם. **יא** מהר"י ווייל דינין ומנהגים אות נו. לבוש סוף ס"ב. מ"א סק"א. **יב** כדלעיל סי' תקכט ס"י וש"נ. **יג** דברים טז, ח: עצרת לה' אלקיך. **יד** במדבר כט, לה: עצרת תהיה לכם. **טו** מהר"י ווייל שם. לבוש שם. **טז** לבוש שם. מ"א שם. **יז** סעיף ל. **יח** הגהות מיימוניות פ"א אות א. אגור סי' תתקכ בשם אגודה פ"ד סי' כא. שו"ע ס"ג. **יט** תרומת הדשן סי' רעה בשם הרב של אחד הגדולים. שו"ע שם. **כ** תרומת הדשן שם. לבוש ס"ב. **כא** האגור שם.

הַקָּדוֹשׁ בָּרוּךְ הוּא בְּרֹאשׁ הַשָּׁנָה,[כב] לְפִיכָךְ יַעֲשֶׂה רְצוֹנוֹ וְיִתְעַנֶּה כָּל שְׁנֵי יָמִים שֶׁל רֹאשׁ הַשָּׁנָה שֶׁהֵן כְּיוֹם אֶחָד אָרֹךְ[כג] כְּמוֹ שֶׁיִּתְבָּאֵר בְּסִימָן ת"ר.[כד] אֲבָל אָסוּר לְהִתְעַנּוֹת בַּלֵּילוֹת שֶׁל רֹאשׁ הַשָּׁנָה כְּמוֹ בִּשְׁאָר יוֹם טוֹב, שֶׁאַף בַּחֲלוֹמוֹ לֹא רָמְזוּ לוֹ אֶלָּא לְהִתְעַנּוֹת בַּיּוֹם,[כה] כְּדֶרֶךְ כָּל תַּעֲנִית חֲלוֹם שֶׁאֵין מִתְעַנִּין אֶלָּא בַּיּוֹם:

blessed be He, on Rosh HaShanah, and that he should therefore carry out His will and fast both days of Rosh HaShanah, for they are considered as one long day, as explained in sec. 600[:3].

However, [he] is forbidden to fast on the nights of Rosh HaShanah, just as on other festivals, for even in his dream it was indicated only that he should fast during the day, as with all fasts undertaken because of a dream: one fasts only during the day.

ו וְאִם הֶרְאוּ לוֹ הַחֲלוֹם בְּיוֹם שֵׁנִי שֶׁל רֹאשׁ הַשָּׁנָה – יִתְעַנֶּה כָּל יָמָיו יוֹם שֵׁנִי בִּלְבַד וְלֹא יוֹם רִאשׁוֹן.[כו]

וּמִכָּל מָקוֹם, מִי שֶׁאֵינוֹ יָרֵא לְנַפְשׁוֹ – אֵינוֹ צָרִיךְ לָחוּשׁ לְקַבָּלָה זוֹ, וְאֵינוֹ צָרִיךְ לְהִתְעַנּוֹת כָּל יָמָיו כְּלָל לֹא בְּיוֹם רִאשׁוֹן וְלֹא בְּיוֹם שֵׁנִי, אַף שֶׁהָיָה הַחֲלוֹם בְּיוֹם רִאשׁוֹן:[כז]

6 If he had the [disturbing] dream on the second [night] of Rosh HaShanah, he should fast on the second day of Rosh HaShanah for the rest of his life, but not on the first day.

Nevertheless, whoever is not anxious for his life need not be concerned about this tradition and need not fast at all throughout his life [on Rosh HaShanah], neither on the first day or the second day, even if he had the [disturbing] dream on the first [night].

ז הַמִּתְעַנֶּה בְּרֹאשׁ הַשָּׁנָה תַּעֲנִית חֲלוֹם – אֵינוֹ צָרִיךְ לֵישֵׁב בְּחֹל תַּעֲנִית עַל תַּעֲנִיתוֹ כְּמוֹ הַמִּתְעַנֶּה בְּשַׁבָּתוֹת וּבְיָמִים טוֹבִים וּכְמוֹ שֶׁנִּתְבָּאֵר בְּסִימָן רפ"ח,[כח] שֶׁהֲרֵי יֵשׁ אוֹמְרִים שֶׁמִּצְוָה לְהִתְעַנּוֹת בְּרֹאשׁ הַשָּׁנָה,[כט,10] וְאַף עַל פִּי שֶׁאֵין הֲלָכָה כֵּן, מִכָּל מָקוֹם כְּדַאי הֵם לִסְמֹךְ עֲלֵיהֶם לְעִנְיָן שֶׁלֹּא נַחֲזִיק תַּעֲנִית זוֹ לַעֲבֵרָה שֶׁיִּצְטָרֵךְ לְהִתְעַנּוֹת בְּחֹל בִּשְׁבִיל כָּךְ:[ל]

7 If one fasts on Rosh HaShanah because of a disturbing dream, he does not have to fast again on a weekday to atone for his fast, as is required if one fasts on *Shabbos* or on another festival, as stated in sec. 288[:3. The rationale is that] there are opinions that it is a *mitzvah* to fast on Rosh HaShanah.[10] Although the *halachah* does not follow this view, it is of sufficient weight to rely upon so that this fast will not be considered a transgression for which a second fast is required during the week [as atonement].

---

10. Similarly, out of deference to those authorities who permit fasting on Rosh HaShanah, the Alter Rebbe rules in sec. 188:10 that if a person forgot to include *Yaaleh VeYavo* in the Grace after Meals, he should not repeat it. (In his *Siddur*, the Alter Rebbe applies this to the daytime meals only.)

כב תרומת הדשן שם. לבוש שם. כג לבוש שם. כד סעיף ג. כה מ"א סק"ג. כו תרומת הדשן שם. שו"ע שם. כז מ"א סק"ה. כח סעיף ג. כט תרומת הדשן שם. רמ"א ס"ג. וכדלעיל ס"א. ל לבוש שם. וראה גם לעיל קפח ריש ס"י, שמטעם זה מי שטעה בברכת המזון ולא הזכיר יעלה ויבוא אינו חוזר לראש.

8 [Ordinarily,] when one undertakes to fast on *Shabbos* or on a festival, his acceptance of the fast is of no consequence, and he may eat without having [his commitment] annulled, as stated in sec. 570.[11] Nevertheless, if one undertakes to fast on Rosh HaShanah, even if he does not make a formal vow, but merely accepts the fast, saying: "I am hereby obligated to fast on Rosh HaShanah," he must have his commitment annulled.

[The rationale is that] since some authorities maintain that it is a *mitzvah* to fast [on Rosh HaShanah], [his acceptance of the fast] does not resemble a commitment to perform a transgression, in which instance the commitment is of no consequence.[12]

ח אַף עַל פִּי שֶׁמִּי שֶׁקִּבֵּל עָלָיו לְהִתְעַנּוֹת בְּשַׁבָּת אוֹ בְּיוֹם טוֹב אֵין קַבָּלָתוֹ כְּלוּם וּמֻתָּר לֶאֱכֹל בְּלֹא הַתָּרָה כְּמוֹ שֶׁנִּתְבָּאֵר בְּסִימָן תק"ע,[לא,11] מִכָּל מָקוֹם מִי שֶׁקִּבֵּל עָלָיו לְהִתְעַנּוֹת בְּרֹאשׁ הַשָּׁנָה, אַף עַל פִּי שֶׁלֹּא הוֹצִיאוֹ בִּלְשׁוֹן נֶדֶר[לב] אֶלָּא בִּלְשׁוֹן קַבָּלַת תַּעֲנִית בְּעָלְמָא[לג] שֶׁאָמַר "הֲרֵי עָלַי לְהִתְעַנּוֹת בְּרֹאשׁ הַשָּׁנָה" — צָרִיךְ הַתָּרָה, מֵאַחַר דְּיֵשׁ אוֹמְרִים[לד] דְּמִצְוָה לְהִתְעַנּוֹת — אֵין זֶה כִּמְקַבֵּל עָלָיו לַעֲבֹר עֲבֵרָה שֶׁאֵין קַבָּלָתוֹ כְּלוּם.[12]

9 People who follow the custom of fasting on Rosh HaShanah should not recite the passage beginning *Aneinu* [in the Afternoon Service], just as we do not recite [it] on Yom Kippur. [The rationale is that] these are days of judgment and it is not appropriate to say [as stated in that passage], "Answer us on our fastday."[13]

ט וְהַנּוֹהֲגִין לְהִתְעַנּוֹת בְּרֹאשׁ הַשָּׁנָה — לֹא יֹאמְרוּ "עֲנֵנוּ", כְּמוֹ שֶׁאֵין אוֹמְרִים "עֲנֵנוּ" בְּיוֹם הַכִּפּוּרִים,[לה] מִפְּנֵי שֶׁהֵן יְמֵי דִּין[לו] וְאֵין שַׁיָּךְ לוֹמַר "בְּיוֹם צוֹם תַּעֲנִיתֵנוּ":[לז,13]

SECTION 598 The Law [Relating to the Recitation of] *Tzidkas'cha* on Rosh HaShanah. (1)

סימן תקצח דִּין צו"צ[א] בְּרֹאשׁ הַשָּׁנָה וּבוֹ סָעִיף אֶחָד:

1 When any other festival falls on *Shabbos*, the passage beginning *Tzidkas'cha* is not recited

א אַף עַל פִּי שֶׁשְּׁאָר יוֹם טוֹב שֶׁחָל בְּשַׁבָּת אֵין אוֹמְרִים "צִדְקָתְךָ"

11. This section of the Alter Rebbe's *Shulchan Aruch* is not extant. See the *Shulchan Aruch* of R. Yosef Caro, sec. 570:1-2.

12. A commitment to fast on *Shabbos* or on another festival would violate Torah law and therefore not be binding. Rosh HaShanah is different, for the reason stated above.

13. The emphasis on Rosh HaShanah and Yom Kippur is the fact that they are days of judgment; the fasting is a secondary aspect. Hence this passage, which is inserted in *Shemoneh Esreh* in the Afternoon Service on other fast-days, is not recited on these days (*Aruch HaShulchan*, sec. 597:5).

לא סימן זה בשוע"ר לא הגיע לידינו, וראה שו"ע שם סעי' א־ב. ואם קיבל בלשון נדר, ראה שם ולעיל סי' תפה ס"ב. סי' תקכז ס"ל. לב קונם אכילת יום פלוני עלי (פרישה סי' תקע אות ב. וראה גם לעיל סי' תפה שם). לג מ"א שם. לד ב"י ד"ה כתב הכלבו. מ"א שם. וכדלעיל ס"א. לה הגהות מנהגים (טירנא) אות קלב, בשם רבי יהודה החסיד. רמ"א ס"ג. לו הגהות מנהגים שם. דרכי משה ס"ק ב. מ"א ס"ק ח. לז לבוש סוף ס"ג. מ"א שם.

סימן תקצח: א שלושת הפסוקים שאומרים במנחה בשבת: צדקתך; וצדקתך; צדקתך.

בְּמִנְחָה,[ב,1] אֲבָל בְּרֹאשׁ הַשָּׁנָה שֶׁחָל בְּשַׁבָּת אוֹמְרִים,[ג] לְפִי שֶׁהוּא יוֹם דִּין וְרָאוּי לוֹמַר צִדּוּק הַדִּין בְּיוֹם דִּין,[ד] וְכָךְ נוֹהֲגִין בִּסְפָרַד.[ה] אֲבָל יֵשׁ אוֹמְרִים[ו] שֶׁאַף בְּרֹאשׁ הַשָּׁנָה שֶׁחָל בְּשַׁבָּת אֵין אוֹמְרִים אוֹתוֹ, מִפְּנֵי שֶׁכָּתוּב בּוֹ[ז,2] "מִשְׁפָּטֶיךָ תְּהוֹם רַבָּה", וְאֵין לְעוֹרֵר הַדִּין בְּיוֹם דִּין,[ח] וְעוֹד שֶׁהַיּוֹם רֹאשׁ חֹדֶשׁ וְאֵין אוֹמְרִים "צִדְקָתְךָ" בְּרֹאשׁ חֹדֶשׁ[ט] כְּמוֹ שֶׁנִּתְבָּאֵר בְּסִימָן רצ"ב.[י] וְכִסְבָרָא זוֹ נוֹהֲגִין בִּמְדִינוֹת אֵלּוּ:[יא,3]

in the Afternoon Service.[1] Nevertheless, when Rosh HaShanah falls on *Shabbos*, it is recited, because [Rosh HaShanah] is the Day of Judgment, and it is appropriate to acknowledge the justice of [G-d's] judgment on the Day of Judgment. This is the custom in the Sephardic [community].

Some authorities, however, maintain that when Rosh HaShanah falls on *Shabbos* this passage should likewise not be recited, because it includes the phrase,[2] "Your judgments extend to the great depths," and it is not appropriate to arouse the attribute of judgment on the Day of Judgment. Moreover, [Rosh HaShanah] is also Rosh Chodesh, and this passage is not recited on Rosh Chodesh, as explained in sec. 292[:7]. This opinion is followed in these lands.[3]

סימן תקצט וּבוֹ סָעִיף אֶחָד:

א לֵיל שֵׁנִי שֶׁל רֹאשׁ הַשָּׁנָה שֶׁחָל לִהְיוֹת בְּמוֹצָאֵי שַׁבָּת[1] אוֹמְרִים "וַתּוֹדִיעֵנוּ"[א] קֹדֶם "וַתִּתֶּן לָנוּ" כְּמוֹ בִּשְׁאָר יוֹם טוֹב שֶׁחָל בְּמוֹצָאֵי שַׁבָּת,[ב] וְאַף עַל פִּי שֶׁמַּזְכִּירִין בּוֹ "חֲגִיגַת הָרֶגֶל" וְרֹאשׁ הַשָּׁנָה אֵינוֹ לֹא חַג וְלֹא רֶגֶל — אֵין בְּכָךְ כְּלוּם, מִשּׁוּם דְּאֵין הַכַּוָּנָה שֶׁהַיּוֹם הוּא רֶגֶל אֶלָּא הוּא מוֹנֶה סֵדֶר הַתִּקּוּן[ג]

SECTION 599 [The Recitation of the Passage *VaTodieinu* on Rosh HaShanah.] (1)

1 When the second night of Rosh HaShanah falls on *Motzaei Shabbos*[1] we recite the passage *VaTodieinu* before the passage *VaTiten Lanu* [in *Shemoneh Esreh*], as is done when any other festival falls on Saturday night. Though *[VaTodieinu]* speaks of "the celebration of the pilgrim festival," and Rosh HaShanah is neither a day of celebration nor a pilgrim festival, this is not significant. For the intent [of the passage] is not [to state] that the day is a pilgrim festival, but to follow the format [that the Sages coined for this

---

1. Its three verses, quoted from *Tehillim* and appearing immediately after the repetition of *Shemoneh Esreh*, speak of the Divine attribute of judgment. See *Siddur Tehillat HaShem* Annotated Edition, p. 266.

2. *Tehillim* 36:7.

3. I.e., within the Ashkenazic community of Eastern Europe. This is also the Lubavitch custom *(Luach Colel Chabad)*.

SECTION 599

1. This law is applicable only with regard to the second day of Rosh HaShanah. Rosh HaShanah can never begin on Saturday night, for according to the fixed calendar we follow, the first day of Rosh HaShanah can never fall on Sunday.

ב כדלעיל סי' רצב ס"ז. ג טור בשם רב עמרם. כל בו סי' סד (ל, א) בשם רב האי. שו"ע ס"א. ד טור. ט"ז סק"א. ה ב"י סוף הסימן. ו ר"ן (ט, א) ד"ה גמרא בשם גאונים. מנהגים (טירנא) מנהגי ר"ה (ע' ק). רמ"א ס"א. ז בצדקתך הא' – תהלים לו, ז. ח לבוש ס"א. וראה גם לקמן סי' תרכב סוף ס"ד. ט ר"ן שם. לבוש. י סעיף ז. יא רמ"א שם.

סימן תקצט: א ראבי"ה ח"א סי' צד. רא"ש פ"ד סי' יד. טור ושו"ע ס"א. וכ"ה בסידור. ב כדלעיל סי' תצא ס"ד. ג ראבי"ה שם. רא"ש שם. טור. לבוש.

blessing, which enumerates] the gifts that the Holy One, blessed be He, has ordained for us — "the sanctity of the *Shabbos,* the glory of the holiday, and the celebration of the pilgrim festivals...."[2]

In *Kiddush* [on that evening, the blessings follow the order whose acronym is] *yaknehaz: [yayin* — wine; *Kiddush; ner* — a candle; *Havdalah;*[3] and *zman* — the blessing *Shehecheyanu],* as [is the practice] whenever a festival falls on Saturday night.

הַמַּתָּנוֹת שֶׁנָּתַן לָנוּ הַקָּדוֹשׁ בָּרוּךְ הוּא "קְדֻשַּׁת שַׁבָּת וּכְבוֹד מוֹעֵד וַחֲגִיגַת הָרֶגֶל וכו'".[2]

וּמְקַדְּשִׁים יקנה"ז[ד,3] כְּבִשְׁאָר יוֹם טוֹב שֶׁחָל בְּמוֹצָאֵי שַׁבָּת:[ה]

SECTION 600 [The Laws Relating to] an Egg Laid on Rosh HaShanah and the Order of *Kiddush.* (1–7)

סימן תר בֵּיצָה שֶׁנּוֹלְדָה בְּרֹאשׁ הַשָּׁנָה וְסֵדֶר הַקִּדּוּשׁ וּבוֹ ז' סְעִיפִים:

1 Even those who live in *Eretz Yisrael* celebrate Rosh HaShanah for two days.[1] The reason they celebrate the other festivals for only one day is that [today] we know how the calculation of the months is determined. We know which day is appropriate to establish as the first day of [each] month,[2] the day from which we calculate the [dates of its] festivals.

א אַף בְּנֵי אֶרֶץ יִשְׂרָאֵל עוֹשִׂין שְׁנֵי יָמִים רֹאשׁ הַשָּׁנָה,[א,1] לְפִי[ב] שֶׁמַּה שֶּׁהֵן אֵין עוֹשִׂין שְׁאָר מוֹעֲדוֹת אֶלָּא יוֹם אֶחָד הַטַּעַם מִשּׁוּם שֶׁאָנוּ בְּקִיאִין בְּחֶשְׁבּוֹן קְבִיעוּת הֶחֳדָשִׁים, וְאָנוּ יוֹדְעִים יוֹם שֶׁרָאוּי לִקְבֹּעַ הַחֹדֶשׁ[2] וְלִמְנוֹת מִמֶּנּוּ הַמּוֹעֲדוֹת,

---

2. The problematic linkage of "the celebration of the pilgrim festival" to Rosh HaShanah is not new. *Ravia,* the medieval author of *Avi HaEzri,* writes that when he confronted his mentors with this anomaly he was told: When any other festival ends on a weekday, the blessing of separation nevertheless speaks of the distinction "between *the Seventh Day* and the six workdays" — because we say that the passage is simply enumerating a series of separations *(Chullin* 26b*).* In the same way, he was told, the standard wording of *VaTodieinu* simply enumerates the series of festivals that were ordained for us. (See: *Piskei HaRosh,* sec. 14, on *Rosh HaShanah,* ch. 4; *Tur,* sec. 599:1. Characteristically, the Alter Rebbe's original phrase *(seder hatikkun — hamatanos)* interweaves elements from all the above-mentioned sources.)

3. Lit., "separation." In this case, the blessing of *Havdalah* demarcates the superior sanctity of the departing *Shabbos* from the lesser sanctity of [the incoming second day of] Rosh HaShanah. Thus, instead of concluding with the usual weekly wording, *hamavdil bein kodesh lechol,* blessing the One "Who makes a distinction between holy and ordinary," the different version on this occasion concludes, *hamavdil bein kodesh lekodesh,* blessing the One "Who makes a distinction between holy and holy."

SECTION 600

1. I.e., according to Scriptural Law *(Vayikra* 23:24*),* Rosh HaShanah should be celebrated for one day only. Nevertheless, it has become the accepted custom — not only for the inhabitants of the Diaspora, who celebrate all one-day holidays for two days, but also in *Eretz Yisrael* — to celebrate Rosh HaShanah for two days. The reasons are set out in this section.

2. During the time of the *Beis HaMikdash,* and for almost three centuries thereafter, the calendar was determined from month to month by the *Sanhedrin,* based on the testimony of witnesses who had sighted the new moon. The Alter Rebbe here considers

ט"ז סק"א. **ד** לבוש. **ה** כדלעיל סי' תעג ס"ו.

סימן תר: א רי"ף ביצה (ג, א). רמב"ם הל' יום טוב פ"א הכ"א, והל' קדוש החדש פ"ה ה"ח. רא"ש ביצה פ"א סי' ד. שו"ע סי' תרא ס"ב. **ב** סיום ביאור הטעם – לקמן סוף ס"ד.

וְאַף בְּנֵי גוֹלָה אֵין עוֹשִׂין שְׁנֵי יָמִים אֶלָּא מִשּׁוּם שֶׁהֵם צְרִיכִין לְקַיֵּם מִנְהַג אֲבוֹתֵיהֶם[ג,3] שֶׁהָיוּ עוֹשִׂים שְׁנֵי יָמִים בִּזְמַן שֶׁהָיוּ מְקַדְּשִׁין עַל פִּי הָרְאִיָּה,[4] שֶׁאֵין הַדָּבָר תָּלוּי בְּחֶשְׁבּוֹן כְּלָל אֶלָּא בִּרְאִיַּת הַלְּבָנָה, וְלֹא הָיוּ בְּנֵי גוֹלָה יוֹדְעִין יוֹם שֶׁהֻקְבַּע בּוֹ הַחֹדֶשׁ בִּירוּשָׁלַיִם וְהָיוּ עוֹשִׂין שְׁנֵי יָמִים מִסָּפֵק, אֲבָל בְּנֵי אֶרֶץ יִשְׂרָאֵל הַקְּרוֹבִים לִירוּשָׁלַיִם לֹא הָיוּ עוֹשִׂין הַמּוֹעֲדוֹת אֶלָּא יוֹם אֶחָד,[ד] לְפִי שֶׁהַבֵּית דִּין שֶׁבִּירוּשָׁלַיִם הָיוּ שׁוֹלְחִים שְׁלוּחִים לְהוֹדִיעַ[5] לָהֶם יוֹם שֶׁנִּקְבַּע בּוֹ הַחֹדֶשׁ[ה] בְּנִיסָן (וּבְסִיוָן[ו]) וּבְתִשְׁרֵי,[ז,6]

[In the present era,] the only reason that even Jews in the Diaspora celebrate [the one-day festivals] for two days is that they are obliged to uphold the custom of their forefathers,[3] who would celebrate [the festivals] for two days during the period when [the day of Rosh Chodesh] was sanctified according to [the testimony of] witnesses.[4] [At that time,] the matter was not dependent on calculations at all, but on the sighting of the [new] moon. The Jews in the Diaspora did not know which day had been established in Jerusalem as [Rosh] Chodesh and would therefore celebrate the holidays for two days because of their doubt. The Jews of *Eretz Yisrael* who were close to Jerusalem would celebrate [each festival] for only one day, for the Rabbinical Court in Jerusalem would send messengers to notify [people elsewhere][5] which day had been established as [Rosh] Chodesh for Nissan and Tishrei.[6] [Accordingly,] in all

---

the predicament of the Jews of those times who lived in outlying communities and outside *Eretz Yisrael.* Even if they knew that a particular festival was to fall, for example, "on the fifteenth of the month," how would they know when to celebrate it? And communications were problematic, as will be explained.

In the time of Hillel II, in the mid-fourth century C.E., the acceptance of a fixed calendar removed doubt for all time. It would now be known in advance whether any particular month in the future would be a short month (i.e., of 29 days), which is described as *chaser* (lit., "lacking"), or a month of 30 days, which is described as *maleh* ("full"). It would likewise be known in advance if any particular year in the future would be a *peshutah,* i.e., a "plain" year of 12 lunar months, or a leap year *(me'uberes* — lit., "a pregnant year"), i.e., comprising 13 lunar months.

3. *Beitzah* 4b. The additional day is known as *Yom-Tov Sheni shel Galuyos* (lit., "the second festival of the exiles").

4. In the original, *al-pi hare'iyah* (lit., "according to the sighting").

5. *Rosh HaShanah* 18a, 22b; *Beitzah, loc. cit.*

6. The standard printed text of the Alter Rebbe's *Shulchan Aruch* mentions also the month of Sivan. *Kuntreis HaShulchan* argues that Sivan should be deleted, as follows: The *Mishnah (Rosh Hashanah* 1:3*)* states that messengers were sent out to notify the people of the day on which Rosh Chodesh was declared for the months of Nissan — because of Pesach, Av — because of Tishah BeAv, Elul — so that the people would be ready for Rosh HaShanah, Tishrei — because of its festivals, Kislev — because of Chanukah, and Adar — because of Purim. While the *Beis HaMikdash* was standing, they would also be sent out in Iyar, because of Pesach Sheni. No messengers would be sent out for Sivan, however, because the celebration of Shavuos depends not on the date in Sivan, but on the counting of the 49 days of the *Omer.* (See *Tosafos* on *Rosh HaShanah* 18a, *s.v. Al Nissan.* See also sec. 494:1, and the essay entitled "When Shavuos Is to be Celebrated," in *Beacons on the Talmud's Sea* (Sichos In English, N.Y., 5757/1997), p. 115ff., where this subject is discussed at length.)

The other months are not mentioned because they are not relevant to the subject at hand.

ג ביצה ד, ב. רמב"ם הל' יום טוב שם והל' קדוש החדש פ"ה ה"ה. וראה גם לעיל סי' תפג ס"ו (שלא לזלזל). סי' תפט סכ"ט. סי' תצ ס"א (תפלות וקידוש ושהחיינו ביום ב') לקמן סי' תרכד ס"י. סי' תרמט סכ"א (שלא לזלזל). ולענין ר"ה ראה גם לקמן סוף ס"ד (אין לזלזל). ד ביצה ד, ב. רמב"ם הל' קדוש החודש שם ה"ד. ה משנה כב, ב. רמב"ם שם פ"ג ה"ח. ו בקונטרס השלחן כתב שהוא ט"ס (ששבועות תלוי בספירת העומר, כדלעיל סי' תצד ס"א). ז ראה

וּבְכָל הַמְּקוֹמוֹת הַקְּרוֹבִים שֶׁהָיוּ הַשְּׁלוּחִים מַגִּיעִין אֲלֵיהֶם קֹדֶם יוֹם טוֹב לֹא הָיוּ עוֹשִׂין אֶלָּא יוֹם אֶחָד, וּלְפִיכָךְ אַף בְּנֵיהֶם אַחֲרֵיהֶם עַכְשָׁו אֵינָן צְרִיכִין לַעֲשׂוֹת שְׁנֵי יָמִים,[ח] כֵּיוָן שֶׁאָנוּ בְּקִיאִים בַּחֶשְׁבּוֹן וְיוֹדְעִים יוֹם שֶׁרָאוּי לִקְבֹּעַ בּוֹ הַחֹדֶשׁ וְלִמְנוֹת מִמֶּנּוּ הַחֹדֶשׁ:[ט]

וְזֶה הַטַּעַם לֹא שַׁיָּךְ אֶלָּא בִּשְׁאָר מוֹעֲדוֹת חוּץ מֵרֹאשׁ הַשָּׁנָה, אֲבָל בְּרֹאשׁ הַשָּׁנָה אַף בְּנֵי אֶרֶץ יִשְׂרָאֵל צְרִיכִים לְקַיֵּם מִנְהַג אֲבוֹתֵיהֶם שֶׁהָיוּ עוֹשִׂין שְׁנֵי יָמִים בִּזְמַן שֶׁהָיוּ מְקַדְּשִׁין עַל פִּי הָרְאִיָּה,[י] שֶׁלֹּא הָיָה הַדָּבָר תָּלוּי בִּידִיעַת הַחֶשְׁבּוֹן אֶלָּא בִּקְבִיעוּת הַבֵּית דִּין שֶׁבִּירוּשָׁלַיִם עַל פִּי רְאִיַּת (הָעֵדִים אֶת)[7] הַלְּבָנָה, וְאַף עַל פִּי שֶׁהַבֵּית דִּין הָיוּ מְשַׁלְּחִין שְׁלוּחִים לְהוֹדִיעַ לַכֹּל, מִכָּל מָקוֹם בְּרֹאשׁ הַשָּׁנָה שֶׁהוּא יוֹם טוֹב אֵין הַשְּׁלוּחִים יְכוֹלִים לָצֵאת[יא] חוּץ לַתְּחוּם:[יב,8]

the nearby places that the messengers would reach before the onset of the festival, it would be observed for only one day. Therefore their descendants today do not have to observe two days, for we know the calculations [on which the calendar is based] and are aware of the day to be established as Rosh Chodesh, from which the [dates of the] month will be marked.

This rationale applies to the festivals other than Rosh HaShanah. On Rosh HaShanah even the inhabitants of *Eretz Yisrael* have to observe the custom of their forefathers, who would celebrate it for two days during the time when [the day of Rosh Chodesh] was sanctified according to the sighting of the moon. For the matter did not depend on a knowledge of the calculations, but on the determination of the Court in Jerusalem based on the sighting of the moon (by witnesses).[7] Although the Court would [normally] dispatch messengers to notify everyone [of the day proclaimed as Rosh Chodesh], the messengers were not able to depart beyond [Jerusalem's Sabbath] limits on Rosh HaShanah, [because it] is a festival.[8]

7. The Alter Rebbe's ruling has its roots (with some differences that will be explained) in the rulings of Rabbeinu Yitzchak Alfasi and *Rambam.* Rabbeinu Asher (see *Piskei HaRosh, Beitzah* 1:4) cites the differing view of Rabbeinu Ephraim and Rabbeinu Zerachyah HaLevi — that Rosh HaShanah should be observed in *Eretz Yisrael* for only one day like the other festivals — and affirms that there were times when this view was actually followed there. (See also subsection 4 below.)

8. On *Shabbos* and on a festival, we are not permitted to proceed more than 2000 cubits beyond the town (or place) at which we are located at the commencement of that holy day and which thus serves as our base for that day. This limit is called *techum Shabbos.* (See sec. 396 and sec. 397.) Since the messengers could not go far from Jerusalem on Rosh HaShanah, only the people in the Holy City and its environs could know for certain whether or not Rosh HaShanah had been declared on the thirtieth day after Rosh Chodesh Elul. And since all the communities outside Jerusalem would observe Rosh HaShanah for two days, they still follow that practice today.

In Jerusalem as well, Rosh HaShanah is celebrated today for two days, because there were times when this was the practice there, too, as stated in subsection 4 below.

משנה יח, סוע"א. שם כא, רע"ב. רמב"ם שם ה"ט וה"י. **ח** רש"י ביצה שם ד"ה ועבדי. רמב"ם שם פ"ה ה"ו. **ט** רמב"ם שם ה"ב וה"ה. **י** רמב"ם שם ה"ז. רא"ש ביצה פ"א סי' ד. וכדלקמן ס"ד. **יא** רמב"ם שם ה"ז. **יב** ראה רא"ש שם בשם רב האי (חוץ לתחום). לבוש (המקומות שהיו רחוקים מירושלים). לקמן ס"ד (חוץ לתחום של ירושלים).

ב וְאַף בַּגּוֹלָה רֹאשׁ הַשָּׁנָה הוּא חָלוּק מִשְּׁאָר מוֹעֲדוֹת,[9] שֶׁשְּׁאָר מוֹעֲדוֹת אַף אֲבוֹתֵיהֶם לֹא הָיוּ עוֹשִׂין שְׁנֵי יָמִים אֶלָּא מֵחֲמַת הַסָּפֵק שֶׁלֹּא הָיוּ יוֹדְעִים יוֹם שֶׁהֻקְבַּע בּוֹ הַחֹדֶשׁ בְּאֶרֶץ יִשְׂרָאֵל,[יג] וּבֵיצָה שֶׁנּוֹלְדָה בְּיוֹם רִאשׁוֹן מֻתֶּרֶת בְּיוֹם שֵׁנִי,[יד,10] שֶׁאִם הַיּוֹם קֹדֶשׁ לְמָחָר הוּא חֹל[טו] וְאֵין בּוֹ אִסּוּר מֻקְצֶה וְנוֹלָד,[טז,11] וְאִם לְמָחָר קֹדֶשׁ הַיּוֹם חֹל וּכְבָר הוּכְנָה הַבֵּיצָה מֵעֶרֶב יוֹם טוֹב,[12] וּלְפִיכָךְ אַף בְּנֵיהֶם אַחֲרֵיהֶם הַיּוֹדְעִים בִּקְבִיעוּת הַחֹדֶשׁ וְיוֹדְעִים שֶׁיּוֹם רִאשׁוֹן הוּא עִקַּר יוֹם טוֹב וְיוֹם שֵׁנִי הוּא גַּם כֵּן יוֹם טוֹב מִדִּבְרֵי סוֹפְרִים,[יז] אַף עַל פִּי כֵן אֵין דִּין בֵּיצָה זוֹ כְּדִין בֵּיצָה שֶׁנּוֹלְדָה בִּשְׁנֵי יָמִים טוֹבִים הַסְּמוּכִים זֶה לָזֶה כְּגוֹן שַׁבָּת וְיוֹם טוֹב שֶׁאִם נוֹלְדָה בָּזֶה אֲסוּרָה בָּזֶה כְּמוֹ שֶׁנִּתְבָּאֵר בְּסִימָן תקי"ג,[יח] דְּכֵיוָן שֶׁהֵן אֵין עוֹשִׂין שְׁנֵי יָמִים אֶלָּא מֵחֲמַת מִנְהַג אֲבוֹתֵיהֶם — אֵין צָרִיךְ לְהַחְמִיר יוֹתֵר מֵאֲבוֹתֵיהֶם[יט] שֶׁהָיָה מֻתָּר לָהֶם מִטַּעַם שֶׁנִּתְבָּאֵר:

2 Even for people in the Diaspora, Rosh HaShanah differs from other festivals.[9] With regard to other festivals, even their forebears would observe two days only because of the doubt, i.e., they did not know which day had been declared Rosh Chodesh in *Eretz Yisrael*. Thus an egg laid on the first day may be used on the second day.[10] [The rationale is that only one of those days is really a festival,] for if [the first day] is holy, [the second day] is ordinary, and the prohibitions of *muktzeh* and *nolad*[11] do not apply. And if it is [the second day] that is holy, and [the first day] is ordinary, the egg was prepared on the day before the holiday.[12]

Now, their descendants know [the correct dates] and are aware that the first day is the essence of the festival and the second day is also a festival [only] by virtue of Rabbinic decree. Nevertheless, the law [now] applying to an egg [laid on the first day of a festival] is not comparable to that of an egg laid on two [Scriptural days of rest] that follow each other, such as a *Shabbos* and a festival, in which instance an egg laid on one may not be eaten on the second, as stated in sec. 513[:9. The rationale for the distinction is that] since they observe two days only because of the custom observed by their forefathers, they are not obliged to be more stringent than their ancestors themselves were. And their ancestors were allowed [to use such an egg] because of the reasons explained above.

---

9. *Beitzah, loc. cit.*

10. According to Scriptural Law, an egg that was laid on a festival that immediately follows *Shabbos*, or on a *Shabbos* that immediately follows a festival, may not be eaten on that day (see sec. 513:1-3.). The rationale is that any food prepared on a *Shabbos* or a festival — even if it was prepared "by the Hand of Heaven" without any human input — may not be eaten on a festival or a *Shabbos* that follows directly thereafter. Nevertheless, as stated in subsection 8 of that section, an egg laid on the first day of a two-day festival observed in the Diaspora may be eaten on the second day, for the reason given in the above text. As the Alter Rebbe proceeds to explain, this does not apply to Rosh HaShanah.

11. On the basis of these two prohibitions (see sec. 495:13), it would be forbidden to use the egg.

12. Hence there is no prohibition involved.

יג רש"י ביצה ד, ב ד"ה של גלויות. רמב"ם שם ה"ד. יד רב בגמרא שם. טור ושו"ע סי' תקיג ס"ה. לעיל שם ס"ח. טו ראה רש"י שם ד"ה מותרת. טז מוקצה בתרנגולת העומדת לגדל ביצים, ונולד בתרנגולת העומדת לאכילה (ראה לעיל סי' תקיג ס"ב). יז ראה רמב"ם שם ה"ו. יח סעיף ט. יט ר"ן ביצה (ט, א) ד"ה

ג אֲבָל בִּשְׁנֵי יָמִים טוֹבִים שֶׁל רֹאשׁ הַשָּׁנָה אֵינוֹ כֵּן, אֶלָּא הֵן נֶחְשָׁבִים כְּיוֹם אֶחָד אָרֹךְ[כ] וּקְדֻשָּׁה אַחַת הֵן[כא] אַף לִבְנֵי אֶרֶץ יִשְׂרָאֵל,[13] וּבֵיצָה שֶׁנּוֹלְדָה בָּרִאשׁוֹן,[כב] אוֹ דָּבָר שֶׁנִּתְלַשׁ מִן הַמְחֻבָּר[14] בָּרִאשׁוֹן, אוֹ דָּבָר שֶׁנִּצַּד בָּרִאשׁוֹן,[כג] כְּשֵׁם שֶׁאָסוּר בּוֹ בַּיּוֹם מִשּׁוּם מֻקְצֶה וְנוֹלָד – כָּךְ אָסוּר בְּיוֹם שֵׁנִי שֶׁהֵם כְּיוֹם אֶחָד אָרֹךְ, חוּץ מִלְּעִנְיַן מֵת בְּיוֹם שֵׁנִי כְּמוֹ שֶׁנִּתְבָּאֵר בְּסִימָן תקכ"ו:[כד,15]

3 [The above concepts do not apply] with regard to the two days of Rosh HaShanah. They are considered as one long day and a single continuum of holiness, even for the inhabitants of *Eretz Yisrael*.[13] [Hence, the following law applies to] an egg that was laid on the first day, to any [produce] that was detached[14] on the first day, or to anything snared on the first day. Just as it is forbidden on [the first day] because of the prohibitions of *muktzeh* and *nolad*, it is forbidden on the second day, because they are considered as one long day.

[There is one] exception: the deceased [may be buried] on the second day, as explained in sec. 526[:6].[15]

ד וְלָמָּה הֵן נֶחְשָׁבִין כְּיוֹם אֶחָד?[16] וַהֲרֵי אָנוּ בְּקִיאִין בִּקְבִיעוּת הַחֹדֶשׁ וְאָנוּ יוֹדְעִין שֶׁרִאשׁוֹן עִקָּר, מִשּׁוּם דְּאַף הַבֵּית דִּין עַצְמָן שֶׁהָיוּ מְקַדְּשִׁין עַל פִּי הָרְאִיָּה הָיוּ עוֹשִׂין לִפְעָמִים שְׁנֵי יָמִים,[כה,17] כֵּיצַד? בָּרִאשׁוֹנָה[כו] כְּשֶׁהִגִּיעַ יוֹם ל' בֶּאֱלוּל[כז] הָיוּ כָל יִשְׂרָאֵל וְהַבֵּית דִּין נוֹהֲגִין אִסּוּר מְלָאכָה וּקְדֻשַּׁת הַיּוֹם

4 Why are [the two days of Rosh HaShanah] considered as one long day?[16] [After all, today] we are aware [of the day] fixed for the new month [to begin], and we know that it is the first day [of Rosh HaShanah] that is of primary importance. [The two days are nevertheless considered as one long day,] because even when the Court would sanctify [the months] on the basis of the sighting [of the new moon], there were times when [this festival] was observed for two days.[17]

How did this come about? Originally, when [the eve of] the thirtieth of Elul arrived, the entire Jewish people and the Court would observe — from nightfall — the prohibitions against forbidden labor and

13. *Beitzah, loc. cit.*

14. E.g., picked, harvested or uprooted.

15. There it is stated that with regard to a burial, the second day of a festival is considered as an ordinary day and all forms of labor may be performed for this purpose. This principle applies also with regard to the second day of Rosh HaShanah.

In practice, for various reasons, this leniency is often not adopted, and burials today are no longer held in many communities on the second day of a festival. Nevertheless, exceptions are occasionally dictated by circumstances.

16. The Alter Rebbe's question is: Why do we not say here, as with the other festivals, that the first and second days are two distinct entities?

17. *Beitzah* 5a.

מניח. הובא ב"י סי' תקכח. וראה שו"ת רשב"א ח"ד סי' קמא וסי' רסג. **כ** רש"י ביצה ד, סוע"ב ד"ה אסורה. רמב"ם הל' יום טוב פ"א הכ"ד. לבוש ריש ס"א. **כא** רש"י שם ה, א סוד"ה עד המנחה. רמב"ם שם. טור ולבוש שם. וראה גם לעיל סי' תצז ס"ט. סי' תקג ס"ג (להחמיר ולא להקל). סי' תקיג ס"ח וס"י. סי' תקטו ס"ו וס"ט. סי' תקכז סכ"ב. וראה. וראה סי' תקא סי"ח וקו"א סק"ב. יגדיל תורה (נ.י.) ב ע' מד. **כב** רב ושמואל שם ד, סוע"ב. טור ושו"ע סי' זה, וסי' תקיג ס"ה. לעיל שם ס"ח. **כג** טור ושו"ע סי' זה. וראה באריכות לעיל סי' תקטו ס"א. **כד** ס"ו. וראה גם לעיל סי' תצו ס"ה. **כה** רש"י ביצה ה, א ד"ה עד המנחה. מ"א סי' תרא סק"א. וראה רמב"ם הל' קידוש החדש פ"ה ה"ח. **כו** משנה ר"ה ל, ב. ביצה ד, סוע"ב. **כז** רש"י ביצה שם ד"ה כל היום. וראה לקו"ש ח"ט ע' 188 הערה 31. שלחן המלך ח"ב ע' רג־רה.

מִבָּעֶרֶב, דְּשֶׁמָּא יָבוֹאוּ עֵדִים לְמָחָר וְיֹאמְרוּ שֶׁרָאוּ הַלְּבָנָה בְּלַיְלָה זוֹ[18] וְיִהְיֶה הַיּוֹם רֹאשׁ חֹדֶשׁ תִּשְׁרֵי וְהוּא רֹאשׁ הַשָּׁנָה וְנִמְצָא שֶׁהַלַּיְלָה הוּא יוֹם טוֹב, וּבַיּוֹם הָיוּ הַבֵּית דִּין יוֹשְׁבִין וּמְצַפִּים לְבִיאַת עֵדִים רוֹאֵי הַלְּבָנָה אוּלַי יָבוֹאוּ וְכָל שָׁעָה שֶׁיָּבוֹאוּ בַּיּוֹם עַד שֶׁתֶּחְשַׁךְ הָיוּ מְקַדְּשִׁין אֶת הַחֹדֶשׁ אוֹתוֹ הַיּוֹם[כח] וְהָיָה רֹאשׁ הַשָּׁנָה בּוֹ בַּיּוֹם, וּמֵאוֹתוֹ יוֹם וָהָלְאָה מוֹנִין לְיוֹם הַכִּפּוּרִים וּלְסֻכּוֹת, וְהָיוּ תָּמִיד רְגִילִין לָבוֹא קֹדֶם זְמַן מִנְחָה,[כט] דְּהַיְנוּ זְמַן הַקְרָבַת תָּמִיד שֶׁל בֵּין הָעַרְבַּיִם,[19] פַּעַם אַחַת נִשְׁתַּהוּ הָעֵדִים מִלָּבוֹא עַד אַחַר הַמִּנְחָה וְהִקְרִיבוּ הַתָּמִיד וְנִתְקַלְקְלוּ הַלְוִיִּם בַּשִּׁיר[ל] וְאָמְרוּ שִׁיר שֶׁל חֹל,[לא] שֶׁהָיוּ סְבוּרִים שֶׁלֹּא יָבוֹאוּ הָעֵדִים עוֹד הַיּוֹם, וּכְשֶׁבָּאוּ — נִמְצָא הַיּוֹם לְמַפְרֵעַ קֹדֶשׁ,[לב] וּמֵאוֹתוֹ הַיּוֹם וָהָלְאָה[20] הִתְקִינוּ חֲכָמִים שֶׁלֹּא יִהְיוּ הַבֵּית דִּין מְקַבְּלִין אֶת הָעֵדִים אֶלָּא עַד הַמִּנְחָה,[לג] וּכְשֶׁיָּבוֹאוּ לְאַחַר הַמִּנְחָה[21] — יִהְיֶה אוֹתוֹ הַיּוֹם מִן

would observe the sanctification of the day, lest witnesses come the following day and testify that they had seen the new moon that night.[18] [Were that to happen,] that day would be declared as Rosh Chodesh Tishrei, which is Rosh HaShanah, and thus the [preceding] night would [have been observed as] a festival.

During the day the Court would be in session, anticipating the possible arrival of witnesses who had sighted the new moon. At whatever hour in the course of the day — until nightfall — they would come [and their testimony would be substantiated], that day would be duly sanctified as the first day of the new month, and Rosh HaShanah would be observed that day. And from that day onward, the days would be calculated [for the observance of] Yom Kippur and Sukkos.

[The witnesses] would always come before *Minchah,* i.e., before the time of the sacrifice of the daily afternoon offering.[19] Once the witnesses were delayed and did not come until after *Minchah.* [The *Kohanim* had already] brought the daily offering and the Levites erred with regard to the psalm, i.e., they sang the psalm associated with the weekday [rather than the song to be recited on Rosh HaShanah], because they did not think that the witnesses would come that day. When they did come, that day was retroactively established as holy.

From that day onward,[20] the Sages ordained that the Court would not receive the testimony of witnesses past *Minchah.* If the witnesses came after *Minchah,*[21] that day would be considered as

18. *Rosh HaShanah* 30b; *Beitzah* 4b.

19. The afternoon offering was brought nine-and-a-half seasonal hours after sunrise. (A seasonal hour is defined as one twelfth of the time between sunrise and sunset.)

20. To prevent such an error from recurring.

21. Certainly, if they did not come at all that day, the following day would be considered as the festival. The remaining concepts mentioned here, however, apply if the witnesses did see the moon on the thirtieth night of Elul.

כח רש"י שם. לבוש שם. כט לבוש שם. ל משנה ר"ה שם. לא גמרא שם. רש"י ביצה ה, רע"א ד"ה ונתקלקלו. לבוש שם. וראה לקו"ש שם. שלחן המלך שם. לב רש"י שם. לבוש שם. לג משנה ר"ה שם. לד רש"י ביצה שם ד"ה עד המנחה. לבוש שם. לה לבוש שם. לו ויקרא כג, ב. לז רש"י ר"ה כה, א ד"ה אתם.

חֹדֶשׁ הֶעָבָר לִמְנוֹת אוֹתוֹ יוֹם ל׳ שֶׁל אֱלוּל וְלִמְנוֹת לְיוֹם הַכִּפּוּרִים וּלְסֻכּוֹת מִיּוֹם הַמָּחֳרָת,[לד, 22] שֶׁיֵּשׁ כֹּחַ בְּיַד בֵּית דִּין לַעֲשׂוֹת דָּבָר זֶה,[לה] שֶׁנֶּאֱמַר[לו, 23] "אֵלֶּה מוֹעֲדֵי ה׳ אֲשֶׁר תִּקְרְאוּ אוֹתָם", "אֹתָם" כְּתִיב בְּלֹא וא"ו[לז] — "אַתֶּם" אֲפִלּוּ מְזִידִין.[לח, 24,25]

וּמִכָּל מָקוֹם, אַף עַל פִּי שֶׁאֵין מוֹנִין לַמּוֹעֲדוֹת מִיּוֹם זֶה וּכְחֹל הוּא חָשׁוּב וְיוֹם טוֹב יִהְיֶה לְמָחָר,[לט] אַף עַל פִּי כֵן לֹא הָיוּ מְזַלְזְלִים בּוֹ וְהָיוּ גּוֹמְרִים אוֹתוֹ בְּאִסּוּרוֹ בִּקְדֻשַּׁת יוֹם טוֹב עַד הַלַּיְלָה מִדִּבְרֵי סוֹפְרִים[מ] כֵּיוָן שֶׁמִּן הַדִּין הָיָה הוּא רָאוּי לִהְיוֹת יוֹם טוֹב מִן הַתּוֹרָה[26]

part of the previous month and would be counted as the thirtieth day of Elul. Yom Kippur and Sukkos would then be counted from the following day.[22]

The Court has the authority to do this, as [implied by] the verse,[23] "These are the festivals of G-d which you shall proclaim." [The word *osam* in the latter phrase, אשר תקראו אתם, here translated as "which,"] is written without the letter *vav*, [and thus can also be read as] *atem* ("you"), [as if to lay stress on the suffix meaning "you" in the preceding verb. From this the Sages understood[24] that the authority for declaring the dates of the festivals is entrusted to] "you," [to the Court]. Even when [the judges] purposely [establish the first of the month on a day other than the day on which the new moon was first seen, their ruling is binding].[25]

Nevertheless, though [the Court] would not begin to calculate the festivals from this day [the thirtieth of Elul], and [in principle] it was to be considered as an ordinary weekday, and the following day would be the festival, they would not treat the day with disrespect. [Instead,] they would complete it until nightfall [in observance of] the prohibitions [of forbidden labor, as befits] the sanctity of the festivals as a result of the Rabbinic decrees. [The rationale is that] according to law, it was fit to be a festival according to Scriptural Law,[26]

---

22. Which was observed as Rosh HaShanah.

23. *Vayikra* 23:37.

24. I.e., an oral tradition received by the Sages uncovered an additional and alternative meaning that is implicit in the unvocalized three-letter Hebrew word. See *Rosh HaShanah* 25a.

25. The Alter Rebbe's position has its roots in the words of the *Tur (Orach Chayim* 600*)*, who differs slightly from *Rambam* in this matter. *Rambam (Hilchos Kiddush HaChodesh* 3:15-19*)* maintains that even if witnesses come after the new moon has been declared and claim to have sighted the new moon on the thirtieth night of the previous month, their testimony is accepted and the dating for that month is retroactively established accordingly. Significantly *(loc. cit.* 2:14*)*, he also interprets the verse from *Vayikra* differently, maintaining that it applies when the judges erred unwittingly; he does not mention their making an intentional mistake. Similarly, when describing why Rosh HaShanah is celebrated for two days *(loc. cit.* 5:8*)*, he does not mention witnesses arriving after *Minchah* on the thirtieth day, but instead speaks of their not coming at all.

What underlies the difference is that the *Tur* and the Alter Rebbe are trying to explain a situation in which Rosh HaShanah was observed on the thirtieth of Elul despite the fact that there was no doubt about the matter at all, and thus there was one day observed because of Scriptural decree and one because of Rabbinic decree.

26. Because the new moon was actually seen on that day.

לבוש שם. **לח** ר"ה שם. לבוש שם. וראה התוועדויות תש"נ ח"ב ע' 182 בהערה. שלחן המלך ח"ב ע' רג הערה 3. **לט** לבוש שם. וראה חידושי הריטב"א עירובין לט, ב. **מ** משנה שם ל, ב ורש"י שם ד"ה נוהגים. ביצה ה, רע"א ורש"י ד"ה עד המנחה. לבוש שם.

אֶלָּא שֶׁנִּתַּן רְשׁוּת לְבֵית דִּין לִדְחוֹת,[מא] וּלְמָחָר עוֹשִׂין יוֹם טוֹב וְרֹאשׁ הַשָּׁנָה שֶׁל תּוֹרָה,[מב] וְאֵלּוּ שְׁנֵי הַיָּמִים הֵן קְדֻשָּׁה אַחַת וּכְיוֹם אֶחָד אָרֹךְ, וּשְׁנֵיהֶם נִקְרָאִים יוֹם טוֹב שֶׁל רֹאשׁ הַשָּׁנָה, יוֹם רִאשׁוֹן מִדִּבְרֵי סוֹפְרִים וְיוֹם שֵׁנִי מִדִּבְרֵי תוֹרָה.[מג, 27]

וְהַמְּקוֹמוֹת שֶׁהֵן חוּץ לַתְּחוּם שֶׁל יְרוּשָׁלַיִם[מד] הָיוּ צְרִיכִין לַעֲשׂוֹת שְׁנֵי יָמִים רֹאשׁ הַשָּׁנָה בְּכָל שָׁנָה וְשָׁנָה, דְּשֶׁמָּא יָבוֹאוּ עֵדִים אַחַר הַמִּנְחָה וְנִמְצָא שֶׁשְּׁנֵי הַיָּמִים הֵן קֹדֶשׁ[מה] וּכְיוֹם אֶחָד הֵן חֲשׁוּבִים, שֶׁהֲרֵי קְדֻשָּׁה אַחַת עֲלֵיהֶם, דְּהַיְנוּ קְדֻשַּׁת רֹאשׁ הַשָּׁנָה, וְאַחַר יוֹם טוֹב כְּשֶׁהָיוּ הַשְּׁלוּחִים יוֹצְאִין וְהָיוּ מוֹדִיעִים לְכָל בְּנֵי אֶרֶץ יִשְׂרָאֵל יוֹם שֶׁהֻקְבַּע בּוֹ הַחֹדֶשׁ,[28] וְהָיוּ הַכֹּל מוֹנִין מִמֶּנּוּ לְיוֹם הַכִּפּוּרִים וּלְסֻכּוֹת.

וְכָךְ הָיָה הַדָּבָר נוֹהֵג תָּמִיד עַד שֶׁבָּטְלוּ סַנְהֶדְרִין וּבָטַל קִדּוּשׁ הַחֹדֶשׁ עַל פִּי הָרְאִיָּה וְהִתְחִילוּ לִקְבֹּעַ הֶחֳדָשִׁים עַל פִּי הַחֶשְׁבּוֹן, וּלְפִיכָךְ הַכֹּל מוֹנִין מִיּוֹם רִאשׁוֹן שֶׁל רֹאשׁ הַשָּׁנָה לְיוֹם הַכִּפּוּרִים וּלְסֻכּוֹת, לְפִי שֶׁעַל פִּי הַחֶשְׁבּוֹן

[and it was not observed as such only because] license was given to the Court to postpone [the observance of the festival].

On the following day, Rosh HaShanah was observed as a festival according to Scriptural Law. These two days represent one continuum of holiness and are like one long day. They are both referred to as the festival of Rosh HaShanah, the first day being of Rabbinic origin and the second, of Scriptural origin.[27]

The communities beyond the *[Shabbos]* limits of Jerusalem would have to observe Rosh HaShanah for two days every year, lest the witnesses come after *Minchah.* Both days would then be holy and would be considered as one [long] day, for a single holiness rests upon them, the holiness of Rosh HaShanah. After the festival, the messengers would depart and would notify all the people of *Eretz Yisrael* which day had been sanctified as the first day of the month.[28] Everyone would then calculate the dates for Yom Kippur and Sukkos from that day.

This was the procedure that was constantly followed until the *Sanhedrin* ceased to function, the practice of sanctifying the first day of the new month according to the sighting [of the new moon] was discontinued, and [the beginnings of] the months were thenceforth established on the basis of a fixed calendar. [Once that calendar was established,] everyone calculates the dates for Yom Kippur and Sukkos from the first day of Rosh HaShanah, because according to [the fixed calendar], Elul

27. This is the opposite of the present custom. At that time, in the above-described scenario, the [end of the] first day was observed as a festival as a token of respect, and the second day was the day declared Rosh HaShanah by the Court. At present, the first day of Rosh HaShanah is the day that must be observed according to Scriptural Law, as the Alter Rebbe proceeds to explain.

28. I.e., whether the thirtieth day after Rosh Chodesh Elul, or the thirty-first day, had been declared as Rosh HaShanah.

מא לבוש שם. מב ראה רש"י שם ושם. לבוש שם. מג לבוש שם. מד כדלעיל סוף ס"א וש"נ. מה רש"י ביצה שם. לבוש שם. מו רמב"ם שם פ"ח ה"ה.

אֱלוּל לְעוֹלָם חָסֵר,[מו,29] וְאַף עַל פִּי כֵן צְרִיכִין הֵן לְקַיֵּם מִנְהַג אֲבוֹתֵיהֶם[מז] שֶׁהָיוּ בִּזְמַן קִדּוּשׁ הַחֹדֶשׁ עַל פִּי הָרְאִיָּה, וְהָיוּ עוֹשִׂין שְׁנֵי יָמִים טוֹבִים שֶׁל רֹאשׁ הַשָּׁנָה אַף בְּאֶרֶץ יִשְׂרָאֵל, וְהָיוּ עוֹשִׂין אוֹתוֹ כְּיוֹם אֶחָד אָרֹךְ, וּקְדֻשָּׁה אַחַת עֲלֵיהֶן, וּבֵיצָה שֶׁנּוֹלְדָה בָּזֶה אֲסוּרָה בָּזֶה מִטַּעַם שֶׁנִּתְבָּאֵר שֶׁמָּא בָּאוּ עֵדִים אַחַר הַמִּנְחָה,[מח] לְפִיכָךְ אַף שֶׁאֵין טַעַם זֶה שַׁיָּךְ לִזְמַן שֶׁקּוֹבְעִין חֳדָשִׁים עַל פִּי הַחֶשְׁבּוֹן וּלְעוֹלָם יוֹם רִאשׁוֹן הוּא עִקָּר וְהוּא יוֹם טוֹב שֶׁל תּוֹרָה,[מט] מִכָּל מָקוֹם אֵין לְזַלְזֵל בְּיוֹם שֵׁנִי וּלְהָקֵל בּוֹ מַה שֶּׁלֹּא הָיוּ מְקִלִּין בּוֹ אֲבוֹתֵינוּ:[נ]

is always a short month.[29] Nevertheless, everyone must maintain the custom of [our] forefathers who lived in the era when the first day of the month was sanctified according to the sighting [of the new moon] and, even in *Eretz Yisrael*, observed Rosh HaShanah as a two-day festival — as one long day and a single continuum of holiness. Thus, too, an egg laid on [the first day] may not be eaten on [the second], for the reason explained — lest the witnesses arrive after *Minchah*.

True, this rationale is not applicable in the [current] era, when the [calendar] is established according to [predetermined] calculations, so that the first day [of Rosh HaShanah] is always of primary importance and it is the festival mandated by Scriptural Law. Nevertheless, the second day may not be treated with disrespect, nor may it be modified with leniencies that our forefathers would not have taken.

ה אַף עַל פִּי שֶׁבְּכָל יוֹם טוֹב שֵׁנִי שֶׁל גָּלֻיּוֹת אוֹמְרִים זְמַן בְּקִדּוּשׁ,[נא] כֵּיוָן שֶׁעוֹשִׂין אוֹתוֹ מֵחֲמַת הַסָּפֵק שֶׁהָיָה לַאֲבוֹתֵינוּ (בִּזְמַן שֶׁהָיוּ מְקַדְּשִׁין עַל פִּי הָרְאִיָּה) שֶׁמָּא הַיּוֹם קֹדֶשׁ וְאֶתְמוֹל חֹל אִם כֵּן לֹא נִפְטַר בִּזְמַן שֶׁל אֶתְמוֹל,[נב] אֲבָל בְּלֵיל שֵׁנִי שֶׁל רֹאשׁ הַשָּׁנָה יֵשׁ אוֹמְרִים[נג] שֶׁאֵין אוֹמְרִים זְמַן,

5 On every festival, on the second day [observed only in] the Diaspora, the blessing *Shehecheyanu* is recited in the course of *Kiddush*, because of the uncertainty that our forefathers had (during the era in which the new month was sanctified according to the sighting [of the moon]). [Their uncertainty was that perhaps it was the second] day that was holy and the previous day an ordinary weekday, in which instance they would not have fulfilled their obligation by reciting *Shehecheyanu* the previous night.

As to the second night of Rosh HaShanah, by contrast, some authorities maintain that *Shehecheyanu* should not be recited. [They argue

29. I.e., comprising 29 days. Though we observe two days of Rosh HaShanah, they are not like the two days of Rosh Chodesh of certain other months. There, the first day of Rosh Chodesh is the last (i.e., thirtieth) day of the past month, and the second day of Rosh Chodesh is the first day of the new month. By contrast, the first of the two days of Rosh HaShanah is the first day of Tishrei.

טור סי׳ תכח. **מז** רמב״ם פ״ה ה״ח (אפילו בירושלים). רא״ש ביצה פ״ד סי׳ א לדעת הרי״ף שם (ג, א). מ״א ס״ק א (אפילו במקום הב״ד). ובזה מסיים מה שהתחיל לעיל ריש ס״א (שאף בני א״י עושין ב׳ ימים ר״ה, לפי כו׳). **מח** רא״ש שם. **מט** ראה רמב״ם שם פ״ה ה״ז. לבוש שם. **נ** ראה ר״ן ביצה (ט, רע״ב). **נא** כדלעיל סי׳ תצ ס״א וש״נ. **נב** רבותיו של רש״י (מחזור ויטרי סי׳ שכ), הובא ברא״ש פ״ד סי׳ יד (מ, א). מרדכי סוכה רמז תשסה. וכדלעיל סי׳ תצ ס״א. **נג** הגאונים, ורבותיו של רש״י שם, הובאו ברא״ש שם, ובהגהות מיימוניות הל׳ שבת פכ״ט הכ״ג אות ז, ובטור.

כֵּיוָן שֶׁשְּׁנֵי הַיָּמִים הֵן קְדֻשָּׁה אַחַת וּכְיוֹם אֶחָד הֵן חֲשׁוּבִין, אִם כֵּן נִפְטַר בִּזְמַן שֶׁל אֶתְמוֹל שֶׁהוּא תְּחִלַּת קְדֻשַּׁת הַיּוֹם, וְלָמָּה יַחֲזֹר לוֹמַר זְמַן בָּאֶמְצַע, וְכֵן בְּיוֹם שֵׁנִי עַל הַשּׁוֹפָר אֵין לוֹמַר זְמַן, שֶׁכְּבָר נִפְטַר בִּזְמַן שֶׁאָמַר אֶתְמוֹל עַל הַשּׁוֹפָר.[נד]

אֲבָל יֵשׁ אוֹמְרִים[נה] שֶׁצָּרִיךְ לוֹמַר זְמַן בֵּין בְּקִדּוּשׁ לֵיל שֵׁנִי בֵּין עַל הַשּׁוֹפָר, מִשּׁוּם שֶׁמַּה שֶּׁהֵן נֶחְשָׁבִין כְּיוֹם אֶחָד אָרֹךְ אֵינוֹ אֶלָּא מֵחֲמַת מִנְהַג אֲבוֹתֵינוּ שֶׁהָיוּ בִּזְמַן קִדּוּשׁ הַחֹדֶשׁ עַל פִּי הָרְאִיָּה וְהָיוּ חוֹשְׁשִׁין שֶׁמָּא בָּאוּ עֵדִים אַחַר הַמִּנְחָה וְנִמְצָא שֶׁשְּׁנֵי הַיָּמִים הֵן יוֹם טוֹב אֶחָד וּקְדֻשָּׁה אַחַת עֲלֵיהֶם, וְכֵיוָן שֶׁאֲבוֹתֵינוּ הָיוּ מְבָרְכִין זְמַן בְּיוֹם שֵׁנִי אַף שֶׁהָיוּ עוֹשִׂין אוֹתָן קְדֻשָּׁה אַחַת וּכְיוֹם אֶחָד, שֶׁהֲרֵי אִם בָּאוּ עֵדִים אַחַר הַמִּנְחָה עִקַּר הַיּוֹם טוֹב שֶׁל תּוֹרָה הוּא לְמָחָר וְיוֹם רִאשׁוֹן אֵינוֹ אֶלָּא מִדִּבְרֵי סוֹפְרִים וּכְחֹל הוּא חָשׁוּב לְגַבֵּי יוֹם שֵׁנִי שֶׁבּוֹ הֻקְבַּע הַחֹדֶשׁ,[נו] לְפִיכָךְ גַּם לָנוּ יֵשׁ לְבָרֵךְ זְמַן בְּלֵיל שֵׁנִי (אַף בְּאֶרֶץ יִשְׂרָאֵל) כְּמוֹ שֶׁמְּבָרְכִין בְּכָל יוֹם טוֹב שֵׁנִי שֶׁל גָּלֻיּוֹת כְּדֵי שֶׁלֹּא לְשַׁנּוֹת מִמִּנְהַג אֲבוֹתֵינוּ:

that] since the two days are a single continuum of holiness and are considered as one [long] day, the obligation was fulfilled by the *Shehecheyanu* that was recited the previous night, when the holiness of the [present] day began. If so, why should the blessing *Shehecheyanu* be recited again in the midst [of this continuum]?

Similarly, with regard to the sounding of the *shofar* on the second day, [these authorities maintain that] the blessing *Shehecheyanu* should not be recited, because [the obligation to recite it] was already filled when this blessing was recited [for the sounding of the *shofar*] on the previous day.

By contrast, other authorities hold that the blessing *Shehecheyanu* should be recited both in the course of *Kiddush* on the second night and before [the sounding of] the *shofar* on the second day. [These authorities argue that the fact that the two days] are considered as one long day is only because of the custom of our forefathers. In the days that Rosh Chodesh was sanctified [when the moon] was sighted, they were concerned that witnesses might have arrived at the Court after *Minchah* and thus the two days would be considered as one festival and one continuum of holiness. [Nevertheless, in such an instance] our forefathers would recite the blessing *Shehecheyanu* on the second day, even though they would observe [the two days] as one continuum of holiness and as one day. For if the witnesses came after *Minchah,* the following day would be the fundamental holiday according to Scriptural Law, and the first day would only be a Rabbinic institution and would be considered as an ordinary weekday when compared to the second day which had been determined as [the beginning of] the month. [These authorities conclude that] we, too, should therefore recite the blessing *Shehecheyanu* on the second night [of Rosh HaShanah] (even in *Eretz Yisrael*), just as it is recited on the other festive second days [observed in] the Diaspora, in order not to deviate from the custom of our forefathers.

נד ראה לקו"ש חל"ז ע' 17 בהערה. נה רש"י בתשובה שם, ורשב"ם, הובאו ברא"ש והגהות מיימוניות שם. טור ושו"ע ס"ב. נו כדלעיל ס"ד. נז שו"ע

ו וַהֲלָכָה כַּסְּבָרָא הָאַחֲרוֹנָה.[נז] מִכָּל מָקוֹם, לְכַתְּחִלָּה טוֹב שֶׁיּוֹצִיא אָדָם אֶת עַצְמוֹ מִידֵי סְפֵק בְּרָכָה,[נח] וְיִלְבַּשׁ מַלְבּוּשׁ חָדָשׁ[נט] בְּעִנְיָן שֶׁצָּרִיךְ לְבָרֵךְ עָלָיו שֶׁהֶחֱיָנוּ בִּשְׁעַת הַלְּבִישָׁה[ס] כְּמוֹ שֶׁנִּתְבָּאֵר בְּסִימָן רכ"ג,[סא, 30] אוֹ יִקַּח פְּרִי חָדָשׁ[31] וְיַנִּיחֶנּוּ לְפָנָיו בְּעֵת הַקִּדּוּשׁ,[סב] וִיבָרֵךְ "שֶׁהֶחֱיָנוּ" וִיהֵא דַּעְתּוֹ גַּם עַל הַמַּלְבּוּשׁ אוֹ עַל הַפְּרִי.[סג] וְאִם יֵשׁ לוֹ תִּירוֹשׁ חָדָשׁ[32] – לֹא יְקַדֵּשׁ עָלָיו כְּדֵי לְבָרֵךְ עָלָיו "שֶׁהֶחֱיָנוּ",[33] דְּמִצְוָה מִן הַמֻּבְחָר לְקַדֵּשׁ עַל יַיִן יָשָׁן[34] כְּמוֹ שֶׁנִּתְבָּאֵר בְּסִימָן רע"ב,[סד] אֶלָּא יְקַדֵּשׁ עַל הַיָּשָׁן וְיַנִּיחַ הַתִּירוֹשׁ לְפָנָיו,[סה] וּכְשֶׁיַּגִּיעַ לְ"שֶׁהֶחֱיָנוּ" יִקַּח הַכּוֹס שֶׁל

6 The *halachah* follows the second opinion. Nevertheless, as an initial and preferred option, it is desirable that one distance himself from [any possibility of] reciting a blessing that may be [unnecessary], by putting on a new garment over which he is required [at that time] to recite the blessing *Shehecheyanu,* as stated in sec. 223.[30] Alternatively, he should take a new fruit[31] and place it before him while [reciting] the *Kiddush* and recite the blessing *Shehecheyanu,* while also keeping in mind the garment or the fruit.

If one has freshly-made grape juice,[32] he should not use it for *Kiddush* in order that the blessing *Shehecheyanu* should [also] relate to it[33] — because, as stated in sec. 272[:2], the most preferable way to perform the *mitzvah* of *Kiddush* is to recite it over aged wine.[34] Instead, he should recite *Kiddush* over the aged wine, while [a cup of the fresh] grape juice is placed before him. When he reaches the blessing *Shehecheyanu* he should raise the cup of

---

30. That section is not extant in the Alter Rebbe's *Shulchan Aruch.* In his *Seder Birkas HaNehenin* (sec. 12:4), the Alter Rebbe writes that the blessing *Shehecheyanu* should be recited as soon as the new garment was purchased. If it was not recited immediately, it may be recited as long as the garment is being worn for the first time, but not at a later wearing. See also sec. 22.

31. I.e., a fruit of the new season that he has not yet tasted. He should look at it while reciting the blessing *Shehecheyanu* (*Piskei HaSiddur*), then drink the wine of *Kiddush.* He should next recite the blessing *borei pri ha'etz* and partake of the new fruit. Only then should he wash his hands and recite the blessing *al netilas yadayim,* in preparation for the blessing *HaMotzi* over the *challah* (*Sefer HaMinhagim: The Book of Chabad-Lubavitch Customs,* p. 118).

The new fruit customarily chosen by the Lubavitcher Rebbes was one of the species with which the Land of Israel was blessed. An amount was eaten that would warrant a *berachah mei'ein shalosh* (*Siddur Tehillat HaShem* Annotated Edition, p. 96), though the wine that had been drunk for *Kiddush* was not included in this blessing. Only then did they wash hands in preparation for *HaMotzi* (see *Otzar Minhagei Chabad: Elul-Tishrei,* p. 82).

32. This does not apply to factory-bottled grape juice, which may date from an earlier season. See *Seder Birkas HaNehenin* 11:15.

33. As an alternative to a fruit of the new season.

34. In contemporary terms: It is better to recite *Kiddush* over wine (or at least a mixture of wine and grape juice) than over grape juice.

שם. **נח** מהר"ם מרוטנבורג בתשב"ץ סי' קכ. הובא ברא"ש והגהות מיימוניות שם, ובטור. **נט** הגהות מיימוניות שם. רמ"א ס"ב. **ס** מ"א סק"א (כשקנה בגד שצריך לתפרו). **סא** סימן זה בשוע"ר לא הגיע לידינו, וראה שו"ע שם ס"ד. סדר ברה"נ פי"ב ה"ד. **סב** רא"ש שם. טור ושו"ע שם. **סג** רא"ש שם. טור ולבוש ס"ג. ובסידור: בליל שני של ר"ה נוהגין להניח פר"ח בפני המקדש ויתן עיניו בו ויאמר שהחיינו. וראה פסקי הסידור אות קעה. ומנהג חב"ד לאכול הפר"ח קודם נטילת ידים לסעודה (ספר המנהגים – חב"ד ע' 56), כדי לסמוך אכילת הפרי לברכת שהחיינו (אג"ק ח"ג ע' רט), ואוכלים כשיעור ומברכים עליו ברכה אחרונה ולא על יין הקידוש (אוצר מנהגי חב"ד ר"ה ע' פב). וראה שלחן המלך ח"ב ע' רה הערה 1. **סד** סעיף ב. **סה** תשב"ץ והגהות מיימוניות שם.

grape juice in his hand, or look at it, and recite that blessing. He should then drink from the cup of aged wine [and after it drink the grape juice].

If one does not have a new garment or a new fruit, he should nevertheless recite the blessing *Shehecheyanu,* for primacy is given to the latter view.[35]

תִּירוֹשׁ בְּיָדוֹ[סו] אוֹ יִתֵּן עֵינָיו בּוֹ[סז] וִיבָרֵךְ "שֶׁהֶחֱיָנוּ", וְיִשְׁתֶּה הַכּוֹס שֶׁל יַיִן יָשָׁן.[סח]

וְאִם אֵין לוֹ בֶּגֶד חָדָשׁ וּפְרִי חָדָשׁ – עִם כָּל זֶה יְבָרֵךְ "שֶׁהֶחֱיָנוּ",[סט] שֶׁהָעִקָּר כַּסְּבָרָא הָאַחֲרוֹנָה:[35]

7 The same applies to the sounding of the *shofar* on the second day [of Rosh HaShanah]. The preferred option is that the person sounding the *shofar* should put on a new garment, and wear it when reciting the blessing *Shehecheyanu.* (The Sephardic custom is not to recite the blessing *Shehecheyanu* [at all on the second day].[36])

If the first day [of Rosh HaShanah] fell on *Shabbos,* and [hence] the *shofar* was not sounded, there is no need to wear a new garment when sounding the *shofar* on the second day, for the blessing *Shehecheyanu* has not yet been recited on the *shofar* [this year].

ז וְכֵן בִּתְקִיעַת שׁוֹפָר שֶׁל יוֹם שֵׁנִי, לְכַתְּחִלָּה יִלְבַּשׁ הַתּוֹקֵעַ בֶּגֶד חָדָשׁ[ע] וְיִהְיֶה עָלָיו בִּשְׁעַת בִּרְכַּת "שֶׁהֶחֱיָנוּ" (וּמִנְהַג סְפָרַד שֶׁלֹּא לְבָרֵךְ "שֶׁהֶחֱיָנוּ"[עא,36]).

וְאִם חָל יוֹם רִאשׁוֹן בְּשַׁבָּת שֶׁלֹּא תָּקְעוּ בַּשּׁוֹפָר[עב] — אֵינוֹ צָרִיךְ לִלְבֹּשׁ בֶּגֶד חָדָשׁ בִּשְׁעַת תְּקִיעוֹת יוֹם שֵׁנִי, כֵּיוָן שֶׁלֹּא בֵּרֵךְ עֲדַיִן "שֶׁהֶחֱיָנוּ" עַל הַשּׁוֹפָר:

SECTION 601 Directives for the Second Day of Rosh HaShanah. (1–2)

סימן תרא סֵדֶר יוֹם שֵׁנִי שֶׁל רֹאשׁ הַשָּׁנָה וּבוֹ ב' סְעִיפִים:

1 On the second day [of Rosh HaShanah], the *Shacharis* and *Mussaf* prayers are recited as on the first day.[1] [The Torah Reading begins with] "…and G-d tested Avraham" until the end of the *parshah,*[2] in order to recall the Binding of Yitzchak.[3] The person called to the Torah as *maftir*[4] reads the same passage from the Torah[5] as on the

א בְּיוֹם שֵׁנִי מִתְפַּלְּלִים שַׁחֲרִית וּמוּסָף כְּמוֹ בְּיוֹם רִאשׁוֹן.[א,1]

וְקוֹרִין מִ"וְהָאֱלֹהִים נִסָּה אֶת אַבְרָהָם"[ב] עַד סוֹף הַסֵּדֶר,[ג,2] כְּדֵי לְהַזְכִּיר עֲקֵדַת יִצְחָק,[ד,3] וּמַפְטִיר[4] קוֹרֵא

---

35. I.e., the latter of the two views presented in subsection 5 above.

36. Unless the first day falls on *Shabbos.*

SECTION 601

1. Except for some differences in the choice of liturgical hymns *(piyyutim)* recited in the repetition of the *Shemoneh Esreh* on these two days.

2. *Bereishis* 22:1-24.

3. I.e., in order that its lasting merit should stand us in good stead on the Day of Judgment *(Rashi* on *Megillah* 31a, *s.v. Maftirin).*

4. In the Hebrew text, the word *maftir* appears twice: first as a noun (signifying the person called to the Torah Reading in addition to the statutory number

סו מנהגים (טירנא) ר"ה (ע' קא). הובא בדרכי משה ס"ק א. מ"א סק"א. סז מ"א שם בשם מטה משה סי' תתכג. סח מנהגים שם (ושם: ומן התירוש). סט האגור סי' תתקכא. שו"ע ורמ"א שם. ע מ"א סק"ג. עא ב"י סוד"ה ולענין. משמעות שו"ע ס"ג. עב טור ושו"ע ס"ג.

סימן תרא: א טור ורמ"א ס"א. ב בראשית כב, א. טור ושו"ע שם. ג טור ושו"ע שם. ד רש"י שם ד"ה מפטירין. לבוש ס"א. ה טור ושו"ע

previous day.[6] Then, for the *haftorah,* he reads from the Book of *Yirmeyahu:* "Thus said G-d..." until [and including] "[Ephraim,] My cherished son."[7] [This passage is chosen] because [among] the obligations of this day is the arousal of [positive] remembrances, and that passage includes the words, "I remember him more and more, therefore My inward parts are moved for him...."

בַּתּוֹרָה[ה] כְּמוֹ אֶתְמוֹל,[ה,6] וּמַפְטִיר בְּיִרְמְיָה[ו] "כֹּה אָמַר וגו' עַד הֲבֵן יַקִּיר וגו'",[7] מִפְּנֵי שֶׁחוֹבַת הַיּוֹם לְהַזְכִּיר זִכְרוֹנוֹת[ז] וּבְאוֹתוֹ עִנְיָן נֶאֱמַר[ח] "זָכֹר אֶזְכְּרֶנּוּ עוֹד עַל כֵּן הָמוּ מֵעַי וגו'":

2 At the conclusion of Rosh HaShanah, *Havdalah* is recited both in the *Shemoneh Esreh* and [later] over a cup of wine, as is done on *Motzaei Shabbos.* As at the conclusion of other festivals, no blessing is made over spices or over fire, as explained in sec. 491[:1]; see that source.[8]

ב וּבְמוֹצָאֵי רֹאשׁ הַשָּׁנָה מַבְדִּילִין[ט] בֵּין בַּתְּפִלָּה בֵּין עַל הַכּוֹס[י] כְּמוֹ בְּמוֹצָאֵי שַׁבָּת, אֶלָּא שֶׁאֵין מְבָרְכִין עַל הַבְּשָׂמִים וְעַל הָאֵשׁ[יא] כְּמוֹ בִּשְׁאָר מוֹצָאֵי יוֹם טוֹב, כְּמוֹ שֶׁנִּתְבָּאֵר בְּסִימָן תצ"א[יב] עַיֵּן שָׁם:[8]

SECTION 602 Directives for the Ten Days of *Teshuvah.*[1] (1–5)

סימן תרב סֵדֶר עֲשֶׂרֶת יְמֵי תְּשׁוּבָה[1] וּבוֹ ה' סְעִיפִים:

1 The day following Rosh HaShanah is a fastday. This is a public fast, as stated in sec. 549, and all the laws governing it are explained in sec. 550;[2] see the details there.[3]

א מִתְעַנִּין לְמָחֳרַת רֹאשׁ הַשָּׁנָה וְהוּא תַּעֲנִית צִבּוּר[א] כְּמוֹ שֶׁנִּתְבָּאֵר בְּסִימָן תקמ"ט;[ב] וְכָל הִלְכוֹתָיו נִתְבָּאֵר בְּסִימָן תק"נ[ג,2] עַיֵּן שָׁם:[3]

of congregants who are given this honor on a *Shabbos* or other festive occasion), and then as a verb (referring to the reading of the *haftorah,* which is the appended passage from the Prophets).

5. See sec. 584, footnote 14 above.

6. *Bamidbar* 29:1-6.

7. *Yirmeyahu* 31:1-19.

8. There the Alter Rebbe explains that we do not recite the blessing over fire, because on festivals — in contrast to *Shabbos* and Yom Kippur — it is not forbidden to make use of fire. Similarly, the custom of smelling spices was instituted to revive one after the departure of the additional soul *(neshamah yeseirah)* that he is granted on *Shabbos,* but not on Rosh HaShanah or on other festivals.

SECTION 602

1. In the original, the above-mentioned ten days are called *Aseres Yemei Teshuvah.*

2. These two sections are not extant in the Alter Rebbe's *Shulchan Aruch.* See the corresponding sections in the *Shulchan Aruch* of R. Yosef Caro.

3. This fast, the Fast of Gedaliah, commemorates the assassination of Gedaliah ben Achikam, the Jewish governor appointed in *Eretz Yisrael* by the Babylonians after the destruction of the First *Beis HaMikdash.* His assassination extinguished the last embers of Jewish independence. See *Yirmeyahu,* ch. 41.

שם. וכדלעיל סי' תקפד ס"ז. **ו** לא א־יט. גמרא שם. טור ושו"ע שם. **ז** רש"י שם ד"ה הבן. ר"ן שם (י, ב) ד"ה גמ'. ב"י ד"ה ומ"ש וקורין. לבוש ס"א. **ח** ירמיה לא, יט. **ט** טור ושו"ע ס"א. **י** ב"י סוף הסי'. לבוש ס"א. **יא** טור ושו"ע שם. **יב** סעיף א.

סימן תרב: א טור ורמ"א. **ב** סימן זה בשוע"ר לא הגיע לידינו, וראה טור ושו"ע שם ס"א (צום גדליה). **ג** סימן זה בשוע"ר לא הגיע לידינו, וראה טור ושו"ע שם סעי' א־ב.

ב וְכָל הַיָּמִים שֶׁבֵּין רֹאשׁ הַשָּׁנָה לְיוֹם הַכִּפּוּרִים מַרְבִּים בִּתְפִלָּה וְתַחֲנוּנִים:[ד] וְנוֹהֲגִים לוֹמַר "אָבִינוּ מַלְכֵּנוּ כו'" עֶרֶב[4] וּבֹקֶר,[ה] מִלְּבַד בְּשַׁבָּת,[ו] וְכֵן בְּעֶרֶב שַׁבָּת אַחַר מִנְחָה אֵין אוֹמְרִים אוֹתוֹ,[ז] כְּמוֹ שֶׁנִּתְבָּאֵר בְּסִימָן (תקצ"ב) [תקפ"ד[ח,5]]:

2 We increase our prayers and supplications during all the days between Rosh HaShanah and Yom Kippur. *Avinu Malkeinu* is customarily recited every evening[4] and morning, but not on *Shabbos*. Similarly, it is not added to the *Minchah* prayer on Friday, as stated in sec. [584:5].[5]

ג וְאוֹמְרִים בְּכָל יוֹם[ט] חוּץ מִשַּׁבָּת[י] ג' פְּעָמִים וִדּוּי קֹדֶם עֲלוֹת הַשַּׁחַר, מִלְּבַד בְּעֶרֶב יוֹם הַכִּפּוּרִים שֶׁאֵין אוֹמְרִים אוֹתוֹ אֶלָּא פַּעַם אַחַת:[יא,6]

3 Every day [between Rosh HaShanah and Yom Kippur], apart from *Shabbos*, the confessional prayer *(Vidui)* is recited three times before dawn, except on the day before Yom Kippur, when it is recited only once.[6]

ד אִם אֵרַע מִילָה בֵּין רֹאשׁ הַשָּׁנָה לְיוֹם הַכִּפּוּרִים אֵין אוֹמְרִים תַּחֲנוּן[יב] וְלֹא "וְהוּא רַחוּם כו'",[יג] אֲבָל אוֹמְרִים "אָבִינוּ מַלְכֵּנוּ"[יד] (וְ"אֵל אֶרֶךְ אַפַּיִם"[טו] וְ"לַמְנַצֵּחַ"[טז,7]):[8]

4 If a circumcision is performed between Rosh HaShanah and Yom Kippur, neither the *Tachanun* prayers nor the passage beginning *VeHu Rachum* are recited [in the course of that day's Morning Service]. *Avinu Malkeinu*, however, is recited (and so, too,[7] the passage beginning *E-l Erech Apayim* and the psalm beginning *LaMenatzeiach*).[8]

---

4. I.e., in the *Minchah* prayer.

5. The reference to sec. 592 in early editions of this work was evidently a printing error.

6. The penitential prayers of *Selichos* are universally recited on a number of mornings before Rosh HaShanah. Here, however, the Alter Rebbe is speaking of the similar custom of continuing to recite such prayers during the Ten Days of *Teshuvah*. Lubavitch custom is to recite them only on the Fast of Gedaliah (after *Shemoneh Esreh*), and only because that day is a communal fastday, not because it is one of the Ten Days of *Teshuvah* — though the *Selichos* of that day do reflect the theme of *teshuvah*.

In contrast to the above text ("three times"), the *AriZal* taught that the confessional prayer should not be recited more than once in the course of any prayer service. (See *Sefer HaMinhagim: The Book of Chabad-Lubavitch Customs,* p. 115, footnote 410.)

7. The parentheses, here and throughout, are part of the original text. In a letter that appears in *Igros Kodesh,* Vol. 2, p. 140, the Rebbe writes that parentheses in this work possibly indicate a matter that the Alter Rebbe desired to reconsider at a later date. (Cf. *She'eris Yehudah,* Responsum 363, and *Shaar HaKollel* 1:2.) *Kuntreis HaShulchan* enumerates many other possible functions of parentheses in this work.

8. Based on *Piskei HaSiddur,* Lubavitch practice follows the Sephardic custom, according to which *E-l Erech Apayim* and *LaMenatzeiach* are not recited on the days on which *Tachanun* is not recited.

On Tishrei 6, 5735, the Rebbe led the communal services. There was a *bris* scheduled after *Shacharis,* and accordingly, he did not recite either *Tachanun* or *Avinu Malkeinu.* At the *farbrengen* that night, he explained that the

ד טור ושו"ע. וראה גם רמב"ם הל' תשובה פ"ג סוף ה"ד. ומנהג חב"ד שלא לומר סליחות בעשי"ת מלבד בצום גדליה (ספר המנהגים – חב"ד ע' 58). ה טור ורמ"א. ו ר"ן ר"ה (ט, א) ד"ה גמ' (בר"ה). שו"ת הריב"ש סי' תקיב. מנהגים (קלויזנר) סי' לא (בעשי"ת). (טירנא) עשי"ת (ע' קד). רמ"א. ז מנהגים (קלויזנר) שם. מהרי"ל הל' עשי"ת (ע' דש). דרכי משה ס"ק א. מ"א סי' תרד ס"ק ב. ח סעיף ה (ר"ה) וש"נ. ט ב"י בשם הרוקח סי' רו. רמ"א. ובסידור לא הובא. י ראה טור. לעיל סי' רפח ס"ח. שער הכולל פל"ו אות ב ואות ח. יא ב"י בשם הרוקח סוס"י ריג ורס"י ריד. רמ"א. יב מנהגים (טירנא) עשי"ת (ע' קד). רמ"א. וכדלעיל סי' קלא ס"ו. יג מנהגים שם. לבוש ס"ב. יד דרכי משה ס"ק א בשם הגהות מנהגים ישנים (שינויי נוסחאות שם ציון 30). רמ"א. וראה

ה אֵין נוֹתְנִים חֵרֶם בֵּין רֹאשׁ הַשָּׁנָה לְיוֹם הַכִּפּוּרִים,[יז] שֶׁלֹּא לְעוֹרֵר כֹּחוֹת הַדִּין בַּזְּמַן הַהוּא.[יח] וְכֵן אֵין מַשְׁבִּיעִין אָדָם בְּבֵית דִּין בַּיָּמִים הָאֵלּוּ,[יט] שֶׁלֹּא לְהָבִיא עֹנֶשׁ שְׁבוּעָה לָעוֹלָם חַס וְשָׁלוֹם.[כ,9] אֲבָל לַעֲשׂוֹת דִּין בֵּין אָדָם לַחֲבֵרוֹ – בְּוַדַּאי מִצְוָה רַבָּה יֵשׁ לָדוּן וּלְהוֹצִיא הַגְּזֵלָה מִתַּחַת יָדוֹ,[כא] שֶׁכְּשֶׁיֵּשׁ דִּין לְמַטָּה – אֵין דִּין לְמַעְלָה.[כב,10] וְאִם יֵשׁ עֵסֶק שְׁבוּעָה בֵּינֵיהֶם – יַנִּיחוּהוּ עַד לְאַחַר יוֹם הַכִּפּוּרִים:[כג]

5 No ban of excommunication *(cherem)* should be declared between Rosh HaShanah and Yom Kippur, in order that the [Divine] attribute of judgment should not be aroused during this time.

Similarly, the Court does not administer an oath during this time, in order that the [severe] punishment associated with [taking an] oath should not be brought into the world, Heaven forbid.[9] By contrast, it is certainly a great *mitzvah* to adjudicate interpersonal cases of law: one should execute judgment and [for example] remove a stolen article from a person's possession — for "if judgment is performed [on this earthly plane] below, there is no judgment Above."[10] If an oath is necessitated, it should be postponed until after Yom Kippur.

סימן תרג וּבוֹ סָעִיף אֶחָד:

SECTION 603 [Additional Stringencies to be Observed During the Ten Days of *Teshuvah*.] (1)

א אַף מִי שֶׁאֵינוֹ נִזְהָר בְּכָל הַשָּׁנָה מִפַּת שֶׁל פַּלְטֵר גּוֹי (עַיֵּן בְּיוֹרֶה דֵעָה סִימָן קי"ב[א,1]), מִכָּל מָקוֹם בַּעֲשֶׂרֶת יְמֵי תְּשׁוּבָה יֵשׁ לוֹ לִזָּהֵר מִמֶּנּוּ.[ב] וְאִם אֵינוֹ יָכוֹל לֶאֱפוֹת בְּעַצְמוֹ – יַכְשִׁיר[2] אֶת הַתַּנּוּר שֶׁאוֹפִין בּוֹ גּוֹיִם,

1 Even a person who throughout the year does not make a point of observing [the restriction against eating] bread baked by a non-Jewish baker (see *Yoreh Deah,* sec. 112[:2])[1] should nevertheless observe this restriction during the Ten Days of *Teshuvah*.

If one cannot bake [his bread] personally, he should *kasher*[2] the oven in which the non-Jews bake

---

two prayers are governed by the same laws. (See the *sichah* delivered by the Rebbe on 6 Tishrei, 5735/1974.)

9. On the retribution aroused by the taking of oaths, even if truthful, see sec. 156:2.

10. *Midrash Tanchuma, Parshas Mishpatim,* sec. 5.

SECTION 603

1. This section of the Alter Rebbe's *Shulchan Aruch* is not extant. See the *Shulchan Aruch* of R. Yosef Caro.

2. The verb "to *kasher*" literally means "to make fit." The intent here is not that simply adding a sliver to the fuel makes the oven kosher in the usual sense, for if the oven was not kosher, the bread could not be eaten at all. Rather, by adding to the wood the Jew is considered to have taken part in baking the bread. Hence it

שיחות קדש ו' תשרי תשל"ה (שלא לומר גם אבינו מלכנו). אוצר מנהגי חב"ד תשרי ע' קסו אות ל. טו וכ"ה בסידור (בסיום תפלת שחרית) לפני אל ארך אפים (שאין אומרים בר"ח וחנוכה ופורים קטן וגדול ב' ימים וערב פסח וט' באב) וש"נ. אבל ראה שיחות קדש שם. אוצר מנהגי חב"ד שם. מנהגי מלך ע' 30. טז מנהגים (טירנא) שם. דרכי משה שם. וראה גם לעיל סי' תכט סי"ב. אבל ראה בסידור שם (לפני למנצח): מנהג ספרד שבכל יום שאין אומרים בו תחנון ונפילת אפים אין אומרים למנצח יענך ולא תפלה לדוד. יז מהרי"ל הל' עשי"ת (ע' דש). רמ"א. וראה גם לעיל סי' תכט סי"ד. יח לבוש סי' תרג. ט"ז. יט מהרי"ל שם. רמ"א. כ ט"ז. כא אחרונים. לבוש סי' תרג. מ"א סק"א. ט"ז. כב מדרש תנחומא משפטים סי' ה. לבוש שם. ט"ז. כג לבוש שם.

סימן תרג: א סימן זה בשוע"ר לא הגיע לידינו, וראה שו"ע ורמ"א שם ס"ב. וראה גם לעיל סי' רמב סי"ג. סי' שכה ס"ו, וש"נ. ב רא"ש פ"ס סוס"י יד. טור ושו"ע.

שֶׁיַּשְׁלִיךְ יִשְׂרָאֵל בְּתוֹךְ הַתַּנּוּר קֵיסָם אֶחָד[ג] כְּמוֹ שֶׁיִּתְבָּאֵר בְּיוֹרֶה דֵעָה סִימָן קי"ב.[ד] מִכָּל מָקוֹם, מִי שֶׁהוֹלֵךְ בַּדֶּרֶךְ אִם אֵין לְפָנָיו פַּת שֶׁל יִשְׂרָאֵל עַד יוֹתֵר מֵאַרְבַּע מִילִין[3] מִמָּקוֹם שֶׁהוּא עוֹמֵד בּוֹ וְרוֹצֶה לֶאֱכֹל – מֻתָּר לוֹ לֶאֱכֹל פַּת שֶׁל פַּלְטֵר גּוֹי אֲפִלּוּ בַּעֲשֶׂרֶת יְמֵי תְשׁוּבָה כְּמוֹ שֶׁמֻּתָּר בִּשְׁאָר יְמוֹת הַשָּׁנָה[ה] כְּמוֹ שֶׁיִּתְבָּאֵר בְּיוֹרֶה דֵעָה שָׁם:[ו]

וְיֵשׁ לְכָל אָדָם לְחַפֵּשׂ וּלְמַשְׁמֵשׁ[ז] בְּמַעֲשָׂיו וְלָשׁוּב מֵהֶם בַּעֲשֶׂרֶת יְמֵי תְשׁוּבָה,[ח] וּסְפֵק עֲבֵרָה צְרִיכָה יוֹתֵר תְּשׁוּבָה מֵעֲבֵרָה וַדָּאִית, כִּי עַל עֲבֵרָה וַדָּאִית אָדָם מִתְחָרֵט בְּכָל לִבּוֹ, אֲבָל סְפֵק עֲבֵרָה הוּא מִתְבָּרֵךְ בִּלְבָבוֹ לוֹמַר שֶׁמָּא לֹא עָשִׂיתִי עֲבֵרָה וְאֵינוֹ מִתְחָרֵט עָלֶיהָ חֲרָטָה גְּמוּרָה[ט] וַהֲרֵי נִשְׁאָר עֹנֶשׁ הָעֲבֵרָה עָלָיו,[י] וּלְכָךְ הָיָה צָרִיךְ קָרְבַּן אָשָׁם[4] תָּלוּי הַבָּא עַל הַסָּפֵק לִהְיוֹת יוֹתֵר בְּיֹקֶר מִקָּרְבַּן חַטָּאת[5] הַבָּא עַל הַוַּדַּאי:[יא]

by throwing a sliver of wood into it, as stated in *Yoreh Deah,* sec. 112[:9].

Nevertheless, one who is traveling on a journey [may take certain leniencies]. If there is no bread that was baked by Jews within four *mil*[3] from his present location and he wishes to eat, he may eat bread baked by a non-Jewish baker even during the Ten Days of *Teshuvah,* just as this is permitted during the remainder of the year, as stated in *Yoreh Deah, loc. cit.*

Every individual should scrutinize and examine his actions and repent for his [conduct] during the Ten Days of *Teshuvah.* [When one is] in doubt [as to whether or not he committed] a particular sin, more serious *teshuvah* is required than when he knows for certain that he sinned. [The rationale is that] when one is certain that he sinned, he regrets [his conduct] with all his heart. When, however, he is in doubt [as to whether he] sinned, he will soothe his heart and say, "Perhaps I did not sin." Hence, he will not regret his sin thoroughly and may thus remain liable for its punishment. For this reason, the sacrifice brought as a conditional guilt-offering[4] [to atone] for the possibility that one sinned had to be more costly than the sin-offering[5] brought [to atone] for a sin that one knows he committed.

---

is no longer considered as having been baked solely by non-Jews.

3. A *mil* is approximately a kilometer.

4. In the original, *korban asham talui.* (See *Vayikra* 5:17ff. and *Zevachim* 48a.)

5. In the original, *korban chatas.*

ג מנהגים (טירנא) עשי"ת (ע' קד). מ"א. לבוש. ד שו"ע ס"ט. ה מ"א. ו שו"ע סט"ז. ז ברמ"א ובלבוש: ולפשפש. וראה עירובין יג, ב. ח רמ"א. לבוש.
ט הרב רבנו יונה ברכות (א, ב) ד"ה והא. כל בו סי' סט (לד, א). רמ"א. י לבוש. יא רבנו יונה שם (מזבחים מח, א ומשנה כריתות כו, ב). רמ"א. לבוש.

הִלְכוֹת יוֹם הַכִּפּוּרִים
THE LAWS OF YOM KIPPUR

SECTION 604 [Conduct] on *Erev* Yom Kippur. (1–7)

1 [It is written,][1] "And you shall afflict your souls on the ninth of the month…." But is it on the ninth of the month that we fast?![2] In fact we fast only on the tenth! For so it is written: "On the tenth of the month you shall afflict your souls,"[3] and "from evening to evening [shall you observe your day of rest]."[4]

The intent of the [first] verse is: Prepare yourself on the ninth [of the month] for the affliction of the tenth. Eat and drink on the ninth, so that you will be able to fast on the tenth.[5]

It is out of G-d's love for the Jewish people that He commanded them to fast only one day in the year.[6] And this is for their good, to atone for their sins. [Moreover,] He commanded them to eat and drink first, so that the fast would not harm them.[7]

סימן תרד סֵדֶר עֶרֶב יוֹם כִּפּוּר וּבוֹ ז' סְעִיפִים:

א "וְעִנִּיתֶם אֶת נַפְשׁוֹתֵיכֶם בְּתִשְׁעָה לַחֹדֶשׁ וגו'",[א,1] וְכִי בְּתִשְׁעָה מִתְעַנִּין?[2] וַהֲלֹא אֵין מִתְעַנִּין אֶלָּא בָּעֲשִׂירִי,[ב] שֶׁנֶּאֱמַר[ג] "בֶּעָשׂוֹר לַחֹדֶשׁ תְּעַנּוּ אֶת נַפְשׁוֹתֵיכֶם",[3] וְנֶאֱמַר[ד] "מֵעֶרֶב עַד עֶרֶב וגו'",[4] אֶלָּא עִנְיַן הַכָּתוּב[ה] הָכִינוּ עַצְמְכֶם בַּתְּשִׁיעִי לְעִנּוּי הָעֲשִׂירִי,[ו] שֶׁתֹּאכְלוּ וְתִשְׁתּוּ בַּתְּשִׁיעִי כְּדֵי שֶׁתּוּכְלוּ לְהִתְעַנּוֹת בָּעֲשִׂירִי,[ז,5] וְהוּא מֵאַהֲבַת הַקָּדוֹשׁ בָּרוּךְ הוּא לְיִשְׂרָאֵל, שֶׁלֹּא צִוָּם לְהִתְעַנּוֹת אֶלָּא יוֹם אֶחָד בַּשָּׁנָה[6] וּלְטוֹבָתָם לְכַפֵּר עֲווֹנוֹתֵיהֶם, וְצִוָּם שֶׁיֹּאכְלוּ וְיִשְׁתּוּ תְּחִלָּה שֶׁלֹּא יַזִּיק לָהֶם הָעִנּוּי.[ח,7]

---

1. *Vayikra* 23:32. The Alter Rebbe's opening passage interpreting this verse is based on *Yoma* 81b, *et al.*, and is found in the *Tur* and *Turei Zahav* 604:1.

2. As explained in sec. 611:2, "afflicting one's soul" is primarily defined as fasting.

3. *Vayikra* 16:29.

4. *Op. cit.* 23:32; i.e., the fast should be observed for one day only *(Turei Zahav, loc. cit.)*.

5. In sec. 608:1 the Alter Rebbe offers another — though not contradictory — interpretation of this verse, which he explains is closer to its simple meaning. There he states that the above interpretation is merely a *smach* (or: *asmachta*), a Biblical allusion cited in support of a Rabbinic ordinance.

6. The other, commemorative fasts were instituted by the Sages, not by Divine fiat.

7. In light of the unique command to eat on the day preceding Yom Kippur, certain *tzadikkim* who habitually ate with only one hand made a point of using both hands on this day. Among them were the Alter Rebbe *(Beis Rebbe,* Hebrew ed., Vol. 1, p. 178*)*, and the Rebbe's father, R. Levi Yitzchak *(Likkutei Sichos,* Vol. 29, p. 319). The Rebbe Rashab did not follow this practice *(Sefer HaSichos 5691,* p. 147*)*.

א ויקרא כג, לב. ב גמרא פא, ב וש"נ. טור ולבוש ס"א. ט"ז ס"ק א. ג שם טז, כט. וראה מ"מ וציונים. ד שם כג, לב. ראה רש"י ר"ה ט, א ד"ה כל. ב"י ריש הסי'. לבוש ס"א. ט"ז סק"א. ה ראה רש"י ברכות שם ד"ה מעלה, ויומא שם ד"ה כל, ורא"ש יומא פ"ח סי' כב (קרא). לבוש ס"א (משמעותא דקרא). וראה לקמן סי' תרח ס"א (במוסגר): שמצות חכמים היא . . . ומצאו להם סמך מן התורה. ו דש"י ברכות שם. טור. ט"ז שם. ז רש"י יומא שם. רא"ש שם. ח רא"ש שם. טור ולבוש שם. וראה לקמן סי' תרח ס"א (להרבות באכילה ושתיה כשיעור ב' ימים). סידור (להרבות בסעודה). שער הכולל פמ"ד אות ג. אוצר מנהגי חב"ד יום הכיפורים ע' קצא.

וּמַה שֶּׁהוֹצִיא הַכָּתוּב אֶת הָאֲכִילָה בִּלְשׁוֹן עִנּוּי[ט] וְלֹא אָמַר בְּפֵרוּשׁ שֶׁיֹּאכְלוּ וְיִשְׁתּוּ בַּתְּשִׁיעִי,[י] לוֹמַר לְךָ שֶׁהָאוֹכֵל וְשׁוֹתֶה בַּתְּשִׁיעִי – מַעֲלֶה עָלָיו הַכָּתוּב כְּאִלּוּ הָיָה מִתְעַנֶּה בּוֹ[יא] מֵחֲמַת מִצְוַת הַקָּדוֹשׁ בָּרוּךְ הוּא שֶׁצִּוָּה לְהִתְעַנּוֹת בּוֹ,[יב] שֶׁאֵין שְׂכַר הָאוֹכֵל וְשׁוֹתֶה מֵחֲמַת מִצְוַת הַקָּדוֹשׁ בָּרוּךְ הוּא דּוֹמֶה לִשְׂכַר הַמִּתְעַנֶּה מֵחֲמַת מִצְוַת הַקָּדוֹשׁ בָּרוּךְ הוּא,[8] אֲבָל זֶה שֶׁאוֹכֵל וְשׁוֹתֶה בַּתְּשִׁיעִי שְׂכָרוֹ הַרְבֵּה מְאֹד כְּאִלּוּ הָיָה מִתְעַנֶּה[יג] (בַּתְּשִׁיעִי וּבָעֲשִׂירִי)[9] מֵחֲמַת מִצְוַת הַקָּדוֹשׁ בָּרוּךְ הוּא שֶׁצִּוָּה לְהִתְעַנּוֹת (בִּשְׁנֵיהֶם).[יד]

דְּכֵיוָן שֶׁיּוֹם הַכִּפּוּרִים בְּעַצְמוֹ אִי אֶפְשָׁר לְכַבְּדוֹ בְּמַאֲכָל וּבְמִשְׁתֶּה כְּדֶרֶךְ שֶׁמְּכַבְּדִין שְׁאָר יוֹם טוֹב[10] – צָרִיךְ לְכַבְּדוֹ בַּיּוֹם שֶׁלְּפָנָיו.[טו]

לְפִיכָךְ אָסוּר לְהִתְעַנּוֹת בּוֹ[טז] אֲפִלּוּ תַּעֲנִית חֲלוֹם,[יז] אַף עַל פִּי שֶׁמֻּתָּר לְהִתְעַנּוֹת תַּעֲנִית חֲלוֹם אֲפִלּוּ בְּשַׁבָּת וְיוֹם טוֹב,[יח,11] מִכָּל מָקוֹם בְּעֶרֶב יוֹם הַכִּפּוּרִים שֶׁהָאֲכִילָה נֶחְשֶׁבֶת כְּעִנּוּי כְּמוֹ שֶׁנִּתְבָּאֵר – אֵין לְהִתְעַנּוֹת בּוֹ,[יט] אֶלָּא יֹאכַל וְיִשְׁתֶּה, וְיֵחָשֵׁב לוֹ כְּאִלּוּ הִתְעַנָּה עַל חֲלוֹמוֹ.[כ]

The reason the verse refers to eating as "affliction" rather than stating explicitly that people should eat and drink on the ninth day is to teach that one who eats and drinks on the ninth is considered by Scripture as if he fasted on it because of G-d's command — that we afflict ourselves on this [day]. And [the verse refers to eating on this day as "affliction," because generally] the reward that one receives for eating and drinking because of G-d's commandment is not comparable to the reward that one receives for fasting because of G-d's commandment.[8]

Nevertheless, one who eats and drinks on the ninth [of Tishrei] receives a great reward as if he fasted (on the ninth and the tenth),[9] because of G-d's command that we fast (on those two days).

[The rationale for this distinction is that] since Yom Kippur itself cannot be honored with food and drink as one honors other festivals,[10] it must be honored on the preceding day.

Accordingly, it is forbidden to fast on the ninth, even on account of a [disturbing] dream. [Such] a fast is permitted on *Shabbos* and on festivals,[11] but on the day preceding Yom Kippur, when eating and drinking is considered as affliction, as explained above, one should not fast. Instead one should eat and drink, and this will be considered as if he fasted because of his dream.

8. For fasting demands greater effort.

9. This could be understood to mean that eating on the ninth is considered as equivalent to two days' fasting, in addition to the actual fast of Yom Kippur. See *Eshel Avraham* (Butchatch), sec. 604; *Shaarei HaMoadim: Yom Kippur,* p. 137.

The Alter Rebbe writes in his *Siddur* (based on a teaching of the *AriZal*) that on the ninth one should "eat the equivalent of two days' food." *Eshel Avraham (loc. cit.)* writes that this is fulfilled by eating a little more than one day's portion.

10. To honor the festivals in this way is a Scriptural command (sec. 629:1).

11. See sec. 288:3.

ט רש"י יומא שם. רא"ש שם. טור ולבוש שם. ט"ז שם. י לבוש וט"ז שם. יא גמרא שם. יב רא"ש שם. טור וב"י ד"ה ומ"ש חשיב. לבוש שם. ט"ז שם. וראה מ"מ וציונים. יג ט"ז שם. לבוש שם. יד ט"ז שם. טו ב"י ד"ה וא"ת. טז הגהות מיימוניות סוף הל' שביתת עשור, מפסחים סח, ב. ב"י שם. יז מהרי"ל הל' ימים נוראים אות י (ע' רסה). רמ"א ס"א. יח כדלעיל סי' רפח ס"ג. יט של"ה מסכת יומא בתחילתו (רכז, ב) ד"ה ובס' מהרי"ל. לבוש שם. ט"ז סק"ב.

Nevertheless, if a person desires to fast because of a dream until the meal before the fast,[12] one should not protest against this. The rationale is that the day preceding Yom Kippur is not like *Shabbos,* concerning which it is said,[13] "And you shall call the *Shabbos* a delight." This is why it is forbidden to fast [on *Shabbos*] for even one moment for the sake of a [ritual] fast, unless the fast is undertaken because of a disturbing dream, as explained in sec. 288[:1, 3]. With regard to the day preceding Yom Kippur, by contrast, "delight" is not mentioned; it is only that it is a *mitzvah* to eat on that day. Thus if one ate once in the course of the day, he has fulfilled his obligation.

2 If one transgressed and erred [by] fasting that entire day, he must undertake a fast after Yom Kippur to atone for having fasted on the day preceding Yom Kippur. If he fasted only until the meal preceding the fast, he is not required to fast [again] after Yom Kippur.

3 [For the laws regarding] one who vows to fast on this day, see sec. 570.[14]

4 According to the letter of the law, it is permitted to eulogize a person on the day preceding Yom Kippur, for it is not a festival at all, and has no distinctive quality other than the obligation to eat on that day. Nevertheless, it is customary to treat it as a festival. On that day, [therefore,] eulogies are not delivered, except for a departed sage

וּמִכָּל מָקוֹם, מִי שֶׁיִּרְצֶה לְהִתְעַנּוֹת עַל חֲלוֹמוֹ עַד סְעוּדָה הַמַּפְסֶקֶת[12] – אֵין לְמַחוֹת בְּיָדוֹ,[כא] לְפִי שֶׁעֶרֶב יוֹם הַכִּפּוּרִים אֵינוֹ דּוֹמֶה לְשַׁבָּת שֶׁנֶּאֱמַר בּוֹ[כב, 13] "וְקָרָאתָ לַשַּׁבָּת עֹנֶג", וּלְפִיכָךְ אָסוּר לְהִתְעַנּוֹת בּוֹ אֲפִלּוּ שָׁעָה אַחַת לְשֵׁם תַּעֲנִית אִם אֵינוֹ תַּעֲנִית חֲלוֹם כְּמוֹ שֶׁנִּתְבָּאֵר בְּסִימָן רפ"ח,[כג] אֲבָל בְּעֶרֶב יוֹם הַכִּפּוּרִים שֶׁלֹּא נֶאֱמַר בּוֹ עֹנֶג אֶלָּא שֶׁמִּצְוָה לֶאֱכֹל בּוֹ, וְאִם אָכַל פַּעַם אַחַת בַּיּוֹם – יָצָא יְדֵי חוֹבָתוֹ:[כד]

ב וְאִם עָבַר וְטָעָה וְהִתְעַנָּה כָּל הַיּוֹם – צָרִיךְ לְהִתְעַנּוֹת[כה] אַחַר יוֹם הַכִּפּוּרִים[כו] תַּעֲנִית א' לְכַפֵּר עַל מַה שֶּׁהִתְעַנָּה בְּעֶרֶב יוֹם הַכִּפּוּרִים. אֲבָל אִם לֹא הִתְעַנָּה אֶלָּא עַד סְעוּדָה הַמַּפְסֶקֶת – אֵינוֹ צָרִיךְ לְהִתְעַנּוֹת אַחַר יוֹם הַכִּפּוּרִים:[כז]

ג אִם נָדַר לְהִתְעַנּוֹת בּוֹ – עַיֵּן בְּסִימָן תק"ע:[כח, 14]

ד אַף עַל פִּי שֶׁמִּן הַדִּין עֶרֶב יוֹם הַכִּפּוּרִים מֻתָּר בְּהֶסְפֵּד שֶׁאֵינוֹ יוֹם טוֹב כְּלָל וְאֵין בּוֹ מַעֲלָה אֶלָּא שֶׁמִּצְוָה לֶאֱכֹל בּוֹ,[כט] מִכָּל מָקוֹם נוֹהֲגִין לַעֲשׂוֹתוֹ יוֹם טוֹב, וְאֵין מַסְפִּידִין בּוֹ אֶלָּא עַל חָכָם

---

12. In the original, *seudah mafsekes.*

13. *Yeshayahu* 58:13.

14. Sec. 570 of the Alter Rebbe's *Shulchan Aruch* is not extant. The *Shulchan Aruch* of R. Yosef Caro (sec. 570:2) states that a person who vows to fast on the day preceding Yom Kippur should have his vow absolved by a sage.

מ"א סק"א. **כ** לבוש שם. ט"ז שם. וראה הער"ב תתח ע' 69. **כא** מנהגים (קלויזנר) סי' פו. מהרי"ל שם ובהל' תענית (ע' רסח). מ"א שם. **כב** ישעיה נח, יג. וכדלעיל סי' רמב ס"א. **כג** סעיף א. **כד** מ"א שם. **כה** ב"י סי' תקסח סוד"ה ומ"ש וא"צ. שו"ע שם ס"ה. מ"א כאן סק"א. לבוש שם ס"ה. משאת בנימין סי' צג. **כו** משאת בנימין שם. מ"א סי' רפח סק"ג. וראה לעיל שם ס"ד. **כז** מ"א סק"א. **כח** סימן זה בשוע"ר לא הגיע לידינו, וראה שו"ע שם ס"א. **כט** מ"א סי' תרו בסופו.

בְּפָנָיו,[ל] אוֹ בְּיוֹם שֶׁבָּאָה שְׁמוּעָתוֹ שֶׁמֵּת שֶׁהוּא כְּמוֹ בְּפָנָיו[לא] כְּמוֹ שֶׁנִּתְבָּאֵר בְּסִימָן תקמ"ז[לב,15] עַיֵּן שָׁם, וְכֵן אֵין אוֹמְרִים צִדּוּק הַדִּין[לג,16] אֶלָּא עַל חָכָם בְּפָנָיו.[לד]

וְכֵן אֵין אוֹמְרִים בּוֹ תַּחֲנוּן,[לה] וְגַם אֵין אוֹמְרִים קֹדֶם עֲלוֹת הַשַּׁחַר הַרְבֵּה סְלִיחוֹת כְּבִשְׁאָר יָמִים.[17] וְיֵשׁ מְקוֹמוֹת נוֹהֲגִין לְהַרְבּוֹת בִּסְלִיחוֹת,[לו] לְפִי שֶׁאֵין חוֹשְׁבִין אוֹתוֹ יוֹם טוֹב אֶלָּא מֵעֲלוֹת הַשַּׁחַר וְאֵילָךְ אֲבָל לֹא בַּלַּיְלָה.[לז] וְהַכֹּל לְפִי הַמִּנְהָג:[לח,18]

ה מִי שֶׁנּוֹהֵג שֶׁלֹּא לֶאֱכֹל בָּשָׂר בְּכָל יְמוֹת הַחֹל כִּי אִם בְּיוֹם שֶׁאֵין אוֹמְרִים בּוֹ תַּחֲנוּן — מֻתָּר לֶאֱכֹל בָּשָׂר אֲפִלּוּ בְּלֵיל עֶרֶב יוֹם הַכִּפּוּרִים, וְכָל שֶׁכֵּן בַּיּוֹם. בַּמֶּה דְּבָרִים אֲמוּרִים? בִּמְקוֹמוֹת שֶׁאֵין אוֹמְרִים הַרְבֵּה סְלִיחוֹת בַּלַּיְלָה, שֶׁהֵן חוֹשְׁבִין לְיוֹם טוֹב גַּם אֶת הַלַּיְלָה, אֲבָל בִּמְקוֹמוֹת שֶׁמַּרְבִּים בִּסְלִיחוֹת שֶׁאֵין חוֹשְׁבִין אֶת הַלַּיְלָה לְיוֹם טוֹב — אֵין לֶאֱכֹל בָּשָׂר בַּלַּיְלָה.[לט]

[while we are] in his presence, or for [a departed sage] on the day that news of his passing first arrives, [for then the mourning is as intense and it is] as if one was in his presence, as explained in sec. 547.[15] Similarly, the passage known as *Tziduk HaDin*[16] is not recited [on this day] except for a sage and in his presence.

Likewise, [the confessional supplications known as] *Tachanun* are not recited on this day, nor are [the penitential prayers called] *Selichos* recited at length before dawn as is customary on the other days.[17] In some communities, however, it is customary to recite *Selichos* at length, because they consider this day as a festival only from dawn onward, not on the preceding night. Everything should follow the [local] custom.[18]

5 One whose custom is not to eat meat on a weekday except on days when *Tachanun* is not recited is permitted to eat meat even on the eve of the ninth of Tishrei. Certainly, this applies during the day.

Where does this apply? In places where it is not customary to recite *Selichos* extensively at night, for they consider the night, too, as part of the festival. By contrast, in regions in which *Selichos* are recited extensively, and the night is not considered as a festival, [such a person] should not eat meat that night.

15. Sec. 547 of the Alter Rebbe's *Shulchan Aruch* is not extant. The *Shulchan Aruch* of R. Yosef Caro (sec. 547:6) equates hearing of a sage's death to being present at the time of his passing. Sec. 547:1 cites the prohibition against eulogizing the deceased on *Chol HaMoed*.

16. Normally recited at a funeral in acceptance (lit., "justification") of the Divine verdict.

17. The Alter Rebbe is referring to the custom of reciting *Selichos* every morning between Rosh HaShanah and Yom Kippur, in contrast to the Lubavitch custom which restricts this to the Fast of Gedaliah. (See sec. 602, footnote 6 above.)

18. The same thinking applies to the inclusion of *Tachanun* in the prayers recited before retiring at night.

ל שו"ע יו"ד סי' תא ס"ה (לענין חול המועד ר"ח חנוכה ופורים). וכ"ה לעיל סי' תכט סוף ס"ח (לענין חדש ניסן). לא מו"ק כז, ב. רמב"ם הל' אבל פי"א ה"ה. שו"ע יו"ד שם. לב סימן זה בשוע"ר לא הגיע לידינו, וראה שו"ע שם ס"ו (לענין קריעה). לג מנהגים (טירנא) מנהג של כל השנה (ע' קסז). רמ"א סי' תכ ס"ב (בכל הימים שאין אומרים בהם תחנון). לד ט"ז שם (בשם הרמ"א, לומר על אדם גדול בימים שאין אומרים תחנון). וראה לעיל סי' תכט ס"ח (לענין חדש ניסן). כף החיים ס"ק כב. מ"מ וציונים. לה מנהגים שם. מהרי"ל הל' ערב יום כיפור (ע' שיב). שו"ע (נפילת אפים) ורמ"א ס"ב (למנצח). וכ"ה לקמן סי' תה ס"ה. סידור (לפני למנצח). לו מהרי"ל שם. רמ"א ס"ב. לז כדלקמן ס"ה וש"נ. לח רמ"א שם. ומנהג חב"ד שלא לומר סליחות בערב יום כיפור (ראה ספר

וַאֲפִלּוּ בִּמְקוֹמוֹת שֶׁאֵין מַרְבִּים בּוֹ בִּסְלִיחוֹת – לֹא יֹאכַל בָּשָׂר קֹדֶם צֵאת הַכּוֹכָבִים שֶׁל לֵיל עֶרֶב יוֹם כִּפּוּר,[19] אַף עַל פִּי שֶׁהִתְפַּלֵּל עַרְבִית מִבְּעוֹד יוֹם,[20] לְפִי שֶׁאֵין חוֹשְׁבִין לְיוֹם טוֹב אֶלָּא לַיְלָה מַמָּשׁ,[מ] שֶׁהֲרֵי אוֹמְרִים תַּחֲנוּן אַחַר תְּפִלַּת הַמִּנְחָה שֶׁל ח' תִּשְׁרֵי,[מא] וּבִשְׁאָר יָמִים[21] שֶׁאֵין אוֹמְרִים בָּהֶם תַּחֲנוּן אֵין אוֹמְרִים תַּחֲנוּן אֲפִלּוּ בְּמִנְחָה שֶׁלִּפְנֵיהֶם, מִכְּלָל שֶׁעֶרֶב יוֹם כִּפּוּר אֵין מַחֲזִיקִין לְיוֹם טוֹב אֶלָּא מִצֵּאת הַכּוֹכָבִים וְאֵילָךְ:[מב]

[Moreover,] even in places where *Selichos* are not recited extensively, [such a person] should not eat meat before the stars appear[19] on the eve of [the ninth of Tishrei] even if he recited the Evening Service before nightfall.[20] The rationale is that only actual nighttime is considered as a festival. [This is evident from the fact that] *Tachanun* is recited after *Shemoneh Esreh* in the Afternoon Service of the eighth of *Tishrei*, whereas with regard to the other days[21] on which *Tachanun* is not recited, it is also omitted even in the Afternoon Service of the preceding day. This indicates that the day preceding Yom Kippur is considered as a festival only from the appearance of the stars onward.

ו אֵין אוֹמְרִים "לַמְנַצֵּחַ יַעַנְךָ וגו'",[מג] שֶׁאֵינוֹ יוֹם צָרָה.[מד,22] וְאֵין אוֹמְרִים בּוֹ "מִזְמוֹר לְתוֹדָה",[מה,23] מִטַּעַם שֶׁנִּתְבָּאֵר בְּסִימָן נ"א[מו] עַיֵּן שָׁם:[24]

6 The psalm *LaMenatzeiach... yaancha* is not recited [on the ninth of Tishrei], for it is not "a day of distress."[22] Nor is the psalm beginning *Mizmor LeTodah*[23] recited on that day, for the reason given in sec. 51[:1].[24]

19. In the original, *tzeis hakochavim* — lit., "when the stars emerge."

20. As is common in certain communities during the summer. In the original, *mibe'od yom* — lit., "while it is yet day."

21. I.e., almost all of the other days.

22. The second verse of that psalm *(Tehillim* 20:2) states, "May G-d answer you on a day of distress."

Though the omission of *Tachanun* has already been discussed, the Alter Rebbe is here addressing the Ashkenazic custom, according to which there are many days on which *Tachanun* is omitted but *LaMenatzeiach* is nevertheless recited (see *Rama,* sec. 132:1). In his *Siddur,* by contrast, the recitation of *LaMenatzeiach* is linked to the recitation of *Tachanun.*

The coexistence of these two rulings accords with the pattern whereby the Alter Rebbe's *Shulchan Aruch* relates to the Ashkenazic prayer rite *(Nussach Ashkenaz),* whereas his *Siddur* follows *Nussach HaAriZal.* This is a variant of the Sephardic prayer rite *(Nussach Sephard).* In the guidelines for the omission of *Tachanun,* for example, the *AriZal* follows the Sephardic custom.

These terms are defined and clarified in sec. 582, footnote 16 above.

23. Hebrew grammar dictates that in specified situations certain consonants should be varied from their accustomed pronunciation. Nevertheless, our transliteration generally seeks to keep familiar Hebrew words recognizable. Hence, as above, *LeTodah* rather than *LeSodah.*

24. The recitation of this psalm *(Tehillim* 100) recalls the *Korban Todah,* the thanksgiving sacrifice, and this was not offered on the day preceding Yom Kippur.

The Torah allows certain sacrifices to be eaten within a fixed timeframe. If it is known that the full span of permissible time will not be available, such sacrifices are not to be offered, for if the sacrificial food was not entirely

המנהגים – חב"ד ע' 58). **לט** של"ה ריש מסכת יומא (רכז, ב) ד"ה וענין ליל. מ"א סק"א. **מ** מ"א שם. **מא** לבוש סי' קלא ס"ו. של"ה שם. מ"א שם. וכ"ה בסידור (לפני למנצח). **מב** של"ה שם. מ"א שם. **מג** מנהגים (טירנא) מנהג עשי"ת (ע' קה). רמ"א ס"ב. ובסידור (לפני למנצח): מנהג ספרד שבכל יום שאין בו תחנון ונפילת אפים אין אומרים למנצח יענך. **מד** לבוש ס"ב. **מה** מנהגים שם. רמ"א שם. וכ"ה בסידור (לפני מזמור לתודה). וראה גם לעיל סי' א מהדו"ק סי"ז גבי פרשת תודה. **מו** ס"א. מפני שלא היתה תודה קריבה ביום זה, וציין לכאן. וראה לבוש ס"ב. וראה חידושי צמח צדק רח, ב. אג"ק ח"ג ע' עא־עב.

ז אֵין אוֹמְרִים בּוֹ "אָבִינוּ מַלְכֵּנוּ", לֹא בִּתְפִלַּת שַׁחֲרִית[מז] וְלֹא בְּמִנְחָה.[מח] וְיֵשׁ מְקוֹמוֹת נוֹהֲגִין כְּשֶׁחָל יוֹם הַכִּפּוּרִים בְּשַׁבָּת שֶׁאֵין אוֹמְרִים בּוֹ אָבִינוּ מַלְכֵּנוּ כְּמוֹ שֶׁיִּתְבָּאֵר בְּסִימָן תרי"ט,[מט, 25] אָז אוֹמְרִים אוֹתוֹ בְּעֶרֶב יוֹם הַכִּפּוּרִים שַׁחֲרִית:[נ]

7 On this day the prayer beginning *Avinu Malkeinu* is not recited in the Morning Service nor in the Afternoon Service. The custom of some communities is to recite *Avinu Malkeinu* at *Shacharis* on the day before Yom Kippur [in years] in which Yom Kippur falls on *Shabbos* and [hence] *Avinu Malkeinu* is not recited, as explained in sec. 619[:23].[25]

סימן תרה מִנְהַג כַּפָּרוֹת בְּעֶרֶב יוֹם כִּפּוּר וּבוֹ ו' סְעִיפִים:

SECTION 605 The Custom of *Kaparos* on Erev Yom Kippur. (1–6)

א נוֹהֲגִין בְּאֵלּוּ הָאֲרָצוֹת[1] לִקַּח בְּעֶרֶב יוֹם הַכִּפּוּרִים[2] תַּרְנְגוֹל כַּפָּרָה[א] לַזָּכָר וְתַרְנְגֹלֶת לַנְּקֵבָה,[ב] וְאוֹמְרִים עָלָיו "זֶה חֲלִיפָתִי זֶה תְּמוּרָתִי זֶה כַּפָּרָתִי וכו'";[ג] (רָאשֵׁי תֵּבוֹת חת"ך) זֶה הַשֵּׁם הַחוֹתֵךְ

1 In these countries,[1] on the day preceding Yom Kippur,[2] it is customary for a male to take a rooster and a female to take a hen, for the ceremony of *kaparah* (atonement).

[While holding the chicken] one says: "This is my exchange; this is my substitute; this is my expiation." ([The acronym comprising the initial letters of the Hebrew words for "exchange," "substitute," and "expiation"] forms the word חתך meaning "cut," [recalling the phrase from

---

consumed this would cause it to be disqualified. Thus, in the present case, a thanksgiving offering may ordinarily be eaten on the day it was offered and on the following night. This would be impossible if it were to be offered on the day that is interrupted by the onset of the Yom Kippur fast.

The *Tzemach Tzedek*, in his novellae to Tractate *Pesachim* (Kehot, N.Y., edition of 5755/1995, p. 415), questions the Alter Rebbe's above ruling. For further discussion, see *Igros Kodesh* (Letters) of the Rebbe, Vol. 3, p. 71ff., and in English translation: *I Will Write it in Their Hearts* (S.I.E., N.Y., 5764), Vol. 4, p. 92.

25. The Lubavitch practice is not to recite *Avinu Malkeinu* on the ninth of Tishrei in all instances *(Luach Colel Chabad,* 5741 and 5744*)*.

SECTION 605

1. I.e., in the Ashkenazic community, where the custom of *kaparos* is well established, having been mentioned in early Responsa and recorded in the *Tur* and the *Rama (Orach Chayim* 605:1*)*. With regard to the Sephardic community, the *Rashba* writes that this practice should be abolished. His view, cited by R. Yosef Caro in his *Shulchan Aruch,* is upheld today by many Sephardim, though others have adopted this custom.

2. *Magen Avraham* (605:1) quotes the *AriZal* and the *Shelah,* who state that this custom should be practiced at dawn, a time of heightened Divine mercy. This concept is quoted by the Alter Rebbe in his *Siddur. Pri Megadim: Eshel Avraham* (605:1) and *Mishnah Berurah* (605:2) advise that if there is a possibility that the slaughter will be disqualified by excessive crowding or by the fatigue of the *shochet,* the custom should be practiced on one of the previous days.

מז דרכי משה (שכן נוהגים בקראקא). מטה משה סי' תתלה (מנהג ארצינו). רמ"א ס"ב. מח דרכי משה סי' תרז אות ג, בשם מנהגים ישנים. רמ"א שם ס"ג. מט סעיף יא. נ דרכי משה ומטה משה שם. רמ"א ס"ב.

סימן תרה: א רא"ש פ"ח סי' כג, וטור, בשם הגאונים. מרדכי רמז תשכג. תשב"ץ סי' קכה. רמ"א (שכן נוהגים בכל מדינות אלו). לבוש ס"א. שער הכוונות ריש דרושי יוה"כ. פע"ח שער כז פ"א. של"ה מסכת יומא ריש פרק תורה אור (רלו, ב). ובסידור: בערב יוה"כ מנהג לשחוט תרנגול לבן הנקרא גבר ושוחטים אותו באשמורת הבקר . . . כי אז חוט של חסד גובר בעולם ואנו שוחטין אותו להכניע הגבורות ומוציאין ממנו דמו כדי להמתיקו ונקרא כפרה כמו שעיר המשתלח, וש"נ. ב תשב"ץ שם. רמ"א. ט"ז סק"ב. וכ"ה בסידור. ג וכ"ה בסידור. ד מנהגים (קלויזנר) סי' לב הג"ה א. הובא במהרי"ל הל' ערב יו"כ (ע' שיג).

the liturgy that praises] G-d "Who apportions [lit., 'cuts'] life for all the living."

The chicken should be circled [over] one's head. One should recite [the passage beginning] *Bnei Adam*. This is done three times.[3]

One should place his hands on [the chicken] in a manner that parallels the practice of *semichah* that was performed for the sacrifices.[4] [The chicken] should be slaughtered immediately thereafter, as the sacrifices were slaughtered directly after *semichah* was performed. There are, however, some who refrain from placing their hands upon [the chicken], so that it will not appear that they are consecrating an animal as an offering and slaughtering it outside [the courtyard of the *Beis HaMikdash*].[5]

[In truth] this is no cause for concern, because chickens are not fit to be offered on the altar. If, however, one does not have chickens [available] and he takes a different creature for a *kaparah*, he should not take turtle-doves or fledgling doves, for they are fit to be offered on the altar. If he were to place his hands on them, it would in fact appear that he was consecrating sacrifices and slaughtering them outside [the courtyard of the *Beis HaMikdash*].

2 White chickens should be chosen, to recall the verse,[6] "[Even] if your sins are like scarlet, they will become as white as snow."

חַיִּים לְכָל חַי,[ד] וּמַחֲזִירוֹ סְבִיב רֹאשׁוֹ,[ה] וְיֹאמַר "בְּנֵי אָדָם כו'",[ו] וְעוֹשִׂין כֵּן ג' פְּעָמִים.[ז,3]

וְסוֹמְכִין עָלָיו יְדֵיהֶם דֻּגְמַת סְמִיכָה בְּקָרְבָּן,[4] וְשׁוֹחֲטִין אוֹתוֹ מִיָּד דִּתֵיכֶף לִסְמִיכָה שְׁחִיטָה.[ח] וְיֵשׁ נִמְנָעִין מִלִּסְמֹךְ עָלָיו יְדֵיהֶם, כְּדֵי שֶׁלֹּא יְהֵא נִרְאֶה כְּמַקְדִּישׁ קָדָשִׁים וְשׁוֹחֲטָן בַּחוּץ.[ט,5] וְאֵין לָחוּשׁ לָזֶה, כֵּיוָן שֶׁהַתַּרְנְגוֹל הוּא דָּבָר שֶׁאֵינוֹ רָאוּי לַמִּזְבֵּחַ.[י] אֲבָל אִם אֵין לוֹ תַּרְנְגוֹלִים וְלוֹקֵחַ שְׁאָר בַּעֲלֵי חַיִּים לְכַפָּרָה – לֹא יִקַּח תּוֹרִים וּבְנֵי יוֹנָה שֶׁהֵם רְאוּיִם לַמִּזְבֵּחַ, וְאִם יִסְמֹךְ יָדָיו עֲלֵיהֶם יְהֵא נִרְאֶה כְּמַקְדִּישׁ קָדָשִׁים וְשׁוֹחֲטָן בַּחוּץ:[יא]

ב וּבוֹחֲרִין בְּתַרְנְגוֹלִים לְבָנִים,[יב] עַל דֶּרֶךְ שֶׁנֶּאֱמַר[יג,6] "אִם יִהְיוּ חֲטָאֵיכֶם כַּשָּׁנִים כַּשֶּׁלֶג יַלְבִּינוּ".

---

3. The *Chabad* custom is as follows: After first reciting the passage beginning *Bnei Adam* once, one recites the sentence beginning *Zeh Chalifasi* once. While doing so, the chicken is circled over one's head once as one says each of the three phrases — *Zeh Chalifasi, Zeh Temurasi, Zeh Kaparasi.*

The above sequence is followed three times. Thus the chicken is circled over one's head nine times in all. (See *Sefer HaMinhagim: The Book of Chabad-Lubavitch Customs,* p. 123.)

4. *Semichah* literally means "leaning." In most cases, the person offering an animal would first lean his hands on it with all his strength (see *Rambam, Hilchos Maaseh HaKorbanos* 3:6-13), thereby identifying with the sacrifice that would atone on his behalf. Significantly, the Alter Rebbe prescribes *semichah* in this context (and it was practiced in many communities), even though it was not performed when a fowl was brought as a sacrifice *(op. cit.,* 3:7).

5. And doing so is forbidden.

From the fact that the custom of *semichah* is not mentioned in the *Siddur,* the author of *Shaar HaKollel* infers that it need not be followed. (In practice, it is not practiced in *Chabad* communities.)

6. *Yeshayahu* 1:18.

שו"ת מהר"י ווייל סי' קצא. דרכי משה ס"ק ג. ט"ז ס"ק ב. מ"א ס"ק ג. **ה** מרדכי שם. לבוש. **ו** רא"ש שם. מהרי"ל שם (ע' שיד). לבוש. **ז** רא"ש שם. טור. לבוש. ובסידור: ויאמר ג' פעמים בני אדם. ומנהג חב"ד לסובב התרנגול מעל הראש ג' פעמים בכל פעם ובסך הכל ט' פעמים (ספר המנהגים – חב"ד ע' 58. וראה שער הכולל פמ"ד אות ב). **ח** רא"ש שם. טור. רמ"א. **ט** ט"ז סק"ג. וכן השמיטו מסידורו. וראה שער הכולל שם ד"ה גם. **י** לבוש. **יא** מ"א סק"ג. **יב** מהרי"ל הל' ערב יו"כ (ע' שיד). רמ"א. שער הכוונות ופע"ח ושל"ה שם. וכ"ה בסידור: מנהג לשחוט תרנגול לבן. **יג** ישעיה א, יח.

בַּמֶּה דְּבָרִים אֲמוּרִים? כְּשֶׁהַלְּבָנִים מְזֻמָּנִים לְפָנָיו אָז יִבְחַר בָּהֶם מִבַּאֲחֵרִים, אֲבָל אִם אֵינָם מְזֻמָּנִים לְפָנָיו – לֹא יְחַזֵּר אַחֲרֵיהֶם בְּדַוְקָא,[7] מִשּׁוּם שֶׁזֶּהוּ כְּעֵין דַּרְכֵי הָאֱמוֹרִי,[יד] שֶׁדַּרְכָּם לְחַזֵּר אַחַר תַּרְנְגוֹלִים לְבָנִים לְהַקְרִיבָן לַעֲבוֹדָה זָרָה,[טו, 8] וּכְתִיב[טז, 9] "וּבְחֻקּוֹתֵיהֶם לֹא תֵלֵכוּ":

When does the above apply? When white ones are at hand; then they should be chosen over others. If they are not presently available one should not seek them out,[7] for this would resemble "the way of the Amorites," who used to seek out white chickens for their idolatrous sacrifice.[8] And [we are commanded],[9] "Do not follow their statutes."

ג יֵשׁ נוֹהֲגִין לִפְטֹר כַּמָּה זְכָרִים בְּתַרְנְגוֹל אֶחָד וְכַמָּה נְקֵבוֹת בְּתַרְנְגֹלֶת אַחַת,[יז] לְפִיכָךְ אֵין לוֹקְחִין לִמְעֻבֶּרֶת אֶלָּא תַּרְנְגוֹל אֶחָד וְתַרְנְגֹלֶת אַחַת,[יח] דְּאִם הָעֻבָּר זָכָר – הֲרֵי יֵשׁ כָּאן תַּרְנְגוֹל אֶחָד, וְאִם הָעֻבָּר נְקֵבָה – דַּי לָהּ וּלְאִמָּהּ בְּתַרְנְגֹלֶת אַחַת.[יט] וְיֵשׁ נוֹהֲגִין[כ] לִקַּח כַּפָּרָה לְכָל אֶחָד וְאֶחָד בִּפְנֵי עַצְמוֹ, לְפִיכָךְ לוֹקְחִין לִמְעֻבֶּרֶת ג' – שְׁתֵּי נְקֵבוֹת וְזָכָר אֶחָד:[10]

3 Some people are accustomed to include several males [in the *kaparos* ceremony performed] with one rooster and several females [in the ceremony performed] with one hen. According to this custom, only one rooster and one hen are taken for a pregnant woman. For if the fetus is male, a rooster was taken, and if it is female, one hen will suffice for the fetus and the mother.

Others follow the custom of taking a *kaparah* for every person individually. According to this view, three chickens should be taken for a pregnant woman, two hens and one rooster.[10]

ד וְנוֹהֲגִין לִתֵּן הַכַּפָּרוֹת לָעֲנִיִּים.[כא] וְיוֹתֵר טוֹב לִפְדּוֹת הַכַּפָּרָה בְּמָמוֹן וּלְחַלֵּק הַמָּמוֹן לָעֲנִיִּים, כְּדֵי שֶׁלֹּא יִתְבַּיְּשׁוּ הָעֲנִיִּים בְּמַה שֶּׁנּוֹתְנִים לָהֶם הַתַּרְנְגוֹלִים שֶׁלָּקְחוּ לְכַפָּרָה:[כב]

4 It is customary to give the [chickens used for] *kaparos* to the poor. However, it is preferable to redeem them with money and to distribute the money among the poor, so that they will not be embarrassed by being given chickens that were used to secure atonement.

7. Black chickens, however, should not be taken, for they reflect the attribute of severity *(Shaar HaKollel).*

8. See *Avodah Zarah* 14a.

9. *Vayikra* 18:3. Based on this verse, both *Sefer HaMitzvos* (negative commandment 30) and *Sefer HaChinuch (mitzvah* 262) include this charge among the 613 commandments. It restricts the imitation of garments, coiffures, or practices that characterize non-Jew cultures for idolatrous or promiscuous motives, or even for no apparent reason. The prohibition is identified with the Amorites, who were among the seven Canaanite nations whose land was conquered and transformed into *Eretz Yisrael.* (See *Talmudic Encyclopedia,* Vol. 17, p. 305ff.)

10. In his *Siddur,* the Alter Rebbe cites only this view.

יד אחרונים. ב"ח סוד"ה ומ"ש ועושה. ט"ז סק"ב. מ"א סק"ג. טו ראה ע"ז יד, א. טז ויקרא יח, ג. וראה גם לעיל מהדו"ב סי' ב ס"ו. אבל ראה סי' שא סל"ג שהביא פסוק (ויקרא כ, כג) "ולא תלכו בחוקות הגוי". יז לבוש. הובא במ"א סק"ב. יח מהרי"ל הל' ערב יו"כ (ע' שיד). רמ"א. לבוש. מ"א שם. יט לבוש. ב"ח ד"ה ומ"ש ועושה. מ"א שם. כ שער הכוונות ופע"ח שם. של"ה שם. ב"ח שם בשם מרדכי קטן. מ"א סק"ב. אליה זוטא סק"ד. וכ"ה בסידור. וראה לקו"ש חכ"ב ע' 60־59. שלחן המלך ח"ב ע' רז"ח. כא מהרי"ל שם. רמ"א. כב מהרי"ל שם. דרכי משה ס"ק ד. רמ"א (או לפדותן). של"ה ריש מסכת יומא

ה וְיֵשׁ מְקוֹמוֹת שֶׁנָּהֲגוּ לֵילֵךְ עַל הַקְּבָרוֹת[כג, 11] לְהַרְבּוֹת שָׁם בִּצְדָקָה, וּמִנְהָג יָפֶה הוּא.[כד, 12] וְהַצְּדָקָה שֶׁנּוֹתְנִים שָׁם הוּא פִּדְיוֹן הַכַּפָּרוֹת,[כה] וּלְכָךְ רָאוּי לָתֵת כְּפִי עֵרֶךְ הַכַּפָּרוֹת שֶׁיֵּשׁ לוֹ בְּבֵיתוֹ.[כו] וְלֹא יֹאמַר שׁוּם תְּחִנָּה, רַק מַה שֶּׁמְּיֻסָּד מִקַּדְמוֹנִים, שֶׁהֲרֵי אֵין אוֹמְרִים תַּחֲנוּן בְּיוֹם זֶה:[כז, 13]

5 In some communities it is customary to visit the cemetery [on the day preceding Yom Kippur][11] and to give *tzedakah* generously there. This is a desirable custom.[12] Since the charity donated there is intended to redeem the *kaparos*, it is appropriate to give an amount equivalent to the value of the chickens that served for *kaparos* in one's home.

[At the cemetery, one] should not recite any supplications other than those instituted by the sages of the early generations, because [the supplicatory prayers collectively called] *Tachanun* are not recited on this date.[13]

ו וְזוֹרְקִין הַבְּנֵי מֵעַיִם[כח] וְהַכָּבֵד וְהַכְּלָיוֹת[כט] שֶׁל הַכַּפָּרוֹת עַל הַגַּגּוֹת אוֹ בֶּחָצֵר מָקוֹם שֶׁהָעוֹפוֹת יְכוֹלִים לָקַחַת מִשָּׁם, לְפִי שֶׁרָאוּי לְרַחֵם עַל הַבְּרִיּוֹת בְּיוֹם זֶה כְּדֵי שֶׁיְּרַחֲמוּ עָלֵינוּ מִן הַשָּׁמַיִם:[ל]

6 The intestines, the liver, and the kidneys of the *kaparos* are customarily strewn on the roofs or in the courtyards, from which they can be taken by birds [of prey]. It is appropriate to show mercy to creatures on this day, so that G-d will show mercy to us.

---

11. In his gloss to sec. 605:1 in the *Shulchan Aruch* of R. Yosef Caro, the *Rama* states that it is customary to visit the cemetery on the day preceding Yom Kippur. His gloss to sec. 581:4 *(op. cit.)* writes similarly regarding the day preceding Rosh HaShanah, and the commentaries there quote the explanation of *Maharil* — that the intent is that one should visit the graves of *tzaddikim*, for at those pure and holy places one's prayers are accepted more readily. Others cite the reason given by the commentaries to the *Rama* on *Shulchan Aruch* 559:10 — that a reminder of one's eventual mortality motivates one to repent.

On the various reasons for visiting the resting places of *tzaddikim*, see the opening passages of a *maamar* attributed to the Mitteler Rebbe — R. DovBer (1773-1827), the second Rebbe of Lubavitch — and entitled *Kuntreis HaHishtat'chus* (Sichos In English, N.Y., 5755/1995). These reasons are summarized in the Publisher's Foreword to *Maaneh Lashon* (English translation; Kehot, N.Y., 5756/1996), pp. vi-vii.

12. Whether or not one visits the cemetery, it is a widespread custom to distribute charity generously before Yom Kippur, in the hope that this expression of compassion will evoke a reciprocal downward flow of Divine compassion, as stated in subsection 6. In this spirit, congregants arriving at *shul* for *Minchah* on the afternoon preceding Yom Kippur commonly find large numbers of plates ranged on the tables before them, each bearing the name of a particular charitable cause. (See *Otzar Minhagei Chabad: Elul-Tishrei,* p. 188.)

13. See sec. 604:4.

(רכז, ב) ד"ה בערב. מ"א סק"ד. **כג** מהרי"ל שם (ע' שיג בשינויי נוסחאות). רמ"א. **כד** רמ"א. וראה אוצר מנהגי חב"ד יוה"כ ע' קפד. **כה** לבוש. מ"א ס"ק ה. **כו** מ"א שם. **כז** מהרי"ל שם. מ"א שם. וראה גם לעיל סי' תרד ס"ד. **כח** תשב"ץ סי' קכו. טור (ושו"ע). רמ"א. **כט** מ"א סק"ו. וראה תשב"ץ שם וטור, מגמרא חולין צה, ב. **ל** תשב"ץ שם. ב"ח ד"ה ומה. ט"ז סוף סק"ד.

סימן תרו שֶׁיְּפַיֵּס אָדָם אֶת חֲבֵרוֹ בְּעֶרֶב יוֹם כִּפּוּר וּבוֹ י״ד סְעִיפִים:

א עֲבֵרָה שֶׁבֵּין אָדָם לַחֲבֵרוֹ – אֵין יוֹם הַכִּפּוּרִים מְכַפֵּר עַד שֶׁיְּרַצֶּה אֶת חֲבֵרוֹ,[א,1] שֶׁנֶּאֱמַר[ב,2] "כִּי בַיּוֹם הַזֶּה יְכַפֵּר עֲלֵיכֶם לְטַהֵר אֶתְכֶם מִכֹּל חַטֹּאתֵיכֶם לִפְנֵי ה' גו'", כְּלוֹמַר חַטֹּאתֵיכֶם שֶׁהֵם לִפְנֵי ה' לְבַד יוֹם הַכִּפּוּרִים מְכַפֵּר, אֲבָל מַה שֶּׁבֵּין אָדָם לַחֲבֵרוֹ אֵין יוֹם הַכִּפּוּרִים מְכַפֵּר עַד שֶׁיְּפַיְּסֶנּוּ.[ג] לְפִיכָךְ יִתֵּן כָּל אָדָם אֶל לִבּוֹ בְּעֶרֶב יוֹם הַכִּפּוּרִים לְפַיֵּס לְכָל מִי שֶׁפָּשַׁע כְּנֶגְדּוֹ,[ד] וַאֲפִלּוּ לֹא הִקְנִיטוֹ אֶלָּא בִּדְבָרִים[3] – צָרִיךְ לֵילֵךְ וּלְפַיְּסוֹ וּלְבַקֵּשׁ מִמֶּנּוּ שֶׁיִּמְחֹל לוֹ,[ה,4] וּבִשְׁעַת בַּקָּשַׁת מְחִילָה צָרִיךְ לְפָרֵט הַחֵטְא שֶׁחָטָא לַחֲבֵרוֹ.[ו] וְאִם חֲבֵרוֹ מִתְבַּיֵּשׁ בָּזֶה – לֹא יְפָרֵט הַחֵטְא:[ז]

ב וְאִם אֵינוֹ מִתְפַּיֵּס בְּפַעַם רִאשׁוֹן – יַחֲזֹר וְיֵלֵךְ לְפַיְּסוֹ פַּעַם שֵׁנִית[ח] בְּמִין רִצּוּי אַחֵר,[ט] וְאִם לֹא נִתְפַּיֵּס – יַחֲזֹר וְיֵלֵךְ פַּעַם שְׁלִישִׁית לְפַיְּסוֹ בְּמִין

SECTION 606 The Requirement that People Appease One Another on *Erev* Yom Kippur. (1–14)

1 Yom Kippur does not atone for sins between a man and his fellow until he has appeased that person.[1] [This concept is derived as follows:] It is written,[2] "Because on this day He will atone for you to purify you, from all your sins before G-d [will you be purified]." The implication is that Yom Kippur atones only for "sins before G-d," whereas [wrongs] between man and man will not be atoned for by Yom Kippur unless one appeases [the other person].

For this reason, on the day before Yom Kippur, everyone should conscientiously appease every individual whom he has wronged. Even if he merely angered someone verbally,[3] he must go and appease him, and request his forgiveness.[4] When asking for forgiveness he should specify the wrong he committed against his fellow, but if this would cause his fellow embarrassment, he should not specify the wrong.

2 If the [offended party] is not appeased the first time, [the offender] should go back and try to appease him a second time with another form of conciliation. If he is still not appeased, he should go to him a third time to

---

1. *Yoma* 85b. Any transgression between man and man is also a transgression between man and G-d, Who has commanded us to respect the property and the feelings of our fellow men. The spiritual influences aroused on Yom Kippur that atone for all transgressions between man and G-d cannot atone for transgressions against one's fellow man until that person is appeased.

2. *Vayikra* 16:30.

3. *Yoma* 87a. Needless to say, if one person wrongs another financially, he must not only appease him for having wronged him, but must also restore the money owed. (See *Rambam, Hilchos Teshuvah* 2:9.)

4. It is preferable that the offender ask for forgiveness personally. If he knows that an agent is more likely to succeed, he may depute an agent *(Bayis Chadash,* cited in *Mishnah Berurah* 606:2).

א משנה פה, ב. טור ושו״ע ס״א. וראה פרדס חב״ד 9 ע' 92. ב ויקרא טז, ל. ג רבי אלעזר בן עזריה במשנה שם. לבוש ס״א. ד רא״ש פ״ח סי' כד. טור ולבוש שם. וראה העו״ב תשטו ע' 18. ה גמרא פז, א. טור ושו״ע שם. ו ב״ח ד״ה מצאתי, בשם דרשות מהר״ש סי' שלג. מ״א ריש הסי'. ז מ״א שם. ח טור ושו״ע שם. רב חסדא ור' יוסי בר חנינא בגמרא שם. ט מהרי״ל הל' ליל יוה״כ (ע' שכה). ב״ח ד״ה ומ״ש וצריך. מ״א סק״א. י רב חסדא בגמרא שם, ורש״י ד״ה

רִצּוּי אַחֵר. וּבְכָל פַּעַם שֶׁהוֹלֵךְ לְפַיְּסוֹ אֲפִלּוּ בַּפַּעַם הָרִאשׁוֹן – יִקַּח עִמּוֹ שְׁלֹשָׁה אֲנָשִׁים וִיפַיְּסֶנּוּ בִּפְנֵיהֶם.[י] וְאִם לֹא נִתְפַּיֵּס בַּפַּעַם הַשְּׁלִישִׁית – שׁוּב אֵין זָקוּק לוֹ,[יא] וּמִכָּל מָקוֹם צָרִיךְ לְהוֹדִיעַ לָרַבִּים דְּהַיְנוּ עֲשָׂרָה אֲנָשִׁים שֶׁהוּא הָלַךְ לְפַיְּסוֹ וְלֹא רָצָה לְהִתְפַּיֵּס,[יב] כְּדֵי שֶׁלֹּא יַחְשְׁדוּהוּ הַבְּרִיּוֹת שֶׁלֹּא רָצָה לְהַכְנִיעַ אֶת עַצְמוֹ לִפְנֵי חֲבֵרוֹ לְבַקֵּשׁ מִמֶּנּוּ מְחִילָה:[יג]

appease him with yet another form of conciliation. Each time he goes to appease him, even the first time, he should take three people with him and try to appease him in their presence.

If the [offended party] is not appeased [even] after the third attempt, one is under no further obligation to him. Nevertheless, one should state publicly — i.e., notify ten people — that he went to appease [that other person] but was refused, so that people at large will not suspect that he was not willing to humble himself before his fellow and ask his forgiveness.

ג בַּמֶּה דְּבָרִים אֲמוּרִים? כְּשֶׁהִקְנִיט אֶת חֲבֵרוֹ, אֲבָל אִם הִקְנִיט אֶת רַבּוֹ,[יד] אֲפִלּוּ אֵינוֹ רַבּוֹ מֻבְהָק[5] רַק שֶׁשָּׁמַע מִמֶּנּוּ דִּבְרֵי תוֹרָה[טו] – צָרִיךְ לֵילֵךְ אֵלָיו כַּמָּה פְּעָמִים עַד שֶׁיִּתְפַּיֵּס. וַאֲפִלּוּ כְּשֶׁהִקְנִיט אֶת חֲבֵרוֹ, אִם רוֹצֶה לְהַחְמִיר עַל עַצְמוֹ וְלֵילֵךְ אֵלָיו כַּמָּה פְּעָמִים – הָרְשׁוּת בְּיָדוֹ,[טז] וּבִלְבַד שֶׁלֹּא יִהְיֶה שָׁם בִּזְיוֹן תּוֹרָה:[יז]

3 When does the above apply? When he angered one of his peers. If, however, he angered his [Torah] teacher, he must go to him repeatedly [to ask forgiveness] until he is appeased. [This applies] not only to one's foremost teacher,[5] but even to a teacher from whom he merely heard words of Torah.

[Moreover,] even if one verbally angered one of his peers, if he desires to be stringent and go to him [to ask forgiveness] many times, he may, provided that doing so will not compromise the respect due to the Torah.

ד וְהַמּוֹחֵל לֹא יִהְיֶה אַכְזָרִי מִלִּמְחֹל[יח,6] אֶלָּא יִמְחֹל לוֹ מִיָּד,[יט] אֶלָּא אִם כֵּן הוּא מִתְכַּוֵּן לְטוֹבַת הַמְבַקֵּשׁ מְחִילָה[כ] כְּדֵי שֶׁיִּכָּנַע לְבָבוֹ הֶעָרֵל,[כא]

4 [One who is asked to] forgive should not be callous and withhold forgiveness.[6] On the contrary, he should forgive immediately, unless his intent is for the benefit of the person asking forgiveness, to humble his brazen heart.

---

5. In the original, *rabo muvhak;* i .e., the mentor from whom he derived most of his learning.

6. Indeed, a person who does so is now considered the sinner *(Rambam, loc. cit.)*. To illustrate this principle, *Rambam* notes in the following law (2:10) that because the Gibeonites did not forgive the family of King Shaul, they were ostracized: "The Gibeonites are not among the Children of Israel" *(II Shmuel* 21:2*)*.

בשלש. טור ושו"ע שם. **יא** רב יוסי בר חנינא בגמרא שם. טור ושו"ע שם. וראה גם תניא אגה"ת פי"א (ק, א). **יב** פסיקתא רבתי (איש שלום) פרשה לח. מדרש תנחומא פרשת וארא סי' ל. מרדכי רמז תשכג. מהרי"ל שם (אחר שהלך ג' פעמים). רמ"א ס"א. **יג** לבוש ס"א. **יד** רי"ף ו, א. רמב"ם הל' תשובה פ"ב ה"ט. רא"ש פ"ח סוס"י יז. טור ושו"ע ס"א. **טו** שו"ת משפט צדק ח"ב סי' מט. כנסת הגדולה הגב"י. מ"א סק"ג. **טז** גמרא שם ע"ב, לפירוש רש"י שם ד"ה רב שאני. ב"ח ד"ה ומ"ש וה"מ. מ"א סק"ב. **יז** ב"ח ומ"א שם. **יח** משנה ב"ק צב, א. רש"י עה"ת במדבר כא, ז. מהרי"ל הל' ליל יום כיפור (ע' שכו). רמ"א ס"א. טור ושו"ע חו"מ סי' תכב ס"א. וראה גם לקמן חו"מ הל' נזקי גו"נ ס"ו (ומציין לכאן). תניא אגה"ת שם. לקו"ש חכ"ח ע' 138 ואילך. **יט** ראה תנחומא חוקת פי"ט. במדב"ר פי"ט, כג. תניא אגה"ת שם. לקו"ש שם ע' 146 הערה 61. לקמן ס"ח. לעיל סי' קנו ס"ג (לענין ת"ח). **כ** רמ"א שם. **כא** ט"ז סק"ב.

אוֹ שֶׁחוֹשֵׁשׁ שֶׁלֹּא יָבוֹא לוֹ לְעַצְמוֹ אֵיזֶה רָעָה עַל יְדֵי שֶׁיִּמְחֹל לוֹ,[כב,7] דְּאָז אֵינוֹ צָרִיךְ לִמְחֹל לוֹ, דְּחַיָּיו קוֹדְמִין לְחַיֵּי חֲבֵרוֹ.[כג]

וְאִם הוֹצִיא עָלָיו שֵׁם רַע[8] — אֵינוֹ צָרִיךְ לִמְחֹל לוֹ[כד] בְּכָל עִנְיָן, אֲפִלּוּ אִם יְבַקֵּשׁ מִמֶּנּוּ כַּמָּה פְּעָמִים,[כה] מִשּׁוּם דְּאֶפְשָׁר שֶׁיֵּשׁ בְּנֵי אָדָם שֶׁשָּׁמְעוּ הוֹצָאַת הַלַּעַז עָלָיו וְלֹא שָׁמְעוּ הַפִּיּוּס וְיִדָּמֶה לָהֶם שֶׁאֶפְשָׁר שֶׁהַלַּעַז הוּא אֱמֶת וְלֹא יָצָא עֲדַיִן אָדָם זֶה נָקִי מֵחֲשָׁד,[כו] וּמִכָּל מָקוֹם מִדַּת עֲנָוָה לִמְחֹל אֲפִלּוּ בְּהוֹצָאַת שֵׁם רַע:[כז]

Alternatively, [one may withhold forgiveness] if he fears that forgiving will cause harm to himself.[7] In such a situation he is not required to forgive, because his own life takes precedence over the life of his fellow.

If one person spread a disparaging report[8] about another, the latter is not required to forgive him under any circumstances, even if he is repeatedly asked for forgiveness, because some people may have heard of the false rumor but not of the appeasement. It will appear to them that the rumor may be true, and that this person has not yet been cleared of unfavorable suspicion.

Nevertheless, [as an expression of] the attribute of humility, it is proper to forgive even one who spread a disparaging report.

ה וְאִם מֵת מִי שֶׁפָּשַׁע כְּנֶגְדּוֹ — מֵבִיא עֲשָׂרָה בְּנֵי אָדָם וּמַעֲמִידָם עַל קִבְרוֹ[7] וְאוֹמֵר בִּפְנֵיהֶם "חָטָאתִי לֵאלֹהֵי יִשְׂרָאֵל וְלִפְלוֹנִי זֶה שֶׁפָּשַׁעְתִּי כְּנֶגְדּוֹ".[כח,9] וְצָרִיךְ שֶׁיֵּלֵךְ לְשָׁם יָחֵף. וְאִם הוּא חוּץ לְשָׁלֹשׁ פַּרְסָאוֹת[10] מִן קִבְרוֹ — אֵינוֹ צָרִיךְ לֵילֵךְ בְּעַצְמוֹ לְשָׁם, אֶלָּא יִשְׁלַח שְׁלוּחוֹ שֶׁיְּבַקֵּשׁ מִמֶּנּוּ מְחִילָה בַּעֲבוּר הַשּׁוֹלְחוֹ בִּפְנֵי עֲשָׂרָה בְּנֵי אָדָם:[כט]

5 If the wronged person died, [the offender] should bring ten people to his grave[7] and say in their presence: "I have sinned against the G-d of Israel and against this person whom I wronged."[9]

He should go there barefoot. If he [lives] more than three *parsaos*[10] from that person's grave, he is not obligated to go personally; he may send an agent who should request forgiveness there on his behalf in the presence of ten people.

ו וַאֲפִלּוּ הוֹצִיא עָלָיו שֵׁם רַע בְּחַיָּיו — מוֹעִיל מַה שֶּׁיְּבַקֵּשׁ מִמֶּנּוּ בִּפְנֵי עֲשָׂרָה בְּנֵי אָדָם, מִשּׁוּם שֶׁאָנוּ אוֹמְדִין דַּעְתּוֹ שֶׁל

6 Even if one spread a disparaging report about [the deceased] in his lifetime, asking his forgiveness in the presence of ten men is sufficient, for we surmise if the

7. *Yoma, loc. cit.*

8. Lit., "gave out a bad reputation."

9. *Maaseh Rokeiach* notes that when the offended party is alive, it is proper to ask forgiveness of him and then of G-d; after his passing, the order is reversed.

10. A *parsah* (parasang) is a Persian measure of distance equivalent to a little more than 2 miles.

כב גמרא פז, ב לפירוש רש"י שם ד"ה חלמא. ב"ח ד"ה ודע דבגמרא. מ"א סק"ד. וראה העו"ב תרמ ע' 23. כג אליה זוטא סק"ג. כד ירושלמי ב"ק פ"ח ה"ז. סמ"ג עשין טז (צט, ג). הגהות מיימוניות הל' תשובה פ"ב אות ט. שו"ת מהר"י ווייל סי' קצא. רמ"א שם. מרדכי רמז תשכג. כה לבוש שם. כו תרומת הדשן ח"ב סי' ריב. לבוש שם. מ"א סק"ה. כז ים של שלמה ב"ק פ"ח סי' סג. מ"א שם. וראה גם ט"ז סק"ג. כח גמרא פז, א. טור ושו"ע ס"ב. כט רש"ל ביש"ש שם סי' נ. מ"א סק"ז. ל ט"ז סק"ג. מ"א (ראה ס"ק ה, שמדת ענוה למחול). לא שלטי הגבורים ב"מ (לג, א), בשם רבנו יחיאל. כנה"ג הגה"ט. מ"א שם. לב רא"ש

הַמֵּת דְּמִן הַסְּתָם אִלּוּ הָיָה קַיָּם הָיָה מוֹחֵל לוֹ:[ל]

deceased were alive, he would probably forgive him.

ז וְאִם חֵרְפוֹ לְאַחַר מִיתָה – אֵינוֹ צָרִיךְ לֵילֵךְ עַל קִבְרוֹ, אֶלָּא מְבַקֵּשׁ מִמֶּנּוּ מְחִילָה בְּמָקוֹם שֶׁבִּיְּשׁוֹ:[לא]

7 If he disgraced him after his death, he does not need to go to his grave. Instead, he should ask his forgiveness in the place where he shamed him.

ח אַף עַל פִּי שֶׁבְּכָל הַשָּׁנָה רָאוּי לְכָל אָדָם לְפַיֵּס תֵּכֶף לְמִי שֶׁפָּשַׁע כְּנֶגְדּוֹ, מִכָּל מָקוֹם בְּעֶרֶב יוֹם הַכִּפּוּרִים צָרִיךְ לִזָּהֵר בָּזֶה בְּיוֹתֵר,[לב] כְּדֵי שֶׁיִּהְיֶה לֵב כָּל יִשְׂרָאֵל שָׁלֵם זֶה עִם זֶה וְלֹא יְהֵא מָקוֹם לַשָּׂטָן לְקַטְרֵג עֲלֵיהֶם:[לג,11]

8 To immediately appease [and ask forgiveness of] a person whom one has wronged is appropriate at any time throughout the year. Nevertheless, on the day before Yom Kippur one should be especially vigilant about this, so that the hearts of the Jewish people will all be at peace with each other, and thus Satan will have no opportunity to level accusations against them.[11]

ט תַּקָּנוֹת קַדְמוֹנִים וְחֵרֶם שֶׁלֹּא לְהוֹצִיא שֵׁם רַע עַל הַמֵּתִים:[לד,12]

9 It is an ordinance instituted by the Sages of the early generations, reinforced by a ban of ostracism, that one may not disparage the reputation of the deceased.[12]

י מִי שֶׁקָּרָא לַחֲבֵרוֹ מַמְזֵר[13] – לֹא פָּגַם בִּכְבוֹד אֲבוֹתָיו, שֶׁיָּכוֹל לוֹמַר אֵלֶיךָ לְבַד נִתְכַּוַּנְתִּי לְבַזּוֹתְךָ, אֶלָּא אִם כֵּן קְרָאוֹ מַמְזֵר בֶּן מַמְזֵר:[לה]

10 If one person called another a *mamzer*,[13] he did not blemish the honor of the latter's parents, because he could explain that he desired only to abuse that particular person himself. [This applies] unless he called him a *mamzer*, the son of a *mamzer*.

יא נוֹהֲגִין לִטְבֹּל בְּעֶרֶב יוֹם הַכִּפּוּרִים.[לו] וְיֵשׁ אוֹמְרִים[לז] שֶׁטַּעַם טְבִילָה זוֹ הוּא מִשּׁוּם קֶרִי,[14] כְּדֵי שֶׁיִּהְיוּ נְקִיִּים וּטְהוֹרִים בְּיוֹם הַכִּפּוּרִים,[15] וּלְפִי טַעַם זֶה

11 It is customary to immerse in a *mikveh* on the day preceding Yom Kippur. Some explain that this immersion was instituted because of *keri*,[14] so that we will be cleansed and pure on Yom Kippur.[15] According

---

11. Moreover, a magnanimous act of forgiveness between man and man prompts a similar dynamic between G-d and man *(Rosh HaShanah* 17b).

12. This is so, even though the dead are unaware of what was said of them *(Aruch HaShulchan* 606:4). Indeed, Moshe Rabbeinu was reprimanded for implying fault in the Patriarchs *(Tanchuma, Parshas Va'eschanan,* sec. 6). See also Mordechai on Tractate *Yoma,* sec. 724.

13. A child born of an adulterous or incestuous relationship.

14. I.e., having had a seminal emission.

15. Ezra instituted the requirement that one who had a seminal emission must immerse

פ"ח סי' כד, מהא דרב בגמרא פז, א. של"ה מסכת יומא עמוד התשובה (רכח, א) ד"ה ואעפ"י. ב"ח ריש הסימן. עטרת זקנים ריש הסימן. לג רא"ש שם. טור. לבוש ס"ב. לד שו"ע ס"ג. מרדכי רמז תשכד, ב"ק רמז קו, בשם ראבי"ה. לה יש"ש ב"ק פ"ח סי' מו. מ"א סק"ו. לו סדר רב עמרם גאון. הרי"ץ גיאת ח"א ע' נט. רא"ש פ"ח סי' כד. טור ולבוש ס"ג. לז רא"ש שם. טור. מהרי"ל הל' ערב יו"כ (ע' שטז), בדעת מהר"ם מרוטנבורג, בתשב"ץ סי' קכב. לבוש ס"ג.

אֵין עִנְיָן כְּלָל לוֹמַר וִדּוּיִים בַּמִּקְוֶה,[16] וְכֵן אֵין צָרִיךְ לִטְבֹּל אֶלָּא פַּעַם אַחַת.[לח]

וּמִי שֶׁטָּבַל בְּעֶרֶב רֹאשׁ הַשָּׁנָה וְלֹא רָאָה קֶרִי אַחַר כָּךְ – אַף עַל פִּי כֵן צָרִיךְ לִטְבֹּל בְּעֶרֶב יוֹם הַכִּפּוּרִים, דְּשֶׁמָּא רָאָה אַחַר כָּךְ מַיִם חֲלוּקִים אוֹ עֲכוּרִים,[לט] שֶׁהָרוֹאֶה אוֹתָן טָמֵא מִשּׁוּם בַּעַל קֶרִי.[מ,17]

וּטְבִילָה זוֹ שֶׁהִיא מִשּׁוּם קֶרִי כְּשֵׁרָה אֲפִלּוּ בְּאַרְבָּעִים סְאָה שְׁאוּבִים[מא,18] כְּשֶׁהֵם בַּקַּרְקַע, אֲבָל לֹא בִּכְלִי.[מב,19]

וּמִי שֶׁהוּא מִצְטַעֵר[מג] בִּטְבִילָה – יָכוֹל לִשְׁפֹּךְ עָלָיו תִּשְׁעָה קַבִּין[20] מַיִם.[מד,21] וְרַשַּׁאי לִשְׁפֹּךְ עָלָיו[22] מִשְּׁנַיִם אוֹ מִשְּׁלֹשָׁה כֵּלִים[מה] זֶה אַחַר זֶה וּבֵין כֻּלָּם יִהְיֶה תִּשְׁעָה קַבִּין, וּבִלְבַד

to this view, there is no point at all in saying confessional prayers in the *mikveh*,[16] nor is there any need to immerse more than once.

One who immersed before Rosh HaShanah and did not have a seminal emission in the interim should nevertheless immerse on the day before Yom Kippur, lest he had discharged a flow of urine that was either intermittent or turbid. For one who has such a discharge is impure, as if he had a seminal emission.[17]

An immersion occasioned by *keri* is valid even in 40 *seah* of drawn water[18] that are collected [in a reservoir] in the ground, but not in a vessel.[19]

One who will suffer discomfort because of this immersion may have nine *kabin*[20] of water[21] poured over [his head and body].[22] This water may be poured from two or three containers in succession, as long as the total quantity is [no less than] nine *kabin*. [In this instance, however,] one must begin pouring from the second container before one has finished pouring from

in a *mikveh* before prayer. Some time later, the Talmudic Sages observed that people on the whole had never fully accepted this standard and ruled that this obligation was no longer binding. (See *Berachos* 22b; see also sec. 88:1 in Vol. 2 of the present work and footnotes there.) Nevertheless, on Yom Kippur, it is appropriate to pray in a state of purity. (Sec. 613:19 below speaks of one who had a seminal emission on Yom Kippur itself.)

16. See *Mateh Ephraim* 606:8.

17. *Mikvaos* 8:2.

18. In the original, *mayim she'uvim.* If a *mikveh* is to be valid for other purposes, the prescribed minimal quantity of water must flow into it naturally; the *mikveh* is invalidated if the water is drawn into it by human intervention. This requirement does not apply to the water in which one who has had a seminal emission must immerse.

19. Hence immersion in a water tank or in a fiberglass fishpond is invalid.

20. A *kav* is a Talmudic fluid measure equal to four *lugin*. To begin with a familiar unit of measure: A *Kiddush* cup must contain at least a *revi'is* (i.e., a quarter of a *lug*) of wine. According to *Shiurei Torah* by R. Avraham Chayim Naeh, this comes to 86 cc. (which is the *gematria* of כוס — "cup"). One *lug* is thus 4 x 86 = 344 cc. There are four *lugim* in one *kav:* 4 x 344 = 1376 cc. Nine *kabin* (the volume required by our text above) is thus 1376 x 9 = 12384 cc. = 12.384 liters. Since one U.S. gallon = 3.785 liters, nine *kabin* is approximately 3 1/4 U.S. gallons. (And since one imperial gallon = 4.546 liters, nine *kabin* is approximately 2 3/4 imperial gallons.)

21. Ordinary tap water, which belongs to the category of *mayim she'uvim,* meets this requirement.

22. *Mikvaos* 3:4.

לח מהר"י ווייל סי' קצא. רמ"א ס"ד. לט מ"א סוף סק"ח. וראה מ"א סי' פח סק"א. לקו"ש ח"ז ע' 315. שלחן המלך ח"א ע' קז־קח. מ מקואות פ"ח מ"ב. רמב"ם הל' אבות הטומאה פ"ה ה"ו. מא משנה מקואות פ"ח מ"א. מ"א סק"ט. ב"י סי' פח ד"ה והוי.לעיל שם סוף ס"א. מב ברייתא ברכות כב, ב כת"ק, ולחד מאן דאמר שם – אף לרבי יהודה. ראב"ד הל' ברכות פ"ו ה"ה (לענין נט"י). ב"י שם. מ"א שם. לעיל שם (במוסגר). סי' קנט סכ"ג. מג מהר"י ווייל שם. מ"א ס"ק ט. מד מהר"ם מרוטנבורג בתשב"ץ שם. רמ"א שם. וראה לעיל שם. מה משנה מקואות פ"ג מ"ד. מ"א סק"ט. וראה גם לעיל שם. מו ב"י שם ד"ה ותשעה,

שֶׁיַּתְחִיל הַשֵּׁנִי עַד שֶׁלֹּא פָּסַק הָרִאשׁוֹן וְכֵן הַשְּׁלִישִׁי עַד שֶׁלֹּא פָּסַק הַשֵּׁנִי.[מו,23] אֲבָל מֵאַרְבָּעָה כֵּלִים – אֵין מִצְטָרְפִין לְתִשְׁעָה קַבִּין.[מז] וַאֲפִלּוּ אִם מְמָרֵק[מח] מִכְּלִי אֶחָד – יִזָּהֵר לְהָרִיק בְּלֹא הַפְסָקָה כְּלָל.[מט,24] וְאִם נִכְנַס חֶצְיוֹ לְתוֹךְ הַמִּקְוֶה וְעַל חֶצְיוֹ שָׁפְכוּ ט׳ קַבִּין – יָצָא.[נ,25]

וְאִשָּׁה שֶׁשִּׁמְּשָׁה תּוֹךְ שְׁלֹשָׁה יָמִים לִטְבִילָה זוֹ – צְרִיכָה לְכַבֵּד בֵּיתָהּ בְּחַמִּין קֹדֶם שֶׁתִּטְבֹּל, כְּדֵי לְהַפְלִיט כָּל הַשִּׁכְבַת זֶרַע שֶׁבִּמְקוֹרָהּ, שֶׁלֹּא תַּפְלִיט אַחַר הַטְּבִילָה וּתְהֵא טְמֵאָה בְּיוֹם הַכִּפּוּרִים[26] – עַיֵּן בְּיוֹרֶה דֵעָה סִימָן קצ״ו.[נא,27] וְאִם שִׁמְּשָׁה סָמוּךְ לִטְבִילָתָהּ אוֹ סָמוּךְ לְוִסְתָּהּ, שֶׁבְּאֵלּוּ הַזְּמַנִּים הִיא רְגִילָה לְהִתְעַבֵּר – לֹא תְּכַבֵּד בֵּיתָהּ בְּחַמִּין, שֶׁמָּא תַּשְׁחִית זֶרַע הַהֵרָיוֹן,[נב] לְפִיכָךְ אֵינָהּ צְרִיכָה לִטְבֹּל כְּלָל בְּעֶרֶב יוֹם הַכִּפּוּרִים:[נג]

the first, and begin pouring from the third before one has finished pouring from the second.[23] Water poured from four containers is never considered as a single quantity of nine *kabin.* [Moreover,] even when pouring from a single container, one must be careful to pour the water without any interruption.[24]

One who immersed half of his body in a *mikveh,* [while] nine *kabin* were poured over the other half, has fulfilled his obligation.[25]

If a woman engaged in relations within three days [before] this immersion, she should wash the private parts with hot water before immersing in order to remove any semen that might be lodged within, lest she discharge it after the immersion and thus be impure on Yom Kippur.[26] See *Shulchan Aruch, Yoreh Deah,* sec. 196.[27]

If she engaged in relations directly following her immersion [after her menstrual cycle] or directly before the onset of her menstrual cycle, at which times she is likely to conceive, she should not wash the private parts with hot water lest she destroy seed [that might have led to] conception. For this reason, she should not immerse at all on the day before Yom Kippur.

---

23. This obviously requires the help of at least one other person.

24. *Taharas Mayim* (sec. 58) states that when there is no alternative, the requirement of pouring nine *kabin* over one's head and body may be fulfilled by taking a shower for two or three minutes, the length of time depending on the water pressure.

25. *Gittin* 16a.

26. Due to the issue raised by the Alter Rebbe and due to additional halachic considerations (e.g., the possibility that this day may fall in the midst of a married woman's seven "clean" days), those women who do observe this practice are usually of maturer years.

27. This section is not extant in the Alter Rebbe's *Shulchan Aruch.* The intent of the above reference is apparently *Yoreh Deah* 196:11, which states that a woman must wait several days before beginning her count of *shivah nekiyim* ("seven clean days") lest she have engaged in relations shortly before the onset of menstruation and discharge semen, in which case the day on which that took place could not be considered as one of those seven days. Once three days have passed, the semen is considered to have decomposed and the above delay is no longer called for.

ממשנה מקואות שם. מ״א שם. **מז** מקואות שם. מ״א שם. וראה לעיל שם, ובנסמן בשוה״ג שם. **מח** בקונטרס השלחן הגיה: מריק. **מט** רבנו יונה ברכות (יג, ב) ד״ה כי. מ״א שם. **נ** בעיא דרב פפא גיטין טז, א (לענין שני לטומאה). רמב״ם הל׳ אבות הטומאה פ״ט ה״ג (לקולא). ב״י שם ד״ה והוי (דבדרבנן נקטינן לקולא). מ״א שם. **נא** סימן זה בשוע״ר לא הגיע לידינו, וראה שו״ע שם סי״א. **נב** מהרי״ל שם. דרכי משה ס״ק ג. מ״א סק״ח. **נג** דרכי משה שם.

12 Other authorities[28] maintain that the reason for this immersion, as also in the case of a convert,[29] is *teshuvah,* and hence one should immerse three times.[30] Accordingly, immersion is also customary even by youths past the age of *bar-mitzvah*[31] and young girls past the age of *bas-mitzvah,*[32] even though the rationale of *keri* is not relevant to them. Likewise, even a person who immersed before Rosh HaShanah and did not have a seminal emission in the interim must still immerse again on the day before Yom Kippur as an act of repentance.

יב אֲבָל יֵשׁ אוֹמְרִים[נד, 28] שֶׁטַּעַם טְבִילָה זוֹ הוּא מִשּׁוּם תְּשׁוּבָה, כְּגֵר הַמִּתְגַּיֵּר.[29] וּלְפִי זֶה יֵשׁ לִטְבֹּל שָׁלֹשׁ פְּעָמִים.[נה, 30] וַאֲפִלּוּ נְעָרִים וּבְתוּלוֹת[32] שֶׁהֵם בְּנֵי מִצְוָה[31] נוֹהֲגִים לִטְבֹּל, אַף עַל פִּי שֶׁאֵין קֶרִי שַׁיָּךְ בָּהֶן.[נו] וַאֲפִלּוּ מִי שֶׁטָּבַל בְּעֶרֶב רֹאשׁ הַשָּׁנָה וְלֹא רָאָה קֶרִי אַחַר כָּךְ — צָרִיךְ לַחֲזֹר וְלִטְבֹּל בְּעֶרֶב יוֹם הַכִּפּוּרִים מִשּׁוּם תְּשׁוּבָה:[נז]

13 One should immerse before the Afternoon Service so that he can recite the confessional prayer (during the Afternoon Service) in a state of purity. There are some who immerse after the meal that precedes the fast[33] so that [their immersion] will be close to [the onset of] Yom Kippur.[34]

יג יֵשׁ לִטְבֹּל קֹדֶם תְּפִלַּת מִנְחָה, כְּדֵי לְהִתְוַדּוֹת (בְּמִנְחָה) בְּטָהֳרָה.[נח] וְיֵשׁ טוֹבְלִין אַחַר סְעוּדָה הַמַּפְסֶקֶת,[33] כְּדֵי שֶׁיְּהֵא סָמוּךְ לְיוֹם הַכִּפּוּרִים:[נט, 34]

14 If a close relative[35] died before Yom Kippur, one is permitted to bathe in hot water and immerse on the day before Yom Kippur. [The rationale is that] Yom Kippur is

יד מִי שֶׁמֵּת לוֹ מֵת[35] קֹדֶם יוֹם הַכִּפּוּרִים — מֻתָּר לוֹ לִרְחֹץ בְּחַמִּין וְלִטְבֹּל בְּעֶרֶב יוֹם הַכִּפּוּרִים, מִפְּנֵי

---

28. Cf. subsection 11 above.

29. Just as a righteous convert (a *ger tzedek*) is required to immerse, the custom is that an apostate Jew who returns to the faith of his fathers also immerses *(Rama, Yoreh Deah* 268:12*)*.

30. I.e., three successive times in the course of a single visit to the *mikveh.* This practice is cited by *Maharil* in the name of *Rokeiach,* and by *Sefer Chassidim* (sec. 394); both sources base it on Biblical allusions.

31. Indeed, according to the accepted custom of Lubavitch (and of many other circles), daily throughout the year.

32. Over the years objections have been raised to this practice, both with regard to young girls and also with regard to women who are presently unmarried, for fear of untoward repercussions. (See *Sdei Chemed, Yom HaKippurim* 1:6, cited in *She'arim HaMetzuyanim BaHalachah* 131:13, and in *Halichos Bas Yisrael,* ch. 19, footnote 61.) Accordingly, this immersion is not very widely practiced today.

33. In the original, *seudah mafsekes.*

34. It is the custom of some *Chabad chassidim* to visit the *mikveh* three times on the day before Yom Kippur: once in the morning, in preparation for *Shacharis,* once before *Minchah,* as explained in the first opinion above, and once after the *seudah mafsekes,* in deference to the second view above.

35. I.e., one's spouse, father, mother, brother, sister, son or daughter, for whom he must observe the seven days of *shivah* mourning during which bathing is prohibited.

נד מהרי"ל שם (ע' שטו). דרכי משה ס"ק ג. מ"א סק"ח בשם ויש אומרים. נה מהרי"ל שם (ע' שטז). דרכי משה שם. מ"א שם. נו מהרי"ל שם (ע' שטו). מ"א שם. נז מהרי"ל שם. דרכי משה שם. מ"א שם. נח מהרי"ל שם ושם. מ"א שם. ט"ז סק"ד. נט מהרי"ל שם. מ"א שם. וראה אוצר מנהגי חב"ד יוה"כ ע' קעח. ס מהרי"ל הל' שמחות (ע' תרה). רמ"א ס"ד. סא סימן זה בשוע"ר לא הגיע לידינו, וראה שו"ע שם סט"ו. סב מ"א סק"י. ולענין טבילת מצוה

considered like a festival which negates the decrees of the *shivah* mourning period, as explained in sec. 548.[36]

However, bathing and immersion should be delayed as late as possible so that they will be close to nightfall, for the reason explained there.[37] The other laws of mourning, e.g., sitting on the ground,[38] must be observed until actual nightfall, for the reason explained there.

שֶׁיּוֹם הַכִּפּוּרִים דִּינוֹ כָּרְגָלִים שֶׁמְּבַטְּלִים מִמֶּנּוּ גְּזֵירַת שִׁבְעָה[ס] כְּמוֹ שֶׁנִּתְבָּאֵר בְּסִימָן תקמ"ח,[סא,36] אֶלָּא דְּיֵשׁ לוֹ לְאַחֵר הָרְחִיצָה וְהַטְּבִילָה כָּל מַה שֶּׁאֶפְשָׁר שֶׁיִּהְיוּ סָמוּךְ לַחֲשֵׁכָה[סב] מִטַּעַם שֶׁנִּתְבָּאֵר שָׁם.[סג,37] וּשְׁאָר דִּינֵי אֲבֵלוּת כְּגוֹן יְשִׁיבָה עַל גַּבֵּי קַרְקַע[38] — צָרִיךְ לִנְהֹג עַד הַלַּיְלָה מַמָּשׁ, מִטַּעַם שֶׁנִּתְבָּאֵר שָׁם:[סד]

SECTION 607 The Order of the Confessional Prayer in the Afternoon Service of *Erev* Yom Kippur. (1–16)

סימן תרז סֵדֶר הַוִּדּוּי בְּמִנְחָה בְּעֶרֶב יוֹם הַכִּפּוּרִים וּבוֹ ט"ז סְעִיפִים:

1 Yom Kippur is a day of forgiveness and atonement,[1] as it is written,[2] "For on this day He will grant atonement…." Accordingly, every individual must confess his sins.[3] [This is derived from a comparison with] all the sacrifices that are offered in order to secure atonement, and concerning them it is written,[4] "And they shall confess [the] sin that they have committed."

According to law, the *mitzvah* of confession applies at the beginning of the time of atonement,[5] i.e., at nightfall on the eve of Yom

א כֵּיוָן שֶׁיּוֹם הַכִּפּוּרִים הוּא יוֹם הַסְּלִיחָה וְכַפָּרָה,[1] כְּמוֹ שֶׁנֶּאֱמַר[א,2] "כִּי בַיּוֹם הַזֶּה יְכַפֵּר וגו'", לְפִיכָךְ צָרִיךְ כָּל אָדָם שֶׁיִּתְוַדֶּה עַל חֲטָאָיו,[3] כִּי כֵּן מָצִינוּ בְּכָל קָרְבָּנוֹת הַבָּאִים לְכַפֵּר,[ב] שֶׁנֶּאֱמַר[ג,4] "וְהִתְוַדּוּ אֶת חַטָּאתָם אֲשֶׁר עָשׂוּ".

וּמִצְוַת וִדּוּי מִן הַדִּין הוּא בְּהַתְחָלַת זְמַן הַכַּפָּרָה,[5] דְּהַיְנוּ מִשֶּׁתֶּחְשַׁךְ[ד] לֵיל

---

36. Sec. 548 of the Alter Rebbe's *Shulchan Aruch* is not extant. In the *Shulchan Aruch* of R. Yosef Caro, this subject is found in sec. 548:7.

37. See *Shulchan Aruch, Orach Chayim* 548:10.

In the year 5725 (1964), on the sixth of Tishrei, the Rebbe's mother passed away. Visited by numerous eminent scholars during the *shivah,* the Rebbe raised the question of whether he would be allowed to immerse before *Minchah* on the afternoon immediately preceding Yom Kippur. The discussion on this subject is recorded in *Toras Menachem — Menachem Zion* (Kehot, N.Y., 1994), Vol. 1, p. 97.

38. Or on a low chair or stool.

SECTION 607

1. *Bava Basra* 122a; cf. *Taanis* 30b.

2. *Vayikra* 16:30.

3. I.e., for the atonement *(kaparah)* to be complete, it must be accompanied by confession *(vidui).*

4. *Bamidbar* 5:7.

5. *Yoma* 87b.

קודם מנחה ראה שיחות קודש תשכ"ה ח"א (ע' 525 ואילך). **סג** ראה שו"ע שם ס"י ובמ"א שם סקי"ד וסקט"ו. ט"ז שם סק"ג. **סד** ראה שם מ"א סקי"ד.

סימן תרז: א ויקרא טז, ל. **ב** לבוש ס"א. וראה לקמן סוף ס"ב (ולשוב בתשובה שלימה). לקוטי באורים לס' התניא ח"ב ע' מ ואילך, וע' סט. שלחן המלך ח"ב ע' רטו הערה 2. **ג** במדבר ה, ז. כ"ה בדפו"ר. וכן הובא בלבוש שם. תניא אגרת התשובה פ"א. ובדפוסים המאוחרים: והתודה אשר חטא עליה (ויקרא ה, ה). וראה רמב"ם הל' תשובה פ"א ה"א (הובאו שניהם). לקוטי באורים שם ע' סח. מ"מ וציונים. **ד** ברייתא פז, ב (עם חשכה). רא"ש פ"ח סי' יט. טור (ושו"ע) ולבוש שם (זמן התחלת הכפרה).

יוֹם הַכִּפּוּרִים, אֶלָּא שֶׁחָשְׁשׁוּ חֲכָמִים[ה] שֶׁמָּא יֶאֱרַע דְּבַר קַלְקָלָה[ו] שֶׁל שִׁכְרוּת[ז] וְכַיּוֹצֵא בּוֹ[ח] בִּסְעוּדָה הַמַּפְסֶקֶת וְלֹא יוּכַל לְהִתְוַדּוֹת[ט] בְּהַתְחָלַת זְמַן הַכַּפָּרָה, לְכָךְ תִּקְנוּ שֶׁיִּתְוַדֶּה כָּל אָדָם בְּעֶרֶב יוֹם הַכִּפּוּרִים בְּמִנְחָה[י] קֹדֶם שֶׁיֹּאכַל בִּסְעוּדָה הַמַּפְסֶקֶת.[יא]

וְאַף עַל פִּי שֶׁהִתְוַדָּה בְּמִנְחָה – צָרִיךְ לַחֲזֹר וּלְהִתְוַדּוֹת בְּעַרְבִית,[יב] שֶׁהִיא הַתְחָלַת זְמַן הַכַּפָּרָה, וְהוּא עִקַּר זְמַן הַוִּדּוּי שֶׁל יוֹם הַכִּפּוּרִים.[יג] וְאַף עַל פִּי שֶׁהִתְוַדָּה עַרְבִית – חוֹזֵר וּמִתְוַדֶּה בִּתְפִלַּת שַׁחֲרִית,[יד] שֶׁמָּא אֵרַע לוֹ דְּבַר עֲבֵרָה אַחַר הַוִּדּוּי שֶׁל עַרְבִית, וּמִטַּעַם הַזֶּה הוּא צָרִיךְ לַחֲזֹר וּלְהִתְוַדּוֹת בְּמוּסָף וּבְמִנְחָה וּבִנְעִילָה[6] שֶׁמָּא אֵרַע לוֹ דְּבַר עֲבֵרָה בְּכָל הַיּוֹם,[טו] שֶׁיּוֹם הַכִּפּוּרִים מְכַפֵּר עַד סוֹפוֹ עִם חֲשֵׁכָה:[טז]

Kippur. Nevertheless, the Sages feared that an undesirable matter such as drunkenness might occur during the meal preceding the fast and one might not be able to confess at the beginning of the time for atonement. They therefore ordained that every individual should confess during the Afternoon Service on the day preceding Yom Kippur, before partaking of the meal preceding the fast.

Even though one confessed during the Afternoon Service, he must confess again during the Evening Service, for this is the beginning of the time of atonement and this is the primary time for the confession of Yom Kippur.

And even though one confessed during the Evening Service, he must confess again during the Morning Service, lest something sinful befell him after the confession during the Evening Service. For the same reason he should repeat the confession during the *Mussaf, Minchah,* and *Neilah* services,[6] lest something sinful befell him in the course of the day, for the atonement granted by Yom Kippur [continues to] take effect until its conclusion, at nightfall.

ב וְיֵשׁ אוֹמְרִים[יז] שֶׁזְּמַן מִצְוַת וִדּוּי מִן הַדִּין הוּא קֹדֶם הַתְחָלַת זְמַן הַכַּפָּרָה, דְּהַיְנוּ עִם חֲשֵׁכָה,[7] כְּדֵי

2 However, some authorities maintain that according to law, the time for the *mitzvah* of confession is before the beginning of the time of atonement, i.e., just before nightfall,[7]

6. The spiritual significance of this repetition is further explained in the teachings of *Chassidus.* The five prayer services of Yom Kippur *(Maariv, Shacharis, Mussaf, Minchah, Ne'ilah)* correspond, in ascending order, to the five levels of the soul *(Nefesh, Ruach, Neshamah, Chayah, Yechidah)* that are cleansed through confession. (See *Likkutei Sichos,* Vol. 4, p. 1154, based on *Likkutei Torah, Bamidbar,* p. 81b; *Sefer HaMaamarim — Melukat,* Vol. 4, p. 17; *op. cit.,* Vol. 5, p. 22. See also: *Hisvaaduyos 5742,* p. 97.

7. I.e., directly before the onset of the holiday, as distinct from the confession after nightfall that appears in the Evening Service.

ה גמרא [ברייתא] שם, לגירסתינו ולגירסת הטור (אבל אמרו חכמים). ו ברייתא שם, לגירסת הרי"ף (ו, א) והרא"ש שם (יארע דבר קלקול בסעודה). מ"א סק"א. ז רש"י שם ד"ה שמא. ר"ן שם ד"ה ת"ר. לבוש שם. ח ר"ן שם. לבוש שם. מ"א שם. ט לבוש שם. י טור ושו"ע ס"א. יא ברייתא שם. טור ושו"ע שם. יב ברייתא שם (לאחר שיאכל וישתה), לפירוש הרמב"ם הל' תשובה פ"ב ה"ז (ערבית). ר"ן שם בשם הראשונים. ב"י שם. יג לבוש שם (כשיכנס יום הדין ויחשך ויתקדש היום). יד ברייתא שם. רי"ף ורא"ש שם. רמב"ם שם. טו ברייתא שם, לפירוש רש"י שם ד"ה דבר קלקלה (לענין אחר סעודה) רמב"ן בחידושיו פז, ב (גם לענין שחרית כו'). הובא בר"ן שם וב"י שם. טז משנה כריתות כה, א. רמב"ן יומא שם. רמב"ם הל' שגגות פ"ג ה"ט. וראה כריתות ז, א וברש"י ד"ה אי נמי דעביד, דהיינו עד שקיעת החמה. יז רמב"ן שם. יח רמב"ן שם (לענין ערבית). יט ראה רמב"ם שם. לעיל ריש ס"א וש"נ. כ ב"י סוד"ה וצריך

so that one will enter the day in a state of penitence and will not have the opportunity to sin between the confession and the beginning of the time of atonement. Nevertheless, the Sages were concerned lest an undesirable matter might occur during the meal and one might not be able to confess before nightfall. They therefore ordained that one should confess during the Afternoon Service.

Although one confessed in the Afternoon Service, he should confess again just before nightfall, for according to law, this is the primary time for confession, since it is possible that something sinful befell him after the Afternoon Service. And even though one confessed before nightfall, he should confess again during the Evening Service and during all the services of the day, for certainly on Yom Kippur itself one is also obligated to confess and repent in complete *teshuvah*.

The *halachah* follows the first view. Nevertheless, it is appropriate for every individual to undertake the stringency of following the second opinion as well. Hence, as he sees twilight approaching, he should stand up[8] and confess.[9]

שֶׁיִּכְנַס לַיּוֹם בִּתְשׁוּבָה וְלֹא יְהֵא שָׁהוּת לַחֲטֹא בֵּין הַוִּדּוּי לְהַתְחָלַת זְמַן הַכַּפָּרָה, אֶלָּא שֶׁחָשְׁשׁוּ חֲכָמִים שֶׁמָּא יֶאֱרַע לוֹ דְּבַר קַלְקָלָה בַּסְּעוּדָה וְלֹא יוּכַל לְהִתְוַדּוֹת עִם חֲשֵׁכָה, לְכָךְ תִּקְּנוּ לְהִתְוַדּוֹת בְּמִנְחָה, וְאַף עַל פִּי שֶׁהִתְוַדָּה בְּמִנְחָה — חוֹזֵר וּמִתְוַדֶּה עִם חֲשֵׁכָה, שֶׁהוּא עִקַּר זְמַן וִדּוּי מִן הַדִּין, שֶׁמָּא אֵרַע לוֹ דְּבַר עֲבֵרָה אַחַר מִנְחָה, וְאַף עַל פִּי שֶׁהִתְוַדָּה עִם חֲשֵׁכָה — חוֹזֵר וּמִתְוַדֶּה בִּתְפִלַּת עַרְבִית וּבְכָל תְּפִלָּה שֶׁל הַיּוֹם, לְפִי שֶׁבְּוַדַּאי גַּם בְּיוֹם הַכִּפּוּרִים עַצְמוֹ חַיָּב לְהִתְוַדּוֹת[יח] וְלָשׁוּב בִּתְשׁוּבָה שְׁלֵמָה.[יט]

וַהֲלָכָה כַּסְּבָרָא הָרִאשׁוֹנָה.[כ] מִכָּל מָקוֹם, רָאוּי לְכָל אָדָם לְהַחְמִיר עַל עַצְמוֹ כַּסְּבָרָא הַשְּׁנִיָּה,[כא] וּכְשֶׁרוֹאֶה בֵּין הַשְּׁמָשׁוֹת מְמַשְׁמֵשׁ וּבָא — יַעֲמֹד[8] וְיִתְוַדֶּה:[כב,9]

3 When one confesses individually,[10] whether during the Afternoon Service on the day before Yom Kippur, or during the Evening, Morning, *Mussaf*, Afternoon, or *Neilah* services of Yom Kippur, he should confess after completing *Shemoneh Esreh*, before leaving the place he was standing. The *sheliach tzibbur*, by contrast,[11] recites the confession on Yom Kippur in the midst of *Shemoneh Esreh*.

ג כְּשֶׁהַיָּחִיד מִתְוַדֶּה,[כג,10] בֵּין בִּתְפִלַּת מִנְחָה שֶׁל עֶרֶב יוֹם הַכִּפּוּרִים בֵּין בְּעַרְבִית שַׁחֲרִית מוּסָף מִנְחָה וּנְעִילָה שֶׁל יוֹם הַכִּפּוּרִים[כד] — הוּא מִתְוַדֶּה אַחַר שֶׁגָּמַר תְּפִלָּתוֹ קֹדֶם שֶׁעָקַר רַגְלָיו, אֲבָל הַשְּׁלִיחַ צִבּוּר[11] אוֹמֵר הַוִּדּוּי בְּיוֹם הַכִּפּוּרִים בְּתוֹךְ הַתְּפִלָּה.[כה]

8. See subsection 7.

9. I.e., at this point *Ashamnu* and *Al Cheit* are recited individually, not communally.

10. *Yoma* 87b.

11. When repeating *Shemoneh Esreh*.

(והעולם לא נהגו כדברי הרמב"ן). **כא** של"ה מסכת יומא עמוד התשובה (רכח, ב) ד"ה בפרק בתרא. מ"א סק"ז. **כב** של"ה שם. וראה אוצר מנהגי חב"ד יוה"כ ע' רא־ב. **כג** גמרא פז, ב. רא"ש פ"ח סי' יט. טור. רמ"א ס"א. **כד** ב"י ד"ה והיכן. **כה** גמרא שם. רא"ש שם. טור. רמ"א שם.

אֲבָל בִּתְפִלַּת הַמִּנְחָה שֶׁל עֶרֶב יוֹם הַכִּפּוּרִים — אֵין הַשְּׁלִיחַ צִבּוּר חוֹזֵר אֶת הַוִּדּוּי בְּקוֹל רָם,[כו,12] דְּכֵיוָן שֶׁלֹּא תִּקְּנוּ הַוִּדּוּי בְּמִנְחָה אֶלָּא מִשּׁוּם חֲשָׁשׁ שֶׁמָּא יֶאֱרַע דְּבַר קַלְקָלָה בַּסְּעוּדָה,[כז] וְהַשְּׁלִיחַ צִבּוּר אֵינוֹ מַחֲזִיר אֶת הַתְּפִלָּה אֶלָּא כְּדֵי לְהוֹצִיא אֶת מִי שֶׁאֵינוֹ בָּקִי — לֹא רָצוּ חֲכָמִים לְתַקֵּן שֶׁיַּחֲזֹר שְׁלִיחַ צִבּוּר אֶת הַוִּדּוּי שֶׁמָּא יֶאֱרַע דְּבַר קַלְקָלָה לְמִי שֶׁאֵינוֹ בָּקִי, שֶׁמּוּעָטִין הֵן שֶׁאֵינָן בְּקִיאִים:[כח]

However, in the Afternoon Service on the day before Yom Kippur, the *sheliach tzibbur* does not repeat the confession aloud.[12] The rationale is that the confession was [placed] in the Afternoon Service only because of a concern that something undesirable might occur during the [following] meal. Now, the *sheliach tzibbur* repeats *Shemoneh Esreh* only to enable one who is not knowledgeable [with regard to prayer] to fulfill his obligation. Hence the Sages did not want to ordain that the *sheliach tzibbur* repeat the confession [only because] it is possible that something undesirable might occur to a person who is not knowledgeable, for [such] people are few.

ד אִם לֹא פֵּרֵט אֶת חֲטָאָיו אֶלָּא אָמַר סְתָם "חָטָאתִי" — יָצָא יְדֵי מִצְוַת וִדּוּי.[כט,13] וּמִכָּל מָקוֹם, לְכַתְּחִלָּה[ל] נָכוֹן לְפָרֵט אֶת הַחֵטְא[לא] שֶׁיֹּאמַר "עָשִׂיתִי כָּךְ וְכָךְ",[לב] מִפְּנֵי (שערב יוה"כ) [שֶׁעַל יְדֵי כֵּן[לג]] הוּא מִתְבַּיֵּשׁ יוֹתֵר לִפְנֵי הַקָּדוֹשׁ בָּרוּךְ הוּא מֵחֲטָאָיו וּמִתְחָרֵט עֲלֵיהֶם מֵעֹמֶק לִבּוֹ.[לד]

וּכְשֶׁהוּא מְפָרֵט חֲטָאָיו — יִתְוַדֶּה בְּלַחַשׁ,[לה] שֶׁאִם יִתְוַדֶּה בְּקוֹל רָם — אָסוּר לוֹ לְפָרֵט חֲטָאָיו בָּרַבִּים,[לו] לְפִי שֶׁאֵין זֶה כְּבוֹד הַמָּקוֹם שֶׁמְּגַלֶּה לָרַבִּים שֶׁחָטָא כְּנֶגְדּוֹ.[לז]

בַּמֶּה דְּבָרִים אֲמוּרִים? בְּחֵטְא שֶׁאֵין מְפֻרְסָם, אֲבָל חֵטְא הַמְפֻרְסָם לָרַבִּים —

4 If one did not enumerate his sins individually, but merely said, "I have sinned," he has fulfilled the *mitzvah* of confession.[13] Initially, however, it is preferable to mention his sins individually, saying, "I did such-and-such," for by doing so he will be more embarrassed [by them] before the Holy One, blessed be He, and will regret them from the depths of his heart.

When one enumerates his sins, he should confess in a whisper. Were he to confess aloud, it would be forbidden for him to enumerate his sins in public, for it would not be respectful to the Omnipresent that one publicly reveal that he sinned against Him.

When does the above apply? To a sin which is not public knowledge. A sin

12. I.e., like the other congregants, he recites it only during the whispered *Shemoneh Esreh*.

13. *Yoma* 86b.

כו טור בשם ראבי"ה סי' תקכח, ובשם הרי"ץ גיאת הל' יוה"כ (ע' נט). מרדכי רמז תשכה. (ושו"ע) רמ"א ס"ה. כז מרדכי שם. טור ולבוש ס"ה. כח ב"י ד"ה וגם כי לא נתקן. לבוש שם. כט גמרא פו, ב. רמב"ם הל' תשובה פ"ב ה"ח. טור ורמ"א ס"ג. וראה לחם משנה שם (אם צריך לומר גם עוינו פשענו). לקו"ש חי"ז ע' 193 ואילך. שלחן המלך ח"ב ע' רט־ריא. ל ב"י ד"ה ולענין הלכה. שו"ע ס"ב, שהלכה כרבי עקיבא פו, ב שאין צריך לפרט החטא. אלא שנכון לפרט בלחש. לא של"ה מסכת יומא עמוד התשובה (רכח, ב) ד"ה בפרק בתרא (שהעיקר כדעת רבי יהודה בן בבא שם, שצריך לפרט). ב"ח ד"ה ומ"ש וכן. לב ראה רמב"ם שם פ"א ה"א. לג כן הגיה בקונטרס השלחן. לד של"ה שם. וראה גם רש"י שם ד"ה בחטא מפורסם. ב"י שם. לה ב"י שם. של"ה שם. לו מ"א סק"ב (גם לדעת רבי יהודה בן בבא). וכדלעיל סי' קא סוף ס"ב וש"נ. לז רש"י שם ד"ה בחטא שאינו מפורסם. ב"ח שם. לח רב שם. מ"א שם.

which is public knowledge, by contrast, may be specifically mentioned in public, even aloud,[14] though there is no obligation to [do so]. One may specify it in a whisper if he so desires.

5 Reciting the confessional prayer *Al Cheit* according to its alphabetical pattern is not considered as enumerating one's sins. Since everyone recites [this confessional] uniformly, it is considered as part of the standard prayer service. It may therefore be recited aloud.

6 The order of the confessions in the *Al Cheit* prayer should be "[And for the sins for which we are obligated to bring] a burnt-offering," then "…a sin-offering," "…an adjustable [guilt-] offering,"[15] and then "…a guilt-offering or a conditional guilt-offering," for the sacrifices are listed in this order in *Parshas Vayikra*.[16]

The sequence that follows is: "for the sins for which we incur [the penalty of] lashing for rebelliousness,"[17] then "…[the penalty of] forty lashes," "…[the penalty of] death by the hand of Heaven," "…[the penalty of] excision and childlessness," and then "…[the penalty of] the four forms of capital punishment." The rationale is that requests should first be modest and only later should be expanded, as explained in sec. 582[:8].[18]

7 As to the wording used [with regard to forgiveness], one should [request] atonement *(kaparah)* with regard to sins *(chata'im)*, forgiveness *(mechilah)* with regard to iniquities *(avonos)*, and pardon *(selichah)* with regard to

מֻתָּר לְפָרְטוֹ בָּרַבִּים אֲפִלּוּ בְּקוֹל רָם.[לח,14] וּמִכָּל מָקוֹם אֵין חוֹבָה לְפָרְטוֹ בְּקוֹל רָם, אֶלָּא יְפָרְטֶנּוּ בְּלַחַשׁ אִם יִרְצֶה:[לט]

ה וּמַה שֶּׁאוֹמְרִים "עַל חֵטְא" עַל סֵדֶר א"ב – אֵין זֶה נִקְרָא פּוֹרֵט חֲטָאָיו, הוֹאִיל וְהַכֹּל אוֹמְרִים בְּשָׁוֶה – אֵינוֹ אֶלָּא כְּנֹסַח תְּפִלָּה, וּלְפִיכָךְ מֻתָּר לְאָמְרוֹ בְּקוֹל רָם:[מ]

ו סֵדֶר הַוִּדּוּי בְּ"עַל חֲטָאִים", שֶׁאָנוּ חַיָּבִים עֲלֵיהֶם עוֹלָה, וְאַחַר כָּךְ חַטָּאת, וְאַחַר כָּךְ קָרְבָּן עוֹלֶה וְיוֹרֵד,[15] וְאַחַר כָּךְ אָשָׁם וַדַּאי וְתָלוּי, לְפִי שֶׁכָּךְ סְדוּרִים הַקָּרְבָּנוֹת בְּפָרָשַׁת וַיִּקְרָא,[16] וְאַחַר כָּךְ שֶׁאָנוּ חַיָּבִים עֲלֵיהֶם מַכַּת מַרְדּוּת,[17] וְאַחַר כָּךְ מַלְקוּת אַרְבָּעִים, וְאַחַר כָּךְ מִיתָה בִּידֵי שָׁמַיִם, וְאַחַר כָּךְ כָּרֵת וַעֲרִירִי, וְאַחַר כָּךְ אַרְבַּע מִיתוֹת בֵּית דִּין, כִּי צָרִיךְ לְבַקֵּשׁ עַל הַקַּל קַל תְּחִלָּה וְאַחַר כָּךְ מוֹסִיף וְהוֹלֵךְ[מא] כְּמוֹ שֶׁנִּתְבָּאֵר בְּסִימָן תקפ"ב:[מב,18]

ז יֹאמַר לְשׁוֹן כַּפָּרָה לַחֲטָאִים וּלְשׁוֹן מְחִילָה לָעֲווֹנוֹת וּלְשׁוֹן סְלִיחָה

14. Indeed, this could even enhance — rather than compromise — G-d's honor.

15. I.e., varying according to one's means.

16. Which is their source in the Torah.

17. In the original, *makas mardus* — the punishment administered for the violation of a Rabbinic commandment.

18. See also sec. 584:3.

לט שו"ע שם (אם רצה). מ"א שם (דמיירי בחטא מפורסם). מ דרכי משה ס"ק ב. רמ"א שם. מא תרומת הדשן ח"ב סי' קיח. הובא בדרכי משה שם. מ"א סק"ג. וכ"ה הנוסח בסידור. מב ס"ח וש"נ.

לַפְּשָׁעִים,[מג, 19] כִּי הַחֵטְא קַל מֵעָוֹן וְעָוֹן קַל מִפֶּשַׁע[מד, 20] וְהַכַּפָּרָה גְּדוֹלָה מֵהַמְּחִילָה וְהַמְּחִילָה גְּדוֹלָה מֵהַסְּלִיחָה,[מה] לְפִיכָךְ הַחֵטְא הוּא מִתְכַּפֵּר וְנִמְחָל הֶעָוֹן וְנִסְלָח הַפֶּשַׁע.[מו, 21]

וְצָרִיךְ לְהִתְוַדּוֹת מְעֻמָּד,[מז, 22] לְפִיכָךְ לֹא יִסְמֹךְ עַל דָּבָר בְּעִנְיָן שֶׁאִם יִנָּטֵל אוֹתוֹ דָּבָר שֶׁהוּא סוֹמֵךְ עָלָיו הָיָה נוֹפֵל[מח] כְּמוֹ שֶׁנִּתְבָּאֵר בְּסִימָן תקפ"ה.[מט, 23] וְטוֹב לִשְׁחוֹת בְּעֵת הַוִּדּוּי כְּמוֹ בְּ"מוֹדִים",[נ] כְּדֵי לְהִתְוַדּוֹת בְּהַכְנָעָה גְּדוֹלָה.[נא]

וּכְשֶׁמִּתְוַדֶּה – יַכֶּה בְּאֶגְרוֹפוֹ עַל הַלֵּב, כְּלוֹמַר אַתָּה גָּרַמְתָּ לִי הַחֵטְא.[נב] וְיֵשׁ נוֹהֲגִין לְהַכּוֹת עַל הֶחָזֶה מִטַּעַם הַיָּדוּעַ לָהֶם:[נג, 24]

transgressions *(pesha'im)*.[19] The rationale is that *cheit* is a lesser offense than *avon*, and *avon* is a lesser offense than *pesha*.[20] *Kaparah* (atonement) is more effective than *mechilah* (forgiveness), and *mechilah* is more effective than *selichah* (pardon). Therefore it is appropriate to speak of sins being atoned, iniquity being forgiven, and transgression being pardoned.[21]

One must stand when confessing.[22] Therefore, one should not lean on any object in such a way that he would fall if it were to be removed, as explained in sec. 585[:1].[23] It is proper to bow when confessing, as is done [while reciting the passage that begins] *Modim*, so that one will confess with profound submissiveness.

When one confesses he should beat his heart with his fist, as if to say, "You caused me to sin." There are those who follow the custom of beating their breasts for reasons known to them.[24]

---

19. In his *Siddur* (see *Siddur Tehillat HaShem* Annotated Edition, p. 144), the Alter Rebbe uses slightly different wording: "forgive us for all our sins, grant us atonement for all our iniquities, and forgive and pardon us for all our transgressions." This resembles the version of *Rambam* and R. David Avudraham (also pronounced: Abudarham).

20. *Yoma* 36b.

21. The sequence here follows the order outlined in subsection 6 above: requests should first be modest and only later should be expanded. Moreover, it is appropriate to pray for the level of atonement that is within reach in the given situation. This explains why the most effective level of forgiveness is paired above with the lightest level of offense, and the minimal level of forgiveness is paired with the most grievous level of offense. Hence regarding a *cheit,* which is an unintentional transgression, we pray that it should be completely erased — as is accomplished by the most effective level of forgiveness, which is *kaparah.* Regarding an *avon,* which is a deliberate transgression ("iniquity"), we ask for forgiveness, *mechilah,* after which a trace may still remain. And we pray that any *pesha,* which is a willfully rebellious transgression, should be cleansed by G-d's *selichah* — the level that manifests the critical Divine attribute of long-suffering patience. (Based on the Alter Rebbe's source: *Shnei Luchos HaBris,* Tractate *Yoma, Amud HaTeshuvah, s.v. Seder HaVidui.*)

22. *Op. cit.* 87b.

23. For if one is leaning in such a manner, he is not considered to be standing.

24. I.e., for Kabbalistic reasons expounded in the writings of the *AriZal.*

On the implied distinction between the two views cited above, see: R. Levi Yitzchok

מג של"ה מסכת יומא עמוד התשובה (רכח, ב) ד"ה סדר הוידוי, בשם עמק ברכה, שכן נהג רמ"א. מ"א סוף סק"ג (אלא שכתב סליחה לעונות, עפ"י מנהגים, טירנא, ערב יום כפור, ע' קו). ובסידור הנוסח (באתה יודע): ותמחול לנו על כל חטאתינו ותכפר לנו על כל עונותינו ותמחול ותסלח לנו על כל פשעינו (כעין נוסח הרמב"ם בנוסח הוידוי שבסוף ס' אהבה. אבודרהם סדר תפלת יוה"כ ד"ה מה נאמר). **מד** כדלקמן סי' תרכא סי"ג וש"נ. וראה גם לעיל סי' תקפד ס"ג. **מה** ראה גם לעיל שם. **מו** של"ה שם. **מז** גמרא פז, ב מעובדא דשמואל. ר"ן (ו, א) ד"ה שמע מינה, בשם הגאונים. רא"ש פ"ח סי' יט. טור ושו"ע ס"ג. **מח** מ"א סק"ד. **מט** סעיף א. **נ** מהרי"ל הל' ליל יוה"כ (ע' שכח). של"ה שם. מ"א סק"ד. **נא** לבוש שם (שלכן צריך בעמידה). **נב** מ"א סק"ג, בשם מדרש קהלת. ט"ז סי' קיד סוף ס"ק ד. **נג** מ"א שם, בשם האריז"ל (שער הכוונות סוף ענין כוונת חזרת העמידה). **נד** טור ושו"ע ס"ג. **נה** ר"ן (ו, א) ד"ה

ח אַף עַל פִּי שֶׁהִתְוַדָּה בִּתְפִלַּת לַחַשׁ, אַף עַל פִּי כֵן כְּשֶׁהַשְּׁלִיחַ צִבּוּר מַגִּיעַ לְוִדּוּי[11] — צָרִיךְ לַחֲזֹר וְלַעֲמֹד[נד] וּלְהִתְוַדּוֹת עִמּוֹ,[נה] וּבְוִדּוּי זֶה אֵינוֹ צָרִיךְ לְפָרֵט הַחֵטְא, אֶלָּא כֵּיוָן שֶׁאָמַר עִם הַשְּׁלִיחַ צִבּוּר אֲבָל אֲנַחְנוּ חָטָאנוּ — דַּי,[נו] וְרַשַּׁאי לֵישֵׁב אַחַר כָּךְ, וּמִכָּל מָקוֹם אֵין לְדַבֵּר[25] בְּשָׁעָה שֶׁהַשְּׁלִיחַ צִבּוּר מִתְוַדֶּה:[נז, 26]

8 Even though one has already confessed when reciting the whispered *Shemoneh Esreh*, when the *sheliach tzibbur* reaches the confession[11] one must stand up and repeat [it] together with him. In this confession one need not enumerate one's sins; it is sufficient to say together with the *sheliach tzibbur*, "Indeed, we... have sinned." He may then sit, but not speak[25] while the *sheliach tzibbur* is confessing.[26]

ט עֲווֹנוֹת שֶׁהִתְוַדָּה עֲלֵיהֶן בְּיוֹם הַכִּפּוּרִים שֶׁעָבַר אַף עַל פִּי שֶׁכְּבָר נִתְכַּפְּרוּ — אַף עַל פִּי כֵן יָכוֹל לַחֲזֹר וּלְפָרְטָן בְּוִדּוּיוֹ,[נח, 27] וְלֹא עוֹד אֶלָּא שֶׁהַחוֹזֵר וּפוֹרְטָן — הֲרֵי זֶה מְשֻׁבָּח,[נט] שֶׁנֶּאֱמַר[ס] "וְחַטָּאתִי נֶגְדִּי תָמִיד",[28] כְּלוֹמַר אֵינִי סָבוּר שֶׁכִּפַּרְתָּ לִי וַהֲרֵי הוּא תָּמִיד כְּאִלּוּ הוּא נֶגְדִּי עוֹמֵד:[סא, 29]

9 Even though sins that one confessed on a previous Yom Kippur were atoned for, one may nevertheless enumerate them again in his present confession.[27] Indeed, it is praiseworthy to [do so], as [indicated by] the verse, "My sin is always before me."[28] [Doing so] implies: "I do not think that You have granted me atonement; it is as if [the sin] is always standing before me."[29]

Raskin, *Siddur Rabbeinu HaZakein im Tziyunim, Mekoros VeHe'aros* (Kehot, N.Y., 2004), *Dinei Lulav*, footnote 15.

The *Chabad* custom is to beat one's breast at each of the verbs in the *Ashamnu* confession, at each of the phrases beginning *Al Cheit*, at each of the phrases beginning *Ve'al Chataim*, and at each of the phrases *selach lanu, mechal lanu*, and *kaper lanu*. (See: *Sefer HaSichos 5701*, p. 151; *Sefer HaSichos 5705*, p. 9; *HaMelech BiMesibo*, Vol. 1, p. 248.)

25. If one prolongs his recitation of the *Shemoneh Esreh* and thus is in the midst of the confession when the *sheliach tzibbur* reaches *Kedushah*, he may join the congregation in responding to *devarim shebikedushah*, i.e.: (a) the verses beginning *Kadosh, Baruch* and *Yimloch;* (b) the *Amen* that follows the blessing ending *HaE-l hakadosh*. (See sec. 122:1 in the present work; see also sec. 66:5.)

On *devarim shebikedushah* (lit., "holy pronouncements"), see sec. 53, footnote 5 in Vol. 1, of the present work.

26. The custom today is to recite both the *Ashamnu* and the *Al Cheit* confessions together with the *sheliach tzibbur*.

27. *Yoma* 86b.

28. *Tehillim* 51:5.

29. Since forgiveness in the wake of earnest repentance is certain, why should one remain aware of early misdeeds? In *Tanya*, ch. 29, the Alter Rebbe explains that successively refined phases of spiritual maturation call for deeper remorse and loftier repentance. However, poising one's past sins before one's eyes could easily cripple any endeavor to serve G-d joyfully. The Alter Rebbe therefore explains that one's awareness of his past sins should face him — but at a distance. This is signified by the Hebrew word for "before me" (viz., *negdi*; see *Tanya — Iggeres HaTeshuvah*, ch. 11).

שמע מינה בשם הגאונים. רמ"א ס"ג. **נו** ראה ב"י ד"ה ועיקר. מ"א סק"ה. וכדלעיל ס"ד. **נז** הגהות מנהגים (ר"ה אות קכ) בשם רב סעדיה גאון. מ"א שם (בשעת הוידוי). **נח** גמרא [ברייתא] פו, ב כרבי אליעזר בן יעקב. רמב"ם הל' תשובה פ"ב ה"ח. טור ושו"ע ס"ד. **נט** רבי אליעזר בן יעקב שם. מ"א סק"ו. **ס** תהלים נא, ה. **סא** רש"י שם ד"ה וחטאתי. וראה תניא אגה"ת סוף פי"א.

10 We do not conclude the confession [with the wording of a blessing].[30] [This applies] both with regard to the confession recited in the Afternoon Service of the day preceding Yom Kippur and with regard to the confessions recited by every individual [at the conclusion of] *Shemoneh Esreh* in the prayer services of Yom Kippur itself.

י אֵין חוֹתְמִין בְּוִדּוּי,[סב,30] בֵּין וִדּוּי שֶׁל עֶרֶב יוֹם הַכִּפּוּרִים שֶׁל מִנְחָה,[סג] בֵּין וִדּוּי שֶׁל הַיָּחִיד אַחַר תְּפִלָּתוֹ בִּתְפִלּוֹת שֶׁל יוֹם הַכִּפּוּרִים עַצְמוֹ:[סד]

11 It is customary that after the Afternoon Service[31] on the day before Yom Kippur, all the congregants receive 39 lashes.[32] Lashes are not effective [in securing expiation for sins] in the present age, since we do not have judges who have been granted [the classical ordination of] *semichah.*[33] Moreover, [a transgressor] is not liable for lashes unless he was warned that the Court would punish him by lashes.[34] Nevertheless, it is customary to give lashes in order that one should take to heart [the task of] repenting for the sins he has committed, and in order to humble his heart and prepare it to serve the revered and awesome G-d with dread and fear.

יא נוֹהֲגִין שֶׁאַחַר תְּפִלַּת הַמִּנְחָה[31] בְּעֶרֶב יוֹם הַכִּפּוּרִים לוֹקִין כָּל הַקָּהָל[סה] ל"ט מַלְקוּת,[סו,32] וְאַף עַל פִּי שֶׁאֵין מַלְקוּת מוֹעִיל בִּזְמַן הַזֶּה שֶׁאֵין לָנוּ דַּיָּנִים סְמוּכִין,[סז,33] וְגַם אֵין חַיָּב מַלְקוּת אֶלָּא אִם כֵּן הִתְרוּ בּוֹ שֶׁהַבֵּית דִּין מַלְקִין אוֹתוֹ,[סח,34] מִכָּל מָקוֹם נוֹהֲגִין לִלְקוֹת, שֶׁמִּתּוֹךְ כָּךְ יִתֵּן אֶל לִבּוֹ לָשׁוּב מֵעֲבֵרוֹת שֶׁבְּיָדוֹ,[סט] וְעוֹד כְּדֵי לְהַכְנִיעַ לְבָבוֹ וּלַהֲכִינָהּ לַעֲבֹד הַשֵּׁם הַנִּכְבָּד וְהַנּוֹרָא בְּאֵימָה וּבְיִרְאָה:[ע]

12 It is customary for the one receiving the lashes to recite the confession while being

יב וְנָהֲגוּ שֶׁהַנִּלְקֶה אוֹמֵר וִדּוּיִים

---

30. This differs from *Rashi's* reading of the *Gemara (Yoma* 87b), that one may conclude the confession with the blessing, "Blessed are You, G-d, the forgiving L-rd."

The confession is followed by the passage beginning *Elokai Netzor,* maintaining its position at the end of every *Shemoneh Esreh* throughout the year *(Minhagei Maharil,* Day of Yom Kippur, sec. 13, cited in *Darchei Moshe* 607:1 and in *Magen Avraham* 607:7).

31. For in the times of the *Beis HaMikdash,* the Court would administer lashes after the Afternoon Service *(Shaar HaKollel).*

In his *Siddur* the Alter Rebbe writes that the lashes should be given before the immersion in the *mikveh* that precedes the Afternoon Service. This sequence, based on the Kabbalistic teachings of *Pri Etz Chayim,* is followed throughout Lubavitch communities today.

32. The nominal lashes administered today are merely symbolic. See also subsections 13 and 14 below, and footnotes there.

33. Lit., "the laying of hands"; i.e., the ordination conferred upon the early sages by their masters in a chain that began with Moshe Rabbeinu and ceased shortly after the era of the *Mishnah,* in approximately 200 C.E. (See *Rambam, Hilchos Sanhedrin,* ch. 4.) Only judges with this ordination can sentence an offender to be lashed.

34. Since such warnings are not given today, there is no one liable to receive lashes.

סב גמרא [ברייתא] פז, ב. ראה גירסת רש"י שם ד"ה וחותם בוידוי. ב"י ד"ה ומ"ש ולפירוש. טור בשם רב עמרם ומנהג ספרד, ושו"ע ס"ה. **סג** שו"ע שם. **סד** לבוש ס"ה. **סה** רא"ש פ"ח סי' כה (שכן נהגו באשכנז). טור ושו"ע ס"ו. ובסידור: מלקות ילקו קודם טבילה ומנחה (עפ"י פע"ח שער כז פ"א ד"ה מע"ח). **סו** טור ושו"ע שם (ארבעים). מ"א סק"ח (ל"ט). **סז** ראה לקמן חו"מ הל' נזקי גו"נ סט"ז. **סח** ב"י סוף הסי'. מ"א סק"ט. **סט** טור ושו"ע שם. **ע** ב"י שם, בשם הכלבו סי' סח (לג, א). **עא** מנהגים (קלויזנר) יום כפור סי' לד. (טירנא) ע' קו. רמ"א ס"ו. ומנהג חב"ד שגם הנלקה אומר והוא רחום ג"פ (ספר

lashed, and for the person administering the lashes to recite the verse *VeHu Rachum*[35] three times. This totals 39 words, paralleling the 39 lashes.[36]

בְּשָׁעָה שֶׁנִּלְקֶה, וְהַמַּלְקֶה אוֹמֵר "וְהוּא רַחוּם יְכַפֵּר עָוֹן וגו'"[עא,35] ג' פְּעָמִים, שֶׁהֵם ל"ט תֵּבוֹת נֶגֶד ל"ט מַלְקוֹת:[עב,36]

13 It is customary to use a strap of any [width], for these are not lashes in the strict sense of the term, requiring a strap a handbreadth wide.

יג וְנָהֲגוּ לְהַלְקוֹת בִּרְצוּעָה כָּל דְּהוּא, שֶׁאֵין זֶה מַלְקוֹת גָּמוּר[עג] שֶׁצְּרִיכָה לִהְיוֹת רְצוּעָה רְחָבָה טֶפַח:[עד]

14 A strap of calf's leather is used; [this] spurs one to repentance by [recalling] the verse, "[Even] an ox knows its master…"[37] However, there is no need to use two straps, one [from an ox and the other] from a donkey,[38] as were used for the actual lashes, for lashes in the present age are not effective [in absolving one of liability].[39]

יד וְלוֹקְחִין רְצוּעָה שֶׁל עֵגֶל,[עה] לְעוֹרְרוֹ בִּתְשׁוּבָה,[עו] עַל דֶּרֶךְ[עז] "יָדַע שׁוֹר קוֹנֵהוּ".[עח,37] אֲבָל אֵין צָרִיךְ לִקַּח שְׁתֵּי רְצוּעוֹת אַחַת שֶׁל חֲמוֹר[עט,38] כְּמוֹ שֶׁהָיוּ בְּמַלְקוֹת גָּמוּר,[פ] כֵּיוָן שֶׁאֵין מַלְקוֹת מוֹעִיל בִּזְמַן הַזֶּה:[פא,39]

15 The person receiving the lashes should neither stand nor sit but should crouch forward, with his back to the south and his face to the north, because a person's sins are primarily due to money, and it is written,[40] "Gold comes from the north." One should therefore humble oneself in that direction, which was the source of his sin.

טו וְהַנִּלְקֶה לֹא יַעֲמֹד וְלֹא יֵשֵׁב רַק מֻטֶּה[פב] אֲחוֹרָיו לַדָּרוֹם וּפָנָיו לַצָּפוֹן,[פג] לְפִי שֶׁעִקַּר חֵטְא הָאָדָם הוּא מֵחֲמַת מָמוֹן, וּכְתִיב[פד,40] "מִצָּפוֹן זָהָב יֶאֱתֶה", עַל כֵּן יַכְנִיעַ אֶת עַצְמוֹ לְאוֹתוֹ רוּחַ לְהוֹדִיעַ שֶׁמִּשָּׁם בָּא לוֹ הַחֵטְא:[פה]

16 Yom Kippur atones only for those who repent and believe in the

טז יוֹם הַכִּפּוּרִים אֵינוֹ מְכַפֵּר אֶלָּא עַל

---

35. *Tehillim* 78:30. According to the direction given in *Sefer HaMinhagim: The Book of Chabad-Lubavitch Customs* (p. 123), the person receiving the lashes also recites this verse three times, [and not the confession].

36. One word accompanies each of the lashes as they touch in turn the back of his right shoulder, the back of his left shoulder, and the middle of his back.

37. *Yeshayahu* 1:3. The verse goes on to say, "...and a donkey [knows] its master's trough — [but] Israel does not know, My people takes no thought."

38. See *Makkos* 22b.

39. See the beginning of subsection 11 above and footnotes there. Today, it is primarily *teshuvah* that secures atonement for one's sins.

40. *Iyov* 37:22.

המנהגים – חב"ד ע' 58). וראה אוצר מנהגי חב"ד יוה"כ ע' קפח סדר המלקות: על כתף ימין, כתף שמאל, תחתיהם באמצע, ובכל הלקאה אומרים תיבת אחת מוהוא רחום. **עב** הגהות מנהגים שם אות קמו. רמ"א שם. **עג** דרכי משה ס"ק ד. רמ"א שם. **עד** משנה מכות כב, ב. מ"א סק"י. **עה** כלבו ומנהגים שם. רמ"א שם. **עו** מ"א סקי"א. **עז** אוצ"ל: על דרך שנאמר (ישעיה א, ג), וכ"ה ברמ"א שם. **עח** רמ"א שם. **עט** כמבואר בכל בו שם. **פ** מכות כב, ב. רמב"ם הל' סנהדרין פט"ז ה"ח. מ"א שם. **פא** ראה דרכי משה ס"ק ד. מ"א שם. **פב** מנהגים שם ושם. רמ"א שם. **פג** מהרי"ל הלק ערב יוה"כ (ע' שיז). רמ"א שם. **פד** איוב לז, כב. וראה ב"ב כה, ב. לעיל סי' צד ס"ג. **פה** ט"ז סק"ד.

הַשָּׁבִים הַמַּאֲמִינִים בְּכַפָּרָתוֹ;[41] אֲבָל הַמְבַעֵט בּוֹ וּמְחַשֵּׁב בְּלִבּוֹ מַה מּוֹעִיל לוֹ יוֹם הַכִּפּוּרִים זֶה — אֵין יוֹם הַכִּפּוּרִים מְכַפֵּר לוֹ:[פו]

atonement it conveys.[41] If a person holds it in disdain and thinks in his heart, "What will Yom Kippur do for [me]?" — Yom Kippur will not atone for him.

סימן תרח סֵדֶר סְעוּדָה הַמַּפְסֶקֶת וּבוֹ י׳ סְעִיפִים:

SECTION 608 The Order of the Meal Preceding the Fast. (1–10)

א מִצְוַת עֲשֵׂה[א] מִן הַתּוֹרָה[ב] לְהוֹסִיף מִן הַחֹל עַל הַקֹּדֶשׁ,[1,ג] בֵּין בְּעִנּוּי[2,ד] בֵּין בְּאִסּוּר מְלָאכָה,[ה] שֶׁנֶּאֱמַר[ו] "וְעִנִּיתֶם אֶת נַפְשֹׁתֵיכֶם בְּתִשְׁעָה לַחֹדֶשׁ בָּעֶרֶב מֵעֶרֶב עַד עֶרֶב תִּשְׁבְּתוּ שַׁבַּתְּכֶם";[3] יָכוֹל יִתְעַנֶּה בְּתִשִׁיעִי לַחֹדֶשׁ? תַּלְמוּד לוֹמַר "בָּעֶרֶב";[4] אִי בָּעֶרֶב יָכוֹל מִשֶּׁתֶּחְשַׁךְ? תַּלְמוּד לוֹמַר "בְּתִשְׁעָה", הָא כֵּיצַד? מַתְחִיל וּמִתְעַנֶּה מִבְּעוֹד יוֹם;[5] מִכָּאן שֶׁמּוֹסִיפִים מֵחֹל עַל הַקֹּדֶשׁ:[ז]

1 It is a positive Scriptural commandment to add [time] from the mundane realm to the realm of holiness,[1] both with regard to afflicting oneself[2] and with regard to the prohibition against work, as it is written, "And you shall afflict your souls on the ninth of the month in the evening; from evening to evening shall you observe your day of rest."[3]

Could [the verse mean] that one should fast on the ninth of the month? [It could not, for] the verse states, "In the evening."[4] If one postulates "in the evening," should [the fast begin] from nightfall? [It could not, for] the verse states, "On the ninth." What, then, is implied? One should begin to fast while it is still day.[5] From this we learn that we must add [time] from the mundane realm to the realm of holiness.

(וְאַף עַל פִּי שֶׁמִּמִּקְרָא זֶה לָמַדְנוּ בְּסִימָן תר"ד[ח] שֶׁמִּצְוָה לֶאֱכֹל בְּעֶרֶב יוֹם כִּפּוּר, מִכָּל מָקוֹם פְּשַׁט הַכָּתוּב מִשּׁוּם תַּעֲנִית מַמָּשׁ[ט] כְּמוֹ שֶׁנִּתְבָּאֵר כָּאן, אֶלָּא שֶׁמִּצְוַת חֲכָמִים

(Sec. 604[:1] states that from the exposition of this [same] verse it was derived that we are commanded to *eat* on the day preceding Yom Kippur. Nevertheless, the simple meaning of the verse is that one must actually fast [on part of that day], as explained here. It is only that the Sages

41. *Kerisos* 7a.

SECTION 608

1. In the original, *lehosif min hachol al hakodesh* — from *Yoma* 81b, which is the source of the following exposition of the verse quoted.

2. I.e., not only fasting, but also refraining from washing, anointing oneself, marital relations, and wearing shoes. See sec. 611:2.

3. *Vayikra* 23:32.

4. Implying that the fast must start in the evening, after the ninth has passed.

5. In the original, *mibe'od yom*.

פו רבי יוחנן בכריתות ז, א. רמב"ם הל' שגגות פ"ג ה"י. רמ"א סוף ס"ו.

סימן תרח: א ראה רש"י סוכה כח, ב ד"ה הואיל. ב ביצה ל, א. שבת קמח, ב. תוס' ר"ה ט, א ד"ה ורבי עקיבא. ב"י ומ"א ריש הסי'. ג גמרא [ברייתא] פא, ב. טור ושו"ע ס"א. ד ברייתא שם (מתענה). רמב"ם הל' שביתת העשור פ"א ה"ו (לצום ולהתענות). טור (באיסור אכילה). לבוש ס"א (באיסור אכילה ושתיה). וראה גם לקמן סי' תריא ס"א (כל הדברים האסורים בעיקר היום). ה משמעות רי"ף (ב, ב). רא"ש פ"ח סי' ח. טור ולבוש שם. שו"ע (סי' רסא ס"א בשם יש אומרים, אף לענין שבת). וראה גם לעיל שם ס"ד (בשם יש אומרים). ו ויקרא כג, לב. ז ברייתא שם. הובא ברי"ף ורא"ש שם. לבוש שם. לעיל שם. ח סעיף א. וכקושיית הלבוש ס"א בהג"ה. ט ראה לקמן ס"ד. י ב"י סי' תיח ד"ה ויחיד. שו"ע סי' תקע ס"ג. יא הגהות מיימוניות סוף הל'

הִיא׳ לְהַרְבּוֹת בִּסְעוּדָה בְּעֶרֶב יוֹם כִּפּוּר[יא] מִטַּעַם שֶׁנִּתְבָּאֵר שָׁם, וּמָצְאוּ לָהֶם סְמָךְ[6] מִן הַתּוֹרָה,[יב] שֶׁנֶּאֱמַר "וְעִנִּיתֶם וגו׳ בְּתִשְׁעָה לַחֹדֶשׁ", וּפֵרְשׁוּ בּוֹ חֲכָמִים שֶׁיָּכִין אֶת עַצְמוֹ בַּאֲכִילַת תְּשִׁיעִי לְעִנּוּי שֶׁל עֲשִׂירִי[יג]).

אֵין לִי אֶלָּא מִלְּפָנָיו, מִלְּאַחֲרָיו מִנַּיִן?[יד] תַּלְמוּד לוֹמַר "מֵעֶרֶב עַד עֶרֶב",[טו] הִקִּישׁ שְׁנֵי הָעֲרָבִים זֶה לָזֶה,[טז] וְאֵין לִי אֶלָּא יוֹם הַכִּפּוּרִים שַׁבָּת מִנַּיִן? תַּלְמוּד לוֹמַר "תִּשְׁבְּתוּ",[7] יוֹם טוֹב מִנַּיִן? תַּלְמוּד לוֹמַר "שַׁבַּתְּכֶם", כָּל שְׁבוּת שֶׁאַתָּה שׁוֹבֵת — אַתָּה מוֹסִיף לָהּ בֵּין מִלְּפָנֶיהָ בֵּין מִלְּאַחֲרֶיהָ.[יז]

יָכוֹל יְהֵא עָנוּשׁ כָּרֵת[9] עַל הַתּוֹסֶפֶת?[8] תַּלְמוּד לוֹמַר[יח,10] "וְכָל הַנֶּפֶשׁ אֲשֶׁר תַּעֲשֶׂה כָּל מְלָאכָה בְּעֶצֶם הַיּוֹם הַזֶּה[11] וְהַאֲבַדְתִּי וגו׳",

commanded that one eat more [than usual] on the day preceding Yom Kippur, for the reason explained there. They found a support[6] [for this practice] in the Torah, as it is written, "And you shall afflict [your souls] on the ninth of the month." The Sages interpreted this to mean that one should prepare oneself for the affliction of the tenth by eating on the ninth.)

[The above teaches only that time must be added] before [the fast]. What source teaches that [time must also be added] after [the fast]? The verse states, "from evening to evening." This establishes an equation between the two evenings. [Just as time must be added in the evening preceding the fast, time must be added in the evening following the fast.]

[The above refers] solely to Yom Kippur. What source teaches that [time should also be added] with regard to *Shabbos?* The above verse continues, "shall you observe [your day of rest]."[7] What is the source that teaches that [an addition should also be made] with regard to festivals? The verse concludes, "[shall you observe] your day of rest." [This implies that] whenever you observe a day of rest, you must add to it from the preceding [day] and the following [day].

Lest one think that [non-observance of] this addition[8] is punishable by *kares,*[9] a [preceding] verse states,[10] "Any [person] who performs any work on that very day,[11] I will cause to perish...." Similarly,

---

6. In the original, *smach* (often: *asmachta*) — the linkage with a Scriptural verse that lends support to a Rabbinic enactment, for verses are sometimes left to the discretionary interpretation of the Sages. (See the *Talmudic Encyclopedia,* Vol. 2, p. 515-522.)

7. Lit., "shall you rest on," in which the verb *tishbesu* (תשבתו) has *Shabbos* (שבת) as its root.

The above passage is paraphrased in sec. 261:4 in support of the same obligation — to observe *Shabbos* for an additional period both before and after the holy day.

8. In the original, *tosefes.*

9. Lit., "excision"; i.e., premature death at the hand of Heaven (*Moed Katan* 28a; *Rashi* on *Vayikra* 23:30) and childlessness (*Rashi, s.v. aririm,* on *Vayikra* 20:20). *Rambam* understands *kares* as signifying that the soul is cut off in the spiritual realms (*Hilchos Teshuvah,* ch. 8).

10. *Vayikra* 23:30.

11. In the original, *be'etzem hayom hazeh.*

שביתת העשור. שו"ע סי' תרד. לעיל שם ס"א (שמצוה לאכול). **יב** ב"י סי' תיח שם, ובסימן תקסח ד"ה ומ"ש ואין צריך. **יג** כדלעיל סי' תרד ס"א, וש"נ. **יד** ברייתא שם, לגירסת הרי"ף ורא"ש שם. וראה לעיל סי' רסא ס"ד (כגירסה שלנו). סי' רצג ס"א (שיעור ההוספה). **טו** ברייתא שם. רמב"ם שם. **טז** קרבן אהרן על הספרא על הפסוק (אמור פי"ד). וראה התמים ע' 620. סופרים וספרים ע' 18. פרדס חב"ד 9 ע' 93. **יז** ברייתא שם לגירסת הרי"ף ורא"ש שם. ולעיל שם: ימים טובים מנין תלמוד לומר תשבתו, שבתות מנין תלמוד לומר שבתכם, הא כיצד כל מקום שנאמר שבות מוסיפים מחול על הקדש מלפניה ולאחריה. **יח** ויקרא כג, ל.

וְכֵן בְּעִנּוּי הוּא אוֹמֵר[יט,12] "כִּי כָל הַנֶּפֶשׁ אֲשֶׁר לֹא תְעֻנֶּה בְּעֶצֶם הַיּוֹם הַזֶּה וְנִכְרְתָה וגו'" – עַל עִצּוּמוֹ שֶׁל יוֹם עָנוּשׁ כָּרֵת, אֲבָל אֵין עֹנֶשׁ כָּרֵת עַל הַתּוֹסֶפֶת:[כ]

with regard to afflicting one's soul, it is written,[12] "Any [person] who will not afflict himself on that very day will be cut off." Thus the punishment of *kares* is administered for [working or eating on] "that very day," but not for [committing these transgressions in] the additional time [appended to the holiday].

ב וְתוֹסֶפֶת זֶה צָרִיךְ שֶׁיְּהֵא קֹדֶם בֵּין הַשְּׁמָשׁוֹת,[כא,13] דְּאִלּוּ בֵּין הַשְּׁמָשׁוֹת עַצְמוֹ (סְפֵק יוֹם) סְפֵק לַיְלָה הוּא וְאֵינוֹ נִקְרָא תּוֹסֶפֶת, וְאַף אִם לֹא הָיָה הַכָּתוּב מַזְהִיר עָלָיו – הָיָה צָרִיךְ לִפְרֹשׁ מִסְּפֵק עֲבֵרָה:[כב]

2 This time must be added before *bein hashmashos,*[13] for [this] period itself is a matter of question: (Is it day) or is it night? Therefore, [observing the prohibitions at this time] is not considered an addition. Indeed, even if Scripture did not forbid [partaking of food or working] at that time, one would still have to refrain because of the possibility of transgression.

ג וְתוֹסֶפֶת זֶה אֵין לוֹ שִׁעוּר,[כג] אֶלָּא שֶׁמִּתְּחִלַּת הַשְּׁקִיעָה שֶׁאֵין הַשֶּׁמֶשׁ נִרְאָה עַל הָאָרֶץ עַד בֵּין הַשְּׁמָשׁוֹת שֶׁהוּא ג' רְבִיעֵי מִילִין קֹדֶם הַלַּיְלָה,[14] וְהַזְּמַן הַזֶּה

3 This additional period does not have a fixed measure. Instead, [the concept can be explained as follows]: There is a period of time [sufficient to walk] three-and-a-quarter *mil* from the beginning of sunset, i.e., when the sun is no longer visible on the earth, until *bein hashmashos. [Bein hashmashos]* itself begins from [the time it takes to walk] three-quarters of a *mil* before nightfall.[14]

---

12. *Loc. cit.*, v. 29.

13. *Bein hashmashos* is the period of twilight between sunset (see subsection 3 below and its footnotes) and the appearance of three stars. As the Alter Rebbe proceeds to explain, the halachic status of this time is much discussed.

14. In this subsection (as also in sec. 261:5 and 331:5), the Alter Rebbe follows the opinion of the *Shulchan Aruch* which, in this source, accepts the view of Rabbeinu Tam. Rabbeinu Tam maintains that it takes 18 minutes to walk a *mil*. According to his view, nightfall is 72 minutes (the time it takes to walk four *mil*) after sunset. The first 58 1/2 minutes is not even considered *bein hashmashos,* but as day. The next 13 1/2 minutes — the time it takes to walk three-quarters of a *mil* — are considered *bein hashmashos.* The addition to Yom Kippur, *Shabbos,* and the festivals must be made in the period that precedes the beginning of *bein hashmashos*. However, this can be after sunset, for according to Rabbeinu Tam, the status of the day has not yet changed.

In *Seder Hachnasas Shabbos* that appears in his *Siddur,* the Alter Rebbe notes that R. Yosef Caro in his *Shulchan Aruch (Yoreh Deah* 262:5) does not accept Rabbeinu Tam's position at all. This is also evident from the statements of *Sifsei Cohen* 262:9. Similarly, many other *Rishonim* do not accept the view of Rabbeinu Tam. Moreover, the Alter Rebbe points out, by 72 minutes after nightfall the sky is filled with stars; it is not merely that three average stars first appear.

Accordingly, he explains that in *Eretz Yisrael* nightfall begins slightly more than 20 minutes after the disappearance of the

יט שם כג, כט. כ ברייתא פא, א. הובא ברי"ף ורא"ש שם. וראה לקו"ש חט"ז ע' 235 הערה 32. כא רא"ש פ"ח סי' ח. טור ושו"ע ס"א. כב רא"ש שם. וראה גם לעיל סי' רסא ס"ה (ספק לילה ואסור בו במלאכה מן התורה בלא מצות תוספת). ושם ס"א (ואם עשה חייב אשם תלוי). וקו"א שם סק"ג (בין השמשות הוא בכלל התוספת בעל כרחו אף אם הוא יום כיון שהוא סמוך לחשכה ממש, ואף שלא קבלו הרי מקובל ועומד הוא מהר סיני). כג רא"ש שם.

If one desires, he may consider this entire time[15] as the addition [to the holy day]. If he desires, he may convey this status on part of that time, provided he adds a certain amount of time that is definitely mundane to the holy [day].

שֶׁהוּא מַהֲלַךְ ג' מִילִין וּרְבִיעַ רָצָה לַעֲשׂוֹת כֻּלּוֹ[15] תּוֹסֶפֶת – עוֹשֶׂה, רָצָה לַעֲשׂוֹת מִקְצָתָהּ – עוֹשֶׂה, וּבִלְבַד שֶׁיּוֹסִיף אֵיזֶה זְמַן שֶׁיִּהְיֶה וַדַּאי מֵחֹל עַל הַקֹּדֶשׁ:[כד]

4 [The following principle applies in a situation in which] women eat and drink until the actual beginning of *bein hashmashos,*[16] unaware that it is a *mitzvah* to add time from the mundane realm to the realm of holiness. If [one] is certain that [his warnings] will not be heeded and they will continue willfully, he should not reprimand them.[17] Better that they [transgress] unknowingly[18] than knowingly.[19]

This principle applies to all prohibitions that are not explicitly stated in the Torah, but [(a)] were derived by the Sages through the

ד נָשִׁים שֶׁאוֹכְלוֹת וְשׁוֹתוֹת[כה] עַד בֵּין הַשְּׁמָשׁוֹת[כו,16] מַמָּשׁ[כז] וְהֵן אֵינָן יוֹדְעוֹת שֶׁמִּצְוָה לְהוֹסִיף מֵחֹל עַל הַקֹּדֶשׁ – אֵין מְמַחִין בְּיָדָן,[17] אִם הוּא יָדוּעַ שֶׁבְּוַדַּאי לֹא יִשְׁמְעוּ לָנוּ[כח] וְיַעֲשׂוּ בְּזָדוֹן, דְּמוּטָב שֶׁיִּהְיוּ שׁוֹגְגִין[18] וְאַל יִהְיוּ מְזִידִים.[כט,19]

וְכֵן הַדִּין בְּכָל דְּבַר אִסּוּר שֶׁאֵינוֹ מְפֹרָשׁ בַּתּוֹרָה[ל] אֶלָּא שֶׁחֲכָמִים

sun on the horizon; i.e., there is a difference of four minutes between the time when the sun is no longer seen (i.e., *shkiah hanireis* — the "visible sunset") and true sunset. The obligation to append time from the mundane realm to the realm of holiness relates to this four-minute margin. This is followed by the period of *bein hashmashos,* which last 18 minutes. (According to this view, it takes 24 minutes to walk a *mil,* and the time it takes to walk three-quarters of a *mil* is 18 minutes.)

This applies only in the months of Nissan and Tishrei. Throughout the year, the time varies slightly according to the angle of the sun's position in relation to earth. In countries located to the north or to the south of *Eretz Yisrael,* the difference in latitude causes this time to be protracted slightly, and *bein hashmashos* lasts for approximately 30 minutes. According to this understanding, the addition for Yom Kippur and *Shabbos* must begin before sunset.

In this context, it is significant to mention the Lubavitch custom of fasting 26 hours on Yom Kippur. (See *HaYom Yom,* entry for Yom Kippur, and *Sefer HaSichos 5705,* p. 21.) The Rebbe writes that the 26th hour need not be complete *(Igros Kodesh,* Vol. 10, p. 297*)*. Thus it is sufficient to fast slightly more than 25 hours.

15. I.e., the time from sunset until the beginning of *bein hashmashos,* as indicated in subsection 2.

16. *Shabbos* 148b.

17. *Magen Avraham* 608:1 states that this principle applies only when one is absolutely certain that his rebuke will not be heeded. Otherwise, he should attempt to influence them.

18. I.e., without having heard that this activity is prohibited.

19. I.e., after having been informed and reprimanded.

טור ושו"ע ס"א. **כד** רמב"ן בתורת האדם שער אבלות ישנה. ר"ן (ב, ב) ד"ה ת"ר ועניתם. שו"ע סי' רסא ס"ב. וכ"ה לעיל סי' רסא ס"ה. וראה בנסמן שם, שבסדר הכנסת שבת פסק כהגאונים שזמן בין השמשות הוא מתחלת השקיעה ועד צאת הכוכבים, ושיעור זמן זה תלוי לפי האקלים וזמני השנה. ועוד שם, ששקיעה האמתית היא בעת סילוק וביאת האור מראשי ההרים הגבוהים שבארץ ישראל, וזמן תוספת שבת היא קודם שקיעה הנראית, שהיא קודם סילוק וביאת האור מראשי האילנות וגגים הגבוהים. **כה** גמרא שבת קמח, ב. ביצה ל, א. רמב"ם הל' שביתת העשור פ"א ה"ז. שו"ע ס"ב. **כו** לבוש ס"ג. ובגמרא וברמב"ם ובשו"ע שם: עד שחשכה. ולענין בין השמשות עצמה, ראה סדר הכנסת שבת – ב' דעות, ושהעיקר להלכה להחמיר בשל תורה. וראה גם לעיל סי' קנו ס"ז (שגם דבר שאיסורו מספק דינו כודאי). **כז** כדלעיל ס"ג, שתוספת זה אין לו שיעור. **כח** תוס' שבת נה, א ד"ה ואע"ג. רא"ש ביצה פ"ד סי' ב. ט"ז סק"ב. מ"א סק"א. וראה גם לעיל סי' קנו סוף ס"ז (לענין בית דין) וש"נ. סדר הכנסת שבת (לענין בין השמשות). **כט** שבת קמח, ב. ביצה ל, א. רמב"ם שם. שו"ע שם. וראה גם לעיל שם (לענין יחיד ולענין רבים ולענין בית דין) וש"נ. **ל** רא"ש שם בשם בעל העיטור הל' יום טוב סי"ג. ר"ן ביצה (טז, ב) ד"ה והך. רמ"א ס"ב. וכ"ה לעיל שם (לענין בית דין) וש"נ.

לְמָדוּהוּ מִמִּדְרַשׁ הַפְּסוּקִים,[לא] אוֹ שֶׁהוּא קַבָּלָה בְּיָדָם הֲלָכָה לְמֹשֶׁה מִסִּינַי,[לב, 20] אוֹ שֶׁהֵן בְּעַצְמָן אָסְרוּ דָבָר[לג] וְאָדָם אֶחָד[לד] עוֹבֵר עַל דִּבְרֵיהֶם בִּשְׁגָגָה שֶׁאֵינוֹ יוֹדֵעַ הָאִסּוּר, וְאַף אִם יוֹדִיעַ לוֹ הָאִסּוּר לֹא יְקַבֵּל מִמֶּנּוּ[לה] — אֵינוֹ צָרִיךְ לִמְחוֹת בְּיָדוֹ, דְּמוּטָב שֶׁיִּהְיֶה שׁוֹגֵג וְלֹא יִהְיֶה מֵזִיד:

ה אֲבָל דָּבָר שֶׁאִסּוּרוֹ מְפֹרָשׁ בַּתּוֹרָה,[לו, 21] אַף עַל פִּי שֶׁיָּדוּעַ לָנוּ שֶׁהַחוֹטֵא הַזֶּה לֹא יְקַבֵּל מִמֶּנּוּ אַף אִם נוֹדִיעַ לוֹ הָאִסּוּר[22] — אַף עַל פִּי כֵן צָרִיךְ לִמְחוֹת בְּיָדוֹ,[לז] לְפִי שֶׁכָּל יִשְׂרָאֵל עֲרֵבִין זֶה בָּזֶה[לח, 23] וְעַל יְדֵי שֶׁמּוֹחֶה בְּיָדוֹ הוּא מוֹצִיא אֶת עַצְמוֹ מֵהָעַרְבוּת.

וּמִכָּל מָקוֹם, לֹא יוֹכִיחֶנּוּ בָּרַבִּים אֶלָּא פַּעַם אַחַת,[24] אֲבָל לֹא יַרְבֶּה בְּתוֹכָחוֹת

principles of exegesis, or [(b)] were received as a tradition passed down to them as laws taught to Moshe [orally] on Mount Sinai,[20] or [(c)] were ordained by the Sages themselves. If a person unwittingly violates a ruling of the Sages because he does not know of the prohibition, and even if he were to be informed he would not stand corrected, there is no obligation to reprimand him. [On the contrary,] it is preferable for him [to transgress] unknowingly than [to transgress] knowingly.

5 With regard to a prohibition explicitly stated in the Torah,[21] by contrast, one is obligated to reprimand a transgressor even if one knows that he will not accept the rebuke when he is informed of the prohibition.[22] [The rationale is that] all of Israel are responsible for each other,[23] and by reprimanding [the transgressor] one frees himself of this liability. Nevertheless, one should not reprimand him publicly more than once.[24] One should not repeatedly reprimand [the

20. In the original, *halachah leMoshe miSinai.*

21. In his *Seder Hachnasas Shabbos, loc. cit.,* the Alter Rebbe cites the ruling of *Magen Avraham* 608:2, that if an explicit Scriptural prohibition is involved, we are commanded to rebuke others even when it is not even certain that they are violating it. For example, as stated above, there is a doubt as to whether *bein hashmashos* is part of the day or part of the night. Hence, if one sees a fellow Jew eating or working during *bein hashmashos* on Yom Kippur, one should certainly rebuke him, for it is possible that he is violating an explicit Scriptural prohibition. In such a case, the leniency stated in subsection 4 does not apply.

22. In sec. 156:7 the Alter Rebbe specifies that this obligation applies only to a fellow Jew with whom one is familiar, for the transgressor will certainly not heed the rebuke of a stranger. Significantly, the Alter Rebbe's ruling there is based on *Magen Avraham* 608:3, yet he makes the above comment in that section, not in the present section to which his source corresponds. The differences between the stances of the Alter Rebbe in these two discussions are analyzed in: R. Levi Yitzchok Raskin, *Siddur Rabbeinu HaZakein im Tziyunim, Mekoros VeHe'aros,* p. 699ff.

23. In this vein, *Shabbos* 54b teaches that one who has the potential to rebuke a fellow Jew for a sin and fails to do so is considered responsible for it, for the transgressor may have desisted in response to a timely word of rebuke. With regard to the mutual responsibility of the Jewish people, see *Shevuos* 39a and *Sanhedrin* 27b. See also sec. 585, footnote 9 above.

24. In sec. 156:7, the Alter Rebbe states that this restriction applies only to an individual; a Rabbinical court *(beis din)* must rebuke transgressors repeatedly.

לא העיטור ורא"ש שם. לב שו"ת מהר"ם אלשקר סי' לה. לג שבת שם. ביצה שם. לד ראה לעיל שם (חילוק בין יחיד לרבים לענין מזיד). לה מ"א סק"א. וכדלעיל בתחלת הסעיף וש"נ. לו רא"ש שם בשם בעל העיטור. ר"ן שם. רמ"א ס"ב. לז וכיון שהודיעו דינו כמזיד, ויש בו מצות הוכחה, שבזה מיירי בהמשך הסעיף. וראה סדר הכנסת שבת (חובה של תורה למחות). תניא פ"א (מי שיש בידו למחות ולא מיחה). לח שיטה מקובצת ביצה שם ד"ה והקשה, בשם

transgressor] publicly[25] once he is certain that [the transgressor] will not accept his rebuke. With regard to such matters it was said,[26] "Just as it is a *mitzvah* to say something that will be heeded, so is it a *mitzvah* not to say something that will not be heeded."

In private, by contrast, one is obligated to reprimand [the transgressor] even 100 times,[27] until the transgressor berates him.[28] Since he informed him of the transgression and he [continued] to willfully violate it, each and every member of the Jewish people is obligated to rebuke him, as it is written,[29] *hocheiach tochiach* — "You shall surely rebuke." [The dual verb implies that one must reiterate a rebuke] even 100 times.

Nevertheless, if the transgression was performed in private, the rebuke should be administered first in private.[30] If, however, [the transgressor] does not amend his conduct, he should be shamed publicly until he repents.[31] If, however, he transgressed overtly, he should be rebuked immediately, so as not to bring about a desecration of G-d's name.[32]

6 If one rebuked a fellow Jew [for committing a transgression], and [he] berated

בָּרַבִּים,[25] מֵאַחַר שֶׁבָּרוּר לוֹ שֶׁלֹּא יְקַבֵּל מִמֶּנּוּ,[לט] וְעַל זֶה אָמְרוּ[מ,26] "כְּשֵׁם שֶׁמִּצְוָה לוֹמַר דָּבָר הַנִּשְׁמָע כָּךְ מִצְוָה שֶׁלֹּא לוֹמַר דָּבָר שֶׁאֵינוֹ נִשְׁמָע".

אֲבָל חַיָּב לְהוֹכִיחוֹ בְּיָחִיד אֲפִלּוּ מֵאָה פְּעָמִים[27] עַד שֶׁיִּנְזֹף בּוֹ הַחוֹטֵא,[מא,28] שֶׁכֵּיוָן שֶׁהוֹדִיעַ לוֹ הָאִסּוּר וְהוּא עוֹבֵר עָלָיו בְּזָדוֹן – חַיָּב כָּל אֶחָד וְאֶחָד מִיִּשְׂרָאֵל לְהוֹכִיחוֹ,[מב] שֶׁנֶּאֱמַר[מג,29] "הוֹכֵחַ תּוֹכִיחַ" – אֲפִלּוּ מֵאָה פְּעָמִים.[מד]

מִכָּל מָקוֹם, אִם הִיא עֲבֵרָה שֶׁבַּסֵּתֶר – יוֹכִיחֶנּוּ בִּתְחִלָּה בַּסֵּתֶר,[30] וְאִם לֹא שָׁב מִדַּרְכּוֹ – מַכְלִימִים אוֹתוֹ בָּרַבִּים עַד שֶׁיָּשׁוּב,[מה,31] אֲבָל אִם עוֹבֵר עֲבֵרָה בְּגָלוּי – מוֹכִיחִין אוֹתוֹ מִיָּד, שֶׁלֹּא יִתְחַלֵּל שֵׁם שָׁמַיִם:[מו,32]

ו מִי שֶׁהוֹכִיחַ אֶת חֲבֵרוֹ וְנָזַף בּוֹ חֲבֵרוֹ

25. *Arachin* 16b.

26. *Yevamos* 65b.

27. I.e., repeatedly.

28. This statement follows the view of R. Yochanan *(Arachin, loc. cit.).* The opposite stance — of Rav — is adopted by *Rambam (Hilchos De'os 6:7),* who makes this obligation extend until the offender strikes the rebuker and declares, "I will not heed!"

The Alter Rebbe quotes these words in sec. 156:8, but not here (608:5), whereas *Rama* (in the corresponding source, *Orach Chayim* 608:2) does. The Alter Rebbe's ruling here follows *Semak,* who is cited in *Magen Avraham,* 608:3.

29. *Vayikra* 19:17, as interpreted by *Bava Metzia* 31a.

30. To spare the transgressor embarrassment.

31. Cf. *Rambam, loc. cit.,* 6:8 (also cited by the Alter Rebbe, *loc. cit.*).

32. I.e., it is a desecration of the honor of G-d's name if a transgression is committed in the presence of people who remain silent and do not protest, thereby implying their acceptance of what they witness.

ריטב"א (לענין מזיד). וכדלעיל סי' קצז ס"ו וש"נ. וראה אסוקי שמעתתא מד, ב ואילך. אבני נזר יו"ד סי' תעג ס"ק ז. חקרי הלכות ח"א לד, א. ח"ב ס, ב. **לט** נמוקי יוסף יבמות כא, רע"ב. רמ"א שם. וראה לעיל סי' קנו ס"ז (שאינו מחלק בזה בין מוכיחו ביחיד למוכיחו ברבים, אלא בין יחיד לרבים), וס"ח (מתי יכול להוכיחנו ברבים). לקמן חו"מ הל' אונאה ס"ל. וראה אבני נזר שם ס"ק ג. **מ** גמרא יבמות סה, ב ובנימוקי יוסף שם. וכ"ה לעיל שם. **מא** ערכין טז, ב כבן עזאי ורבי יוחנן. סמ"ק סי' קיב. מ"א סק"ג. וכ"ה לקמן ס"ו. אבל לעיל שם (כרמ"א כאן): עד שיכנו החוטא או יקללנו, וש"נ. **מב** ולעיל שם: ואינו מחוייב להוכיח אלא עמיתו שהוא חבירו שהוא גם בו, אבל איש אחר שאם יוכיחנו ישנאנו וינקום ממנו אינו צריך להוכיחו כיון שבודאי לא ישמע לו, אבל חבירו אפילו אם יודע שלא ישמע לו חייב להוכיחו. וראה תניא ח"א פל"ב: הוכח תוכיח את עמיתך עם שאתך בתורה ומצות. **מג** ויקרא יט, יז. **מד** ב"מ לא, א. וראה גם לעיל שם. **מה** רמב"ם הל' דעות פ"ו ה"ח. סמ"ג ל"ת ו. וכ"ה לעיל שם (בדברי שמים). לקמן חו"מ שם. **מו** סמ"ק שם. מ"א שם. וכ"ה לעיל שם.

הַחוֹטֵא – לֹא יוֹכִיחֶנּוּ עוֹד[מז] עַל עֲבֵרָה זוֹ, שֶׁנֶּאֱמַר[מח,33] "אַל תּוֹכַח לֵץ וגו'":

him, he should not rebuke him again for the same transgression, as it is written,[33] "Do not rebuke a mocker."

ז אִם הִפְסִיק מֵאֲכִילָתוֹ בְּעוֹד הַיּוֹם גָּדוֹל,[מט] אַף עַל פִּי שֶׁהִסְכִּים בְּדַעְתּוֹ שֶׁלֹּא לֶאֱכֹל עוֹד הַיּוֹם[נ] – אַף עַל פִּי כֵן מֻתָּר לוֹ לַחֲזֹר וְלֶאֱכֹל, כֵּיוָן שֶׁלֹּא הוֹצִיא כֵן בִּשְׂפָתָיו, דִּדְבָרִים שֶׁבַּלֵּב אֵינָן דְּבָרִים.[נא] וְאִם הוֹצִיא כֵן בִּשְׂפָתָיו – אָסוּר לוֹ לֶאֱכֹל[נב] מִדִּין נֶדֶר[נג] (וְלֹא מֵחֲמַת אִסּוּר יוֹם הַכִּפּוּרִים), כֵּיוָן שֶׁאָמַר בְּפֵרוּשׁ שֶׁלֹּא יֹאכַל עוֹד הַיּוֹם.[34]

7 If one stopped eating while it was [obviously] still daytime, he may eat again even though he had resolved not to eat any more that day, because he did not articulate [this intent], and the designs of one's heart are not binding.

If one did articulate [this intent] he is forbidden to eat, (not because of the prohibition of [eating on] Yom Kippur, but) because [he is considered to have taken] a vow, for he explicitly said that he would not eat again that day.[34]

אֲבָל אִם קִבֵּל עָלָיו תַּעֲנִית שֶׁל יוֹם הַכִּפּוּרִים בִּסְתָם וְלֹא אָמַר בְּפֵרוּשׁ שֶׁלֹּא יֹאכַל עוֹד, אִם הוּא עֲדַיִן קֹדֶם פְּלַג הַמִּנְחָה,[35] – אֵין קַבָּלָתוֹ כְּלוּם[נד] וּמֻתָּר לַחֲזֹר וְלֶאֱכֹל, וְאִם (עַיֵּן סִימָן רס"א[נה,36] טַעַם עַל זֶה) הוּא אַחַר פְּלַג הַמִּנְחָה – אֲזַי מוֹעֶלֶת קַבָּלָתוֹ וְחָל עָלָיו כָּל חֹמֶר שֶׁל יוֹם הַכִּפּוּרִים[נו] וְאָסוּר בִּמְלָאכָה וּבִרְחִיצָה וְסִיכָה,[נז] חוּץ מִנְּעִילַת הַסַּנְדָּל[נח] כְּמוֹ שֶׁנִּתְבָּאֵר בְּסִימָן

[Different principles apply,] however, if one undertook the fast of Yom Kippur without further qualification, not stating explicitly that he would no longer eat. If it is before *plag haminchah,*[35] his acceptance is of no consequence, and he may eat again. If, however, (for the reason, see sec. 261[:5],[36]) it is after *plag haminchah,* his acceptance is significant and the full stringency of Yom Kippur applies to him. [Besides being forbidden to eat,] he is forbidden to work, to wash, or to anoint himself. He is, however, allowed to wear shoes, as stated in sec. 553.[37]

---

33. *Mishlei* 9:8.

34. In a situation of necessity, he can have the vow annulled by the appropriate procedure *(hataras nedarim).*

35. I.e., one-and-a-quarter seasonal hours before sunset.

36. The Alter Rebbe refers there to sec. 263:6, which states that one should not light *Shabbos* candles before *plag haminchah,* because at that early hour it is not obvious that this is being done in honor of *Shabbos.* Similarly, it might be said, undertaking the fast well before the approach of the holy day does not make one's motivation evident.

37. Sec. 553 of the Alter Rebbe's *Shulchan Aruch* is not extant. In his gloss to the *Shulchan Aruch* of R. Yosef Caro, *Turei Zahav* 553:1 writes that since a person in this situation continues to wear his shoes, it as if he explicitly stated that he has undertaken all the restrictions of Yom Kippur except for this one.

מז כדלעיל ס"ה וש"נ. **מח** משלי ט, ח. מ"א שם. וראה יבמות סה, ב. **מט** תוס' עירובין מא, א ד"ה אי, בשם איכה רבתי (ג, ו). רא"ש פ"ח סוס"י כה. טור ושו"ע ס"ג. **נ** מ"מ הל' תענית פ"ג ה"ג בשם ויש מן האחרונים. ב"י סי' תקנג ד"ה ומ"ש רבנו וכ"כ הרי"ף. רמ"א סי' תקנג ס"א. לבוש שם ס"א. **נא** רמ"א שם. לבוש שם. **נב** רי"ף תענית (ג, ב), ורמב"ם שם, לפירוש המ"מ שם. שו"ע ורמ"א שם ס"א. לבוש שם. מ"א כאן סק"ד. **נג** משמעות מ"א שם, שלמד כן מדין שבסימן תקסב סי"א. וראה לבוש שם. **נד** ב"י סוס"י תקנג, בשם הרמב"ן בתורת האדם (ענין אבלות ישנה ד"ה עד כאן פירשנו בשיעורי בין השמשות). רבנו ירוחם נתיב ז ח"א (נא, א). מ"א שם. **נה** ס"ה ובקו"א סוף סק"ג. **נו** מדין עצומו של יום ולא רק מדין תוספת (ראה לעיל קו"א שם). **נז** ראה ב"ח סי' תקנג ד"ה

תקנ"ג,[נט,37] וְשָׁם נִתְבָּאֵר דְּטוֹב לְהַחְמִיר וּלְהַתְנוֹת[38] בִּסְעוּדָה הַמַּפְסֶקֶת שֶׁיְּהֵא רַשַּׁאי לֶאֱכֹל וְלִשְׁתּוֹת עוֹד אַחַר הַסְּעוּדָה:[ס]

There it is explained that it is advisable to be stringent and to stipulate[38] at [the conclusion of] the meal preceding the fast that one will still be permitted to eat and drink after the meal.

ח בְּעֶרֶב יוֹם כִּפּוּר[סא] אֲפִלּוּ בִּסְעוּדַת שַׁחֲרִית[סב] – אֵין לֶאֱכֹל אֶלָּא מַאֲכָלִים קַלִּים לְהִתְעַכֵּל[סג] (כְּדֵי שֶׁלֹּא יִהְיֶה שָׂבֵעַ)[39] כְּגוֹן בְּשַׂר עוֹפוֹת וְדָגִים,[סד] כְּדֵי שֶׁלֹּא יְהֵא שָׂבֵעַ וּמִתְגָּאֶה כְּשֶׁיִּתְפַּלֵּל[סה] בְּיוֹם הַכִּפּוּרִים.

וְכֵן אֵין אוֹכְלִים דְּבָרִים הַמַּרְבִּים זֶרַע אֲפִלּוּ בִּסְעוּדַת שַׁחֲרִית, כְּגוֹן שׁוּמִים וּבֵיצִים.[סו] אֲבָל מַאַכְלֵי חָלָב[סז] וְחֶמְאָה[סח,40] אַף עַל פִּי שֶׁהֵן מַרְבִּין זֶרַע – מִכָּל מָקוֹם נוֹהֲגִין לְאָכְלָם בְּשַׁחֲרִית,[סט] כֵּיוָן שֶׁהֵם מַאֲכָלִים קַלִּים[ע] לְהִתְעַכֵּל.

אֲבָל בִּסְעוּדָה הַמַּפְסֶקֶת שֶׁהוּא סָמוּךְ לַלַּיְלָה – אֵין לֶאֱכֹל אוֹתָם. וְכֵן אֵין לֶאֱכֹל בִּסְעוּדָה הַמַּפְסֶקֶת דְּבָרִים הַמְחַמְּמִים אֶת הַגּוּף [כְּגוֹן] בְּשָׂמִים וְכַרְכֹּם, שֶׁמָּא יָבוֹא לִידֵי קֶרִי[עא] בַּלַּיְלָה:

8 On the day preceding Yom Kippur, even during the morning meal, one should eat only foods that are readily digestible (so that he will not be [overly] satiated),[39] e.g., fowl and fish, so that he will not be satisfied and proud while praying on the day preceding Yom Kippur.

Additionally, one should not eat foods that spur [the production of] semen, e.g., garlic and eggs, even in the morning meal. Milk products and butter,[40] by contrast, although they [too] spur the production of semen, are customarily eaten in the morning, since they are easily digestible. One should not, however, partake of them at the meal before the fast that is close to nightfall. Similarly, at that meal one should not partake of foods such as spices and saffron that arouse the body's natural heat, lest that lead to a nocturnal emission.

ט אִם אָכַל הַרְבֵּה בְּעֶרֶב יוֹם כִּפּוּר – לֹא יָשִׂים אֶצְבָּעוֹ בְּפִיו[עב,41] לְהָקִיא, שֶׁמָּא יִבְלַע מִן הַקִּיאָה:[עג]

9 One who overate on the day before Yom Kippur should not put his finger down his throat [on Yom Kippur][41] in order to vomit, lest he swallow part of his vomit.

---

38. Either verbally or in thought *(Machtzis HaShekel* 553:2*)*.

39. This phrase is enclosed by parentheses in the original text, and its repetition shortly afterwards suggests that it is a printing error. Alternatively, the first phrase may refer to physical satiation, while the second may signify the smugness that glut may bring.

40. See *Yoma* 18a; see also *Igros Kodesh* of the Rebbe, Vol. 3, p. 210.

41. Bracketed phrase added by *Kuntreis HaShulchan,* following *Magen Avraham.*

ומ"ש רבנו אדברי הראב"ד. ט"ז שם ס"ק א. מ"א שם סק"ד (לענין רחיצה בתשעה באב). **נח** ט"ז סי' תקנג שם. **נט** סימן זה בשוע"ר לא הגיע לידינו, וראה ב"ח וט"ז ומ"א שם. **ס** מ"א שם ס"ק ב, להחמיר לדעת הפוסקים (הובאו בב"ח כאן ושם, ובמ"א כאן ס"ק ד) שקבלה בלב הוי קבלה. **סא** כלבו סי' סח (לג, א) בשם הר"מ (ראה תשב"ץ סי' קכז). שו"ע ס"ד. **סב** ב"ח בסוף הסימן, ממשמעות התוס' ע"ז ה, ב ד"ה וכדברי. **סג** כלבו שם. שו"ע שם. **סד** תוס' שם. **סה** כלבו שם. שו"ע שם. **סו** ט"ז סק"ג. **סז** מהרי"ל הל' ערב יוה"כ (ע' שיט). רמ"א ס"ד. **סח** ראה מ"א סק"ו. וראה אג"ק ח"ג ע' רי. שלחן המלך ח"ב ע' ריב. **סט** מהרי"ל שם. רמ"א שם. **ע** מ"א סק"ז. **עא** מהרי"ל שם. רמ"א שם ומ"א סק"ה. **עב** בקונטרס השלחן הגיה: בפיו ביוה"כ להקיא. **עג** ס' החסידים סי' תשסט. מ"א סוף סק"ז.

10 One should not eat sesame seeds on the day preceding Yom Kippur, [lest] they cause regurgitation on Yom Kippur.

י לֹא יֹאכַל שֻׁמְשְׁמִין בְּעֶרֶב יוֹם כִּפּוּר, מִפְּנֵי שֶׁמַּעֲלֶה גֵּרָה[עד] בְּיוֹם הַכִּפּוּרִים:

SECTION 609 Insulation of Hot [Foods or Beverages] on *Erev* Yom Kippur. (1)

סימן תרט הַטְמָנַת חַמִּין בְּעֶרֶב יוֹם כִּפּוּר וּבוֹ סְעִיף אֶחָד:

1 Some authorities forbid the insulation[1] of hot food or beverages on the day before Yom Kippur so that they will be warm on the night following Yom Kippur. [They maintain that] insulating hot [food or drink] was permitted [by the Sages] only in honor of *Shabbos*.[2] In this instance, one is insulating [the food or drink] to be consumed on the night following Yom Kippur, which is an ordinary weekday. [According to these authorities] this was not permitted at all, because the food would be warming on Yom Kippur, and thus Yom Kippur would be preparing for an ordinary weekday.

Other authorities maintain that insulating [hot food or beverages] on the day before Yom Kippur is permissible, for [it is activity performed on] a weekday that is preparing for [another] weekday. Although the food remains on the cooking range on Yom Kippur, this is not considered as preparing [for the following day] since one is not performing any activity on Yom Kippur itself.

The *halachah* follows the latter opinion. Nevertheless, in these lands, it is customary to follow the stringency of the first opinion.[3]

א יֵשׁ אוֹסְרִים[א] לְהַטְמִין[1] חַמִּין מֵעֶרֶב יוֹם כִּפּוּר לְמוֹצָאֵי יוֹם הַכִּפּוּרִים, מִפְּנֵי שֶׁלֹּא הִתִּירוּ לְהַטְמִין חַמִּין אֶלָּא לִכְבוֹד הַשַּׁבָּת,[ב,2] אֲבָל זֶה שֶׁהוּא מַטְמִין לְמוֹצָאֵי יוֹם הַכִּפּוּרִים שֶׁהוּא חֹל – לֹא הִתִּירוּ לוֹ כְּלָל, לְפִי שֶׁהַתַּבְשִׁיל מִתְחַמֵּם בְּיוֹם הַכִּפּוּרִים, וְנִמְצָא יוֹם הַכִּפּוּרִים מֵכִין לְחֹל.[ג]

וְיֵשׁ מַתִּירִים[ד] לְהַטְמִין בְּעֶרֶב יוֹם כִּפּוּר, מִפְּנֵי שֶׁהוּא מֵכִין מֵחֹל לְחֹל, וְאַף עַל פִּי שֶׁשּׁוֹהֶה עַל הַכִּירָה בְּיוֹם הַכִּפּוּרִים – אֵין זוֹ חֲשׁוּבָה הֲכָנָה, כֵּיוָן שֶׁאֵינוֹ עוֹשֶׂה מַעֲשֶׂה בְּיוֹם הַכִּפּוּרִים.

וַהֲלָכָה כִּסְבָרָא הָאַחֲרוֹנָה. מִכָּל מָקוֹם, נוֹהֲגִין בְּאֵלּוּ הַמְּדִינוֹת לְהַחְמִיר כִּסְבָרָא הָרִאשׁוֹנָה:[ה,3]

---

1. In the original, *hatmanah* — the wrapping or covering of hot food or beverages to preserve their heat. See sec. 253ff. where this subject is discussed.

2. I.e., to enable one to enjoy the *Shabbos* meals.

3. If one did not follow this stringency, he is still permitted to partake of the food directly after the conclusion of Yom Kippur. There is no need to wait until the food could have been warmed (*Pri Megadim: Eshel Avraham* 609:1).

עד ס' החסידים שם. מ"א שם. וראה עוד לעיל סי' – סי"ד.
סימן תרט: א גאונים, הובאו ברא"ש פ"ח סי' כו, טור ורמ"א. ב כדלעיל סי' רנז סי"ג. ולצורך מוצאי שבת – ראה לעיל סי' רנד סי"א. ג בנימין זאב סי' רטז. מ"א סק"א. ד רא"ש שם בשם רב שרירא גאון. טור ושו"ע שם. ה מהרי"ל הל' ערב יוה"כ (ע' שכא). רמ"א.

SECTION 610 Kindling Lights on Yom Kippur. (1–10)

1 Yom Kippur must be honored by [the kindling of] lights, as is required with regard to other festivals, as will be explained.[1] In certain regions, however, the custom is to prohibit the kindling of lights on the night of Yom Kippur in a house in which one lives together with his wife.[2] This [safeguard] was ordained lest a man desire his wife when he sees her by candlelight and thus [be motivated to] engage in marital relations.[3] In other regions [it is customary to] kindle lights in the house, for since relations are forbidden in the presence of a light, this will not come about.[4]

In those places where it is customary to kindle lights, one should recite the blessing [that praises G-d] "Who sanctified us with His commandments and commanded us to kindle the light of Yom Kippur," for it is a *mitzvah* to kindle lights [in honor of] that day as it is on *Shabbos* and the festivals.[5]

2 If there is a lamp burning in the house, a light should be kindled in the bedroom that a man shares with his wife. [This applies both] in regions in which it is customary to kindle lights and in regions in which [this] is not customary, for it is feared that the sight of one's wife by the light [burning] in the house will be conducive to marital relations in a room in which no light is burning.[6]

סימן תרי הַדְלָקַת הַנֵּרוֹת בְּיוֹם הַכִּפּוּרִים וּבוֹ י׳ סְעִיפִים:

א יוֹם הַכִּפּוּרִים צָרִיךְ לְכַבְּדוֹ בְּנֵרוֹת[א] כְּמוֹ בִּשְׁאָר יָמִים טוֹבִים[ב] כְּמוֹ שֶׁיִּתְבָּאֵר,[ג,1] אֶלָּא שֶׁיֵּשׁ מְקוֹמוֹת שֶׁנּוֹהֲגִין אִסּוּר בְּהַדְלָקַת נֵר בְּלֵיל יוֹם הַכִּפּוּרִים[ד] בְּבַיִת שֶׁאִישׁ וְאִשְׁתּוֹ דָּרִים בּוֹ,[2] גְּזֵרָה שֶׁמָּא יִתְאַוֶּה לְאִשְׁתּוֹ כְּשֶׁיִּרְאֶנָּה לְאוֹר הַנֵּר וְיָבוֹא לִידֵי תַּשְׁמִישׁ,[ה,3] אֲבָל יֵשׁ מְקוֹמוֹת שֶׁמַּדְלִיקִין[ו] בַּבַּיִת, שֶׁכֵּיוָן שֶׁאָסוּר לְשַׁמֵּשׁ לְאוֹר הַנֵּר – בְּוַדַּאי לֹא יָבוֹא לִידֵי תַּשְׁמִישׁ.[ז,4]

וְאוֹתָן מְקוֹמוֹת שֶׁמַּדְלִיקִין צְרִיכִין לְבָרֵךְ[ח] "אֲשֶׁר קִדְּשָׁנוּ בְּמִצְוֹתָיו וְצִוָּנוּ לְהַדְלִיק נֵר שֶׁל יוֹם הַכִּפּוּרִים",[ט] שֶׁהֲרֵי יוֹם הַכִּפּוּרִים מִצְוָה לְהַדְלִיק בּוֹ נֵרוֹת[י] כְּמוֹ בְּשַׁבָּתוֹת[יא] וְיָמִים טוֹבִים:[יב,5]

ב אִם יֵשׁ לוֹ נֵר דָּלוּק בַּבַּיִת – צָרִיךְ לְהַדְלִיק נֵר בַּחֶדֶר שֶׁלָּן בּוֹ עִם אִשְׁתּוֹ,[יג] בֵּין בְּמָקוֹם שֶׁנּוֹהֲגִין לְהַדְלִיק[יד] בֵּין בְּמָקוֹם שֶׁאֵין נוֹהֲגִין לְהַדְלִיק, שֶׁכֵּיוָן שֶׁרוֹאֶה אֶת אִשְׁתּוֹ לְאוֹר הַנֵּר שֶׁבַּבַּיִת אִם כֵּן יֵשׁ לָחוּשׁ שֶׁמָּא יָבוֹא לִידֵי תַּשְׁמִישׁ בַּחֶדֶר שֶׁאֵין שָׁם נֵר דּוֹלֵק:[טו,6]

---

1. Subsection 4.

2. *Pesachim* 53b.

3. Which are forbidden on Yom Kippur (sec. 611:2). Sec. 615:1 lists additional safeguards.

4. See the *Shulchan Aruch* of R. Yosef Caro, sec. 240:11.

5. The Lubavitch custom is to kindle lights. In addition to the above blessing, the blessing *Shehecheyanu* is recited. See sec. 619, footnote 24 below.

6. On the kindling of a light as a safeguard, see subsection 1 above.

א רא"ש פ"ח סי' ט (ראה ב"ח בסוף הסימן). מרדכי רמז תשכה. הובא מ"א סק"ב. **ב** ראה לעיל סי' תקיד סי"ג וסכ"ה. **ג** סוף ס"ח. **ד** משנה פסחים נג, ב. טור ושו"ע ס"א. **ה** ברייתא שם ורש"י ד"ה בין. **ו** משנה שם. טור ושו"ע שם. **ז** ברייתא ורש"י שם. וראה גם ירושלמי פסחים פ"ד ה"ד. הובא ב"י ריש הסי'. **ח** רא"ש פ"ח סי' כז. מנהגים (טירנא) ערב יום כפור (ע' קז). טור ושו"ע ורמ"א ס"ב. **ט** ראה רמ"א סוף ס"א. פר"ח סוף ס"ב. **י** ראה רא"ש שם (משום שלום בית). מ"א סי' רסג סקי"ג. **יא** כדלעיל סי' רסג ס"א. **יב** כדלעיל סי' תקיד סכ"ד. **יג** מהרי"ל הל' ערב יוה"כ (ע' שכא). רמ"א ס"א. **יד** ראה מ"א סק"ב. **טו** מהרי"ל שם. רמ"א שם.

ג אֲפִלּוּ בִּמְקוֹמוֹת שֶׁאֵין מַדְלִיקִין בַּבַּיִת, מִכָּל מָקוֹם מַדְלִיקִין בְּבָתֵּי כְנֵסִיּוֹת וּבְבָתֵּי מִדְרָשׁוֹת וּבִמְבוֹאוֹת הָאֲפֵלוֹת וְעַל גַּבֵּי הַחוֹלִים.[טז,7]

וְכֵן אִם חָל יוֹם הַכִּפּוּרִים בְּשַׁבָּת — חַיָּבִין הַכֹּל לְהַדְלִיק אַף בְּבֵיתוֹ,[יז] וּמְבָרְכִין "אֲשֶׁר קִדְּשָׁנוּ בְּמִצְוֹתָיו וְצִוָּנוּ לְהַדְלִיק נֵר שֶׁל שַׁבָּת וְשֶׁל יוֹם הַכִּפּוּרִים":[יח]

3 Even in regions in which it is customary not to kindle lights in the home, lights are kindled in synagogues and in Houses of Study, in dark alleyways, and over a [sick-bed].[7] In addition, when Yom Kippur falls on *Shabbos,* everyone is obligated to kindle lights at home as well. One then recites the blessing [that praises G-d] "Who sanctified us with His commandments and commanded us to kindle the light of *Shabbos* and of Yom Kippur."

ד נוֹהֲגִין בְּכָל מָקוֹם לְהַצִּיעַ בְּגָדִים נָאִים בְּבֵית הַכְּנֶסֶת,[יט] וְגַם בַּבָּתִּים לְהַצִּיעַ מַפָּה יָפָה עַל הַשֻּׁלְחָן כְּמוֹ בְּשַׁבָּת[כ] וְיוֹם טוֹב.

וְכֵן נוֹהֲגִים לְהַרְבּוֹת בְּנֵרוֹת בְּבֵית הַכְּנֶסֶת,[כא] שֶׁנֶּאֱמַר[כב,8] "עַל כֵּן בָּאֻרִים כַּבְּדוּ ה'", וּמְתַרְגְּמִינָן[כג] "בְּפַנָּסַיָּא יְקָרוּ ה'".[כד,9] וְטוֹב לַעֲשׂוֹת פְּתִילוֹת עָבוֹת בְּבֵית הַכְּנֶסֶת, לְהַרְבּוֹת אוֹרָן.[כה]

וְנָהֲגוּ שֶׁכָּל אִישׁ גָּדוֹל וְקָטָן עוֹשִׂין בִּשְׁבִילוֹ נֵר[כו] לְבֵית הַכְּנֶסֶת.[כז] וְעַכְשָׁו נוֹהֲגִין שֶׁאֵין עוֹשִׂין נֵר אֶלָּא לִנְשׂוּאִי בִּלְבַד:[כח,10]

4 It is a universal custom to spread fine cloths in the synagogue. Similarly, it is customary to cover the table at home with an attractive tablecloth, as is done on *Shabbos* and festivals.

Similarly, it is customary to kindle numerous lights in the synagogue [in honor of Yom Kippur], in allusion to the phrase,[8] "Therefore honor G-d *ba'urim,*" which the *Targum* renders as "…honor G-d with lights."[9] It is desirable to make thick wicks [for the lamps] in the synagogue to increase their light.

It was once customary that a candle was kindled in the synagogue for every man, both for an adult and a minor. The present custom is to kindle a light for a married man only.[10]

---

7. *Pesachim, loc. cit.* Blessings should not be recited when kindling these lights *(Bach, Pri Chadash).*

8. *Yeshayahu* 24:15.

9. Others understand this word as meaning crevices, trenches, or valleys.

10. The Lubavitch custom, before sunset on the eve of Yom Kippur, is to light one 24-hour candle in the synagogue for the entire household. This is known as a *lebedige licht* — "a living light." Also, a 24-hour candle is kindled at home as a memorial for one's departed parents. (A number of souls may be commemorated by one candle. See *Mateh Ephraim* 603:8.)

Sefer HaMinhagim records that on the preceding Friday, on the eve of *Shabbos Teshuvah* (which is also known as *Shabbos Shuvah*), it was customary in the household of each of the respective Rebbes to light a *teshuvah licht* — "a *teshuvah* light." A large candle was plaited of several wicks, one for each member of the family. In other households, this practice is rarely — if at all — observed at present.

טז משנה שם. טור ושו"ע ס"ג. יז גמרא [ברייתא] שם, כרבי שמעון בן אלעזר. רמב"ם פ"ג ה"י. שו"ע ס"א. יח רמ"א סוף ס"א. יט טור ושו"ע ס"ד. וראה גם לקמן סוף ס"ח. כ מרדכי רמז תשכה. מנהגים (טירנא) ערב יום כפור (ע' קז). רמ"א ס"ד. וכדלעיל סי' רסב ס"א. כא רא"ש פ"ח סי' ט. טור ושו"ע שם. וראה גם לעיל סי' תקיד סי"ד. כב ישעיה כד, טו. כג ראה ילקוט שמעוני ישעיה רמז תכה. כד רא"ש שם. טור. כה מ"א סוף הסי', בשם ילקוט שמעוני שופטים רמז מב. כו מרדכי רמז תשכג. מהרי"ל הל' ערב יוה"כ (ע' שכב). מהר"י וייל סי' קצא. רמ"א ס"ד. כז לבוש ס"ג. כח מ"א סק"ג. כט כלבו סי' סח (לג, א). רמ"א ס"ד.

ה גַּם נָהֲגוּ לַעֲשׂוֹת נֵר נְשָׁמָה לְאָבִיו וּלְאִמּוֹ שֶׁמֵּתוּ:[כט,11]

5 In addition, candles are customarily lit for the souls of one's departed father and mother.[11]

ו וְאִם כָּבוּ נֵרוֹת אֵלּוּ בְּיוֹם הַכִּפּוּרִים – אֵין לוֹמַר לְנָכְרִי שֶׁיַּחֲזֹר לְהַדְלִיקָן.[ל] וַאֲפִלּוּ לִרְמֹז לוֹ אָסוּר.[לא] וְלֹא עוֹד אֶלָּא שֶׁאִם בָּא לְהַדְלִיק מֵעַצְמוֹ – צָרִיךְ לִמְחוֹת בְּיָדוֹ כְּמוֹ שֶׁנִּתְבָּאֵר בְּסִימָן רע"ו.[לב] וְכֵן אֵין לוֹמַר לְנָכְרִי לְקַבֵּל שַׁעֲוָה הַנּוֹטֵף מִן הַנֵּרוֹת,[לג] מִפְּנֵי שֶׁהַיִּשְׂרָאֵל אָסוּר לוֹ לְטַלְטֵל הַשַּׁעֲוָה מִפְּנֵי שֶׁהִיא מֻקְצָה כְּמוֹ שֶׁנִּתְבָּאֵר בְּסִימָן רס"ה,[לד,12] וְכָל שֶׁאֵין הֶתֵּר לְהַיִּשְׂרָאֵל לְטַלְטְלוֹ – אָסוּר לוֹמַר לְנָכְרִי לְטַלְטְלוֹ כְּמוֹ שֶׁנִּתְבָּאֵר בְּסִימָן רע"ו,[לה] עַיֵּן שָׁם:

6 If the candles went out on Yom Kippur, one should not tell a non-Jew to rekindle them. It is forbidden even to hint to him [to do so]. Indeed, if he wants to take the initiative of rekindling them one should object, as stated in sec. 276[:3].

Similarly, one may not instruct a non-Jew to collect the wax that drips from the candles, because a Jew is forbidden to move [it] since it is *muktzeh,* as stated in sec. 265[:3].[12] And whenever an object may not be moved by a Jew, it is forbidden to tell a non-Jew to move it, as explained in sec. 276[:9-10].

ז וְנָהֲגוּ לִקַּח נָכְרִי לִשְׁמֹר הַנֵּרוֹת שֶׁלֹּא יָבוֹא חָס וְשָׁלוֹם לִידֵי דְלֵקָה, וּמִכֹּחַ זֶה נָהֲגוּ הֶהָמוֹן לוֹמַר לוֹ לְכַבּוֹת וּלְהַדְלִיק, וְאֵין לָזֶה הֶתֵּר כְּלָל, וְיֵשׁ לִמְחוֹת בְּיָדָם, וּבִפְרָט בְּיוֹם הַדִּין:[לו]

7 It has become customary to [hire] a non-Jew to watch the candles so that they will not cause a fire, Heaven forbid. As a result of this practice, unlettered people customarily instruct him to extinguish [the candles] and relight them. There is no license for this at all. They should be reprimanded for doing so, in particular on the Day of Judgment.

ח מִי שֶׁכָּבָה נֵרוֹ בְּיוֹם הַכִּפּוּרִים – סִימָן רַע לוֹ.[לז] וְתַקָּנָתוֹ, שֶׁיַּחֲזֹר וְיַדְלִיקֶנּוּ בְּמוֹצָאֵי יוֹם הַכִּפּוּרִים, וְלֹא יְכַבֶּנּוּ עוֹד אֶלָּא יַנִּיחֶנּוּ לִדְלֹק עַד גְּמִירָא, וְגַם יְקַבֵּל עָלָיו שֶׁכָּל יָמָיו לֹא יְכַבֶּה נֵרוֹ בְּמוֹצָאֵי יוֹם הַכִּפּוּרִים לֹא הוּא וְלֹא אַחֵר אֶלָּא יַנִּיחֶנּוּ לִדְלֹק עַד גְּמִירָא.[לח]

8 It is an unfavorable omen if one's candle goes out on Yom Kippur. This may be rectified by relighting it on the night following Yom Kippur and not extinguishing it, but letting it remain alight until it burns out. Also, a person [in this situation] should resolve that for the rest of his life neither he nor anyone else will extinguish his candle on the night following Yom Kippur, and that instead, it will be left alight until it burns out.

---

11. This confers atonement upon them (*Mishnah Berurah* 610:12).

12. The Alter Rebbe refers there to sec. 279:2, which explains that since it was forbidden to partake of the oil in a lamp during *bein hashmashos* (the time between sunset and nightfall), it is forbidden to partake of it and to move it throughout *Shabbos.* The drippings are thus *muktzeh.*

וראה אליה רבה ס"ק ד. **ל** מהרי"ל הל' ליל יוה"כ (ע' של). רמ"א שם. **לא** דרכי משה ס"ק ד. וראה גם לעיל סי' שז ס"ז. **לב** סעיף ג. **לג** הגהות מנהגים יו"כ אות קעט. מ"א סק"ד. **לד** ראה שם ס"ה. **לה** ס"י ובקו"א סק"ג. **לו** מהרי"ל שם. מ"א שם. **לז** ראה הוריות יב, א. **לח** הגהות מנהגים שם, בשם מנהגים ישנים. רמ"א שם.

("לִקְדוֹשׁ ה' מְכֻבָּד"[לט,14] — זֶה יוֹם הַכִּפּוּרִים שֶׁאֵין בּוֹ אֲכִילָה וּשְׁתִיָּה,[13,15] אָמְרָה תּוֹרָה כַּבְּדוּהוּ בִּכְסוּת נְקִיָּה[מ] וּבְנֵרוֹת,[מא] לְפִיכָךְ נוֹהֲגִין לְהַצִּיעַ בְּגָדִים נָאִים בְּבֵית הַכְּנֶסֶת[מב]):

([Our Sages[13] interpret the phrase],[14] "the holy [day] of G-d, honored," as referring to Yom Kippur, on which there is neither eating or drinking.[15] The Torah [therefore] says: "Honor it with clean clothing and lights." [In this spirit,] it is customary to spread fine cloths in the synagogue.)

ט יֵשׁ נוֹהֲגִין לִלְבֹּשׁ בְּגָדִים לְבָנִים נְקִיִּים בְּיוֹם הַכִּפּוּרִים, כְּדֵי לִהְיוֹת דֻּגְמַת מַלְאֲכֵי הַשָּׁרֵת.[מג,16] וְכֵן נוֹהֲגִין בִּמְדִינוֹת אֵלּוּ לִלְבֹּשׁ הַקִּיטְל,[17] שֶׁהוּא בֶּגֶד לָבָן וְנָקִי.[מד] וְיֵשׁ עוֹד טַעַם בִּלְבִישַׁת הַקִּיטְל, מִפְּנֵי שֶׁהוּא בֶּגֶד מֵתִים וְעַל יְדֵי זֶה נִכְנָע לֵב אָדָם[מה] לַעֲשׂוֹת תְּשׁוּבָה שְׁלֵמָה,[מו] וּלְפִיכָךְ[18] גַּם מִי שֶׁהוּא אָבֵל מֻתָּר לִלְבֹּשׁ הַקִּיטְל.[מז]

וְכֵן הַנָּשִׁים יְכוֹלוֹת לִלְבֹּשׁ הַקִּיטְל כְּדֵי לְהַכְנִיעַ לִבָּן,[מח,19] אֲבָל שְׁאָר בְּגָדִים לְבָנִים

9 It is the custom of some people to wear clean white clothes on Yom Kippur in order to resemble the ministering angels.[16] Indeed, the custom in these countries is to wear a *kittel*,[17] which is a clean white garment.

There is another reason for wearing a *kittel:* since it [resembles] a shroud, it humbles one's heart toward full repentance. For this reason,[18] even a mourner may wear a *kittel.*

Similarly, women may wear a *kittel* to humble their hearts,[19] but should not wear

---

13. *Shabbos* 119a.

14. *Yeshayahu* 58:11.

15. This is implied by the term "holy," i.e., removed from all ordinary mundane activity.

16. Since the angels in *Yechezkel* 9:2 and in *Daniel* 12:5 are depicted as being garbed in linen, *Darchei Moshe* 610:5 writes that the *kittel* should be made of linen.

17. Yiddish name for a simple, lightweight, white outer garment (from Middle High German, "a small coat") worn on specified occasions, and also used as a shroud.

According to Lubavitch custom it is worn on Yom Kippur only by married men, and not by younger men, for one is not punishable at the hands of Heaven before age twenty, and in former times young men were typically married by that age. After marriage, "a bridegroom who wore a *kittel* at his wedding does not wear one on the first Yom Kippur thereafter" *(Sefer HaMinhagim: The Book of Chabad-Lubavitch Customs,* p. 124*)*, "since he already wore it on his personal Yom Kippur that year, namely, his wedding day" *(Igros Kodesh* of the Rebbe, Vol. 5, p. 87*)*.

Since a *kittel* (like a *gartl*) is designated as a garment of prayer, it should be removed before one enters a lavatory (sec. 21:3 in Vol. 1 of the present work).

18. Unlike the previous reason (regarding the garb of angels), whereby the *kittel* is perceived as a fine garment that would not suit a person in his year of mourning. See *Aruch HaShulchan,* sec. 610:2.

19. This custom is not practiced today. In some communities, though not in Lubavitch, the headkerchiefs or other women's garments worn on Yom Kippur are white *(Mateh Ephraim* 610:9*)*. This source also notes that wearing jewelry on Yom Kippur detracts from the awe and reverence that should characterize the Day of Judgment. It is a widespread custom to refrain in particular from wearing gold ornaments. This recalls the plain white linen garb, unadorned by any gold ornament, that the *Kohen Gadol* wore on this

לט ישעיה נח, יג. **מ** גמרא שבת קיט, א. רא"ש פ"ח סי' ט. טור. וראה גם לעיל ס"ד. לקמן סי' תריד ס"ח. **מא** ראה ב"ח סוף הסימן. לעיל שם. **מב** טור ושו"ע ס"ד. לעיל ס"ד. **מג** מרדכי רמז תשכג. רמ"א ס"ד. וראה לעיל סי' יח ס"ג שמטעם זה מתעטפים בטלית ביוה"כ ואפילו בלילה. **מד** דרכי משה ס"ק ה. רמ"א שם. וראה לעיל סי' כא ס"ג שההולך לפנות צריך לפשוט הקיטל. **מה** דרכי משה שם. רמ"א שם. וראה גם לעיל סי' תעב ס"ד. **מו** לבוש ס"ד. **מז** ט"ז סק"ג.

other white clothes in order to resemble the angels, for they cannot resemble them. This is hinted at in [the Hebrew wording of] the phrase,[20] "The wise man ascended to the city of the mighty." In that verse, the word for "the mighty" (גבורים) is spelled גברים, [which can also mean "the men"].[21]

אֵין לָהֶן לִלְבֹּשׁ כְּדֵי לִהְיוֹת דֻּגְמַת מַלְאֲכֵי הַשָּׁרֵת, שֶׁאֵין יְכוֹלוֹת לִהְיוֹת כְּמַלְאָכִים,[מט] שֶׁנֶּאֱמַר[נ,20] "עִיר גִּבֹּרִים עָלָה חָכָם וגו'", "גְּבָרִים" כְּתִיב:[נא,21]

10 One who wears sackcloth for the sake of repentance should [exchange it for festive clothing in honor of] Yom Kippur, because it is a festival and must be honored with clean clothing, as explained [above].

י הַלּוֹבֵשׁ שַׂק מֵחֲמַת תְּשׁוּבָה – צָרִיךְ לְפָשְׁטוֹ בְּיוֹם הַכִּפּוּרִים,[נב] מִפְּנֵי שֶׁהוּא יוֹם טוֹב[נג] וְצָרִיךְ לְכַבְּדוֹ בִּכְסוּת נְקִיָּה כְּמוֹ שֶׁנִּתְבָּאֵר:[נד]

SECTION 611 [The Restrictions Observed on] the Night of Yom Kippur, [which is Governed by] the Same Laws as the Day of Yom Kippur. (1–10)

סימן תריא לֵיל יוֹם הַכִּפּוּרִים דִּינוֹ כְּיוֹמוֹ וּבוֹ י' סְעִיפִים:

1 The night of Yom Kippur [is governed by the same laws] as the day [of Yom Kippur] in all respects:[1] whatever is forbidden by day is also forbidden at night. [Moreover,] whatever is forbidden on the festival itself is also forbidden even during the additional time that is appended from the mundane realm to the realm of holiness, both before and after [the festival].[2]

א לֵיל יוֹם הַכִּפּוּרִים הֲרֵי הוּא כְּיוֹמוֹ לְכָל דָּבָר,[א,1] שֶׁכָּל דְּבָרִים הָאֲסוּרִים בַּיּוֹם – אֲסוּרִים בַּלַּיְלָה. וַאֲפִלּוּ בַּתּוֹסֶפֶת שֶׁמּוֹסִיפִין מֵחֹל עַל הַקֹּדֶשׁ בֵּין מִלְּפָנָיו[ב] בֵּין מִלְּאַחֲרָיו[ג] – אֲסוּרִים כָּל הַדְּבָרִים הָאֲסוּרִים בְּעִקַּר הַיּוֹם:[2]

2 What activities are forbidden? Performing work, eating and drinking, washing, anointing

ב וּמָה הֵן הַדְּבָרִים הָאֲסוּרִים? מְלָאכָה, אֲכִילָה וּשְׁתִיָּה, רְחִיצָה וְסִיכָה, נְעִילַת הַסַּנְדָּל,

---

day when he entered the Holy of Holies *(Elef LaMateh* on *Mateh Ephraim, loc. cit.*, note 7*)*.

20. *Mishlei* 21:22. The verse alludes to Moshe's ascent to Heaven, "the city of the mighty [angels]," to receive the Torah.

21. Implying that the angels manifest male qualities. See *Yalkut Shimoni* on this verse.

SECTION 611

1. With the exception of Tishah BeAv, the commemorative fasts ordained by the Sages are observed from dawn until the appearance of the stars. Yom Kippur is observed from sunset on the ninth of Tishrei until the appearance of the stars on the tenth of Tishrei: "From evening until evening shall you observe your day of rest" *(Vayikra* 23:32*)*.

2. See sec. 608:1-3.

וראה גם לעיל סי' תעב ס"ד. **מח** מ"א סק"ה. **מט** ראה גם לקמן סי' תריט סי"ז. **נ** משלי כא, כב. **נא** מ"א שם (ע"פ ויקרא רבה פל"א, ה). **נב** ספר חסידים סי' תרטו. מ"א שם. **נג** ספר חסידים שם. וראה לעיל סי' תקכט סוף ס"ז. מ"מ וציונים. **נד** סוף ס"ח. וראה גם לעיל סי' קכח סנ"ז (וכבוד היום במלבושים נאים). לקו"ש חכ"ט ע' 203 ואילך. שלחן המלך ח"ב ע' רטו.

סימן תריא: א רמב"ם הל' שביתת העשור פ"א ה"ו. טור ושו"ע ס"א. **ב** כדלעיל סי' תרח ס"א וש"נ. וראה שם סוף ס"ז. **ג** כדלעיל שם (הוקשו זה לזה). ראה לשון הרמב"ם שם: שוהה בעינויו. וראה גם לקמן סי' תרכד סט"ו.

תַּשְׁמִישׁ הַמִּטָּה.[ד,3] אֲבָל אֵין חִיּוּב כָּרֵת[4] אֶלָּא עַל מְלָאכָה וַאֲכִילָה וּשְׁתִיָּה,[ה] שֶׁנֶּאֱמַר[ו,5] "וְכָל הַנֶּפֶשׁ[6] אֲשֶׁר תַּעֲשֶׂה כָּל מְלָאכָה[ז] וְהַאֲבַדְתִּי וגו'", וְנֶאֱמַר[ח,7] "כִּי כָל הַנֶּפֶשׁ אֲשֶׁר לֹא תְעֻנֶּה[ט] וְנִכְרְתָה וגו'", וּסְתַם עִנּוּי הוּא[8] מְנִיעַת אֲכִילָה וּשְׁתִיָּה,[י] כְּמוֹ שֶׁנֶּאֱמַר[יא,9] "וַיְעַנְּךָ וַיַּרְעִבֶךָ וַיַּאֲכִלְךָ וגו'", וּשְׁתִיָּה בִּכְלַל אֲכִילָה.[יב]

אֲבָל רְחִיצָה וְסִיכָה וּנְעִילַת הַסַּנְדָּל וְתַשְׁמִישׁ הַמִּטָּה, אַף עַל פִּי שֶׁגַּם הֵם נִקְרָאִים עִנּוּי לִפְעָמִים כְּמוֹ שֶׁלָּמְדוּ חֲכָמִים[יג] מִמִּדְרַשׁ הַפְּסוּקִים,[10] מִכָּל מָקוֹם סְתַם עִנּוּי לֹא נֶאֱמַר בְּרֹב הַפְּעָמִים אֶלָּא עַל מְנִיעַת אֲכִילָה

oneself, wearing shoes, and marital relations.[3] One is liable for *kares*,[4] however, only for performing work, eating, or drinking.

[These concepts are derived as follows:] It is written,[5] "[As to] any person[6] who will perform any work [on that very day], I will cause [that person] to perish [from among his people]." It is also written,[7] "For any person who will not afflict himself [on that very day] will be cut off [from his people]." And the term "affliction," when unqualified,[8] refers to withholding food and drink, as is evident from the verse,[9] "And He afflicted you and subjected you to hunger, and fed you [the manna]." Eating includes drinking.

Washing, anointing oneself, and marital relations are also sometimes called "affliction," as our Sages derived through the interpretation of Scriptural verses.[10] Nevertheless, when the term "affliction" is used without qualification, in most cases it signifies abstention from food

3. *Yoma* 73b. These activities are discussed presently: work — in subsection 4ff. below; eating and drinking — sec. 612; washing — sec. 613; anointing — sec. 614; marital relations — sec. 615.

4. Lit., "excision"; i.e., premature death at the hand of Heaven *(Moed Katan* 28a; *Rashi* on *Vayikra* 23:30*)* and childlessness *(Rashi, s.v. aririm,* on *Vayikra* 20:20*)*. *Rambam* understands *kares* as signifying that the soul is cut off in the spiritual realms *(Hilchos Teshuvah,* ch. 8*)*.

5. *Vayikra* 23:30.

6. Lit., "soul." (Throughout this Biblical passage, the Aramaic *Targum* of Onkelos translates the Hebrew phrase *kol hanefesh* as *kol anasha* or *kol enash.)*

7. *Vayikra* 23:29.

8. In the original, *stam inui*.

9. *Devarim* 8:3.

10. *Yoma* 76b quotes *Daniel* 10:3: "I ate no desirable bread, nor did meat or wine enter my mouth, nor did I anoint myself for three whole weeks." And speaking of this period, a later passage (v. 12) adds, "From the time you set your heart to understand and afflict yourself...." Evidently, refraining from anointing oneself is considered affliction.

Yoma 77a derives the fact that refraining from washing and wearing shoes is considered an "affliction" from King Shlomo's words to Evyasar the Priest *(I Melachim* 2:26*)*: "...because you were afflicted in all that my father was afflicted." When describing his father David's flight from Avshalom, *II Shmuel* 17:29 states that "the people are hungry, and weary, and thirsty, in the desert" — and "weary" is understood there to mean that they were unable to wash. And when David departed from Jerusalem during that rebellion, he "ascended with his head covered, going barefoot" *(op. cit.* 15:30*)*. Thus, among the afflictions Evyasar suffered were the inability to wash and the necessity of going barefoot.

Finally, abstention from marital relations is also considered "affliction." This the Sages learn from *Bereishis* 31:50: "If you afflict my daughters..." *(Yoma, loc. cit.)*.

ד משנה עג, ב. טור ושו"ע ס"א. ה ברייתא עד, א. טור ושו"ע שם. ו ויקרא כג, ל. לבוש ס"א. ז אוצ"ל: וגו'. ח שם כג, כט. ט אוצ"ל: וגו'. י ברייתא עד, ב. לבוש שם (מעונה ממש). יא דברים ח, ג. תנא דבי רבי ישמעאל שם עד, ב ורש"י ד"ה ונאמר. לבוש שם. יב גמרא עו, א. יג ראה גמרא עו, ב. עז, א־ב. לבוש שם. יד ר"ן (א, א) ד"ה יום הכיפורים, בדעת הרמב"ם פ"א ה"ה. לבוש שם. ב"ח ד"ה ואע"ג. מ"א ריש הסי'. וראה גם לקמן סי' תריג ס"א (רחיצה). סי'

and drink alone. At the same time, since [these other activities] are also occasionally called "affliction," they are also forbidden on Yom Kippur according to Scriptural Law.[11] [This is derived from the description of Yom Kippur as][12] "a *Shabbos* of absolute rest," for the Sages[13] received the tradition that this signifies the cessation of any activity [whose deprivation] is sometimes termed "affliction."

3 The Torah entrusted [the interpretation of] the prohibition of these matters to the Sages, who allowed certain leniencies as appeared appropriate to them, as will be explained below,[14] with G-d's help.

4 What does [the prohibition against] work imply? Any [activity] for which one is liable[15] on *Shabbos,* one is liable for on Yom Kippur. Any activity for which one is not liable if it is performed on *Shabbos,* but which is nevertheless forbidden,[16] is in the same category on Yom Kippur. [One difference is that a person who] intentionally performs [a forbidden labor on] *Shabbos* is liable for execution by stoning, while with regard to Yom Kippur he is liable for *kares.*[17]

[In addition], all the prohibitions against transferring [articles from one domain to another] that apply on *Shabbos*[18] apply as well on

וּשְׁתִיָּה בִּלְבַד. וּמִכָּל מָקוֹם כֵּיוָן שֶׁגַּם הֵם נִקְרָאִים עִנּוּי לִפְעָמִים, לְפִיכָךְ גַּם הֵם אֲסוּרִים בְּיוֹם הַכִּפּוּרִים מִן הַתּוֹרָה,[יד, 11] שֶׁנֶּאֱמַר[טו, 12] "שַׁבַּת שַׁבָּתוֹן", וְקִבְּלוּ חֲכָמִים[טז, 13] בְּפֵרוּשׁ הַפָּסוּק שְׁבוּת מִכָּל דָּבָר שֶׁנִּקְרָא עִנּוּי לִפְעָמִים:

ג וְאִסּוּר דְּבָרִים אֵלּוּ[יז] מָסַר הַכָּתוּב לַחֲכָמִים, וְהֵם הֵקֵלּוּ בָּהֶם כַּמָּה קֻלּוֹת כְּמוֹ שֶׁהָיָה נִרְאֶה בְּעֵינֵיהֶם לְהָקֵל,[יח] וּכְמוֹ שֶׁיִּתְבָּאֵר לְפָנֵינוּ[יט, 14] בְּעֶזְרַת ה':

ד מְלָאכָה כֵּיצַד?[כ] כָּל מְלָאכָה שֶׁחַיָּבִים[15] עָלֶיהָ בְּשַׁבָּת – חַיָּבִים עָלֶיהָ בְּיוֹם הַכִּפּוּרִים, וְכָל שֶׁבְּשַׁבָּת פָּטוּר אֲבָל אָסוּר[16] – הוּא גַּם כֵּן בְּיוֹם הַכִּפּוּרִים, אֶלָּא שֶׁשַּׁבָּת זְדוֹנוֹ סְקִילָה וְיוֹם הַכִּפּוּרִים זְדוֹנוֹ כָּרֵת.[כא, 17] וְכָל אִסּוּרֵי הוֹצָאוֹת שַׁבָּת[18] נוֹהֲגִין גַּם כֵּן

11. I.e., the prohibition is not an ordinance of the Sages for which they found a support *(asmachta)* in the Torah, as is the view of certain *Rishonim,* but is of Scriptural origin.

12. In the original, *Shabbas Shabboson (Vayikra* 16:31, 23:32*).*

13. *Yoma* 74a.

14. E.g., sec. 613:1 (concerning washing) and sec. 614:5-7 (concerning the wearing of shoes).

15. In this context, the term "liable" *(chayav)* means liable for *kares* (see footnote 4) if the activity was performed intentionally *(meizid),* liable for execution if the activity was performed in the view of witnesses who gave a warning *(be'eidim vehasraah),* or liable to bring a sacrifice if the activity was performed without willful intent *(shogeg).* (See *Rambam, Hilchos Shabbos* 1:2.)

16. In the original, *patur aval assur* (lit., "not liable, but forbidden"); e.g., an activity that is by nature destructive, an activity performed without intent, or a forbidden activity that is not performed in full.

17. *Megillah* 7b.

18. In the original, "the prohibitions against transferring [articles from one domain to another] that apply on *Shabbos*" appears as *issurei hotzaos Shabbos.*

תריד ס"ט (נעילת הסנדל). **טו** ויקרא טז, יא. **טז** גמרא עד, א. רמב"ם שם. ר"ן שם. לבוש שם. **יז** של רחיצה, סיכה, נעילת הסנדל ותשמיש המטה. **יח** ר"ן שם. לבוש סוף ס"א. **יט** סי' תריג ס"א (רחיצה). סי' תריד ס"א (סיכה). שם ס"ו־ז (נעילת הסנדל). **כ** לבוש ס"ב. **כא** משנה מגילה ז, ב. טור ושו"ע ס"ב.

בְּיוֹם הַכִּפּוּרִים.[כב,19] וְכָל דָּבָר שֶׁאָסוּר לְטַלְטְלוֹ[20] בְּשַׁבָּת – אָסוּר לְטַלְטְלוֹ בְּיוֹם הַכִּפּוּרִים:[כג]

ה אֶלָּא שֶׁבָּזֶה הֵקֵלּוּ בוֹ,[21] שֶׁהִתִּירוּ לִקְנֹב יָרָק,[כד] דְּהַיְנוּ לְנַתֵּק הֶעָלִים מִן הַקְּלָחִים כְּדֵי לְהַשְׁווֹתָם שֶׁיִּהְיוּ מוּכָנִים לַחְתְּכָם,[כה] וְכֵן לְהָדִיחַ אוֹתוֹ[כו] שֶׁיִּהְיֶה מוּכָן לְבַשְּׁלוֹ בָּעֶרֶב מִיָּד,[22] וְכֵן לִפְצֹעַ אֱגוֹזִים[כז,23] כְּדֵי שֶׁיִּהְיוּ מוּכָנִים לַאֲכִילַת עֶרֶב,[כח] וְלֹא יִצְטָרֵךְ לִטְרֹחַ בָּהֶן בָּעֶרֶב. וְכָל דְּבָרִים אֵלּוּ אַף עַל פִּי שֶׁאֲסוּרִים בְּשַׁבָּת, שֶׁהֲרֵי הוּא טוֹרֵחַ וּמֵכִין מִשַּׁבָּת לְחֹל[כט] כֵּיוָן שֶׁאֵין צְרִיכִים הַיּוֹם עַד לָעֶרֶב, מִכָּל מָקוֹם בְּיוֹם הַכִּפּוּרִים הִתִּירוּ מִשּׁוּם פִּקּוּחַ נֶפֶשׁ,[ל,24] שֶׁלֹּא יִצְטָרֵךְ לִטְרֹחַ בִּדְבָרִים אֵלּוּ בָּעֶרֶב קֹדֶם אֲכִילָתוֹ וְיִהְיֶה לוֹ עָגְמַת

Yom Kippur.[19] And any article that may not be moved [within one's own domain][20] on *Shabbos* may not be moved on Yom Kippur.

5 [The Sages,] however, granted [several] leniencies [on Yom Kippur],[21] allowing one to prepare a vegetable, i.e., to remove the leaves from the stalk to make them even, so that they will be ready to cut. Similarly, they may be rinsed so that they will be ready to cook immediately in the evening.[22] Similarly, nuts may be cracked open[23] so that they will ready to eat in the evening and there will be no need to take the trouble [to prepare them] in the evening.

All of these activities are forbidden on *Shabbos* because one would be taking the trouble of preparing for a weekday on *Shabbos,* [and] these foods are not needed that day until the evening. Nevertheless, [the Sages] permitted these activities on Yom Kippur because they are essential to life[24] — so that one would not have to take the trouble of doing these tasks on the night [following Yom Kippur] before he eats, for it would cause him

19. I.e., unlike the contrary possibility that is mooted in *Kerisos* 14a.

20. I.e., the prohibitions against *muktzeh*.

21. *Shabbos* 114b. These leniencies are not practiced today; see subsection 8 below.

22. Removing the leaves and rinsing them are both interpretations of the Talmudic term *lekanev yerek*. The Alter Rebbe considers the difference of opinion as merely semantic and rules that both of these preparatory activities are permitted.

23. Elsewhere, however, the Alter Rebbe cautions that nuts should not be cracked on *Shabbos* [and hence also not on Yom Kippur], lest while doing so one inadvertently separates a broken shell from the peeled nuts — and this would constitute the Scripturally forbidden labor called *borer* (*Hilchesa Rabsa LeShabbata; Siddur Tehillat HaShem* Annotated Edition, p. 599ff.).

24. In the original, *pikuach nefesh,* which normally signifies "saving from mortal danger" in situations that supersede even weighty Scriptural prohibitions. The classic Talmudic case is the permission — and the obligation — to desecrate *Shabbos* by digging through a pile of rubble to save a life in jeopardy. (Indeed, the Hebrew term literally means "clearing away"; see *HaMetargem* on *Shabbos* 150a.) Our text, permitting the early preparation of vegetables, does not appear to be speaking of any comparable urgency. Accordingly, it has been suggested that there is a printing error and the text should read *agmas nefesh* — lit., "the soul's distress," as is the wording of *Shabbos* 115a cited immediately below.

כב טור. לבוש שם. וראה כריתות יד, א. רמב"ם הל' עירובין פ"ח ה"ד. כג רמב"ם פ"א ה"ב. טור ושו"ע שם. כד גמרא שבת קיד, ב. טור ושו"ע ס"ב. כה רש"י שם ד"ה וליתקע. הובא ב"י ד"ה ומ"ש אלא. כו מ"מ הל' שביתת העשור פ"א ה"ג, בשם הרמב"ן שם ד"ה אי, ורשב"א שם ד"ה יוה"כ. ב"י שם. כז גמרא שם קטו, רע"א. טור ושו"ע שם. כח טור. לבוש ס"ב. כט רש"י שם קיד, ב ד"ה אסור. לבוש שם. ל אוצ"ל: עגמת נפש. וראה ירושלמי פסחים

נֶפֶשׁ[לא,25] בְּעִנּוּת נַפְשׁוֹ בַּעֲשִׂיַּת דְּבָרִים אֵלּוּ כְּשֶׁהוּא מְעֻנֶּה:

anguish[25] to do them while [still] fasting.

ו וְלֹא הִתִּירוּ דְּבָרִים אֵלּוּ אֶלָּא כְּשֶׁחָל יוֹם הַכִּפּוּרִים בְּחֹל,[26] אֲבָל כְּשֶׁחָל בְּשַׁבָּת – לֹא הִתִּירוּ דְּבָרִים אֵלּוּ,[לב] גְּזֵרָה שֶׁמָּא יַעֲשֶׂה כֵּן בִּשְׁאָר שַׁבְּתוֹת הַשָּׁנָה[לג] שֶׁיָּכִין בַּיּוֹם מַה שֶּׁצָּרִיךְ לַאֲכִילַת עֶרֶב, שֶׁלֹּא יַבְחִין שֶׁהִתִּירוּ לוֹ בְּיוֹם הַכִּפּוּרִים מִשּׁוּם עָגְמַת נֶפֶשׁ:

6 The Sages permitted these activities only when Yom Kippur falls on a weekday;[26] they did not permit them when [it] falls on *Shabbos.* They enacted this ordinance lest one do these activities on the other *Shabbasos* of the year, preparing [food] during the day [of *Shabbos*] to be eaten at night, not realizing that permission was granted on Yom Kippur [only] in order to spare anguish.

ז אֲפִלּוּ בְּיוֹם הַכִּפּוּרִים שֶׁחָל בְּחֹל לֹא הִתִּירוּ אֶלָּא מִן הַמִּנְחָה וּלְמַעְלָה,[לד,27] מִשּׁוּם שֶׁאָז אֵין לָחוּשׁ שֶׁמָּא עַל יְדֵי הִתְעַסְּקוּתוֹ בְּתִקּוּן הַמַּאֲכָל יִשְׁכַּח שֶׁהוּא יוֹם הַכִּפּוּרִים וְיֹאכַל מִמֶּנּוּ, כֵּיוָן שֶׁהוּא אַחַר הַמִּנְחָה שֶׁהוּא קָרוֹב לְעֵת הֶתֵּר אֲכִילָה דְּהַיְנוּ צֵאת הַכּוֹכָבִים וְדוֹמֶה לוֹ כְּמִי שֶׁיֵּשׁ לוֹ פַּת בְּסַלּוֹ.[28] אֲבָל קֹדֶם הַמִּנְחָה – אָסוּר לוֹ לְהִתְעַסֵּק בְּתִקּוּנֵי הַמַּאֲכָל שֶׁל עֶרֶב, שֶׁמָּא יִשְׁכַּח וְיֹאכַל מִמֶּנּוּ:[לה]

7 Even when Yom Kippur falls on a weekday, this permission was granted only from the late afternoon[27] onward. At that time, there is no reason to be concerned lest one's involvement with the preparation of food will cause him to forget that it is Yom Kippur and partake of it. For since it is in the late afternoon, close to the time when it is permitted to eat, i.e., the appearance of the stars, one will have the feeling that food is at hand.[28] Before the late afternoon, by contrast, it is forbidden to become involved in the preparation of food for the night, lest one forget and partake of it.

ח עַכְשָׁו נָהֲגוּ כָּל יִשְׂרָאֵל לֶאֱסֹר קְנִיבַת יָרָק וְהַפְצָעַת אֱגוֹזִים,[לו] וְהוּא הַדִּין

8 In the present era, it has become universal Jewish custom to forbid the preparation of vegetables and the cracking of nuts. This also applies to other ways of

---

25. In the original, *agmas nefesh*.

26. *Shabbos* 114b.

27. *Op. cit.* 115a. In the original, *min haminchah u'lemaalah;* i.e., *minchah ketanah,* which is nine-and-a-half seasonal hours after sunrise. See *Mishnah Berurah* 611:7.

Shaar HaTziyun, sec. 9, notes that shelling nuts and peeling vegetables for delayed use on *Shabbos* is a Scriptural offense (see the *Shulchan Aruch* of R. Yosef Caro, sec. 321:19; this section is not extant in the present work). In keeping with this principle, Scriptural Law permits these activities in the late afternoon of Yom Kippur only because the food is to be eaten shortly thereafter.

28. *Yoma* 18b. Lit., "...that he has bread in his basket." I.e., drives are less powerful when relief is imminent.

פ"ד ה"ד (מפני הסכנה). **לא** שבת קטו, רע"א. לפירוש בעל המאור (מב, א). ר"ן שם (מב, ב) ד"ה גרסי׳. מ"מ שם. מ"א סק"ב. **לב** גמרא שם קיד, ב כרב הונא. רמב"ם שם. טור ושו"ע שם. **לג** רבנו מנוח על הרמב"ם שם. **לד** גמרא שם קטו, א. טור ושו"ע שם. **לה** בעל המאור שם (מב, א). ר"ן שם בשם יש מי שאומר. מ"מ שם. מ"א שם. **לו** ר"ח שם עה"ג. רמב"ם שם. טור ושו"ע שם.

שְׁאָר תִּקּוּנֵי מַאֲכָלִים שֶׁל עֶרֶב, אֲפִלּוּ אַחַר הַמִּנְחָה, לְפִי שֶׁבְּדוֹרוֹת אַחֲרוֹנִים הִתְחִילוּ לְקַלְקֵל לְמַהֵר וְלַעֲשׂוֹת דְּבָרִים אֵלּוּ קֹדֶם הַמִּנְחָה,[29] לְפִיכָךְ הֶחְמִירוּ עֲלֵיהֶם וְאָסְרוּ אֲפִלּוּ לְאַחַר הַמִּנְחָה:[לז]

preparing food for the evening, even in the late afternoon. [The rationale for this stringency is that] in the later generations, people wrongfully began to rush and perform these activities even before the late afternoon.[29] [The Sages] therefore ruled stringently and forbade these activities even in the late afternoon.

ט בַּמֶּה דְּבָרִים אֲמוּרִים? בְּהִתְעַסְּקוּת בְּתִקּוּנֵי הַמַּאֲכָל,[לח] אֲבָל לִגַּע בָּאֳכָלִין — מֻתָּר כָּל הַיּוֹם,[לט,30] וְאֵינוֹ דּוֹמֶה לְחָמֵץ[31] שֶׁאָסוּר לִגַּע בּוֹ בְּפֶסַח,[מ] לְפִי שֶׁבְּפֶסַח הוּא אוֹכֵל שְׁאָר דְּבָרִים — חוֹשְׁשִׁין שֶׁמָּא יִשְׁכַּח אִסּוּר חָמֵץ בְּפֶסַח וְיֹאכַל גַּם אֶת זֶה שֶׁנּוֹגֵעַ, כֵּיוָן שֶׁבְּיָמִים אֵלּוּ אֵינֶנּוּ פָּרוּשׁ וּמֻבְדָּל כְּלָל מֵאֲכִילָה, מַה שֶּׁאֵין כֵּן בְּיוֹם הַכִּפּוּרִים שֶׁהוּא פָּרוּשׁ וּמֻבְדָּל מֵאֲכִילָה לְגַמְרֵי — אֵין חוֹשְׁשִׁין שֶׁמָּא יִשְׁכַּח וְיֹאכַל,[מא] אֶלָּא אִם כֵּן הוּא מִתְעַסֵּק בְּתִקּוּן הַמַּאֲכָל לְתַקְּנוֹ וּלְהַכְשִׁירוֹ לַאֲכִילָה, אֲבָל בִּנְגִיעָה בְּעָלְמָא — אֵין חוֹשְׁשִׁין לְכָךְ.

וּלְפִיכָךְ מֻתָּר לִתֵּן לַקְּטַנִּים לֶאֱכֹל,[מב] אַף עַל פִּי שֶׁהַקְּטַנִּים יְכוֹלִים לִטֹּל בְּעַצְמָן מִבְּלִי שֶׁיִּגְּעוּ הַגְּדוֹלִים בַּמַּאֲכָל.[מג] וְאִם אֵין הַקָּטָן יָכוֹל לֶאֱכֹל אֶלָּא אִם כֵּן יִתְעַסֵּק הַגָּדוֹל בְּתִקּוּן הַמַּאֲכָל לְהַכְשִׁירוֹ וּלְתַקְּנוֹ לַאֲכִילַת הַקָּטָן — מֻתָּר לוֹ לְתַקְּנוֹ,[32] כֵּיוָן שֶׁאִי אֶפְשָׁר לַקָּטָן לְאָכְלוֹ מִבַּלְעֲדֵי תִּקּוּן זֶה:

9 To what does [this prohibition] apply? To activities that involve the preparation of food. Throughout the day, however, food may be touched[30] — unlike *chametz,*[31] which may not be touched on Pesach. Since on Pesach one is allowed to eat other foods, there is reason for concern that [if he is allowed to] touch *chametz* he will forget the prohibition against it and partake of it, too, for during those days he is not at all withdrawn and isolated from eating.

On Yom Kippur, by contrast, since one is entirely withdrawn and isolated from eating, there is no cause for concern lest he forget and eat, unless he is involved in preparing food for consumption. When, by contrast, one merely touches food, this is no cause for concern.

For this reason it is permitted to serve children food, even though they could take it alone without the adults having to touch it. If a child cannot eat unless an adult prepares the food for him, the adult is allowed to prepare it,[32] since it is impossible for the child to eat without this preparation.

---

29. And doing so sometimes involves a Scriptural offense; see footnote 27 above.

30. And served to children, as the Alter Rebbe goes on to explain.

31. Leaven, which is forbidden on Pesach.

32. I.e., despite the above concern that he might partake of it.

לז גמרא שם קטו, רע"א. מלחמות לרמב"ן שם (מב, א). ר"ן שם. ט"ז סק"ב. לח מ"א סי' תריב סוף הסימן. לט תרומת הדשן סי' קמז. רמ"א שם ס"י. מ כדלעיל סי' תמו ס"ז. וראה לעיל סי' תעא סי"ג. מא תרומת הדשן שם, בשם מהר"ח אור זרוע סי' מט (בשאר התעניות). הובא ב"י ריש סי' תרטז, ובדרכי משה סי' תריב אות ב. מ"א שם סק"ו. מב תרומת הדשן שם. רמ"א שם. מג מ"א שם. מד מהרי"ל שם הל' יום כפור (ע' שלז). רמ"א ס"ב. מה מ"א ס"ק

10 It is customary to allow young children to play with nuts on a table, as spoken of in sec. 338[:6].[33] One should not raise any objection to this, even [if they play in this manner] before the late afternoon.

י וְנָהֲגוּ שֶׁהַתִּינוֹקוֹת מְשַׂחֲקִין בָּאֱגוֹזִים[מד] עַל הַשֻּׁלְחָן,[מה] עַיֵּן סִימָן של"ח,[מו,33] וְאֵין לִמְחוֹת בְּיָדָם אֲפִלּוּ קֹדֶם מִנְחָה:[מז]

SECTION 612 The [Prohibition][1] of Eating on Yom Kippur and the [Minimum] Quantity [for which one is Liable]. (1–16)

סימן תריב שִׁעוּר[1] אֲכִילָה בְּיוֹם הַכִּפּוּרִים וְשִׁעוּר כַּמּוּתָהּ וּבוֹ ט"ז סְעִיפִים:

1 What does [the prohibition against] eating involve? If, on Yom Kippur, one eats a quantity[2] of food that puts his mind at ease when hungry,[3] he is liable for *kares*,[4] as it is written,[5] "Any person who will not afflict himself [on that very day will be cut off from his people]." And after eating this quantity of food, one will not feel afflicted."[6]

Our Sages received the tradition as a *halachah* transmitted to Moshe at Sinai that this quantity is the size of a large date,[7] which is slightly less than

א אֲכִילָה כֵּיצַד?[א] הָאוֹכֵל בְּיוֹם הַכִּפּוּרִים שִׁעוּר[2] שֶׁכְּשֶׁהוּא רָעֵב תִּתְיַשֵּׁב עָלָיו דַּעְתּוֹ בַּאֲכִילָה זוֹ[ב,3] — חַיָּב[ג] כָּרֵת,[ד,4] שֶׁנֶּאֱמַר[ה,5] "כִּי כָל הַנֶּפֶשׁ אֲשֶׁר לֹא תְעֻנֶּה וגו'", וּכְשֶׁאוֹכֵל כְּשִׁעוּר הַזֶּה — הֲרֵי אֵינוֹ מְעֻנֶּה,[ו,6] וְקִבְּלוּ חֲכָמִים הֲלָכָה לְמֹשֶׁה מִסִּינַי[ז] שֶׁשִּׁעוּר זֶה הוּא כְּכוֹתֶבֶת[ח] הַגַּסָּה,[ט,7] וְהוּא פָּחוֹת[י] מְעַט[יא]

33. In that source the Alter Rebbe forbids playing such games on the floor, even if it is paved.

SECTION 612

1. Since the repetitious wording of the heading in the Hebrew original is problematic, it would appear that its first word — *shiur* ("quantity") — is an early copyist's or printer's slip for *issur* ("prohibition"). Indeed, the latter is the wording of the corresponding heading in the parent *Shulchan Aruch* of R. Yosef Caro. Hence the tentative English translation proposed above.

2. The quantities *(shiurim)* that appear in this context are expressed above in terms of volume. However, due to the difficulty of accurately measuring the volume of various foods, the present foot notes quote contemporary authorities who have translated the various quantities into their approximate equivalents in weight. The size of a date is thus represented either as 30 cc. or as 30 grams. (See R. Avraham Chayim Naeh, *Shiurei Torah,* Foreword, and p. 189.)

3. *Yoma* 80b.

4. Lit., "excision"; i.e., premature death at the hand of Heaven *(Moed Katan* 28a; *Rashi* on *Vayikra* 23:30) and childlessness *(Rashi, s.v. aririm,* on *Vayikra* 20:20*). Rambam* understands *kares* as signifying that the soul is cut off in the spiritual realms *(Hilchos Teshuvah,* ch. 8*).*

5. *Vayikra* 23:29.

6. In the case of all forbidden substances, one is liable once one has eaten even as little as a *kezayis,* the volume of an olive. The Alter Rebbe therefore explains here that Yom Kippur is different, for the Torah does not speak of "not eating," but of "affliction." And as long as one has not eaten the quantity stated, the size of a large date, he still feels "afflicted."

7. In the original, *koseves hagassah* (*Yoma* 73b; see also sec. 618:13

ג. מו סעיף ו (משא"כ על גבי קרקע, שמא ישווה גומות, ומ"מ אין למחות בהם). מז דרכי משה ס"ק ב. רמ"א שם.

סימן תריב: א לבוש ס"א. ב גמרא פ, ב. לבוש שם. וראה לעיל סי' קפד ס"ג. ג משנה עג, ב. טור ושו"ע ס"א. ד גמרא שם. ה ויקרא כג, כט. ו רש"י עט, א ד"ה קים. לבוש שם. ז גמרא פ, א. וראה גם לקמן סי' תרלא סוף ס"ז וש"נ. ח תמרה (רש"י ריש ביצה). ט משנה עג, ב. טור ושו"ע שם. י מסקנת הגמרא עט, סוע"ב. טור ושו"ע שם. יא רמב"ם פ"ב ה"א. שו"ע שם.

מִכַּבֵּיצָה.[8] וְשִׁעוּר זֶה שָׁוֶה לְכָל אָדָם, בֵּין לְנַנָּס בֵּין לְעוֹג מֶלֶךְ הַבָּשָׁן,[9] לְפִי שֶׁכָּל אָדָם כְּשֶׁיִּרְעַב תִּתְיַשֵּׁב עָלָיו דַּעְתּוֹ בַּאֲכִילָה כַּשִּׁעוּר הַזֶּה, אֶלָּא שֶׁעוֹג מֶלֶךְ הַבָּשָׁן תִּתְיַשֵּׁב דַּעְתּוֹ מְעַט וּשְׁאָר כָּל אָדָם מִתְיַשֶּׁבֶת דַּעְתָּם הַרְבֵּה:[יב]

the size of an egg.[8] This measure applies for everyone, whether a dwarf, or Og, King of Bashan.[9] For whenever anyone is hungry, his mind will be put at ease by eating this amount, except that the mind of Og, King of Bashan, will be less at ease and the mind of any other person will be more at ease.

ב כָּל הָאֳכָלִין[10] מִצְטָרְפִין זֶה עִם זֶה לְהַשְׁלִים לְשִׁעוּר זֶה.[יג,11] אֲבָל אֳכָלִין וּמַשְׁקִין[יד] שֶׁאָכַל חֲצִי שִׁעוּר וְשָׁתָה חֲצִי שִׁעוּר[טו,12] — אֵין מִצְטָרְפִין, לְפִי שֶׁאֵין דַּעְתּוֹ מִתְיַשֶּׁבֶת בְּכָךְ.[טז] אֲבָל הָאוֹכֵל יָרָק עִם הַצִּיר שֶׁעָלָיו, וְכֵן בָּשָׂר עִם הַמֶּלַח שֶׁעָלָיו — הֲרֵי הַצִּיר וְהַמֶּלַח מִצְטָרְפִין לְהַשְׁלִים לְכַשִּׁעוּר,[יז] לְפִי שֶׁכָּל מַשְׁקֶה הַבָּא לְהַכְשִׁיר אֶת הָאֹכֶל — הֲרֵי הוּא כְּאֹכֶל:[יח]

2 All foods[10] combine together to complete this measure,[11] but not food and drink. If one ate half a measure [of food] and drank half a measure [of a liquid],[12] [the two] do not combine, because his mind will not be set at ease in this manner.

Nevertheless, if one [ate] a vegetable with its brine or meat with salt on it, the brine and the salt are counted as part of the [minimum] measure, for any liquid used to prepare food [for consumption] is considered as the food itself.

ג שְׁתֵּי אֲכִילוֹת מִצְטָרְפוֹת, כְּגוֹן שֶׁאָכַל מְעַט וְהִפְסִיק וְחָזַר וְאָכַל מְעַט עַד שֶׁהִשְׁלִים לְכַשִּׁיעוּר — מִצְטָרְפִין, וְהוּא שֶׁלֹּא שָׁהָ[ה] מִתְּחִלַּת אֲכִילָה רִאשׁוֹנָה עַד סוֹף אֲכִילָה אַחֲרוֹנָה יוֹתֵר מִכְּדֵי אֲכִילַת פְּרָס (פֵּרוּשׁ[יט] חֲצִי כִּכַּר לֶחֶם),

3 If one ate twice, the two times are both counted [toward the minimum measure]; e.g., if one ate a small amount, stopped, and then ate a small amount again, [and continued doing this] until he had eaten the minimum measure, [everything he ate] is counted [toward the total and he is liable].

[The above applies only] when the [total] time he ate, from beginning to end, did not extend over more than *kdei achilas pras,* the time it takes to eat a *pras* (i.e., half a

---

below). As to its current equivalent, R. Avraham Chayim Naeh cites views ranging from 30 grams, the most stringent view, to 38 and 48 grams *(Shiurei Torah,* ch. 3:10-11).

8. I.e., an egg without its shell. R. Avraham Chayim Naeh defines this measure as 43 grams or 53.8 grams *(op. cit.,* 3:9-10). Generally, 57.6 grams is given as the average weight of an egg, but that includes its shell.

9. A giant of the early Biblical era.

10. Both kosher and non-kosher foods *(Tur, Orach Chayim* 612).

11. I.e., one who eats 25 grams of one type of food and 25 grams of another type of food is liable for *kares.*

12. The measure of drink for which one is liable is a cheekful, as stated in subsection 12.

יב אביי בגמרא פ, ב. וראה לקו"ש חכ"ו ע' 105 ואילך. שלחן המלך ח"ב ע' רטז ואילך. יג משנה עג, ב. טור ושו"ע ס"ב. ולענין צירוף משקים ראה לקמן סי"ג. יד משנה שם. טור ושו"ע שם. טו לבוש ס"ב. טז גמרא פא, א. לבוש שם. יז גמרא פ, ב. טור ושו"ע שם. יח גמרא שם. רמב"ם שם פ"ב ה"ז. לבוש שם. ט"ז ס"ק ג. יט רש"י פ, ב ד"ה כזית. כ משנה כריתות יב, ב (בשאר איסורים). תוספתא פ"ד ה"ד (ביום כיפור). גמרא שם. רמב"ם פ"ב ה"ד. טור ושו"ע

אֲבָל אִם שָׁהָ[ה] יוֹתֵר מִכְּדֵי אֲכִילַת פְּרָס – אֵין מִצְטָרְפִין,[כ] לְפִי שֶׁאֵין דַּעְתּוֹ מִתְיַשֶּׁבֶת בַּאֲכִילָה מְפְסֶקֶת כָּזוֹ:[כא]

loaf of bread). If, however, [his eating] extended over more than the time it takes to eat half a loaf of bread, [the two or more times he ate] are not counted together, because one's mind will not be set at ease by eating interruptedly in this manner

ד שִׁעוּר אֲכִילַת פְּרָס שֶׁאָמְרוּ בְּיוֹם הַכִּפּוּרִים וּבְכָל אִסּוּרֵי תוֹרָה, בֵּין שֶׁהֵן מִן הַתּוֹרָה בֵּין שֶׁהֵן מִדִּבְרֵי סוֹפְרִים, יֵשׁ אוֹמְרִים[כב] שֶׁהוּא כְּמוֹ ד' בֵּיצִים, וְיֵשׁ אוֹמְרִים[כג] שֶׁהוּא כְּמוֹ ג' בֵּיצִים שׁוֹחֲקוֹת,[כד] כְּלוֹמַר בְּמִלּוּי וּבְרֶוַח וְלֹא בְּצִמְצוּם.[כה] וּלְעִנְיַן הֲלָכָה, כָּל שֶׁהוּא בְּשֶׁל תּוֹרָה – הַלֵּךְ אַחַר הַמַּחְמִיר,[כו] וְכָל שֶׁהוּא בְּשֶׁל דִּבְרֵיהֶם – הַלֵּךְ אַחַר הַמֵּקֵל:[כז,13]

4 This measure [of time — the time it takes to eat] half a loaf of bread — which [relates to the prohibition against eating on] Yom Kippur and to all Torah prohibitions [involving eating], whether of Scriptural or Rabbinic authority, is [a matter of dispute]. According to some authorities, [half a loaf of bread is] equivalent to four eggs, while according to others, it is equivalent to three amply-sized eggs; i.e., [the volume of the contents of the eggs is estimated] generously, not scantily. With regard to actual practice, in questions of Scriptural Law one should follow the more stringent view, and in questions of Rabbinic Law one should follow the more lenient view.[13]

ה הָאוֹכֵל בְּיוֹם הַכִּפּוּרִים אֲכִילָה גַּסָּה,[כח,14] כְּגוֹן שֶׁלְּאַחַר שֶׁאָכַל הַרְבֵּה בְּעֶרֶב יוֹם הַכִּפּוּרִים[15] אָכַל מִיָּד בְּיוֹם הַכִּפּוּרִים בִּתְחִלַּת הַלַּיְלָה כְּשֶׁהָיָה עֲדַיִן שָׂבֵעַ וּמָלֵא מֵאֲכִילַת עֶרֶב יוֹם הַכִּפּוּרִים,[כט] וְאֵינוֹ נֶהֱנֶה כְּלָל

5 [Suppose] a person overate [grossly][14] on Yom Kippur; for example, after eating substantially during the day before the onset of Yom Kippur,[15] he ate again immediately at the beginning of the night of Yom Kippur, while still satisfied and full from eating during the day of *erev* Yom Kippur. Since he does not benefit at all

13. The halachic definitions of this measure vary from 3 to 9 minutes. See notes in *Sefer HaMinhagim*, p. 45. Based on *Shiurei Torah* (ch. 3:15), the accepted Lubavitch practice is to consider *kdei achilas pras* as 4 minutes when defining the timeframe within which one must eat the statutory *kezayis* of *matzah* at the *Seder* of Pesach, but as 9 minutes with regard to eating on Yom Kippur. This measure is significant with regard to the intervals at which certain quantities of food may be served to a sick person (see sec. 618:13).

14. In the original, *achilah gassah* (see *Yoma* 80b).

15. Overeating on Yom Kippur is defined thus, for otherwise, before beginning to overeat, one would be subject to the usual liability for eating an ordinary quantity of food on Yom Kippur.

ס"ג. וראה גם לעיל סי' תמב ס"א. סי' תעה ס"ח. סדר ברכת הנהנין פ"ח ה"ב (לענין ברכת המזון). **כא** גמרא שם, ורש"י שם ד"ה בטפי. **כב** רש"י פ, ב ד"ה חצי פרס, וכר"ש במשנה עירובין פב, ב. טור. דעה הא' בשו"ע שם. **כג** רמב"ם פ"ב ה"ד כריב"ב בעירובין שם. רשב"א בתורת הבית ב"ד ש"א (יב, א). דעה הב' בשו"ע שם. וראה גם לעיל סי' תמב ס"א. סי' תעה ס"ח. סדר ברה"נ פ"ח ה"ב. ולענין שיעור ב' סעודות ראה לעיל סי' שסח ס"ג, וסי' תפו ס"א וש"נ. **כד** רשב"א שם. רמ"א ס"ד. **כה** ראה רמב"ם הל' שבת פי"ז הל"ו. רש"י עירובין ג, סע"ב. ערוך ערך סחק. באר הגולה לרמ"א שם. **כו** ראה לקמן סי' תריח סוף סי"ג. **כז** שיעורו בזמן (לקט הדעות) ראה ס' המנהגים – חב"ד ע' 45. **כח** ריש לקיש בגמרא פ, ב. טור ושו"ע ס"ו. וראה גם לעיל סי' קצז ס"ט (לענין ברכת המזון). סי' רד סט"ו (ברכה). סי' תעו ס"ה (אכילת מצה). **כט** רש"י שם ד"ה אכילה גסה. טור ושו"ע שם.

מֵאֲכִילָה גַּסָּה זוֹ,[ל] וְהִיא מַזֶּקֶת לְגוּפוֹ,[לא] לְפִיכָךְ הוּא פָּטוּר מִכָּרֵת,[16] שֶׁנֶּאֱמַר[לב] "אֲשֶׁר לֹא תְעֻנֶּה" — פְּרָט לְמַזִּיק[לג] גּוּפוֹ בַּאֲכִילָה,[לד] שֶׁהוּא מְעֻנֶּה:[לה]

from overeating in this manner and it harms his body, he is not liable for *kares*.[16]

[The rationale: the above-quoted verse concerning] "any person who will not afflict himself" implies that [the punishment of *kares*] does not apply to one who harms his body through eating, for he *is* afflicted.

ו בַּמֶּה דְּבָרִים אֲמוּרִים? כְּשֶׁאָכַל מַאֲכָלִים שֶׁאֵינָם רְאוּיִים אֶלָּא לְמִי שֶׁהוּא רָעֵב, אֲבָל אִם אָכַל מַאֲכָלִים הָרְאוּיִים אַף לְמִי שֶׁהוּא שָׂבֵעַ,[לו] כְּגוֹן מַאֲכָלִים הַמְתֻבָּלִים וְהַמְבֻשָּׂמִים[לז] שֶׁיֵּשׁ בָּהֶם הֲנָאָה לַגּוּף אַף לַשָּׂבֵעַ — חַיָּב אַף עַל פִּי שֶׁאֲכָלָן עַל הַשֹּׂבַע,[לח] דְּרַוְחָא לְבִיסוּמָא שְׁכִיחַ.[לט, 17] וְהוּא שֶׁלֹּא אָכַל הַרְבֵּה כָּל כָּךְ בְּעֶרֶב יוֹם הַכִּפּוּרִים עַד שֶׁיָּקוּץ בְּכָל מִינֵי מָזוֹן, אֲבָל אִם קָץ בִּמְזוֹנוֹ אַף עַל פִּי שֶׁאָכַל מַאֲכָל מְבֻשָּׂם — פָּטוּר,[מ, 16] וְאֵין דָּבָר זֶה תָּלוּי אֶלָּא לְפִי מַה שֶּׁמַּרְגִּישׁ בְּנַפְשׁוֹ[מא] אִם יֵשׁ לוֹ הֲנָאָה בַּאֲכִילָה גַּסָּה זוֹ:

6 When does the above apply? When one ate foods that are appropriate only for a person who is hungry. If, however, one ate foods that are also fit for a person who is sated, e.g., spiced and seasoned foods that give the body pleasure even when he is satisfied, he is liable even though he ate when sated, for "the stomach always makes room for a delicacy."[17]

[The above applies] provided one did not eat so much on the day before Yom Kippur that he would find all kinds of food nauseating. If, however, he is nauseated by food, he is not liable[16] even if he ate seasoned foods. There is no objective criterion as to whether any particular individual derives pleasure from overeating in this way.

ז הֲנָאַת אֲכִילָה וּשְׁתִיָּה אֲסוּרָה בְּיוֹם הַכִּפּוּרִים אַף עַל פִּי שֶׁאֵינוֹ אוֹכְלוֹ וְשׁוֹתֵהוּ,[18] כְּגוֹן שֶׁטּוֹעֵם לַחֵךְ וּפוֹלֵט,[מב] וַאֲפִלּוּ דְּבָרִים שֶׁאֵינָם רְאוּיִים לַאֲכִילָה, כְּגוֹן עֲצֵי בְּשָׂמִים וְעֵץ מָתוֹק — אָסוּר לִטְעֹם[19]

7 Deriving pleasure from eating and drinking on Yom Kippur is forbidden even when one does not actually eat or drink;[18] for example, he tastes food with his palate and then spits it out. This applies even with regard to substances that are not fit to be eaten. For example, it is forbidden to taste wood with a spicy or sweet taste[19]

16. I.e., doing so is *patur aval assur:* though he is not liable for the punishment of *kares*, overeating remains forbidden. (See *Pri Megadim: Mishbetzos Zahav* 612:2.)

17. *Megillah* 7b.

18. *Rosh* on *Taanis* 1:15, and see the sources to the law quoted in footnote 20 below; cf. *Berachos* 14a.

19. This applies regardless of whether the flavor is natural or man-made.

ל רש"י שם. כלבו סי' סט (לד, ב) בשם הר"ש. לבוש ס"ו. לא כלבו שם. לבוש שם. וראה גם רש"י שם ד"ה פרט. לב ויקרא כג, כט. לג ריש לקיש שם. לבוש שם. לד רש"י שם. לבוש שם. לה ר"ח שם עה"ג. לו כלבו שם. לבוש שם. לז כלבו שם. רמ"א ס"ו. לבוש שם. לח כלבו שם. לבוש שם. לט עירובין פב, ב. כלבו שם. רמ"א שם. לבוש שם. מ ב"ח ד"ה אכל. מ"א סק"ג. מא מ"א שם. מב רא"ש תענית פ"א סי' טו, בשם הר"י ברצלוני. טור ושו"ע סי' תקסז ס"א. וראה לעיל סי' — סי"ד. סי' תרח ס"י. לקמן סי' תריג ס"ז. מג ראבי"ה סי' תתסא. מרדכי תענית רמז תרכז. רמ"א ס"ו, ובסימן תקסז ס"ג. מד סימן זה

in order to moisten one's throat [even though] one spits it out afterwards, as stated in sec. 567.[20]

By contrast, it is permissible to smell all types of fragrances on Yom Kippur, because fragrance is not a substance from which the body derives any pleasure;[21] only the soul derives pleasure from it. Hence it is not forbidden on Yom Kippur. Indeed, it is desirable to smell [fragrances] on Yom Kippur in order to complete the sum of 100 blessings.[22]

8 One who eats foods that are not fit for human consumption is not liable for *kares*,[23] even if he ate a large amount. He is, however, given lashes for rebellious conduct.[24]

9 9. If one ate the leaves that sprout from reeds, he is not liable, for these are not food for humans.[25]

10 If one ate the buds of vines that budded before Rosh HaShanah, he is not liable,[25] for they are considered as mere wood [and not food]. If they budded after Rosh HaShanah, they will still be soft on Yom Kippur and will be fit for human consumption. Therefore, if one ate them on Yom Kippur, he is liable.

כְּדֵי לְלַחְלֵחַ גְּרוֹנוֹ וְלִפְלֹט[מג] כְּמוֹ שֶׁנִּתְבָּאֵר בְּסִימָן תקס"ז.[מד, 20]

אֲבָל מֻתָּר לְהָרִיחַ כָּל מִינֵי רֵיחַ בְּיוֹם הַכִּפּוּרִים,[מה] לְפִי שֶׁהָרֵיחַ הוּא דָּבָר שֶׁאֵין הַגּוּף נֶהֱנֶה מִמֶּנּוּ כְּלָל[21] אֶלָּא הַנְּשָׁמָה בִּלְבַד נֶהֱנֵית מִמֶּנּוּ,[מו] לְפִיכָךְ לֹא נֶאֱסַר בְּיוֹם הַכִּפּוּרִים, וְאַדְּרַבָּא טוֹב לְהָרִיחַ כְּדֵי לְמַלְּאוֹת מִנְיַן מֵאָה בְּרָכוֹת:[מז, 22]

ח אָכַל אֳכָלִים שֶׁאֵינָם רְאוּיִים[מח] לַאֲכִילַת אָדָם, אַף עַל פִּי שֶׁאָכַל הַרְבֵּה מֵהֶם – פָּטוּר מִן הַכָּרֵת,[23] אֲבָל מַכִּין אוֹתוֹ מַכַּת מַרְדּוּת:[מט, 24]

ט אָכַל עָלֵי קָנִים – פָּטוּר,[נ] לְפִי שֶׁאֵינָן מַאֲכַל אָדָם:[נא, 25]

י אָכַל לוּלְבֵי גְּפָנִים שֶׁלִּבְלְבוּ קֹדֶם רֹאשׁ הַשָּׁנָה – פָּטוּר[25][נב] דְּעֵץ בְּעָלְמָא הֵם,[נג] וְאִם לִבְלְבוּ אַחַר רֹאשׁ הַשָּׁנָה[נג] עֲדַיִן הֵם רַכִּים בְּיוֹם הַכִּפּוּרִים וּרְאוּיִים לַאֲכִילַת אָדָם,[נד] וּלְפִיכָךְ אִם אֲכָלָן בְּיוֹם הַכִּפּוּרִים – חַיָּב:[נה]

---

20. Sec. 567 of the Alter Rebbe's *Shulchan Aruch* is not extant. The *Shulchan Aruch* of R. Yosef Caro states: "One who is fasting may taste... provided he spits out. On Yom Kippur and *Tishah BeAv*, however, this is forbidden" (sec. 647:1).

21. *Berachos* 43b.

22. In sec. 46:1, the Alter Rebbe describes the obligation to recite no fewer than 100 blessings every day. (See Vol. 1 of the present work, sec. 46.) Since no blessings over foods are recited on Yom Kippur, it is recommended that one fill the quota by reciting blessings over fragrances.

The laws involving the incidence of these blessings and their wording are found in *Seder Birkas HaNehenim,* ch. 11 (see Vol. 3 of the present work).

23. *Yoma* 81a, and see footnote 4 above.

24. In the original, *makas mardus.* See sec. 607, footnote 17 above.

25. *Yoma* 81b.

בשועה"ר לא הגיע לידינו, וראה טור ושו"ע ורמ"א שם. **מה** מ"א סק"ד. **מו** ברכות מג, ב. וראה לקו"ש חי"ד ע' 149 הערה *8 ובשוה"ג. שלחן המלך ח"ב ע' ריח. **מז** מ"א שם. וראה גם לעיל סי' מו סוף ס"א, ושם: אך אי אפשר לברך על כל פעם אם לא בהיסח הדעת. **מח** משנה פא, א. טור ושו"ע ס"ו. **מט** רמב"ם פ"ב ה"ה. **נ** גמרא [ברייתא] פא, ב. טור ושו"ע ס"ז. **נא** ראה רבנו מנוח על הרמב"ם פ"ב ה"ו. **נב** רש"י שם ד"ה מר"ה. טור ושו"ע שם. **נג** גמרא שם. טור ושו"ע שם. **נד** טור ולבוש ס"ז. **נה** ברייתא שם. טור ושו"ע שם.

11 If one ate dried peppers or dry ginger he is not liable, because they are not fit to eat.[26] If he ate them while they were moist, when they are fit to be eaten, he is liable.

יא אָכַל פִּלְפְּלִין יְבֵשִׁים וְזַנְגְּבִיל יָבֵשׁ — פָּטוּר,[נו] לְפִי שֶׁאֵינָן רְאוּיִים לַאֲכִילָה.[נז, 26] אֲכָלָן כְּשֶׁהֵן רְטֻבִּין,[נח] שֶׁאָז הֵן רְאוּיִים לַאֲכִילָה[נט] — חַיָּב:

12 One who drinks a cheekful[27] on Yom Kippur is liable.[28] The measure of a cheekful is calculated for each person individually,[29] a larger person according to his size, and a smaller person, according to his size.

The intent is not an entire cheekful, but an amount such that if moved to one side of one's mouth, it would look like a cheekful. For a person of average size, this comes to less than a quarter *(revi'is)* of a *lug.*[30]

יב הַשּׁוֹתֶה בְּיוֹם הַכִּפּוּרִים כִּמְלֹא לֻגְמָיו[27] — חַיָּב,[ס, 28] וּמְשַׁעֲרִין בִּמְלֹא לֻגְמָיו שֶׁל הַשּׁוֹתֶה עַצְמוֹ[29] כָּל אָדָם לְפִי מַה שֶּׁהוּא,[סא] הַגָּדוֹל לְפִי גָּדְלוֹ וְהַקָּטָן לְפִי קָטְנוֹ,[סב] וְלֹא מְלֹא לֻגְמָיו מַמָּשׁ, אֶלָּא כָּל שֶׁאִלּוּ מְסַלְּקוֹ לְצַד אֶחָד מִפִּיו וְיֵרָאֶה כִּמְלֹא לֻגְמָיו,[סג] וְהוּא פָּחוֹת מֵרְבִיעִית הַלֹּג בְּאָדָם בֵּינוֹנִי:[סד, 30]

13 All liquids combine together to complete [the measure of] a cheekful.[31]

יג כָּל הַמַּשְׁקִין מִצְטָרְפִין זֶה עִם זֶה לְהַשְׁלִים כִּמְלֹא לֻגְמָיו:[סה, 31]

14 (If one drank liquids that are not fit to drink, e.g., brine, fish-brine, or undiluted vinegar that is so strong that if poured on the ground it will bubble, he is not liable for *kares*[32] even if he drank a large amount,

יד (שָׁתָה מַשְׁקִין שֶׁאֵינָם רְאוּיִים לִשְׁתִיָּה, כְּגוֹן צִיר אוֹ מוּרְיָס[סו] (פֵּרוּשׁ[סז] צִיר שֶׁל דָּגִים), אוֹ חֹמֶץ חַי[סח] (פֵּרוּשׁ[סט] שֶׁאֵינוֹ מָזוּג בְּמַיִם) שֶׁהוּא חָזָק כָּל כָּךְ שֶׁאִם יַשְׁלִיכוּ אוֹתוֹ עַל הָאָרֶץ יְבַעְבֵּעַ,[ע] אַף עַל פִּי שֶׁשָּׁתָה הַרְבֵּה מֵהֶן[עא] — פָּטוּר מִן הַכָּרֵת,[32] אֲבָל מַכִּין

---

26. *Yoma* 81b. Although they are spices, they are not food.

27. In the original, *melo lugmav.*

28. *Yoma* 73b.

29. *Keilim* 17:11; *Yoma* 80b.

30. The name of this fluid measure is sometimes pronounced *log.*

According to *Shiurei Torah,* a *revi'is* is 86 cc. Though a cheekful is not a standard measure, *Shiurei Torah* (3:14) maintains that for an average person, a cheekful can safely be considered as 42 cc., approximately half a *revi'is.*

A person who anticipates the possibility that he will need to drink in small amounts *(leshiurin)* on Yom Kippur should make appropriate preparations beforehand. He should empty his bloated cheekful of water into an empty glass and mark the level of the water. Liquids beneath the line will be within his quota (see footnotes in *Shiurei Torah, loc. cit.*).

31. *Yoma* 73b.

32. *Op. cit.* 81a.

נו גמרא שם. טור ושו"ע שם. נז טור ושו"ע ס"ח (כם). וראה גם לעיל סי' רב סכ"ב (לענין ברכה). נח גמרא שם. טור ושו"ע שם. נט טור ולבוש ס"ז. וראה גם לעיל שם סכ"א. סי' רג ס"ד. ס משנה עג, ב. טור ושו"ע ס"ט. סא כלים פי"ז מי"א. גמרא פ, רע"ב. טור ושו"ע שם. סב ב"י ד"ה ומ"ש ומשערין. שו"ע שם. סג שמואל בגמרא פ, א. טור ושו"ע שם. סד משמעות הגמרא שם. רמב"ם שם ה"א. טור ושו"ע שם. וראה לעיל סי' קצ ס"ו, וסי' רעא סכ"ד, וסי' תעב סי"ט, שהוא רוב רביעית. סה משנה עג, ב. טור ושו"ע שם. ולענין צירוף אוכלים ראה לעיל ס"ב. סו משנה פא, א. רמב"ם פ"ב ה"ה. טור ורמ"א ס"ט. וראה תוס' יום טוב על המשנה שם. סז ראה רש"י נדרים נא, ב ד"ה ובציר (ציר מקרבי דגים ומוריים משומן דגים). לעיל סי' שכא ס"ג (לכבוש בו דגים). סי' תמב ס"ו (שומן דגים). מ"מ וציונים. סח גמרא פא, סוע"ב. רמב"ם שם. טור ורמ"א שם. סט ראה גמרא שם ורש"י ד"ה מזגו. ע מ"א סק"ה.

though he is punishable[33] by lashes for rebellious conduct. If, by contrast, he drank vinegar diluted with water, even if he drank only a cheekful, he is liable [for *kares*].)[34]

15 Drinking at intervals is counted collectively [as contributing to the minimum measure]. For example, if one drank a little, paused briefly, and then drank again, and the combined measure of both drinks is a cheekful, he is liable.

When does the above apply? When the [total] time he drank, from beginning to end, was not longer than the time it takes to drink a *revi'is* of a *lug*.[35] If, however, [his drinking] extended over a longer [time], the [two times he drank] are not counted together [and he is not liable].

Some authorities maintain that [these times] do count together [and the individual is held liable], unless the [total] time he drank, from beginning to end, extended over longer than the time it takes to eat half a loaf of bread, as is the law with regard to counting sporadic eating [toward the minimum measure].[36]

With regard to actual practice, the initial and preferred option is to be stringent and rule according to the latter view, as will be explained in sec. 618;[37] see that source.

16 All of the measures mentioned in this section, whether for eating or for

אוֹתוֹ[33] מַכּוֹת מַרְדּוּת.[עב] אֲבָל אִם שָׁתָה חֹמֶץ מָזוּג בְּמַיִם,[עג] אֲפִלּוּ לֹא שָׁתָה אֶלָּא כִּמְלֹא לֻגְמָיו[עד] — חַיָּב):[34]

טו שְׁתִיּוֹת מִצְטָרְפוֹת זוֹ עִם זוֹ, כְּגוֹן שֶׁשָּׁתָה מְעַט וְהִפְסִיק מְעַט וְחָזַר וְשָׁתָה מְעַט וּבֵין שְׁתֵּיהֶן יֵשׁ כִּמְלֹא לֻגְמָיו — חַיָּב.[עה] בַּמֶּה דְּבָרִים אֲמוּרִים? כְּשֶׁלֹּא שָׁהָה מִתְּחִלַּת שְׁתִיָּה רִאשׁוֹנָה עַד סוֹף שְׁתִיָּה אַחֲרוֹנָה יוֹתֵר מִכְּדֵי שְׁתִיַּת רְבִיעִית הַלֹּג.[35] אֲבָל, אִם שָׁהָה יוֹתֵר מִכְּדֵי שְׁתִיַּת רְבִיעִית — אֵין מִצְטָרְפִין.[עו]

וְיֵשׁ אוֹמְרִים[עז] שֶׁלְּעוֹלָם הֵן מִצְטָרְפִין אֶלָּא אִם כֵּן שָׁהָה מִתְּחִלַּת שְׁתִיָּה רִאשׁוֹנָה עַד סוֹף שְׁתִיָּה אַחֲרוֹנָה יוֹתֵר מִכְּדֵי אֲכִילַת פְּרָס, כְּמוֹ בְּצֵרוּף שְׁתֵּי אֲכִילוֹת.[עח,36]

וּלְעִנְיַן הֲלָכָה, יֵשׁ לְהַחְמִיר לְכַתְּחִלָּה וְלִפְסֹק כִּסְבָרָא הָאַחֲרוֹנָה[עט] כְּמוֹ שֶׁיִּתְבָּאֵר בְּסִימָן תרי"ח,[פ,37] עַיֵּן שָׁם:

טז כָּל שִׁעוּרִין הַלָּלוּ שֶׁנִּתְבָּאֲרוּ בְּסִימָן זֶה, בֵּין שִׁעוּר אֲכִילָה בֵּין

33. Some printings of the Alter Rebbe's *Shulchan Aruch* insert in parentheses the phrase "in the era of the *Beis HaMikdash*." This phrase, however, was added only to appease the censor, for the idea that a Jewish court could administer punishment could have antagonized certain governments.

34. *Yoma* 81b.

35. In the original, *kdei shesiyas revi'is halug*.

36. See subsection 3 above.

37. Which describes the laws pertaining to feeding a patient who is dangerously ill.

וראה גם לעיל סי' רד ס"ב. **עא** רמב"ם שם. מ"א שם. **עב** רמב"ם שם. **עג** רמב"ם שם ממשמעות הגמרא שם. טור. וראה לעיל שם לענין ברכה. **עד** ב"ח ד"ה ומ"ש אכל בדעת הרמב"ם והטור. **עה** משנה עג, ב (כל המשקין מצטרפין למלא לוגמיו). **עו** הרי"ץ גיאת הל' יוה"כ (ע' ג). רמב"ם פ"ב ה"ד, והל' מאכלות אסורות פי"ד ה"ט, והל' תרומות פ"י ה"ג, עפ"י גירסתו בתוספתא פ"ד ה"ד. דעה הא' בטור ושו"ע ס"י. וראה גם לעיל סי' תעב ס"כ. **עז** ראב"ד הל' תרומות שם, עפ"י כריתות יג, א. דעה הב' בטור ושו"ע שם. וראה גם לעיל שם. **עח** דלעיל ס"ג. **עט** ראה פר"ח ס"י. לעיל שם. סדר ברה"נ פ"ח ה"ו (לענין ברכה אחרונה), ושו"נ. **פ** סעיף יד.

שִׁעוּר שְׁתִיָּה — לֹא נֶאֶמְרוּ אֶלָּא לְעִנְיַן חִיּוּב חַטָּאת[פא,38] (וְגַם לָנוּ יֵשׁ נָפְקָא מִנַּהּ לְעִנְיַן חוֹלֶה שֶׁיֵּשׁ בּוֹ סַכָּנָה[פב,39] כְּמוֹ שֶׁיִּתְבָּאֵר שָׁם[פג]), אֲבָל לְעִנְיַן אִסּוּר[פד] אֲפִלּוּ אָכַל כָּל שֶׁהוּא וְשָׁתָה כָּל שֶׁהוּא[פה] — הֲרֵי עָשָׂה אִסּוּר מִן הַתּוֹרָה,[40] וְכֵן הַדִּין בְּכָל אִסּוּרִין שֶׁבַּתּוֹרָה[פו] שֶׁנֶּאֱמַר בָּהֶם שִׁעוּרִים, שֶׁאֲפִלּוּ בְּמַשֶּׁהוּ[פז] מֵהֶן יֵשׁ אִסּוּר מִן הַתּוֹרָה:

drinking, were discussed [in the *Talmud*] only with regard to the obligation of bringing a sin-offering.[38] (Today, too, they are significant, with regard to [feeding] a sick person whose life is in danger,[39] as explained [in sec. 618:13-14].) As far as the prohibition itself is concerned, even if one ate or drank the smallest amount he has violated a Scriptural prohibition.[40]

This law applies to all the Torah's prohibitions regarding which a measure was mentioned: there is a Scriptural prohibition against partaking of even the slightest amount [of such a substance].

סימן תריג אִסּוּר רְחִיצָה בְּיוֹם הַכִּפּוּרִים וּבוֹ כ"א סְעִיפִים:

א רְחִיצָה כֵּיצַד?[א] כָּל רְחִיצָה שֶׁל תַּעֲנוּג[ב] אֲסוּרָה בְּיוֹם הַכִּפּוּרִים, מִשּׁוּם[1] "אֲשֶׁר לֹא תְעֻנֶּה וגו'",[ג] לְפִיכָךְ אָסוּר לִרְחֹץ מִקְצָת גּוּפוֹ כְּכָל גּוּפוֹ[ד,2] בֵּין בְּחַמִּין בֵּין בְּצוֹנֵן,[ה] וַאֲפִלּוּ לְהוֹשִׁיט אֶצְבָּעוֹ בְּמַיִם אָסוּר.[ו]

אֲבָל אִם הָיוּ יָדָיו[ז] אוֹ רַגְלָיו[ח] אוֹ שְׁאָר מָקוֹם בְּכָל גּוּפוֹ[ט] מְלֻכְלָךְ בְּטִיט אוֹ בְצוֹאָה, אוֹ שֶׁנָּטַף דָּם מֵחָטְמוֹ[י] — מֻתָּר לִרְחֲצוֹ, כֵּיוָן שֶׁאֵינוֹ מִתְכַּוֵּן

SECTION 613 The Prohibition against Washing Oneself on Yom Kippur. (1–21)

1 What does [the prohibition against] washing oneself involve? Any washing for pleasure is forbidden on Yom Kippur, in fulfillment [of the verse],[1] "[Any person] who will not afflict himself [on that very day]…." Accordingly, it is forbidden to wash part of one's body just as [it is forbidden to wash] the entire body,[2] whether with hot water or cold. It is even forbidden to dip one's finger in water.

However, if one's hands, feet, or another part of his body were soiled with mud or excrement, or if his nose bled, he may wash [that part], for he does not intend to derive pleasure

---

38. In the original, *chiyuv chatas.*

39. In the original, *choleh sheyesh bo sakanah.*

40. This is the view of R. Yochanan (in *Yoma* 73b), that although punishment is meted out only if one partakes of the standard measure, eating even the slightest amount violates a Scriptural prohibition. Resh Lakish *(ibid.)* maintains that this prohibition is Rabbinic in origin.

SECTION 613

1. *Vayikra* 23:29. See sec. 611:2 above.

2. *Yoma* 87b.

פא גמרא עג, ב. טור ושו"ע ס"ה. **פב** ב"י ד"ה אבל. ט"ז סק"א. **פג** סי' תריח סעי' יג־יד. **פד** רבי יוחנן בגמרא שם. טור ושו"ע שם. **פה** טור ושו"ע שם. **פו** ראה לעיל סי' תמב קו"א ס"ק יז. לקמן חו"מ הל' גזילה וגניבה ס"א. העו"ב תשלח ע' 87. **פז** תוס' שבועות כג, ב ד"ה דמוקי. וראה גם לעיל סי' שב קו"א סק"א ד"ה והנה. וראה פס"ד צמח צדק קמט, ג. יגדיל תורה (נ.י.) לח ע' כט ואילך. אהלי שם ב ע' קסא. כללי הפוסקים וההוראה כלל יח.

סימן תריג: א לבוש ס"א. **ב** טור ושו"ע ס"א. **ג** ויקרא כג, כט. גמרא עו, ב (דאקרי עינוי). לבוש שם. וראה לעיל סי' תריא ס"ב. **ד** גמרא [ברייתא] עז, ב. טור ולבוש שם. **ה** גמרא עז, א (מים קרים). יראים השלם סי' תכ. טור ושו"ע שם. **ו** פסחים נד, ב. טור ושו"ע שם. **ז** ברייתא עז, ב לגירסת הרא"ש פ"ח סי' ב. טור ושו"ע שם. **ח** תוספתא פ"ד ה"ו. סמ"ג ל"ת סט (כד, ב). שו"ע שם. **ט** הגהות מיימוניות פ"ג אות ב. שו"ע שם. **י** רוקח ריש סי' ריז. שו"ע שם. **יא** רוקח

לְתַעֲנוּג,[יא] רַק שֶׁיִּזָּהֵר שֶׁלֹּא יִרְחַץ אֶלָּא מָקוֹם הַמְטֻנָּף בִּלְבַד:[יב]

[from this washing]. He must, however, be careful to wash only the part [of his body] that is soiled.

ב וְכֵן בַּבֹּקֶר כְּשֶׁנֵּעוֹר מִשְּׁנָתוֹ — נוֹטֵל יָדָיו[יג] ג' פְּעָמִים כְּמוֹ שֶׁנִּתְבָּאֵר בְּסִימָן ד'[יד] (מִטַּעַם שֶׁנִּתְבָּאֵר בְּסִימָן תקנ"ד[טו,3]), וִיבָרֵךְ "עַל נְטִילַת יָדָיִם".[טז] וְיִזָּהֵר שֶׁלֹּא יִטֹּל אֶלָּא עַד סוֹף קִשְׁרֵי אֶצְבְּעוֹתָיו,[יז,4] וְלֹא יְכַוֵּן לַהֲנָאַת רְחִיצָה[יח] רַק לְהַעֲבִיר הָרוּחַ רָעָה מֵעַל הַיָּדַיִם.[יט] וּלְאַחַר שֶׁנִּגֵּב יָדָיו בַּמַּפָּה — מַעֲבִיר הַמַּפָּה עַל גַּבֵּי עֵינָיו, לְהַעֲבִיר מֵהֶם חֶבְלֵי שֵׁנָה:[כ,5]

2 Similarly, when rising from sleep in the morning, one should wash his hands three times [alternately] as stated in sec. 4[:4], for the reason stated in sec. 554,[3] and recite the blessing *al netilas yadayim.* He should be careful not to wash beyond his fingers.[4] He should not intend to derive pleasure from the washing, but only to remove the spirit of impurity from his hands.

After drying the hands with a towel, one should wipe his eyes with it in order to remove "the bonds of sleep."[5]

ג וְאִם יֵשׁ לִכְלוּךְ עַל גַּבֵּי עֵינָיו[כא] וְדַרְכּוֹ לְרָחְצָם בְּכָל יְמוֹת הַשָּׁנָה[כב] — רוֹחֵץ אוֹתָם כְּדַרְכּוֹ וְאֵינוֹ חוֹשֵׁשׁ. וְכֵן מִי שֶׁהוּא

3 If one's eyes are soiled and he is accustomed to washing them through out the year, he may wash them in his ordinary manner without concern. Similarly,

3. Sec. 554, which enumerates the laws of Tishah BeAv, is not extant in the Alter Rebbe's *Shulchan Aruch*. The *Shulchan Aruch* of R. Yosef Caro (sec. 554:10) states that one may wash his hands in the morning, and its commentaries explain that this washing, to remove the spirit of impurity that rests on one's hands after sleep, is equivalent to washing to remove dirt.

4. According to Rabbinic Law, the rationale for this restriction can be explained as follows. One authority holds that the entire hand must be washed, until the wrist; another holds that only the fingers must be washed. Throughout the year we follow the more stringent opinion, for there is no difficulty with washing an additional part of the body. On Yom Kippur, when doing so would violate a prohibition, we wash only the fingers.

And from a mystical perspective: The holiness of Yom Kippur restricts the power of the forces of impurity so that it does not extend beyond one's fingers. (See the gloss of *Mikdash Melech* to the *Zohar,* Vol. II, p. 173a, cited in *Likkutei Sichos,* Vol. 9, p. 385.)

On the handwashing that precedes the Priestly Blessing *(Birkas Kohanim),* see subsection 6 below and footnotes there.

At the close of Yom Kippur, before *Havdalah,* one pours water over each hand three times alternately, as at *netilas yadayim* on a regular morning, but without reciting the blessing *(Sefer HaMinhagim: The Book of Chabad-Lubavitch Customs,* p. 126*)*. Those who will recite *Havdalah* at home, and thus *Kiddush Levanah* precedes *Havdalah,* should wash their hands as above before *Kiddush Levanah.*

5. From the blessing *HaMapil* that is recited before retiring at night. From a comparison to subsection 3 below ("If one's eyes are soiled..."), the intent here appears to be feelings of drowsiness.

שם. שו"ע שם. וראה גם לקמן סי' תריד ס"א (לענין סיכה). **יב** רמב"ם פ"ג ה"ב. מ"א סק"א. **יג** ר"ת בתוס' עז, ב ד"ה משום. רא"ש פ"ח סי' ג. טור ושו"ע ס"ב. **יד** ס"ד (מהדו"ק). וראה גם מהדו"ת שם ריש ס"ב. **טו** סימן זה בשוע"ר לא הגיע לידינו. **טז** רא"ש פ"ח סי' ג, בשם בעל העיטור (הל' יוה"כ קו, ג). ר"ן (ב, א) ד"ה והוי. שו"ע שם. **יז** רא"ש שם. רבנו ירוחם נתיב ז ח"ב (נא, ב). טור ושו"ע שם. וכ"ה מנהג חב"ד (ספר המנהגים – חב"ד ע' 59). וראה אג"ק ח"ג ע' קמח. ח"כ ע' רפד. לעיל סי' ד מהדו"ב סוף ס"א, וש"נ. **יח** הגהות מיימוניות פ"ג אות ב. רמ"א ס"ב. **יט** רמ"א שם. **כ** ירושלמי פ"ח ה"א. כלבו סי' פג (לד, ג). הובא ב"י ד"ה ומ"ש ואפילו. **כא** הרי"ץ גיאת (ע' נב). הובא ברא"ש פ"ח סי' ז, ובטור. **כב** ר"ן (ב, א) ד"ה והוי. ב"ח שם ד"ה וכתב גאון.

אִסְטְנִיס וְאֵין דַּעְתּוֹ מְיֻשֶּׁבֶת עָלָיו עַד שֶׁיְּקַנֵּחַ פָּנָיו בְּמַיִם – מֻתָּר לוֹ לְקַנֵּחַ בְּמַיִם בְּיוֹם הַכִּפּוּרִים.[כג] אֲבָל הַמִּנְהָג לְהַחְמִיר שֶׁאֲפִלּוּ מִי שֶׁהוּא אִסְטְנִיס אֵין מְקַנֵּחַ פָּנָיו וְלֹא עֵינָיו בְּמַיִם,[כד] אֶלָּא אִם כֵּן יֵשׁ לִכְלוּךְ עַל פָּנָיו אוֹ עַל גַּבֵּי עֵינָיו, שֶׁאָז מֻתָּר לְכָל אָדָם לִרְחֹץ[כה] כְּדַרְכּוֹ בְּכָל הַשָּׁנָה:

one who is delicate and will not feel at ease unless he cleans his face with water may [do so] on Yom Kippur. Nevertheless, the custom is to be stringent. Thus even a delicate person should not clean his face or his eyes with water unless [they] are soiled. Indeed, in such an instance, any person may wash [his face and eyes] in the manner that he does throughout the year.

ד אִם הֵטִיל מֵי רַגְלַיִם וְשִׁפְשֵׁף בְּיָדָיו לְהַעֲבִיר הַנִּיצוֹצוֹת מֵעַל רַגְלָיו, אוֹ שֶׁעָשָׂה צְרָכָיו[כו] וְקִנַּח בְּיָדוֹ[כז] – מֻתָּר לוֹ לִרְחֹץ יָדָיו עַד סוֹף קִשְׁרֵי אֶצְבְּעוֹתָיו[כח] לְהַעֲבִיר מֵהֶן הַלִּכְלוּךְ,[כט] וּכְדֵי לְבָרֵךְ "אֲשֶׁר יָצַר" בְּיָדַיִם נְקִיּוֹת.[ל] אֲבָל אִם לֹא שִׁפְשֵׁף וְלֹא קִנַּח בְּיָדוֹ – לֹא יִטֹּל יָדָיו כְּלָל, שֶׁמֻּתָּר לְבָרֵךְ "אֲשֶׁר יָצַר" בְּלֹא נְטִילַת יָדַיִם, כֵּיוָן שֶׁלֹּא נִתְלַכְלְכוּ יָדָיו.[לא] וְהָרוֹצֶה לִטֹּל יָדָיו קֹדֶם שֶׁיְּבָרֵךְ "אֲשֶׁר יָצַר" – יְשַׁפְשֵׁף בְּיָדוֹ וִיקַנֵּחַ כְּדֵי שֶׁיִּצְטָרֵךְ לִטֹּל יָדָיו,[לב] וְכֵן נָכוֹן לַעֲשׂוֹת כְּדֵי לְבָרֵךְ "אֲשֶׁר יָצַר" בְּיָדַיִם נְקִיּוֹת וּטְהוֹרוֹת:[לג,6]

4 If after urinating one used his hands to brush off drops of urine from his feet, or to cleanse himself after defecating, he may remove the dirt from his hands by washing them [only] for the length of his fingers. This will also enable him to recite the blessing *Asher Yatzar* with clean hands.

If he did not use his hands to brush away [the drops of urine] or to cleanse himself, he should not wash his hands at all, for it is permitted to recite the blessing *Asher Yatzar* without washing one's hands, since one's hands have not been soiled.

One who desires to wash his hands before reciting the blessing *Asher Yatzar* should brush away [the drops of urine] or cleanse himself [with his hands] so that he will be required to wash his hands. It is proper to conduct oneself in this manner so that one will be able to recite the blessing *Asher Yatzar* with clean and pure hands.[6]

ה בַּמֶּה דְּבָרִים אֲמוּרִים? בְּלֵיל יוֹם הַכִּפּוּרִים[לד] אַחַר הַתְּפִלָּה, אֲבָל קֹדֶם הַתְּפִלָּה,[לה] אוֹ בַּיּוֹם שֶׁמִּתְפַּלְלִין

5 When do the above [restrictions against washing] apply? On the night of Yom Kippur after prayer. [At night,] before prayer, or during the day — since we pray throughout

6. Alternatively, one can touch part of the body that is normally covered and thus be required to wash his hands before reciting the blessing. See *Siddur Derech HaChayim*, sec. 162:1 (in *Siddur Torah Or*).

כג רא"ש שם וטור בשם גאון (הרי"ץ גיאת שם). שו"ע ס"ד. כד הלכות ומנהגי מהר"ש סי' ריד אות א. מהרי"ל הל' יום כפור (ע' שלב). דרכי משה ס"ק ב. רמ"א ס"ד. כה ב"ח שם. אליה זוטא סק"ד. כו רא"ש פ"ח סי' ג. טור ושו"ע ס"ג. כז טור ושו"ע שם. כח רא"ש שם. טור ורמ"א ולבוש ס"ג. כט ראה רא"ש ושו"ע שם. ל ב"ח ד"ה ומ"ש וכן, בדעת הרא"ש והטור. לא ב"ח שם. מ"א סק"ב. לב ב"ח שם בדעתם. לג כדלעיל סי' ז ס"ב. וראה ט"ז ס"ק ב. לד מ"א שם. לה ב"י ד"ה ומ"ש וכן. שו"ע ס"ג. לו מ"א שם. לז הגהות מיימוניות פ"ג אות ב, בשם רשב"[ם], ריב"א, ר[א]ב"ן (קסט, א), ר"[ש], רבנו

כָּל הַיּוֹם,[לו] אִם הֵטִיל מַיִם אַף עַל פִּי שֶׁלֹּא שִׁפְשֵׁף בְּיָדָיו, אוֹ שֶׁעָשָׂה צְרָכָיו אַף עַל פִּי שֶׁלֹּא קִנַּח בְּיָדוֹ – מֻתָּר לִטֹּל יָדָיו[לז] עַד סוֹף קִשְׁרֵי אֶצְבְּעוֹתָיו,[לח] שֶׁמִּצְוָה לְהִתְפַּלֵּל בְּיָדַיִם טְהוֹרוֹת בִּרְחִיצָה,[לט] שֶׁנֶּאֱמַר[מ,7] "הִכּוֹן לִקְרַאת אֱלֹהֶיךָ יִשְׂרָאֵל":

the day — one may wash his hands until the ends of his fingers after urinating even if he did not brush away [the drops of urine] with his hands, or after defecating even if he did not clean himself with his hands. [The rationale is that] it is a *mitzvah* to pray with hands that have been purified through washing, as it is written,[7] "Prepare yourself before your G-d, O Israel."

ו וְכֵן כֹּהֵן הָעוֹלֶה לַדּוּכָן – נוֹטֵל יָדָיו,[מא] אַף עַל פִּי שֶׁנָּטַל יָדָיו קֹדֶם הַתְּפִלָּה.[מב,8] וְכֵן הַלֵּוִי[מג] בְּמָקוֹם שֶׁנּוֹהֲגִין שֶׁהַלֵּוִי נוֹטֵל יָדָיו קֹדֶם שֶׁיּוֹצֵק מַיִם עַל יְדֵי הַכֹּהֵן[מד,9] – מֻתָּר לוֹ לִטֹּל בְּיוֹם הַכִּפּוּרִים, כֵּיוָן שֶׁאֵינוֹ מִתְכַּוֵּן לְתַעֲנוּג.[מה]

וּלְפִיכָךְ הַבָּא מִן הַדֶּרֶךְ וְרַגְלָיו כֵּהוֹת – מֻתָּר לִרְחָצָן,[מו] כֵּיוָן שֶׁאֵינוֹ מִתְכַּוֵּן אֶלָּא לִרְפוּאָה,[10] וְכֵן כָּל כְּיוֹצֵא בָּזֶה:

6 Similarly, a *kohen* who ascends the dais [before the Ark] should wash his hands [before the Priestly Blessing] even though he already washed his hands in the morning.[8] A Levite as well — in places where Levites wash their own hands [alternately] before pouring water over the hands of the *kohanim*[9] — may wash his hands [at this time] on Yom Kippur, since his intent is not to derive pleasure.

For this reason, one who has just arrived from a long trek and whose feet are weary may wash them, for his intent is solely for healing.[10] Similar laws apply in all analogous situations.

---

7. *Amos* 4:12, translated here in the spirit of the present context. Sec. 92:1 cites the same verse as a charge to prepare one's body for prayer.

8. The *Kitzur Shulchan Aruch* (sec. 133:4) states that before blessing the people, the *kohanim* should wash their hands as far as the wrist (cf. the present work, sec. 128:8), even on Yom Kippur. Unlike certain other authorities, the *Kitzur Shulchan Aruch* continues that, lest a question regarding the blessing arise, it is proper that the *kohanim* also wash their hands in this manner in the morning. The Rebbe is reported to have advised individuals to follow this ruling of the *Kitzur* (see *Otzar Minhagei Chabad,* p. 217). On *Motzaei* Yom Kippur, at the close of the holy day, the *kohanim* should nevertheless wash their hands — as at *netilas yadayim* on a regular morning — again. (See *Likkutei Sichos,* Vol. 9, p. 386ff.)

9. In sec. 128:10, the Alter Rebbe writes that it is proper for the Levites to follow this practice, but that it is customary in these countries to rely on the washing carried out before prayer. Nevertheless, many *levi'im* do wash their hands first, presumably because of the concern that the Alter Rebbe raises there — that they may have inadvertently touched an unclean part of the body. (See *Kaf HaChayim,* sec. 128:40 and 128:42.)

10. *Talmud Yerushalmi, Yoma* 5:1.

יהודה (משום הכון). ר"ן (ב, א) ד"ה והוי (לתפלה). שו"ע שם. לח מהרי"ל הל' יום כפור (ע' שלב). שו"ע שם. לט ראב"ן ור"ן שם. וראה גם רא"ש שם. מ עמוס ד, יב. הגהות מיימוניות שם בשמם. וראה גם לעיל סי' ז ס"ב. תהלה לדוד סי' ז ס"ק א. מא יראים השלם סי' תכ. הובא בהגהות מיימוניות שם. מהרי"ל שם. רמ"א ס"ד. וראה לקו"ש ח"ט ע' 386, דהיינו עד פרק הזרוע (מהרי"ל שם. מטה משה סי' תתנא. שיירי כנסת הגדולה הגב"י אות א). בדי השלחן סי' ב ס"ק י. חדות יהושע. אוצר מנהגי חב"ד יוה"כ ע' ריז. מב מהרי"ל שם. רמ"א שם. מג שו"ת הר"ש הלוי סי' ט. מ"א סק"ג. מד כדלעיל סי' קכח ס"י. מה רמ"א שם. מו ירושלמי פ"ח ה"א. הגהות מיימוניות פ"ג אות ד. ב"י ד"ה כתב הרמב"ם. רמ"א שם.

ז אָסוּר לִרְחֹץ פִּיו בְּיוֹם הַכִּפּוּרִים[מז] כְּמוֹ שֶׁנִּתְבָּאֵר בְּסִימָן תקס"ז,[מח] עַיֵּן שָׁם:[11]

7 It is forbidden to rinse one's mouth on Yom Kippur, as explained in sec. 567. Note [the ruling] there.[11]

ח הַהוֹלֵךְ לְבֵית הַמִּדְרָשׁ,[מט] אוֹ לְהַקְבִּיל פְּנֵי אָבִיו אוֹ פְּנֵי רַבּוֹ אוֹ מִי שֶׁגָּדוֹל מִמֶּנּוּ בְּחָכְמָה,[נ] אוֹ לְצָרְכֵי שְׁאָר מִצְוֹת[נא] – יָכוֹל לַעֲבֹר בַּמַּיִם עַד צַוָּארוֹ,[12] בֵּין בַּהֲלִיכָה בֵּין בַּחֲזָרָה,[13] וְאֵין חוֹשֵׁשׁ מִשּׁוּם אִסּוּר רְחִיצָה[נב] בְּיוֹם הַכִּפּוּרִים, כֵּיוָן שֶׁהוֹלֵךְ לִדְבַר מִצְוָה,[נג] וְעוֹד שֶׁאֵינוֹ מִתְכַּוֵּן לְתַעֲנוּג.[נד] וּבִלְבַד שֶׁיַּעֲשֶׂה שִׁנּוּי[נה] מִכָּל עוֹבֵר בַּמַּיִם בְּחֹל, דְּהַיְנוּ שֶׁלֹּא יוֹצִיא יָדָיו מִתַּחַת שְׂפַת חֲלוּקוֹ[נו] כְּדֵי לְהַגְבִּיהַּ חֲלוּקוֹ מְעַט[נז] כְּמוֹ שֶׁעוֹשִׂין כָּל עוֹבְרֵי בַּמַּיִם בְּחֹל, כְּדֵי שֶׁעַל יְדֵי הַשִּׁנּוּי יִזְכֹּר שֶׁהַיּוֹם אֵינוֹ חֹל וְלֹא יָבוֹא לִסְחֹט אֶת בְּגָדָיו.[נח]

וְאַף עַל פִּי שֶׁבֶּגֶד שְׁרִיָּתוֹ בְּמַיִם זֶהוּ כִּבּוּסוֹ אַף עַל פִּי שֶׁאֵינוֹ סוֹחֲטוֹ כְּמוֹ שֶׁנִּתְבָּאֵר בְּסִימָן ש"ב,[נט] אַף עַל פִּי כֵן הִתִּירוּ לַעֲבֹר בַּמַּיִם בְּיוֹם הַכִּפּוּרִים, מִשּׁוּם שֶׁלֹּא אָמְרִינָן שְׁרִיָּתוֹ זֶהוּ כִּבּוּסוֹ אֶלָּא אִם כֵּן הָיָה מְלֻכְלָךְ קֹדֶם הַשְּׁרִיָּה[ס] כְּמוֹ שֶׁנִּתְבָּאֵר בְּסִימָן ש"ב,[סא] עַיֵּן שָׁם:

8 One who goes out to the House of Study, or to welcome his father or teacher or someone whose scholarship surpasses his own, or to attend to the needs of another *mitzvah,* may wade through water up to his neck.[12] [This applies] both when going and when returning.[13] He need not be concerned about the prohibition against bathing on Yom Kippur, because he is going out in order to perform a *mitzvah*. Moreover, he is not [entering the water] for the sake of pleasure.

However, he must deviate from the manner in which people commonly cross the water on a weekday; [for example,] he should not raise his hands under the hem of his cloak in order to lift it a little, as is done by anyone who wades through water on a weekday. Through this deviation he will recall that this is not a weekday and hence will not wring out his clothes inadvertently.

Soaking clothes in water is considered laundering even if they are not wrung out, as stated in sec. 302[:20-21]. Wading through water on Yom Kippur was nevertheless permitted, because soaking clothes is considered equivalent to laundering only if they were soiled before being soaked, as stated in sec. 302. Note the explanation there.

---

11. Sec. 567 of the Alter Rebbe's *Shulchan Aruch* is not extant. The *Shulchan Aruch* of R. Yosef Caro (sec. 567:3) states: "It is not proper to follow the practice of rinsing one's mouth on a public fast day. By contrast, on a fast that an individual voluntarily accepts, since he spits out [the water] he may rinse his mouth."

12. *Yoma* 77b.

13. For if he is not allowed to return, the *mitzvah* will be left undone.

מז רמ"א ס"ד. מח סימן זה בשוע"ר לא הגיע לידינו, וראה שו"ע שם ס"ג. מט גמרא עז, ב (לפירקא כו' למשאל שמעתא). טור ושו"ע ס"ה. נ ברייתא שם. טור ושו"ע שם. נא טור ושו"ע שם. לבוש ס"ה. נב רש"י שם ד"ה ואינו. נג רמב"ם פ"ג ה"ו. ר"ן (א, ב) ד"ה לנטורי. נד לבוש ס"ח. וראה גם לקמן ס"י. נה טור ולבוש שם. נו גמרא שם. טור ושו"ע שם. נז שאז אין בזה איסור משוי, כדלעיל סי' שא סל"ו וש"נ. נח רא"ש פ"ח סי' ד. טור ולבוש ס"ה. ט"ז סק"ד. וראה גם לעיל סי' שא קו"א סק"א. נט סעיף כא. ס רא"ש שם. סא שם בדעה הא' (ולדעה הב' שם, הביא טעם ההיתר כאן, כיון שזה דרך לכלוך). סב

9 When does the above apply? To an irrigation channel whose water does not flow fast.[12] A river whose swift current sweeps [things] away, even if it is not much more than waist high, may not be crossed even on a weekday, because of the danger that the water carry one away.

ט בַּמֶּה דְּבָרִים אֲמוּרִים? בְּאַמַּת הַמַּיִם שֶׁאֵין מֵימָיו רוֹדְפִים מַהֵר,[12] אֲבָל נַחַל שֶׁמֵּימָיו רוֹדְפִין[סב] מַהֵר וְשׁוֹטְפִין[סג] — אַף בְּחֹל אָסוּר לַעֲבֹר בּוֹ, אֲפִלּוּ אֵין הַמַּיִם מַגִּיעִין לוֹ אֶלָּא מְעַט לְמַעְלָה מִמָּתְנָיו,[סד] מִפְּנֵי הַסַּכָּנָה[סה] שֶׁלֹּא יִשְׁטְפוּהוּ הַמַּיִם:[סו]

10 There is no license to wade through water for the sake of performing a *mitzvah* except when one passes through the water itself. By contrast, it is forbidden to pass [over water] on a small boat, even for the sake of a *mitzvah*. For the sake of a *mitzvah,* license was granted only [to supersede] the prohibition against bathing, because one does not [wade through the water] with the intent of [deriving] pleasure. Crossing [water] by boat, by contrast, involves [the performance of an activity] forbidden by the Sages as an absolute *shvus,*[14] as explained in sec. 248[:9][15] and sec. 339[:10]. Hence, the Sages upheld their decree even though it causes one to remain passive[16] and thus nullify [the observance of] a *mitzvah.*[12]

י אֵין הֶתֵּר לַעֲבֹר בַּמַּיִם לִדְבַר מִצְוָה אֶלָּא כְּשֶׁעוֹבֵר בַּמַּיִם עַצְמָן, אֲבָל לַעֲבֹר בִּסְפִינָה קְטַנָּה — אָסוּר אֲפִלּוּ לִדְבַר מִצְוָה,[סז] לְפִי שֶׁלֹּא הִתִּירוּ לִדְבַר מִצְוָה אֶלָּא אִסּוּר רְחִיצָה כֵּיוָן שֶׁאֵין מִתְכַּוֵּן לְתַעֲנוּג, אֲבָל לַעֲבֹר בִּסְפִינָה שֶׁיֵּשׁ בָּזֶה שְׁבוּת גָּמוּר[14] מִדִּבְרֵי סוֹפְרִים[סח] כְּמוֹ שֶׁנִּתְבָּאֵר בְּסִימָן רמ"ח[סט,15] וְשל"ט[ע] — הֶעֱמִידוּ חֲכָמִים אֶת דִּבְרֵיהֶם לְבַטֵּל מִצְוָה[12] בְּשֵׁב וְאַל תַּעֲשֶׂה:[עא,16]

11 A Torah teacher is forbidden to wade through water to welcome his student. It is even forbidden for him [to wade through water] to welcome a colleague, unless that colleague is a greater scholar than himself. However, he is permitted to cross through water and return if he seeks to ask a point of law of his colleague, or of one of his own students who also studied under other sages. Needless to say, [this also applies] if he is going

יא הָרַב אָסוּר לַעֲבֹר בַּמַּיִם כְּדֵי לְקַבֵּל פְּנֵי תַּלְמִידוֹ.[עב] וַאֲפִלּוּ לְהַקְבִּיל פְּנֵי חֲבֵרוֹ אָסוּר, אִם אֵין חֲבֵרוֹ גָּדוֹל מִמֶּנּוּ בְּחָכְמָה.[עג] אֲבָל אִם רוֹצֶה לִשְׁאֹל דְּבַר הֲלָכָה[עד] מֵחֲבֵרוֹ אוֹ מִתַּלְמִידוֹ שֶׁלָּמַד גַּם אֵצֶל חֲכָמִים אֲחֵרִים,[עה] וְאֵין צָרִיךְ לוֹמַר אִם הוֹלֵךְ

---

14. Defined in sec. 595, footnote 6 above.

15. There it is explained that this was forbidden because it resembles swimming.

16. In the original, *shev ve'al taaseh* — lit., "[Just] sit, and do not take action." (See sec. 586:22 above.)

אביי עז, ב. שו"ע ס"ה. **סג** רש"י ד"ה שאני. שו"ע ס"ה. **סד** מ"א סק"ו. וראה ט"ז ס"ק ה. **סה** שו"ע שם. **סו** ב"י ד"ה והא דשרינן. **סז** טור בשם הלכות גדולות הל' יוה"כ (לא, א). שו"ע ס"ו. **סח** ב"ח ד"ה וכתב בה"ג. מ"א סק"ח. **סט** סעיף ט. **ע** סעיף י. **עא** יבמות צ, סע"א. לבוש סוף ס"ו. וכדלעיל סי' קכח ס"ג וש"נ. **עב** בעיא בגמרא עז, ב ולחומרא. רי"ף (א, ב). טור ושו"ע ס"ז. **עג** תרומת הדשן סי' עז. מ"א סק"ה. **עד** גמרא שם (למשאל שמעתא). ב"י ד"ה ההולך. **עה** ט"ז סי' שא סק"ב.

לִלְמֹד עִם תַּלְמִידִים כְּגוֹן שֶׁאֵין הַתַּלְמִיד יָכוֹל לָבוֹא אֶצְלוֹ[עו] — מֻתָּר לוֹ לַעֲבֹר בַּמַּיִם בַּהֲלִיכָה וּבַחֲזָרָה:[עז]

to study with his students in circumstances under which [they] cannot come to him.

יב הַהוֹלֵךְ לִשְׁמֹר פֵּרוֹתָיו — מֻתָּר לוֹ לַעֲבֹר בַּמַּיִם,[עח,12] אַף עַל פִּי שֶׁאֵין מִצְוָה בַּהֲלִיכָתוֹ,[עט] מִכָּל מָקוֹם מִשּׁוּם הֶפְסֵד מָמוֹנוֹ הִתִּירוּ לוֹ לַעֲבֹר.[פ,17] אֲבָל בַּחֲזָרָתוֹ — אָסוּר לַעֲבֹר,[פא] שֶׁאֵין בְּכָךְ הֶפְסֵד מָמוֹן אִם לֹא יַחֲזֹר לִמְקוֹמוֹ עַד לְאַחַר יוֹם הַכִּפּוּרִים:

12 One who is going to guard his produce may wade through water.[12] Though there is no *mitzvah* involved in his going, he was given license to pass through because of the financial loss [he might suffer].[17] However, he may not wade through water to return, for no financial loss will be incurred if he does not return to his [original] place until after Yom Kippur.

יג אַף בְּמָקוֹם שֶׁהִתִּירוּ לוֹ לַעֲבֹר בְּמַיִם — לֹא יַעֲבֹר אֶלָּא אִם כֵּן אֵין לוֹ דֶּרֶךְ אַחֶרֶת שֶׁיָּכוֹל לְהַגִּיעַ לִמְחוֹז חֶפְצוֹ אִם לֹא יַעֲבֹר בַּמַּיִם,[פב] אֲבָל אִם יֵשׁ לוֹ דֶּרֶךְ אַחֶרֶת לְהַקִּיף אֶת הַמַּיִם אֲפִלּוּ הִיא אֲרֻכָּה מִזּוֹ — מוּטָב שֶׁיַּרְבֶּה בְּהִלּוּךְ לְהַקִּיף אֶת הַמַּיִם וְאַל יַעֲבֹר בַּמַּיִם, שֶׁיֵּשׁ כָּאן חֲשַׁשׁ רְחִיצָה, וְעוֹד שֶׁהוּא קָרוֹב לָבוֹא לִידֵי סְחִיטָה:[פג]

13 Even in a situation in which one was given license to wade through water, he should not do so unless he has no other way to reach his desired destination. If there is another way [to reach it] without passing through water, [he should follow it] even if it is longer. Better that he make a long detour around the water than wade through it, for there is room for concern [that the prohibition against] washing [will be violated]. Moreover, it is likely that he will inadvertently wring out [his clothes].

יד מֻתָּר לְהִצְטַנֵּן בְּטִיט אַף עַל פִּי שֶׁיֵּשׁ בּוֹ קְצָת לַחְלוּחִית,[פד,18] וְאֵין בּוֹ מִשּׁוּם אִסּוּר רְחִיצָה, אֲבָל אִם יֵשׁ בּוֹ כָּל כָּךְ לַחוּת[פה] עַד שֶׁאִם יַנִּיחַ עָלָיו יָדוֹ תַּעֲלֶה בָּהּ לַחוּת כָּל כָּךְ עַד שֶׁאִם יַדְבִּיקֶנָּה לְיָדוֹ אַחֶרֶת תִּדְבַּק בָּהּ הַלַּחוּת שֶׁקִּבְּלָה מִן הַטִּיט,[פו] וְזֶהוּ נִקְרָא טוֹפֵחַ עַל מְנַת לְהַטְפִּיחַ[פז,19] — אָסוּר

14 It is permitted to cool off with clay, even though it is still somewhat moist.[18] This does not violate the prohibition against washing. [Different laws apply,] however, if [the clay] is moist enough to enable a hand that has touched it to moisten his other hand. This [degree of moisture] is what is meant by the expression *tofeiach al-menas lehatpiach*.[19]

---

17. Since one's livelihood was involved, no restriction was imposed.

18. *Yoma* 78a.

19. Popularly pronounced *lehatfiach*.

עו ט"ז סק"ו. עז ראה גמרא שם. עח גמרא [ברייתא] עז, ב. טור ושו"ע ס"ח. עט ראה לעיל סי' סג קו"א סק"א. סי' רמח סי"ב. פ ר"ן (א, סוע"ב) ד"ה לנטורי. מ"א סק"ט. פא טור ושו"ע שם. פב רש"ל בביאורו לסמג הל' שבת מלאכת דש. ב"ח סוד"ה גרסינן. ט"ז סק"ח. מ"א סק"י. פג מ"א שם. וראה לעיל סי' שא קו"א ס"ק א. פד טור ממשמעות הגמרא עח, א. לבוש ס"ט. פה רבי יהושע בן לוי בגמרא שם. טור ושו"ע ס"ט. פו רמב"ם פ"ג ה"ד. טור. פז אביי שם. שו"ע

לְהִצְטַנֵּן בּוֹ, מִפְּנֵי שֶׁזֶּהוּ כְּרוֹחֵץ בְּמַיִם:[פח]

Cooling off in [clay so moist] is forbidden, because it falls in the category of washing in water.

טו וּמֻתָּר לְהִצְטַנֵּן בְּכָל מִינֵי פֵּרוֹת, וּבְתִינוֹק,[20] וּבְכָל מִינֵי כֵּלִים הָרֵיקִים,[פט] בֵּין שֶׁהֵם שֶׁל כֶּסֶף וְזָהָב בֵּין שֶׁהֵם שֶׁל חֶרֶס,[צ] שֶׁלֹּא אָסְרוּ אֶלָּא רְחִיצָה בְּמַיִם, אֲבָל אָסוּר לְהִצְטַנֵּן בְּכֵלִים שֶׁיֵּשׁ בָּהֶם מַיִם אֲפִלּוּ אֵינָן מְלֵאִים,[צא] שֶׁמָּא יִתְנַעְנְעוּ הַכֵּלִים וְיִשָּׁפְכוּ הַמַּיִם שֶׁבָּהֶן עַל גּוּפוֹ,[צב] וְנִמְצָא רוֹחֵץ בְּיוֹם הַכִּפּוּרִים:

15 It is permitted to cool off by contact with any kind of fruit, or with an infant,[20] or with any kind of empty vessel, whether of silver, gold, or earthenware. All that was forbidden was washing in water. It is forbidden to cool off with vessels that contain water, even if they are not full, lest they be shaken and the water they contain spill over one's body. Thus one would be washing on Yom Kippur.

טז אַף עַל פִּי שֶׁמִּן הַדִּין[21] מֻתָּר לִשְׁרוֹת מַפָּה בְּמַיִם בְּעֶרֶב יוֹם הַכִּפּוּרִים[צג] וּמוֹצִיאָהּ מִן הַמַּיִם קֹדֶם יוֹם הַכִּפּוּרִים וּמִתְנַגֶּבֶת וְהוֹלֶכֶת[צד] עַד שֶׁלֹּא יְהֵא בָּהּ טוֹפֵחַ עַל מְנָת לְהַטְפִּיחַ[צה,22] וְאָז מְקַנֵּחַ בָּהּ פָּנָיו יָדָיו וְרַגְלָיו[צו] כְּדֵי לְהִצְטַנֵּן,[צז] אַף עַל פִּי שֶׁאֵינוֹ עוֹשֶׂה לְהַעֲבִיר הַלִּכְלוּךְ אֶלָּא כְּדֵי לְהִתְעַנֵּג, אַף עַל פִּי כֵן מֻתָּר מִן הַדִּין כֵּיוָן שֶׁהִיא נְגוּבָה מִן הַמַּיִם,[צח] כְּמוֹ שֶׁנִּתְבָּאֵר בְּסִימָן תקנ"ד[צט] לְעִנְיַן תִּשְׁעָה בְּאָב,[23] מִכָּל מָקוֹם בְּיוֹם הַכִּפּוּרִים יֵשׁ לְהַחְמִיר,[ק] לְפִי שֶׁאִם הָיָה מְקַנֵּחַ בְּמַפָּה שֶׁאֵינָהּ נְגוּבָה מִן הַמַּיִם – יֵשׁ בְּכָאן אִסּוּר מִן הַתּוֹרָה מִשּׁוּם

16 According to the letter of the law,[21] it is permitted to soak a cloth in water on the day preceding Yom Kippur, remove it from the water before Yom Kippur, and leave it to dry gradually so that it will no longer be as moist as *tofeiach al-menas lehatpiach.*[22] It may then be used for cooling off by wiping one's face, hands, and feet. Even if this is not done in order to remove dirt, but for pleasure, it is permitted according to the letter of the law, since [the cloth] is dry, without water, as explained in sec. 554 with regard to *Tishah BeAv.*[23]

Nevertheless, on Yom Kippur, one should be stringent [and refrain from doing so], because if one was wiping himself with a cloth from which water has not dried out, he would be [violating] the Scriptural

20. *Ibid.* I.e., an adult may hold the infant, whose body temperature may be lower than his own.

21. In the original, *min hadin.*

22. Defined in subsection 14 above.

23. Sec. 554 of the Alter Rebbe's *Shulchan Aruch* is not extant. This advice is given with regard to *Tishah BeAv* by the *Tur* and *Rama* (*Orach Chayim* 554:14).

שם. **פח** ראה רש"י שם ד"ה ע"ג טינא. **פט** גמרא שם. טור ושו"ע שם. **צ** דעה הא' בטור. שו"ע שם. ב"ח ד"ה ומ"ש ויש. אליה זוטא סק"ח. **צא** גמרא שם. טור ושו"ע שם. **צב** רי"ף (ב, א). לבוש ס"ט. וראה רש"י שם ד"ה דמזדריב. ט"ז ס"ק ט. **צג** גמרא עח, א. **צד** רא"ש תענית פ"ד סוס"י לח. ר"ן (ב, א) ד"ה זעירא וד"ה אבל. רמב"ם פ"ג ה"ה. **צה** הגהות מיימוניות שם אות ח. ב"י ד"ה ומ"ש ואפילו כל אדם. מ"א סי' תקנד ס"ק טו. **צו** גמרא שם (לגירסא שלפנינו לענין תשעה באב (ולאחד הלשונות אף לענין יוה"כ). רא"ש ור"ן שם. רמב"ם שם (על פניו). טור ורמ"א סי' תקנד סי"ד (לענין תשעה באב). **צז** רא"ש ור"ן וטור שם. הגהות מיימוניות שם. **צח** טור ורמ"א שם. ב"י שם ד"ה בפרק. **צט** סימן זה בשוע"ר לא הגיע לידינו, וראה טור וב"י ורמ"א ומ"א שם. **ק** ר"ן שם (שאוסר רק באופן הנ"ל). הגהות מיימוניות שם, לפירוש הדרכי משה ס"ק ג (דמשמע שאוסר לגמרי). רמ"א ס"ט.

סְחִיטָה,[קא, 24] לְפִיכָךְ יֵשׁ לְהַחְמִיר אַף בִּנְגוּבָה מִן הַמַּיִם שֶׁהָיוּ עָלֶיהָ מִבְּעוֹד יוֹם, גְּזֵרָה שֶׁמָּא לֹא תִּתְנַגֵּב יָפֶה וִיקַנֵּחַ בָּהּ וְיָבוֹא לִידֵי סְחִיטָה:[קב]

prohibition against wringing [out water].[24] For this reason one should be stringent and [refrain from using] even a cloth that is dry from the water that was upon it the previous day. This [safeguard] was ordained lest the cloth not be thoroughly dry, and the person wipe himself with it and thus [inadvertently violate the prohibition against] wringing out water.

יז חוֹלֶה[קג] אַף עַל פִּי שֶׁאֵין בּוֹ סַכָּנָה[קד, 25] — מֻתָּר לִרְחֹץ כְּדַרְכּוֹ בְּיוֹם הַכִּפּוּרִים:

17 A person who is sick, even though he is not in danger,[25] may wash as usual on Yom Kippur.

יח הַכַּלָּה אַחַר נִשּׂוּאֶיהָ — מֻתֶּרֶת לִרְחֹץ פָּנֶיהָ בְּיוֹם הַכִּפּוּרִים,[קה, 26] לְפִי שֶׁהִיא צְרִיכָה לְהִתְנָאוֹת עַד שֶׁתִּתְחַבֵּב עַל בַּעְלָהּ.[קו, 27] וְכָל שְׁלֹשִׁים יוֹם לְחֻפָּתָהּ הִיא קְרוּיָה כַּלָּה:[קז]

18 After marriage, a bride may wash her face on Yom Kippur,[26] since she must look attractive and thus endear herself to her husband.[27] She is called a bride for the 30 days following her wedding.

יט מִי שֶׁרָאָה קֶרִי[28] בְּיוֹם הַכִּפּוּרִים בַּזְּמַן הַזֶּה,[קח] שֶׁבָּטְלָה תַּקָּנַת עֶזְרָא[קט] שֶׁתִּקֵּן טְבִילָה לְבַעַל קֶרִי[קי, 29] — אָסוּר לוֹ לִטְבֹּל אוֹ לִשְׁפֹּךְ עָלָיו

19 [The following directives apply if] one had a seminal emission on Yom Kippur[28] in the present age, i.e., [in the era] since Ezra's ordinance — that one who had a seminal emission must immerse [in the *mikveh*] — was nullified.[29] It is forbidden for him to immerse [in a *mikveh*] or to pour nine *kabin* [of water]

---

24. Sec. 301:56 states that since squeezing water from a garment is equivalent to laundering, it is prohibited as a derivative of the forbidden labor of bleaching wool. A further issue is involved if one desires the liquid that will be extracted through squeezing (see sec. 320:21). For this reason, many contemporary authorities rule that baby-wipes may not be used on *Shabbos*.

25. In the original, *choleh she'ein bo sakanah.*

26. *Yoma* 73a.

27. *Op. cit.* 78b.

28. See also sec. 615:2.

29. Scriptural Law allows one who had a seminal emission to study Torah and pray. Ezra instituted the requirement that one who had a seminal emission must immerse in a *mikveh* before prayer, so that "scholars will not frequent their wives like roosters." Some time later, the Talmudic Sages observed that people on the whole had never fully accepted this standard and ruled that this obligation was no longer binding. (See *Berachos* 22b; see also sec. 88:1 in Vol. 2 of the present work, and footnotes there, and sec. 606:11 in the present volume, and footnotes there.)

Nevertheless, though the obligation to immerse was nullified, the purification that immersion brings was not. Thus it was — and is — customary for many to observe this practice (though not, of course, on Yom Kippur).

קא גמרא שם (ואותבינך סחיטה), ורש"י סד"ה איפכא (דכמין כלים נגובים עדיין יש כדי לסחוט). הגהות מיימוניות שם. דרכי משה ורמ"א שם. וראה לעיל סי' שא סנ"ו. קב דרכי משה ס"ק ג. רמ"א שם. קג רמב"ם פ"ג ה"ב. רמ"א שם. קד כדלקמן סי' תריד ס"א לענין סיכה, וש"נ. קה משנה עג, ב כרבי אליעזר. רמב"ם פ"ג ה"א. טור ושו"ע ס"י. קו רש"י שם ד"ה והכלה. וראה גמרא עח, ב. רמב"ם שם. קז גמרא שם. רש"י במשנה שם. טור ושו"ע שם. קח רמב"ם פ"ג ה"ג (שלא אמרו שטובל (ברייתא פח, א) אלא קודם שבטלה התקנה). הגהות מיימוניות שם, ומרדכי רמז תשכה, וטור, בשם ר"ת. שו"ע ס"א. קט ברכות כב, א. וכלעיל סי' פח ס"א. קי ב"ק פב, א. קיא רמב"ם שם. קיב רמב"ם שם. שו"ע שם. קיג רמב"ם שם. קיד תוס' ביצה יח, ב ד"ה כל. טור

over his [head and body].[30] Even one who follows this practice throughout the year may not do so on Yom Kippur, because "a custom does not [have the power] to release the forbidden, only to restrict what is permitted."[31]

If the semen is still moist, it is sufficient to wipe it off with a cloth.[32] If it has dried or his skin is soiled, he should wash the soiled areas alone, and then pray.

תִּשְׁעָה קַבִּין,[30] אֲפִלּוּ מִי שֶׁנּוֹהֵג כָּךְ בְּכָל יְמוֹת הַשָּׁנָה — לֹא יִנְהַג כֵּן בְּיוֹם הַכִּפּוּרִים,[קי"א] שֶׁאֵין מִנְהָג לְהַתִּיר אֶת הָאָסוּר אֶלָּא לֶאֱסֹר אֶת הַמֻּתָּר,[קי"ב, 31] אֶלָּא אִם הַקֶּרִי עֲדַיִן הוּא לַח — מְקַנְּחוֹ בְּמַפָּה וְדַיּוֹ,[32] וְאִם נִתְיַבֵּשׁ כְּבָר אוֹ שֶׁנִּתְלַכְלֵךְ בְּשָׂרוֹ — רוֹחֵץ בַּמְּקוֹמוֹת הַמְלֻכְלָכִין שֶׁבּוֹ לְבַד וּמִתְפַּלֵּל:[קי"ג]

20 A woman may not immerse [in a *mikveh*] on the night of Yom Kippur,[33] even if that night is the appropriate time for her immersion; since marital relations are forbidden on this night, there is no *mitzvah* at all in her immersion. For, as stated in *Yoreh Deah,* sec. 197, there is no *mitzvah* for a woman to immerse at the appropriate time[34] unless her husband is with her, and [failing to immerse] would restrict [the *mitzvah* of] procreation.

כ אָסוּר לְאִשָּׁה לִטְבֹּל בְּלֵיל יוֹם הַכִּפּוּרִים[33] אֲפִלּוּ הִגִּיעַ זְמַן טְבִילָתָהּ בְּלַיְלָה זוֹ,[קי"ד] כֵּיוָן שֶׁאֲסוּרָה לְשַׁמֵּשׁ בְּלַיְלָה זוֹ[קטו] — אֵין בִּטְבִילָתָהּ מִצְוָה כְּלָל, לְפִי מַה שֶּׁיִּתְבָּאֵר בְּיוֹרֶה דֵעָה סִימָן קצ"ז[קטז] דִּטְבִילָה בִּזְמַנָּהּ לָאו מִצְוָה הִיא[34] אֶלָּא אִם כֵּן בַּעְלָהּ עִמָּהּ וּמִשּׁוּם בִּטּוּל פְּרִיָּה וּרְבִיָּה:[קי"ז]

21 In contrast, a woman who on Yom Kippur begins wearing white undergarments [in preparation for her immersion][35] may wash slightly between the

כא אֲבָל אִשָּׁה הַלּוֹבֶשֶׁת לְבָנִים בְּיוֹם הַכִּפּוּרִים[35] — מֻתֶּרֶת לִרְחֹץ קְצָת

---

30. The conditions under which this can serve men as an emergency substitute for immersion in a *mikveh* are outlined in sec. 606:11.

31. I.e., on the basis of a custom one may choose to restrict his own conduct; on an ordinary day, he may undertake to observe Ezra's ordinance and refrain from praying until he has immersed. However, he cannot use his adherence to a custom as a basis for overriding a prohibition, in this instance the prohibition against bathing on Yom Kippur. (See *Rambam, Hilchos Shvisas Asor* 3:3, based on *Rosh HaShanah* 15b.)

32. See sec. 76:4.

33. I.e., the night of the fast. On the night at the end of the fast, immersion is permitted.

34. In the era of the *Beis HaMikdash,* when the laws of ritual purity were observed more inclusively than is now possible, it was a *mitzvah* for a woman to immerse herself as soon as possible to attain a state of purity, even if her husband was out of town. In the present era, the only *mitzvah* involved in hastening immersion is to enable procreation.

See also the notes to *Likkutei Sichos,* Vol. 14, p. 58.

35. In preparation for her immersion in the *mikveh* a woman counts *shivah neki'im,* seven spotless days, during which she wears white undergarments.

ושו"ע סי"ב. קטו תוס' שם בסופו. קטז סימן זה בשוע"ר לא הגיע לידינו, וראה טור ושו"ע שם ס"ב וט"ז סק"ב. לעיל סי' שכו ס"ז. אבל ראה לקמן הל' נדה סי' קפו בסופו (שאסור לאשה לעמוד בימי טומאתה אפילו אין בעלה בעיר, כדלקמן סי' קצז). לקו"ש חי"ד ע' 27 הערה 58. יגדיל תורה (נ.י.) כא ע' תקלז. כג ע' תרפג. כח ע' קצ. ל ע' שו. שלחן המלך ח"ב ע' רכ־רכא. קובץ דברי תורה טו ע' לה. קיז ראה פס"ד צמח צדק יו"ד סי' קצו ס"ו.

בֵּין יַרְכוֹתֶיהָ,[קיח] בֵּין בְּחַמִּין[36] בֵּין בְּצוֹנֵן, דְּכֵיוָן שֶׁעַל יְדֵי רְחִיצָה זוֹ הִיא מְמַהֶרֶת לִטְבֹּל וּלְשַׁמֵּשׁ אִם כֵּן הִיא רְחִיצָה שֶׁל מִצְוָה,[קיט, 37] וּכְבָר נִתְבָּאֵר[קכ, 38] שֶׁכָּל רְחִיצָה שֶׁל מִצְוָה מֻתֶּרֶת בְּיוֹם הַכִּפּוּרִים וְלֹא אָסְרוּ אֶלָּא כְּשֶׁמִּתְכַּוֵּן לְתַעֲנוּג:[קכא]

thighs, whether with hot water[36] or with cold water [to prepare for making a *hefsek taharah*]. Since this washing enables her to immerse and engage in relations without delay, it is considered washing for the sake of a *mitzvah*.[37] As explained above,[38] any washing for the sake of a *mitzvah* is permitted on Yom Kippur; only [washing] with the intent of deriving pleasure is forbidden.

סימן תריד דִּינֵי סִיכָה וּנְעִילַת הַסַּנְדָּל בְּיוֹם הַכִּפּוּרִים וּבוֹ י״א סְעִיפִים:

SECTION 614 Laws Relating to Anointing Oneself and Wearing Shoes on Yom Kippur. (1–11)

א סִיכָה כֵּיצַד?[א] אָסוּר לָסוּךְ מִקְצָת גּוּפוֹ כְּכָל גּוּפוֹ.[ב, 1] וְאִם הָיָה חוֹלֶה[ג] אֲפִלּוּ אֵין בּוֹ סַכָּנָה,[ד] אוֹ שֶׁיֵּשׁ לוֹ חֲטָטִין בְּרֹאשׁוֹ — סָךְ כְּדַרְכּוֹ וְאֵינוֹ חוֹשֵׁשׁ,[ה] שֶׁלֹּא אָסְרוּ אֶלָּא סִיכָה שֶׁל תַּעֲנוּג.[ו, 2] אֲבָל בְּלֹא שׁוּם חֹלִי, אֲפִלּוּ אֵינוֹ מִתְכַּוֵּן לְתַעֲנוּג[ז] אֶלָּא לְהַעֲבִיר אֶת הַזֻּהֲמָא — אָסוּר.[ח, 3] וְאֵינוֹ

1 What does [the prohibition against] anointing oneself involve? It is forbidden to anoint part of one's body just as [it is forbidden to anoint] the entire body.[1]

If one is sick, even though he is not in danger, or if there are scabs on his scalp, he may anoint himself as usual without hesitation, for all that was forbidden was anointing for pleasure.[2]

However, one who is not sick at all is forbidden [to anoint himself], even if he does not seek to derive pleasure but only to remove dirt.[3]

---

36. Needless to say, the hot water would have to have been warmed before Yom Kippur. It is forbidden to warm it on this holy day, or to use hot water from a tap, or to use a washcloth or sponge.

37. A woman may not, however, wash on Yom Kippur in preparation for her immersion on the night following the fast, for this washing could be done either on the day preceding Yom Kippur or on the night following it.

38. Subsection 8.

SECTION 614

1. *Yoma* 77b.

2. In sec. 327:1, the Alter Rebbe writes that "in these regions" it is not customary to anoint oneself with oil except for medical reasons, and therefore on *Shabbos* one may not anoint his head when there are scabs, for the Sages banned the use of medicaments on *Shabbos* for ailments that are not severe.

It must, therefore, be assumed that here the Alter Rebbe is speaking about the practice in countries where even healthy people customarily anoint themselves during the week. It is therefore permitted to anoint oneself on *Shabbos,* because it is not obvious that this is being done for medical reasons. See also *Mishnah Berurah* 614:2.

3. The application of any form of deodorant, and certainly of perfume, is similarly forbidden on Yom Kippur.

קיח שו״ת משאת בנימין סי׳ ה. מ״א סקי״ג. קיט משאת בנימין שם. קכ סעיף ח. קכא כדלעיל ס״א.

סימן תריד: א לבוש ס״א. ב גמרא [ברייתא] עז, ב. טור ושו״ע ס״א. ג ברייתא שם. טור ושו״ע שם. ד רמב״ם פ״ג ה״ט. רא״ש פ״ח סי׳ ג. טור ושו״ע שם. וראה גם לעיל סי׳ תריג סי״ז (לענין רחיצה). לקמן ס״ה (לענין סנדל). ה ברייתא שם. טור ושו״ע שם. ו ירושלמי פ״ח ה״א, לגירסת הסמ״ג ל״ת סט (כד, סוע״ב) והגהות מיימוניות שם אות מ. הובא ב״י ד״ה ומ״ש אבל. ז רמב״ם שם. טור ולבוש ס״א. ח טור ושו״ע ס״א. ט כדלעיל סי׳ תריג ס״א. י מ״א סק״א.

דּוֹמֶה לִרְחִיצָה שֶׁכָּל שֶׁאֵינוֹ מִתְכַּוֵּן לְתַעֲנוּג מֻתָּר,[ט] לְפִי שֶׁהַסִּיכָה מִתְעַנְּגִין בָּהּ יוֹתֵר מִתַּעֲנוּג רְחִיצָה,[י] לְפִיכָךְ הֶחְמִירוּ בָּהּ יוֹתֵר (וְאָסְרוּ אַף בְּשֶׁאֵינוֹ מִתְכַּוֵּן לְתַעֲנוּג), אֶלָּא אִם כֵּן שֶׁהַסִּיכָה אֵינָהּ שֶׁל תַּעֲנוּג כְּלָל, כְּגוֹן שֶׁסָּךְ לִרְפוּאָה:[יא]

[This prohibition] does not resemble [the prohibition against] washing, which is permitted so long as it is not done for pleasure. Since anointing oneself is more pleasurable than washing, [the Sages] were more stringent (and forbade it even when it is not done for pleasure) — unless it is done without any pleasurable intent at all, such as for medical reasons.

ב נְעִילַת הַסַּנְדָּל כֵּיצַד?[יב] אָסוּר לִנְעֹל מִנְעָל שֶׁל עוֹר וְסַנְדָּל שֶׁל עוֹר[יג] אֲפִלּוּ בְּרַגְלוֹ אַחַת,[יד] וְאֵין חִלּוּק בֵּין בֵּיתוֹ לִרְשׁוּת הָרַבִּים – בְּכָל מָקוֹם אָסוּר.[טו,4]

וַאֲפִלּוּ סַנְדָּל שֶׁל עֵץ וּמְחֻפֶּה עוֹר – אָסוּר.[טז,5] וַאֲפִלּוּ מִי שֶׁהוּא קִטֵּעַ – אָסוּר לוֹ לִלְבֹּשׁ קַב שֶׁלּוֹ[יז] (פֵּרוּשׁ[יח] מִי שֶׁנִּקְטְעוּ רַגְלָיו עוֹשֶׂה לוֹ דְּפוּס כְּמִין רֶגֶל וְחוֹקֵק בּוֹ בֵּית קִבּוּל וּמַנִּיחַ רֹאשׁ שׁוֹקוֹ בְּתוֹכוֹ) אִם הוּא מְחֻפֶּה עוֹר.[יט,6] וּמִי שֶׁאֶפְשָׁר לוֹ – טוֹב לְהַחְמִיר בְּסַנְדָּל שֶׁל עֵץ אֲפִלּוּ אֵינוֹ מְחֻפֶּה עוֹר:[כ,7]

2 What does [the prohibition against] wearing shoes involve? It is forbidden to wear leather shoes or leather sandals, even on one foot, regardless of whether one is at home or in the public domain. The prohibition applies everywhere.[4]

It is even forbidden to wear a wooden shoe that is lined with leather.[5] Even an amputee may not wear his prosthetic limb if it is lined with leather.[6] (I.e., if one's leg was amputated, an artificial limb is made with a cavity [to fit] the stump.)

If possible, one should be stringent and not wear a wooden shoe, even if it is not lined with leather.[7]

---

4. *Yevamos* 102b. In *Maamarei Admur HaZakein HaKetzarim,* p. 337, the Alter Rebbe explains the mystical basis for this prohibition. Leather shoes serve as an intermediary through which man comes in contact with the earth. Thus, on ordinary days, they enable him to perform his life work of elevating materiality and transforming it into a medium for holiness. On Yom Kippur, the material world is elevated by the spiritual influence of the day itself. Leather shoes are then no longer necessary. Indeed, they interfere, and dull one's appreciation of this day's unique power.

5. Similarly, it is forbidden to wear a shoe with leather uppers even if the sole is made of other substances. Some authorities permit wearing shoes made of other substances that are coated with leather *(Kaf HaChayim,* sec. 554:75*),* while others forbid this *(Maharam Shik,* Responsum 316*).*

6. *Yoma* 78b; *Yevamos* 103a.

7. Because when wearing a wooden shoe, unlike a shoe made of one of the substances listed in the next subsection, one does not feel the earth.

לבוש ס"א. וראה גם ט"ז סי' תריג ס"ק א. **יא** ראה מ"מ וציונים. יגדיל תורה (נ.י) נה ע' שנז. **יב** לבוש ס"ב. **יג** רבא ביבמות קב, ב. רי"ף (ב, ב), לפירוש הר"ן שם ד"ה הלכך. רא"ש פ"ח סי' ז. טור ושו"ע ס"ב. וראה גם לעיל סי' שא קו"א ריש סק"ה. **יד** רמב"ם פ"ג ה"ז. ב"י ד"ה ומ"ש וכן מותר. לבוש ס"ב. **טו** גמרא יבמות קב, ב. **טז** תורת האדם להרמב"ן ענין האבלות ד"ה בנעילת הסנדל, בשם הגאונים (לענין אבל). טור ושו"ע יו"ד סי' שפב ס"א. כל בו סי' סט (לד, ד), בשם בעל ההשלמה (עח, ב), בשם ר' אשר (לענין יוה"כ). שו"ע ס"ב. וראה גם לעיל סי' שא סי"ב (במוסגר). **יז** ברייתא עח, ב. טור ושו"ע שם. **יח** תוס' שם ד"ה הקיטע (הב') בשם רש"י. וראה גם לעיל סי' שא סי"ב. **יט** ראה יבמות קג, א. שו"ע שם. **כ** אליה זוטא סק"א, לחוש לדעת רבנו ירוחם נ"ז ח"ב (נא, ג), וריא"ז (שלטי הגבורים ב, א אות ג), שאוסרים בשל עץ. ראה לעיל בקו"א שם (דלא קיי"ל הכי).

ג אֲבָל מֻתָּר לִנְעֹל סַנְדָּל אוֹ מִנְעָל שֶׁל גֶּמִי וְשֶׁל קַשׁ וְשֶׁל בֶּגֶד אוֹ שֶׁל שְׁאָר מִינִים,[כא, 8] שֶׁהֲרֵי גּוּשֵׁי הָאָרֶץ מַגִּיעַ לְרַגְלָיו וּמַרְגִּישׁ שֶׁהוּא יָחֵף,[כב] וְעוֹד שֶׁלֹּא אָסְרוּ אֶלָּא מִנְעָל וְכָל שֶׁאֵינוֹ שֶׁל עוֹר אֵינוֹ נִקְרָא מִנְעָל[כג] אֶלָּא מַלְבּוּשׁ:[כד]

3 It is, however, permissible to wear sandals or shoes made of reeds, straw, cloth, or other substances,[8] because [then] one's feet feel the bumps on the ground; [indeed,] he feels as if he is barefoot. Moreover, [the Sages] forbade only a shoe, and [a foot-covering] that is not made of leather is considered a garment, not a shoe.

ד וְכֵן מֻתָּר לִכְרֹךְ בֶּגֶד[כה] קָשֶׁה[כו] סְבִיב רַגְלָיו. וּמֻתָּר לָצֵאת בּוֹ אֲפִלּוּ לִרְשׁוּת הָרַבִּים,[כז, 9] אַף עַל פִּי שֶׁבְּכָל שַׁבְּתוֹת הַשָּׁנָה אָסוּר לָצֵאת בּוֹ לִרְשׁוּת הָרַבִּים כֵּיוָן שֶׁאֵינוֹ דֶּרֶךְ מַלְבּוּשׁ,[כח, 10] מִכָּל מָקוֹם בְּיוֹם הַכִּפּוּרִים כֵּיוָן שֶׁאָסוּר בִּנְעִילַת הַסַּנְדָּל וְאִי אֶפְשָׁר לוֹ לִנְעֹל מִנְעָל שֶׁל עוֹר[כט] — נִקְרָא זֶה דֶּרֶךְ מַלְבּוּשׁ לְאוֹתוֹ הַיּוֹם:[ל]

וְיֵשׁ אוֹסְרִין[לא] לָצֵאת בּוֹ לִרְשׁוּת הָרַבִּים, אֶלָּא אִם כֵּן הוֹלֵךְ לִדְבַר מִצְוָה, אוֹ לִשְׁאָר דָּבָר הֶכְרֵחִי לוֹ בַּיּוֹם הַהוּא, וְהוּא מְפֻנָּק וְאֵין דַּי לוֹ בִּלְבִישַׁת אַנְפִּילָאוֹת מִפְּנֵי שֶׁהֵן עֲשׂוּיִין מִבֶּגֶד רַךְ — אָז הִתִּירוּ לוֹ לָצֵאת לִרְשׁוּת הָרַבִּים בְּבֶגֶד קָשֶׁה וְכָרוּךְ סְבִיב רַגְלָיו. וְטוֹב לְהַחְמִיר כִּסְבָרָא זוֹ.

4 Similarly, one is permitted to wind a stiff cloth around one's feet and go out wearing this even to the public domain.[9] On all the *Shabbasos* of the year it is forbidden to wear [such a footcovering] in the public domain, since this is not the ordinary manner of dress.[10] On Yom Kippur, however, one may not wear sandals, nor can one wear leather shoes; hence [such a footcovering] is considered an ordinary manner of dress for that day.

However, some authorities forbid wearing such a footcovering in the public domain unless one is going somewhere for the sake of a *mitzvah* or another matter that he must attend to on that day, and he is pampered, so that socks alone will not suffice because they are made of soft fabric. [The latter authorities argue that only] in such a situation was license granted to go out to the public domain wearing a stiff cloth wound around one's feet. It is preferable to be stringent and follow the [latter] opinion.

---

8. Including synthetic substances. Such shoes are customarily worn on Yom Kippur, in contrast to the practice of those who observe the stringency of wearing only socks *(Sefer HaMinhagim: The Book of Chabad-Lubavitch Customs,* p. 96, with regard to Tishah BeAv*)*. See *Pri Etz Chayim (Shaar Yom HaKippurim* 4*)*.

9. In the original, *reshus harabim (Yoma, loc. cit.)*.

10. And hence would be considered equivalent to carrying there. See related concepts in sec. 301:3, 12.

כא גמרא עח, ב. רמב"ם פ"ג ה"ז. טור ושו"ע ס"ב. לבוש שם (קושי הארץ. וראה לקו"ש ח"ד ע' 1360־1). **כב** רמב"ם שם. **כג** הרמב"ן במלחמות (ב, א־ב). ר"ן (ב, ב) סוף דבור הא' בדעת הרי"ף. וראה גם לעיל סי' שא סי"ב ובקו"א סק"ה. **כד** ראה לבוש שם. וראה ט"ז סק"ב. **כה** גמרא עח, ב. רמב"ם פ"ג ה"ז. ט"ז שם. **כו** ט"ז שם. **כז** רא"ש פ"ח סוס"י ז. ר"ן (ב, ב) ד"ה ומיהו וד"ה ואיכא. שו"ע ס"ב. ט"ז שם. **כח** ר"ן שם (בכל הני דלעיל ס"ג). לבוש ס"ב. ט"ז שם (כשכורך בגד קשה שאינו דרך מלבוש). וראה לעיל סי' שא סוף סי"ב ובקו"א רסק"ה לענין מנעלים של עץ. **כט** ר"ן שם. ב"י ד"ה וכתב הר"ן. לבוש שם. **ל** ט"ז שם. וראה גם לבוש שם. **לא** בה"ג הל' יוה"כ (לא, ב). הובא בטור. לפירוש הט"ז שם. **לב** ט"ז שם (שבזה מודה בה"ג). מ"א סק"ב (שנוהגין

All authorities agree that it is permitted to go out to the public domain wearing cloth socks, for they are being worn in the ordinary manner. Similarly, it is permitted to go out, even to the public domain, wearing any kind of shoes made of any substance other than leather.

On Yom Kippur, it is permitted to stand on cushions and bedding, even if made of leather, for doing so is not considered as deriving the kind of comfort that comes from wearing shoes. It was forbidden only to wear [leather] when clasped around one's feet. Nevertheless, may blessings light upon one who is stringent [and does not stand] on leather cushions and bedding.

When does the above apply? At times other than when reciting the *Shemoneh Esreh* prayer. When one is reciting the *Shemoneh Esreh* prayer, it is forbidden to stand on cushions and bedding even if they are not made of leather, for [doing so] during prayer appears prideful.

However, it is permitted to stand on objects other than cushions and bedding, [e.g., rugs or straw mats,] even when reciting *Shemoneh Esreh,* provided that [their upper surface] is not more than three handbreadths above the ground, as stated in sec. 90[:1-2].

5 A woman who has given birth may wear [leather] shoes on Yom Kippur for 30 days after giving birth[11] because the cold is harmful for her. Similarly, [leather] shoes may be worn by one who is sick, even though he is not in danger, but cold is

אֲבָל לָצֵאת לִרְשׁוּת הָרַבִּים בְּאַנְפִּילָאוֹת שֶׁל בֶּגֶד – מֻתָּר בְּכָל עִנְיָן לְדִבְרֵי הַכֹּל,[לב] כֵּיוָן שֶׁלּוֹבְשָׁן דֶּרֶךְ לְבִישָׁה.[לג] וְהוּא הַדִּין שֶׁמֻּתָּר לָצֵאת בְּכָל מִין מִנְעָל שֶׁאֵינוֹ שֶׁל עוֹר[לד] אֲפִלּוּ לִרְשׁוּת הָרַבִּים.[לה]

מֻתָּר לַעֲמֹד בְּיוֹם הַכִּפּוּרִים עַל גַּבֵּי כָּרִים וּכְסָתוֹת[לו] אֲפִלּוּ הֵן שֶׁל עוֹר,[לז] שֶׁאֵין זֶה הֲנָאַת דֶּרֶךְ נְעִילָה, וְלֹא אָסְרוּ אֶלָּא כְּשֶׁהוּא מַנְעִיל בְּרַגְלָיו.[לח] מִכָּל מָקוֹם הַמַּחְמִיר בְּכָרִים וּכְסָתוֹת שֶׁל עוֹר – תָּבוֹא עָלָיו בְּרָכָה.[לט]

בַּמֶּה דְּבָרִים אֲמוּרִים? שֶׁלֹּא בִּשְׁעַת תְּפִלַּת שְׁמוֹנֶה עֶשְׂרֵה, אֲבָל בְּשָׁעָה שֶׁמִּתְפַּלֵּל תְּפִלַּת שְׁמוֹנֶה עֶשְׂרֵה – אָסוּר לַעֲמֹד עַל גַּבֵּי כָּרִים וּכְסָתוֹת אֲפִלּוּ אֵינָן שֶׁל עוֹר,[מ] מִשּׁוּם שֶׁנִּרְאֶה כְּמִתְגָּאֶה אִם יַעֲמֹד עַל כָּרִים בִּשְׁעַת תְּפִלָּה.[מא] אֲבָל מֻתָּר לַעֲמֹד עַל שְׁאָר דְּבָרִים חוּץ מִן כָּרִים וּכְסָתוֹת אֲפִלּוּ בְּשָׁעָה שֶׁמִּתְפַּלֵּל תְּפִלַּת שְׁמוֹנֶה עֶשְׂרֵה אִם אֵינוֹ גָּבוֹהַּ שְׁלֹשָׁה טְפָחִים מִן הָאָרֶץ, כְּמוֹ שֶׁנִּתְבָּאֵר בְּסִימָן צ׳:[מב]

ה חַיָּה[מג] כָּל שְׁלֹשִׁים יוֹם אַחַר לֵדָתָהּ[מד] – מֻתֶּרֶת לִנְעֹל אֲפִלּוּ בְּיוֹם הַכִּפּוּרִים,[11] מִפְּנֵי שֶׁהַצִּנָּה[מה] קָשָׁה לָהּ.[מו] וְכֵן חוֹלֶה אֲפִלּוּ אֵין בּוֹ סַכָּנָה[מז] אֶלָּא שֶׁהַצִּנָּה

11. *Yoma* 73b.

להקל כדעת הר"ן דלעיל). **לג** ט"ז שם. **לד** גמרא עח, ב. **לה** ר"ן שם. ט"ז סק"א. **לו** מרדכי רמז תשכו. ב"ח סוף הסי' בשם מהרי"ש. **לז** מהרי"ל הל' ליל יו"כ (ע' שכד). תרומת הדשן סי' קמט. רמ"א ס"ב. לבוש סוף ס"ד. **לח** לבוש שם. וראה גם תרומת הדשן שם. **לט** תרומת הדשן שם. רמ"א שם. **מ** ב"ח בשם מהרי"ש שם. מ"א סק"ג. לבוש סי' תריט סוף ס"א. **מא** לבוש שם. מ"א שם. **מב** סעיף ב. **מג** משנה עג, ב וכרבי אליעזר. רמב"ם פ"ג ה"ח. טור ושו"ע ס"ג. חיה – יולדת (רש"י שם). **מד** רמב"ם שם. ר"ן (א, א) ד"ה ולענין (שנלמד משבת קכט, א). טור ושו"ע שם. וראה לעיל סי' של ס"ה. **מה** גמרא עח, ב. רמב"ם שם. טור. **מו** רש"י במשנה שם ד"ה תנעול. לבוש ס"ג. **מז** רמב"ם שם. שו"ע שם. וכדלעיל ס"א לענין סיכה, וש"נ.

קָשֶׁה לוֹ,[מח] וְכֵן מִי שֶׁיֵּשׁ לוֹ מַכָּה בְּרַגְלָיו[מט] — מֻתָּרִים לִנְעֹל:

harmful for him, and similarly by one whose [foot] is wounded.

ו וְכֵן אִם יָרְדוּ גְשָׁמִים וְרוֹצֶה לֵילֵךְ מִבֵּית הַכְּנֶסֶת לְבֵיתוֹ אוֹ לְהֵפֶךְ וְהוּא אָדָם מְפֻנָּק[נ] וּמִצְטַעֵר[נא] בְּלִכְלוּךְ רַגְלָיו בְּמֵי גְשָׁמִים[נב] — מֻתָּר לוֹ לִנְעֹל, וּכְשֶׁיַּגִּיעַ לְבֵיתוֹ אוֹ לְבֵית הַכְּנֶסֶת יַחְלְצֵם.[נג] אֲבָל מִי שֶׁאֵינוֹ מְפֻנָּק — אָסוּר.[נד]

אֲבָל אִם יֵשׁ שָׁם רֶפֶשׁ וָטִיט — מֻתָּר לְכָל אָדָם לִנְעֹל, לְפִי שֶׁהַכֹּל חֲשׁוּבִין מְפֻנָּקִין לְעִנְיָן זֶה[נה] (וְיֵשׁ אוֹמְרִים[נו] דְּאַף בְּטִיט וָרֶפֶשׁ אֵין הֶתֵּר אֶלָּא לְמִי שֶׁיָּדוּעַ שֶׁהוּא מְפֻנָּק, אֲבָל אֵין כָּל אָדָם יָכוֹל לוֹמַר מְפֻנָּק אֲנִי. אֲבָל הַמִּנְהָג כַּסְּבָרָא הָרִאשׁוֹנָה).

אֲבָל לֹא כְּמוֹ שֶׁנּוֹהֲגִין רַבִּים מֵהֲמוֹן עַם שֶׁהוֹלְכִים בָּרְחוֹב בְּמִנְעָלִים אַף שֶׁאֵין שָׁם רֶפֶשׁ וָטִיט וּכְשֶׁבָּאִין לְבֵית הַכְּנֶסֶת הֵם הוֹלְכִים גַּם כֵּן בְּמִנְעָלִים רַק בְּהַגִּיעוֹ לִמְקוֹמוֹ חוֹלֵץ, וְאֵלּוּ בַּחֲשֵׁכָה יִתְהַלְּכוּ[12] וּפוֹשְׁעִים נִקְרְאוּ אִם אֵינָן שׁוֹמְעִים לְקוֹל מוֹרֵיהֶם:[נז]

6 Similarly, if it rains and one desires to walk from the synagogue to his home or vice versa, then if he is pampered and is distressed when his feet become soiled because of the rain, he may wear [leather] shoes. Once he reaches home or the synagogue, he should remove them. One who is not pampered, however, is not given such license.

Nevertheless, if the streets are filled with sludge and mud, any person is permitted to wear [leather] shoes, for in this regard everyone is considered as pampered. (Some authorities maintain that even when [the streets are filled with] mud and sludge, license is granted only to one who is known to be pampered — but not everyone has the right to say, "I am pampered." The custom, however, is to follow the first opinion.)

There is no [license to follow] the practice of many of the common people who walk in the street with [leather] shoes even though there is no sludge or mud. When they reach the synagogue, they continue to walk with their shoes; they do not remove them until they reach their place. Such people "walk in darkness"[12] and may be termed transgressors, if they do not listen to the voice of those who instruct them.

ז הַהוֹלֵךְ בְּמָקוֹם שֶׁמְּצוּיִים עַקְרַבִּים אוֹ שְׁאָר דְּבָרִים הַנּוֹשְׁכִין — מֻתָּר לוֹ לִנְעֹל אֲפִלּוּ מִנְעָל שֶׁל עוֹר,[נח,11] וַאֲפִלּוּ אֵינוֹ הוֹלֵךְ לִדְבַר מִצְוָה[נט] אֶלָּא לְטַיֵּל[ס] מֻתָּר לִנְעֹל כְּדֵי שֶׁלֹּא יִשְׁכֶנּוּ עַקְרָב וְכַיּוֹצֵא בּוֹ:

7 If one walks in a place where there are scorpions or other creatures that bite, he may wear even leather [shoes].[11] This license applies even when one is not going for a purpose associated with a *mitzvah,* but is merely strolling, lest he be bitten by a scorpion or the like.

---

12. Cf. *Koheles* 2:14.

מח לבוש ס"ג. **מט** רבנו ירוחם נ"ז ח"ב (נא, ג). שו"ע שם. **נ** מהרי"ל הל' ליל יו"כ (ע' שכד). רמ"א ס"ד. **נא** לבוש ס"ג. **נב** ב"ח סוף הסי'. ט"ז סוף סק"ב. **נג** מהרי"ל שם. רמ"א שם. **נד** נמוקי יוסף יבמות (לג, א) ד"ה גרסי', בשם הרשב"א. מטה משה סי' תתנח. ב"ח שם. **נה** ט"ז סק"ג. של"ה מסכת יומא עמוד

ח כְּשֶׁהוֹלֵךְ מִבֵּיתוֹ לְבֵית הַכְּנֶסֶת בְּמִנְעָלִים – לֹא יֵלֵךְ בָּהֶן בְּבֵית הַכְּנֶסֶת. וְכֵן לֹא יַנִּיחֵם בְּבֵית הַכְּנֶסֶת בְּגָלוּי,[סא] לְפִי שֶׁלִּכְלוּךְ שֶׁעַל גַּבֵּי הַמִּנְעָלִים הוּא זִלְזוּל לְבֵית הַכְּנֶסֶת בְּיוֹם קָדוֹשׁ כָּזֶה שֶׁחַיָּבִים לְכַבְּדוֹ בִּכְסוּת נְקִיָּה[סב] וּבְכָל דְּבַר טָהֳרָה,[סג] אֶלָּא יַנִּיחֵם בְּמָקוֹם מֻצְנָע בְּבֵית הַכְּנֶסֶת שֶׁלֹּא יֵרָאוּ, אוֹ יְשַׁלְּחֵם לְבֵיתוֹ[סד] אִם אֶפְשָׁר לוֹ:[סה,13]

8 If one walks from his home to the synagogue in shoes, he should not wear them in the synagogue, nor should he leave them [there] in a visible place, because the dirt on [them] compromises the dignity of the synagogue. [This applies in particular] on this holy day, which should be honored with clean clothes and all matters associated with purity. Hence, one should leave [his shoes] in a discreet place in the synagogue so they will not be seen. If possible,[13] he should send them home.

ט הַמְהַלֵּךְ בַּדֶּרֶךְ, אַף עַל פִּי שֶׁבְּתִשְׁעָה בְּאָב מֻתָּר בִּנְעִילַת הַסַּנְדָּל[סו] – בְּיוֹם הַכִּפּוּרִים אָסוּר,[סז] לְפִי שֶׁעִקַּר אִסּוּר נְעִילַת הַסַּנְדָּל בְּיוֹם הַכִּפּוּרִים הוּא מִן הַתּוֹרָה כְּמוֹ שֶׁנִּתְבָּאֵר בְּסִימָן תרי״א[סח] עַיֵּן שָׁם, לְפִיכָךְ הֶחְמִירוּ בּוֹ יוֹתֵר מִבְּתִשְׁעָה בְּאָב:

9 A person walking on a journey is forbidden to wear shoes on Yom Kippur even though this is permitted on Tishah BeAv, because the prohibition against wearing shoes on Yom Kippur is basically Scriptural in origin, as stated in sec. 611[:2]; see that source. Therefore [the Sages] ruled more stringently than with regard to Tishah BeAv.

י וְכֵן מִטַּעַם זֶה הַהוֹלֵךְ בֵּין הַנָּכְרִים וְחוֹשֵׁשׁ שֶׁלֹּא יַלְעִיגוּ עָלָיו, אַף עַל פִּי שֶׁבְּתִשְׁעָה בְּאָב מֻתָּר לִנְעֹל[סט] – בְּיוֹם הַכִּפּוּרִים אָסוּר:[ע]

10 For the same reason, a person walking among non-Jews who fears that they will mock him is forbidden to wear [leather] shoes on Yom Kippur, even though on Tishah BeAv one is permitted to wear [leather] shoes [in such circumstances].

יא כָּל מָקוֹם שֶׁמֻּתָּר לִנְעֹל – טוֹב שֶׁיַּחֲלִיף מִנְעָל שֶׁל שְׂמֹאל בְּיָמִין וְשֶׁל יָמִין לִשְׂמֹאל:[עא]

11 Whenever one is permitted to wear [leather] shoes [on Yom Kippur], it is advisable to switch [shoes], wearing his left shoe on his right foot and his right shoe on his left foot.

---

13. I.e., if he has a non-Jew servant, or if he lives in a community with an *eruv*.

התשובה (רכח, ב) ד״ה אמר מהרי״ל. **נו** מ״א סק״ה. **נז** ט״ז סוף סק״ב. **נח** שמואל בגמרא עח, סוע״ב ורש״י ד״ה אם. רמב״ם פ״ג ה״ח. טור ושו״ע ס״ד. לבוש ס״ג. **נט** טור. ב״י ד״ה כתב בה״ג. לבוש שם. **ס** לבוש שם. **סא** מהרי״ל הל׳ ליל יוה״כ (ע׳ שכג). של״ה מסכת יומא עמוד התשובה (רכח, ב) ד״ה אמר מהרי״ל. מ״א סק״ז. **סב** כדלעיל סי׳ תרי סוף ס״ח. **סג** מהרי״ל שם. **סד** מהרי״ל שם. של״ה שם. מ״א שם. **סה** ראה של״ה שם. **סו** ראה שו״ע סי׳ תקנד סי״ז. **סז** מ״א סק״ז. **סח** סעיף ב. **סט** ראה סי׳ תקנד שם ברמ״א. **ע** מ״א שם. **עא** של״ה שם. מ״א סק״ו.

סימן תרטו דִּין תַּשְׁמִישׁ הַמִּטָּה בְּיוֹם הַכִּפּוּרִים וּבוֹ ב׳ סְעִיפִים:

א כְּבָר בֵּאַרְנוּ[א] שֶׁיּוֹם הַכִּפּוּרִים אָסוּר בְּתַשְׁמִישׁ הַמִּטָּה,[1] וּלְפִי שֶׁלִּבּוֹ שֶׁל אָדָם גַּס עִם אִשְׁתּוֹ וּבְקַל יוּכַל לָבוֹא עִמָּהּ לִידֵי הֶרְגֵּל דָּבָר, לְפִיכָךְ צָרִיךְ לִנְהֹג עִמָּהּ בְּיוֹם הַכִּפּוּרִים כָּל הַרְחָקוֹת שֶׁנּוֹהֵג עִמָּהּ בִּימֵי טֻמְאַת נִדָּתָהּ,[ב,2] דְּהַיְנוּ שֶׁלֹּא יִגַּע בָּהּ,[ג] וְאֵין צָרִיךְ לוֹמַר[ד] שֶׁלֹּא יִישַׁן עִמָּהּ בְּמִטָּה אַחַת[ה] אֲפִלּוּ הוּא בְּבִגְדוֹ וְהִיא בְּבִגְדָהּ,[ו] וְכֵן לֹא יַרְבֶּה עִמָּהּ בִּדְבָרִים,[ז] וְכֵן בְּכָל הַפְּרָטִים שֶׁנִּתְבָּאֲרוּ בְּיוֹרֶה דֵעָה סִימָן קצ״ה.[ח,3]

וּבְכָל דְּבָרִים אֵלּוּ צָרִיךְ לְהִזָּהֵר בֵּין בְּלֵיל יוֹם הַכִּפּוּרִים בֵּין בַּיּוֹם:[ט]

ב הָרוֹאֶה קֶרִי[י] בְּלֵיל[יא] יוֹם הַכִּפּוּרִים[4] – יִדְאַג[יב] כָּל הַשָּׁנָה,[5] שֶׁמָּא לֹא קִבְּלוּ תַּעֲנִיתוֹ[יג] וְהִשְׂבִּיעוּהוּ בְּמַה שֶּׁבְּיָדָם לְהַשְׂבִּיעוֹ, כְּעֶבֶד[6] שֶׁבָּא לִמְזֹג כּוֹס לְרַבּוֹ[7] וְשׁוֹפֵךְ לוֹ רַבּוֹ הַקִּיתוֹן[יד]

SECTION 615 Laws Relating to [the Prohibition against] Marital Relations on Yom Kippur. (1–2)

1 We have already explained[1] that marital relations are forbidden on Yom Kippur. A person feels little restraint with regard to his wife, and it is very possible that they will engage in what is familiar to them, [i.e., relations]. Accordingly, [as a safeguard,] he should conduct himself with her on Yom Kippur according to all the restrictions[2] that he observes when she is in a state of *niddah* impurity.

Accordingly, he should not touch her. Needless to say, they should not sleep in the same bed, even if they are both clothed. Similarly, he should not converse with her extensively — and so on, following all the particulars stated in *Yoreh Deah,* sec. 195.[3] All of these restrictions should be upheld on the day of Yom Kippur as well as at night.

2 A man who had a seminal emission on the night of Yom Kippur[4] should be concerned the entire year:[5] perhaps his fast was not accepted and instead he was granted satisfaction in [an alternative] way. He may be likened[6] to a servant who came to prepare a cup of wine for his master,[7] and his master poured the pitcher (i.e., the pitcher of water used to dilute

1. Sec. 611:2.

2. In the original, *harchakos*.

3. This section of the Alter Rebbe's *Shulchan Aruch* is not extant; see the corresponding section in the *Shulchan Aruch* of R. Yosef Caro.

4. Sec. 613:19 states that one may not immerse in a *mikveh* on Yom Kippur.

5. *Yoma* 88a and *Rashi* there; i.e., he should strive to attain a higher level of *teshuvah (Likkutei Sichos,* Vol. 17, p. 191*)*.

6. The analogy is borrowed from *Sukkah* 28b-29a.

7. The strong wines of the Talmudic era were served only after being diluted.

א סי׳ תריא ס״ב. **ב** מהרי״ל הל׳ ערב יוה״כ (ע׳ שכא). של״ה מסכת יומא עמוד התשובה (רכח, ב) ד״ה אסור. מ״א סק״א. **ג** אגודה פסחים סי׳ נב, בשם רבנו שמחה. מהרי״ל שם. שו״ע ס״א. **ד** ט״ז סק״א. **ה** הגהות מרדכי מועד קטן רמז תתקלד. שו״ע שם. וראה לקמן יו״ד סי׳ קפד סוף סק״ו ובקו״א רסק״ב. **ו** ראה שו״ע יו״ד סי׳ קצה ס״ו. וראה לקמן שם סק״ו ובקו״א סק״א. **ז** מהרי״ל ושל״ה שם. מ״א שם. **ח** סימן זה בשוע״ר לא הגיע לידינו, וראה שו״ע שם. **ט** מהרי״ל שם. של״ה שם. מ״א שם. וראה לעיל סי׳ מ קו״א סק״ב. **י** תנא דבי רבי ישמעאל בגמרא פח, א. טור ושו״ע ס״ב. **יא** שו״ת מהרי״ל סי׳ קמא. ב״י ד״ה הרואה. שו״ע שם. **יב** ראה לקו״ש חי״ז ע׳ 191. **יג** ראה שו״ת צמח צדק או״ח סי׳ קיא בשם רבנו (שהאמור כאן הוא לאנשים גדולים מאד שמצד הרהורי לבם רחוקים מזה מאד). אג״ק ח״ד ע׳ נח. חי״ד ע׳ לא וע׳ רעו. **יד** רש״י שם ד״ה ידאג. טור ולבוש ס״ב. **טו** רש״י סוכה כח, ב ד״ה ושפך. **טז** סוכה

(פֵּרוּשׁ קִיתוֹן שֶׁל מַיִם[טו] שֶׁמְּמַנָּה מוֹזֵג הַכּוֹס שֶׁל יַיִן) עַל פָּנָיו, כְּלוֹמַר אִי אֶפְשִׁי בְּשִׁמּוּשְׁךָ,[טז,8] וְאִם עָלְתָה לוֹ שָׁנָה – מֻבְטָח לוֹ שֶׁהוּא בֶּן עוֹלָם הַבָּא,[יז] שֶׁבְּוַדַּאי יֵשׁ לוֹ זְכֻיּוֹת הַרְבֵּה שֶׁהֵגֵנּוּ עָלָיו,[יח] וְהוּא יַאֲרִיךְ יָמִים,[יט,9] שֶׁכָּךְ הַסִּימָן "יִרְאֶה זֶרַע[10] – יַאֲרִיךְ יָמִים":[כ]

the cup of wine) in his face, as if to say, "I do not desire your service."[8]

If a person in that situation lives through the ensuing year, he may rest assured that he has a share in the World to Come, for he certainly possesses numerous merits that protected him. Moreover, his days will be prolonged, as it is written,[9] "He will see offspring[10] and will live long."

סימן תרטז הַקְּטַנִּים מָתַי יַתְחִילוּ לְהִתְעַנּוֹת וּבוֹ י"א סְעִיפִים:

SECTION 616 At What Age Should Children Begin to Fast. (1–11)

א כָּל הַדְּבָרִים הָאֲסוּרִים בְּיוֹם הַכִּפּוּרִים מִשּׁוּם מִצְוַת עִנּוּי[א] בִּלְבַד[ב] – לֹא גָּזְרוּ עַל הַקְּטַנִּים, לְפִיכָךְ מֻתָּר לְגָדוֹל לְהַאֲכִיל אֶת הַקָּטָן[ג] וּלְהַשְׁקוֹתוֹ וּלְסוּכוֹ וּלְרָחְצוֹ[ד] בְּצוֹנֵן, אֲבָל לֹא יַרְחִיצֶנּוּ בְּחַמִּין[ה] כָּל גּוּפוֹ,[ו] אֲפִלּוּ הוּחַמּוּ מִבְּעוֹד יוֹם,[1] שֶׁהָרְחִיצָה בְּחַמִּין אֵינָהּ אֲסוּרָה מִשּׁוּם מִצְוַת עִנּוּי

1 It was not ordained that children [are required to refrain from] any of the activities that are prohibited on Yom Kippur solely because they involve "affliction." Accordingly, an adult is permitted to give a child food and drink, to anoint him, and to wash him – [but only] with cold water.

However, he may not wash his entire body with hot water, even if that water was heated before the beginning of Yom Kippur.[1] [The rationale is that] washing in hot water is forbidden not only because of the *mitzvah* that one must

---

8. The Alter Rebbe advised on several occasions that the foregoing passage applies to pure-minded individuals of whom it would never be expected that such a thing occur. Concerning a person of such stature it can be said that since his fast was not accepted, from Heaven he was granted satisfaction in another way. Any other person should "divert his attention from the matter entirely and be happy and glad of heart." (Recorded by the *Tzemach Tzedek* in *Shaar HaMiluim*, Responsum 62; in the new edition, see *Orach Chayim*, Responsum 111.)

In a letter suggesting how one should respond to such an occurrence, the Rebbe quotes the *Tzemach Tzedek* and also suggests that every day until the following Rosh HaShanah one should recite chapters 103 and 104 of *Tehillim* and a chapter of *Tanya — Iggeres HaTeshuvah (Igros Kodesh,* Vol. 4, p. 58*)*.

9. *Yeshayahu* 53:10.

10. In the original — *zera,* which means both "offspring" and "seed" (i.e., semen). Hence, echoing the last words of Tractate *Yoma* as explained by *Rashi,* the Alter Rebbe concludes with the reassurance that he who sees seed will live long.

SECTION 616

1. In the original, *mibe'od yom* (lit., "while it was yet day").

כט, א. וראה גם לקמן סי' תרלט סכ"ד. וראה שלחן המלך ח"ב ע' רכו הערה 15. יז תנא דבי רבי ישמעאל יומא שם. טור ושו"ע שם. יח רש"י שם ד"ה ואם. טו[ר]. לבוש שם. יט רב דימי בגמרא שם. כ ישעיה נג, י. רש"י שם ד"ה סגי. תוס' שם ד"ה מפיש. וראה לקו"ש חי"ז ע' 182־3. שלחן המלך ח"ב ע' רכב־ז.
סימן תרטז: א ברייתא עח, ב. טור ושו"ע ס"א. ב מ"א סק"א. ג משמעות הגמרא שם. רש"י שם ד"ה הא. ר"ן (ב, ב) ד"ה התינוקת. טור ורמ"א ס"א. וראה לעיל סי' רסט ס"ג, וסי' תעא ס"י (משום שהמאכל מותר מחמת עצמו אלא שהוא זמן האסור באכילה), וש"נ. לקמן ס"ד וסוף ס"ו. ד משמעות הגמרא שם. רש"י שם. ר"ן שם. מ"א שם. ה מ"א שם. ו כדלעיל סי' שכו ס"א (או רובו).

בִּלְבַד, שֶׁהֲרֵי בְּכָל שַׁבְּתוֹת הַשָּׁנָה אָסוּר לִרְחֹץ בְּחַמִּין, אֶלָּא יֵשׁ בָּהּ גַּם מִשּׁוּם גְּזֵרַת מֶרְחָץ (פֵּרוּשׁ שֶׁהַבַּלָּנִים הֵם חֲשׁוּדִים לְהָחֵם מַיִם בְּשַׁבָּת,[2] וּלְכָךְ אָסְרוּ לִכְנֹס לַמֶּרְחָץ בְּשַׁבָּת) כְּמוֹ שֶׁנִּתְבָּאֵר בְּסִימָן שכ"ו;[ז] וּלְפִיכָךְ אָסוּר לַעֲשׂוֹתָהּ לְקָטָן בְּיָדַיִם,[ח] כְּמוֹ שֶׁאָסוּר לְהַאֲכִילוֹ בְּיָדַיִם כָּל הָאִסּוּרִין שֶׁל דִּבְרֵיהֶם כְּמוֹ שֶׁנִּתְבָּאֵר בְּסִימָן שמ"ג:[ט]

afflict oneself, for washing with hot water is forbidden on all the *Shabbasos* throughout the year. As explained in sec. 326[:1], a [safeguard] was also ordained against [entering a] bathhouse [on *Shabbos* or on a festival]. (Since it was suspected that bathhouse attendants would heat water on *Shabbos*,[2] [the Sages] forbade entering a bathhouse on *Shabbos*.) Hence it is forbidden [for an adult] to [bathe] a child [in hot water], just as it is forbidden to feed him by hand anything that is forbidden by Rabbinic ordinance, as stated in sec. 343[:5].

ב וְכֵן אָסוּר לְגָדוֹל לִנְעֹל אֶת הַסַּנְדָּל לַקָּטָן,[י,3] לְפִי שֶׁאֵין זֶה עִנּוּי לְהַקָּטָן שֶׁאֵינוֹ חוֹשֵׁשׁ כָּל כָּךְ אִם לֹא יִנְעֹל,[יא,4] אֲבָל אִם הַקָּטָן נוֹעֵל מֵעַצְמוֹ — אִם צָרִיךְ לִמְחוֹת בְּיָדוֹ נִתְבָּאֵר בְּסִימָן שמ"ג,[יב,5] עַיֵּן שָׁם:

2 Similarly, an adult is forbidden to put [leather] shoes on a child.[3] [The rationale is that] this is not a great affliction for a child, for a child does not really mind if he does not wear shoes.[4] [The question of whether] an adult must reprimand a child who puts on shoes on his own initiative is explained in sec. 343[:1].[5] Note [the explanation] there.

ג וְעַכְשָׁו שֶׁאֵין נוֹהֲגִין לִרְחֹץ וְלָסוּךְ אֶת הַקָּטָן בְּכָל יוֹם, וְאֵין מְנִיעַת הָרְחִיצָה וְהַסִּיכָה בְּיוֹם הַכִּפּוּרִים נֶחְשֶׁבֶת לוֹ לְעִנּוּי כְּלָל — אֵין לְרָחְצוֹ וּלְסוּכוֹ בְּיוֹם הַכִּפּוּרִים. וְכֵן הוּא הַמִּנְהָג:[יג,6]

3 In the present era, when it is not customary to wash and anoint a child every day, refraining from washing and anointing him on Yom Kippur is not considered affliction at all. Hence a child should not be washed and anointed on Yom Kippur. This is the [prevailing] custom.[6]

---

2. As the Alter Rebbe explains in the source cited, the intent was not that the attendants would kindle fires on *Shabbos*, but that they would kindle fires before *Shabbos* that would hopefully continue to heat the cold water throughout the day. Nevertheless, even this was forbidden, lest they forget and stoke the fires on *Shabbos*.

3. *Yoma* 78b.

4. I.e., since children sometimes run barefoot and being without leather shoes on Yom Kippur will not disturb them, they can observe this restriction like adults. In fact, it is customary on Yom Kippur for them to wear shoes made of substances other than leather.

5. There the Alter Rebbe explains that a child who does something prohibited should be rebuked only if adults are likely to learn from his example and relax their own observance. This proviso does not exempt the child's father from training him (see subsection 4 below).

6. This applies even if it is possible to have a non-Jew wash and anoint him *(Mishnah Berurah* 616:3*)*. Needless to say, if a child has soiled himself he may be cleaned, for even adults may wash themselves to remove filth.

ז סעיף א. ח ראה לעיל סי' שלא סי"א. סי' תקיא ס"א. ט סעיף ה. י ברייתא וגמרא עח, ב. טור ושו"ע ס"א. יא גמרא שם. טור ולבוש ס"א. יב ס"א (כשלא הגיע לחנוך). יג לבוש סוף ס"ב. מ"א סוף סק"א. וראה גם לעיל סי' תקיא ס"א. יד שיתבאר לקמן ס"ה ואילך. טו מ"א סק"ב. טז כדלקמן ס"ז שגם בזה

ד וְכָל זֶה בְּקָטָן שֶׁלֹּא הִגִּיעַ לְחִנּוּךְ מִצְוַת עִנּוּי,[יד] אֲבָל אִם הִגִּיעַ לְחִנּוּךְ — אָסוּר לְהַאֲכִילוֹ[טו] וּלְהַשְׁקוֹתוֹ וּלְסוּכוֹ וּלְרָחְצוֹ[טז] בְּיָדַיִם וְעַל דֶּרֶךְ שֶׁנִּתְבָּאֵר.[יז] וְאִם הוּא מֵעַצְמוֹ עוֹשֶׂה אֶחָד מִדְּבָרִים אֵלּוּ — אֵין צָרִיךְ לִמְחוֹת בְּיָדוֹ, חוּץ מֵאָבִיו שֶׁצָּרִיךְ לִמְחוֹת בְּיָדוֹ וּלְחַנֵּךְ אֶת בְּנוֹ בְּמִצְווֹת,[יח,7] אֲבָל אִמּוֹ אֵינָהּ מְצֻוָּה עַל כָּךְ,[יט,8] אֲבָל מִכָּל מָקוֹם אָסוּר לָהּ לִתֵּן לְפָנָיו לֶאֱכֹל, דַּהֲרֵי זֶה כְּאִלּוּ מַאֲכִילָתוֹ בְּיָדַיִם:[כ]

ה וְכֵיצַד הוּא חִנּוּכוֹ?[כא,9] קָטָן הַבָּרִיא[כב] בֶּן תֵּשַׁע שָׁנִים[כג] שְׁלֵמוֹת[כד] (פֵּרוּשׁ[כה] שֶׁנִּשְׁלְמוּ לוֹ תֵּשַׁע שָׁנִים לִפְנֵי יוֹם הַכִּפּוּרִים),[10] אוֹ בֶּן עֶשֶׂר שָׁנִים[כו] שְׁלֵמוֹת אֲפִלּוּ הוּא כָּחוּשׁ וּתְשׁוּשׁ כֹּחַ[כז] — מְחַנְּכִין אוֹתוֹ לְשָׁעוֹת מִדִּבְרֵי סוֹפְרִים.[11] כֵּיצַד? אִם הָיָה רָגִיל לֶאֱכֹל בִּשְׁתֵּי שָׁעוֹת עַל הַיּוֹם[12] — מַאֲכִילִין אוֹתוֹ בְּשָׁלֹשׁ, הָיָה רָגִיל לֶאֱכֹל בְּשָׁלֹשׁ — מַאֲכִילִין אוֹתוֹ בְּאַרְבַּע,[כח] לְפִי כֹּחַ הַבֵּן מוֹסִיפִין לְעַנּוֹת אוֹתוֹ בְּשָׁעוֹת.[כט,13] וְכֵן הַדִּין בִּקְטַנָּה

4 All of the above applies with regard to a young child who has not [matured and] reached an age at which he can be educated to observe the *mitzvah* of afflicting oneself [on Yom Kippur]. If he has reached an educable age, it is forbidden to give him food and drink, to anoint him, or to wash him oneself, as explained [above].

If [the child] performs any of these activities on his own initiative, no one except for his father is obligated to object to his doing so, for [only] a father is obligated to raise an objection to his [misconduct] and to educate his son in [the observance of] the *mitzvos*.[7] His mother is not commanded to do this.[8] Nevertheless, it is forbidden for her to place food before him, because that is equivalent to feeding him by hand.

5 How should a child be educated [in the observance of this *mitzvah*]?[9] A healthy boy who is a full nine years of age (i.e., he [reached his ninth birthday] before Yom Kippur[10]), or who is ten years old, even if he is frail and weak, should be trained [to fast] hour by hour, progressively. This is a Rabbinic obligation.[11]

What is implied? If he normally eats at 8 AM,[12] he should be given food [no earlier than] at 9 AM. If he normally eats at 9, he should be given food [no earlier than] at 10. Hours of affliction are added according to the son's strength.[13]

Similar principles apply with regard to a

---

7. See sec. 343:2.

8. *Loc. cit.*, subsection 4.

9. *Yoma* 82a.

10. Or on the day of Yom Kippur, as stated in subsection 8.

11. Devolving on his father.

12. Lit., "at two hours"; i.e., two hours after sunrise, when the sun rises at 6 AM and sets at 6 PM.

13. R. Yosef Yitzchak Schneersohn, the sixth Lubavitcher

צריך לחנכו, וש"נ. **יז** ס"א־ב (בדברים האסורים אף בלא הגיע לחנוך, וכ"ה כאן באכילה כשהגיע לחנוך). וראה עד"ז לעיל סי' תעא סוף ס"י. **יח** תוס' ישנים פב, א ד"ה בן בשם ר"י. הגהות מיימוניות פ"ב אות כ. מ"א שם. וכדלעיל סי' שמג סעי' ב־ג. **יט** תוס' ישנים שם. וכדלעיל שם ס"ד. **כ** מ"א שם (ושם גם הטעם דלא דמי להא דלקמן סי' תר"מ ס"ד). וראה גם לעיל סי' שמג ס"י (במוסגר). **כא** משנה פב, רע"א. **כב** רב חסדא שם. ר"ן (ג, ב) ד"ה ופסק. רמ"א ס"ב. **כג** גמרא שם כרב נחמן, לגירסת ופירוש הרי"ף (ג, ב. ראה ר"ן שם ד"ה ופסק), ורמב"ם פ"ב ה"י (ראה מ"מ שם). שו"ע ס"ב. **כד** ר"ן שם. מ"מ שם. שו"ע שם. וראה לקמן הל' תלמוד תורה קו"א ס"ק א (קרוב לסוף) מתי שנים האמורות בתלמוד הן שלימות. **כה** ר"ן (ג, א) ד"ה אמר. **כו** רב נחמן שם. רי"ף שם. רמב"ם שם. שו"ע שם. **כז** רש"י שם ד"ה בחולה. **כח** ברייתא שם. רמב"ם שם. טור ושו"ע שם (ראה ט"ז ס"ק ב). **כט** רמב"ם שם. שו"ע שם.

הַבְּרִיאָה אִם הִיא בַּת ט' שָׁנִים שְׁלֵמוֹת,[14] אוֹ בַּת עֶשֶׂר שָׁנִים שְׁלֵמוֹת אֲפִלּוּ אֵינָהּ בְּרִיאָה:[ל]

healthy daughter who is nine years old[14] or one who is ten, even if she is not robust.

ו בֶּן י"א שָׁנִים[לא] שְׁלֵמוֹת,[לב] בֵּין זָכָר וּבֵין נְקֵבָה[לג] – מִתְעַנִּין וּמַשְׁלִימִין[15] מִדִּבְרֵי סוֹפְרִים, כְּדֵי לְחַנְּכָן בְּמִצְוֹת.

וְיֵשׁ אוֹמְרִים[לד] שֶׁאֲפִלּוּ בְּנוֹת י"א שָׁנִים שְׁלֵמוֹת וּבֵן זָכָר בֶּן י"ב שָׁנִים שְׁלֵמוֹת אֵינָן צְרִיכִין לְהַשְׁלִים כְּלָל אֲפִלּוּ מִדִּבְרֵי סוֹפְרִים, אֶלָּא מְחַנְּכִין אוֹתָן לְשָׁעוֹת וְעַל דֶּרֶךְ שֶׁנִּתְבָּאֵר,[לה] דְּכֵיוָן שֶׁהַחִנּוּךְ אֵינוֹ אֶלָּא מִדִּבְרֵי סוֹפְרִים[לו,16] – לֹא רָצוּ חֲכָמִים לְהַחְמִיר עֲלֵיהֶם כָּל כָּךְ שֶׁיִּתְעַנּ[וּ] עַד הַלַּיְלָה, וְדַי לָהֶם בְּחִנּוּךְ שָׁעוֹת לְפִי כֹּחָם.

וְאַף עַל פִּי שֶׁהָעִקָּר כַּסְּבָרָא הָרִאשׁוֹנָה, מִכָּל מָקוֹם בְּנַעַר שֶׁהוּא כָּחוּשׁ וּתְשׁוּשׁ כֹּחַ וְאֵינוֹ חָזָק לִסְבֹּל הַתַּעֲנִית – יֵשׁ לִסְמֹךְ עַל סְבָרָא הָאַחֲרוֹנָה,[לז] וּמֻתָּר לְהַאֲכִילוֹ[לח] אַף שֶׁאֵין שׁוּם חֲשַׁשׁ סַכָּנָה אִם יַשְׁלִים:[לט]

6 A child who is a full eleven years of age, whether male or female, should complete the fast [on Yom Kippur].[15] [This is] a Rabbinic ordinance that was instituted in order to train them in [the observance of] the *mitzvos*.

Some authorities, however, maintain that even girls who are a full eleven years of age and boys who are a full twelve years of age are under no obligation whatever — even Rabbinic — to complete [the fast]. Instead, they should be trained to fast by hourly stages, as explained above. [Their rationale is that] since this training is only a Rabbinic ordinance,[16] the Sages did not wish to be stringent and require that [children] fast until nightfall; it is sufficient that they be trained [to fast] by hourly stages, according to their strength.

Though primacy is given to the first opinion, if a child is frail and weak, and not strong enough to bear the fast, one may rely on the latter view. He may be given food even if completing the fast involves no risk.

ז וּכְדֶרֶךְ שֶׁמְּחַנְּכִין אוֹתָן בְּאִסּוּר אֲכִילָה וּשְׁתִיָּה הֵן לְשָׁעוֹת וְהֵן לְהַשְׁלִים וּכְמוֹ שֶׁנִּתְבָּאֵר – כָּךְ צָרִיךְ לְחַנְּכָ[ן]

7 Just as [a child] is trained, as explained above, [to observe] the prohibitions against eating and drinking by hourly stages and [ultimately] to complete [the fast], so, too, he should be trained [to observe] the

---

Rebbe, writes in a letter that children who do not fast should not overindulge when eating on Yom Kippur and should take care to recite the blessings before and after eating (the *Igros Kodesh* of the Rebbe Rayatz, Vol. 7, p. 2).

With regard to the text of the Grace after Meals to be recited in such a case, see sec. 618:18.

14. Although a girl becomes obligated by the *mitzvos* a year earlier than a boy, she is not trained to observe this *mitzvah* any earlier (*Mishnah Berurah* 616:6).

15. *Yoma, loc. cit.*

16. *Sukkah* 28b; *Nazir* 29a. See also sec. 343:2, and *Hilchos Talmud Torah* 1:1.

ל רב נחמן שם, לגירסת הרי"ף שם. ראה ר"ן שם (ג, ב) ד"ה ופסק. רמ"א שם. לא רב נחמן בגמרא שם. רי"ף שם. רמב"ם שם. שו"ע שם. לב מ"מ שם. לג רב נחמן שם, לגירסת ופירוש הרי"ף והרמב"ם שם. שו"ע שם. לד רבי יוחנן בגמרא שם. הלכות גדולות הל' יוה"כ (לא, ג). הרי"ץ גיאת הל' יוה"כ (ע' נה). תוס' כתובות נ, א ד"ה ובת. אור זרוע ח"ב סוס"י רעה. רוקח סי' ריז. יראים השלם סוס"י נא. הגהות מיימוניות פ"ב אות י. רמ"א ס"ב בשם ויש אומרים. לה סעיף ה. לו כדלעיל סי' שמג ס"ב, וש"נ. לז תרומת הדשן סי' קנה. רמ"א שם. לח כדלעיל ס"א. לט ראה גם לעיל סי' רסט ס"ג. סי' תעא

prohibitions against washing and anointing oneself. This is a Talmudic requirement, not only a matter of custom.

8 Once a male who is a full thirteen years of age and a female who is a full twelve years of age have manifested signs of physical maturity,[17] they are considered as adults with regard to [the observance of] all the *mitzvos*[18] and are obligated by Scriptural Law to complete the fast. If they [have reached this age but] have not manifested signs of physical maturity, they are still considered as minors, and Scriptural Law does not obligate them to complete the fast. However, according to the first — and primary — view cited above, they are obligated to complete the fast by Rabbinic Law.

[Moreover, in this instance,] even in the case of a boy who is frail and weak it is not appropriate to rely on the latter and more lenient view cited above. Once a boy is fully thirteen years of age, the possibility must be considered that he has produced signs of physical maturity, but they are no longer present.[19] [This surmise is reasonable, because a child] commonly manifests signs of physical maturity as soon as he turns thirteen, and if so, his obligation to complete the fast could possibly be of Scriptural authority.

Even if he completes his thirteenth year on Yom Kippur itself, i.e., Yom Kippur was his birthday, he is obligated to complete [the fast] even if he is frail and weak, because he [is considered to have] completed his thirteenth year when the beginning of the night of Yom

בְּאִסּוּר רְחִיצָה וְסִיכָה[מ] אֲפִלּוּ מִדִּין הַתַּלְמוּד[מא] וְלֹא מֵחֲמַת הַמִּנְהָג בִּלְבַד:[מב]

ח בֶּן י"ג שָׁנִים שְׁלֵמוֹת וּנְקֵבָה בַּת י"ב שְׁלֵמוֹת, אִם הֵבִיאוּ שְׁתֵּי שְׂעָרוֹת[17] – הֲרֵי הֵם כִּגְדוֹלִים לְכָל הַמִּצְווֹת[מג,18] וְחַיָּבִים לְהַשְׁלִים הַתַּעֲנִית מִן הַתּוֹרָה,[מד] אֲבָל אִם עֲדַיִן לֹא הֵבִיאוּ שְׁתֵּי שְׂעָרוֹת – עֲדַיִן הֵן קְטַנִּים וְאֵין חַיָּבִין לְהַשְׁלִים מִן הַתּוֹרָה, אֲבָל חַיָּבִים לְהַשְׁלִים מִדִּבְרֵי סוֹפְרִים[מה] לְפִי סְבָרָא הָרִאשׁוֹנָה שֶׁבֵּאַרְנוּ[מו] שֶׁהִיא עִקָּר.

וַאֲפִלּוּ בְּנַעַר שֶׁהוּא כָּחוּשׁ וְתַשׁ כֹּחַ – אֵין לְהָקֵל לִסְמֹךְ עַל סְבָרָא הָאַחֲרוֹנָה שֶׁבֵּאַרְנוּ, דְּכֵיוָן שֶׁעָבְרוּ לוֹ י"ג שָׁנִים אָנוּ חוֹשְׁשִׁין שֶׁמָּא הֵבִיא כְּבָר שְׁתֵּי שְׂעָרוֹת וְנָשְׁרוּ,[מז,19] לְפִי שֶׁדֶּרֶךְ הוּא לְהָבִיא שְׁתֵּי שְׂעָרוֹת מִיָּד אַחַר י"ג שָׁנִים,[מח] וְאִם כֵּן הֲרֵי יֵשׁ כָּאן סָפֵק שֶׁמָּא הוּא חַיָּב לְהַשְׁלִים מִן הַתּוֹרָה.[מט]

וַאֲפִלּוּ נִשְׁלְמוּ לוֹ הַי"ג שָׁנִים בְּיוֹם הַכִּפּוּרִים עַצְמוֹ שֶׁנּוֹלַד בְּיוֹם הַכִּפּוּרִים – אַף עַל פִּי כֵן חַיָּב לְהַשְׁלִים, אֲפִלּוּ הוּא כָּחוּשׁ וְתַשׁ כֹּחַ,[נ] לְפִי שֶׁבִּתְחִלַּת כְּנִיסַת לֵיל יוֹם הַכִּפּוּרִים כְּבָר נִשְׁלְמוּ

17. Lit., "produced two [pubic] hairs."

18. *Yoma, loc. cit.*

19. Lit., "they [the hairs] fell out."

ס"י. מ טור. רמ"א ס"ב. וראה גם לעיל ס"ד. מא מדאמרינן במשנה פב, א אין מענין כו' אבל מחנכין (סתם). מב המוזכר לעיל ס"ג. מג כדלעיל סי' נה ס"ו וסי"ב וש"נ. מד גמרא פב, א כרבי יוחנן. רי"ף (ג, ב). רמב"ם פ"ב הי"א. שו"ע ס"ב. מה רמב"ם שם. שו"ע שם. מו סעיף ו. מז נדה מו, א. טור ושו"ע אהע"ז סי' קנה ס"כ. וראה שו"ת צמח צדק או"ח סי' סב ד"ה אך ורק. מח כדלעיל סי' נה ס"ו. מט תרומת הדשן סי' קנה. רמ"א ס"ב וט"ז סק"ה. ולענין פחות מכשיעור, ראה שו"ת צמח צדק שם ד"ה מעתה (שרבנו עשה מעשה בילד קטן וחלוש שהי' לו חום ונתרפא כו'). לעיל סי' תריב סט"ז (שגם פחות מכשיעור אסור מהתורה). נ מ"א סק"ג.

לוֹ י״ג שָׁנִים,[נא,20] וְיֵשׁ לָחוּשׁ שֶׁמָּא הֵבִיא שְׁתֵּי שְׂעָרוֹת בְּיוֹם הַכִּפּוּרִים וְנָשְׁרוּ בְּיוֹם הַכִּפּוּרִים,[נב] וְכָל סָפֵק שֶׁל תּוֹרָה הוֹלְכִין בּוֹ לְהַחְמִיר:

Kippur arrives.[20] Thus it is possible that he manifested signs of physical maturity on Yom Kippur, but they disappeared on that day — and whenever a Scriptural [obligation] is in the balance, the more stringent approach is to be followed.

ט בַּמֶּה דְּבָרִים אֲמוּרִים? בְּיוֹם הַכִּפּוּרִים שֶׁהוּא מִן הַתּוֹרָה, אֲבָל בִּשְׁאָר תַּעֲנִיּוֹת[21] שֶׁאֵינָן אֶלָּא מִדִּבְרֵי סוֹפְרִים — אֵין צְרִיכִין לְהִתְעַנּוֹת אֶלָּא אִם כֵּן יָדוּעַ שֶׁהֵבִיאוּ שְׁתֵּי שְׂעָרוֹת:[נג]

9 When does the above apply? With regard to Yom Kippur, when [the obligation to fast] is of Scriptural origin. On other fastdays,[21] which are of Rabbinic origin alone, [a child] need not fast unless it is known that he has manifested signs of physical maturity.

י קָטָן שֶׁהוּא פָּחוֹת מִבֶּן תֵּשַׁע שָׁנִים שְׁלֵמוֹת — אֵין מְעַנִּין אוֹתוֹ בְּיוֹם הַכִּפּוּרִים.[נד] וַאֲפִלּוּ אִם הַקָּטָן רוֹצֶה לְהַחְמִיר עַל עַצְמוֹ — מוֹחִין בְּיָדוֹ,[נה] כְּדֵי שֶׁלֹּא יָבוֹא לִידֵי סַכָּנָה:[נו]

10 When a child is less than nine full years of age, he should not be required to afflict himself on Yom Kippur. Even if a child seeks to undertake the stringency [of refraining from eating], he should be reprimanded, lest he endanger himself.

יא מַה שֶּׁאֵין מְדַקְדְּקִים עַכְשָׁו שֶׁיִּתְעַנֶּה קָטָן כְּשֶׁהוּא בֶּן י״א שָׁנִים שְׁלֵמוֹת, לְפִי שֶׁהַכֹּל לוֹמְדִים עַכְשָׁו[נז] וְהַתּוֹרָה מַתֶּשֶׁת כֹּחָם[נח,22] וּלְכָךְ אֵינָן חֲשׁוּבִין כִּבְרִיאִין לְעִנְיָן זֶה, וּכְבָר נִתְבָּאֵר[נט,23] שֶׁכָּל שֶׁאֵינוֹ בָּרִיא אֵינוֹ צָרִיךְ לְהַשְׁלִים לְפִי שֶׁיֵּשׁ לִסְמֹךְ עַל סְבָרָא הָאַחֲרוֹנָה שֶׁבֵּאַרְנוּ, וְעוֹד דִּבַזְּמַן הַזֶּה שֶׁיָּרְדָה חֻלְשָׁה לָעוֹלָם[ס,24] מִן הַסְּתָם כָּל קָטָן אֵינוֹ נֶחְשָׁב כְּבָרִיא לְעִנְיָן זֶה,[סא] אֶלָּא אִם כֵּן יָדוּעַ שֶׁהוּא בָּרִיא וְחָזָק לִסְבֹּל:

11 At present we are not particular that a child who is eleven full years of age should fast, because today all [children] study, and the [study of] Torah weakens them.[22] In this context, therefore, they are not considered robust and, as explained above,[23] whenever a child is not robust, he does not have to complete [the fast], because we can rely on the second opinion cited. Moreover, in the present age, after "weakness descended to the world,"[24] it may be assumed that a child is not considered robust in this regard unless it is known that he is healthy and strong enough to bear [the fast].

---

20. See the last paragraph of sec. 53:13, in Vol. 1 of the present work.

21. Including Tishah BeAv.

22. As *Sanhedrin* 26b states, "[Torah study] weakens one's strength."

23. Subsection 6.

24. Cf. *Horayos* 13b.

נא כדלעיל סי' נג סוף סי"ג, וש"נ. **נב** ראה תרומת הדשן שם בסופו. ב"י שם. **נג** מ"א שם. וראה לקמן יו"ד סי' קצ ס"ק ד (לענין כתמים דרבנן, שדוקא כשבדקוה ולא מצאו אין חוששין שמא נשרו). הוספות למנחת פתים או"ח. **נד** רמב"ם פ"ב הי"א. שו"ע ס"ב. **נה** כלבו סי' סט (לד, ג). רמ"א סוף ס"ב. **נו** רמב"ם שם. שו"ע שם. **נז** ב"ח סוף הסי'. מ"א סוף סק"ב. **נח** סנהדרין כו, ב. וראה גם רש"י כתובות נ, א ד"ה ובתינוקת. **נט** סעיף ו. **ס** ראה הוריות יג, ב. וראה לעיל סי' מו ס"ו. **סא** ב"ח שם. מ"א שם.

SECTION 617 Laws Relating to Pregnant and Nursing Women, and Women after Recent Childbirth, on Yom Kippur. (1–5)

1 Pregnant and nursing women must complete the fast on Yom Kippur.[1]

2 [The following laws apply if] a pregnant woman smells [the aroma of] a delicacy, [and desires it so intensely] that if she is not given the food she may miscarry.[2] For the fetus [also] smelled the aroma of the food and desires it, and if [the mother] does not partake of it, [the fetus] may break loose [from the placenta in an endeavor] to leave [the womb], thus endangering the lives of them both.

[In such a situation,] someone should whisper in her ear that this day is Yom Kippur, for perhaps [this awareness will] enable her to restrain herself. If her mind becomes settled, and the fetus ceases its desire because of this reminder, well and good. If her mind remains unsettled and she says, "I need to eat" (see the explanation of this statement in sec. 618[:1]), or if her face began to change [color] even if she did not say, "I need to eat," one should dip a stalk[3] in sauce and place it in her mouth [for her to suck], in the [hope] that this will settle her.[4]

If she remains unsettled and her face remains different from its usual appearance, or if she still says, "I need [to eat]," she should be given some of the sauce itself (in small amounts, each less than the minimum measure[5] [for

סימן תריז דִּין עֻבָּרָה וּמְנִיקָה וְיוֹלֶדֶת בְּיוֹם הַכִּפּוּרִים וּבוֹ ה' סְעִיפִים:

א עֻבָּרוֹת וּמְנִיקוֹת – מִתְעַנּוֹת וּמַשְׁלִימוֹת בְּיוֹם הַכִּפּוּרִים:[א,1]

ב עֻבָּרָה שֶׁהֵרִיחָה מַאֲכָל[ב] וְאִם לֹא יִתְּנוּ לָהּ מֵהַמַּאֲכָל אֶפְשָׁר שֶׁתַּפִּיל עֻבָּרָהּ,[ג,2] לְפִי שֶׁהָעֻבָּר הֵרִיחַ רֵיחַ הַמַּאֲכָל וּמִתְאַוֶּה לוֹ, וְאִם לֹא תֹּאכַל מִמֶּנּוּ אֶפְשָׁר שֶׁיִּתְעַקֵּר לָצֵאת וְנִמְצָא שְׁנֵיהֶם מְסֻכָּנִים[ד] – לוֹחֲשִׁין לָהּ בְּאָזְנָהּ שֶׁהַיּוֹם הוּא יוֹם הַכִּפּוּרִים[ה] אוּלַי תּוּכַל לְהִתְאַפֵּק,[ו] וְאִם נִתְיַשְּׁבָה דַּעְתָּהּ[ז] שֶׁפָּסַק הָעֻבָּר מִתַּאֲוָתוֹ[ח] עַל יְדֵי זִכָּרוֹן זֶה[ט] – מוּטָב.

וְאִם לֹא נִתְיַשְּׁבָה דַּעְתָּהּ בָּזֶה אֶלָּא אוֹמֶרֶת צְרִיכָה אֲנִי לֶאֱכֹל[י] (עַיֵּן בֵּאוּר דָּבָר זֶה בְּסִימָן תרי"ח[יא]), אוֹ שֶׁהִתְחִילוּ פָּנֶיהָ מִשְׁתַּנִּים אַף עַל פִּי שֶׁלֹּא אָמְרָה צְרִיכָה אֲנִי לֶאֱכֹל[יב] – תּוֹחֲבִין כּוּשׁ בָּרֹטֶב[3] וְנוֹתְנִין לְתוֹךְ פִּיהָ, שֶׁמָּא תִּתְיַשֵּׁב דַּעְתָּהּ בָּזֶה.[4] וְאִם לֹא נִתְיַשְּׁבָה דַּעְתָּהּ בְּכָךְ וַעֲדַיִן פָּנֶיהָ מְשֻׁנִּים אוֹ שֶׁעֲדַיִן אוֹמֶרֶת צְרִיכָה אֲנִי – נוֹתְנִין לָהּ מִן הָרֹטֶב עַצְמוֹ[יג] (פָּחוֹת פָּחוֹת מִכְּשִׁעוּר,[5]

---

1. *Pesachim* 54a.

2. *Yoma* 82a, and *Rashi* there.

3. Lit., "a spindle" or "a reed."

4. Since a pregnant woman may be subject to drastic changes in appetite that are not necessarily dependent on an actual need for food, a mere taste will possibly satisfy her.

5. I.e., the size of a date, i.e., at least 30 grams. On the

א רבא בגמרא פסחים נד, א. טור ושו"ע ס"א. ב משנה פב, א. טור ושו"ע ס"ב. ג בה"ג הל' יוה"כ (לא, ג). הובא ברא"ש פ"ח סי' יג, ור"ן (ג, ב) ד"ה וכתוב בה"ג. ד רש"י שם ד"ה עוברה. וראה רא"ש ור"ן שם. ה גמרא פב, ב. טור ושו"ע ס"ב. ו רש"י שם ד"ה לחושו. ז טור. לבוש ס"ב. וראה גם רמב"ם פ"ב ה"ט ושו"ע שם (אם נתקררה דעתה). ח רש"י שם ד"ה ואלחישה. ט רמב"ם שם. שו"ע שם. י מ"א סק"א, בדעת הטור ורבנו ירוחם נתיב כ ח"א (רכז, ג). יא סעיף א. יב רבנו ירוחם שם, בשם הרמב"ן בתורת האדם שער הסכנה ד"ה ובהלכות גדולות. רמ"א ס"א. יג גמרא [ברייתא] פב, א (באיסור). טור לפירוש הב' בב"י ד"ה ומ"ש רבנו ואם (דמיירי אף בהיתר ביוה"כ). לבוש ס"ב. ב"ח ד"ה ומ"ש רבנו נותנין. מ"א סק"ב.

כְּמוֹ שֶׁיִּתְבָּאֵר בְּסִימָן תרי"ח[יד]).

וְאִם גַּם בָּזֶה לֹא נִתְיַשְּׁבָה דַּעְתָּהּ – נוֹתְנִין לָהּ מִן הַמַּאֲכָל עַצְמוֹ[טו] (פָּחוֹת פָּחוֹת מִכְּשִׁעוּר) עַד שֶׁתִּתְיַשֵּׁב דַּעְתָּהּ:[טז,6]

which one is liable], as will be explained in sec. 618[:13]).

If this, too, is not sufficient to settle her, she should be given some of the food itself (in small amounts, each less than the minimum measure) until she feels settled.[6]

ג וְלֹא מְעֻבֶּרֶת בִּלְבַד, אֶלָּא אֲפִלּוּ כָּל אָדָם שֶׁהֵרִיחַ מַאֲכָל וְנִשְׁתַּנּוּ פָּנָיו – מְסֻכָּן הוּא אִם לֹא יִתְּנוּ לוֹ לִטְעֹם מֵהַמַּאֲכָל, לְפִיכָךְ מַאֲכִילִין אוֹתוֹ בְּיוֹם הַכִּפּוּרִים[יז] כְּדֶרֶךְ שֶׁמַּאֲכִילִין אֶת הַמְעֻבֶּרֶת שֶׁהֵרִיחָה,[יח] אֲבָל אִם לֹא נִשְׁתַּנּוּ פָּנָיו[יט] אַף עַל פִּי שֶׁאוֹמֵר צָרִיךְ אֲנִי לֶאֱכֹל[כ] – אֵין מַאֲכִילִין אוֹתוֹ.

אֶלָּא אִם כֵּן הוּא חוֹלֶה, שֶׁאָז אֲפִלּוּ לֹא הֵרִיחַ רֵיחַ מַאֲכָל וְהוּא אוֹמֵר צָרִיךְ אֲנִי,[כא] אוֹ שֶׁהָרוֹפְאִים אוֹמְרִים שֶׁהוּא צָרִיךְ לֶאֱכֹל[כב] – מַאֲכִילִין אוֹתוֹ מִיָּד שֶׁצָּרִיךְ לוֹ, כְּדֵי הַצָּרִיךְ לוֹ. וְלֹא אָמְרוּ לִתֵּן לוֹ תְּחִלָּה מִן הָרֹטֶב, אֶלָּא בִּמְעֻבֶּרֶת אוֹ מִי שֶׁהֵרִיחַ רֵיחַ הַמַּאֲכָל, שֶׁאֵין לָהֶם וְלֹא לָנוּ אֹמֶד בְּיִשּׁוּב דַּעְתָּם, פְּעָמִים מִתְיַשֵּׁב בְּרֹטֶב וּפְעָמִים שֶׁצְּרִיכִין לְהַמַּאֲכָל עַצְמוֹ, לְפִיכָךְ מְדַקְדְּקִין עִמָּהֶם בְּכָל מַה שֶּׁאֶפְשָׁר, אֲבָל חוֹלֶה שֶׁמַּאֲכִילִין אוֹתוֹ עַל פִּי רוֹפְאִים בְּקִיאִים – נוֹתְנִים לוֹ כְּפִי מַה שֶּׁאוֹמְרִים

3 [These laws] apply not only to a pregnant woman. Any person who smells [the aroma of] food, and [desires it so intensely that] his face changes [color], is [considered to be] in mortal danger if he is not given the opportunity to taste the food. He should therefore be given food on Yom Kippur in the same manner as a pregnant woman is given.

If his face did not change [color] he should not be given food even though he says, "I need to eat," unless he is sick. [If he is sick] and says, "I need [to eat]," or if doctors say that he must eat, then even if he did not smell [the aroma of] food he should be given the amount he needs as soon as he needs it. [The procedure of] first giving some of the sauce was stated only with regard to a pregnant woman or to a person who smelled the aroma of food, for neither they, nor we, are able to estimate when their minds will be settled. Sometimes the sauce itself will suffice, and sometimes they need the food itself. We are therefore particular, [when feeding] them, to whatever extent possible.

With regard to a sick person, by contrast, [since] he is given food on the advice of knowledgeable doctors, he should be given

---

relationship between units of volume and units of weight, see sec. 612:1 and footnote 1 there. See also sec. 618, footnote 15 below.

6. Though the pregnant woman is allowed to eat the food she desires, once her mind is settled she is not allowed to eat again on Yom Kippur. It is not argued that since she has already broken her fast, she may now eat whatever she wishes *(Mishnah Berurah* 617:7, citing Rabbeinu Mano'ach*)*.

יד סעיף יג. טו ברייתא שם. טור וב"י שם. מ"א שם. טז משנה שם (שתשיב נפשה). רמב"ם שם (שתתיישב נפשה). ב"י שם (בהעתקת לשון הרמב"ם). שו"ע שם. יז רא"ש פ"ח סי' יג. טור ושו"ע ס"ג. יח ראה לבוש ס"ג. יט ב"ח ד"ה ומ"ש וכן. כ מ"א סוף סק"א. כא כדלקמן סי' תריח ס"א. כב כדלקמן שם ס"ב.

הַבְּקִיאִים.[כג] וְכֵן אִם מַאֲכִילִין אוֹתוֹ עַל פִּי עַצְמוֹ שֶׁאוֹמֵר צָרִיךְ אֲנִי – נוֹתְנִים לוֹ עַד שֶׁיֹּאמַר דַּי.[כד]

אֶלָּא שֶׁצָּרִיךְ לִזָּהֵר לְהַאֲכִיל אוֹתוֹ פָּחוֹת פָּחוֹת מִכְּשִׁעוּר, כְּמוֹ שֶׁיִּתְבָּאֵר בְּסִימָן תרי"ח:[כה]

ד יוֹלֶדֶת תּוֹךְ שְׁלֹשָׁה יָמִים – לֹא תִתְעַנֶּה כְּלָל,[כו] אֲפִלּוּ אוֹמֶרֶת אֵינִי צְרִיכָה – מַאֲכִילִין אוֹתָהּ[כז] בְּעַל כָּרְחָהּ.[כח] וּמִכָּל מָקוֹם יֵשׁ לְהַאֲכִילָהּ פָּחוֹת פָּחוֹת מִכְּשִׁעוּר,[כט] כְּמוֹ שֶׁיִּתְבָּאֵר בְּסִימָן תרי"ח.[ל]

מִשְּׁלֹשָׁה יָמִים עַד סוֹף שִׁבְעַת יָמִים לְלֵדָתָהּ, אִם אָמְרָה צְרִיכָה אֲנִי לֶאֱכֹל[לא] אַף עַל פִּי שֶׁחַבְרוֹתֶיהָ[לב] וְכֵן הָרוֹפְאִים[לג] אוֹמְרִים שֶׁאֵינָהּ צְרִיכָה – אַף עַל פִּי כֵן מַאֲכִילִין אוֹתָהּ מִיָּד[לד,7] פָּחוֹת פָּחוֹת מִכְּשִׁעוּר, כְּמוֹ שֶׁיִּתְבָּאֵר שָׁם.[לה]

מִכָּאן וְאֵילָךְ – הֲרֵי הִיא כִּשְׁאָר חוֹלֶה שֶׁאֵין בּוֹ סַכָּנָה,[לו] לְפִי שֶׁבְּוַדַּאי אֵין שׁוּם סַכָּנָה מֵחֲמַת הַלֵּדָה לְאַחַר שִׁבְעָה יָמִים לְלֵדָתָהּ. לְפִיכָךְ אֲפִלּוּ אִם אָמְרָה צְרִיכָה אֲנִי לֶאֱכֹל מֵחֲמַת צַעַר הַלֵּדָה – אֵין מַאֲכִילִין אוֹתָהּ, כֵּיוָן שֶׁאֵין סַכָּנָה בַּדָּבָר. אֲבָל אִם אָמְרָה צְרִיכָה אֲנִי לֶאֱכֹל מֵחֲמַת שֶׁמִּתְכַּבֵּד עָלַי חָלְיִי – מַאֲכִילִין אוֹתָהּ[לז]

what [they] recommend. Similarly, when food is given to [a sick person because] he himself says, "I need [to eat]," it should be given until he says that it is sufficient. One must be particular, however, to give it in small amounts, each less than the minimum measure [for which one is liable], as will be explained in sec. 618[:13].

4 Within three days of childbirth, a woman should not fast at all. Even if she says, "I do not need [to eat]," she should be served food against her will. Nevertheless, it should be given to her in small amounts, each less than the minimum measure [for which one is liable], as will be explained in sec. 618[:13].

[The following procedure applies] between the end of the third day and the end of the seventh day after childbirth. If she says, "I need to eat," then even though her peers and the doctors likewise say that there is no need for this, she should immediately be given food[7] (in small amounts, each less than the minimum measure [for which one is liable], as explained there).

Beyond [seven days after childbirth] she is considered as any sick person whose condition is not dangerous, for after seven days she is certainly not in any danger arising from the birth. Therefore, even if she said, "Because of the suffering of the birth I must eat," she should not be given food, because no risk is involved.

However, if she said, "I must eat because illness is overcoming me," she should

---

7. In this matter, the requests of a sick person should likewise be granted even in the face of contrary medical opinion (sec. 618:1).

כג רמב"ן בתורת האדם שער הסכנה ד"ה עוברה. רא"ש שם. ר"ן (ג, ב) ד"ה גמ׳. טור ולבוש ס"ג. מ"א סק"ב. כד כדלקמן שם ס"א. כה סי"ג, וש"נ. כו רמב"ן בתורת האדם שער הסכנה ד"ה ובשאלתות. רא"ש פ"ח סי׳ י. ר"ן (א, א) ד"ה ולענין. טור ושו"ע ס"ד. כז ב"ח סוף הסי׳. מ"א סק"ג. וכדלעיל סי׳ של ס"ד לענין חילול שבת. וראה שם אם גם הרופא אומר שאינה צריכה. כח כדלקמן סי׳ תריח סי"ב. כט מ"א שם. ל סעיף יג. לא רמב"ן שם. רא"ש שם. טור ושו"ע שם. לב ב"ח סי׳ של ד"ה ומ"ש כל. לג אליה זוטא שם סק"ב (אפילו מאה רופאים). וכ"ה לעיל שם ס"ה. וראה גם לקמן סי׳ תריח סוף ס"א (בחולה). לד ובסתמא ובאינה יודעת, ראה לקמן סוף ס"ה. לה סעיף יג. לו שבת קכט, א. וראה גם לעיל סי׳ של ס"ה. לז איסור והיתר כלל ס סי׳ ב. אליה זוטא סק"א.

כְּדֶרֶךְ שֶׁמַּאֲכִילִין כָּל חוֹלֶה שֶׁאוֹמֵר צָרִיךְ אֲנִי, כְּמוֹ שֶׁיִּתְבָּאֵר שָׁם,[לח] עַיֵּן שָׁם:

be given food in the same manner that it is given to any sick person who says, "I must [eat]," as explained in [sec. 618:1].

ה שְׁלֹשֶׁת יָמִים אֵלּוּ, וְכֵן שִׁבְעַת יָמִים אֵלּוּ – אֵין מוֹנִין אוֹתָם מֵעֵת לְעֵת, כְּגוֹן אִם יָלְדָה בְּז' בְּתִשְׁרֵי אַחַר חֲצוֹת הַיּוֹם – אֵין מְחַשְּׁבִין הַשְּׁלֹשָׁה יָמִים עַד אַחַר חֲצוֹת הַיּוֹם שֶׁל יוֹם הַכִּפּוּרִים, אֶלָּא מְחַשְּׁבִין אוֹתָם לְפִי סֵדֶר יְמֵי בְּרֵאשִׁית,[8] וְיוֹם הַכִּפּוּרִים הוּא יוֹם רְבִיעִי לְלֵדָתָהּ.[לט]

וְאִם[מ,9] אָמְרָה אֵינִי צְרִיכָה – אֵין מַאֲכִילִין אוֹתָהּ כְּלָל.[מא] אֲבָל בִּסְתָם שֶׁאֵינָהּ אוֹמֶרֶת כְּלוּם,[מב] אוֹ שֶׁאוֹמֶרֶת שֶׁאֵינָהּ יוֹדַעַת אִם הִיא צְרִיכָה – מַאֲכִילִין אוֹתָהּ, אֶלָּא אִם כֵּן שֶׁחַבְרוֹתֶיהָ אוֹ הָרוֹפְאִים אוֹמְרִים שֶׁאֵינָהּ צְרִיכָה, שֶׁאָז אֵין מַאֲכִילִין אוֹתָהּ,[מג] אֶלָּא אִם כֵּן אָמְרָה בְּפֵרוּשׁ צְרִיכָה אֲנִי לֶאֱכֹל:[מד]

5 The three days and the seven days [referred to above in subsection 4] are not counted from hour to hour. For example, if a woman gave birth on the seventh of Tishrei after midday, the three days are not counted as continuing until after midday on Yom Kippur, but according to the days of the week.[8] Thus, [in the above situation,] Yom Kippur is considered the fourth day after she gave birth.

If, [between the end of the third day and the end of the seventh day after childbirth,[9]] she said, "I do not need [to eat]," she should not be given food at all. If she simply said nothing, or if she said that she did not know whether she needed [to eat], she should be given food, unless her friends or doctors say that she does not need [to eat]. In such a case she should not be given food unless she explicitly says, "I need to eat."

סימן תריח דִּין חוֹלֶה בְּיוֹם הַכִּפּוּרִים וּבוֹ י"ח סְעִיפִים:

SECTION 618 Laws Relating to a Sick Person on Yom Kippur. (1–18)

א חוֹלֶה שֶׁהוּא אוֹמֵר צָרִיךְ אֲנִי לֶאֱכֹל,[א,1] אַף עַל פִּי שֶׁאֵינוֹ אוֹמֵר שֶׁאִם לֹא יֹאכַל אֶפְשָׁר שֶׁיִּסְתַּכֵּן,[ב,2] אֶלָּא

1 [The following principles apply with regard to] a sick person who says, "I need to eat"[1] — even when he does not say that if he does not eat, [his life] might be endangered.[2]

---

8. Lit., "the days of creation," implying that each day begins at nightfall and ends the following evening.

9. This paragraph reverts to the subject of the second paragraph of subsection 4 above.

SECTION 618

1. *Yoma* 82a, 83a.

2. A sick person is permitted to eat only when his life is endangered, not merely because he feels severe discomfort. Nevertheless, there is no need for him to explicitly state that he feels mortal danger. As long as he knows that it is Yom Kippur, it is assumed that unless he felt such danger he would not request food.

לח סעיף א. לט תרומת הדשן סי' קמח. שו"ע ס"ד. וכ"ה לעיל סי' של ס"ו. וראה שו"ת צמח צדק או"ח סי' סג, בשם מהרי"ל, להקל ברכה וענוגה פחות מכשיעור. מ חוזר לדין משלשה עד סוף שבעה, דלעיל ס"ד. מא רמב"ן בתורת האדם שער הסכנה ד"ה ובשאלתות. ר"ן (א, א) ד"ה ולענין. מב משמעות הרמב"ן והר"ן שם. וכדלעיל סי' של ס"ה לענין חילול שבת. מג ראה לעיל שם, וש"נ. מד כדלעיל ס"ד.

סימן תריח: א משנה פב, א. טור ושו"ע ס"א. ב הגהת סמ"ק סי' רכא אות ב, בשם ר"י. הגהות מיימוניות פ"ב אות ה, בשם ר"ת. טור, לפירוש הב"ח

לְאַחַר שֶׁהוֹדִיעוּהוּ שֶׁהַיּוֹם הוּא יוֹם הַכִּפּוּרִים[ג] אוֹ שֶׁיּוֹדֵעַ מֵעַצְמוֹ שֶׁהַיּוֹם הוּא יוֹם הַכִּפּוּרִים[ד] וְאוֹמֵר תְּנוּ לִי לֶאֱכֹל,[ה] אוֹ שֶׁאוֹמֵר אֵינִי יָכוֹל לִסְבֹּל הַתַּעֲנִית מֵחֲמַת חֳלִי,[ו] וְכַיּוֹצֵא בִּלְשׁוֹנוֹת אֵלּוּ שֶׁנִּרְאֶה מֵהֶם כַּוָּנָתוֹ שֶׁאַף עַל פִּי שֶׁהוּא יוֹדֵעַ שֶׁהַיּוֹם הוּא יוֹם הַכִּפּוּרִים אַף עַל פִּי כֵן רְצוֹנוֹ לֶאֱכֹל – מַאֲכִילִין אוֹתוֹ מִיָּד, עַד שֶׁיֹּאמַר דַּי,[ז] לְפִי שֶׁאֵין אָנוּ מַחֲזִיקִים אוֹתוֹ לְרָשָׁע,[ח] וּמִן הַסְּתָם הוּא מַרְגִּישׁ בְּעַצְמוֹ שֶׁהוּא צָרִיךְ לְכָךְ, שֶׁ"הַלֵּב יוֹדֵעַ מָרַת נַפְשׁוֹ".[ט,3]

וּלְפִיכָךְ אֲפִלּוּ מֵאָה רוֹפְאִים אוֹמְרִים שֶׁאֵינוֹ צָרִיךְ לֶאֱכֹל,[י] וַאֲפִלּוּ הֵם אוֹמְרִים שֶׁהַמַּאֲכָל מַזִּיק לוֹ[יא] – שׁוֹמְעִין לַחוֹלֶה,[4] שֶׁבְּוַדַּאי הוּא צָרִיךְ לְכָךְ, כֵּיוָן שֶׁהוּא יוֹדֵעַ שֶׁהַיּוֹם יוֹם הַכִּפּוּרִים וְאַף עַל פִּי כֵן הוּא מְבַקֵּשׁ לֶאֱכֹל:

If, after he is informed that it is Yom Kippur, or [it is obvious] that he himself knows that it is Yom Kippur, he [nevertheless] says "Give me [food] to eat," or "I cannot bear the fast because of my sickness," or any similar expression indicating that even though he knows it is Yom Kippur he wishes to eat, he should immediately be given food until he says, "Enough."

[The rationale:] It is not assumed that he is a wicked person [who desires to violate the prohibition]. The assumption is that he feels that he requires this [food], for a person's own heart knows the bitterness of his soul.[3] Therefore, even if a hundred doctors say that he does not need to eat, and even if they say that food will harm him, it is the words of the patient that are to be heeded.[4] [It is assumed that] he certainly needs [to eat], because he knows that it is Yom Kippur, and he nevertheless requests food.

ב וַאֲפִלּוּ אִם הַחוֹלֶה אוֹמֵר אֵינִי צָרִיךְ לֶאֱכֹל וְיֵשׁ שָׁם רוֹפֵא[יב] אֲפִלּוּ הוּא נָכְרִי[יג] וְאוֹמֵר שֶׁהוּא צָרִיךְ לֶאֱכֹל[יד] – מַאֲכִילִין אוֹתוֹ עַל פִּיו, וְהוּא שֶׁיְּהֵא בָּקִי.[טו,5] וְאַף עַל פִּי שֶׁאֵין

2 Even though the patient himself says that [he] does not have to eat, but there is a doctor — even a non-Jew — who says that he must eat, the patient should be given food as directed by the doctor, provided he is an expert.[5]

---

3. Cf. *Mishlei* 14:10.

4. *Yoma* 83a. *Radvaz* (Vol. 4, Responsum 66) maintains that the patient's word is accepted against the doctor's only with regard to food, but not with regard to medicines. Sec. 328:12 in the present work discusses similar issues with regard to the prohibition of taking medication on *Shabbos*. If a patient requests medicine on *Shabbos*, then even if a doctor thinks that it is unnecessary, the patient's request is respected. If, however, the doctor deems the medicine to be harmful, his warning should be heeded.

The author of *Aruch HaShulchan* (618:5-6) disagrees with the distinction drawn by *Radvaz*. He maintains that if a patient is so ill as to be bedridden, we do not rely on the principle that he is more knowledgeable about his condition than the doctor.

5. *Yoma* 83a.

ד"ה ומ"ש שמאחר. הובא בב"י ריש הסימן. **ג** סמ"ק שם. טור. לבוש ס"א. **ד** הגהות מיימוניות שם בשם ר"ת. ב"ח שם. אליה זוטא סק"ב. **ה** סמ"ק שם. ב"ח שם. **ו** הגהות מיימוניות שם. ב"ח שם. עטרת זקנים ס"ק א. **ז** משנה שם. **ח** לבוש סוף ס"א. **ט** משלי יד, י. גמרא פג, א. לבוש שם. וראה גם לעיל סי' שכח סי"ב. **י** גמרא שם. טור ושו"ע שם. וראה גם לעיל סי' תריז ס"ד (ביולדת). **יא** שו"ת רדב"ז ח"ד סי' סו. כנסת הגדולה הגה"ט. מ"א סק"ג. וראה לעיל שם (לענין תרופה בשבת). **יב** משנה פב, א (ע"פ בקיאין). גמרא פג, א (רופא אומר צריך כו'). טור ושו"ע ס"א. **יג** מהרי"ק שורש קנט. שו"ע שם. וכ"ה לקמן ס"ו וש"נ. וראה לקמן הל' נדה סי' קפז סקל"ו. שו"ת צמח צדק יו"ד סי' קמח אות ב. **יד** רא"ש פ"ח סי' יג (דאין לך רופא שיאמר אם לא יאכל שמא ימות). **טו** משנה פב, א. רמב"ם פ"ב ה"ח. טור ושו"ע שם.

הָרוֹפֵא אוֹמֵר שֶׁאִם לֹא יֹאכַל יִסְתַּכֵּן, רַק שֶׁאוֹמֵר שֶׁאֶפְשָׁר שֶׁיַּכְבִּיד עָלָיו חָלְיוֹ – מַאֲכִילִין אוֹתוֹ, לְפִי שֶׁאָנוּ חוֹשְׁשִׁין שֶׁמָּא יַכְבִּיד עָלָיו חָלְיוֹ וְיִסְתַּכֵּן.[טז] וְאַף עַל פִּי שֶׁהַחוֹלֶה בְּעַצְמוֹ אוֹמֵר שֶׁאֵינוֹ צָרִיךְ – אֵין אֲמִירָתוֹ נֶחְשֶׁבֶת לִכְלוּם כְּדֵי שֶׁנַּחְמִיר עָלָיו בִּשְׁבִיל אֲמִירָתוֹ, דְּשֶׁמָּא מֵחֲמַת טֵרוּף הַדַּעַת הוּא אוֹמֵר כֵּן,[יז] שֶׁאֵינוֹ מַרְגִּישׁ בְּחָלְיוֹ מֵחֲמַת רֹב חֻלְשָׁה,[יח] וּסְפֵק נְפָשׁוֹת לְהָקֵל:[יט,6]

[Moreover,] even if the doctor does not say that if the patient does not eat he will be endangered, but merely that his illness might possibly intensify, the patient should be given food, for fear that such deterioration may lead to mortal danger. Even though the patient says that he does not have to eat, his statement carries no weight in justifying a stringent ruling, for he may have spoken out of confusion and distress, being so weak that he is unaware of [the severity of] his illness. [Hence the rule applies:] Whenever a question of life and death is in the balance, the lenient ruling is to be followed.[6]

ג רוֹפֵא אֶחָד אוֹמֵר שֶׁהוּא צָרִיךְ לֶאֱכֹל וְרוֹפֵא אֶחָד אוֹמֵר שֶׁאֵינוֹ צָרִיךְ לֶאֱכֹל,[כ] אִם הַחוֹלֶה אֵינוֹ אוֹמֵר כְּלוּם אוֹ שֶׁאוֹמֵר אֵינִי יוֹדֵעַ[כא] – מַאֲכִילִין אוֹתוֹ, שֶׁסְּפֵק נְפָשׁוֹת לְהָקֵל,[כב,6] אֲבָל אִם גַּם הַחוֹלֶה אוֹמֵר אֵינִי צָרִיךְ – אֵין מַאֲכִילִין אוֹתוֹ,[כג] כֵּיוָן שֶׁיֵּשׁ רוֹפֵא אֶחָד שֶׁאוֹמֵר כְּמוֹתוֹ – אֵין אָנוּ תּוֹלִים אֲמִירָתוֹ בְּטֵרוּף הַדַּעַת:[כד]

3 [The following principles apply if] one doctor says that [the patient] must eat and another doctor says that it is not necessary. If the sick person does not say anything, or if he says that he does not know, he should be given food, for whenever a question of life and death is in the balance, the lenient ruling is to be followed.[6]

If, however, the patient himself also says that he does not need [to eat], he should not be given food. Since one doctor shares his opinion, it is not assumed that he spoke out of confusion and distress.

ד אִם הַחוֹלֶה אֵין אוֹמֵר כְּלוּם אוֹ שֶׁאוֹמֵר אֵינִי יוֹדֵעַ, וְרוֹפֵא אֶחָד אוֹמֵר שֶׁהוּא צָרִיךְ לֶאֱכֹל וּשְׁנֵי רוֹפְאִים אוֹמְרִים שֶׁאֵינוֹ צָרִיךְ – אֵין מַאֲכִילִין אוֹתוֹ,[כה] לְפִי שֶׁאֵין דְּבָרָיו שֶׁל אֶחָד בִּמְקוֹם שְׁנַיִם.[כו] וְאִם הָאֶחָד הוּא מֻפְלָג

4 If the patient says nothing or if he says that he does not know, and one doctor says that he needs to eat, and two doctors say that he does not need [to eat], the patient should not be given food, because one voice does not outweigh two.

If, however, the first [doctor] is distinguished for his expertise when compared to

---

6. In the original *(ibid.), safek nefashos — lehakel.*

טז רא"ש שם. ב"ח ריש הסי'. מ"א סק"ב. יז גמרא פג, א לפרש"י ד"ה תונבא. לבוש ס"א. ט"ז סק"ב. יח לבוש שם. יט גמרא שם. ב"י ד"ה ומ"ש אם. לבוש שם. וראה גם לעיל סי' שכח ס"י. סי' שכט ס"ב. כ רמב"ם פ"ב ה"ח. שו"ע ס"ב. וראה גם לעיל סי' שכח ס"י. כא מ"מ שם. אליה זוטא סק"ג. כב גמרא שם. לבוש ס"ב. ט"ז סק"ד. כג גמרא שם. טור ושו"ע ס"ג. כד רמב"ן בתורת האדם שער הסכנה ד"ה חולה. הובא ברא"ש פ"ח סי' יג (ואין דבריו של אחד במקום שנים, כדלקמן ס"ד). כה משמעות הגמרא שם (בהא דלעיל ס"ג). טור ושו"ע שם. כו רמב"ן ורא"ש שם. ב"י שם. לבוש שם. כז רמב"ן שם. טור ולבוש

the two [doctors] who say that the patient need not eat, his words should be respected: the ruling should be lenient and the patient should be given food, because a question of life and death is involved.

בְּחָכְמָה נֶגֶד שְׁנַיִם הָאוֹמְרִים שֶׁאֵינוֹ צָרִיךְ – חוֹשְׁשִׁין לִדְבָרָיו לְהָקֵל וּלְהַאֲכִילוֹ,[כז] כֵּיוָן שֶׁהוּא סְפֵק סַכָּנַת נְפָשׁוֹת:[כח]

5 If, however, two doctors state that the patient must eat,[5] then even if a hundred doctors say that he does not have to eat, and even if the patient himself says that he does not have to eat, he should be given food. [This applies] even when the hundred who say that he does not have to eat are greater experts and are more distinguished for their knowledge than the two [who rule leniently. For] in an uncertainty involving life and death, a stringent ruling is not determined by greater wisdom or greater numbers. Instead, since two [doctors] who are knowledgeable in this discipline say that the patient must eat, they are considered as distinguished experts. We see [a parallel] to this in [the laws of] testimony. There, by Scriptural decree, two witnesses are considered equivalent to a hundred.

ה אֲבָל אִם שְׁנֵי רוֹפְאִים אוֹמְרִים שֶׁהוּא צָרִיךְ לֶאֱכֹל,[5] אֲפִלּוּ מֵאָה אוֹמְרִים שֶׁאֵינוֹ צָרִיךְ, וַאֲפִלּוּ אִם גַּם הַחוֹלֶה אוֹמֵר שֶׁאֵינוֹ צָרִיךְ – מַאֲכִילִין אוֹתוֹ.[כט] וַאֲפִלּוּ אִם הָאוֹמְרִים שֶׁאֵינוֹ צָרִיךְ הֵם יוֹתֵר מֻמְחִים וְהֵן מֻפְלָגִים בְּחָכְמָה נֶגֶד אֵלּוּ הַשְּׁנַיִם[ל] – אֵין הוֹלְכִין בִּסְפֵק נְפָשׁוֹת אַחַר רֹב חָכְמָה וְלֹא אַחַר רֹב מִנְיַן דֵּעוֹת לְהַחְמִיר,[לא] אֶלָּא כֵּיוָן שֶׁשְּׁנַיִם אוֹמְרִים שֶׁהוּא צָרִיךְ לֶאֱכֹל וְהֵן בְּקִיאִים בְּחָכְמָה – הֲרֵי הֵן חֲשׁוּבִין כְּמוֹ חֲכָמִים מֻפְלָגִים, כְּמוֹ שֶׁמָּצִינוּ לְעִנְיַן עֵדוּת שֶׁשְּׁנַיִם חֲשׁוּבִים כְּמֵאָה[לב] מִגְּזֵרַת הַכָּתוּב:[לג]

6 In this context, a doctor who is a woman or a non-Jew is equivalent to the most legally competent Jewish male,[7] whether [that doctor's] opinion is more lenient or more stringent. [That doctor's] word is trusted to outweigh the opinion of the most legally competent Jewish doctor, according to the guidelines discussed above.

ו אִם הָרוֹפֵא הוּא אִשָּׁה אוֹ נָכְרִי – הֲרֵי הוּא כְּכָשֵׁר שֶׁבְּיִשְׂרָאֵל לְעִנְיָן זֶה,[7] בֵּין לְהָקֵל בֵּין לְהַחְמִיר, וְנֶאֱמָן לְהַכְחִישׁ רוֹפֵא הַכָּשֵׁר שֶׁבְּיִשְׂרָאֵל,[לד] וְעַל דֶּרֶךְ שֶׁנִּתְבָּאֵר:[לה]

7 [Even] if the patient says that he does not need [to eat] and [even if] a doctor says that he does not know whether he must

ז אִם הַחוֹלֶה אוֹמֵר שֶׁאֵינוֹ צָרִיךְ וְהָרוֹפֵא אוֹמֵר שֶׁאֵינוֹ יוֹדֵעַ אִם הוּא

---

7. Witnesses in court must be Jewish, male, and not have disqualifying character faults. None of these restrictions apply to doctors. Here the critical criterion is medical proficiency.

ס"ג. ט"ז ומ"א סק"ה. כח רמב"ן שם. לבוש שם. כט גמרא שם כאוקימתא בתרא. מסקנת הרמב"ן שם. רא"ש פ"ח סי' יג. טור ושו"ע ס"ד. ל משמעות רא"ש שם וטור. רמ"א ס"ב. ראה מ"א ס"ק ד. לא רמב"ן שם. רא"ש שם (לענין רוב דעות). ב"ח ד"ה ומ"ש ולא נהירא (בדעת הרא"ש והטור, לענין רוב חכמה). לב גמרא שם. לג ראה משנה מכות ה, ב. רמב"ם הל' עדות פי"ח ה"ג. לד רא"ש פ"ח סי' יד בשם ריב"א. מ"א סק"א. וראה גם לעיל ס"ב וש"נ. לה סעי' ג־ה.

צָרִיךְ לֶאֱכֹל,[לו] שֶׁאֶפְשָׁר שֶׁאֵין שׁוּם חֲשָׁשׁ וְסָפֵק כְּלָל שֶׁיַּכְבִּיד עָלָיו חָלְיוֹ מֵחֲמַת מְנִיעַת הָאֲכִילָה[לז] – מַאֲכִילִין אוֹתוֹ, לְפִי שֶׁאִם הָיָה הָרוֹפֵא אוֹמֵר שֶׁיּוֹדֵעַ לוֹ שֶׁיֵּשׁ חֲשַׁשׁ סָפֵק בַּדָּבָר שֶׁמָּא יַכְבִּיד עָלָיו חָלְיוֹ הָיוּ מַאֲכִילִים אוֹתוֹ,[לח] לָכֵן גַּם עַכְשָׁו שֶׁהוּא מְסֻפָּק בָּזֶה מַאֲכִילִין אוֹתוֹ, שֶׁכָּל סְפֵק נְפָשׁוֹת הוֹלְכִין לְהָקֵל[לט] אֲפִלּוּ בְּכַמָּה וְכַמָּה סְפֵקוֹת:[מ]

eat, since possibly there is no [reason] whatever for concern or doubt that the illness will intensify because food was withheld, food should be given to him. [The rationale is that] if the doctor had said that he knew that there was [reason] for concern or doubt that the illness would intensify, the patient would have been given food. Therefore even now, when the doctor is undecided, [the patient] should be given food. For whenever a question of life and death is in the balance, the lenient ruling is to be followed, even if there are many cumulative doubts involved.

ח אֲבָל אִם הָרוֹפֵא אוֹמֵר שֶׁאֵינוֹ צָרִיךְ וְהַחוֹלֶה אֵינוֹ יוֹדֵעַ – אֵין מַאֲכִילִין אוֹתוֹ,[מא, 8] לְפִי שֶׁאֵינוֹ יוֹדֵעַ שֶׁל חוֹלֶה לָאו כְּלוּם הוּא, שֶׁרֻבָּן שֶׁל חוֹלִים אֵינָן יוֹדְעִין וּבְקִיאִין בְּחָלְיֵי שֶׁלָּהֶן.[מב] אֲבָל אִם הַחוֹלֶה הוּא בְּעַצְמוֹ גַּם כֵּן רוֹפֵא בָּקִי וְהוּא מַכִּיר בְּחָלְיוֹ וְאוֹמֵר אֵינִי יוֹדֵעַ אִם צָרִיךְ לֶאֱכֹל בְּיוֹם הַכִּפּוּרִים – מַאֲכִילִין אוֹתוֹ,[מג] לְפִי שֶׁאִלּוּ הָיָה אוֹמֵר צָרִיךְ הָיוּ מַאֲכִילִין אוֹתוֹ, לָכֵן גַּם עַכְשָׁו שֶׁאוֹמֵר אֵינִי יוֹדֵעַ מַאֲכִילִין אוֹתוֹ מִסָּפֵק:

8 If, however, a doctor says that there is no need for [the patient to eat] and the patient himself does not know, he should not be given food.[8] The patient's statement that he does not know is of no consequence, for most patients do not know, nor are they knowledgeable with regard to their illness.

[The ruling is different] if the patient is himself an expert doctor and is knowledgeable with regard to his illness. If he says that he does not know whether he must eat on Yom Kippur, he should be given food. The rationale is that if he had said that he must eat, he would be given food. Therefore even now, when he says that he does not know, he should be given food because of the doubt involved.

ט וְאִם הָרוֹפֵא[9] אוֹמֵר שֶׁאֵינוֹ מַכִּיר אֶת חָלְיוֹ – הֲרֵי הוּא כִּשְׁאָר כָּל אָדָם, וְאֵין דְּבָרָיו מַעֲלִין כְּשֶׁאוֹמֵר צָרִיךְ אוֹ שֶׁאוֹמֵר אֵינִי יוֹדֵעַ שֶׁיֹּאכַל עַל פִּיו. וְכֵן כְּשֶׁאוֹמֵר אֵינוֹ צָרִיךְ – אֵין דְּבָרָיו

9 If a doctor[9] says that he is not knowledgeable about the patient's illness, he is like any other person and his opinion is of no consequence when he says that the sick person must eat or that he does not know.

Similarly, if [such a doctor] says that there

---

8. *Talmud Yerushalmi, Yoma* 8:4.

9. For example, the opinion of a dermatologist is of no consequence where the judgment of a cardiologist is required.

לו רבי יוחנן בירושלמי פ"ח ה"ד. טור ושו"ע ס"ה. לז ראה ב"ח ד"ה ואם חולה. ט"ז סק"ז. לח לבוש ס"ה. וכדלעיל ס"ב. לט ירושלמי שם. מ ראה לעיל סי' שכט ס"ג, וש"נ. מא רמב"ן בתורת האדם שער הסכנה ד"ה חולה. רא"ש פ"ח סי' יג. ר"ן (ד, ב) ד"ה ירושלמי. טור ושו"ע ס"ה. מב רמב"ן שם. לבוש ס"ה. ט"ז סק"ח. מג ט"ז שם. מד רבנו ירוחם נ"ז ח"ב (נא, ד). שו"ע ס"ו. מה איסור והיתר הארוך כלל ס אות א. רמ"א ס"ו. מו בראשית ט, ה. איסור

מוֹרִידִין כְּלָל.[מד] וְאִם הַחוֹלֶה (אוֹמֵר אֵינִי יוֹדֵעַ אוֹ שֶׁהַחוֹלֶה) אוֹמֵר אֵינִי צָרִיךְ וְרוֹפֵא אֶחָד אוֹמֵר צָרִיךְ – מַאֲכִילִין אוֹתוֹ, וְאֵין מַשְׁגִּיחִין בְּדִבְרֵי רוֹפֵא זֶה שֶׁאוֹמֵר אֵינוֹ צָרִיךְ, כֵּיוָן שֶׁאֵינוֹ מַכִּיר אֶת הַחֹלִי:

is no need for the patient to eat, his words are of no consequence. [Thus,] if the patient says (that [he] does not know or) that he does not have to [eat], and one [other] doctor says that he must [eat], the patient should be given food. No attention is paid to the words of the doctor who says that the patient need not [eat], since he is not familiar with this illness.

י אֲפִלּוּ בְּמָקוֹם שֶׁאֵין שָׁם רוֹפְאִים בְּקִיאִין שֶׁיַּאַמְדוּהוּ אִם הוּא צָרִיךְ לֶאֱכֹל, מִכָּל מָקוֹם אִם נֶחֱלַשׁ הַרְבֵּה עַד שֶׁנִּרְאֶה לְרֹב בְּנֵי אָדָם שֶׁאֶצְלוֹ שֶׁהוּא מְסֻכָּן – מַאֲכִילִין אוֹתוֹ:[מה]

10 Even in a place where there are no expert doctors to evaluate whether [the patient] must eat, if he becomes so weak that most of the people around him regard him as dangerously ill, he should be given food.

יא אִם הַחוֹלֶה יוֹדֵעַ בְּעַצְמוֹ שֶׁצָּרִיךְ לֶאֱכֹל וּמַחְמִיר עַל עַצְמוֹ וְאֵינוֹ אוֹכֵל – עָלָיו הַכָּתוּב אוֹמֵר[מו,10] "וְאַךְ אֶת דִּמְכֶם לְנַפְשֹׁתֵיכֶם אֶדְרֹשׁ וגו'":[11]

11 As to a patient who knows himself that he must eat, but is stringent with himself and does not eat, of him Scripture says,[10] "But I will demand the blood of your souls..."[11]

יב כָּל מָקוֹם שֶׁמֻּתָּר לֶאֱכֹל וְאֵינוֹ רוֹצֶה לֶאֱכֹל – מַאֲכִילִין אוֹתוֹ בְּעַל כָּרְחוֹ:[מז]

12 Whenever it is permitted for one to eat [on Yom Kippur] and he does not wish to eat, he should be fed against his will.

יג כְּשֶׁמַּאֲכִילִין אֶת הַחוֹלֶה[מח] שֶׁאֵינוֹ אוֹמֵר צָרִיךְ אֲנִי לֶאֱכֹל[מט] וּמַאֲכִילִין אוֹתוֹ עַל פִּי בְּקִיאִים,[נ,12] וְכֵן כְּשֶׁמַּאֲכִילִין אֶת הַמְעֻבֶּרֶת שֶׁהֵרִיחָה מַאֲכָל וְנִשְׁתַּנּוּ פָּנֶיהָ[נא,13] אוֹ כָּל אָדָם שֶׁנִּשְׁתַּנּוּ פָּנָיו מֵרֵיחַ הַמַּאֲכָל[נב]

13 [The following rules apply when,] following the advice of experts, food is given to a patient who does not say that he must eat.[12] They also apply to a pregnant woman who smells [the aroma of] food and her face begins to change [color][13] — or to any other person whose face changes color because he [smells] the aroma of food

10. *Bereishis* 9:5.

11. Since in his misguided piety he is exposing himself to danger, G-d will hold him answerable for the consequences.

12. Since the patient did not say that he must eat and he is being fed because of a doubt, efforts are made to minimize the extent of the prohibition involved. However, if he said he must eat or if doctors said he must eat, he is given food accordingly, regardless of the restrictions described below.

13. See sec. 617:2.

והיתר שם אות ח. שיירי כנסת הגדולה הגה"ט ס"ק ב. אליה זוטא סק"ב. **מז** שו"ת רדב"ז ח"ד סי' סז. שיירי כנסת הגדולה שם. אליה זוטא שם. וראה גם לעיל סי' שכח סי"א. בה"ג הל' יוה"כ (לב, א). רמב"ן בתורת האדם שער הסכנה ד"ה עוברה (אף בחולה). רא"ש פ"ח סי' יג. טור ושו"ע ס"ז. **מח** כריתות יג, א (במעוברת). **מט** שזה יתבאר לקמן סט"ו. **נ** כדלעיל ס"ב. **נא** כדלעיל סי' תריז ס"ב. **נב** כדלעיל שם ס"ג.

וְלֹא נִתְיַשְּׁבָה דַּעְתָּם בִּטְעִימַת הָרֹטֶב,[נג] וְכֵן כְּשֶׁמַּאֲכִילִין אֶת הַיּוֹלֶדֶת שֶׁאֵינָהּ אוֹמֶרֶת צְרִיכָה אֲנִי לֶאֱכֹל כְּגוֹן תּוֹךְ שְׁלֹשָׁה יָמִים לְלִדְתָּהּ[נד] — כָּל אֵלּוּ מַאֲכִילִין אוֹתָן מְעַט מְעַט כְּדֵי שֶׁלֹּא יִצְטָרֵף לְכְשִׁעוּר שֶׁנִּתְבָּאֵר בְּסִימָן תרי"ב[נה] שֶׁחַיָּבִים עָלָיו כָּרֵת וּמַלְקוֹת,[14] כְּדֵי לְהָקֵל מֵעֲלֵיהֶם מֵאִסּוּר כָּרֵת וּמַלְקוֹת לְאִסּוּר בִּלְבַד,[נו] לְכָךְ מַאֲכִילִין אוֹתוֹ בַּתְּחִלָּה פָּחוֹת מִכְּכוֹתֶבֶת[15] דְּהַיְנוּ כִּשְׁנֵי שְׁלִישֵׁי בֵּיצָה בֵּינוֹנִית[נז] אוֹ מְעַט יוֹתֵר, רַק שֶׁלֹּא יִהְיֶה קָרוֹב לְכְבֵיצָה[נח,16] שֶׁזֶּהוּ שִׁעוּר כְּכוֹתֶבֶת,[נט] וְאַחַר כָּךְ יִשְׁהוּ כְּדֵי אֲכִילַת אַרְבַּע בֵּיצִים,[ס] וּלְפָחוֹת יִשְׁהוּ כְּדֵי אֲכִילַת שָׁלֹשׁ בֵּיצִים[סא] (עַיֵּן סִימָן תרי"ב[סב,17]), וְיַחְזְרוּ וְיַאֲכִילוּהוּ כְּשִׁעוּר אֲכִילָה רִאשׁוֹנָה:[סג]

יד וְהַשְּׁתִיָּה[18] — יִבְדְּקוּ בַּחוֹלֶה עַצְמוֹ

— who was not satisfied when given a taste of the sauce. They apply similarly to a woman within three days of childbirth, who does not say that [she] must eat.

A person in any of these situations should be given small portions at a time, so that when combined they will not add up to the measure defined in sec. 612[:1], for which one is liable for *kares* and lashes.[14] [In this way,] this person's liability will be reduced from [that associated with a violation punishable by] *kares* or lashes to the mere violation of the prohibition [against eating even less than the required measure].

For this reason, such a person is initially given less than the size of a date,[15] i.e., two-thirds the size of an average-sized egg or slightly more, but not approaching the size of an egg;[16] this is the measure of the size of a date. Afterwards, [his attendants] should wait the time it takes to eat four eggs, or at least the time it takes to eat three eggs (see sec. 612[:4]),[17] and then give him the initial measure again.

14 With regard to drinking,[18] it should first be determined how much a particular

14. The violation of Yom Kippur is punishable by *kares*. And a person whose brazen transgression incurs *kares* is given lashes *(Rambam, Hilchos Sanhedrin* 1:18*)*.

15. The strictest measure given for the size of a date *(kekoseves)* is 30 grams/cc. (R. Avraham Chayim Naeh, *Shiurei Torah*). If that is not sufficient, one may rely on the opinions that calculate this measure as 38 or even 48 grams/cc.

16. I.e., an egg without its shell. R. Avraham Chayim Naeh defines this measure — *kebeitzah*, the size of an egg — as 43 grams according to the stricter opinion, and otherwise as 53.8 grams *(op. cit.* 3:9-10*)*. Generally, 57.6 grams is given as the average weight of an egg, but that includes its shell.

17. The unit of time called *kdei achilas pras*, the time it takes to eat half a loaf of bread, is variously held to equal the time it takes to eat four eggs, or three. The halachic definitions of this unit of time vary from 3 to 9 minutes. (See *Sefer HaMinhagim: The Book of Chabad-Lubavitch Customs*, p. 93, footnote 343.) Based on *Shiurei Torah* (3:15), the accepted Lubavitch practice is to consider *kdei achilas pras* as 4 minutes when defining the timeframe within which one must eat the statutory *kezayis* of *matzah* at the *Seder* of Pesach, but as 9 minutes with regard to eating on Yom Kippur.

18. As stated in sec. 612:2 above, the measure for which one is liable for drinking on Yom Kippur is

נג לבוש ס"ז. וראה לעיל שם סוף ס"ב (במוסגר) שגם את הרוטב יתנו פחות פחות מכשיעור. נד מ"א סי' תריז סק"ג. וכ"ה לעיל שם רס"ד. נה סעי' א, ג, ד שהוא ככותבת בכדי אכילת פרס. נו בה"ג ורמב"ן ורא"ש שם. וראה גם לעיל סי' תריב סט"ז. נז ר"ן (ג, א) ד"ה ונמצינו. שו"ע שם. וראה לקו"ש ח"ז ע' 112 בשוה"ג. נח מ"א סק"ו. נט כדלעיל סי' תריב ס"א. ס ר"ן שם. שו"ע שם. סא מ"א סק"ז. סב סעיף ד. סג לבוש סוף ס"ז. סד ר"ן שם. שו"ע שם. סה שו"ע

כַּמָּה הִיא כְּדֵי שֶׁיְּסַלְּקֶנּוּ לְצַד אֶחָד וְיֵרָאֶה כִּמְלֹא לֻגְמָיו[סד] וְיַשְׁקוּהוּ פָּחוֹת מֵאוֹתוֹ שִׁעוּר,[סה] וְיִשְׁהוּ כְּדֵי אֲכִילַת אַרְבַּע בֵּיצִים,[סו] וּלְפָחוֹת יִשְׁהוּ כְּדֵי אֲכִילַת שָׁלֹשׁ בֵּיצִים,[סז] וּלְכָל הַפָּחוֹת לֹא יִפְחֲתוּ מִלִּשְׁתּוֹת כְּדֵי שְׁתִיַּת רְבִיעִית (עַיֵּן סִימָן תרי"ב[סח]), וְיַחְזְרוּ וְיַשְׁקוּהוּ כְּשִׁעוּר שְׁתִיָּה רִאשׁוֹנָה.

וְאִם אֲמָדוּהוּ הָרוֹפְאִים[סט] אוֹ שְׁאָר בְּקִיאִין (כְּגוֹן בְּיוֹלֶדֶת שֶׁרֹב נָשִׁים בְּקִיאוֹת בְּצָרְכֵיהֶן וְיֵשׁ לָהֶן נֶאֱמָנוּת[ע] כְּמוֹ שֶׁנִּתְבָּאֵר בְּסִימָן ש"ל[עא]) שֶׁאֵין שִׁעוּרִים הַלָּלוּ מַסְפִּיקִין לוֹ, אוֹ שֶׁנִּסְתַּפְּקוּ בַּדָּבָר[עב] — מַאֲכִילִין וּמַשְׁקִין אוֹתָן כָּל צָרְכָּן מִיָּד כְּפִי מַה שֶּׁיֹּאמְרוּ הַבְּקִיאִין:

patient's cheekful contains; [i.e., not an entire cheekful, but the amount of liquid which] if moved to one side of his mouth would look like a cheekful. He should be given less than this amount. [His attendants] should then wait the amount of time necessary to eat four eggs, or at least the amount of time necessary to eat three eggs, or at the very least the amount of time necessary to drink a *revi'is* (see sec. 612[:15]). He should then be given the same measure to drink again.

If, however, doctors or other knowledgeable people (for example, most women know the needs of a woman after childbirth, and their word can be relied upon, as stated in sec. 330[:4-5]) assess that these limited quantities are insufficient or if they are unsure about this, the patient should immediately be given all the food and drink he needs, as prescribed by these knowledgeable individuals.

טו אֲבָל אִם הַמְעֻבֶּרֶת אוֹ הַיּוֹלֶדֶת בְּתוֹךְ שִׁבְעָה יָמִים אוֹ הַחוֹלֶה יוֹדְעִים בְּעַצְמָם שֶׁצְּרִיכִים לֶאֱכֹל[עג] — אֲזַי אֵין מְדַקְדְּקִים עִמָּהֶם בְּכָל שִׁעוּרִים הַלָּלוּ, אֶלָּא נוֹתְנִים לִפְנֵיהֶם מַאֲכָל, וְאוֹמְרִים לוֹ יוֹם כִּפּוּר הוּא[עד] וְאִם אַתָּה יוֹדֵעַ[עה] אוֹ שֶׁמִּסְתַּפֵּק לְךָ[עו] שֶׁמָּא יֵשׁ חֲשַׁשׁ סַכָּנָה אִם לֹא תֹּאכַל כְּשִׁעוּר — אֱכֹל כְּשִׁעוּר, וְאִם לָאו — אֱכֹל פָּחוֹת מִכְּשִׁעוּר,[עז] וְהוּא יֹאכַל כְּפִי מַה שֶּׁיֵּרָאֶה בְּעֵינָיו:

15 If a patient — a pregnant woman, or a woman who is within seven days of childbirth, or a sick person — knows himself that he must eat, we do not show concern for any of these measures. Instead, we place food before him and say: "Today is Yom Kippur. If you know — or if you think it is possible — that you will be in [mortal] danger if you do not eat more than the minimum quantity [for which one is held liable], eat [that quantity, or more]. If not, eat less than that quantity at recurring intervals." The person will then eat in whatever way appears appropriate in his own eyes.

---

a cheekful *(melo lugmav)*. Though this is not a standard measure, the Sages gave general guidelines. On that basis, *Shiurei Torah* (3:14) maintains that for an average person, a cheekful can be considered as 42 cc., which is approximately half a *revi'is* (a full *revi'is* being calculated as 86 cc.). See sec. 612:12 above. A person who anticipates the possibility that he will need to drink in small amounts *(leshiurin)* on Yom Kippur is referred to sec. 612, footnote 30 there.

ס"ח. וראה גם ר"ן שם. **סו** ר"ן שם. שו"ע שם. **סז** ראה ר"ן שם. **סח** סעיף טו. **סט** רמב"ן ורא"ש ור"ן שם. טור ושו"ע ס"ח. **ע** הלכות ומנהגי מהר"ש סי' ריג אות ב. מהרי"ל הל' יום כפור (ע' שלה). ב"ח סוף הסימן. מ"א סוף סק"ח. **עא** סעיף ד. **עב** ר"ן שם. שו"ע שם. **עג** ר"ן ושו"ע שם (שהחולה אומר כן). **עד** מהר"ש שם. מהרי"ל שם (ע' שלד). ב"ח שם. ט"ז ס"ק ט. מ"א ס"ק ח. **עה** ט"ז שם. **עו** לבוש ס"ח. **עז** ט"ז שם.

טז מִי שֶׁאֲחָזוֹ בֻּלְמוּס,[עח] וְהוּא חֳלִי הַבָּא מֵחֲמַת רְעָבוֹן וְסִימָנוֹ שֶׁעֵינָיו כֵּהוֹת וְאֵינוֹ יָכוֹל לִרְאוֹת[עט] – מַאֲכִילִין אוֹתוֹ עַד שֶׁיֵּאוֹרוּ עֵינָיו.[19] וְאִם אֵין שָׁם מַאֲכָל שֶׁל הֶתֵּר – מַאֲכִילִין אוֹתוֹ מַאֲכָל שֶׁל אִסּוּר.[פ] וְאִם יֵשׁ כָּאן שְׁנֵי מִינֵי אִסּוּרִים אֶחָד חָמוּר מֵחֲבֵרוֹ – מַאֲכִילִין אוֹתוֹ הַקַּל תְּחִלָּה,[פא] שֶׁמָּא יַסְפִּיק לוֹ זֶה בִּלְבַד:

16 If a person is seized by *bulmus,* an ailment caused by hunger whose symptom is that his vision is dimmed and he cannot see, he should be given food until his sight is restored.[19] If there is no kosher food available, he may be given non-kosher food. If there are two types of forbidden food, one governed by a more serious prohibition than the other, we give him the one governed by the lesser prohibition first, [in the hope that] it alone will be sufficient for him.

יז אִם צָרִיךְ לְבָשָׂר וְיֵשׁ כָּאן בְּהֵמָה שֶׁצְּרִיכִים לְשָׁחֲטָהּ[20] וּבְשַׂר נְבֵלָה מוּכֶנֶת[פב, 21] – עַיֵּן בְּסִימָן שכ"ח:[פג, 22]

17 [The laws that apply when a patient] requires meat, there is an animal that must be slaughtered,[20] and meat is also available from an animal that was not ritually slaughtered,[21] [are discussed in] sec. 328[:16].[22]

יח חוֹלֶה שֶׁאָכַל בְּיוֹם הַכִּפּוּרִים וְנִתְיַשְּׁבָה דַּעְתּוֹ בְּעִנְיָן שֶׁיָּכוֹל לְבָרֵךְ בִּרְכַּת הַמָּזוֹן[23] – צָרִיךְ לְהַזְכִּיר שֶׁל יוֹם הַכִּפּוּרִים בְּבִרְכַּת הַמָּזוֹן, שֶׁיֹּאמַר "יַעֲלֶה וְיָבוֹא" בְּ"בוֹנֵה יְרוּשָׁלָיִם".[פד, 24] וְאִם חָל בְּשַׁבָּת – יֹאמַר גַּם כֵּן "רְצֵה".[פה] אֲבָל אֵינוֹ צָרִיךְ לִבְצֹעַ עַל שְׁתֵּי כִּכָּרוֹת, וְגַם אֵינוֹ צָרִיךְ לְקַדֵּשׁ עַל הַיַּיִן וְלֹא עַל הַפַּת, מִשּׁוּם שֶׁלֹּא תִּקְּנוּ חֲכָמִים דְּבָרִים אֵלּוּ בְּיוֹם הַכִּפּוּרִים:[פו]

18 When a patient who ate [out of necessity] on Yom Kippur becomes composed and is able to recite the Grace After Meals,[23] he should mention Yom Kippur in the Grace; i.e., he should add the passage *Yaaleh VeYavo* in the blessing *Boneh Yerushalayim.*[24] If Yom Kippur falls on *Shabbos,* he should also add the passage beginning *Retzeh.* He is not, however, required to recite a blessing over two loaves of bread, nor is he required to recite *Kiddush* over wine or over bread, because the Sages did not ordain such matters for Yom Kippur.

19. *Yoma* 83a.

20. This would involve the performance of a labor that is forbidden on this day.

21. This would involve eating forbidden food.

22. There the Alter Rebbe states that the patient should be given the kosher meat.

23. Concentration is an essential requirement for the Grace after Meals. Now, having eaten, he will have the requisite composure.

24. This ruling also appears in sec. 188:11. The author of *Shaar HaKollel* 34:9 argues that the fact that the Alter Rebbe did not mention the recitation of *Yaaleh VeYavo* in his *Siddur* indicates that he later reversed his opinion and held that it should be omitted. R. Avraham Chayim Naeh differs and maintains that the Alter Rebbe nevertheless holds that the passage should be recited. (See Rav Chayim Naeh's *Piskei Siddur,* sec. 185.)

עח משנה פג, א. טור ושו"ע ס"ט. **עט** רש"י שם ד"ה מי. טור ושו"ע שם. **פ** משנה שם. טור ושו"ע שם. **פא** גמרא [ברייתא] שם. טור ושו"ע שם. **פב** רמ"א ס"ט. **פג** סעיף טז. **פד** שו"ת מהר"ם מרוטנבורג (פראג) סי' עא. רא"ש הובא בטור. שו"ע ס"י. וראה לעיל סי' קפח סוף סי"א שהביא דעת רבנו אביגדור שבשבלי הלקט (סי' שיב) שאין צריך להזכיר יעלה ויבוא ביוה"כ (ומציין לכאן, שהובאה דעה זו במ"א ס"ק י), ושלכן אם שכח ונזכר קודם ברכת הטוב והמטיב לא יברך אשר נתן. וגם בסידור לא נזכרה ברכה זו ביוה"כ. וראה שער הכולל פל"ד אות ט. פסקי הסידור אות קפה. **פה** כנסת הגדולה הגה"ט. מ"א סקי"א. **פו** מ"א סק"י.

סימן תריט סֵדֶר לֵיל יוֹם הַכִּפּוּרִים וּבוֹ י״ח סְעִיפִים:

א לֵיל יוֹם הַכִּפּוּרִים נוֹהֲגִין שֶׁקֹּדֶם שֶׁמִּתְפַּלְּלִין מַתִּירִים[1] לְכָל הָעֲבַרְיָנִים,[א] וְהֵן הָעוֹבְרִים עַל גְּזֵירוֹת וְחֶרְמוֹת הַקָּהָל[ב] מַתִּירִין לָהֶן כְּדֵי שֶׁנּוּכַל לְהִתְפַּלֵּל עִמָּהֶם[ג,2] בַּאֲגֻדָּה אַחַת,[ד,3] שֶׁאָמְרוּ חֲכָמִים[ה,4] כָּל תַּעֲנִית צִבּוּר שֶׁאֵין בּוֹ מִפּוֹשְׁעֵי יִשְׂרָאֵל — אֵינוֹ תַּעֲנִית, שֶׁהֲרֵי חֶלְבְּנָה רֵיחָהּ רַע וּמְנָאָהּ הַכָּתוּב[ו,5] עִם סַמָּנֵי הַקְּטֹרֶת.[6]

וְכֵיצַד מַתִּירִין לָהֶם? הַגָּדוֹל שֶׁבַּקָּהָל מְצָרֵף עִמּוֹ שְׁנֵי אֲנָשִׁים, כְּדֵי שֶׁהֵם יִהְיוּ מְשֻׁלָּחִים שֶׁל כָּל הַקָּהָל לְהַתִּיר לָהֶם.[7] וְאִם הַגָּדוֹל שֶׁבַּקָּהָל

SECTION 619 The Order of [the Prayers on] the Night of Yom Kippur. (1–18)

1 Before the prayer service on the night of Yom Kippur, a limited reprieve[1] is customarily granted to all the transgressors — i.e., to those who have violated the decrees and bans imposed by the community — so that we can pray together with them[2] as one united group.[3] As our Sages taught,[4] "Any communal fast that does not include the sinners of Israel is not a fast [that evokes G-d's mercy] — for galbanum has an unpleasant odor, yet the Torah lists it[5] among the spices of the incense offering."[6]

How is this limited reprieve granted to them? The congregant of the highest spiritual standing has two members of the congregation join him to represent the entire congregation to grant the reprieve [to the transgressors].[7] If the congregant of the highest spiritual standing is

---

1. This concept cannot be translated by one unequivocal word, because some of the classical authorities, including the *Bach,* understand it (minimally) as granting no more than license to join the congregational service, whereas others, including the Alter Rebbe, understand it (maximally) as granting a certain degree of reprieve. The phrase "limited reprieve" (or "permissive remission") attempts to span that range of meanings.

2. As to praying together with a person who was excommunicated, see *Yoreh Deah* 334:11, and sec. 55:14 in Vol. 1 of the present work.

3. In the original, "one united group" is *agudah achas.* The noun *agudah* is borrowed here from the phrase, *Vaagudaso al eretz yesadah (Amos* 9:6*).* As understood by *Rashi* at the straightforward level of interpretation known as *pshat,* this phrase means that G-d established the community of His creatures on the earth. On the non-literal level of interpretation known as *derush,* Abbaye learns from this phrase (as spelled out by *Rashi* on *Kerisos* 6b) that only when all His creatures are together, as one *agudah,* are they lastingly established on the earth *(al eretz yesadah).*

4. *Kerisos, loc. cit.*

5. *Shmos* 30:35.

6. Likewise, the willow represents those individuals who are distinguished neither for their study of the Torah nor for their observance of the commandments. Yet the *mitzvah* that also includes the prestigious *lulav* and *esrog* and *hadassim* cannot be observed unless they join forces with the humble willow *(Perishah, Orach Chayim* 619:1*).*

7. As is the practice in many other circles, three (or, according to Lubavitch custom, three or more) Torah scrolls are taken out of the Ark, and the congregants holding them stand around the *sheliach tzibbur,* together constituting a *beis din.* (On the number of scrolls taken out, see *HaMelech BiMesibo,* Vol. 2, p. 21.)

The *sheliach tzibbur* recites the statement beginning *Al-Daas HaMakom* three times in an undertone *(Sefer HaMinhagim: The Book of Chabad-Lubavitch Customs,* p.

א טור ושו״ע ס״א. ב מרדכי רמז תשכה. לבוש ס״א. ג מרדכי שם. תשב״ץ סי׳ קלא. טור. ד אביי כריתות ו, ב (ואגודתו). מרדכי שם. ה רב שמעון חסידא כריתות שם. מרדכי שם. טור. ו שמות ל, לז.

הוּא שְׁלִיחַ צִבּוּר[8] (קָבוּעַ בָּעִיר) – אֵינוֹ צָרִיךְ לְצָרֵף עִמּוֹ שׁוּם אָדָם לְהַתִּיר לָהֶם, לְפִי שֶׁיָּדוּעַ שֶׁהוּא שְׁלִיחַ הַצִּבּוּר, וַהֲרֵי זֶה כְּאִלּוּ כָּל הַקָּהָל הִתִּירוּ לָהֶם:[ז] וְיֹאמַר בְּזֶה הַלָּשׁוֹן "בִּישִׁיבָה שֶׁל מַעְלָה וּבִישִׁיבָה שֶׁל מַטָּה, עַל דַּעַת הַמָּקוֹם וְעַל דַּעַת הַקָּהָל, אָנוּ מַתִּירִין לְהִתְפַּלֵּל עִם הָעֲבַרְיָנִים",[ח] כְּלוֹמַר שֶׁהַיְשִׁיבוֹת מַסְכִּימוֹת לְצָרֵף דַּעַת הַמָּקוֹם לְדַעַת הַקָּהָל לְהַתִּיר לָהֶם. וְלֹא יֹאמַר[ט] בַּתְּחִלָּה "עַל דַּעַת הַמָּקוֹם וְעַל דַּעַת הַקָּהָל" וְאַחַר כָּךְ "בִּישִׁיבָה שֶׁל מַעְלָה כו'":[י,9]

also the (town's permanent) *sheliach tzibbur*,[8] he does not need to have others join him to grant the remission, for it is known that he is the emissary of the congregation. Thus it is as if the entire congregation granted it to them.

He should say the following words: "By the authority of the Heavenly tribunal and by the authority of the earthly tribunal, with the sanction of the Omnipresent and with the sanction of the congregation, we grant license to pray together with the sinners"; i.e., the tribunals agree to join G-d's sanction to that of the congregation to grant [the sinners] license.

One should not begin by saying "With the sanction of the Omnipresent and with the sanction of the congregation" and only then say "By the authority of the Heavenly tribunal…."[9]

ב וְאַחַר כָּךְ אוֹמֵר הַשְּׁלִיחַ צִבּוּר "כָּל נִדְרֵי כו'".[יא] וְיֹאמַר "מִיּוֹם הַכִּפּוּרִים זֶה עַד יוֹם כִּפּוּרִים הַבָּא עָלֵינוּ לְטוֹבָה כו'",[יב] וְנוֹהֲגִין כֵּן כְּדֵי לְהַתְנוֹת עַל כָּל נְדָרִים שֶׁיִּדְּרוּ בְּשָׁנָה הַבָּאָה שֶׁיִּהְיוּ בְּטֵלִים,[יג,10] לְפִי שֶׁאֵין הָעוֹלָם נִזְהָרִים

2 The *sheliach tzibbur* then recites *Kol Nidrei*. The expression he should use is "from this Yom Kippur until the next Yom Kippur (may it come to us favorably)…," because the intent of this traditional wording is to stipulate that all the vows to be undertaken in the coming year are to be of no effect.[10] [The rationale for this is that] people are not

124), but loudly enough to be heard by the three people around him who constitute the *ad hoc* Rabbinical Court.

8. Throughout this context, the terms *chazzan* and *sheliach tzibbur* are used interchangeably. In common parlance, the appelation *chazzan* is sometimes reserved for a professional with superior musical sophistication.

9. Notwithstanding the above, the *machzor* of *Chabad* — like generic *machzorim* — differs (see *Likkutei Mahariach*).

Today's *machzor* of *Chabad* evolved by gradual stages. In 5701 (1941), Agudas Chabad appended *Machzor Berditchev*, 5673 (1913), ed. R. Chaim Eliezer Bichovsky — one of the many existing *machzorim* that followed the liturgical rite known as *Nussach Ari* — to the classic *Siddur Torah Or*. A paperback edition compiled by the Rebbe, including only the prayers that are unique to the Days of Awe, first appeared in 5709 (1949). It was intended for use together with a *Siddur*, where the reader would find all the other, more familiar passages. The current self-contained edition entitled *Machzor HaShalem* first appeared in 5713 (1953), and has since been amplified and translated.

10. And not to release any vows (*nedarim*) undertaken in the past year (*Tosafos* on *Nedarim* 23b, *s.v. Ve'es*).

ז ט"ז סק"א. ח תשב"ץ שם (בנוסח שלנו). טור ושו"ע שם. ט ט"ז ס"ק ב. י שכן הנוסח בתשב"ץ המובא בב"י ריש הסימן, ובמחזורים, וכ"ה נוסח חב"ד (ראה אוצר מנהגי חב"ד יוה"כ ע' רה). ונוהגים לאמרו שלש פעמים ובקול נמוך (ספר המנהגים – חב"ד ע' 58), אך באופן שגם ב' האנשים העומדים עמו ישמעו (אוצר מנהגי חב"ד שם). יא הרי"ץ גיאת (ע' ס) בשם הגאונים (מיום כיפורים שעבר עד היום הזה). ראבי"ה סוס"י תקכח. רא"ש פ"ח סי' כח. טור ושו"ע ס"א. יב רבנו תם בספר הישר סי' קמד (חלק החידושים סי' ק), ובתוס' נדרים כג, ב ד"ה ואת. הובא ברא"ש פ"ח סי' כח וטור. לבוש ס"א. ולענין התרת נדרים של ערב ר"ה, ראה סדור (סדר התרת נדרים) שעושים שניהם (התרה על העבר ומסירת מודעה על העתיד), וש"נ. יג ר"ת שם, ע"פ נדרים כג.

בִּנְדָרִים וְעוֹבְרִים עַל[11] "לֹא יַחֵל דְּבָרוֹ",[יד] לְכָךְ מְבַטְּלִין אוֹתָן בַּתְּחִלָּה קֹדֶם שֶׁיָּחוּלוּ, שֶׁהַתְּנַאי מוֹעִיל לְבַטֵּל הַנֶּדֶר שֶׁלֹּא יָחוּל כְּלָל כְּמוֹ שֶׁיִּתְבָּאֵר בְּיוֹרֶה דֵעָה סִימָן רי"א[טו, 12] (וְעַיֵּן שָׁם כָּל דִּינֵי בִּטּוּל הַנֶּדֶר), וּלְכָךְ צָרִיךְ לוֹמַר "אִיחֲרַטְנָא בְּהוֹן כו'",[טז] כְּלוֹמַר כָּל הַנְּדָרִים שֶׁאֶדֹּר בַּשָּׁנָה הַבָּאָה אֲנִי מִתְחָרֵט עֲלֵיהֶן מֵעַכְשָׁו וּמַתְנֶה עֲלֵיהֶן שֶׁיִּהְיוּ בְּטֵלִין:[יז, 13]

mindful with regard to vows and thus they transgress the prohibition,[11] "He shall not desecrate his word." Vows are therefore nullified at the outset, before they take effect — for a stipulation can nullify a vow so that it should not take effect at all, as stated in *Yoreh Deah,* sec. 211[12] (where all the laws governing the nullification of vows may be found). For this reason, the wording to be used is *icharatna behon,* implying that as to "all the vows that I will take in the coming year, I regret them from the present time and stipulate that they will be of no effect."[13]

ג וְגַם כָּל הַקָּהָל יֹאמְרוּ "כָּל נִדְרֵי כו'" בְּלַחַשׁ עִם הַשְּׁלִיחַ צִבּוּר[יח] (וְעַיֵּן בְּיוֹרֶה דֵעָה שָׁם[יט] דְּצָרִיךְ לוֹמַר בְּקוֹל רָם מְעַט בְּעִנְיָן שֶׁיְּהֵא נִשְׁמָע לְהָעוֹמְדִים אֶצְלוֹ), כְּדֵי שֶׁיַּתְנֶה כָּל אֶחָד וְאֶחָד בִּפְנֵי עַצְמוֹ עַל נְדָרָיו שֶׁיִּדֹּר בַּשָּׁנָה הַבָּאָה,[כ] שֶׁאֵין תְּנַאי הַשְּׁלִיחַ צִבּוּר מוֹעִיל לַאֲחֵרִים,[כא] וּלְכָךְ נִתַּקֵּן בִּלְשׁוֹן יָחִיד "דְּאִינְדַּרְנָא",[כב] אוֹ "דִּי נְדַרְנָא",[כג] אוֹ "דִּנְדַרְנָא",[כד, 14]

3 The entire congregation should also recite *Kol Nidrei* in a whisper together with the *sheliach tzibbur.* (See *Yoreh Deah, loc. cit.,* [which states that] one should recite it in a slightly raised voice so that it may be heard by the people standing nearby.) Every individual will [thus] make a stipulation concerning the vows he will undertake in the coming year, for the stipulation made by the *sheliach tzibbur* is not effective with regard to other individuals. This is why it was ordained that [the operative verbs] should be expressed in the singular: *de'indarna, di nedarna, dinedarna,*[14]

---

11. *Bamidbar* 30:3.

12. This section is not extant in the Alter Rebbe's *Shulchan Aruch;* see the *Shulchan Aruch* of R. Yosef Caro, sec. 211:2, and *Rama, ad loc.,* gloss #1.

13. Early texts for the annulment of vows on the eve of Yom Kippur addressed vows that were made from the preceding Yom Kippur until the present Yom Kippur. Rabbeinu Tam *(Tosafos, loc. cit.)* objects to this on a number of grounds, and maintains that this annulment is a form of notice relating to vows that may be declared in the coming year. Accordingly, the wording of this passage was changed from the past tense to the future or infinitive tense. But then, as the *Tur* asks, how could the term "regret" be used here, which surely relates to the past? This the Alter Rebbe explains here: One means that if he should vow during the coming year, his regret is already in place as of now, before the fact.

A further nuance: *Tosafos (loc. cit.)* writes *"de'icharatna,"* which could mean (as clarified by the *Bach*) "provided that I regret." The Alter Rebbe, however, follows *Magen Avraham* (619:2), and keeps the traditional term *"icharatna,"* which implies a regret from now on future vows, not being contingent upon whether or not there will actually be a later regret.

14. These are three variants of the same term.

ב (וגם יוה"כ נקרא ר"ה). **יד** במדבר כט, ג. לבוש שם. **טו** סימן זה בשוע"ר לא הגיע לידינו, וראה שו"ע שם ס"ב. רמ"א שם ס"א. **טז** רא"ש וטור שם בשם ר"ת. רבנו ירוחם נתיב ז ח"א (נ, ד). מ"א סק"ב. **יז** רא"ש וטור שם בשם ר"ת. וכ"ה הנוסח בהתרת נדרים (מסירת המודעה) שבסדור. **יח** רא"ש שם (בנוסח כל נדרי שעל העבר). לבוש ס"א (גם בנוסח שלנו שעל להבא). מ"א סק"ו. **יט** ש"ך סי' ריא סק"ב. **כ** לבוש שם. **כא** לבוש שם. מ"א שם. **כב** ב"ח סוד"ה ומ"ש כבר. לבוש שם. **כג** דרכי משה הארוך אות א. מ"א סק"ב. **כד** רא"ש שם. ב"ח שם.

"אוֹ דְּאִשְׁתַּבַּעְנָא",[כה] "אוֹ דְּאַחֲרִימְנָא[כו] כו'", כְּלוֹמַר מַה שֶּׁאֶדּוֹר וְאֶשָּׁבַע וְאַחֲרִים וְאֶאֱסוֹר נְכָסַי, בֵּין עַל נַפְשִׁי בֵּין עַל נְפָשׁוֹת אֲחֵרוֹת, "מִיּוֹם כִּפּוּרִים זֶה עַד יוֹם הַכִּפּוּרִים כו'"[15] (וְלֹא יֹאמַר דִּי נָדַרְנָא בְּקָמָ"ץ תַּחַת נוּ"ן רִאשׁוֹנָה, לְפִי שֶׁמַּשְׁמָעוּתָהּ הוּא שֶׁנָּדַרְתִּי כְּבָר[כז]):

de'ishtabana, or *de'acharimna.* [That is to say:] "Whatever vows and oaths that I undertake, or commitments to dedicate [property] for sacred use or to forbid its use by myself or by others, from this Yom Kippur until the coming Yom Kippur — [may they be nullified]."[15]

(In the phrase *di nedarna,* the first *nun* should not be vocalized with a *kamatz,* for that would imply "[those] that I have already vowed.")

ד וְנוֹהֲגִין לְהַתְחִיל "כָּל נִדְרֵי" מִבְּעוֹד יוֹם,[כח,16] דְּאֵין מַתִּירִין נְדָרִים בְּשַׁבָּת וְיוֹם טוֹב,[כט,17] וְאַף עַל פִּי שֶׁאֵין אָנוּ מַתִּירִין הַנְּדָרִים שֶׁלְּעָבַר אֶלָּא אָנוּ מְבַטְּלִין הַנְּדָרִים שֶׁלְּהַבָּא,[ל] מִכָּל מָקוֹם הוּא דּוֹמֶה קְצָת לְהַתָּרַת נְדָרִים,[לא] וְיֵשׁ לָחוּשׁ שֶׁמָּא יִטְעוּ לוֹמַר מַתִּירִין נְדָרִים בְּשַׁבָּת וְיוֹם טוֹב. וּמִטַּעַם זֶה נוֹהֲגִין לְהַעֲמִיד שְׁנֵי אֲנָשִׁים אֵצֶל הַשְּׁלִיחַ צִבּוּר בְּשָׁעָה שֶׁאוֹמֵר "כָּל נִדְרֵי", כְּדֵי שֶׁלֹּא יִטְעוּ לוֹמַר מַתִּירִין נְדָרִים בְּיָחִיד:[לב]

4 It is customary to begin *Kol Nidrei* while it is still day,[16] because vows are not released on *Shabbos* and festivals.[17] Though we are not releasing past vows but are nullifying future vows, [the statement] somewhat resembles the release of vows. Thus there is cause for concern that people may mistakenly think that vows may be released on *Shabbos* and festivals. [Indeed,] it is for this reason that two men are customarily instructed to stand next to the *sheliach tzibbur* when he recites *Kol Nidrei,* so that [people] will not mistakenly think that vows can be released by one [judge].

ה וְנוֹהֲגִין שֶׁהַשְּׁלִיחַ צִבּוּר אוֹמֵר אוֹתוֹ ג' פְּעָמִים,[לג] וְכָל פַּעַם מַגְבִּיהַּ הַקּוֹל יוֹתֵר מִבָּרִאשׁוֹנָה,[לד] לְפִי שֶׁבְּדֶרֶךְ זוֹ נִשְׁמָע בְּאֵימָה וּבְיִרְאָה.[לה]

5 It is customary for the *sheliach tzibbur* to recite *[Kol Nidrei]* three times, each time in a louder voice. In this manner, it will be listened to with awe and reverence.

---

15. In the foregoing explanation, the Alter Rebbe addresses an apparent anomaly noted by the *Levush* (619:1): *de'indarna* ("vows… that I undertake" or "that I shall vow") is in the singular, whereas *nafshasana* ("upon ourselves") is in the plural. In resolution, the Alter Rebbe explains that each individual's declaration ("I vow") relates to any or all of us ("upon ourselves"), for one individual may have vowed to forbid himself the use of our assets.

16. Thus it would actually be recited before the onset of Yom Kippur. This was not the practice of the Rebbes. (See *Otzar Minhagei Chabad,* p. 202.)

17. See sec. 341:1.

כה רא"ש שם. לבוש שם. כו לבוש שם. כז ראה לבוש שם. כח מהרי"ל הל' ליל יום כפור (ע' שכו). רמ"א ס"א. ומנהג חב"ד שאין מדקדקין בזה (אוצר מנהגי חב"ד יוה"כ ע' רב אות קכא). כט רא"ש פ"ח סי' כח, וטור (שלכן אומרים אותו קודם ברכו). מהרי"ל שם. וכדלעיל סי' שמא ס"א. ל כדלעיל ס"ב. לא ב"ח ד"ה ומ"ש וכבר. מ"א סק"ה. אליה זוטא סק"ב. לב ב"ח שם. אליה זוטא שם. לג רא"ש פ"ח סי' כח. מרדכי רמז תשכו. רמ"א ס"א. לד מהרי"ל שם (ע' שכז). רמ"א שם. לה מהרי"ל שם. דרכי משה ס"ק ב. לו מהרי"ל שם (ע' שכו). רמ"א שם. לז מ"א סק"ו. וראה לעיל סי' רסז ס"ב. לח הרי"ץ גיאת (ע'

He should then continue chanting until nightfall so that the Evening Service will [begin] at the appropriate time.

6 The *sheliach tzibbur* then recites the verse beginning *VeNislach*[18] three times and the congregation recites the verse *VaYomer A-donai*[19] three times.[20]

One should not deviate from a town's local custom, even with regard to the liturgical hymns or melodies,[21] so that he will not disturb the concentration of the congregants.

7 The *sheliach tzibbur* should then recite the blessing *Shehecheyanu* without a cup [of wine].[22] [The rationale is that] Yom Kippur is a [festival] that comes at appointed intervals, and hence the blessing *Shehecheyanu* should be recited, as is done on all the festivals. Nevertheless, the blessing cannot be recited over a cup [of wine,[23] even] while it is still day, for by reciting the blessing [that praises G-d for] "enabling us to reach this season," the individual has accepted Yom Kippur upon himself,[24] and thus may not drink from the cup. Nor may he recite the blessing over the cup of wine and

וּמַמְשִׁיךְ בְּנִגּוּנִים עַד הַלַּיְלָה,[לו] כְּדֵי לְהִתְפַּלֵּל עַרְבִית בִּזְמַנָּהּ:[לז]

ו וְאַחַר כָּךְ אוֹמֵר הַשְּׁלִיחַ צִבּוּר[לח] ג' פְּעָמִים[לט] "וְנִסְלַח כו'",[מ, 18] וְהַקָּהָל אוֹמְרִים ג' פְּעָמִים[20] "וַיֹּאמֶר ה' כו'".[מא, 19]

וְאַל יְשַׁנֶּה אָדָם מִמִּנְהַג הָעִיר אֲפִלּוּ בְּפִיּוּטִים אוֹ בְּנִגּוּנִים שֶׁמְּנַגְּנִים שָׁם,[מב, 21] שֶׁלֹּא יְבַלְבֵּל דַּעַת הַקָּהָל:[מג]

ז וְאַחַר כָּךְ אוֹמֵר הַשְּׁלִיחַ צִבּוּר "שֶׁהֶחֱיָנוּ" בְּלֹא כוֹס,[מד, 22] לְפִי שֶׁיּוֹם הַכִּפּוּרִים הוּא דָּבָר הַבָּא מִזְּמַן לִזְמַן וְצָרִיךְ לְבָרֵךְ "שֶׁהֶחֱיָנוּ" כְּמוֹ בְּכָל הָרְגָלִים,[מה] אֶלָּא שֶׁאִי אֶפְשָׁר לְבָרֵךְ עַל הַכּוֹס[23] מִבְּעוֹד יוֹם, מִשּׁוּם שֶׁכֵּיוָן שֶׁבֵּרַךְ שֶׁ"הִגִּיעָנוּ לִזְמַן הַזֶּה" – הֲרֵי קִבֵּל עָלָיו יוֹם הַכִּפּוּרִים,[24] וְאָסוּר לוֹ לִשְׁתּוֹת מִן הַכּוֹס, וְגַם אִי אֶפְשָׁר לְבָרֵךְ עַל הַכּוֹס

---

18. *Bamidbar* 15:26.

19. *Ibid.* 14:20.

20. In practice, according to the *machzor* of *Chabad,* the sequence is as follows: The verse beginning *VeNislach* is first recited three times by the *sheliach tzibbur* and then three times by the congregants. The *sheliach tzibbur* then recites the verse beginning *Slach Na (Bamidbar* 14:19*)*, followed by the two words *vesham ne'emar.* The congregants respond by reciting the following verse, beginning *VaYomer A-donai,* three times. Finally, the *sheliach tzibbur* repeats the same verse three times.

21. Which are not integral components of the prayer service.

22. *Eruvin* 40b.

23. As would be appropriate, and as is the practice on other festivals when *Shehecheyanu* is recited in the course of *Kiddush*.

24. By saying this, he has indicated that he is already in the midst of the festival.

A practical corollary: Though a woman usually accepts the incoming *Shabbos* at candlelighting, in exceptional circumstances she may have in mind that this should not yet take effect (see sec. 263:7). However, should she wish to do the same on the eve of *Yom-Tov* or of Yom Kippur, she should not recite the blessing *Shehecheyanu* at candlelighting, for by doing so she will already have accepted the sanctity of that day.

ס) בשם הגאונים. ראבי"ה סוס"י תקכח. טור. מהרי"ל הל' ליל יום כפור (ע' שכח). **לט** מנהגים (טירנא) מנהג יוה"כ (ע' קט). רמ"א ס"א. **מ** במדבר טו, כו. **מא** במדבר יד, כ (סלחתי כדבריך). מנהגים ורמ"א שם. ומנהג חב"ד שאומר החזן פסוק (שם יד, יט) סלח נא לעון גו' (מנהגים, טירנא, שם), והחזן והקהל אומרים ג"פ ויאמר ה' גו' (אוצר מנהגי חב"ד יוה"כ ע' רה אות קלו). **מב** מהרי"ל הל' תפלת שחרית דיוה"כ (ע' שלט). רמ"א שם. **מג** מ"א סק"ז. **מד** גמרא עירובין מ, ב. טור ושו"ע ס"א. **מה** גמרא שם. רמב"ם הל' ברכות פי"א ה"ט. לבוש ס"א. וכדלעיל סי' תלב ס"ג וש"נ.

וְלִתֵּן מִמֶּנּוּ לְתִינוֹק,[מו] מִטַּעַם שֶׁנִּתְבָּאֵר בְּסִימָן תקנ"ו,[מז] עַיֵּן שָׁם:[25]

give it to a child [to drink], for the reason explained in sec. 556. Note [the explanation] there.[25]

ח וּמִן הַדִּין הָיָה נָכוֹן שֶׁכָּל הַקָּהָל יֵצְאוּ יְדֵי חוֹבָתָן בְּבִרְכַּת הַשְּׁלִיחַ צִבּוּר וְלֹא יְבָרֵךְ כָּל אֶחָד וְאֶחָד בִּפְנֵי עַצְמוֹ[מח, 26] לְפִי שֶׁ"בְּרָב עָם הַדְרַת מֶלֶךְ"[מט] כְּמוֹ שֶׁנִּתְבָּאֵר בְּסִימָן רצ"ח,[נ, 27] אֶלָּא שֶׁעַכְשָׁו עַל הָרֹב אֵין הַשְּׁלִיחַ צִבּוּר מְכַוֵּן כְּלָל לְהוֹצִיא אֲחֵרִים, לָכֵן יְבָרֵךְ כָּל אֶחָד וְאֶחָד לְעַצְמוֹ[נא] בְּלַחַשׁ,[28] וְיִזָּהֵר לְסַיֵּם קֹדֶם שֶׁיְּסַיֵּם הַשְּׁלִיחַ צִבּוּר כְּדֵי שֶׁיּוּכַל לַעֲנוֹת אָמֵן אַחַר בִּרְכַּת הַשְּׁלִיחַ צִבּוּר.[נב] וְכֵן הַדִּין בְּבִרְכַּת הַלֵּל.[נג, 29] וְכֵן הַדִּין בְּבִרְכַּת

8 According to the letter of the law, it would be appropriate for the entire congregation to fulfill their obligation with the blessing *[Shehecheyanu]* recited by the *sheliach tzibbur* instead of each one reciting it individually, for[26] "a king's glory is seen amidst a multitude of people," as stated in sec. 298[:20].[27] At present, however, since a *sheliach tzibbur* does not generally intend to fulfill the obligation on behalf of others, every individual should recite the blessing himself in a whisper,[28] [but] should take care to complete [the blessing] before the *sheliach tzibbur* does, so that he can respond *Amen* to his blessing.

A similar principle also applies to the recitation of the blessing before *Hallel*[29] and the blessing [recited before performing the

25. Sec. 556 of the Alter Rebbe's *Shulchan Aruch* is not extant. The corresponding section in the *Shulchan Aruch* of R. Yosef Caro states that when the fast of *Tishah BeAv* begins on *Motzaei Shabbos, Havdalah* should not be recited until Sunday night, when the fast ends. In a gloss at that point, *Magen Avraham* explains why we do not recite *Havdalah* on *Motzaei Shabbos* and let a child drink the wine: we fear that when he grows older he may rely on this recollection, and drink. See also sec. 621:4-6 below and footnotes.

26. *Mishlei* 14:28.

27. There the Alter Rebbe writes that when many people are present in a synagogue at the end of the Evening Service on *Motzaei Shabbos* and fire is brought in for *Havdalah,* one person should recite the blessing on behalf of them all.

28. Women and girls who recited the blessing *Shehecheyanu* at home when lighting the candles for the festival should not recite the blessing again now. This point should be publicized for it is the subject of a common mistake, whereby G-d's name is uttered in vain. (See *Sefer HaMinhagim: The Book of Chabad-Lubavitch Customs,* p. 134.)

29. On the festivals on which the entire *Hallel* is recited, the Lubavitch custom is that the congregants listen to the recitation of the blessing by the *sheliach tzibbur,* respond *Amen,* and then recite the blessing individually. On days when Half-*Hallel* is recited, the Alter Rebbe writes in his *Siddur* that the congregation should fulfill their obligation to recite the blessing by listening to the blessing recited by the *sheliach tzibbur*. However, the Rebbe once related that on Rosh Chodesh, the chassidim of former times would make a point of quietly reciting the blessing before *Hallel* individually *(Sichas Shabbos Parshas Masei,* 5741/1981*)*.

מו גמרא שם. טור. לבוש שם. מ"א סק"ד. מז סימן זה בשוע"ר לא הגיע לידינו, וראה מ"א שם ריש הסי'. וראה גם לקמן סי' תרכא ס"ד. מח ב"י סוד"ה כתב הכלבו. דרכי משה הארוך אות ד. של"ה מסכת יומא עמוד התשובה (רכח, רע"ב) ד"ה הלכתא. הובאו במ"א סק"ג. מט משלי יד, כח. ברכות נג, א כבית הלל. של"ה שם. נ סעיף כ. וראה לעיל סי' ריג ס"ו, שזהו במצות שמקיימים כולם ביחד (משא"כ בברכת תפילין וציצית, אם רצו אחד מברך לכולם כדי לקיים ברוב עם הדרת מלך ואם רצו כל אחד מברך לעצמו). וראה העו"ב תתה ע' 72. נא מ"א שם. ואלו שברכו שהחיינו בשעת הדלקת נרות לא יברכו עכשיו (ס' המנהגים – חב"ד ע' 63). נב מלבושי יום טוב (בלבוש סוף ס"א). אליה זוטא סק"ו. וכדלעיל סי' נא ס"ג. סי' נט ס"ד. סי' קפג ס"י. נג מ"א שם (שיברך לעצמו). וראה סידור סדר הלל, ובנסמן שם. נד מ"א שם (שיברך לעצמו). וראה לעיל סי' נט ס"ד שלא לענות אמן לאחר ברכת המצות או ברכת הנהנין.

mitzvah of] *lulav* [and *esrog*] in the synagogue.[30]

9 On both the night and the day of Yom Kippur, we say *Baruch Shem Kevod Malchuso LeOlam Vaed* in a loud voice. [The rationale for this is] that the *Midrash*[31] relates that "when Moshe ascended on high [to receive the Torah], he heard the angels praising the Holy One, blessed be He, [by saying] *Baruch Shem Kevod Malchuso LeOlam Vaed.* He brought [this expression of praise] down for the Jewish people, but commanded them to say it quietly — just like the man who stole a beautiful object from the king's palace and gave it to his wife, but told her, 'Do not adorn yourself with it except in the privacy of your home.' "

This is why throughout the year we say *[Baruch Shem Kevod Malchuso LeOlam Vaed]* in a whisper, but on Yom Kippur — when we resemble the angels, as stated in sec. 610[:9] — we say it aloud and publicly.

10 If [Yom Kippur] falls on *Shabbos,* the passage beginning *Vaychulu* is recited after *Shemoneh Esreh.* The *sheliach tzibbur* then recites the single blessing that summarizes the seven blessings of *Shemoneh Esreh,* and should conclude it with the words *Mekadesh HaShabbos.*[32] He does not mention Yom Kippur in this blessing, for the reason explained in sec. 268[:14].

We do not recite the passages of *Kabbalas Shabbos,*[33] but we do say *Mizmor Shir LeYom*

הַלּוּלָב[נד] שֶׁבְּבֵית הַכְּנֶסֶת:[נה, 30]

ט לֵיל יוֹם הַכִּפּוּרִים וּמָחֳרָתוֹ אוֹמְרִים "בָּרוּךְ שֵׁם כְּבוֹד מַלְכוּתוֹ לְעוֹלָם וָעֶד" בְּקוֹל רָם,[נו] לְפִי שֶׁאָמְרוּ בַּמִּדְרָשׁ[נז, 31] כְּשֶׁעָלָה מֹשֶׁה לַמָּרוֹם שָׁמַע לְמַלְאֲכֵי הַשָּׁרֵת שֶׁהָיוּ מְקַלְּסִין לְהַקָּדוֹשׁ בָּרוּךְ הוּא "בָּרוּךְ שֵׁם כְּבוֹד מַלְכוּתוֹ לְעוֹלָם וָעֶד", וְהוֹרִידוֹ לְיִשְׂרָאֵל, וְצִוָּה לָהֶם לְאָמְרוֹ בַּחֲשַׁאי, מָשָׁל לְאָדָם שֶׁגָּנַב חֵפֶץ נָאֶה מִתּוֹךְ פַּלְטֵרִין שֶׁל מֶלֶךְ וּנְתָנָהּ לְאִשְׁתּוֹ וְאָמַר לָהּ אַל תִּתְקַשְּׁטִי בּוֹ אֶלָּא בִּצְנִעָא בְּתוֹךְ בֵּיתֵךְ, לָכֵן כָּל הַשָּׁנָה אוֹמְרִים אוֹתוֹ בְּלַחַשׁ,[נח] אֲבָל בְּיוֹם הַכִּפּוּרִים שֶׁאָנוּ דּוֹמִין לְמַלְאָכִים כְּמוֹ שֶׁנִּתְבָּאֵר בְּסִימָן תר"י[נט] — אָנוּ אוֹמְרִים אוֹתוֹ בְּקוֹל רָם בְּפַרְהֶסְיָא:

י אִם חָל בְּשַׁבָּת אוֹמְרִים "וַיְכֻלּוּ" אַחַר תְּפִלַּת עַרְבִית, וְהַשְּׁלִיחַ צִבּוּר אוֹמֵר בְּרָכָה אַחַת מֵעֵין שֶׁבַע[ס] וְחוֹתֵם "מְקַדֵּשׁ הַשַּׁבָּת",[32] וְאֵינוֹ מַזְכִּיר יוֹם הַכִּפּוּרִים בִּבְרָכָה זוֹ[סא] מִטַּעַם שֶׁנִּתְבָּאֵר בְּסִימָן רס"ח.[סב]

וְאֵין אוֹמְרִים קַבָּלַת שַׁבָּת,[33] אֲבָל

30. The text refers to the practice of fulfilling the *mitzvah* of *lulav* and *esrog* in the synagogue immediately before *Hallel.* Contemporary Lubavitch practice is to fulfill this *mitzvah* in the *sukkah* before beginning the morning prayers, as the Alter Rebbe writes in his *Siddur.*

31. *Devarim Rabbah* 2:36.

32. See *Shabbos* 24b.

33. With which the incoming *Shabbos* is normally welcomed.

נה כדלקמן סי' תרמד. וראה בסידור דיני נטילת לולב שמצוה מן המובחר לברך על הלולב בסוכה (קודם התפלה). נו טור ושו"ע ס"ב. וראה לעיל סי' סג ס"ג שיש נוהגין לאמרו מעומד. נז דברים רבה פרשה ב, לו. הובא בטור. מ"א סק"ח. נח ראה לעיל סי' סא סי"ג טעם נוסף לאמירתו בלחש. נט סעיף ט. ס טור ושו"ע ס"ג. סא גמרא שבת כד, ב. טור ושו"ע שם. סב סי"ד (לענין יום טוב שחל בשבת). וראה לעיל סי' תקפב ס"ד שצריך לומר המלך הקדוש.

"מִזְמוֹר שִׁיר לְיוֹם הַשַּׁבָּת"[34] יֵשׁ לְאָמְרוֹ[סג] קֹדֶם "בָּרְכוּ":[סד,35]

HaShabbos[34] before *Barchu.*[35]

יא וְאֵין אוֹמְרִים "אָבִינוּ מַלְכֵּנוּ" כְּשֶׁחָל בְּשַׁבָּת,[סה] מִלְּבַד בִּתְפִלַּת נְעִילָה כְּמוֹ שֶׁיִּתְבָּאֵר בְּסִימָן תרכ"ג,[סו] אֲבָל שְׁאָר הַסְּלִיחוֹת[36] וְהַתְּחִנּוֹת[37] אוֹמְרִים כְּמוֹ כְּשֶׁחָל בְּחֹל:[סז]

11 When [Yom Kippur] falls on *Shabbos,* the prayer beginning *Avinu Malkeinu* is not recited except in the course of the *Neilah* service, as will be explained in sec. 623[:9]. However, the other penitential prayers[36] and the other supplications[37] are recited, as is done when [Yom Kippur] falls on a weekday.

יב אֵין אוֹמְרִים "בְּאַהֲבָה מִקְרָא קֹדֶשׁ"[38] אֲפִלּוּ כְּשֶׁחָל בְּשַׁבָּת,[סח] אֲבָל "בְּאַהֲבָה" הָרִאשׁוֹן אוֹמְרִים[סט] אֲפִלּוּ בְּחֹל:[ע]

12 Even when [Yom Kippur] falls on *Shabbos,* we do not recite the phrase *be'ahavah mikra kodesh* [in the middle blessing of *Shemoneh Esreh*].[38] We do, however, say *be'ahavah* the first time this word appears in this passage *[VaTiten lanu... be'ahavah],* even if [Yom Kippur] falls on a weekday.

יג וְנוֹהֲגִין שֶׁאֵין אוֹמְרִים "אֱלֹקֵינוּ וֵאלֹקֵי אֲבוֹתֵינוּ רְצֵה בִמְנוּחָתֵנוּ"

13 [In the course of that middle blessing,] it is customary not to say *Elokeinu V'Elokei Avoseinu, Retzeh BiMenuchaseinu...* ("Our G-d, and G-d of our ancestors, please find favor in our rest...") when [Yom Kippur] falls

---

34. Psalm 92.

35. The *machzor* of *Chabad* specifies that when Yom Kippur falls on *Shabbos,* instead of beginning as usual with *Lechu Neranenah,* we recite the psalm *Mizmor LeDavid* (psalm 29), and then proceed as always — with the passage *Ana BeCho'ach,* the hymn *Lechah Dodi,* psalms 92 and 93, the Mourners' *Kaddish,* and the passage from the *Zohar* beginning *Kegavna* — before Half-*Kaddish* and *Barchu.* (See *Shaar HaKollel* 17:6, and *Sefer HaMinhagim: The Book of Chabad-Lubavitch Customs,* p. 124.)

Some authorities hold that the hymn beginning *Lechah Dodi* should be omitted, because it is associated with greeting the *neshamah yeseirah,* the additional soul that a Jew is granted on *Shabbos.* Since Yom Kippur, they argue, is a fast day, a day of affliction for the soul, it is not appropriate that an extra soul be granted *(Eliyah Rabbah* 262:5*).* Others authorities question how the influence of the holiest day of the year could possibly be said to minimize the augmented spiritual potential with which a Jew is endowed on *Shabbos.* Rather, they maintain, an additional soul is granted and *Lechah Dodi* should accordingly be recited *(Shyarei Knesses HaGedolah* on *Tur* 262, gloss #4, cited in *Kaf HaChaim* 619:38 and *Ketzeh HaMateh* 618:32*).*

36. In the original, *selichos.*

37. In the original, *techinos.*

38. This phrase means, "[You... have given us... this day...] in love..., as a holy assembly." It is customarily inserted on every festival that coincides with *Shabbos,* since it alludes to the Jewish people's willing acceptance of the *Shabbos* even before they were given the entire Torah *(Levush,* sec. 487*).*

In his *Siddur,* notwithstanding the above text, the Alter Rebbe includes this addition for Yom Kippur as well.

סג שיירי כנה"ג בהגה"ט אות ח. אליה זוטא סק"י. ומנהג חב"ד להתחיל ממזמור לדוד כמו בכל יום טוב שחל בשבת (ספר המנהגים – חב"ד ע' 59. וראה גם שער הכולל פי"ז אות ו. אוצר מנהגי חב"ד שם ע' רו־רז). **סד** ראה לעיל סי' רסא ס"ז. **סה** ריב"ש סי' תקיב. מנהגים (טירנא) מנהג יוה"כ (ע' קי). רמ"א ס"ג. וראה גם לעיל סי' תקפד ס"ה. סי' תרב ס"ב. **סו** סעיף ט. **סז** ריב"ש שם. רמ"א שם. **סח** מ"א סק"ז. לבוש ס"ב. והיינו אף שאומרים כן בשבת יום טוב, כדלעיל סי' תפז ס"ו. וכ"ה לעיל סי' תקפב סט"ו לענין ר"ה. אבל בסידור הנוסח לאמרו בשבת (ראה אליה רבה סקי"ד, בשם אבודרהם סדר תפלת יוה"כ סד"ה ערבית, לומר כן בכל יוה"כ). **סט** לבוש שם. **ע** כדלעיל סי' תפז ס"ו (בשאר יום טוב). **עא** לבוש שם, ובסימן תקפב ס"ח. מ"א שם. ובסידור כתב

כְּשֶׁחָל בְּשַׁבָּת,[עא, 39] דְּכֵיוָן שֶׁהוּא יוֹם עִנּוּי אֵין לָנוּ רָצוֹן כָּל כָּךְ בִּמְנוּחָתֵנוּ,[עב] וְאֵיךְ נִתְפַּלֵּל שֶׁיִּרְצֶה הַקָּדוֹשׁ בָּרוּךְ הוּא בִּמְנוּחָתֵנוּ שֶׁאֵינָהּ מְנוּחָה גְּמוּרָה,[עג] אֲבָל אוֹמְרִים "וְהַנְחִילֵנוּ[עד] בְּאַהֲבָה וּבְרָצוֹן שַׁבַּת קָדְשֶׁךָ כו'", שֶׁזֶּהוּ בַּקָּשָׁה עַל כָּל שַׁבְּתוֹת הַשָּׁנָה[עה] שֶׁאֵינָן יוֹם הַכִּפּוּרִים, וְאַחַר כָּךְ אוֹמְרִים "וְטַהֵר לִבֵּנוּ לְעָבְדְּךָ בֶּאֱמֶת כִּי אַתָּה סָלְחָן כו'", כְּלוֹמַר שֶׁעַל יְדֵי הַסְּלִיחָה מְטַהֵר לִבֵּנוּ[עו] (וּדְלֹא כְּמוֹ שֶׁכָּתוּב בִּקְצָת מַחֲזוֹרִים בִּתְפִלַּת רֹאשׁ הַשָּׁנָה וְיוֹם הַכִּפּוּרִים "וְטַהֵר לִבֵּנוּ כו'" קֹדֶם "וְהַנְחִילֵנוּ כו'", שֶׁאֵיךְ שַׁיָּךְ לוֹמַר אַחַר כָּךְ "כִּי אַתָּה סָלְחָן כו'", אוֹ "כִּי אַתָּה אֱלֹהִים אֱמֶת"[עז, 40]):

on *Shabbos*.[39] Since this is a day of affliction and we do not derive so much satisfaction from our rest, how can we pray that the Holy One, blessed be He, should derive satisfaction from our rest when it is not complete?

We do, however, say *vehanchileinu... be'ahavah uveratzon Shabbas kodshecha...* ("Grant us... as a heritage with love and desire Your holy *Shabbos...*,"), for this request relates to all the *Shabbasos* of the year that are not Yom Kippur. After that we say *vetaheir libeinu...* ("Purify our hearts so that we will serve You in truth, for You are the One Who forgives..."); that is, He purifies our hearts by means of forgiveness.

(This order differs from that found in certain *machzorim* which maintain that in the prayers of Rosh HaShanah and Yom Kippur, *vetaheir libeinu* should be recited before *vehanchileinu*. For how is it appropriate to say *ki Atah salchan* ("for You are the One Who forgives") or *ki Atah Elokim emes...* ("for You are the true G-d") after that [request]?)[40]

יד בְּכָל תְּפִלּוֹת יוֹם הַכִּפּוּרִים צָרִיךְ לְהַעֲמִיד שְׁנֵי אֲנָשִׁים אֵצֶל הַשְּׁלִיחַ צִבּוּר אֶחָד מִימִינוֹ וְאֶחָד מִשְּׂמֹאלוֹ,[עח] כְּמוֹ בְּכָל תַּעֲנִית צִבּוּר כְּמוֹ שֶׁנִּתְבָּאֵר בְּסִימָן תקס"ו[עט] עַיֵּן שָׁם, וְעַכְשָׁו אֵין נוֹהֲגִין כְּלָל לְהַעֲמִיד שְׁנֵי אֲנָשִׁים אֵצֶל הַשְּׁלִיחַ צִבּוּר בְּכָל תַּעֲנִית צִבּוּר

14 During all the prayer services of Yom Kippur, [following longstanding custom,] we should have two people stand next to the *sheliach tzibbur*, one to his right and one to his left, as is the practice on all communal fasts and as is stated in sec. 566; see that source. At present, the custom of having two men stand next to the *sheliach tzibbur* is not followed at all on any of the communal fasts,

---

39. This phrase, too, the Alter Rebbe includes in his *Siddur* (inserting as well the word *Na* after *Retzeh*).

40. I.e., there is an apparent incongruity between (a) the request that G-d "grant us... as a heritage... [His] holy *Shabbos...*," and (b) the reasons given in support of that request ("for You are the One Who forgives," or "for You are the true G-d"). This is not the case when "purify our hearts" is followed by "for You are the One Who forgives."

לאמרו (כבסידור האריז"ל וסידור השל"ה, ובגדי ישע (וינר) סי' תקפב), ושם הנוסח: רצה נא במנוחתנו. **עב** לבוש שם. **עג** לבוש סי' תקפ[ב] ס"ח. **עד** ה' אלקינו. **עה** לבוש ס"ב. **עו** לבוש ס"ג. **עז** ראה לבוש ס"ב. **עח** טור מפרקי דרבי אליעזר פמ"ד. הגהות מיימוניות בסוף הל' שביתת העשור ד"ה אין, ממכילתא פ' ויבא עמלק סוף פ"א. שו"ע ס"ד. **עט** סימן זה בשוע"ר לא הגיע לידינו, וראה שו"ע שם ס"ז.

מִטַּעַם שֶׁנִּתְבָּאֵר שָׁם,[פ, 41] וְלָכֵן גַּם בְּיוֹם הַכִּפּוּרִים אֵין צָרִיךְ לְהַעֲמִיד,[פא] וְלָכֵן נוֹהֲגִין שֶׁתֵּכֶף אַחַר "בָּרְכוּ"[42] הוֹלְכִין מֵעַל הַשְּׁלִיחַ צִבּוּר הָאֲנָשִׁים שֶׁעָמְדוּ אֶצְלוֹ בִּשְׁעַת אֲמִירַת "כָּל נִדְרֵי":[פב]

for the reason[s] explained in that section.[41] Hence, it is not necessary to do so on Yom Kippur either. It is therefore customary that the men who stood near the *sheliach tzibbur* during the recitation of *Kol Nidrei* leave [their place next to] him immediately after *Barchu*.[42]

טו יֵשׁ נוֹהֲגִין לַעֲמֹד עַל רַגְלֵיהֶם כָּל הַיּוֹם וְכָל הַלַּיְלָה,[פג] דְּהַיְנוּ כָּל זְמַן שֶׁהֵם נֵעוֹרִים בַּלַּיְלָה אֵין יוֹשְׁבִין.[פד] אֲבָל מִכָּל מָקוֹם צְרִיכִין לִישֹׁן בַּלַּיְלָה, כְּדֵי שֶׁיּוּכְלוּ לְהִתְפַּלֵּל בַּיּוֹם בְּכַוָּנָה וְלֹא יִתְנַמְנְמוּ בִּתְפִלָּתָם:[פה, 43]

15 Some people follow the custom of standing on their feet for the entire day and night [of Yom Kippur]; i.e., as long as they are awake at night, they do not sit down. However, they should sleep at night, so that they will be able to pray with concentration during the day without dozing off during their prayers.[43]

טז וְאִם נֶחֱלְשׁוּ – יְכוֹלִים לִסְמֹךְ לְשׁוּם דָּבָר.[פו] וּמִי שֶׁעָמַד פַּעַם אַחַת כָּל יוֹם הַכִּפּוּרִים וְהָיָה בְּדַעְתּוֹ לִנְהֹג כֵּן לְעוֹלָם, אִם רוֹצֶה לְשַׁנּוֹת מִנְהָגוֹ – צָרִיךְ הַתָּרָה כְּמוֹ נֶדֶר,[פז] כְּמוֹ שֶׁיִּתְבָּאֵר

16 If [people who stand throughout] feel weak, they may lean on something [for support].

If one stood throughout Yom Kippur once and intended to do so indefinitely, but then desired to change his custom, he must request a formal absolution [of his commitment] as with the release of a vow, as stated

---

41. Sec. 566 in the Alter Rebbe's *Shulchan Aruch* is not extant. The *Shulchan Aruch* of R. Yosef Caro (sec. 566:7) states that two men should stand next to the *sheliach tzibbur* to recite the *Selichos* together with him. *Magen Avraham* explains that this practice has its roots in the fast that Moshe undertook during the war against Amalek. There, Aharon and Hur stood by him all day long, supporting his arms as he stretched them out to G-d in prayer (*Shmos* 17:12).

Despite these ancient origins, *Magen Avraham* continues, this practice is not followed today. He gives two possible explanations: (a) since the concept of *tzibbur,* community, does not apply fully in the Diaspora, there is no true concept of a communal fast; (b) since today we all recite the *Selichos* together with the *sheliach tzibbur,* there is no need to designate two individuals for that purpose.

42. At this point they return the Torah scrolls to the Ark and return to their places.

According to Lubavitch custom, this is done before *Barchu* (in fact, immediately after the blessing *Shehecheyanu,* whether on a weekday or on *Shabbos*).

43. In his *Siddur* the Alter Rebbe writes that it is commendable not to sleep that night, but to engage in Torah study. The prevailing Lubavitch custom, however, is to sleep on the night of Yom Kippur. Indeed, when outlining the schedule for the supplementary recitation of *Tehillim* during Elul and the Days of Awe, the Rebbe, R. Yosef Yitzchak Schneersohn, writes in the name of the Baal Shem Tov that before going to sleep that night one should recite psalms 124-132.

פ ראה מ"א שם סק"י. **פא** מ"א סק"ט ובסימן תקסו שם. **פב** מ"א ס"ק ט. ט"ז סוף סק"א. **פג** טור ושו"ע ס"ה. **פד** ראה מ"מ וציונים. **פה** ב"י ד"ה ועוד. כנסת הגדולה הגה"ט. ט"ז סק"ה. מ"א סק"י. וראה גם לקמן סי"ח. ובסידור: וטוב שלא לישן בליל יוה"כ אלא לעסוק בתורה, וש"נ. **פו** מהרי"ל הל' ליל יוה"כ (ע' שכה). דרכי משה ס"ק י. מ"א שם. **פז** מהר"י ווייל סי' קצא. כנסת הגדולה הגה"ט. אליה זוטא סק"ז. **פח** סימן זה בשוע"ר לא הגיע לידינו, וראה שו"ע שם סי' ריד ס"א. לעיל סי' רמט סי"ג. **פט** מטה משה אות תתסט. מ"א סק"י. **צ** ראה פרקי דרבי אליעזר פמ"ו. הובא בטור סי' תרו ובהגהות מיימוניות סוף

in *Yoreh Deah*, sec. 215.[44]

17 Women should not stand throughout Yom Kippur. To do so would be pointless, because the primary reason for standing is to resemble the angels who are called "the ones who stand."[45] This is not relevant with regard to women, as stated in sec. 610[:9].

18 Though throughout the year it is forbidden to sleep in a synagogue, it is customary to sleep there on the night of Yom Kippur, because hymns and praises are recited there for most of the night. Besides, some people sleep there to watch [in turn] over the candles. Thus there is no question of a prohibition, since this done for the sake of the synagogue, as explained in sec. 151.[46] However, one should make a point of sleeping on the west side of the synagogue, distant from the Holy Ark, or in the women's section of the synagogue if there are no women there. People who do not intend to recite hymns and praises in the synagogue should not sleep there at all.

The *chazzanim*[47] who are due to lead the prayers during the day should not remain awake throughout the night, because not sleeping at night will affect their voices. Indeed, everyone would do well not to remain awake the entire night, as

בְּיוֹרֶה דֵעָה סִימָן רט״ו:[פח,44]

יז הַנָּשִׁים אֵין לָהֶם לַעֲמֹד כָּל יוֹם הַכִּפּוּרִים,[פט] לְפִי שֶׁאֵין תּוֹעֶלֶת בַּעֲמִידָתָם, שֶׁעִקַּר טַעַם הָעֲמִידָה הוּא כְּדֵי לִהְיוֹת דֻּגְמַת הַמַּלְאָכִים שֶׁנִּקְרָאִים "עוֹמְדִים",[צ,45] וְזֶה אֵין שַׁיָּךְ בַּנָּשִׁים כְּמוֹ שֶׁנִּתְבָּאֵר בְּסִימָן תר״י:[צא]

יח אַף עַל פִּי שֶׁבְּכָל הַשָּׁנָה אָסוּר לִישֹׁן בְּבֵית הַכְּנֶסֶת,[צב] מִכָּל מָקוֹם בְּלֵיל יוֹם הַכִּפּוּרִים נוֹהֲגִין לִישֹׁן בְּבֵית הַכְּנֶסֶת, לְפִי שֶׁאוֹמְרִים שָׁם שִׁירוֹת וְתִשְׁבָּחוֹת רֹב הַלַּיְלָה, וְיֵשׁ יְשֵׁנִים שָׁם כְּדֵי לִשְׁמֹר אֶת הַנֵּרוֹת, וְאֵין כָּאן חֲשַׁשׁ אִסּוּר[צג] כֵּיוָן שֶׁהוּא צֹרֶךְ בֵּית הַכְּנֶסֶת[צד] כְּמוֹ שֶׁנִּתְבָּאֵר בְּסִימָן קנ״א.[צה,46] אַךְ יִזָּהֲרוּ לִישֹׁן בְּמַעֲרָב[צו] רָחוֹק מִן הָאָרוֹן,[צז] אוֹ בְּבֵית הַכְּנֶסֶת שֶׁל נָשִׁים אִם אֵין שָׁם נָשִׁים.[צח] אֲבָל אוֹתָם שֶׁאֵינָם רוֹצִים לוֹמַר שָׁם שִׁירוֹת וְתִשְׁבָּחוֹת — לֹא יִישְׁנוּ כְּלָל בְּבֵית הַכְּנֶסֶת.[צט] וְהַחַזָּנִים[47] הַמִּתְפַּלְּלִים בַּיּוֹם — לֹא יָעוּרוּ כָּל הַלַּיְלָה, לְפִי שֶׁמַּפְסִידִים אֶת קוֹלָם כְּשֶׁאֵינָם יְשֵׁנִים בַּלַּיְלָה.[ק] וַאֲפִלּוּ כָּל אָדָם — טוֹב לוֹ שֶׁלֹּא יָעוּר כָּל הַלַּיְלָה,[קא] כְּמוֹ

44. This section in the Alter Rebbe's *Shulchan Aruch* is not extant. See the *Shulchan Aruch* of R Yosef Caro, sec. 214:1, and sec. 249:13 in the present work.

45. *Zechariah* 3:7.

46. Sec. 151 in the Alter Rebbe's *Shulchan Aruch* is not extant. See the *Shulchan Aruch* of R. Yosef Caro, sec. 151:4.

47. Throughout this context, the terms *chazzan* and *sheliach tzibbur* are used interchangeably. In common parlance, the appelation *chazzan* is sometimes reserved for a professional with superior musical sophistication.

הל' שביתת העשור ד"ה מה. **צא** סעיף ט. **צב** תוספתא מגילה פ"ב הי"א. תוס' ב"ב ג, ב ד"ה ועייליה. שו"ע סי' קנא ס"ג. **צג** הגהות מיימוניות שם סוד"ה כל. ב"י ד"ה ועוד נהגו ללון. **צד** ראה מרדכי מגילה רמז תתכט. ב"ב רמז תסה. הגהות מיימוניות הל' תפלה פי"א אות ה. טור ושו"ע סי' קנא ס"ד. **צה** סימן זה בשוע"ר לא הגיע לידינו, וראה שו"ע שם ס"ד. **צו** הגהות מיימוניות שם בשם מהר"מ. מהרי"ל הל' ליל יום כפור (ע' שלא). מטה משה סי' תתעא. אליה רבה ס"ק כ. **צז** מהר"י ווייל סי' קצא. רמ"א ס"ו. **צח** הגהות מיימוניות שם. מהרי"ל הל' ליל יו"כ אות יב. מטה משה שם. אליה רבה שם. **צט** מהר"י ווייל שם. רמ"א שם. **ק** מהרי"ל שם. רמ"א שם. **קא** לבוש ס"ד. מ"א סקי"א.

שֶׁנִּתְבָּאֵר לְמַעְלָה.[קב]

וְטוֹב לוֹמַר קֹדֶם הַשֵּׁנָה ד׳ מִזְמוֹרִים הָרִאשׁוֹנִים שֶׁל תְּהִלִּים,[קג] שֶׁהֵם שְׁמִירָה לְקֶרִי.[קד, 48] וְגַם טוֹב לִזָּהֵר שֶׁלֹּא יַעֲטֹף אֶת עַצְמוֹ בְּכָרִים וּכְסָתוֹת, שֶׁלֹּא יָבוֹא לִידֵי חִמּוּם, וְעַל כָּל פָּנִים יִזָּהֵר שֶׁלֹּא לְכַסּוֹת רַגְלָיו, זֵכֶר לַדָּבָר "וַתְּגַל מַרְגְּלֹתָיו"[קה] שֶׁל בֹּעַז,[49] שֶׁלֹּא יָבוֹא לִידֵי חִמּוּם:[קו]

stated [in subsection 15] above.

Before going to sleep, it is advisable to recite the first four psalms of the book of *Tehillim,* for they are a safeguard against having a nocturnal seminal emission.[48] In addition, one should make a point of not covering himself with [so many] blankets and spreads that [his body] will be excessively warmed. One should at least leave his legs uncovered, as alluded to by the uncovering of Boaz' legs,[49] so that one's body will not become excessively warmed.

סימן תרכ מִנְהָג יָפֶה לְקַצֵּר בִּתְפִלַּת שַׁחֲרִית וּבוֹ ב׳ סְעִיפִים:

SECTION 620 The Desirable Custom of Shortening the Morning Service [on Yom Kippur]. (1–2)

א טוֹב שֶׁלֹּא לְהַאֲרִיךְ בִּתְפִלַּת שַׁחֲרִית, כְּדֵי לְמַהֵר בְּעִנְיָן שֶׁיּוּכַל לְהִתְפַּלֵּל מוּסָף[א] קֹדֶם ו׳ שָׁעוֹת וּמֶחֱצָה.[ב] וְאִם הֶאֱרִיךְ הַחַזָּן יוֹתֵר מִדַּאי, וְאִי אֶפְשָׁר שֶׁלֹּא יְאַחֲרוּ מוּסָף עַד לְאַחַר ו׳ שָׁעוֹת וּמֶחֱצָה — יֵשׁ לְדַלֵּג סְלִיחוֹת[ג] וְ"אָבִינוּ מַלְכֵּנוּ"[ד] כְּדֵי לְהַתְחִיל תְּפִלַּת מוּסָף קֹדֶם שֶׁיַּגִּיעַ זְמַן

1 It is preferable not to prolong *Shacharis,* the Morning Service, so that [the congregation] will make haste and will be able to recite the *Mussaf* prayers before six-and-a-half [seasonal] hours [have passed since sunrise]. If the *sheliach tzibbur* prolonged [his prayers] excessively and the *Mussaf* service will inevitably be delayed until after six-and-a-half [seasonal] hours have passed, [the congregation] should skip the *Selichos* supplications and the *Avinu Malkeinu* prayer in order to begin *Mussaf* before the time

---

48. As mentioned above, the Alter Rebbe writes in his *Siddur* that it is preferable not to sleep on the night of Yom Kippur, but to engage in Torah study. There he recommends that one should recite these four psalms, but does not connect them with sleep. According to the *machzor* of *Chabad,* these psalms are recited communally after the Evening Service and are followed by *Kaddish.*

The Alter Rebbe also writes in his *Siddur* that these psalms should be recited because they comprise 310 words, the numerical equivalent of the word קרי (seminal emission), and the first and last letters of the psalms are numerically equivalent to 131, which is the equivalent of סמא-ל (Samae-l, another name for Satan).

Shaar HaKollel, quoting *Shaar HaKavanos,* notes that to reach 310 one must add the four psalms themselves, and to reach 131 one must also add the *hei* of the word *ha'ish.* The author of *Shaar HaKollel* holds that the latter total is reached instead by adding the five letters of בברית ("in the covenant"), a word with Kabbalistic connotations.

49. *Rus* 3:7.

קב סעיף טו. קג אבודרהם סדר תפלת יוה"כ. קד של"ה מסכת יומא עמוד התשובה (רכט, א) ד"ה אמנם מי, בשם סדר היום ליל יוה"כ. מ"א שם. ובסידור: אחר ערבית יש לומר ארבעה מזמורים הראשונים שבתהלים (כי יש בהם ש"י תיבות כמנין קרי, וראשי תיבות וסופי תיבות מהמזמורים מנין קל"א כמנין סמא"ל) כדי להנצל מקרי, וגם יכוין בשם הוי' בניקוד בברית [חיריק, שב"א, חיריק]. קה רות ג, ז. קו של"ה שם. אליה זוטא סקי"א.

סימן תרכ: א הגהות מיימוניות הל' שביתת העשור בסופו ד"ה צריך. טור ושו"ע ס"א. ב הגהות מיימוניות שם. מהרי"ל הל' יו"כ (ע' שלח). וראה גם לעיל סי' רפו ס"ה. ג לבוש. ד הגהות מיימוניות שם בשם מהר"מ. מהרי"ל שם. לבוש. מ"א. ה סעיף ה. ו מ"א סי' תרכב סוף סק"ב. וראה גם לעיל סי' א מהדו"ב

תְּפִלַּת הַמִּנְחָה, דְּהַיְנוּ ו' שָׁעוֹת וּמֶחֱצָה, שֶׁאָז מִן הַדִּין צָרִיךְ לְהִתְפַּלֵּל מִנְחָה תְּחִלָּה כְּמוֹ שֶׁנִּתְבָּאֵר בְּסִימָן רפ"ו.[ה,1]

וּמִכָּל מָקוֹם אִם אֵרַע שֶׁאֵחֲרוּ לְהִתְפַּלֵּל מוּסָף עַד ו' שָׁעוֹת וּמֶחֱצָה – אַף עַל פִּי כֵן יִתְפַּלְּלוּ מוּסָף תְּחִלָּה קֹדֶם מִנְחָה,[2] מִטַּעַם שֶׁנִּתְבָּאֵר שָׁם,[3] עַיֵּן שָׁם:

arrives for *Minchah,* the Afternoon Service, which is after six-and-a-half hours [have passed since sunrise. The rationale is that] once that time arrives, the law prescribes that the Afternoon Service must be recited first, as is stated in sec. 286[:5].[1]

Nevertheless, if it happened that the recitation of the *Mussaf* service was delayed until six-and-a-half hours had passed, the *Mussaf* service should still be recited before the Afternoon Service,[2] for the reason explained there.[3]

ב טוֹב לוֹמַר מְעַט סְלִיחוֹת בְּנַחַת מֵהַרְבֵּה בִּמְרוּצָה:[ו,4]

2 It is better to recite fewer penitential prayers deliberately than to recite many in haste.[4]

סימן תרכא סֵדֶר קְרִיאַת הַתּוֹרָה וּמִילָה בְּיוֹם כִּפּוּר וּבוֹ י"ז סְעִיפִים:[1]

SECTION 621 The Order of the Torah Reading and [the Laws Relating to] a Circumcision on Yom Kippur. (1–17)

א מוֹצִיאִין שְׁנֵי סְפָרִים,[א] וְקוֹרִים בָּרִאשׁוֹן שִׁשָּׁה[2] אֲנָשִׁים[ב,3] בְּפָרָשַׁת "אַחֲרֵי מוֹת"[ג] עַד "וַיַּעַשׂ

1 [After[1] the Morning Service,] two Torah scrolls are taken out [of the Ark]. From the first [scroll], six[2] men read[3] [passages] from [the beginning of] *Parshas Acharei Mos* until *vayaas*

SECTION 620

1. As explained there, the Afternoon Service is given precedence because it is recited more frequently than the *Mussaf* service.

2. Moreover, it is not customary to omit the *Selichos* and the *Avinu Malkeinu* prayers, even though their recitation will prolong the prayer service.

3. The subsection cited states that a congregation should always recite the *Mussaf* service first, lest the impression be created that the Afternoon Service should precede *Mussaf,* even before noon. In contrast, an individual praying alone should recite the Afternoon Service first, if six-and-a-half seasonal hours have elapsed since sunrise.

4. Likewise, with regard to the midnight devotions of *Tikkun Chatzos,* the Alter Rebbe cites the words of the *Tur* — that a modest measure recited with genuine intent is preferable to a greater quantity with less earnest feelings. (Cited in *Mahadura Basra,* sec. 1:2, in Vol. 1 of the present work.)

SECTION 621

1. The above heading relates only to subsections 1-6; most of the present section deals with *Mussaf,* the *Avodah,* and related subjects.

2. Five *aliyos* are apportioned on all other festivals; the superior holiness of Yom Kippur is marked by an additional *aliyah.* (This term means both the honor of being called to the Reading of the Torah, and the passage read for each such individual.) *Mateh Ephraim* advises that one should endeavor to receive an *aliyah* in the course of the High Holidays (in the original, *Yamim Nora'im* — lit., "Days of Awe").

3. In earlier ages, each congregant honored with an *aliyah* to the Torah would read his passage from the scroll himself. See sec. 584, footnote 14.

ס"ב ומהדו"ק ס"ט: טוב מעט בכוונה מהרבות שלא בכוונה.

סימן תרכא: א רמב"ם הל' תפלה פי"ג הי"ד. טור ושו"ע ס"א. ב משנה מגילה כא, א. טור ושו"ע שם. וראה גם לעיל סי' רפב ס"א. ג משנה שם ל, ב. טור ושו"ע שם.

כַּאֲשֶׁר צִוָּה ה'",[ד,4] וְאִם חָל בְּשַׁבָּת קוֹרִין שִׁבְעָה,[ה] וּמַפְטִיר[5] קוֹרֵא[3] בְּסֵפֶר שֵׁנִי בְּפִינְחָס "וּבֶעָשׂוֹר לַחֹדֶשׁ",[ו,6] וּמַפְטִיר בִּישַׁעְיָה "וְאָמַר סֹלּוּ סֹלּוּ"[ז] עַד "כִּי פִּי ה' דִּבֵּר",[ח,7] לְפִי שֶׁבְּפָרָשָׁה זוֹ נִתְבָּאֵר עִנְיַן תְּשׁוּבָה וְתַעֲנִית:[ט]

ב בְּבִרְכוֹת הַפְטָרָה אֵין חוֹתְמִין "בָּרוּךְ אַתָּה ה' מֶלֶךְ מוֹחֵל וְסוֹלֵחַ",[י] אֶלָּא יֹאמַר "וּדְבָרְךָ אֱמֶת[יא,8] וְקַיָּם לָעַד בָּרוּךְ אַתָּה ה' מֶלֶךְ עַל כָּל הָאָרֶץ מְקַדֵּשׁ כו'":[9]

ג אִם יֵשׁ מִילָה בְּיוֹם הַכִּפּוּרִים – מָלִין בֵּין קְרִיאַת הַתּוֹרָה לְמוּסָף,[יב] וְאַחַר הַמִּילָה אוֹמְרִים "אַשְׁרֵי".[יג] וְיֵשׁ נוֹהֲגִין לָמוּל אַחַר

kaasher tzivah A-donai ("And he did as G-d commanded…").[4] If [Yom Kippur] falls on *Shabbos*, the reading [is divided between] seven [men]. The *maftir*[5] then reads[3] [a passage] from *Parshas Pinchas* beginning, *Uve'asor lachodesh* ("And on the tenth of the month…"),[6] from the second scroll. For the *Haftarah*, he recites the passage from *Yeshayahu* that begins *Ve'amar: Solu, solu…* ("He declares: 'Pave, pave…' ") and that ends *ki pi A-donai dibeir* ("for the Mouth of G-d has spoken"),[7] for this passage speaks of repentance and fasting.

2 The blessings for the *Haftorah* do not conclude with the words, *Baruch Atah A-donai, Melech mochel vesoleiach…* ("Blessed are You, G-d, King Who forgives and pardons…"), but should conclude with the words, *U'dvarcha emes*[8] *vekayam laad; Baruch Atah A-donai, Melech al kol haaretz, mekadesh…* ("And Your word is true and everlasting; blessed are You, G-d, King of the entire earth, Who sanctifies…").[9]

3 On Yom Kippur, a circumcision should be performed between the Reading of the Torah and the *Mussaf* service. *Ashrei* is recited after the circumcision, though there are some whose custom is to perform the circumcision after the recitation of

4. I.e., *Vayikra* 16:1-34, as specified in *Megillah* 30b.

5. Lit., "the one who concludes"; i.e., the additional (in this case, the seventh) congregant, for whom a brief passage concerning the festival is now read from the second Torah scroll. He will then be honored with the reading of the *Haftarah,* which is a passage from the Prophets whose theme is related to that day's Torah reading.

6. I.e., *Bamidbar* 29:7-11, which describes the *Mussaf* offerings brought on Yom Kippur. This passage is always read, regardless of whether Yom Kippur falls on *Shabbos* or on a weekday.

7. I.e., *Yeshayahu* 57:14-58:14, as specified in *Megillah* 31a.

8. As mentioned in the notes to sec. 582:11, in his *Siddur* the Alter Rebbe chooses the version, *U'dvarcha malkeinu emes* ("And Your word, our King, is true").

9. Since the *Haftorah* is not a request for forgiveness, it is not appropriate in this blessing to praise G-d as "the King Who forgives…" *(Kol-Bo).*

In practice, the version chosen by the Alter Rebbe in his *Siddur* — originating in the *Rokeiach* and found in all the *Siddurim* that follow the teachings of the *AriZal* as well as in many Ashkenazic *Siddurim* — combines the text of both versions, incorporating references to "the King Who forgives."

ד ויקרא טז, לד. טור ושו"ע שם. ה טור ושו"ע שם. וראה לעיל סי' רפב ס"ב שטוב שלא להוסיף מעל שבעה קרואים. ו במדבר כט, ז. תוספתא מגילה פ"ג ה"ג. רמב"ם שם. טור ושו"ע שם. ז נז, יד. ברייתא שם לא, א ורש"י ד"ה כי. טור ושו"ע שם. ח נח, יד. טור ושו"ע שם. ט רש"י שם. ב"י ריש הסי'. לבוש ס"א. י כלבו סי' ע (לה, ד), בשם ה"ר נתן. מנהגים (טירנא) מנהג יוה"כ (ע' קיג). דרכי משה ס"ק ב. לבוש סוף ס"א. מ"א ריש הסי'. אבל בסידור (אצל שחרית של שבת) הנוסח (עפ"י רוקח קרוב לסוס"י ריז. הובא בב"י): ברוך אתה ה' מלך מוחל וסולח כו'. יא וכ"ה לעיל בר"ה סי' תקפב סי"א. ובסידור: ודברך מלכנו אמת. יב רוקח סי' ריז ד"ה ומה שפוסקין. מרדכי סוף רמז תשכז. הגהות מרדכי שבת רמז תע, בשם מהר"ם מרוטנבורג. שו"ע ס"ב. יג הגהות מרדכי שם. שו"ע שם. מ"א סק"ב. יד מנהגים (טירנא) ע' קיג. רמ"א ס"ב. טו הגהות מרדכי שם. שו"ע שם. טז לבוש ס"ב. יז הגהות מרדכי שם. שו"ע

Ashrei.[10]

In regions in which a circumcision is customarily held in the home of the child and not in the synagogue,[11] it is not performed until the Torah scrolls have been returned to the Ark, for it would be a disgrace to a Torah scroll to leave it [unattended] and to leave [the synagogue]. After the circumcision [the congregants] return to the synagogue, and the *Kaddish* that precedes the *Mussaf* service is recited.[12]

"אַשְׁרֵי".[יד,10] וְאִם הוּא בְּמָקוֹם שֶׁמָּלִין הַתִּינוֹק בְּבֵיתוֹ וְלֹא בְּבֵית הַכְּנֶסֶת[11] – אֵין מָלִין עַד חֲזָרַת סִפְרֵי תוֹרָה לַהֵיכָל,[טו] מִשּׁוּם שֶׁהוּא בִּזָּיוֹן סֵפֶר תּוֹרָה לְהַנִּיחוֹ וְלָצֵאת לַחוּץ,[טז] וְאַחַר הַמִּילָה חוֹזְרִין לְבֵית הַכְּנֶסֶת וְאוֹמְרִים קַדִּישׁ שֶׁלִּפְנֵי תְּפִלַּת מוּסָף:[יז,12]

4 After the circumcision, there are those who follow the custom of reciting the blessing for the circumcision without a cup [of wine], because one may not drink from it, nor may one give it to a child to taste.[13] This [safeguard] was ordained[14] for fear that the child become accustomed to drinking this [wine associated] with a *mitzvah,* and hence will grant himself license to partake of [some other] cup of wine associated with a blessing[15] even after he attains majority.

We do have a child taste [a cup of wine in such a situation] on Tishah BeAv, and the above reservation is no cause for concern, because this is an infrequent situation, as explained in sec. 559.[16]

ד וְאַחַר הַמִּילָה, יֵשׁ נוֹהֲגִין לְבָרֵךְ בִּרְכַּת הַמִּילָה בְּלֹא כוֹס,[יח] לְפִי שֶׁאִי אֶפְשָׁר לִטְעֹם מִמֶּנּוּ, וְגַם אֵין מַטְעִימִים לַתִּינוֹק,[13] גְּזֵרָה[14] שֶׁמָּא יִהְיֶה הַתִּינוֹק רָגִיל בִּשְׁתִיָּה זוֹ שֶׁל מִצְוָה וְיוֹרֶה הֶתֵּר לְעַצְמוֹ לִשְׁתּוֹת מִכּוֹס שֶׁל בְּרָכָה[15] אַף לִכְשֶׁיִּגְדַּל.[יט] וְאַף עַל פִּי שֶׁבְּתִשְׁעָה בְּאָב מַטְעִימִים לַתִּינוֹק וְאֵין חוֹשְׁשִׁין לְכָךְ מִפְּנֵי שֶׁהוּא דָּבָר שֶׁאֵינוֹ מָצוּי כְּמוֹ שֶׁנִּתְבָּאֵר בְּסִימָן תקנ"ט,[כ,16]

---

10. In his *Shulchan Aruch* (621:2), R. Yosef Caro writes that the circumcision should precede the recitation of *Ashrei,* so that it will follow directly after the Reading of the Torah *(Rokeiach* sec. 217*)*. The *Rama* holds that the circumcision should follow *Ashrei* and the return of the Torah scrolls to the Ark. In this instance, *Magen Avraham* (621:2), *Eliyah Rabbah* (591:2), and other Ashkenazic authorities suggest following the position of R. Yosef Caro. *(Eliyah Rabbah* explains that this sequence averts a pause between *Ashrei* and the subsequent *Kaddish.)* In practice, this is the prevailing custom throughout the Jewish world.

11. Either because of the weather (see sec. 131:6) or because there is no *eruv (Mishnah Berurah* 621:8*)*.

12. If the circumcision is held outside the synagogue, the Rebbe in *Likkutei Sichos* (Vol. 19, p. 458) recommends that a chapter of *Tehillim* be recited before the Half-*Kaddish* that precedes *Mussaf,* for *Kaddish* may be recited only immediately after a psalm or other prayer. (See sec. 54:4 in Vol. 1 of the present work.

13. I.e., a child other than the infant being circumcised.

14. See *Eruvin* 40b.

15. In the original, *kos shel berachah.*

16. Sec. 559 in the Alter Rebbe's *Shulchan Aruch* is not extant. The *Shulchan Aruch* of R. Yosef Caro (sec. 559:7) speaks of circumstances in which the wine is given to a child, and *Magen Avraham* explains in a gloss (on sec. 559:9) that there is no need to be concerned about the child's possible mistake in future years, because not every year does a circumcision take place on Tishah BeAv.

שם. ולפני הקדיש יאמר איזה מזמור (לקו"ש חי"ט ע' 458). **יח** מרדכי סוף רמז תשכז, בשם רבנו יעקב ב"ר שמשון. ר"ן שבת (נז, א) ד"ה וכתבו, בשם הגאונים. אבודרהם הל' ברכת מילה, בשם הרי"ץ גיאת והרמב"ם. שו"ע ס"ג. **יט** מרדכי ואבודרהם שם. וראה רש"י עירובין מ, ב ד"ה דאתי. ט"ז סק"א וסי' תריט סק"ג. לעיל סי' שמג ס"ח. סי' תריט ס"ז. **כ** סימן זה בשוע"ר לא הגיע לידינו, וראה טור ושו"ע שם ס"ז ומ"א סק"ט.

מִכָּל מָקוֹם בְּיוֹם הַכִּפּוּרִים שֶׁהוּא מִן הַתּוֹרָה וְעָנוּשׁ כָּרֵת – הֶחְמִירוּ יוֹתֵר[כא] וְחָשְׁשׁוּ אַף לְדָבָר שֶׁאֵינוֹ מָצוּי:

Concerning Yom Kippur, by contrast, when [the prohibition against eating or drinking] is of Scriptural origin, and [its violation] is punishable by *kares,* [the Sages] were more stringent and regarded even an infrequent situation as a cause for concern.

ה וְיֵשׁ נוֹהֲגִין לְבָרֵךְ עַל הַכּוֹס וּלְהַטְעִים מִמֶּנּוּ לַתִּינוֹק הַנִּמּוֹל,[כב] שֶׁבְּקָטָן כָּזֶה אֵין לִגְזוֹר שֶׁמָּא יִשְׁתֶּה אַף לִכְשֶׁיִּגְדַּל.[כג,17] וְאַף עַל פִּי שֶׁכָּל כּוֹס שֶׁל בְּרָכָה צָרִיךְ לְהַטְעִים מִמֶּנּוּ לְקָטָן שֶׁהִגִּיעַ לִכְלַל חִנּוּךְ בְּרָכוֹת כְּמוֹ שֶׁנִּתְבָּאֵר בְּסִימָן רס"ט[כד] וְתקנ"ט,[כה,18] מִכָּל מָקוֹם כּוֹס שֶׁל מִילָה שֶׁהַבְּרָכָה נִתְקְנָה בִּשְׁבִיל תִּינוֹק הַנִּמּוֹל לָכֵן דַּי כְּשֶׁנּוֹתְנִים לוֹ לִשְׁתּוֹת.[כו] וּמִכָּל מָקוֹם, צָרִיךְ לִזָּהֵר שֶׁיִּתְּנוּ לוֹ לִשְׁתּוֹת קְצָת מֵהַכּוֹס, מִלְּבַד מַה שֶּׁנּוֹתְנִים לְפִיו כְּשֶׁאוֹמֵר "בְּדָמַיִךְ חֲיִי":[כז,19]

5 There are others who follow the custom of reciting the blessing over the cup of wine and giving a taste of it to the infant who was just circumcised, because for a child of that age there is no need to ordain [a safeguard] lest he drink after he attains majority.[17]

In all [other] instances, whenever a cup [of wine] associated with a blessing is given to a child to taste, [the cup] must be given to a child who is mature enough to be educated to recite blessings, as stated in sec. 269[:3] and 559.[18] Nevertheless, since [in this instance] the blessing recited over the cup [of wine] was ordained for the sake of the infant being circumcised, it is sufficient that he be given [a taste of the wine] to drink. However, care must be taken that he be given wine from the cup, in addition to the wine that is placed in his mouth during the recitation of the words *bedamayich chayi* ("By your blood you shall live").[19]

---

17. As stated in *Luach Colel Chabad,* this is the practice followed at present.

18. In sec. 269:3, the Alter Rebbe discusses the practice of reciting *Kiddush* on Friday night in the synagogue, despite the fact that the person reciting it will not partake of a meal there. To avoid the halachic difficulties involved, he writes that the wine should be given to a child — but only to a child mature enough to be trained in the recitation of blessings.

The reason for this proviso, as the Alter Rebbe writes in sec. 273:6, is that one may recite *Kiddush* on behalf of others, even though he is not fulfilling his own obligation for *Kiddush* at that time. Why? The Jewish people share bonds of mutual responsibility (*areivus* — lit., "guarantorship"). Hence, when one individual has not fulfilled a particular *mitzvah,* every other Jew — even one who has already fulfilled the *mitzvah* — is responsible that this fellow Jew fulfill it. (Cf. *Rashi* on *Rosh HaShanah* 29a, *s.v. Af-al-pi.*) Accordingly, if the listener does not know how to recite the blessing himself, one may recite the blessing on his behalf. (See sec. 187:23 above.)

When there is no obligation to train a child due to his present immaturity, the guarantorship obviously does not apply. In such a case, not only is there no license to recite such a blessing, but to do so would be considered reciting a blessing in vain.

19. *Yechezkel* 16:6 (*Siddur Tehillat HaShem,* p. 411).

כא מרדכי שם. לבוש ס"ג. וראה מ"מ וציונים. כב מרדכי השלם רמז תשכז ע' פח. הובא בב"י סי' תקנט ד"ה ואם יש תינוק. רמ"א ס"ג. כג מרדכי שם. כד ס"ג. וראה סי' קצ ס"ד ב' דעות בזה. כה ראה מ"א שם סוף סק"ט. כו מ"א סי' רסט סק"א. וראה לעיל סי' קצ ס"ד, שבמילה ביום הכיפורים סומכים על הדעה הב' שם, שאפשר להטעים כוס של ברכה לתינוק שלא הגיע לחנוך, ומציין לכאן. כז מ"א סק"ג. כח תוס' שבת קלט, א ד"ה וליתן בשם ר"ת. עירובין

6 There are those who follow the custom of reciting the blessing over a cup [of wine] and then giving it to children to taste, as is the practice on Tishah BeAv. Though initially this should not be done on Yom Kippur for the reason stated above, those who practice this leniency should not be rebuked.

ו וְיֵשׁ נוֹהֲגִים[כח] שֶׁמְּבָרְכִים עַל הַכּוֹס וּמַטְעִימִים לַתִּינוֹקוֹת, כְּמוֹ בְּתִשְׁעָה בְּאָב. וְאַף עַל פִּי שֶׁאֵין לִנְהֹג כֵּן לְכַתְּחִלָּה בְּיוֹם הַכִּפּוּרִים מִטַּעַם שֶׁנִּתְבָּאֵר לְמַעְלָה,[כט] מִכָּל מָקוֹם אֵין לִמְחוֹת בְּיַד הַנּוֹהֲגִין הֶתֵּר:[ל]

7 In the *Mussaf* service, the *sheliach tzibbur* recounts the order of [that day's] Temple service,[20] for the service of the High Priest[21] on Yom Kippur primarily involved the *Mussaf* sacrifices, and in the midst of offering them he would perform all the [other] components of that day's [distinctive] service as prescribed in *Parshas Acharei Mos.*

ז בְּמוּסָף אוֹמֵר הַשְּׁלִיחַ צִבּוּר סֵדֶר הָעֲבוֹדָה,[לא,20] לְפִי שֶׁעִקַּר עֲבוֹדַת כֹּהֵן גָּדוֹל[21] בְּיוֹם הַכִּפּוּרִים הָיְתָה בְּקָרְבְּנוֹת הַמּוּסָפִים,[לב] שֶׁבְּאֶמְצַע הַקְרָבָתָם הָיָה עוֹבֵד כָּל עֲבוֹדַת הַיּוֹם הָאֲמוּרִים בְּפָרָשַׁת "אַחֲרֵי מוֹת":[לג]

8 Ten times in the course of Yom Kippur[22] the High Priest would utter the Four-Letter name of G-d[23] as it is written — three times in his first confessional: "Please, *HaShem,* I have sinned…; please, *HaShem,* atone…; 'before *HaShem*[24] you will be purified' "; three times in each of the second and third confessionals; and once at the lottery [concerning the goats to be offered], when he said [concerning one of them], "A sin-offering for *HaShem.*"

ח עֲשָׂרָה פְּעָמִים הָיָה כֹּהֵן גָּדוֹל מַזְכִּיר אֶת הַשֵּׁם הַמְּפֹרָשׁ[23] כִּכְתָבוֹ בְּיוֹם הַכִּפּוּרִים,[22] ג' פְּעָמִים בְּוִדּוּי רִאשׁוֹן "אָנָּא ה' חָטָאתִי כו', אָנָּא ה' כַּפֶּר כו', לִפְנֵי ה'[24] תִּטְהָרוּ", וְכֵן ג' פְּעָמִים בְּוִדּוּי שֵׁנִי, וְכֵן ג' פְּעָמִים בְּוִדּוּי שְׁלִישִׁי, וּפַעַם אַחַת בְּגוֹרָלוֹת כְּשֶׁאוֹמֵר "לַה' חַטָּאת".[לד]

---

20. In the original, *Seder HaAvodah.*

21. In the original, *Kohen Gadol.*

22. *Yoma* 39b.

23. In the original, *Shem HaMeforash* (lit., "the explicit name"), i.e., the name י-ה-ו-ה which the *Kohen Gadol* would pronounce as it is written ("explicitly") only in the course of the service in the *Beis HaMikdash* on that day. In the prayers, and when one is quoting a complete Biblical verse, this name is pronounced *A-donai* (lit., "my L-rd"). At all other times, out of reverence, it is merely alluded to as *HaShem* (lit., "the name").

The above explanation of the term *Shem HaMeforash* conveys the Alter Rebbe's understanding of it, following *Rambam (Hilchos Tefillah* 14:10, *et al.);* hence his choice of the word *kiksavo* ("as it is written"). Other authorities understand the term *Shem HaMeforash* differently in this context (see the *Reshimos* of the Rebbe, Booklet #41).

24. *Vayikra* 16:30.

מ, ב ד"ה דלמא בשם רבנו שמואל. הובא במרדכי ובר"ן ובאבודרהם שם. לבוש ס"ג בשם מנהגים (טירנא) הל' יום כפור (ע' קיג, לאחת הגירסאות). מ"א סק"ג. **כט** סעיף ד. **ל** לבוש שם. מ"א שם. **לא** משמעות הגמרא לו, ב; נו, ב. הובא בר"ן (ו, א) ד"ה ומהא. טור ושו"ע ס"ד. **לב** סדר רב עמרם (בתפלת המנחה), בשם רב נטרונאי. הובא במרדכי רמז תשכז. ב"י ד"ה וכתב המרדכי. לבוש ס"ד. ט"ז סק"ב. **לג** ראה רא"ש יומא סדר עבודת יוה"כ בסופו. **לד** גמרא [ברייתא] לט, ב ורש"י ד"ה שלשה וד"ה ואחד. רמב"ם הל' עבודת יוה"כ פ"ב ה"ו. טור. ט"ז ס"ק ב.

וְכָל מָקוֹם שֶׁהַכֹּהֵן גָּדוֹל הָיָה מַזְכִּיר שֵׁם הַמְפֹרָשׁ[לה] — אָנוּ אוֹמְרִים "הַשֵּׁם",[25] וְאֵין אוֹמְרִים "אֲדֹנָי" כְּמוֹ בְּכָל תְּפִלּוֹתֵינוּ, כְּדֵי שֶׁלֹּא יְהֵא נִרְאֶה שֶׁגַּם הַכֹּהֵן גָּדוֹל הָיָה אוֹמֵר בְּכִנּוּי[26] אַדְנוּת כְּמוֹ שֶׁאָנוּ אוֹמְרִים, לְפִיכָךְ אָנוּ אוֹמְרִים הַשֵּׁם סְתָם בְּרֶמֶז, לְהוֹרוֹת שֶׁהַכֹּהֵן גָּדוֹל הָיָה מַזְכִּיר כָּאן שֵׁם הַמְפֹרָשׁ, חוּץ מִן "לִפְנֵי ה' תִּטְהָרוּ", שֶׁאָנוּ אוֹמְרִים בְּכִנּוּי שֵׁם אַדְנוּת, לְפִי שֶׁאֵין אָנוּ בָּאִין בְּכָאן לוֹמַר אֵיךְ הָיָה הַכֹּהֵן גָּדוֹל מַזְכִּיר אֶת הַשֵּׁם, אֶלָּא כַּוָּנָתֵנוּ לִקְרוֹת הַפָּסוּק[לו] כְּמוֹ שֶׁדַּרְכֵּנוּ לִקְרוֹת בַּתּוֹרָה, דְּהַיְנוּ בְּכִנּוּי אַדְנוּת.[לז]

וְכֵן כְּשֶׁאָנוּ אוֹמְרִים "לַה' חַטָּאת"[לח] אָנוּ אוֹמְרִים בְּכִנּוּי אַדְנוּת, כְּמוֹ שֶׁדַּרְכֵּנוּ לִקְרוֹת בַּתּוֹרָה, שֶׁנֶּאֱמַר בַּתּוֹרָה[לט, 27] "אֲשֶׁר עָלָה עָלָיו הַגּוֹרָל לַה' וְעָשָׂהוּ חַטָּאת". וּמִכָּל מָקוֹם, כֵּיוָן שֶׁבַּתּוֹרָה אָנוּ קוֹרִין קְצָת בְּשִׁנּוּי מִמַּה שֶּׁאוֹמְרִים בְּיוֹם הַכִּפּוּרִים, שֶׁהֲרֵי בְּיוֹם הַכִּפּוּרִים אֵין אוֹמְרִים תֵּבַת "וְעָשָׂהוּ", לָכֵן נָכוֹן לַעֲשׂוֹת עַל צַד הַיּוֹתֵר טוֹב וְלוֹמַר "לְהַשֵּׁם חַטָּאת":[מ, 28]

ט אֲבָל כְּשֶׁאוֹמְרִים הַבַּקָּשָׁה שֶׁל כֹּהֵן גָּדוֹל,[29] דְּהַיְנוּ "יְהִי רָצוֹן מִלְּפָנֶיךָ ה'

[On Yom Kippur, as we read the description of that day's service,] whenever the High Priest would mention the Four-Letter Divine name we say *HaShem*,[25] and not *A-donai* as we say in all our prayers, so that it will not appear that the High Priest would use the appellation[26] *A-donai* as we do. [To make that distinction] we say *HaShem*, alluding to the fact that at this point the High Priest would utter the Four-Letter Divine name.

An exception is made in the phrase *lifnei A-donai tit'haru* ("before G-d you will be purified"). Here we use the appellation *A-donai*, for in this case we are not relating how the High Priest would utter G-d's name: our intention is to read the verse just as we read other verses from the Torah, and [hence] we use the appellation *A-donai*.

Similarly, when we say [the Hebrew words for] "a sin-offering for G-d," we use the appellation *A-donai*, as we customarily say when we read the Torah, as [indeed,] it is written in the Torah:[27] "...upon which the lot 'for G-d' fell, and he shall offer it as a sin-offering." Nevertheless, the reading in the Torah slightly differs from the way we describe [the offerings] on Yom Kippur, for on Yom Kippur we do not say the word *ve'asahu* ("and he shall offer it"). Hence it is proper to follow the most desirable course of action and say "a sin-offering for *HaShem*."[28]

9 [In the course of the *Avodah*,] we cite the request made by the High Priest[29] [after departing from the Holy of Holies], *Yehi ratzon*

25. Lit., "the name."

26. In the original, *kinui;* i.e., a mere appellation, as distinct from an actual name.

27. *Vayikra* 16:9.

28. In his *Siddur,* following the *AriZal,* the Alter Rebbe does not write *laHaShem* ("for *HaShem*"). The phrase is therefore pronounced *laA-donai chatas.*

29. See *Machzor for Yom Kippur* Annotated Edition, p. 252.

לה רא"ש פ"ח סי' יט (ככתבו, ולא של מ"ב). טור (ושו"ע). ט"ז ס"ק ב. מ"א ס"ק ד. לו ויקרא טז, ל. לז טור בשם הרי"ץ גיאת הל' יוה"כ (ע' סג). שו"ת הריב"ש סי' ריט, בשם רבותיו. ב"י ד"ה כתב רב סעדיה. לבוש ס"ו. מ"א ס"ק ד. ט"ז סק"ב. לח מ"א שם. לט ויקרא טז, ט. מ ט"ז שם. ובסדר עבודה

אֱלֹקֵינוּ וֵאלֹקֵי אֲבוֹתֵינוּ כו׳, וְעַל אַנְשֵׁי הַשָּׁרוֹן[30] הוּא אוֹמֵר[מא] "יְהִי רָצוֹן מִלְּפָנֶיךָ ה׳ אֱלֹקֵינוּ וֵאלֹקֵי אֲבוֹתֵינוּ כו׳"[31] — אוֹמְרִים כָּל הָאַזְכָּרוֹת שֶׁבָּהּ בְּכִנּוּי אַדְנוּת, שֶׁגַּם הַכֹּהֵן גָּדוֹל הָיָה אוֹמֵר כָּאן בְּכִנּוּי אַדְנוּת:[מב]

milfanecha A-donai Elokeinu v'Elokei Avoseinu... ("May it be Your will, G-d, our L-rd, and L-rd of our forefathers"), and the prayer he would recite for the inhabitants of the Sharon[30] [which likewise begins], *Yehi ratzon milfanecha A-donai Elokeinu v'Elokei avoseinu*....[31] Here, in contrast to the above contexts, G-d is repeatedly addressed by the appellation *A-donai,* for even the High Priest would use that appellation in these prayers.

י וְאַף עַל פִּי שֶׁכַּוָּנָתֵנוּ בַּאֲמִירַת בַּקָּשָׁה זוֹ לְסַפֵּר הֵיאַךְ הָיָה הַכֹּהֵן גָּדוֹל מְבַקֵּשׁ[מג] — אַף עַל פִּי כֵן אֵין כָּאן הַזְכָּרַת שֵׁם שָׁמַיִם לְבַטָּלָה, כֵּיוָן שֶׁגַּם כַּוָּנָתֵנוּ הוּא לְהִתְפַּלֵּל עַל עַצְמֵנוּ,[מד] שֶׁהֲרֵי אָנוּ מוֹסִיפִין בָּהּ כַּמָּה בַּקָּשׁוֹת שֶׁלֹּא הָיָה הַכֹּהֵן גָּדוֹל אוֹמְרָם כְּלָל,[מה] כְּמוֹ "שֶׁתַּעֲלֵנוּ בְּשִׂמְחָה לְאַרְצֵנוּ"[מו, 32] וְכַיּוֹצֵא בָּזֶה:

10 Our intent in reciting this request is to describe how the High Priest would make his request. Nevertheless, there is no [question] here of mentioning G-d's name in vain, because our intent is also to pray for ourselves. [This is obvious] from the fact that we add several requests that the High Priest would not make at all; for example, "[a year in which] You will cause us to ascend to our land with joy,"[32] and the like.

יא וּבְכָל שְׁלֹשֶׁת וִדּוּיִים אֵלּוּ אוֹמְרִים בַּתְּחִלָּה "אָנָּא הַ[שֵּׁם] וכו׳" וְאַחַר כָּךְ "אָנָּא בְּשֵׁם כַּפֶּר נָא כו׳",[מז] שֶׁכְּשֶׁמְּבַקֵּשׁ רַחֲמִים עַל הַכַּפָּרָה יֵשׁ לוֹמַר "אָנָּא בְּשֵׁם", כְּלוֹמַר שֶׁהַקָּדוֹשׁ

11 In all three above-mentioned confessionals, we first say *Ana HaShem*... ("We beseech You, *HaShem*..."), and then we say *Ana beShem, kaper na*... ("We beseech You, through the name *HaShem*, grant atonement..."). When requesting G-d's mercy in granting atonement, we say *Ana beShem,* i.e., "We beseech You, for the sake of Your name *HaShem*" — [the intent

---

30. This extensive plain, lying between the mountains of central *Eretz Yisrael* and the coast, was prone to flooding when there were heavy rains (see *Talmud Yerushalmi, Yoma* 5:2, and *Korban HaEdah* there).

31. This prayer is included in the description of the *Avodah* that appears in the *machzorim* that follow *Nussach Ashkenaz*, but, despite its mention above, is not included by the Alter Rebbe in his *Siddur*.

This seeming ambivalence accords with the pattern whereby the Alter Rebbe's *Shulchan Aruch* is geared to the Ashkenazic prayer rite *(Nussach Ashkenaz),* whereas his *Siddur* follows *Nussach HaAriZal.* The latter is a variant of the Sephardic prayer rite *(Nussach Sephard).* These terms are defined and clarified in sec. 582, footnote 16 above.

32. This phrase, too, is included in the version of the *Avodah* that appears in *Nussach Ashkenaz,* but is not included by the Alter Rebbe in his *Siddur.* Obviously, this request was not made by the High Priest when praying in the *Beis HaMikdash.*

שבסידור – בשם הוי׳ (שקוראים בשם אדנות). **מא** בנוסח הסדור ליתא. **מב** מ״א שם. ט״ז שם. **מג** ב״ח סוף הסי׳. **מד** ט״ז שם. **מה** מ״א שם. **מו** ט״ז שם (שלא אמר כהן גדול שהרי יושב בא״י). **מז** ירושלמי יומא פ״ג ה״ז. ראבי״ה סי׳ תקל. רא״ש פ״ח סי׳ יט. טור ולבוש ס״ו. ט״ז סק״ב.

בָּרוּךְ הוּא יוֹשִׁיעַ עַל יְדֵי שֵׁם הָעֶצֶם שֶׁהוּא רַחֲמִים גְּמוּרִים (בְּלִי תַּעֲרוֹבוֹת דִּין כְּלָל):מח, 33

being] that the Holy One, blessed be He, should deliver [us] through the medium of His essential name, which represents utter mercy (with no judgmental component whatever).[33]

יב וְנוֹהֲגִין לִפֹּל עַל פְּנֵיהֶם[34] כְּשֶׁאוֹמְרִים "וְהַכֹּהֲנִים וְהָעָם כו'",מט, 35 וְגַם בְּ"עָלֵינוּ לְשַׁבֵּחַ".נ אֲבָל הַשְּׁלִיחַ צִבּוּר אָסוּר לוֹ לַעֲקֹר מִמְּקוֹמוֹ בִּשְׁעַת הַתְּפִלָּה וְלֵילֵךְ לַאֲחוֹרָיו כְּדֵי לִפֹּל עַל פָּנָיו,נא וְיֵשׁ לִמְחוֹת בְּיַד הָעוֹשִׂים כֵּן.נב וְנוֹהֲגִין שֶׁהַשְּׁלִיחַ צִבּוּר עוֹמֵד בַּתְּחִלָּה רָחוֹק קְצָת מִן הַתֵּבָה בְּעִנְיָן שֶׁלֹּא יִצְטָרֵךְ לַעֲקֹר רַגְלָיו כְּדֵי לִפֹּל עַל פָּנָיו:נג, 36

12 It is customary to prostrate ourselves on our faces[34] when we recite the passage beginning *Vehakohanim vehaam...* ("And the priests and the people standing in the courtyard... would prostrate themselves... when they heard the name...."),[35] and also when reciting the prayer *Aleinu LeShabeiach.*

[Since he is in the midst of repeating *Shemoneh Esreh,*] the *sheliach tzibbur* may not move from his place while praying and step back in order to prostrate himself. [Indeed,] those who do so should be rebuked. It is [therefore] customary for the *sheliach tzibbur* to stand from the outset at a slight distance from the lectern, so that he will not have to move from his place in order to prostrate himself.[36]

יג סֵדֶר הַוִּדּוּי "חָטָאתִי עָוִיתִי פָּשַׁעְתִּי",נד, 37 לְפִי שֶׁהַחֲטָאִים הֵם הַשְּׁגָגוֹת, וַעֲוֹנוֹת הֵם הַזְּדוֹנוֹת,נה

13 The order of [the verbs in] the confession is *chatasi, avisi, pashati* ("I have sinned, I have transgressed, I have committed iniquity").[37] [The rationale is that] *chata'im* ("sins") implies unintentional violations; *avonos* ("transgressions")

---

33. As taught in the *Kabbalah,* the Four-Letter name of G-d expresses the quality of mercy, while the name *Elokim* expresses the quality of judgment.

34. When prostrating themselves, it was the practice of the Rebbes to kneel on the floor, bend forward, support themselves on the hands as well, and touch the floor with their foreheads. (See also: *Megillah* 22b; *Otzar Minhagei Chabad,* p. 132, #320-321.)

In synagogues with stone floors, one should place a cloth between his face and the floor, for prostrating oneself on a stone floor outside the *Beis HaMikdash* violates a Scriptural prohibition. *Sefer HaMinhagim: The Book of Chabad-Lubavitch Customs* (p. 120) cites the *Shulchan Aruch* of R. Yosef Caro, *Orach Chayim,* end of sec. 131, and speaks of "a floor of stone or of similar material." Some other sources do not restrict this prohibition to stone flooring. (See, e.g.: *Mishnah Berurah,* gloss #5 to *Orach Chayim,* sec. 621:4; *Kitzur Shulchan Aruch,* sec. 133:23.)

35. In his *Siddur,* the Alter Rebbe notes that the second time this passage appears, at the description of the drawing of lots for the goats, we do not prostrate ourselves (*Machzor for Yom Kippur* Annotated Edition, p. 249).

36. Today, in many synagogues, the lectern has a retractable shelf on which the *sheliach tzibbur* places his *machzor* when repeating *Shemoneh Esreh,* and which is pushed in when the time comes for him to prostrate himself. Alternatively, he is provided with an additional, movable lectern for the repetition of *Shemoneh Esreh.*

37. *Yoma* 36b.

מח ט"ז שם. **מט** טור בשם ראבי"ה סי' תקל. מרדכי רמז תשכז. רמ"א ס"ד. וראה סידור, דהיינו רק בוהכהנים של הוידויים, משא"כ בוהכהנים של גורלות אין צריך לכרוע. וראה שעה"כ פמ"ד אות יז. אוצר מנהגי חב"ד ע' רכז. אופן הכריעה, ראה לעיל סי' קלא ס"א (כל השנה). פס"ד צמח צדק שמב, א. אוצר מנהגי חב"ד ע' קלב (בר"ה ויוה"כ). **נ** רמ"א שם. **נא** דרכי משה ס"ק ו, בשם ריב"ש סי' שלב. רמ"א שם. **נב** רמ"א שם. **נג** אליה זוטא סק"ה. **נד** גמרא

refers to intentional breaches that the individual knew were forbidden yet proceeded with them for his self-gratification; and *psha'im* ("iniquitous acts") refers to rebellious deeds that were done in order to arouse [G-d's] wrath, not for gratification. One should confess first over lighter offenses and then over weightier ones.

כְּלוֹמַר הָעֲבֵרוֹת שֶׁעָשָׂה אוֹתָם בְּמֵזִיד שֶׁיָּדַע שֶׁאָסוּר לַעֲשׂוֹתָן וְעָשָׂה אוֹתָם לַהֲנָאָתוֹ,[נו] וּפְשָׁעִים הֵם הַמּוֹרְדִים,[נז] כְּלוֹמַר שֶׁעוֹשֶׂה לְהַכְעִיס[נח] וְלֹא בִּשְׁבִיל הֲנָאָתוֹ, וְצָרִיךְ לְהִתְוַדּוֹת תְּחִלָּה עַל הַקַּל וְאַחַר כָּךְ עַל הֶחָמוּר:[נט]

14 It is customary to verbally recall the souls [of the departed] on Yom Kippur[38] and to solemnly pledge to contribute *tzedakah* on their behalf, for the dead are also granted atonement on Yom Kippur. [Indeed,] for that reason, [in the Holy Tongue] this day is called *Yom HaKippurim,* the plural suffix signifying atonement for the living and for the dead.

The *tzedakah* which is promised on their behalf is effective in securing atonement for them, for the Holy One, blessed be He, examines hearts, and knows that if they were alive, they would also give *tzedakah*. If, however, one undertakes to give *tzedakah* on behalf of a wicked person,[39] [the gift] is of no avail to him.

יד וְנוֹהֲגִין לְהַזְכִּיר נְשָׁמוֹת בְּיוֹם הַכִּפּוּרִים[ס, 38] וְנוֹדְרִים צְדָקָה בַּעֲבוּרָם,[סא] לְפִי שֶׁהַמֵּתִים יֵשׁ לָהֶם גַּם כֵּן כַּפָּרָה בְּיוֹם הַכִּפּוּרִים,[סב] וְעַל כֵּן הוּא נִקְרָא "כִּפּוּרִים" לְשׁוֹן רַבִּים, לַחַיִּים וְלַמֵּתִים,[סג] וּכְשֶׁנּוֹדְרִים צְדָקָה בַּעֲבוּרָם – מוֹעִיל לָהֶם לְכַפֵּר בַּעֲדָם, לְפִי שֶׁהַקָּדוֹשׁ בָּרוּךְ הוּא בּוֹחֵן לִבּוֹת וְיוֹדֵעַ שֶׁאִלּוּ הָיוּ בַּחַיִּים הָיוּ גַּם כֵּן נוֹתְנִים צְדָקָה.[סד] אֲבָל אִם נוֹדֵר צְדָקָה בַּעֲבוּר מִי שֶׁהָיָה רָשָׁע[39] – אֵין מוֹעִיל לוֹ כְּלוּם:[סה]

15 If one feels sorrow over the death of the sons of Aharon and sheds tears over their [death] on Yom Kippur, his sins are pardoned and [he is assured that] his sons will not die in his lifetime.[40]

טו הַמִּצְטַעֵר עַל מִיתַת בְּנֵי אַהֲרֹן וּמוֹרִיד דְּמָעוֹת עֲלֵיהֶם בְּיוֹם הַכִּפּוּרִים – מוֹחֲלִים עֲוֹנוֹתָיו וּבָנָיו אֵינָם מֵתִים בְּחַיָּיו:[סו, 40]

---

38. Their names are mentioned in the prayer called *Hazkaras Neshamos,* which is commonly known by its initial word as *Yizkor* ("May [G-d] remember..."). See *Machzor for Yom Kippur* Annotated Edition, pp. 210-11.

39. Who would not give himself.

40. *Zohar,* Vol. III, p. 57b. *Mateh Ephraim* explains the connection between Yom Kippur and Aharon's sons as follows: We should calculate that if G-d punished Aharon's sons, who were on such a high spiritual level, we should surely make a reckoning of our own spiritual standing and repent accordingly.

On a positive note, *Chassidus* observes that *Vayikra* 16:1 prefaces the commandments concerning the Yom Kippur sacrificial worship with the words, "G-d spoke to Moshe after the death of Aharon's two sons, when

[ברייתא] לו, ב כחכמים. רי"ף (ו, א). רמב"ם הל' עבודת יוה"כ פ"ד ה"א. טור ושו"ע ס"ה. וכ"ה הנוסח בסידור (בוידוי שבסדר עבודה). **נה** ברייתא שם. לבוש ס"ה. מ"א ס"ק ה. **נו** לבוש שם. **נז** ברייתא שם. **נח** רש"י שם ד"ה המרדים. לבוש שם. **נט** לבוש שם. מ"א שם. וכדלעיל סי' תרז ס"ו וש"נ. **ס** כלבו סי' ע (לה, ג). רמ"א ס"ו. ובסידור בא נוסח הזכרת נשמות לפני מוסף לשלש רגלים. ולענין הזכרת נשמות בשבת ראה לעיל סי' רפד סי"ד. **סא** רוקח סי' ריז ד"ה ומה שפוסקין. מרדכי ריש רמז תשכז. שו"ע ס"ו. **סב** מרדכי שם. רמ"א שם. **סג** מהר"י ווייל סי' קצא. דרכי משה ס"ק ח. **סד** רוקח שם. ב"י סוף הסי'. ט"ז סק"ד. מ"א סק"ו. **סה** רוקח שם. ב"י שם. מ"א שם. **סו** זהר ח"ג נז, ב. מ"א ריש הסי'.

טז וּמִצְוָה[41] לִלְמֹד בְּיוֹם הַכִּפּוּרִים מִשְׁנָיוֹת יוֹמָא,[42] כְּדֵי שֶׁתַּעֲלֶה הָאֲמִירָה בִּמְקוֹם הַקָּרְבָּה,[43] גַּם בַּגְּמָרָא סוֹף יוֹמָא מַאֲמָרִים הַמְדַבְּרִים בְּמַעֲלוֹת הַתְּשׁוּבָה:[סז]

16 On Yom Kippur, it is a *mitzvah*[41] to study the *Mishnayos* of Tractate *Yoma*,[42] so that the mention [of the sacrificial offerings] will be counted as taking the place of the actual offering.[43] One should also study the *Gemara* at the end of this tractate, which includes teachings that speak of the virtues of *teshuvah*.

יז וְאֵין לְתַלְמִיד חָכָם לַעֲסֹק בַּתּוֹרָה וּלְהַשְׁמִיט אֶת עַצְמוֹ מִלְּהִתְפַּלֵּל הַתְּפִלּוֹת וְהַסְּלִיחוֹת וְהַבַּקָּשׁוֹת עִם הַצִּבּוּר:[סח]

17 A Torah scholar should not occupy himself with his study and withdraw from reciting the prayers, requests for atonement, and supplications, together with the congregation.

סִימָן תרכב סֵדֶר תְּפִלַּת מִנְחָה וּבוֹ ו' סְעִיפִים:

SECTION 622 The Order of the Afternoon Service. (1–6)

א אֵין אוֹמְרִים "אֵין כֵּאלֹהֵינוּ"[א] אַחַר תְּפִלַּת מוּסָף, כְּמוֹ שֶׁאוֹמְרִים בִּשְׁאָר שַׁבָּת וְיוֹם טוֹב, לְפִי שֶׁעִקָּרוֹ לֹא נִתַּקֵּן אֶלָּא כְּנֶגֶד בְּרָכוֹת אֶמְצָעִיּוֹת שֶׁל תְּפִלַּת שְׁמוֹנֶה עֶשְׂרֵה שֶׁאֵין אוֹמְרִים אוֹתָן בְּשַׁבָּת וְיוֹם טוֹב,[ב] אֲבָל בְּיוֹם הַכִּפּוּרִים כְּבָר אָמְרוּ פִּיּוּטִים שֶׁיֵּשׁ בָּהֶם הַזְכָּרוֹת בְּרָכוֹת אֵלּוּ כְּגוֹן "אֲהַלֶּלְךָ כו'".[ג,1]

1 The hymn *Ein k'Elokeinu* is not recited after the *Mussaf* prayers as is done on other *Shabbasos* and festivals. The rationale is that [this hymn] was instituted primarily to take the place of the intermediate blessings of *Shemoneh Esreh* that are not recited on *Shabbos* and festivals. On Yom Kippur [this is unnecessary, because] we have already recited *piyyutim* that recall these blessings, such as *Ahalelcha*.[1]

---

they came close before G-d, and died." Aharon's sons died because their Divine service was impelled only by *ratzo,* the rapturous desire of the soul to *run forward* and cleave to its Source, without being grounded by *shov,* the soul's sober determination to *return* and fulfill its mission in the physical body and material world. On Yom Kippur, paralleling this dual dynamic, we tap these same intense spiritual energies, but focus them on maintaining our worldly framework. (See *Likkutei Sichos,* Vol. 3, p. 987ff.; Vol. 32, p. 98ff.)

41. In addition to its formal meaning, referring to a positive or prohibitive commandment, this term sometimes signifies a praiseworthy action.

42. The Aramaic name of this tractate means "the day," i.e., the day *par excellence.* Its subjects include the sacrificial offerings of Yom Kippur.

43. The Rebbe writes that he has not seen this practice being widely observed. (See *Otzar Minhagei Chabad,* p. 232.)

SECTION 622

1. In the *Machzor for Yom Kippur Annotated Edition,* this hymn is found in the *Shacharis* service (p. 186), preceded by the phrase *Mi E-l Kamocha.*

סז של"ה מסכת יומא עמוד התשובה בסופו (רכט, סע"א) ד"ה משום. אליה זוטא סק"א. וראה אוצר מנהגי חב"ד ע' רלב (שלא ראינו נוהגין כן). **סח** כנסת הגדולה הגה"ט. אליה זוטא שם. וראה גם לעיל סי' סח ס"א.

סימן תרכב: א מהרי"ל הל' מוסף דיום כפור (ע' שנא). רמ"א ס"א. **ב** מהרי"ל שם, בשם מחזור ויטרי (ע' 106). ובנוסח הסדור אומרים כן אף בחול. וראה שער הכולל פי"א אות ל. **ג** מהרי"ל שם. לבוש סי' תרכא בסופו. מ"א סק"א. **ד** ט"ז סק"ג. **ה** ט"ז שם (ביחידות). מ"א שם. **ו** ומנהג חב"ד לאמר אחר

By contrast, the passage describing the incense compounded [for the twice-daily offering] should be recited after *Mussaf,* for though this offering is mentioned in [the description of] the *Avodah,* the particular herbs it comprises are not enumerated there [as they are in this passage].[2]

2 It is customary in some regions to recite *Ashrei* and *U'Va LeTziyon* before the Afternoon Service [on Yom Kippur], as is customary on every *Shabbos* and festival.[3] In these countries,[4] however, we do not recite *Ashrei* and *U'Va LeTziyon* until before the *Neilah* service, so as to make a distinction between the Afternoon Service and *Neilah*. Since the Torah Reading[5] intervenes between *Mussaf* and the Afternoon Service, there is no need to make any further break by reciting *Ashrei* and *U'Va LeTziyon* at that point.

We should hasten the recitation of the *Minchah* service as much as possible.[6]

3 Even if [Yom Kippur] falls on *Shabbos,* we do not recite the verse beginning *Vaani sefilasi*[7] [before taking out the Torah, as is done on other *Shabbasos*. The rationale is] that on other *Shabbasos* this verse is recited in praise of the Jewish people, who read the Torah and pray even though they have eaten and drunk, unlike the nations of the world, who "eat and

אֲבָל "פִּטּוּם הַקְּטֹרֶת", אַף עַל פִּי שֶׁגַּם הִיא נִזְכְּרָה בָּעֲבוֹדָה, מִכָּל מָקוֹם פְּרָטֵי סַמְמָנֵי הַקְּטֹרֶת לֹא הֻזְכְּרוּ שָׁם;[ד] וְלָכֵן יֵשׁ לְאָמְרָם[ה] אַחַר תְּפִלַּת מוּסָף:[ו,2]

ב יֵשׁ מְקוֹמוֹת נוֹהֲגִים לוֹמַר "אַשְׁרֵי וּבָא לְצִיּוֹן" קֹדֶם תְּפִלַּת הַמִּנְחָה[ז] כְּמוֹ בְּכָל שַׁבָּת וְיוֹם טוֹב,[ח,3] אֲבָל בִּמְדִינוֹת אֵלּוּ[4] אֵין אוֹמְרִים "אַשְׁרֵי וּבָא לְצִיּוֹן" עַד קֹדֶם נְעִילָה,[ט] כְּדֵי לְהַפְסִיק בֵּין תְּפִלַּת מִנְחָה לִנְעִילָה בַּאֲמִירַת "אַשְׁרֵי וּבָא לְצִיּוֹן", אֲבָל בֵּין מוּסָף לְמִנְחָה מַפְסִיקִין בִּקְרִיאַת הַתּוֹרָה,[5] לְפִיכָךְ אֵין צָרִיךְ לְהַפְסִיק עוֹד בְּ"אַשְׁרֵי וּבָא לְצִיּוֹן";[י] וְיֵשׁ לָנוּ לְמַהֵר תְּפִלַּת הַמִּנְחָה בְּכָל מַה דְּאֶפְשָׁר:[יא,6]

ג אֵין אוֹמְרִים "וַאֲנִי תְפִלָּתִי"[7] אֲפִלּוּ אִם חָל לִהְיוֹת בְּשַׁבָּת,[יב] לְפִי שֶׁבְּכָל הַשַּׁבָּתוֹת אוֹמְרִים אוֹתוֹ לְשַׁבֵּחַ יִשְׂרָאֵל שֶׁאַף עַל פִּי שֶׁאָכְלוּ וְשָׁתוּ אַף עַל פִּי כֵן הֵם קוֹרִין בַּתּוֹרָה וּמִתְפַּלְּלִין אַחַר כָּךְ מַה שֶּׁאֵין כֵּן אֻמּוֹת הָעוֹלָם שֶׁאוֹכְלִין

2. According to Lubavitch custom, *Ein k'Eilokeinu* and the passage concerning the incense offering are recited not after *Mussaf,* but after *Neilah.*

3. This follows the ruling of R. Yosef Caro, *Orach Chayim* 622:1.

4. I.e., throughout the predominantly Ashkenazic communities of Europe, following the ruling of *Rama (loc. cit.).*

5. I.e., the second Torah Reading that precedes the *Shemoneh Esreh* of *Minchah.*

6. So that *Neilah* may be started by day.

7. *Tehillim* 69:14.

נעילה: קוה, אין כאלקינו, פיטום הקטורת ועלינו (ראה ספר המנהגים – חב"ד ע' 59. אוצר מנהגי חב"ד ע' רל וע' רמד). **ז** רמב"ם הל' תפלה פי"ב הכ"א. טור ושו"ע ס"א. וראה לקמן סי' תרכג ס"א. **ח** לבוש ס"ב. וכדלעיל סי' רצב ס"א. **ט** מרדכי רמז תשכז. הגהות מיימוניות שם אות ת, ובסוף הל' שביתת עשור ד"ה כשאומר. כלבו סי' ע (לה, ד) בשם ה"ר נתן. מנהגים (טירנא) ע' קטז. רמ"א ס"א. **י** כלבו שם. הובא ב"י ריש הסי'. לבוש ס"א. ובסידור: תפלת מנחה וידבר וקטורת ואחר כך מתפללים שמונה עשרה . . . תפלת נעילה אומרים אשרי ובא לציון. וראה שער הכולל פמ"ד אות יט. **יא** ב"י ריש הסימן בשם המרדכי. לבוש שם. ט"ז סק"ב. **יב** טור ושו"ע ס"א. וכ"ה מנהג חב"ד (ספר המנהגים – חב"ד ע' 63. וראה שם הערה 35).

וְשׁוֹתִין וּפוֹחֲזִין,[יג,8] אֲבָל בְּיוֹם הַכִּפּוּרִים אֵין שַׁיָּךְ זֶה:[יד]

ד וּמוֹצִיאִין סֵפֶר תּוֹרָה וְקוֹרִין שְׁלֹשָׁה אֲנָשִׁים[טו,9] בְּפָרָשַׁת עֲרָיוֹת[טז] עַד סוֹף הַפָּרָשָׁה,[יז,10] שֶׁמִּי שֶׁיֵּשׁ עֲבֵרָה בְּיָדוֹ יִפְרֹשׁ מֵהֶן, לְפִי שֶׁהָעֲרָיוֹת עֲבֵרָה מְצוּיָה שֶׁנַּפְשׁוֹ שֶׁל אָדָם מְחַמַּדְתָּן וְיִצְרוֹ תּוֹקְפוֹ,[יח] וְהַשְּׁלִישִׁי מַפְטִיר[יט] בְּיוֹנָה,[כ] לְפִי שֶׁיֵּשׁ בּוֹ כֹּחַ הַתְּשׁוּבָה[כא] וְשֶׁאֵין יְכוֹלִין לִבְרֹחַ מֵאֵת פְּנֵי הַקָּדוֹשׁ בָּרוּךְ הוּא,[כב,11] וְנוֹהֲגִים לְסַיֵּם הַהַפְטָרָה בְּמִיכָה[כג] "מִי אֵל כָּמוֹךָ כו'".[12]

וְאַחַר הַהַפְטָרָה נוֹהֲגִין בִּמְדִינוֹת אֵלּוּ שֶׁלֹּא לְבָרֵךְ רַק שָׁלֹשׁ בְּרָכוֹת, אֲבָל אֵין אוֹמְרִים "עַל הַתּוֹרָה וְעַל הָעֲבוֹדָה",[כד] לְפִי שֶׁכְּבָר נִגְמְרָה עֲבוֹדַת הַיּוֹם קֹדֶם הַמִּנְחָה.[כה]

וְנוֹהֲגִים בִּמְדִינוֹת אֵלּוּ שֶׁאֵין אוֹמְרִים

drink and [then] act wantonly."[8] On Yom Kippur this [contrast] is not applicable.

4 [Before *Shemoneh Esreh*] a Torah scroll is taken out [of the Ark], and three men read[9] the text concerning forbidden relations until the end of that passage,[10] so that anyone who has been sinful should distance himself from [such relations. This passage was chosen] because forbidden relations are a common sin, for a person has an innate desire for them and his natural inclination thrusts him [in that direction].

The congregant who received the third *aliyah* [also] reads the *Haftarah* — which is [the Book of] *Yonah,* because it [exemplifies] the power of *teshuvah* and shows that no man can flee from the Presence of the Holy One, blessed be He.[11] The *Haftarah* customarily concludes with [the three verses from the Book of] *Michah* beginning *Mi E-l kamocha.*[12]

It is customary in these regions to recite only three blessings after the *Haftarah.* We do not recite the blessing [beginning] *Al haTorah ve'al haAvodah,* because the *Avodah,* [that day's unique service in the *Beis HaMikdash,*] was completed before the Afternoon Service.

When [Yom Kippur] falls on *Shabbos,* it is not customary in these countries to recite the

8. The quoted phrase is from *Bereishis Rabbah* 39:8; the teaching appears at greater length in sec. 292:3 of the present work.

The last 14 words of the Alter Rebbe's above text were deleted — evidently by ecclesiastical censors — from the editions of his *Shulchan Aruch* that were originally published in Europe.

9. I.e., three congregants are called to the Reading of the Torah. See sec. 584, footnote 14 above.

10. I.e., they read successive passages from *Vayikra,* ch. 18 (see *Megillah* 31a).

11. This Book tells how Yonah, who had sought to flee from the burden of prophecy, was compelled by Divinely-engineered circumstances to accept his mission, and how his earnest message moved the (non-Jew) inhabitants of Nineveh to repent and thereby avert destruction.

12. *Michah* 7:18-20, whose theme is G-d's compassion and forgiveness. The thirteen phrases that comprise this quotation correspond to the Thirteen Attributes of Mercy enumerated in *Shmos* 34:6-7.

יג כדלעיל סי' רצב ס"ג. יד טור ולבוש סוף ס"ב. ט"ז ס"ק א. טו רמב"ם הל' תפלה פי"ב הט"ז. טור ושו"ע ס"ב. וכמו בשבת מנחה, דלעיל סי' רצב ס"ב, וש"נ. טז גמרא [ברייתא] מגילה לא, א. טור ושו"ע שם. יז טור ושו"ע שם. יח רש"י שם ד"ה קורין. ט"ז ס"ק ד. יט טור ושו"ע שם. והטעם נתבאר לעיל סי' רפב סוף סי"א. כ ברייתא שם. טור ושו"ע שם. כא ב"י ד"ה וקורין. לבוש ס"ב. כב אבודרהם סדר תפלת יוה"כ. אליה זוטא סק"ב. כג ז, יח־כ. טור ושו"ע שם. כד רמ"א ס"ב. וכ"ה בהגהות מיימוניות סוף הל' שביתת העשור ד"ה המפטיר בשם ראב"ן. מהרי"ל הל' תפלת מנחה דיום כפור (ע' שנב). רמ"א ס"ב. כה הגהות מיימוניות שם. לבוש ס"ב. כו ר"ן ר"ה (ט, א) ד"ה גמרא מכלל, בשם הר"י ברצלוני. דרכי משה ס"ק ד. רמ"א ס"ג. כז תהלים לו, ז.

passage beginning *Tzidkas'cha* [in the Afternoon Service], because it includes the phrase,[13] "Your judgments extend to the great depths." And on Yom Kippur we ask for mercy rather than judgment, [asking G-d to go] beyond the limits of the law, as in the verse,[14] "Do not enter into judgment [with Your servant]."

"צִדְקָתְךָ" כְּשֶׁחָל בְּשַׁבָּת,[כו] לְפִי שֶׁכָּתוּב בּוֹ[13] "מִשְׁפָּטֶיךָ תְּהוֹם רַבָּה",[כז] וְאֵין אָנוּ מְבַקְּשִׁין מִשְׁפָּט בְּיוֹם הַכִּפּוּרִים אֶלָּא רַחֲמִים וְלִפְנִים מִשּׁוּרַת הַדִּין, כְּעֵין שֶׁנֶּאֱמַר[כח] "וְאַל תָּבוֹא בְמִשְׁפָּט כו'":[כט,14]

5 If time is pressing, *Avinu Malkeinu* should be omitted so that *Neilah* will start on time, as stated in sec. 623[:2].[15]

ה אִם הַשָּׁעָה דְּחוּקָה – יְדַלְּגוּ "אָבִינוּ מַלְכֵּנוּ", כְּדֵי לְהַתְחִיל נְעִילָה בִּזְמַנָּהּ[ל] שֶׁיִּתְבָּאֵר בְּסִימָן תרכ"ג:[לא,15]

6 The *Kohanim* do not bless the people during the Afternoon Service on Yom Kippur, as stated in sec. 129[:1]; see that source. Nevertheless, the *sheliach tzibbur* should recite [the passage beginning *Elokeinu v'Elokei avoseinu* which quotes] the Priestly Blessing, and also *Sim shalom*,[16] for the reason stated there.[17]

ו אַף עַל פִּי שֶׁאֵין נְשִׂיאַת כַּפַּיִם בְּמִנְחָה בְּיוֹם הַכִּפּוּרִים[לב] כְּמוֹ שֶׁנִּתְבָּאֵר בְּסִימָן קכ"ט[לג] עַיֵּן שָׁם, אַף עַל פִּי כֵן יֹאמַר הַשְּׁלִיחַ צִבּוּר בִּרְכַּת כֹּהֲנִים[לד] וְ"שִׂים שָׁלוֹם"[לה,16] מִטַּעַם שֶׁנִּתְבָּאֵר שָׁם,[לו,17] עַיֵּן שָׁם:

SECTION 623 The Order of the *Neilah* Service. (1–[12])

סימן תרכג סֵדֶר תְּפִלַּת נְעִילָה וּבוֹ י"[ב] סְעִיפִים:

1 In communities in which *Ashrei* and *U'Va LeTziyon* are recited before the Afternoon Service, *Ashrei* should be repeated before [the concluding service called] *Neilah*, in order to signify a break between

א בִּמְקוֹמוֹת שֶׁאוֹמְרִים "אַשְׁרֵי וּבָא לְצִיּוֹן" קֹדֶם תְּפִלַּת מִנְחָה[א] – צְרִיכִים לַחֲזֹר וְלוֹמַר "אַשְׁרֵי" קֹדֶם תְּפִלַּת נְעִילָה,[ב] כְּדֵי לְהַפְסִיק בֵּין מִנְחָה לִנְעִילָה,[ג]

---

13. *Tehillim* 36:7.

14. *Ibid.* 143:2.

15. Lubavitch custom is not to omit *Avinu Malkeinu* even though this may delay the beginning of *Neilah*.

16. The custom of some Ashkenazic communities is to begin the final blessing of the *Shemoneh Esreh* with the phrase *Shalom rav* instead of *Sim shalom*, in every prayer service that does not include the Priestly Blessing. Since the Priestly Blessing may be recited in the Afternoon Service, the version *Sim Shalom* is appropriate. In his *Siddur*, the Alter Rebbe uses the version *Sim Shalom* in the *Shemoneh Esreh* at all times, even when the Priestly Blessing is not recited.

17. In sec. 129:2, the Alter Rebbe writes that although the *Kohanim* would not bless the people in the Afternoon Service on Yom Kippur, nevertheless, if a priest did go up to bless the people then, he should recite the blessing. Hence the passage beginning *Elokeinu v'Elokei avoseinu* is appropriate at this time.

כח תהלים קמג, ב. כט לבוש שם. וראה גם לעיל סי' תקצה גבי ר"ה (ואין לעורר הדין ביום דין). ל הגהות מיימוניות שם ד"ה צריך. הובא ב"י סוף הסי'. מ"א סק"ב. וראה גם לעיל סי' תרכ ס"א. לא סעיף ב. לב טור בשם רב עמרם. שו"ע ס"ד. לג סעיף א. לד דרכי משה ס"ק ה, בשם מנהגים (טירנא) מנהג יוה"כ (ע' קטז). לבוש ס"ג. לה ולא שלום רב (ראה ב"י סוף הסימן בשם המרדכי. לעיל סי' קכז ס"ג). ובסידור הנוסח שים שלום בכל התפלות. לו סעיף ב.
סימן תרכג: א כדלעיל סי' תרכב ס"ב, שיש מקומות נוהגים כן. ב טור ושו"ע ס"א. וראה לעיל שם, המנהג במדינות אלו, שלא לומר אשרי ובא לציון עד קודם נעילה. ג ראה גם לעיל שם.

מִטַּעַם שֶׁנִּתְבָּאֵר בְּסִימָן ק"ח[ד,1] וק"ה:[ה,2]

the Afternoon Service and *Neilah,* for the reason stated in sec. 108[:5][1] and sec. 105[:1].[2]

ב הַתְחָלַת זְמַן תְּפִלַּת נְעִילָה הוּא כְּשֶׁהַחַמָּה בְּרֹאשׁ הָאִילָנוֹת,[ו] דְּהַיְנוּ קָרוֹב לְהַתְחָלַת הַשְּׁקִיעָה,[ז] וְנִמְשָׁךְ זְמַנָּהּ עַד סָמוּךְ לְצֵאת הַכּוֹכָבִים.[ח] לְפִיכָךְ צָרִיךְ הַשְּׁלִיחַ צִבּוּר לְקַצֵּר בִּסְלִיחוֹת וּפִיּוּטִים שֶׁבְּאֶמְצַע הַתְּפִלָּה, וְגַם אֵין לוֹ לִמְשֹׁךְ בִּתְפִלַּת נְעִילָה כָּל תֵּבָה וְתֵבָה כְּדֶרֶךְ שֶׁמּוֹשֵׁךְ בִּשְׁאָר תְּפִלּוֹת,[ט] כְּדֵי שֶׁיִּגְמֹר קֹדֶם צֵאת הַכּוֹכָבִים, לְפִי שֶׁתְּפִלָּה זוֹ הִיא בְּתַעֲנִית צִבּוּר[י,3] כְּנֶגֶד נְעִילַת[4] שַׁעֲרֵי הֵיכָל שֶׁבַּמִּקְדָּשׁ[יא,5] שֶׁהָיָה בַּיּוֹם אַחַר הַדְלָקַת נֵרוֹת שֶׁל בֵּין הָעַרְבַּיִם,[יב,6] כְּעֶבֶד הָרוֹצֶה לָצֵאת מִן הַמֶּלֶךְ וּמִקֹּדֶם שֶׁיֵּצֵא הוּא מְבַקֵּשׁ פְּרָס וּמְנַת הַמֶּלֶךְ וְיוֹצֵא וְנוֹעֵל הַשַּׁעַר אַחֲרָיו:[יג]

2 The time for the *Neilah* prayer begins when the sun is at the treetops, i.e., shortly before the beginning of sunset, and continues until shortly before the appearance of the stars. The *sheliach tzibbur* should therefore be brief in the recitation of the *Selichos* and hymns in the midst of this service. He should not extend every word of the *Neilah* service as he does in the other prayer services, so that he will be able to complete *[Neilah]* before the stars appear.

[The rationale is that] this prayer was instituted on communal fastdays[3] to correspond to the locking[4] of the gates of the Sanctuary in the *[Beis Ha]Mikdash*[5] which took place during the day, after the kindling [of the *Menorah*] in the [late] afternoon.[6] In this [we] resemble a servant who seeks to take his leave of the king, but before departing he requests a reward or a gift, and then departs and locks the gate behind him.

ג אֲבָל יֵשׁ אוֹמְרִים[יד] שֶׁיְּכוֹלִין לְהַאֲרִיךְ וּלְהַמְשִׁיךְ בִּתְפִלַּת נְעִילָה גַּם בַּלַּיְלָה, וְאַף עַל פִּי שֶׁהוּא אַחַר נְעִילַת שַׁעֲרֵי הֵיכָל, לְפִי שֶׁלֹּא תִּקְּנוּ כְּלָל לְהִתְפַּלֵּל

3 Some authorities, however, maintain that the *Neilah* service can be extended and continued into the night, even though this is after the time that the gates of the Sanctuary were locked. [They argue that] it was not at all ordained that this service should be

1. There the Alter Rebbe states that one who has to recite *Shemoneh Esreh* twice should separate the two prayers by reciting *Ashrei,* so that the second *Shemoneh Esreh* will begin amidst consolatory words of Torah.

2. There the Alter Rebbe states that a person who recites *Shemoneh Esreh* twice in succession should interpose a quiet moment during which to compose himself.

3. See *Pesachim* 54b.

4. For *Neilah* means "locking."

5. *Talmud Yerushalmi, Berachos* 4:2, *Taanis* 4:4.

6. *Pnei Moshe* on *Taanis, loc. cit.*

ד ס"ה (לעמוד מדברי תחנונים של תורה). וראה שער הכולל פמ"ד אות יט. ה שתהא דעתו מיושבת. ו ר(מב)"ן (ו, ב) ד"ה ירושלמי, בשם הירושלמי ברכות פ"ד ה"א (שגם רב התחיל אז). מהר"ם מרוטנבורג (שיש להתפלל כולה ביום), הובא בר"ן שם ד"ה והוי, ובהגהות מיימוניות הל' תפלה פ"ג אות ה. רא"ש פ"ח סי' כ. טור ושו"ע ס"ב. ז כדלעיל סי' רסא ס"ו (במוסגר). ולפי שיטת הגאונים, ראה סדר הכנסת שבת בתחלתו, שזמן זה (כשהחמה בראש האילנות) היא שקיעה הנראית, שהוא זמן קצר לפני השקיעה האמיתית (כשהשמש בראשי ההרים), וש"נ. ח מ"א ס"ק א (בפירוש דברי הרמב"ם הל' תפלה פ"ג ה"ו, ושו"ע כאן ס"א: שישלים אותה סמוך לשקיעת החמה). כרבי יוחנן בירושלמי שם (שיש להתפלל כולה ביום). וראה גם לקמן סי' תרכד ס"א (כרבי יוחנן). ט ב"י סוד"ה ומאריכין. שו"ע שם. י ראה פסחים נד, ב ורש"י ד"ה לתפלת. משנה תענית כו, א ורש"י ד"ה נעילת. רמב"ם הל' תעניות פ"ה ה"ה. טור סי' תקעט בסופו. לבוש ס"ב. לעיל סי' קכט ס"א. יא ירושלמי שם כרבי יוחנן. לבוש שם. יב רא"ש שם. ר"ן שם ד"ה ירושלמי. לבוש שם. יג לבוש שם. יד ר"ן

recited at the time that the Sanctuary gates were locked, but that it is called *Neilah* because it is recited at the end of the day; it concludes the day's prayers, and is recited just before the gates of Heaven are locked at the end of the prayers.[7]

4 The *halachah* follows the former view.[8] Nevertheless, nowadays that it is customary to follow the latter view,[9] those who do so should not be rebuked. *[Neilah]* must however be started while it is still well before sunset. Also, care should be taken to recite the hymn beginning *Hayom yifneh* ("The day wanes") before sunset, for otherwise one would [seemingly] be uttering a falsehood in G-d's Presence.[10]

5 [At *Neilah,* in the phrases inserted in *Shemoneh Esreh,* and in *Avinu Malkeinu,* the wording of our requests is modified:] We say *chasmeinu* ("seal us") instead of *kasveinu* ("inscribe us"), *vachasom* ("seal") instead of *uchesov* ("inscribe"), and *veneichaseim* (" may we be sealed") instead of *venikaseiv* ("may we be inscribed").[11]

6 If [Yom Kippur falls on] *Shabbos,* one should mention *Shabbos* in this service,[12] just as it [was] mentioned in the other prayer services in the course of the day, for it is still *Shabbos.* Even those who extend [the *Neilah*] service into the night

תְּפִלָּה זוֹ בְּעֵת נְעִילַת שַׁעֲרֵי הֵיכָל, וּמַה שֶּׁנִּקְרָא תְּפִלַּת נְעִילָה, הַיְנוּ לְפִי שֶׁמִּתְפַּלְּלִין אוֹתָהּ בְּסוֹף הַיּוֹם וְהִיא גְּמַר תְּפִלּוֹת שֶׁל הַיּוֹם, וּמִתְפַּלְּלִין אוֹתָהּ סָמוּךְ לִנְעִילַת שַׁעֲרֵי שָׁמַיִם[טו] שֶׁנּוֹעֲלִין אוֹתָם בִּגְמַר הַתְּפִלּוֹת:[טז,7]

ד וְאַף עַל פִּי שֶׁהָעִקָּר כַּסְּבָרָא הָרִאשׁוֹנָה,[8] מִכָּל מָקוֹם עַכְשָׁו שֶׁנּוֹהֲגִין כַּסְּבָרָא הָאַחֲרוֹנָה[9] — אֵין לִמְחוֹת בְּיָדָם, וּמִכָּל מָקוֹם צְרִיכִין לְהַתְחִיל בְּעוֹד הַיּוֹם גָּדוֹל, וְגַם יִזָּהֲרוּ לוֹמַר חָרוּז "הַיּוֹם יִפְנֶה כו'" קֹדֶם הַעֲרֵב שֶׁמֶשׁ, דְּאִם לֹא כֵן הוּא דּוֹבֵר שְׁקָרִים לִפְנֵי ה':[יז,10]

ה וְאוֹמְרִים בִּמְקוֹם "כָּתְבֵנוּ" — "חָתְמֵנוּ",[יח] וּבִמְקוֹם "וּכְתֹב" — "וַחֲתֹם", וּבִמְקוֹם "וְנִכָּתֵב" — "וְנֵחָתֵם":[יט,11]

ו וְאִם הוּא שַׁבָּת — מַזְכִּיר שֶׁל שַׁבָּת בִּתְפִלָּה זוֹ[כ,12] כְּדֶרֶךְ שֶׁמַּזְכִּיר בִּשְׁאָר תְּפִלּוֹת הַיּוֹם,[כא] שֶׁהֲרֵי עֲדַיִן יוֹם שַׁבָּת הוּא,[כב] וַאֲפִלּוּ אוֹתָם הַמַּמְשִׁיכִים תְּפִלָּה זוֹ בַּלַּיְלָה, מִכָּל מָקוֹם כֵּיוָן שֶׁהִתְחִילוּ מִבְּעוֹד

7. On another level, it has been taught that this service is called *Neilah* because at that crucial hour every individual Jew is (so to speak) locked in, alone with his Maker. (See *Likkutei Sichos,* Vol. 4, p. 1154.)

8. I.e., that *Neilah* should end by the time the stars appear (as in subsection 2 above).

9. I.e., that *Neilah* may be extended into the night (as in subsection 3 above).

10. *Sefer HaMinhagim: The Book of Chabad-Lubavitch Customs,* p. 125, states that this phrase may nevertheless be recited even after sunset. In fact, it is recited even after dark.

11. For at this time the judgment for the coming year is sealed.

12. *Shabbos* 24b.

(ו, ב) ד"ה והוי בדעת הרי"ף שם, כרב בירושלמי שם. ב"ח בדעת הרא"ש שם. **טו** רב בירושלמי שם. **טז** רש"י תענית דף כו, א ד"ה נעילת. **יז** ב"ח סד"ה ולענין הלכה. מ"א סק"א. ומנהג חב"ד לאמרו גם אם כבר העריב היום (ספר המנהגים – חב"ד ע' 59). **יח** רוקח סי' ריז ד"ה אשרי. מרדכי רמז תשכז. טור. רמ"א ס"ב. **יט** רוקח שם. טור. לבוש סוף ס"ב. **כ** גמרא שבת כד, רע"ב. טור ושו"ע ס"ג. וראה גם לעיל סי' רסח סי"ד. **כא** ראה גמרא שם. **כב** לבוש ס"ג.

יוֹם – צָרִיךְ לְהַזְכִּיר שֶׁל שַׁבָּת (כְּמוֹ שֶׁנִּתְבָּאֵר בְּסִימָן קפ"ח[כג, 13]).

אֲבָל בְּוִדּוּי שֶׁלְּאַחַר הַתְּפִלָּה[14] – אֵין מַזְכִּירִין בּוֹ שֶׁל שַׁבָּת,[כד] כֵּיוָן שֶׁכְּבָר סִיֵּם בִּרְכַּת שַׁבָּת (דְּהַיְנוּ "אַתָּה בְחַרְתָּנוּ" שֶׁחוֹתְמִין "מְקַדֵּשׁ הַשַּׁבָּת") וְלֹא מָצִינוּ הַזְכָּרָה אַחַר סִיּוּם הַבְּרָכָה,[כה] כְּמוֹ שֶׁנִּתְבָּאֵר בְּסִימָן תכ"ה,[כו, 15] עַיֵּן שָׁם.

בַּמֶּה דְּבָרִים אֲמוּרִים? בְּיָחִיד, אֲבָל הַשְּׁלִיחַ צִבּוּר כֵּיוָן שֶׁאוֹמֵר הַוִּדּוּי בְּתוֹךְ הַתְּפִלָּה – צָרִיךְ לְהַזְכִּיר שֶׁל שַׁבָּת[כז] בְּ"אַתָּה הִבְדַּלְתָּ אֱנוֹשׁ כו'" כְּדֶרֶךְ שֶׁמַּזְכִּיר בּוֹ שֶׁל יוֹם הַכִּפּוּרִים, שֶׁהֲרֵי בִּרְכַּת "אַתָּה בְחַרְתָּנוּ" הִיא מְיֻחֶדֶת לְשַׁבָּת וּלְיוֹם הַכִּפּוּרִים, שֶׁהֲרֵי מַזְכִּיר בָּהּ שֶׁל שַׁבָּת בַּתְּחִלָּה "וַתִּתֶּן לָנוּ אֶת יוֹם הַשַּׁבָּת הַזֶּה וכו'" וּבַסּוֹף חוֹתֵם "מְקַדֵּשׁ הַשַּׁבָּת כו'".[כח] וּמִכָּל מָקוֹם, אִם לֹא הִזְכִּיר שֶׁל שַׁבָּת בְּתוֹךְ הַוִּדּוּי – אֵין מַחֲזִירִין אוֹתוֹ,[כט] כֵּיוָן שֶׁהִזְכִּירוֹ בְּתוֹךְ הַתְּפִלָּה.[ל] אֲבָל אִם לֹא

must still mention *Shabbos,* because they began it while it was still day (as stated in sec. 188[:17]).[13] In the confessional that follows *Shemoneh Esreh,*[14] however, one should not mention *Shabbos,* because the blessing concerning *Shabbos* has already ended. (["The blessing concerning *Shabbos*" is] the passage that begins *Atah bechartanu,* and that concludes with the words *mekadesh haShabbos* [which praise G-d for sanctifying the *Shabbos*].) And we have never found a mention [of *Shabbos*] after the end of that blessing, as stated in sec. 425.[15]

To whom does the above apply? To an individual [who recites *Shemoneh Esreh*]. As to the *sheliach tzibbur,* by contrast, since he recites the confessional in the midst of [repeating] *Shemoneh Esreh,* he must mention *Shabbos* in the passage beginning *Atah hivdalta enosh,* just as he mentions Yom Kippur there. For the blessing [beginning] *Atah bechartanu* relates specifically to both *Shabbos* and Yom Kippur, since *Shabbos* is mentioned [both] in the beginning, namely, *Vatiten lanu... es yom haShabbos hazeh* ("and You gave us... this *Shabbos* day"), and in the concluding phrase [that begins] *mekadesh haShabbos....* Nevertheless, if the *sheliach tzibbur* [erred and] did not mention *Shabbos* in the confessional, he is not required to repeat [the blessing], since he has already mentioned the *Shabbos* in [this] prayer. If, however, one did not

13. There the Alter Rebbe speaks about a meal that began on *Shabbos* and continued after nightfall (as is frequently the case with *seudah shelishis*). He explains that the obligation to mention the uniqueness of the day takes effect at the beginning of the meal. Hence, since it was *Shabbos* when the meal began, *Shabbos* must be mentioned in the Grace after Meals even if it was recited after *Shabbos* ended.

14. I.e., the confessional that an individual worshiper recites after the main body of *Shemoneh Esreh.*

15. Sec. 425 in the Alter Rebbe's *Shulchan Aruch* is not extant. The *Shulchan Aruch* of R. Yosef Caro (sec. 425:1) states that when Rosh Chodesh falls on *Shabbos,* we do not mention *Shabbos* in the passage known as *Yaaleh veyavo,* because it was already mentioned in the fourth blessing of *Shemoneh Esreh.*

כג סעיף יז. וראה מ"מ וציונים. כד רא"ש שבת פ"ב סי' טז. מרדכי שם רמז רפב. טור ושו"ע שם. לבוש ס"ג. כו סימן זה בשוע"ר לא הגיע לידינו, וראה טור ושו"ע שם ס"א. כז שבלי הלקט סי' קעח. שו"ת מהרי"ל סי' ג. ב"י ד"ה ומ"ש אבל. שו"ע שם. כח ראה לבוש שם. כט ב"י שם. שו"ע שם. ל לבוש שם. מ"א סק"ב. לא הגהות מרדכי שבת רמז תנו (עט, א). הובא ב"י ד"ה ואם, ובדרכי משה הארוך אות ג. מ"א שם. לב טור ושו"ע ס"ד.

הִזְכִּיר שֶׁל שַׁבָּת כְּלָל אֲפִלּוּ בְּתוֹךְ הַתְּפִלָּה[16] — מַחֲזִירִין אוֹתוֹ,[לא,17] בֵּין יָחִיד בֵּין שְׁלִיחַ צִבּוּר:

mention the *Shabbos* at all, even in the midst of *Shemoneh Esreh,*[16] he is required to repeat [the blessing or the *Shemoneh Esreh*].[17] [This applies] both to an individual worshiper and to a *sheliach tzibbur*.

ז בְּמָקוֹם שֶׁאוֹמְרִים "כֶּתֶר" בְּמוּסָף — אוֹמְרִים גַּם כֵּן בִּנְעִילָה,[לב] וּבִמְקוֹמוֹת שֶׁאוֹמְרִים "נַעֲרִיצְךָ" בְּמוּסָף — אוֹמְרִים גַּם כֵּן בִּנְעִילָה:[לג]

7 Wherever *Kesser* is customarily said [at the beginning of *Kedushah*] at *Mussaf,* it is also said at *Neilah.* Wherever *Naaritzcha* is customarily said at *Mussaf,* it is also said at *Neilah.*

ח נוֹשְׂאִים כַּפַּיִם[18] בִּנְעִילָה.[לד,19] וּלְפִי שֶׁנְּשִׂיאַת כַּפַּיִם הֻקְּשָׁה לַעֲבוֹדָה[20] כְּמוֹ שֶׁנִּתְבָּאֵר בְּסִימָן קכ"ח[לה] וַעֲבוֹדָה אֵינָהּ אֶלָּא בַּיּוֹם,[לו] לְפִיכָךְ צָרִיךְ הַשְּׁלִיחַ צִבּוּר לְמַהֵר בִּתְפִלַּת נְעִילָה וּלְדַלֵּג הַסְּלִיחוֹת אִם אֵין שְׁהוּת בַּיּוֹם בְּעִנְיָן שֶׁתְּהֵא נְשִׂיאַת כַּפַּיִם בַּיּוֹם[לז] קֹדֶם צֵאת הַכּוֹכָבִים.[לח]

אֲבָל בִּמְדִינוֹת אֵלּוּ אֵין נוֹהֲגִין כֵּן, אֶלָּא אֵין הַכֹּהֲנִים עוֹלִין לַדּוּכָן[21] כְּלָל בִּנְעִילָה,[לט] לְפִי שֶׁמַּאֲרִיכִין בִּסְלִיחוֹת וּפִזְמוֹנִים עַד הַלַּיְלָה וְאֵין נְשִׂיאַת כַּפַּיִם בַּלַּיְלָה.[מ] אֲבָל מִכָּל מָקוֹם אוֹמֵר הַשְּׁלִיחַ צִבּוּר "אֱלֹקֵינוּ וֵאלֹקֵי אֲבוֹתֵינוּ בָּרְכֵנוּ כו'" אַף עַל פִּי שֶׁהוּא לַיְלָה, שֶׁבָּזֶה אֵין קְפִידָא כָּל כָּךְ,[מא]

8 [The *Kohanim* customarily] bless the people[18] at *Neilah.*[19] An equation exists between the Priestly Blessing and the sacrificial service [in the *Beis HaMikdash*],[20] as stated in sec. 128[:44], and the sacrificial service takes place only during the day. The *sheliach tzibbur* must therefore be brief in the *Neilah* service and omit the *Selichos,* if not enough time will be left in the day to enable the Priestly Blessing to be recited before the stars appear.

This is not, however, the practice in these countries. The *Kohanim* do not bless the people[21] at all during the *Neilah* service, for it is customary to extend it [by reciting] *Selichos* and hymns until the night, and the Priestly Blessing is not given at night.

Nevertheless, the *sheliach tzibbur* should recite [the passage beginning] *Elokeinu v'Elokei avoseinu barcheinu* [which quotes the Priestly Blessing]. This is not really problematic even though it is already night,

16. I.e., at the conclusion of the intermediate blessing.

17. I.e., if one became aware of his omission before completing *Shemoneh Esreh,* he must repeat from the intermediate blessing onward. If he realized his mistake only after completing *Shemoneh Esreh,* he must repeat the entire *Shemoneh Esreh.*

18. Lit., "raise their hands."

19. *Taanis* 26a.

20. *Sotah* 38a.

21. Lit., "ascend the dais."

לג ב"ח סוף הסימן. עטרת זקנים ס"ק ג. לד משנה תענית כו, א. טור ושו"ע ס"ה. וראה גם לעיל סי' קכח ס"א וסנ"ז. סי' קכט ס"א. והיינו אף במדינות אלו שאין נשיאות כפים אלא ביום טוב, כדלעיל סי' קכח סנ"ז, ושם נתבאר הטעם. לה סכ"ג וסמ"ד וסנ"א. לו הגהות מיימוניות הל' תפלה פ"ג אות ה (לענין נשיאת כפים). מהרי"ל הל' תפלת שחרית דיו"כ (ע' שלט). לבוש ס"ה. וכדלעיל סי' א מהדו"ב ס"ט וש"נ. לז הגהות מיימוניות סוף הל' שביתת העשור ד"ה צריך, בשם מהר"מ. ב"י סוד"ה ומאריכין. לבוש סוף ס"ד. מ"א סק"ג. לח לבוש שם. לט מנהגים (טירנא) מנהג יוה"כ (ע' קיז). רמ"א ס"ה. וכ"ה מנהג חב"ד אפילו עוד היום גדול (ספר המנהגים – חב"ד ע' 59. אג"ק ח"ח ע' ע). מ לבוש ס"ה. ב"ח סוף הסי'. מא מ"א סק"ג.

כֵּיוָן שֶׁתְּפִלָּה זוֹ רְאוּיָה לִנְשִׂיאַת כַּפַּיִם, שֶׁהֲרֵי הַתְחָלַת זְמַנָּהּ הִיא מִבְּעוֹד יוֹם:[מב, 22]

since [in principle] the Priestly Blessing is appropriate in [the *Neilah*] prayer, for the time of its recitation begins while it is yet day.[22]

ט וְאַחַר הַתְּפִלָּה אוֹמְרִים "אָבִינוּ מַלְכֵּנוּ"[מג, 23] אֲפִלּוּ כְּשֶׁחָל בְּשַׁבָּת,[מד] וַאֲפִלּוּ עֲדַיִן הוּא יוֹם,[מה] וְאַף עַל פִּי שֶׁבְּכָל הַיּוֹם אֵין אוֹמְרִים "אָבִינוּ מַלְכֵּנוּ" כְּשֶׁהוּא שַׁבָּת, מִכָּל מָקוֹם עַכְשָׁו יֵשׁ לְאָמְרוֹ, לְפִי שֶׁעַכְשָׁו הוּא גְּמַר הַחֲתִימָה וְאָנוּ צְרִיכִין לְבַקֵּשׁ רַחֲמִים, וְאִם לֹא עַכְשָׁו – אֵימָתַי:[מו, 24]

9 After [the repetition of] *Shemoneh Esreh* we recite the prayer *Avinu Malkeinu*,[23] even when Yom Kippur falls on *Shabbos*, and even if it is still day. Although throughout the day we do not recite *Avinu Malkeinu* on *Shabbos*, we should recite it at this time, for at this time the sealing [of the Divine decree for the coming year] is made final. We need to request mercy, "and if not now, when?"[24]

י בְּסוֹף הַסְּלִיחוֹת[מז] אוֹמְרִים "שְׁמַע יִשְׂרָאֵל" פַּעַם אַחַת, וְשָׁלֹשׁ פְּעָמִים "בָּרוּךְ שֵׁם כְּבוֹד מַלְכוּתוֹ לְעוֹלָם וָעֶד",[מח] וְאַחַר כָּךְ אוֹמְרִים שֶׁבַע פְּעָמִים "ה' הוּא הָאֱלֹהִים"[מט] לְלַוּוֹת הַשְּׁכִינָה שֶׁתַּעֲלֶה וְתִסְתַּלֵּק עַכְשָׁו לְמַעְלָה מִשִּׁבְעָה רְקִיעִים, שֶׁבִּשְׁעַת הַתְּפִלָּה הָיְתָה הַשְּׁכִינָה שְׁרוּיָה בֵּינֵינוּ וְעַכְשָׁו תַּעֲלֶה לִמְקוֹמָהּ:[נ]

10 After concluding the penitential prayers we say the verse beginning *Shema Yisrael* once, *Baruch shem kevod malchuso leolam vaed* three times, and then *A-donai hu haElokim* seven times, to escort the Divine Presence that now departs and ascends beyond the seven heavens. For during the prayers, the Divine Presence abided in our midst; now it ascends to its place.

יא וְאוֹמְרִים קַדִּישׁ[נא] שָׁלֵם,[נב] וְאַחַר כָּךְ[נג] תּוֹקְעִין תְּקִיעָה אַחַת,[נד, 25] וְיֵשׁ נוֹהֲגִין

11 At this point [the *sheliach tzibbur*] recites the complete *Kaddish* and then one *tekiah* is sounded.[25] The custom

22. In Lubavitch practice the *Kohanim* do not bless the people at *Neilah*, even before sunset (*Sefer HaMinhagim: The Book of Chabad-Lubavitch Customs*, p. 126). Instead, as above, the *sheliach tzibbur* recites the passage *Elokeinu v'Elokei avoseinu*, which quotes the Priestly Blessing.

23. As stated in subsection 5 above, at this point we substitute *chasmeinu* ("seal us") wherever our previous request was worded *kasveinu* ("inscribe us").

24. The quoted phrase is borrowed from *Avos* 1:14.

25. According to Lubavitch custom (noted in *Machzor HaShalem*), this *tekiah* is sounded in the middle of *Kaddish*, before the sentence beginning *Tiskabel*. Immediately before the *shofar* is sounded, as an expression of trust that our sins have been forgiven, and that the newly-launched year will indeed be a happy one, the congregation breaks out into singing the exultant rhythms of "Napoleon's March," which is sometimes accompanied by exuberant dancing. After the *shofar* is sounded, the congregation proclaims: *Leshanah habaah biYerushalayim* — "Next year in Jerusalem!"

מב מהרי"ל שם (אף לענין איחר עד הלילה). וכדלעיל ס"ב. מג מהרי"ל הל' יוה"כ ע' שמג). דרכי משה ס"ק ג. רמ"א ס"ה. מד מהרי"ל שם. דרכי משה ס"ק ב. מ"א ס"ק ג. מה מ"א שם. מו ר"ן ר"ה (ט, א) ד"ה מכלל. ב"י סי' תרכב ד"ה ואם חל. מ"א שם. מז שו"ע ס"ו. במחזור חב"ד הוא אחר אבינו מלכנו. מח מנהגים (טירנא) מנהג יוה"כ (ע' קיז). רמ"א ס"ו. וראה לעיל סי' סא ס"ט וסי"ב. מט תוס' ברכות לד, א ד"ה אמר. סמ"ג ל"ת סט בשם מורו. שו"ע שם. וראה לעיל שם ס"י. נ לבוש ס"ה. וראה לעיל שם. נא מנהגים (טירנא) יום כפור (ע' קיז). רמ"א ס"ו. נב מנהגים שם. לבוש ס"ה. נג מנהגים שם. רמ"א שם. ועוד שם, שבקצת

in some regions is to sound a series of *tekiah-shevarim-teruah-tekiah [shofar* blasts*]*.

Although we have not yet recited *Havdalah* in *Shemoneh Esreh,* there is no prohibition whatever [against sounding the *shofar*], for [doing so] does not involve [the performance of] a forbidden labor.[26] It is not even forbidden as a *shvus*[27] in a complete sense, as stated in sec. 588[:4]. It is forbidden on *Shabbos* and festivals only because of the prohibition against mundane activities,[28] as explained in that section. Hence, one may allow sounding [the *shofar*] even [as early as] *bein hashmashos,*[29] if the *Neilah* service has already been completed. (See sec. 342[:1].)[30]

[Subsections 12 and 13 are not extant.][31]

14 The reason for this *shofar* blast is that it signifies the ascent and withdrawal of the Divine Presence — just as, at the Giving of the Torah, the Divine Presence ascended "at the sounding of the extended *shofar* blast."[32] And elsewhere it is written,[33] "G-d ascended with the *shofar* blast."

לִתְקֹעַ תשר״ת.[נה]

וְאַף עַל פִּי שֶׁעֲדַיִן לֹא הִבְדִּילוּ בַּתְּפִלָּה[נו] — אַף עַל פִּי כֵן אֵין כָּאן אִסּוּר כְּלָל, כֵּיוָן שֶׁהַתְּקִיעָה אֵינָהּ מְלָאכָה[26] כְּלָל[נז] וְאֵין בָּהּ אֲפִלּוּ מִשּׁוּם שְׁבוּת[27] גָּמוּר כְּמוֹ שֶׁנִּתְבָּאֵר בְּסִימָן תקפ״[ח],[נח] וְלֹא אָסְרוּ בְּשַׁבָּת וְיוֹם טוֹב אֶלָּא מִשּׁוּם עוּבְדִין דְּחֹל[28] כְּמוֹ שֶׁנִּתְבָּאֵר שָׁם, לְפִיכָךְ יֵשׁ לְהַתִּיר תְּקִיעָה זוֹ אֲפִלּוּ בֵּין הַשְּׁמָשׁוֹת[נט,29] אִם כְּבָר גָּמְרוּ תְּפִלַּת נְעִילָה (וְעַיֵּן בְּסִימָן שמ״ב[ס,30]):

יד [יב] וְטַעַם תְּקִיעָה זוֹ הִיא סִימָן לְסִלּוּק שְׁכִינָה לְמַעְלָה,[סא] כְּמוֹ שֶׁהָיָה בְּמַתַּן תּוֹרָה שֶׁכְּשֶׁעָלְתָה הַשְּׁכִינָה נֶאֱמַר[סב] "בִּמְשֹׁךְ הַיֹּבֵל וכו'",[32] וְנֶאֱמַר[סג,33] "עָלָה אֱלֹהִים בִּתְרוּעָה כו'".

26. In the original, *melachah.*

27. A Rabbinic prohibition enacted because an activity resembles — or may lead to the performance of — an activity forbidden by Scriptural Law *(Rambam, Hilchos Shabbos* 21:1*).*

28. In the original, *uvdin dechol.*

29. *Bein hashmashos* is the twilight period between sunset and the appearance of the stars. The various views as to its precise definition and as to whether it is considered as day or as night are clarified in sec. 608:2-3 and footnotes 593 and 594.

30. There the Alter Rebbe writes that all the prohibitions instituted because of a Rabbinic decree on *Shabbos* and on festivals can be relaxed at the time of *bein hashmashos* if performing the forbidden activity is connected with a *mitzvah.* The reasons the Alter Rebbe gives in subsection 14 below satisfy that requirement.

31. Since the heading of sec. 624 mentions 14 subsections, it would appear that two of them were lost before publication. In sec. 586 the missing subsections are ignored, and the numbering continues in sequence — unlike here, where the numbers skip the two missing subsections. Alternatively, the number 14 could well be a printing error, especially since that final subsection appears to follow naturally after subsection 11.

32. *Shmos* 19:13.

33. *Tehillim* 47:6.

מקומות נהגו לתקוע קודם קדיש. ומנהג חב״ד שתוקעין באמצע הקדיש לפני תתקבל – אחר שמנגנים ״מארש״ (ספר המנהגים – חב״ד ע׳ 59). **נד** תוס׳ מגילה ד, ב ד״ה ויעבירנה (הב׳). מרדכי רמז תשכז. הגהות מיימוניות סוף הל׳ שביתת העשור ד״ה מה שנהגו לתקוע. האגור סי׳ תתקנא. רמ״א שם. וכ״ה מנהג חב״ד (ראה אוצר מנהגי חב״ד יוה״כ ע׳ רמג אות רפב), ואחר התקיעה אומרים: לשנה הבאה בירושלים (מחזור), ואחר כך משלימים הקדיש (ספר המנהגים – חב״ד שם). **נה** הגהות מיימוניות שם בשם רב פלטוי גאון ורב עמרם. טור סי׳ תרכד. שו״ע ס״ו. **נו** ראה לעיל סי׳ רצט סוף סט״ו ולקמן סי׳ תרכד סט״ו (לענין מוסיף מחול על הקדש). **נז** תוס׳ שם. מרדכי שם. הגהות מיימוניות שם. טור שם. מנהגים שם. מ״א סק״ד. **נח** סעיף ד. **נט** מ״א שם. אליה רבה סק״ו. וראה אוצר מנהגי חב״ד שם ע׳ רמב אות רפ. **ס** וציין שם לכאן (לענין בין השמשות). **סא** סמ״ג סוף ל״ת סט. לבוש ס״ה. ט״ז סק״ב. **סב** שמות י, יט. **סג** תהלים מז, ו.

וְעוֹד יֵשׁ טַעַם בִּתְקִיעָה זוֹ, לְהַרְאוֹת שֶׁהוּא יוֹם טוֹב[34] וּלְהַרְבּוֹת בִּסְעוּדָה,[סד, 35] מִפְּנֵי שֶׁאֵין יוֹם טוֹב זֶה מְפֻרְסָם — עָשׂוּ בוֹ תַּקָּנָה לְפַרְסְמוֹ,[סה] לָכֵן יִפְקְדוּ אִישׁ אֶת רֵעֵהוּ בְּצֵאתוֹ מִבֵּית הַכְּנֶסֶת כְּדֶרֶךְ שֶׁאוֹמְרִים בְּשַׁבָּת וְיוֹם טוֹב:[סו, 36]

Another reason for this *shofar* blast is to [publicize that this night] is a festive time,[34] so that people should [celebrate with] an ample festive meal.[35] Since this festive time is not widely known, [this *shofar* blast] was ordained to publicize it. When leaving the synagogue, therefore, people should exchange festive greetings as is the custom on *Shabbos* and festivals.[36]

סִימָן תרכד סֵדֶר מוֹצָאֵי יוֹם הַכִּפּוּרִים וּבוֹ ט"ו סְעִיפִים:

SECTION 624 The Order [to be Followed] on the Night at the Close of Yom Kippur. (1–15)

א וּמִתְפַּלְּלִין תְּפִלַּת עַרְבִית,[1] שֶׁאֵין תְּפִלַּת נְעִילָה פּוֹטֶרֶת שֶׁל עַרְבִית[א] אֲפִלּוּ אוֹתָם הַמַּמְשִׁיכִים בָּהּ בַּלַּיְלָה,[ב] כֵּיוָן שֶׁהִזְכִּירוּ בָהּ שֶׁל יוֹם הַכִּפּוּרִים.[ג]

וְאוֹמְרִים הַבְדָּלָה בְּ"חוֹנֵן הַדַּעַת"[ד] כְּמוֹ בְּכָל מוֹצָאֵי שַׁבָּת וְיוֹם טוֹב:[ה]

1 [After *Neilah*] the Evening Service is recited.[1] That obligation is not discharged by *Neilah,* even for those who extend its recitation into the night, because in it they mentioned Yom Kippur.

[In the *Shemoneh Esreh* of the Evening Service,] *Havdalah* is included in [the blessing] *Chonen hadaas,* as is done at the close of every *Shabbos* and festival.

ב וְצָרִיךְ לְהוֹסִיף מִן הַחֹל עַל הַקֹּדֶשׁ בִּיצִיאָתוֹ[ו] כְּמוֹ בִּכְנִיסָתוֹ[2] כְּמוֹ שֶׁנִּתְבָּאֵר בְּסִימָן תר"ח,[ז, 3] דְּהַיְנוּ שֶׁיַּמְתִּינוּ[4] מְעַט אַחַר צֵאת הַכּוֹכָבִים.[ח]

2 At the close of the festival one must add [time] from the mundane realm to the realm of holiness, just as is done at its entry,[2] as stated in sec. 608[:1].[3] Thus, [before relaxing any of the prohibitions of Yom Kippur,[4]] one must wait a short time after the appearance of the stars.

---

34. In the original, *Yom-Tov* — though obviously this term is used here as a metaphor, and not in its strict halachic sense. (See sec. 624:9.)

35. See sec. 624:9.

36. It was the Rebbe's custom to wish all those present *Gut Yom-Tov* three times, before leaving the synagogue after the Evening Service at the end of Yom Kippur.

SECTION 624

1. The Hebrew phrase *Motzaei Yom Kippur* is translated in the above heading as "the night at the close of Yom Kippur." This is the meaning intended by the briefer phrase used throughout the following text — "the night after Yom Kippur."

2. *Yoma* 81b.

3. As stated there, there is no minimum measure of time that must be added.

4. See subsection 15 below.

סד תוס' שבת קיד, ב ד"ה ואמאי. סמ"ג שם. אליה זוטא סק"ג. וכדלקמן סי' תרכד ס"ט. סה תוס' וסמ"ג שם. אליה זוטא שם. סו מטה משה סוס"י תתפה. אליה זוטא שם.

סימן תרכד: א גמרא פז, סע"ב (ברייתא דלא כרב). ירושלמי ברכות פ"ד ה"א כרבי יוחנן. רי"ף (ו, ב). רא"ש פ"ח סי' כ בשם מהר"מ מרוטנברג (דקיי"ל כרבי יוחנן). ב כדעת הרי"ף (ו, ב) דלעיל סי' תרכג ס"ג, מ"מ כותב שנוהגים להתפלל ערבית. ב"ח סי' תרכג (בדעת הטור). ט"ז סק"א (בדעת הרי"ף). ג לבוש ס"א. ד ברייתא פח, רע"א כרבי חנינא בן גמליאל משום אבותיו. טור ושו"ע ס"א. ה לבוש שם. ו ברייתא פא, ב. טור ושו"ע ס"ב. ז סעיף א. ח רא"ש פ"ח סי' ח. טור ושו"ע שם. ט מ"א ריש הסי'. י ס"ד (במוסגר): אבל אם משקה ממנו לתינוקות אין שום אדם יכול לצאת י"ח בהבדלה זו כיון שלא שתה אדם

וּבִמְקוֹמוֹת שֶׁמַּבְדִּילִין עַל הַכּוֹס בְּבֵית הַכְּנֶסֶת בְּכָל מוֹצָאֵי שַׁבָּת וְיוֹם טוֹב — גַּם עַכְשָׁו יַבְדִּיל הַשְּׁלִיחַ צִבּוּר, וְיַטְעִים מִן הַכּוֹס לְקָטָן, אוֹ לְגָדוֹל אִם מִתְכַּוֵּן לָצֵאת בְּהַבְדָּלָה זוֹ.[ט,5] וְעַיֵּן בְּסִימָן רצ"ה:[י,6]

In places where *Havdalah* is recited over a cup [of wine] in the synagogue on the night after every *Shabbos* and festival, the *sheliach tzibbur* should likewise recite *Havdalah* [on the night after Yom Kippur]. He should give the cup to a minor or to an adult to drink, if [that adult] intends to fulfill his obligation with this *Havdalah*.[5] See sec. 295[:4].[6]

ג הַמַּבְדִּיל עַל הַכּוֹס בְּמוֹצָאֵי יוֹם הַכִּפּוּרִים — אֵינוֹ מְבָרֵךְ עַל הַבְּשָׂמִים,[יא] שֶׁלֹּא תִקְּנוּ אֶלָּא בְּמוֹצָאֵי שַׁבָּת כְּדֵי לְהָשִׁיב אֶת הַנֶּפֶשׁ יְתֵרָה שֶׁהָלְכָה לָהּ.[יב]

אֲבָל אִם חָל יוֹם הַכִּפּוּרִים בְּשַׁבָּת — מְבָרְכִין עַל הַבְּשָׂמִים כְּמוֹ בְּכָל מוֹצָאֵי שַׁבָּת:[יג]

3 When reciting *Havdalah* over a cup [of wine] on the night after Yom Kippur, one should not recite a blessing over spices, for this was instituted only for the night after *Shabbos,* in order to counter [the faintness experienced at that time] when the additional soul [of *Shabbos*] takes its leave. If, however, Yom Kippur falls on *Shabbos,* the blessing over spices is recited, as is done at the close of every *Shabbos.*

ד אֲבָל עַל הָאוּר צָרִיךְ לְבָרֵךְ[7] אֲפִלּוּ כְּשֶׁחָל בְּחֹל,[יד] לְפִי שֶׁהוּא דָּבָר חָדָשׁ שֶׁלֹּא נֶהֱנָה מִמֶּנּוּ בְּיוֹם הַכִּפּוּרִים[טו] שֶׁאָסוּר בְּהַבְעָרָה,[8] לְפִיכָךְ אֵינוֹ דוֹמֶה לִשְׁאָר מוֹצָאֵי יוֹם טוֹב שֶׁאֵין מְבָרְכִין עָלָיו,[טז] לְפִי שֶׁאֵין מְבָרְכִין עַל הָאוּר אֶלָּא

4 However, a blessing must be recited over fire,[7] even when [Yom Kippur] falls on a weekday, [thereby indicating that] it is a new entity from which we did not benefit on Yom Kippur, for it is forbidden to light fire [on that day].[8] Therefore [the night after Yom Kippur] is different from the night after any other festival, when a blessing is not recited over [fire].

[The rationale is that] a blessing is recited

---

5. If the *sheliach tzibbur* desires to fulfill his own obligation by reciting *Havdalah* at this time, rather than at home, he may do so and drink himself.

6. There the Alter Rebbe explains that if *Havdalah* is being recited as a mere formality, the cup of wine may be given to a child to drink. If, however, there are adults who seek to fulfill their obligation with this *Havdalah,* one of those adults must drink of the wine.

7. *Pesachim* 54a. The Alter Rebbe writes (in sec. 298:1-2) that on the night after *Shabbos* there is no obligation to seek out fire over which to recite a blessing. If none is available, the blessing may be omitted. The night at the end of Yom Kippur is different: some authorities maintain that one must seek out fire for this blessing, for it is comparable to the blessing of *Havdalah* itself.

8. On the other festivals, by contrast, although it is forbidden to kindle a new fire (sec. 502:1), it is permitted to light a fire from an existing fire (sec. 495:5; sec. 511:1; sec. 514:13-14).

שיוצא י"ח בהבדלה זו, וש"נ. **יא** רמב"ם הל' שבת פכ"ט הכ"ח. טור ושו"ע ס"ד. וראה ט"ז ס"ק ב, ולעיל סי' רצט סוף ס"ט, שאם מברך הוי הפסק בין ברכת היין לשתייתו. **יב** כל סי' מא. הובא בב"י ד"ה ומבדילין. וראה לעיל סי' רצז ס"א. סי' תצא סוף ס"א. **יג** אחרונים. אבודרהם סדר תפלת נעילה ד"ה וחוזר (ע' רצ). שו"ת מהרי"ל סי' לד. ב"ח ד"ה ומבדילין בשם מהרש"ל. ט"ז סק"ב. מ"א סק"א. וראה לעיל סי' רצז ס"ב שציין לכאן. **יד** רבי יוחנן בגמרא פסחים נד, א. טור ושו"ע ס"ד. וראה לעיל סי' רחצ ס"ב שבמוצאי יוה"כ יש אומרים שצריך לחזר אחר ברכת האור לפי שהיא כברכת הבדלה . . . שהבדיל לנו זה היום משאר יום טוב שנאסר בו להבעיר אור עד עתה בלילה. **טו** רש"י שם ד"ה באור ששבת. טור ולבוש ס"ד. **טז** כדלעיל סי' תצא ס"א.

בִּשְׁעַת חִדּוּשׁוֹ,[יז] דְּהַיְנוּ בְּמוֹצָאֵי שַׁבָּת שֶׁהוּא תְּחִלַּת בְּרִיָּתוֹ,[יח, 9] אוֹ בְּמוֹצָאֵי יוֹם הַכִּפּוּרִים שֶׁהוּא כְּמוֹ דָּבָר חָדָשׁ לָנוּ כְּמוֹ שֶׁנִּתְבָּאֵר:

over fire only at the time when it was brought into being, i.e., on the night after *Shabbos,* when fire was first created,[9] or on the night after Yom Kippur, when fire is like a new entity for us, as was explained above.

ה וְאֵין מְבָרְכִין בְּמוֹצָאֵי יוֹם הַכִּפּוּרִים עַל הָאוּר שֶׁהוֹצִיאוּהוּ עַתָּה בְּמוֹצָאֵי יוֹם הַכִּפּוּרִים מִן הָאֲבָנִים אוֹ מִן הָעֵצִים,[יט, 10] וְלֹא עַל הָאוּר שֶׁהֻדְלַק מֵאוּר זֶה,[כ, 11] אֶלָּא עַל אוּר שֶׁשָּׁבַת[כא, 12] מִמְּלָאכָה, כְּגוֹן עֲשָׁשִׁית שֶׁהָיְתָה דּוֹלֶקֶת וְהוֹלֶכֶת מֵעֶרֶב יוֹם כִּפּוּר.[כב]

וְאַף עַל פִּי שֶׁבְּמוֹצָאֵי שַׁבָּת מְבָרְכִין עַל הָאוּר הַיּוֹצֵא מִן הָאֲבָנִים וְעֵצִים,[כג] הַיְנוּ לְפִי שֶׁתְּחִלַּת בְּרִיָּתוֹ בְּמוֹצָאֵי שַׁבָּת הָיְתָה עַל דֶּרֶךְ זֶה, שֶׁנָּטַל אָדָם הָרִאשׁוֹן שְׁנֵי אֲבָנִים וְהִקִּישָׁן זֶה בָּזֶה וְיָצָא אוּר[כד] וּבֵרַךְ עָלָיו "בּוֹרֵא מְאוֹרֵי הָאֵשׁ",[כה, 13] לָכֵן מְבָרְכִין בְּמוֹצָאֵי שַׁבָּת עַל כָּל אוּר שֶׁבָּעוֹלָם (אֶלָּא אִם כֵּן נַעֲשָׂה בּוֹ מְלָאכָה בְּשַׁבָּת כְּמוֹ שֶׁנִּתְבָּאֵר בְּסִימָן רח"צ[כו]) אֲפִלּוּ יָצָא עַתָּה מִן הָאֲבָנִים, לְפִי שֶׁזֶּהוּ כְּעֵין בְּרִיָּתוֹ, אֲבָל בְּמוֹצָאֵי יוֹם הַכִּפּוּרִים שֶׁטַּעַם בִּרְכָתוֹ הוּא לְפִי שֶׁפָּסְקָה הֲנָאָתוֹ בּוֹ בַּיּוֹם

5 On the night after Yom Kippur, the blessing is not recited over fire that was produced [that night] from flint or wood,[10] nor over fire that was kindled from such fire,[11] but only over fire that "rested"[12] from work, such as a lamp that has been alight since the eve of Yom Kippur.

On the night after [any] *Shabbos,* a blessing may be recited over fire that was produced from flint or wood, because it was in this manner that fire was originally created on the night after [the first] *Shabbos.* As [our Sages relate,[13] on the night after the first *Shabbos* of creation] Adam took two stones, struck them together, brought forth fire, and recited the blessing *borei meorei ha'esh,* [praising G-d as "the Creator of the lights of fire"]. Hence on the night following [any] *Shabbos,* the blessing may be recited over any fire (unless it was used for forbidden labor on *Shabbos,* as stated in sec. 298[:7]) — even over fire produced at that time from flint, for this resembles the way it was originally brought into being.

On the night after Yom Kippur, by contrast, the reason for this blessing is that one was unable to benefit [from fire] on that day,

9. See subsection 5 below.

10. Nor on fire produced that night from any other source. See *Pesachim, loc. cit.*

11. This law applies even after the event *(bediavad);* i.e., even if the blessing had already been recited over fire lit after Yom Kippur, it must now be repeated over a fire that "rested."

12. In the original, *ur sheshavas.* (A 24-hour candle that has "rested" from work since the eve of Yom Kippur is called *ner sheshavas.*)

13. *Pesachim* 54a; see sec. 298:2 in the present work.

יז שו"ת רשב"א ח"א סי' קנט. וכדלעיל סי' רחצ סוף ס"א. יח ברייתא שם. יט ברייתא וגמרא פסחים שם ורש"י ד"ה באור היוצא. טור ושו"ע ס"ד. כ מ"א ס"ק ג (בפירוש דעה הא' בכל בו סי' ע (לו, ג), ובשו"ע ס"ד) וס"ק ד (ממשמעות רבנו יונה ברכות (מ, א) ד"ה לא). כא גמרא שם. רמב"ם שם פכ"ט הכ"ז. כלבו שם. לבוש ס"ד. מ"א סק"ב. כב רש"י שם ד"ה באור ששבת. כלבו שם. לבוש שם. כג ברייתא שם. וכדלעיל סי' רחצ סי"ד. כד רבי יוסי בברייתא פסחים שם. וכדלעיל שם ס"א וסי"ד. כה ירושלמי ברכות פ"ח ה"ה. הובא בכל בו שם. לבוש שם. כו סעיף ז. כז כלבו שם. כח מ"מ פכ"ט הכ"ז. כט רש"י שם ד"ה

וְעַכְשָׁו הֻתַּר לוֹ — אֵין לְבָרֵךְ אֶלָּא עַל אוֹר שֶׁשָּׁבַת[כז] מַמָּשׁ,[כח] דְּהַיְנוּ שֶׁהֻדְלַק מֵעֶרֶב יוֹם כִּפּוּר וְשָׁבַת כָּל יוֹם הַכִּפּוּרִים.[כט]

וַאֲפִלּוּ אִם חָל יוֹם הַכִּפּוּרִים בְּשַׁבָּת — אֵין מְבָרֵךְ בְּמוֹצָאֵי שַׁבָּת אֶלָּא עַל הָאוֹר שֶׁהֻדְלַק מֵעֶרֶב יוֹם כִּפּוּר וְשָׁבַת כָּל יוֹם הַכִּפּוּרִים, כְּדֵי לְהַרְאוֹת שֶׁיּוֹם זֶה הוּא מְקֻדָּשׁ שֶׁשָּׁבַת מִן הָאוֹר:[ל]

ו יִשְׂרָאֵל שֶׁהִדְלִיק מִגּוֹי בְּמוֹצָאֵי יוֹם הַכִּפּוּרִים — אֵין מְבָרְכִין עָלָיו,[לא] מִפְּנֵי שֶׁאוּרוֹ שֶׁל גּוֹי נַעֲשָׂה בּוֹ מְלָאכָה שֶׁהֻדְלַק בְּיוֹם הַכִּפּוּרִים.[לב] וְאַף עַל פִּי שֶׁבְּמוֹצָאֵי שַׁבָּת מְבָרְכִין עָלָיו,[לג] לְפִי שֶׁהוּא מְבָרֵךְ עַל תּוֹסֶפֶת שַׁלְהֶבֶת שֶׁל הֶתֵּר שֶׁנִּתּוֹסֵף בְּנֵרוֹ שֶׁל יִשְׂרָאֵל,[לד] מִכָּל מָקוֹם בְּמוֹצָאֵי יוֹם הַכִּפּוּרִים — אֵין מְבָרֵךְ עָלָיו, לְפִי שֶׁתּוֹסֶפֶת שַׁלְהֶבֶת זוֹ הִיא נוֹלְדָה עַכְשָׁו, וְדוֹמֶה לְאוֹר הַיּוֹצֵא מִן הָאֲבָנִים בְּמוֹצָאֵי יוֹם כִּפּוּר שֶׁאֵין מְבָרְכִין עָלָיו, וְלֹא עַל הָאוֹר שֶׁהֻדְלַק מִמֶּנּוּ,[לה] אֶלָּא עַל הָאוֹר שֶׁדָּלַק מֵעֶרֶב יוֹם כִּפּוּר אוֹ עַל הָאוֹר שֶׁהֻדְלַק מִמֶּנּוּ. וְלָכֵן נוֹהֲגִין לְהַדְלִיק נֵר לַהַבְדָּלָה מֵעַשָּׁשִׁיּוֹת שֶׁל בֵּית הַכְּנֶסֶת שֶׁדָּלְקוּ מֵעֶרֶב יוֹם כִּפּוּר:[לו,14]

and now this is permitted. Hence, the blessing should be recited only over fire that actually "rested," i.e., that was kindled on the day before Yom Kippur and "rested" throughout the day of Yom Kippur. Even when Yom Kippur falls on *Shabbos,* the blessing should be recited — at night, at the close of the holy day — only over fire that was kindled on the day before Yom Kippur and "rested" throughout the day of Yom Kippur, to show that this day was sanctified in that fire was not kindled during that time.

6 A blessing may not be recited over fire that a Jew lit from [the fire of] a non-Jew on the night after Yom Kippur, because labor had been performed with the non-Jew's fire, for it was kindled on Yom Kippur. On the night after *Shabbos,* [by contrast,] a blessing may be recited over such [fire], because the blessing is recited over the flame that was [now] added — permissibly — to the Jew's lamp. On the night after Yom Kippur, however, a blessing should not be recited over such [fire], because this additional flame came into being at the present time. Thus it resembles light that was produced from flint on the night after Yom Kippur over which — or over light kindled from such fire — a blessing may not be recited. Rather, the blessing is recited only over fire that has been alight from the day before Yom Kippur, or over fire kindled from such fire.

For this reason, it is customary to light a candle for *Havdalah* from the lamps in the synagogue that were alight since the day before Yom Kippur.[14]

---

14. Or from one of the 24-hour candles kindled at home. See sec. 610, footnote 10 above.

באור ששבת. ל מ"א סק"ז. לא רמב"ן ברכות סופ"ח. מ"מ הל' שבת פכ"ט הכ"ז. שו"ע ס"ה. לב לבוש ריש ס"ה. לג ברייתא ברכות נג, א. וכדלעיל סי' רחצ ס"ט. לד גמרא שם. וכדלעיל שם. לה כדלעיל ריש ס"ה וש"נ. לו רמב"ן שם. מ"מ שם. שו"ע שם.

ז וּמִכָּל מָקוֹם אֲפִלּוּ אוּר שֶׁהֻדְלַק בְּיוֹם כִּפּוּר עַצְמוֹ, אִם הֻדְלַק בְּהֶתֵּר כְּגוֹן לַחוֹלֶה – יְכוֹלִים לְבָרֵךְ עָלָיו בְּמוֹצָאֵי יוֹם הַכִּפּוּרִים[לז,15] כְּמוֹ שֶׁמְּבָרְכִין עָלָיו בְּמוֹצָאֵי שַׁבָּת כְּמוֹ שֶׁנִּתְבָּאֵר בְּסִימָן רח"צ:[לח,16]

7 Nevertheless, even if fire was kindled on Yom Kippur itself — in a permissible manner, such as for a patient — a blessing may be recited over it on the night after Yom Kippur,[15] just as a blessing may be recited over it on the night after *Shabbos*, as explained in sec. 298[:7].[16]

ח אַף עַל פִּי שֶׁמִּן הַדִּין מֻתָּר לְבָרֵךְ בְּמוֹצָאֵי יוֹם הַכִּפּוּרִים עַל הָאוּר שֶׁהֻדְלַק מִן הָאוּר שֶׁשָּׁבַת, דְּהַיְנוּ שֶׁהֻדְלַק מֵעֶרֶב יוֹם כִּפּוּר כְּמוֹ שֶׁנִּתְבָּאֵר,[לט] מִכָּל מָקוֹם טוֹב לְהַחְמִיר וּלְבָרֵךְ עַל אוּר שֶׁשָּׁבַת מִבְּעוֹד יוֹם מַמָּשׁ.[מ]

וּמִכָּל מָקוֹם לֹא יְבָרֵךְ עַל נֵרוֹת[17] שֶׁל בֵּית הַכְּנֶסֶת בְּעַצְמָן[מא] אַף עַל פִּי שֶׁהֻדְלְקוּ מִבְּעוֹד יוֹם, לְפִי שֶׁלֹּא הֻדְלְקוּ רַק לִכְבוֹד הַיּוֹם[מב] וְלִכְבוֹד בֵּית הַכְּנֶסֶת[מג] וְלֹא בִּשְׁבִיל לְהָאִיר, וְאֵין מְבָרְכִין אֶלָּא עַל הָאוּר שֶׁהֻדְלַק לְהָאִיר[מד] כְּמוֹ שֶׁנִּתְבָּאֵר בְּסִימָן רח"צ,[מה,18] אֶלָּא מַדְלִיק נֵר אֶחָד מִנֵּר שֶׁל בֵּית הַכְּנֶסֶת הַדּוֹלֵק מֵעֶרֶב יוֹם כִּפּוּר וִיבָרֵךְ עַל שְׁנֵיהֶם בְּיַחַד.[מו]

וְאִם אִי אֶפְשָׁר לוֹ לְהַבְדִּיל עַל שְׁנֵיהֶם בְּיַחַד – יַבְדִּיל עַל נֵר שֶׁהִדְלִיק מִן נֵרוֹת

8 According to [the letter of] the law, a blessing may be recited on the night after Yom Kippur over fire that was kindled from fire that "rested," i.e., that was kindled before Yom Kippur. Nevertheless, it is desirable to be stringent and to recite the blessing over the actual fire that "rested" from daytime [on the eve of Yom Kippur].

Nevertheless, the blessing should not be recited over the synagogue candles[17] themselves, even though they were kindled during the [previous] day, because they were kindled [primarily] in honor of the day and in honor of the synagogue, and not for illumination. And this blessing should be recited only over fire that was kindled for illumination, as stated in sec. 298[:15].[18]

Rather, one should kindle a lamp from a synagogue lamp that was kindled on the day before Yom Kippur and recite the blessing [of *Havdalah*] over both of them together. If it is impossible to recite *Havdalah* over both [flames] together, *Havdalah* should be recited over the lamp that was kindled from the

15. *Pesachim, loc. cit.*

16. I.e., because no transgression was involved in kindling it.

17. In the original, *neros,* which signifies both candles and lamps, varying according to context.

18. There and in the subsequent laws, the Alter Rebbe gives several examples of this principle, such as the fire lit in a hearth or in an oven for its heat and not for its light, and a lamp kindled in honor of a funeral.

In a parallel discussion to the present one, in sec. 298:17, the Alter Rebbe points out that lamps are lit in a synagogue both in honor of the Divine Presence that abides there, and in order to provide light for the worshipers.

לז גמרא פסחים נד, א לפירוש רש"י שם ד"ה באור ששבת. טור ושו"ע שם. לח סעיף ז. לט סוף ס"ו. מ לחוש לדעת אור זרוע (הל' מוצ"ש סי' צה), שהיא דעה הא' שברמ"א ס"ה, ומ"א סק"ה. מא דרכי משה ס"ק ב בשם אגודה סוף יומא. מהר"י ווייל סי' קצא. דעה הב' ברמ"א שם. אחרונים. מב מהרי"ל הל' תפלת נעילה דיו"כ (ע' שנח). דרכי משה שם (לכבוד). מ"א ס"ק ו. ט"ז סק"ד (לכבוד היום). וראה לעיל סי' תרי ס"ד וסוף ס"ח. מג תוס' ברכות נג, א ד"ה הא, בשם ר"ח. וראה גם לעיל סי' רחצ סי"ז (לכבוד שכינה). סי' תקיד סי"ד (לכבוד המקום). מד לבוש ס"ד. מה סעי' טו־יח. מו מהרי"ל שם. רמ"א שם.

שֶׁל בֵּית הַכְּנֶסֶת שֶׁהֻדְלְקוּ מִבְּעוֹד יוֹם, וְלֹא יַבְדִּיל עַל נֵרוֹת שֶׁל בֵּית הַכְּנֶסֶת בִּלְבַד.[מז]

lamps of the synagogue which were kindled on the previous day; one should not recite the blessing over the lamps of the synagogue alone.

וְאִם עָבַר וּבֵרַךְ עַל נֵרוֹת שֶׁל בֵּית הַכְּנֶסֶת בִּלְבַד אַף עַל פִּי שֶׁהֻדְלְקוּ לְכָבוֹד – אַף עַל פִּי כֵן אֵין צָרִיךְ לַחֲזֹר וּלְבָרֵךְ עַל נֵר אַחֵר, כֵּיוָן שֶׁעֲשׂוּיִין גַּם לְהָאִיר, שֶׁהֲרֵי מִתְפַּלְּלִין לְאוֹרָן:[מח,19]

[After the fact,] one who wrongly recited the blessing over the synagogue lights alone does not have to recite a repeated blessing over another lamp, because though they are kindled [primarily] in honor [of the synagogue], they are also kindled for illumination, for people pray by their light.[19]

ט וְאוֹכְלִין וּשְׂמֵחִין בְּמוֹצָאֵי יוֹם כִּפּוּר,[מט] מִשּׁוּם שֶׁהוּא קְצָת יוֹם טוֹב[נ,20] כְּמוֹ שֶׁנִּתְבָּאֵר בְּסִימָן תרכ"ג,[נא,21] וּבַת קוֹל יוֹצֵאת בְּמוֹצָאֵי יוֹם כִּפּוּר וְאוֹמֶרֶת "לֵךְ אֱכֹל בְּשִׂמְחָה":[נב,22]

9 It is customary to eat [a festive meal] and be joyful on the night after Yom Kippur because it is a somewhat festive time,[20] as stated in sec. 623[:14].[21]

A Heavenly voice resounds on the night after Yom Kippur proclaiming, "Go and eat in joy."[22]

י יֵשׁ אַנְשֵׁי מַעֲשֶׂה שֶׁמַּחְמִירִין לַעֲשׂוֹת יוֹם כִּפּוּר שְׁנֵי יָמִים[נג] כְּמוֹ שֶׁאָנוּ עוֹשִׂים שְׁנֵי יָמִים טוֹבִים בַּגּוֹלָה בִּשְׁאָר כָּל הַמּוֹעֲדוֹת, וּמִי שֶׁנָּהַג חֻמְרָא זוֹ וְרוֹצֶה לְשַׁנּוֹת מִנְהָגוֹ – צָרִיךְ הַתָּרָה[23] כְּמוֹ נֶדֶר:[נד]

10 Certain conscientious individuals undertake the stringency of observing Yom Kippur for two days, just as we observe all the festivals for two days in the Diaspora. If one observed this stringency and then desired to change his practice, he must go through [a process of] absolution,[23] as would be necessary to release a vow.

---

19. The Alter Rebbe is speaking about synagogues of past centuries that were illuminated by oil lamps and candles. At present, the lights that burn throughout the day are usually the *yahrzeit* candles lit at home in honor of the departed, the candles kindled by every head of a family in the synagogue (see sec. 610, footnote 10 above), and the lights kindled over the lectern of the *sheliach tzibbur.* These candles are not kindled for their light and hence, even after the fact, the blessing should not be recited on them alone. If, however, a candle was kindled at home for the purpose of providing light, e.g. in the bedroom (see sec. 610:2), a blessing may be recited over it alone.

20. In the original, *ktzas Yom-Tov* (lit., "something of a festival").

21. The Rebbe Rashab taught that preparing an ample meal at this time is a conduit for material blessings throughout the year to come. See *Otzar Minhagei Chabad,* p. 251.

22. *Koheles* 9:7, as expounded in *Koheles Rabbah.* The verse in full reads: "Go and eat your bread in joy and drink your wine with a gladsome heart, for G-d has favored your deeds."

23. In the original, *hatarah.*

מז רמ"א שם, לפירוש מ"א סק"ז. **מח** ראה לעיל סי' רחצ סוף סי"ז (במוסגר). **מט** טור. מהר"י ווייל סי' קצא. רמ"א ס"ה. **נ** תוס' פז, ב ד"ה והאמר (כעין יום טוב). רמ"א שם. **נא** סעיף י[ב]. **נב** קהלת ט, ז. מדרש קהלת רבה ט, ז. הובא בתוס' שם. טור וב"י ד"ה ואוכלין. וראה התוועדויות תנש"א ח"א ע' 86. **נג** סמ"ק סוס"י רכא, והגהות מיימוניות סוף הל' שביתת העשור ד"ה תרי יומי, בשם הרבה גדולים, כרבא ר"ה כא, א. טור. רמ"א ס"ה. **נד** הגהות סמ"ק שם, בשם מהר"ם בתשב"ץ סי' קלז (שקיבל עליו וצריך להתענות לעולם). טור בשם הרא"ש (שיש לזה התרה). רמ"א שם.

אֲבָל אֵין לִנְהֹג חֻמְרָא זוֹ, מִשּׁוּם שֶׁיֵּשׁ לָחוּשׁ לְסַכָּנָה,[נה,24] וְעוֹד שֶׁהֲרֵי עַכְשָׁו שֶׁבָּטֵל קִדּוּשׁ הַחֹדֶשׁ עַל פִּי הָרְאִיָּה[25] אָנוּ בְּקִיאִים בְּחֶשְׁבּוֹן קְבִיעוּת הֶחֳדָשִׁים,[נו] וְאָנוּ אוֹמְרִים שֶׁאֱלוּל לְעוֹלָם חָסֵר וְיוֹם רִאשׁוֹן שֶׁל רֹאשׁ הַשָּׁנָה הוּא רֹאשׁ חֹדֶשׁ תִּשְׁרֵי[נז] וּבֶעָשׂוֹר לַחֹדֶשׁ הוּא יוֹם הַכִּפּוּרִים שֶׁלָּנוּ, וְאֵין אָנוּ עוֹשִׂין שְׁאָר כָּל הַמּוֹעֲדוֹת שְׁנֵי יָמִים אֶלָּא כְּדֵי שֶׁלֹּא לְשַׁנּוֹת מִמִּנְהַג אֲבוֹתֵינוּ שֶׁהָיוּ בִּזְמַן שֶׁהָיוּ מְקַדְּשִׁים הֶחֳדָשִׁים עַל פִּי הָרְאִיָּה וְלֹא הָיוּ יוֹדְעִים יוֹם שֶׁנִּרְאֵית בּוֹ הַלְּבָנָה וְנִקְבַּע בּוֹ רֹאשׁ הַשָּׁנָה בְּאֶרֶץ יִשְׂרָאֵל, וְאִם כֵּן בְּיוֹם הַכִּפּוּרִים אַף[נח] אֲבוֹתֵינוּ לֹא עָשׂוּ אֶלָּא יוֹם אֶחָד[נט] מֵחֲמַת חֲשַׁשׁ סַכָּנָה,[ס] שֶׁאֵין גּוֹזְרִין עַל הַצִּבּוּר אֶלָּא אִם כֵּן רֹב הַצִּבּוּר יְכוֹלִין לַעֲמֹד בָּהּ,[סא,26] אִם כֵּן[סב] לָמָּה לָנוּ לְהַחְמִיר וּלְהִתְעַנּוֹת בְּחִנָּם:[סג]

This stringency should not be followed because of the risk involved.[24] Moreover, at present, when the sanctification of the month [based on the testimony of witnesses who] sighted [the newborn moon][25] has been discontinued, we know the calculations according to which the months are determined. [It has been determined] that Elul is always a "short" month [i.e., of 29 days]; [the thirtieth day is] the first day of Rosh HaShanah, which is the first of Tishrei; and the tenth day of the month is Yom Kippur for us. [There is no longer any doubt about the matter.] We observe all the other festivals for two days only in order that we should not depart from the custom of our forefathers in the era in which the moon was sanctified [based on the testimony of witnesses who] sighted [the moon. The people living in the outlying Diaspora] did not know when the moon was sighted and which day had been established as Rosh HaShanah in *Eretz Yisrael*. Our forefathers, too, observed Yom Kippur for only one day, because of the risk involved, for a decree is not imposed on the community unless the majority of the community can uphold it.[26] Why, then, should we undertake this stringency and fast unnecessarily?

יא וְאוֹתָן הָעוֹשִׂין שְׁנֵי יָמִים יוֹם הַכִּפּוּרִים אֲפִלּוּ הֵם עֲשָׂרָה בְּיַחַד – אַף עַל פִּי כֵן לֹא יְשַׁנּוּ מִתְּפִלּוֹת שֶׁל חֹל,[סד] שֶׁכָּל הַמִּתְפַּלֵּל תְּפִלָּה שֶׁלֹּא תִּקְּנוּהוּ חֲכָמִים לַזְּמַן הַהוּא – הֲרֵי זֶה מְבָרֵךְ לְבַטָּלָה,[סה]

11 People — even ten [praying] together — who observe [Yom Kippur] for two days should not deviate from the weekday prayers, for anyone who recites a *Shemoneh Esreh* that was not ordained by our Sages for a particular time is reciting blessings in vain.

24. I.e., a two-day fast might be life-threatening.

25. In the original, *kiddush hachodesh al-pi hare'iyah* (lit., "the sanctification of the moon according to the sighting"). See sec. 600:4 above and footnotes there.

26. Hence the Sages did not institute a second day of Yom Kippur.

נה אוז זרוע הל' יוה"כ סוס"י רפא, ע"פ ירושלמי חלה פ"א ה"א. הגהות מיימוניות שם. רמ"א שם. **נו** סמ"ק שם. **נז** כדלעיל סי' תר ס"ד. **נח** בקונטרס השלחן הגיה: שאף. **נט** הגהות מיימוניות שם. ב"י ד"ה וחסידים. לבוש ס"ה. מ"א סוף סק"ז. **ס** ירושלמי שם. הגהות מיימוניות שם. ב"י שם. **סא** ב"ב ס, ב וש"נ. וראה לבוש שם. **סב** בקונטרס השלחן הגיה שתיבת א"כ מיותרת. **סג** ראה הגהות מיימוניות שם. לבוש שם. מ"א שם. **סד** טור בשם הרא"ש. ב"י ד"ה ואדוני אבי ז"ל היה מוחה, בשם האגודה סוף יומא. שו"ת מהרי"ל סי' קפד. מ"א סק"ז. **סה** ב"ח ד"ה ומ"ש וא"א. מ"א שם. **סו** מהרי"ל שם. מ"א שם. **סז** מ"א שם.

The *Selichos* and hymns [of Yom Kippur], however, may be recited as they desire, because they include no blessings [that would be recited] in vain — but only after they have completed *Shemoneh Esreh*. They may not interrupt the *Shemoneh Esreh* to recite them even if they are praying with their own quorum.

12 If Yom Kippur falls on Thursday, they may not prepare any of their *Shabbos* needs [on Friday, which is their second day] — even through other people, nor [even] through a non-Jew — because they consider that day as Yom Kippur.[27]

On *Shabbos*, they may eat with other people who did not cook additional [food] for them. If, however, a non-Jew cooked food for himself on that day, and he knows [these individuals who are observing a second day of Yom Kippur], they may not eat what he cooked, even if a Jew helped [the non-Jew] and thus the prohibition against eating food cooked by non-Jews does not apply. This [safeguard] was ordained for fear that the non-Jew prepare additional food for them in the coming year[s]. When, by contrast, a Jew prepares food for himself, there is no cause for concern that he might cook more for these [individuals in the coming years], for he will presumably not transgress the prohibition against placing a stumbling block before the blind.[28] [No Jew] would serve [these individuals who are observing a second day of Yom Kippur] food he has cooked, because they consider this day to be Yom Kippur.

אַךְ בִּסְלִיחוֹת וּפִיּוּטִים יֹאמְרוּ כִּרְצוֹנָם,[סו] כֵּיוָן שֶׁאֵין שָׁם בְּרָכָה לְבַטָּלָה, וּבִלְבַד שֶׁיֹּאמְרוּ אוֹתָם אַחַר סִיּוּם תְּפִלָּתָם, אֲבָל לֹא יַפְסִיקוּ בַּאֲמִירָתָם בְּאֶמְצַע הַתְּפִלָּה[סז] אֲפִלּוּ כְּשֶׁמִּתְפַּלְּלִין בְּצִבּוּר שֶׁלָּהֶם:

יב וּכְשֶׁחָל יוֹם הַכִּפּוּרִים בְּיוֹם חֲמִישִׁי – אָסוּר לָהֶם לְהָכִין צָרְכֵי שַׁבָּת אֲפִלּוּ עַל יְדֵי אֲחֵרִים אוֹ עַל יְדֵי גּוֹי, כֵּיוָן שֶׁהֵן מַחֲזִיקִין יוֹם זֶה לְיוֹם הַכִּפּוּרִים.[27] אַךְ יֹאכְלוּ בְּשַׁבָּת עִם אֲחֵרִים שֶׁלֹּא הִרְבּוּ לְבַשֵּׁל בִּשְׁבִילָם,[סח] אֲבָל אִם גּוֹי בִּשֵּׁל בְּיוֹם זֶה לְצָרְכּוֹ אִם הוּא מַכִּיר אוֹתָם אֲסוּרִים לֶאֱכֹל מִבִּשּׁוּלוֹ,[סט] אֲפִלּוּ אִם סִיַּע עִמּוֹ יִשְׂרָאֵל בְּעִנְיָן שֶׁאֵין בּוֹ מִשּׁוּם בִּשּׁוּלֵי גוֹיִם, גְּזֵרָה שֶׁמָּא יַרְבֶּה הַגּוֹי בְּשָׁנָה הַבָּאָה לְבַשֵּׁל גַּם בִּשְׁבִילָם,[ע] אֲבָל יִשְׂרָאֵל הַמְבַשֵּׁל בִּשְׁבִיל עַצְמוֹ – אֵין לָחוּשׁ שֶׁמָּא יַרְבֶּה לְבַשֵּׁל גַּם בִּשְׁבִילָם, שֶׁמִּן הַסְּתָם לֹא יַעֲבֹר עַל לָאו דְּ"לִפְנֵי עִוֵּר לֹא תִתֵּן מִכְשׁוֹל",[עא, 28] וְלֹא יַאֲכִיל אוֹתָם מִבִּשּׁוּלוֹ,[עב] כֵּיוָן שֶׁהֵם מַחֲזִיקִין יוֹם זֶה לְיוֹם כִּפּוּר:

27. And they may not benefit from labor performed for them on that day, just as one may not benefit from labor performed for him on *Shabbos*.

28. I.e., he would not want to cause them to unwittingly violate their standards. The metaphor is borrowed from *Vayikra* 19:14.

סח הגהות מיימוניות שם, בשם שו"ת מהר"מ מרוטנבורג (פראג) סי' עו. לבוש ס"ה. מ"א שם. סט מהר"מ מרוטנבורג שם. מ"א שם. ע כדלעיל סי' שכה סט"ז וש"נ. עא ויקרא יט, יד. עב מהר"מ שם. מ"א שם.

יג הַיָּמִים שֶׁבֵּין יוֹם הַכִּפּוּרִים לְסֻכּוֹת הֵן יְמֵי שִׂמְחָה, שֶׁבָּהֶן הָיוּ מְחַנְּכִין אֶת הַמִּזְבֵּחַ בִּימֵי שְׁלֹמֹה,[עג] לְפִיכָךְ אֵין מִתְעַנִּין בָּהֶן אֲפִלּוּ יוֹם מִיתַת אָב וָאֵם,[עד, 29] וְאֵין אוֹמְרִים תַּחֲנוּן:[עה, 30]

13 The days between Yom Kippur and Sukkos are days of rejoicing, for in this period the Altar [in the *Beis HaMikdash*] was inaugurated at the time of [King] Shlomo. Therefore we do not fast during these days, even on the anniversary of the passing of one's father or mother,[29] nor is *Tachanun* recited.[30]

יד בַּיּוֹם שֶׁאַחַר יוֹם הַכִּפּוּרִים – מַשְׁכִּימִין לְבֵית הַכְּנֶסֶת:[עו, 31]

14 It is customary on the day after Yom Kippur to rise early for [the Morning Service in] the synagogue.[31]

טו (כָּל הַדְּבָרִים הָאֲסוּרִים בְּיוֹם הַכִּפּוּרִים מֵחֲמַת מִצְוַת עִנּוּי, כְּגוֹן רְחִיצָה וְסִיכָה וּנְעִילַת הַסַּנְדָּל – מֻתָּרִים מִיָּד אַחַר שֶׁהוֹסִיף מְעַט מֵחֹל עַל הַקֹּדֶשׁ,[עז, 32] אֲפִלּוּ לֹא הִבְדִּיל עֲדַיִן[עח] בַּתְּפִלָּה,[עט] חוּץ מֵאֲכִילָה וּשְׁתִיָּה, שֶׁלֹּא אָסְרוּ קֹדֶם הַבְדָּלָה אֶלָּא אֲכִילָה וּשְׁתִיָּה וַעֲשִׂיַּת מְלָאכָה מַמָּשׁ, כְּמוֹ שֶׁנִּתְבָּאֵר בְּסִימָן רצ"ט,[פ] עַיֵּן שָׁם):[33]

15 (All the [activities] prohibited on Yom Kippur because of the *mitzvah* to afflict oneself — such as washing, anointing oneself, and wearing shoes — are permitted immediately after one has added a little [time] from the mundane realm to the realm of holiness,[32] even though *Havdalah* has not yet been recited in the course of *Shemoneh Esreh*. The only exceptions are eating and drinking, for only eating, drinking, and the performance of actual work were forbidden before *Havdalah*, as was explained in sec. 299. Note the explanation there.)[33]

---

29. When it is customary in many communities to fast *(Rama, Yoreh Deah* 376:4*)*.

30. The Alter Rebbe states in his *Siddur* that *Tachanun* is customarily omitted until the end of the month of Tishrei, for since these four days are followed by the festival of Sukkos, the remainder of the month remains festive.

31. This shows that we are eager to pray for reasons other than requesting a favorable judgment *(Mishnah Berurah* 624:14*)*.

In Yiddish, the day following Yom Kippur is called *G-tt's nommen* ("G-d's name"), in alluion to the transcendent levels of Divinity that are revealed on that day *(Sefer HaMinhagim: The Book of Chabad-Lubavitch Customs,* p. 126). In the Holy Tongue, this date is rendered as *BeShem HaShem.*

32. See subsection 2 above.

33. Subsection 1 there refers to sec. 271:9, which states that one may not eat or drink before *Kiddush* or *Havdalah,* for the time limit for the observance of these *mitzvos* may pass while one is engrossed in a meal. In sec. 299:15, likewise in the context of *Shabbos,* the Alter Rebbe states that no forbidden labor may be performed until one has first recited *Havdalah,* whether in the course of *Shemoneh Esreh* or over a cup of wine, thereby deferentially escorting the departing King.

עג מהרי"ל הל' יוה"כ (ע' שנז, וע' שנט בשינויי נוסחאות). מ"א סק"ז. וראה הגהות מיימוניות הל' תפלה פ"ה אות ש. עד מ"א שם בשם הגהות מנהגים יו"כ אות קפג. עה הגהות מיימוניות שם. מנהגים (טירנא) ע' קיט. רמ"א ס"ה. עו מנהגים. מ"א סק"ז, בשם מעגלי צדק ומהרי"ל (שם ע' שנח בשינויי נוסחאות). עז כדלעיל ס"ב. עח מ"א ריש הסי'. עט ראה גם לעיל סי' תצא ס"ג (לענין אכילת חמץ במוצאי פסח). פ ס"א וסט"ו.

הִלְכוֹת סֻכָּה
LAWS REGARDING THE SUKKAH

SECTION 625 [The *Mitzvah* to Dwell in a *Sukkah*]. (1)

1 It is written:[1] "You shall dwell in *sukkos* for seven days, ... so that your [coming] generations shall know that I caused the Children of Israel to dwell in *sukkos* when I took them out of the Land of Egypt." [The term *sukkos* in the latter context] refers to the Clouds of [G-d's] Glory[2] that encompassed [the Jewish people and provided] them with shade so that they would not be smitten by scorching heat and sun.[3]

In emulation of this, [G-d] commanded us to make *sukkos* that are made for shade[4] so that we will recall His wondrous and awesome deeds. When dwelling in the *sukkah,* everyone should therefore have the intent[5] that he is dwelling in it in order to

סימן תרכה

א "בַּסֻּכֹּת תֵּשְׁבוּ שִׁבְעַת יָמִים [גו'], לְמַעַן יֵדְעוּ דֹרֹתֵיכֶם כִּי בַסֻּכּוֹת הוֹשַׁבְתִּי אֶת בְּנֵי יִשְׂרָאֵל בְּהוֹצִיאִי אוֹתָם מֵאֶרֶץ מִצְרָיִם"[א,1] – הֵם הָיוּ עַנְנֵי כְבוֹדוֹ[ב,2] שֶׁהִקִּיפָם בָּהֶם לְצֵל לְבַל יַכֶּה בָהֶם שָׁרָב וָשֶׁמֶשׁ.[ג,3] וְדֻגְמָא לָזֶה צִוָּנוּ לַעֲשׂוֹת סֻכּוֹת הָעֲשׂוּיוֹת לְצֵל,[ד,4] כְּדֵי שֶׁנִּזְכֹּר נִפְלְאוֹתָיו וְנוֹרְאוֹתָיו.[ה]

וְלָכֵן[ו] צָרִיךְ כָּל אָדָם לְכַוֵּן[5] בִּישִׁיבָתוֹ בַּסֻּכָּה, שֶׁיּוֹשֵׁב בָּהּ כְּדֵי

---

1. *Vayikra* 23:42-43.

2. *Sukkah* 11b.

3. The Rebbe explains how the Alter Rebbe's wording, which modifies the language of his source, the *Tur,* distinguishes between two halachically significant facets of the *mitzvah:* (a) *the structural function* of the *s'chach,* that it must be intended for the purpose of shade, and (b) that it *provide benefit for man,* sheltering him from the sun. (See *Likkutei Sichos,* Vol. 32, p. 140ff.)

On a related question, the *Bach (Orach Chayim* 625*)* asks why the Clouds of Glory were singled out from all the miracles that G-d worked for the Jewish people in their journey through the desert (e.g., the manna, Miriam's Well) and a *mitzvah* was instituted only in connection with this miracle.

The author of *Beis Elokim (Shaar HaYesodos,* ch. 37*)* offers a resolution. The other miracles provided food and water, indispensable necessities. The Clouds of Glory were not a necessity, for journeying under the desert sun would have been possible, though uncomfortable. By miraculously sheltering His people with the Clouds of Glory, G-d showed His loving care for them — and this love is highlighted by the *mitzvah* of *sukkah.* See *Likkutei Sichos,* Vol. 18, p. 258 (and footnote 53 there), and Vol. 32, p. 147.

4. See sec. 626:1-2 below.

5. The word translated here as "therefore" is copied in this edition from the first printing of the present work. In this spirit, the Rebbe notes that generally the intent associated with a *mitzvah* is secondary to its actual performance. In this instance, however, since the commandment to dwell in the *sukkah* specifies "that your [coming] generations shall know," the intent is an integral component of the *mitzvah.* (See *Likkutei Sichos,* Vol. 9, p. 231, and Vol. 32, p. 140ff., elaborating on the *Bach, loc. cit.,* and other sources.)

Hence the Rebbe's custom of glancing at the *s'chach* while saying the closing words of the blessing *leishev basukkah* (*Otzar Minhagei Chabad,* p. 299).

א ויקרא כג, מב־ג. ב רבי אליעזר בברייתא יא, ב (ענני כבוד). טור (כבודו) ושו״ע ס״א. וראה גם לעיל סי׳ תכט ס״ד. ג טור ושו״ע שם. ד כדלקמן סי׳ תרכו ס״א וש״נ. וראה לקו״ש חל״ב ע׳ 140 ואילך. שלחן המלך ח״ב ע׳ רכח. ה טור ולבוש. ו כן הוא בדפו״ר. אמנם ברוב הדפוסים: וכן. וראה לקו״ש שם. שלחן המלך שם ע׳ רלג.

לְקַיֵּם מִצְוַת הַקָּדוֹשׁ בָּרוּךְ הוּא שֶׁצִּוָּנוּ לֵישֵׁב בַּסֻּכָּה זֵכֶר לִיצִיאַת מִצְרַיִם:[ז,6]

וּמִצְוָה לְתַקֵּן הַסֻּכָּה[ח] וְלִבְנוֹתָהּ כֻּלָּהּ מִיָּד לְמָחֳרַת יוֹם הַכִּפּוּרִים[ט] אַחַר יְצִיאָה מִבֵּית הַכְּנֶסֶת,[7] מִצְוָה הַבָּאָה לְיָדוֹ אַל יַחְמִיצֶנָּה:[י,8]

fulfill the *mitzvah* of the Holy One, blessed be He, Who commanded us to dwell in a *sukkah* in commemoration of the Exodus from Egypt.[6]

It is a *mitzvah* to prepare the *sukkah* and to complete its construction immediately, on the day following Yom Kippur, after departing from the synagogue.[7] A *mitzvah* that comes to hand should not be delayed.[8]

סימן תרכו הָעוֹשֶׂה סֻכָּה תַּחַת הָאִילָן אוֹ תַּחַת הַגַּג וּבוֹ כ"א סְעִיפִים:

SECTION 626 Laws Relating to the Construction of a *Sukkah* under a Tree or under a Roof. (1–21)

א אֵין אָדָם יוֹצֵא יְדֵי חוֹבָתוֹ אֶלָּא בְּסֻכָּה שֶׁאֵינָהּ עֲשׂוּיָה אֶלָּא לְצֵל[א,1] בִּלְבַד דֻּגְמַת עַנְנֵי כָבוֹד,[2] אֲבָל אִם הִיא עֲשׂוּיָה גַּם לְדִירָה דְּהַיְנוּ לָדוּר בָּהּ בִּקְבִיעוּת[ב] וְלֹא לְהִסְתּוֹפֵף בְּצִלָּהּ בִּלְבַד, אוֹ שֶׁעֲשׂוּיָה גַּם לְהִשְׁתַּמֵּשׁ בָּהּ תַּשְׁמִישׁ שֶׁל צְנִיעוּת[ג] כְּגוֹן לְאוֹצָר,[ד] אוֹ שְׁאָר

1 One can fulfill his obligation [to dwell in a *sukkah*] only with a *sukkah* that is made for the purpose of shade alone,[1] like the Clouds of Glory.[2] If, however, it is also made with the intent of serving as a dwelling, i.e., to enable one to live there in a permanent manner and not only to take shelter in its shade, or if it is also intended for private use, such as for a storehouse, or for another function that

---

6. Nevertheless, as the *Tur* explains, we do not celebrate Sukkos directly after Pesach, because it would not be apparent that we are dwelling in the *sukkah* in observance of a *mitzvah*. After all, people commonly live in such structures during the summer. However, since Sukkos is celebrated (in the Northern Hemisphere) after the summer has ended and it has begun to become cool, it is clear that we are dwelling in the *sukkah* in observance of G-d's command.

7. Though the intent here is that one should build the *sukkah* on the morning of the eleventh of Tishrei, many meticulous individuals make at least preliminary preparations at night, at the end of Yom Kippur (see *Rama, Orach Chayim* 624:5). This is Lubavitch custom, as noted in *Sefer HaMinhagim: The Book of Chabad-Lubavitch Customs* (Kehot, N.Y., 5750/1990), p. 126.

The custom in some other communities is to complete most of the construction before Yom Kippur so that one will have acquired an additional merit before the judgment of that day (see *Shaarei Teshuvah* 625:1).

8. Cf. *Mechilta, Parshas Bo.*

SECTION 626

1. *Sukkah* 8b; see also 2b.

The Rebbe explains that the Alter Rebbe departs from the structure of the corresponding section in the *Tur* and the *Shulchan Aruch* and begins with this law, because it defines the nature of the *mitzvah* of *sukkah* (see sec. 625, footnote 3 above).

2. See sec. 625 above and footnotes 2-5.

ז מ"א ריש הסי'. ב"ח ד"ה תלה. ועד"ז ראה לעיל סי' ח סי"ז (בציצית). סי' כה סי"א (בתפילין). ח מהרי"ל ריש הל' סוכות. רמ"א. ט מ"א סק"א, בשם מהרי"ל שם. וראה רמ"א סוס"י תרכד, להתחיל מיד במוצאי יוה"כ, וכ"ה מנהג חב"ד, עכ"פ בדיבור (ס' המנהגים — חב"ד ע' 59. אוצר מנהגי חב"ד ע' רנה). י מהרי"ל שם, בשם מהר"ם סג"ל. רמ"א. ע"פ מכילתא בא פ"ט ד"ה ושמרתם. רש"י מגילה ו, סע"ב, ושמות יב, יז. וראה לעיל סי' צד סוף ס"ה. סי' רמח קו"א ס"ק א.

סימן תרכו: א רב חסדא גמרא ח, ב ורש"י שם ד"ה אמר רב חסדא. טור ושו"ע סי' תרלה ס"א. וכדלעיל סי' תרכה וש"נ. ב ר"ן (ד, א) ד"ה סוכת. ט"ז ומ"א סי' תרלה סק"א (גם בדעת רש"י). וראה גם לקמן סי' תרלא סי"ב. ואם עשויה רק לצל ודר בה כל השנה, ראה לקמן סי' תרלו ס"ב. ג רש"י שם. מ"א שם. ד ר"ן שם. ט"ז ומ"א שם. ועד"ז לעיל סי' תקיח סי"ב (עצים שהכניסן לאוצר להצניען). וראה העו"ב תתנט ע' 59. ה ראבי"ה סי' תריא, בשם ר"ת. הגהות

תַּשְׁמִישׁ שֶׁצָּרִיךְ לַעֲשׂוֹתוֹ בְּמָקוֹם צָנוּעַ, אוֹ שֶׁהִיא עֲשׂוּיָה גַּם לְמַחְסֶה וּלְמִסְתּוֹר מִזֶּרֶם וּמִמָּטָר,[ה,3] כָּל שֶׁאֵינָהּ עֲשׂוּיָה לְצֵל בִּלְבַד – אֵין זוֹ סֻכָּה אֶלָּא בַּיִת,[ו] שֶׁהֲרֵי הַבַּיִת הוּא מְיֻחָד לְכָל דְּבָרִים אֵלּוּ, וְהַתּוֹרָה אָמְרָה סֻכָּה וְלֹא בַּיִת:[ז]

requires a secluded place, or if it was also made "as a protective haven from downpours of rain,"[3] [it is not halachically acceptable].

Any structure that was not made for shade alone is not deemed a *sukkah* but a house. A house is designated for all of these purposes, but the Torah specified a *sukkah,* not a house.

ב וּצְרִיכָה שֶׁתְּהֵא הַסֻּכָּה תַּחַת אֲוִיר הַשָּׁמַיִם[ח] דֻּגְמַת עַנְנֵי הַכָּבוֹד,[ט] אֲבָל אִם עֲשָׂאָהּ בְּתוֹךְ הַבַּיִת – פְּסוּלָה,[י,4] לְפִי שֶׁאֵין צֵל הַסֻּכָּה מְשַׁמֵּשׁ כְּלוּם,[יא] שֶׁאַף בִּלְעֲדֵי הַסְּכָךְ[5] יֵשׁ כָּאן צֵל מֵחֲמַת תִּקְרַת הַבַּיִת. וְכֵן הַדִּין בְּעוֹשֶׂה סֻכָּה תַּחַת הָאִילָן,[יב,4] אוֹ תַּחַת שְׁאָר דְּבָרִים הַפְּסוּלִים לִסְכָךְ שֶׁיִּתְבָּאֵר בְּסִימָן תרל"א,[יג,6] בֵּין שֶׁקָּדְמָה הַסֻּכָּה לַדָּבָר הַפָּסוּל הַמַּאֲהִיל עָלֶיהָ בֵּין שֶׁקָּדַם הַדָּבָר הַפָּסוּל לְהַסֻּכָּה,[יד] שֶׁמִּכָּל מָקוֹם עַכְשָׁו אֵין צֵל הַסֻּכָּה מְשַׁמֵּשׁ כְּלוּם, כֵּיוָן שֶׁהַצֵּל הָעֶלְיוֹן עָלָיו:

2 A *sukkah* must be under the open sky, as were the Clouds of Glory. If a *sukkah* was constructed within a house it is invalid,[4] because [its] shade serves no purpose; even without the *s'chach,*[5] there is shade because of the roof of the house.

The same law applies if a *sukkah* is made under a tree,[4] or under any other materials that are unacceptable as *s'chach,* as explained in sec. 631.[6] [This restriction applies] whether the *sukkah* existed before it was covered by the material whose shade is halachically unacceptable, or whether that invalid [covering] was present before the *sukkah* was constructed. In either case [the *sukkah* is invalid] because the shade brought about by the *sukkah* now serves no purpose, for the shade brought about by the other material is above it.

ג לְפִיכָךְ אֲפִלּוּ אִם צֵל הַסֻּכָּה[7] מְרֻבָּה מֵחַמָּתָהּ[8] בְּלֹא צֵרוּף צֵל הָעֶלְיוֹן

3 Such a *sukkah* is therefore invalid, even if the shadow that [its *s'chach*[7]] casts [on the floor] exceeds the sunlit area,[8] without including at all the shade from the higher, [invalid]

3. Cf. *Yeshayahu* 4:6.

4. *Sukkah* 9b.

5. Lit., "covering." (See sec. 629 and 631 below.) The key term *s'chach* is the source of the noun *Sukkah* (see *Rashi* on *Sukkah* 2a), which sometimes serves in the above Hebrew text as a synonym for it.

6. Subsections 11 and 12 of that section begin to speak of this subject, but, as noted at the end of that section, the surviving text as printed is incomplete.

7. Lit., "the *sukkah.*" See footnote 5 above.

8. A *sukkah* is invalid if its *s'chach* casts a shadow over less than half of its floor area (lit., "if its sun [sunlit area] is more extensive than its shade"; *Sukkah* 1:1). Accordingly, the term חמתה (lit., "its sun") is generally translated here as "its sunlit area." The balance between sunlit and shaded

מיימוניות פ"ה אות ט. ט"ז שם. והוא לשון הפסוק ישעיה ד, ו. וראה לקו"ש חל"ב ע' 142 הערה 30. לקמן סי' תרלא ס"ה. שו"ת אבני נזר או"ח סי' תעד. פתחא זוטא לסי' תרלה ס"א. ו ט"ז שם. וראה גם לקמן סי' תרכט ס"י. סי' תרלא ס"ה. ז רש"י יד, א ד"ה רבי מאיר. מ"א סק"א. ט"ז סי' תרכט סקי"ח. וראה לקמן שם סכ"ט. ח טור ולבוש ס"א. ט"ז ס"ק א. ט לבוש שם. י משנה וברייתא ט, ב. טור ורמ"א ס"א. יא ר"ן (ה, רע"א). וראה לקו"ש שם הערה 31. שלחן המלך שם ע' רלח. יב משנה וברייתא ט, ב. טור ושו"ע ס"א. יג אוצ"ל: סי' תרכט ס"א. יד ראבי"ה סי' תריג. הובא ברא"ש פ"א סי' יד וטור. ר"ן שם. שו"ע שם.

כְּלָל, דְּהַיְנוּ שֶׁאֲפִלּוּ אִם יִנָּטֵל צֵל הָעֶלְיוֹן מִכָּאן יִהְיֶה צִלָּתָהּ מְרֻבָּה מֵחַמָּתָהּ — אַף עַל פִּי כֵן פְּסוּלָה. וַאֲפִלּוּ אִם צֵל הָעֶלְיוֹן בִּלְבַד הוּא מְעַט מִזְעָר, בְּעִנְיָן שֶׁאִם יִנָּטֵל צֵל הַתַּחְתּוֹן דְּהַיְנוּ צֵל הַסְּכָךְ שֶׁעַל גַּבֵּי הַסֻּכָּה תִּהְיֶה חַמָּתוֹ שֶׁל הָעֶלְיוֹן מְרֻבָּה מִצִּלָּתוֹ — אַף עַל פִּי כֵן פְּסוּלָה,[טו] דְּכֵיוָן שֶׁצֵּל הָעֶלְיוֹן שֶׁהוּא פָּסוּל עוֹמֵד לְמַעְלָה — הֲרֵי הוּא מְבַטֵּל צֵל הַסְּכָךְ שֶׁתַּחְתָּיו כְּנֶגְדּוֹ מַמָּשׁ, שֶׁהֲרֵי אֵינוֹ מְשַׁמֵּשׁ כְּלוּם, כֵּיוָן שֶׁהָעֶלְיוֹן מֵצֵל עַל מָקוֹם שֶׁהוּא מֵצֵל,[טז] וּלְפִיכָךְ אָנוּ רוֹאִים כְּאִלּוּ נִטַּל וְנֶחְסַר מִן צֵל הַסְּכָךְ הַכָּשֵׁר[יז] כְּשִׁעוּר צֵל הָעֶלְיוֹן שֶׁמֵּצֵל עַל הַסֻּכָּה, וּכְאִלּוּ הָיָה הַמָּקוֹם הַזֶּה שֶׁהָעֶלְיוֹן מֵצֵל עָלָיו מְקוֹם חַמָּה, וְתִהְיֶה הַסֻּכָּה חַמָּתָהּ מְרֻבָּה מִצִּלָּתָהּ:[יח,9]

covering; i.e., even if the shadow cast by the higher covering were removed, the shadow cast by [the *sukkah*] would exceed its sunlit area.

[Moreover,] even if the shade from the higher, [invalid] covering alone is so limited that if the shade from the lower [covering] — i.e., the *s'chach* of the *sukkah* — was removed, the [floor] area remaining open to the sunlight admitted by the higher [covering] would exceed its shaded area, the *sukkah* is nevertheless invalid. [The rationale is that] the shade from the higher, invalid [covering] nullifies the shade produced by the *s'chach* directly beneath it; [that *s'chach*] serves no purpose, since the higher, invalid [covering] produces shade over the same place over which [the *s'chach*] produces shade. [See fig. 1.] We therefore consider the shade [on the floor] caused by the valid *s'chach* as if it were reduced to the same extent as the area [of *s'chach*] that is shaded by the higher, [invalid] covering. Hence this is as if the [latter] area [of *s'chach*], which is shaded by the higher, [invalid] covering, was [open to the sky, and the corresponding floor area was] sunlit. The sunlit area of the *sukkah* [may] thus exceed its shaded part [thus invalidating the *sukkah*].[9]

ד אֲבָל אִם צֵל הַסֻּכָּה הוּא מְרֻבֶּה מְאֹד, בְּעִנְיָן שֶׁאֲפִלּוּ אִם יִנָּטֵל מִמֶּנָּה כְּשִׁעוּר צֵל הָעֶלְיוֹן וְיִהְיֶה

4 If, however, the shade produced by [the *s'chach* of] the *sukkah* is so extensive that even if an area [of *s'chach*] equivalent to the part shaded by the higher, [invalid covering] were

areas is calculated according to what is seen on the *sukkah* floor, not according to the gaps in the *s'chach* that admit the sunlight. The Sages express the difference in terms of small and large silver coins that were current in the Talmudic era: In the *s'chach* above, a gap as small as a *zuz* admits sunlight which on the floor diffuses to the size of an *istera* (*Sukkah* 22b).

As evident from the continuation of the section (see also *Tur, Orach Chayim* 626), when the branches of a tree produce so much shade that there is more shade than sun under them, a valid *sukkah* can never be constructed there. When, however, there is more sun than shade under a tree, a valid *sukkah* may be constructed there in certain circumstances, even without detaching or moving the branches, as the Alter Rebbe proceeds to explain.

9. In certain circumstances, however, a *sukkah* may be valid even when it is partly covered by invalid substances, as the Alter Rebbe states in subsection 4 below.

טו ראבי"ה שם, בשם הריב"א. רא"ש שם. ר"ן שם. דעה הב' בטור ושו"ע שם. טז ר"ן שם. וכדלעיל ס"ב. יז טור ור"ן שם. לבוש סוף ס"ב. יח טור ולבוש

הַמָּקוֹם שֶׁהָעֶלְיוֹן מֵצֵל עָלָיו מְקוֹם חַמָּה וְאַף עַל פִּי כֵן תִּהְיֶה הַסֻּכָּה צִלָּתָהּ מְרֻבָּה מֵחַמָּתָהּ — כְּשֵׁרָה:[יט]

ה וְכָל זֶה כְּשֶׁהָיָה הַסְּכָךְ פָּסוּל לְמַעְלָה עַל הַסְּכָךְ כָּשֵׁר, אֲבָל אִם הָיוּ מְעֹרָבִים זֶה בָּזֶה, כְּגוֹן אִילָן שֶׁהָיָה מֵצֵל עַל הַסֻּכָּה שֶׁלְּמַטָּה מִמֶּנּוּ וְהִשְׁפִּיל עֲנָפָיו לְמַטָּה[כ] וְעֵרְבָן, אִם הַסְּכָךְ הַכָּשֵׁר הוּא מְרֻבֶּה הַרְבֵּה[10] מִן הַסְּכָךְ הַפָּסוּל

to be removed and the remaining area were open to sunlight, the shaded part of the *sukkah* would nevertheless exceed its sunlit area, the *sukkah* is valid. [See fig. 2.]

5 The above applies when the material that is invalid as *s'chach* was positioned above the valid *s'chach*. [Different rules apply] if [the two] were intermingled; for example, if there was a tree that cast a shadow over a *sukkah*, and one lowered its branches and mixed them together [with the acceptable *s'chach*. See p. 252, fig. 3.]

If there is much more[10] of the valid *s'chach* than of the material that is invalid for *s'chach*,

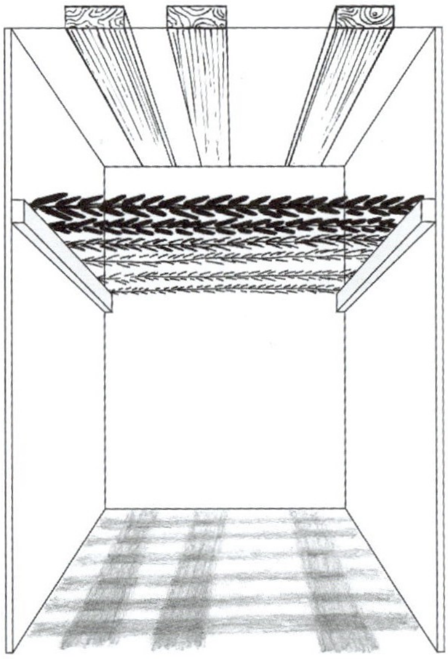

Fig. 1:
In this diagram, 60% of the floor area is shaded by valid *s'chach*. However, the uppermost covering is invalid, since it is made of boards that are more than four *tefachim* wide (see sec. 629:29). The shadow it casts - overlapping (say) 30% of the area - nullifies the shade produced by the corresponding amount of valid *s'chach* directly beneath it. Hence only [60% - 30% =] 30% of the floor area is now shaded by valid *s'chach*. Since this is less than half of the floor area, this *sukkah* is invalid. (See sec. 626:3.)

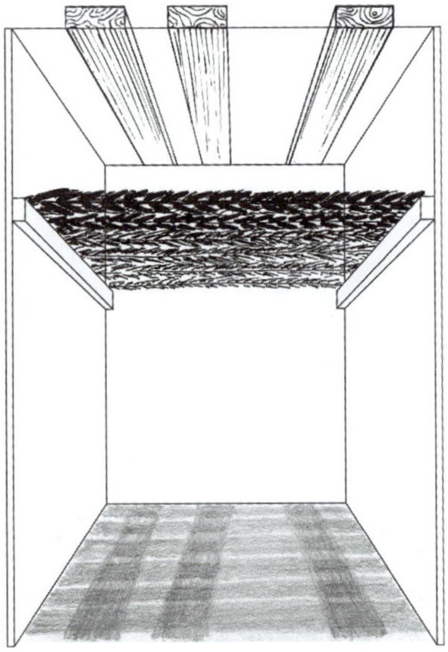

Fig. 2:
Since the valid *s'chach* here is thicker, it casts a shade over (say) 85% of the floor area. Even if one now deducts the amount of shade produced by the overlapping invalid material, the floor area that is shaded by valid *s'chach* still exceeds the sunlit area. (85% - 30% = 55%.) This *sukkah* is thus valid. (See sec. 626:4.)

10. In this passage (subsection 5), "much more valid *s'chach*" signifies an overall majority (e.g., 60% valid coverage *vis-à-vis* 30% invalid, the remaining 10% being open space). In subsection 6, by contrast, the valid *s'chach* has only a simple majority (e.g., 40% valid coverage *vis-à-vis* 30% invalid).

שם. יט ראבי"ה שם (כשענפי האילן על מקום חמה). רא"ש וטור שם (כשינטל כנגד האילן ישאר כשיעור). ר"ן שם. רמ"א סוף ס"א. כ רב פפא ט, ב.

הַמְעֹרָב בּוֹ – הֲרֵי הַפָּסוּל נִתְבַּטֵּל בָּרֹב,[כא] אַף אִם הִנִּיחַ סְכַךְ הַכָּשֵׁר עַל סְכַךְ הַפָּסוּל – נִקְרָא עִרְבּוּב וּבָטֵל בָּרֹב,[כב,11] וְאַף עַל פִּי שֶׁסְּכַךְ הַפָּסוּל הוּא נִכָּר בֵּין הַכָּשֵׁר וְאֵינוֹ מְעֹרָב יָפֶה וְהוּא יָכוֹל לַהֲסִירוֹ מִשָּׁם – אַף עַל פִּי כֵן הוּא בָּטֵל.[כג]

וְאַף עַל פִּי שֶׁבְּכָל אִסּוּרִין שֶׁבַּתּוֹרָה אִם הוּא מַכִּיר אֶת הָאִסּוּר וְיָכוֹל לַהֲסִירוֹ מִן הַתַּעֲרוֹבוֹת אֵינוֹ

the invalid material becomes *batel* — insignificant and [therefore] nullified — *vis-à-vis* the majority [of the valid *s'chach*]. Moreover, even if the valid *s'chach* is placed upon the material that is invalid as *s'chach,* it is considered as intermingled and is nullified *vis-à-vis* the majority [of the valid *s'chach*].[11]

[In this instance,] the material that is invalid as *s'chach* is distinct from the valid *[s'chach];* it is not completely intermingled, and could be removed. Nevertheless, it is nullified. [This represents an exception to the accepted pattern.] With regard to all the prohibitions of the Torah, [we follow the principle that] if the forbidden substance is recognizable and can be removed from the mixture, it does not

Fig. 3:
Sec. 626:5 describes a case in which the shade over 60% of the floor area remains valid, despite the presence of 30% shade produced by the intermingled, invalid covering. The *sukkah* is thus valid.

Fig. 4:
In this *sukkah,* the valid *s'chach* is so sparse that its shade covers only (say) 40% of the floor area. Since in this case the shade (say 30%) produced by the invalid material is disregarded (see sec. 626:6), the *sukkah* is invalid, because less than half of its floor area is shaded by valid *s'chach.*

11. The new concept introduced by this law is that because the invalid *s'chach* is mixed together with the valid *s'chach,* one may fulfill one's obligation to dwell in a *sukkah* by sitting under that mixture. In the situation described in the previous subsection, although the *sukkah* as a whole is not disqualified, one may not sit under the part covered by invalid *s'chach* if that *s'chach* exceeds four handbreadths. (See the *Shulchan Aruch* of R. Yosef Caro, sec. 632:1).

כא רש"י שם ד"ה בשחבטן (אף לענין להצטרף, כדלקמן ס"ט). ר"ן שם (לענין שלא יפסול). וראה גם לקמן סי' תרכט סט"ז. **כב** ראבי"ה סי' תרטז. מרדכי השלם רמז תשלח. רמ"א ס"א. **כג** ר"ן שם. מ"א סק"ד. **כד** קושית הר"ן שם (יכול להתירו ולעמוד עליו). מ"א ס"ק ג (שיכול להסירו). **כה** כדלעיל סי' תקז וש"נ. ולענין

בָּטֵל[כד] אֲפִלּוּ בְּאֶלֶף,[כה, 12] הַיְנוּ שֶׁאָסוּר לֶאֱכֹל אֶת הַתַּעֲרוֹבוֹת, שֶׁלֹּא יִפְגַּע בְּגוּף הָאִסּוּר עַצְמוֹ, שֶׁלֹּא נִתְבַּטֵּל כֵּיוָן שֶׁיָּכוֹל לַהֲסִירוֹ מִשָּׁם, אֲבָל כָּאן אֵינוֹ נֶהֱנֶה כְּלָל מִן הָאִסּוּר, שֶׁהֲרֵי אַף אִם יִנָּטֵל סְכָךְ הַפָּסוּל מִן הַסֻּכָּה יִהְיֶה צִלָּתָהּ מְרֻבָּה מֵחַמָּתָהּ מֵחֲמַת סְכָךְ הַכָּשֵׁר,[כו] וְאֵין אָנוּ צְרִיכִים לְבַטֵּל אֶת הַפָּסוּל בְּרֹב אֶלָּא כְּדֵי שֶׁלֹּא יִהְיֶה לוֹ כֹּחַ לִפְסֹל אֶת הַסְּכָךְ הַכָּשֵׁר הַמְעֹרָב עִמּוֹ:[כז]

become nullified, even if there is 1000 times more of the permitted substance.[12] [In the case of food, for example,] such a mixture may not be eaten, lest one encounter the actual forbidden substance whose existence was not nullified, because it could have been removed. In this instance, however, [that principle is not followed]. For no benefit is gained from the forbidden material; even if the substance that is invalid as *s'chach* were to be removed from the *sukkah,* there would be enough valid *s'chach* for the shade of the *sukkah* to exceed its sunlit area. We must nullify the invalid material *vis-à-vis* the large amount [of the valid *s'chach*] only so that [the invalid material] will not disqualify the valid *s'chach* with which it is combined.

ו אֲבָל אִם צֵל הַכָּשֵׁר הוּא מְעַט בְּעִנְיָן שֶׁאִם יִנָּטֵל צֵל הַפָּסוּל מִן הַסֻּכָּה לֹא יְהֵא צִלָּתָהּ מְרֻבָּה מֵחַמָּתָהּ — הֲרֵי הִיא פְּסוּלָה, לְפִי שֶׁאֵין צֵל הַפָּסוּל מִצְטָרֵף לְהַשְׁלִים הַשִּׁעוּר לְצֵל הַכָּשֵׁר, כֵּיוָן שֶׁלֹּא נִתְבַּטֵּל עֲדַיִן בִּטּוּל גָּמוּר, שֶׁהֲרֵי יָכוֹל לַהֲסִירוֹ מִשָּׁם:[כח]

6 However, if so little shade is produced by valid *[s'chach]* that when the shade produced by the [intermingled] invalid material is removed from the *sukkah,* the shade [on the floor] will not exceed the sunlit area, [the *sukkah*] is invalid. [See fig. 4.] For the shade produced by the invalid material cannot be combined with the shade produced by valid *[s'chach]* to complete its minimum measure. The rationale [for this stringency] is that [the invalid material] has not yet been entirely nullified, for it could be removed.

ז וְכָל זֶה כְּשֶׁהַסְּכָךְ הַפָּסוּל הַמְעֹרָב בַּכָּשֵׁר הוּא בְּעַצְמוֹ קַל וְקָלוּשׁ בְּעִנְיָן שֶׁחַמָּתוֹ מְרֻבָּה מִצִּלָּתוֹ,[13] אֲבָל אִם צִלָּתוֹ מְרֻבָּה מֵחַמָּתוֹ — אֵין בִּטּוּל בְּרֹב מוֹעִיל לוֹ שֶׁלֹּא יִפְסֹל אֶת הַסֻּכָּה בְּצִלּוֹ,[כט] כֵּיוָן שֶׁצֵּל הַכָּשֵׁר אֵינוֹ

7 All of the above applies when the invalid material that is intermingled with the valid *s'chach* is so flimsy and insubstantial that the sunlit area [in the *sukkah*] exceeds the shaded area.[13] If, however, [the invalid material] causes the shade to exceed the sunlit area, its nullification *vis-à-vis* the greater quantity [of valid *s'chach*] is not effective in preventing its shade from disqualifying the *sukkah.* For the valid *s'chach* serves

---

12. See Rabbeinu Nissim, *Beitzah* 4b. Since the forbidden substance is distinguishable, it is not appropriate to say that it can become *batel.* See also *Shulchan Aruch, Yoreh Deah* 92:3, and sec. 507:5 in the present work.

13. *Sukkah* 9b.

פירור המעורב בקמח, ראה לעיל סי' תמז קו"א סק"ט. סי' תסו ס"ט. **כו** ר"ן שם. מ"מ פ"ה הי"ב בשם הרמב"ן. רבנו ירוחם נתיב ח ח"א (נה, ב) בדעת ראבי"ה. הובא במ"א סק"ד. **כז** מ"א שם. וראה קובץ כינוס תורה ד ע' כו. **כח** מ"א שם. **כט** רבא בגמרא ט, ב. לפירוש רב פפא (דמיירי בחבטן). וראה גם לקמן ס"ט (לדעה הב').

מְשַׁמֵּשׁ כְּלוּם[ל] בְּמָקוֹם שֶׁהַפָּסוּל הָיָה יָכוֹל לִהְיוֹת מֵצֵל שָׁם אִם לֹא נִתְעָרֵב שָׁם, כֵּיוָן שֶׁצִּלָּתוֹ מְרֻבָּה מֵחַמָּתוֹ, וְלָכֵן אֵין הַסֻּכָּה כְּשֵׁרָה, אֶלָּא אִם כֵּן יֵשׁ בָּהּ סְכָךְ כָּשֵׁר הַרְבֵּה כָּל כָּךְ עַד שֶׁאִם יִנָּטֵל מֵהַסְּכָךְ הַכָּשֵׁר כְּשִׁעוּר הַסְּכָךְ הַפָּסוּל הַמְעֹרָב בּוֹ הָיְתָה הַסֻּכָּה צִלָּתָהּ מְרֻבָּה מֵחַמָּתָהּ:[לא,14]

no function in the place where the invalid material would provide shade [even] if [the valid *s'chach*] were not mixed with it, for the shade [produced by the invalid material] exceeds the sunlit area [of the *sukkah*. See fig. 5.]

Such a *sukkah* is therefore acceptable only if it has so much valid *s'chach* that if we would remove [from it] an amount that is equivalent to the invalid material that is intermingled with it, the shaded area within the *sukkah* would still exceed its sunlit area.[14] [See fig. 6.]

Fig. 5:
In this *sukkah,* described in the first paragraph of sec. 626:7, there is enough valid *s'chach* to cast a shadow over (say) 90% of the floor area. However, so much invalid material is intermingled with it that it alone would be able to cast a shadow over (say) 60% of the floor area. This invalid material is therefore not nullified *vis-à-vis* the greater quantity of valid *s'chach* (90% - 60% = 30%). The *sukkah* is thus invalid..

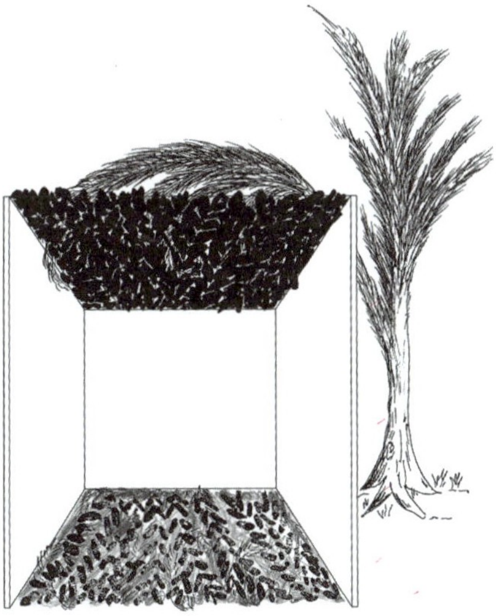

Fig. 6:
The second paragraph of sec. 626:7 explains why this *sukkah* is valid. Its *s'chach* is so plentiful that even if we were to remove an amount equivalent to the invalid material intermingled with it (150% - 60% = 90%), the greater part of the floor area would still be shaded.

14. In the above ruling — and similarly, in subsections 9-10 — the Alter Rebbe's wording provokes an obvious question: Since the invalid material covers more than half of the *sukkah,* how is it possible that if an equivalent amount of valid *s'chach* was removed, the shade in the *sukkah* would still exceed the sunlit area? Since the majority of the material is acceptable, leniency can be taken with regard to the shade it produces.

Evidently the above calculations concerning the *s'chach* address its volume, not only its area. In this the Alter Rebbe's *Shulchan Aruch* differs with the approach of the *Tur* and *Bach.* See also: R. Sholom Ber Levin, *Dover Shalom* (Kehot, N.Y., 5763/2003), p. 240ff.

ל ר"ן שם. ב"י ד"ה ואם האילן. לא ראה יגדיל תורה (נ.י.) נה ע' שנח. העו"ב תתנט ע' 62. לב ר"ן שם, ממשנה טו, א. מ"מ שם בשם הרמב"ן. מ"א ס"ק

8 When does the above apply? When the valid *s'chach* and the invalid material are intermingled, or when the invalid material is positioned below the valid *s'chach.* [In such an instance,] the valid *s'chach* must exceed the invalid material so that [the latter] will be [outweighed and hence] nullified and [thus] will not disqualify the *sukkah* by its shade.

If, however, both [the valid *s'chach* and the invalid material] were placed on the *sukkah* separately, one next to the other, without being mixed together at all, there is no need that the valid *s'chach* exceed the invalid material. Even if they are equal in amount the *sukkah* is valid, for, as explained in sec. 631[:10], this is a *halachah* transmitted to Moshe at Sinai.[15]

9 ([16]Some authorities differ with this entire approach. They maintain that if the invalid material is intermingled with valid *s'chach* and they are both of the same type, and thus the invalid material is not at all distinct, [there is room for leniency]. For example: one built a *sukkah* under a tree, bent down [its] branches, and lowered them [so that he could] mix them together with the detached *s'chach* on top of the *sukkah.* Although it is possible for him to remove the prohibited material by raising the branches up to the trunk of the tree, as long as they are mixed together [with the valid *s'chach*] and are not distinct, they are nullified *vis-à-vis* the majority [of valid *s'chach.* Moreover,] they may be combined together with it to fill the [required] measure, [so that] the shade [within the *sukkah*] will exceed the sunlit area.[17] (This differs from the first

ח בַּמֶּה דְּבָרִים אֲמוּרִים? כְּשֶׁהַכָּשֵׁר וְהַפָּסוּל הֵן מְעֹרָבִין, אוֹ שֶׁהַפָּסוּל הוּא מֻנָּח לְמַטָּה מִן הַכָּשֵׁר, שֶׁאָז צָרִיךְ שֶׁיְּהֵא בַּכָּשֵׁר רֹב כְּנֶגֶד הַפָּסוּל כְּדֵי לְבַטְּלוֹ שֶׁלֹּא יִפְסֹל אֶת הַסֻּכָּה בְּצִלּוֹ, אֲבָל אִם הָיוּ מֻנָּחִין עַל הַסֻּכָּה כָּל אֶחָד וְאֶחָד בִּפְנֵי עַצְמוֹ זֶה בְּצַד זֶה וְאֵינָן מְעֹרָבִין כְּלָל – אֵין צָרִיךְ שֶׁיִּהְיֶה בַּכָּשֵׁר רֹב כְּנֶגֶד הַפָּסוּל, אֶלָּא אֲפִלּוּ אִם הֵם מֶחֱצָה עַל מֶחֱצָה גַּם כֵּן – הַסֻּכָּה הִיא כְּשֵׁרָה,[לב] שֶׁכָּךְ הִיא הֲלָכָה לְמֹשֶׁה מִסִּינַי[לג, 15] כְּמוֹ שֶׁיִּתְבָּאֵר בְּסִימָן תרל"א,[לד] עַיֵּן שָׁם:

ט (וְיֵשׁ[16] חוֹלְקִין עַל כָּל זֶה[לה] וְאוֹמְרִים שֶׁאִם הַפָּסוּל מְעֹרָב בַּכָּשֵׁר וּשְׁנֵיהֶן הֵן מִין אֶחָד שֶׁאֵין הַפָּסוּל נִכָּר כְּלָל, כְּגוֹן הָעוֹשֶׂה סֻכָּתוֹ תַּחַת הָאִילָן וְהִשְׁפִּיל עַנְפֵי הָאִילָן וְהוֹרִידָן לְמַטָּה וְעֵרְבָן עִם הַסְּכָךְ הַתָּלוּשׁ שֶׁעַל גַּבֵּי הַסֻּכָּה,[לו] אַף עַל פִּי שֶׁהוּא יָכוֹל לְהָסִיר אֶת הָאִסּוּר, דְּהַיְנוּ שֶׁיַּגְבִּיהַּ אֶת הָעֲנָפִים לְעִקַּר הָאִילָן, מִכָּל מָקוֹם כָּל זְמַן שֶׁהֵן מְעֹרָבִין יַחַד וְאֵין נִכָּרִין[לז] – הֵן בְּטֵלִים בְּרֹב הַכָּשֵׁר, וּמִצְטָרְפִין עִמּוֹ לְהַשְׁלִים לְשִׁעוּר צִלָּתָהּ מְרֻבָּה מֵחַמָּתָהּ[17] (דְּלֹא כְּמוֹ שֶׁנִּתְבָּאֵר

15. See sec. 631, footnote 9 below.

16. In the standard printed text of the Alter Rebbe's *Shulchan Aruch*, there is no closing parenthesis.

17. Thus, for example, 40% valid *s'chach* plus 20% invalid material = 60% acceptable coverage.

ד. לג רשב"א חולין כט, א ד"ה אי. ר"ן שם. מ"א סק"ג. לד סעיף י וש"נ. לה רש"י ט, ב ד"ה הא קא מצטרף (דמהני להשלים) וד"ה בשחבטן (דמהני כשבטל ברוב), לפי מה שביאר בדבריו בראבי"ה סי' ריג. ר"ת הובא במרדכי רמז תשלד (שאם הכשר צלתו מרובה מחמתו אין הפסול פוסל אף בלא עירוב, א"כ מהני עירוב אף להשלים). תוס' ט, ב ד"ה הא. דעה הא' בטור שו"ע ס"א. לו רב פפא בגמרא שם לפירוש רש"י שם. לז רש"י שם ד"ה בשחבטן. תוס' טו, ב ד"ה והא. סמ"ג עשין מג (קכ, ב). ב"י ד"ה ומ"ש רבנו וה"ר יחיאל.

בַּדֵּעָה הָרִאשׁוֹנָה[18]).*

וְהוּא שֶׁיְּהֵא סְכָךְ פָּסוּל הַמְעֹרָב דַּק וְקָלוּשׁ בְּעִנְיָן שֶׁיְּהֵא חַמָּתוֹ מְרֻבָּה מִצִּלָּתוֹ, אֲבָל אִם צִלָּתוֹ מְרֻבָּה מֵחַמָּתוֹ – אֵינוֹ מִצְטָרֵף לְהַשְׁלִים לְשִׁעוּר צִלָּתָהּ מְרֻבָּה מֵחַמָּתָהּ.[לח,19] אֲבָל אִם הַסֻּכָּה הִיא צִלָּתָהּ מְרֻבָּה מֵחַמָּתָהּ בְּלֹא צֵרוּף צֵל סְכָךְ הַפָּסוּל – אֵינָהּ נִפְסֶלֶת לְעוֹלָם מֵחֲמַת צֵל סְכָךְ הַפָּסוּל, אַף עַל פִּי שֶׁצִּלָּתוֹ מְרֻבָּה מֵחַמָּתוֹ:[לט,20]

opinion.)[18]

[In this situation,] the invalid material that is mixed [with the valid *s'chach*] must be so flimsy and insubstantial that the sunlit area [within the *sukkah*] exceeds its shade. If, however, the shade [from the invalid material] exceeds the sunlit area [within the *sukkah*], it cannot be combined [as part of the valid *s'chach*] and be counted towards the measure that is required to make the shade [within the *sukkah*] exceed its sunlit area.[19]

Nevertheless, if the shade [within] the *sukkah* exceeds its sunlit area without counting the shade cast by the invalid material, [the *sukkah*] is never disqualified by the invalid material, even though [its quantity alone would suffice to make] the shade exceed the sunlit area.[20]

* וְאַף עַל פִּי שֶׁבְּכָל אִסּוּרִים שֶׁבַּתּוֹרָה אִם יָכוֹל לְהָסִיר אֶת הָאִסּוּר אֵינוֹ מִתְבַּטֵּל בְּרֹב, אֲבָל כָּאן הֲלָכָה לְמֹשֶׁה מִסִּינַי הוּא שֶׁאֵין צָרִיךְ לִהְיוֹת כָּל הַסְּכָךְ הַצָּרִיךְ לַסֻּכָּה שֶׁיְּהֵא סְכָךְ כָּשֵׁר אֶלָּא שֶׁיִּהְיֶה הָרֹב כָּשֵׁר,[מ] וְהַשְּׁאָר אַף עַל פִּי שֶׁהוּא פָּסוּל – אַף עַל פִּי כֵן הַסֻּכָּה מִתְכַּשֶּׁרֶת בּוֹ, וְאִם כֵּן אֵין עַל הַמִּעוּט שֵׁם סְכָךְ פָּסוּל, אֶלָּא גַּם הוּא חוֹזֵר לִהְיוֹת סְכָךְ כָּשֵׁר עַל יְדֵי רֹב הַכָּשֵׁר שֶׁעִמּוֹ.[מא] וּלְפִיכָךְ מֻתָּר לְעָרֵב וּלְבַטֵּל סְכָךְ פָּסוּל בְּכָשֵׁר לְכַתְּחִלָּה,[מב] מַה שֶּׁאֵין כֵּן בִּשְׁאָר אִסּוּרִין שֶׁאֵין מְבַטְּלִין אִסּוּר לְכַתְּחִלָּה,[מג] לְפִי שֶׁאֵין שֵׁם אִסּוּר כְּלָל עַל הַמִּעוּט הַפָּסוּל הַמְעֹרָב בְּכָשֵׁר.

18. The first opinion maintains that since the invalid material is still attached to the tree and thus a distinct entity, it can never be considered as part of the valid *s'chach* and can never be counted towards the measure that is required to make the shade within the *sukkah* exceed its sunlit area.

At this point in the Hebrew text, a marginal note explains the Alter Rebbe's rationale for the lenient ruling. The rule in all other contexts is that if a forbidden substance can be removed from a mixture, it is never nullified by the presence of a greater amount of a permitted substance. In this instance, exceptionally, a *halachah* transmitted to Moshe at Sinai states that it is not necessary for the entire *s'chach* of a *sukkah* to be valid. Rather, as long as the majority is permissible, the *sukkah* is valid even though part of its *s'chach* is not.

That minority of *s'chach* is therefore not considered as invalid. Because it is mixed together with the valid substances, the entire mixture is considered as valid *s'chach*. Moreover, it is even permitted initially to make such a mixture and thus nullify the presence of the material which alone would have been invalid as *s'chach*. It is true that as a rule, it is initially forbidden to mix small amounts of a forbidden substance into a permitted substance so that the existence of the forbidden substance will become nullified. That rule does not apply in this instance, however, because the invalid *s'chach* is not forbidden. Hence, it is not distinguished as an entity that cannot be nullified.

(The above explanation, summarized from the above-mentioned marginal note, varies from the explanations given in *Magen Avraham* 626:3.)

19. Thus, for example, 45% valid *s'chach* despite 55% invalid material = 45% coverage = unacceptable.

20. Thus, for example, 60% valid s'chach despite 60% invalid material = 60% valid = acceptable.

As in footnote 14 above, the Alter Rebbe's statements raise questions, for here, too, the *sukkah* is deemed valid even though there is enough invalid material to cover the majority of its area. One solution was offered there. For an

לח רבא בגמרא ט, ב. לפירוש רב פפא (דמיירי בחבטן). וראה גם לעיל ס"ז (לדעה הא'). לט וכ"ה לקמן סוף ס"י, אף בלא מעורב. וראה העו"ב תתנט ע' 63. מ ר"ן שם. מ"א סק"ג (שמבאר תירוץ ר"ן לשיטת רש"י. וראה לעיל ס"ה, התירוץ לשיטת הר"ן וסיעתו). וראה שו"ת צמח צדק יו"ד סי' ע אות ה. סי'

10 [These authorities also differ] when the invalid material is not intermingled with the valid *s'chach*, but is positioned overhead and casts its shadow over [it]. If the shade [within] the *sukkah* does not exceed its sunlit area without counting the shade [from] the invalid material — even when the sunlit area [within the *sukkah*] exceeds its shade if the invalid material alone is [considered] — the *sukkah* is invalid.[21] [The rationale is that it is] the invalid material that completes the [required] measure [of shade].

If, however, the shade [from the valid *s'chach*] exceeds the sunlit area without the addition of the shade from the invalid material, [the *sukkah*] is valid.[22] [This applies] even when the shade from the invalid material exceeds the sunlit area [within the *sukkah*].

Primacy should be given to the first opinion with regard to all of the above. Nevertheless, in a pressing situation in which one does not have another *sukkah* and he cannot correct such a *sukkah* and make it valid, he may rely on the latter opinion[23] so that he will not negate [the observance of] the *mitzvah* of *sukkah*.[24]

י וְאִם סְכַךְ הַפָּסוּל אֵינוֹ מְעֹרָב עִם סְכַךְ הַכָּשֵׁר אֶלָּא הוּא עוֹמֵד לְמַעְלָה וּמֵצֵל עַל הַכָּשֵׁר, אִם אֵין צֵל הַסֻּכָּה מְרֻבֶּה מֵחַמָּתָהּ בְּלֹא צֵרוּף צֵל הַפָּסוּל, אַף עַל פִּי שֶׁהַפָּסוּל חַמָּתוֹ מְרֻבָּה מִצִּלָּתוֹ – אַף עַל פִּי כֵן הֲרֵי זוֹ פְּסוּלָה,[21] שֶׁהֲרֵי סְכַךְ פָּסוּל מַשְׁלִימָהּ לְשִׁעוּרָהּ,[מד] אֲבָל אִם צִלָּתָהּ מְרֻבָּה מֵחַמָּתָהּ בְּלֹא צֵרוּף צֵל הַפָּסוּל,[מה] אַף עַל פִּי שֶׁהַפָּסוּל צִלָּתוֹ מְרֻבָּה מֵחַמָּתוֹ – הֲרֵי זוֹ כְּשֵׁרָה.[מו,22]

וְהָעִקָּר כַּסְּבָרָא הָרִאשׁוֹנָה בְּכָל זֶה.[מז] וּמִכָּל מָקוֹם, בִּשְׁעַת הַדְּחָק[מח] שֶׁאֵין לוֹ סֻכָּה אַחֶרֶת, וְגַם אִי אֶפְשָׁר לוֹ לְתַקֵּן סֻכָּה זוֹ וּלְהַכְשִׁירָהּ – יֵשׁ לִסְמֹךְ עַל סְבָרָא הָאַחֲרוֹנָה,[23] שֶׁלֹּא לְהִתְבַּטֵּל מִמִּצְוַת סֻכָּה:[24]

---

alternative explanation see *Dover Shalom* (cited in that footnote).

21. Thus, for example, 40% valid *s'chach* despite 20% invalid material = 40% coverage = unacceptable.

22. Thus, for example, 60% valid *s'chach* despite 60% invalid material = 60% coverage = acceptable.

23. Most authorities (see *Tur* and *Shulchan Aruch, Orach Chayim* 626:1) disqualify a *sukkah* constructed under a tree whose shade covers the majority of the area of the *sukkah,* in all situations. Nevertheless, the Alter Rebbe here is granting a leniency for a person who would be unable to observe the *mitzvah* otherwise, relying on the view of *Korban Nesanel (Sukkah* 1:14).

24. The following table summarizes the opinions outlined in the foregoing subsections:

	If the valid *s'chach* is separate:	If the valid *s'chach* is mixed with invalid material:
1st VIEW	It cancels out the equivalent area (subsection 3)	The invalid material does not count toward the required quantity (subsection 6)
2nd VIEW	It does not cancel out the equivalent area (subsection 10)	The invalid material counts toward the required quantity (subsection 9)

קסה אות י. **מא** ראה ריטב"א סוכה שם. **מב** מ"א שם. וראה לעיל סי' תמב קו"א סק"ג (כבר תירץ שם המ"א בשם הר"ן בטוב טעם ודעת). **מג** ביצה ד, ב. טור ושו"ע יו"ד סי' צט ס"ה. וכדלעיל שם ס"ה וש"נ. **מד** רש"י שם סוד"ה הא. **מה** ראבי"ה ורא"ש שם בדעת רש"י. תוס' שם. מרדכי שם בדעת רש"י ור"ת. דעה הא' בטור ושו"ע שם. **מו** קרבן נתנאל פ"א סי' יד אות ע, בדעת הרא"ש. ועד"ז לקמן סי' תרכח ס"ב, בסוכה ע"ג סוכה למעלה מכ', לכל הדעות. וראה קובץ יגדיל תורה שם. העו"ב שם. **מז** שכן דעת ריב"א, הובא בראבי"ה שם. טור בשם הרמב"ן. ר"ן שם. מ"מ שם. מרדכי שם בשם רבנו פרץ בהגהת סמ"ק סי' צג (ע' נה). רבנו יחיאל, הובא בטור. רבנו שמשון מקוצי, הובא במרדכי שם. **מח** אליה רבה אות ה.

יא אִם רוֹצֶה לִקְצֹץ אֶת הָאִילָן לְהַכְשִׁירוֹ לְסִכּוּךְ – יִתְבָּאֵר בְּסִימָן תרכ"ט[מט] שֶׁצָּרִיךְ לְנַעֲנֵעַ אֶת כָּל הָאִילָן, עַיֵּן שָׁם הַטַּעַם:[25]

11 If one desires to cut off [the branches of] a tree [that had been placed on a *sukkah*] to make them valid for *s'chach,* as will be explained in sec. 629[:20], he must move all [the branches of] the tree. Note the rationale explained there.[25]

יב מֻתָּר לַעֲשׂוֹת סֻכָּה לְמַטָּה בַּבַּיִת תַּחַת הַגָּג שֶׁהֵסִירוּ הָרְעָפִים מִמֶּנּוּ כְּדֵי לַעֲשׂוֹת סֻכָּה, אַף עַל פִּי שֶׁנִּשְׁאֲרוּ עֲדַיִן הָעֵצִים אוֹ הַקּוֹרוֹת שֶׁהָרְעָפִים מֻנָּחִים עֲלֵיהֶם:[נ]

וּמֻתָּר לֵישֵׁב תַּחַת הָעֵצִים אוֹ הַקּוֹרוֹת עַצְמָן[נא] אַף עַל פִּי שֶׁהֵם סְכָךְ פָּסוּל, שֶׁהֲרֵי לֹא נִקְבְּעוּ בַּגָּג לְשֵׁם צֵל בִּלְבַד אֶלָּא כְּדֵי לָתֵת עֲלֵיהֶם אֶת הָרְעָפִים,[נב] מִכָּל מָקוֹם כֵּיוָן שֶׁעָשָׂה מַעֲשֶׂה וְהֵסִיר אֶת הָרְעָפִים[נג] לְשֵׁם עֲשִׂיַּת סֻכָּה לְצֵל — הֲרֵי זֶה כְּאִלּוּ עָשָׂה מַעֲשֶׂה בְּגוּף הָעֵצִים אוֹ הַקּוֹרוֹת וְהִתְקִינָם לְשֵׁם סֻכָּה,[נד] שֶׁהֲרֵי הֵם כְּשֵׁרִים לְסִכּוּךְ, שֶׁהֵן גְּדֵלִים מִן הָאָרֶץ וְאֵין מְקַבְּלִין טֻמְאָה, וְאַף עַל פִּי שֶׁהֵן מְחֻבָּרִים[26] — אֵין בְּכָךְ כְּלוּם, דְּתָלוּשׁ וּלְבַסּוֹף חִבְּרוֹ כָּשֵׁר לְסֻכָּה[נה] כְּמוֹ שֶׁיִּתְבָּאֵר בְּסִימָן תרכ"ט,[נו, 27] וְכֵיוָן

12 It is permitted to make a *sukkah* in a house below a roof from which the shingles were removed so that a *sukkah* be made there, even if the wood or the beams on which the shingles rest remain. [It would appear that] the wood and the beams are not valid as *s'chach,* since they were affixed in the roof to support the shingles and not for the purpose of shade alone. Nevertheless, one may sit under the wood or the beams themselves. [The rationale is that] since one performed an action and removed the shingles with the intent of making a *sukkah* for shade, it is considered as if he performed an action with regard to the wood or the beams themselves and prepared them for the sake of the *sukkah.* And they are acceptable for use as *s'chach,* for they are products of the earth and are not susceptible to ritual impurity. The fact that they are attached[26] is not significant. For an entity that was detached and then attached [to the ground] is acceptable for [the *s'chach* of] a *sukkah,* as explained in sec. 629.[27]

The act [of removing the shingles] makes [the remaining beams or supports of wood]

---

25. That section states that invalid material that was already in place cannot serve for *s'chach;* present action is required. And moving the branches is considered as equivalent to placing them there for the first time.

26. To be valid for use as *s'chach,* a substance must have grown from the ground and be presently detached (see sec. 629:1, 20); i.e., it may not be naturally attached to the ground, in the way that a tree is naturally attached. The rafters here are attached to the house, and the house is halachically continuous with the ground — but since this attachment is artificial, they are valid as *s'chach.*

27. The Alter Rebbe is apparently referring to one of the missing components of sec. 629. A parallel concept appears at the end of the gloss of *Beis Yosef* to the corresponding section in the *Tur,* and is cited by *Magen Avraham,* sec. 629:11.

מט סעיף כ. נ בעל העיטור הל' סוכה שער הרביעי (פג, ג). טור ושו"ע ס"ג. נא מ"א סק"ו. נב לבוש ס"ג. נג בעל העיטור שם, לפירוש המ"א שם, וחדושי הגהות מהרל"ח. נד מהרל"ח שם. נה תרומת הדשן סי' פט. הובא ב"י סוף הסי'. לבוש שם. נו ראה לבוש שם ס"ח, ומ"א שם סקי"א. נז ראה לקמן

שֶׁהֵן עַצְמָן כְּשֵׁרִים לִסְכָךְ עַל יְדֵי מַעֲשֶׂה זוֹ וְיָכוֹל לְהַנִּיחַ עֲלֵיהֶם עוֹד סְכָךְ כָּשֵׁר וְהֵן מִצְטָרְפִין עִם סְכָךְ זֶה לְהַשְׁלִים לְשִׁעוּר צִלָּתָהּ מְרֻבָּה מֵחַמָּתָהּ, וְלָכֵן גַּם עַכְשָׁו שֶׁלֹּא הִנִּיחַ הַסְּכָךְ עֲלֵיהֶם אֶלָּא תַּחְתֵּיהֶן לְמַטָּה בַּבַּיִת – מֻתָּר לֵישֵׁב תַּחְתֵּיהֶן מַמָּשׁ, כֵּיוָן שֶׁהֵם סְכָךְ כָּשֵׁר:[נז]

themselves valid as *s'chach.* [Additional] valid *s'chach* could therefore be placed upon them and they may be counted together with [it] to make up the quantity required to make the shade [within the *sukkah*] exceed its sunlit area. Therefore even when — as in the present instance — the *s'chach* was not placed upon them, but under them, in the house, one may sit directly under them, for they are valid *s'chach.*

יג אֲבָל אִם לֹא הֵסִיר אֶת הָרְעָפִים כְּדֵי לַעֲשׂוֹת שָׁם סֻכָּה אֶלָּא כָּךְ הָיְתָה מִקֹּדֶם בְּנוּיָה בְּלֹא גַג, כֵּיוָן שֶׁלֹּא עָשָׂה שׁוּם מַעֲשֶׂה בַּגַּג לְשֵׁם עֲשִׂיַּת סֻכָּה לְצֵל, אִם כֵּן הָעֵצִים אוֹ הַקּוֹרוֹת הֵן סְכָךְ פָּסוּל, וְדִינוֹ כְּדִין סְכָךְ פָּסוּל הַמַּאֲהִיל עַל גַּבֵּי הַסְּכָךְ כָּשֵׁר[נח] וְעַל דֶּרֶךְ שֶׁנִּתְבָּאֵר[נט, 28] (פֵּרוּשׁ שֶׁכָּל שֶׁאֵין סְכָךְ הַכָּשֵׁר הַרְבֵּה כָּל כָּךְ עַד שֶׁאִם יִנָּטֵל מִמֶּנּוּ כְּשִׁעוּר סְכָךְ הַפָּסוּל הַמֵּצֵל עָלָיו יִהְיֶה עֲדַיִן צֵל הַסֻּכָּה מְרֻבָּה מֵחַמָּתָהּ – פָּסוּל[ס]):

13 [Different rules apply,] however, if one did not remove the shingles for the sake of making a *sukkah* there, but the structure was initially built [with beams, though] without a roof. Since [in such a case] no action was taken with [the beams of] the roof for the sake of making a *sukkah* for shade, the wood or the beams are invalid as *s'chach,* and hence are governed by the laws that apply when invalid material covers valid *s'chach,* as explained [above].[28] (I.e., whenever the valid *s'chach* is not so ample that if one removed an amount equivalent to the invalid material that casts a shadow over it, the shade [within the *sukkah*] would [still] exceed its sunlit area, [the *sukkah*] is invalid.)

יד בַּמֶּה דְּבָרִים אֲמוּרִים? כְּשֶׁמְּסַכֵּךְ תַּחַת הַגָּג, אֲבָל אִם מְסַכֵּךְ עַל גַּבֵּי הָעֵצִים אוֹ הַקּוֹרוֹת, אַף עַל פִּי שֶׁהֵן סְמוּכִין זֶה לָזֶה בְּפָחוֹת מִשְּׁלֹשָׁה טְפָחִים – הֲרֵי זוֹ כְּשֵׁרָה, וְאֵין אוֹמְרִים כָּאן לָבוּד[29] שֶׁיִּצְטָרְפוּ כָּל הָעֵצִים וְיִהְיוּ נֶחְשָׁבִין כְּעֵץ אֶחָד רָחָב מִסְּכָךְ הַפָּסוּל

14 When does the above apply? When the *s'chach* was placed below [the exposed frame of] the roof. If, however, the *s'chach* was placed upon the wood or the beams, then even if there was less than three handbreadths' space between [the beams], [the *sukkah*] is valid.

We do not apply the principle of *lavud*[29] and regard all the pieces of wood as joined, and thus they would be considered as one piece of wood that was invalid as *s'chach* and

28. Subsection 3.

29. *Lavud* (lit., "joined") is a common halachic construct whereby two entities separated by a space of less than three handbreadths are considered as constituting a single continuum. See *Eruvin* 9a, *et al.*

סי' תרכח ס"א. נח מהרי"ל הל' סוכה (ע' שסה). מ"א סק"ו. נט סעיף ג ואילך. ס לדעה הא' דלעיל ס"ג־ד, ובשעת הדחק סומכים על דעה הב' דלעיל ס"י.

יוֹתֵר מֵאַרְבָּעָה טְפָחִים שֶׁהוּא פּוֹסֵל אֶת הַסֻּכָּה כְּמוֹ שֶׁיִּתְבָּאֵר בְּסִימָן תרל"ב,סא,30 שֶׁכֵּיוָן שֶׁסְּכָךְ כָּשֵׁר מֻנָּח בֵּין עֵץ לַחֲבֵירוֹ – הוּא מַפְסִיק בֵּינֵיהֶם שֶׁלֹּא יִצְטָרְפוּ,סב וְאֵין אוֹמְרִים לָבוּד אֶלָּא אִם כֵּן אֵין שׁוּם דָּבָר מַפְסִיק בֵּינְתַיִם:

טו וְאִם מֻתָּר לֵישֵׁב תַּחַת הָעֵצִים – יִתְבָּאֵר בְּסִימָן תרל"א:סג,31

טז אִם הִנִּיחַ סְכָךְ פָּסוּל עַל גַּבֵּי הַסֻּכָּה שֶׁלֹּא הָיָה עָלֶיהָ שׁוּם סְכָךְ וְאַחַר כָּךְ הִנִּיחַ עָלֶיהָ סְכָךְ כָּשֵׁר עַל גַּבֵּי סְכָךְ הַפָּסוּל וְאַחַר כָּךְ הֵסִיר סְכָךְ הַפָּסוּל מֵעַל גַּבֵּי הַסֻּכָּה וְנִשְׁאַר סְכָךְ הָעֶלְיוֹן הַכָּשֵׁר בִּלְבַדּוֹ מֵצֵל עַל גַּבֵּי הַסֻּכָּה, וְכֵן הָעוֹשֶׂה דָּפְנוֹת הַסֻּכָּה תַּחַת גַּג הַבַּיִת וְהִנִּיחַ סְכָךְ כָּשֵׁר עַל גַּבֵּי הַגָּג וְאַחַר כָּךְ הֵסִיר אֶת הַגָּג מִתַּחַת הַסְּכָךְ הַמֻּנָּח עָלֶיהָ – הֲרֵי זוֹ פְּסוּלָה,סד לְפִי שֶׁבְּשָׁעָה שֶׁעָשָׂה אֶת הַסֻּכָּה, דְּהַיְנוּ בְּשָׁעָה שֶׁהִנִּיחַ סְכָךְ הַכָּשֵׁר שֶׁהוּא עִקַּר הַסֻּכָּה, הָיְתָה הַסֻּכָּה פְּסוּלָה מֵחֲמַת סְכָךְ הַפָּסוּל שֶׁעָלֶיהָ, וְאַחַר כָּךְ כְּשֶׁהֵסִיר אֶת הַפָּסוּל לֹא עָשָׂה מַעֲשֶׂה בְּגוּף הַסֻּכָּה32 לְהַכְשִׁירָהּ אֶלָּא מֵאֵלֶיהָ נִתְכַּשְּׁרָה עַל יְדֵי הֲסָרַת הַפְּסוּל,

wider than four handbreadths, and hence would disqualify the *sukkah,* as will be explained in sec. 632.[30] The reason [we do not follow this principle] is that the valid *s'chach* that is placed between one piece of wood and another disrupts their [halachic] continuity. The principle of *lavud* can apply only when nothing interposes between the neighboring entities.

15 [The question of] whether [or not] it is permissible to sit under the wood is explained in sec. 631.[31]

16 [One halachic principle applies in both of the following situations. A person first] placed material that is invalid as *s'chach* on a *sukkah* that had no *s'chach.* He then placed valid *s'chach* above the invalid material. Finally, he removed the invalid material, leaving only the upper, valid *s'chach* casting shade on the [floor of the] *sukkah.* Similarly, a person built the walls of the *sukkah* below the roof of his house, placed valid *s'chach* above the roof, and then removed the roof that was under the *s'chach.* [In both instances, the *sukkah*] is invalid, because at the time he made the *sukkah* — i.e., at the time he put the valid *s'chach* in place, which is the essence of [making] the *sukkah* — the *sukkah* was invalid because of the invalid material that covered it [directly]. Afterwards, when he removed this invalid material, he did not perform an act involving the *sukkah* itself[32] to make it acceptable; it was validated [so to speak] as a matter of course, by the removal of the invalid material.

30. Sec. 632 of the Alter Rebbe's *Shulchan Aruch* is not extant. See *Magen Avraham,* sec. 632:5.

31. The end of sec. 631 is also not extant.

32. I.e., he did not perform an act involving the *s'chach* itself, but only the invalid material.

סא סימן זה בשוע"ר לא הגיע לידינו, וראה טור ושו"ע שם ס"א. סב מ"א ס"ק ו. סג ראה שם סי"ב, אך סוף הסעיף לא הגיע לידינו, וראה מ"א שם סק"ז־ח.
סד שלטי הגבורים (ח, א אות א), בשם פסקי ריא"ז. מ"א סוף סק"[ז]. סה דברים טז, יב. סו ברייתא יא, ב וש"נ. וראה גם לקמן סי' תרכט ס"כ ואילך. וכ"ה

וְהַתּוֹרָה אָמְרָה[סה,33] "חַג הַסֻּכּוֹת תַּעֲשֶׂה לְךָ וגו'", וְלֹא מִן הֶעָשׂוּי[סו] מֵאֵלָיו,[סז,34] שֶׁהָעֲשִׂיָּה הָרִאשׁוֹנָה שֶׁהָיְתָה בִּפְסוּל – אֵינָהּ נֶחְשֶׁבֶת עֲשִׂיָּה כְּלָל:[35]

The Torah, however, states,[33] "Make the Sukkos festival for yourself." [Implied is that the *sukkah* must be *made.*] We may not [use] something which is already made, [but which later became suitable] as a matter of course[34] — for the initial act of making, which was invalid, is not considered "making" at all.[35]

יז בַּמֶּה דְּבָרִים אֲמוּרִים? שֶׁפְּסוּל הַסֻּכָּה הָיָה מֵחֲמַת עַצְמָהּ, כְּגוֹן בְּנִדּוֹן שֶׁאָמַרְנוּ שֶׁהִנִּיחַ סְכָךְ הַכָּשֵׁר עַל גַּבֵּי הַפָּסוּל, שֶׁגּוּף הַסֻּכָּה דְּהַיְנוּ סְכָךְ הַכָּשֵׁר נַעֲשָׂה בִּפְסוּל מֵחֲמַת עַצְמוֹ, שֶׁאֵינוֹ נִקְרָא סְכָךְ כְּלָל כֵּיוָן שֶׁיֵּשׁ דָּבָר מַפְסִיק בֵּינוֹ לְהַדְּפָנוֹת, שֶׁהֲרֵי אֵין צִלּוֹ מוֹעִיל כְּלוּם.[סח,36]

17 When does the above apply? When the disqualifying factor was inherent in the *sukkah;* for example, in the instance above when valid *s'chach* was placed over invalid material. In this instance, the *sukkah* itself — i.e., [what should have been] the valid *s'chach* — was made in an inherently invalid manner. It could not be called *s'chach* at all, because some other entity interposed between it and the walls, and [thus] the shade it produces is of no consequence whatever.[36]

אֲבָל אִם פְּסוּל הַסֻּכָּה הוּא מֵחֲמַת דָּבָר אַחֵר הַפּוֹסֵל אוֹתָהּ, כְּגוֹן הָעוֹשֶׂה סֻכָּתוֹ תַּחַת גַּג הַבַּיִת וְאַחַר שֶׁסִּכְּכָהּ כְּהִלְכָתָהּ הֵסִיר אֶת הַגָּג מֵעַל גַּבֵּי הַסֻּכָּה – הֲרֵי זוֹ כְּשֵׁרָה[סט] אַף עַל פִּי שֶׁלֹּא עָשָׂה מַעֲשֶׂה בְּגוּפָהּ לְהַכְשִׁירָהּ, כֵּיוָן שֶׁאֵין פְּסוּלָהּ אֶלָּא מֵחֲמַת דָּבָר אַחֵר דְּהַיְנוּ גַּג הַבַּיִת שֶׁמֵּצֵל עָלָיו וְלֹא מֵחֲמַת עַצְמָהּ, שֶׁהֲרֵי הִיא מְסֻכֶּכֶת כְּהִלְכָתָהּ בִּסְכָךְ כָּשֵׁר[ע] הַמֻּנָּח עַל

If, however, [the *s'chach*] is disqualified by an external factor — e.g., one constructed his *sukkah* under the roof of a house and, after placing *s'chach* upon it as required by law, removed the roof [of the house] that was above the *sukkah* — it is valid, even though no action was taken with [the *s'chach*] itself to make it valid. [The rationale is that] it was disqualified only by an external factor, namely, the roof of the house that cast shade over it; it is not inherently invalid. [On the contrary, the *sukkah*] was covered as required by law, with valid *s'chach* placed

33. *Devarim* 16:13.

34. *Sukkah* 11b. This requirement does not apply to the walls of the *sukkah,* but only to the *s'chach.*

35. This principle has many parallels. For example, *Devarim* 22:12 states: "You shall *make* braided threads on the four corners of your garment." Hence the Sages taught that *tzitzis* must initially be made for the purpose of fulfilling this commandment. *tzitzis* that were made previously in an unacceptable manner cannot be corrected to serve this purpose (see sec. 10:10, 11:15, *et al.,* in Vol. 1 of the present work). Sec. 629:20 below also elaborates on this principle.

36. In the above instance the structure is simply not a *sukkah,* because there is no connection between the *s'chach* and the walls. In the instance that follows, by contrast, the *sukkah* is essentially valid; it is just not functional because there is a roof overhead, and when that disqualifying factor is removed, the *sukkah* is valid.

לענין ציצית כדלעיל סי' י ס"י וש"נ. **סז** רש"י שם יא, א ד"ה אכשורי. **סח** ראה לעיל ס"ב וש"נ. **סט** אור זרוע ח"ב הל' סוכה סי' רפט, בשם ר"י הלבן. הובא בהגהות אשרי פ"א סי' כד. ארחות חיים הל' סוכה סי' כו. מהרי"ל ה"ל סוכות (ע' שסה). רמ"א ס"ב. **ע** אור זרוע והגהות אשרי שם. רמ"א שם.

גַּבֵּי דָּפְנוֹתֶיהָ, לָכֵן כֵּיוָן שֶׁעָשָׂה מַעֲשֶׂה הַכָּשֵׁר בְּדָבָר הַפּוֹסְלָהּ,[עא] דְּהַיְנוּ שֶׁהֵסִיר אֶת עֲצֵי הַגָּג שֶׁהָיוּ קְבוּעִין שָׁם לְשֵׁם דִּירָה וְלֹא לְשֵׁם צֵל, וּלְפִיכָךְ הָיָה עָלֶיהָ שֵׁם סְכָךְ פָּסוּל, וְעַכְשָׁו שֶׁהֱסִירָן מִשָּׁם לְגַמְרֵי[37] — נִקְרָא עֲלֵיהֶם שֵׁם סְכָךְ כָּשֵׁר, וַאֲפִלּוּ עַל הָעֵצִים הַנִּשְׁאָרִים נִקְרָא עֲלֵיהֶם שֵׁם סְכָךְ כָּשֵׁר כְּמוֹ שֶׁבֵּאַרְנוּ לְמַעְלָה,[עב] לְפִיכָךְ מוֹעִיל מַעֲשֶׂה הַכָּשֵׁר זֶה לְהַכְשִׁיר אֶת הַסֻּכָּה, כֵּיוָן שֶׁלֹּא הָיְתָה פְּסוּלָה אֶלָּא מֵחֲמַת הַגָּג וּכְבָר עָשָׂה בּוֹ מַעֲשֶׂה הַכָּשֵׁר:

over its walls. Hence, [the *sukkah*] becomes valid when this was brought about by a validating action taken with the disqualifying factor; i.e., one removed the wooden pieces of the roof that had been affixed there to create a dwelling and not to generate shade, and hence had been deemed invalid as *s'chach*. When, however, they have been entirely removed from there, [the *s'chach* of the *sukkah*][37] — so, too, even the remaining beams — is now also considered as valid *s'chach*, as explained [in subsection 12] above. The action is effective in rendering the *sukkah* valid, because it had been disqualified only by the roof, and something was [since] done to [the roof] to rectify that factor.

יח אֲבָל אִם לֹא עָשָׂה מַעֲשֶׂה הַכָּשֵׁר בְּדָבָר הַפּוֹסְלָהּ, כְּגוֹן שֶׁלֹּא הֵסִיר אֶת הַגָּג לְגַמְרֵי מִמְּקוֹם קְבִיעוּתוֹ, אֶלָּא עָשָׂה אוֹתוֹ כְּעֵין דֶּלֶת לִפְתֹּחַ וְלִסְגֹּר בְּעֵת הַגֶּשֶׁם, כֵּיוָן שֶׁלֹּא הֱסִירוֹ מִשָּׁם לְגַמְרֵי — אֵין זֶה מַעֲשֶׂה[עג] גָּמוּר, וּלְפִיכָךְ אֵינוֹ מוֹעִיל לְהַכְשִׁיר אֶת הָעֵצִים הַנִּשְׁאָרִים וְלֹא אֶת הַסֻּכָּה שֶׁנִּפְסְלָה מֵחֲמָתָהּ (כְּשֶׁעֲדַיִן לֹא נִפְתְּחָה הַדֶּלֶת וְהָיְתָה מַאֲהֶלֶת עַל הַסֻּכָּה):

18 [Different rules apply] if one did not perform an action to validate the *sukkah* [by changing] the disqualifying factor itself; e.g., he did not remove the roof entirely from the place where it was fixed, but [placed it on hinges, so that] it served as a door, to be opened and closed during the rain.

In such a situation, since the roof was not removed entirely, the above action is not sufficient to validate the remaining [supporting] beams and the *[s'chach]* which was disqualified because of it ([and which was already in place] when the hinged roof[38] was not yet opened, but overhung the *sukkah*).

יט בַּמֶּה דְּבָרִים אֲמוּרִים? כְּשֶׁסִּכֵּךְ אֶת הַסֻּכָּה קֹדֶם שֶׁפָּתַח אֶת הַדֶּלֶת[38] בַּגָּג, אוֹ אֲפִלּוּ לְאַחַר שֶׁפָּתַח אֶלָּא שֶׁבִּשְׁעַת הַסִּכּוּךְ הָיְתָה הַדֶּלֶת[38] סְגוּרָה

19 When is [the *sukkah* disqualified] because of this? When the *s'chach* was placed on the *sukkah* before he made an opening for the hinged cover[38] in the roof — or even after [that opening] was made, except that when the *s'chach* was put in place, the hinged cover[38] was closed and overhung

37. The first appearance of the Hebrew phrase *nikra aleihem* ("they are considered," in the plural) is problematic. Hence the bracketed phrase in the above translation.

38. Lit., "the door."

עא ארחות חיים שם. **עב** סעיף יב. **עג** מ"א סק"ז, בדעת המחמיר (מהר"א) שהובא במהרי"ל שם, ובדעת פסקי הריא"ז ושלטי הגבורים שם. **עד** מ"א שם,

the *sukkah*. Since the *sukkah* was constructed [i.e., since the *s'chach* was put in place] invalidly, the fact that the hinged cover was later opened is not sufficient to render it valid, for no action was taken [to change] the *sukkah* itself.

If, however, at the time one covered the *sukkah* with *s'chach*, the hinged roof was open as required by law and did not overhang it, [the *sukkah* is valid]. Even if it is later closed, and thus the *sukkah* was disqualified while the hinged roof was closed, the *sukkah* becomes valid again when the hinged roof is opened. For the *sukkah* was initially made [i.e., the *s'chach* was put in place] validly, since the door was then open.[39]

וְהָיְתָה מַאֲהֶלֶת עַל הַסֻּכָּה, דְּכֵיוָן שֶׁעֲשִׂיַּת הַסֻּכָּה הָיְתָה בִּפְסוּל – שׁוּב אֵין מוֹעִיל לָהּ מַה שֶּׁאַחַר כָּךְ פָּתַח אֶת הַדֶּלֶת, כֵּיוָן שֶׁלֹּא עָשָׂה מַעֲשֶׂה בְּגוּף הַסֻּכָּה. אֲבָל אִם בְּשָׁעָה שֶׁסִּיכְּכָהּ הָיְתָה הַדֶּלֶת פְּתוּחָה כְּהִלְכָתָהּ וְלֹא הָיְתָה מַאֲהֶלֶת עַל הַסֻּכָּה, אַף עַל פִּי שֶׁאַחַר כָּךְ סְגָרָהּ וְנִפְסְלָה הַסֻּכָּה בְּשָׁעָה שֶׁהַדֶּלֶת סְגוּרָה, מִכָּל מָקוֹם כְּשֶׁהוּא פּוֹתֵחַ אֶת הַדֶּלֶת – הַסֻּכָּה חוֹזֶרֶת לְהֶכְשֵׁרָהּ, כֵּיוָן שֶׁתְּחִלַּת עֲשִׂיָּתָהּ הָיְתָה בְּכַשְׁרוּת בְּשָׁעָה שֶׁהַדֶּלֶת הָיְתָה פְּתוּחָה:עד, 39

20 If this [retractable roof][38] has hinges that enable it to be opened and closed, it completely fits the halachic definition of an entrance and may be closed and opened on *Shabbos* and the festivals. [Doing so] does not involve the forbidden [labors] of demolishing or building.[40]

כ וְאִם יֵשׁ לְדֶלֶת זוֹ[38] צִירִים שֶׁסּוֹגֵר וּפוֹתֵחַ בָּהֶם[עה] – הֲרֵי הִיא כְּפֶתַח[עו] גָּמוּר, וּמֻתָּר לְסָגְרָהּ וּלְפָתְחָהּ בְּשַׁבָּת וְיוֹם טוֹב, וְאֵין בָּזֶה מִשּׁוּם אִסּוּר סְתִירָה וּבִנְיָן:עז, 40

21 When [the hinged roof] is closed, one must be careful not to sit under it with the intent of fulfilling the *mitzvah* of the *sukkah*, for at that time the *sukkah* is not valid and one does not fulfill his obligation by dwelling in it.*

כא וְצָרִיךְ שֶׁיִּזָּהֵר שֶׁלֹּא יֵשֵׁב תַּחְתֶּיהָ לְשֵׁם מִצְוַת סֻכָּה כְּשֶׁהִיא סְגוּרָה, שֶׁאָז הִיא פְּסוּלָה,[עח] וְאֵינוֹ יוֹצֵא יְדֵי חוֹבָתוֹ בִּישִׁיבָה זוֹ:

39. This *sukkah* is not disqualified on the grounds that one must initially *make* a *sukkah*, and not merely make use of something that became suitable as a matter of course (see subsection 16 above) — because at the outset, this *sukkah* was made validly. Thereafter, its temporary disqualification is of no consequence.

Subsection 19, incidentally, is not an academic abstraction; an awning or other covering is often used to keep a *sukkah* neat and dry.

40. Sec. 313:8 discusses the use of unhinged doors on *Shabbos*.

* For a summary of sec. 626, see p. 448.

שבזה יודו גם המחמירים הנ"ל. **עה** דרכי משה ס"ק א. רמ"א ס"ג. **עו** מ"א סק"ח. **עז** רמ"א שם. וכדלעיל סי' שיג ס"ח וש"נ. **עח** רמ"א שם.

סימן תרכז דִּין הַיָּשֵׁן בַּסֻּכָּה וּבוֹ ז' סְעִיפִים:

SECTION 627 Laws Relating to One who Sleeps in a *Sukkah*. (1–7)

א צָרִיךְ[1] לֵישֵׁב תַּחַת אֲוִיר הַסְּכָךְ[א] שֶׁלֹּא יְהֵא אֹהֶל[2] אַחֵר מַפְסִיק בֵּינוֹ לְהַסְּכָךְ,[ב] כְּדֵי שֶׁיִּהְיֶה יוֹשֵׁב בְּצֵל סֻכָּה וְלֹא בְּצֵל אֹהֶל;[ג] וְאֵינוֹ נִקְרָא אֹהֶל אֶלָּא דָּבָר שֶׁהוּא[3] גָּבוֹהַּ עֲשָׂרָה טְפָחִים[ד,4] מִן הָאָרֶץ,[ה,5] וְאַף עַל פִּי שֶׁאֵין לוֹ דְּפָנוֹת[ו] אָסוּר לֵישֵׁב תַּחְתָּיו;[6] לְפִיכָךְ הַיָּשֵׁן תַּחַת הַמִּטָּה בַּסֻּכָּה[ז] אִם הִיא גְּבוֹהָ[ה] עֲשָׂרָה טְפָחִים[ח] — לֹא יָצָא יְדֵי חוֹבָתוֹ:[7]

1 One[1] is required to dwell [directly] under the space of the *s'chach;* i.e., there should no other shelter *(ohel)*[2] intervening between the person and the *s'chach*. In this manner, he will be dwelling in the shade of the *sukkah* and not in the shade of [another] shelter.

The term *ohel* is used only for a [structure] that is [at least][3] ten handbreadths[4] above the ground.[5] Even if it has no walls, it is forbidden to dwell under it.[6] Therefore a person who sleeps in a *sukkah* under a bed that is ten handbreadths high has not fulfilled his obligation.[7]

ב וְכֵן הַיָּשֵׁן תַּחַת הַכִּלָּה[ט] הַפְּרוּסָה סְבִיבוֹת הַמִּטָּה[י] בְּשִׁפּוּעַ,[יא] אִם יֵשׁ לָהּ גַּג[יב,8] טֶפַח,[יג] דְּהַיְנוּ שֶׁרֹחַב טֶפַח מִמֶּנּוּ פָּרוּס בְּיֹשֶׁר עַל גַּבֵּי הַמִּטָּה וְלֹא בְּשִׁפּוּעַ,[יד] כְּגוֹן שֶׁהַכְּלוֹנָס שֶׁהוּא תָּלוּי בּוֹ וּפְרוּסָה עַל גַּבָּיו יֵשׁ בּוֹ רֹחַב טֶפַח, וְיֵשׁ עֲשָׂרָה טְפָחִים[טו] מִן גַּג טֶפַח זֶה עַד הָאָרֶץ,[טז] אַף עַל פִּי שֶׁמִּמֶּנּוּ עַד הַמִּטָּה שֶׁיָּשֵׁן עָלֶיהָ אֵין שָׁם עֲשָׂרָה טְפָחִים —

2 Similar laws apply if one sleeps under a slanting canopy that surrounds a bed. If the highest part[8] of the canopy over the bed is a handbreadth wide and is not slanted, but spread out horizontally, one has not fulfilled his obligation. This is the case, for example, if the beam upon which [the canopy] hangs and over which it is spread is a handbreadth wide and [is] ten handbreadths from the ground, even though it is not ten handbreadths above the bed on which the person is lying. Since any roof that is a handbreadth wide and ten

---

1. This section deals with the placing of a bed in the *sukkah,* including the halachic problems raised by the canopy beds that were common in the Talmudic era. On the obligation to sleep in the *sukkah* and the current *Chabad* practice not to do so, see sec. 639:7-9 and their footnotes.

2. Lit., "tent."

3. Throughout this passage, the dimensions cited are minimal. "A handbreadth" should thus be understood to mean "at least a handbreadth" and "ten handbreadths" should be understood to mean "at least ten handbreadths."

4. A handbreadth *(tefach)* is defined in *Shiurei Torah* as 8 cm. Ten handbreadths thus come to approx. 31.5 inches.

5. *Sukkah* 10b.

6. I.e., no *mitzvah* would be fulfilled by doing so.

7. *Op. cit.,* 20b.

8. Lit., "the roof."

א טור ורמ"א ס"א. **ב** רש"י י, א ד"ה פסולה. כ, ב ד"ה הישן. **ג** בעל המאור (י, א) ד"ה תרגמה. ר"ן שם ד"ה תרגמא. ט"ז סק"א. **ד** גמרא י, ב ורש"י ד"ה והוא. תוס' כ, ב ד"ה הישן. בעל המאור שם. וראה גם תוס' שבת קלח, ב ד"ה שאין (משא"כ לענין שבת דלעיל סי' שטו ס"א ואילך, ויו"ט דלעיל סי' תקכב ס"ה). **ה** כדלקמן ס"ב. **ו** רמב"ם פ"ה הכ"ג. וראה לעיל סי' שטו ס"א. משנה ברורה שעה"צ ס"ק ד. **ז** משנה כ, ב. טור ושו"ע ס"א. **ח** שמואל בגמרא שם. טור ושו"ע שם. **ט** גמרא שם. רש"י שם ד"ה כילה. **י** רש"י שם ד"ה כילה. **יא** רש"י יא, א ד"ה כילת חתנים. **יב** גמרא יא, א. **יג** רמב"ם פ"ה הכ"ג. טור ושו"ע שם. וכדלעיל סי' שטו ס"ב וסט"ז וש"נ. **יד** רש"י יט, ב ד"ה בכילת. וכדלעיל שם. **טו** גמרא שם. רמב"ם שם. טור ושו"ע שם. **טז** מ"א סק"ג, ממשמעות התוס' כא, סע"ב. עטרת זקנים ס"ק א. וראה לקמן ס"ה ובהגהה. **יז** אגודה סי' ט. ב"ח ד"ה ומ"ש אבל. מ"א סק"א. וראה גם לעיל סי' שטו

handbreadths above the ground is defined as an *ohel,* this person is not sleeping under the shade of the *sukkah,* but under the shade of the *ohel.*[9]

3 [In certain instances, stringency is required] even when [the canopy] does not have a roof that is a handbreadth wide. If within three handbreadths of the roof, there is a part that is a handbreadth wide — i.e., if as [the canopy descends and] spreads out from the beam on either side, there is a horizontal span of a handbreadth within three handbreadths of the beam — it is forbidden to sleep under it,[6] even when one is not [lying] directly under that handbreadth (see the end of sec. 631).[10]

[The rationale is that] any space within three handbreadths is governed by the principle of *lavud,*[11] [according to which the entire space is considered as if on the same level]. Thus it is as if the roof of the canopy was a handbreadth wide. And whenever a [structure] has a roof that is a handbreadth wide, that entire [structure] is called an *ohel* — and this now interposes between the person and the *s'chach.*

4 [The following rules apply if a person] spreads a sheet over a *kinof;* i.e., he affixes [horizontal] rods *(klonsos)* to [connect the tops of] the four bedposts *(kundasin)* that extend from [the corners of] the bed[12] and spreads a sheet over them. It is forbidden by Rabbinic decree to sleep under it[6] even if the tops of these bedposts are less than ten handbreadths above the ground,[5] because the sheet spread

אף על פי כן לא יצא ידי חובתו, שכל גג טפח הגבוה עשרה טפחים מן הארץ – נקרא אהל, ונמצא שאינו ישן בצל סכה אלא בצל אהל:[9]

ג ואפלו אין לה גג טפח, אם יש בפחות משלשה טפחים סמוך לגג רחב טפח,[יז] דהינו לאחר שירדה מעל הכלונס מכאן ומכאן ונתרחבו טפח אין שם מן טפח זה עד הכלונס שלשה טפחים ביושר – אסור לישן תחתיו[6] אפלו שלא כנגד טפח זה (עין סוף סימן תרל"א[יח,10]), לפי שכל פחות משלשה טפחים הוא כלבוד[יט,11] וכאלו יש בגגה רחב טפח,[כ] וכל דבר שיש לו גג רחב טפח כלו נקרא אהל,[כא] ונמצא אהל מפסיק בינו להסכך:

ד מי שפרס סדין על גבי קינוף,[כב] דהינו ארבעה קונדסין הבולטין מארבעת רגלי המטה[12] ומניח כלונסות מזה לזה ופורס עליהן סדין[כג] – אסור לישן תחתיו מדברי סופרים,[כד,6] אפלו אם ראשי קונדסין אלו אינן גבוהין עשרה טפחים[כה] מן הארץ,[5] כיון שיש להם גג רחב טפח ביושר, דהינו הסדין

9. As clarified at the end of subsection 3 below, the flat roof that is a handbreadth wide causes the remainder of the canopy to be considered as part of an *ohel* and this disqualifies the space under it.

10. The passage referred to is not extant. See the *Shulchan Aruch* of R. Yosef Caro, sec. 631:10.

11. *Lavud* (lit., "joined") is a common halachic construct whereby two entities separated by a space of less than three handbreadths are considered as constituting a single continuum. See *Eruvin* 9a, *et al.*

12. The resultant frame is called a *kinof (Sukkah* 10a*)*. See fig. 7 on the following page.

סט"ו. **יח** סוף הסי' לא הגיע לידינו. **יט** מ"א סי' תרלא סק"ט. וכדלעיל שם. **כ** רש"י עירובין קב, סוע"א. **כא** רא"ש פ"א סי' לז. **כב** משנה י, א. **כג** רש"י שם ד"ה על גבי קינוף. טור ושו"ע ס"ג. **כד** ראה תוס' י, ב ד"ה ובלבד (מדרבנן). **כה** גמרא י, ב. טור ושו"ע שם.

שֶׁפָּרוּס עַל גַּבָּיו מִלְמַעְלָה:

ה אֲבָל אִם קוֹנְדֵּס אֶחָד בּוֹלֵט בְּאֶמְצַע הַמִּטָּה מֵרַאֲשׁוֹתֶיהָ וְהַשֵּׁנִי בּוֹלֵט כְּנֶגְדּוֹ בְּמַרְגְּלוֹתֶיהָ[13] וּמַנִּיחַ כְּלוֹנָס מִזֶּה לָזֶה וּפוֹרֵס עָלָיו סָדִין,[כו] כֵּיוָן שֶׁהַסָּדִין פָּרוּס בְּשִׁפּוּעַ וְאֵין לוֹ גַּג רָחָב טֶפַח[כז] בְּיֹשֶׁר[כח] — מֻתָּר לִישֹׁן תַּחְתָּיו, וְהוּא שֶׁאֵין הַכְּלוֹנָס גָּבוֹהַּ עֲשָׂרָה טְפָחִים[כט] מִן הַמִּטָּה,[ל,5] אֲבָל אִם הוּא גָּבוֹהַּ עֲשָׂרָה טְפָחִים מִן הַמִּטָּה* — אָסוּר לִישֹׁן[6] תַּחַת הַסָּדִין:[לא,14]

over the bed [serves as] a horizontal roof that is [more than] a handbreadth wide.

5 [Different rules apply,] however, if a sheet is spread over a rod connecting [the top of] one post that projects from the middle of the head of the bed and the opposite post that projects from [the middle of] the foot of the bed.[13] [See fig. 8.] Since the sheet is spread at a [sharp] incline and does not have a level roof that is one handbreadth wide, it is permitted to sleep under it provided the rod is less than ten handbreadths above the bed.[5] If it is ten handbreadths above the bed, it is forbidden to sleep[6] below the sheet.[14]

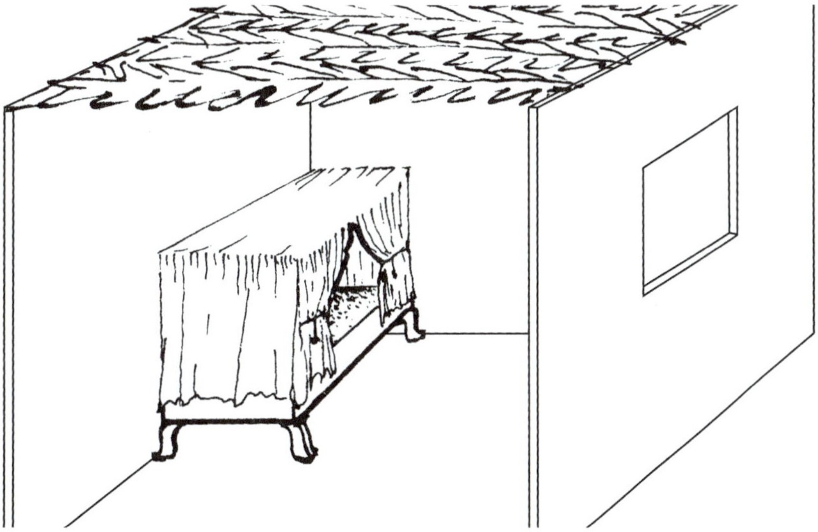

Fig. 7:
The frame *(kinof)* of this canopy bed is described in sec. 627:4.

13. *Sukkah* 10a.

14. This restriction parallels the Rabbinic prohibition that appears in subsection 4. A note appended to the Hebrew text calls attention to the difference between subsection 2, where the measurement was made from the ground, and the present subsection, in which the measurement is made from the bed. The difference is explained as follows: The canopy described in the earlier subsection is not attached to the bed, but stands on the ground; hence the measurement is made from the ground. In this subsection, the frame from which the sheet is suspended is attached to the bed; hence the measurement is made from the bed.

The note gives the source for this distinction as sec. 630, which is not extant in the present work. See the *Shulchan Aruch* of R. Yosef Caro, sec. 630:13.

כו משנה י, א ורש"י ד"ה אבל פורס. טור ושו"ע ס"ג. כז רש"י שם. שו"ע שם. כח כדלעיל ס"ב וש"נ. כט גמרא [ברייתא] י, ב. טור ושו"ע שם. ל גמרא

ו מֻתָּר לִפְרֹס בַּסֻּכָּה קְרָמִים הַמְצֻיָּרִים וּסְדִינִין הַמְצֻיָּרִים כְּדֵי לְנָאוֹתָהּ,[15] בֵּין סְבִיב הַכְּתָלִים,[לד] בֵּין תַּחַת הַסְּכָךְ,[לה,14] וְאַף עַל פִּי שֶׁהֵן מְקַבְּלִין טֻמְאָה וּפְסוּלִין לְסִכּוּךְ[לו] כְּמוֹ שֶׁיִּתְבָּאֵר בְּסִימָן תרכ"ט[לז] – אַף עַל פִּי כֵן אֵין פּוֹסְלִין אֶת הַסֻּכָּה בְּאַרְבָּעָה טְפָחִים[לח] כְּדִין סְכָךְ פָּסוּל, וּכְמוֹ שֶׁיִּתְבָּאֵר בְּסִימָן תרל"ב.[לט,16]

6 It is permitted to hang fabrics and sheets with designs in a *sukkah* as decorations,[15] both on the walls or under the *s'chach*.[14] These hangings are subject to contracting ritual impurity and [thus] are not acceptable for *s'chach*, as will be explained in sec. 629[:1]. Nevertheless, [even] a four-handbreadth piece of such fabric does not disqualify the *sukkah*, as is done by other materials that are invalid as *s'chach*, as will be explained in sec. 632.[16]

* וּמַה שֶּׁבַּכִּלָּה מוֹדְדִין הָעֲשָׂרָה טְפָחִים מִן הָאָרֶץ[לב] וְכָאן מוֹדְדִין אוֹתָן מִן הַמִּטָּה, הַיְנוּ לְפִי שֶׁהַכְּלוֹנָס שֶׁהַכִּלָּה פְּרוּסָה עַל גַּבָּהּ אֵינֶנּוּ קָבוּעַ בַּמִּטָּה וְאִם תִּנָּטֵל הַמִּטָּה לֹא תִּנָּטֵל הַכִּלָּה, אֲבָל כָּאן הַכְּלוֹנָס קָבוּעַ בְּקוּנְדְּסִין הַבּוֹלְטִין מִן הַמִּטָּה וְאִם תִּנָּטֵל הַמִּטָּה יִנָּטֵל הַסָּדִין, וְטַעַם לְחִלּוּק זֶה יִתְבָּאֵר בְּסוֹף סִימָן תר"ל,[לג] עַיֵּן שָׁם הַטַּעַם.

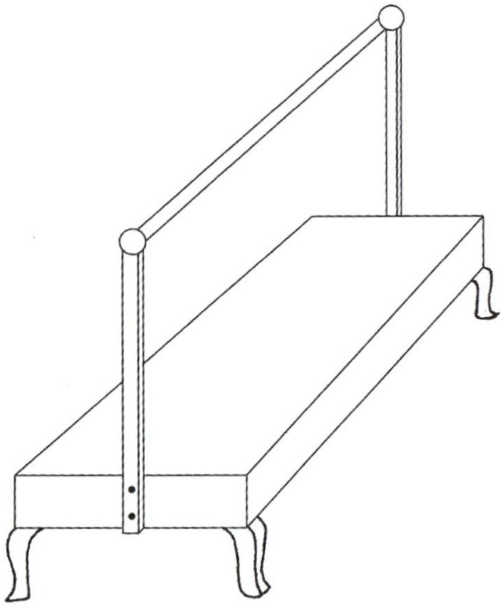

Fig. 8:
Here, the vertical posts *(naklitin)* are connected by a single, narrow, horizontal rod *(klonas)*. See sec. 627:5.

15. Notwithstanding the above, it is not Lubavitch custom to decorate a *sukkah* at all (see *Sefer HaMinhagim: The Book of Chabad-Lubavitch Customs*, p. 139, based on a *sichah* of Sukkos, 5704; see also *Otzar Minhagei Chabad*, p. 267).

16. Sec. 632 of the present work is not extant. The *Shulchan Aruch* of R. Yosef Caro (sec. 632:1) discusses situations in which a sukkah is disqualified by four handbreadths of invalid covering.

[ברייתא] שם. לא ברייתא שם. טור. לב לעיל ס"ב. לג סימן זה בשוע"ר לא הגיע לידינו, וראה שו"ע שם סי"ג. לד גמרא י, רע"ב. רמב"ם פ"ה הי"ז. וראה גם לקמן סי' תרלח ס"ו. לה רב חסדא י, א. טור ושו"ע ס"ד, וסי' תרכט סי"ט. וראה גם לקמן שם. לו רש"י שם. ד"ה הנשר. לבוש ס"ד. לז ס"א ואילך (והיינו אפילו כשהסדין נעשה מדבר הצומח מן הארץ). לח משמעות מ"א ס"ק ד (שגם כשאינו לנוי לא אסרינן מדינא אלא ברחב ד' טפחים). אליה רבה סק"ז.
לט סימן זה בשוע"ר לא הגיע לידינו, וראה טור ושו"ע שם ס"א.

וְלֹא עוֹד[מ] אֶלָּא שֶׁמֻּתָּר אֲפִלּוּ לֵישֵׁב תַּחְתֵּיהֶן מַמָּשׁ,[17] אַף עַל פִּי שֶׁהֵן גְּבוֹהִין עֲשָׂרָה טְפָחִים מִן הָאָרֶץ – אֵינָן חֲשׁוּבִין אֹהֶל לְהַפְסִיק בֵּינוֹ לְהַסְּכָךְ, לְפִי שֶׁהֵן בְּטֵלִים לְגַבֵּי הַסְּכָךְ,[מא] כֵּיוָן שֶׁנַּעֲשׂוּ לְצֹרֶךְ הַסְּכָךְ דְּהַיְנוּ לְנָאוֹתוֹ,[מב] וְעוֹד שֶׁכָּל שֶׁלֹּא נַעֲשָׂה לְצֵל[מג] אֵין שֵׁם סְכָךְ עֲלֵיהֶם,[מד] וּלְכָךְ אֵין פּוֹסְלִין אֶת הַסֻּכָּה מִשּׁוּם סְכָךְ פָּסוּל, וּמֻתָּר לֵישֵׁב תַּחְתֵּיהֶן, לְפִי שֶׁהֵן בְּטֵלִין[18] לְגַבֵּי הַסְּכָךְ.[מה]

בַּמֶּה דְּבָרִים אֲמוּרִים? כְּשֶׁהֵן סְמוּכִין בְּתוֹךְ אַרְבָּעָה טְפָחִים לְהַסְּכָךְ,[5] וְאָז הֵן בְּטֵלִין אֶצְלוֹ, אֲבָל אִם הֵם מֻפְלָגִין מִמֶּנּוּ אַרְבָּעָה טְפָחִים – אֵינָן בְּטֵלִין אֶצְלוֹ, וּפוֹסְלִין אֶת הַסֻּכָּה[מו] כְּדִין סְכָךְ פָּסוּל,[מז] וְעַל דֶּרֶךְ שֶׁיִּתְבָּאֵר בְּסִימָן תרל"ב.[מח, 17]

וּמִכָּל מָקוֹם, אַף עַל פִּי שֶׁסְּכָךְ פָּסוּל אֵינוֹ פּוֹסֵל אֶת הַסֻּכָּה אֶלָּא אִם כֵּן יֵשׁ בּוֹ אַרְבָּעָה טְפָחִים[19] אֲבָל אִם אֵין בּוֹ אַרְבָּעָה טְפָחִים מֻתָּר אֲפִלּוּ לֵישֵׁב תַּחְתָּיו,[מט] אַף עַל פִּי כֵן יֵשׁ לִזָּהֵר שֶׁלֹּא לְהַרְחִיק נוֹיֵי הַסֻּכָּה מִן הַסְּכָךְ אַרְבָּעָה טְפָחִים[נ] אַף עַל פִּי שֶׁאֵין בָּהֶן אַרְבָּעָה טְפָחִים,[נא] גְּזֵרָה שֶׁמָּא יִהְיֶה בָּהֶן אַרְבָּעָה טְפָחִים, שֶׁאָז אָסוּר לֵישֵׁב תַּחְתֵּיהֶן:[נב, 6]

Moreover, it is even permitted to sit directly below these [decorative hangings].[17] Although they are more than ten handbreadths from the ground, they are not considered as an *ohel* that interposes between the person and the *s'chach,* because they are subservient to the *s'chach:* they were hung for its sake, in order to decorate it. Furthermore, since they were not hung for the purpose of shade, they are not considered as *s'chach* at all. Hence, they do not disqualify the *sukkah* as unacceptable *s'chach* would, and it is permitted to sit under them, because they are subservient[18] to the *s'chach.*

When does the above apply? When they are within four handbreadths of the *s'chach,*[5] for then they are subservient to it. If, however, they are positioned [lower] than four handbreadths from the *s'chach,* they are not considered as subservient to it and they disqualify the *sukkah,* as is the case with other materials that are invalid as *s'chach,* as will be explained in sec. 632.[17]

Material that is invalid as *s'chach* does not disqualify a *sukkah* unless it measures four handbreadths[19] [or more]. If there are less than four handbreadths, one may even sit under it. Nevertheless, one should be careful not to hang the decorations [lower] than four handbreadths from the *s'chach,* even if they measure less than four handbreadths. This [safeguard] was ordained lest one use [decorations] that are four handbreadths in size, in which instance it would be forbidden to sit under them.[6]

---

17. And to fulfill one's obligation thereby.

18. In the original, *beteilim* (pl. of *batel*).

19. The *Mishnah Berurah* 632:2 states that this restriction applies only if this invalid material extends over the entire width of the *sukkah.*

מ שסכך פסול פוסל כל הסוכה, ואהל להפסיק פוסל רק לישב תחתיו, כדלעיל ס"א, ומבאר הטעם שלנאותה אינו נפסל מב' הטעמים. **מא** רש"י י, ב ד"ה פסולה. טור ולבוש ס"ד. וראה גם לקמן סי' תרנא ס"ד (לענין לולב). **מב** מרדכי רמז תשלו, בשם רבנו פרץ. לבוש סי' תרכט סי"ט (כשעשוי לנוי, לדעה הב' שבלבוש שם). **מג** לבוש כאן ס"ד. **מד** רש"י י, א ד"ה אבל לנאותה. לבוש שם (כשעשוי לנוי). ב"ח סי' תרכט ד"ה אפילו, ומ"א סי' תרכט סקכ"ג (אף כשפורס להגן מפני החמה והעלין, לדעה הב' שבשו"ע שם). **מה** לבוש כאן ס"ד (לענין סכך פסול ולענין אהל). ב"ח ומ"א שם (לענין סכך פסול). **מו** רב

7 All the above applies to decorations of the *sukkah*. If an object is hung under the *s'chach* for purposes other than decorating the *sukkah*, [different laws apply,] as will be explained in sec. 629.[20]

ז וְכָל זֶה בְּנוֹיֵי הַסֻּכָּה, אֲבָל אִם פֵּרֵס תַּחַת הַסְּכָךְ דָּבָר שֶׁאֵינוֹ נוֹי לַסֻּכָּה – יִתְבָּאֵר בְּסִימָן תרכ"ט,[נג] עַיֵּן שָׁם:[20]

SECTION 628 Laws Relating to a *Sukkah* [Constructed] Under another *Sukkah*. (1–9)

סימן תרכח דִּינֵי סֻכָּה שֶׁתַּחַת סֻכָּה וּבוֹ ט' סְעִיפִים:

1 [The following laws apply when] one *sukkah* [is constructed] under another *sukkah*,[1] i.e., the *s'chach* of the lower *sukkah* is the floor of the upper *sukkah*. [See fig. 9, p. 270.] If there are at least ten handbreadths — the minimum acceptable height for a *sukkah*, as will be explained in sec. 633[2] — between the lower *s'chach* and the upper *s'chach*, and [the floor of] the upper *[sukkah* is strong enough to support a person who*]* uses it [together with his] pillows and mattresses without falling into the lower *sukkah*, the upper *sukkah* is valid and the lower *sukkah* is invalid. [This concept is derived[1] from] the verse,[3] "And you shall dwell in *sukkos* (בסוכת)." [This word is written] without a *vav* [in the third syllable],[4] implying [that one must dwell under] one *sukkah* and not under two levels of *s'chach*.

If, however, it is impossible for [the floor of] the upper *[sukkah* to support a person together with his*]* pillows and mattresses even with

א סֻכָּה שֶׁעַל גַּבֵּי סֻכָּה[א,1] שֶׁסְּכָכָהּ שֶׁל תַּחְתּוֹנָה הִיא קַרְקָעִיתָהּ שֶׁל עֶלְיוֹנָה,[ב] אִם יֵשׁ בֵּין סְכָךְ הַתַּחְתּוֹן לִסְכָךְ הָעֶלְיוֹן עֲשָׂרָה טְפָחִים,[ג] שֶׁזֶּהוּ שִׁעוּר הֶכְשֵׁר גֹּבַהּ הַסֻּכָּה[ד] כְּמוֹ שֶׁיִּתְבָּאֵר בְּסִימָן תרל"ג,[ה,2] וְיָכוֹל לְהִשְׁתַּמֵּשׁ בָּעֶלְיוֹנָה בְּכָרִים וּכְסָתוֹת[ו] וְלֹא תִּפֹּל בַּסֻּכָּה הַתַּחְתּוֹנָה – הָעֶלְיוֹנָה כְּשֵׁרָה וְהַתַּחְתּוֹנָה פְּסוּלָה,[1] שֶׁנֶּאֱמַר[ז,3] "בַּסֻּכֹּת תֵּשְׁבוּ וגו'", חָסֵר וא"ו שְׁנִיָּה,[4] מַשְׁמַע סֻכָּה אַחַת, וְלֹא תַּחַת שְׁנֵי סְכָכִים.[ח]

אֲבָל אִם אֵינוֹ יָכוֹל לְהִשְׁתַּמֵּשׁ בְּכָרִים וּכְסָתוֹת בָּעֶלְיוֹנָה אֲפִלּוּ עַל יְדֵי הַדְּחָק,[ט] כֵּיוָן שֶׁהָעֶלְיוֹנָה אֵינָהּ

---

20. The end of sec. 629 of the present work is not extant. See the *Shulchan Aruch* of R. Yosef Caro, sec. 629:19.

* For a summary of sec. 627, see p. 449.

SECTION 628

1. *Sukkah* 9b.

2. Sec. 633 of the present work is not extant. See the *Shulchan Aruch* of R. Yosef Caro, sec. 633:8.

3. *Vayikra* 23:42.

4. I.e., the plural suffix does not appear in full.

חסדא ורב בר רב הונא בגמרא י, ב. רמב"ם פ"ה הי"ח. רא"ש פ"א סי' יח. טור ושו"ע ס"ד. **מז** רא"ש פ"א סי' טו. ר"ן (ה, ב) ד"ה ולענין. וראה לקמן בסוף הסעיף שמ"מ לא יאסר (מדינא) אלא לישב תחתיהן. **מח** שו"ע ס"א. **מט** ראה שו"ע שם. **נ** מהרי"ל הל' סוכה (ע' שסז). רמ"א ס"ד. **נא** מ"א סק"ד. **נב** ט"ז סק"ה. **נג** סיום סימן זה בשוע"ר לא הגיע לידינו, וראה ב' הדעות בשו"ע שם סי"ט.

סימן תרכח: א משנה ט, ב. טור ושו"ע ס"א. **ב** רש"י י, א ד"ה שתיהן וד"ה וקיימא. **ג** שמואל בגמרא י, א. רא"ש פ"א סי' טו. טור ושו"ע שם. **ד** גמרא שם בטעמא דשמואל. **ה** סימן זה בשוע"ר לא הגיע לידינו, וראה טור ושו"ע שם ס"ח. **ו** רב דימי בגמרא שם, בשם אמרי במערבא. טור ושו"ע שם. **ז** ויקרא כג, מב. ברייתא ט, ב. **ח** רב נחמן בר יצחק שם. ר"ח שם עה"ג. לבוש סי' תרכו ס"א. **ט** גמרא י, א אליבא דת"ק. טור ושו"ע שם.

רְאוּיָה כְּלָל אֲפִלּוּ לְדִירַת אַרְעַי, שֶׁהֲרֵי אֲפִלּוּ עַל יְדֵי הַדְּחָק אֵינוֹ יָכוֹל לְהִשְׁתַּמֵּשׁ בָּהּ בְּכָרִים וּכְסָתוֹת – אֵינָהּ נִקְרֵאת סֻכָּה כְּלָל,[יא,5] וְאֵינָהּ פּוֹסֶלֶת אֶת הַתַּחְתּוֹנָה מִשּׁוּם סֻכָּה שֶׁתַּחַת סֻכָּה.

וְכֵן אִם הָעֶלְיוֹנָה אֵינָהּ גְּבוֹהָה עֲשָׂרָה טְפָחִים,[יב] אוֹ שֶׁחַמָּתָהּ מְרֻבָּה מִצִּלָּתָהּ[יג,6] – אֵינָהּ נִקְרֵאת סֻכָּה כְּלָל לִפְסֹל אֶת הַתַּחְתּוֹנָה:

difficulty, the upper *sukkah* is not fit to be dwelt in even temporarily. Since it cannot [support a person together with his] pillows and mattresses even with difficulty, it is not called a *sukkah* at all.[5] Hence, the lower *sukkah* is not considered a *sukkah* beneath a *sukkah* and thus is not disqualified by it.

Similarly, if the upper *sukkah* is less than ten handbreadths high or the sunlit area [of its floor] exceeds its shaded area,[6] it is not called a *sukkah* at all [and hence does not] disqualify the lower *sukkah*.

ב לְפִיכָךְ אִם הַתַּחְתּוֹנָה הִיא צִלָּתָהּ מְרֻבָּה מֵחַמָּתָהּ בְּלִי צֵרוּף צֵל סְכַךְ הָעֶלְיוֹנָה, אָז הִיא כְּשֵׁרָה בְּכָל עִנְיָן, אֲפִלּוּ אִם סְכַךְ הָעֶלְיוֹנָה גָּבוֹהַּ יוֹתֵר מֵעֶשְׂרִים

2 Therefore, [in the latter situations,] if the shaded part of the lower *[sukkah]* exceeds its sunlit area without including the shadow cast by the upper *s'chach*, [the lower *sukkah*] is valid without question, even if the *s'chach* of the upper *sukkah* is more than 20

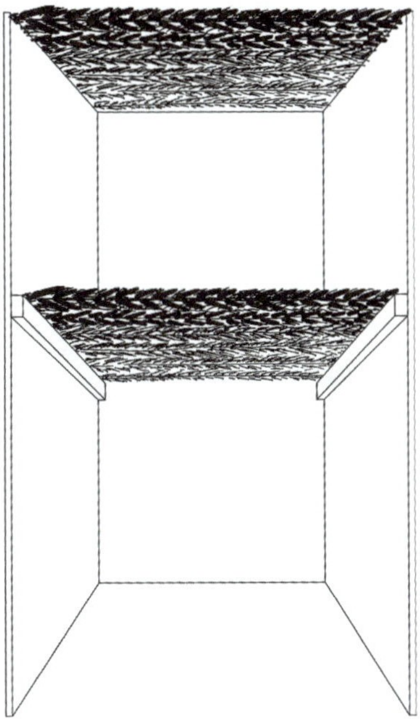

Fig. 9: See sec. 628:1.

5. And no obligation would be fulfilled by dwelling in it *(Kessef Mishneh).*

6. See sec. 626:3.

י ראה ר"ן (ה, רע"א). ב"י סוד"ה סוכה. לבוש ס"א. ט"ז סק"א. יא ראה רש"י י, א ד"ה ומשני. לבוש שם. יב שמואל שם. טור ושו"ע שם. יג גמרא שם.

אַמָּה[יד,7] מִקַּרְקָעִית הַתַּחְתּוֹנָה.[טו] וְאַף עַל פִּי שֶׁסְּכָךְ הָעֶלְיוֹנָה הוּא פָּסוּל לַסֻּכָּה הַתַּחְתּוֹנָה מִפְּנֵי שֶׁהוּא לְמַעְלָה מֵעֶשְׂרִים אַמָּה, וְנִמְצָא שֶׁסְּכָךְ פָּסוּל מֵצֵל עַל הַתַּחְתּוֹנָה, וּכְבָר נִתְבָּאֵר בְּסִימָן תרכ"ו[טז] שֶׁכָּל סְכָךְ פָּסוּל פּוֹסֵל סְכָךְ כָּשֵׁר שֶׁתַּחְתָּיו[8] — אַף עַל פִּי כֵן הַתַּחְתּוֹנָה כְּשֵׁרָה, אֲפִלּוּ אִם סְכָךְ הָעֶלְיוֹן צִלָּתָהּ מְרֻבָּה מֵחַמָּתָהּ,[יז] שֶׁלֹּא אָמְרוּ שֶׁסְּכָךְ פָּסוּל פּוֹסֵל סְכָךְ כָּשֵׁר שֶׁתַּחְתָּיו אֶלָּא בִּסְכָךְ שֶׁפְּסוּלוֹ הוּא מֵחֲמַת עַצְמוֹ, כְּגוֹן מְחֻבָּר אוֹ דָּבָר שֶׁרָאוּי לְקַבֵּל טֻמְאָה, אֲבָל סְכָךְ שֶׁכָּשֵׁר מֵחֲמַת עַצְמוֹ אֶלָּא שֶׁדָּבָר אַחֵר גּוֹרֵם לוֹ לִפְסֹל, כְּגוֹן שֶׁמֻּנָּח לְמַעְלָה מֵעֶשְׂרִים אַמָּה — אֵינוֹ פּוֹסֵל סְכָךְ כָּשֵׁר שֶׁתַּחְתָּיו,[יח] כֵּיוָן שֶׁהוּא בְּעַצְמוֹ רָאוּי לִסְכּוֹךְ בַּסֻּכָּה שֶׁתַּחְתָּיו:[יט]

ג אֲבָל אִם הַתַּחְתּוֹנָה אֵין צִלָּתָהּ מְרֻבָּה מֵחַמָּתָהּ[1] אֶלָּא עַל יְדֵי צֵרוּף צֵל סְכַךְ הָעֶלְיוֹנָה, אִם סְכַךְ הָעֶלְיוֹנָה הוּא לְמַעְלָה מֵעֶשְׂרִים אַמָּה מִקַּרְקָעִית הַתַּחְתּוֹנָה — הַתַּחְתּוֹנָה פְּסוּלָה,[כ] שֶׁאֵין סְכָךְ פָּסוּל[9] מִצְטָרֵף לִסְכָךְ כָּשֵׁר לְהַשְׁלִים לְכַשִּׁעוּר:

cubits[7] higher than the floor of the lower *sukkah.*

[Theoretically, this situation could present a problem,] because the *s'chach* of the upper *sukkah* is invalid for the lower *sukkah,* being more than 20 cubits [above ground level].[7] Here, then, is a situation in which material that is invalid as *s'chach* is casting a shadow over the lower *sukkah,* and, as explained in sec. 626[:2-3], material that is invalid as *s'chach* disqualifies valid *s'chach* that is placed under it.[8] Nevertheless, in this instance, the lower *sukkah* is valid, even if the shadow cast by the upper *s'chach* exceeds the sunlit area [on the ground]. For the principle that invalid material disqualifies the valid *s'chach* below it applies only when the invalid material is inherently unsatisfactory; e.g., it is still connected to the ground or it is susceptible to contracting ritual impurity. When, however, the *s'chach* is inherently valid but is rendered unacceptable by an external factor — for example, by being situated more than 20 cubits above [ground level] — it does not disqualify the valid *s'chach* that is below it, for it is inherently suitable for use as *s'chach* for the lower *sukkah.*

3 [A different rule applies,] however, when the shade [on the floor] of the lower *sukkah* does not exceed its sunlit area[1] unless the *s'chach* of the upper *sukkah* is also taken into account. [In such a situation,] if the *s'chach* of the upper *sukkah* is more than 20 cubits from the floor of the lower *sukkah,* the lower *sukkah* is invalid, for invalid material[9] cannot be counted together with valid *s'chach* to make up the required measure.

7. See the *Shulchan Aruch* of R. Yosef Caro, sec. 633:1. (The corresponding section of the present work is not extant.)

8. As explained there, in such a situation the valid *s'chach* no longer produces shade, for it is not exposed to the sun.

9. I.e., it is invalid because of its height.

יד ר"ת בתוס' ט, ב ד"ה הא, ובמרדכי רמז תשלה. רמב"ם פ"ה סוף הכ"ב, לפירוש הכסף משנה שם. טור ושו"ע ס"א. **טו** לבוש ס"א. וראה גם רש"י י, א סוף דבור הא'. **טז** לדעה הא' דלעיל שם ס"ג־ח. **יז** ט"ז סק"ב. וראה לעיל שם ס"י, שכ"ה לדעה הב' שם אף בסוכה תחת האילן. **יח** ר"ת שם. **יט** מרדכי שם. **כ** גמרא ט, סוע"ב. ר"ת ורמב"ם שם. טור ושו"ע ס"א.

ד הָעוֹשֶׂה סֻכָּתוֹ בְּרֹאשׁ הָעֲגָלָה אוֹ בְּרֹאשׁ הַסְּפִינָה,[כא,10] אִם אֵינָהּ יְכוֹלָה לַעֲמֹד בְּרוּחַ מְצוּיָה דְּיַבָּשָׁה[11] — פְּסוּלָה,[כב,12] וְהַיּוֹשֵׁב בָּהּ אֲפִלּוּ בְּשָׁעָה שֶׁאֵין שָׁם רוּחַ כְּלָל[כג] — לֹא יָצָא יְדֵי חוֹבָתוֹ, לְפִי שֶׁאֵינָהּ דִּירָה כְּלָל.[כד,13] אֲבָל אִם יְכוֹלָה לַעֲמֹד בְּרוּחַ מְצוּיָה דְּיַבָּשָׁה אַף עַל פִּי שֶׁאֵינָהּ יְכוֹלָה לַעֲמֹד בְּרוּחַ מְצוּיָה דְּיָם — כְּשֵׁרָה,[כה] וְהַיּוֹשֵׁב בָּהּ אֲפִלּוּ בְּשָׁעָה שֶׁהַסְּפִינָה מְהַלֶּכֶת[כו] — יוֹצֵא יְדֵי חוֹבָתוֹ, שֶׁהַסֻּכָּה אֵינָהּ צְרִיכָה לִהְיוֹת דִּירַת קֶבַע (שֶׁתְּהֵא רְאוּיָה לְיָמִים הַרְבֵּה) אֶלָּא דִּירַת עֲרַאי:[כז,14]

4 If a *sukkah* constructed upon a wagon or upon a boat[10] cannot withstand ordinary land winds,[11] it is invalid.[12] A person who dwells in it — even when there is no wind at all — does not fulfill his obligation, because it is not deemed a dwelling at all.[13] However, if [the *sukkah*] could withstand the winds common on land, then even if it could not withstand the winds common at sea, one fulfills his obligation, even if he dwells in it while the ship is at sea. [The rationale is that] a *sukkah* does not have to be a permanent dwelling (which is fit to live in for an extended period), but a temporary dwelling.[14]

ה הָעוֹשֶׂה סֻכָּתוֹ בְּרֹאשׁ הַגָּמָל אוֹ בְּרֹאשׁ הָאִילָן,[כח] שֶׁרֹאשׁ הָאִילָן הוּא קַרְקָעִית סֻכָּתוֹ,[כט] וְעָשָׂה שָׁם מְחִצּוֹת וְסִכֵּךְ עַל גַּבֵּיהֶן[ל] — כְּשֵׁרָה.[10]

וְאֵין עוֹלִין לָהּ בְּשַׁבָּת וְיוֹם טוֹב,[לא,15] שֶׁאָסוּר לְהִשְׁתַּמֵּשׁ בְּבַעֲלֵי חַיִּים וּבִמְחֻבָּר לַקַּרְקַע[16] בְּשַׁבָּת וְיוֹם טוֹב[לב] כְּמוֹ שֶׁנִּתְבָּאֵר בְּסִימָן של"ו,[לג,17] וְאֵין דּוֹחִין אֲפִלּוּ שְׁבוּת[18]

5 [If a person] constructs his *sukkah* on a camel [see fig. 10] or on top of a tree, i.e., the treetop serves as the base of the *sukkah* and he builds walls and places *s'chach* over them [see fig. 11], it is valid.[10] One may not, however, climb up to it on *Shabbos* or on a festival,[15] for [at such times] it is forbidden to make use of any living creature or of any plant connected to the ground,[16] as stated in sec. 336.[17] We do not override even a *shvus*[18] —

10. *Sukkah* 22b.

11. Which are usually milder than winds on the open sea.

12. *op. cit.*, 23a.

13. See the *Shulchan Aruch* of R. Yosef Caro, 630:10. (The corresponding section of the present work is not extant.)

14. Thus, even though the *sukkah* is transported, it is valid. This principle serves as the halachic basis for the Lubavitch *sukkah*-mobiles that bring this *mitzvah* to thousands of Jews who would otherwise not be exposed to it.

15. I.e., it may be used on *Chol HaMoed,* but not on the first day of Sukkos in *Eretz Yisrael* or on the first two days of the festival in the Diaspora.

16. *Beitzah* 36b.

17. That section details the prohibition against climbing a tree or making use of other growing plants. The laws on the use of animals on *Shabbos* are found in sec. 305 and sec. 339.

18. The above prohibitions are examples of a *shvus,* which is a Rabbinic prohibition instituted because the action in question resembles a Scriptural prohibition or might lead one to transgress a

כא משנה כב, ב. טור ושו"ע ס"ב. **כב** גמרא כג, א. טור ושו"ע שם. **כג** ראה מ"א סי' תרל סקט"ז. **כד** רש"י שם ד"ה לא כלום היא. לבוש ס"ב. **כה** ברייתא וגמרא כג, א וכר"ע. טור ושו"ע שם. **כו** מ"א סק"ד, ממשמעות הגמרא שם. **כז** גמרא שם אליבא דר"ע. **כח** משנה כב, ב. טור ושו"ע ס"ג. **כט** רש"י שם ד"ה בראש האילן. **ל** רש"י שם. ר"ן (י, א) ד"ה מתני' הסומך, בשם הרמב"ן במלחמות שם. הובא ב"י סי' תרל קרוב לסופו. מ"א סק"ה. וכדלקמן סוף ס"ז, וסי' תרכט סי"א־ב, שלכתחלה לא יסמוך הסכך על דבר הפסול לסכך. **לא** משנה שם. טור ושו"ע שם. **לב** ר"ן (י, ב) ד"ה מתני' וב"י סוף הסי' ולבוש ס"ג וט"ז

which was ordained by the Sages — in order to enable the observance of the *mitzvah* of *sukkah,* for the reasons explained in sec. 586[:22].[19]

שֶׁל דִּבְרֵי סוֹפְרִים מִפְּנֵי קִיּוּם מִצְוַת סֻכָּה, מִטַּעַם שֶׁנִּתְבָּאֵר בְּסִימָן תקפ"ו,[לד] עַיֵּן שָׁם:[19]

6 Even if the base of the *sukkah* is on the ground, but the canes of the *s'chach* are resting on a tree, it is forbidden to enter it on *Shabbos* or on a festival. This [safeguard] was ordained lest one use the *s'chach* by placing something on it or hanging something from it. Thus one would be making use of the appendages of a tree, for this is how the *s'chach* that is leaning on the tree is categorized, and it is forbidden to make use of such an entity on *Shabbos* or on a festival,[20] as stated in sec. 336[:20].

ו וַאֲפִלּוּ אִם הַסֻּכָּה הִיא עַל הָאָרֶץ אֶלָּא שֶׁהַקָּנִים שֶׁל סְכָךְ מְסֻמָּכִין עַל הָאִילָן — אָסוּר לִכָּנֵס לְתוֹכָהּ בְּשַׁבָּת וְיוֹם טוֹב, גְּזֵרָה שֶׁמָּא יִשְׁתַּמֵּשׁ בְּהַסְּכָךְ שֶׁיַּנִּיחַ שָׁם חֲפָצָיו,[לה] אוֹ יִתְלֶה בּוֹ שׁוּם דָּבָר[לו] וְנִמְצָא מִשְׁתַּמֵּשׁ בְּצִדְדֵי הָאִילָן,[לז] דְּהַיְנוּ הַסְּכָךְ שֶׁסָּמוּךְ עַל הָאִילָן נִקְרָא צִדְדֵי הָאִילָן, וְאָסוּר לְהִשְׁתַּמֵּשׁ בּוֹ בְּשַׁבָּת וְיוֹם טוֹב[20] כְּמוֹ שֶׁנִּתְבָּאֵר בְּסִימָן של"ו:[לח]

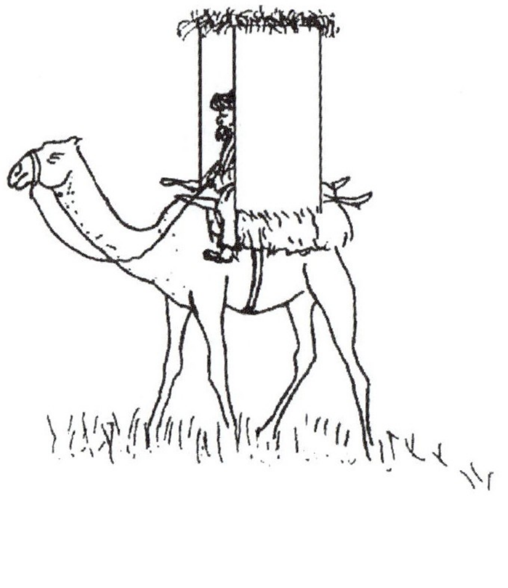

Fig. 10: See sec. 628:5.

Fig. 11: See sec. 628:5.

Scriptural prohibition *(Rambam, Hilchos Shabbos* 21:1).

19. There the Alter Rebbe states: "For the Sages equated their rulings with those [stemming] from Scriptural Law and buttressed the authority of their rulings even though they led to the negation of Scriptural Law, in cases in which one remains inactive and [simply] refrains from performing [an action required of him by the Torah]."

20. *Shabbos* 154b.

סק"ג מביצה לו, ב. לג ס"א (אילן), וסי' שה סכ"ג (בהמה). לד סכ"ב. וראה גם לקמן סי' תרמ ס"י. לה רא"ש פ"ב סי' ד, כפירוש רש"י שבת קנד, ב ד"ה שתים, וכפירוש הא' בתוס' שם ד"ה שתים. מ"א סק"ו. לו מ"מ פ"ד ה"ו. לז מסקנת הגמרא שבת שם. וראה רש"י שם ד"ה דחק. לח סעיף כ.

ז בַּמֶּה דְּבָרִים אֲמוּרִים? בַּיָּמִים הָרִאשׁוֹנִים שֶׁהָיוּ רְגִילִים לְהִשְׁתַּמֵּשׁ בַּסְּכָךְ לְהַנִּיחַ וְלִתְלוֹת שָׁם חֶפְצֵיהֶם,[לט] אֲבָל עַכְשָׁו שֶׁאֵין רְגִילִין בְּכָךְ – אֵין חוֹשְׁשִׁין לְכָךְ, וּלְפִיכָךְ יֵשׁ לְהַתִּיר לִכָּנֵס לְתוֹכָהּ בְּשַׁבָּת וְיוֹם טוֹב.[מ]

וּמִכָּל מָקוֹם, לְכַתְּחִלָּה אֵין לִסְמֹךְ אֶת הַסְּכָךְ עַל הָאִילָן, שֶׁאֵין מַעֲמִידִין אֶת הַסְּכָךְ לְכַתְּחִלָּה אֶלָּא בְּדָבָר הָרָאוּי לְסִכּוּךְ[מא] כְּמוֹ שֶׁיִּתְבָּאֵר בְּסִימָן תרכ"ט,[מב] עַיֵּן שָׁם הַטַּעַם:[21]

7 When did the above apply? In earlier eras, when people would frequently use the *s'chach*, placing their articles on it and hanging them from it. In the present era, by contrast, when people are not accustomed to doing so, we do not have to take this possibility into account. Hence, permission may be granted to enter [such a *sukkah*] on *Shabbos* or on a festival. Nevertheless, as an initial preference, a tree should not be used as support for the *s'chach*, because [for this purpose] one should preferably use only objects that are fit to serve as *s'chach*, as will be explained in sec. 629[:11]. Note the explanation given there.[21]

ח וְאִם רָאשֵׁי הַקָּנִים שֶׁל הַסְּכָךְ נִסְמָכִים עַל רֹאשׁ הַגָּמָל – אֲפִלּוּ בְּדִיעֲבַד פְּסוּלָה, לְפִי שֶׁאֵין לָהּ קֶבַע, שֶׁהֲרֵי הַגָּמָל סוֹפוֹ לֵילֵךְ מִכָּאן וְיִפֹּל הַסְּכָךְ.[מג, 22] וְלֹא הִכְשִׁירוּ סֻכָּה בְּרֹאשׁ הַגָּמָל אֶלָּא אִם כֵּן סִכֵּךְ עַל גַּבֵּי מְחִצּוֹת שֶׁעַל גַּבֵּי הַגָּמָל,[מד] שֶׁהַסֻּכָּה מִטַּלְטֶלֶת עִם הַגָּמָל:

8 If the ends of the canes of *s'chach* are resting on top of a camel, [the *sukkah*] is invalid, even after the fact, because it has no permanence. Ultimately, the camel will move from [that place] and the *s'chach* will fall.[22] A *sukkah* constructed on top of a camel was permitted only when the *s'chach* was placed on walls that were built on the camel and thus the *sukkah* is carried with the camel.

ט הָעוֹשֶׂה מִקְצָת קַרְקָעִית סֻכָּתוֹ וּמִקְצָת דָּפְנוֹתֶיהָ עַל רֹאשׁ הָאִילָן וּמִקְצָת קַרְקָעִיתָהּ וּמִקְצָת דָּפְנוֹתֶיהָ עַל דָּבָר אַחֵר[מה] וְסִכֵּךְ עַל גַּבֵּי הַדְּפָנוֹת,[מו, 10] אִם הִיא עֲשׂוּיָה בְּעִנְיָן שֶׁאִם יִנָּטֵל הָאִילָן תִּשָּׁאֵר הִיא עוֹמֶדֶת עַל הַדָּבָר אַחֵר וְלֹא תִּפֹּל[23]

9 [The following rule applies if] a person built part of the base for his *sukkah* and part of its walls on top of a tree and part of its base and walls on something else, and then placed *s'chach* on the walls.[10] If [the *sukkah*] is constructed in such a manner that if the tree was removed, it would still stand on the other support without falling,[23]

21. There the Alter Rebbe explains that this safeguard was ordained lest a person err and use such objects as *s'chach*.

22. Theoretically, an animal may serve as a wall of a *sukkah* if it is not being used to support the *s'chach*, as stated in the *Shulchan Aruch* of R. Yosef Caro, sec. 630:11. (The corresponding section of the present work is not extant.)

23. I.e., the remaining support is wide enough and strong enough to support the entire *sukkah*.

לט מ"א שם, ממשמעות המ"מ שם. וראה גם תוס' שם. **מ** מ"א שם. **מא** מ"א סי' תרכט סק"ט. **מב** סעיף יא. **מג** ע"פ ר"ן (י, א) ד"ה מתני' הסומך, בשם הראב"ד בהשגות שם (לענין כרעי המטה). מ"א סי' תרל סקי"ד. **מד** כדלעיל ס"ה. **מה** רש"י כב, ב ד"ה שתים. טור ושו"ע ס"ג. **מו** ר"ן (יא, א) ד"ה שתים (וכדלעיל ס"ה).

one may enter it on *Shabbos* and on the festivals using a ladder that is not [supported by] the tree. If not [see fig. 12], one may not climb up to it on *Shabbos* and on the festivals. Since [in the latter instance] it is supported by the tree, a person entering it is making use of the appendages of a tree, as explained above.[24]

– מֻתָּר לַעֲלוֹת לָהּ בְּשַׁבָּת וְיוֹם טוֹב[מז] בְּסֻלָּם שֶׁלֹּא עַל דֶּרֶךְ הָאִילָן,[מח] וְאִם לָאו – אֵין עוֹלִין לָהּ בְּשַׁבָּת וְיוֹם טוֹב, דְּכֵיוָן שֶׁסְּמִיכָתָהּ עַל הָאִילָן – נִמְצָא כְּשֶׁנִּכְנָס לְתוֹכָהּ מִשְׁתַּמֵּשׁ בְּצִדְדֵי הָאִילָן כְּמוֹ שֶׁבֵּאַרְנוּ לְמַעְלָה:[מט,24]

SECTION 629 What Materials May Be Used as *S'chach*. (1–33)

סימן תרכט מַה צָּרִיךְ לִהְיוֹת הַסְּכָךְ וּבוֹ ל"ג סְעִיפִים:

1 To be valid for use as *s'chach*, a substance must:

[a] have grown from the ground;

[b] be [presently] detached from the ground; and

[c] not be susceptible to ritual impurity.[1]

If [a substance] does not grow from the ground, then even though it is not susceptible to ritual impurity — e.g., unprocessed animal hides,

א אֵין מְסַכְּכִין אֶלָּא בְּדָבָר שֶׁהוּא צוֹמֵחַ מִן הָאָרֶץ וְהוּא תָּלוּשׁ מִן הַקַּרְקַע[א] וְאֵינוֹ מְקַבֵּל טֻמְאָה.[ב,1] אֲבָל אִם אֵינוֹ צוֹמֵחַ מִן הָאָרֶץ אַף עַל פִּי שֶׁאֵינוֹ מְקַבֵּל טֻמְאָה, כְּגוֹן עוֹרוֹת

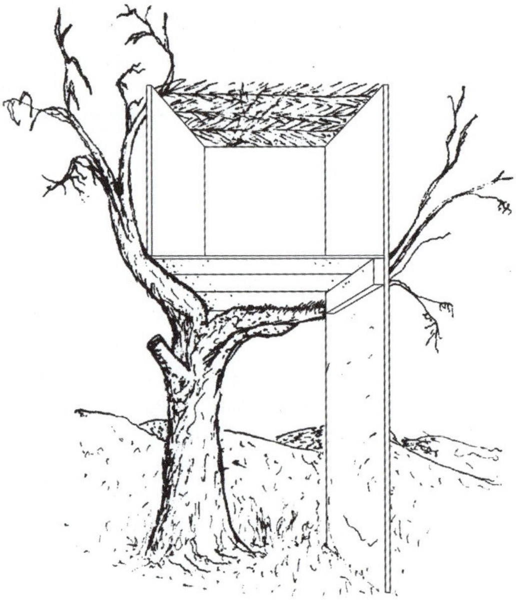

Fig. 12: See sec. 628:9.
As evident from this diagram, the leaves of a tree on which a *sukkah* was built should not cover the *s'chach*.

24. In subsection 6.

* For a summary of sec. 628, see p. 450.)

SECTION 629

1. *Sukkah* 11a.

מז משנה כג, רע"א. טור ושו"ע שם. **מח** שזה אסור, כדלעיל סי' שלו ס"כ וש"נ. **מט** סעיף ו.
סימן תרכט: א יתבאר לקמן ס"כ. **ב** משנה יא, א. טור ושו"ע ס"א.

בְּהֵמָה שֶׁלֹּא נֶעֶבְדוּ שֶׁאֵינָן מְקַבְּלִין טֻמְאָה,[ג] אוֹ עָפָר,[ד] אוֹ מִינֵי מַתָּכוֹת[ה] אַף עַל פִּי שֶׁלֹּא עָשָׂה מֵהֶן כֵּלִים שֶׁאֵינָן מְקַבְּלִין טֻמְאָה, וְכֵן כָּל דָּבָר שֶׁרָאוּי לְקַבֵּל טֻמְאָה[ו] אַף עַל פִּי שֶׁהוּא צוֹמֵחַ מִן הָאָרֶץ,[1] כְּגוֹן כָּל מִינֵי אֳכָלִין[ז,2] אַף עַל פִּי שֶׁלֹּא הֻכְשְׁרוּ,[ח,3] וְכָל מִינֵי כֵּלִים אֲפִלּוּ שֶׁל עֵץ[ט] שֶׁיֵּשׁ לָהֶן בֵּית קִבּוּל[י] שֶׁהֵן מְקַבְּלִין טֻמְאָה[4] — אֵין מְסַכְּכִין בָּהֶן, שֶׁנֶּאֱמַר[יא,5] "חַג הַסֻּכֹּת תַּעֲשֶׂה לְךָ בְּאָסְפְּךָ מִגָּרְנְךָ וּמִיִּקְבֶךָ", בִּפְסֹלֶת גֹּרֶן וָיֶקֶב הַכָּתוּב מְדַבֵּר,[יב,6] דְּהַיְנוּ קַשִּׁין[יג] אוֹ שִׁבֹּלֶת וְקָנִין[יד] שֶׁאוֹסְפִים אוֹתָן מִן הַגֹּרֶן וְהַיֶּקֶב, וּמֵהֶן וְכַיּוֹצֵא בָּהֶן שֶׁצּוֹמְחִין מִן הָאָרֶץ וְאֵינוֹ מְקַבֵּל טֻמְאָה — תַּעֲשֶׂה לְךָ סֻכּוֹת,[טו] וְלֹא מִדְּבָרִים אֲחֵרִים:[טז]

which are not susceptible to ritual impurity, or earth, or metal, even if it was not fashioned into a utensil and [hence] is not susceptible to ritual impurity — it may not be used as *s'chach*.

[The same applies to] any substance that is susceptible to ritual impurity, even though it grows from the ground,[1] such as all kinds of food[2] even if they were not readied [to actually contract ritual impurity],[3] and to all kinds of utensils — even wooden ones — that have a receptacle, and are thus susceptible to ritual impurity.[4]

[This restriction is derived from] the verse,[5] "Make the Sukkos festival for yourself, when you gather from your threshing floor and your winepress." [Implied[6] is that] the verse is speaking of the remnants left on the threshing floor and in the winepress, i.e., straw, stalks, and reeds that can be collected from the threshing floor and the winepress. [The verse is implying that] *sukkos* should be made of these and of other such things that grow from the ground and are not susceptible to ritual impurity; they should not be made of anything else.

2. *Op. cit.*, 13b.

3. This is the second of two distinct stages of susceptibility to ritual impurity:

(a) Anything that belongs to one of the many categories of objects that in principle are susceptible to ritual impurity is described as being *mekabel tumah* or *ra'ui lekabel tumah*.

(b) Foodstuffs belong to such a category. However, such an object is readied to actually contract ritual impurity (e.g., by contact with a dead reptile) only if it was first moistened by water or by certain other liquids. (See *Rambam, Hilchos Tumas Ochalin* 1:1.) Any foodstuff that has thereby been readied to actually contract ritual impurity is described as being *muchshar lekabel tumah*.

The emphasis here is that even if produce has not reached the stage at which it is readied to contract ritual impurity, it is still considered as susceptible to ritual impurity and hence disqualified as *s'chach*.

4. See subsections 3 and 14 with regard to utensils that do not have a receptacle.

5. *Devarim* 16:13.

6. *Sukkah* 12a.

ג רש"י שם ד"ה ואין. טור ושו"ע שם. ד ר"ן (ז, ב) ד"ה מתני'. רמ"א ס"א. ה רמב"ם פ"ה ה"ב. טור ושו"ע שם. ו משנה שם (שהוא מקבל טומאה). ט"ז ס"ק ב (ראוי). מ"א ס"ק יא (אפילו חדשים שידוע שלא נטמאו). וראה גם לקמן ס"ז וש"נ. ז ברייתא יג, ב וכת"ק. רמב"ם פ"ה ה"ג. רא"ש פ"א סי' כז. טור ושו"ע ס"ט. ח רש"י יג, ב ד"ה ופוסלין (כדלקמן סי"ט), לפירוש התוס' שם ד"ה ירקות (דמיירי שלא הוכשרו). תוס' רי"ד שם. ט רמב"ם שם ה"ב. לבוש ס"ב. י משא"כ פשוטי כלי עץ, שאם הם רחבים קצת נאסרו רק מדרבנן (כדלקמן סי"ד וש"נ), ואם אינם רחבים לא נאסרו אף מדרבנן (ט"ז סק"ה. מ"א סק"א. וכדלקמן ס"ג). יא דברים טז, יד. יב רבי יוחנן בגמרא יב, א. לבוש ס"א. יג רש"י שם ד"ה פסולת. יד ברש"י שם: ואשכולות ריקנים. וכ"ה בט"ז ס"ק א. ואולי צ"ל כן גם כאן. טו רש"י ר"ה יג, א ד"ה ואמר מר. טז ראה פרדס חב"ד 9 ע' 95. יז גמרא טז, א. רמב"ם פ"ה ה"ב. טור ושו"ע ס"ב. יח גמרא שם. רמב"ם שם. יט ראה שבת כו, ב. רמב"ם הל' כלים פכ"ב ה"א. וראה גם לעיל סי' רסד סט"ו. כ ב"ח ד"ה סככה. מ"א סק"ב, בפירוש דברי השלטי גבורים ו, ב אות ג, בשם הריא"ז. וראה לקמן ס"ג וש"נ. כא תוס' שבת כו, א ד"ה אין בו. כב רש"י טו, ב ד"ה בבלאי. וראה גם רמב"ם שם. כג משמעות הגמרא שם. וראה חקרי הלכות ח"א לד, ב.

ב כָּל דָּבָר שֶׁהָיָה רָאוּי לְקַבֵּל טֻמְאָה שָׁעָה אַחַת אַף עַל פִּי שֶׁאַחַר כָּךְ נִטַּהֵר מִלְּקַבֵּל טֻמְאָה, כְּגוֹן כֵּלִים שֶׁנִּשְׁבְּרוּ וְאֵין בְּשִׁבְרֵיהֶן כַּשִּׁעוּר הָרָאוּי לְקַבָּלַת טֻמְאָה,[ז,7] וְכֵן מַטְלָנִיּוֹת שֶׁבָּלוּ וְלֹא נִשְׁתַּיֵּר בָּהֶן שָׁלֹשׁ אֶצְבָּעוֹת עַל שָׁלֹשׁ אֶצְבָּעוֹת[יח] שֶׁשּׁוּב אֵין מְקַבְּלִין טֻמְאָה,[יט,8] וְכֵן בֵּית יָד שֶׁל כְּלִי שֶׁנִּשְׁבַּר מִן הַכְּלִי[כ] שֶׁבְּעוֹדוֹ מְחֻבָּר לַכְּלִי הָיָה מְקַבֵּל טֻמְאָה כָּמוֹהוּ וְעַכְשָׁו נִטַּהֵר מִלְּקַבֵּל שׁוּם טֻמְאָה,[9] כָּל אֵלּוּ כֵּיוָן שֶׁפַּעַם אַחַת הָיוּ רְאוּיִין לְקַבָּלַת טֻמְאָה[כא] — גָּזְרוּ חֲכָמִים עֲלֵיהֶם[כב,10] שֶׁלֹּא לְסַכֵּךְ בָּהֶן לְעוֹלָם. וְאִם עָבַר וְסִכֵּךְ — סֻכָּתוֹ פְּסוּלָה, כְּמוֹ הַמְסַכֵּךְ בִּסְכָךְ שֶׁהוּא פָּסוּל מִן הַתּוֹרָה:[כג]

2 Anything that was susceptible to ritual impurity even briefly [may not be used for *s'chach*], even though later [its status changed and] it was no longer susceptible to ritual impurity. For example:

[a] utensils that were broken, when their broken pieces are not large enough to be considered susceptible to ritual impurity;[7]

[b] pieces of cloth that became so tattered that less than three fingerbreadths by three fingerbreadths remain, in which instance they are no longer susceptible to ritual impurity;[8] or

[c] the handle of a utensil which, like the utensil itself, was susceptible to ritual impurity while it was connected to the utensil, but when broken off is no longer susceptible to any ritual impurity.[9]

Since any such objects were once susceptible to ritual impurity, the Sages ordained[10] that they should never be used for *s'chach*. If a person transgressed and used them to cover his *sukkah*, it is invalid, just as if he had used *s'chach* that is invalid according to Scriptural Law.

ג הַבֵּית יָד שֶׁל חִצִּים יֵשׁ עוֹשִׂין אוֹתָן זְכָרִים, דְּהַיְנוּ שֶׁאֵין נוֹקְבִין בָּהֶן שׁוּם נֶקֶב אֶלָּא עוֹשִׂין בַּחֵץ כְּעֵין בֵּית קִבּוּל וְתוֹחֲבִין אֶת הַבֵּית יָד לְשָׁם, וְיֵשׁ עוֹשִׂין אוֹתָן נְקֵבוֹת, דְּהַיְנוּ שֶׁעוֹשִׂין נֶקֶב בְּרֹאשָׁן וְהַחֵץ עָשׂוּי כְּמַרְצֵעַ[11] וְנִכְנָס לְתוֹךְ הַנֶּקֶב,[12]

3 [The ruling on whether] shafts for arrowheads [can be used as *s'chach* depends on the way the arrows were made]. Some are made "male"; i.e., a hole is made not in the shaft but in the arrowhead, and the shaft is pressed into it. Others are made "female"; i.e., a hole is made in the end of the shaft and [the back of] the arrowhead is made like an awl[11] that is inserted in the hole.[12]

Fig. 13: Male arrow (left) and female arrow (right). See sec. 629:3.

7. Op. cit., 16a. If a utensil breaks and becomes useless, its status changes and it is no longer susceptible to ritual impurity. If its remnants are large enough to be useful as containers, they may be considered utensils in their own right — but only if they are large enough to hold a significant amount. See *Keilim* 2:2.

8. For such a piece of cloth is too small to be considered a significant entity.

9. See *Shabbos* 26b.

10. I.e., according to Scriptural Law these objects would be acceptable as *s'chach*, but the Sages forbade their use.

11. I.e., with a screwlike base.

12. *Sukkah* 12b. See fig. 13.

The "male" shafts are not susceptible to ritual impurity, because they have no receptacle. Therefore, if they have never been inserted in an arrowhead,[13] they may be used for *s'chach*. The "female" shafts, by contrast, [may not be used for *s'chach*], since they have a receptacle. Even though the receptacle is intended to be permanently filled by [the back of] the arrowhead and never to be emptied, [the shaft] is nevertheless susceptible to ritual impurity. Therefore, if it is used as *s'chach*, the *sukkah* is invalid.

וְהַזְּכָרִים אֵין מְקַבְּלִין טֻמְאָה, לְפִי שֶׁאֵין לָהֶם בֵּית קִבּוּל,[כד] וּלְפִיכָךְ מֻתָּר לְסַכֵּךְ בָּהֶן[כה] אִם עֲדַיִן לֹא הָיוּ קְבוּעִין בְּהַחֵץ מֵעוֹלָם,[כו,13] אֲבָל הַנְּקֵבוֹת כֵּיוָן שֶׁיֵּשׁ בָּהֶן בֵּית קִבּוּל, אַף עַל פִּי שֶׁהַבֵּית קִבּוּל עָשׂוּי לְמַלְּאוֹת עַל יְדֵי הַחֵץ[כז] מִלּוּי עוֹלָם שֶׁלֹּא לְהִתְרוֹקֵן עוֹד[כח] — אַף עַל פִּי כֵן הוּא מְקַבֵּל טֻמְאָה, וּלְפִיכָךְ אִם סִכֵּךְ בָּהֶן — סְכָכוֹ פְּסוּלָה:[כט]

4 Reeds that grow hollow are not susceptible to ritual impurity even though they have a receptacle, because it was not made to serve [man] as a receptacle. They may therefore be used as *s'chach*. Similarly, a [wooden] gutter may be used as *s'chach*, because it was not made to serve as a receptacle.[14]

ד קָנִים הַנִּבְרָאִים חֲלוּלִים אַף עַל פִּי שֶׁיֵּשׁ לָהֶן בֵּית קִבּוּל — אֵין מְקַבְּלִין טֻמְאָה, לְפִי שֶׁלֹּא נַעֲשָׂה לְקַבָּלָה, וּלְפִיכָךְ מֻתָּר לְסַכֵּךְ בָּהֶם.[ל] וְכֵן מֻתָּר לְסַכֵּךְ בְּצִנּוֹר, לְפִי שֶׁלֹּא נַעֲשָׂה לְקַבָּלָה:[לא,14]

5 If one used stalks of flax that are yet to be crushed in a mortar[15] and brushed out with a comb,[16] they are valid [as *s'chach*],[17] because they are still recognizable as plants.[18] If, however, the fibers have been crushed in a mortar, even though they have not been brushed out with a comb, they are invalid by a Rabbinic ordinance, because they have been so transformed that they [no longer] appear to be products of the earth.

Similarly, cotton or hemp that has been

ה סִיכְּכָהּ בְּפִשְׁתֵּי הָעֵץ, שֶׁלֹּא דָּךְ אוֹתָן בְּמַכְתֶּשֶׁת[15] וְלֹא נִפֵּץ אוֹתָן בְּמַסְרֵק[16] — כְּשֵׁרָה,[לב,17] שֶׁעֲדַיִן נִכָּרִים שֶׁהֵן עֵץ.[לג,18] אֲבָל אִם דָּךְ אוֹתָן בְּמַכְתֶּשֶׁת, אַף עַל פִּי שֶׁלֹּא נִפֵּץ אוֹתָן בְּמַסְרֵק — פְּסוּלָה[לד] מִדִּבְרֵי סוֹפְרִים,[לה] לְפִי שֶׁנִּשְׁתַּנֵּית צוּרָתָן וּכְאִלּוּ אֵינָ[ן] מִגִּדּוּלֵי קַרְקַע.[לו] וְהוּא הַדִּין צֶמֶר גֶּפֶן אוֹ קַנָּבוֹס שֶׁנִּפֵּץ אוֹתָן —

13. If they have been inserted into the arrowhead, they are considered as its handle, and hence are susceptible to ritual impurity and invalid as *s'chach*.

14. *Mikvaos* 4:3.

15. Presumably an elongated mortar.

16. I.e., unprocessed flax, such as that in which Rachav hid the spies in Jericho *(Yehoshua* 2:6*)*.

17. *Sukkah, loc. cit.*

18. Lit., "wood."

כד רש"י יב, ב ד"ה סככה וד"ה זכרים וד"ה נקבות. **כה** גמרא שם. טור ושו"ע ס"ג. **כו** מ"א שם. ב"ח ד"ה סככה, בפירוש דברי השלטי גבורים שם, בשם הריא"ז (שאם יש בהם ברזל מקבלים טומאה ע"י הברזל). **כז** גמרא שם. וראה לקמן סי"א (בסולם). **כח** רש"י שם ד"ה העשוי. **כט** גמרא שם. טור ושו"ע שם. **ל** שו"ת הרא"ש כלל כד סי' יב. הובא ב"י ד"ה סככה. לבוש ס"ג. מ"א סוף סק"ב. **לא** מקוואות פ"ד מ"ג. רא"ש שם. ב"י ומ"א שם. וראה גם לקמן ס"ח (במוסגר). **לב** גמרא יב, ב. רי"ף (ו, ב). רמב"ם פ"ה ה"ד. רא"ש פ"א סי' כד. טור ושו"ע ס"ד. **לג** רי"ף ורמב"ם ורא"ש שם (דעדיין עץ הוא). וכדלקמן בסמוך, שתלוי אם ניכר ולא נשתנית צורתה. **לד** ספק דרבה בר בר חנה שם. אליה זוטא סק"ג בשם תניא רבתא סי' פב (ענין הסוכה). **לה** תוס' שם ד"ה באניצי. ב"י ד"ה בפשתן. הגהת הלבוש שם. מ"א סק"ג. **לו** רמב"ם שם. ט"ז ס"ק ו. **לז** ב"ח סוד"ה בפשתן. מ"א שם. **לח** מ"א שם.

combed out may not be used as *s'chach.* Neither may husks of flax broken off as the flax [was crushed] be used as *s'chach.*

6 Ropes made of reed-grass or palm-tree bast may be used as *s'chach,*[19] because ropes are not susceptible to ritual impurity, having no receptacle. Ropes made of flax or hemp, by contrast, may not be used as *s'chach,* because they have been so transformed that they [no longer] appear to be products of the earth.

7 [The following rules apply with regard to covering a *sukkah* with] a mat made of reeds, straw, grass, or rushes,[20] whether or not the mat is smooth and thus fit to lie on.

If [a mat] is small, i.e., it is only large enough to lie on, it is presumably intended to be used for [that purpose]. Thus it is susceptible to ritual impurity[21] if a *zav*[22] would lie on it. Hence it may not be used as *s'chach* even if a *zav* has not yet lain on it.

An exception is made if [such a mat] was made with the intent that it be used as a covering. [It is also permissible] if it was purchased with that intent from a craftsman, because [he] makes mats without any specific intent, seeking to sell them to whoever needs them, each person for his own particular need. Therefore, it is the purchaser's intent at the time of acquisition that defines its purpose. If he intended to use it for shade,

אֵין מְסַכְּכִין בָּהֶם.[לז] וְכֵן נְעֹרֶת שֶׁל פִּשְׁתָּן הַנִּדָּק מִן הַפִּשְׁתָּן – אֵין מְסַכְּכִין בּוֹ:[לח]

ו מְסַכְּכִין בַּחֲבָלִים שֶׁל גֶּמִי וְשֶׁל סִיב,[לט] לְפִי שֶׁהַחֲבָלִים אֵין מְקַבְּלִין טֻמְאָה, שֶׁאֵין לָהֶם בֵּית קִבּוּל,[מ,19] אֲבָל חֲבָלִים שֶׁל פִּשְׁתָּן וְשֶׁל קַנְבּוֹס – אֵין מְסַכְּכִין בָּהֶן,[מא] מִפְּנֵי שֶׁנִּשְׁתַּנָּה צוּרָתוֹ וּכְאִלּוּ אֵינוֹ מִגִּדּוּלֵי קַרְקַע:[מב]

ז מַחֲצֶלֶת שֶׁל קָנִים[מג] וְשֶׁל קַשׁ[מד] וְשֶׁל גֶּמִי וְשֶׁל שִׁפָּה,[מה,20] בֵּין שֶׁהִיא חֲלָקָה שֶׁרְאוּיָה לִשְׁכִיבָה, בֵּין שֶׁאֵינָהּ חֲלָקָה,[מו] אִם הִיא קְטַנָּה,[מז] דְּהַיְנוּ שֶׁאֵין בָּהּ אֶלָּא כְּדֵי שְׁכִיבָה[מח] – סְתָמָא עוֹמֶדֶת לִשְׁכִיבָה[מט] וּרְאוּיָה לְקַבֵּל טֻמְאָה[21] אִם יִשְׁכַּב עָלֶיהָ הַזָּב,[22] וּלְפִיכָךְ אֵין מְסַכְּכִין בָּהּ אֲפִלּוּ עֲדַיִן לֹא שָׁכַב עָלֶיהָ הַזָּב;[נ] אֶלָּא אִם כֵּן עֲשָׂאָהּ לְסִכּוּךְ,[נא] אוֹ שֶׁלְּקָחָהּ מִן הָאֻמָּן כְּדֵי לְסַכֵּךְ בָּהּ, שֶׁהָאֻמָּן עוֹשֶׂה בִּסְתָם לְמָכְרָן לְמִי שֶׁצָּרִיךְ לָהֶן כָּל אֶחָד וְאֶחָד לְפִי צָרְכּוֹ, וְאִם כֵּן יֵשׁ לֵילֵךְ אַחַר דַּעַת הַלּוֹקֵחַ בְּעֵת קְנִיָּתוֹ,[נב] וְאִם דַּעְתּוֹ לְסִכּוּךְ, אַף עַל פִּי שֶׁיֵּשׁ לָהּ שָׂפָה[נג] בְּעִנְיַן

19. *Talmud Yerushalmi, Sukkah* 1:5.

20. *Sukkah* 19b-20a.

21. Of the category called *midras,* which is defined by *Rambam* in *Hilchos Metam'ei Mishkav U'Moshav* 7:1.

22. I.e., a male who has a discharge resembling gonorrhea and whose ritual impurity is imparted to various substances. (See *Vayikra,* ch. 15, and commentaries.)

לט ירושלמי פ"א ה"ה. רמב"ם פ"ה ה"ד. טור ושו"ע ס"ה. מ מ"מ שם. ב"י ד"ה בחבלים. מא ירושלמי שם. מ"מ שם. טור ושו"ע שם. מב מ"מ שם. ב"י שם. מ"א סק"ד. מג משנה יט, ב. טור ושו"ע ס"ו. מד רא"ש פ"א סי' לז. טור ושו"ע שם. מה ברייתא כ, א. טור ושו"ע שם. מו כרבי יוסי ורבי דוסא בברייתא שם. רא"ש שם בדעת הרי"ף. טור ושו"ע שם. מז רב פפא בגמרא שם אליבא דכו"ע. טור ושו"ע שם. מח ר"ן (ט, ב) ד"ה גמרא אסקה. ב"י ד"ה ומ"ש מחצלת. לבוש ס"ו. מט רב פפא שם. טור ושו"ע שם. נ ר"ן שם. ב"י שם. וכדלעיל ס"א (שראוי). נא רש"י שם ד"ה אלא. טור ושו"ע שם. נב רא"ש פ"א סי' לז, וטור, בשם ה"ר ישעיה (אף במקום שהמנהג להשתמש בהם לשכיבה, ובזה חולקים עליו). ט"ז ס"ק ז (במקום שאין מנהג מבורר, לדברי הכל). וראה לקמן ס"ט. נג שו"ת רדב"ז ח"א סי' צז [ח"ד סי' א'קסח]. מ"א סק"ו.

שֶׁרְאוּיָה לְקַבָּלָה – אַף עַל פִּי כֵן אֵינָהּ מְקַבֶּלֶת טֻמְאָה, וְקִבּוּל זֶה אֵינוֹ חָשׁוּב כְּלוּם, כֵּיוָן שֶׁהַמַּחְצֶלֶת אֵינָהּ עֲשׂוּיָה לְקַבָּלָה:[נד]

it is not susceptible to ritual impurity, even if it has a rim and could thus serve as a receptacle. This factor is not significant, since this mat was not intended for use as a container.

ח אֲבָל אִם הִיא גְּדוֹלָה יוֹתֵר מִכְּדֵי שְׁכִיבָה – סְתָמָא עוֹמֶדֶת לְסִכּוּךְ,[נה] וַאֲפִלּוּ אִם יִשְׁכַּב עָלֶיהָ הַזָּב – אֵינָהּ מְקַבֶּלֶת טֻמְאָה[נו] כֵּיוָן שֶׁאֵינָהּ מְיֻחֶדֶת לִשְׁכִיבָה, וְלָכֵן מְסַכְּכִין בָּהּ.

בַּמֶּה דְּבָרִים אֲמוּרִים? כְּשֶׁאֵין לָהּ שָׂפָה מְקֻפֶּת, אֲבָל אִם יֵשׁ לָהּ שָׂפָה מְקֻפֶּת[נז] (מֵאַרְבַּע רוּחוֹתֶיהָ[נח]) בְּעִנְיָן שֶׁרְאוּיָה לְקַבָּלָה – אֵין מְסַכְּכִין בָּהּ,[23] לְפִי שֶׁסְּתָמָא עֲשׂוּיָה גַּם לְתַשְׁמִישׁ לִתֵּן פֵּרוֹת עַל גַּבָּהּ[נט] (וַאֲפִלּוּ אִם נִטַּל שְׂפָתָהּ – אֵין מְסַכְּכִין בָּהּ,[ס] כְּמוֹ שֶׁאֵין מְסַכְּכִים בְּשִׁבְרֵי כֵלִים[סא] כְּמוֹ שֶׁנִּתְבָּאֵר[סב]):

8 If, by contrast, a mat is larger than what a person would lie on, it was presumably intended to be used for shade. It would therefore not contract ritual impurity even if a *zav* would lie on it, because it was not designated [for that purpose]. It may therefore be used as *s'chach*.

When does the above apply? When it is not surrounded by a rim. If, however, it has a rim (around all its four sides), so that it is fit for use as a receptacle, it may not be used as *s'chach*,[23] because it was presumably intended to serve a function, [e.g.,] for fruit to be laid on it [to dry]. (Moreover, even if that rim is removed, the mat may not be used as *s'chach*, just as broken utensils may not be used for that purpose, as explained [in subsection 2 above].)

ט וְכָל זֶה בְּמָקוֹם שֶׁאֵין מִנְהָג מְבֹרָר בְּתַשְׁמִישֵׁי הַמַּחְצָלָאוֹת,[סג] אֲבָל בְּמָקוֹם שֶׁהַמִּנְהָג שֶׁל רֹב בְּנֵי הָעִיר לְהִשְׁתַּמֵּשׁ בְּמַחְצָלָאוֹת קְטַנּוֹת לְסִכּוּךְ – מֻתָּר לְסַכֵּךְ בָּהֶן אֲפִלּוּ בִּסְתָם מַחְצֶלֶת קְטַנָּה,[סד] אֶלָּא אִם כֵּן יָדוּעַ שֶׁנַּעֲשׂוּ לִשְׁכִיבָה. וּבְמָקוֹם שֶׁמִּנְהַג רֹב בְּנֵי הָעִיר לְהִשְׁתַּמֵּשׁ בְּמַחְצָלָאוֹת גְּדוֹלוֹת לִשְׁכִיבָה[סה] כְּמוֹ שֶׁהַמִּנְהָג הוּא בִּמְקוֹמוֹת הָאֵלּוּ[סו, 24] – אֵין מְסַכְּכִין בְּמַחְצֶלֶת גְּדוֹלָה.

9 All the above [principles] apply in a place that has no clearly fixed custom with regard to the use of mats. In a place where the custom of most of the townsmen is to use [even] small mats for shade, such mats may be used as *s'chach*. [This applies even] to a small mat of undefined purpose, unless it is known that it was made to be lain upon.

In a place where most of the townsmen are accustomed to using large mats to lie upon, as is the custom in these regions,[24] a large mat may not be used for *s'chach*, even

---

23. *Sukkah* 20b.

24. I.e., in Europe.

נד רדב"ז שם. נה רב פפא כ, א בדעת בדעת תנא קמא במשנה יט, ב. טור ושו"ע ס"ו. נו ר"ן (ט, ב) ד"ה גמרא אסקה. ב"י ד"ה ומ"ש מחצלת. נז גמרא כ, ב. רש"י שם ד"ה גדנפא. טור ושו"ע שם. נח ראה מקוואות פ"ד מ"ב, ופירוש הרא"ש שם. שו"ע יו"ד סי' רא ריש סל"ו. וכדלעיל סוף ס"ד וש"נ. נט רש"י שם. ס טור ושו"ע שם. סא ב"י ד"ה ומ"ש שאפילו. לבוש ס"ו. סב סעיף ב. סג ט"ז סק"ז. וראה גם מ"א ס"ק ז. סד רא"ש פ"א סי' לז. רמ"א ס"ו. לבוש שם. סה ב"ח ד"ה כתב ה"ר ישעיה. סה רא"ש שם. טור. לבוש שם. סו מ"א סק"ה, בשם מעגלי צדק (קצת דיני סוכה בקצור). סז טור בשם רא"ש שם. לבוש שם.

if it is known that this mat was made for the purpose of shade, because of the impression that might be created.[25] Not everyone will know [the purpose for which it was made, and people] will say that it was made to lie upon, as is the prevailing custom in the city.[26]

וַאֲפִלּוּ אִם יָדוּעַ שֶׁמַּחְצֶלֶת זוֹ נַעֲשֵׂית לְסִכּוּךְ — אֵין לְסַכֵּךְ בָּהּ, מִפְּנֵי מַרְאִית הָעַיִן[25] שֶׁאֵין הַכֹּל יוֹדְעִין בָּזֶה וְיֹאמְרוּ שֶׁנַּעֲשֵׂית לִשְׁכִיבָה כְּמוֹ שֶׁהוּא מִנְהַג רֹב בְּנֵי הָעִיר:[סז,26]

10 Similarly, in a place where it is customary to fix mats in a roof to serve as a ceiling, mats may not be used as *s'chach*, even if they were made for use as *s'chach* and thus are not susceptible to ritual impurity. [This safeguard] was enacted lest a person sit [in his house] under the ceiling that is made of mats and say, "What is the difference between these mats and those?" And the mats used for the ceiling of a house are invalid according to Scriptural Law, for they were not affixed in place for the purpose of shade, but rather [to complete] a dwelling.

י וְכֵן בְּמָקוֹם שֶׁנּוֹהֲגִים לִקְבֹּעַ מַחְצְלָאוֹת בַּגַּגִּין כְּעֵין תִּקְרָה — אֵין מְסַכְּכִין בָּהֶן,[סח] אֲפִלּוּ נַעֲשׂוּ לְסִכּוּךְ שֶׁאֵינָן מְקַבְּלִין טֻמְאָה, גְּזֵרָה שֶׁמָּא יֵשֵׁב תַּחַת תִּקְרַת הַבַּיִת[סט] הָעֲשׂוּיָה מִמַּחְצְלָאוֹת, שֶׁיֹּאמַר מַה בֵּין מַחְצְלָאוֹת אֵלּוּ לְמַחְצְלָאוֹת אֵלּוּ,[ע] וּמַחְצְלָאוֹת שֶׁל תִּקְרַת הַבַּיִת פְּסוּלִין מִן הַתּוֹרָה, שֶׁלֹּא הֻקְבְּעוּ שָׁם לְשֵׁם צֵל אֶלָּא לְשֵׁם דִּירָה:[עא]

11 There is a question as to whether a ladder is susceptible to ritual impurity. [It might be argued that since] it has no receptacle, it is like all flat wooden implements,[27] which are not susceptible to ritual impurity.[28] Alternatively, it is possible that the holes into which the rungs of the ladder are wedged resemble receptacles, in which case [a ladder] may not be used as *s'chach*.

[Furthermore,] as the initial and preferred option,[29] one should be careful not to lay [a ladder] on the roof so that the *s'chach*

יא הַסֻּלָּם — יֵשׁ לְהִסְתַּפֵּק בּוֹ[עב] אִם הוּא מְקַבֵּל טֻמְאָה, לְפִי שֶׁאֵין בּוֹ בֵּית קִבּוּל וַהֲרֵי הוּא כִּשְׁאָר כָּל פְּשׁוּטֵי כְלֵי עֵץ[27] שֶׁאֵינָן מְקַבְּלִין טֻמְאָה,[28] אוֹ אֶפְשָׁר שֶׁהַנְּקָבִים שֶׁהַשְּׁלִיבוֹת תְּקוּעוֹת בָּהֶן הֵן דּוֹמִין לְבֵית קִבּוּל, וּלְפִיכָךְ אֵין לְסַכֵּךְ בּוֹ.[עג]

וּלְכַתְּחִלָּה[29] יֵשׁ לִזָּהֵר שֶׁלֹּא לְהַנִּיחָהּ עַל גַּבֵּי הַגָּג כְּדֵי לְהַנִּיחַ עָלָיו הַסְּכָךְ,[עד]

---

25. In the original, *mipnei maris haayin* (lit., "because of what the eye sees").

26. Some communities today use mats made specifically for *s'chach*. This does not contradict the above ruling, because: (a) mats are not commonly used today as they once were, so it is not appropriate to assume that they are used primarily to lie upon; (b) it is well known that such mats are made for use as *s'chach*, so it is less likely that a mistaken impression will be created.

27. In the original, *peshutei klei etz*. (*Keli* can also mean: object, utensil, or piece of equipment.)

28. *Keilim* 15:1.

29. In the original, *lechat'chilah*.

סח כלבו סי' עא (לז, ב). רמ"א ס"ו. **סט** ט"ז סק"ח. **ע** כמו בנסרים ד' טפחים, דלקמן סכ"ט וש"נ. **עא** כדלעיל סי' תרכו ס"א. לקמן שם. **עב** שו"ת הרשב"א ח"א סי' קצו, ובמיוחסות סי' רטו. הובא בתרומת הדשן סי' צ. שו"ע ס"ז. **עג** ט"ז סק"ז. מ"א ס"ק ח. שו"ת הרשב"א ח"א רס"י קצה. וכדלעיל ס"ג (בבית יד הנקבות של חצים). **עד** תרומת הדשן שם, בדעת הרשב"א שם. שו"ע שם.

וְכֵן שֶׁלֹּא לְהַנִּיחוֹ עַל גַּבֵּי הַסְּכָךְ כְּדֵי לְהַחֲזִיקוֹ[עה] שֶׁלֹּא יְפַזְּרֶנּוּ הָרוּחַ. וְהוּא הַדִּין שֶׁאֵין מְחַזְּקִין[עו] וְאֵין מַעֲמִידִין[עז] אֶת הַסְּכָךְ לְכַתְּחִלָּה בְּכָל דָּבָר שֶׁרָאוּי לְקַבֵּל טֻמְאָה כְּגוֹן כִּסֵּא וְסַפְסָל,[עח,30] גְּזֵרָה שֶׁמָּא יְסַכֵּךְ בָּהֶן:[עט]

can be placed upon it, nor to lay it on the *s'chach* in order to hold it in place so that it will not be scattered by the wind. Similarly, as an initial and preferred option, no [other] object that is susceptible to ritual impurity, such as a chair or a bench, should be used to hold the *s'chach* in place or to support it.[30] This [safeguard] was ordained lest [such objects] be used for the actual *s'chach*.

יב בַּמֶּה דְּבָרִים אֲמוּרִים? כְּשֶׁהַסִּכּוּךְ בְּעַצְמוֹ מֻנָּח עַל גַּבֵּי דָּבָר שֶׁמְּקַבֵּל טֻמְאָה, אוֹ שֶׁדָּבָר הַמְקַבֵּל טֻמְאָה מֻנָּח עַל גַּבֵּי הַסְּכָךְ מַמָּשׁ וּמַחֲזִיקוֹ, אֲבָל אִם הַסְּכָךְ מֻנָּח עַל גַּבֵּי כְּלוֹנְסָאוֹת אוֹ עַל גַּבֵּי יְתֵדוֹת וְהֵן מֻנָּחִים עַל גַּבֵּי דָּבָר הַמְקַבֵּל טֻמְאָה — אֵין בְּכָךְ כְּלוּם,[פ] וּמֻתָּר לַעֲשׂוֹת כֵּן לְכַתְּחִלָּה,[פא] וְאַף עַל פִּי שֶׁדָּבָר הַמַּעֲמִיד וּמַחֲזִיק אֶת הַסְּכָךְ נִסְמָךְ עַל גַּבֵּי דָּבָר הַפָּסוּל לְסִכּוּךְ — אֵין בְּכָךְ כְּלוּם, שֶׁהֲרֵי כָּל סֻכָּה שֶׁבָּעוֹלָם מַעֲמִידֵי הַסְּכָךְ הֵן נִסְמָכִים עַל גַּבֵּי קַרְקַע עוֹלָם[פב] הַפְּסוּלָה לְסִכּוּךְ:[פג]

12 When does the above apply? When the *s'chach* itself was placed on an object that is susceptible to ritual impurity, or when [such an object] was placed on the *s'chach* itself to hold it in place. By contrast, [no problem is involved] if the *s'chach* is placed on beams or pegs, and they are placed on an object that is susceptible to ritual impurity. It is permitted to do this [even] as an initial and preferred option. It is of no consequence that the object that supports the *s'chach* or holds it in place is supported by something that is invalid as *s'chach* — for the supports for the *s'chach* of every *sukkah* in the world are supported by the ground, which is invalid as *s'chach*.

יג וְכָל זֶה לְכַתְּחִלָּה,[29] אֲבָל בְּדִיעֲבַד[פד,31] שֶׁכְּבָר הֶעֱמִיד אֶת הַסְּכָךְ עַצְמוֹ בְּדָבָר הַמְקַבֵּל טֻמְאָה — מֻתָּר לֵישֵׁב בָּהּ[32] לְכַתְּחִלָּה.[פה,33]

13 All of this applies at the outset.[29] After the fact,[31] if one already supported the *s'chach* itself with something that is susceptible to ritual impurity, one may sit in [such a *sukkah*][32] [even] as an initial and preferred option.[33]

---

30. Similarly, ropes should not be used to support the *s'chach* directly, nor to hold it down (*Mishnah Berurah* 629:26). However, ropes may be used to secure pieces of wood which will in turn hold the *s'chach* in place.

31. In the original Aramaic, *bediavad* (often loosely pronounced *bedieved*).

32. And fulfill one's obligation thereby.

33. I.e., even if the above preference was not observed when the *sukkah* was being constructed, there is no need to hesitate about using the *sukkah* afterwards.

עה מהרי"ל הל' סוכה (ע' שסג). רמ"א ס"ז. מ"א סוף סק"ט. **עו** מהרי"ל שם. רמ"א שם. **עז** ר"ן (י, א) ד"ה ולענין הלכה כיון. מ"א סק"ט. וראה גם לעיל סי' תרכח ס"ז. **עח** מהרי"ל שם. רמ"א שם. **עט** ר"ן שם. מ"א שם. **פ** ריטב"א כא, ב ד"ה וחד אמר. ר"ן (י, א) ד"ה מתני' הסומך, בשם הרמב"ן במלחמות שם. הובא ב"י סוס"י תרל. מ"א סוף סק"ט. **פא** מ"א שם. **פב** ראה רמב"ן שם. ריטב"א שם. **פג** כדלעיל ס"א (עפר). **פד** מ"א סוף סק"ט. **פה** משמעות

וַאֲפִלּוּ לְכַתְּחִלָּה מֻתָּר לְהַנִּיחַ אֶת הַסְּכָךְ עַצְמוֹ עַל גַּבֵּי הַדְּפָנוֹת[פו] אֲפִלּוּ אִם הֵן מִן הַפָּסוּל לְסִכּוּךְ,[פז] כְּגוֹן חוֹמַת אֲבָנִים,[34] לְפִי שֶׁאֵין לִגְזֹר שֶׁמָּא יְסַכֵּךְ סֻכָּתוֹ בַּאֲבָנִים, שֶׁהַכֹּל יוֹדְעִין שֶׁהָאֲבָנִים פְּסוּלִין לְסִכּוּךְ,[פח] שֶׁהֲרֵי אֵין זוֹ סֻכָּה כְּלָל אֶלָּא כְּעֵין בֵּית דִּירַת קֶבַע.[פט, 35]

Moreover, even as an initial and preferred option, it is permitted to rest the *s'chach* itself on the walls of the *sukkah* even though they are made of materials that are invalid as *s'chach*, as is the case with a stone wall.[34] [The rationale is that] there is no need to ordain such [a safeguard] for fear that someone might use stones as *s'chach;* everyone knows that stones are invalid as *s'chach*, for this would not be a *sukkah* at all, but a kind of permanent dwelling.[35]

וְכֵן מֻתָּר לְכַתְּחִלָּה לְחַבֵּר כְּלוֹנְסָאוֹת הַסֻּכָּה שֶׁהַסְּכָךְ מֻנָּח עָלֶיהָ לְדָפְנוֹת הַסֻּכָּה עַל יְדֵי מַסְמְרִים שֶׁל בַּרְזֶל, אוֹ לְקָשְׁרָן בַּחֲתִיכוֹת בְּגָדִים הַמְקַבְּלִין טֻמְאָה,[צ] כֵּיוָן שֶׁהַסְּכָךְ עַצְמוֹ מֻנָּח עַל גַּבֵּי כְּלוֹנְסָאוֹת שֶׁאֵינָן מְקַבְּלִין טֻמְאָה וּכְשֵׁרִים לְסִכּוּךְ:[צא]

Similarly, [even] as an initial and preferred option, it is permitted to attach the beams — on which the *s'chach* rests — to the walls of the *sukkah* with iron nails or tie them with pieces of cloth that are susceptible to ritual impurity. [This is permitted,] because the *s'chach* itself is placed on beams which are not susceptible to ritual impurity and which are valid as *s'chach*.

יד כָּל פְּשׁוּטֵי כְּלֵי עֵץ הָרְחָבִים קְצָת וְרָאוּי לְהַנִּיחַ עֲלֵיהֶם דָּבָר, כְּגוֹן שֻׁלְחָן וּמַגְרֵפָה וּמַרְדֶּה – גָּזְרוּ חֲכָמִים עֲלֵיהֶם טֻמְאָה, לְפִי שֶׁהֵן דּוֹמִין לְבֵית קִבּוּל, לְפִיכָךְ אֵין לְסַכֵּךְ בָּהֶן,[צב, 36] וְכֵן אֵין לְהַנִּיחָן עַל גַּבֵּי הַסְּכָךְ לְהַחֲזִיקוֹ, אֲפִלּוּ אִם נִשְׁבְּרוּ,[צג] כֵּיוָן שֶׁהָיוּ רְאוּיִים לְקַבֵּל טֻמְאָה שָׁעָה אַחַת – גָּזְרוּ עֲלֵיהֶן:[צד]

14 The Sages ordained that any flat wooden objects of minimal width on which something could be placed, such as a table, a spade, or a baker's trowel, are susceptible to ritual impurity, because they resemble receptacles. Therefore, they may not be used as *s'chach*,[36] nor may they be laid on the *s'chach* to hold it in place, even if they are broken. Since there was a time when they were susceptible to ritual impurity, it was ordained [that they should never be used for *s'chach*].

---

34. According to the version of some *Rishonim*, the *Talmud Yerushalmi (Sukkah*, end of 1:6*)* rules that even the walls of a *sukkah* must be made of material that is not susceptible to contract ritual impurity. (See: *Hagahos Ashri, Sukkah* 1:24; *Bach* and *Pri Megadim: Mishbetzos Zahav*, beginning of sec. 630. However, is not customary to make a point of using only materials that are valid as *s'chach* when constructing the *sukkah* walls. (See *Sefer HaMinhagim: The Book of Chabad-Lubavitch Customs*, p. 139.)

Based in subsection 13, it could be argued that *s'chach* may be laid directly on *sukkah* walls made of plastic, for example. Common practice, however, is to lay the *s'chach* on wooden beams that are placed atop the walls. (See Responsa *Minchas Yitzchak*, Vol. 4, sec. 45.)

35. See sec. 626:1.

36. See subsection 2 above.

הטור והשו"ע סוס"י תרל, עיין מ"א שם. וראה עד"ז לקמן סוף סכ"א. **פו** ריטב"א שם. ר"ן שם. רמב"ן שם. מ"א סק"ט. **פז** מ"א שם. **פח** ר"ן שם. מ"א שם. **פט** ראה לעיל סי' תרכו ס"א. **צ** תרומת הדשן סי' צא. שו"ע ס"ח. **צא** מ"א סוף סק"ט. **צב** תוס' סוכה ה, א סוד"ה מסגרתו. מ"א סוף סקי"א. וראה גם ט"ז ס"ק ה. ואם אינן מיוחדין לתשמיש, ראה לקמן סל"א. **צג** מ"א שם. **צד** כדלעיל ס"ב.

15 All the accessories[37] to food — such as the straw of ears of grain, the twigs to which grapes [are attached], and the branches to which dates [are attached] — are susceptible to ritual impurity[38] at the time they are attached to the food. [This concept is derived as follows:] From the verse,[39] "It shall be impure *for you*," the Sages inferred[40] that anything that is necessary *for you* with regard to this food, i.e., [even] the accessories, is susceptible to ritual impurity like the food itself.

The term "accessory" is applied only to [a maximum of] three handbreadths of the straw[41] of ears of grain that belong to the kinds that are harvested with a sickle; four handbreadths of date branches; and two handbreadths of the twigs to which grapes [are attached], i.e., one handbreadth to the right of the cluster [of grapes] that hangs from the branch and one handbreadth to the left. If the branches are longer than these measures, all that is susceptible to ritual impurity is the part that is within these [maximum] distances from the food.

([Different rules apply with regard to] the straw of ears of grain that belong to those varieties that are not harvested with a sickle, but are uprooted by hand. Their definition as "accessories" is not limited by their length; even if they are very long, they are considered as "accessories" and are susceptible to ritual impurity.)

טו כָּל יְדוֹת הָאֳכָלִים[צה, 37] כְּגוֹן קַשִּׁין שֶׁל שִׁבֳּלִים וּזְמוֹרוֹת שֶׁל עֲנָבִים וּמַכְבְּדוֹת שֶׁל תְּמָרִים[צו] — מְקַבְּלִין טֻמְאָה[38] בְּשָׁעָה שֶׁהֵן מְחֻבָּרִין[צז] לְהָאֹכֶל, שֶׁנֶּאֱמַר[צח, 39] "טָמֵא הוּא לָכֶם", וְדָרְשׁוּ חֲכָמִים[צט, 40] "לָכֶם" — לְכָל דָּבָר שֶׁהוּא צָרִיךְ לָכֶם בָּאֹכֶל הַזֶּה,[ק] דְּהַיְנוּ יָדוֹת,[קא] הוּא מְקַבֵּל טֻמְאָה כְּאֹכֶל עַצְמוֹ.[קב]

וְאֵינוֹ נִקְרָא יָד אֶלָּא שְׁלֹשָׁה טְפָחִים בְּקַשִּׁין שֶׁל מִין שִׁבֳּלִים[קג, 41] הַנִּקְצָרִין בְּמַגָּל (אֲבָל מִין שִׁבֳּלִים שֶׁאֵין דַּרְכָּן לְהִקָּצֵר בְּמַגָּל אֶלָּא עוֹקְרִין אוֹתָן בַּיָּד — אֵין שִׁעוּר לִידוֹתֵיהֶן,[קד] שֶׁאֲפִלּוּ הֵן אֲרֻכִּין הַרְבֵּה הֵן מְקַבְּלִים טֻמְאָה מִשּׁוּם יָד), וְאַרְבָּעָה טְפָחִים בְּמַכְבְּדוֹת שֶׁל תְּמָרִים,[קה] וּשְׁנֵי טְפָחִים בִּזְמוֹרוֹת שֶׁל עֲנָבִים, דְּהַיְנוּ טֶפַח אֶחָד מִימִין הָאֶשְׁכּוֹל הַתָּלוּי בַּזְּמוֹרָה וְטֶפַח אֶחָד מִשְּׂמֹאלוֹ.[קו] אֲבָל אִם הֵן אֲרֻכִּים יוֹתֵר מִשִּׁעוּר הַזֶּה — אֵין מְקַבֵּל טֻמְאָה אֶלָּא מַה שֶּׁהוּא סָמוּךְ לְהָאֹכֶל כַּשִּׁעוּר הַזֶּה:[קז]

16 Therefore, [the following law applies if] a person covered his *sukkah* with the straw of ears of grain, twigs to which grapes [are attached], and branches [laden] with dates.

טז לְפִיכָךְ הַמְסַכֵּךְ סֻכָּתוֹ בְּקַשִּׁין שֶׁל שִׁבֳּלִים וּבִזְמוֹרוֹת וּבָהֶן עֲנָבִים וּבְמַכְבְּדוֹת וּבָהֶן תְּמָרִים,

37. In the original, *yados* (lit., "handles").

38. *Uktzin* 1:1; *Sukkah* 13b.

39. *Vayikra* 11:38.

40. *Chullin* 118a.

41. *Uktzin* 1:3.

צה משנה עוקצין פ"א מ"א. רמב"ם הל' טומאת אוכלין פ"ה ה"א. צו גמרא [ברייתא] יג, ב (שם גם: סוכי תאנים. ולא נתפרש שיעורו במשנה דלקמן). צז רמב"ם שם ה"ה. צח ויקרא יא, לח. צט חולין קיח, א. רמב"ם שם. ק רש"י שם ד"ה טמא הוא לכם. קא חולין שם. קב רש"י שם ד"ה טמא. קג משנה שם מ"ג. רמב"ם שם ה"כ. שו"ת הרא"ש כלל כד סי' יד. מ"א ס"ק יב. קד משנה שם. רמב"ם שם. מ"א שם. קה משנה שם. רמב"ם שם. קו משנה שם ופירוש ר"ש שם. והיינו כשכרת את האשכולות עם הזמורה. קז מ"א שם. וראה גם רש"י יג, ב ד"ה על הידות. קח גמרא [ברייתא] יג, ב כת"ק. רא"ש פ"א סי' כז.

אִם אֵין הַקַּשִּׁין וְהַזְּמוֹרוֹת וְהַמַּכְבְּדוֹת אֲרֻכִּין כָּל כָּךְ עַד שֶׁיְּהֵא בָּהֶן רֹב נֶגֶד הָאֹכֶל וְהַיָּד שֶׁלּוֹ — הֲרֵי הִיא פְּסוּלָה.[קח,42]

בַּמֶּה דְּבָרִים אֲמוּרִים? כְּשֶׁקָּצַר אוֹ בָּצַר אוֹתָן לַאֲכִילָה,[קט] שֶׁאָז צָרִיךְ חִבּוּר הַיָּד עִם הָאֹכֶל לֶאֱחֹז בּוֹ אֶת הָאֹכֶל,[קי,43] אֲבָל אִם קְצָרָן וּבְצָרָן לְסִכּוּךְ,[קיא] שֶׁאָז אֵין נוֹחַ לוֹ חִבּוּר הַיָּד עִם הָאֹכֶל, שֶׁהֲרֵי הָאֹכֶל פּוֹסֵל סֻכָּתוֹ,[קיב,44] וְלָכֵן אֵין הַיָּד מְקַבֵּל טֻמְאָה, שֶׁאֵין הַיָּד מְקַבֵּל טֻמְאָה אֶלָּא מֵחֲמַת שֶׁהוּא טָפֵל וּמְשַׁמֵּשׁ לָאֹכֶל וְנֶחְשָׁב כָּאֹכֶל עַצְמוֹ,[קיג] מַה שֶּׁאֵין כֵּן אֹכֶל זֶה שֶׁאֵין צָרִיךְ לוֹ כְּלָל לְסִכּוּךְ שֶׁבִּשְׁבִילוֹ קְצָרוֹ וְאֵין הַיָּד טָפֵל אֵלָיו, וּלְפִיכָךְ הַיָּד מִצְטָרֵף עִם שְׁאָר אֹרֶךְ הַקַּשִּׁין וְהַזְּמוֹרוֹת לְבַטֵּל אֶת הָאֹכֶל בְּרֹב:[קיד]

If the straw, the twigs, and the branches are not long enough to constitute a majority when compared to the food and to [that part of the straw, twigs, or branches that is considered] its "accessory," [the *s'chach*] is invalid.[42]

When does the above apply? When the grain was reaped or the fruit was harvested for food. In such a situation, the "accessory" must be connected to the food so that the food can be held.[43]

If, by contrast, one reaped or harvested [the grain or the fruit] for the purpose of *s'chach,* he is not happy to have the "accessory" connected to the food, for the food will disqualify his *sukkah.*[44] The "accessory" is therefore not susceptible to ritual impurity, for it is [ordinarily] susceptible to ritual impurity only because it is a subordinate auxiliary to food, and hence is considered to be like the food itself. In this instance, by contrast, the food is not at all needed for use as *s'chach,* and that was the purpose for which this person reaped. Hence, the "accessory" is not considered as subordinate to [the food. That part of the straw and the twigs that is considered as] an "accessory" therefore combines with the remainder of the length of the straw and the twigs to make the food *batel* — insignificant and therefore nullified — *vis-à-vis* the majority [of valid *s'chach*].

יז וְאִם מִתְּחִלָּה קְצָרָן וּבְצָרָן לַאֲכִילָה וְאַחַר כָּךְ נִמְלַךְ עֲלֵיהֶן לְסִכּוּךְ[קטו] — אֵין הַמַּחֲשָׁבָה מוֹצִיאָה אֶת הַיָּדוֹת מִידֵי קַבָּלַת טֻמְאָה,[42] עַד שֶׁיַּעֲשֶׂה בָּהֶן מַעֲשֶׂה שֶׁנִּכָּר[קטז] כְּשֶׁקָּצַר אוֹ בָּצַר[קיז] שֶׁרוֹצֶה אוֹתָם לְסִכּוּךְ וְלֹא לַאֲכִילָה, כְּגוֹן

17 If at the outset, a person harvested and reaped [the grain or fruit] with the intent of using them for food, and then changed his mind, and decided to use [the branches] for *s'chach,* his [change of] intent does not change the status of the accessories and remove their susceptibility to ritual impurity.[42] [To do that,] he must do something to them that indicates that when he reaped or harvested, it was with the intent of using them for *s'chach* and not for food; e.g.,

---

42. *Sukkah* 13b.

43. I.e., by its stem.

44. It is invalid as *s'chach;* see subsection 1 above.

טור ושו"ע ס"י. **קט** גמרא שם. רא"ש שם. טור ושו"ע שם. **קי** ראה רש"י שם ד"ה הבוצר. **קיא** רב מנשיא בר גדא אמר רב הונא שם. **קיב** רש"י שם ד"ה הקוצר. **קיג** ראה רא"ש שם (חשיבי כאוכל). רמב"ם שם הי"ד (נחשב כאוכל). **קיד** ברייתא שם כת"ק. טור ושו"ע שם. וראה לעיל סי' תרכו ס"ה ואילך (אופני ביטולו ברוב). **קטו** גמרא שם. טור ושו"ע שם. **קטז** טור ושו"ע שם. **קיז** משא"כ אח"כ לא מהני, כדעיל ס"ב. וראה דברי נחמי' סוכה שם. מ"מ וציונים.

שֶׁיָּדוּשׁ אוֹתָן בְּמַקָּבוֹת אוֹ בְּרַגְלֵי בְּהֵמָה:[קיח, 45]

he must thresh them with mallets or with animal hooves.[45]

יח כָּל שֶׁהוּא מַאֲכַל בְּהֵמָה וְאֵין בְּנֵי אָדָם אוֹכְלִין אוֹתָן אֶלָּא לִרְפוּאָה,[קיט] כְּגוֹן פינו"גי הַנִּקְרָא בְּעַרְבִי שׁוּמ"ר[46] — מְסַכְּכִין בּוֹ לְכַתְּחִלָּה:[קכ]

18 Any [plant] that is primarily used as animal fodder and is consumed by humans only for medicinal purposes, such as *finugee,* which is called *shumar* in Arabic,[46] may be used for *s'chach* as an initial and preferred option.

יט סִכֵּךְ בִּירָקוֹת שֶׁמְּמַהֲרִים לְהִתְיַבֵּשׁ[קכא] תּוֹךְ שִׁבְעָה יָמִים[קכב, 47] וְלִפֹּל הֶעָלִין עַד שֶׁיִּשָּׁאֵר אֲוִיר[קכג, 42] — הֲרֵי הֵן חֲשׁוּבִין כְּאִלּוּ נָפְלוּ מִיָּד[קכד] אַף עַל פִּי שֶׁעֲדַיִן לֹא יָבְשׁוּ,[קכה] וּפוֹסְלִין אֶת הַסֻּכָּה[קכו] אֲפִלּוּ מִן הַצַּד בִּשְׁלֹשָׁה טְפָחִים[קכז] כְּדִין אֲוִיר, כְּמוֹ שֶׁיִּתְבָּאֵר בְּסִימָן תרל"ב.[קכח, 48]

19 If one used for *s'chach* vegetables that will dry within seven days,[47] and their leaves will fall, leaving open space,[42] [the leaves] are considered from the outset as if they have [already] fallen, even though they have not yet dried. Hence, [an area of] three handbreadths of them – even if they are at the side [of the *sukkah*] – disqualifies the *sukkah* as empty space would, as will be explained in sec. 632.[48]

---

45. In which instance the stalks are no longer effective as "handles" to the food.

The Alter Rebbe's ruling reflects the principle that to change the status of an object that was established through thought (the intent of the person while reaping), a change of mind, i.e., another thought (the intent later to use it for *s'chach*), is not sufficient. A deed (threshing the food) must be performed.

However, the Alter Rebbe's wording differs somewhat from that of the *Tur* and the *Shulchan Aruch* of R. Yosef Caro (629:10). The *Shulchan Aruch* states: "If one reaped them to eat, and changed one's mind and decided to use them for *s'chach,* the intent does not negate the categorization of the accessories as food. [This cannot occur] until one performs a deed that indicates that one desires them for *s'chach….*"

By contrast, the Alter Rebbe writes that "he must do something to them that indicates that when he reaped or harvested, it was with the intent of using them for *s'chach….*" The Alter Rebbe's meaning here is unclear: Since at the time these stalks were harvested for food, how could a later action redefine the original intent?

The author of *Divrei Nechemiah,* R. Nechemiah of Dubrovna, in his glosses on *Sukkah* 13b, understands that the Alter Rebbe intended here to address a problem with which generations of commentators have grappled: Earlier we learned (subsection 2) that materials that were once susceptible to ritual impurity continue to remain invalid for *s'chach* even if they were later broken and thus became immune to ritual impurity — yet here an invalid form of *s'chach* is being rehabilitated! Evidently, concludes the author of *Divrei Nechemiah,* the Alter Rebbe has solved this problem in the above passage, but the exact solution remains unclear.

46. And fennel in English.

47. The length of time for which the *sukkah* is required.

48. Sec. 632 of the Alter Rebbe's *Shulchan Aruch* is not extant. The *Shulchan Aruch* of R. Yosef Caro states that when there are three handbreadths of empty space in a *sukkah,* whether at the sides or in the center, the *sukkah* may be disqualified, but this also depends on its size. (See sec 632:2 there for details.)

קיח רש"י יד, א ד"ה אלא למאן. ב"י ד"ה ומ"ש ואם קצרו. קיט ארחות חיים הל' סוכה סי' יד, בשם ה"ר יחיאל וה"ר שמואל מאיוור"א. רבנו ירוחם נ"ח ח"א (נו, א) בטעם הב'. רמ"א סי"א. קכ שו"ת הרא"ש כלל כד סי' יד (מטעם אחר). ארחות חיים ורבנו ירוחם שם. שו"ע סי"א. קכא גמרא יג, ב. טור ושו"ע סי"ב. קכב ר"ן (ז, א) ד"ה גרסי'. רמ"א סי"ב. ט"ז ס"ק יד. קכג ב"ח ד"ה ואם סיכך. מ"א סקי"ג. ט"ז שם. קכד לבוש סי"ב. קכה ב"ח שם. קכו גמרא ורש"י שם ד"ה ופוסלין. טור ושו"ע שם. קכז רש"י שם. הגהות מיימוניות פ"ה ה"ג אות ב. רמ"א שם. קכח סימן זה בשוע"ר לא הגיע לידינו, וראה טור ושו"ע

וְאַף עַל פִּי שֶׁהֵן מְקַבְּלִין טֻמְאָה — אֵין דִּינָן כִּסְכָךְ פָּסוּל[49] שֶׁאֵינוֹ פּוֹסֵל אֶלָּא בְּאַרְבָּעָה טְפָחִים בְּאֶמְצַע הַסְּכָךְ,[קכט,50] דְּכֵיוָן שֶׁסּוֹפָן לִבֹּל וְלִפֹּל תּוֹךְ הֶחָג[קל] — אֵין שֵׁם סְכָךְ עֲלֵיהֶן,[קלא] וּכְאִלּוּ אֵינָן כְּלָל:[קלב]

Though they are susceptible to ritual impurity they are not considered as invalid *s'chach,*[49] which does not disqualify the *sukkah* unless there are four handbreadths of it in the midst of the *s'chach.*[50] [The rationale is that] since ultimately [the leaves] will wilt and fall in the course of the festival, they are not considered as *s'chach.* It is as if they do not exist.

כ כָּל דָּבָר הַמְחֻבָּר לַקַּרְקַע — אֵין מְסַכְּכִין בּוֹ,[קלג,1] לְפִי שֶׁאֵינוֹ דּוֹמֶה לִפְסֹלֶת גֹּרֶן וָיֶקֶב[51] שֶׁהֵם תְּלוּשִׁים מִן הַקַּרְקַע.[קלד] וְאִם סִכֵּךְ בִּמְחֻבָּר וְאַחַר כָּךְ קְצָצוֹ — פָּסוּל,[קלה,52] שֶׁנֶּאֱמַר[קלו,5] "חַג הַסֻּכֹּת תַּעֲשֶׂה כו'", "תַּעֲשֶׂה" — וְלֹא מִן הֶעָשׂוּי[קלז] בִּפְסוּל,[קלח,53] שֶׁהָעֲשִׂיָּה הָרִאשׁוֹנָה שֶׁהִיא בִּפְסוּל אֵינָהּ חֲשׁוּבָה עֲשִׂיָּה כְּלָל, כְּאִלּוּ לֹא עָשָׂה מְאוּמָה,[קלט] וּמַה שֶּׁאַחַר כָּךְ מַכְשִׁירוֹ[54] עַל יְדֵי קְצִיצַת הָאִילָן — אֵין זוֹ חֲשׁוּבָה עֲשִׂיָּה,[קמ] כֵּיוָן שֶׁאֵינוֹ עוֹשֶׂה מַעֲשֶׂה חָדָשׁ בְּהַסְּכָךְ, דְּהַיְנוּ שֶׁאֵינוֹ סוֹתְרָהּ כְּלָל,[קמא] לְפִיכָךְ אֵין לוֹ תַּקָּנָה אֶלָּא אִם כֵּן יְנַעְנַע[קמב] כָּל הַסְּכָךְ הַפָּסוּל

20 One may not use a substance that is [still] connected to the ground as *s'chach,*[1] because it does not resemble "the remnants of the threshing floor and the winepress,"[51] which have been detached from the ground.

[Moreover,] if one covered a *sukkah* with [branches] that were connected [to the ground] and then detached [them], [the *s'chach*] is invalid.[52] [This is derived from] the verse,[5] "Make the Sukkos festival...." [Implied is that] one must *make* [the *sukkah*], and not [use] something which was already made in an unacceptable manner.[53] Since the *sukkah* was originally made in an unacceptable manner, it is not considered to have been made at all. It is as if nothing was done. The fact that one later made the *sukkah* valid[54] by detaching the tree [from the ground] is not considered as performing an action, for nothing new was done to the *s'chach;* i.e., he did not undo [his previous action] at all.

Therefore there is no way to correct [such a *sukkah*] unless one moves about all the invalid

49. I.e., viewing the vegetables as open space leads to a more stringent ruling than considering them as invalid for *s'chach.*

50. As opposed to the edge of the *s'chach,* in which case the *sukkah* is not disqualified unless the invalid *s'chach* extends over at least four cubits. Instead, it is considered as a *dofen akumah* — "a bent wall"; i.e., it is as if the wall, which need not be made of valid *s'chach,* was bent over horizontally along its upper edge, until it became part of the ceiling. (See the *Shulchan Aruch* of R. Yosef Caro, sec. 632:1.)

51. See subsection 1 above.

52. *Sukkah* 11b.

53. And which later became suitable as a matter of course. The above principle is also discussed in sec. 626:16.

54. I.e., sought to make the *sukkah* valid.

שם ס"ב. קכט רש"י שם. קל לבוש שם. קלא ראה מ"מ וציונים. קלב גמרא שם. לבוש שם. קלג משנה יא, א. טור ושו"ע סי"ג. קלד רש"י ט, ב ד"ה הא קמצטרף סכך. לבוש ס"א. וראה לעיל ס"א. קלה ברייתא וגמרא יא, ב. טור ושו"ע סי' תרכו ס"ב. קלו דברים טז, יג. קלז ברייתא שם. וראה גם לעיל שם סט"ז. קלח רש"י יא, א ד"ה ויתיב. קלט ראה גם לעיל סי' י סי"ד, וש"נ. קמ גמרא יא, ב. טור שם. קמא ראה רש"י שם. קמב גמרא יא, א. טור ושו"ע שם.

שֶׁקְּצָצוֹ,[קמג] דְּהַיְנוּ שֶׁמַּגְבִּיהוֹ מְעַט[קמד] וְחוֹזֵר וּמַנִּיחוֹ,[קמה] שֶׁבְּשָׁעָה שֶׁמַּגְבִּיהוֹ נִתְבַּטְּלָה עֲשִׂיָּה הָרִאשׁוֹנָה[קמו] שֶׁהָיְתָה בִּפְסוּל, וְאַחַר כָּךְ כְּשֶׁמַּנִּיחָן הוּא עוֹשֶׂה מַעֲשֶׂה חָדָשׁ בְּגוּף הַסֻּכָּה:

s'chach that was detached; i.e., one must lift it up slightly and then put it down again. For at the time it was lifted, the first act — [putting it in place] when it was invalid — was nullified. When he now puts it in place, he is doing something new to the *sukkah* itself.

כא יֵשׁ דְּבָרִים שֶׁאָסְרוּ חֲכָמִים לְסַכֵּךְ בָּהֶן[קמז] לְכַתְּחִלָּה,[קמח] וְהֵם מִינֵי עֲשָׂבִים שֶׁרֵיחָם רַע,[קמט] אַף עַל פִּי שֶׁאֵינָן רְאוּיִין לַאֲכִילָה וְאֵין מְקַבְּלִין טֻמְאָה,[קנ, 55] וְכֵן מִינֵי סְנֶה שֶׁעֲלֵיהֶן נוֹשְׁרִין[קנא] תָּמִיד אַף עַל פִּי שֶׁלֹּא בִּשְׁעַת הָרוּחַ,[קנב, 56] לְפִי שֶׁאָנוּ חוֹשְׁשִׁין שֶׁמָּא מִתּוֹךְ שֶׁרֵיחָן רַע אוֹ מִתּוֹךְ שֶׁעֲלֵיהֶן נוֹשְׁרִין יֵצֵא מִן הַסֻּכָּה.[קנג] וְאִם עָבַר וְסִכֵּךְ בָּהֶן — כְּשֵׁרָה,[קנד] וּמֻתָּר לֵישֵׁב בָּהּ[32] לְכַתְּחִלָּה:[קנה]

21 There are certain substances that our Sages forbade using as *s'chach* as an initial preference. Among them are: [a] grasses with an unpleasant smell, [which are invalid] even though they are not edible and are not susceptible to ritual impurity;[55] and also [b] certain kinds of brambles whose leaves fall at all times, even when there is no wind.[56]

[The rationale is that] we are apprehensive that a person may leave the *sukkah* because of the unpleasant smell or because of the falling leaves. Nevertheless, if one transgressed and used these materials as *s'chach,* [the *sukkah*] is valid and one may dwell in it[32] as an initial and preferred option.

כב חֲבִילֵי קַשׁ וַחֲבִילֵי עֵצִים — אֵין מְסַכְּכִין בָּהֶן[קנו] כְּשֶׁהֵן אֲגוּדִין,[קנז, 6] מִפְּנֵי שֶׁפְּעָמִים שֶׁאָדָם בָּא מִן הַשָּׂדֶה בָּעֶרֶב[קנח] בְּכָל יְמוֹת הַחַמָּה[קנט] וַחֲבִילָתוֹ עַל כְּתֵפוֹ וּמַנִּיחָהּ עַל גַּבֵּי סֻכָּתוֹ[קס] שֶׁיֵּשׁ לוֹ כָּל יְמוֹת הַחַמָּה לְמִקְנֵהוּ[קסא] כְּדֵי לְיַבְּשָׁהּ[קסב] וְלֹא לְשֵׁם סְכָךְ,[קסג] וּכְשֶׁמַּגִּיעַ הֶחָג[57] נִמְלָךְ עָלֶיהָ לְסִכּוּךְ,[קסד] וְהַתּוֹרָה

22 Bundles of straw or bundles of wood may not be used for *s'chach* while they are bound together.[6] [The rationale is that] on any summer evening a person will sometimes come from the fields with his bundle on his shoulder and place it to dry on the *sukkah* that he uses throughout the summer for his herds. [Thus he will] not [have placed it there] for the purpose of shade. When Sukkos[57] comes, he will change his mind [and desire to use it] for *s'chach.* [This is not

---

55. *Sukkah* 13a. If the odor is so unpleasant that it would be difficult to bear, the *sukkah* is invalid by Scriptural Law *(Mishnah Berurah* 629:38*)*.

56. If they fall only in the wind, they are valid *(op. cit.,* 629:39*)*.

57. In the original, *hachag* — "the festival." Throughout the *Tanach* and the *Talmud,* this term often signifies the festival *par excellence,* i.e., Sukkos.

קמג ר"ן (ו, א) ד"ה אוקימנא. קמד רש"י שם. קמה רש"י ושו"ע שם. וראה מ"מ וציונים. קמו רש"י שם (ניענוע קרוב לסתירה הוא). קמז גמרא יב, סוע"ב. טור ושו"ע סי"ד. קמח רא"ש פ"א סי' כה. טור ושו"ע שם. קמט גמרא יג, רע"א. טור ושו"ע שם. קנ רש"י יב, סוע"ב ד"ה מסככין. טור ושו"ע שם. קנא גמרא יג, רע"א. טור ושו"ע שם. קנב ב"ח סוף הסי'. מ"א סקט"ו. קנג גמרא שם. טור ושו"ע שם. קנד רמב"ם פ"ה ה"ב. רא"ש שם. מ"א סקי"ד. קנה מ"א שם ממשמעות לשון הרמב"ם שם. וראה עד"ז לעיל סי"ג. קנו משנה יב, א. רמב"ם פ"ה ה"י. טור ושו"ע סט"ו. קנז רש"י שם ד"ה אין מסככין. קנח רבי יוחנן בגמרא שם. טור ושו"ע שם. קנט רש"י שם ד"ה פעמים. קס גמרא שם. טור ושו"ע שם. קסא רש"י שם ד"ה ומניחה. קסב גמרא שם. טור ושו"ע שם.

acceptable,] for [with regard to the *sukkah*] the Torah states,[58] "Make [the Sukkos festival...]." [Implied is that] one must *make* [the *sukkah*], and not [use] something that was already made in an unacceptable manner.

Now, this bundle was not placed there for *s'chach,* [nor] even for shade, but to dry. Hence, it is not considered as *s'chach* and this *sukkah* will have been made in an unacceptable manner. The Sages therefore ordained that bundles should never be used as *s'chach* even when they were placed on the *sukkah* in order to fulfill the *mitzvah* of *sukkah* for the festival. [See fig. 14.] This ordinance [is a safeguard to forestall the possibility of error] involving bundles [that may have been placed there] throughout the summer.

23 Since this prohibition was enacted only because of this ordinance, it was necessary to prohibit [the use of] only bundles [of the kind] which

אָמְרָה[קסה,58] "תַּעֲשֶׂה" – וְלֹא מִן הֶעָשׂוּי[קסו] בִּפְסוּל,[קסז] וַחֲבִילָה זוֹ שֶׁהֻנְּחָה שָׁם שֶׁלֹּא לְשֵׁם סְכָךְ אֲפִלּוּ לְצֵל[קסח] אֶלָּא כְּדֵי לְיַבְּשָׁהּ – אֵין שֵׁם סְכָךְ עָלֶיהָ,[קסט] וְנִמְצָא שֶׁעֲשִׂיָּתָהּ שֶׁל סֻכָּה זוֹ הִיא בִּפְסוּל, לְפִיכָךְ גָּזְרוּ חֲכָמִים[קע] שֶׁלֹּא יְסַכְּכָהּ בַּחֲבִילוֹת אֲפִלּוּ הוּא מְטִילָהּ עַל הַסֻּכָּה לְשֵׁם מִצְוַת סֻכַּת הֶחָג, גְּזֵרָה מִשּׁוּם חֲבִילוֹת שֶׁל כָּל יְמוֹת הַחַמָּה:[קעא]

כג וְכֵיוָן שֶׁלֹּא אָסְרוּ אֶלָּא מִפְּנֵי גְּזֵרָה זוֹ, לֹא הֻצְרְכוּ לֶאֱסֹר אֶלָּא בַּחֲבִילָה שֶׁדֶּרֶךְ

Fig. 14: See sec. 629:22.

58. *Devarim, op. cit.* See subsection 20 above.

קסג רש"י שם. טור. קסד רש"י שם. קסה דברים טז, יג. קסו גמרא שם. טור ושו"ע שם. קסז רש"י שם ד"ה והתורה. טור ושו"ע שם. קסח רש"י שם. טור. לבוש סט"ו. מ"א סקט"ז. וכלקמן סכ"ח שפסולה מהתורה. קסט רש"י שם. קע גמרא שם. טור ושו"ע שם. קעא רש"י שם.

לַיִּבָּשָׁה,[קעב] דְּהַיְנוּ שֶׁיֵּשׁ בָּהּ לֹא פָּחוֹת מִן עֶשְׂרִים וַחֲמִשָּׁה קָנִים,[קעג,59] אֲבָל חֲבִילָה שֶׁאֵין בָּהּ עֶשְׂרִים וַחֲמִשָּׁה קָנִים – מֻתָּר לְסַכֵּךְ בָּהּ:[קעד]

are commonly left to dry out, i.e., which have no fewer than 25 canes in them.[59] Bundles of fewer than 25 canes may be used as *s'chach.*

כד וְאִם עֶשְׂרִים וַחֲמִשָּׁה קָנִים אוֹ יוֹתֵר[קעה] יוֹצְאִין מִגֶּזַע אֶחָד וְהֵן מִפֹּרָדִין בְּרֹאשָׁן הַשֵּׁנִי וַאֲגָדָן שָׁם[קעו] – אַף עַל פִּי כֵן כֵּיוָן שֶׁעִקָּרָן אֶחָד אֵינוֹ דּוֹמֶה לַחֲבִילָה שֶׁדֶּרֶךְ לַיִּבָּשָׁה וְלָכֵן מֻתָּר לְסַכֵּךְ בָּהּ.[60] וְאִם אָגַד עִמָּהֶן קָנֶה אֶחָד[קעז] שֶׁאֵינָהּ מְחֻבֶּרֶת עִמָּהֶן בְּעִקָּר אֶחָד, אִם יֵשׁ בַּחֲבִילָה זוֹ עִם קָנֶה זֶה עֶשְׂרִים וַחֲמִשָּׁה קָנִים – נִקְרֵאת חֲבִילָה, וְאֵין מְסַכְּכִין בָּהּ:[קעח]

24 [Moreover,] even if there are 25 or more canes coming out of one stem, but they are separate at the other end and bound together there, they may be used as *s'chach,*[60] for since they [emerge from] the same stem, they do not resemble a bundle that is left to dry. If, however, a person tied one cane that did not emerge from the same stem together with them, it is considered as [such] a bundle if there are 25 canes together with the additional one, and it may not be used as *s'chach.*

כה קָנִים שֶׁעוֹשִׂין אוֹתָן חֲבִילוֹת חֲבִילוֹת כְּדֵי לְמָכְרָן בַּשּׁוּק בְּמִנְיָן[קעט,2] וּכְשֶׁקּוֹנֶה אוֹתָן הַלּוֹקֵחַ מַתִּיר אֲגוּדָן מִיָּד[קפ] – מֻתָּר לְסַכֵּךְ בָּהֶן, וְאֵין בָּהֶן מִשּׁוּם גְּזֵרַת חֲבִילָה שֶׁל כָּל יְמוֹת הַחַמָּה, כֵּיוָן שֶׁחֲבִילָה זוֹ אֵין דֶּרֶךְ לְהַצְנִיעָהּ בַּאֲגֻדָּה,[קפא] וְהַלּוֹקְחָהּ כְּדֵי לַיִּבָּשָׁה מַתִּיר אֲגֻדָּתָהּ[קפב] מִיָּד:

25 As to canes that are bound together in bundles to be sold in the marketplace by number,[2] a purchaser unties them as soon as he buys them. One may [therefore] use them as *s'chach.* The ordinance forbidding the use of bundles bound throughout the summer months is not applied [in this context], because such a bundle is not ordinarily set aside while bound. [Even one who] purchases it to dry out [the wood] unties it immediately.

כו חֲבִילוֹת שֶׁעוֹשִׂין מֵעֲרָבָה וְרָאשֵׁיהֶן הַגַּסִּים לְצַד אֶחָד וְרָאשֵׁיהֶן הַדַּקִּין לְצַד אַחֵר[2] וְדַרְכָּן לְקָשְׁרָן בִּשְׁנֵי רָאשֵׁיהֶן, כֵּיוָן שֶׁהִתִּיר קֶשֶׁר שֶׁבְּרֹאשׁ הַגַּס – מֻתָּר לְסַכֵּךְ בָּהֶן,[קפג] מִשּׁוּם שֶׁהַקֶּשֶׁר שֶׁלַּצַּד הָאַחֵר אֵינוֹ

26 [The following law applies to] bundles of willow branches whose thick ends are tied together at one extremity and whose thin ends are tied together at the other.[2] As soon as one unties the knot at the thick end, [the

---

59. *Talmud Yerushalmi, Sukkah* 1:6. **60.** *Sukkah* 13a.

קעב טור ושו"ע שם. **קעג** ירושלמי פ"א ה"ו. רמב"ם שם. רא"ש פ"א סי' כד. טור ושו"ע שם. **קעד** טור ושו"ע שם. **קעה** טור ושו"ע סט"ו. **קעו** גמרא יג, א. טור ושו"ע שם. **קעז** רב חסדא בגמרא שם אליבא דרבנן. רא"ש פ"א סי' כה. טור ושו"ע שם. **קעח** רא"ש שם. טור ושו"ע שם. **קעט** מרימר בגמרא יג, רע"ב. טור ושו"ע סט"ז. **קפ** רש"י שם ד"ה מסככין. **קפא** רש"י שם ד"ה אלא. טור ושו"ע שם. **קפב** רש"י שם ד"ה אלא. וראה יגדיל תורה (נ.י) ח ע' פב. **קפג** רבי אבא בגמרא שם. לפירוש הר"ן (ז, א) ד"ה הני. הובא בב"י ד"ה גרסינן. **קפד** רב הונא בריה דרב יהושע שם. ב"י שם. [ר]מ"א סט"ו. **קפה** לבוש

חָזָק כָּל כָּךְ שֶׁיִּתְקַיֵּם אִם יְטַלְטֵל אֶת הַחֲבִילָה, וְכָל אֶגֶד שֶׁאֵינוֹ עָשׂוּי לְטַלְטְלוֹ בְּאֶגְדּוֹ – אֵינוֹ נִקְרָא אֶגֶד כְּלָל:[קפד]

bundle] may be used as *s'chach,* because the knot at the [thin] end is not so strong that it will hold if the bundle is carried. And any bundle that is not fit to be carried while bound is not considered a bundle at all.

כז אֲבָל אִם קָשַׁר אֶת הַחֲבִילָה בְּאֶמְצָעָהּ בִּלְבַד – אֵין מְסַכְּכִין בָּהּ, מִפְּנֵי שֶׁהִיא מִטַּלְטֶלֶת בְּאֶגֶד זֶה:[קפה]

27 If [such] a bundle was tied only in the middle, it may not be used as *s'chach,* because it could be carried when bound in this way.

כח אִם עָבַר וְסִכֵּךְ בַּחֲבִילָה – מַתִּיר אֲגֻדָּה וְהִיא כְּשֵׁרָה.[קפו,6] וְאַף עַל פִּי שֶׁתְּחִלַּת עֲשִׂיַּת סֻכָּה זוֹ הָיְתָה בְּפָסוּל – אֵין לְפָסְלָהּ מִשּׁוּם "תַּעֲשֶׂה וְלֹא מִן הֶעָשׂוּי בְּפָסוּל",[61] כֵּיוָן שֶׁאֵין פְּסוּלָהּ אֶלָּא מֵחֲמַת גְּזֵרָה בְּעָלְמָא[קפז] כְּמוֹ שֶׁנִּתְבָּאֵר.[קפח,62]

אֲבָל חֲבִילָה שֶׁהֶעֱלָה אוֹתָהּ לְיַבְּשָׁהּ וּכְשֶׁהִגִּיעַ הֶחָג נִמְלַךְ עָלֶיהָ לְסַכּוֹךְ שֶׁפְּסוּלָה מִן הַתּוֹרָה,[קפט] שֶׁהֲרֵי לֹא הִנִּיחָהּ שָׁם לְשֵׁם צֵל[קצ] – אֵין מוֹעִיל לָהּ הַתָּרַת הָאֶגֶד לְהַכְשִׁירָהּ,[קצא] כֵּיוָן שֶׁפְּסוּלָהּ לֹא הָיָה מֵחֲמַת הָאֶגֶד בִּלְבַד, אֶלָּא הֲנָחָתָהּ שֶׁלֹּא לְשֵׁם צֵל גָּרַם לָהּ לְהִפָּסֵל מִן הַתּוֹרָה, לְפִיכָךְ צָרִיךְ לַעֲשׂוֹת מַעֲשֶׂה חָדָשׁ לַהֲנָחָתָהּ, דְּהַיְנוּ שֶׁיַּגְבִּיהֶנּוּ מְעַט וְיַחֲזֹר וְיַנִּיחֵהוּ[קצב] לְשֵׁם צֵל,[קצג] וְגַם צָרִיךְ לְהַתִּיר אֲגֻדָּה,[קצד] שֶׁאֵין מְסַכְּכִין בַּחֲבִילָה גְּזֵרָה מִשּׁוּם חֲבִילָה שֶׁל כָּל יְמוֹת הַחַמָּה כְּמוֹ שֶׁנִּתְבָּאֵר:[62]

28 If one transgressed and used a bundle as *s'chach,* he may untie [it] and thus [render the *s'chach*] valid.[6] Though the *sukkah* was originally made in an unacceptable manner, it should not be disqualified because of [the above requirement to] *"make,* rather than [use] what was already made in an unacceptable manner."[61] [This leniency is granted] because [bundles are] deemed invalid only by Rabbinic ordinance, as explained above.[62]

If, however, one placed a bundle [on the *sukkah*] to dry, and when Sukkos arrived he changed his mind and decided to use it for *s'chach,* it is invalid by Scriptural Law, for it was not put there for shade. Hence, untying it is not sufficient to render it valid. [The rationale is that] it was not disqualified merely because it was tied together; rather, the fact that it was not laid in place for shade caused it to be disqualified by Scriptural Law. Something new must therefore be done to [the way] it was laid down. It must be lifted up slightly and then put back in place with the intent that it provide shade.

The bundle must also be untied, for a bundle may not be used as *s'chach* because of the [safeguard] that was ordained [to forestall the possibility of error] involving a bundle [that may have been placed there] throughout the summer, as was explained above.[62]

61. See subsection 20 above. **62.** In subsection 22.

סי"ז. מ"א ס"ק יז. **קפו** משנה יב, א. טור ושו"ע סי"ז. ט"ז סקי"ז. **קפז** טור ושו"ע שם. **קפח** סעיף כב. **קפט** גמרא שם. טור ושו"ע שם. **קצ** רש"י שם ד"ה והתורה. וכדלעיל סי' תרכו ס"א. **קצא** טור ושו"ע שם. **קצב** ראה מרדכי רמז תשלח בשם ר"ת. ר"ן (ו, ב) ד"ה גמרא. טור ושו"ע שם (נענוע). רש"י יא, א ד"ה ויתיב (שמגביה ומניחו). וכדלעיל ס"כ. **קצג** ראה מ"א סי' תרכו סק"ה. **קצד** ב"ח ד"ה ומ"ש הר"ן. מ"א סקי"ט.

כט נְסָרִים שֶׁרָחְבָּן אַרְבָּעָה טְפָחִים — אָסוּר לְסַכֵּךְ בָּהֶן,[קצה, 63] לְפִי שֶׁרֹב תִּקְרוֹת הַבַּיִת עֲשׂוּיוֹת מֵהֶן,[קצו] וְיֵשׁ לָחוּשׁ שֶׁמָּא יֵשֵׁב תַּחַת תִּקְרַת בֵּיתוֹ וְיֹאמַר מַה לִּי לְסַכֵּךְ בִּנְסָרִים אֵלּוּ מַה לִּי לֵישֵׁב תַּחַת תִּקְרַת בֵּיתִי אַף הִיא מִנְּסָרִים עֲשׂוּיָה,[קצז] וְתִקְרַת הַבַּיִת הִיא פְּסוּלָה מִן הַתּוֹרָה מִטַּעַם שֶׁנִּתְבָּאֵר בְּסִימָן תרכ"ו:[קצח, 64]

29 Boards that are [at least] four handbreadths wide may not be used as *s'chach*,[63] because the ceilings of most homes are made of [such boards]. Thus, [were they to be used,] there would be cause for concern that someone might sit under the ceiling of his home and say, "What difference is there between covering my *sukkah* with such boards — and sitting under the ceiling of my home? It, too, is made of boards!" And the ceiling of a home is invalid [as *s'chach*] according to Scriptural Law, for the reason explained in sec. 626.[64]

ל וַאֲפִלּוּ אִם לֹא הֵטִיל רֹחַב הַנְּסָרִים עַל גַּבֵּי הַסֻּכָּה אֶלָּא הֲפָכָן וְהִשְׁכִּיבָן עַל צִדָּן שֶׁהוּא פָּחוֹת מֵאַרְבָּעָה טְפָחִים — אַף עַל פִּי כֵן פְּסוּלָה,[קצט, 63] דְּכֵיוָן שֶׁיֵּשׁ שֵׁם פְּסוּל עֲלֵיהֶן[ר] — נַעֲשׂוּ כְּשַׁפּוּדִין שֶׁל מַתֶּכֶת[רא] הַפְּסוּלִין לְסַכֵּךְ בְּכָל עִנְיָן שֶׁהוֹפְכָן:[רב]

30 Even if one did not place the width of the boards on the *sukkah*, but turned them and laid them on their sides, which were less than four handbreadths wide, they are, nevertheless, invalid.[63] Once they have been deemed invalid, they are like metal spits that are invalid as *s'chach*, regardless of which way they are turned.

לא אֲבָל מֻתָּר לְסַכֵּךְ בִּנְסָרִים שֶׁאֵין רָחְבָּן אַרְבָּעָה טְפָחִים,[רג] וַאֲפִלּוּ אִם הֵם מְשֻׁפִּין[רד] וְדוֹמִין לְכֵלִים,[רה, 65] וְאַף עַל פִּי שֶׁהֵן רְאוּיִים לִישִׁיבָה,[66] גַּם הֵן רְאוּיִין לְהִשְׁתַּמֵּשׁ בָּהֶן לְהַנִּיחַ פֵּרוֹת וְכִכָּרוֹת עַל גַּבֵּיהֶן[67] שֶׁהֲרֵי הֵן רְחָבִין קְצָת — אַף עַל פִּי כֵן אֵינָן מְקַבְּלִין טֻמְאָה אִם אֵינָן מְיֻחָדִין לֹא לִישִׁיבָה וְלֹא לְשׁוּם תַּשְׁמִישׁ,[רו] אֶלָּא

31 However, boards that are less than four handbreadths wide may be used as *s'chach* even if they have been planed and resemble utensils,[65] despite the fact that they are wide enough to be fit for use as seats[66] [and] are also fit to have fruit and loaves placed on them.[67] Nevertheless, they are not susceptible to ritual impurity, for they were not set aside to be sat upon nor to be used for any other purpose, but

---

63. *Sukkah* 14a.

64. As stated in sec. 626:1, even if the ceiling would otherwise be valid, it is disqualified, because the covering of a *sukkah* must be made only for shade, not for a dwelling.

65. *Sukkah* 15a.

66. In which instance they would be susceptible to contracting ritual impurity of the category called *midras*. (See footnote 21 above.)

67. In which instance they could be compared to other utensils that serve as receptacles and hence are susceptible to ritual impurity. (See subsection 14 above.)

קצה משנה וגמרא יד, א. טור ושו"ע סי"ח. קצו רש"י שם ד"ה ר' מאיר. קצז רש"י שם ד"ה מחלוקת. קצח סעיף א. קצט רב הונא ורב נחמן בגמרא יד, ב. טור ושו"ע שם. ר רש"י שם ד"ה פסולה. ט"ז סקי"ט. רא רב נחמן שם. רב רש"י שם. וכדלעיל ס"א. רג גמרא יד, א. טור ושו"ע שם. רד גמרא טו, א. טור ושו"ע שם. רה טור ושו"ע שם. רו מ"א סקכ"א. ואם עשויין להניח עליהן פירות, ראה לעיל סי"ד. רז ט"ז סק"כ, בשם הלבוש. רח אוצ"ל: לסחורה. רט הגהות [מיימוניות] פ"ה הכ"א אות א. דרכי משה ס"ק ט. מ"א סקכ"ב. רי ב"ח ד"ה ומ"ש ואפילו. מ"א שם. ריא סעיף ה. ריב ב"ח שם, בשם הגהות

עוֹמְדִין לְבִנְיָן[רז] אוֹ לִסְתִירָה:[רח, 68]

are intended for construction or for destroying a building.[68]

לב וְעַכְשָׁו בַּזְּמַן הַזֶּה שֶׁמְּסַכְּכִין הַבָּתִּים בִּנְסָרִים שֶׁאֵין בָּהֶן שְׁלֹשָׁה טְפָחִים – יֵשׁ לִפְסֹל סֻכָּה הַמְסֻכֶּכֶת אֲפִלּוּ בִּנְסָרִים שֶׁאֵין בְּרָחְבָּן שְׁלֹשָׁה טְפָחִים,[רט] מִשּׁוּם גְּזֵרָה שֶׁמָּא יֵשֵׁב תַּחַת תִּקְרַת בֵּיתוֹ הָעֲשׂוּיָה מִנְּסָרִים כָּאֵלּוּ.[69]

אֲבָל מֻתָּר לְסַכֵּךְ בִּנְסָרִים קְצָרִים מְאֹד שֶׁקּוֹרִין (לאיטי"ש או שינדלי"ן),[70] שֶׁאֵין דֶּרֶךְ לַעֲשׂוֹת תִּקְרַת הַבַּיִת מִנְּסָרִים קְצָרִים כָּאֵלּוּ.[ר'] וּמִכָּל מָקוֹם, צָרִיךְ לִזָּהֵר לַעֲשׂוֹת הַסְּכָךְ עֲרַאי וְקַל בְּעִנְיָן שֶׁיּוּכְלוּ הַגְּשָׁמִים לֵירֵד בְּתוֹכוֹ כְּמוֹ שֶׁיִּתְבָּאֵר בְּסִימָן תרל"א.[ריא] וּלְפִיכָךְ נָהֲגוּ הָעוֹלָם שֶׁלֹּא לְסַכֵּךְ בָּהֶן כְּלָל, שֶׁמָּא יִטְעוּ לְסַכֵּךְ בְּעִנְיַן קְבִיעוּת שֶׁלֹּא יוּכְלוּ הַגְּשָׁמִים לֵירֵד בְּתוֹכוֹ:[ריב]

32 Today, when homes are roofed by boards that are less than three handbreadths wide, a *sukkah* should be disqualified even if boards less than three handbreadths wide are used as *s'chach*, because of the [safeguard] that was ordained lest one sit under the ceiling of his home that is made of such boards.[69]

However, one may use very narrow boards, such as lattices and shingles,[70] for it is not common to make the ceiling of a home out of such narrow boards. Nevertheless, one must be careful to make the *s'chach* temporary and light so that rain can penetrate [the *sukkah*], as stated in sec. 631[:5]. It has therefore become customary not to use [boards] for *s'chach* at all, lest someone err and [build] a permanent [roof] that rain could not penetrate.

לג וּבִשְׁעַת הַדְּחָק שֶׁאֵין לָהֶם בַּמֶּה לְסַכֵּךְ – מְסַכְּכִין בִּנְסָרִים אֲפִלּוּ יֵשׁ בָּהֶם אַרְבָּעָה טְפָחִים אִם אִי אֶפְשָׁר בְּעִנְיָן אַחֵר.[ריג, 71] וְהוּא הַדִּין בְּכָל דָּבָר הָאָסוּר מִשּׁוּם גְּזֵרָה:[ריד]

חָסֵר[רטו, 72]

33 In a pressing situation, where people lack materials to use as *s'chach*, one may use boards as *s'chach*, even if they are [more than] four handbreadths wide, if there is no other alternative.[71] This principle applies to all materials prohibited [as *s'chach*] because of a Rabbinic ordinance.*

[The end of sec. 629[72]
and the entire sec. 630 are not extant.]

---

68. This translation follows the standard printed text (לסתירה), which is almost certainly a printing error. The correct version should evidently read לסחורה ("as merchandise"). See *Mishnah Berurah* 629:48.

69. See subsection 29 above.

70. Evidently it was common for shingles to be made of wood. However, the mention here of shingles is somewhat problematic, for though they are not used for ceilings, they are used for roofing. The Alter Rebbe's source *(Magen Avraham* 629:22) mentions shingles only as something not to be used as *s'chach*.

71. Once, in order to circumvent a Roman edict against *sukkos*, the Sages constructed — and used — a *sukkah* roofed with boards *(Sukkah* 14b).

72. Some of the points referred to at the end of the corresponding section in the *Shulchan Aruch* of R. Yosef Caro are spoken of in sec. 640:10 in the present work.

* For a summary of sec. 629, see p. 450.

סמ"ק סי' צג (ע' נה) אות לב. מ"א שם. **ריג** שלטי גבורים (ז, ב) אות ב. מ"א סקכ"ב (ממשמעות הגמרא יד, ב: מעשה בשעת הסכנה כו'). **ריד** מ"א שם.
רטו סיום הסי' (סי"ט משו"ע. וראה לקמן סי' תרמ סוף ס"י). וסי' תרל (דיני דפנות הסוכה).

SECTION 631 [A *Sukkah*] whose Sunlit Area Exceeds its Shaded Area, and Other Laws Governing the *S'chach*. (1–12)

1 If the *s'chach* is a very light covering with much empty space, but no one place has three handbreadths of empty space,[1] [the *sukkah*] is valid,[2] [provided] the overall shaded part [of its floor] exceeds its sunlit area;[3] i.e., there is more *s'chach* than open space.

2 If the *s'chach* does not exceed the open space, but they are equal, [the *sukkah*] is invalid.[4] The reason is that when the sunlight coming through the space[s] in the *s'chach* reaches the floor of the *sukkah,* it diffuses [over an area] greater than the open space[s] in the *s'chach* above. On the floor of the *sukkah,* the sunlit area thus exceeds the shaded part.

3 However, if on the *sukkah* floor the sunlit area is equal to its shaded part, the *sukkah* is valid,[4] for it is certain that above, at [the level of] the covering, there is less open space than *s'chach.* Since the above area of *[s'chach* that casts a*]* shadow thus exceeds the area [that admits] sunlight, such *s'chach* is completely valid.[5]

סימן תרלא סֻכָּה שֶׁחַמָּתָהּ מְרֻבָּה מִצִּלָּתָהּ וְיֶתֶר דִּינֵי הַסְּכָךְ וּבוֹ י"ב סְעִיפִים:

א הָיָה הַסְּכָךְ כִּסּוּי דַּק מְאֹד שֶׁיֵּשׁ בּוֹ אֲוִיר הַרְבֵּה,[א] אֶלָּא שֶׁאֵין שְׁלֹשָׁה טְפָחִים אֲוִיר בְּמָקוֹם אֶחָד,[ב,1] וּבֵין הַכֹּל צִלָּתוֹ מְרֻבָּה מֵחַמָּתוֹ[ג,3] שֶׁהַסְּכָךְ הִיא מְרֻבָּה מִן הָאֲוִיר[ד] – הֲרֵי זוֹ כְּשֵׁרָה:[2]

ב אֲבָל אִם אֵין הַסְּכָךְ מְרֻבֶּה מִן הָאֲוִיר אֶלָּא הֵן שָׁוִין – פְּסוּלָה,[ה,4] לְפִי שֶׁהַחַמָּה הַנִּכְנֶסֶת בַּאֲוִיר הַסִּכּוּךְ כְּשֶׁהִיא מַגִּיעָה לְקַרְקָעִית הַסֻּכָּה הִיא מִתְפַּשֶּׁטֶת יוֹתֵר מִמַּה שֶּׁהִיא לְמַעְלָה בַּאֲוִיר הַסִּכּוּךְ, וְנִמְצָא שֶׁהַסֻּכָּה לְמַטָּה בְּקַרְקָעִיתָהּ הִיא חַמָּתָהּ מְרֻבָּה מִצִּלָּתָהּ:[ו]

ג אֲבָל אִם לְמַטָּה בְּקַרְקָעִיתָהּ הִיא חַמָּתָהּ וְצִלָּתָהּ שָׁוִין – כְּשֵׁרָה,[ז,4] לְפִי שֶׁיָּדוּעַ שֶׁלְּמַעְלָה בְּהַסְּכָךְ הָאֲוִיר הוּא מוּעָט מִן הַסִּכּוּךְ[ח] וְצִלָּתָהּ לְמַעְלָה הִיא מְרֻבָּה מֵחַמָּתָהּ,[ט] וַהֲרֵי זֶה סְכָךְ גָּמוּר:[י,5]

---

1. For details of the situations in which such space disqualifies a *sukkah,* see the *Shulchan Aruch* of R. Yosef Caro, sec. 632:2 (sec. 632 of the Alter Rebbe's *Shulchan Aruch* is not extant).

2. *Sukkah* 22a.

3. This concept is clarified in sec. 626, footnote 8 above.

4. *Sukkah* 22b.

5. The Rebbe points to an apparent contradiction between the present subsection and subsection 2. The present subsection requires that the shaded area *exceed* the sunlit area; from subsection 2 it appears that it would suffice if they were *equal,* if not for the problem caused by the diffusion of the sun's rays.

In resolution, the Rebbe distinguishes between two issues:

(a) The requirement relating to the *s'chach* itself is the focus of subsection 3. Here the *s'chach* exceeds the area that admits sunlight, and hence is described as "completely valid."

(b) The effect of the *s'chach* — how the quantity of its shade affects the person inside the *sukkah.* This is the focus of subsection 2, which requires that this person should not be exposed to

א משנה כב, א לפירוש רב בגמרא שם ורש"י ד"ה ענייה. טור ושו"ע ס"ד. **ב** רש"י שם. טור ושו"ע שם. **ג** משנה וגמרא שם. טור ושו"ע שם. **ד** רמב"ם פ"ה הי"ט. **ה** גמרא כב, ב. טור ושו"ע ס"א. **ו** גמרא שם, לפירוש רש"י שם ד"ה כאן. רי"ף (י, ב). רמב"ם פ"ה הי"ט, כפירוש הגהות מיימוניות שם אות ש, ומ"מ שם הט"ז. רא"ש פ"ב סי' ג. ר"ן שם סוד"ה גמרא. טור ושו"ע שם. **ח** רש"י שם. **ט** רי"ף שם. לבוש ס"א. **ז** גמרא שם. טור ושו"ע ס"א. **י** ראה לקו"ש חל"ב ע'

ד וְאִם רֹב סְכַךְ צִלָּתָהּ מְרֻבָּה מֵחַמָּתָהּ שְׁתֵּי מַשֶּׁהוּיִין, שֶׁהָאֲוִיר שֶׁבּוֹ הוּא מוּעָט מְאֹד, וּמִעוּט הַסְּכָךְ חַמָּתוֹ מְרֻבָּה מִצִּלָּתוֹ מַשֶּׁהוּ,[7] בְּעִנְיָן שֶׁאִם נִצְרָף הַחַמָּה וְהַצֵּל שֶׁל כָּל הַסִּכּוּךְ יִהְיֶה צִלָּתוֹ מְרֻבָּה מֵחַמָּתוֹ מַשֶּׁהוּ — הֲרֵי זוֹ כְּשֵׁרָה,[יא,6] וּמֻתָּר לֵישֵׁב אֲפִלּוּ תַּחַת מִעוּט הַסְּכָךְ שֶׁחַמָּתוֹ מְרֻבָּה,[יב] לְפִי שֶׁהוּא בָּטֵל לְגַבֵּי רֹב הַסְּכָךְ שֶׁצִּלָּתוֹ מְרֻבָּה. מִכָּל מָקוֹם, אִם מִעוּט הַסְּכָךְ שֶׁחַמָּתוֹ מְרֻבָּה יֵשׁ בּוֹ שִׁבְעָה טְפָחִים עַל שִׁבְעָה טְפָחִים[יג] כְּדֵי שִׁעוּר הֶכְשֵׁר סֻכָּה[יד,8] — אֵין לֵישֵׁב תַּחְתָּיו,[טו,9] לְפִי שֶׁהוּא מָקוֹם חָשׁוּב[10] וְאֵינוֹ בָּטֵל לְגַבֵּי שְׁאָר הַסְּכָךְ שֶׁצִּלָּתוֹ מְרֻבָּה:

4 [A *sukkah*] is valid if the majority of the *s'chach* casts a shadow whose area is two small measures[6] greater than the sunlit area, and hence the empty space in the *s'chach* is [considered as] very little, while [under] a smaller part of the *s'chach*, the sunlit area exceeds the shaded part by a small measure. Thus when the sunlit area and the shaded area [under] the entire *s'chach* are added together, the shaded area will exceed the sunlit area by a small measure.[7]

One may even dwell under the smaller part of the *s'chach*, [under which] the sunlit area exceeds [the shade], for this part is *batel* — insignificant and therefore nullified — *vis-à-vis* the majority of *s'chach*, [under which] the shade exceeds [the sunlit area].

Nevertheless, if the smaller part of *s'chach*, [under which] the sunlit area exceeds [the shade], is seven handbreadths by seven handbreadths [or more], which is the minimum valid size for a *sukkah*,[8] one should not sit under this [part of the *s'chach*].[9] [The rationale is that] it is a significant area.[10] Hence it is not *batel* — insignificant and therefore nullified — *vis-à-vis* the remainder of the *s'chach*, [under which] the shade exceeds [the sunlit area].

ה לְכַתְּחִלָּה[11] צָרִיךְ לַעֲשׂוֹת אֶת הַסִּכּוּךְ קַל וְקָלוּשׁ בְּעִנְיָן שֶׁיִּהְיוּ הַכּוֹכָבִים[טז] הַגְּדוֹלִים[יז] נִרְאִים מִתּוֹכוֹ בַּלַּיְלָה,[יח,12] וּבְדִיעֲבַד[13] אֲפִלּוּ

5 As an initial and preferred option,[11] the *s'chach* should be light and sparse enough for large stars to be seen through it at night.[12] After the fact,[13]

---

more sunlight than shade. Had the shade been equal to the sunlight, the *sukkah* may not have met the optimum standards, but it would have been acceptable. (See *Likkutei Sichos*, Vol. 32, p. 140ff.)

6. This phrase is not intended to signify any particular dimension. In fact, the original uses a plural form of the indeterminate term *mashehu* (lit., "a [mere] something").

7. *Sukkah* 19a.

8. In the original, *shiur hechsher sukkah.* See the *Shulchan Aruch* of R. Yosef Caro, sec. 634:1 (sec. 634 of the Alter Rebbe's *Shulchan Aruch* is not extant).

9. Though it does not invalidate the *sukkah*, one may not (for example) eat while seated under this part of the *s'chach.*

10. In the original, *makom chashuv.*

11. In the original, *lechat'chilah.*

12. *Talmud Yerushalmi, Sukkah* 2:3.

13. In the original Aramaic, *bediavad* (often loosely pronounced *bedieved*).

143. שלחן המלך ח"ב ע' רלט. קובץ כינוס תורה א ע' לג. העו"ב תצג ע' 6. **יא** ברייתא יט, א, לפירוש רבי יוחנן בגמרא שם. רא"ש פ"א סי' לה. טור ושו"ע ס"ב. **יב** רא"ש שם סי' ג. ר"ן (ט, א) ד"ה גרסי'. לבוש ס"ב. ט"ז סק"א. **יג** ר"ן שם. רמ"א ס"ב. **יד** ראה טור ושו"ע סי' תרלד ס"א. **טו** ט"ז שם. **טז** ירושלמי פ"ב ה"ג. רא"ש פ"ב סוס"י ג. טור ושו"ע ס"ג. ומנהג חב"ד להרבות בסכך (ספר המנהגים — חב"ד ע' 65. וראה המלך במסיבו ח"ב ע' קצב. לקו"ש ח"ט ע' 231 בשוה"ג. אוצר מנהגי חב"ד חה"ס ע' רסו). **יז** רמב"ם פ"ה הכ"א. שו"ע שם. **יח** ב"ח ד"ה וצריך. מ"א סק"א.

הָיְתָה מְעֻבָּה כְּמִין בַּיִת[יט] עַד שֶׁאֵין זַהֲרוּרֵי שֶׁמֶשׁ נִרְאִים מִתּוֹכָהּ[כ] — כְּשֵׁרָה.[14] וְהוּא שֶׁיָּכוֹל הַמָּטָר לֵירֵד בְּתוֹכָהּ, אֲבָל אִם הָיָה הַסְּכָךְ מְעֻבֶּה כָּל כָּךְ עַד שֶׁאֵין הַמָּטָר יָכוֹל לֵירֵד בְּתוֹכָהּ — פְּסוּלָה,[כא,15] לְפִי שֶׁאֵין נִקְרֵאת סֻכָּה אֶלָּא אִם כֵּן אֵינָהּ מְגִנָּה אֶלָּא מִן הַצֵּל בִּלְבַד, אֲבָל אִם מְגִנָּה גַּם מִן הַמָּטָר — אֵין נִקְרֵאת סֻכָּה, אֶלָּא כְּמִין בַּיִת הִיא זוֹ:[כב,16]

even if [the s'chach] was very thick, [making it seem] like [the roof of] a house and not allowing the rays of the sun to be visible from within, it is valid.[14]

[The above applies] provided rain can come into [the sukkah]. If the s'chach is so thick that rain cannot penetrate, the sukkah is invalid,[15] for [a structure] is called a sukkah only when it offers shelter from [sunlight] alone, [providing] shade. If it also offers shelter from rain, it cannot be called a sukkah; it is like a house.[16]

ו הָיָה הַסִּכּוּךְ מְבֻלְבָּל, דְּהַיְנוּ שֶׁמִּקְצָתוֹ עוֹלֶה מְעַט לְמַעְלָה וּמִקְצָתוֹ יוֹרֵד מְעַט לְמַטָּה,[כג] אַף עַל פִּי שֶׁמִּתּוֹךְ כָּךְ חַמָּתָהּ מְרֻבָּה מִצִּלָּתָהּ[כד] — כְּשֵׁרָה,[2] שֶׁכֵּיוָן שֶׁאִם תַּעֲמֹד הַחַמָּה בְּאֶמְצַע הָרָקִיעַ כְּנֶגֶד רֹאשׁ כָּל אָדָם יִהְיֶה צִלָּתָהּ מְרֻבָּה מֵחַמָּתָהּ[כה] — אֵין לִפְסֹל אוֹתָהּ מֵחֲמַת חַמָּה הַבָּאָה מִן הַצַּד בַּאֲלַכְסוֹן:[כו]

6 If the *s'chach* was irregular, i.e., parts of it were on a somewhat higher level and parts were on a somewhat lower level, [the *sukkah*] is valid,[2] even though [at times] the sunlit area [on the floor] appears to exceed its shaded area. [The rationale is that] since when the sun is at its zenith, directly overhead, the shaded part [of the *sukkah* floor] does exceed its sunlit area, [the *sukkah*] should not be disqualified because of sunlight that comes in [at other times] from the side, at an angle.

ז בַּמֶּה דְּבָרִים אֲמוּרִים? כְּשֶׁאֵין בַּגֹּבַהּ שֶׁבֵּין הָעוֹלֶה לְהַיּוֹרֵד ג' טְפָחִים,[כז,2] שֶׁכָּל פָּחוֹת מִג' טְפָחִים הֲרֵי הוּא כְּלָבוּד[כח,17] וּמִצְטָרְפִין זֶה עִם זֶה לִהְיוֹת נִקְרָאִים סְכָךְ אֶחָד,[כט] אֲבָל אִם יֵשׁ בֵּינֵיהֶם

7 When does the above apply? When the vertical distance between the higher level and the lower level [of the *s'chach*] is less than three handbreadths,[2] for any gap smaller than three handbreadths is governed by the principle of *lavud*.[17] Hence, [the two levels of *s'chach*] are combined and considered as a single covering of *s'chach*. If there are three

14. *Sukkah* 22a-b. *Sefer HaMinhagim: The Book of Chabad-Lubavitch Customs* (p. 139) states that the Lubavitch custom is to use an abundance of *s'chach.* This was always the custom in the household of the Rebbes. See also *Otzar Minhagei Chabad,* p. 266.

15. *Pri Megadim: Eshel Avraham* (631:2) states that if, in the midst of the *sukkah,* there is a patch of *s'chach* whose area is four handbreadths square, and it is so thick that the rain cannot penetrate it, that part of the *sukkah* is invalid.

16. See sec. 626:1.

17. *Lavud* (lit., "joined") is a common halachic construct whereby two entities separated by a space

יט משנה כב, א. טור ושו"ע שם. כ ברייתא כב, ב כבית הלל, ורש"י שם ד"ה כוכבי. ב"ח סוד"ה וצריך בדעת הטור. ט"ז סק"ב. כא טור בשם ר"ת. הגהות מיימוניות פ"ה ה"ה אות ט. מרדכי רמז תשלב. מ"א סק"ב. ב"ח ד"ה ומ"ש ור"ת, ובסי' תרלה ד"ה ולענין. לבוש ס"ג. כב כדלעיל סי' תרכו ס"א. וראה פתחא זוטא סי' תרלא ס"ג. סי' תרלה ס"א. כג משנה כב, א לפירוש שמואל בגמרא שם. טור ושו"ע ס"ה. כד רש"י שם ד"ה קנה. טור. רמ"א ס"ה. כה תוס' שם ד"ה קנה. טור. כו תוס' שם. ב"י סוד"ה היה בדעת רש"י ותוס'. כז אביי בגמרא שם. טור ושו"ע שם. כח תוס' שם בסופו. לבוש ס"ה. וראה גם לעיל סי' שסג סכ"ד. כט רש"י שם ד"ה אלא. תוס' שם. ל תוס' שם. לא רבא בגמרא שם ורש"י ד"ה שאין. טור ושו"ע שם. לב ראה רש"י שם. לג ראה רש"י נדה

שְׁלֹשָׁה טְפָחִים — אֵין מִצְטָרְפִין זֶה עִם זֶה, וְאֵין זֶה חָשׁוּב סְכָךְ כְּלָל.[ל]

וְאִם יֵשׁ בְּרֹחַב הַסִּכּוּךְ הָעוֹלֶה[לא] כְּשִׁעוּר גַּג[לב] דְּהַיְנוּ טֶפַח עַל טֶפַח[לג] אוֹ יוֹתֵר וְהוּא מְכֻוָּן כְּנֶגֶד הָאֲוִיר שֶׁבֵּין הַתַּחְתּוֹן,[לד,18] אַף עַל פִּי שֶׁיֵּשׁ בֵּינֵיהֶם יוֹתֵר מִג' טְפָחִים — כְּשֵׁרָה, לְפִי שֶׁאָנוּ רוֹאִים אֶת הָעוֹלֶה כְּאִלּוּ יָרַד לְמַטָּה[19] וּמֻנָּח בָּאֲוִיר שֶׁכְּנֶגְדּוֹ.[לה] וְהוּא שֶׁיְּהֵא רֹחַב הָאֲוִיר כְּרֹחַב הָעוֹלֶה[לו] אוֹ יוֹתֵר מִמֶּנּוּ,[לז] אֲבָל אִם הָיָה פָּחוֹת מִמֶּנּוּ,[לח] וְכֵן אִם הָעוֹלֶה אֵינוֹ מְכֻוָּן מַמָּשׁ כְּנֶגֶד

handbreadths [or more] between them, they are not combined and they are not considered as a covering of *s'chach* at all.

If the width of the higher level of *s'chach* meets at least the minimum requirement [to be called] a roof, a handbreadth by a handbreadth, and it is positioned exactly over the open space on the lower level,[18] the *sukkah* is valid, even though there are more than three handbreadths between the two. We consider [the *s'chach* on] the higher level as if it had descended[19] and was positioned in the empty space under it. [See fig. 15.]

[The above applies] if the width of the empty space [between the strips of *s'chach*] is the same as the area of the upper level [of *s'chach*] or more than it. If it was less than it, or if the higher level [of *s'chach*] was not positioned exactly over the

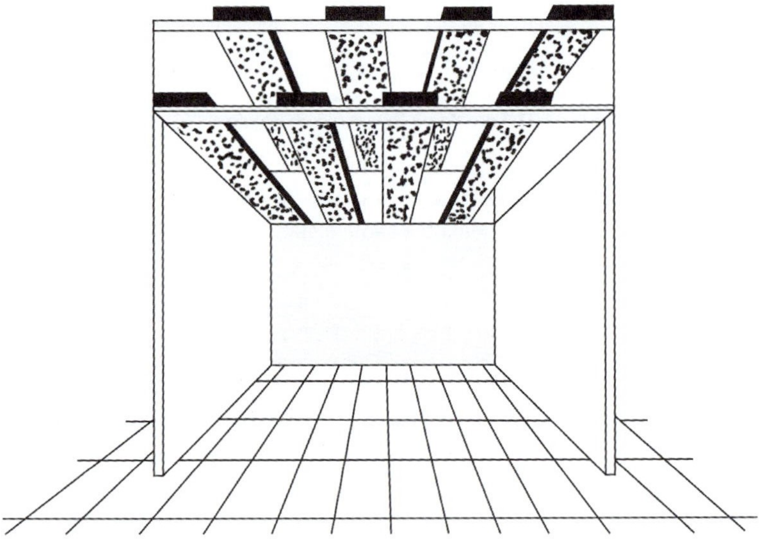

Fig. 15: See sec. 631:7.

of less than three handbreadths are considered as constituting a single continuum. See *Eruvin* 9a, *et al.*

18. Cf. *Ohalos* 12:5.

19. This principle, known as *chavot rami* (Hebrew/Aramaic; lit., "throw it downward"; *Sukkah* 22a, *Eruvin* 9a), also applies to the laws that define the domains in which one may carry on *Shabbos* (see *Rambam, Hilchos Shabbos* 17:25) and to the laws of ritual impurity (see *Rambam, Hilchos Tumas Meis* 16:5; *et al.*).

20. Here, and very often

כו, א ד"ה טפח. רמב"ם הל' טומאת מת פי"ב ה"א. וראה גם לעיל סי' שא סמ"ח. סי' שטו ס"ב. סי' שסג סכ"ד. לקמן סי' תרלו ס"ב. לד רמב"ם פ"ה הכ"א. שו"ע שם. לה רבא שם (חבוט רמי). וראה לשון הרמב"ם והשו"ע שם. לבוש שם. לקמן בהמשך הסעיף. לו ר"ן (י, ב) ד"ה הא' ממשמעות הרמב"ם שם, ראה כ"מ שם. רמ"א ס"ה. לז לחם משנה שם, ע"ש. וראה כס"מ שם. לח ר"ן שם.

הָאֲוִיר שֶׁתַּחְתָּיו, בְּעִנְיָן שֶׁאִם הָיָה יוֹרֵד לְמַטָּה כְּנֶגְדּוֹ מַמָּשׁ הָיָה מִקְצָתוֹ נוֹגֵעַ בַּסְּכָךְ הַתַּחְתּוֹן – אֵין אָנוּ רוֹאִין אוֹתוֹ[20] כְּאִלּוּ יָרַד לְמַטָּה.[לט]

וְכָל שִׁעוּרִין הַלָּלוּ הֵן הֲלָכָה לְמֹשֶׁה מִסִּינַי:[מ, 21]

ח קָנִים הַיּוֹצְאִים מֵאֲחוֹרֵי הַסֻּכָּה[מא] וּשְׁתֵּי דְּפָנוֹת נִמְשָׁכִים עִמָּהֶם,[מב, 22] כְּגוֹן שֶׁאֲחוֹרֵי דֹּפֶן אֶמְצָעִי שֶׁל הַסֻּכָּה בּוֹלְטִין קָנִים מֵהַסְּכָךְ,[23] וְיֵשׁ בָּהֶן הֶכְשֵׁר סֻכָּה דְּהַיְנוּ שִׁבְעָה טְפָחִים עַל שִׁבְעָה טְפָחִים,[מג, 8] וְצִלָּתָן מְרֻבָּה מֵחַמָּתָן, וְיֵשׁ לָהֶם שָׁלֹשׁ דְּפָנוֹת

empty space below it, but instead, were it to be lowered, part of it would touch the lower level of *s'chach,* the higher level is not considered[20] as if it had come down to the lower [level]. All of these measures are *halachos* transmitted to Moshe at Sinai.[21]

8 [The following laws apply when] canes [from the *s'chach*] project outward behind the *sukkah* and two of the walls extend together with them,[22] as is the case when the canes of the *s'chach* extend behind the middle wall.[23] If [a] these canes extend over the minimum area of a *sukkah,* which is seven handbreadths square,[8] and [b] the shaded area [under them] exceeds the sunlit area, and [c] there are three walls,

throughout this work, the original Hebrew employs the common Rabbinic wording, "*we* do not consider...," as if the speakers are the halachic authorities who were consulted on the question at hand.

21. See: *Yoma* 80a; *Sukkah* 5b; and sec. 612:1 in the present work.

22. I.e., in the same direction and to at least the same distance.

23. I.e., two parallel walls continue beyond the wall that joins them (hence called the "middle" wall), and the space between them is covered by the projecting *s'chach.* See *Sukkah* 19a; see also fig. 16.

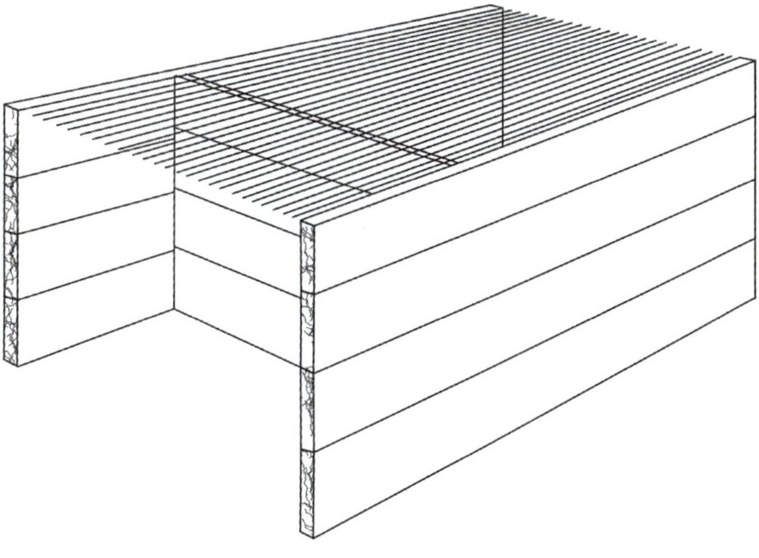

Fig. 16: See sec. 631:8.

לט לחם משנה שם. מ ראה יומא פ, א. סוכה ה, ב. רש"י יז, ב ד"ה משום. לעיל סי' תריב ס"א. מא ברייתא יט, א לפירוש עולא בגמרא שם. טור ושו"ע ס"ו. מב ריטב"א שם. וראה רש"י שם ד"ה לבראי. מג רש"י שם ד"ה והא בעינן. וכמבואר בשו"ע סי' תרלד. מד גמרא שם ורש"י ד"ה לבראי. טור ושו"ע שם.

דְּהַיְנוּ דֹּפֶן הָאֶמְצָעִי שֶׁל הַסֻּכָּה וְכָל דְּפָנוֹת הָאֲרֻכּוֹת הַנִּמְשָׁכוֹת עִמָּהֶם – הֲרֵי זוֹ סֻכָּה גְּמוּרָה וּכְשֵׁרָה, אַף עַל פִּי שֶׁדֹּפֶן הָאֶמְצָעִי לֹא נַעֲשָׂה בִּשְׁבִילָהּ אֶלָּא בִּשְׁבִיל עִקַּר הַסֻּכָּה:[מד, 24]

i.e., the middle wall and the whole of the two long walls that extend together [with the canes], this is a completely valid *sukkah.* [This is true] even though the middle wall was not constructed with this intent, but to serve the main *sukkah.*[24]

ט וְכֵן קָנִים הַבּוֹלְטִים מֵהַסְּכָךְ לְצַד רוּחַ רְבִיעִית הַסֻּכָּה[25] שֶׁהוּא פָּרוּץ וְאֵין בּוֹ דֹּפֶן[26] וְדֹפֶן אֶחָד נִמְשָׁךְ מֵהַסֻּכָּה עִם[22] קָנִים אֵלּוּ[מה, 7] שֶׁיֵּשׁ בָּהֶם הֶכְשֵׁר סֻכָּה[מו] – הֲרֵי מָקוֹם זֶה נֶחְשָׁב גַּם כֵּן מִן הַסֻּכָּה, וּמֻתָּר לֵישֵׁב שָׁם[27] אַף עַל פִּי שֶׁאֵין שָׁם אֶלָּא דֹּפֶן אֶחָד. וַאֲפִלּוּ אִם בַּעַל הַסֻּכָּה גִּלָּה דַּעְתּוֹ

9 A similar [law applies] if the canes of the *s'chach* project beyond the fourth side of the *sukkah,*[25] which is open and not enclosed by a wall,[26] and one of the [parallel] walls extends outward with[22] those canes.[7] If the canes [covering this addition] extend over the minimum dimensions of a *sukkah,* this [additional] area is also considered as part of the *sukkah* and one may sit there[27] even though it has only one wall.

[These laws apply] even [when it is possible to say that] the owner of the

---

24. One's intent is significant only while putting the *s'chach* in place, not while constructing the walls. See the *Shulchan Aruch* of R. Yosef Caro, sec. 635:1 (sec. 635 of the Alter Rebbe's *Shulchan Aruch* is not extant).

25. See fig. 17.

26. A *sukkah* is valid even with three walls; see the *Shulchan Aruch* of R. Yosef Caro, sec. 630 (sec. 630 of the Alter Rebbe's *Shulchan Aruch* is not extant).

27. And thereby fulfill one's obligation.

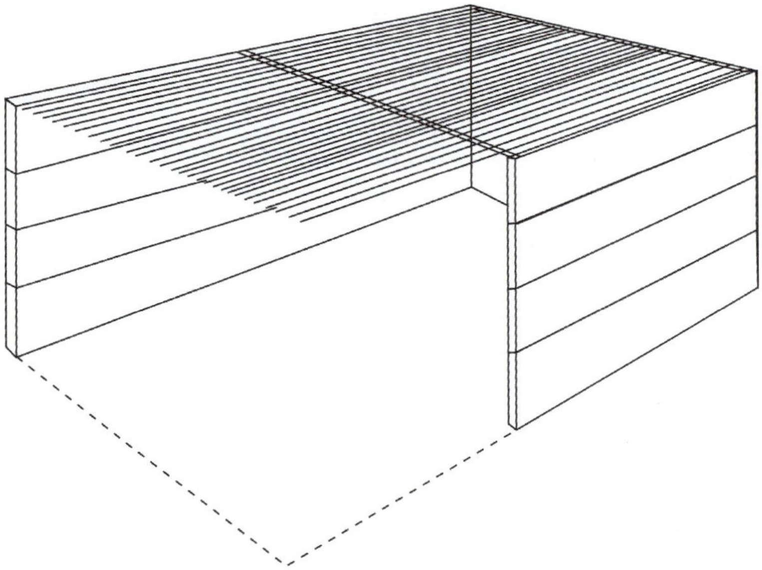

Fig. 17: See sec. 631:9.

מה ברייתא יט, א לפירוש רבה ורב יוסף בגמרא שם. טור ושו"ע ס"ז. מו ראה רש"י שם ד"ה מהו דתימא ובמהרש"א שם.

שֶׁכַּוָּנָתוֹ הָיְתָה לַעֲשׂוֹת כָּל הַסֻּכָּה בִּדְפָנוֹת אֲרֻכּוֹת[28] הַנִּמְשָׁכוֹת עִם כָּל אֹרֶךְ הַסְּכָךְ, כְּגוֹן שֶׁלְּאַחַר שֶׁעָשָׂה דֹּפֶן אֶחָד אָרֹךְ בְּאֹרֶךְ כָּל הַסְּכָךְ עָשָׂה דֹּפֶן שֶׁכְּנֶגְדּוֹ אָרֹךְ יוֹתֵר מִשִּׁבְעָה טְפָחִים[29] – אֵין אוֹמְרִים כֵּיוָן שֶׁהָיָה דַּי לַדֹּפֶן שְׁלִישִׁי הַזֶּה לַעֲשׂוֹתוֹ שִׁבְעָה טְפָחִים בִּלְבַד וְזֶה שֶׁהֶאֱרִיכוֹ יוֹתֵר גִּלָּה דַּעְתּוֹ שֶׁכַּוָּנָתוֹ לְהַמְשִׁיךְ הַדְּפָנוֹת עִם הַסְּכָךְ שֶׁלֹּא לֵישֵׁב תַּחַת הַסְּכָךְ הַפָּרוּץ שֶׁאֵין שְׁתֵּי דְּפָנוֹת נִמְשָׁכוֹת עִמָּהּ, וְאִם כֵּן דֹּפֶן זֶה הַנִּמְשָׁךְ עִם קָנִים אֵלּוּ הַבּוֹלְטִים מִן הַסְּכָךְ אֵין נֶחְשָׁב כְּלָל מִן הַסֻּכָּה אֶלָּא בִּפְנֵי עַצְמוֹ הוּא עוֹמֵד, וְנִמְצָא שֶׁאֵין לְקָנִים אֵלּוּ רַק דֹּפֶן אֶחָד דְּהַיְנוּ דֹּפֶן הַנִּמְשָׁךְ עִמָּהֶם[מז] – אֵין אָנוּ אוֹמְרִים כֵּן, מִשּׁוּם שֶׁאֵין אָנוּ הוֹלְכִין אַחַר גִּלּוּי דַּעְתּוֹ בָּזֶה (לְפִי שֶׁעֲשִׂיַּת הַסֻּכָּה אֵינָהּ צְרִיכָה כַּוָּנָה כְּמוֹ שֶׁיִּתְבָּאֵר בְּסִימָן תרל"ה[מח,30]), וּכְאִלּוּ לֹא גִּלָּה דַּעְתּוֹ כְּלָל, שֶׁכָּל הַסְּכָךְ מִתְכַּשֵּׁר בַּדֹּפֶן הַשְּׁלִישִׁי הַזֶּה הַקָּצָר אַף עַל פִּי שֶׁאֵינוֹ נִמְשָׁךְ עִם

sukkah revealed his intent to construct the entire *sukkah* with long walls,[28] flanking the full length of the *s'chach*. [How could one assert that this intent could be discerned?] For example, after he had built one *sukkah* wall as long as the entire length of the *s'chach*, he made the opposite wall longer than seven handbreadths.[29]

[This supposition is not accepted.] We do not say that since the third wall could have been only seven handbreadths long, by extending it beyond [that minimum] he revealed his intent that the walls of the *sukkah* should extend together with the *s'chach* so that he would not be sitting under the *s'chach* in the open area which does not have both walls extend outward with it. Following that logic, [one would say that] this wall which extends outward [together] with the canes extending from the *s'chach* should not at all be considered as part of the *sukkah*, but rather as a distinct entity. Thus these canes [are flanked] by only one wall, the wall that extends with them [and thus cannot be considered as part of the *sukkah*].

We do not say this. For [even if the latter were to be the builder's intent,] we are not concerned with his intent (for there is no requirement that a *sukkah* be built with the intent [that it be used for a *mitzvah*], as explained in sec. 635[30]). Thus it is as if he did not reveal his intent at all. [Rather,] the entire length of the *s'chach* is rendered valid by the third, short wall, even if it does not extend

28. For the third wall need not extend across the entire length of the *sukkah*. By making it the minimum length, the owner implied that he desired the extension to be part of the *sukkah* even if the wall does not extend together with it. In contrast, in the situation to be described, there is a plausible assumption to invalidate the *sukkah*, as the Alter Rebbe proceeds to explain: One could say that the owner desired that the *sukkah* should not extend beyond the walls. For were that not to have been his intent, there would have been no need for him to extend the wall beyond its minimum measure. Nevertheless, we do not accept that argument and instead we rule that the *sukkah* is valid *(Turei Zahav* 631:5*)*.

29. The minimum length for the walls of a *sukkah*.

30. See the *Shulchan Aruch* of R. Yosef Caro, sec. 635:1 (sec. 635 of the Alter Rebbe's *Shulchan Aruch* is not extant).

מז רא"ש פ"א סי' לה. טור ושו"ע שם. ט"ז סק"ה. מ"א ס"ק ד. מח סימן זה בשוע"ר לא הגיע לידינו, וראה טור ושו"ע שם ס"א. מט ראה רש"י שם ד"ה קמ"ל. נ סימן

כָּל אֹרֶךְ הַסְּכָךְ כְּמוֹ שֶׁנִּמְשַׁךְ דֹּפֶן שֶׁכְּנֶגְדּוֹ,[מט] וּכְמוֹ שֶׁנִּתְבָּאֵר בְּסִימָן תר"ל:[נ,31]

the entire length of the *s'chach* as does the opposite wall, as stated in sec. 630.[31]

י כְּבָר בֵּאַרְנוּ בְּסִימָן תרכ"ו[נא] שֶׁאִם סִכֵּךְ בִּסְכָךְ פָּסוּל וּבִסְכָךְ כָּשֵׁר וְאֵינָן מְעֹרָבִין זֶה עִם זֶה אֶלָּא כָּל אֶחָד וְאֶחָד מֻנָּח עַל הַסֻּכָּה בִּפְנֵי עַצְמוֹ זֶה בְּצַד זֶה — אֵינוֹ צָרִיךְ שֶׁיִּהְיֶה בַּסְּכָךְ הַכָּשֵׁר רֹב כְּנֶגֶד הַפָּסוּל, אֶלָּא אֲפִלּוּ אִם הֵן מֶחֱצָה עַל מֶחֱצָה גַּם כֵּן הַסֻּכָּה כְּשֵׁרָה,[נב,32] שֶׁכָּךְ הוּא הֲלָכָה לְמֹשֶׁה מִסִּינַי שֶׁהַסְּכָךְ הַצָּרִיךְ לְהַסֻּכָּה אֵינוֹ צָרִיךְ לִהְיוֹת רֹב מִן הַכָּשֵׁר לִסְכּוּךְ אֶלָּא חֲצִי הַסְּכָךְ בִּלְבַד.[נג] וְהוּא שֶׁלֹּא יִהְיֶה מִסְּכָךְ הַפָּסוּל אַרְבָּעָה טְפָחִים בְּמָקוֹם אֶחָד[נד] בְּסֻכָּה גְּדוֹלָה,[33] אוֹ שְׁלֹשָׁה

10 As explained in sec. 626[:8], if one covered [the *sukkah*] partly with valid *s'chach* and partly with materials that are invalid as *s'chach,* and did not mix them together, but placed them separately on the *sukkah* next to each other, there need not be more valid *s'chach* than invalid covering. Even if they are of equal amounts, the *sukkah* is valid,[32] for it is a *halachah* transmitted to Moshe at Sinai that the valid *s'chach* required for a *sukkah* need not constitute a majority; half is sufficient.

[This applies] provided there is not [a strip of] four handbreadths of invalid covering in one place in a large *sukkah,*[33]

---

31. Sec. 630 of the Alter Rebbe's *Shulchan Aruch* is not extant. See *Rama (Orach Chayim* 630:2*)*.

32. See *Sukkah* 15a.

33. I.e., any *sukkah* that exceeds the minimum area of seven handbreadths square. See fig. 18.

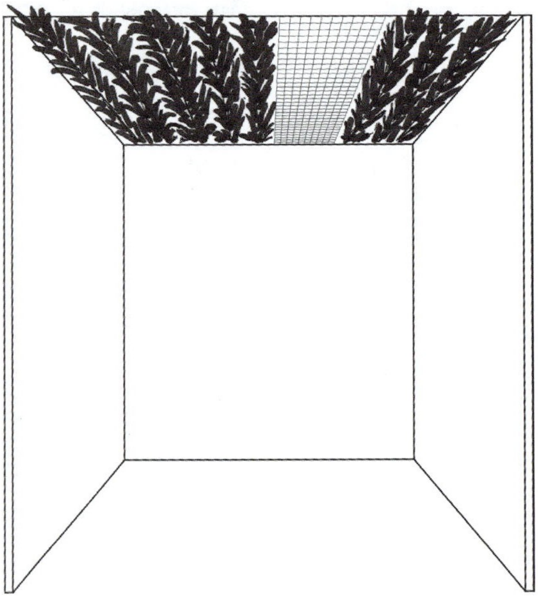

Fig. 18: Here, the invalid material is less than four *tefachim* wide and covers less than half of the area of the *sukkah*. This *sukkah* is thus valid. See sec. 631:10.

זה בשוע"ר לא הגיע לידינו, וראה טור ושו"ע שם ס"ב שמספיק שתי דפנות ושלישית טפח. **נא** סעיף ח. **נב** ר"ן (ה, א) דיבור הראשון וד"ה ונמצא, ומ"מ פ"ה הי"ב, בשם הרמב"ן, ממשנה טו, א. **נג** ר"ן שם דיבור הראשון. מ"א סי' תרכו סק"ג. וכדלעיל סי' שסב סי"ח לענין מחיצות. וכ"ה לקמן סי' תרמח ס"כ. **נד** טור ושו"ע ס"ח.

טְפָחִים בְּסֻכָּה קְטַנָּה[נה] שֶׁאֵין בָּהּ כִּי אִם שִׁבְעָה טְפָחִים עַל שִׁבְעָה טְפָחִים, כְּמוֹ שֶׁיִּתְבָּאֵר בְּסִימָן תרל"ב,[נו] עַיֵּן שָׁם:[34]

יא וַאֲפִלּוּ אִם סְכָךְ הַכָּשֵׁר הוּא קַל וְקָלוּשׁ כְּדִינוֹ בְּעִנְיָן שֶׁהַכּוֹכָבִים נִרְאִים מִתּוֹכוֹ[נז] וּסְכָךְ הַפָּסוּל אֵין הַכּוֹכָבִים נִרְאִים מִתּוֹכוֹ (כֵּיצַד? כְּגוֹן שֶׁסִּכֵּךְ בְּשַׁפּוּדִין שֶׁהֵן סְכָךְ פָּסוּל[36] וְהִנִּיחַ רֶוַח בֵּין שַׁפּוּד לְשַׁפּוּד כִּמְלֹא שַׁפּוּד וְנָתַן שָׁם סְכָךְ כָּשֵׁר[נח] קַל וְקָלוּשׁ כְּדִינוֹ, וְנִמְצָא שֶׁסְּכָךְ הַפָּסוּל הוּא מְרֻבֶּה עַל הַכָּשֵׁר כְּשִׁעוּר הָאֹרֶךְ[37] שֶׁבִּסְכָךְ הַכָּשֵׁר שֶׁהַכּוֹכָבִים נִרְאִים מִתּוֹכָהּ, מִכָּל מָקוֹם כֵּיוָן שֶׁאֹרֶךְ וְרֹחַב מְקוֹם הַמְסֻכָּךְ בִּסְכָךְ כָּשֵׁר הוּא כְּאֹרֶךְ וְרֹחַב מְקוֹם הַמְסֻכָּךְ בִּסְכָךְ פָּסוּל) — הֲרֵי זוֹ כְּשֵׁרָה מִן הַתּוֹרָה.[נט, 35]

אֶלָּא שֶׁלְּפִי שֶׁהָאָדָם אִי אֶפְשָׁר לוֹ לְצַמְצֵם[ס] לְמַלְּאוֹת כָּל הָאֲוִיר שֶׁבֵּין שַׁפּוּד לְשַׁפּוּד בִּסְכָךְ כָּשֵׁר[סא] שֶׁלֹּא יִהְיֶה שׁוּם אֲוִיר מַשֶּׁהוּ בֵּין הַשַּׁפּוּד לִסְכָךְ הַכָּשֵׁר,[סב] וְנִמְצָא

or of three handbreadths in a small *sukkah* that is only seven handbreadths square, as will be explained in sec. 632.[34]

11 Even if the valid *s'chach* is sufficiently light and sparse — as is required — to enable the stars to be seen through it, and they cannot be seen through the material that is invalid for *s'chach*, the *sukkah* is valid according to Scriptural Law.[35]

(What is implied? A person covered [the top of the *sukkah*] with [metal] spits, which are invalid as *s'chach*.[36] He left a space the width of a spit between each pair of spits and filled those spaces with light and sparse valid *s'chach* as required by law. Thus the invalid *s'chach* exceeds the valid *s'chach* by the measure of the [empty space[37]] in the valid *s'chach* through which the stars are visible. Nevertheless, since the length and the width of the area covered by valid *s'chach* are equivalent to the length and width of the area covered by invalid *s'chach*), the *sukkah* is valid according to Scriptural Law.

Nonetheless, it is impossible for a person to be exact and fill all the empty space between the spits with valid *s'chach* without leaving any space whatever between [any] spit and the [adjoining] valid *s'chach*. Thus

34. See the *Shulchan Aruch* of R. Yosef Caro, sec. 632:1 (sec. 632 of the Alter Rebbe's *Shulchan Aruch* is not extant). As evident from that source, when a strip of invalid *s'chach* runs from one wall to the other in the midst of a *sukkah* that exceeds the minimum area of seven handbreadths square, it divides the *sukkah* in half and the area beneath the invalid *s'chach* may not be used. If such a strip of invalid *s'chach* runs across a *sukkah* with only three valid walls, the *sukkah* is invalidated because it is considered as if divided into two parts, each with only two valid walls. If this invalid *s'chach* was placed at the side, however, the *sukkah* is valid — by virtue of the principle of *dofen akumah* (lit., "a bent wall") that is explained in sec. 629, footnote 50 above.

35. *Sukkah* 15a.

36. These spits are less than four handbreadths wide. Otherwise, they would disqualify the *sukkah* (see end of subsection 10 above).

37. In the Hebrew original: אורך ("length"), but possibly this should read אויר ("space"), as is the wording here in earlier codifiers. Hence the above bracketed translation.

נה ב"י ד"ה ומ"ש ואין בהם. דרכי משה ס"ק ג בשם הגהות מהר"א מפראג. רמ"א ס"ח. **נו** סימן זה בשוע"ר לא הגיע לידינו, וראה טור ושו"ע שם ס"א. **נז** כדלעיל ס"ה. **נח** משנה טו, סוע"א ורש"י שם. טור ושו"ע ס"ח. **נט** ראה אבני נזר או"ח סי' תסד אות א ואילך. **ס** גמרא טו, רע"ב כגירסת ר"ח ור"ת בתוס' ד"ה פרוץ. רא"ש פ"א סי' כט. טור ושו"ע שם. **סא** תוס' שם. רא"ש שם. טור ושו"ע שם. **סב** תוס' שם. **סג** רא"ש שם (לרב פפא). טור ושו"ע שם.

the invalid *s'chach* will exceed the valid *s'chach,*[38] for the space between one spit and another is no more than exactly the width of a spit. Moreover, this space is not even filled entirely with valid *s'chach;* there is a minimal space between it and the invalid *s'chach.* Hence, such a *sukkah* is not valid unless one placed on it a little additional valid *s'chach* to overlap the invalid *s'chach,* for then, all the empty space between the spits will certainly be covered.

Similarly, [such a *sukkah* is valid] if the spits were placed like the warp, i.e., lengthwise over the *sukkah,* and the canes of valid *s'chach* were placed like the woof, i.e., across the width of the *sukkah.* In such a situation, if one did not place the ends of the canes on the spits, they would certainly fall to the ground. Thus, inevitably, all the empty space is certainly covered and not even a minimal space is left between the spits and the valid *s'chach.*

שֶׁסְּכָךְ הַפָּסוּל הוּא מְרֻבֶּה עַל הַכָּשֵׁר,[סג, 38] שֶׁהֲרֵי אֵין בֵּין שַׁפּוּד לְשַׁפּוּד אֶלָּא כִּמְלֹא שַׁפּוּד בְּצִמְצוּם,[סד] וְגַם מָקוֹם זֶה אֵינוֹ מָלֵא מִסְּכָךְ כָּשֵׁר אֶלָּא נִשְׁאָר אֲוִיר מַשֶּׁהוּ בֵּינוֹ לַסְּכָךְ הַפָּסוּל, לְפִיכָךְ אֵין סֻכָּה זוֹ כְּשֵׁרָה אֶלָּא אִם כֵּן הֶעְדִּיף מְעַט סְכָךְ הַכָּשֵׁר וּנְתָנוֹ עַל הַפָּסוּל,[סה] שֶׁאָז בְּוַדַּאי נִתְכַּסָּה כָּל הָאֲוִיר שֶׁבֵּין שַׁפּוּד לְשַׁפּוּד.[סו]

וְכֵן אִם הָיוּ הַשַּׁפּוּדִין נְתוּנִין שְׁתִי דְּהַיְנוּ לְאֹרֶךְ הַסֻּכָּה וְהַקָּנִים שֶׁל סְכָךְ הַכָּשֵׁר נְתוּנִים עֵרֶב[סז] דְּהַיְנוּ לְרֹחַב הַסֻּכָּה, שֶׁאָז עַל כָּרְחָךְ אִם אֵינוֹ נוֹתֵן רָאשֵׁי הַקָּנִים עַל הַשַּׁפּוּד הֲרֵי הֵן נוֹפְלִים לָאָרֶץ,[סח] וְאִם כֵּן עַל כָּרְחָךְ בְּוַדַּאי מִתְכַּסֶּה כָּל הָאֲוִיר[סט] וְלֹא נִשְׁאָר אֲפִלּוּ אֲוִיר מַשֶּׁהוּ בֵּין הַשַּׁפּוּדִין לַסְּכָךְ הַכָּשֵׁר:

12 [The following applies to] a house roofed with boards that are not covered by a *maazivah* (i.e., a clay floor that [sometimes] overlays them),[35] and [one desires] to make [the house] valid so that he can dwell under [the boards] for the sake of [the *mitzvah* of] a *sukkah.* Now, these boards are invalid as *s'chach,* even if they are less than four handbreadths wide,[39] because they were not put in place for the purpose of shade, but for the sake of a dwelling. How can they be made valid? Every alternate board must be removed and valid *s'chach* must be put in its place. In this way, the en-

יב בַּיִת הַמְקֹרֶה בִּנְסָרִים שֶׁאֵין עֲלֵיהֶם מַעֲזִיבָה[ע] (פֵּרוּשׁ[עא] רִצְפַּת טִיט שֶׁמְּשִׁימִין עֲלֵיהֶם[35]) וּבָא לְהַכְשִׁירוֹ לֵישֵׁב תַּחְתֵּיהֶן לְשֵׁם סֻכָּה,[עב] שֶׁהֲרֵי נְסָרִים אֵלּוּ הֵם פְּסוּלִים לְסִכּוּךְ אֲפִלּוּ אֵין בְּרָחְבָּן אַרְבָּעָה טְפָחִים,[39] לְפִי שֶׁלֹּא הֻנְּחוּ כָּאן לְשֵׁם צֵל אֶלָּא לְשֵׁם דִּירָה,[עג] כֵּיצַד מַכְשִׁירָן? נוֹטֵל נֶסֶר אֶחָד[עד] מִבֵּין שְׁנַיִם[עה] וְיִתֵּן סְכָךְ כָּשֵׁר בִּמְקוֹמָהּ,[עו] וְחוֹזֵר וְנוֹטֵל נֶסֶר אֶחָד[עז] וְיִתֵּן סְכָךְ כָּשֵׁר בִּמְקוֹמָהּ, וְתִהְיֶה כְּשֵׁרָה

38. See the rationale given in *Tosafos* (*Sukkah* 15b).

39. See sec. 629:29.

סד רא"ש שם (לרב פפא). **סה** רבי אמי בגמרא שם לפירוש התוס' שם. טור ושו"ע שם. **סו** תוס' שם. טור ושו"ע שם. **סז** רבא בגמרא שם. טור ושו"ע שם. **סח** רש"י שם ד"ה רבא. וראה גם תוס' שם. **סט** תוס' שם. טור ושו"ע שם. **ע** משנה טו, רע"א. טור ושו"ע ס"ט. **עא** רש"י שם ד"ה מעזיבה. **עב** רמב"ם פ"ה ה"ח. רש"י שם ד"ה ב"ש. **עג** רמב"ם פ"ה ה"ח. וכדלעיל סי' תרכו ס"א. **עד** רבי יהודה במשנה שם אליבא דבית הלל. רמב"ם שם. טור ושו"ע שם. **עה** פירוש המשניות לרמב"ם שם. טור ושו"ע שם. **עו** רמב"ם שם. טור ושו"ע שם. **עז** רא"ש פ"א סי' כט. טור. לבוש שם.

כָּל הַסֻּכָּה:[עח,40]

חָסֵר[עט,41]

tire *sukkah* will be valid.[40]

[The end of sec. 631 and the whole of sec. 632-635 are not extant.[41]]

סימן תרלו דִּין סֻכָּה יְשָׁנָה וּבוֹ ג' סְעִיפִים:

SECTION 636 Laws Relating to an Old *Sukkah.* (1–3)

א סֻכָּה יְשָׁנָה,[א] דְּהַיְנוּ שֶׁעֲשָׂאָהּ קֹדֶם שְׁלֹשִׁים יוֹם שֶׁלִּפְנֵי הֶחָג[ב] – כְּשֵׁרָה,[1] וּבִלְבַד שֶׁיְּחַדֵּשׁ בָּהּ לְשֵׁם הֶחָג.[ג,2] וְאִם עֲשָׂאָהּ לְשֵׁם חַג[3] אֲפִלּוּ מִתְּחִלַּת הַשָּׁנָה[4] – אֵין צָרִיךְ לְחַדֵּשׁ בָּהּ דָּבָר:[ד,5]

1 1. An old *sukkah* — i.e., one that was made more than 30 days before Sukkos — is valid, provided[1] something new was done to it for the sake of the festival.[2] If it was constructed for the sake of the festival,[3] even at the beginning of the year,[4] nothing new need be done to it.[5]

ב חִדּוּשׁ זֶה שֶׁאָמַרְנוּ – צָרִיךְ שֶׁיְּהֵא בְּגוּף הַסְּכָךְ,[ה] דְּהַיְנוּ שֶׁיַּנִּיחַ סְכָךְ חָדָשׁ לְשֵׁם הֶחָג, וַאֲפִלּוּ אֵין בַּסְּכָךְ הַמְחֻדָּשׁ אֶלָּא

2 This new activity must involve the *s'chach* itself, i.e., some new *s'chach* must be put in place for the purpose of the festival. For this, even a handbreadth by a

---

40. Unlike subsection 11, this subsection makes no mention of a need for overlapping, for even the boards that were not moved are also deemed valid *s'chach.* See *Mishnah Berurah* 631:23, and sec. 626:12 above.

* For a summary of sec. 631, see p. 452.

41. The corresponding sections in the *Shulchan Aruch* of R. Yosef Caro deal with factors that invalidate *s'chach,* with the height and area of a *sukkah,* and with *sukkos* built in a variety of unconventional situations.

SECTION 636

1. *Sukkah* 9a. According to *Magen Avraham* 636:1 and *Mishnah Berurah* 636:4, the directive that follows — that something new be done to the *sukkah* for the sake of the festival — is not an absolute requirement: it merely upgrades the level at which the *mitzvah* is fulfilled. These authorities hold that after the fact, even if nothing new was done, the *sukkah* is still valid, provided its *s'chach* was put in place for the purpose of shelter.

2. *Talmud Yerushalmi, Sukkah* 1:2.

3. The issue is thus not the date of construction, but the builder's intent at the time. And since the laws of the festival are commonly studied 30 days beforehand, it may be assumed that people are already aware of its advent, and that whoever constructs a *sukkah* at that time constructs it with the festival in mind. See parallels in sec. 436:1.

4. I.e., Rosh Chodesh Nissan, which is considered the beginning of the year in certain contexts. *Shaar HaTziyun* 336:9, however, states that it refers to Rosh HaShanah a year earlier.

In the context of the search for *chametz* on the eve of Pesach, "the beginning of the year" means "after last Pesach" (see sec. 436:8 in the present work). Accordingly, that phrase here would mean "after last Sukkos" (as in the commentary of R. Pinchas Kehati on *Sukkah* 1:1).

5. Some authorities hold that if the same *sukkah* is used every year, a small part of it must be covered with new *s'chach,* as stated in subsection 2 below. (See *Mishnah Berurah* 636:7, citing *Chayei Adam,* based on *Magen Avraham* 638:2, which is restated by the Alter Rebbe, sec. 638:16.) *Aruch HaShulchan* 636:1 questions this ruling.

עח רמב"ם שם. טור ושו"ע שם. **עט** סיום ס"ט וס"י שבשו"ע, וסי' תרלב (דברים הפוסלים בסכך) תרלג (דין גובה הסוכה) תרלד (שלא תהיה פחות מן שבעה על שבעה) תרלה (דין סוכת גנב"ך ורקב"ש).

סימן תרלו: א משנה ט, א וכבית הלל. טור ושו"ע ס"א. **ב** רש"י שם ד"ב בית שמאי. ר"ן (א, א) ד"ה איזו. שו"ע שם. **ג** ירושלמי פ"א ה"ב. תוס' שם ד"ה סוכה. רא"ש פ"א סי' יג. טור ושו"ע שם. **ד** משנה שם. תוס' שם ד"ה ואם (דהיינו אפילו לבית הלל, לענין שאין צריך לחדש בה דבר). הגהות אשרי שם בשם אור זרוע סי' רפו. טור ושו"ע שם. **ה** רא"ש שם בשם בעל העיטור ריש הל' סוכה. טור וב"י ד"ה ומ"ש ובלבד. **ו** ירושלמי שם. תוס' שם ד"ה סוכה. רא"ש שם. טור ושו"ע

טֶפַח[ו] עַל טֶפַח[ז] מְרֻבָּע[ח] – דַּי בְּכָךְ.[6] וְאִם אֹרֶךְ הֶחָדוּשׁ הוּא הוֹלֵךְ עַל פְּנֵי כָּל אֹרֶךְ אוֹ לְרֹחַב הַסֻּכָּה, אֲפִלּוּ אֵין בְּרָחְבּוֹ אֶלָּא כָּל שֶׁהוּא – דַּי בְּכָךְ.[ט]

וְכָל זֶה בִּסְכָךְ, אֲבָל בִּדְפָנוֹת[י] אֲפִלּוּ עֲשָׂאָן מִתְּחִלַּת הַשָּׁנָה בְּבֵרוּר שֶׁלֹּא לְשֵׁם הֶחָג – אֵינוֹ צָרִיךְ לְחַדֵּשׁ בָּהֶם דָּבָר:

handbreadth is sufficient.[6] Alternatively, if the new *s'chach* extends along the entire length or across the entire width of the *sukkah,* even [a strip of] the slightest width is sufficient.

All of the above applies to the *s'chach.* With regard to the walls, [the *sukkah* is valid] even if they were made at the beginning of the year explicitly for a purpose other than the festival. Nothing new need be done to them.

ג יוֹצֵר כְּלֵי חֶרֶס שֶׁיֵּשׁ לוֹ שְׁתֵּי סֻכּוֹת זוֹ לִפְנִים מִזּוֹ[יא] וּשְׁתֵּיהֶן עֲשׂוּיוֹת לְצֵל[יב,7] וְעוֹשֶׂה קְדֵרוֹתָיו בַּפְּנִימִית וּמוֹכְרָם בַּחִיצוֹנָה[יג] – הַפְּנִימִית אֵינוֹ יוֹצֵא בָהּ יְדֵי סֻכָּה,[יד] אַף עַל פִּי שֶׁהִיא עֲשׂוּיָה לְצֵל, מִכָּל מָקוֹם כֵּיוָן שֶׁהִיא דִּירָתוֹ כָּל הַשָּׁנָה שֶׁהוּא אוֹכֵל וְיָשֵׁן בָּהּ וְעוֹשֶׂה בָהּ רֹב תַּשְׁמִישָׁיו – אֵין נִכָּר שֶׁהוּא דָר בָּהּ עַתָּה לְשֵׁם מִצְוָה,[טו] אֲבָל הַחִיצוֹנָה יוֹצֵא בָהּ יְדֵי סֻכָּה,[טז] שֶׁהֲרֵי אֵינוֹ דָר בָּהּ כָּל הַשָּׁנָה,[יז,8] וַאֲפִלּוּ הַפְּנִימִית אִם מַגְבִּיהַּ אֶת הַסְּכָךְ וְחוֹזֵר וּמַנִּיחוֹ לְשֵׁם סֻכָּה – כְּשֵׁרָה,[יח,9] שֶׁהֲרֵי אֲפִלּוּ תִּקְרַת הַבַּיִת מִתְכַּשֶּׁרֶת לִסְכּוֹךְ עַל יְדֵי מַעֲשֶׂה זוֹ כְּמוֹ שֶׁנִּתְבָּאֵר בְּסִימָן תרל"א:[יט,10]

3 [The following laws apply with regard to] a potter [whose workplace is comprised] of two [adjoining] *sukkos,* one of which gives access to the other, and both of which were constructed for shade.[7] He fashions his pots in the inner *[sukkah]* and sells them in the outer *[sukkah].*

Though the inner *sukkah* was built for shade, he does not fulfill [the obligation to dwell] in the *sukkah* with it, because it serves as his dwelling throughout the year. Since he eats, sleeps, and performs most of his activities there, it would not be evident [during the festival] that he is now doing these things for the sake of the *mitzvah.* He may, however, fulfill his obligation using the outer *[sukkah],* for he does not dwell in it throughout the year.[8]

Moreover, even the inner *[sukkah]* is valid if he raises the *s'chach* and then puts it back for the sake [of the *mitzvah*] of *sukkah,*[9] for even the roof of a house can be validated for *s'chach* through such an action, as explained in sec. 631.[10]

---

6. *Talmud Yerushalmi, loc. cit.*

7. *Sukkah* 8a.

8. The *Mishnah Berurah* 636:10 stipulates that even the outer *sukkah* requires some new *s'chach,* as in subsection 2 above.

9. Since this inner *sukkah* is used as a dwelling throughout the year, merely covering a small part of it with new *s'chach* will not suffice. A more significant activity is required to make the necessary distinction *(Mishnah Berurah* 636:9).

10. The end of sec. 631 of the Alter Rebbe's *Shulchan Aruch* is not extant. See *Magen Avraham* 631:6 and 8, and sec. 629:20 above.

שם. **ז** טור ושו"ע שם. וראה גם לעיל סי' תרלא ס"ז. **ח** מ"א סק"ב. **ט** ירושלמי שם. תוס' שם. רא"ש שם. טור ושו"ע שם. **י** ט"ז סק"א. **יא** גמרא ח, ב ורש"י ד"ה שתי. טור ושו"ע ס"ב. **יב** מ"א סי' תרלא סק"א. ואם עשויה גם לדור בה בקביעות, ראה לעיל סי' תרכו ס"א. **יג** טור ושו"ע שם. וראה רש"י שם. **יד** גמרא שם. טור ושו"ע שם. **טו** רש"י שם ד"ה פנימית. טור ושו"ע שם. **טז** גמרא שם. טור ושו"ע שם. **יז** רש"י שם ד"ה החיצונה. טור ושו"ע שם. **יח** מ"א סק"ג. **יט** סעיף יב.

סימן תרלז דִּין סֻכָּה שְׁאוּלָה וּגְזוּלָה וּבוֹ י״ב סְעִיפִים:

א מִי שֶׁלֹּא עָשָׂה סֻכָּה קֹדֶם הֶחָג,[א] בֵּין בְּשׁוֹגֵג[1] בֵּין בְּמֵזִיד[ב,2] — הֲרֵי זֶה עוֹשֶׂה סֻכָּה בְּחֻלּוֹ שֶׁל מוֹעֵד[ג,3] וְיוֹשֵׁב בָּהּ.[ד,4] וְאַף עַל פִּי שֶׁנֶּאֱמַר[ה,5] "חַג הַסֻּכֹּת תַּעֲשֶׂה לְךָ שִׁבְעַת יָמִים", אֵין כַּוָּנַת הַכָּתוּב לַעֲשׂוֹת סֻכָּה הָרְאוּיָה לְשִׁבְעָה יָמִים[ו] פְּרָט לְחֻלּוֹ שֶׁל מוֹעֵד שֶׁאֵינָהּ רְאוּיָה לְשִׁבְעָה יָמִים;[ז] אֶלָּא כַּוָּנַת הַכָּתוּב כָּל שִׁבְעַת הַיָּמִים תַּעֲשֶׂה סֻכָּה,[ח] אִם לֹא עָשִׂיתָ בְּיוֹם רִאשׁוֹן — תַּעֲשֶׂה בְּיוֹם שֵׁנִי, וַאֲפִלּוּ בְּסוֹף יוֹם הַשְּׁבִיעִי:[ט,6]

ב וְכֵן מֻתָּר לָצֵאת מִסֻּכָּה זוֹ וְלֵישֵׁב בְּסֻכָּה אַחֶרֶת,[י,4] וְאֵין צָרִיךְ לֵישֵׁב כָּל שִׁבְעַת הַיָּמִים בְּסֻכָּה אַחַת:[יא]

ג אַף עַל פִּי שֶׁאָמְרָה תוֹרָה "חַג הַסֻּכֹּת תַּעֲשֶׂה לְךָ", "לְךָ" — "מִשֶּׁלְּךָ",[יב] כְּלוֹמַר שֶׁתְּהֵא הַסֻּכָּה שֶׁלְּךָ וְלֹא שֶׁל חֲבֵרְךָ — אַף עַל פִּי כֵן יוֹצֵא אָדָם יְדֵי חוֹבָתוֹ בְּסֻכָּה

SECTION 637 Laws Relating to a Borrowed or Stolen *Sukkah*. (1–12)

1 A person who did not build a *sukkah* before the festival, whether unintentionally[1] or intentionally,[2] should build a *sukkah* during *Chol HaMoed*[3] and dwell in it.[4] Though it is written,[5] "Make the Sukkos festival for yourself for seven days," the intent is not that one must build a *sukkah* fit to be used for seven days, thus excluding [one built during] *Chol HaMoed* which would not be fit to be used for seven days, but rather — throughout the seven days you should make a *sukkah*. If you did not make it on the first day, make it on the second, or even towards the close of the seventh day.[6]

2 Similarly, it is permitted to leave one *sukkah* and dwell in another *sukkah*.[4] There is no requirement to dwell in the same *sukkah* for all seven days.

3 The Torah states, "Make the Sukkos festival for yourself," [implying that] the *sukkah* must be your own and not your friend's. Nevertheless, one may fulfill his obligation with a borrowed

---

1. In the original, *beshogeg*.

2. In the original, *bemeizid*.

3. The intermediate days of Sukkos (and Pesach). One cannot build a *sukkah* on the first day (and in the Diaspora: on the first two days) of Sukkos, because building is one of the labors forbidden on *Shabbos* and *Yom-Tov*. *Mishnah Berurah* 637:1 speaks of the laws that apply if the *s'chach* is blown off by wind or rain on the festival.

If a *sukkah* is built during *Chol HaMoed,* some authorities permit this to be done at the usual professional standards. However, it is preferable to limit oneself to less. See: *Biur Halachah* 637, *s.v. Oseh;* R. Yekusiel Farkash, *Chol HaMoed KeHilchaso* (Jerusalem, 5747), sec. 8:25, p. 280; R. Yehoshua Neuwirth, *Shemiras Shabbos KeHilchaso,* Vol. 2, sec. 67:40.

4. *Sukkah* 27b.

5. *Devarim* 16:13.

6. Unlike Pesach, whose seventh day is a fully-fledged *Yom-Tov,* the seventh day of Sukkos *(Hoshana Rabbah)* shares the laws of the preceding semi-festive days of *Chol HaMoed,* during which a *sukkah* may be built.

א רש״י כז, ב ד״ה ורבנן. רמב״ם פ״ו הט״ו. טור ושו״ע ס״א. ב רמב״ם שם. שו״ע שם. ג גמרא [ברייתא] כז, ב כחכמים. רמב״ם שם. טור ושו״ע שם. ד אף שאינו יושב בה שבעת ימים, וכדלקמן ס״ב. ה דברים טז, יג. ו כדעת רבי אליעזר בברייתא שם. ז רש״י שם ד״ה עשה. ח גמרא שם (עשה סוכה בחג). רבנו מנוח על הרמב״ם שם. ב״י ריש הסי׳. לבוש ס״א. ט״ז ס״ק א. ט רמב״ם שם. שו״ע שם. ט״ז שם. וראה פרדס חב״ד 9 ע׳ 97. י גמרא [ברייתא] כז, ב כחכמים. טור ושו״ע שם. יא טור ולבוש סוף ס״א. יב ברייתא כז, ב. וכדלקמן סי׳ תרמט ס״א לענין לולב. יג גמרא [ברייתא] שם כחכמים. טור ושו״ע ס״ב. יד לבוש

שְׁאוּלָה,[יג,7] דְּכֵיוָן שֶׁנִּכְנַס לָהּ בִּרְשׁוּת – הֲרֵי הִיא כְּשֶׁלּוֹ,[יד,8] וְלֹא נֶאֱמַר "לְךָ מִשֶּׁלְּךָ", אֶלָּא לְהוֹצִיא אֶת הַגְּזוּלָה[טו] וְעַל דֶּרֶךְ שֶׁיִּתְבָּאֵר.[טז]

וְכֵן יוֹצֵא אָדָם יְדֵי חוֹבָתוֹ בְּסֻכָּה שֶׁיֵּשׁ לוֹ שֻׁתָּפוּת בָּהּ עִם חֲבֵרוֹ,[יז] אֲפִלּוּ אִם נִכְנָס לָהּ שֶׁלֹּא בִּרְשׁוּת חֲבֵרוֹ, וְאֵין זֶה נִקְרָא גָּזֵל,[יח] כֵּיוָן שֶׁעַל דַּעַת כֵּן נִשְׁתַּתְּפוּ שֶׁכָּל אֶחָד מֵהֶם יִשְׁתַּמֵּשׁ בָּהּ כִּרְצוֹנוֹ:[יט]

ד וַאֲפִלּוּ סֻכָּה הַגְּזוּלָה פְּעָמִים שֶׁהִיא כְּשֵׁרָה.[9] כֵּיצַד? הֲרֵי שֶׁתִּקֵּן יִשְׂרָאֵל סֻכָּתוֹ וּבָא חֲבֵרוֹ וְהוֹצִיאוֹ מִסֻּכָּתוֹ וּגְזָלָהּ

sukkah,[7] because, since he enters it with permission, it is considered as his own.[8] The phrase "for yourself," implying that the *sukkah* must be one's own, was stated only to exclude a stolen *sukkah,* as will be explained.

Similarly, one may fulfill his obligation with a *sukkah* that he owns in partnership with a friend, even if one of the partners enters without the permission of the other. This is not considered as theft, for the partnership was established with the intent that each partner may use [the *sukkah*] as he desires.

4 There are situations in which even a stolen *sukkah* is valid.[9]

What is implied? When a Jew assembles his *sukkah* and someone comes along and forces him to leave and [uses it], that person

7. The Alter Rebbe is explaining here that the term "for yourself" does not merely rule out the validity of a stolen *sukkah* (as might be inferred from *Tosafos* on *Sukkah* 27b), but rather it defines the *mitzvah:* the *sukkah* must be one's own. (See *Rivash,* Responsum 347, cited in *Likkutei Sichos,* Vol. 19, p. 348-350. See also footnote 8 below.)

8. The Sages note a similar restriction with regard to the Four Species used for the *mitzvah* of *lulav* and *esrog.* They, too, must be "your own"; the *mitzvah* cannot be fulfilled if any of the Four Species belong to another (see sec. 649:1 below). In that instance, however, a person may not fulfill his obligation with a borrowed *lulav.* (The word *lulav* often signifies the species collectively.) Why then is a borrowed *sukkah* permitted?

In response, the Sages explain that the verse *(Vayikra* 23:42), "Every individual [within] Israel shall dwell in *sukkos,"* teaches that it would be appropriate that the entire Jewish people dwell in a single *sukkah.* In such a situation, there will certainly be individuals dwelling in a borrowed *sukkah* *(Sukkah* 27b and *Rashi* there).

In *Likkutei Sichos,* Vol. 19, pp. 348ff., the Rebbe further clarifies why a borrowed *sukkah* is considered one's own, but not a borrowed *lulav.* The *mitzvah* of dwelling in the *sukkah* involves considering the *sukkah* as one's permanent dwelling. Thus when a person lends his *sukkah* to a friend, his intent is that his friend will regard it as actually his, for only with such an intent can the *mitzvah* be fulfilled.

By contrast, the concept that an individual must personally own the Four Species does not *define* that commandment. It is a requirement that must be met, but not an integral part of the *mitzvah.* For a borrowed *lulav* to be valid, therefore, the owner should explicitly specify that he is giving it as a gift with the intent that it be returned. (See the *Shulchan Aruch* of R. Yosef Caro, 658:4; *Sefer HaMinhagim: The Book of Chabad-Lubavitch Customs,* p. 142.) Unlike the law regarding a *sukkah,* this is not a presumption one can take for granted.

The complete discussion of this subject is outlined in *Beacons on the Talmud's Sea* (Sichos In English, N.Y., 1997), pp. 67ff.

9. Needless to say, the following laws do not condone theft in any form; they deal with the status of the stolen items after the fact.

ס"ב. וכ"ה לקמן סי"א (שכשמשאילה מדעתו הוי כשלו ממש, משא"כ בלאו הכי יוצא רק בדיעבד). וראה לקו"ש חי"ט ע' 350-348. חידושים וביאורים בש"ס ח"ב ע' פו-פט. שלחן המלך ח"ב ע' רמב-ו. יגדיל תורה (נ.י.) יח ע' שלד. כב ע' תריא. כט ע' רכא. כינוס תורה יד ע' סט. שערי שלום סי' לא אות יט. העו"ב תקיג ע' 10. **טו** גמרא שם אליבא דחכמים. **טז** סעי' ה ואילך. **יז** תוס' שם ד"ה כל. ריב"ש שם סי' שמז (גם לדעת רש"י שם ד"ה כל האזרח, ור"ן שם (יב, ב) ד"ה דכתיב). שו"ע שם. **יח** שיאסר עכ"פ לכתחלה, כדלקמן סי"א. **יט** ריב"ש שם. ב"י ד"ה וכתב הר"ן.

has fulfilled his obligation.[10] [The rationale is that] land can never be stolen;[11] i.e., unlike movable property, it is never considered as stolen property that enters the possession of the thief and becomes his property in every respect. For example, if the value [of landed property] increased while it was in the hands of the thief, the increase in value does not belong to him, as it would were movable property to be involved.[12]

Rather, [landed property] is always considered to be in the possession of its [rightful] owner and lent out, as it were, to the thief. Any object attached to such landed property is considered as the landed property itself. It [too] is not acquired by the thief, but rather is "lent out" to him. Hence, this *sukkah* which is built on the ground is considered as being "lent out" to the thief, and he may fulfill his obligation with it as one may with a borrowed *sukkah*.[10]

וְיָשַׁב בָּהּ — יָצָא,[כ,10] שֶׁאֵין הַקַּרְקַע נִגְזֶלֶת,[כא,11] כְּלוֹמַר שֶׁאֵין עָלֶיהָ תּוֹרַת גָּזֵל כִּמְטַּלְטְלִין לַעֲמֹד בְּחֶזְקַת הַגַּזְלָן[כב] וּבִרְשׁוּתוֹ לְכָל דָּבָר, כְּגוֹן שֶׁאִם הִשְׁבִּיחָה בִּרְשׁוּת הַגַּזְלָן — אֵין הַשֶּׁבַח שֶׁלּוֹ[כג] כְּמוֹ בִּמְטַּלְטְלִין,[כד,12] אֶלָּא לְעוֹלָם הִיא בְּחֶזְקַת בְּעָלֶיהָ, וַהֲרֵי הִיא כִּשְׁאוּלָה בְּיַד הַגַּזְלָן,[כה] וְכָל הַמְחֻבָּר לַקַּרְקַע — הֲרֵי הוּא כְּקַרְקַע,[כו] שֶׁאֵינוֹ נִקְנֶה לְהַגַּזְלָן אֶלָּא הֲרֵי הוּא כְּשָׁאוּל בְּיָדוֹ, וּלְפִיכָךְ סֻכָּה זוֹ שֶׁהִיא בְּנוּיָה עַל הַקַּרְקַע — הֲרֵי הִיא כִּשְׁאוּלָה בְּיַד הַגַּזְלָן, וְיוֹצֵא הוּא בָּהּ יְדֵי חוֹבָתוֹ כְּמוֹ שֶׁיּוֹצְאִין בְּסֻכָּה שְׁאוּלָה:[כז,10]

5 If a person stole pieces of wood and used them as *s'chach* for his *sukkah*, [the *sukkah* may be valid].[10] Even though he did not attach them to his *sukkah*[13] but merely placed them on it, and even though he did not change them in any way, [they are considered his]. During the other days of the year, in such a situation, [the thief] would be obligated to return the same pieces of wood to the person from whom he stole, for

ה וְאִם גָּזַל עֵצִים וְסִכֵּךְ בָּהֶם סֻכָּתוֹ,[כח,10] אַף עַל פִּי שֶׁלֹּא חִבְּרָן לְסֻכָּתוֹ[13] אֶלָּא הִנִּיחָן עַל גַּבֵּי סֻכָּתוֹ,[כט] וְלֹא עָשָׂה בָּהֶן שׁוּם שִׁנּוּי בְּעִנְיָן שֶׁבִּשְׁאָר יְמוֹת הַשָּׁנָה חַיָּב לְהַחֲזִיר הָעֵצִים עַצְמָן לְהַנִּגְזָל,[ל] שֶׁהֲרֵי לֹא קָנָה

---

10. *Sukkah* 31a.

11. *Bava Kama* 117a.

12. The *Shulchan Aruch* of R. Yosef Caro *(Choshen Mishpat*, sec. 354*)* discusses the laws involving movable property whose value increases after being stolen.

13. Different laws apply to stolen property used for other purposes. Ordinarily, a piece of wood that was stolen and is still unmodified must be returned to its owner. If it was altered, e.g., by being fashioned into a chair, the original owner has no claim on the actual wood, but only on its monetary value. (See the *Shulchan Aruch* of R. Yosef Caro, *Choshen Mishpat* 360:1.) If a piece of wood was not altered, but was built into a house, the thief need only pay the value of the wood. The Sages did not require him to demolish his building in order to return the stolen article itself, because of *takkanas hashavim* — "the ordinance for penitents," whereby they sought to encourage thieves to repent. (See *Bava Kama* 95a.)

כ רב נחמן לא, א וכחכמים בברייתא שם. טור ושו"ע ס"ג. כא ברייתא ב"ק קיז, א כחכמים. טור ושו"ע חו"מ סי' שעא ס"א. וראה גם לקמן סי' תרמט ס"ח. הל' גזילה סי"א. כב רש"י סוכה שם ד"ה אי קרקע. כג טור ורמ"א חו"מ שם. סמ"ע שם ס"ק ב. וראה לקמן סי' תרמט ס"ח (להתחייב באחריותה). כד ראה טור ושו"ע שם סי' שנד ס"א וסי' שסב ס"ב. כה רש"י סוכה שם ד"ה ואי אינה. מ"א סק"ב. כו רש"י שם ד"ה מחלוקת. תירוץ הא' שבמ"א ס"ק ז, כדעה הב' שברמ"א חו"מ סי' צה ס"א. וראה גם לקמן ס"ח. כז גמרא שם. וראה לקמן סי"א דהיינו רק בדיעבד. כח גמרא לא, א. טור ושו"ע ס"ג. כט גמרא שם (לענין גזל קורה, אפילו לא חיברו בטיט). רמב"ם פ"ה הכ"ה. שו"ע שם. ל גמרא שם (לבתר שבעה הדר בעיניה). טור ושו"ע חו"מ סי' שם ס"א. לא רש"י

אוֹתָם כְּלָל כֵּיוָן שֶׁלֹּא עָשָׂה בָהֶם שׁוּם שִׁנּוּי,[14] מִכָּל מָקוֹם מִשּׁוּם מִצְוַת סֻכָּה[לא] תִּקְּנוּ חֲכָמִים שֶׁאֵין לְהַנִּגְזָל אֶלָּא דְּמֵי הָעֵצִים בִּלְבַד,[לב] וְאֵינוֹ צָרִיךְ לִסְתֹּר סֻכָּתוֹ כְּדֵי לְהַחֲזִיר לוֹ הָעֵצִים עַצְמָן,[לג] וּמֻתָּר לֵישֵׁב בְּסֻכָּה זוֹ וַאֲפִלּוּ לְכַתְּחִלָּה.[לד]

וְאִם אֵין הַגַּזְלָן רוֹצֶה לָתֵת לוֹ דְּמֵי הָעֵצִים – אֵינוֹ יוֹצֵא יְדֵי חוֹבָתוֹ בְּסֻכָּה זוֹ,[15] שֶׁהֲרֵי גְּזוּלָה הִיא בְּיָדוֹ:[לה,16]

he has not acquired them at all, since he did not change them in any way.[14] Nevertheless, [to allow the thief to observe] the *mitzvah* of *sukkah*, the Sages ordained that the person from whom the wood was stolen is owed only its value. [The thief] is not required to dismantle his *sukkah* and return the actual pieces of wood. He is permitted to dwell in this *sukkah*, even as an initial option.

If, however, the thief is not willing to pay [the original owner] the value of the wood, he cannot fulfill his obligation with this *sukkah*,[15] for it is stolen property that he is holding.[16]

ו וְכֵן אִם גָּזַל סֻכָּה שֶׁאֵינָהּ מְחֻבֶּרֶת לַקַּרְקַע, כְּגוֹן שֶׁעֲשׂוּיָה בְּרֹאשׁ הָעֲגָלָה אוֹ בְּרֹאשׁ הַסְּפִינָה,[לו] שֶׁהֲרֵי הִיא כִּמְטַלְטְלִין וְיֵשׁ עָלֶיהָ תּוֹרַת גָּזֵל לִהְיוֹת עוֹמֶדֶת בְּחֶזְקַת הַגַּזְלָן[לז] לְכָל דָּבָר, וְאֵינָהּ כִּשְׁאוּלָה בְּיָדוֹ[17] אֶלָּא הֲרֵי הִיא גְּזוּלָה תַּחַת יָדוֹ, וּלְפִיכָךְ אִם יָשַׁב בָּהּ בֶּחָג – לֹא יָצָא יְדֵי חוֹבָתוֹ.

וַאֲפִלּוּ אִם רוֹצֶה לָתֵת לְהַנִּגְזָל דְּמֵי סֻכָּתוֹ – אֵין מוֹעִיל לוֹ כְּלוּם,[לח] שֶׁלֹּא תִּקְּנוּ חֲכָמִים כֵּן אֶלָּא אִם כֵּן טָרַח עָלֶיהָ לִבְנוֹתָהּ לְשֵׁם מִצְוָה, כְּגוֹן שֶׁגָּזַל עֵצִים וְסִכֵּךְ בָּהֶן,[לט,18] אֲבָל זֶה שֶׁגָּזַל סֻכָּה כְּשֵׁרָה וְלֹא טָרַח עָלֶיהָ

6 Similar [laws apply when] a person steals a *sukkah* that is not attached to the ground, e.g., it was built on top of a wagon or on top of a ship. Such [a *sukkah*] is considered as movable property. Thus it can be considered as stolen property and can be considered as entering the possession of the thief in every respect. Thus it is not considered as a borrowed object,[17] but as stolen property that he is holding.

Accordingly, if [the thief] dwells in the *sukkah* on the festival, he has not fulfilled his obligation. Even if he desires to give the person from whom he stole [the *sukkah*] financial recompense for it, this is of no avail, for the Sages instituted such an ordinance only when one labored to build [a *sukkah*] for the sake of the *mitzvah*, e.g., when he stole pieces of wood and used them for *s'chach*.[18] In this instance, however, [the thief] stole a valid *sukkah*. He did

---

14. See the *Shulchan Aruch* of R. Yosef Caro, *Choshen Mishpat*, sec. 360 and sec. 362. Sec. 649 below discusses parallel laws with regard to a stolen *lulav* and *esrog*.

15. It is invalid even if he intends to return the stolen property after the festival (*Biur Halachah* 637, *s.v. Yatza*).

16. Hence, if one cuts down branches growing on other people's property (or on public property) and does not intend to pay for them, they are considered stolen, and thus are invalid as *s'chach*.

17. As explained in subsection 4 above.

18. As in sec. 5 above.

שם ד"ה מפני (דמצוה משוי ליה כל שבעה כבנין קבע). סמ"ע שם סק"ד. לב גמרא שם. רמב"ם שם. טור ושו"ע ס"ג. לג רש"י שם. לד מ"א סק"ד. לה טור בשם בעל העיטור הל' סוכה סוף שער ד (פה, ד). מ"א סק"ה. לו רש"י לא, א ד"ה אבל. טור ושו"ע ס"ג. לז רש"י שם ד"ה אי קרקע. לח רש"י שם ד"ה אבל. לט כדלעיל ס"ה.

וְלֹא הוֹצִיא עָלֶיהָ הוֹצָאוֹת לְהַכְשִׁירָהּ – צָרִיךְ לְהַחֲזִירָהּ בְּעֵינֶיהָ לְבַעְלָהּ:[מ]

not invest any effort or money in it. [Hence,] he is required to return it to its owner intact.

ז וְכֵן אִם רְאוּבֵן בָּנָה סֻכָּה בְּקַרְקָעִיתוֹ שֶׁל שִׁמְעוֹן[מא] שֶׁלֹּא מִדַּעְתּוֹ[מב] וְשִׁמְעוֹן תָּקַף עַל רְאוּבֵן וְהוֹצִיאוֹ מִסֻּכָּתוֹ הַבְּנוּיָה בַּקַּרְקַע שֶׁלּוֹ וְיָשַׁב בָּהּ – לֹא יָצָא יְדֵי חוֹבָתוֹ, שֶׁהֲרֵי גְּזוּלָה הִיא תַּחַת יָדוֹ, וְאֵינָהּ כִּשְׁאוּלָה, כֵּיוָן שֶׁאֵינָהּ עוֹמֶדֶת עַל קַרְקַע שֶׁל רְאוּבֵן.[19]

וְאַף עַל פִּי שֶׁכָּל הַמְחֻבָּר לַקַּרְקַע הֲרֵי הוּא כְּקַרְקַע, וְקַרְקַע אֵין עָלֶיהָ תּוֹרַת גְּזֵלָה אֶלָּא תּוֹרַת שְׁאֵלָה, מִכָּל מָקוֹם כֵּיוָן שֶׁאֵין הַסֻּכָּה עוֹמֶדֶת עַל קַרְקַע שֶׁל נִגְזָל אֶלָּא עַל קַרְקַע שֶׁל הַגַּזְלָן – הֲרֵי הִיא בְּחֶזְקָתוֹ שֶׁל הַגַּזְלָן לְכָל דָּבָר, כְּמוֹ שְׁאָר מִטַּלְטְלִין, שֶׁכֵּיוָן שֶׁנִּכְנַס לִרְשׁוּת הַגַּזְלָן – הֲרֵי הִיא בְּחֶזְקָתוֹ לְכָל דָּבָר וְאֵינָהּ כִּשְׁאוּלָה בְּיָדוֹ, אֶלָּא הֲרֵי הֵן גְּזוּלִין תַּחַת יָדוֹ:[מג]

7 Similar [laws apply in the following instance]. Reuven built a *sukkah* on Shimon's land without Shimon's consent. Shimon overpowered Reuven, removed him from the *sukkah* on his land, and then dwelled in the *sukkah*. [By dwelling there, however, Shimon] has not fulfilled his obligation, because the *sukkah* is considered as stolen property in his hands; it is not considered as borrowed property, for [the *sukkah*] is not standing on Reuven's land.[19]

[One might argue that] anything attached to landed property is considered as the landed property itself and hence is not considered as stolen property, but rather as a borrowed article. Nevertheless, [in this situation, that reasoning does not apply] because the *sukkah* is not standing on the land of the person from whom it was stolen, but on the land of the thief. [Hence,] it is in the possession of the thief in all respects, as is all movable property. Once it enters his possession, it is in his domain in all respects. It is not considered as a borrowed object, but as stolen property in his hands.

ח אֲבָל אִם רְאוּבֵן בָּנָה סֻכָּתוֹ בְּקַרְקָעוֹ שֶׁל שִׁמְעוֹן מִדַּעְתּוֹ שֶׁהִשְׁאִיל לוֹ הַקַּרְקַע לְשִׁבְעַת יְמֵי הֶחָג וְאַחַר כָּךְ גָּזַל מִמֶּנּוּ סֻכָּתוֹ וְיָשַׁב בָּהּ – יָצָא יְדֵי חוֹבָתוֹ, שֶׁכָּל שִׁבְעַת יְמֵי הֶחָג הַקַּרְקַע שֶׁל רְאוּבֵן[20] וְסֻכָּתוֹ עוֹמֶדֶת בְּחֶזְקָתוֹ אַף לְאַחַר שֶׁגְּזָלָהּ שִׁמְעוֹן

8 [Different rules apply if] Reuven built his *sukkah* on Shimon's property with the consent of Shimon, who lent the land to him for the seven days of the festival, and then Shimon stole [Reuven's] *sukkah* from him. [If Shimon now] dwells in it, he has fulfilled his obligation.

[The rationale is that] throughout the seven days of the festival the land belongs to Reuven[20] and his *sukkah* remains in his possession, even after Shimon stole it from him, for everything

19. Hence the *sukkah* is governed by the laws applying to movable property, rather than those applying to land.

20. For Shimon lent it to him.

מ רש"י שם. הגהות אשרי פ"ב סי' טז. רמ"א ס"ג. מא תוס' לא, א סוד"ה אבל. אור זרוע ח"ב סי' שב. הגהות אשרי שם. רמ"א שם. מב תוס' שם, לגירסת (רשב"א) [מהרש"א] והגהות הב"ח שם, וכאן בסוף הסימן. אור זרוע והגהות אשרי שם. דרכי משה ס"ק א. מ"א סק"ז. מג מ"א שם. מד ב"ח שם.

attached to landed property is considered as the landed property itself. Thus [the *sukkah*] is not considered as stolen property but rather as a borrowed article, as was explained [in subsection 4] above.

9 All of the above applies after the fact; if [a thief] dwelt in [a stolen *sukkah*], he has fulfilled his obligation. Initially, however, one should not [use] another's *sukkah* without his consent, even when he does not intend to steal it from him, because its owner may object to having someone watch him unawares as he eats and goes about his affairs.

One may, however, enter and [use] another's *sukkah* when its owner is not present; he certainly will not object to this,[21] for a person is pleased when a *mitzvah* is performed with his resources if this does not entail financial loss, as was explained in sec. 14[:9].[22]

10 Similarly, one should initially not build his *sukkah* on another's land without his consent, for perhaps the owner would object to his establishing a dwelling on his property without his consent. The presumption that a person is pleased when a *mitzvah* is performed with his resources applies only when this happens on occasion, not when someone uses his resources consistently, as was explained in sec. 14[:10].

11 Similarly, as an initial and preferred option, a *sukkah* should not be constructed on land belonging to people at large,[23] such as a public place or thorough-

מִמֶּנּוּ,[מד] שֶׁכָּל הַמְחֻבָּר לַקַּרְקַע – הֲרֵי הוּא כְּקַרְקַע,[מה] שֶׁאֵין עָלֶיהָ תּוֹרַת גְּזֵלָה אֶלָּא תּוֹרַת שְׁאֵלָה כְּמוֹ שֶׁנִּתְבָּאֵר:[מו]

ט וְכָל זֶה בְּדִיעֲבַד שֶׁכְּבָר יָשַׁב בָּהּ – יָצָא יְדֵי חוֹבָתוֹ, אֲבָל לְכַתְּחִלָּה אֵין לֵישֵׁב בְּסֻכָּתוֹ שֶׁל חֲבֵרוֹ שֶׁלֹּא מִדַּעְתּוֹ, אַף עַל פִּי שֶׁאֵין דַּעְתּוֹ לְגָזְלָהּ מִמֶּנּוּ,[מז] שֶׁמָּא בַּעַל הַסֻּכָּה הוּא מַקְפִּיד עַל זֶה שֶׁלֹּא יִרְאֶה חֲבֵרוֹ אֶת אֲכִילָתוֹ וְאֶת עֲסָקָיו בְּלִי יְדִיעָתוֹ.[מח]

אֲבָל מֻתָּר לִכָּנֵס וְלֵישֵׁב בְּסֻכַּת חֲבֵרוֹ בְּשָׁעָה שֶׁאֵין בַּעַל הַסֻּכָּה שָׁם בְּסֻכָּתוֹ, שֶׁבְּוַדַּאי לֹא יַקְפִּיד עַל זֶה,[21] שֶׁנּוֹחַ לוֹ לְאָדָם שֶׁתֵּעָשֶׂה מִצְוָה בְּמָמוֹנוֹ[מט] בְּדָבָר שֶׁאֵין בּוֹ חֶסְרוֹן כִּיס כְּמוֹ שֶׁנִּתְבָּאֵר בְּסִימָן י"ד:[נ, 22]

י וְכֵן אֵין לַעֲשׂוֹת סֻכָּה לְכַתְּחִלָּה בְּקַרְקַע שֶׁל חֲבֵרוֹ שֶׁלֹּא מִדַּעְתּוֹ,[נא] דְּשֶׁמָּא בַּעַל הַקַּרְקַע הוּא מַקְפִּיד עַל שֶׁהוּא קוֹבֵעַ דִּירָתוֹ בִּרְשׁוּתוֹ בְּלִי יְדִיעָתוֹ, וְאֵין אוֹמְרִים נוֹחַ לוֹ לְאָדָם שֶׁיֵּעָשׂוּ מִצְוָה בְּמָמוֹנוֹ אֶלָּא כְּשֶׁעוֹשִׂין בְּאַקְרַאי בְּעָלְמָא, אֲבָל לֹא כְּשֶׁמִּשְׁתַּמֵּשׁ בְּמָמוֹנוֹ בִּקְבִיעוּת כְּמוֹ שֶׁנִּתְבָּאֵר בְּסִימָן י"ד:[נב]

יא וְכֵן אֵין לַעֲשׂוֹת סֻכָּה לְכַתְּחִלָּה בְּקַרְקַע שֶׁל רַבִּים,[נג, 23] כְּגוֹן בִּרְחוֹב

---

21. And hence, this is considered as if he had granted his permission.

22. It is thus obvious that the visitor must leave the *sukkah* clean and tidy.

23. *Talmud Yerushalmi, Sukkah* 3:1.

מ"א שם. **מה** תירוץ הא' שבמ"א שם, וכדלעיל ס"ד וש"נ. **מו** סעיף ד. **מז** רמ"א ס"ג. **מח** ט"ז סק"ד. **מט** ט"ז שם. **נ** ס"ט, וש"נ. **נא** רמ"א שם. **נב** סעיף י. **נג** ירושלמי פ"ג ה"א. לפירוש אור זרוע סי' שב בסופו (דאיירי בלכתחלה). דרכי משה ס"ק א. [ר]מ"א ס"ג.

fare. Even though the entire city belongs to Jews and the Jews would certainly waive [any objections], one should not construct a *sukkah* in the public domain — for everyone has the right to walk in the city, as stated in [the *Shulchan Aruch,] Choshen Mishpat,* sec. 162[:2], and the non-Jews will not waive [their objections]. Hence, such a *sukkah* would be considered a stolen *sukkah.*[24]

After the fact, one has fulfilled his obligation with a stolen *sukkah* that is standing on land [used without its owner's consent], as explained.[25] Nevertheless, as an initial and preferred option, one should not [use] a *sukkah* standing on another's property, because [such a *sukkah*] is not quite considered his own. And the Torah states, "Make... for yourself," [implying that the *sukkah* must be] "your own."[26] [Such a *sukkah*] is not entirely similar to a borrowed *[sukkah],* for this is given with [the owner's] consent, and hence is considered as actually belonging to the borrower. [This does not apply to a stolen *sukkah*.] Accordingly, people who construct their *sukkos* in the public domain should be rebuked.

If one transgressed and built his *sukkah* in any of the locations that we explained should not be [used] as an initial and preferred option, he should not recite a blessing over it[27] even though it is acceptable, as explained above.

הָעִיר וְכַיּוֹצֵא בוֹ בְּמָקוֹם שֶׁהָרַבִּים עוֹבְרִים שָׁם, וַאֲפִלּוּ אִם כָּל הָעִיר הִיא שֶׁל יִשְׂרָאֵל וְהַיִּשְׂרָאֵל הוּא בְּוַדַּאי מוֹחֵל לוֹ עַל כָּךְ, מִכָּל מָקוֹם אֵין לַעֲשׂוֹת סֻכָּה בִּרְשׁוּת הָרַבִּים, שֶׁהֲרֵי יֵשׁ לְכָל הָעוֹלָם הִלּוּךְ בּוֹ[נד] כְּמוֹ שֶׁכָּתוּב בְּחֹשֶׁן מִשְׁפָּט סִימָן [ק]ס"ב,[נה] וְהַגּוֹיִם אֵינָן מוֹחֲלִין עַל כָּךְ, וַהֲרֵי הִיא סֻכָּה גְּזוּלָה.[נו,24]

וְאַף עַל פִּי שֶׁבְּדִיעֲבַד יוֹצֵא בְּסֻכָּה גְּזוּלָה הָעוֹמֶדֶת בְּקַרְקַע [הַנִּגְזָל[נז]] כְּמוֹ שֶׁנִּתְבָּאֵר,[נח,25] מִכָּל מָקוֹם לְכַתְּחִלָּה אֵין לֵישֵׁב בְּסֻכָּה הָעוֹמֶדֶת בְּקַרְקַע שֶׁל חֲבֵרוֹ, מִפְּנֵי שֶׁאֵינָהּ נִקְרֵאת שֶׁלּוֹ מַמָּשׁ, וְהַתּוֹרָה אָמְרָה[נט] "תַּעֲשֶׂה לְךָ" — "מִשֶּׁלְּךָ",[26] וְאֵינָהּ דּוֹמָה לִשְׁאֵלָה מַמָּשׁ שֶׁהִשְׁאִילָהּ לוֹ מִדַּעְתּוֹ וַהֲרֵי הִיא כְּשֶׁלּוֹ מַמָּשׁ;[ס] וּלְכָךְ יֵשׁ לִמְחוֹת בְּהָעוֹשִׂים סֻכָּה בִּרְשׁוּת הָרַבִּים.

וְכָל מָקוֹם שֶׁבֵּאַרְנוּ שֶׁאֵין לַעֲשׂוֹת שָׁם סֻכָּה לְכַתְּחִלָּה, וְעָבַר וְעָשָׂה, אַף עַל פִּי שֶׁהִיא כְּשֵׁרָה כְּמוֹ שֶׁנִּתְבָּאֵר, מִכָּל מָקוֹם אֵין לְבָרֵךְ עָלֶיהָ,[סא,27]

24. I.e., the place on which it is located is being misappropriated.

25. See above, subsections 4, 7, 10.

26. See subsection 3 above.

27. These concepts are of contemporary relevance, for restaurant owners (and private citizens) often construct their *sukkos* in the public domain. Also, in an apartment complex or condominium, *sukkos* are often built on land that does not belong to each of the tenants/homeowners individually. Similarly, Lubavitch volunteers commonly construct *sukkos* in the public domain, in outreach endeavors to enable passersby to fulfill the *mitzvah.* In the latter instance (and this also applies with regard to some restaurants), the municipal authorities grant permission for such structures to be built. In the absence of such permission, the issue is halachically problematic. Thus, for both halachic and practical reasons, one should be careful that such a *sukkah* should not obstruct the flow of pedestrian traffic.

The Alter Rebbe's ruling draws on *Magen Avraham* 637:2, and

נד מ"א סק"ג. **נה** ס"ב. וראה גם לקמן חו"מ הל' גזילה סל"ג. **נו** מ"א שם. וראה לקמן סי' תרמט ס"א (בין מישראל בין מנכרי), וש"נ. **נז** כן תיקן בקונטרס השלחן. **נח** ס"ד וס"ז. **נט** דברים טז, יג. וכדלעיל ס"ג. **ס** כדלעיל שם, וש"נ. **סא** מ"א סוף סק"ג. **סב** ב"ק צד, א. וכדלעיל סי' יא סוף סי"ב, וש"נ. **סג** מהרי"ל

Since [building it] involved a transgression, one would be considered as blaspheming G-d rather than blessing Him.[28]

כֵּיוָן שֶׁעַל יְדֵי עֲבֵרָה בָּאָה סֻכָּה זוֹ לְיָדוֹ – אֵין זֶה מְבָרֵךְ אֶלָּא מְנָאֵץ:[סב, 28]

12 A Jew should not cut down *s'chach* by himself from a forest belonging to a non-Jew, even with his consent. Instead, the non-Jew should cut it down and give it to the Jew. Alternatively, it should be cut down by another Jew who is not intending to dwell in the *sukkah* to be made with this *s'chach* and then given to the Jew who owns this *sukkah*.

The rationale [for these safeguards] will be explained in sec. 649[:8-10]. All the particulars applying to this law will be explained there.[29]

יב לֹא יְקַצֵּץ הַיִּשְׂרָאֵל בְּעַצְמוֹ אֶת הַסְּכָךְ מִיַּעַר שֶׁל גּוֹי[סג] אֲפִלּוּ מִדַּעַת הַגּוֹי,[סד] אֶלָּא יְקַצְּצֶנּוּ הַגּוֹי וְיִתְּנֶנּוּ לְיַד הַיִּשְׂרָאֵל, אוֹ יְקַצְּצֶנּוּ יִשְׂרָאֵל אַחֵר[סה] שֶׁלֹּא יִהְיֶה יוֹשֵׁב בְּסֻכָּה זוֹ שֶׁיַּעֲשׂוּ מִסְּכָךְ זֶה וְיִתְּנֶנּוּ לְיִשְׂרָאֵל בַּעַל הַסֻּכָּה, מִטַּעַם שֶׁיִּתְבָּאֵר בְּסִימָן תרמ"ט,[סו] עַיֵּן שָׁם, וְשָׁם יִתְבָּאֵר כָּל פְּרָטֵי דִּין זֶה:[29]

SECTION 638 A *Sukkah* and its Decorations are Forbidden [for Mundane Use] Throughout the Seven [Days of the Festival]. (1–21)

סימן תרלח סֻכָּה וְנוֹיָהּ אֲסוּרִין כָּל שִׁבְעָה וּבוֹ כ"א סְעִיפִים:

1 [Our Sages state:][1] Just as G-d's holy name[2]

א כְּשֵׁם[1] שֶׁחָל שֵׁם שָׁמַיִם[2] עַל

since then this issue has been much discussed by halachic authorities, for a public area was often the only place where a Jew had the option of building his *sukkah*. For example: *Mishnah Berurah* 637:10 (see also *Biur Halachah*) cites the Responsa of *Shoel U'Meishiv, Mahadura* 1, Responsum 128, condoning the construction of a *sukkah* on the sidewalk in front of one's own home. Others, however, maintain that this responsum would justify the use of the area in front of one's entrance that may be used for loading and unloading, but not the use of any further public area. See also sec. 640:6 below.

28. On the non-literal level of *derush, Bava Kama* 94a interprets *Tehillim* 10:3 to mean that "a robber who recites a blessing blasphemes G-d," and rules that a blessing should not be recited over *mitzvos* when they are performed with stolen objects.

29. There the Alter Rebbe explains that the prohibition was instituted because we fear that the non-Jew laid hands on the property. Nevertheless, since in halachic terms land cannot be stolen, as explained above, the property and the trees growing on it still belong to the original owner. Accordingly, one would be taking the branches without permission from the owner, i.e., stealing. When, however, another person — either the presumed owner or a friend — took the branches, the person making the *lulav* or building the *sukkah* acquired the branches according to law. For we assume that the rightful owner despairs of ever getting them back, and despair *(yiush)* followed by a change of possession *(shinui reshus)* makes it possible for a person to acquire a stolen object.

In the present age, when the ownership of land is regulated by law and registered in the deeds office, the above difficulty is far less prevalent.

* For a summary of sec. 637, see p. 454.

SECTION 638

1. See: *Sukkah* 9a; *Beitzah* 30b; and *Rashi* there.

2. In the original, *Shem Shamayim* — lit., "the name of [the One in] Heaven."

הל' סוכות (ע' שסג). רמ"א ס"ג. **סד** אליה זוטא סק"א. **סה** ט"ז סי' תרסד סק"ו. מ"א סי' תרמט סק"ו. עטרת זקנים שם. וראה גם לעיל סי' יא קו"א ס"ק ג. לקמן סי' תרמט ס"ח. **סו** סעיף ח.

הַקֳּדָשִׁים,[א,3] וּלְכָךְ הֵן אֲסוּרִים[ב] בַּהֲנָאָה — כָּךְ חָל שֵׁם שָׁמַיִם עַל הַסֻּכָּה, שֶׁנֶּאֱמַר[ג,4] "חַג הַסֻּכּוֹת שִׁבְעַת יָמִים לַה'", מַה חַג דְּהַיְנוּ חֲגִיגָה[ד,5] לַה' — אַף סֻכָּה לַה':[6]

abides upon things that are consecrated,[3] and hence it is forbidden to derive benefit from them, so, too, His holy name abides upon the *sukkah,* as it is written,[4] "... the Sukkos festival for seven days unto G-d." Just as the festival — i.e., the festive *chagigah* offering[5] — is consecrated unto G-d, so, too, is the *sukkah* consecrated unto G-d.[6]

וְאֵין נִקְרָא סֻכָּה אֶלָּא הַסְּכָךְ בִּלְבַד;[ה] לְפִיכָךְ אָסוּר לְהִסְתַּפֵּק מֵעֲצֵי[7] הַסְּכָךְ כָּל שִׁבְעַת יְמֵי הֶחָג מִן הַתּוֹרָה;[ו] בֵּין מֵהַסְּכָךְ הַצָּרִיךְ לְהֶכְשֵׁר סֻכָּה, דְּהַיְנוּ ז' טְפָחִים עַל ז' טְפָחִים, בֵּין מֵהַסְּכָךְ הַיָּתֵר עַל הֶכְשֵׁר סֻכָּה.

[In this context,] the term *sukkah* refers to the *s'chach* alone. Therefore there is a Scriptural prohibition against making use of the branches[7] used for the *s'chach* throughout the seven days of the festival. [This applies] both to the minimum quantity of *s'chach* required to render the *sukkah* valid, i.e., the amount that covers an area seven handbreadths by seven handbreadths, and to any *s'chach* added beyond this minimum requirement.

וַאֲפִלּוּ נָפְלָה הַסֻּכָּה וְנִתְבַּטְּלָה מִצְוָתָהּ — אַף עַל פִּי כֵן אָסוּר לְהִסְתַּפֵּק מֵעֲצֵי הַסְּכָךְ כָּל שִׁבְעַת יְמֵי הֶחָג מִן הַתּוֹרָה:[ז,8]

Even if the *sukkah* collapsed and can no longer be used for the *mitzvah,* there is still a Scriptural prohibition against making use of the branches of the *s'chach* throughout the seven days of the festival.[8]

ב וּמִדִּבְרֵי סוֹפְרִים[ח] אָסוּר לְהִסְתַּפֵּק אֲפִלּוּ מֵעֲצֵי[9] הַדְּפָנוֹת כָּל שִׁבְעַת יְמֵי הֶחָג,[ט,10] אֲפִלּוּ אִם נָפְלָה הַסֻּכָּה,[י,11]

2 According to Rabbinic Law, it is also forbidden to make use of the wood[9] used for the walls [of the *sukkah*] throughout the seven days of the festival,[10] even if the *sukkah* collapsed.[11]

---

3. In the original, *kodashim;* e.g., animals designated for a sacrificial offering.

4. *Vayikra* 23:34.

5. See *Sukkah* 9a; *Beitzah* 30b; and *Rashi* there.

6. I.e., the sanctity of a *sukkah* surpasses that of many other objects that are used for *mitzvos.* For example, *tzitzis* (see sec. 21:1 in Vol. 1 of the present work) are considered as *tashmishei mitzvah,* objects used for a *mitzvah,* and must be treated with respect. Nevertheless, they are not categorized as "holy." By contrast, the *s'chach* and (by extension) the walls of a *sukkah* are invested with a degree of holiness similar to that conveyed upon a sacrificial animal. (Even the decorations of a *sukkah* may not be used for other purposes; see subsection 6 below.) This concept is explained at length in *Or HaTorah (Sukkos,* p. 1705*)* and *Likkutei Sichos,* Vol. 19, p. 357. See also the footnotes to subsections 15 and 19 below.

7. Or pieces of wood.

8. They may, however, be used to cover another *sukkah.*

9. Or other materials.

10. A note appended to the original states that the prohibition against making use of the *s'chach,* the walls, and the decorations continues to apply on Shemini Atzeres, the eighth day of the festival. In the Diaspora, the prohibition applies

א גמרא [ברייתא] סוכה ט, א. ביצה ל, ב. ב רש"י שם ושם ד"ה על החגיגה. וראה מ"מ וציונים. ג ויקרא כג, לד. ברייתא שם ושם. ד רש"י שם ושם ד"ה חג. ה רש"י יב, א ד"ה כשרין. ט"ז סי' תרל ס"ק א. ו רא"ש פ"א סי' יג. רמב"ם פ"ו הט"ו, לפירוש הט"ז סק"א. וראה אור התורה דברים ע' א'תשה, החילוק בין קדושה זו לציצית דלעיל סי' כא ס"א. ז ט"ז שם, בדעת הרמב"ם שם (דלא ס"ל כב' התירוצים שבתוס' שם ד"ה מנין, לחלק בין הצריך להכשר סוכה לבין היתר, או בין עודה קיימת לבין נפלה). ח ב"י ד"ה ויש לדקדק, וט"ז שם, בדעת הרמב"ם שם. ט רמב"ם שם. שו"ע ס"א (שמונת ימי החג, וראה לקמן

The walls are not the fundamental component of the *sukkah.* Nevertheless, since they were designated for the *mitzvah* of the *sukkah,* the sanctity of the *sukkah* abides upon them, and hence one may not benefit from them, as with [the *s'chach*] itself.

[In certain situations, this prohibition is extended to include] walls that are not required to make the *sukkah* valid. For example, if one made four complete walls for a *sukkah*[12] without specifying which wall[s] were intended to fulfill the minimum requirement and which one was intended to be the fourth wall that [merely] endowed the *mitzvah* with its optimal status, all of the walls are [considered as being] designated for the *mitzvah* of the *sukkah,* and the sanctity of the *sukkah* abides upon them. If, however, one added another wall after bringing the [three] walls to the dimensions that are required to render the *sukkah* valid, it is apparent that his intent in making this wall is merely to perform the *mitzvah* in the optimal manner. [Hence, the use of] this wall was never prohibited and the sanctity of the *sukkah* never abided upon it.

וְאַף עַל פִּי שֶׁהַדְּפָנוֹת אֵינָן עִקַּר הַסֻּכָּה, מִכָּל מָקוֹם הוֹאִיל וְהֻקְצוּ לְמִצְוַת סֻכָּה – חָל עֲלֵיהֶם קְדֻשַּׁת הַסֻּכָּה לְהֵאָסֵר בַּהֲנָאָה כְּמוֹתָהּ.[יא] וַאֲפִלּוּ הַדְּפָנוֹת שֶׁאֵין צָרִיךְ לְהֶכְשֵׁר סֻכָּה, כְּגוֹן שֶׁעָשָׂה אַרְבַּע דְּפָנוֹת שְׁלֵמוֹת,[12] אִם עָשָׂה אַרְבַּעְתָּן בִּסְתָם, שֶׁלֹּא פֵּרֵשׁ עַל אֵיזֶה דֹּפֶן כַּוָּנָתוֹ לְהֶכְשֵׁר סֻכָּה וְעַל אֵיזֶה דֹּפֶן כַּוָּנָתוֹ לַעֲשׂוֹתוֹ דֹּפֶן רְבִיעִי לְמִצְוָה מִן הַמֻּבְחָר בְּעָלְמָא – הֲרֵי כָּל הַדְּפָנוֹת מֻקְצוֹת לְמִצְוַת הַסֻּכָּה וְחָל עֲלֵיהֶם קְדֻשַּׁת הַסֻּכָּה. אֲבָל אִם לְאַחַר שֶׁעָשָׂה מִן הַדְּפָנוֹת שִׁעוּר הַצָּרִיךְ לְהֶכְשֵׁר סֻכָּה הוֹסִיף עוֹד דֹּפֶן,[יב] שֶׁנִּרְאֶה מִכַּוָּנָתוֹ בַּעֲשִׂיַּת זֶה הַדֹּפֶן שֶׁאֵינוֹ אֶלָּא לְמִצְוָה מִן הַמֻּבְחָר בְּעָלְמָא – לֹא נֶאֱסַר כְּלָל זֶה הַדֹּפֶן וְלֹא חָלָה עָלָיו קְדֻשַּׁת הַסֻּכָּה מֵעוֹלָם:[יג]*

* וְעַיֵּן בְּסִימָן תרס"ז[יד] שָׁם נִתְבָּאֵר דְּבֵין עֲצֵי הַסְּכָךְ וּבֵין עֲצֵי הַדְּפָנוֹת וּבֵין נוֹי הַסֻּכָּה אֲסוּרִין גַּם בִּשְׁמִינִי עֲצֶרֶת בְּאֶרֶץ יִשְׂרָאֵל, וּבְחוּץ לָאָרֶץ אֲסוּרִים אַף בַּתְּשִׁיעִי, עַיֵּן שָׁם הַטַּעַם.

3 If one added more reeds to make the *s'chach* thicker after placing all of the *s'chach* that his *sukkah* needed,

ג אִם לְאַחַר שֶׁסִּכֵּךְ כָּל סְכָךְ הַצָּרִיךְ לְסֻכָּתוֹ הוֹסִיף עָלָיו עוֹד קָנִים בְּעֳבִי הַסְּכָךְ –

also on Simchas Torah, the ninth day. (That note refers the reader to the explanation given in sec. 667 of the Alter Rebbe's *Shulchan Aruch,* which is not extant; see the corresponding section of the *Shulchan Aruch* of R. Yosef Caro.)

The rationale is that it is forbidden to make use of these objects *bein hashmashos* — from sunset until the appearance of the stars — at the close of the seventh day of Sukkos. And since the prohibition was in force at that time, it is extended throughout the following festive day(s).

11. See *Beitzah* 30b.

12. The minimum requirement for a *sukkah* is three walls (see the *Shulchan Aruch* of R. Yosef Caro, sec. 630). Building a fourth wall is considered a *mitzvah min hamuvchar,* the optimal fulfillment of the *mitzvah.*

בהגהה). י ביצה ל, ב (בסוכה נופלת, שבסוכת החג אסורה). רמ"א ס"א (אף בדעת התוס' שם, דעכ"פ מדברי סופרים אסור). וראה לקמן סי"ב (דאף בזה לא מהני תנאי). יא ב"י ד"ה ויש לדקדק. יב ר"ן ביצה (יז, א) ד"ה ועצי. שו"ע שם. יג ראה יגדיל תורה (נ.י.) ח ע' פז. יד סימן זה בשוע"ר לא הגיע לידינו, וראה טור ושו"ע שם ס"א. ולענין הסכך אחר שעברו ימי החג, ראה לקמן סי"ט.

הֲרֵי קָנִים אֵלּוּ שֶׁהוֹסִיף הֵן בְּטֵלִים לְגַבֵּי הַסְּכָךְ וְחָל עֲלֵיהֶן קְדֻשַּׁת הַסֻּכָּה. אֲבָל אִם הִנִּיחַ עַל הַסְּכָךְ חֲבִילוֹת שֶׁל קָנִים מְקֻשָּׁרִים, כֵּיוָן שֶׁלֹּא הִתִּיר אֲגֻדָּן[טו] — נִכָּר הַדָּבָר שֶׁאֵינוֹ מִתְכַּוֵּן עֲלֵיהֶם לִסְכּוֹךְ, שֶׁהֲרֵי דֶּרֶךְ הָעוֹלָם שֶׁכָּל הַמְסַכֵּךְ בְּקָנִים הוּא מַתִּיר אֲגֻדָּן, וְזֶה שֶׁלֹּא הִתִּיר נִכָּר הַדָּבָר שֶׁאֵינוֹ מִתְכַּוֵּן בָּהֶן לְהוֹסִיף בְּעֳבִי הַסְּכָךְ,[13] וּלְפִיכָךְ אֵינָן בְּטֵלִים לְגַבֵּי הַסְּכָךְ[14] וְלֹא חָלָה עֲלֵיהֶם קְדֻשַּׁת הַסֻּכָּה:[טז]

these additional reeds are considered subordinate to the s'chach and the holiness of the *sukkah* abides upon them.

[Different rules apply] if, however, one placed bound bundles of reeds on the *s'chach*. Since he did not untie them, it is evident that he did not intend that they should serve as *s'chach*,[13] for people who use reeds to provide shade normally untie the bundles. The fact that this individual did not untie them indicates that he did not intend that they should serve to make the *s'chach* thicker. Hence they are not considered subordinate to the *s'chach*[14] and the holiness of the *sukkah* does not abide upon them.

ד אֲבָל אִם הוֹסִיף קָנִים בְּעֳבִי הַדְּפָנוֹת, דְּהַיְנוּ שֶׁזָּקַף קָנִים אֵצֶל הַדֹּפֶן סָמוּךְ לַדֹּפֶן, בֵּין שֶׁהַקָּנִים הֵן אֲגוּדִים יַחַד כְּעֵין חֲבִילָה, בֵּין שֶׁהֵן מְפֹרָדִין זֶה מִזֶּה,[יז] אִם נִתְכַּוֵּן בִּסְמִיכַת הַקָּנִים לַדֹּפֶן[יח] כְּדֵי לְחַזֵּק אֶת הַדֹּפֶן[יט] אוֹ כְּדֵי לְהוֹסִיף בְּעָבְיוֹ[כ] — הֲרֵי הֵן בְּטֵלִים לְגַבֵּי הַדֹּפֶן אַף עַל פִּי שֶׁאֵינָן מְחֻבָּרִין לַדֹּפֶן, וְחָל עֲלֵיהֶם קְדֻשַּׁת הַסֻּכָּה כְּמוֹ עַל הַדֹּפֶן עַצְמוֹ:

4 If one adds reeds to the thickness of the walls, i.e., he erected reeds next to the wall, [the same rules apply,] whether they are bound together like a bundle or they are separate. If in placing the reeds next to the wall he intended to support it or to increase its thickness, they are considered as subordinate to the wall, even though they are not connected to it. [Hence] the holiness of the *sukkah* abides upon them as upon the wall itself.

ה וַאֲפִלּוּ עֲצֵי הַסְּכָךְ וְהַדְּפָנוֹת עַצְמָן אֵינָן אֲסוּרִים אֶלָּא לְהִסְתַּפֵּק מֵהֶן,[כא] דְּהַיְנוּ שֶׁלֹּא יִטֹּל מֵהֶן שׁוּם דָּבָר, אֲפִלּוּ קֵיסָם לַחְצוֹץ בּוֹ שִׁנָּיו,[כב] שֶׁהֲרֵי כְּשֶׁמַּפְרִיד

5 The prohibition against making use of the branches of the *s'chach* and the walls themselves involves only taking any part [of them for one's own purposes], even a sliver to use as a toothpick, for by separating

---

13. Needless to say, they must be placed in a manner that does not disqualify the *sukkah*, as stated above in sec. 629:22ff.

14. See sec. 518:17-19. Moreover, it would appear that since these bundles were not placed atop the *sukkah* for the purpose of shade, they are not valid *s'chach*, and if they were not removed, they should invalidate that area of the *sukkah*.

טו באופן שאינו פוסל הסכך, כדלעיל סי׳ תרכט סכ״ב ואילך. טז ט״ז סי׳ תקיח סוף סק״ו (כדלעיל סי׳ תקיח סי״ח־ט בסוכה שאינה של מצוה, וש״נ. ושכן יש לחלק אף לענין סוכת החג). יז כדלעיל סי׳ תקיח סי״ז, לענין סוכה שאינה של מצוה, שאין חילוק בין חבילה למפורדים. יח (רא״ש). מ״א סק״א (שגם בסוכת מצוה תלוי בכוונתו, כמו בסוכה שאינה של מצוה, דלעיל שם). יט ט״ז סי׳ תקי[ח] שם (שאף שלענין סוכה שאינה של מצוה מתירין בזה, כדלעיל שם סי״ז, בזה חמורה סוכת מצוה, כסברת הב״י שם ד״ה וכתוב בהג״א). כ שבזה נאסר אף בסוכה שאינה של מצוה, כדלעיל שם סט״ז. כא ט״ז סק״ג. וראה גם תוס׳ שבת כב, א ד״ה אבוהון. כב מהרי״ל הל׳ סוכות (ע׳ שסז). רמ״א ס״א. כג ט״ז שם. כד גמרא שבת קנו (כנראה שייך לקמן ס״ו). ריטב״א לז, ב ד״ה

הַקֵּיסָם מֵהַסֻּכָּה מַפְקִיעַ הוּא מֵעָלָיו קְדֻשַּׁת הַסֻּכָּה. אֲבָל מֻתָּר לֵהָנוֹת מֵהֶן הֲנָאָה לְהִשְׁתַּמֵּשׁ בָּהֶם כָּל תַּשְׁמִישׁ כָּל שֶׁאֵינוֹ מַפְקִיעַ מֵעֲלֵיהֶם קְדֻשַּׁת הַסֻּכָּה, כְּגוֹן לְהַנִּיחַ עֲלֵיהֶם חֲפָצָיו,[כג] וּלְהָרִיחַ בָּהֶם אִם הֵם עֲצֵי בְשָׂמִים,[כד] וְכָל כַּיּוֹצֵא בָּזֶה:

it from the *sukkah,* one removes the holiness of the *sukkah* from it. It is, however, permitted to derive any benefit from them by using them in a manner that does not remove the holiness of the *sukkah* from them, e.g., placing one's articles upon them, smelling them if they are fragrant kinds of wood, or the like.

ו נוֹיֵי הַסֻּכָּה, דְּהַיְנוּ מִינֵי פֵּרוֹת וּמִינֵי מְגָדִים שֶׁתּוֹלִים בַּסֻּכָּה כְּדֵי לְנָאוֹתָהּ,[כה] בֵּין שֶׁהֵן תַּחַת הַסְּכָךְ, בֵּין שֶׁהֵן סְבִיב הַדְּפָנוֹת[כו, 15] — אָסוּר לְהִסְתַּפֵּק מֵהֶם כָּל יְמֵי הֶחָג, וַאֲפִלּוּ אִם נָפְלוּ מֵהַסֻּכָּה,[כז] מִפְּנֵי שֶׁהוּא בִּזּוּי לַמִּצְוָה כְּשֶׁמִּסְתַּפֵּק מִנּוֹיָהּ.[כח, 16] וְכֵיוָן שֶׁהֵן אֲסוּרִין בַּאֲכִילָה — אֲסוּרִין גַּם בְּטִלְטוּל בְּשַׁבָּת וְיוֹם טוֹב,[כט, 17] שֶׁהֲרֵי אֵינָן רְאוּיִים לִכְלוּם כָּל יְמֵי הֶחָג,[ל] וַאֲפִלּוּ מִפְּנֵי הַגַּנָּבִים אוֹ מִפְּנֵי הַגְּשָׁמִים[לא] אֲסוּרִים לְטַלְטְלָם:[לב]

6 It is forbidden throughout the festival to make use of the decorations of the *sukkah,* i.e., various fruits or delicacies that are hung in the *sukkah,* whether under the *s'chach* or around the walls, to adorn it.[15] [This applies] even when they have fallen from the *sukkah,* for making [mundane] use of the decorations of a *mitzvah* is disrespectful to the *mitzvah.*[16]

Moreover, since these articles may not be eaten, it is also forbidden to move them on *Shabbos* and on *Yom-Tov,*[17] for they are not fit to be used for any purpose throughout the festival. It is forbidden to move them even to protect them from thieves or rain.

ז וְאִם הִתְנָה עֲלֵיהֶם[לג] מֵעֶרֶב יוֹם טוֹב[11] קֹדֶם כְּנִיסַת יוֹם טוֹב, דְּהַיְנוּ קֹדֶם בֵּין הַשְּׁמָשׁוֹת,[לד, 18] וְאָמַר אֵין אֲנִי בּוֹדֵל

7 [Different laws apply if a person] made a stipulation [concerning the decorations] on the day before the festival;[10] i.e., before the festival began, meaning before *bein hashmashos,*[18] he said, "I will not refrain

---

15. *Sukkah* 10a-b. As stated above (see sec. 627, footnote 15), it is not Lubavitch custom to decorate the *sukkah.* Drapes that were hung to make the *sukkah* more comfortable will acquire the status of "*sukkah* decorations" discussed above. This is not the case with a plain electric light that was used in the *sukkah:* it may be removed and used elsewhere (Responsa *Chelkas Yaakov* by R. Yaakov Breisch, Vol. 2, #127).

16. *Shabbos* 22a.

17. I.e., on the first and eighth days of the festival in *Eretz Yisrael,* and on the first, second, eighth and ninth days of the festival in the Diaspora. See also sec. 513:3 and 515:1.

18. The twilight period between sunset and the appearance of three stars.

הדם, בשם רבו. דעה הב׳ בר״ן (יח, א) ד״ה הדם. דעה הא׳ ברמ״א סוף ס״ב. ט״ז שם. **כה** גמרא [ברייתא] י, א. רמב״ם פ״ו הט״ז. שו״ע ס״ב. **כו** גמרא שם ע״ב (דילמא מן הצד). ט״ז ס״ק ח. מ״א ס״ק ט. **כז** שו״ת הרא״ש כלל כד סי׳ ט. ר״ן ביצה (יז, א) ד״ה ומיהו. טור ושו״ע שם. **כח** גמרא שבת כב, א. ר״ן שם (גם אחר שנפלו). ב״י ד״ה ומ״ש ולפי. וראה לעיל סי׳ כא ס״א. סי׳ מב ס״ו. **כט** בה״ג פ׳ הישן (לג, א). הובא במרדכי רמז תשלח (לענין שבת). טור (אף לענין יו״ט). הר״א מזרחי בביאורו לסמ״ג (יז, ג), שהוכיח כן מ[גמרא שבת קנו, ב]. רמ״א ס״ב. **ל** ראה גם לעיל סי׳ תקיג ס״ג ובקו״א סק״א. סי׳ תקטו ס״א. **לא** שהיתה סברה להתיר מטעם אנן סהדי, כדלקמן סי״א וש״נ. **לב** ב״י ד״ה ומ״ש בשם שו״ת הרא״ש כלל כד סי׳ ט. **לג** גמרא [ברייתא] ביצה ל, ב. טור ושו״ע ס״ב. **לד** רש״י שם ד״ה אביי ורבא. דרכי משה ס״ק ג. רמ״א ס״ב.

מִלְּהִסְתַּפֵּק מֵהֶם כָּל שְׁהוּת אֹרֶךְ בֵּין הַשְּׁמָשׁוֹת[לה] שֶׁל כָּל שְׁמוֹנַת הַיָּמִים,[לו] וְנִמְצָא בְּשָׁעָה שֶׁהָיְתָה הַקְּדֻשָּׁה צְרִיכָה לָחוּל עֲלֵיהֶם, דְּהַיְנוּ בְּבֵין הַשְּׁמָשׁוֹת שֶׁהִיא תְּחִלַּת כְּנִיסַת הַיּוֹם, בְּשָׁעָה זוֹ לֹא חָלָה עֲלֵיהֶם כְּלָל, שֶׁהֲרֵי הִתְנָה עֲלֵיהֶם שֶׁיִּהְיֶה כֹּחוֹ וּזְכוּתוֹ בָּהֶם, וְאִם כֵּן לֹא הֻקְצוּ כְּלָל לְמִצְוָה,[לז] וּלְפִיכָךְ מֻתָּר לְהִסְתַּפֵּק מֵהֶם בְּכָל הֶחָג אֵימָתַי שֶׁיִּרְצֶה, וְאַף עַל פִּי שֶׁהֵן תְּלוּיִים בַּסֻּכָּה – אֵין בָּזֶה מִשּׁוּם בִּזּוּי מִצְוָה,[לח] כֵּיוָן שֶׁלֹּא הֻקְצוּ כְּלָל לְמִצְוָה:

ח אֲבָל אִם אֵינוֹ מַתְנֶה עֲלֵיהֶם בְּלָשׁוֹן זֶה שֶׁבֵּאַרְנוּ, רַק אוֹמֵר אֲנִי מַתְנֶה עֲלֵיהֶם שֶׁאֱהֵא מֻתָּר לְהִסְתַּפֵּק מֵהֶם כְּשֶׁיִּפְּלוּ מֵהַסֻּכָּה – אֵין תְּנַאי זֶה מוֹעִיל כְּלוּם,[לט] שֶׁהֲרֵי לֹא הִתְנָה אֶלָּא עַל שָׁעָה שֶׁלֹּא יִהְיוּ תְּלוּיִים בַּסֻּכָּה, וְאִם כֵּן בְּבֵין הַשְּׁמָשׁוֹת שֶׁהָיוּ תְּלוּיִים בַּסֻּכָּה – חָלָה עֲלֵיהֶן קְדֻשַּׁת הַסֻּכָּה, וְכֵיוָן שֶׁחָלָה – שׁוּב אֵינָהּ נִפְקַעַת עַל יְדֵי מַה שֶּׁהִתְנָה מִתְּחִלָּה,[מ] שֶׁאֵין תְּנַאי מוֹעִיל אֶלָּא לְשֶׁלֹּא תָּחוּל הַקְּדֻשָּׁה, אֲבָל כֵּיוָן שֶׁחָלָה – שׁוּב אֵינָהּ נִפְקַעַת, וּלְפִיכָךְ אֲפִלּוּ אִם נָפְלָה מֵהַסֻּכָּה – אָסוּר לְהִסְתַּפֵּק מֵהֶם:

ט וְכֵן אִם אָמַר אֵינִי בּוֹדֵל מֵהֶם כָּל שְׁהוּת אֹרֶךְ בֵּין הַשְּׁמָשׁוֹת שֶׁל יוֹם הָרִאשׁוֹן בִּלְבַד, וְלֹא הִתְנָה עַל בֵּין

from making use of them throughout the time of *bein hashmashos* on all the eight days [of the festival]." Thus, at the time the holiness would rest upon them, *bein hashmashos,* which is the beginning of the onset of the day, [the holiness] did not rest upon them at all, for he [explicitly] stipulated that he would have the power and the right [to use] them. Hence they were never set aside for the *mitzvah* at all. He is therefore permitted to make use of them whenever he desires throughout the festival. Though they are hanging in the *sukkah,* [making use of them] is not considered as disrespectful to the *mitzvah,* since they were never set aside for the *mitzvah*.

8 If, however, one does not use the above wording when making his stipulation, but merely says, "I stipulate that I will be permitted to benefit from [the decorations] if they fall from the *sukkah,*" this stipulation is not effective at all, for it relates only to the time that they will not be hanging in the *sukkah*. At the time of *bein hashmashos,* therefore, when they are hanging in the *sukkah,* its holiness rests upon them. And once it is invested [upon them], it is never dislodged by his earlier stipulation, for a stipulation is effective in preventing holiness from resting [upon an object], but once it is invested it is never dislodged. Therefore, even if they fell from the *sukkah,* it is forbidden to benefit from them.

9 Similarly, if one stipulated that he will not refrain from using [the decorations] throughout *bein hashmashos* of the first day alone and does not make a stipulation with

לה אביי ורבא בגמרא שם ורש"י שם. טור ושו"ע שם. לו ארחות חיים הל' סוכה סי' מא בשם הרמב"ן. רמ"א שם. לז רש"י שם. לח שו"ת הרא"ש כלל כד סי' ט. לט הגהות מיימוניות פ"ו הט"ז (דפוס קושטא) בשם הגהת סמ"ק סי' צג (ע' נד). טור ושו"ע ס"ב. מ ב"י ד"ה ומ"ש ודוקא. לבוש ס"ב. מא ארחות

הַשְּׁמָשׁוֹת שֶׁל שְׁאָר הַיָּמִים[מא] — אָסוּר לְהִסְתַּפֵּק מֵהֶם מִיּוֹם שֵׁנִי וְאֵילָךְ, לְפִי שֶׁכָּל יוֹם וָיוֹם נֶחְשָׁב לִקְדֻשָּׁה בִּפְנֵי עַצְמָהּ[מב,19] וְחָלָה עֲלֵיהֶם הַקְּדֻשָּׁה בִּתְחִלַּת כְּנִיסַת כָּל יוֹם שֶׁלֹּא הִתְנָה עָלָיו.[מג]

וְאִם הִתְנָה עֲלֵיהֶם שֶׁאֵינוֹ בּוֹדֵל מֵהֶם כָּל שְׁהוּת בֵּין הַשְּׁמָשׁוֹת שֶׁמִּיּוֹם שֵׁנִי וְאֵילָךְ וְלֹא הִתְנָה עַל בֵּין הַשְּׁמָשׁוֹת שֶׁל יוֹם הָרִאשׁוֹן — אָסוּר לְהִסְתַּפֵּק מֵהֶם אֲפִלּוּ מִיּוֹם שֵׁנִי וְאֵילָךְ, שֶׁכֵּיוָן שֶׁחָלָה עֲלֵיהֶם הַקְּדֻשָּׁה בְּבֵין הַשְּׁמָשׁוֹת הָרִאשׁוֹן — שׁוּב אֵינָהּ נִפְקַעַת כָּל יְמֵי הֶחָג, לְפִי שֶׁהֵן יוֹם אֶחָד אָרֹךְ[מד] לְעִנְיָן זֶה[מה] לְהַחְמִיר אֲבָל לֹא לְהָקֵל.[11]

אֲבָל אִם הִתְנָה וְאָמַר אֵינִי בּוֹדֵל מֵהֶן כָּל בֵּין הַשְּׁמָשׁוֹת בִּסְתָם, דְּהַיְנוּ שֶׁלֹּא הִזְכִּיר בְּפֵרוּשׁ לַיּוֹם הָרִאשׁוֹן וְלֹא לִשְׁאָר יָמִים — הָיְתָה כַּוָּנָתוֹ עַל בֵּין הַשְּׁמָשׁוֹת שֶׁל כָּל יְמֵי הֶחָג,[מו] וַהֲרֵי זֶה מֻתָּר לְהִסְתַּפֵּק מֵהֶן אֵימָתַי שֶׁיִּרְצֶה, בֵּין בַּיּוֹם הָרִאשׁוֹן בֵּין בִּשְׁאָר יָמִים:

י וְכֵן אִם לֹא הִזְכִּיר כְּלָל בֵּין הַשְּׁמָשׁוֹת, אֶלָּא אָמַר אֵינִי בּוֹדֵל אֶת עַצְמִי מִלְּהִסְתַּפֵּק מֵהֶם בְּכָל עֵת שֶׁאֶרְצֶה[מז] — הֲרֵי זֶה מִסְתַּפֵּק מֵהֶן אֵימָתַי שֶׁיִּרְצֶה, שֶׁכֵּיוָן שֶׁהִתְנָה לְהִסְתַּפֵּק מֵהֶן בְּכָל עֵת

regard to *bein hashmashos* of the subsequent days, he may not make use of them from *bein hashmashos* [at the onset] of the second day and onward.

[The rationale is that] each individual day is considered as a separate unit of holiness.[19] [Hence] this holiness rests upon [the decorations of the *sukkah*] at the beginning of the onset of each day for which no stipulation was made.

If one stipulated that he is not refraining from using them throughout *bein hashmashos* of the second day and of the subsequent days, but made no stipulation concerning *bein hashmashos* of the first day, he may not make use [of them] even from the second day and onward. Once the holiness rested upon them during *bein hashmashos* of the first day, it is not dislodged throughout all the days of the festival, for in this regard — to establish a stringency, but not a leniency — they are considered as one long day.[10]

However, if one stipulates, "I will not refrain from using them throughout *bein hashmashos*," without specifying his intent, mentioning explicitly neither the first day nor any of the subsequent days, [it is assumed that] he had in mind all the days of the festival. He is therefore permitted to use [the decorations] whenever he desires, whether on the first day or on the other days.

10 Similarly, if he does not mention *bein hashmashos* at all, but says, "I will not refrain from making use of [the decorations] whenever I desire," he may make use of them whenever he desires. Since he stipulated that he could make use of them whenever he

---

19. As explained in sec. 644.

חיים שם בשם הרמב״ן. הובא ב״י שם. רמ״א שם. **מב** כדלקמן סי׳ תרמד. **מג** ארחות חיים ורמב״ן שם. ב״י שם. לבוש ס״ב. ט״ז סק״ה. **מד** ביצה ל, סוע״ב. ארחות חיים ורמב״ן שם. ב״י שם. לבוש שם. ט״ז ס״ק ו. וראה גם לקמן סי׳ תרמט ס״כ (לענין אתרוג. אלא ששם מועיל תנאי, וש״נ). **מה** ט״ז שם. **מו** יש״ש ביצה פ״ד סי׳ ג. מ״א סק״ז. אליה זוטא סק״ג. **מז** בה״ג פ׳ הישן (לג, א). טור ושו״ע סוף ס״ב.

שֶׁיִּרְצֶה – הֲרֵי גַּם בֵּין הַשְּׁמָשׁוֹת הוּא בִּכְלַל הַתְּנַאי, וְנִמְצָא שֶׁלֹּא חָלָה עֲלֵיהֶם הַקְּדֻשָּׁה מֵעוֹלָם:[מח]

desired, *bein hashmashos* is also included in his stipulation. Thus the holiness [of the *sukkah*] never rested upon them.

יא וְנָהֲגוּ הָעוֹלָם שֶׁכָּל דָּבָר חָשׁוּב תּוֹלִין בַּסֻּכָּה לְנוֹי,[מט] כְּגוֹן סְדִינִין הַמְצֻיָּרִים וְכַיּוֹצֵא בָּהֶן, וּמְסִירִין אוֹתָן מִן הַסֻּכָּה בְּכָל עֵת שֶׁיִּרְצוּ, כְּגוֹן [מִ]פְּנֵי הַגְּשָׁמִים אוֹ [מִ]פְּנֵי הַגַּנָּבִים, אֲפִלּוּ אִם לֹא הִתְנָה עֲלֵיהֶם מֵעֶרֶב יוֹם טוֹב.[נ,20] וְיֵשׁ שֶׁנָּתְנוּ טַעַם לַמִּנְהָג, דְּכֵיוָן שֶׁמִּנְהַג הָעוֹלָם לַהֲסִירָן מֵהַסֻּכָּה מֵחֲמַת חֲשַׁשׁ הַגַּנָּבִים אוֹ [מִ]פְּנֵי הַגְּשָׁמִים, אִם כֵּן כָּל אָדָם שֶׁתּוֹלֶה דְּבָרִים חֲשׁוּבִים בַּסֻּכָּה לְנוֹי וַדַּאי אֵין דַּעְתּוֹ אֶלָּא עַל דֶּרֶךְ הַמִּנְהָג, דְּהַיְנוּ לַהֲסִירָן מִשָּׁם בְּעֵת הַצֹּרֶךְ, וַהֲרֵי זֶה כְּאִלּוּ הִתְנָה עֲלֵיהֶם[נא] בְּפֵרוּשׁ תְּנַאי הַמּוֹעִיל לַהֲסִירָן מִשָּׁם כְּשֶׁיִּצְטָרֵךְ, דְּהַיְנוּ שֶׁאֵינוֹ בּוֹדֵל מֵהֶם כָּל שְׁהוּת בֵּין הַשְּׁמָשׁוֹת שֶׁל כָּל יְמֵי הֶחָג, וּלְפִיכָךְ מֻתָּר לַהֲסִירָן מִשָּׁם אֵימָתַי שֶׁיִּרְצֶה, וַאֲפִלּוּ שֶׁלֹּא בִּשְׁעַת הַגֶּשֶׁם, וַאֲפִלּוּ אֵין שָׁם חֲשַׁשׁ מֵהַגַּנָּבִים, שֶׁהֲרֵי לֹא חָלָה עֲלֵיהֶם קְדֻשַּׁת הַסֻּכָּה מֵעוֹלָם.

וּמִכָּל מָקוֹם, לְכַתְּחִלָּה נָכוֹן הַדָּבָר לְהִתְנוֹת עֲלֵיהֶם מֵעֶרֶב יוֹם טוֹב:[נב]

11 People customarily decorate their *sukkah* by hanging all kinds of valuable objects in it, such as sheets with designs or pictures, and remove them at will from the *sukkah* — e.g., because of rain or because of thieves — even though they did not make a stipulation before the festival began.[20] Some have justified this practice. They argue that since it has become customary to remove them from the *sukkah* because of possible theft or rain, whoever hangs valuable articles in the *sukkah* as decorations does so only with the intent of following the [prevalent] custom, i.e., to remove them when necessary. [Hence,] it is as if one made a stipulation that is effective [in allowing him] to remove them when necessary. [Thus it is as if he said that] he will not refrain from using them throughout *bein hashmashos* on all the days of the festival.

Accordingly, he may remove them whenever he desires, even when there is no rain or concern over theft, for the holiness of the *sukkah* never rested upon them. Nevertheless, as an initial and preferred option, one ought to make a stipulation concerning these objects before the onset of the festival.

20. Though the basic restriction is that the decorations not be used for other purposes, here we see an objection to merely removing them from the *sukkah*. Plausibly, the aim of the current discussion is to justify their removal even on *Shabbos* or *Yom-Tov*. If they are subservient to the *sukkah*, they become *muktzeh* (see subsection 6), and by virtue of the above-described stipulation they are not annexed to the sanctity of the *sukkah*, and will not be subject to the restrictions of being *muktzeh*. (See: R. Eliyahu Weissfish, *Sefer HaSukkah HaShalem* (Jerusalem, 5753/1903), p. 449, citing R. Shlomo Zalman Auerbach.)

מח ב״י ד״ה ומ״ש אבל. מט ראה ספר המנהגים — חב״ד ע׳ 65 (שאין מנהג חב״ד לתלות נויי סוכה). אוצר מנהגי חב״ד חג הסוכות ע׳ רסז. נ דרכי משה ס״ק ה. רמ״א ס״ב. נא ט״ז ס״ק ח. נב דרכי משה ורמ״א שם. נג גמרא ביצה ל, ב לפירוש רש״י שם ד״ה אביי. טור ורמ״א ס״א. מ״א ריש הסימן. נד ר״י

12 All of the above [leniencies] apply [only] to the decorations of the *sukkah,* but not to the branches used for the actual *s'chach.*[11] A stipulation to make use of them is never effective, even if the *sukkah* collapses during the eight days of the festival, for the prohibition against [using] them is of Scriptural origin, as stated above.[21]

[Moreover, this stringency applies] even to the walls of the *sukkah,* although their [use is] prohibited only by Rabbinic decree. Since they were designated to be used for the *mitzvah* of the *sukkah,* the holiness of the *sukkah* rests upon them and a stipulation to make use of them is of no consequence. [This applies] even if the *sukkah* falls during the festival.[22]

[The rationale for this restriction can be explained as follows:] As stated above,[23] whenever one does not stipulate that he will not refrain from making use [of something] throughout the duration of *bein hashmashos,* the stipulation is not effective at all. [Now,] he must refrain from making use of the *[sukkah]* walls throughout the duration of *bein hashmashos* on the first day, for it is a festival. Thus he may not take any part of the wood of the actual walls, for that would constitute the demolition of a structure on the festival.[24] Therefore, regardless of his intent, the holiness [of the *sukkah*] is invested upon the walls from the first day onward and is not dislodged throughout the days of the festival, even if the *sukkah* collapsed in the course of the festival.

13 [Different rules apply] if, after completing the construction of a wall, one increased its thickness [by adding] reeds that

יב וְכָל זֶה בְּנוֹיֵי הַסֻּכָּה, אֲבָל עֲצֵי הַסְּכָךְ עַצְמָם[11] — אֵין מוֹעִיל לָהֶם שׁוּם תְּנַאי[נג] לְהִסְתַּפֵּק מֵהֶן, אֲפִלּוּ לִכְשֶׁתִּפֹּל הַסֻּכָּה[נד] בְּתוֹךְ שְׁמוֹנַת יְמֵי הֶחָג, שֶׁהֲרֵי אִסּוּרָן הוּא מִן הַתּוֹרָה[נה] כְּמוֹ שֶׁנִּתְבָּאֵר לְמַעְלָה.[נו,21]

וַאֲפִלּוּ עֲצֵי הַדְּפָנוֹת שֶׁאִסּוּרָן אֵינוֹ אֶלָּא מִדִּבְרֵי סוֹפְרִים, הוֹאִיל וְהֻקְצוּ לְמִצְוַת סֻכָּה חָלָה עֲלֵיהֶם קְדֻשַּׁת הַסֻּכָּה[נז] — אַף עַל פִּי כֵן אֵין מוֹעִיל לָהֶם הַתְּנַאי לְהִסְתַּפֵּק מֵהֶן אֲפִלּוּ לִכְשֶׁתִּפֹּל הַסֻּכָּה בְּתוֹךְ הֶחָג,[22] שֶׁהֲרֵי כָּל שֶׁאֵינוֹ מַתְנֶה שֶׁאֵינוֹ בּוֹדֵל מֵהֶן כָּל שְׁהוּת שֶׁל בֵּין הַשְּׁמָשׁוֹת — אֵינוֹ תְּנַאי כְּלָל כְּמוֹ שֶׁנִּתְבָּאֵר,[נח,23] וּמֵעֲצֵי הַדְּפָנוֹת עַל כָּרְחוֹ הוּא צָרִיךְ לִהְיוֹת מֻבְדָּל מֵהֶן כָּל שְׁהוּת בֵּין הַשְּׁמָשׁוֹת שֶׁל יוֹם הָרִאשׁוֹן שֶׁהוּא יוֹם טוֹב,[24] וְאִי אֶפְשָׁר לוֹ לִטֹּל שׁוּם דָּבָר מֵעֲצֵי הַדְּפָנוֹת עַצְמָן מִשּׁוּם סְתִירַת אֹהֶל בְּיוֹם טוֹב, וְאִם כֵּן בְּעַל כָּרְחוֹ חָלָה עֲלֵיהֶם הַקְּדֻשָּׁה מִיּוֹם הָרִאשׁוֹן, וְשׁוּב אֵינָהּ נִפְקַעַת כָּל יְמֵי הֶחָג,[נט] אֲפִלּוּ אִם נָפְלָה הַסֻּכָּה בְּתוֹךְ הֶחָג:

יג אֲבָל אִם לְאַחַר שֶׁגָּמַר עֲשִׂיַּת הַדֹּפֶן הוֹסִיף בְּעָבְיוֹ קָנִים זְקוּפִים

---

21. Subsection 1.

22. As stated in subsection 2.

23. Subsection 8.

24. This is a forbidden labor. Sec. 518:15-20 describes in detail how this prohibition applies to a *sukkah.*

בתוס' ט, א ד"ה מנין. רמ"א שם. וראה לעיל ס"ב. נה ר"ן ביצה (יז, א) סוד"ה אבל. הובא במ"א ריש הסי'. נו סעיף א. נז כדלעיל ס"ב. נח סעיף ח. נט רש"י ור"י שם. לבוש סוף ס"ב. מ"א ריש הסי'. וראה העו"ב תרא ע' 15.

סְמוּכִים לַדֹּפֶן כְּדֵי לְחַזְּקוֹ, וְאֵינָן מְחֻבָּרִין עִם הַדֹּפֶן בְּעִנְיָן שֶׁמֻּתָּר לִטֹּל קָנִים אֵלּוּ מֵהַדֹּפֶן בְּיוֹם טוֹב וְאֵין בָּזֶה מִשּׁוּם סְתִירַת אֹהֶל כֵּיוָן שֶׁאֵינָן מְחֻבָּרִין לְהַדֹּפֶן, וּכְמוֹ שֶׁנִּתְבָּאֵר בְּסִימָן תקי״ח,[ס] וְהִתְנָה[סא] עַל קָנִים אֵלּוּ תְּנַאי הַמּוֹעִיל לְהִסְתַּפֵּק בְּכָל עֵת שֶׁיִּרְצֶה וְעַל דֶּרֶךְ שֶׁנִּתְבָּאֵר[סב] — הֲרֵי זֶה מִסְתַּפֵּק מֵהֶן בְּכָל עֵת שֶׁיִּרְצֶה, שֶׁהֲרֵי בְּבֵין הַשְּׁמָשׁוֹת הָרִאשׁוֹן הָיָה יָכוֹל לְהִסְתַּפֵּק מֵהֶן, וְנִמְצָא שֶׁלֹּא חָלָה עֲלֵיהֶם קְדֻשַּׁת הַסֻּכָּה מֵעוֹלָם:

stand erect next to it to bolster it. They are not connected to the wall and so it is permitted to take them away from the wall on the festival. This is not considered tearing down a structure, since [the reeds] are not connected to the wall, as explained in sec. 518[:17].

[Hence,] if one made a stipulation that allows him to make use of [these reeds] whenever he desires, as explained above, he may make use of them whenever he desires, because during *bein hashmashos* on the first [day of the festival] he was permitted to use them. The holiness of the *sukkah* thus never rested upon them.

יד וְאִם עָשָׂה סֻכָּה בְּחֹל הַמּוֹעֵד[סג] וְהִתְנָה עַל עֲצֵי הַדְּפָנוֹת בִּתְנַאי הַמּוֹעִיל לְהִסְתַּפֵּק מֵהֶן בְּכָל עֵת שֶׁיִּרְצֶה — הֲרֵי זֶה מִסְתַּפֵּק מֵהֶן בְּכָל עֵת שֶׁיִּרְצֶה, אֲפִלּוּ בְּשָׁעָה שֶׁהַסֻּכָּה קַיֶּמֶת וְיוֹשֵׁב בָּהּ לְשֵׁם מִצְוָה,[25] וְאֵין בָּזֶה מִשּׁוּם בִּזּוּי מִצְוָה, כֵּיוָן שֶׁהַדְּפָנוֹת לֹא הֻקְצוּ כְּלָל לַמִּצְוָה, שֶׁהֲרֵי הִתְנָה עֲלֵיהֶם מִתְּחִלָּה שֶׁיְּהֵא רַשַּׁאי לְהִסְתַּפֵּק מֵהֶן, וְנִמְצָא שֶׁלֹּא חָלָה עֲלֵיהֶם קְדֻשַּׁת הַסֻּכָּה מֵעוֹלָם:

14 If one built a *sukkah* on *Chol HaMoed* and made a stipulation concerning the wood of its walls that enables him to make use of it whenever he desires, he may make use of it whenever he desires, even while the *sukkah* is standing and he is dwelling in it for the sake of the *mitzvah*.[25] This is not considered disrespectful to the *mitzvah* because these walls were never set aside for the *mitzvah,* since at the outset he stipulated that he could make use of them. Thus the holiness of the *sukkah* never rested upon them.

טו וְכָל אִסּוּרִים הָאֵלּוּ שֶׁבֵּאַרְנוּ בְּסִימָן זֶה נוֹהֲגִין אֲפִלּוּ בְּסֻכָּה שֶׁלֹּא נַעֲשֵׂית לְשֵׁם מִצְוָה, וַאֲפִלּוּ לֹא חִדֵּשׁ בָּהּ דָּבָר,[סד] וְהוּא שֶׁיָּשַׁב בָּהּ פַּעַם אַחַת לְשֵׁם מִצְוַת סֻכָּה.[סה] אֲבָל קֹדֶם שֶׁיֵּשֵׁב בָּהּ[סו] לְשֵׁם

15 All the prohibitions that we have explained in this section apply even when a *sukkah* was not constructed for the sake of the *mitzvah,* and even if one did not bring about any changes [in an existing *sukkah*] — provided that he sat in it [at least] once for the sake of the *mitzvah* of *sukkah.*

Before one sits in the *sukkah* for the sake

25. The stipulation can be effective in this instance, because on *Chol HaMoed* there is no prohibition against demolishing the walls of a *sukkah.*

ס סעיף יז. סא מ״א שם. וראה מ״מ וציונים. סב ס״ז. סג רש״ל ביש״ש ביצה פ״ד סי׳ ג. מ״א ריש הסי׳. סד רבנו ירוחם נ״ח ח״ב (נז, ג). מ״א סק״ב. סה מ״א שם. סו שאילתות דרב אחאי פ׳ שלח שאילתא קכו. אור זרוע ח״ב סי׳ שם. הגהות אשרי ביצה פ״ד סי׳ ג. רמ״א סוף ס״א. וראה העו״ב תשפב ע׳

of the *mitzvah,* by contrast, it has no holiness at all, even if it was made for the sake of the *mitzvah* of *sukkah.* It is even permitted to make use of the branches of the *s'chach.* Needless to say, [this] also [applies to] the wood used for the walls and to the decorations, for any [object associated with a] *mitzvah* that has not yet been used for the *mitzvah* is not invested with holiness at all, as was stated in sec. 42[:4, 6].[26]

מִצְוַת סֻכָּה[סז] — אֵין עָלֶיהָ קְדֻשָּׁה כְּלָל, אֲפִלּוּ עֲשָׂאָהּ לְשֵׁם מִצְוַת סֻכָּה, וּמֻתָּר לְהִסְתַּפֵּק אֲפִלּוּ מֵעֲצֵי הַסְּכָךְ, וְאֵין צָרִיךְ לוֹמַר מֵעֲצֵי הַדְּפָנוֹת וּמִנּוֹיֵי הַסֻּכָּה, שֶׁכָּל מִצְוָה שֶׁעֲדַיִן לֹא נִשְׁתַּמְּשׁוּ בָּהּ לְשֵׁם מִצְוָה — אֵין עָלֶיהָ קְדֻשָּׁה כְּלָל, כְּמוֹ שֶׁנִּתְבָּאֵר בְּסִימָן מ"ב:[סח, 26]

16 [Similar concepts apply] even to a person who has a *sukkah* that remains standing from year to year. Though he dwelt in it [in observance of the *mitzvah*] in the previous year, making use of it is not prohibited until he dwells in it on Sukkos in the present year. For the holiness of the *sukkah* departs with the conclusion of the festival in the previous year and does not revert to it until one dwells in it once for the sake of [observing] the *mitzvah.*

טז וַאֲפִלּוּ מִי שֶׁיֵּשׁ לוֹ סֻכָּה בְּנוּיָה מִשָּׁנָה לְשָׁנָה, אַף עַל פִּי שֶׁיָּשַׁב בָּהּ בְּשָׁנָה שֶׁעָבְרָה — אַף עַל פִּי כֵן אֵינָהּ אֲסוּרָה עַד שֶׁיֵּשֵׁב בָּהּ בֶּחָג שֶׁל שָׁנָה זוֹ, דְּכֵיוָן שֶׁעָבַר הֶחָג שֶׁל שָׁנָה שֶׁעָבְרָה — בָּטְלָה קְדֻשַּׁת הַסֻּכָּה, וְאֵין הַקְּדֻשָּׁה חָלָה עָלֶיהָ עַד שֶׁיֵּשֵׁב בָּהּ פַּעַם אַחַת לְשֵׁם מִצְוָה:[סט]

17 A person who desires to remove the decorations of a *sukkah* on *Yom-Tov*[17] because of rain or because of thieves[27] should be careful not to tie the decorations to the *sukkah* with a [halachically-defined] knot, for it is forbidden to untie such knots on a festival. Instead, he should tie [the decorations] with a bow.[28]

יז מִי שֶׁרוֹצֶה לְהָסִיר נוֹיֵי הַסֻּכָּה בְּיוֹם טוֹב[17] מִפְּנֵי הַגְּשָׁמִים וְהַגַּנָּבִים[27] — יִזָּהֵר שֶׁלֹּא יִקְשֹׁר הַנּוֹיִין בַּסֻּכָּה בְּקֶשֶׁר גָּמוּר, שֶׁהֲרֵי אָסוּר לְהַתִּירָן בְּיוֹם טוֹב, אֶלָּא יַעַנְבֵם:[ע, 28]

18 Even when one does not intend to remove

יח אַף מִי שֶׁאֵין דַּעְתּוֹ לְהָסִיר

---

26. Significantly, in subsection 6 of that section, the Alter Rebbe cites a stringent view concerning "something that was designated to become a sacred object itself. For example, it is forbidden to write mundane matters on parchment that was processed for a Torah scroll, *tefillin,* or *mezuzos,* unless a stipulation was specified to this effect [at the outset]." He then proceeds to cite another view that allows leniency with regard to such sacred objects. With regard to *s'chach,* however, the Alter Rebbe does not mention the more stringent opinion.

This subsection reflects the intermediate status of the holiness of a *sukkah.* On one hand, even when it was not designated for the *mitzvah,* once used for the *mitzvah* it becomes sanctified (in contrast to a satchel used to carry *tefillin,* as stated in sec. 42). On the other hand, merely designating it for the *mitzvah* itself is not significant.

27. As stated in subsection 11.

28. In which instance such a prohibition does not exist. See sec. 317.

74. סז לבוש סוף ס"א. סח ס"ד וס"ו. סט מ"א סק"ב. ע אגודה פ"א סי' ט. דרכי משה ס"ק ה. מ"א סק"ט. וראה לעיל סי' שיז ס"ג. לקמן סי' תרנא ס"ו.

הַנּוֹיִין מֵהַסֻּכָּה כָּל יְמֵי הֶחָג, מִכָּל מָקוֹם אִם יוֹדֵעַ שֶׁהַיְלָדִים יֹאכְלוּ מֵהַנּוֹיִין בְּתוֹךְ הֶחָג – יַתְנֶה עֲלֵיהֶם מֵעֶרֶב יוֹם טוֹב:[עא, 29]

[edible] decorations from the *sukkah* throughout the days of the festival, if he knows that children will partake of them during [that time], he should make a stipulation before the onset of the festival.[29]

יט עֲצֵי הַסְּכָךְ[30] אַחַר שֶׁעָבְרוּ יְמֵי הֶחָג, אַף עַל פִּי שֶׁאֵין צָרִיךְ לְגָנְזָן[7] וּמֻתָּר לְהִסְתַּפֵּק מֵהֶן וּלְהִשְׁתַּמֵּשׁ בָּהֶן לְכָל מַה שֶּׁיִּרְצֶה, מִכָּל מָקוֹם נָכוֹן לִזָּהֵר שֶׁלֹּא לְהִשְׁתַּמֵּשׁ בָּהֶן תַּשְׁמִישׁ בִּזָּיוֹן, שֶׁאֵינָהּ כָּבוֹד לַמִּצְוָה שֶׁעָבְרָה,[עב, 31] וְאֵין צָרִיךְ לוֹמַר שֶׁאֵין לִפְסֹעַ עֲלֵיהֶם,[עג] שֶׁלֹּא יִנְהֹג בָּהֶם מִנְהַג בִּזָּיוֹן:

19 After the days of the festival have passed, there is no need to entomb the branches[7] used for *s'chach;*[30] they may be taken and used for whatever one desires. Nevertheless, it is proper not to use them for a degrading purpose that would be disrespectful to the *mitzvah* for which they had been used.[31] Needless to say, one should not tread on them, so as not to treat them disrespectfully.

כ אוֹתָן אֲנָשִׁים שֶׁחוֹקְקִים פָּסוּק[עד] "בַּסֻּכֹּת תֵּשְׁבוּ כו'" עַל הַדְּלַעַת[32] וְתוֹלִים בַּסֻּכָּה לְנוֹי[עה] – צָרִיךְ לִמְחוֹת בְּיָדָם, לְפִי שֶׁאָסוּר לִכְתֹּב פְּסוּקִים מִן הַתּוֹרָה אֶלָּא אִם כֵּן יֵשׁ בָּהֶם סֵפֶר שָׁלֵם[33] כְּמוֹ שֶׁנִּתְבָּאֵר בְּיוֹרֶה דֵעָה סִימָן רפ"ג,[עו, 34] וַחֲקִיקָה הִיא כִּכְתִיבָה לְעִנְיָן זֶה:[עז]

20 People who engrave a gourd with the verse,[32] "You shall dwell in *Sukkos...*," and hang it in the *sukkah* as a decoration, should be rebuked. [The rationale is] that it is forbidden to write any verses from the Torah unless one writes out an entire scroll,[33] as stated in *Yoreh Deah,* sec. 283.[34] In this context, engraving is equivalent to writing.

---

29. As stated in subsection 7. The holiness of the *sukkah* will thus not rest upon the decorations and no transgression will be involved.

30. Unlike a damaged segment of a Torah scroll or of *tefillin,* whose sacred status remains even after they can no longer be used for their respective *mitzvos.*

31. During the festival their holiness is higher than that of *tashmishei mitzvah,* objects used for the performance of a *mitzvah,* as stated in the footnotes to subsection 1 above. After the festival their status declines and they are bound by the same laws that apply to *tashmishei mitzvah.* See sec. 21:1 in Vol. 1 of the present work.

32. *Vayikra* 23:42.

33. Classrooms are commonly decorated with posters that include Biblical quotations. Their message, as *Bikurei Yaakov* (638:18) points out, can be preserved respectfully, unlike the engravings in the perishable gourd.

34. This section of *Yoreh Deah* is not extant in the Alter Rebbe's *Shulchan Aruch.* The *Shulchan Aruch* of R. Yosef Caro *(Yoreh Deah,* sec. 283:2) states that a scroll should not be written with selections from the Torah. *Turei Zahav* 283:1 states that such scrolls may be written to facilitate study, but not for use as amulets.

To relate this to the concept at hand: Though it has become widely accepted to print passages from the Torah and from the *Tanach,* such leniency is allowed only for the sake of Torah study or prayer. To write a verse for decorative purposes is forbidden.

עא מ"א סק"ד. **עב** ט"ז סי' כא סק"ב. וכדלעיל שם ס"א. **עג** מ"א סוף סק"ט. **עד** ויקרא כג, מב. **עה** מ"א סק"ט. **עו** סימן זה בשוע"ר לא הגיע לידינו, וראה שו"ע שם ס"ב וס"ד. ט"ז שם סק"א וסק"ג וש"ך סק"ו. לעיל סי' רפד ס"ד. סי' שלד סי"ג. **עז** כדלעיל סי' שמ ס"ז. **עח** מהרי"ל הל' סוכות (ע' שסב). מ"א

כא אֵין לִתְלוֹת שַׁעַטְנֵז סְבִיב הַדְּפָנוֹת שֶׁל הַסֻּכָּה לְנוֹי אֶלָּא אִם כֵּן הוּא לְמַעְלָה מְרַאֲשׁוֹתָיו שֶׁל אָדָם,[עח] מִטַּעַם שֶׁנִּתְבָּאֵר בְּיוֹרֶה דֵעָה סִימָן ש"א:[עט, 35]

21 [Fabrics that are] *shaatnez* [which is a forbidden combination of wool and linen] may not be hung around the walls of a *sukkah* as decorations unless they are hung higher than a person's head. The rationale [for this restriction] is explained in *Yoreh Deah,* sec. 301.[35]

סימן תרלט דִּינֵי יְשִׁיבַת סֻכָּה וּבוֹ כ"ו סְעִיפִים:

SECTION 639 Laws Relating to Dwelling in the *Sukkah.* (1–26)

א "בַּסֻּכֹּת תֵּשְׁבוּ שִׁבְעַת יָמִים",[א, 1] וְלָמְדוּ מִפִּי הַשְּׁמוּעָה[ב, 2] "תֵּשְׁבוּ" – כְּעֵין תָּדוּרוּ, כְּלוֹמַר כְּדֶרֶךְ שֶׁהוּא דָּר כָּל הַשָּׁנָה בְּבֵיתוֹ – הִזְקִיקַתּוּ תּוֹרָה לְהַנִּיחַ דִּירָתוֹ וְלָדוּר כָּאן בַּסֻּכָּה עִם מִטּוֹתָיו וּמַצְּעוֹתָיו וּכְלֵי תַשְׁמִישׁוֹ,[ג] מִכָּאן אָמְרוּ חֲכָמִים:[ד, 2] כָּל שִׁבְעַת הַיָּמִים אָדָם עוֹשֶׂה בֵּיתוֹ עֲרַאי וְסֻכָּתוֹ קֶבַע. כֵּיצַד? הָיָה לוֹ מַצָּעוֹת נָאוֹת וְכֵלִים נָאִים – מַעֲלָן[3] לַסֻּכָּה,[ה] וְכֵן כָּל כְּלֵי שְׁתִיָּה[ו] הַצְּרִיכִים לוֹ[ז] – יִהְיוּ עִמּוֹ בַּסֻּכָּה[4] כְּדֶרֶךְ שֶׁהֵן עִמּוֹ בְּבֵיתוֹ בְּכָל הַשָּׁנָה. אֲבָל כֵּלִים שֶׁמַּשְׁהִין בָּהֶן קֶמַח[ח] וְהָעֲרֵבוֹת[ט]

1 It is written,[1] "You shall dwell in *sukkos* for seven days." Based on the Oral Tradition, [the Sages] commented:[2] "You must dwell [in the *sukkah*] as you reside" — i.e., in the manner that one resides in his home throughout the year. The Torah requires that one leave his home and dwell in the *sukkah* with his beds, his bedcovers, and all his household articles. On this basis our Sages said:[2] Throughout these seven days, a person should treat his home as his temporary dwelling and his *sukkah* as his permanent dwelling.

What is implied? If a person has attractive bedcovers and attractive utensils, he should bring them[3] to the *sukkah*. Similarly, all the drinking utensils that he requires should be with him in the *sukkah,*[4] just as he has them at hand in his home throughout the year. By contrast, containers used to store flour, kneading troughs,

---

35. This section of *Yoreh Deah* is not extant in the Alter Rebbe's *Shulchan Aruch*. The *Shulchan Aruch* of R. Yosef Caro (*Yoreh Deah,* sec. 301:11) states that it is forbidden to hang a soft curtain made of *shaatnez,* because sometimes an attendant will use it to warm himself. However, *shaatnez* may be used as a decoration when there is no likelihood that this will happen for, as *Sifsei Kohen* (301:11) notes, even though a person derives benefit from using the forbidden fabric (as a curtain or, in the law at hand, as a decoration), there is no prohibition involved here since he does not wear it as a garment.

* For a summary of sec. 638, see p. 454.

SECTION 639

1. *Vayikra* 23:42.

2. *Sukkah* 28b.

3. Lit., "bring them *up* to the *sukkah,*" for a *sukkah* in the Talmudic era was commonly built on the householder's flat roof. See *Rashi* on *Shabbos* 154b, s.v. *Shtayim.*

4. *Sukkah* 29a.

סק"ט (מתשמיש אדם). **עט** סימן זה בשוע"ר לא הגיע לידינו, וראה שו"ע שם סי"א. ט"ז וש"ך שם סקי"א. לעיל סי' שח ספ"ה. סי' תקטז ס"ב.

סימן תרלט: א ויקרא כג, מב. **ב** גמרא [ברייתא] כח, ב. **ג** רש"י דף כו, א ד"ה כעין תדורו. **ד** משנה כח, ב. טור ושו"ע ס"א. **ה** ברייתא שם. טור ושו"ע שם. **ו** רבא כט, רע"א. רמב"ם פ"ו ה"ה. שו"ע שם. **ז** למעט כלי שאיבה, דלקמן סעיף ב. **ח** בה"ג הל' סוכה (לב, ב). שבלי הלקט סי' שדמ (בהג"ה משבלי הלקט הקצר). מ"א סק"א. **ט** בה"ג שם. תוס' כט, א ד"ה מנא. מרדכי רמז תשמה בשם ויש מפרשים. מ"א שם.

וְכֵלִים שֶׁל מַיִם[י] – אֵינָן צְרִיכִין לִהְיוֹת בַּסֻּכָּה, שֶׁאַף בְּכָל הַשָּׁנָה אֵין דְּבָרִים אֵלּוּ רְגִילִים לִהְיוֹת עִמּוֹ בְּבֵית דִּירָתוֹ,[5] אֶלָּא בַּיִת יֵשׁ לָהֶם בִּלְבָדָם:[יא]

and water containers need not be kept in the *sukkah,* for one does not [necessarily] keep such articles in his home[5] throughout the year; they are kept is separate [store]houses.

ב כְּלֵי אֲכִילָה[יב] לְאַחַר אֲכִילָה,[יג] כְּגוֹן קְדֵרוֹת[יד] וּקְעָרוֹת[טו] שֶׁאַחַר הָאֲכִילָה הֵן מְאוּסִין[טז] – צָרִיךְ לְהוֹצִיאָן מִן הַסֻּכָּה.[יז,6] וְכֵן דְּלִי אוֹ כַּד שֶׁשּׁוֹאֲבִין בּוֹ מַיִם – לֹא יַכְנִיסֵם לְתוֹךְ הַסֻּכָּה.[יח] וְכֵן לֹא יַעֲשֶׂה שׁוּם תַּשְׁמִישׁ בָּזוּי בַּסֻּכָּה,[יט] כְּגוֹן שְׁטִיפַת קְדֵרוֹת וּקְעָרוֹת,[כ] כְּדֵי שֶׁלֹּא יִהְיוּ מִצְוֹת בְּזוּיוֹת עָלָיו.[כא] אֲבָל מֻתָּר לִשְׁטֹף כְּלֵי הַשְּׁתִיָּה[כב] כְּגוֹן כּוֹסוֹת וְצִנְצָנִיּוֹת בַּסֻּכָּה:

2 After a meal, vessels that were used for food, such as pots and plates, are offensive. Hence they must be removed from the *sukkah.*[6] Similarly, a bucket or a jug that serves to draw water [from a well] should not be brought into the *sukkah.* Nor should the *sukkah* be used for any lowly task, such as washing pots and plates, so that *mitzvos* will not be held in disdain. Drinking utensils, however, such as glasses and jars, may be washed in the *sukkah.*

ג הַמְּנוֹרָה[כג] בְּשָׁעָה שֶׁהִיא דוֹלֶקֶת[כד] – צְרִיכָה לִהְיוֹת בְּתוֹךְ הַסֻּכָּה.[4] וְאִם הַסֻּכָּה קְטַנָּה[כה] בְּעִנְיָן שֶׁיֵּשׁ לָחוּשׁ[כו] שֶׁמָּא יִתְקָרֵב הַנֵּר לְדָפְנֵי הַסֻּכָּה[כז] אוֹ לְהַסְּכָךְ וְתֶאֱחַז בָּהֶן הָאוּר וְתִשְׂרֹף סֻכָּתוֹ[כח] – צָרִיךְ לְהַנִּיחָהּ חוּץ לַסֻּכָּה, אֲפִלּוּ הִיא שֶׁל זָהָב.[כט]

וְנוֹהֲגִין שֶׁלֹּא לְהַכְנִיס נֵר שֶׁל חֶרֶס אֲפִלּוּ לְסֻכָּה גְּדוֹלָה:[ל,7]

3 While a lamp is lit, it should be placed in the *sukkah.*[4] If the *sukkah* is so small that there is reason for concern that it may be placed close to the wall or the *s'chach* and the *sukkah* will catch fire, it should be placed outside the *sukkah,* even if the lamp is golden.

It is customary not to bring an earthenware lamp into a *sukkah,* even if the *sukkah* is large.[7]

ד כֵּיצַד מִצְוַת יְשִׁיבָה בַּסֻּכָּה[לא]? שֶׁיִּהְיֶה אוֹכֵל וְשׁוֹתֶה[לב] וְיָשֵׁן[לג,8] וּמְטַיֵּל[לד] וְדָר בַּסֻּכָּה

4 How is the *mitzvah* of dwelling in the *sukkah* [observed]? A person should eat, drink, sleep,[8] relax, and dwell in the *sukkah* for all these seven

5. Today, *bayis* means "home" or "house"; in Talmudic and halachic usage it sometimes signifies "room," or "the main room of the house."

6. Just as they are removed from any room in which one eats.

7. Since an earthenware lamp blackens with use, it is out of place in the *sukkah.*

8. *Sukkah* 20b, 28b.

י בשבלי הלקט ובמ"א שם: של בשמים. ולענין כלים ששואבים בהם מים, ראה לקמן ס"ב. יא תוס' שם. מרדכי שם. יב רבא בגמרא כט, א. רמב"ם פ"ו ה"ה. שו"ע ס"א. יג רש"י שם ד"ה מאני מיכלא. טור ורמ"א ס"א. יד רמב"ם ושו"ע שם. טו רש"י שם. רמב"ם ושו"ע שם. טז תוס' שם ד"ה מנא בדעת רש"י שם. הגהות מיימוניות שם אות ז. טור. מ"א סק"ג. יז רש"י שם. יח רבא שם. (ר)מ"א סק"א. יט ארחות חיים הל' סוכה סי' לד. רמ"א ס"א. כ ארחות חיים שם. לבוש סוף ס"א. מ"א ס"ק ג. כא ארחות חיים ורמ"א שם. כב מ"א שם. כג גמרא כט, א. טור ושו"ע ס"א. כד תוס' שם ד"ה ואמרי. טור ולבוש ס"א (מותר. וראה שו"ע סי' תרסו). כה גמרא שם. טור ושו"ע שם. כו ט"ז סוף ס"ק ג. כז רא"ש פ"ב סי' יט. לבוש שם. כח תוס' שם. ר"ן (יג, א) ד"ה שרגא. מ"א סק"ב. כט אור זרוע הל' סוכה סי' דש. ראבי"ה סי' תרמא. הגהות אשרי שם. ב"י ד"ה כתב בהג"א. ל רוקח הל' סוכות סי' ריט. ב"י שם. (ר)מ"א סק"ב. לא רמב"ם פ"ו ה"ה. שו"ע ס"א. לב גמרא [ברייתא] כח, ב. רמב"ם שם. טור ושו"ע שם. לג משנה כ, ב (ורש"י שם ד"ה לא יצא. וכדלעיל סי' תרכז). ברייתא כו, א.

כָּל שִׁבְעַת הַיָּמִים,[9] בֵּין בַּיּוֹם בֵּין בַּלַּיְלָה, כְּדֶרֶךְ שֶׁהוּא דָּר בְּבֵיתוֹ בִּשְׁאָר יְמוֹת הַשָּׁנָה.[לה] וְאִם הוּא צָרִיךְ לְסַפֵּר עִם חֲבֵרוֹ – יְסַפֵּר עִמּוֹ בַּסֻּכָּה.[לו] כְּלָלוֹ שֶׁל דָּבָר, לְעוֹלָם יְדַמֶּה עָלָיו סֻכָּתוֹ כְּאִלּוּ הִיא בֵּיתוֹ,[לז] וְכָל דָּבָר שֶׁלֹּא הָיָה עוֹשֶׂה חוּץ לְבֵיתוֹ – לֹא יַעֲשֶׂה חוּץ לְסֻכָּתוֹ.[10]

לְפִיכָךְ, כָּל שִׁבְעַת הַיָּמִים צָרִיךְ לִקְרוֹת[לח] וְלִלְמֹד[לט,11] בְּתוֹךְ הַסֻּכָּה[2] (אֶלָּא אִם כֵּן קוֹרֵא וְלוֹמֵד בְּבֵית הַמִּדְרָשׁ[מ,12]). וְאִם הוּא מֵבִין וּמְדַקְדֵּק כְּשֶׁלּוֹמֵד – יָכוֹל לִלְמֹד חוּץ לַסֻּכָּה,[מא,13] כְּדֵי שֶׁתְּהֵא דַּעְתּוֹ מְיֻשֶּׁבֶת עָלָיו,[מב] שֶׁרֹחַב הָאֲוִיר יָפֶה לוֹ לְהַרְחִיב דַּעְתּוֹ.[מג] וּמִכָּל מָקוֹם, הַכֹּל לְפִי הָעִנְיָן, שֶׁאִם יֵשׁ לוֹ מְנוּחָה בַּסֻּכָּה – צָרִיךְ לִלְמֹד בַּסֻּכָּה.

וְאִם צָרִיךְ לִלְמֹד מִתּוֹךְ סְפָרִים הַרְבֵּה,[מד] אִם אֶפְשָׁר לוֹ לְהָכִין לָהֶם מָקוֹם בְּסֻכָּתוֹ בְּעִנְיָן שֶׁלֹּא יִצְטָרֵךְ לְפַנּוֹתָם מִסֻּכָּתוֹ בְּעֵת הָאֲכִילָה וְהַשֵּׁנָה וְלַחֲזֹר וּלְהַכְנִיסָן בְּעֵת הַלִּמּוּד – צָרִיךְ לִלְמֹד בְּתוֹךְ הַסֻּכָּה,[מה] אֲבָל אִם אִי אֶפְשָׁר לוֹ לְהָכִין לָהֶם מָקוֹם בְּקַל בְּלֹא טֹרַח רַב וְיֵשׁ לוֹ טֹרַח[מו] רַב לְפַנּוֹתָם

days,[9] during the day and at night as he dwells in his own home throughout the year. If he wants to speak to a friend, he should speak with him in the *sukkah*. To summarize: A person should regard the *sukkah* as his home. Whatever he would not do outside his home, he should not do outside his *sukkah*.[10]

For this reason, throughout these seven days, he should read and study[11] in the *sukkah*[1] (unless he reads and studies in the House of Study[12]). If he studies in depth and with careful scrutiny, he may do so outside the *sukkah*[13] so that his mind will be settled, for ample space broadens one's thinking.

Nevertheless, every situation should be judged individually. If a person is at ease in the *sukkah*, he should study in the *sukkah*. If his study requires many books, and he can prepare a place for them in his *sukkah* so that he will not have to remove them when he eats and sleeps and bring them back when he studies, he should study in the *sukkah*. However, if he cannot prepare a place for [his books] easily, without much difficulty, and he finds it very troublesome to take them out and

---

9. As stated in the *Shulchan Aruch* of R. Yosef Caro, sec. 668:1, in the Diaspora we dwell in the *sukkah* on Shemini Atzeres as well, but no blessing is recited at this time.

10. The *Shelah* highlights the holiness of the *sukkah:* though it houses one's mundane activities, those activities should all be suffused with holiness. One should be particularly vigilant with his speech, avoiding gossip, *lashon hara,* and the like. It is recounted that the Rebbe Maharash (R. Shmuel, the fourth Lubavitcher Rebbe) once overheard an irritated remark in his *sukkah*. He gently corrected the speaker: "You know, in the presence of the *s'chach* one ought to show respect. The *s'chach* doesn't *like* anger." [See *Sefer HaSichos 5704* (1944), p. 12.]

11. In the original, "read" relates to the Written Law (i.e., Scripture), and "study" relates to the Oral Law.

12. I.e., the communal *beis midrash.*

13. I.e., at home.

טור ורמ"א ס"א. שו"ע ס"ב. וכדלקמן ס"ח־ט וש"נ. וראה לקו"ש חכ"ט 215. שלחן המלך ח"ב ע' רמו־ז. **לד** ברייתא כח, ב. טור ורמ"א ס"א. **לה** רמב"ם שם. שו"ע שם. **לו** מהרי"ל הל' סוכות (ע' שע). דרכי משה ס"ק א. ט"ז סק"א. **לז** דרכי משה שם. **לח** רבא כח, סוע"ב. רמב"ם פ"ו ה"ט. שו"ע ס"ד. **לט** ברייתא וגמרא שם. טור ורמ"א ס"ד. **מ** כדלקמן ס"ה (בתפלה) וש"נ. **מא** גמרא שם, לפירוש רש"י שם ותנוי. רמב"ם שם. טור ושו"ע שם. **מב** רמב"ם שם. שו"ע שם. **מג** רש"י שם ד"ה בר. **מד** מ"א סקי"ג. **מה** אליה רבה סק"ב. **מו** מ"א שם.

וְלַחֲזוֹר וּלְהַכְנִיסָם – יָכוֹל לִלְמֹד חוּץ לַסֻּכָּה, לְפִי שֶׁכָּל טִרְחָא יְתֵרָה שֶׁאֵין הָאָדָם[מז] מִצְטַעֵר וּמוֹנֵעַ אֶת עַצְמוֹ מִטִּרְחָא זוֹ כְּדֵי לֵישֵׁב בְּבֵיתוֹ בִּקְבִיעוּת – אֵין מְחֻיָּב לִטְרֹחַ כְּדֵי לֵישֵׁב בְּסֻכָּתוֹ בִּקְבִיעוּת:[מח,14]

bring them into the *sukkah,* he may study outside the *sukkah.* If dwelling in one's home as people normally do required such a burdensome effort that one would refrain from undertaking it, one is likewise not obligated to undertake such an effort in order to be able to dwell in this manner in his *sukkah.*[14]

ה הַמִּתְפַּלֵּל, אִם יֵשׁ לוֹ מְנוּחָה בַּסֻּכָּה שֶׁיּוּכַל לְהִתְפַּלֵּל שָׁם בְּכַוָּנָה – צָרִיךְ לִכָּנֵס לַסֻּכָּה וּלְהִתְפַּלֵּל,[מט] שֶׁהֲרֵי בִּשְׁאָר יְמוֹת הַשָּׁנָה כְּשֶׁאֵינוֹ מִתְפַּלֵּל בְּבֵית הַכְּנֶסֶת הוּא נִכְנָס לְבֵיתוֹ וּמִתְפַּלֵּל.

בַּמֶּה דְּבָרִים אֲמוּרִים? בְּמָקוֹם שֶׁאֵין שָׁם בֵּית הַכְּנֶסֶת, אוֹ שֶׁאִי אֶפְשָׁר לוֹ לֵילֵךְ לְבֵית הַכְּנֶסֶת, אֲבָל אִם אֶפְשָׁר לוֹ לֵילֵךְ לְבֵית הַכְּנֶסֶת – יֵלֵךְ, וְאֵינוֹ צָרִיךְ לְהִתְפַּלֵּל בַּסֻּכָּה:[נ]

5 If one feels at ease when praying in the *sukkah* and can concentrate there on his prayers, he should enter the *sukkah* to pray, for at other times during the year, when he does not pray in a synagogue, he enters his home to pray.

When does the above apply? In a place where there is no synagogue or where it is impossible for him to go to the synagogue. If, however, he can go to the synagogue, he should go; he need not pray in the *sukkah.*

ו הַמַּבְדִּיל עַל הַכּוֹס – צָרִיךְ לִכָּנֵס לַסֻּכָּה לְהַבְדִּיל שָׁם,[15] שֶׁהֲרֵי בִּשְׁאָר יְמוֹת הַשָּׁנָה נִכְנָס לְבֵיתוֹ לְהַבְדִּיל שָׁם:[נא]

6 When one recites *Havdalah* over a cup [of wine], he should enter the *sukkah* to recite it,[15] for at other times during the year, he would enter his home to recite *Havdalah.*

ז אוֹכְלִין אֲכִילַת עֲרַאי[16] חוּץ לַסֻּכָּה,[נב,17] אֲבָל אָסוּר לִישֹׁן אֲפִלּוּ שְׁנַת עֲרַאי חוּץ לַסֻּכָּה,[נג,18] לְפִי שֶׁבְּשֵׁנָה אֵין לְחַלֵּק בֵּין עֲרַאי לְקֶבַע,[19] שֶׁלִּפְעָמִים שֶׁאֵינוֹ מְנַמְנֵם אֶלָּא מְעַט

7 One may take a snack[16] outside the *sukkah.*[17] One may not, however, take even a short nap outside the *sukkah.*[18] With regard to sleep, no distinction should be drawn between a nap and sound sleep,[19] since sometimes a person will doze off

---

14. Lit., "For any great effort that would cause such discomfort that one would refrain from undertaking it in order to be able to dwell in his home in a permanent manner, one is not obligated to undertake in order to be able to dwell in his *Sukkah* in a permanent manner."

15. The Lubavitch custom is to also recite the blessing *leishev basukkah* when reciting *Havdalah.* See the footnotes to subsection 15 below.

16. *Sukkah* 25a. A snack *(achilas arai)* is defined in subsection 11 below.

17. Just as a snack is eaten outside one's home.

18. *Op. cit.,* 26a.

19. "Sound sleep" translates *shnas keva,* and "nap" translates *shnas arai.* The Sages term a sleep of more than 60 breaths *shnas keva,* i.e., a sleep that lasts a significant

מז אוצ"ל: שהאדם. מח כדלקמן סי' תרמ ס"ה וש"נ. מט ב"ח ד"ה כתב הרמב"ם. אליה זוטא סק"ב. מ"א סקי"ד. נ שלטי גבורים יג, א אות ב בשם ריא"ז. הובא בב"ח ומ"א וא"ז שם. נא ט"ז סקי"ד. נב משנה כה, א. טור ושו"ע שם. נג ברייתא כו, א. טור ושו"ע ס"ב. נד רבא בגמרא שם ורש"י ד"ה רבא. לבוש

briefly and that will suffice. Hence for him,[20] this is considered as sound sleep that obligates him to enter the *sukkah*.

וְדַיּוֹ בְּכָךְ, לְפִיכָךְ זוֹ הִיא שְׁנַת קֶבַע שֶׁלּוֹ[נד,20] שֶׁחַיָּב לִכְנֹס לַסֻּכָּה בִּשְׁבִילָהּ:

8 In cold regions, where the [weather] will make sleeping in the *sukkah* uncomfortable if one does not have enough pillows and blankets, there is no requirement to sleep in the *sukkah*. Moreover, [there is room for leniency] even if one has sufficient bedding, but he cannot prepare a place for it in the *sukkah* for all seven days of the festival so that he will not have to go to the trouble of removing it from the *sukkah* at mealtimes and then returning it to the *sukkah* for sleeping. [If] this entails so much trouble that were he to be faced by such a difficulty at home, he would not sleep at home,[21] he is not obligated to sleep in the *sukkah*, for whoever suffers discomfort while dwelling in the *sukkah* is not obligated to dwell in it, as stated in sec. 640[:5ff.].

ח בַּמְּקוֹמוֹת הַקָּרִים[נה] שֶׁיֵּשׁ צַעַר לִישֹׁן בַּסֻּכָּה מֵחֲמַת הַקֹּר[נו] וְאֵין לוֹ כָּרִים וּכְסָתוֹת כָּרָאוּי[נז] אֵין צָרִיךְ לִישֹׁן בַּסֻּכָּה וַאֲפִלּוּ יֵשׁ לוֹ כָּרִים אֶלָּא שֶׁאִי אֶפְשָׁר לוֹ לְהָכִין לָהֶם מָקוֹם בַּסֻּכָּה לְכָל שִׁבְעַת יְמֵי הֶחָג בְּעִנְיָן שֶׁיִּצְטָרֵךְ לִטְרֹחַ לְהוֹצִיאָן מֵהַסֻּכָּה בִּשְׁעַת הָאֲכִילָה וְלַחֲזֹר וּלְהַכְנִיסָן בְּעֵת הַשֵּׁנָה וְהִיא טִרְחָא יְתֵרָה וּמִצְטַעֵר בְּטִרְחָא זוֹ[נח] בְּעִנְיָן שֶׁאִם הָיָה לוֹ טִרְחָא כָּזוֹ לִישֹׁן בְּבֵיתוֹ לֹא הָיָה יָשֵׁן בְּבֵיתוֹ[נט,21] אֵינוֹ צָרִיךְ לִישֹׁן בַּסֻּכָּה שֶׁכָּל הַמִּצְטַעֵר בִּישִׁיבַת הַסֻּכָּה פָּטוּר מִישִׁיבָתָהּ כְּמוֹ שֶׁיִּתְבָּאֵר בְּסִימָן תר"מ:[ס]

9 At present, people at large have adopted the practice of following a lenient approach when it comes to sleeping [in the *sukkah*]. Only those who are punctilious in their observance of *mitzvos* sleep in the *sukkah*.[22]

There are those who have offered

ט וְעַכְשָׁו נָהֲגוּ הָעוֹלָם לְהָקֵל בְּשֵׁנָה, שֶׁאֵין יְשֵׁנִים בַּסֻּכָּה רַק הַמְדַקְדְּקִים בְּמִצְווֹת.[סא,22] וְיֵשׁ שֶׁלִּמְּדוּ

---

period. This is variously held to indicate a time period as short as three minutes or as long as 72 minutes. *Sefer HaMaamarim 5568*, p. 543, speaks of periods of 12 minutes and one hour. *Ketzos HaShulchan (Badei HaShulchan* 2:1) adopts the average time of approximately half an hour.

20. Since it composes him.

21. But would seek alternative accommodations. See also subsection 4.

22. The Rebbe notes that the sixth Lubavitcher Rebbe, R. Yosef Yitzchak Schneersohn, made a point of never eating or drinking anything, even water, outside the *sukkah*, and yet he did not sleep in the *sukkah*. The Rebbe explains that we cannot say that the Rebbe Rayatz relied on the leniency stated in this or the previous subsection, for he never allowed physical discomfort to interfere with his observance of the *mitzvos*. On the contrary, he would eat in the *sukkah* despite the rain (see subsections. 19 and 21 and their footnotes).

In explanation, the Rebbe relates this conduct to a statement by the Mitteler Rebbe, R. DovBer, the second Lubavitcher Rebbe: "How is it possible to sleep in a *sukkah*? The transcendent lights *(makkifim)* of the

ס"ב. ט"ז סק"ה. מ"א סק"ד. **נה** רמ"א ס"ב. ב"ח סי' תרמ ד"ה ומ"ש ונראה (בארץ רוסיא. וראה לעיל סי' תקז קו"א סק"ד ד"ה כתב: ובמדינתנו שאין הקור גדול כ"כ בימי פסח וסוכות). **נו** מרדכי רמז תשמא. רמ"א שם. **נז** לבוש סי' תרמ ס"ד. מ"א סק"ז. **נח** לבוש שם. **נט** ראה גם לעיל סוף ס"ד. **ס** סעיף ה. **סא** דרכי משה ס"ק ג. רמ"א ס"ב. ומנהג חב"ד שאין ישנים בסוכה. ראה ספר השיחות תרצט ע' 295. לקו"ש חכ"ט ע' 211 ואילך. אג"ק חי"א ע' תיד. המלך במסיבו ח"א ע' סג. ח"ב ע' לג. אוצר מנהגי חב"ד חה"ס ע' שא־שב.

עֲלֵיהֶם זְכוּת,[סב] לְמִי שֶׁנָּשׂוּי אִשָּׁה שֶׁחַיָּב לְשַׂמֵּחַ אֶת אִשְׁתּוֹ בָּרֶגֶל,[סג, 23] וְנָשִׁים פְּטוּרוֹת מִן הַסֻּכָּה,[סד, 24] אִם כֵּן אִם אֵינוֹ רוֹצֶה לִפְרֹשׁ מֵאִשְׁתּוֹ — מִקְרֵי דְּבַר מִצְוָה,[25] וְכָל הָעוֹסֵק בַּמִּצְוָה — פָּטוּר מִמִּצְוָה אַחֶרֶת[26] כְּמוֹ שֶׁיִּתְבָּאֵר בְּסִימָן תר"מ,[סה] וְעַל כֵּן הוּא פָּטוּר מִשֵּׁנָה בַּסֻּכָּה בַּלַּיְלָה, וַאֲפִלּוּ אִם אִשְׁתּוֹ אֵינָהּ טְהוֹרָה, מִכָּל מָקוֹם שַׁיָּךְ שִׂמְחָה כְּשֶׁבַּעְלָהּ מִתְיַחֵד עִמָּהּ בְּחֶדֶר אֶחָד[סו] כְּמוֹ שֶׁיִּתְבָּאֵר.[סז, 27]

וּמִכָּל מָקוֹם, טוֹב לְהַחְמִיר שֶׁיִּהְיֶה לוֹ סֻכָּה מְיֻחֶדֶת שֶׁיּוּכַל לִישֹׁן שָׁם עִם אִשְׁתּוֹ וִיקַיֵּם שְׁתֵּי הַמִּצְווֹת:[סח]

י [סט] הַנּוֹשֵׂא[ע] בְּתוּלָה[עא, 28] שְׁנַיִם אוֹ

rationalizations for married men, [explaining] that they are obligated to bring happiness to their wives during the festivals[23] and women are not obligated [to observe the *mitzvah* of] *sukkah*.[24] Hence the fact that a person does not desire to separate from his wife is considered a matter associated with a *mitzvah*,[25] and whoever is occupied with the performance of a *mitzvah* is exempt from performing a different *mitzvah*,[26] as explained in sec. 640[:18]. Thus [a married man] is not obligated to sleep in the *sukkah* at night. [The above line of thought applies] even if one's wife is not ritually pure, for she is happy when her husband shares the privacy of their room with her, as will be explained.[27] Nevertheless, it is desirable that one follow the stringent approach and have a private *sukkah* where he can sleep together with his wife, and thus perform both *mitzvos*.

10 [The following laws apply when a man] marries a virgin bride[28] two or three days

Sefirah of *Binah* shine there!" [See *Sefer HaSichos*, 5699 (1938-1939), p. 295.] Because of the intense spiritual lights that shine in a *sukkah*, the Mitteler Rebbe could not conceive of sleeping there. Hence the halachic exemption that applies to a person who is uncomfortable in the *sukkah*, for whatever reason,

Now, the practice of not sleeping in the *sukkah* is observed not only by spiritual giants like the Mitteler Rebbe and the Rebbe Yosef Yitzchak, but also by their followers, including many who certainly do not sense — and hence are not made uncomfortable by — the intense spiritual energy that is manifest there. Why do they not observe the obligation as prescribed?

The Rebbe resolves that question by explaining that a chassid, whose souls are bonded with his Rebbe, seeks to observe his practices. A chassid would be sorely distressed if he observed a *mitzvah* in a manner that was different from that of his Rebbe. Moreover, he is distressed by the very fact that he would find it possible to sleep in a *sukkah*, despite the intense spiritual lights. And this distress exempts him from the obligation to sleep in the *sukkah*. (See *Likkutei Sichos*, Vol. 29, pp. 211ff.)

23. See: *Pesachim* 109a; sec. 529:6-7 in the present work.

24. See sec. 640:1.

25. In the original, *dvar mitzvah*.

26. Cf. *Sukkah* 25a.

27. See subsection 10 below. See also *Turei Zahav* 639:9, based on *Eruvin* 63b.

28. In *Kuntreis HaShulchan*, R. Avraham Chayim Naeh suggests that this subsection should be included in sec. 640, which deals with those who are exempt from dwelling in the *sukkah*, and indeed, the *Shulchan Aruch* of R. Yosef Caro deals with these laws in that section. From sec. 249:8, it would appear that the Alter Rebbe once thought to do so as well. However, the reference in subsection 9 in the present section ("as will be explained") suggests that his inclusion of this point here is part of his structure for this section.

סב ט"ז סק"ט. וראה דרכי משה ורמ"א שם. סג פסחים קט, א. וראה לעיל סי' תקכט ס"ו-ז. סד כדלקמן סי' תרמ ס"א. סה סעיף יח. סו דרכי משה וט"ז שם, מגמרא עירובין סג, ב. סז לקמן ס"י. סח רמ"א שם. סט בקונטרס השלחן כתב שמקומו בסי' תרמ (כמו בשו"ע הב"י), וכן מציין אליו לעיל סי' רמט

שְׁלֹשָׁה יָמִים קֹדֶם הֶחָג[עב, 29] בְּעִנְיָן שֶׁנִּמְשְׁכוּ שִׁבְעַת יְמֵי הַמִּשְׁתֶּה שֶׁלּוֹ בְּתוֹךְ הֶחָג[עג] (דְּאִלּוּ בֶּחָג עַצְמוֹ אֵין נוֹשְׂאִין נָשִׁים[עד] כְּמוֹ שֶׁנִּתְבָּאֵר בְּסִימָן תקמ"ו[עה, 30]), בַּיָּמִים הָרִאשׁוֹנִים שֶׁהָיוּ נוֹהֲגִים שֶׁכָּל שִׁבְעַת יְמֵי הַמִּשְׁתֶּה הָיוּ מִתְיַחֲדִין הֶחָתָן וְהַכַּלָּה בְּחֶדֶר מְיֻחָד, וְאֵין שׁוּם אָדָם נִכְנָס אֶצְלָם רַק בְּעֵת שֶׁרוֹצִים לִשְׂמֹחַ אוֹתָן וְלֶאֱכֹל וְלִשְׁתּוֹת עִמָּהֶם,[עו] וְזֶה הַחֶדֶר נִקְרָא חֻפָּה[עז] — הֲרֵי הֶחָתָן וְהַשּׁוֹשְׁבִינִין וְכָל בְּנֵי הַחֻפָּה[עח] דְּהַיְנוּ אוֹתָם אֲנָשִׁים שֶׁאוֹכְלִים עִם הֶחָתָן פְּטוּרִים מִן הַסֻּכָּה כָּל שִׁבְעַת יְמֵי הַמִּשְׁתֶּה, וּמֻתָּרִים לֶאֱכֹל וְלִשְׁתּוֹת וְלִשְׂמֹחַ חוּץ לַסֻּכָּה, דְּהַיְנוּ בְּחֶדֶר הַנִּקְרָא חֻפָּה, לְפִי שֶׁאִי אֶפְשָׁר לִשְׂמֹחַ כָּרָאוּי בְּתוֹךְ הַסֻּכָּה,[31] שֶׁאֵין עִקַּר הַשִּׂמְחָה אֶלָּא בַּחֻפָּה,[עט] שֶׁהוּא עִקַּר יְשִׁיבַת הֶחָתָן וְכַלָּה,[פ] דְּהַיְנוּ מָקוֹם שֶׁהֵם מִתְיַחֲדִין שָׁם, וְאִי אֶפְשָׁר לַעֲשׂוֹת עִקַּר יְשִׁיבַת הֶחָתָן וְכַלָּה בְּתוֹךְ הַסֻּכָּה,[פא] לְפִי שֶׁכָּל סֻכָּה אֵין לָהּ רַק שְׁלֹשָׁה דְּפָנוֹת וּפְרוּצָה בְּרוּחַ רְבִיעִית וּבוֹשׁ שָׁם הֶחָתָן לְשַׂחֵק עִם כַּלָּתוֹ.[פב]

וְלָכֵן עַכְשָׁו שֶׁנּוֹהֲגִין לַעֲשׂוֹת אַרְבַּע מְחִיצוֹת לַסֻּכָּה[פג, 32] — אַף הֶחָתָן חַיָּב

before the festival[29] and thus the seven days of the [wedding] celebrations extend into the festival. (Weddings are not held on Sukkos itself, as stated in sec. 546.[30]) In earlier generations, it was customary for the bride and groom to spend all seven days of the [marriage] celebrations secluded in a private room called a *chuppah*. Other people would join them only at times when they wanted to celebrate with them and eat and drink with them.

The groom, his attendants, and all the bridal company — i.e., the men who eat with the groom — are exempt from [the *mitzvah* of] the *sukkah* for all seven days of the [wedding] celebrations. They are permitted to eat, drink, and celebrate outside the *sukkah*, i.e., in the room called the *chuppah*. One cannot celebrate properly in a *sukkah*,[31] because one can truly rejoice only in the *chuppah*, which is essentially where the bride and groom dwell; it is here that they are alone. The essential dwelling place of the bride and the groom cannot be in a *sukkah*, for a [typical] *sukkah* has only three walls and is open on the fourth side. A groom would be embarrassed to rejoice with his bride in such a place.

Today, therefore, when a *sukkah* is customarily built with four walls,[32] even a groom is obligated [to observe the *mitzvah*

29. *Sukkah* 25b.

30. Sec. 546 of the Alter Rebbe's *Shulchan Aruch* is not extant. See the *Shulchan Aruch* of R. Yosef Caro, sec. 546:1.

31. This celebration is a *mitzvah* and since the members of the wedding party are involved in the observance of that *mitzvah*, they are not obligated by the *mitzvah* of *Sukkah* at that time.

32. See sec. 638:2.

סוף ס"ח "כמ"ש בסי' תר"מ". אבל ראה לעיל ס"ט שמציין לכאן "כמ"ש" (כמו שיתבאר). **ע** גמרא כה, ב (חתן). שו"ע סי' תרמ ס"ו. **עא** ראה לעיל סי' ע ס"ג (לענין פטור קריאת שמע). וראה אהע"ז סי' סב ס"ב וס"ו וסי"ג (שבעולה אין לה שבעת ימי המשתה). **עב** רש"י שם ד"ה תרתי. מ"א סי' תרמ סקי"א (ערב הרגל), וסי' תקמו סק"ד (הטעם שלא לישא בערב יו"ט). **עג** לבוש סי' תרמ ס"ו. **עד** רש"י שם (ממשנה מו"ק ח, ב). מ"א שם. **עה** סימן זה בשוע"ר לא הגיע לידינו, וראה טור ושו"ע שם ס"א. **עו** טורי זהב אבן העזר סי' סב סק"ז קרוב לסופו. **עז** תוס' כה, ב ד"ה אין. **עח** רב אבא בר זבדא אמר רב שם. רמב"ם פ"ו ה"ג. שו"ע שם. **עט** גמרא שם. מ"א שם. **פ** תוס' שם סוד"ה אין. רא"ש פ"ב סי' ח. **פא** גמרא שם וכרבא. **פב** רש"י שם ד"ה צער. מ"א שם. **פג** ראה רמ"א סי' תרל ס"ה. לעיל סי' תרלח ס"ב.

בַּסֻּכָּה:[פד, 33]

יא כְּבָר אָמַרְנוּ[פה, 34] שֶׁמֻּתָּר לֶאֱכֹל אֲכִילַת עֲרַאי חוּץ לַסֻּכָּה.[35] וְכַמָּה הִיא אֲכִילַת עֲרַאי? כַּבֵּיצָה,[פו, 36] שֶׁכֵּן דֶּרֶךְ הָאָדָם לִטְעֹם פַּעַם אַחַת מְלֹא פִּיו חוּץ לְבֵיתוֹ,[פז] וּמְלֹא פִּיו הוּא כְּבֵיצָה,[פח] שֶׁאֵין בֵּית הַבְּלִיעָה[38] מַחֲזִיק יוֹתֵר מִכְּבֵיצָה.[פט, 37]

בַּמֶּה דְּבָרִים אֲמוּרִים? בְּפַת[צ] הָעֲשׂוּיָה מֵחֲמֵשֶׁת הַמִּינִים[39] אוֹ בְּתַבְשִׁיל[40] הֶעָשׂוּי מֵחֲמֵשֶׁת הַמִּינִים,[צא, 41] אֲבָל שְׁאָר מִינֵי מַאֲכָלִים,[צב] וְאֵין צָרִיךְ לוֹמַר מִינֵי פֵּרוֹת,[צג] אֲפִלּוּ אוֹכֵל מֵהֶם הַרְבֵּה,[צד] וַאֲפִלּוּ קוֹבֵעַ עֲלֵיהֶן סְעוּדָתוֹ[צה] — מֻתָּר לְאָכְלָן חוּץ לַסֻּכָּה, לְפִי שֶׁקְּבִיעַת מִינִים אֵלּוּ

of] *sukkah*.[33]

11 We have already stated[34] that it is permitted to eat a snack outside the *sukkah*.[35] What is meant by a snack? [An amount of food no greater than] the size of an egg *(kebeitzah)*,[36] for one commonly eats [up to] a mouthful at a time outside his home. And a mouthful is equivalent to the size of an egg, for [our Sages taught[37] that] the mouth[38] does not contain a quantity [of food] exceeding the size of an egg.

With regard to what does the above apply? With regard to bread made of [one of] the five types of grain,[39] or to cooked[40] food made of these types of grain.[41] With regard to other types of food, and needless to say, with regard to fruit, [greater leniency applies]. Even if one eats a large amount, and even if he bases a meal on these foods, he may eat them outside the *sukkah*, because basing a meal on such foods

33. Today, our entire conception of the seven days of wedding celebrations has changed and most of the customs mentioned in this subsection are no longer followed. During Sukkos, the post-wedding celebratory meals known as *sheva berachos* (from the seven blessings appended to the Grace after Meals) are held in a *sukkah*.

34. Subsection 7.

35. The practice in *Chabad,* as in other chassidic circles, is not to rely on this leniency and to eat and drink solely inside a *sukkah* throughout the festival. See: subsection 12 below; *Likkutei Sichos, loc. cit.; Sefer HaMinhagim: The Book of Chabad-Lubavitch Customs,* p. 143.

36. *Sukkah* 26a. This refers to an egg without its shell, and is slightly less than two ounces (53.8 grams) according to *Shiurei Torah* (p. 185ff.).

37. *Yoma* 80a.

38. In the original, *beis habeliah* (from the word for "swallowing") — i.e., the space that contains a mouthful that can be swallowed at once.

39. Wheat, barley, oats, spelt, and rye. See the Alter Rebbe's *Seder Birkas HaNehenin* 1:6.

40. Or baked.

41. *Yoma* 79b. According to the above, the blessing *leishev basukkah* should be recited only when partaking of more than a *kebeitzah* of food made of one of these five grains. However, since some authorities hold that eating food of this kind (popularly known as *mezonos*) is considered as more than a mere snack, it is advisable to remain seated for a short while in the *sukkah,* for this alone warrants the recitation of the blessing *leishev basukkah.* (See *Mishnah Berurah* 639:16, based on the *Shulchan Aruch* of R. Yosef Caro 639:2.)

פד מ"א שם. **פה** סעיף ז. **פו** אביי בגמרא כו, א (כדטעים בר בי רב ועייל לכלה). תוס' שם ד"ה תרתי (שזה מלא פיו דהיינו כביצה). רש"י כז, א ד"ה ואביי. רא"ש פ"ב סי' יג. טור ושו"ע ס"ב. וכ"ה לעיל סי' עדר ס"ו. סי' רצא ס"א. וראה גם לעיל סי' רפו ס"ד. **פז** ריטב"א כה, א ד"ה אוכלין. **פח** תוס' שם. **פט** יומא פ, א. תוס' סוכה שם. רא"ש שם. **צ** יומא עט, ב. טור ושו"ע שם. תוס' סוכה שם. **צא** ברייתא כז, א (במיני תרגימא). לפירוש הרא"ש שם. שו"ע שם. מ"א סוף ס"ק ו (דהיינו כשאוכל יותר מכביצה, אפילו לא קבע עליו סעודתו). וראה גם לעיל סי' תעא ס"ב, וש"נ (שמיני תרגימא הוי תבשיל העשוי מחמשת המינים). **צב** רא"ש שם (שחולק על רבנו פרץ, שמצריך אף בבשר וגבינה). **צג** גמרא יומא עט, ב כרבא. טור ושו"ע שם. **צד** גמרא שם (שתי כותבות). מ"א ס"ק ו. **צה** גמרא שם לדעת רבא. אור זרוע הל' סוכה סי' שא. הגהות אשרי שם. דרכי משה ס"ק ד ממשמעות הפוסקים. רמ"א ס"ב. מ"א שם. ומנהג חב"ד להחמיר בזה (ראה לקמן סי"ב בשתיה, וראה תשב"ץ סי' קמד שמהר"ם מרוטנבורג חשש בפירות לאידך לישנא בגמרא שם, ומבואר במ"א שם, דהיינו

אֵינָהּ חֲשׁוּבָה אֶלָּא כַּאֲכִילַת עֲרַאי שֶׁל פַּת:[צו]

יב מֻתָּר לִשְׁתּוֹת[צז] כָּל הַמַּשְׁקִין[42] חוּץ לַסֻּכָּה, אֲפִלּוּ יַיִן,[צח] וַאֲפִלּוּ שׁוֹתֶה יוֹתֵר מֵרְבִיעִית,[צט, 43] וְכָל הַמַּחְמִיר עַל עַצְמוֹ שֶׁלֹּא לִשְׁתּוֹת חוּץ לַסֻּכָּה אֲפִלּוּ מַיִם – הֲרֵי זֶה מְשֻׁבָּח.[ק, 42]

בַּמֶּה דְּבָרִים אֲמוּרִים? כְּשֶׁשּׁוֹתֶה דֶּרֶךְ עֲרַאי, אֲבָל אִם קוֹבֵעַ אֶת עַצְמוֹ לִשְׁתּוֹת יַיִן,[קא, 44] אוֹ שְׁאָר מַשְׁקִין שֶׁדֶּרֶךְ לִקְבֹּעַ עֲלֵיהֶן, כְּגוֹן מֵי דְּבַשׁ וְשֵׁכָר[קב] בִּמְדִינוֹת אֵלּוּ שֶׁרְגִילִין לִקְבֹּעַ עֲלֵיהֶן לִשְׁתּוֹת בְּלֹא סְעוּדָה[קג] – צָרִיךְ לִכָּנֵס לְתוֹךְ הַסֻּכָּה.

אֲבָל אֵין צָרִיךְ לְבָרֵךְ "לֵישֵׁב בַּסֻּכָּה", לְפִי שֶׁהַשְּׁתִיָּה הִיא טְפֵלָה לָאֲכִילָה וּבִרְכַּת "לֵישֵׁב בַּסֻּכָּה" שֶׁבֵּרַךְ עַל אֲכִילַת שַׁחֲרִית הִיא פּוֹטֶרֶת אֶת הַשְּׁתִיָּה שֶׁל כָּל הַיּוֹם,[קד] וְכֵן הִיא פּוֹטֶרֶת אֶת הַשֵּׁנָה וְטִיּוּל בַּסֻּכָּה[קה] כָּל הַיּוֹם, שֶׁאֵין צָרִיךְ לְבָרֵךְ עֲלֵיהֶם, שֶׁאֲפִלּוּ יָצָא חוּץ לְסֻכָּתוֹ אַחַר הָאֲכִילָה וְהִפְסִיק הַרְבֵּה בֵּין הָאֲכִילָה לְהַשְּׁתִיָּה וְשֵׁנָה וְטִיּוּל,[קו] מִכָּל מָקוֹם כֵּיוָן שֶׁכֻּלָּם נִמְשָׁכִים וּטְפֵלִים לָאֲכִילָה שֶׁהִיא עִקַּר מִצְוַת הַיְשִׁיבָה

is accorded no more [halachic] significance than eating a snack of bread.

12 It is permitted to drink any beverage,[42] even wine, outside the *sukkah*, even if one drinks more than a *revi'is*.[43] [Nevertheless,] one who is stringent with himself and drinks no beverage, even water, outside the *sukkah* is praiseworthy.[42]

When does [the above leniency] apply? When one drinks in a casual manner. By contrast, one is required to enter a *sukkah* if he [intends to sit down] to drink wine[44] or other beverages that one commonly sits down to drink, such as mead or beer in these countries, [even] when a meal is not [served].

[In such situations], however, there is no need to recite the blessing *leishev basukkah*, because the drinking is secondary to eating and [this] blessing that one recited in the morning covers his drinking throughout the day. Similarly, it covers sleeping and relaxing in the *sukkah* throughout the day. There is no need to recite a blessing over [these activities], even if after eating one leaves the *sukkah* and [then] makes a long interruption before drinking, sleeping, or relaxing. Since [these activities] are all subordinate to eating, which is the main component of the *mitzvah* of

---

42. *Sukkah* 26b.

43. Drinking a *revi'is*, which is 86 cc. according to *Shiurei Torah*, is considered significant enough to require the recitation of a blessing afterwards (*Seder Birkas HaNehenin* 8:1).

44. In the original, *im koveia es atzmo lishtos yayin*. The first verb suggests permanence; hence, settling down comfortably before drinking wine, as opposed to a hasty thirst-quencher.

אפילו לא קבע עליו). **צו** גמרא שם. רא"ש שם. לבוש ס"ב. מ"א שם. **צז** גמרא כו, סע"ב (דלי של מים, שהוא רק כדי להחמיר על עצמו). רמב"ם פ"ו ה"ו (מים). טור ושו"ע ס"ב. **צח** רא"ש פ"ב סי' יג. טור ושו"ע שם. **צט** גמרא שם (דלי). וכדלקמן בסמוך, שלא אסרו אלא כשקובע עצמו. **ק** משנה וגמרא כו, ב. רמב"ם שם. טור ושו"ע שם. וכן הוא מנהג חב"ד (ספר המנהגים — חב"ד ע' 67. אוצר מנהגי חב"ד חה"ס ע' ש). **קא** אור זרוע הל' סוכה סוס"י שא (שמסתפק בזה). הגהות אשרי שם. שבלי הלקט סי' שדמ בשם ה"ר אביגדור כהן (בשבת ויו"ט). אגור סי' תתקעה. דרכי משה ס"ק ד. לבוש שם. ב"ח ד"ה ומ"ש ושתיית. מ"א סק"ה. ט"ז ס"ק ו. **קב** אור זרוע והגהות אשרי ודרכי משה וט"ז שם. וראה לקמן סוף סט"ו שיש מפקפקין, וש"נ. **קג** מ"א סי' רי[ג] סק"ו. ט"ז שם ס"ק ב. לעיל שם סוף ס"א. **קד** ט"ז ס"ק ז וס"ק כ. **קה** תוס' ברכות יא, ב ד"ה שכבר ורא"ש פ"ק דברכות סי' יג. ט"ז שם ושם. **קו** שדוקא בזה צריך לברך על האכילה, כדלקמן סי"ג וש"נ.

בַּסֻּכָּה[45] — בִּרְכַּת הָאֲכִילָה פּוֹטַרְתָּם.[קז]

וַאֲפִלּוּ שׁוֹתֶה וְיָשֵׁן וּמְטַיֵּל קֹדֶם הָאֲכִילָה — אֵין צָרִיךְ לְבָרֵךְ, לְפִי שֶׁהֵן טְפֵלִים לְהָאֲכִילָה שֶׁלְּאַחֲרֵיהֶם:[קח]

יג וְאִם הָיָה קָבוּעַ לִשְׁתִיָּה בַּסֻּכָּה[46] וְנִמְלַךְ לֶאֱכֹל, אַף עַל פִּי שֶׁלֹּא הָיָה צָרִיךְ לְבָרֵךְ "לֵישֵׁב בַּסֻּכָּה" עַל הַשְּׁתִיָּה לְפִי שֶׁבִּרְכַּת הָאֲכִילָה שֶׁלְּפָנֶיהָ פּוֹטַרְתָּהּ — אַף עַל פִּי כֵן צָרִיךְ לְבָרֵךְ "לֵישֵׁב בַּסֻּכָּה" עַל אֲכִילָה זוֹ הָאַחֲרוֹנָה, שֶׁאֵין אֲכִילָה זוֹ טְפֵלָה לָאֲכִילָה הָרִאשׁוֹנָה, אֶלָּא הִיא חֲשׁוּבָה בִּפְנֵי עַצְמָהּ.[קט]

בַּמֶּה דְּבָרִים אֲמוּרִים? כְּשֶׁיָּצָא[קי] מִן הַסֻּכָּה בֵּין גְּמַר אֲכִילָה רִאשׁוֹנָה לְהַתְחָלַת אֲכִילָה אַחֲרוֹנָה וְשָׁהָה שָׁם חוּץ לַסֻּכָּה וְלֹא חָזַר לְאַלְתַּר[קיא] אֶלָּא לְאַחַר שָׁעָה וּשְׁתַּיִם,[קיב, 47] אוֹ אֲפִלּוּ אִם חָזַר לְאַלְתַּר אֶלָּא שֶׁבְּשָׁעָה שֶׁיָּצָא מִן הַסֻּכָּה הָיָה דַּעְתּוֹ לִשְׁהוֹת הַרְבֵּה חוּץ לַסֻּכָּה

dwelling in the *sukkah*,[45] they are covered by the blessing recited over eating. Even if one drinks, sleeps, or relaxes [in the *sukkah*] before he eats, he is not required to recite a blessing, for [these activities] are subordinate to the eating that follows them.

13 If one went and sat down in the *sukkah* in order to drink,[46] and changed his mind and decided to eat [bread], he must now recite the blessing *leishev basukkah*. He was not required to recite the blessing *leishev basukkah* for drinking, because it was covered by the blessing he had earlier recited over eating. [With regard to eating, by contrast,] a [later] meal is not considered as subordinate to a previous meal, but is considered a significant entity in its own right.

When does the above apply? When one left the *sukkah* between the end of the previous meal and the beginning of the later meal, and tarried for an hour or two outside the *sukkah*[47] [instead of] returning immediately. Alternatively, it applies even when one returned immediately, but at the time he left the *sukkah* he intended to remain outside it

---

45. *Tzafnas Paneiach* (gloss to *Hilchos Sukkos* 6:2) cites support for this statement from *Eruvin* 4b, which states that one's basic dwelling place is determined according to where he eats, not where he sleeps. Accordingly, subsection 17 rules that on the first night of *Yom-Tov*, the essential obligation to observe the *mitzvah* of *Sukkah* involves eating — and not any other activity — in the *sukkah* (*Likkutei Sichos, loc. cit.*).

46. See footnote 44 above.

47. The Rebbe notes that with regard to *tefillin*, the Alter Rebbe considers two to three hours a significant interruption (sec. 25:29), and questions why a different measure is given with regard to a *sukkah*.

In each case, the Rebbe's criterion for an interruption is the length of time the *mitzvah* in question requires. Eating a meal usually takes an hour and can extend to two hours. Hence, with regard to the *mitzvah* of *Sukkah*, the Alter Rebbe speaks of an interruption of an hour or two. The weekday morning prayers should take an hour and a half (see *Tanya — Iggeres HaKodesh*, Epistle 1). The *tefillin* are thus worn for about two hours or, for those who pray at length, three hours. Therefore, in the context of *tefillin*, the Alter Rebbe speaks of an interruption of between two and three hours. (See *Likkutei Sichos*, Vol. 4, pp. 1363ff.)

קז ר"ת הובא ברא"ש פ"ד סי' ג. שו"ע ס"ח (שאין מברכין אלא בשעת אכילה). ט"ז סק"כ. וראה לקו"ש חכ"ט ע' 217. שלחן המלך ח"ב ע' רנ. קח ט"ז סוף סק"ז (לענין שתיה) וסוף ס"ק כ (אף בשינה וטיול). קט ט"ז ס"ק כ. קי מ"א סקי"ז. לבוש סוף ס"ב. דלא כט"ז שם, וב"ח סוס"י תרמג. קיא מ"א שם. קיב רש"י יומא ל, א ד"ה נוטל (ששעה או שתים הוי היסח הפסק לסעודה). וראה לעיל סי' ח סכ"ג (לענין ציצית) כמה שעות. סי' כה סכ"ט (לענין תפילין)

וְשֶׁלֹּא לַחֲזֹר לַסֻּכָּה לְאַלְתַּר,[קיג] שֶׁאָז אֵין הַבְּרָכָה שֶׁבֵּרַךְ עַל אֲכִילָה הָרִאשׁוֹנָה פּוֹטֶרֶת אֲכִילָה אַחֲרוֹנָה, כֵּיוָן שֶׁהִפְסִיק בֵּינֵיהֶן בִּיצִיאָה גְּמוּרָה עַל דַּעַת שֶׁלֹּא לַחֲזֹר לְאַלְתַּר.

אֲבָל אִם לֹא הִפְסִיק בֵּינֵיהֶם בִּיצִיאָה גְּמוּרָה[קיד] שֶׁלֹּא לַחֲזֹר לְאַלְתַּר[קטו] — אֵינוֹ צָרִיךְ לְבָרֵךְ עַל אֲכִילָה אַחֲרוֹנָה. וַאֲפִלּוּ הוּא כָּל ז' יָמִים בְּתוֹךְ הַסֻּכָּה, אִם לֹא יָצָא מִמֶּנָּה יְצִיאָה גְּמוּרָה שֶׁלֹּא לַחֲזֹר לְאַלְתַּר — אֵין צָרִיךְ לְבָרֵךְ "לֵישֵׁב בַּסֻּכָּה", רַק בַּפַּעַם הָרִאשׁוֹן שֶׁנִּכְנַס לַסֻּכָּה:[קטז]

יד וְכָל זֶה כְּשֶׁנִּכְנָס לְאוֹתָהּ סֻכָּה שֶׁבֵּרַךְ בָּהּ בַּאֲכִילָה רִאשׁוֹנָה, אֲבָל אִם נִכְנָס לְסֻכָּה אַחֶרֶת,[קיז] אֲפִלּוּ הִיא בְּאוֹתוֹ חָצֵר[קיח] סְמוּכָה לַסֻּכָּה שֶׁבֵּרַךְ בָּהּ בַּאֲכִילָה רִאשׁוֹנָה, כְּשֶׁרוֹצֶה לֶאֱכֹל בְּסֻכָּה זוֹ דָּבָר שֶׁאָסוּר לְאָכְלוֹ חוּץ לַסֻּכָּה — צָרִיךְ לַחֲזֹר וּלְבָרֵךְ "לֵישֵׁב בַּסֻּכָּה", אֲפִלּוּ אִם הִיא בְּעִנְיָן שֶׁאֵין צָרִיךְ לְבָרֵךְ בִּרְכַּת הַנֶּהֱנִין[48] עַל אֲכִילָה זוֹ, כְּגוֹן שֶׁהוּא עוֹמֵד בְּאֶמְצַע סְעוּדָתוֹ[קיט] שֶׁאָכַל בַּסֻּכָּה שֶׁבֵּרַךְ בָּהּ וּפוֹסֵק סְעוּדָתוֹ וְהָלַךְ לֶאֱכֹל בְּסֻכָּה אַחֶרֶת[49] — צָרִיךְ לַחֲזֹר וּלְבָרֵךְ:

for a long time and not to return immediately. In these situations, the blessing one recited over the first meal does not cover the second meal, since he made an interruption between them by making what is unquestionably a departure with no intent to return immediately.

If, however, one did not make an interruption by making [such] a departure with no intent of returning immediately, he is not required to recite a second blessing on the later meal. [Moreover,] even if one spends all seven days [of the festival] in the *sukkah* without making a complete departure from which he does not intend to return immediately, he is not required to recite the blessing *leishev basukkah* [at any time other than] the first time he enters the *sukkah*.

14 The above applies when one reenters the same *sukkah* in which he ate his first meal. [Different rules apply,] however, if he enters another *sukkah,* even if it is located in the same courtyard, close to the *sukkah* in which he recited the blessing for his first meal. If, when in the [second] *sukkah,* he desires to eat something that may not be eaten outside a *sukkah,* he is required to recite the blessing *leishev basukkah* again. [This applies] even when he would not be required to recite a blessing[48] before eating this food. For example, in the middle of the meal that he ate in the *sukkah* in which he recited the blessing, he interrupted his meal and went to eat in the other *sukkah.* [Although in such a case he does not have to recite a blessing before eating,][49] he must recite the blessing *[leishev basukkah]* again.

48. I.e., one of the preliminary blessings *(birchos hanehenin)* over food, such as *HaMotzi* or *Borei Minei Mezonos.*

49. Suppose a person ate one of the foods that require him to recite a thanksgiving blessing thereafter (such as the Grace after Meals or

ב' או ג' שעות. אג"ק ח"ג ע' רי־ריב. רכג. קיג ראבי"ה סי' תרמד. הובא במ"מ פ"ו הי"ב. ריטב"א מה, ב סד"ה ורבה. מ"א שם (לענין סוכה), ובסי' ח סקי"ח (אף לענין ציצית). וכ"ה לעיל שם סכ"ג. קיד לבוש שם. מ"א סקי"ז. קטו ראבי"ה ומ"מ וריטב"א שם. מ"א שם. קטז מ"א שם. ולענין שיחה בסוכה — ראה לעיל סי' תלב ס"ז, וסי' תקצב סוף ס"ז, שאינה הפסק. קיז מ"א סקי"ז. קיח מ"א סי' ח סקי"ז (לענין טלית אחר, שמבית לבית באותה חצר הוי הפסק. וכ"ה לעיל שם סכ"ב וקו"א ס"ק ה). וראה גם לעיל רס"י קעח (לענין בין ברכה לאכילה). סי' רעג סוף ס"ד (לענין קידוש במקום סעודה). סי' תלב ס"ח (לענין בין ברכה למצוה). קיט כדלעיל סי' קעח ס"ג (שבאמצע סעודה לא הוי הליכה מבית לבית הפסק).

טו וַאֲפִלּוּ אִם אֵינוֹ רוֹצֶה לֶאֱכֹל בְּסֻכָּה זוֹ אֶלָּא שֶׁנִּכְנָס לְתוֹכָהּ לִישֹׁן וּלְטַיֵּל – צָרִיךְ לְבָרֵךְ "לֵישֵׁב בַּסֻּכָּה", שֶׁאֵין שֵׁנָה וְטִיּוּל שֶׁבְּסֻכָּה זוֹ נִפְטָרִין בַּבְּרָכָה שֶׁבֵּרַךְ בְּסֻכָּה אַחֶרֶת.[קכ] אֲבָל אִם נִכְנָס לְתוֹכָהּ לֶאֱכֹל בְּתוֹכָהּ מִינֵי מַאֲכָלִים שֶׁמֻּתָּר לְאָכְלָן חוּץ לַסֻּכָּה – אֵין צָרִיךְ לְבָרֵךְ.

וְאִם רוֹצֶה לִקְבֹּעַ אֶת עַצְמוֹ שָׁם לִשְׁתּוֹת יַיִן[44] וּשְׁאָר מַשְׁקִים שֶׁדֶּרֶךְ לִקְבֹּעַ עֲלֵיהֶם מִן הַדִּין – צָרִיךְ לְבָרֵךְ, שֶׁהֲרֵי אָסוּר לִשְׁתּוֹתָן חוּץ לַסֻּכָּה.[קכא, 50] וּמִכָּל מָקוֹם, לְפִי שֶׁיֵּשׁ מְפַקְפְּקִין[קכב] עַל בְּרָכָה זוֹ, לָכֵן נָכוֹן הַדָּבָר שֶׁלֹּא לִקְבֹּעַ אֶת עַצְמוֹ בִּשְׁתִיָּה, רַק בְּסֻכָּה שֶׁאָכַל בָּהּ הַיּוֹם וּבֵרַךְ עָלֶיהָ "לֵישֵׁב בַּסֻּכָּה":[קכג, 51]

15 Even if one does not desire to eat in the [second] *sukkah,* but enters there to sleep or to relax, he must recite the blessing *leishev basukkah,* for the sleeping and relaxation in this *sukkah* are not covered by the blessing that he recited in the [first] *sukkah.* If, however, he entered [the second *sukkah*] to partake of types of food that may be eaten outside the *sukkah,* it is not necessary to recite the blessing *[leishev basukkah* again*].*

If one [intended to take a seat in the second *sukkah*] in order to drink wine[44] or other beverages that one commonly sits down to drink, the letter of the law requires him to recite the blessing *[leishev basukkah* again*],* for these beverages may not be drunk outside the *sukkah.*[50] Nevertheless, since some authorities raise questions about [the recitation of] this blessing, it is proper not to [decide to sit down and] drink [such beverages] except in a *sukkah* in which one ate that day and within which one recited the blessing *leishev basukkah.*[51]

טז אִם שָׁכַח לְבָרֵךְ "לֵישֵׁב בַּסֻּכָּה" עַד שֶׁגָּמַר סְעוּדָתוֹ – יְבָרֵךְ לְאַחַר סְעוּדָתוֹ.[קכד] וְאַף עַל פִּי שֶׁכָּל הַמִּצְוֹת צָרִיךְ לְבָרֵךְ עֲלֵיהֶן עוֹבֵר לַעֲשִׂיָּתָן,[קכה, 52] מִכָּל מָקוֹם הֲרֵי גַּם הַיְשִׁיבָה שֶׁיּוֹשֵׁב בַּסֻּכָּה אַחַר הַסְּעוּדָה הוּא גַּם כֵּן בִּכְלַל

16 If one forgot to recite the blessing *leishev basukkah* until he had completed his meal, he should [nevertheless] recite the blessing after the meal. Though the blessings for the observance of *mitzvos* should be recited before performing the deed,[52] sitting in the *sukkah* after the meal is also included in

Al HaMichyah) in the place where he ate. If he departed before reciting that blessing, he is not considered to have concluded his meal. Hence he is not required to recite a preliminary blessing before continuing the meal elsewhere. (See sec. 178:3.)

50. As stated in subsection 12.

51. The Lubavitch practice is to recite the blessing *leishev basukkah* when drinking wine even when one does not partake of a meal or pastries. Specifically this refers to: (a) the recitation of *Havdalah,* regarding which it can be explained that the *mitzvah* endows the situation with significance; and (b) when sitting with friends, and certainly at a chassidic *farbrengen,* even if one does not partake of pastries. (See *Sefer HaSichos 5696-5700,* p. 295.)

52. In the original, *over laasiyasan (Pesachim* 7b; see sec. 46:3 in Vol. 1 of the present work*).*

קכ רא"ש פ"ד סי' ג, בשם רב האי גאון. ט"ז סוף ס"ק כ. קכא כדלעיל סי"ב. קכב ב"י ד"ה ומ"ש רבנו ושתיית (שדינו כדין קבע על הפירות, דלעיל סי"א). דרכי משה סוף ס"ק ד (דלא מקרי קביעות). רמ"א ס"ב (אפילו קבע עלייהו). ב"ח ד"ה ומ"ש ושתיית (לאפוקי נפשיה מפלוגתא). מ"א סק"ה. קכג כדלעיל שם. קכד

הַמִּצְוָה,[קכו,53] וְאִם כֵּן הֲרֵי הוּא מְבָרֵךְ קֹדֶם עֲשִׂיַּת הַמִּצְוָה:[קכז]

the *mitzvah*.[53] Hence, one is [still] reciting the blessing before performing the *mitzvah*.

יז אֵין קִצְבָּה לִסְעוּדוֹת שֶׁל סֻכָּה,[קכח,54] אֶלָּא אִם יִרְצֶה יֹאכַל בַּסֻּכָּה, וְאִם יִרְצֶה לֹא יֹאכַל רַק מִינֵי מַאֲכָלִים שֶׁמֻּתָּר לְאָכְלָן חוּץ לַסֻּכָּה,[קכט,55] שֶׁאֵין הַמִּצְוָה אֶלָּא שֶׁאִם יֹאכַל לֹא יֹאכַל חוּץ לַסֻּכָּה.[קל]

בַּמֶּה דְּבָרִים אֲמוּרִים? בְּחֻלּוֹ שֶׁל מוֹעֵד,[קלא] אֲבָל בְּיוֹם טוֹב[56] וּבְשַׁבָּת שֶׁהוּא בְּתוֹךְ הֶחָג שֶׁחַיָּב לֶאֱכֹל פַּת יוֹתֵר מִכַּבֵּיצָה[קלב,57] כְּמוֹ שֶׁנִּתְבָּאֵר בְּסִימָן רצ"[א][קלג] — צָרִיךְ לֶאֱכֹל בְּתוֹךְ הַסֻּכָּה.

וְאִם יָרְדוּ גְשָׁמִים — הֲרֵי זֶה נִכְנָס לְתוֹךְ הַבַּיִת,[קלד] וְעַל דֶּרֶךְ שֶׁיִּתְבָּאֵר.[קלה]

בַּמֶּה דְּבָרִים אֲמוּרִים? מִלַּיְלָה הָרִאשׁוֹנָה שֶׁל חַג וְאֵילָךְ,[54] אֲבָל בַּלַּיְלָה הָרִאשׁוֹנָה שֶׁל חַג,[קלו] דְּהַיְנוּ לֵיל ט"ו בְּתִשְׁרֵי,[קלז,58] — צָרִיךְ לֶאֱכֹל בְּתוֹךְ הַסֻּכָּה אֲפִלּוּ בִּשְׁעַת הַגֶּשֶׁם,[קלח] וְאַף עַל פִּי שֶׁהוּא מִצְטַעֵר מֵחֲמַת הַגֶּשֶׁם,

17 There is no fixed number of meals that one must eat in the *sukkah*.[54] If one desires, he may eat in the *sukkah*, and if he so desires, he may eat only foods that may be eaten outside the *sukkah*[55] — for the *mitzvah* is only that if one eats [a significant meal], he may not eat outside the *sukkah*.

When does the above apply? On *Chol HaMoed*. On *Yom-Tov*,[56] and on *Shabbos* that falls within the festival, when one must eat more than a *kebeitzah*[57] of bread as stated in sec. 291[:1, and sec. 274:6], one must eat in a *sukkah*. If it rains, however, he may enter his home, as will be explained [in subsection 21 below].

When does this apply? After the first night of *Yom-Tov*.[54] On the first night of *Yom-Tov*, i.e., the eve of the fifteenth of Tishrei,[58] one must eat in the *sukkah* even if it is raining and the rain causes discomfort.

53. See subsection 4 above. In this spirit, sec. 592:7 states that one fulfills a *mitzvah* every moment that he sits in the *sukkah*.

54. *Sukkah* 27a.

55. On Pesach, similarly, one is obligated to eat *matzah* only on the first night; during the remainder of the festival, he may prefer to eat other foods. At this point, however, the similarity ends. Eating in a *sukkah* is a *mitzvah* at any time throughout the festival; hence, the blessing *leishev basukkah* is recited every time that *mitzvah* is observed. Eating *matzah* is a *mitzvah* only on the first night; hence, the blessing *al achilas matzah* is recited only then.

56. In *Eretz Yisrael*, on the first day of the festival; in the Diaspora, on the first two days. Regarding the eighth day, see footnote 9 above.

57. A quantity defined in subsection 11.

58. I.e., the night between Tishrei 14 and Tishrei 15. With regard to the second night of the festival, see the end of subsection 19.

מ"א סוף סקי"ז. **קכה** פסחים ז, ב. וכדלעיל סי' מו ס"ג וש"נ. **קכו** מ"א שם. וכדלעיל ס"ד. וראה גם לעיל סי' תקצב סוף ס"ז: שכל רגע ורגע שהוא יושב בסוכה . . . הוא מקיים מצות הקב"ה. **קכז** ראה לקמן סי' תרמג ס"ב. **קכח** משנה כז, א וכחכמים. טור ושו"ע ס"ג. **קכט** רמב"ם פ"ו ה"ז. שו"ע שם. **קל** רש"י שם ד"ה אין. טור. לבוש ס"ג. **קלא** ראה גם לעיל סי' קפח ס"י. **קלב** טור ושו"ע רס"י רצא (כביצה). מ"א סי' רצא סק"א (שהכוונה יותר מכביצה). **קלג** דעה הא' שבס"א (ומסתפק שם אם הכוונה לכביצה או ליותר מכביצה). וראה גם דעה הא' שבסי' עדר ס"ו. סי' תקכט ס"ד. דעה הב' — לקמן סי"ט. **קלד** תוס' רבנו יהודה ברכות מט, ב ד"ה ברכת המזון (שבזה מיירי משנה דידן, שאין קצבה אף ביו"ט ושבת). הובא בתוס' שם ד"ה אי בעי. הגהות סמ"ק סי' צג (נז, א). רא"ש ברכות פ"ז סי' כג. **קלה** סעיף כא. **קלו** משנה שם כחכמים (חוץ מלילי יו"ט ראשון של חג. וראה לקמן סי"ט שבליל ב' סומכים על דעה ב' דלקמן שם, וש"נ). טור ושו"ע ס"ג. **קלז** ראה לקו"ש חכ"ב ע' 129 הערה 50 ובשוה"ג. **קלח** הגהות סמ"[ק] שם. רא"ש שם. ר"ן (יב, ב) ד"ה מתני' ר"א בשם אחרים. טור. רמ"א ס"ה. וראה גם לקמן סי' תרמ ס"ה.

וְכָל הַמִּצְטַעֵר פָּטוּר מִן הַסֻּכָּה,[קלט] מִכָּל מָקוֹם בַּלַּיְלָה הָרִאשׁוֹנָה — חַיָּב לֶאֱכֹל בַּסֻּכָּה, לְפִי שֶׁאָנוּ לְמֵדִין בִּגְזֵרָה שָׁוָה[קמ, 59] מֵחַג הַמַּצּוֹת: נֶאֱמַר כָּאן בְּחַג הַסֻּכּוֹת[קמא, 60] "בַּחֲמִשָּׁה עָשָׂר יוֹם לַחֹדֶשׁ", וְנֶאֱמַר לְהַלָּן בְּחַג הַמַּצּוֹת[קמב, 61] "בַּחֲמִשָּׁה עָשָׂר יוֹם לַחֹדֶשׁ", מַה ט"ו יוֹם הָאָמוּר לְהַלָּן לַיְלָה הָרִאשׁוֹנָה חוֹבָה לֶאֱכֹל כַּזַּיִת[62] מַצָּה כְּמוֹ שֶׁנִּתְבָּאֵר בְּסִימָן תע"ה[קמג] — אַף ט"ו הָאָמוּר כָּאן חוֹבָה לֶאֱכֹל בַּסֻּכָּה.[63]

וּבַאֲכִילַת כַּזַּיִת בְּתוֹךְ הַסֻּכָּה יוֹצֵא יְדֵי חוֹבָה, כְּמוֹ שֶׁיּוֹצֵא בַּאֲכִילַת כַּזַּיִת מַצָּה.[קמד, 64] אֲבָל מִכָּל מָקוֹם, חַיָּב לֶאֱכֹל עוֹד פַּת בַּבַּיִת, שֶׁהֲרֵי בְּכָל סְעוּדַת יוֹם טוֹב חוֹבָה לֶאֱכֹל יוֹתֵר מִכַּבֵּיצָה פַּת,[קמה] אֶלָּא שֶׁבְּתוֹךְ הַסֻּכָּה בִּשְׁעַת הַגֶּשֶׁם — אֵין חוֹבָה לֶאֱכֹל יוֹתֵר מִכַּזַּיִת, כְּמוֹ בַּאֲכִילַת מַצָּה.

[Generally,] whenever one feels discomfort, he is released from [the obligation of dwelling in] the *sukkah*. Nevertheless, the first night [of *Yom-Tov* is an exception and] one is obligated to eat in the *sukkah*. We derive [this concept] through a verbal association[59] with the festival of Pesach. With regard to the festival of Sukkos it is written,[60] "On the fifteenth day of the... month." And with regard to the festival of Pesach it is later written,[61] "On the fifteenth day of the... month." Just as with regard to the fifteenth day stated later, there is an obligation on the first night to eat at least a *kezayis*[62] of *matzah*, as stated in sec. 475[:32], so, too, with regard to the fifteenth day [stated concerning Sukkos], there is an obligation to eat in the *sukkah*.[63] One fulfills his obligation by eating a *kezayis* [of bread] in the *sukkah*, just as he fulfills his obligation by eating a *kezayis* of *matzah* [on the night of Pesach].[64]

Nevertheless, [if one leaves the *sukkah*,] he is still obligated to eat more bread at home. For at every *Yom-Tov* meal there is an obligation to eat more than a *kebeitzah* of bread, except that when it is raining in the *sukkah*, one is required to eat no more than a *kezayis* there — the same [minimum quantity that is required to fulfill the *mitzvah* of] eating *matzah* [on Pesach].

59. In the original, *gezeirah shavah* — a halachic analogy based on a Biblical expression that appears identically in two different contexts.

60. *Vayikra* 23:34.

61. *Bamidbar* 33:3.

62. Lit., "the size of an olive" — approximately an ounce, according to *Shiurei Torah*.

63. The Rebbe explains the emphasis on eating in the *sukkah* on the first night of *Yom-Tov* as follows: Pesach is celebrated on Nissan 15, the anniversary of the Exodus. Hence, though Pesach is characterized by the *mitzvah* of eating *matzah*, a certain dimension of the festival exists independent of the *mitzvah*. Sukkos is not celebrated at the time the Jews were first protected by the Clouds of Glory. The significance of the holiday depends, rather, on our observance. To borrow the wording of the verse *(Vayikra* 23:42-43*)*: Through our "dwelling in the *sukkah* for seven days," "your [future] generations will know that I caused the Children of Israel to dwell in *sukkos*...." Hence, even when the weather is unfavorable, the *Yom-Tov* must be inaugurated with the observance of the *mitzvah*. (See *Likkutei Sichos*, Vol. 22, p. 129.)

64. *Talmud Yerushalmi, Sukkah* 2:7.

קלט כדלקמן שם. קמ רבי יוחנן משום ר' שמעון בן יהוצדק שם. לבוש ס"ג. קמא ויקרא כג, לד. במדבר כט, יב קמב ויקרא כג, ו. במדבר כח, יז. קמג סעיף לב. קמד רב זעירא בירושלמי פ"ב ה"ז. הובא בתוס' שם ד"ה תשבו. רא"ש ור"ן שם. טור ושו"ע שם. רמ"א ס"ה. קמה כדלעיל בתחלת הסעיף. קמו ראה ב"י

Moreover, even when it is not raining, if one desires to eat a *kezayis* in the *sukkah* and eat precisely a *kebeitzah*[65] at home, he may do so.[66] Nevertheless, a person who is stringent and eats his entire meal in the *sukkah* when it is not raining is praiseworthy, as stated above.[67]

וַאֲפִלּוּ שֶׁלֹּא בִּשְׁעַת הַגֶּשֶׁם, אִם יִרְצֶה לֶאֱכֹל כַּזַּיִת בַּסֻּכָּה וּכַבֵּיצָה מְצֻמְצֶמֶת[65] תּוֹךְ הַבַּיִת[קמו] – הָרְשׁוּת בְּיָדוֹ,[66] אֶלָּא שֶׁהַמַּחְמִיר לֶאֱכֹל כָּל הַסְּעוּדָה בְּתוֹךְ הַסֻּכָּה שֶׁלֹּא בִּשְׁעַת הַגֶּשֶׁם – הֲרֵי זֶה מְשֻׁבָּח כְּמוֹ שֶׁנִּתְבָּאֵר לְמַעְלָה:[קמז, 67]

18 When a person eats in the *sukkah* when it is raining, he must also recite *Kiddush* over wine in the *sukkah*, for *Kiddush* may only be recited in the place where one eats his meal.[68] [In such a situation, one] should recite the blessing *leishev basukkah* before [the blessing] *Shehecheyanu*,[69] just as if it was not raining.

יח כְּשֶׁאוֹכֵל בִּשְׁעַת הַגֶּשֶׁם בַּסֻּכָּה – צָרִיךְ גַּם כֵּן לְקַדֵּשׁ עַל הַיַּיִן בְּתוֹךְ הַסֻּכָּה,[קמח] שֶׁהֲרֵי אֵין קִדּוּשׁ אֶלָּא בִּמְקוֹם סְעוּדָה,[קמט, 68] וִיבָרֵךְ "לֵישֵׁב בַּסֻּכָּה"[קנ] קֹדֶם "שֶׁהֶחֱיָנוּ"[קנא, 69] כְּמוֹ אִם לֹא הָיָה גֶּשֶׁם:

19 Some authorities differ with the above and maintain that at all the meals of *Shabbos* and *Yom-Tov*, one is not required to eat more than a *kezayis* of bread. Hence, [these authorities argue,] if one desires to eat only a *kezayis* on *Yom-Tov*, or on the *Shabbos* during the festival, and to eat it outside the *sukkah*, he may do so.

[These authorities agree that] from the association with Pesach, we derive that it is an obligation to eat in the *sukkah* on the first night [of *Yom-Tov*. They maintain, however, that] this association does not teach

יט וְיֵשׁ חוֹלְקִין עַל כָּל זֶה[קנב] וְאוֹמְרִים שֶׁבְּכָל סְעוּדוֹת שַׁבָּת וְיוֹם טוֹב אֵין צָרִיךְ לֶאֱכֹל פַּת רַק כַּזַּיִת, וְאִם כֵּן בְּיוֹם טוֹב וְשַׁבָּת שֶׁבְּתוֹךְ הֶחָג אִם יִרְצֶה שֶׁלֹּא לֶאֱכֹל רַק כַּזַּיִת וּלְאָכְלוֹ חוּץ לַסֻּכָּה – הָרְשׁוּת בְּיָדוֹ.

וְדָבָר זֶה אָנוּ לְמֵדִין בִּגְזֵרָה שָׁוָה מֵחַג הַמַּצּוֹת שֶׁחוֹבָה לֶאֱכֹל בַּסֻּכָּה בַּלַּיְלָה הָרִאשׁוֹנָה, אֲבָל אֵין לְמֵדִין בִּגְזֵרָה שָׁוָה

65. In the original, *kebeitzah metzumtzemes*.

66. For, as stated in subsection 11, a *kebeitzah* or less is considered a snack and may be eaten outside the *sukkah*. If one were to eat more than a *kebeitzah*, he would be required to do so in the *sukkah*.

67. Subsection 12.

68. As stated in sec. 273:1. Hence it would not be acceptable to recite *Kiddush* inside and then partake of bread in the *sukkah*. Nor is it desirable to recite *Kiddush* and eat inside, and then go out to the *sukkah* and eat a *kezayis* of bread. This would cause one to recite a blessing unnecessarily, since he would be required to recite the blessing *Shehecheyanu* twice: once at *Kiddush* in connection with the observance of the festival and again in the *sukkah* for the observance of that *mitzvah* (*Mishnah Berurah* 639:36).

69. See sec. 643:1.

ד"ה ומ"ש רבנו אע"ג, שגם בלילה הראשון אין איסור לאכול חוץ מסוכה פחות מכשיעור. וע"י אכילת הכביצה בבית והכזית בסוכה יוצא ידי חובת סעודת יו"ט. **קמז** סעיף יב (אפילו לענין שתיית מים). **קמח** תרומת הדשן סי' צה. רמ"א סוף ס"ה. **קמט** כדלעיל סי' רעג ס"א. ומיירי שאוכל כל הסעודה בסוכה, כדלעיל סוף סי"ז. וראה לבוש ס"ג. מ"מ וציונים. **קנ** מ"א סוף סק"ט. ט"ז ס"ק יז. וראה חקרי הלכות א לה, ב. **קנא** כדלקמן סי' תרמג ס"א, שברכת שהחיינו היא גם על הסוכה. וראה גם תרומת הדשן ורמ"א שם. **קנב** ריטב"א כז, א ד"ה הא. ר"ן (יב, ב) ד"ה מתני' ר"א (שבזה מיירי משנה דידן, שאין קצבה אף ביו"ט ושבת). הובא במ"א סי' קפח סק"ט, וכאן סק"י. והיא דעה הב' דלעיל סי' עדר ס"ו. סי' רצא ס"א. וראה העו"ב תתו ע' 71.

זוֹ שֶׁיִּהְיֶה חוֹבָה לֶאֱכֹל אַף בִּשְׁעַת הַגֶּשֶׁם,[קנג] שֶׁכֵּיוָן שֶׁהוּא מִצְטַעֵר מֵחֲמַת הַגְּשָׁמִים הוּא פָּטוּר מִן הַסֻּכָּה אַף בַּלַּיְלָה הָרִאשׁוֹנָה.[קנד]

וְאַף עַל פִּי שֶׁהָעִקָּר כַּסְּבָרָא הָרִאשׁוֹנָה[קנה] בְּכָל זֶה, מִכָּל מָקוֹם בְּלֵיל שֵׁנִי שֶׁל גָּלֻיּוֹת כֵּיוָן שֶׁאֵינוֹ אֶלָּא מִנְהָג שֶׁהֲרֵי אָנוּ בְּקִיאִים בִּקְבִיעוּת הַחֹדֶשׁ[קנו, 70] – יֵשׁ לִסְמֹךְ עַל סְבָרָא הָאַחֲרוֹנָה וְאֵינוֹ צָרִיךְ לֶאֱכֹל בַּסֻּכָּה בִּשְׁעַת הַגֶּשֶׁם.[קנז] וּמִי שֶׁרוֹצֶה לְהַחְמִיר עַל עַצְמוֹ גַּם בְּלֵיל שֵׁנִי כַּסְּבָרָא הָרִאשׁוֹנָה – אֵינוֹ צָרִיךְ לְקַדֵּשׁ בַּסֻּכָּה, אֶלָּא יְקַדֵּשׁ וְיֹאכַל כָּל סְעוּדָתוֹ בְּתוֹךְ הַבַּיִת, וְאַחַר הָאֲכִילָה יִכָּנֵס לַסֻּכָּה וְיֹאכַל שָׁם כַּזַּיִת[קנח] וְלֹא יְבָרֵךְ "לֵישֵׁב בַּסֻּכָּה":[קנט, 71]

that we are obligated to eat [in the *sukkah*] while it is raining. [They maintain that] since [a person] feels discomfort because of the rain, he is exempt from the *[mitzvah* of*] sukkah* even on the first night.

The *halachah* follows the first view. Nevertheless, [different rules apply] on the eve of the second day [observed in the] Diaspora. Since we know the dates of the month[70] and thus [the observance of the second day] is merely a custom, one may rely on [the leniency of] the second opinion; one is not required to eat in the *sukkah* [on the second night] if it is raining.

If one desires to undertake the stringency of following the first opinion on the second night as well, he need not recite *Kiddush* in the *sukkah*. Instead, he should recite *Kiddush* and eat his entire meal at home. After he has eaten he should enter the *sukkah* and eat a *kezayis* there, [but] should not recite the blessing *leishev basukkah*.[71]

כ וְכֵיוָן שֶׁאֲכִילַת לַיְלָה הָרִאשׁוֹנָה נִלְמַד בִּגְזֵרָה שָׁוָה מֵאֲכִילַת מַצָּה – צָרִיךְ לִהְיוֹת דּוֹמֶה לָהּ בְּכָל דָּבָר, דְּהַיְנוּ שֶׁלֹּא יֹאכַל בְּעֶרֶב יוֹם טוֹב[קס] מִן הַמִּנְחָה וּלְמַעְלָה[קסא, 72] כְּדֵי שֶׁיֹּאכַל

20 Since [the obligation to] eat [in the *sukkah*] on the first night is derived from the association with eating *matzah*, [its observance] must resemble [the observance of the *mitzvah* of eating *matzah*] in all its particulars: During the day, before the onset of *Yom-Tov*, one should not eat from the [late] afternoon[72] onward, so that one will eat in the

70. Because we follow a fixed calendar. See sec. 600:1.

71. The rationale is that since one is not obligated to eat in the *sukkah* when it is raining, doing so does not fulfill a *mitzvah* and hence does not require a blessing. Even though on the first night a blessing is required in this situation, it should not be recited on the second night, in deference to the second opinion. Similarly, there is no difficulty with regard to the recitation of the blessing *Shehecheyanu* (as in footnote 68 above), for one has fulfilled his obligation by reciting that blessing on the first day.

As mentioned above, it is Lubavitch custom to eat in the *sukkah* even when it is raining vigorously, and a blessing is recited. See footnote 22; *Likkutei Sichos, loc. cit.;* and *Otzar Minhagei Chabad*, p. 302ff.

72. This is a free translation of the Alter Rebbe's term, which means the middle of the tenth seasonal hour of the day (i.e., 3:30 PM, if the sun rises and sets at 6:00). Scholars have debated why the term used here is not identical with

קנג שו"ת רשב"א ח"ד סי' עח. ב"י ד"ה ובכתבי, ממשמעות סמ"ג עשין מג (קכ, ג), ואור זרוע ח"ב סי' שא. וראה גם תוס' ברכות מט, ב ד"ה אי. קנד רשב"א שם. קנה ט"ז סקי"ז (לענין ליל ראשון בגשם, שלכן מברכים לישב בסוכה, כדלעיל סי"ח). וכן פסק לעיל סי' תקכט ס"ד (לענין סעודת יו"ט, שצריך יותר מכביצה). קנו כדלעיל סי' תר ס"א. קנז תרומת הדשן שם. רמ"א ס"ה. ט"ז שם בדעת הרמ"א ס"ה. מ"א סקט"ו. וראה לקו"ש חכ"ב ע' 31 הערה 13.

sukkah with an appetite;[64] one should not eat in the *sukkah* until after the appearance of the stars;[73] and one should be careful to eat before midnight. In all these particulars, [this *mitzvah*] resembles [the obligation of] eating *matzah,* as stated in the laws of Pesach.[74]

בַּסֻּכָּה לְתֵאָבוֹן,[קסב,64] וְלֹא יֹאכַל בַּסֻּכָּה עַד לְאַחַר צֵאת הַכּוֹכָבִים,[קסג,73] וְיִזָּהֵר לֶאֱכֹל קֹדֶם חֲצוֹת לַיְלָה,[קסד] הַכֹּל כְּמוֹ בַּאֲכִילַת מַצָּה כְּמוֹ שֶׁנִּתְבָּאֵר בְּהִלְכוֹת פֶּסַח:[קסה,74]

21 When is it permitted to leave the *sukkah* because of rain with regard to the meals of the festival other than on the first night? When so many drops of rain descend into the *sukkah* that, were they to fall into a cooked dish of beans which spoils quickly if only a small amount of water is added to it, that dish would spoil.[75] In such a situation, a person may leave the *sukkah* even though he does not have cooked food in the *sukkah* at this time.

A person who does not know how to calculate such a measure should reckon: If this same quantity of rain would come down into his house, he would leave his house, he may leave the *sukkah.*

כא מֵאֵימָתַי מֻתָּר לְפַנּוֹת מִן הַסֻּכָּה מִפְּנֵי הַגְּשָׁמִים?[קסו] בִּשְׁאָר סְעוּדוֹת הֶחָג, חוּץ מִלַּיְלָה הָרִאשׁוֹנָה,[קסז] מִשָּׁעָה שֶׁיֵּרְדוּ כָּל כָּךְ טִפּוֹת לְתוֹךְ הַסֻּכָּה שֶׁאִם הָיוּ נוֹפְלִים[קסח] לְתוֹךְ תַּבְשִׁיל שֶׁל פּוֹל[קסט] שֶׁדַּרְכּוֹ לְמַהֵר לְהִתְקַלְקֵל בְּמַיִם מוּעָטִים[קע] הָיָה הַתַּבְשִׁיל מִתְקַלְקֵל[75] — הֲרֵי זֶה יוֹצֵא מִן הַסֻּכָּה, אַף עַל פִּי שֶׁאֵין לְפָנָיו תַּבְשִׁיל בַּסֻּכָּה.[קעא] וּמִי שֶׁאֵינוֹ בָּקִי בְּשִׁעוּר זֶה — יְשַׁעֵר אִם הָיוּ יוֹרְדִים כָּל כָּךְ גְּשָׁמִים לְתוֹךְ הַבַּיִת אִם הָיָה יוֹצֵא מִן הַבַּיִת יוֹצֵא גַּם כֵּן מִן הַסֻּכָּה:[קעב]

22 All of the above applies with regard to eating. With regard to sleeping, there is no need to assess whether enough rain has come down to cause cooked food to spoil, for sleeping even in a light rain is distressful. [In such a situation] one may leave the *sukkah,* for anyone who feels discomfort is exempt from the *[mitzvah* of] *sukkah.*[76]

כב וְכָל זֶה בַּאֲכִילָה, אֲבָל בְּשֵׁנָה אֵין צָרִיךְ לְשַׁעֵר בִּכְדֵי שֶׁיִּתְקַלְקֵל הַתַּבְשִׁיל, שֶׁבִּגְשָׁמִים מוּעָטִים יֵשׁ צַעַר לִישֹׁן שָׁם, וְיוּכַל לָצֵאת מֵהַסֻּכָּה,[קעג] שֶׁכָּל הַמִּצְטַעֵר פָּטוּר מִן הַסֻּכָּה.[קעד,76]

---

the term that appears in the Alter Rebbe's source *(Magen Avraham* 639:12*)*, nor with the term that appears in sec. 471:1 above.

73. In the original, *tzeis hakochavim.*

74. See sec. 471:1, sec. 472:2, and sec. 477:6, respectively.

75. *Sukkah* 28b-29a; *Talmud Yerushalmi, Sukkah* 2:10.

76. As stated in sec. 640:5.

קנח תרומת הדשן שם. דרכי משה ס"ק ה. ט"ז ומ"א שם. קנט ט"ז שם. קס מהרי"ל הל' סוכות (ע' שע). רמ"א ס"ג. קסא מ"א סקי"ב (משעה עשירית, וכדלעיל סי' תעא ס"א). קסב ירושלמי פ"ב ה"ז. הובא בתוס' כז, א ד"ה תשבו. אור זרוע ח"ב סי' שא. מהרי"ל שם. רמ"א שם. קסג ארחות חיים הל' סוכה סי' לו. מהרי"ל שם. רמ"א שם. קסד מהר"י וייל סי' קצא. מהרי"ל שם. רמ"א שם. קסה סי' תעא ס"א לענין אכילה בע"פ. סי' תעב ס"ב לענין אכילה בלילה. סי' תעז ס"ו לענין אכילה לפני חצות. קסו משנה כח, ב. רמב"ם פ"ו ה"י. שו"ע ס"ה. קסז לדעה הא' דלעיל סי"ז, שהיא העיקר (כדלעיל סי"ט). קסח ירושלמי פ"ב ה"י. רמב"ם שם. טור בשם סמ"ג עשין מג (קכ, ד). שו"ע שם. קסט גמרא כט, א (של גריסין). רמב"ם שם. שו"ע שם. קע רש"י שם ד"ה מקפה. פיה"מ להרמב"ם. ט"ז סקט"ו. קעא אור זרוע הל' סוכה סי' שה. הגהות אשרי פ"ב סי' כ. טור ורמ"א ס"ה. קעב יראים השלם סי' תכא. מרדכי רמז תשמ. מהרי"ל הל' סוכות (ע' שע). רמ"א שם. קעג מהר"י וייל סי' קצא. רמ"א ס"ז. קעד כדלקמן סי' תרמ ס"ה.

וּכְשֵׁם שֶׁמֻּתָּר לִפָּנוֹת מִן הַסֻּכָּה מִפְּנֵי הַגְּשָׁמִים — כָּךְ מֻתָּר לִפָּנוֹת מִפְּנֵי הַשָּׁרָב אוֹ מִפְּנֵי הַיַּתּוּשִׁים,[קעה] אֲפִלּוּ אֵין הָאָדָם מִצְטַעֵר בְּכָךְ אֶלָּא שֶׁהַתַּבְשִׁיל מִתְקַלְקֵל בְּכָךְ,[קעו] וְכֵן אִם הָעֵת קַר שֶׁהַמַּאֲכָלִים הַשְּׁמֵנִים נִקְרָשִׁים בַּסֻּכָּה[קעז] — אוֹכֵל כָּל סְעוּדָתוֹ בַּבַּיִת:[קעח]

Just as it is permissible to leave the *sukkah* because of rain, so, too, one may leave it because of excessive heat or because of mosquitoes. [This applies] even if they do not cause one discomfort, but they spoil his food. Similarly, if it is so cold that fatty foods congeal, one may eat his whole meal at home.

כג כָּל הַפָּטוּר מִיְּשִׁיבַת הַסֻּכָּה וְאֵינוֹ יוֹצֵא מֵהַסֻּכָּה — אֵינוֹ מְקַבֵּל שָׂכָר עַל אוֹתוֹ יְשִׁיבָה, וְאֵינוֹ אֶלָּא מִן הַהֶדְיוֹטוֹת:[קעט, 77]

23 Whenever one is exempt from [the *mitzvah*] of *sukkah*, but does not leave the *sukkah*, he is not rewarded for dwelling there [at that time]. Instead, he is considered a commoner.[77]

כד הַיּוֹצֵא מֵהַסֻּכָּה מִפְּנֵי הַגְּשָׁמִים — אַל יִבְעַט וְיֵצֵא, אֶלָּא יֵצֵא בְּהַכְנָעָה,[קפ, 78] כְּעֶבֶד שֶׁבָּא לִמְזֹג כּוֹס לְרַבּוֹ וְשׁוֹפְכוֹ לוֹ[קפא] רַבּוֹ עַל פָּנָיו, כְּלוֹמַר אֵינִי חָפֵץ בְּשִׁמּוּשְׁךָ:[קפב, 79]

24 When one leaves the *sukkah* because of rain, he should not leave brazenly, but submissively,[78] like a servant who came to pour a drink for his master, and his master poured it out on his face, as if to say, "I do not desire your service."[79]

כה הָיָה אוֹכֵל בַּסֻּכָּה וְיָרְדוּ גְשָׁמִים וְהָלַךְ לְבֵיתוֹ[קפג] לִגְמֹר סְעוּדָתוֹ וּכְשֶׁיָּשַׁב לוֹ לֶאֱכֹל פָּסְקוּ הַגְּשָׁמִים[קפד] — אֵין מְחַיְּבִין אוֹתוֹ לַחֲזֹר לַסֻּכָּה לִגְמֹר סְעוּדָתוֹ,[קפה] אֶלָּא גּוֹמֵר סְעוּדָתוֹ בְּבֵיתוֹ:[80]

25 If one was eating in a *sukkah*, it rained, and he entered his home to complete his meal, he may complete that meal at home.[80] [Even] if it stopped raining when he sat down to eat, he is not required to return to the *sukkah*.

כו הָיָה יָשֵׁן בְּתוֹךְ הַסֻּכָּה וְיָרְדוּ גְשָׁמִים וְנִכְנַס לְתוֹךְ הַבַּיִת[קפו] לִגְמֹר שְׁנָתוֹ וְעַד

26 If one was sleeping in the *sukkah*, it rained, and he entered his home to finish sleeping and before he

77. I.e., according to law, remaining in the *sukkah* when this is not required is not considered a more punctilious observance of the *mitzvah*, but is rather the conduct of an unlearned individual. Nevertheless, chassidim would say, "Be a commoner — but eat in the *sukkah!*" See *Otzar Minhagei Chabad*, pp. 302-306.

78. See *Avodah Zarah* 3b.

79. *Sukkah* 28b-29a. The person leaving the *sukkah* will feel humbled and disturbed that he was deprived of the opportunity to fulfill the *mitzvah*.

80. *Ibid.*

קעה ירושלמי שם. אור זרוע שם. הגהות אשרי שם. ב"י ד"ה גרסינן. מ"א סקט"ו. **קעו** ב"ח ד"ה היה אוכל. מ"א שם. **קעז** לבוש סוף ס"ה. ב"ח שם. מ"א שם. **קעח** מ"א שם. **קעט** הגהות מיימוניות פ"ו אות ב בשם ר' שמחה. רמ"א ס"ז. וכדלעיל סי' תעב סי"ג וש"נ. וראה מנחת אלעזר ח"ד סוס"י לא (שתלמידי הבעש"ט דור אחר דור נהגו לישב בסוכה ז' ימי החג גם אם ירדו גשמים). לקו"ש חכ"ט ע' 211. אוצר מנהגי חב"ד חה"ס ע' שב. **קפ** מהרי"ל הל' סוכות (ע' שעא). ורמ"א סוף ס"ז. גמרא ע"ז דף ג רע"ב. **קפא** משנה כח, ב. **קפב** ברייתא כט, א. וראה גם לעיל סי' תריד ס"ב. ולעיל סי' קיד ס"א: לפי שהגשמים הם סימן קללה בחג הסוכות שאי אפשר לישב בסוכה בשעת הגשם אין מזכירין הגשם עד עבור ז' ימי ישיבה בסוכה. וראה לקו"ש חי"ד ע' 433. **קפג** גמרא [ברייתא] כט, א. רמב"ם פ"ו ה"י. שו"ע ס"ו. **קפד** רש"י שם ד"ה וירדו. **קפה** ברייתא שם. רמב"ם שם. טור ושו"ע שם. **קפו** ברייתא שם. טור ושו"ע ס"ז.

שֶׁלֹּא שָׁכַב פָּסְקוּ הַגְּשָׁמִים – צָרִיךְ לַחֲזוֹר לַסֻּכָּה.[קפז] אֲבָל אִם כְּבָר שָׁכַב בְּתוֹךְ הַבַּיִת וְאַחַר כָּךְ פָּסְקוּ הַגְּשָׁמִים – אֵינוֹ צָרִיךְ לַחֲזוֹר לַסֻּכָּה, אֶלָּא יָשֵׁן בְּבֵיתוֹ כָּל אוֹתוֹ הַלַּיְלָה. וַאֲפִלּוּ הֵקִיץ מִשְּׁנָתוֹ קֹדֶם שֶׁעָלָה עַמּוּד הַשַּׁחַר – אֵין מַטְרִיחִין אוֹתוֹ לַחֲזוֹר לַסֻּכָּה לִגְמֹר שָׁם שְׁנָתוֹ,[76] אֶלָּא מֻתָּר לוֹ לִגְמֹר שְׁנָתוֹ בְּבֵיתוֹ.[קפח] וַאֲפִלּוּ כְּבָר עָלָה עַמּוּד הַשַּׁחַר וְהוּא עֲדַיִן יָשֵׁן בְּתוֹךְ הַבַּיִת – אֵין צְרִיכִים לַהֲקִיצוֹ מִשְּׁנָתוֹ,[קפט] אֶלָּא מַנִּיחִין אוֹתוֹ לִישַׁן עַד שֶׁיִּנָּעֵר מֵאֵלָיו.[קצ] וְאִם הֵקִיץ מִשְּׁנָתוֹ לְאַחַר שֶׁעָלָה עַמּוּד הַשַּׁחַר וְרוֹצֶה לַחֲזוֹר וְלִישַׁן – צָרִיךְ לֵילֵךְ לְתוֹךְ הַסֻּכָּה וְלִישַׁן שָׁם, כֵּיוָן שֶׁכְּבָר עָלָה עַמּוּד הַשַּׁחַר:[קצא,81]

lay down the rain ceased, he must return to the *sukkah.* If, however, he already lay down inside his home and then the rain ceased, he need not return to the *sukkah,* but may sleep at home that entire night. Even if he woke up before dawn [and wanted to go back to sleep], he is not required to take the trouble of returning to the *sukkah* to finish sleeping,[76] but may finish sleeping at home.

[Moreover,] even if dawn has passed and he is still sleeping at home, there is no need to wake him up [to go to the *sukkah*]. Rather, he should be allowed to sleep until he wakes up on his own accord. If, however, he wakes up after dawn and desires to go back to sleep, he must go to the *sukkah* and sleep there, for it is already after dawn.[81]

סימן תרמ מִי הֵם הַפְּטוּרִים מִיְּשִׁיבַת סֻכָּה וּבוֹ כ"ב סְעִיפִים:

SECTION 640 Individuals who are Exempt from Dwelling in a *Sukkah.* (1–22)

א נָשִׁים וַעֲבָדִים פְּטוּרִים מִן הַסֻּכָּה,[א,1] מִפְּנֵי שֶׁהוּא מִצְוַת עֲשֵׂה שֶׁהַזְּמַן גְּרָמָא.[ב,2] אֲבָל מִי שֶׁחֶצְיוֹ עֶבֶד וְחֶצְיוֹ בֶּן חוֹרִין[3] – חַיָּב בְּסֻכָּה,[ג] מֵחֲמַת צַד חֵרוּת שֶׁבּוֹ:[ד,4]

1 Women and bondmen are exempt from the *mitzvah* of *sukkah*[1] because it is a positive *mitzvah* whose observance is associated with a specific time.[2] A person who is half a bondman and half a free man,[3] by contrast, is obligated, because in part he is a free man.[4]

---

81. *Ibid.* Thus the leniency granted him during the night no longer applies.

SECTION 640

1. *Sukkah* 28a. See also sec. 17:1.

2. In the original, *mitzvas aseh shehazman grama (Sukkah, loc. cit.).*

3. I.e., a Canaanite bondman who had been jointly owned by two Jewish masters and was then freed by only one of them.

4. Lit., "because of his free dimension," by virtue of which he is obligated to observe the *mitzvos* that bind any Jew. See also sec. 589:1.

קפז מ"א סקט"ז. **קפח** גמרא שם ורש"י ד"ה אלא. טור ושו"ע שם. וראה אג"ק אדמו"ר מוהרש"ב ח"א ע' שסב. **קפט** רש"י שם ד"ה אלא. משמעות טור ורמ"א ס"ז. לבוש ס"ז. ט"ז סקי"ח. **קצ** לבוש שם. ט"ז שם. **קצא** גמרא שם. טור ושו"ע שם.

סימן תרמ: א משנה כח, א. טור ושו"ע ס"א. **ב** גמרא כח, סע"א. לבוש ס"א. ט"ז סק"א. וכדלעיל סי' יז ס"א וש"נ. **ג** רמב"ם פ"ו ה"א. שו"ע שם. וכדלעיל סי' תקפט ס"א (לענין שופר). **ד** לבוש סוף ס"א.

ב טֻמְטוּם[5] וְאַנְדְּרוֹגִינוּס[6] — חַיָּבִים בְּסֻכָּה מִסָּפֵק[ה] שֶׁמָּא הוּא זָכָר,[ו,7] אֲבָל אֵינָם צְרִיכִים לְבָרֵךְ "לֵישֵׁב בַּסֻּכָּה",[ז] שֶׁכָּל סְפֵק בְּרָכוֹת לְהָקֵל,[ח,8] אֲבָל אִם יִרְצוּ לְבָרֵךְ — הָרְשׁוּת בְּיָדָם[ט] כְּמוֹ שֶׁנִּתְבָּאֵר בְּסִימָן י"ז,[י] עַיֵּן שָׁם.[9]

וַאֲפִלּוּ נְקֵבוֹת וַדָּאוֹת אִם יִרְצוּ לֵישֵׁב בַּסֻּכָּה וּלְבָרֵךְ — הָרְשׁוּת בְּיָדָם.[יא] אֲבָל מִי שֶׁכְּבָר בֵּרַךְ "לֵישֵׁב בַּסֻּכָּה" — לֹא יַחֲזֹר וִיבָרֵךְ כְּדֵי לְהוֹצִיא אֶת הַנָּשִׁים,[יב] כֵּיוָן שֶׁאֵין הַנָּשִׁים חַיָּבוֹת בִּבְרָכָה זוֹ — הֲרֵי זוֹ בְּרָכָה לְבַטָּלָה,[10] כְּמוֹ שֶׁנִּתְבָּאֵר בְּסִימָן תקפ"ט,[יג] עַיֵּן שָׁם:

2 A *tumtum*[5] and a hermaphrodite[6] are obligated [to observe the *mitzvah* of] *sukkah,* because possibly they are males.[7] They are not required to recite the blessing *leishev basukkah,* for whenever there is a doubt as to [whether] a blessing [should be recited], the lenient perspective is taken.[8] If, however, they desire to recite the blessing, they have that option, as explained in sec. 17[:3].[9]

Indeed, even women who desire to dwell in a *sukkah* and recite a blessing have that option. Nevertheless, a person who already recited the blessing *leishev basukkah* should not recite it a second time to fulfill the obligation on behalf of women. Since they are exempt from this blessing, [to recite] it [on their behalf] is to recite a blessing in vain,[10] as explained in sec. 589[:2].

ג אַף עַל פִּי שֶׁהַקְּטַנִּים פְּטוּרִים מִן הַסֻּכָּה[יד] מִן הַתּוֹרָה עַד שֶׁיִּהְיוּ בְּנֵי י"ג שָׁנִים, מִכָּל מָקוֹם מִדִּבְרֵי סוֹפְרִים[טו] כָּל קָטָן שֶׁאֵינוֹ צָרִיךְ לְאִמּוֹ,[טז] דְּהַיְנוּ בֶּן שֵׁשׁ שָׁנִים[יז] שְׁלֵמוֹת,[יח,12] וְאִם הַקָּטָן חָכָם[יט] וְחָרִיף[כ] בְּעִנְיָן שֶׁאֵינוֹ צָרִיךְ לְאִמּוֹ אֲפִלּוּ כְּשֶׁהוּא בֶּן חָמֵשׁ שָׁנִים שְׁלֵמוֹת — חַיָּב בְּסֻכָּה כְּדֵי לְחַנְּכוֹ בְּמִצְוֹת.[11]

3 Although, according to Scriptural Law, minors are exempt from the *mitzvah* of *sukkah* until they reach the age of thirteen, any boy who does not require his mother's [attention] is obligated by Rabbinic Law [to dwell] in the *sukkah,* so that he will be trained to observe the *mitzvos.*[11] [At what age is he considered sufficiently independent?] From the time he is fully six years old,[12] or, if he is bright and precocious and does not require his mother's attention, from the time he is fully five years old.

---

5. A person of masked and indeterminate gender.

6. In the original, *androgynus.*

7. The nature of the doubt differs. With regard to a *tumtum,* surgery could prove the person to be either male or female. With regard to an *androgynus,* the doubt is a question of halachic status, for the Sages did not issue a definitive ruling as whether such a person is considered male or female.

8. In the original, *safek berachos — lehakel;* i.e., a Rabbinically-ordained blessing is not recited. See sec. 167:12.

9. That subsection states that women who observe the *mitzvah* of *tzitzis* may recite a blessing, praising G-d for "commanding us to put on *tzitzis,*" for "though they themselves are not commanded [to observe that *mitzvah*], men are so commanded."

10. In the original, *berachah levatalah.*

11. In the original, *kdei lechancho bemitzvos; cf. Sukkah* 28a-b.

12. See *Eruvin* 82b.

ה רמב"ם שם. שו"ע שם. וכדלעיל יז ס"ב (לענין ציצית). סי' תקפח ס"ט (לענין שופר). ו לבוש סוף ס"א. ז כדלעיל סי' יז ס"ב (לענין ציצית). ח ראה לעיל סי' קסז סי"ב ושו"נ. ט רמ"א סי' יז ס"ב. י סעיף ג, ושו"נ. יא ראה תוס' ר"ה לג, א ד"ה הא. רא"ש שם פ"ד סי' ז. ר"ן שם (ט, ב) ד"ה ומ"מ. רמ"א שם. לעיל שם. יב מ"א סק"א. יג סעיף ב. יד משנה כח, א. טור ושו"ע ס"א. טו גמרא כח, ב. טור ושו"ע ס"ב. טז משנה שם. טור ושו"ע שם. יז גמרא עירובין פב, ב (רב אסי, לענין עירוב, בן

If a child still needs his mother, just as she is exempt [from observing the *mitzvah*], so, too, is the child exempt even according to Rabbinic Law, for he requires her [attention].

אֲבָל כְּשֶׁעֲדַיִן הוּא צָרִיךְ לְאִמּוֹ, כְּשֵׁם שֶׁאִמּוֹ פְּטוּרָה – כָּךְ הוּא פָּטוּר אֲפִלּוּ מִדִּבְרֵי סוֹפְרִים, כֵּיוָן שֶׁהוּא צָרִיךְ לָהּ:[כא]

4 Even though a child who does not require his mother's [attention] is obligated [to dwell] in the *sukkah,* if he eats and sleeps outside the *sukkah* others are not required to rebuke or scold him, as stated in sec. 343[:1]. His father, by contrast, is obligated to scold and rebuke him, and bring him into the *sukkah* to train him in the observance of the *mitzvos.*[13]

His mother is not obligated to train him in the observance of the *mitzvos.*[14] In relation to him she is considered as any other person. [Moreover,] she is permitted to place food before him outside the *sukkah* even though she knows that he will certainly not enter the *sukkah* to eat, but will eat in the place in which she placed the food. This is not a cause for concern, because she is not telling him to eat outside the *sukkah.*[15]

ד אַף עַל פִּי שֶׁהַקָּטָן שֶׁאֵינוֹ צָרִיךְ לְאִמּוֹ חַיָּב בְּסֻכָּה, מִכָּל מָקוֹם אִם הוּא אוֹכֵל וְיָשֵׁן חוּץ לַסֻּכָּה – אֵין צְרִיכִין לִמְחוֹת בְּיָדוֹ וְלִגְעֹר בּוֹ כְּמוֹ שֶׁנִּתְבָּאֵר בְּסִימָן שמ"ג.[כב] אֲבָל אָבִיו חַיָּב לִגְעֹר בּוֹ וְלִמְחוֹת בְּיָדוֹ וּלְהַכְנִיסוֹ לְתוֹךְ הַסֻּכָּה, כְּדֵי לְחַנְּכוֹ בְּמִצְוֹת.[כג,13] אֲבָל אִמּוֹ אֵינָהּ חַיֶּבֶת לְחַנְּכוֹ בְּמִצְוֹת,[כד,14] וַהֲרֵי הִיא אֶצְלוֹ כִּשְׁאָר כָּל אָדָם.[כה] וּמֻתָּר לָהּ לִתֵּן לְפָנָיו לֶאֱכֹל חוּץ לַסֻּכָּה, אַף עַל פִּי שֶׁיּוֹדַעַת שֶׁבְּוַדַּאי לֹא יִכָּנֵס לַסֻּכָּה לֶאֱכֹל אֶלָּא יֹאכַל בְּמָקוֹם שֶׁנְּתָנָה לְפָנָיו – אֵין בְּכָךְ כְּלוּם, כֵּיוָן שֶׁאֵינָהּ אוֹמֶרֶת לוֹ שֶׁיֹּאכַל חוּץ לַסֻּכָּה:[כו,15]

5 The Torah obligated [us] to dwell in the *sukkah* only to the extent that one normally dwells in his home throughout the year. Therefore a person who feels discomfort when dwelling in the *sukkah* and would free himself of that discomfort by leaving the *sukkah* is

ה לֹא חִיְּבָה תּוֹרָה לֵישֵׁב בַּסֻּכָּה אֶלָּא כְּדֶרֶךְ שֶׁאָדָם דָּר בְּבֵיתוֹ כָּל הַשָּׁנָה, לְפִיכָךְ[כז] מִי שֶׁהוּא מִצְטַעֵר[כח] בִּישִׁיבַת הַסֻּכָּה וּכְשֶׁיֵּצֵא מִמֶּנָּה יִנָּצֵל מִן הַצַּעַר[כט]

---

13. Sec. 343:2.

14. *Loc. cit.,* subsection 4.

15. For the mother, as stated above, training her child to observe *mitzvos* is not a formal halachic obligation. (See sec. 343:10.)

However, over and beyond the minimal formal obligations, scores of classical sources testify to the mother's critical role in molding young Jewish lives. The Rebbe's frequent expositions of these sources are summarized and documented in *A Partner in the Dynamic of Creation: Womanhood in the Teachings of the Lubavitcher Rebbe* (S.I.E., N.Y., 1994); see, for example, p. 57ff.

שש. ולדעת ריש לקיש, כבר ארבע כבר חמש). רמב"ם פ"ו ה"א (לגירסת כמה דפוסים: כבן שש. ולגירסת מ"מ וכ"מ: כבן חמש כבן שש). וראה הל' ת"ת לרבנו פ"א קו"א סק"א קרוב לסופו (שם נתבארה ההלכה לב' הגירסות). **יח** ברייתא וגמרא שם ע"ב (עד בן שש ועד בכלל), לפירוש שבקו"א שם (דהיינו על שנה ששית בכלל ולא על שביעית). וכן מבואר במ"מ שם (לגירסתו). ט"ז סק"ב. **יט** לבוש ס"ב. **כ** רש"י שם סע"א (לענין כבר ארבע כבר חמש). אחרונים. ט"ז ריש סק"ב. מ"א סק"ב (וראה גמרא שם, שלדעת ריש לקיש היינו כשאיתיה לאבוה במתא. ובקו"א שם, דבסוכה ודאי איתיה לאבוה, שהרי מצות חנוך היא על האב לבדו; כדלקמן ס"ד). **כא** ר"ן (יג, א) ד"ה מתני' נשים. לבוש שם. **כב** ס"א, וש"נ. **כג** כדלעיל שם ס"ב, וש"נ. **כד** מ"א סק"ג. וכדלעיל שם ס"ד, וש"נ. **כה** ראה הערות וציונים להל' ת"ת ח"ב ע' 692. **כו** מ"א סי' תרטז סק"ב (ושם גם הטעם דלא דמי להא דלעיל שם ס"ד). וראה לעיל סי' שמג ס"י וש"נ. **כז** תוס' כו, א ד"ה הולכי. יראים השלם סי' תכא. מרדכי רמז תשמ. לבוש ס"ג. ט"ז סק"ז. **כח** רבא בגמרא כו, א. טור ושו"ע ס"ד. **כט** יראים ומרדכי שם. רמ"א סוף ס"ד.

– פָּטוּר מִן הַסֻּכָּה,[16] שֶׁאַף בְּכָל הַשָּׁנָה אֵין אָדָם דָּר בְּמָקוֹם שֶׁהוּא מִצְטַעֵר. בַּמֶּה דְּבָרִים אֲמוּרִים? בִּשְׁאָר סְעוּדוֹת הֶחָג, אֲבָל בַּלַּיְלָה הָרִאשׁוֹנָה אַף הַמִּצְטַעֵר חַיָּב לֶאֱכֹל כַּזַּיִת בַּסֻּכָּה[ל] כְּמוֹ שֶׁנִּתְבָּאֵר בְּסִימָן תרל"ט:[לא]

exempt from dwelling in it,[16] for throughout the year one does not dwell in a place that causes him discomfort.

When does this apply? With regard to the meals of the festival other than on the first night. At that time, even a person who suffers discomfort is obligated to eat [at least] a *kezayis* in the *sukkah,* as explained in sec. 639[:17].

ו אֵיזֶהוּ מִצְטַעֵר[לב]? זֶה שֶׁאֵינוֹ יָכוֹל לֶאֱכֹל[לג] אוֹ לִישֹׁן[לד] בַּסֻּכָּה מִפְּנֵי הָרוּחַ שֶׁמְּצַעֲרוֹ, אוֹ מִפְּנֵי הַזְּבוּבִים וְהַפַּרְעוֹשִׁים[לה] וְכַיּוֹצֵא בָּהֶן, אוֹ מִפְּנֵי רֵיחַ רַע[לו] שֶׁמְּרִיחִין בְּתוֹךְ הַסֻּכָּה, וּכְשֶׁיֵּצֵא מִמֶּנָּה יִנָּצֵל מִכָּל אֵלּוּ.[לז,16]

בַּמֶּה דְּבָרִים אֲמוּרִים? שֶׁנּוֹלַד לוֹ הַצַּעַר בְּמִקְרֶה אַחַר שֶׁעָשָׂה שָׁם הַסֻּכָּה, אֲבָל אִם עָשָׂה סֻכָּה בְּמָקוֹם שֶׁיָּדוּעַ לוֹ שֶׁיִּצְטַעֵר אַחַר כָּךְ בָּהּ,[לח] כְּגוֹן שֶׁעָשָׂה בְּמָקוֹם שֶׁהָרוּחַ מְצוּיָה וְשׁוֹלֶטֶת שָׁם,[לט] וַאֲפִלּוּ עָשָׂה בְּמָקוֹם שֶׁלֹּא יִהְיֶה לוֹ צַעַר בַּאֲכִילָה אֶלָּא שֶׁיִּהְיֶה לוֹ צַעַר בַּשֵּׁנָה,[מ] כְּגוֹן שֶׁעָשָׂה בָּרְחוֹב[מא] שֶׁאִי אֶפְשָׁר לוֹ לִישֹׁן שָׁם בְּנַחַת מֵחֲמַת מוֹרָא הַגַּנָּבִים וְהַלִּסְטִים – הֲרֵי סֻכָּה זוֹ פְּסוּלָה, וְאֵינוֹ יוֹצֵא בָהּ אֲפִלּוּ בַּאֲכִילָה אַף עַל פִּי שֶׁאֵין לוֹ צַעַר כְּלָל בָּהּ, לְפִי שֶׁכָּל סֻכָּה שֶׁאֵינוֹ יָכוֹל לֶאֱכֹל וְלִשְׁתּוֹת וּלְטַיֵּל וְלִישֹׁן בָּהּ בְּנַחַת בְּלֹא שׁוּם צַעַר – אֵינָהּ נִקְרֵאת דִּירָה כְּלָל, לְפִי

6 What is meant by discomfort? The inability to eat or sleep in the *sukkah* because of a distressing wind, or because of flies or fleas or the like, or because of an unpleasant odor in the *sukkah,* when it is possible for him to free himself from these discomforts by departing.[16]

When does the above apply? When the distressing factor arose incidentally, after he made the *sukkah* in its present location. A *sukkah* is invalid if it was made in a place where one knows that he will later suffer discomfort, such as if he built it in a place that he knows to be windy.

[Moreover,] a *sukkah* is invalid even if it was built in a place where one will not suffer discomfort while eating, but will suffer discomfort while sleeping; e.g., he built his *sukkah* in the street, where he cannot sleep tranquilly for fear of thieves and robbers. One does not fulfill his obligation with [such a *sukkah*] even while eating, even though at that time he feels no discomfort at all. [The rationale is that] whenever a person cannot eat, drink, relax, and sleep in a *sukkah* tranquilly, without aggravation, it is not considered a dwelling at all, because

---

16. See *Sukkah* 26a.

ל כלבו סי' עא (לח, א) בשם ה"ר שלמיה. רמ"א רס"ד. לא דעה הא' דלעיל שם סי"ז, שכן עיקר (שם סי"ט). לב רמב"ם פ"ו ה"ב. שו"ע ס"ד. לג רא"ש פ"ב סי' יב. ארחות חיים הל' סוכה אות לב בשם רוב הפוסקים. טור ומ"א סק"ה. לד רבא כו, א. רמב"ם שם. טור ושו"ע שם. לה רב שם (משום בקי), לפירוש הערוך ערך בק (הג'). רמב"ם ושו"ע שם. לו רבא שם. רמב"ם ושו"ע שם. לז כדלעיל ס"ה. לח יראים השלם סי' תכא. מרדכי רמז תשמ. הגהות מיימוניות פ"ו אות א. הגהות אשרי פ"ב סי' יב. רמ"א ס"ד. לט לבוש ס"ד. מ יראים השלם שם. מרדכי שם. הגהות אשרי שם. לבוש שם. מא לבוש שם. מ"א סק"ז.

it does not resemble his home where he can meet all his needs comfortably.

However, if one builds his *sukkah* in the street and can sleep there at night without being fearful for his own safety, even if he is afraid that his utensils may be stolen from the *sukkah,* the *sukkah* is valid — for it is fit to serve him as a dwelling since he is not afraid to sleep in it, and he can return his utensils to his home at night. Nevertheless, as an initial and preferred option, one should not build a *sukkah* in the street; for explanation, see sec. 637[:11].

7 If one built a small *sukkah* in which he cannot sleep comfortably because he cannot stretch out his arms and legs, it is [nevertheless] valid. He is obligated to sleep in it and to bend his arms and legs. This does not qualify as discomfort, for sometimes a person will sleep with his body and his limbs bent.

If one feels discomfort, he alone is exempt from the obligation [to dwell in] the *sukkah.* His attendants are obligated [to dwell in] the *sukkah;* i.e., if they desire to eat or to sleep, they must enter it. If, by contrast, one is sick — even if he is not dangerously ill, indeed, even if he merely suffers pain in his head or eyes and it is difficult for him to dwell in the *sukkah* — his attendants too are exempt [from dwelling in] the *sukkah,*[17] for they are occupied with the observance of a *mitzvah.*[18] And whoever is occupied with the performance of a *mitzvah* is exempt

שֶׁאֵינוֹ דוֹמֶה לְבֵיתוֹ שֶׁיָּכוֹל לַעֲשׂוֹת שָׁם כָּל צָרְכּוֹ בְּנַחַת.[מב]

אֲבָל מִי שֶׁעָשָׂה סֻכָּה בָּרְחוֹב וְאֵינוֹ מִתְיָרֵא בְּנַפְשׁוֹ לִישַׁן שָׁם בַּלַּיְלָה, אַף עַל פִּי שֶׁמִּתְיָרֵא שֶׁלֹּא יִגְנְבוּ כְּלֵי תַּשְׁמִישׁוֹ שֶׁבַּסֻּכָּה – הֲרֵי זוֹ כְּשֵׁרָה, שֶׁהֲרֵי הִיא רְאוּיָה לוֹ לְדִירָה כֵּיוָן שֶׁאֵינוֹ מִתְיָרֵא לִישַׁן בָּהּ, וּכְלֵי תַּשְׁמִישׁוֹ יָכוֹל לְהַכְנִיסָן בַּלַּיְלָה לְתוֹךְ הַבַּיִת.[מג]

וּמִכָּל מָקוֹם, לְכַתְּחִלָּה אֵין לַעֲשׂוֹת סֻכָּה בָּרְחוֹב כְּמוֹ שֶׁנִּתְבָּאֵר בְּסִימָן תרל"ז,[מד] עַיֵּן שָׁם:

ז מִי שֶׁעָשָׂה סֻכָּה קְטַנָּה בְּעִנְיָן שֶׁמִּצְטַעֵר בָּהּ בַּשֵּׁנָה שֶׁלֹּא יוּכַל לִפְשֹׁט בָּהּ יָדָיו וְרַגְלָיו[מה] – הֲרֵי זוֹ כְּשֵׁרָה,[מו] וְחַיָּב לִישַׁן בָּהּ וְלִכְפֹּף יָדָיו וְרַגְלָיו,[מז] לְפִי שֶׁאֵין חָשׁוּב צַעַר, שֶׁכֵּן דֶּרֶךְ הָאָדָם שֶׁלִּפְעָמִים יָשֵׁן בִּכְפִיפַת גּוּפוֹ וְאֵיבָרָיו.[מח]

הַמִּצְטַעֵר אֵין פָּטוּר מִן הַסֻּכָּה אֶלָּא הוּא בְּעַצְמוֹ, אֲבָל מְשַׁמְּשָׁיו חַיָּבִים בַּסֻּכָּה,[מט] דְּהַיְנוּ שֶׁאִם הֵם רוֹצִים לֶאֱכֹל אוֹ לִישַׁן – חַיָּבִים לִכְנֹס לְתוֹךְ הַסֻּכָּה.

אֲבָל מִי שֶׁהוּא חוֹלֶה[נ] אֲפִלּוּ אֵין בּוֹ סַכָּנָה, אֲפִלּוּ אֵין לוֹ אֶלָּא מֵחוֹשׁ בְּרֹאשׁוֹ אוֹ בְּעֵינָיו[נא] וִישִׁיבַת הַסֻּכָּה קָשָׁה לוֹ[נב] – גַּם מְשַׁמְּשָׁיו פְּטוּרִין מִן הַסֻּכָּה,[17] לְפִי שֶׁהֵן עוֹסְקִין בְּמִצְוָה,[18] וְכָל הָעוֹסֵק בְּמִצְוָה – פָּטוּר

17. *Op. cit.,* 25a.

18. Tending to this sick person.

מב יראים השלם שם. מרדכי שם. הגהות אשרי שם. רמ"א שם. וראה חקרי הלכות ח"א לו, א. **מג** שו"ת רמ"א סי' כט. דרכי משה ס"ק ד. מ"א סק"ז. **מד** סעיף יא. **מה** תרומת הדשן סי' צב. רמ"א ס"ד. **מו** ראה ט"ז סק"ה. **מז** תרומת הדשן שם. רמ"א שם. מ"א סק"ט. **מח** תרומת הדשן שם. לבוש שם. **מט** גמרא כו, א. טור ושו"ע ס"ד. **נ** משנה כה, א. טור ושו"ע ס"ג. **נא** ברייתא כו, א. טור ושו"ע שם. **נב** ריטב"א כה, א ד"ה חולין (ומצטער בה). לבוש ס"ג (דשמא תזיק לו טרחת עלייתו או ישיבתו בסוכה).

מִמִּצְוָה אַחֶרֶת,[נג,19] לְפִיכָךְ אֵינָן פְּטוּרִין אֶלָּא בְּשָׁעָה שֶׁהֵם מְשַׁמְּשִׁים אוֹתָן,[נד] שֶׁאָז הֵן עוֹסְקִין בְּמִצְוָה:[20]

from performing a different *mitzvah*.[19] Accordingly, the attendants are exempt [from dwelling in the *sukkah*] only while they are caring for him, for that is when they are occupied in the observance of a *mitzvah*.[20]

ח מִי שֶׁמַּקִּיז דָּם – חַיָּב בַּסֻּכָּה,[נה] שֶׁאֵינוֹ מִצְטַעֵר כְּלָל, וְאַדְּרַבָּה הוּא שָׂמֵחַ וּמַרְבֶּה בַּאֲכִילָה וּשְׁתִיָּה.[נו] בַּמֶּה דְּבָרִים אֲמוּרִים? כְּשֶׁאֵינוֹ מַקִּיז אֶלָּא כְּדֵי לִשְׁמֹר בְּרִיאוּתוֹ[21] וְאֵינוֹ מַרְגִּישׁ שׁוּם חֹלִי בְּעַצְמוֹ, אֲבָל אִם מַרְגִּישׁ בּוֹ חֹלִי (מֵחֲמַת הַקָּזָה) וְיֵשׁ שָׁם קְצָת קְרִירוּת – הֲרֵי זֶה פָּטוּר מִן הַסֻּכָּה.[נז]

מִכָּל מָקוֹם, לְכַתְּחִלָּה אֵין לְהַקִּיז דָּם בְּתוֹךְ הֶחָג אִם אֶפְשָׁר לוֹ לְהַקִּיז קֹדֶם הֶחָג אוֹ לְהִתְאַחֵר עַד אַחַר הֶחָג,[נח] שֶׁאֵין לָאָדָם לְהָבִיא אֶת עַצְמוֹ לִידֵי צַעַר בֶּחָג בְּעִנְיָן שֶׁיִּפָּטֵר מִן הַסֻּכָּה.

וּמִטַּעַם זֶה אֵין לִשְׁתּוֹת סַם הַמְשַׁלְשֵׁל בְּתוֹךְ הֶחָג כָּל שֶׁאֶפְשָׁר לוֹ לְהַקְדִּים אוֹ לְאַחֵר. וְאִם עָבַר וְשָׁתָה – פָּטוּר מִן הַסֻּכָּה,[נט] כֵּיוָן שֶׁהַקְּרִירוּת קָשָׁה לוֹ:[ס]

8 A person who let blood is obligated [to dwell in] the *sukkah*, for he suffers no discomfort at all. On the contrary, he is happy and eats and drinks more than usual.

When does the above apply? When he lets blood only in order to protect his health,[21] and he does not feel sick at all. If, however, he feels sick (because of letting blood) and it is slightly chilly, he is exempt from [dwelling in] the *sukkah*.

Initially, however, it is preferable not to let blood during the festival if it is possible to do so beforehand or to postpone doing so until after the festival, for one should not cause himself discomfort that may exempt him from the obligation [to dwell in] the *sukkah*. For this reason, it is forbidden for a person to imbibe a diarrhetic agent during Sukkos if he could undergo [this treatment] before or after [the festival]. If he transgressed and imbibed [such a substance], he is exempt [from dwelling in] the *sukkah*, because the cold is difficult for him to bear.

ט מִי שֶׁכָּבוּ לוֹ נֵרוֹתָיו בַּסֻּכָּה בְּלֵיל שַׁבָּת[סא] שֶׁבְּתוֹךְ הֶחָג[סב,22] וְיֵשׁ לוֹ נֵר דּוֹלֵק בְּתוֹךְ

9 If the lamps illuminating one's *sukkah* went out on Friday night during the festival,[22] and he has a lamp burning in

19. *Ibid.;* see also subsection 18 below.

20. *Ibid.;* see also *Berachos* 11a, 16a.

Moreover, two attendants who are not needed constantly should alternate during meals so that each of them will have the opportunity to eat in the *sukkah* (*Shaarei Teshuvah* 640:3).

21. I.e., as a preventive measure, not as a remedy.

22. This is the only day on which such a question could arise, for even on the first two days of *Yom-Tov,* if it is not *Shabbos,* the light may be kindled from an existing light or brought in from outside the *sukkah*. (The above law refers only to candlelight. Electric lights may not be relit on *Yom-Tov.*)

See subsection 5 above, from which it is apparent that if the lights

נג לבוש שם. וכדלעיל סי' לח ס"ז וש"נ. וראה גם לקמן סי"ח. נד ארחות חיים הל' סוכה אות לב. שו"ע שם בשם ויש מי שאומר. וראה פתחא זוטא ס"ג. ערוך השלחן ס"ג. נה אור זרוע הל' סוכה סי' רצט. הגהות אשרי פ"ב סי' יב. דמ"א ס"ג. נו אור זרוע שם. הגהות אשרי שם. דרכי משה ס"ק ב. ט"ז סק"ג. מ"א סק"ד. נז ט"ז שם. וראה גם לעיל סי' שכח סכ"ד וש"נ. נח אור זרוע שם. הגהות אשרי שם. דרכי משה שם. מ"א וט"ז שם. נט מ"א שם. ס ראה מ"א

his home, he may leave the *sukkah* and eat at home where the lamp is burning, for it is uncomfortable to eat in the dark without a lamp.

Even if he has a friend who has a lamp in his *sukkah,* we do not obligate the person whose lamp went out to bring his meal to his friend's *sukkah* so that he can eat by the light of the lamp. [The rationale is that] to eat in a friend's *sukkah* is also uncomfortable, for a man finds pleasure only in his own domain.

Nevertheless, if he can go to his friend's *sukkah* without much difficulty, no leniency should be taken regarding this matter, for the above reason does not fully qualify as a discomfort that should exempt him from the obligation [to dwell] in the *sukkah.*

בֵּיתוֹ – מֻתָּר לוֹ לָצֵאת מֵהַסֻּכָּה וְלֶאֱכֹל בְּתוֹךְ בֵּיתוֹ בִּמְקוֹם הַנֵּר, לְפִי שֶׁצַּעַר הוּא לָאָדָם לֶאֱכֹל בַּחֹשֶׁךְ בְּלֹא נֵר.[סג] וַאֲפִלּוּ יֵשׁ לַחֲבֵרוֹ נֵר בְּסֻכָּתוֹ – אֵין אוֹמְרִים לָזֶה שֶׁכָּבוּ נֵרוֹתָיו הָבֵא סְעוּדָתְךָ לְסֻכַּת חֲבֵרְךָ וֶאֱכֹל שָׁם לְאוֹר הַנֵּר,[סד] לְפִי שֶׁזֶּהוּ גַּם כֵּן צַעַר לָאָדָם לֶאֱכֹל בְּסֻכַּת חֲבֵרוֹ, שֶׁאֵין עָרֵב לָאָדָם אֶלָּא בְּשֶׁלּוֹ.[סה] מִכָּל מָקוֹם, אִם אֶפְשָׁר לוֹ לָבוֹא לְסֻכַּת חֲבֵרוֹ בְּלֹא טֹרַח גָּדוֹל – אֵין לְהָקֵל בַּדָּבָר,[סו] לְפִי שֶׁאֵין זֶה מִצְטַעֵר גָּמוּר שֶׁיִּפָּטֵר מִן הַסֻּכָּה בִּשְׁבִיל כָּךְ:

10 It is permitted to hang a cloth or sheet on the sides of a *sukkah* on *Shabbos* or on *Yom-Tov*[23] to protect the candles from being extinguished by the wind. This does not constitute [a transgression of] the prohibition against constructing a tent[24] on *Shabbos* and on *Yom-Tov,* because a partition[25] is not considered a tent, as stated in sec. 315[:3].[26] It is, however, forbidden to hang [such an object] under the *s'chach,*[27]

י מֻתָּר לִפְרֹשׂ בֶּגֶד אוֹ סָדִין בַּסֻּכָּה מִן הַצַּד בְּשַׁבָּת אוֹ בְּיוֹם טוֹב[23] לְהָגֵן מִפְּנֵי הָרוּחַ שֶׁלֹּא יְכַבֶּה אֶת הַנֵּרוֹת,[סז] וְאֵין אִסּוּר מִשּׁוּם עֲשִׂיַּת אֹהֶל[24] בְּשַׁבָּת וּבְיוֹם טוֹב, שֶׁאֵין בִּמְחִצָּה[25] מִשּׁוּם אֹהֶל כְּמוֹ שֶׁנִּתְבָּאֵר בְּסִימָן שט"ו.[סח,26]

אֲבָל אָסוּר לִפְרֹס תַּחַת הַסְּכָךְ,[סט,27]

went out on the first night of Sukkos that fell on *Shabbos,* one is obligated to eat a *kezayis* of bread in the *sukkah* even if one feels discomfort.

23. In *Eretz Yisrael,* on the first day of the festival; in the Diaspora, on the first two days.

24. In the original, *ohel.*

25. In the original, *mechitzah.*

26. There the Alter Rebbe writes that one may hang a temporary curtain on *Shabbos* and on *Yom-Tov,* provided it does not serve as a partition for a ritual purpose, e.g., serve as a wall that makes a *sukkah* valid (see the commentaries to the *Shulchan Aruch* of R. Yosef Caro, sec. 630:12), or to permit carrying in an enclosure (see the present work, sec. 362:14), and the like.

27. Since the cloth is being extended under the *s'chach,* it is not considered as the strengthening of an existing tent, but rather the construction of a new one, and as such is forbidden by Rabbinic law.

Coverings are commonly used to protect the *s'chach* from rain. Unless these coverings are opened up for at least a handbreadth before *Shabbos,* extending them on the holiday is considered comparable to the construction of a tent and hence forbidden (see sec. 315). If, however, a covering is attached to a frame, e.g., an awning, it may be spread out on *Shabbos* (see sec. 315:15).

שם (דהא סכנה הוא לו). **סא** תרומת הדשן סי' צג, ופסקים סי' קנח. רמ"א ס"ד. **סב** משא"כ בליל א' דיו"ט שחל בשבת, שאף המצטער חייב לאכול כזית בסוכה, כדלעיל ס"ה. **סג** תרומת הדשן שם. לבוש ס"ד. וראה גם לעיל סי' רסג ס"ד. סי' תקכז סכ"ט. **סד** תרומת הדשן שם. רמ"א שם. **סה** תרומת הדשן שם. לבוש שם. **סו** תרומת הדשן שם. רמ"א שם. **סז** אור זרוע הל' שבת סי' עח סוף אות ו. רמ"א ס"ד. **סח** סעיף ג. **סט** אור זרוע שם. רמ"א שם.

אֲפִלּוּ אִם הוּא בְּעִנְיָן שֶׁאִם לֹא יַעֲשֶׂה כָּךְ לֹא יוּכַל לֶאֱכֹל כְּלָל בַּסֻּכָּה מֵחֲמַת הָרוּחַ שֶׁיְּכַבֶּה אֶת הַנֵּרוֹת בְּלֵיל שַׁבָּת, לְפִי שֶׁאֵין מִצְוַת סֻכָּה דּוֹחָה אֶת שׁוּם אִסּוּר אֲפִלּוּ שֶׁל דִּבְרֵיהֶם,[ע,28] מִטַּעַם שֶׁנִּתְבָּאֵר בְּסוֹף סִימָן תקפ"ו,[עא] עַיֵּן שָׁם.[29]

אֲבָל מֻתָּר לִפְרֹס עַל גַּבֵּי הַסְּכָךְ, אִם (עַיֵּן סִימָן תרכט מָגֵן אַבְרָהָם[עב]) הוּא[עג] שֶׁאִם לֹא יַעֲשֶׂה כָּךְ לֹא יוּכַל לֶאֱכֹל בַּסֻּכָּה, לְפִי שֶׁאֵין כָּאן אֹהֶל כְּלָל, כֵּיוָן שֶׁאֵין גֹּבַהּ טֶפַח בֵּין הַסָּדִין לַסְּכָךְ שֶׁתַּחְתָּיו.[עד]

אֲבָל אִם אֵין בָּרוּר לוֹ שֶׁאִם לֹא יִפְרֹס שָׁם סָדִין לֹא יוּכַל לֶאֱכֹל בַּסֻּכָּה אֲפִלּוּ בְּחֹל – אָסוּר לִפְרֹס סָדִין תַּחַת הַסְּכָךְ אוֹ עַל גַּבֵּי הַסְּכָךְ, מִטַּעַם שֶׁנִּתְבָּאֵר בְּסוֹף סִימָן תרכ"ט:[עה,30]

even when — if this is not done — it will be impossible to eat in the *sukkah* at all, because the wind will extinguish the candles on Friday night. For [the observance of] the *mitzvah* of *sukkah* does not override any prohibition, even a prohibition of Rabbinic origin,[28] for the reason explained [in] sec. 586[:22].[29]

It is, however, permitted to spread [such an object] on the *s'chach* if it would be impossible otherwise to eat in the *sukkah* (see *Magen Avraham* 629[:25]). The rationale is that there is no tent at all, because there is not a handbreadth of space between the sheet and the *s'chach* beneath it. If, however, one is not certain that if he does not spread out a sheet he will not be able to eat in the *sukkah*, it is forbidden to spread out a sheet even on a weekday, whether below or above the *s'chach*, for the reason explained at the end of sec. 629.[30]

יא אֵין הַמִּצְטַעֵר פָּטוּר מִן הַסֻּכָּה אֶלָּא אִם כֵּן הוּא מִצְטַעֵר בְּדָבָר שֶׁדֶּרֶךְ בְּנֵי אָדָם לְהִצְטַעֵר בּוֹ,[עו] אֲבָל אִם הוּא

11 A person who suffers discomfort is exempt from the obligation [to dwell] in the *sukkah* only if he feels discomfort from a factor that ordinarily causes people discomfort. If he feels

28. In this case, the Rabbinic prohibition against constructing a temporary shelter (see sec. 315:1).

29. There the Alter Rebbe writes that "the Sages equated their rulings with those [stemming] from Scriptural Law and buttressed the authority of their rulings even though they led to the negation of Scriptural Law, in cases in which one remains inactive and [simply] refrains from performing [an action required of him by the Torah]." See another application of this principle in sec. 628:5.

30. The end of sec. 629 of the Alter Rebbe's *Shulchan Aruch* is not extant. In the *Shulchan Aruch* of R. Yosef Caro, the last subsection of sec. 629 speaks of hanging a sheet under or over the *s'chach* because of heat or because the leaves of the *s'chach* may fall. Some authorities maintain that this disqualifies the *sukkah* because the sheet is considered as a separate entity. Others maintain that the sheet is considered as subordinate to the *s'chach*, and that hence the *sukkah* remains valid. *Magen Avraham* 629:25 cites the ruling of *Beis Yosef*, that it is forbidden to eat under such a sheet, but adds that if it is raining, it is preferable to eat under such a covering than not to eat in a *sukkah* at all. Similarly, in the instance at hand, if spreading out the sheet under or over the *s'chach* will enable one to eat in the *sukkah*, and otherwise he will not, there is room for leniency.

ע עשיית אהל ארעי ביו"ט, וכדלעיל שם ס"א. עא סכ"ב. וראה גם לעיל סי' תרכח ס"ה. עב סקכ"ה (מחלוקת אם מותר לאכול תחתיו). עג בקונטרס השלחן הגיה: בענין. עד מ"א ס"ק ח. עה סוף סימן זה בשוע"ר לא הגיע לידינו, וראה שו"ע שם סי"ט. עו טור. רמ"א ס"ד. עז ט"ז סק"ו. עח גמרא כט, א. רי"ף

discomfort because of something that ordinarily does not cause people discomfort, his feelings are [halachically] insignificant because of those of the majority.

[An exception applies when one] is known to be delicate.[31] [He is exempt from the obligation to dwell in the *sukkah*] if he feels discomfort from a cause that makes all delicate people feel uncomfortable. One may not, however, claim to be delicate [and thus be exempt from the *mitzvah* of *sukkah*] unless this is known to be his nature.

מִצְטַעֵר בְּדָבָר שֶׁאֵין דַּרְכָּן שֶׁל בְּנֵי אָדָם לְהִצְטַעֵר מֵחֲמַת דָּבָר זֶה — בְּטֵלָה דַּעְתּוֹ אֵצֶל כָּל אָדָם,[עז] אֶלָּא אִם כֵּן יָדוּעַ שֶׁהוּא מֵאֲנִינֵי הַדַּעַת[עח,31] וְהוּא מִצְטַעֵר בְּדָבָר שֶׁכָּל אֲנִינֵי הַדַּעַת מִצְטַעֲרִין מֵחֲמַת דָּבָר זֶה,[עט] אֲבָל אֵין כָּל אָדָם יָכוֹל לוֹמַר מֵאֲנִינֵי הַדַּעַת אֲנִי, אֶלָּא אִם כֵּן יָדוּעַ שֶׁהוּא מֵאֲנִינֵי הַדַּעַת:[פ]

12 A person who sleeps in the *sukkah* in a canopy bed which has a roof at least a handbreadth wide and which is at least ten handbreadths high does not fulfill his obligation.[32] Nevertheless, if there are mosquitoes in the *sukkah* that annoy him, it is preferable that he sleep in such a canopy bed than outside the *sukkah,*[16] for there is [an opinion] that allows one outright to sleep in such a bed, even if there are no mosquitoes.[33] Though the *halachah* does not follow this opinion, [it can be relied on when one would otherwise leave the *sukkah*].

יב אַף עַל פִּי שֶׁהַיָּשֵׁן בַּסֻּכָּה בְּכִלָּה שֶׁיֵּשׁ לָהּ גַּג רָחָב טֶפַח וְגָבוֹהַּ עֲשָׂרָה טְפָחִים לֹא יָצָא יְדֵי חוֹבָתוֹ,[פא,32] מִכָּל מָקוֹם אִם יֵשׁ יַתּוּשִׁין בַּסֻּכָּה שֶׁמְּצַעֲרִין אוֹתוֹ — מוּטָב שֶׁיִּישַׁן בְּכִלָּה זֶה[פב] מִשֶּׁיִּישַׁן חוּץ לַסֻּכָּה,[פג,16] לְפִי שֶׁיֵּשׁ מִי שֶׁמַּתִּיר לְכַתְּחִלָּה[פד] לִישֹׁן בְּכִלָּה זוֹ[פה] אֲפִלּוּ בְּמָקוֹם שֶׁאֵין שָׁם יַתּוּשִׁין,[33] אַף עַל פִּי שֶׁאֵין הֲלָכָה כִּדְבָרָיו בְּדָבָר זֶה:

13 A mourner is obligated [to dwell] in the *sukkah,*[34] even on the first day [of mourning]. It is distressing[35] for him to dwell in the *sukkah,* for a mourner desires to be

יג אָבֵל חַיָּב בְּסֻכָּה[פו,34] אֲפִלּוּ בְּיוֹם רִאשׁוֹן,[פז] וְאַף עַל פִּי שֶׁצַּעַר הוּא[35] לוֹ לֵישֵׁב בַּסֻּכָּה, שֶׁהָאָבֵל חָפֵץ לִהְיוֹת

31. *Sukkah* 29a.

32. For this bed is considered as a tent, as stated in sec. 627:2. A person sleeping in such a bed is not considered to be sleeping in the *sukkah*.

33. *Op. cit.,* 11a.

34. *op. cit.,* 25b. Overt mourning is postponed until after the festival, unlike the more private aspects of mourning. (See *Shulchan Aruch, Yoreh Deah* 399:2.) From the time of demise until after the burial, during the initial stage of acute grief during which the mourner is termed an *onen,* he is exempt from the *mitzvah* of *sukkah,* as with all the positive commandments. (See: *Meiri, loc. cit.; Mishnah Berurah* 640:31.)

35. Thus there is a difference between situations in which the discomfort is caused by factors related to the *sukkah* (in which instance the person is exempt), and circumstances in which one feels discomfort for personal reasons (in which instance he is obligated).

(יג, א). רא"ש פ"ב סי' כ. **עט** ב"ח ד"ה ומ"ש ונראה. ט"ז שם. **פ** מ"א סק"ט. **פא** כדלעיל סי' תרכז ס"ב. **פב** בקונטרס השלחן מגיה: זו. **פג** מ"א סק"ט, ממשמעות הגמרא כו, א: רב שרא לרב אחא כו'. **פד** רבה בר רב הונא בגמרא יא, א כרבי יהודה במשנה כ, ב. **פה** מ"א שם. **פו** גמרא כה, ב. טור ושו"ע ס"ה. **פז** גמרא שם (שביום הראשון פטור מתפילין וחייב בסוכה). וראה מ"א סי' תקמח סק"ה. לעיל סי' תעב ס"ג־ד.

מִתְבּוֹדֵד[36] לִהְיוֹת טָרוּד בְּצַעֲרוֹ וּבְאֶבְלוֹ[פח] – אַף עַל פִּי כֵן חַיָּב לֵישֵׁב בַּסֻּכָּה, וּלְהָסִיר הָאֲבֵלוּת מִלִּבּוֹ[פט] בְּעִנְיָן שֶׁלֹּא יִהְיֶה לוֹ צַעַר כְּלָל בִּישִׁיבָה בַּסֻּכָּה. אֲבָל אִם אֵינוֹ יָכוֹל לְהָסִיר הָאֲבֵלוּת מִלִּבּוֹ, כְּגוֹן שֶׁהַמֵּת חָבִיב לוֹ מְאֹד,[צ] וְיֵשׁ לוֹ צַעַר בַּסֻּכָּה[צא] שֶׁאֵינוֹ יָכוֹל לִהְיוֹת טָרוּד שָׁם בָּאֲבֵלוּת כְּמוֹ בְּבֵיתוֹ שֶׁיֵּשֵׁב שָׁם בָּדָד – פָּטוּר מִן הַסֻּכָּה:

alone,[36] [so that he can] be preoccupied with his pain and mourning. He is nevertheless obligated to dwell in the *sukkah,* and to remove the mourning from his heart so that he will not feel any discomfort from dwelling in the *sukkah.*

If, however, he cannot clear his heart from mourning, because the deceased was very dear to him, and he feels discomfort in the *sukkah* because he cannot be preoccupied with his mourning as he would be at home where he would sit alone, he is exempt from dwelling in the *sukkah*.

יד סְעוּדַת בְּרִית מִילָה, וְכֵן הַסְּעוּדָה שֶׁאוֹכְלִין אֵצֶל הַיּוֹלֶדֶת[צב] (כָּךְ הָיָה הַמִּנְהָג בַּיָּמִים הָרִאשׁוֹנִים[צג,37]) – חַיָּבִים בַּסֻּכָּה,[38] אַף עַל פִּי שֶׁצַּר לָהֶם הַמָּקוֹם לָשֶׁבֶת שָׁם וְאִי אֶפְשָׁר לָהֶם לִשְׂמֹחַ כָּרָאוּי – אַף עַל פִּי כֵן יֹאכְלוּ בַּסֻּכָּה, וְאוֹתָם אֲנָשִׁים שֶׁצַּר לָהֶם – לֹא יֹאכְלוּ כְּלָל בִּסְעוּדָה זוֹ,[צד] אַף עַל פִּי שֶׁסְּעוּדַת בְּרִית מִילָה הִיא סְעוּדַת מִצְוָה,[צה,39] מִכָּל מָקוֹם אֵינָהּ מִצְוָה גְּדוֹלָה כָּל כָּךְ[צו] לִדְחוֹת מִצְוַת סֻכָּה בִּשְׁבִילָהּ, שֶׁהִיא מִצְוַת עֲשֵׂה שֶׁל תּוֹרָה:

14 The festive meal celebrating a circumcision and the festive meal held in honor of a woman who gave birth (as was the custom in former times[37]) must be held in a *sukkah,*[38] even though the space is restricted and people will not be able to celebrate appropriately. Nevertheless, [the festive meal should be held] in a *sukkah* and those people who are held back by the constrictions [of space] should not participate in this feast.

Though the festive meal celebrating a circumcision is considered a festive meal associated with a *mitzvah,*[39] it is not a *mitzvah* of such standing that it should override the *mitzvah* of [eating in] the *sukkah,* which is a positive commandment of Scriptural authority.

טו הַמְהַלֵּךְ בַּדֶּרֶךְ בִּימֵי הַסֻּכּוֹת,[צז,16] אִם הוּא אוֹכֵל וְיָשֵׁן עַל פְּנֵי הַשָּׂדֶה בְּמָקוֹם שֶׁאֵין שָׁם יִשּׁוּב כְּלָל[צח]

15 [The following laws apply when] a person travels on a journey during Sukkos.[16] If he eats and sleeps in open places, in areas where there is no settlement at all,

36. And the *sukkah* may be exposed to public view or may be frequented by others.

37. See *Luach Birkas HaNehenin* 4:16.

38. With regard to a *sheva berachos* celebration, see sec. 639:10 and its footnotes.

39. In the original, a *seudas mitzvah.* See the gloss of *Rama* to the *Shulchan Aruch* of R. Yosef Caro, *Yoreh Deah* 265:12.

פח רא"ש פ"ב סי' ז. מ"א סק"י. פט גמרא שם (ליתובי דעתיה). רא"ש שם. מ"א שם. צ תניא סי' פג. מ"א שם. צא מ"א שם. צב מהרי"ק שורש קעח. רמ"א ס"ו. צג בלילה שלפני המילה. וראה לוח ברכת הנהנין פ"ד הט"ז (סעודת בן זכר), וש"נ. "כפר חב"ד" 1017 ע' 14. 1019 ע' 14. צד מ"א ס"ק יג (די להם בי' אנשים). צה רמ"א יו"ד סי' רסה סי"ב. וראה גם לעיל סי' רמט ס"ו. סי' תמד סט"ו. צו מהרי"ק שם. מ"א שם. צז ברייתא כו, א. צח ר"ן (יב, א)

he does not have to take the trouble of building a *sukkah*. Even if he dwells in one place in a field throughout the holiday and he has the potential to make a *sukkah* in this place, he is still not required to take the trouble [of making a *sukkah*] there.[40] Instead, if a *sukkah* that was made for shade is available in the place where he was camping, he should dwell in it. If not, he may eat, drink, and sleep in an open space, for a *sukkah* is like the home in which he lives throughout the year, and a person will not establish his dwelling in a place where there is no settlement whatever.

16 However, when he reaches an inhabited place, even if it is inhabited by non-Jews, and desires to eat and sleep there, he is obligated to build a *sukkah* and enter it to eat and sleep.[40]

When does the above apply? When one has the opportunity to build a *sukkah* during the interval between the time he arrived at that settlement and the time at which travelers in a comparable situation eat and sleep. I.e., if he travels during the day and spends the night in a settlement, [travelers in his situation] eat and sleep at the beginning of the night so that they can rise early in the morning to resume their journey; [hence,] if he has enough time to build a *sukkah* before the above-described time for eating and sleeping, [he is obligated to build a *sukkah*].

[Different rules apply if] one reaches a settlement near the time at which travelers in his situation eat and sleep. If he must take the trouble to build a *sukkah* before the

– אֵינוֹ צָרִיךְ לִטְרֹחַ וְלַעֲשׂוֹת לוֹ סֻכָּה, אֲפִלּוּ הוּא יוֹשֵׁב כָּל הֶחָג בְּמָקוֹם אֶחָד בַּשָּׂדֶה[צט] וְיֵשׁ לוֹ סִפּוּק לַעֲשׂוֹת לוֹ סֻכָּה בַּמָּקוֹם הַזֶּה – אַף עַל פִּי כֵן אֵינוֹ צָרִיךְ לִטְרֹחַ בִּשְׁבִיל כָּךְ,[ק,40] אֶלָּא אִם יֵשׁ שָׁם בִּמְקוֹם חֲנִיָּתוֹ סֻכָּה מוּכֶנֶת עֲשׂוּיָה לְשֵׁם צֵל – הֲרֵי זֶה יוֹשֵׁב בָּהּ,[קא] וְאִם לָאו – אוֹכֵל וְשׁוֹתֶה וְיָשֵׁן עַל פְּנֵי הַשָּׂדֶה, לְפִי שֶׁהַסֻּכָּה הִיא כְּעֵין דִּירַת בֵּיתוֹ בְּכָל הַשָּׁנָה, וְאֵין אָדָם קוֹבֵעַ דִּירָתוֹ בְּמָקוֹם שֶׁאֵין שָׁם יִשּׁוּב כְּלָל:[קב]

טז אֲבָל כְּשֶׁהִגִּיעַ לִמְקוֹם יִשּׁוּב,[קג] אֲפִלּוּ הוּא יִשּׁוּב גּוֹיִם וְרוֹצֶה לֶאֱכֹל אוֹ לִישֹׁן שָׁם – חַיָּב לַעֲשׂוֹת לוֹ סֻכָּה,[קד] וְיִכָּנֵס לְתוֹכָהּ לֶאֱכֹל וְלִישֹׁן.[קה,40]

בַּמֶּה דְּבָרִים אֲמוּרִים? כְּשֶׁיֵּשׁ לוֹ פְּנַאי לַעֲשׂוֹת סֻכָּה מִשָּׁעָה שֶׁהִגִּיעַ לַיִּשּׁוּב עַד שְׁעַת הָאֲכִילָה[קו] וְהַשֵּׁנָה שֶׁל עוֹבְרֵי דְרָכִים כַּיּוֹצֵא בּוֹ, דְּהַיְנוּ שֶׁאִם הוּא מְהַלֵּךְ בַּיּוֹם וְלָן בַּלַּיְלָה בְּיִשּׁוּב[קז] וְיֵשׁ פְּנַאי לַעֲשׂוֹת סֻכָּה מִשֶּׁהִגִּיעַ לַיִּשּׁוּב עַד עֵת הָאֲכִילָה וְהַשֵּׁנָה שֶׁל עוֹבְרֵי דְרָכִים הַמְהַלְּכִים בַּיּוֹם וְלָנִין בַּיִּשּׁוּב וּמְמַהֲרִין לֶאֱכֹל וְלִישֹׁן בִּתְחִלַּת הַלַּיְלָה בְּעִנְיָן שֶׁיּוּכְלוּ לָקוּם בְּהַשְׁכָּמָה לֵילֵךְ לְדַרְכָּם. אֲבָל אִם הִגִּיעַ לַיִּשּׁוּב סָמוּךְ לְעֵת הָאֹכֶל[קח] אוֹ לְעֵת הַשֵּׁנָה שֶׁל עוֹבְרֵי דְרָכִים כַּיּוֹצֵא בּוֹ, בְּעִנְיָן שֶׁאִם יַטְרִיחַ לַעֲשׂוֹת סֻכָּה

---

40. *Sukkah* 47a.

דיבור הא'. ארחות חיים הל' סוכה אות לג. מ"א סוף סקט"ו. **צט** גמרא מז, א ורש"י ותוס' ד"ה גמירי. מ"א שם. **ק** מ"א שם. **קא** תוס' דף מז שם. **קב** ראה ארחות חיים שם. **קג** תוס' כו, א ד"ה וחייבין. ר"ן (יב, א) דבור הא'. מ"א סקט"ו. **קד** מ"א שם. **קה** גמרא [ברייתא] שם (וחייבין בלילה). טור ושו"ע ס"ז. **קו** מ"א שם. **קז** תוס' שם. מ"א שם. **קח** מ"א שם.

קֹדֶם עֵת הָאֲכִילָה וְהַשֵּׁנָה שֶׁל עוֹבְרֵי דְרָכִים כַּיּוֹצֵא בוֹ יִהְיֶה לוֹ עִכּוּב בְּדַרְכּוֹ שֶׁלֹּא יוּכַל לֵילֵךְ לְמָחָר בְּהַשְׁכָּמָה לְדַרְכּוֹ – אֵינוֹ צָרִיךְ לִטְרֹחַ וְלַעֲשׂוֹת סֻכָּה, וּמֻתָּר לוֹ לֶאֱכֹל וְלִישֹׁן בְּבַיִת.

וְאֵין צָרִיךְ לוֹמַר שֶׁאִם אֵינוֹ רוֹצֶה לְהִתְעַכֵּב כְּלָל בַּיִּשּׁוּב[קט] רַק לֶאֱכֹל וְלִישֹׁן וּלְמַהֵר לֵילֵךְ לְדַרְכּוֹ, שֶׁאֵינוֹ צָרִיךְ לִטְרֹחַ וְלַעֲשׂוֹת סֻכָּה, כֵּיוָן שֶׁמֵּחֲמַת זֶה יִהְיֶה לוֹ עִכּוּב בְּדַרְכּוֹ.[41] וַאֲפִלּוּ אִם הוּא הוֹלֵךְ לִדְבַר הָרְשׁוּת,[42] מִכָּל מָקוֹם אֵינוֹ מְחֻיָּב לָדוּר בַּסֻּכָּה בִּקְבִיעוּת יְמֵי הֶחָג יוֹתֵר מִמַּה שֶּׁהוּא דָר בִּקְבִיעוּת בְּבֵיתוֹ כָּל הַשָּׁנָה, וּכְשֵׁם שֶׁהוּא מַנִּיחַ אֶת בֵּיתוֹ בְּכָל הַשָּׁנָה וְהוֹלֵךְ לַדֶּרֶךְ – כָּךְ מֻתָּר לוֹ לְהַנִּיחַ סֻכָּתוֹ וְלֵילֵךְ לַדֶּרֶךְ,[קי] וּכְשֵׁם שֶׁבְּכָל הַשָּׁנָה כְּשֶׁהוּא בַּדֶּרֶךְ לִפְעָמִים אֵינוֹ אוֹכֵל בְּתוֹךְ הַבַּיִת כְּדֵי שֶׁלֹּא יִהְיֶה לוֹ עִכּוּב בְּדַרְכּוֹ – כָּךְ מֻתָּר לוֹ לֶאֱכֹל וְלִישֹׁן חוּץ לַסֻּכָּה מִפְּנֵי אִחוּר דַּרְכּוֹ:

יז אוֹתָן הַהוֹלְכִים לַכְּפָרִים לִתְבֹּעַ חוֹבוֹתֵיהֶם[קיא] וְלָנִים שָׁם בַּכְּפָר, כֵּיוָן שֶׁמִּן הַדִּין הֵם חַיָּבִים לַעֲשׂוֹת שָׁם סֻכָּה,[קיב] כֵּיוָן שֶׁהֵם שׁוֹהִים וּמִתְעַכְּבִים הַרְבֵּה בְּכָל כְּפָר וּכְפָר, לָכֵן אִם אֵינָן עוֹשִׂים שָׁם סֻכָּה – אָסוּר לָהֶם לֶאֱכֹל וְלִישֹׁן שָׁם,

time at which travelers similar to himself eat and sleep, his journey will be delayed and he will not be able to rise early the next morning and continue traveling. [Hence] he is not required to take the trouble to build a *sukkah,* but may eat and sleep in a house. Needless to say, when one does not desire to tarry in the settlement at all, but only to eat and sleep and quickly resume his journey, he is not required to take the trouble of building a *sukkah*, because this will delay his journey.[41]

[The above applies] even if one is traveling for his own mundane affairs.[42] Nevertheless, he is not obligated to regard the *sukkah* as his permanent dwelling during Sukkos more than he regards his home as his permanent dwelling throughout the year. Just as throughout the year he sometimes leaves his home and undertakes a journey, so, too, he is permitted to leave his *sukkah* and undertake a journey. And just as occasionally, when he is traveling throughout the year, he does not eat indoors so that his journey will not be delayed, so, too, he is permitted [at this time] to eat and sleep outside the *sukkah* so that his journey will not be delayed.

17 People who travel to villages to collect debts, and [usually] stay overnight in the village, are obligated by law to build a *sukkah* there, because they abide in each village for a long time. Hence, if they do not build a *sukkah* there, they are forbidden to eat and sleep [in the village],

---

41. The preceding sentences evidently related to a new arrival who may possibly spend a few days in the settlement.

42. In the original, *dvar hareshus;* in the more common plural form, *divrei reshus* — lit., "matters that are permissible," as opposed to matters that are obligatory, viz., *mitzvos.*

קט מ"א שם. קי רש"י ותוס' שם ד"ה הולכי. רמ"א ס"ח. קיא ארחות חיים שם. הובא ב"י שם. רמ"א שם. מ"א סקט"ו. קיב מ"א שם. קיג ארחות חיים

but must return to their homes every night to eat and sleep in a *sukkah.*

18 The above [laws] apply to a person who travels for his own mundane affairs. When, by contrast, one travels to [fulfill] a *mitzvah*[43] — e.g., to meet his Torah teacher,[44] to redeem captives, or the like — and he reaches a settlement before he performs the *mitzvah,* he is not required to take the trouble to build a *sukkah.* [Moreover,] even if there is an existing *sukkah* there, if it is not readily accessible to him he does not have to take the trouble and seek after it, but is permitted to eat and sleep in a house.

[The rationale is that] whenever a person is not in his own home and is preoccupied with the *mitzvah* and how it should be carried out, he is considered as being occupied with the performance of a *mitzvah.* And whenever one is involved in the performance of one *mitzvah,* he does not have to seek out another *mitzvah* while he is occupied in the performance of the first.[45] Though he can fulfill both *mitzvos* without delaying or hindering the *mitzvah* which he is occupied with, the Torah exempted him from taking the trouble to seek out a different *mitzvah,* as explained in sec. 38[:7].

When, by contrast, no trouble is involved in seeking out a *sukkah,* such as when there is an accessible *sukkah* at hand, he is obligated to enter it to eat and sleep. If he cannot eat and sleep as well in a *sukkah* as he could in a house and thus will be weary

וּצְרִיכִין הֵם לָשׁוּב לְבָתֵּיהֶם בְּכָל לַיְלָה לֶאֱכֹל וְלִישֹׁן בַּסֻּכָּה:[קיג]

יח וְכָל זֶה בְּמִי שֶׁהוֹלֵךְ לִדְבַר הָרְשׁוּת, אֲבָל מִי שֶׁהוֹלֵךְ לִדְבַר מִצְוָה,[קיד, 43] כְּגוֹן לְהַקְבִּיל פְּנֵי רַבּוֹ[קטו, 44] אוֹ לְפִדְיוֹן שְׁבוּיִים[קטז] וְכַיּוֹצֵא בָּזֶה,[קיז] וְהִגִּיעַ לַיִּשּׁוּב בְּעוֹד שֶׁלֹּא עָשָׂה מִצְוָתוֹ[קיח] — אֵינוֹ צָרִיךְ לִטְרֹחַ וְלַעֲשׂוֹת סֻכָּה. וַאֲפִלּוּ אִם יֵשׁ שָׁם סֻכָּה בְּנוּיָה, אִם אֵינָהּ מְזֻמֶּנֶת לְפָנָיו — אֵינוֹ צָרִיךְ לִטְרֹחַ[קיט] וְלַחֲזֹר אַחֲרֶיהָ,[קכ] וּמֻתָּר לוֹ לֶאֱכֹל וְלִישֹׁן בַּבַּיִת, שֶׁכָּל זְמַן שֶׁאֵינוֹ בְּבֵיתוֹ וְהוּא טָרוּד בְּמַחֲשֶׁבֶת הַמִּצְוָה וּבְתִקּוּנֶיהָ[קכא] — הֲרֵי זֶה נִקְרָא עוֹסֵק בְּמִצְוָה, וְכָל הָעוֹסֵק בְּמִצְוָה[קכב] אַחַת, אֵין צָרִיךְ לִטְרֹחַ וּלְחַזֵּר אַחַר מִצְוָה אַחֶרֶת בְּעוֹד שֶׁהוּא עוֹסֵק בְּמִצְוָה זוֹ.[45] וְאַף עַל פִּי שֶׁאֶפְשָׁר לוֹ לְקַיֵּם שְׁתֵּי הַמִּצְוֹת בְּלִי שׁוּם שִׁהוּי וְעִכּוּב לַהַמִּצְוָה שֶׁעוֹסֵק בָּהּ, מִכָּל מָקוֹם הַתּוֹרָה פְּטָרַתּוּ מִלִּטְרֹחַ וּלְחַזֵּר אַחַר מִצְוָה אַחֶרֶת[קכג] כְּמוֹ שֶׁנִּתְבָּאֵר בְּסִימָן ל"ח.[קכד]

אֲבָל אִם אֵינוֹ צָרִיךְ לִטְרֹחַ וּלְחַזֵּר אַחַר סֻכָּה, כְּגוֹן שֶׁיֵּשׁ סֻכָּה מְזֻמֶּנֶת לְפָנָיו — חַיָּב לִכָּנֵס לְתוֹכָהּ לֶאֱכֹל וְלִישֹׁן.[קכה]

וְאִם אֵינוֹ יָכוֹל לֶאֱכֹל וְלִישֹׁן כָּל כָּךְ בְּטוֹב בַּסֻּכָּה כְּמוֹ בַּבַּיִת וְיִהְיֶה יָגֵעַ לְמָחָר

---

43. In the original, *dvar mitzvah* (*op. cit.,* 25a).

44. And there is an obligation to go out and greet one's Torah teacher, especially during a festival (*op. cit.,* 27b).

45. Cf. *op. cit.,* 25a.

וב"י ורמ"א (המחמיר תע"ב). מ"א שם. קיד משנה כה, א. טור ושו"ע ס"ז. קטו גמרא כו, א. רש"י ותוס' כה, א ד"ה שלוחי. טור ולבוש ס"ז. קטז רש"י ותוס' שם. טור ולבוש שם (ושם גם: גם ללמוד תורה. וראה לעיל סי' תמד סי"ח וש"נ). קיז טור ולבוש שם. קיח אור זרוע הל' סוכה סי' רצט. הגהות אשרי פ"ב סי' ו. קיט מ"א סקי"ד. קכ רא"ש פ"ב סי' ו. קכא רש"י כו, א ד"ה הולכים. קכב גמרא כה, א. וראה גם לעיל ס"ז. קכג ר"ן (יא, א) ד"ה ואיכא. מ"א ס"ק יד. קכד סעיף ז, וש"נ. קכה ר"ן שם ד"ה ומיהו. מ"א שם. וכ"ה לעיל שם.

מֵחֲמַת מְנִיעַת הַשֵּׁנָה וְלֹא יוּכַל לַעֲסֹק בַּמִּצְוָה כָּרָאוּי — פָּטוּר מִלִּישֹׁן בַּסֻּכָּה:[קכו]

on the following day for lack of sleep and will not be able to carry out the *mitzvah* appropriately, he is exempt from sleeping in the *sukkah*.

יט שׁוֹמְרֵי הָעִיר בַּיּוֹם,[קכז] דְּהַיְנוּ כָּל הַיּוֹם הֵן מְהַלְּכִין סְבִיב הָעִיר[קכח] לְשָׁמְרָהּ מִגְּיָסוֹת הַבָּאוֹת עָלֶיהָ[קכט,46] — פְּטוּרִין מִן הַסֻּכָּה כָּל הַיּוֹם,[16] וּמֻתָּר לָהֶם לֶאֱכֹל חוּץ לַסֻּכָּה, וַאֲפִלּוּ אִם יֵשׁ שָׁם סֻכָּה מוּכֶנֶת — אֵינָם צְרִיכִים לִכְנֹס לְתוֹכָהּ לֶאֱכֹל אִם הוּא בְּעִנְיָן שֶׁעַל יְדֵי כֵּן יִתְבַּטְּלוּ מִשְּׁמִירָתָן,[קל] אֲבָל חַיָּבִים בַּסֻּכָּה בַּלַּיְלָה, שֶׁאָז אֵינָן שׁוֹמְרִים אֶת הָעִיר. וְאִם הֵם שׁוֹמְרִים בַּלַּיְלָה וְלֹא בַּיּוֹם — פְּטוּרִים בַּלַּיְלָה וְחַיָּבִים בַּיּוֹם:[קלא]

19 A city's day-guards, i.e., those who patrol the city limits all day long to protect it from attacking troops,[46] are exempt from [the *mitzvah* of] *sukkah* throughout the day,[16] and may eat outside a *sukkah*. Even if there is a *sukkah* ready for them, they are not required to enter it to eat if doing so will [even temporarily] prevent them from guarding. At night they are obligated [to observe the *mitzvah* of] *sukkah,* for at that time they are not guarding the city.

If they are on guard at night, but not by day, they are exempt [from the *mitzvah* of *sukkah*] at night but are obligated by day.

כ שׁוֹמְרֵי גַּנּוֹת וּפַרְדֵּסִים[קלב] שֶׁהֵן קְבוּעִין שָׁם[קלג] בַּיּוֹם וּבַלַּיְלָה — פְּטוּרִין מִן הַסֻּכָּה[16] בֵּין בַּיּוֹם בֵּין בַּלַּיְלָה. וְאַף עַל פִּי שֶׁהֵן קְבוּעִין בְּמָקוֹם אֶחָד כָּל יְמֵי הֶחָג — אַף עַל פִּי כֵן אֵין מְחַיְּבִין אוֹתוֹ לַעֲשׂוֹת סֻכָּה בַּמָּקוֹם הַהוּא, לְפִי שֶׁאִם יַעֲשֶׂה הַשּׁוֹמֵר סֻכָּה בְּמָקוֹם אֶחָד יֵדַע הַגַּנָּב שֶׁיֵּשׁ לוֹ לַשּׁוֹמֵר מָקוֹם קָבוּעַ וְיָבוֹא וְיִגְנֹב מִמָּקוֹם אַחֵר,[קלד] וְנִמְצָא שֶׁעַל יְדֵי הַסֻּכָּה אֵין שְׁמִירָתוֹ כְּלוּם, וְהַתּוֹרָה לֹא חִיְּבָה לַעֲשׂוֹת סֻכָּה אֶלָּא כְּמוֹ שֶׁדָּר בְּבֵיתוֹ, וְזֶה שֶׁמַּנִּיחַ דִּירַת בֵּיתוֹ בִּשְׁבִיל שְׁמִירַת מָמוֹנוֹ מֵהֶפְסֵד — אֵין מְחַיְּבִין אוֹתוֹ לֵישֵׁב בַּסֻּכָּה, שֶׁעַל יְדֵי זֶה יַגִּיעַ לוֹ הֶפְסֵד לְמָמוֹנוֹ.

20 People who guard gardens and orchards and remain there by day and by night are exempt from [the *mitzvah* of] *sukkah*[16] both by day and by night. Even if they remain in one place throughout all the days of the festival, they are not required to build a *sukkah* there, because if a guard makes a *sukkah* in one place, a thief will know that the guard has a fixed place and will attempt to steal from another place. Thus the *sukkah* makes his guarding worthless. [Now,] the Torah has obligated him to build a *sukkah* [to serve him as a dwelling place] only to the extent that his home is his dwelling place. Since [this person] would leave his home to protect himself from financial loss, he is not required to dwell in the *sukkah* when doing so would cause him financial loss.

---

46. *Talmud Yerushalmi, Sukkah* 2:5.

קכו ראבי"ה סי' תרלה. מרדכי רמז תשמ. הגהות מיימוניות פ"ו אות ד. מ"א שם. קכז גמרא [ברייתא] כו, א. טור ושו"ע ס"ט. קכח מ"א סקט"ז. קכט ירושלמי פ"ב ה"ה. מ"א שם. קל ליישב תמיהת הפרי מגדים ולבושי שרד על המ"א שם (משא"כ בשומרי גנות דלקמן ס"כ, לא פטרוהו אלא מלעשות סוכה). קלא ברייתא שם. טור ושו"ע שם. קלב גמרא [ברייתא] שם. טור ושו"ע ס"י. קלג רש"י שם ד"ה שומרי. קלד רבא בגמרא שם ורש"י ד"ה פרצה.

אֲבָל אִם הָיָה שׁוֹמֵר כְּרִי שֶׁל תְּבוּאָה, שֶׁיָּכוֹל לִשְׁמֹר כָּל הַכְּרִי מִמְּקוֹם קְבִיעָתוֹ – חַיָּב לַעֲשׂוֹת לוֹ סֻכָּה בִּמְקוֹם קְבִיעָתוֹ,[קלה] כֵּיוָן שֶׁלֹּא יַגִּיעַ לוֹ שׁוּם הֶפְסֵד עַל יְדֵי כָּךְ, אַף עַל פִּי שֶׁסֻּכָּה זוֹ תִּהְיֶה רְחוֹקָה מִן הָעִיר בְּעִנְיָן שֶׁאִי אֶפְשָׁר לוֹ לְהָבִיא לְשָׁם כָּל כְּלֵי תַשְׁמִישׁוֹ שֶׁהוּא מִשְׁתַּמֵּשׁ בָּהֶן בְּבֵיתוֹ, מִכָּל מָקוֹם כֵּיוָן שֶׁמְּנִיעָה זוֹ אֵינָהּ מֵחֲמַת הַסֻּכָּה, שֶׁהֲרֵי אַף אִם לֹא יַעֲשֶׂה בְּכָאן סֻכָּה לֹא יִשְׁתַּמֵּשׁ בִּכְלֵי תַּשְׁמִישׁוֹ שֶׁבְּבֵיתוֹ, לְכָךְ אֵינוֹ נִפְטָר מִן הַסֻּכָּה בִּשְׁבִיל כָּךְ:[קלו, 47]

If, however, a person is guarding a grainheap, in which instance he is able to guard the entire grainheap while remaining in his fixed place, he is obligated to make himself a *sukkah* at his fixed place, for this will not entail any loss. Though this *sukkah* will be distant from the city, and thus he will not be able to bring all of the utensils that he uses at home, this does not exempt him from [the obligation to dwell in] the *sukkah*,[47] because this inconvenience does not arise from the *sukkah*. Even if he would not build a *sukkah* here, [while guarding the grainheap,] he would likewise not use [all] the utensils in his home.

כא וְכֵן אוֹתָן הַיּוֹשְׁבִין בַּחֲנוּת כָּל הַיּוֹם, אֲפִלּוּ אִם דָּרִים חוּץ לָעִיר רָחוֹק מִן חֲנֻיּוֹתֵיהֶם שֶׁבְּתוֹךְ הָעִיר – אַף עַל פִּי כֵן חַיָּבִים לַעֲשׂוֹת סֻכָּה אֵצֶל חֲנֻיּוֹתֵיהֶם לֶאֱכֹל שָׁם, וְאָסוּר לָהֶם לֶאֱכֹל בְּתוֹךְ הַחֲנוּת.[קלז] וְאִם אִי אֶפְשָׁר לָהֶם לַעֲשׂוֹת סֻכָּה אֵצֶל הַחֲנוּת – צְרִיכִים לָשׁוּב לְבָתֵּיהֶם לֶאֱכֹל בַּסֻּכָּה:[קלח, 48]

21 Similar [laws apply] with regard to people who sit in stores throughout the day. Even if they live outside the city, far from their stores in the city, they are obligated to build a *sukkah* near their stores to eat. It is forbidden for them to eat inside the store. If they cannot make a *sukkah* near the store, they must return home to eat within the *sukkah*.[48]

כב יִשְׂרְאֵלִים הַשְּׂכוּרִים אֵצֶל נָכְרִי בְּחַג הַסֻּכּוֹת לַעֲשׂוֹת בְּתוֹךְ כַּרְמוֹ אֶת יֵינוֹ – פְּטוּרִין מִן הַסֻּכָּה בֵּין בַּיּוֹם וּבֵין בַּלַּיְלָה, לְפִי שֶׁהֵן צְרִיכִים לִשְׁמֹר תָּמִיד אֶת הַיַּיִן מִמַּגַּע נָכְרִי.[קלט, 49]

22 If Jews are hired by a non-Jew on Sukkos to make [kosher] wine in his vineyard, they are exempt from [the *mitzvah* of] *sukkah* both by day and by night, because they are required to guard the wine at all times from being touched by the non-Jew.[49]

---

47. The individual exempted at the end of subsection 15 was far removed from any human habitation. The individual obligated in the present subsection is in a rural setting; while it is not close to a town, it is not far away.

48. As stated in subsection 17. According to the letter of the law, people in this situation could also eat foods other than bread and grain products (or even a small quantity of the latter) in the store, for there is no obligation to eat such foods in a *sukkah*. Nevertheless, as mentioned above, the Lubavitch custom is not to eat or drink anything, even water, outside the *sukkah*. See sec. 639, footnote 35 above.

49. If he were to touch it, it would

טור ושו"ע שם. קלה גמרא שם אליבא דרבא ורש"י ד"ה כריא. טור ושו"ע השם. קלו ראה ר"ן (יב, א) ד"ה רבא אמר. מ"א סקי"ז וראה לעיל סי' תרלט ס"ד וס"ח. קלז מ"א סקט"ז. קלח כדלעיל סי"ז. וראה מסגרת השלחן סי' קלה ס"ק יט. יגדיל תורה (נ.י.) ב ע' נט. קלט הגהת סמ"ק סי' צג אות נג. הגהות מיימוניות (קושטא) פ"ו ה"ד. כלבו הל' סוכה סי' עא (לח, א). רמ"א ס"י.

אֲבָל אִם הוּא בְּעִנְיָן שֶׁאֵין צָרִיךְ לִשְׁמֹר תָּמִיד, כְּגוֹן שֶׁהַיַּיִן כְּבָר נַעֲשָׂה בְּהֶכְשֵׁר וּמֻנָּח בַּחֲצֵרוֹ[קמ] שֶׁל הַנָּכְרִי, שֶׁאֵין הַיִּשְׂרָאֵל צָרִיךְ לִהְיוֹת יוֹשֵׁב וּמְשַׁמֵּר תָּמִיד, אֶלָּא כְּשֶׁהַיִּשְׂרָאֵל דָּר בֶּחָצֵר זוֹ שֶׁהַיַּיִן בְּתוֹכוֹ דַּי בְּכָךְ כְּמוֹ שֶׁיִּתְבָּאֵר בְּיוֹרֶה דֵעָה בְּסִימָן קל"א,[קמא,50] וּלְכָךְ חַיָּב הוּא לַעֲשׂוֹת סֻכָּה בְּחָצֵר זוֹ וְלָדוּר בְּתוֹכָהּ כָּל יְמֵי הֶחָג:

[Different rules apply] if there is no need for them to guard [the wine] continuously; for example, the wine was already made in a kosher manner and was placed in the non-Jew's courtyard, in which instance a Jew need not sit there and guard it at all times. It is sufficient merely for him to dwell in this courtyard, as stated in *Yoreh Deah,* sec. 131.[50] In such a situation he must make a *sukkah* in this courtyard, and dwell in it throughout all the days of the festival.

סימן תרמא שֶׁאֵין מְבָרְכִין שֶׁהֶחֱיָנוּ עַל עֲשִׂיַּת הַסֻּכָּה וּבוֹ ב' סְעִיפִים:

SECTION 641 The Blessing *Shehecheyanu* is Not Recited over the Construction of a *Sukkah.* (1–2)

א הָעוֹשֶׂה סֻכָּה,[א] בֵּין לְעַצְמוֹ שֶׁיֵּשֵׁב בָּהּ הוּא עַצְמוֹ בֶּחָג וּבֵין לַאֲחֵרִים[ב] שֶׁיֵּשְׁבוּ בָהּ בֶּחָג – אֵינוֹ מְבָרֵךְ עַל עֲשִׂיָּתוֹ,[1] דְּהַיְנוּ שֶׁאֵינוֹ מְבָרֵךְ "אֲשֶׁר קִדְּשָׁנוּ בְּמִצְוֹתָיו וְצִוָּנוּ לַעֲשׂוֹת סֻכָּה"[ג] כְּמוֹ שֶׁמְּבָרְכִים עַל עֲשִׂיַּת שְׁאָר כָּל הַמִּצְוֹת,[2] לְפִי שֶׁעֲשִׂיָּתָהּ אֵינָהּ גְּמַר הַמִּצְוָה,[ד,3] שֶׁעִקַּר הַמִּצְוָה הוּא לֵישֵׁב בָּהּ בֶּחָג.

1 Whether one constructs a *sukkah* for himself, so that he himself can dwell in it during the festival, or for others, so that they can dwell in it during the festival, he should not recite a blessing over its construction;[1] i.e., he does not recite a *berachah* blessing Him "Who sanctified us with His commandments and commanded us to build a *sukkah,*" as is done when one performs all the other *mitzvos.*[2] [The rationale is] that constructing the *sukkah* is not the consummation of the *mitzvah,*[3] for the core of the *mitzvah* is to dwell in [the *sukkah*] during the festival.

---

not be called *yein nesech* — lit., "wine poured [in idolatrous worship]." It would, however, now be classified as *stam yeinam* — lit., "their ordinary wine" (i.e., any wine of non-Jews). And "because of their daughters," the Sages forbade the drinking of this wine, too, in order to discourage socializing that could lead to intermarriage and hence to idolatry *(Avodah Zarah* 36b*).*

50. Sec. 131 of the Alter Rebbe's *Shulchan Aruch* is not extant. This law is found in the *Shulchan Aruch* of R. Yosef Caro, *Yoreh Deah* 131:1.

SECTION 641

1. *Menachos* 42a-b.

2. I.e., almost all the other *mitzvos* have similar blessings.

3. Constructing it is thus merely a preparatory phase in the observance of the *mitzvah.*

In *Likkutei Sichos,* Vol. 29, p. 496, the Rebbe distinguishes between preparatory phases that exist at different levels:

(a) Constructing the *sukkah* is a *mitzvah* in its own right. This is the stance of the *Talmud Yerushalmi (Sukkah* 1:2*),* which rules accordingly — though the *halachah* does

קמ מ"א סקי"ח. קמא סימן זה בשוע"ר לא הגיע לידינו, וראה שו"ע שם ס"א (שדוקא בנתנו בחצרו סגי במה שדר בחצר, משא"כ בעושה יינו).
סימן תרמא: א גמרא מנחות מב, א־ב. רמב"ם הל' ברכות פי"א ה"ח. טור ושו"ע. ב תוס' סוכה מו, א ד"ה העושה (הא'). שו"ע. ג שכך היה מקום לברך כשעושה לעצמו (ראה תוס' שם בשם הירושלמי ברכות פ"ט ה"ג. רמב"ם שם). וראה לעיל סי' תלב ס"ד. ד מסקנת הגמרא מנחות שם ע"ב. רמב"ם שם.

אֲבָל "שֶׁהֶחֱיָנוּ" הָיָה רָאוּי לְבָרֵךְ בִּשְׁעַת עֲשִׂיָּה אִם עוֹשֶׂה אוֹתָהּ לְעַצְמוֹ,[ה,4] שֶׁהֲרֵי הִיא מִצְוָה הַבָּאָה מִזְּמַן לִזְמַן;[ו] וְאִם עוֹשֶׂה אוֹתָהּ לַאֲחֵרִים – הָיָה רָאוּי שֶׁבַּעַל הַסֻּכָּה[ז] שֶׁיֵּשֵׁב בָּהּ בֶּחָג יְבָרֵךְ "שֶׁהֶחֱיָנוּ" בִּשְׁעַת עֲשִׂיָּתָהּ, שֶׁעִקַּר הַבְּרָכָה נִתְקְנָה עַל הַשִּׂמְחָה שֶׁיֵּשׁ לָאָדָם מִן הַמִּצְוָה[ח] שֶׁאֵינָהּ תְּדִירָה וּבָאָה מִזְּמַן לִזְמַן, וְעִקַּר הַשִּׂמְחָה הִיא לְבַעַל הַסֻּכָּה וְלֹא לְהָעוֹשֶׂה הַסֻּכָּה.[ט]

אֲבָל אֵין אָנוּ מְבָרְכִין כְּלָל "שֶׁהֶחֱיָנוּ" בִּשְׁעַת עֲשִׂיָּה אֲפִלּוּ אִם עוֹשֶׂה סֻכָּה לְעַצְמוֹ, לְפִי שֶׁאָנוּ סוֹמְכִין עַל בִּרְכַּת "שֶׁהֶחֱיָנוּ" שֶׁאוֹמְרִים בְּקִדּוּשׁ הַיּוֹם[י,5] שֶׁבְּלֵיל יוֹם טוֹב בִּשְׁבִיל מִצְוַת קִדּוּשׁ הַיּוֹם שֶׁהִיא גַּם כֵּן מִצְוָה הַבָּאָה

Nevertheless, it would seem appropriate to recite the blessing *Shehecheyanu* when constructing the *sukkah* if one is making it for oneself,[4] for this is a *mitzvah* that presents itself periodically. Likewise, if one is constructing the *sukkah* for someone else, it would seem appropriate for the owner of the *sukkah,* who will dwell in it during the festival, to recite the blessing *Shehecheyanu* at the time of its construction. For in essence, this blessing was ordained to mark the joy experienced at the performance of a *mitzvah* that is infrequent but presents itself periodically, and the one who primarily experiences this joy is the owner of the *sukkah,* not the person building it.

However, we do not recite the blessing *Shehecheyanu* at the time of construction at all, even if one builds a *sukkah* for himself. [The rationale:] We rely on the blessing *Shehecheyanu* that we recite during *Kiddush*[5] on the [first] night of *Yom-Tov* that [is recited] because of the *mitzvah* of sanctifying the festival, which is also a

---

not follow this ruling — that a blessing should be recited at the time of construction. This stance somewhat resembles an *avodah sheyesh achareha avodah* ("an *avodah* that is followed by an[other] *avodah*"), i.e., a phase in the sacrificial service in the *Beis HaMikdash* that is brought to completion only by certain supplementary activities, as opposed to an *avodah tamah* (lit., "a consummated service"). See *Yoma* 24a.

(b) Constructing the *sukkah* is considered part of the *mitzvah.* This is the view of the *Talmud Bavli (Menachos* 42b*),* which the Alter Rebbe follows in our text.

(c) Further removed and less connected kinds of preparation are called *machshirei mitzvah* — preparatory activities that enable a *mitzvah* to be ultimately performed, e.g., chopping wood to make coals for fashioning a knife for circumcision (see *Shabbos* 130a).

(d) Some other preparations are so distantly related to their respective *mitzvos* that the question of reciting a *berachah* over them does not even arise.

In the same source the Rebbe also contrasts the above cases with the preparation of a *lulav.* The latter case is not mentioned at all by the Alter Rebbe in connection with the blessing *Shehecheyanu,* though *Rambam* equates it with building a *sukkah* and requires that this blessing be recited at that time (see *Mishneh Torah, Hilchos Berachos* 11:8, 9).

4. *Sukkah* 46a.

5. In the original, *Kiddush HaYom* (lit., "the *Kiddush* of the day"). This does not mean "the daytime *Kiddush,*" but "the sanctification of the [festive] day."

טעם הא' בלבוש. וראה גם לעיל סי' יט ס"א (בציצית). סי' רסג קו"א ס"ק ג (שבמסקנא נשאר רק טעם זה). לקו"ש חי"ז ע' 188 הערה 56. שלחן המלך ח"ב ע' רנח. ה ברייתא מו, א. טור ושו"ע. ו רמב"ם שם ה"ט. וכדלעיל סי' תלב ס"ג וש"נ. וראה גם לעיל סי' תקפה ס"ה. ז מ"א סק"א. ח ראה תוס' מו, א ד"ה העושה (הב'). הגהות מיימוניות הל' מילה פ"ג אות ד. לבוש סוף הסי'. וראה לקו"ש חי"ט ע' 372 הערה 12. שלחן המלך ח"ב רנט. יגדיל תורה ב ע' ס. ט ראה מרדכי רמז תשסט. לבוש שם. י רב כהנא בגמרא מו, א. טור ושו"ע. ועד"ז לעיל סי' תלב ס"ג.

מִזְּמַן לִזְמַן,[יא,6] וּבְרָכָה אַחַת עוֹלָה לְכָאן וּלְכָאן:[יב,7]

mitzvah that comes [only] periodically.[6] The one blessing covers both requirements.[7]

ב בַּמֶּה דְּבָרִים אֲמוּרִים?[8] כְּשֶׁמְּקַדֵּשׁ קִדּוּשׁ הַיּוֹם בְּתוֹךְ הַסֻּכָּה, אֲבָל אִם בְּלֵיל יוֹם טוֹב קִדֵּשׁ בְּתוֹךְ הַבַּיִת – אֵינוֹ יוֹצֵא בְּבִרְכַּת "שֶׁהֶחֱיָנוּ" שֶׁצָּרִיךְ לְבָרֵךְ עַל מִצְוַת יְשִׁיבַת הַסֻּכָּה[יג,9] בִּבְרָכָה זוֹ שֶׁאוֹמֵר בַּבַּיִת, וּלְפִיכָךְ כְּשֶׁיִּכָּנֵס לַסֻּכָּה לֶאֱכֹל סְעוּדָה אַחֶרֶת מִשְּׁאָר סְעוּדוֹת הֶחָג – צָרִיךְ לְבָרֵךְ "שֶׁהֶחֱיָנוּ"[יד] אַחַר[10] בִּרְכַּת "לֵישֵׁב בַּסֻּכָּה",[טו] אֲפִלּוּ אֵין הַסֻּכָּה שֶׁלּוֹ:[טז,11]

2 When does the above[8] apply? When one recites *Kiddush* in the *sukkah*. If, however, on the night of *Yom-Tov*, one made *Kiddush* inside his home, reciting the blessing *Shehecheyanu* in his home does not enable him to fulfill the obligation to recite it for the *mitzvah* of dwelling in the *sukkah*.[9]

Therefore when he enters the *sukkah* to eat one of the other meals of the festival, he must recite the blessing *Shehecheyanu*, after[10] reciting the blessing *leishev basukkah*, even if the *sukkah* is not his.[11]

סִימָן תרמב דִּין לַיְלָה רִאשׁוֹנָה שֶׁחָלָה בְּשַׁבָּת וּבוֹ ב' סְעִיפִים:

SECTION 642 The Laws that Apply when the First Night [of Sukkos] Falls on *Shabbos*. (1–2)

א אִם חָל יוֹם רִאשׁוֹן שֶׁל סֻכּוֹת[1] לִהְיוֹת בְּשַׁבָּת – אוֹמֵר הַשְּׁלִיחַ צִבּוּר בְּעַרְבִית בְּרָכָה אַחַת מֵעֵין שֶׁבַע, וּמַזְכִּיר בָּהּ שַׁבָּת וְאֵינוֹ מַזְכִּיר בָּהּ יוֹם טוֹב,[א,2] כְּמוֹ שֶׁנִּתְבָּאֵר בְּסִימָן רס"ח;[ב] עַיֵּן שָׁם:

1 When the first night of Sukkos[1] falls on *Shabbos*, the *sheliach tzibbur* recites the one blessing that summarizes the seven blessings of *Shemoneh Esreh*. In it he mentions the *Shabbos*, but not the festival,[2] for the reason given in sec. 268[:14].

---

6. *Eruvin* 40b.

7. I.e., the *mitzvah* of reciting *Kiddush* for the festival, and the *mitzvah* of building the *sukkah*. It also includes the *mitzvah* of dwelling in the *sukkah*.

Likkutei Sichos (Vol. 22, p. 127, note 42) notes the view of certain authorities that if one recited the blessing *Shehecheyanu* when building the *sukkah*, he should not recite it again at the beginning of the festival — because "the essence of the festival is for the sake of the *sukkah*."

8. That the blessing *Shehecheyanu* recited during *Kiddush* also covers the *mitzvah* of *sukkah*.

9. For he is not fulfilling the *mitzvah* of dwelling in the *sukkah* at the time he recites the blessing.

10. On this sequence, see sec. 643, footnote 5 below.

11. For one may fulfill the *mitzvah* of dwelling in a *sukkah* in a *sukkah* that is not his own, as stated in sec. 637:3.

SECTION 642

1. According to the fixed calendar employed at present, it is impossible for the second night of Sukkos to fall on *Shabbos*.

2. See *Shabbos* 24b.

יא עירובין מ, ב. וראה גם לעיל סי' תריט ס"ז. לקו"ש חל"ז ע' 15 הערה 12. יב רא"ש פסחים פ"א סי' י. טור. והיינו שעולה גם על מצות ישיבת סוכה (כדלקמן ס"ב). וראה אג"ק חט"ו ע' מ. לקו"ש כב ע' 128 בשוה"ג. שלחן המלך ח"ב ע' לז. יג ראה לעיל סוף ס"א, לקמן סוף הסעיף. יד ר"ן (כב, ב) ד"ה ואם, בשם הראב"ד. רמ"א. טו כדלקמן סי' תרמג ס"א. טז שמקיים מצות ישיבת הסוכה גם בסוכה שאינו שלו, כדלעיל סי' תרלז ס"ג.

סימן תרמב: א רבא שבת כד, ב. טור ושו"ע ס"א. ב סעיף יד. ג פיוטים שאומרים בתפלת ערבית של לילות יו"ט. בסידור לא הובאו כלל פיוטים אלו.

2 When the first night [of Sukkos] falls on *Shabbos,* the *Maaravis* hymns[3] are not recited. [Instead,] the *Maaravis* of the first night are recited on the second night.

ב אֵין אוֹמְרִים "מַעֲרָבִית"[ג,3] בְּלֵיל רִאשׁוֹן שֶׁחָל בְּשַׁבָּת,[ד] וּבְלֵיל שֵׁנִי אוֹמְרִים "מַעֲרָבִית" שֶׁל לֵיל רִאשׁוֹן:[ה]

SECTION 643 The Order of *Kiddush.* (1–5)

סימן תרמג סֵדֶר הַקִּדּוּשׁ וּבוֹ ה' סְעִיפִים:

1 [This is] the sequence [of the blessings] when reciting *Kiddush* on the first night of Sukkos.[1] First, one recites a blessing over the wine,[2] then one recites the blessing that sanctifies the festival,[3] then the blessing *leishev basukkah,*[4] and then the blessing *Shehecheyanu.*[5]

[The blessing sanctifying the festival precedes the blessing *leishev basukkah*] because the day must [obviously] be sanctified before one is obligated [to dwell in] a *sukkah.* [The blessing *Shehecheyanu* is recited last,] because it relates to the previously-mentioned sanctification of the day and also to the *mitzvah* of the *sukkah,*[6] as explained in sec. 641[:1].

א סֵדֶר הַקִּדּוּשׁ[א] בְּלֵיל א' שֶׁל סֻכּוֹת,[ב,1] בַּתְּחִלָּה מְבָרֵךְ עַל הַיַּיִן,[2] וְאַחַר כָּךְ אוֹמֵר קִדּוּשׁ הַיּוֹם,[ג,3] וְאַחַר כָּךְ יְבָרֵךְ "לֵישֵׁב בַּסֻּכָּה",[ד,4] שֶׁהֲרֵי עַל כָּרְחֵךְ צָרִיךְ הַיּוֹם לְהִתְקַדֵּשׁ תְּחִלָּה קֹדֶם שֶׁיִּתְחַיֵּב בְּסֻכָּה,[ה] וְאַחַר כָּךְ מְבָרֵךְ "שֶׁהֶחֱיָנוּ"[ו,5] בָּאַחֲרוֹנָה, לְפִי שֶׁבְּרָכָה זוֹ חוֹזֶרֶת עַל קִדּוּשׁ הַיּוֹם וְעַל מִצְוַת סֻכָּה,[ז,6] כְּמוֹ שֶׁנִּתְבָּאֵר בְּסִימָן תרמ"א,[ח] עַיֵּן שָׁם:

2 It is customary not to make a point of stand-

ב וְנוֹהֲגִים שֶׁאֵין מְדַקְדְּקִים לַעֲמֹד

3. Medieval liturgical hymns *(piyyutim)* of this genre — i.e., those composed for the *Yom-Tov* Evening Service — are customarily recited in some Ashkenazic communities. They do not appear in Lubavitch practice at all. See sec. 275:3.

SECTION 643

1. *Sukkah* 56a.

2. I.e., *...borei pri hagafen.*

3. In the original, *Kiddush HaYom;* i.e., the blessing that ends, *...mekadesh Yisrael vehazmanim.*

4. The words mean "to dwell... in the *sukkah.*" See subsection 2 below.

5. On the second night of Sukkos, the order of the blessings *leishev basukkah* and *Shehecheyanu* is reversed *(Shulchan Aruch* of R. Yosef Caro, sec. 661; see also *Sefer HaMinhagim: The Book of Chabad-Lubavitch Customs,* p. 144*).* The blessing *Shehecheyanu* is recited on the second night only because of *Kiddush,* so that the second day of *Yom-Tov* should not be perceived as less significant than the first. It is therefore recited directly after *Kiddush.* By contrast, at that moment the *mitzvah* of *sukkah* does not warrant the blessing *Shehecheyanu,* for — as mentioned in sec. 641 — that blessing would be appropriate even if it was recited before the festival, when constructing the *sukkah.* Therefore, even if the first day were to be viewed as a weekday, there would be no need to repeat the blessing *Shehecheyanu* over the *sukkah* itself.

6. This includes both the *mitzvah* of building the *sukkah* and the *mitzvah* of dwelling in it.

ד כדלעיל סי' ערה ס"ג. ה לבוש. מ"א. וכדלעיל סי' תפט סכ"ח.

סימן תרמג: א מסקנת הגמרא נו, א (סוכה ואח"כ זמן). טור שו"ע ס"א. ב משא"כ בליל ב' — זמן ואח"כ סוכה. רא"ש פ"ד סי' ד. הגהות מיימוניות פ"ו אות ש, בשם רבנו יעקב ברבנו שמשון. טור ורמ"א סי' תרסא. וראה גם הגהות אדמו"ר מוהרש"ב לסידור תורה אור. ספר המנהגים — חב"ד ע' 67. אג"ק ח"ה ע' ז. ג כבית הלל בברייתא נו, א. טור ושו"ע שם. וראה לעיל סי' תעג ס"ו. ד טור ושו"ע שם. ה לבוש ס"א. ו מסקנת הגמרא שם. טור ושו"ע שם. ז טור ושו"ע שם. ונתבאר בט"ז ס"ק א. ח סעיף א.

בִּשְׁעַת הַקִּדּוּשׁ[7] אֶלָּא מְקַדְּשִׁין אֲפִלּוּ מְיֻשָּׁב,[ט] וְאַף בִּרְכַּת "לֵישֵׁב בַּסֻּכָּה" אוֹמְרִים אֲפִלּוּ מְיֻשָּׁב:[י]

וְאַף עַל פִּי שֶׁכָּל הַמִּצְווֹת מְבָרֵךְ עֲלֵיהֶם עוֹבֵר לַעֲשִׂיָּתָן,[יא,8] וְהָיָה נָכוֹן לְבָרֵךְ "לֵישֵׁב בַּסֻּכָּה" קֹדֶם שֶׁיֵּשֵׁב לֶאֱכֹל,[יב] שֶׁהַיְשִׁיבָה הִיא הַמִּצְוָה,[יג] שֶׁנֶּאֱמַר[יד,9] "בַּסֻּכֹּת תֵּשְׁבוּ",[10] וְאַף עַל פִּי שֶׁאֵין מִצְוָה כְּלָל לֵישֵׁב מַמָּשׁ,[טו] שֶׁ"תֵּשְׁבוּ" הוּא לָשׁוֹן תִּתְעַכְּבוּ,[טז,11] כְּמוֹ שֶׁנֶּאֱמַר[יז,12] "וַתֵּשְׁבוּ[11] בְקָדֵשׁ יָמִים רַבִּים", מִכָּל מָקוֹם אֵין לְבָרֵךְ אֶלָּא בְּשָׁעָה שֶׁנִּכָּר הָעַכָּבָה וְהַקְּבִיעוּת, דְּהַיְנוּ בִּישִׁיבָה מַמָּשׁ, שֶׁבָּזֶה מַרְאֶה עַצְמוֹ שֶׁרוֹצֶה לְהִתְעַכֵּב שָׁם, אֲבָל כָּל שֶׁעוֹמֵד אֵין נִכָּר כְּלָל הָעַכָּבָה וְהַקְּבִיעוּת שֶׁאֶפְשָׁר שֶׁתֵּכֶף יַחֲזֹר וְיֵצֵא.[יח]

וְכֵיוָן שֶׁעִקַּר הַמִּצְוָה הִיא הָעַכָּבָה וְהַקְּבִיעוּת הָיָה רָאוּי לְבָרֵךְ קֹדֶם הָעַכָּבָה וְהַקְּבִיעוּת, דְּהַיְנוּ קֹדֶם הַיְשִׁיבָה,[יט] אֶלָּא שֶׁלְּפִי שֶׁעִקַּר הַמִּצְוָה שֶׁאָנוּ מְבָרְכִין עָלֶיהָ הִיא הָאֲכִילָה,[כ] שֶׁהֲרֵי אִם יוֹשֵׁב

ing while [reciting] *Kiddush;*[7] it is recited even while one is seated. Moreover, even the blessing *leishev basukkah* may be recited while sitting. Now, all of the blessings that were ordained over the performance of the *mitzvos* are recited before one fulfills them.[8] It would thus be appropriate to recite the blessing *leishev basukkah* before one sits down to eat, for sitting down [to eat] constitutes the *mitzvah,* as it is written,[9] "And you shall dwell[10] in *sukkos.*"

The *mitzvah* is not that one should actually sit, for תשבו [in that verse] means "you shall dwell,"[11] as in the verse,[12] "And you dwelt[11] (ותשבו) in Kadesh for many days." Nevertheless, it is proper to recite the blessing only when it is evident that one is abiding [in the *sukkah*] more than momentarily. This is evident when one actually sits; taking a seat shows that one intends to remain there for some time. When, by contrast, a person stands, it is not evident that he intends to remain [in the *sukkah*] more than momentarily, for he may take his leave at any time.

Thus, since the core of the *mitzvah* is to remain [in the *sukkah*] in more than a transient manner, it would be appropriate to recite the blessing before one [does this], i.e. before one sits. Nonetheless, since the essence of the *mitzvah* over which we recite the blessing is eating —

7. Based on the teachings of the *AriZal*, Lubavitch custom is to stand when reciting *Kiddush* on Sukkos and throughout the year *(Sefer HaMinhagim: The Book of Chabad-Lubavitch Customs,* p. 55*).*

8. In the original, *over laasiyasan (Pesachim* 7b*).*

9. *Vayikra* 23:43.

10. The root ישב means both "sit" and "dwell."

11. The word here implies remaining in one place.

12. *Devarim* 1:46, as quoted in *Megillah* 21a.

ט רא"ש פ"ד סי' ג (שאפשר גם אחר שישב). טור. רמ"א ס"ב (שנוהגין לקדש מיושב). מ"א סק"א. ולענין עמידה בקידוש בשבת ויו"ט, ראה לעיל סי' רעא סי"ט וש"נ. י רא"ש שם. טור. לבוש ס"ב. וראה לעיל סי' ח ס"ג (כל ברכת המצות צריך להיות מעומד). פרמ"ג שם אשל אברהם סוף סק"ב. יא פסחים ז, ב. וכדלעיל סי' מו ס"ג וש"נ. יב רא"ש שם, ומ"מ פ"ו הי"ב, בדעת הרמב"ם שם (שהצריך לברך קודם שישב). יג ב"י ד"ה והרמב"ם, בדעת הרמב"ם שם. יד ויקרא כג, מב. ב"ח ד"ה ומ"ש והרמב"ם, בדעת הרמב"ם שם. טו מגיד משנה שם. ב"ח שם לדעת הרא"ש. ט"ז סק"ב אף לדעת הרמב"ם שם. טז רא"ש שם. טור. לבוש שם. ט"ז שם. יז דברים א, מו. מגילה כא, סוע"א (ברא"ש וטור הביאו הפסוק שבבמדבר כ, א: וישב העם בקדש). יח ט"ז שם. יט ט"ז שם. כ ט"ז שם לדעת הרא"ש שם. מ"א שם. כא סי"ב. וראה שם סט"ז. כב ט"ז שם. כג רמ"א ס"ג. כד ט"ז סק"ד. ומנהג חב"ד בקידוש היום של יו"ט ושבת חוהמ"ס

בַּסֻּכָּה וְאֵינוֹ אוֹכֵל אֵינוֹ מְבָרֵךְ כְּמוֹ שֶׁנִּתְבָּאֵר בְּסִימָן תרל"ט,[כא] לְפִיכָךְ אֵין אָנוּ חוֹשְׁשִׁין אֶלָּא לְהַקְדִּים הַבְּרָכָה לְהָאֲכִילָה שֶׁהִיא עִקַּר הַמִּצְוָה שֶׁעָלֶיהָ מְבָרְכִין,[כב] אֲבָל לֹא לְהַקְדִּימָהּ לִפְנֵי הַיְשִׁיבָה וְהַקְּבִיעוּת, לְפִי שֶׁהִיא לְבַדָּהּ בְּלֹא אֲכִילָה אֵינָהּ עִקַּר הַמִּצְוָה שֶׁעָלֶיהָ מְבָרְכִין:[13]

for if a person sits in a *sukkah* and does not eat, he should not recite a blessing, as explained in sec. 639[:12] — we are concerned only that the blessing [over the *sukkah*] should be recited before one eats, for this is the essence of the *mitzvah* over which the blessing is recited, and not before remaining [in the *sukkah*] in more than a transient manner. For [the latter instance] alone, i.e., when one does not eat, is not the essence of the *mitzvah* over which a blessing is recited.[13]

ג וְכָל זֶה[כג] בְּלֵיל יוֹם טוֹב אוֹ בְּלֵיל שַׁבָּת שֶׁיֵּשׁ בָּהֶן קִדּוּשׁ הַיּוֹם לְכָךְ הוּא סוֹמֵךְ בִּרְכַּת הַסֻּכָּה לְקִדּוּשׁ הַיּוֹם, אֲבָל בִּשְׁאָר סְעוּדוֹת הֶחָג, אֲפִלּוּ בִּסְעוּדַּת שַׁבָּת וְיוֹם טוֹב שַׁחֲרִית שֶׁמְּבָרֵךְ עַל הַכּוֹס, כֵּיוָן שֶׁאֵינוֹ אוֹמֵר קִדּוּשׁ הַיּוֹם[14] — אֵינוֹ אוֹמֵר "לֵישֵׁב בַּסֻּכָּה" קֹדֶם שְׁתִיַּת הַכּוֹס,[15] לְפִי שֶׁצָּרִיךְ לִסְמֹךְ בְּרָכָה זוֹ לְהָאֲכִילָה שֶׁהִיא עִקַּר הַמִּצְוָה שֶׁעָלֶיהָ מְבָרְכִין:[כד]

3 All of the above applies on the night of *Yom-Tov* or on Friday night, when one sanctifies the day [by reciting *Kiddush*], and hence the blessing over the *sukkah* immediately follows the blessing sanctifying the day. It does not apply at the meals [eaten] on the other [days of] Sukkos, nor even at the morning meals eaten on *Shabbos* and *Yom-Tov* [before which] one recites a blessing over a cup [of wine]. At those times, since one is not reciting a blessing sanctifying the day,[14] one should not recite the blessing *leishev basukkah* before drinking the cup [of wine],[15] in order that it should be recited directly before eating, for this is the essence of the *mitzvah* over which the blessing is being recited.

ד וּמִן הַדִּין הָיָה רָאוּי לְבָרֵךְ בְּרָכָה זוֹ קֹדֶם בִּרְכַּת "הַמּוֹצִיא",[כה] שֶׁהֲרֵי חוֹבַת בְּרָכָה זוֹ חָל עָלָיו מִתְּחִלָּה מִיָּד שֶׁיֵּשֵׁב לֶאֱכֹל וְרָאוּי לְהַקְדִּימָהּ לְבִרְכַּת הַמּוֹצִיא שֶׁאֵינָהּ

4 According to the law it would be appropriate to recite this blessing before the blessing *HaMotzi,* since the obligation to recite this blessing applies as soon as one sits down to eat. Therefore it would be fitting to recite it before the blessing *HaMotzi,* which he is not required

---

13. When the blessing *leishev basukkah* appears in the course of *Kiddush,* Lubavitch custom is to recite it while standing (see footnote 7 above). Otherwise it is recited while sitting, as is the universal Ashkenazic custom.

14. I.e., in the daytime *Kiddush* one recites only the blessing *borei pri hagafen* over the wine, and not the blessing sanctifying the day.

15. On the *Yom-Tov* days of Sukkos and on *Shabbos,* Lubavitch custom is to recite the blessing *leishev basukkah* after *Kiddush* and before partaking of the wine, both at night and by day *(Sefer HaMinhagim: The Book of Chabad-Lubavitch Customs,* p. 143*)*.

שמברכין לישב בסוכה אחר הקידוש (ספר המנהגים — חב"ד ע' 67. אוצר מנהגי חב"ד סוכות ע' שח). כמו כן נוהגים לברך לישב בסוכה בהבדלה (ראה אוצר מנהגי חב"ד ע' שם ע' שכד. וראה לעיל סי' תרלט ס"ו). **כה** מהר"מ מרוטנבורג בתשב"ץ סי' קמב (שכן יש לנהוג). הובא ברא"ש פ"ד סי' ג וטור.

חוֹבָה עָלָיו עַד שֶׁרוֹצֶה לִטְעֹם.[כו]

וּמִכָּל מָקוֹם נוֹהֲגִים הָעוֹלָם לְבָרֵךְ בְּרָכָה זוֹ אַחַר בִּרְכַּת "הַמּוֹצִיא",[כז] לְפִי שֶׁבִּרְכַּת "הַמּוֹצִיא" הִיא הַתְחָלַת הַסְּעוּדָה, וְרָאוּ הָעוֹלָם לְהַתְחִיל בִּסְעוּדָה קֹדֶם בִּרְכַּת הַסֻּכָּה, לְפִי שֶׁאֵין מְבָרְכִין בִּרְכַּת הַסֻּכָּה אֶלָּא בִּשְׁעַת סְעוּדָה,[כח] וְאֵין בִּרְכַּת הַסֻּכָּה חֲשׁוּבָה הֶפְסֵק בֵּין בִּרְכַּת "הַמּוֹצִיא" לַאֲכִילָה, כֵּיוָן שֶׁבְּרָכָה זוֹ הִיא מִצָּרְכֵי הַסְּעוּדָה[כט] וְכָל שֶׁהוּא לְצֹרֶךְ הַסְּעוּדָה אֵינוֹ חָשׁוּב הֶפְסֵק, כְּמוֹ שֶׁנִּתְבָּאֵר בְּסִימָן קס"[ז]:[ל]

ה אִם לֹא בֵּרַךְ "שֶׁהֶחֱיָנוּ" בְּלֵיל הָרִאשׁוֹן וְנִזְכַּר לְמָחָר – אוֹמֵר בְּשָׁעָה שֶׁנִּזְכַּר[לא,16] אֲפִלּוּ שֶׁלֹּא עַל הַכּוֹס.[לב,17] וְאִם לֹא נִזְכַּר לְמָחָר, וְגַם בְּלֵיל שֵׁנִי שָׁכַח וְלֹא בֵּרַךְ "שֶׁהֶחֱיָנוּ", וְנִזְכַּר בְּאֶחָד מִשְּׁאָר יְמֵי הֶחָג – יְבָרֵךְ אֵימָתַי שֶׁנִּזְכַּר, שֶׁבִּרְכַּת "שֶׁהֶחֱיָנוּ" יֵשׁ לָהּ תַּשְׁלוּמִין כָּל שִׁבְעָה,[לג] כְּמוֹ שֶׁנִּתְבָּאֵר בְּסִימָן תע"ג[לד] לְעִנְיַן פֶּסַח, אֶלָּא שֶׁבְּחַג הַסֻּכּוֹת כְּשֶׁהוּא מְבָרֵךְ "שֶׁהֶחֱיָנוּ" – צָרִיךְ לְבָרֵךְ תּוֹךְ הַסֻּכָּה,[18] כְּדֵי לִפְטֹר גַּם אֶת הַסֻּכָּה,[19] כְּמוֹ שֶׁנִּתְבָּאֵר בְּסִימָן תרמ"א:[לה]

to recite until he desires to partake [of the bread].

Nevertheless, it has become universal custom to recite this blessing after the blessing *HaMotzi,* because the blessing *HaMotzi* marks the beginning of the meal, and people at large saw it fitting to begin the meal before reciting the blessing over the *sukkah,* because that blessing is recited only at the time of a meal.

The blessing over the *sukkah* is not considered an interruption between the blessing *HaMotzi* and eating, because this blessing is an integral necessity for the meal, and whenever an activity is necessary for a meal, it is not considered an interruption, as explained in sec. 167[:9].

5 If one did not recite the blessing *Shehecheyanu* on the first night [of *Yom-Tov*] and remembered the next day, he should recite it when he remembers,[16] even though he will not be reciting it over a cup of wine.[17] If he does not remember on the following day and also forgets [when reciting *Kiddush*] on the second night, and remembers during one of the other days of the festival, he should recite the blessing whenever he remembers. For one may compensate for [the failure to recite] the blessing *Shehecheyanu* throughout the seven days [of the festival], as explained in sec. 473[:2], with regard to Pesach. On Sukkos, however, the blessing *Shehecheyanu* must be recited in the *sukkah,*[18] in order that the blessing should fulfill one's obligation to relate it to the *sukkah* as well,[19] as explained in sec. 641[:1-2].

16. *Sukkah* 47b.

17. I.e., even though he will be reciting the blessing *Shehecheyanu* on the second day of the holiday, he should not wait until then, but should recite it as soon as he remembers. See also sec. 619:7.

18. As opposed to the blessing *Shehecheyanu* on Pesach, which can be recited "in the marketplace" (sec. 473:2).

19. And not only to the festival.

כו ב"י סוף הסי' (לסמוך ברכה לישיבה). ט"ז סק"ד (כדאמרינן בגמרא נו, א: חובא דיומא עדיף). כז הגהת הר"פ בתשב"ץ שם. רא"ש שם. טור ושו"ע ס"ג. כח רא"ש שם. טור. כט ב"י שם. לבוש ס"ג. מ"א סק"ב. וכמו בכל קידוש והבדלה, כדלעיל סי' קצ ס"א. סי' רצו ס"א. סי' תעג ס"ו. ל סעיף ט. לא גמרא מז, ב. מ"א ריש הסי'. לב רב נחמן שם. וראה גם לעיל סי' תריט ס"ז. לג גמרא שם. מ"א שם. וראה לקו"ש חל"ז ע' 15־16. שלחן המלך ח"ב ע' קכ־קכא. לד סעיף ב. לה ס"ב.

SECTION 644 The Order Followed for *Hallel* on All the Days of the Festival. (1)

1 After the *sheliach tzibbur* repeats the morning *Shemoneh Esreh,* we take [in hand] the *lulav* and the other species in order to fulfill the positive Scriptural commandment,[1] "And you shall take for yourselves on the first day...."[2] [Before observing this commandment,] we recite the blessings *Al Netilas Lulav* and *Shehecheyanu.* The manner in which the *lulav* is taken, the blessings recited, and the *naanuim,*[3] will be described in sec. 651.[4]

It is a positive *mitzvah* of Rabbinic origin to recite the whole of *Hallel* on all eight days of the festival because each day is considered as a *Yom-Tov* in its own right, for the sacrifices offered on each day are different from those of all the other days. On Pesach, by contrast, since the sacrifices offered on all the days of the festival are the same, the Sages ordained that the complete *Hallel* should be recited only on the first day.[5] All the

סימן תרמד סֵדֶר הַהַלֵּל כָּל יְמֵי הֶחָג וּבוֹ סָעִיף אֶחָד:

א אַחַר שֶׁחָזַר שְׁלִיחַ צִבּוּר תְּפִלַּת הַשַּׁחַר – נוֹטְלִין הַלּוּלָב וּמִינָיו[א] לְקַיֵּם מִצְוַת עֲשֵׂה שֶׁל תּוֹרָה,[1] שֶׁנֶּאֱמַר[ב] "וּלְקַחְתֶּם לָכֶם בַּיּוֹם הָרִאשׁוֹן וגו'",[2] וּמְבָרְכִין "עַל נְטִילַת לוּלָב"[ג] וְ"שֶׁהֶחֱיָנוּ".[ד] וְסֵדֶר נְטִילָתוֹ וּבִרְכוֹתָיו וְנִעְנוּעוֹ[3] – יִתְבָּאֵר בְּסִימָן תרנ"א.[ה,4]

וּמִצְוַת עֲשֵׂה מִדִּבְרֵי סוֹפְרִים[ו] לִגְמֹר הַהַלֵּל כָּל שְׁמוֹנַת יְמֵי הֶחָג,[ז] לְפִי שֶׁכָּל יוֹם וָיוֹם נֶחְשָׁב לְיוֹם טוֹב בִּפְנֵי עַצְמוֹ,[ח] כֵּיוָן שֶׁחָלוּק בְּקָרְבְּנוֹתָיו מִשְּׁאָר יָמִים, מַה שֶּׁאֵין כֵּן בְּפֶסַח שֶׁכָּל קָרְבְּנוֹת שֶׁל כָּל הַיָּמִים הֵן שָׁוִין, לְפִיכָךְ לֹא תִקְּנוּ לִגְמֹר הַהַלֵּל אֶלָּא בְּיוֹם רִאשׁוֹן בִּלְבַד.[ט,5] וְכָל מִשְׁפַּט

1. *Vayikra* 23:40.

2. Based on the teachings of the *AriZal,* the Alter Rebbe recommends in his *Siddur* that one should fulfill this *mitzvah* early in the morning, before beginning one's prayers (and before eating). In this way, the *mitzvah* can be fulfilled in the *sukkah,* enabling the spiritual influence of the *sukkah* to enhance the performance of the *mitzvah.* (See *Siddur Tehillat HaShem* Annotated Edition, p. 306; *Likkutei Sichos,* Vol. 22, p. 124ff.) *Otzar Minhagei Chabad,* p. 293, states in the name of the Rebbe that it is preferable to associate the fulfillment of the *mitzvah* of *lulav* and *esrog* in the *sukkah* with the recitation of the blessing *leishev basukkah.* Hence, after fulfilling that *mitzvah,* it is desirable to partake of an amount of cake or the like that requires that blessing (see sec. 639:11).

On the question of refreshments before the morning prayers, see the footnotes to sec. 89:5.

3. I.e., the moving or shaking of the *lulav.*

4. It appears that only part of that section was ever published in the Alter Rebbe's *Shulchan Aruch.* The remaining laws of that section and the later sections are not extant. The very last subsection printed in that section speaks of reciting the blessing before performing the *mitzvah.*

5. The entire *Hallel* is also recited on the second day of Pesach in the Diaspora, where it is comparable to the first day. On the remaining days, both in *Eretz Yisrael* and in the Diaspora, two of its passages are omitted, as on Rosh Chodesh (see sec. 490:6-7).

א טור ושו"ע ס"א. ובסידור (דיני הלולב): ומן הדין יש לברך על הלולב אחר התפלה קודם ההלל אלא שמצות נטילתו בסוכה הוא מצוה מן המובחר ואי אפשר לצאת מבית הכנסת מפני הרואים, לפיכך בבוקר קודם שיתפלל בעודו בסוכה יברך. וראה לקו"ש חכ"ב ע' 124 ואילך. ב ויקרא כג, מ. ג כדלקמן סי' תרנא סי"ז וש"נ. ד רא"ש פ"ד סי' ב. טור ושו"ע שם. ה רובו של סי' זה לא הגיע לידינו, וראה שו"ע שם ונו"כ ס"ה ואילך. סידור שם. ו רמב"ם הל' חנוכה פ"ג ה"ו. ב"י ד"ה ומברכין. לבוש ס"א. וראה לעיל סי' תפח ס"ב: מצוה מדברי סופרים מתקנת הנביאים, וש"נ. ז תענית כח, ב. ערכין י, א. טור ושו"ע שם. ח רש"י תענית כח, ב ד"ה יחיד. תוס' שם ד"ה ויום טוב. טור. לבוש ס"א. וראה גם לעיל סי' תצ ס"ו וסוף סט"ז. ט גמרא ערכין י, רע"ב. רש"י ותוס' שם. וראה גם לעיל סי' תצ ס"ו.

הַהַלֵּל וְהִלְכוֹתָיו וְיָמִים שֶׁגּוֹמְרִין אוֹתוֹ – כְּבָר נִתְבָּאֵר בְּסִימָן תפ"ח, עַיֵּן שָׁם וּבְסִימָן תכ"[ב].[יא,6]

principles governing [the recitation of] *Hallel,* its laws, and the days on which *Hallel* is completed, have already been explained in sec. 488[:2-4] and 422.[6]

וְאֵין אוֹמְרִים "אֵל נָא לְעוֹלָם תְּעֻרַץ" בַּפִּיּוּטִים שֶׁל יוֹם רִאשׁוֹן שֶׁל סֻכּוֹת:[יב,7]

[The hymn] *E-l Na LeOlam Tuaratz* is not recited among the liturgical hymns of the first day of Sukkos.[7]

---

6. This section of the Alter Rebbe's *Shulchan Aruch* is not extant. In the *Shulchan Aruch* of R. Yosef Caro, this section describes the prayers recited on Rosh Chodesh and the custom of reciting *Hallel* on that day.

7. No *piyyutim* for Sukkos appear in the Alter Rebbe's *Siddur*.

י סעי' ב־ד. **יא** סימן זה בשוע"ר לא הגיע לידינו, וראה שו"ע שם ס"ב ואילך. **יב** לבוש שם. מ"א סוף הסי'. בסידור לא הובא שום פיוט לסוכות.

הִלְכוֹת לוּלָב
LAWS REGARDING THE LULAV

סימן תרמה דִּינֵי לוּלָב וּבוֹ כ"א סְעִיפִים:

SECTION 645 Laws Relating to the *Lulav*. (1–21)

א "וּלְקַחְתֶּם[א] לָכֶם בַּיּוֹם הָרִאשׁוֹן פְּרִי עֵץ הָדָר כַּפֹּת תְּמָרִים וַעֲנַף עֵץ עָבֹת וְעַרְבֵי נָחַל וגו'",[ב,1] וְדָרְשׁוּ[3] חֲכָמִים[ג,3] "פְּרִי עֵץ"[2] – שֶׁהָעֵץ כְּפִרְיוֹ בְּטַעַם שָׁוֶה,[ד] וְאֵיזֶה? זֶה אֶתְרוֹג שֶׁטַּעַם עֵצוֹ וּפִרְיוֹ שָׁוֶה:[4]

1 [It is written:] "And on the first day, you shall take for yourselves the fruit of a beautiful tree, fronds of a date-palm, a branch of a braided tree, and willows of the brook."[1]

From the words "the fruit of a tree,"[2] the Sages extrapolated[3] that the verse alludes to a tree whose wood has the same flavor as its fruit. Which [species] is that? A citron *(esrog)*, for its wood and its fruit share the same taste.[4]

ב "הָדָר"[5] – שֶׁיִּהְיֶה נָאֶה,[ה,6] וְ"הָדָר" בְּתָאֳרוֹ וּבְגִדּוּלוֹ, וְעַל דֶּרֶךְ שֶׁיִּתְבָּאֵר בְּסִימָן תרמ"ח.

וּלְפִי שֶׁכָּל אַרְבָּעָה מִינִים[7] אֵלּוּ כְּתוּבִים בְּפָסוּק אֶחָד[ו] – הֲרֵי הֻקְּשׁוּ זֶה לָזֶה[8] וּלְמֵדִין זֶה מִזֶּה, לְפִיכָךְ כָּל ד' מִינִים אֵלּוּ צְרִיכִים לִהְיוֹת נָאִים וּמְהֻדָּרִים[ז] בְּתָאֳרָם וּבְגִדּוּלָם, וְעַל דֶּרֶךְ שֶׁיִּתְבָּאֵר:

2 The word "beautiful"[5] implies that [this fruit] must be attractive[6] and comely in its appearance and shape, as will be explained in sec. 648. And, since all of the four species[7] appear in the same verse, they are likened to one another by a textual association,[8] and the characteristics of one are also applied to the others. Hence all these Four Species must be attractive and comely in their appearance and shape, as will be explained.

---

1. *Vayikra* 23:40. As will be explained in the forthcoming sections, the last four phrases allude respectively to the *esrog* (a citron), the *lulav* (a closed palm frond), the *hadassim* (myrtle twigs), and the *aravos* (willow twigs).

2. In the original, *pri etz.*

3. *Sukkah* 35a.

4. Commenting on *Sukkah* 35a, the source for this statement, the *Chasam Sofer (Orach Chayim,* Responsum 207) cites the following explanation in the name of *Maharam* Chaviv: The sap of any other citrus tree — the flavor of the tree — tastes the same as the peel of its fruit; the fruit itself has a different flavor. In the case of the *esrog,* the actual flesh of its fruit — i.e., the innermost clusters of juice-bearing sacs among which the seeds are embedded — is so minimal as to be insignificant. These clusters (or fruity seed compartments) are surrounded by an extremely thick mass of white, pulpy material. (Fig. 28 on p. 186 below shows an *esrog* in cross-section.) Since it is this mass that is edible, it can certainly be called "the fruit" of the *esrog* tree. And its taste is the same as that of the sap.

5. In the original, *hadar.*

6. *Sukkah* 31a.

7. In the original, *daled minim* (often: *arbaah minim*).

8. I.e., by a *hekesh.*

א לכללות הסימנים תרמה-תרנא, ראה ארבעת המינים ע"פ שו"ע אדמו"ר הזקן (ויינר). **ב** ויקרא כג, מ. **ג** גמרא [ברייתא] לה, א. רי"ף שם (יז, א). רא"ש פ"ג סי' טו. **ד** רש"י שם ד"ה פרי. **ה** גמרא לא, א (בעי הדר). לבוש ס"א (הדר ויפה). **ו** תוס' שם ד"ה ור"י סבר. לבוש שם. **ז** רבא שם לרבי יהודה (לענין לולב). ר"ן (יג, ב) ד"ה לולב (וילפינן שאר מינין מאתרוג). לבוש שם.

3 The term "fronds of a date-palm" denotes a *lulav* that grows on a date-palm.[9] Since the Torah used the term [כַּפֹּת [תְּמָרִים — *kapos [tmarim]* — instead of the "leaves of a date-palm" *(alei tmarim)*, we learn that the leaves must be such that can be brought together and bound together[10] with the *shidrah* (the spine),[11] because they are still pliable. [This concept is derived,] because vowel points[12] are not written in the Torah, and the term כַּפֹּת *(kapos)* could be interpreted as if it was written כָּפוּת *(kafus)*, meaning "bound."[13]

If, however, the *lulav* remains on the date-palm until its leaves became as stiff as wood and they spread out and became separated from the spine, [difficulties arise]. The stiffer they become, the more do they spread away from the spine. If they have become so firm that they can no longer be bound together with the spine, [the *lulav*] is invalid.[13]

4 If [the leaves] have not stiffened to that extent, [the *lulav*] is valid, even if when they are not bound together they would stand separate and apart from each other.[13] [See fig. 19.] Indeed, [it is valid] even if they are not actually bound together,[14] because the Torah

ג "כַּפֹּת תְּמָרִים" — זֶה לוּלָב שֶׁהוּא גָּדֵל עַל אִילָן שֶׁל תְּמָרִים,[9] וּמִתּוֹךְ שֶׁכָּתְבָה הַתּוֹרָה לְשׁוֹן "כַּפֹּת" וְלֹא כָּתְבָה "עֲלֵי תְמָרִים", מִכָּאן אַתָּה לָמֵד שֶׁצָּרִיךְ שֶׁיִּהְיֶה אוֹתָן עָלִים הָרְאוּיִין לְאָגְדָן וְלִכְפּוֹתָן[10] עִם הַשִּׁדְרָה[ח,11] מֵחֲמַת שֶׁהֵן עֲדַיִן רַכִּים, שֶׁהֲרֵי לֹא נִכְתְּבוּ נְקֻדּוֹת בַּתּוֹרָה,[12] וּפֵרוּשׁוֹ הוּא "כָּפוּת."[ט,13] אֲבָל אִם שָׁהָה הַלּוּלָב עַל הַדֶּקֶל עַד שֶׁנִּתְקַשּׁוּ עָלָיו כְּעֵץ וְנִתְרַחֲקוּ וְנִתְפָּרְדוּ מֵהַשִּׁדְרָה, שֶׁכֵּן הוּא דַּרְכָּן שֶׁכָּל מַה שֶּׁהֵן מוֹסִיפִים לְהִתְקַשּׁוֹת הֵן מִתְרַחֲקִים מֵהַשִּׁדְרָה, וְאִם נִתְקַשּׁוּ כָּל כָּךְ עַד שֶׁאִי אֶפְשָׁר לִכְפּוֹתָן וּלְאָגְדָן עִם הַשִּׁדְרָה[י] — הֲרֵי זֶה פָּסוּל:[יא,13]

ד אֲבָל אִם לֹא נִתְקַשּׁוּ כָּל כָּךְ, אַף עַל פִּי שֶׁכָּל זְמַן שֶׁאֵינָן כְּפוּתִין הֵן עוֹמְדִין מְפֹרָדִין וּמְרֻחָקִין זֶה מִזֶּה[13] — אַף עַל פִּי כֵן הוּא כָּשֵׁר[יב] אֲפִלּוּ אִם לֹא כְּפָתוּ כְּלָל,[יג,14] שֶׁלֹּא הִקְפִּידָה תּוֹרָה

9. Hence the debate in *Minchas Elazar* (Vol. 5, Responsum 8) on the status of a *lulav* taken from a date-palm that itself does not bear dates (e.g., due to the climate). A more recent debate revolves around *lulavim* taken from a Canary palm, which is readily distinguishable because its leaves emerge from the spine of each branch at much closer intervals than those of the date-palm. *Igros Moshe (Orach Chayim,* Vol. 4, Responsum 123) and other sources maintain that this is a totally different species and cannot be used for the *mitzvah* at all. Other contemporary authorities rule that such *lulavim* are perfectly acceptable (see *Piskei Teshuvos* 645, footnote 3). Common practice today is to use *lulavim* from palms that produce edible dates.

10. In the original, *kafus* ("bound"). This requirement relates not to the present state of the leaves, but to their potential state.

11. The smooth central shaft is so called, for just as one's ribs fan out from either side of the spine, the leaves of the *lulav* branch out from either side of the *shidrah*.

12. In the original, *nekudos* (lit., "dots").

13. *Sukkah* 32a.

14. *op. cit.,* 29b.

ח ראה ארבעת המינים (ויינר) ע׳ מד. ט גמרא לב, א (כפות אם היה פרוד יכפתנו. והיינו לרבי יהודה. ולת״ק במשנה כט, ב סגי בראויין, כדלקמן ס״ד). לבוש שם. י גמרא שם (חרותא בעינא כפות וליכא). רש״י ד״ה חרות וד״ה חרותא וד״ה בעינן כפות (לפירוש הב״י ד״ה ומ״ש אבל). טור ורמ״א ס״ב. וראה דברי נחמיה סי׳ מז (מח, ג ואילך). יא גמרא [ברייתא] שם (חרות פסול). טור ורמ״א שם. יב גמרא [ברייתא] שם. רש״י שם ד״ה דומה לחרות (התחיל להתקשות ועדיין לא נעשה עץ). טור (שדוקא נעשה כעץ פסול). ט״ז ס״ק ג. יג משנה כט, ב וכת״ק. טור ושו״ע ס״א. יד ריטב״א ור״ן במשנה שם ד״ה נפרדו. ב״ח ריש

אֶלָּא שֶׁיְּהֵא רָאוּי לְכְפּוֹתָהּ אֲבָל לֹא שֶׁיְּהֵא כָּפוּת מַמָּשׁ,[יד] שֶׁהֲרֵי אֵין אָנוּ קוֹרִין "כָּפוּת" אֶלָּא "כַּפּוֹת":

ה וּמִכָּל מָקוֹם, מִצְוָה מִן הַמֻּבְחָר שֶׁלֹּא לִטֹּל לוּלָב שֶׁעָלָיו פְּרוּדוֹת זֶה מִזֶּה[טו] אֲפִלּוּ אִם לֹא נִתְקַשּׁוּ כְּלָל, אֶלָּא שֶׁמֵּחֲמַת שֶׁנֶּעֶקְרוּ מְעַט בִּמְקוֹם חִבּוּרָם בַּשִּׁדְרָה נִתְפָּרְדוּ זֶה מִזֶּה מְעַט, אַף עַל פִּי שֶׁאֵין תְּלוּיִין לְמַטָּה כְּלָל אֶלָּא הֵן עוֹלִין לְמַעְלָה עִם הַשִּׁדְרָה:[טז]

ו אֲבָל אִם הֵן תְּלוּיִין וְאֵינָן עוֹלִין עִם הַשִּׁדְרָה[יז] אֶלָּא אִם כֵּן אוֹגְדִין אוֹתָן עִמּוֹ — הֲרֵי לוּלָב זֶה פָּסוּל מִן הַתּוֹרָה,[יח, 15] אֲפִלּוּ אִם לֹא נֶעֶקְרוּ הֶעָלִים לְגַמְרֵי[יט] מֵהַשִּׁדְרָה אֶלָּא הֵן מְחֻבָּרִים עִמּוֹ מְעַט, וַאֲפִלּוּ אָגַד אוֹתָן עִם הַשִּׁדְרָה[כ] — אֵין זֶה הִדּוּר:[כא]

ז פְּסוּלִים הַלָּלוּ שֶׁבֶּעָלִין שֶׁבֵּאַרְנוּ — אֵינָן פּוֹסְלִין אֶלָּא אִם כֵּן הֵן רֹב

required only that they be capable of being bound together, not that they actually be bound together — for [in fact] we do not read the term as כָּפוּת (*kafus* — "bound"), but as כַּפּוֹת (*kapos* — "fronds").

5 Nevertheless, the preferred way to perform the *mitzvah* is not to take a *lulav* whose leaves are separated from each other, even if they have not stiffened at all. [Indeed, a *lulav* should not be taken] even if its leaves have become somewhat detached from the point at which they are connected to the spine and hence have separated slightly — even though they are not [bent over and] hanging downward at all, but point upward together with the spine.

6 If, by contrast, [the leaves] are hanging [downward] and do not point upward together with the spine unless they are bound together, this *lulav* is invalid according to Scriptural Law.[15] [See fig. 20.] [This applies] even if the leaves were not entirely detached from the spine but remained connected to it slightly, and even if one bound them together with the spine, [because such a *lulav*] is not considered "beautiful."

7 The factors explained above that disqualify [a *lulav*] because of its leaves do not apply unless they characterize the majority of the

Fig. 19: See sec. 645:4.

Fig. 20: See sec. 645:6.

15. *Ibid.* The Alter Rebbe's ruling is based on his interpretation of the gloss by *Turei Zahav* on sec. 645:1. Some authorities interpret that gloss differently.

הסי'. **טו** מגיד משנה פ"ח ה"ג, בשם הגאונים. רמ"א ס"א. ב"י ריש הסי'. **טז** מגיד משנה שם (דמיירי בעולין למעלה מאליהן). רמ"א שם (שלא יהיו פרודות לגמרי). נהר שלום ס"ק א. וראה דברי נחמיה סי' מז (מט, סע"ד ואילך). מ"מ וציונים. **יז** משנה שם, לפירוש הרי"ף (טו, א: שנתרו מן השדרה והן תלויין בה), והרמב"ם שם (שידלדלו משדרו), לפי' המ"מ שם (ואפילו לא נדלדלו מעיקר חבוריהן כיון שתלויות למטה פסול). שו"ע ס"ב (כלשון הרמב"ם) ורמ"א שם (כפירוש המ"מ). **יח** ראה מ"מ וציונים. **יט** רבנו ירוחם נתיב ח ח"ג (נ, ד) בדעת הרי"ף שם. וראה דברי נחמיה שם. ארבעת המינים (ויינר) ע' מו ואילך. **כ** ריטב"א לב, א ד"ה אמר רב פפא. **כא** רש"י במשנה שם ד"ה נפרצו. רבנו ירוחם נתיב ח ח"ג (נח, ד). עטרת צבי ס"ק א. מ"א ס"ק ו. וראה גם לקמן ס"ט.

הֶעָלִין שֶׁל הַלּוּלָב,[כב] אֲבָל אִם מִעוּט הֶעָלִין נַעֲשׂוּ כָּךְ וְרֹב הֶעָלִין נִשְׁאֲרוּ מְחֻבָּרִין בַּשִּׁדְרָה וּמְכַסִּין אֶת רֹב הַשִּׁדְרָה[כג] וְעַל דֶּרֶךְ שֶׁיִּתְבָּאֵר[כד,16] — הֲרֵי זֶה כָּשֵׁר, לְפִי שֶׁהַכֹּל הוֹלֵךְ אַחַר הָרֹב:[17]

leaves. If a minority of the leaves were affected in this way, but the majority of the leaves remained connected to the spine and covered most of it in the manner to be explained,[16] [the *lulav*] is valid, for everything depends on the majority.[17]

ח אִם הַשִּׁדְרָה עַצְמָהּ נִשְׁבְּרָה בְּאֶמְצָעִיתָהּ, וְלֹא נִשְׁבְּרָה לְגַמְרֵי לִשְׁנֵי חֲלָקִים אֶלָּא נִתְקַפְּלָה לִשְׁנַיִם שֶׁחֵלֶק הָעֶלְיוֹן תָּלוּי לְמַטָּה — כָּשֵׁר, וּמִכָּל מָקוֹם צָרִיךְ לְאַגְּדוֹ שָׁם בִּמְקוֹם הַקֵּפֶל שֶׁלֹּא יִהְיֶה רֹאשׁוֹ תָּלוּי לְמַטָּה:[כה]

8 [A *lulav*] is valid [even] if the spine itself was broken in the middle — not broken in two, but bent over [so that now it appears] as two because the upper part hangs downward. Nevertheless, it must be bound up at the point at which it is bent over so that its top will not be hanging downward.

ט דֶּרֶךְ בְּרִיַּת הֶעָלִין שֶׁל לוּלָב כָּךְ הִיא, כְּשֶׁהֵן גְּדֵלִים גְּדֵלִים שְׁנַיִם שְׁנַיִם זֶה לְעֻמַּת זֶה מִשְּׁנֵי צִדֵּי הַשִּׁדְרָה, וְכָל עָלֶה וְעָלֶה כָּפוּל לִשְׁנַיִם, וְהוּא דָּבוּק מִגַּבּוֹ וּפָתוּחַ מִלְּפָנָיו,[כו] וְאִם נֶחְלְקוּ[כז] רֹב הֶעָלִין[כח] שֶׁל הַלּוּלָב לִשְׁנַיִם בְּרֹב אָרְכָּן,[כט] דְּהַיְנוּ שֶׁרֹב עֲלֵי הַלּוּלָב נִסְדְּקוּ מִגַּבָּן בִּמְקוֹם הַקֵּפֶל, בְּעִנְיָן שֶׁכָּל עָלֶה מֵהֶן נֶחֱלַק בְּרֹב אָרְכּוֹ לִשְׁנַיִם — הֲרֵי לוּלָב זֶה פָּסוּל, לְפִי שֶׁאֵינוֹ מְהֻדָּר.[ל,13] וְכֵן אִם מִתְּחִלַּת בְּרִיָּתוֹ[לא] לֹא הָיוּ רֹב עָלָיו[לב] כְּפוּלִים לִשְׁנַיִם בְּרֹב אָרְכָּן — הֲרֵי זֶה פָּסוּל:

9 The normal pattern of growth for the leaves of a *lulav* is as follows: As the leaves grow, they grow in pairs, one opposite the other on either side of the spine. Each leaf is in fact a double leaf, connected at the back and open at the front.

If most of the leaves of a *lulav* become split in two along most of their length — i.e., most of the leaves of the *lulav* become split along the crease at the back and thus each leaf is divided in two for most of its length — this *lulav* is invalid, because it is not considered "beautiful."[13]

Similarly, if [a *lulav*] naturally grew in such a way that most of its leaves were not double over most of their length, it is not valid.

16. See subsection. 13.

17. At present, the prevailing custom is not to use a *lulav* whose leaves are separated at all.

כב תוספתא פ"ב ה"ח. הובא בתוס' כט, ב ד"ה נפרצו. ר"ן (יד, ב דיבור הראשון). רמ"א שם (אף לפירוש הנ"ל בנפרצו). וראה גם לקמן ס"ט. סי' תרמז ס"ו (לענין ערבה). **כג** ראה עד"ז לקמן סי' תרמו ס"ג־ד, לענין הדס. **כד** לקמן סי"ג ואילך — אופן כיסוי השדרה. **כה** מ"א ס"ק ב. **כו** רמב"ם שם פ"ח ה"ד. שו"ע ס"ג. לבוש ס"ג. **כז** גמרא לב, א (נחלקה התיומת), לפי' הרי"ף שם (טו, א). רמב"ם פ"ח ה"ד. סמ"ג עשין מד (קכא, א), וסמ"ק סי' קצג (ע' קנט), בשם רבנו חננאל שם. מ"מ שם, בשם הרמב"ן ד"ה ענין נפרצו, ממשמעות הירושלמי פ"ג ה"א. שו"ע שם. **כח** תוס' כט, ב ד"ה נפרצו (לפירושו שמפרש כן נפרצו). רא"ש פ"ג סי' ו, וטור (בדעת הרי"ף). רמ"א ס"ג. וכדלעיל ס"ז מהתוספתא פ"ב ה"ח. **כט** רא"ש שם וטור (בדעת הרי"ף). מ"מ שם. לבוש ס"ג. מ"א ס"ק ג. **ל** רבנו ירוחם נתיב ח ח"ג (נח, ד). מ"א ס"ק ו. וכדלעיל ס"ו. **לא** רבא שם (לולבא דסליק בחד הוצא), לפירוש הרמב"ם שם, כפירוש הרא"ש פ"ג סי' ה. טור ושו"ע שם. **לב** ר"ן (טו, א) ד"ה תניא. ריטב"א שם ד"ה אמר רבא. לבוש שם. **לג** רש"י ב"ק צו, א ד"ה התיומת. ר"ן (טו, רע"א). ריטב"א לא, ב ד"ה אמר ר"ה. מ"מ פ"ח ה"ד, בשם יש מי שפירש. **לד** כדלקמן סי"ז (לענין נקטם) וש"נ. **לה** פירוש אחר ברש"י (ראה רש"י שם), שהובא בהגהת סמ"ק סי' קצג

10 The above applies to all the leaves other than the topmost, middle leaf,[18] which is the tallest of the leaves and is called "the head of the *lulav*." This leaf is normally double, like the other leaves of the *lulav*. If it did not grow as a double leaf, [the *lulav*] is invalid, even if all the other leaves are double.

So, too, [the *lulav*] is invalid if [this leaf] was double at the outset, and then became split over its entire length, i.e., from its tip until the place from which the leaves emerge. (From this place downward, it is no longer called the "middle leaf"; it is the spine proper.)

In the above instances involving the topmost leaf, the *lulav* is not disqualified because it is not considered "beautiful," but because of the [interpretation of the verb in the above-quoted] verse: ולקחתם — "And you shall take." From this word the Sages learned that [what is taken] should be perfect and complete.[19] Now, the middle leaf is the essential component of the lulav, for it is seen at first glance, and it is normally double. Hence, if it is split in half, it is obvious and apparent that it is not "perfect and complete" in the place where it is split.[20]

11 When does the above apply? When it is split along its entire length. If

י וְכָל זֶה בִּשְׁאָר עֲלֵי הַלּוּלָב חוּץ מֵעָלֶה הָעֶלְיוֹן הָאֶמְצָעִי,[18] אֲבָל עָלֶה הָעֶלְיוֹן הָאֶמְצָעִי שֶׁהוּא גָּבוֹהַּ מִכָּל הֶעָלִין,[לג] וְהוּא נִקְרָא רֹאשׁ הַלּוּלָב,[לד] וְדֶרֶךְ עָלֶה זֶה לִהְיוֹת כָּפוּל כִּשְׁאָר עֲלֵי הַלּוּלָב,[לה] וְאִם לֹא הָיָה כָּפוּל מִתְּחִלַּת בְּרִיָּתוֹ — הֲרֵי זֶה פָּסוּל,[לו] אֲפִלּוּ אִם כָּל הֶעָלִין חוּץ מִזֶּה הֵן כְּפוּלִין. וְכֵן אִם הָיָה כָּפוּל מִתְּחִלַּת בְּרִיָּתוֹ וְאַחַר כָּךְ נֶחְלַק לִשְׁנַיִם בְּכָל אָרְכּוֹ, דְּהַיְנוּ מֵרֹאשׁוֹ עַד מָקוֹם שֶׁעָלִין יוֹצְאִין מִשָּׁם[לז] (שֶׁמִּמָּקוֹם זֶה וּלְמַטָּה אֵינוֹ נִקְרָא עָלֶה הָאֶמְצָעִי אֶלָּא גּוּף הַשִּׁדְרָה[לח]) — פָּסוּל.

וּפְסוּלִים אֵלּוּ שֶׁבְּעָלֶה הָעֶלְיוֹן אֵינוֹ מִשּׁוּם הִדּוּר הַלּוּלָב,[לט] אֶלָּא מִשּׁוּם שֶׁנֶּאֱמַר "וּלְקַחְתֶּם", וְדָרְשׁוּ חֲכָמִים[מ] לְקִיחָה תַּמָּה וּשְׁלֵמָה,[מא,19] וְזֶה הֶעָלֶה שֶׁהוּא עִקַּר הַלּוּלָב שֶׁהָאָדָם רוֹאֶה אוֹתוֹ בִּתְחִלַּת הַשְׁקָפָתוֹ,[מב] וְדַרְכּוֹ לִהְיוֹת כָּפוּל בְּכָל הַלּוּלָבִין, וְאִם הוּא חָלוּק לִשְׁנַיִם — הֲרֵי נִכָּר וְנִרְאֶה שֶׁאֵינוֹ תָּם וְשָׁלֵם בִּמְקוֹם הַסֶּדֶק:[20]

יא בַּמֶּה דְּבָרִים אֲמוּרִים? בְּנֶחְלַק בְּכָל

18. This leaf is the continuation of the spine. All the other leaves grow in pairs, each having an identical counterpart on the other side of the spine. This leaf, uniquely, has no partner.

19. The first four Hebrew letters (ולקח) denote taking; the last two Hebrew letters (תם) spell the word *tam* — "perfect." See *Sukkah* 34b.

20. There are thus two main reasons for disqualifying any of the Four Species: (a) lack of beauty, and (b) incompleteness. The latter objection applies only on the first day; the former applies throughout the festival. See sec. 649:17ff.

(ע' קנט) אות ג. תרומת הדשן סי' צו. דרכי משה ס"ק ה. מ"א ס"ק ד. וראה העו"ב תתם ע' 57. **לו** כל בו סי' עב (מ, ג), לדעת רש"י. רמ"א ס"ג. **לז** רש"י לב, א ד"ה נחלקה (בפירושו הא', דמיירי בשני עלין: עד העלין שלמטה מהם). הגהת סמ"ק שם (שפירש כן אף בפירוש הב' של רש"י). אור זרוע ח"ב סוס"י שו (על פרש"י אני סומך למעשה). תרומת הדשן שם. דרכי משה שם. רמ"א שם (והכי נוהגין). **לח** ראה לקמן סי' תרנ ס"א. **לט** רבנו ירוחם נתיב ח ח"ג (נח, ד). מ"א ס"ק ו. וכ"ה לקמן סי"ב. **מ** גמרא לד, ב (לענין שד' המינים מעכבין זא"ז). וראה גם לקמן סי' תרמח סי"ד (לענין אתרוג). **מא** רש"י שם ד"ה תמה. וראה לקמן סי' תרמט סי"ז-ט, שמטעם זה (בלבד) פסול ביום הראשון בלבד. **מב** כדלקמן סי' תרמח סכ"א (לענין חוטמו של אתרוג, וש"נ). ר"ן (יד, סע"א), וריטב"א כט, ב, סד"ה נקטם ראשו (שעשו ראשו של לולב כחוטמו של אתרוג).

אָרְכּוֹ,[מג] אֲבָל אִם לֹא נֶחֱלַק אֶלָּא מִקְצָתוֹ[מד] – כָּשֵׁר.

וְכָל זֶה בְּדִיעֲבַד,[21] אוֹ שֶׁאֵין לוֹ לוּלָב אַחֵר – אֵינוֹ צָרִיךְ לְבָרֵךְ עַל לוּלָב שֶׁל חֲבֵרוֹ בְּיוֹם א׳ שֶׁל סֻכּוֹת, אֲבָל לְכַתְּחִלָּה[22] מִצְוָה מִן הַמֻּבְחָר[23] לַחֲזֹר[מה] אַחַר לוּלָב שֶׁלֹּא נֶחֱלַק עָלֶה הָעֶלְיוֹן שֶׁלּוֹ כְּלָל אֶלָּא הוּא כָּפוּל מֵרֹאשׁוֹ עַד מָקוֹם שֶׁעָלִין יוֹצְאִין מִשָּׁם, לְפִי שֶׁיֵּשׁ פּוֹסְלִין אֲפִלּוּ אִם לֹא נֶחֱלַק אֶלָּא מִקְצָת עָלֶה זֶה הָעֶלְיוֹן, וְאַף עַל פִּי שֶׁאֵין הֲלָכָה כְּדִבְרֵיהֶם, מִכָּל מָקוֹם טוֹב לָחוּשׁ לְדִבְרֵיהֶם אִם אֶפְשָׁר:[מו]

only part of it is split, [the *lulav*] is valid.

All the above applies only after the fact[21] or when one does not have another *lulav;* in such a case one does not have to recite the blessing over a *lulav* belonging to a friend on the first day of Sukkos. As the initial and preferred option,[22] the optimal way of performing the *mitzvah*[23] is to seek a *lulav* whose topmost leaf is not split at all, but which is double from its tip until the place [on the spine] from which the leaves emerge — for some authorities disqualify [a *lulav*] even if only a [small] part of this middle leaf is split. Though the *halachah* does not follow their opinion, it is desirable to respect it if possible.

יב וְאִם נִסְדְּקָה הַשִּׁדְרָה[מז] תַּחַת עָלֶה זֶה הָעֶלְיוֹן, דְּהַיְנוּ מִמָּקוֹם שֶׁעָלֶיהָ יוֹצְאִים וּלְמַטָּה,[מח] אִם נִתְרַחֲקוּ שְׁנֵי צִדֵּי הַסֶּדֶק זֶה מִזֶּה עַד שֶׁיֵּרָאוּ כִּשְׁנַיִם – פָּסוּל,[24,מט] לְפִי שֶׁחֶסְרוֹנוֹ נִרְאֶה וְנִכָּר שֶׁאֵינוֹ תָּם וְשָׁלֵם:[נ]

12 If the spine is split from below this topmost leaf, i.e., from the point the leaves emerge and downward, [the *lulav*] is invalid.[24] This applies if the two sides of the crack become separated to the extent that they appear as two entities, for then the fault is apparent, and it is obvious that [the *lulav*] is not perfect and complete.

יג דֶּרֶךְ גִּדּוּל הַלּוּלָב כָּךְ הוּא:[נא] לְאַחַר שֶׁיּוֹצֵא עָלֶה אֶחָד מֵהַשִּׁדְרָה מִיָּד כְּשִׁעוּר שְׁתֵּי אֶצְבָּעוֹת עוֹלֶה עוֹד אֶחָד וְכֵן הַרְבֵּה זֶה עַל גַּבֵּי זֶה עַד שֶׁמִּתְכַּסֶּה כֻּלּוֹ בְּעָלִין[נב] מִצַּד אֶחָד, וְכֵן מִצַּד הַשֵּׁנִי, וְאִם מִצַּד אֶחָד הוּא מְכֻסֶּה כֻּלּוֹ בְּעָלִין וְצַד הַשֵּׁנִי הוּא עָרֹם בְּלֹא עָלִין – פָּסוּל,[נג] לְפִי שֶׁאֵינוֹ מְהֻדָּר:[20,נד]

13 A *lulav* normally grows in the following manner: After one leaf emerges from the spine, another emerges close by, at a distance of about two fingerbreadths. Similarly, many follow, one above the other, until the entire *[lulav]* is covered with leaves on both sides. If one side is entirely covered with leaves and the other side is bare, without leaves, [the *lulav*] is invalid, because it is not considered "beautiful."[20]

---

21. In the original Aramaic, *bediavad* (popularly mispronounced *bedieved*).

22. In the original Hebrew, *lechat'chilah.*

23. In the original Hebrew, *mitzvah min hamuvchar.*

מג כדלעיל ס"י בדעת רש"י. מד ולא רובו. ר"ן (טו, רע"א), וריטב"א לא, ב ד"ה אמר ר"ה, בתי' הא'. מגיד משנה פ"ח ה"ד (לב' הדעות). מה ראה לעיל סי' תעג ס"ל (לקנותו בדמים יקרים). מו ריטב"א ור"ן שם. רמ"א ס"ג. מז ברייתא לב, א (סדוק כו' פסול). גמרא שם (דעביד כהימנק), לפי' הראב"ד בתמים דעים סי' רלא. הובא ברא"ש פ"ג ס"ב (על שדרה קאמר). מח רבנו ירוחם נתיב ח ח"ג (נח, ג: ושני העלין האמצעיים לא נחלקו). רמ"א ס"ז. מט רמב"ם פ"ח ה"ג. שו"ע

14 Similarly, if [a *lulav*] does not have many leaves above each other, but on either side one leaf emerges from near the base [of the *lulav*] and ascends until its tip, [the *lulav*] is invalid, for this, too, is not considered "beautiful."[20]

יד וְכֵן אִם אֵין לוֹ עָלִין הַרְבֵּה זֶה עַל גַּבֵּי זֶה, אֶלָּא מִכָּל צַד יוֹצֵא עָלֶה אֶחָד לְמַטָּה סָמוּךְ לְעִקָּרוֹ וְעוֹלֶה עַד רֹאשׁוֹ — פָּסוּל,[נה] שֶׁגַּם זֶה אֵינוֹ הִדּוּר:[נו,20]

15 Similarly, [difficulties can arise] if [a *lulav*] has many leaves, but they do not [lie] on top of each other; [the base of] one leaf is so much lower [on the spine] than [the base of] the leaf above it that the [outer] leaf does not lie at all on the leaf [that should be covered by it].[25] If the tip of the leaf [that is lower on the spine] reaches the base of the leaf that is higher than it and thus the entire spine of the *lulav* is covered with leaves, [the *lulav*] is valid. [See fig. 21.] If the tip of the [lower] leaf does not reach the base of the leaf [above it], [the *lulav*] is invalid,[14] for this is not considered "beautiful." [See fig. 22.]

טו וְכֵן אִם הָיוּ לוֹ הַרְבֵּה עָלִין וְלֹא הָיוּ מֻנָּחִין זֶה עַל גַּבֵּי זֶה אֶלָּא זֶה תַּחַת זֶה, דְּהַיְנוּ שֶׁהֵן מְרֻחָקִין זֶה לְמַעְלָה מִזֶּה הַרְבֵּה בְּעִנְיָן שֶׁאֵין הָעֶלְיוֹן מֻנָּח כְּלָל עַל גַּבֵּי הַתַּחְתּוֹן שֶׁלְּמַטָּה מִמֶּנּוּ,[25] אִם רֹאשׁ עָלֶה זֶה מַגִּיעַ לְעִקַּר עָלֶה זֶה שֶׁלְּמַעְלָה מִמֶּנּוּ עַד שֶׁנִּמְצָא כָּל הַשִּׁדְרָה שֶׁל לוּלָב מְכֻסָּה בֶּעָלִין — כָּשֵׁר, אֲבָל אִם אֵין רֹאשׁוֹ שֶׁל זֶה מַגִּיעַ לְעִקָּרוֹ שֶׁל זֶה — פָּסוּל,[נז,14] שֶׁאֵין זֶה הִדּוּר:[נח]

Fig. 21: A valid *lulav*.

Fig. 22: An invalid *lulav*.

24. *Sukkah* 32b.

25. In a kosher *lulav*, every leaf that emerges from a lower point on the shaft of the *lulav* should overlap [part of] the leaf that emerges from a higher point on the shaft of the *lulav*. Here, therefore, "the [outer] leaf" (lit., "the upper leaf") does not signify a leaf that emerges from a higher rung on the shaft, but a leaf that should lie on top of — and partly cover — another leaf which is closer to the shaft.

ס"ז. נ רבנו ירוחם שם (נח, ד). מ"א ס"ק ו. וכדלעיל ס"י וש"נ. נא ראה גמרא שם. נב טור ולבוש ס"ד. נג רבא בגמרא שם (לולבא דסליק בחד הוצא), לפירוש רש"י שם ד"ה דסליק. רא"ש פ"ג ס"ה בשמו. טור ושו"ע ס"ג. נד רבנו ירוחם נתיב ח (נח, ד). לבוש ס"ד. מ"א ס"ק ו. לבוש ס"ג. וראה ר"ן (טו, ב) ד"ה תניא בשם י"א. נה רבא בגמרא שם (לולבא דסליק בחד הוצא), לפירוש הרא"ש שם בשם רב שר שלום (שו"ת הגאונים שערי תשובה סי' שו). טור ושו"ע ס"ד. נו לבוש ס"ד. עטרת צבי ס"ק ז. נז משנה כט, ב (ציני הר הברזל). כאוקימתא דאביי לב, א. רש"י שם ד"ה ציני. טור ושו"ע שם. נח לבוש שם. עטרת צבי שם.

טז לוּלָב שֶׁיָּבְשָׁה[נט] רֹב שִׁדְרָתוֹ[ס] אוֹ שֶׁיָּבְשׁוּ רֹב עָלָיו[סא] — פָּסוּל, שֶׁאֵין זֶה נִקְרָא הָדוּר.[סב,14] וְכַמָּה שִׁעוּר יַבְשׁוּת הַפּוֹסֵל[סג]? יֵשׁ אוֹמְרִים[סד] מִשֶּׁנִּפְרָךְ בַּצִּפֹּרֶן כְּשֶׁמְּמַשְׁמְשִׁין בּוֹ.[סה] וְיֵשׁ אוֹמְרִים[סו] מִשֶּׁיִּכְלֶה כָּל מַרְאֵה יַרְקוּת שֶׁבּוֹ וְהִלְבִּינוּ פָּנָיו — הֲרֵי הוּא נִקְרָא יָבֵשׁ, אַף עַל פִּי שֶׁאֵינוֹ נִפְרָךְ בַּצִּפֹּרֶן, לְפִי שֶׁזֶּהוּ סִימָן שֶׁכָּלָה הַלַּחְלוּחִית שֶׁבּוֹ. וַהֲלָכָה כַּסְּבָרָא הָאַחֲרוֹנָה.[סז] וּמִכָּל מָקוֹם, בִּשְׁעַת הַדְּחָק כְּגוֹן בִּמְדִינוֹת אֵלּוּ שֶׁאֵין לוּלָבִין מְצוּיִין — יֵשׁ לִסְמֹךְ עַל סְבָרָא הָרִאשׁוֹנָה[סח] (אִם אִי אֶפְשָׁר לִמְצֹא לוּלָב אַחֵר,[26] עַיֵּן בֵּית יוֹסֵף סִימָן תרמ"ט[סט,27]):

16 When the majority of the spine of a *lulav* or most of its leaves become dried out, [the *lulav*] is invalid, because it is not considered "beautiful."[14]

What degree of dryness invalidates a *lulav?* Some authorities hold [that it must become so dry that] it crumbles when fingered by one's nail. Others hold that once [the *lulav*] entirely loses its greenish color and becomes white, it is considered as dried out even if it will not crumble when touched with a nail, for this is a sign that all of its [natural] moisture has been drained.

The *halachah* follows the latter opinion. Nevertheless, in a pressing situation — such as in these countries, where palm fronds are not common — one may rely on the first opinion (if it is impossible to find another *lulav;*[26] see the gloss of *Beis Yosef* to sec. 649).[27]

יז נִקְטַם רֹאשׁוֹ — פָּסוּל,[ע,14] לְפִי שֶׁאֵין זֶה הָדוּר.[עא] וְאֵיזֶהוּ רֹאשׁוֹ? זֶה עָלֶה הָעֶלְיוֹן הָאֶמְצָעִי שֶׁהוּא גָּבוֹהַּ מִכָּל הֶעָלִין,[עב] וְאִם עָלֶה זֶה נִקְטַם בְּרֹאשׁוֹ אֲפִלּוּ כָּל שֶׁהוּא[עג] — פָּסוּל. וְיֵשׁ אוֹמְרִים[עד] שֶׁאֵינוֹ פָּסוּל אֶלָּא אִם כֵּן נִקְטַם רֹב אָרְכּוֹ שֶׁל עָלֶה זֶה הָעֶלְיוֹן. וְיֵשׁ לְהַחְמִיר

17 If the tip [of the *lulav*] has been clipped off, [the *lulav*] is invalid,[14] for it is not considered "beautiful."

What is meant by its tip? The tallest, middle leaf, which is higher than all the other leaves. If even the smallest amount of this leaf is clipped off, [the *lulav*] is invalid.

Some authorities maintain that [a *lulav*] is not disqualified unless most of the length of this tallest leaf has been cut off. One should be

26. In Eastern Europe, before the modern advances in travel and communications, this law had far greater relevance than at present. In those times *lulavim* were sometimes saved for months, even for years. Today, when a *lulav* can be shipped anywhere in the world with relative ease, there is less room for leniency.

27. That gloss cites authorities who maintain that greater leniency is granted with regard to a *lulav* that has become dried out than with regard to other disqualifying factors.

נט משנה כט, ב. טור ושו"ע ס"ה. **ס** טור ורמ"א ס"ה. **סא** רא"ש פ"ג סוף ס"ב. טור ושו"ע שם. **סב** גמרא כט, ב. לא, א. לבוש ס"ה. **סג** לענין הדס, ראה לקמן סי' תרמו ס"ח. ולענין ערבה, לקמן סי' תרמז ס"ו. ולענין אתרוג, לקמן סי' תרמח ס"א. **סד** תוס' כט, ב ד"ה לולב. פירוש הא' ברא"ש שם סי' א, ובטור. דרכי משה ס"ק ג, בשם הגהות מיימוניות (קושטא) פ"ח ה"ד. רמ"א שם. **סה** רש"י בכורות לז, א ד"ה נפרכת (לענין בכור). וראה גם לקמן סי' תרמו ס"ח (לענין הדס). **סו** ראב"ד בתמים דעים סי' רלב. רא"ש שם בשמו. ריטב"א כט, ב ד"ה והיבש. ר"ן (יג, ב) ד"ה לולב. מגיד משנה פ"ח ה"א. טור ושו"ע שם. **סז** טור (וכן עיקר). ט"ז ס"ק ה. **סח** הגהות מיימוניות שם. רמ"א שם. ט"ז שם. **סט** ד"ה וכל הפסולים בשם המרדכי רמז תשנ. רמ"א סי' תרמט ס"ו. לקמן שם סכ"ג־ד. **ע** משנה כט, ב. טור ושו"ע ס"ו. **עא** ירושלמי פ"ג ה"א. הובא ברא"ש פ"ג ס"ב. מ"א ס"ק ו. **עב** ריטב"א כט, ב סד"ה נקטם ראשו. מ"מ פ"ח ה"ג. וראה גם לעיל ס"י. **עג** תוס' כט, ב ד"ה נקטם (בשני עלים האמצעיים). רא"ש שם (כנ"ל, וראה טור וב"י סד"ה ומ"ש ופי'). ריטב"א שם. ר"ן (יד, א) ד"ה נקטם. מגיד משנה פ"ח ה"ג. **עד** ריטב"א שם בשם רבנו יונה. ר"ן ומ"מ שם בשם י"א. ב"י שם בדעת הטור (אופן הא'). עטרת צבי ס"ק ט. **עה** מנהגים (טירנא) ריש הל' סוכות (לגירסת הדפוסים שלנו,

כַּסְּבָרָא הָרִאשׁוֹנָה. וּמִכָּל מָקוֹם, בִּשְׁעַת הַדְּחָק שֶׁאִי אֶפְשָׁר לִמְצֹא לוּלָב אַחֵר – יֵשׁ לִסְמֹךְ עַל סְבָרָא הָאַחֲרוֹנָה. וּמֻתָּר לְבָרֵךְ עַל לוּלָב שֶׁנִּקְטַם מִעוּט שֶׁל עָלֶה הָעֶלְיוֹן,[עה] אֲבָל אִם נִקְטַם רֻבּוֹ – אֵין לְבָרֵךְ עָלָיו אֲפִלּוּ בִּשְׁעַת הַדְּחָק,[עו] אֶלָּא אִם כֵּן בְּמָקוֹם שֶׁנּוֹהֲגִים לְבָרֵךְ עַל כָּל הַפְּסוּלִין גְּמוּרִים בִּשְׁעַת הַדְּחָק, וּכְמוֹ שֶׁיִּתְבָּאֵר בְּסִימָן תרמ"ט,[עז] עַיֵּן שָׁם:[28]

stringent and follow the first opinion, but in a pressing situation, when no other *lulav* can be found, one may rely on the latter opinion, and use such a *lulav,* reciting a blessing over it, even though less than half of its tallest leaf has been cut off. If, however, the majority of this leaf has been cut off, a blessing should not be recited over such [a *lulav*], even in a pressing situation. [The only exception] is a place where it is customary to recite a blessing [over the Four Species] even though they are entirely invalid even in a pressing situation, as will be explained in sec. 649[:22-23].[28]

יח אִם יֵשׁ לוֹ כְּמִין קוֹצִים יוֹצְאִים מִשִּׁדְרָתוֹ,[עח,29] וְכֵן אִם נִצְמַת וְנִכְוַץ,[עט,13] וְכֵן אִם נֶעֱקַם לְפָנָיו,[פ] דְּהַיְנוּ הַצַּד שֶׁכְּנֶגֶד הַשִּׁדְרָה נֶעֱקַם וְנִכְפַּף[פא] עַד שֶׁנַּעֲשֵׂית שִׁדְרָתוֹ כְּגַב בַּעַל חֲטוֹטָרוֹת[30] – פָּסוּל,[פב] שֶׁאֵין זֶה הִדּוּר.[פג] וְכֵן אִם נֶעֱקַם לְאֶחָד מִצְּדָדָיו – פָּסוּל:[פד]

18 [A *lulav*] is invalid if it has thorn-like projections emerging from its spine,[29] or if it is contracted or shrunk,[13] or if it is bent over frontward, i.e., the side opposite the spine is bent over until the spine appears like a hunchback[30] — for [such *lulavim*] are not considered "beautiful." Similarly, [a *lulav*] is invalid if it is bent over to either side.

יט אֲבָל אִם נֶעֱקַם לַאֲחוֹרָיו,[פה] דְּהַיְנוּ שֶׁשִּׁדְרָתוֹ נֶעֶקְמָה וְנִכְפְּפָה בְּאֶמְצָעִיתָהּ לְצַד פָּנָיו[פו] – כָּשֵׁר, שֶׁזֶּהוּ דֶּרֶךְ בְּרִיָּתוֹ[פז] וַהֲדָרוֹ.[פח,30]

בַּמֶּה דְּבָרִים אֲמוּרִים? כְּשֶׁנֶּעֶקְמָה וְנִכְפְּפָה בְּאֶמְצָעִיתָהּ,[פט] אֲבָל אִם נִכְפְּפָה

19 If [the *lulav*] is bent back, so that the middle of the spine bends inward, it is valid, for this is the way it grows and is considered "beautiful."[30]

When does the above apply? When the middle of the spine is bent over. If, however, the top [of the spine] is bent

---

28. As explained there, this opinion is not accepted.

29. The *Gemara* supports this objection by quoting a verse from the Book of *Mishlei* (3:17) that extols the Torah: "Its ways are pleasant ways, and all its paths are peace" *(Sukkah* 32a).

30. Ordinarily, the fronds of a palm emerge from its trunk with the central shaft (the spine) facing downward. The spine is commonly arched, with a slight concave curve. Hence, such a *lulav* is valid. A convex curve is abnormal, and invalidates the *lulav.*

שהתיר רק בנקטם כל שהוא). וגם בריטב"א ומ"א לא כתבו אלא לחשוש לדעת הפוסלים בכל שהוא. וראה גם לקמן סי' תרמו סי"א. תרמח ס"ו וס"ח וסי"ח וס"כ. סי' תרמט סי"ט. **עו** ב"י שם. ב"ח סד"ה ומ"ש בשם. מ"א ס"ק ו (שלא התירו בזה אלא בהדס, כדלקמן סי' תרמו סי"א). **עז** סכ"ב־ג. **עח** גמרא [ברייתא] לב, רע"א, לגירסת ופירוש רש"י שם ד"ה קווץ. טור ושו"ע ס"ח. **עט** ברייתא שם לגירסת ר"ח ורי"ף (טו, א: כווץ). ערוך ערך קווץ הא'. הובא בתוס' ד"ה קווץ. רא"ש פ"ג ס"ד, בשם הערוך (ערך קווץ הא'). טור ושו"ע שם. **פ** ברייתא שם, כאוקימתא דרבא שם. טור ושו"ע שם. **פא** רש"י שם ד"ה מלפניו. **פב** רמב"ם פ"ח ה"ג. שו"ע שם. **פג** לבוש ס"ח. וראה גם מ"א ס"ק ו. **פד** רב נחמן שם וכלישנא קמא. רי"ף שם. רא"ש פ"ג סי' ד. טור ושו"ע שם. **פה** רבא בגמרא שם. טור ושו"ע שם. **פו** ראה ב"י סד"ה יש לו (שיש מפרשים דפניו היינו צד השדרה). **פז** רבא שם. שו"ע ולבוש שם. **פח** לבוש שם. **פט** טור ולבוש שם.

בְּרֹאשׁוֹ[צ] כְּאַגְמוֹן[31] שֶׁרֹאשׁוֹ כָּפוּף וְשָׁחוּחַ לְמַטָּה,[צא] בֵּין שֶׁנִּכְפְּפָה לְצַד פָּנָיו בֵּין שֶׁנִּכְפְּפָה לְצַד אֲחוֹרָיו – פָּסוּל,[צב,32] שֶׁאֵין זֶה הִדּוּר:[צג]

over like a bullrush[31] whose head is bent over and bowed downward, [the *lulav*] is invalid.[32] [This applies] whether it is bent forward or backward, for this is not considered "beautiful."

כ וְכָל זֶה כְּשֶׁהַשִּׁדְרָה בְּעַצְמָהּ הִיא כְּפוּפָה, אֲבָל אִם הֶעָלִין בִּלְבַד הֵן כְּפוּפִים, אֲפִלּוּ נִכְפַּף גַּם הֶעָלֶה הָעֶלְיוֹן הָאֶמְצָעִי – הֲרֵי זֶה כָּשֵׁר, לְפִי שֶׁכֵּן דֶּרֶךְ הַרְבֵּה לוּלָבִין שֶׁעֲלֵיהֶן הֵן כְּפוּפִים.[צד] וְיֵשׁ פּוֹסְלִין[צה] אִם רֹב עֲלֵי הַלּוּלָב הֵן כְּפוּפִין בְּרָאשֵׁיהֶן אֲפִלּוּ כָּל שֶׁהוּא. וְיֵשׁ לְהַחְמִיר כְּדִבְרֵיהֶם.[33] אֲבָל אִם הוּא שְׁעַת הַדְּחָק שֶׁאִי אֶפְשָׁר לִמְצֹא לוּלָב אַחֵר – יֵשׁ לִסְמֹךְ עַל סְבָרָא הָרִאשׁוֹנָה,[צו] וּמֻתָּר לְבָרֵךְ עַל לוּלָב זֶה[צז] אֲפִלּוּ אִם כָּל עָלָיו הֵן כְּפוּפִין. וְכֵן מִיּוֹם שֵׁנִי שֶׁל חַג וְאֵילָךְ שֶׁאֵין חִיּוּב נְטִילַת לוּלָב[34] בָּהֶן מִדִּבְרֵי תּוֹרָה אֶלָּא מִדִּבְרֵי סוֹפְרִים[צח,35] – יֵשׁ לְהָקֵל כִּסְבָרָא

20 The above [disqualifications] apply when the spine itself is bent over. If, however, only the leaves are bent over — even if the topmost, middle leaf is also bent over — [the *lulav*] is valid, for this is the way many *lulavim* grow, with their leaves bent over.

Some authorities disqualify a *lulav* if the tops of most of its leaves are even slightly bent over. One should be stringent and follow their ruling.[33] In a pressing situation when another *lulav* cannot be found, one may rely on the first opinion and recite a blessing on such a *lulav*, even if all its leaves are bent over.

Similarly, from the second day of the festival onward, when the obligation to take a *lulav* in hand[34] is not of Scriptural authority, but is a Rabbinic ordinance,[35] one may be lenient and follow the first

---

31. Cf. *Yeshayahu* 58:5.

32. *Sukkah* 31b.

33. The contemporary *Chabad* practice is to seek *lulavim* that have no bent leaves *(Sefer HaMinhagim: The Book of Chabad-Lubavitch Customs,* p. 140*)*.

34. The word *lulav* is often used to indicate all of the Four Species (see sec. 651:17 below).

35. *Vayikra* 23:40 states: "And on the first day, you shall take for yourselves the fruit of a beautiful tree, fronds of a date-palm, a branch of a braided tree, and willows of the brook, and you shall rejoice before G-d, your L-rd, for seven days." As explained by the commentaries to *Sukkah* 3:12, this verse reflects two requirements of the *mitzvah:*

(a) To take a *lulav* in hand on the first day of the festival, as it is written, "On the first day, you shall take...." This obligation applies wherever a Jew lives.

(b) To take a *lulav* in hand for seven days in the *Beis HaMikdash,* as it is written, "And you shall rejoice before G-d [i.e., in the *Beis HaMikdash*] for seven days."

After the destruction of the Second *Beis HaMikdash,* Rabban Yochanan ben Zakkai ordained that even outside that holy site, the *lulav* should be taken in hand during all seven days of the holiday (with the exception of *Shabbos*). The authority for this requirement is thus *midivrei sofrim,* a Rabbinic ordinance.

צ ברייתא לא, ב (כפוף). רש״י שם ד״ה כפוף (ראשו). טור ושו״ע ס״ט. **צא** רש״י שם. **צב** לבוש ס״ט. **צג** ריטב״א כט, ב סד״ה נקטם. לבוש שם. **צד** רא״ש כלל כד סי׳ י. רבנו ירוחם נתיב ח ח״ג (נח, ג). טור ושו״ע ס״ט. דרכי משה ס״ק ו (שכן נוהגין). **צה** לבוש ס״ט. מ״א ס״ק ח. וראה ספר המנהגים — חב״ד עמ׳ 65: לוקחין לולב שאין עליו כפופין (הנק׳ כפתורים־קנעפלאך). **צו** ט״ז ס״ק י. **צז** ראה לעיל סי״ז וש״נ. **צח** כדלקמן סי׳ תרמט ס״ב. **צט** סעיף י (לענין

opinion if another *lulav* cannot readily be found, as stated in sec. 646[:10].

הָרִאשׁוֹנָה אִם אִי אֶפְשָׁר לוֹ לִמְצֹא בְּקַל לוּלָב אַחֵר. עַיֵּן סִימָן תרמ"ו:[צט]

21 The above applies when only the tops of the leaves were bent over and the major part of the leaves remained unbent. If, however, the body of the leaves is so bent over towards the middle that it appears that [they are] bent in half, [the *lulav*] is invalid, for this is not at all "beautiful."

כא וְכָל זֶה כְּשֶׁלֹּא נִכְפְּפוּ אֶלָּא רָאשֵׁי הֶעָלִין וְנִשְׁאַר הַגּוּף גָּדוֹל מֵהֶעָלִין בְּלִי כְּפִיפָה, אֲבָל אִם גּוּף הֶעָלִין נִכְפְּפוּ הַרְבֵּה מְאֹד לְאֶמְצָעָן וְנִרְאֶה כְּמוֹ שֶׁנִּכְפַּף הֶעָלֶה לִשְׁנַיִם – פָּסוּל, שֶׁאֵין זֶה הִדּוּר כְּלָל:[ק]

SECTION 646 Laws Relating to the Myrtle. (1–14)

סימן תרמו דִּינֵי הֲדַס וּבוֹ י"ד סְעִיפִים:

1 [The Torah speaks of] "a branch of a braided tree."[1] The Sages[2] interpreted this as referring to [a species] whose "branches" (i.e., its leaves[3]) cover its "tree" [i.e., its twig]. The words *va'anaf etz* imply that the entire twig [of the tree] is leaves; i.e., it is covered with leaves because they (are braided and)[4] lie on their faces. The term *avos* implies that the leaves are braided; i.e., they overlap one another like [the links of] a chain.[5]

To what [species] does this [description] apply? To the myrtle.

א "וַעֲנַף עֵץ עָבֹת",[א,1] דָּרְשׁוּ חֲכָמִים[ב,2] שֶׁעֲנָפָיו (פֵּרוּשׁ עָלָיו[ג,3]) חוֹפִין אֶת עֵצָיו, שֶׁכֵּן הוּא מַשְׁמָעוּת הַכָּתוּב "וַעֲנַף עֵץ", כְּלוֹמַר שֶׁכָּל הָעֵץ הוּא עָנָף, דְּהַיְנוּ שֶׁהוּא מְחֻפֶּה בְּעָלִין, עַל יְדֵי שֶׁהֵן (עֲשׂוּיִין בִּקְלִיעָה[4]) שׁוֹכְבִין עַל אַפֵּיהֶן;[ד] "עָבֹת" – שֶׁעָלָיו קְלוּעִין כְּמִין קְלִיעָה,[ה] דְּהַיְנוּ שֶׁהֵן מֻרְכָּבִין זֶה עַל זֶה כְּעֵין שַׁלְשֶׁלֶת,[5] וְאֵיזֶה הוּא? הֱוֵי אוֹמֵר זֶה הֲדַס:[ו]

2 [A twig] is not considered "braided" unless at least three leaves emerge

ב וְאֵינוֹ נִקְרָא "עָבֹת" אֶלָּא אִם כֵּן יוֹצְאִין מִמֶּנּוּ לְפָחוֹת שְׁלֹשָׁה עָלִין

---

1. In the original, *anaf etz avos (Vayikra 23:40)*; popularly, *hadassim*. See sec. 645:1 and footnote 1 of that section.

2. *Sukkah* 32b.

3. See: *Rashi* there; *Rambam, Hilchos Lulav* 7:2.

4. The parentheses in this case evidently indicate that the enclosed phrase should be omitted, because this sentence focuses on *anaf etz*, whereas the term *avos* ("braided") is discussed in the following sentence. This use of parentheses — to indicate a proposed variant wording (Aramaic: *girsa*) — is one of the *nine* distinct possible functions of parentheses in this work, as enumerated by R. Chayim Avraham Naeh in the Introduction to his *Kuntreis HaShulchan*.

5. *Shmos* 28:22 uses the same word *avos* to describe the braided chains attached to the breastplate of the *Kohen Gadol* (see *Divrei Nechemiah, Orach Chayim*, p. 50d).

הדס). וראה גם לקמן סי' תרמט סי"ט (נכפפו רוב ראשי העלין שבלולב). ק ט"ז שם. אליה רבה ס"ק ט.

סימן תרמו: א ויקרא כג, מ. ב גמרא לב, ב. טור ושו"ע ס"ג. ג רש"י שם ד"ה ענף. רמב"ם פ"ז ה"ב. שו"ע שם. לבוש ס"א. ד רש"י שם. וראה דברי נחמיה סי' מח (נא, ג). ה גמרא [ברייתא] שם. ו רש"י שם ד"ה בעינן. יב, א ד"ה היינו.

מִקֵּן אֶחָד,[ז,6] כְּלוֹמַר שֶׁיּוֹצְאִין שְׁלֹשָׁה עָלִין אוֹ יוֹתֵר סְמוּכִין זֶה לָזֶה בְּעִגּוּל אֶחָד, שֶׁאֵין אֶחָד מֵהֶם נָמוּךְ מֵחֲבֵרוֹ, אַף עַל פִּי שֶׁאֵין כָּל הַשְּׁלֹשָׁה עָלִין יוֹצְאִין מֵעֹקֶץ אֶחָד, כֵּיוָן שֶׁהֵן דְּבוּקִין זֶה בָּזֶה וְעוֹמְדִין בְּשָׁוֶה בְּעִגּוּל אֶחָד – הֲרֵי זֶה עָבֹת.[ח] אֲבָל אִם שְׁנֵי עָלִין הֵן עוֹמְדִין בְּשָׁוֶה דְּבוּקִים זֶה בָּזֶה וְעָלֶה הַשְּׁלִישִׁי הוּא לְמַעְלָה מֵהֶם,[ט] אוֹ שֶׁהַשְּׁלִישִׁי יוֹצֵא לְמַטָּה מֵהַשְּׁנַיִם וְעוֹלֶה וְרוֹכֵב עַל גַּבֵּי הַשְּׁנַיִם[י] – אֵין זֶה "עָבֹת", אֶלָּא[6] נִקְרָא "הֲדַס שׁוֹטֶה",[יא,7] וּפָסוּל כָּל שִׁבְעָה,[יב] אֲפִלּוּ בִּשְׁעַת הַדְּחָק שֶׁאִי אֶפְשָׁר לִמְצֹא הֲדַס אַחֵר,[יג] וְאֵין לִטֹּל אוֹתוֹ אֲפִלּוּ בְּלֹא בְּרָכָה, כֵּיוָן שֶׁאֵינוֹ מִין הֲדַס הַכָּשֵׁר כְּלָל.[יד] עַיֵּן סִימָן תרמ"ט:[טו]

ג וּלְכַתְּחִלָּה מִצְוָה לְחַזֵּר אַחַר הֲדַס

from a single "nest";[6] i.e., three or more leaves are positioned next to each other in a circle [around the stem], none of them being lower than the other. Even though they do not emerge from a single stem, since they are very close to each other and stand on an equal plane in one circle they are considered as "braided." [See fig. 23.]

If, however, two leaves stand on an equal plane, very close to each other, and the third leaf emerges on a higher level than the other two or emerges on a lower level than the other two and ascends and lies on them, this is not considered "braided." [See fig. 24.] Rather,[6] such a species is called a deviant myrtle.[7] It is invalid throughout the seven days of the festival, even in a pressing situation when no other myrtle twig can be found. It should not be used even without reciting a blessing, for it does not belong to the same species as a valid myrtle. See sec. 649[:23].

3 As an initial preference, it is a *mitzvah* to seek out a myrtle [twig] that is

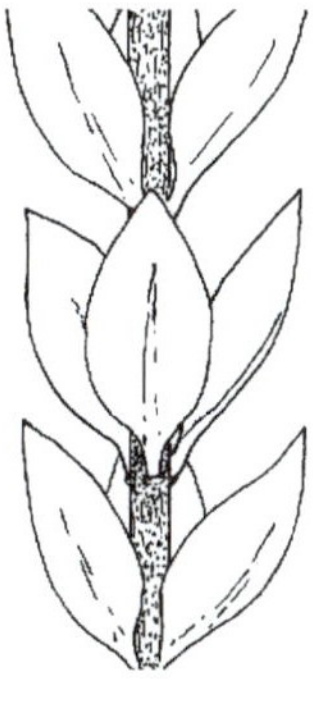

Fig. 23:
Three stems sprouting from the same "nest"
(see sec. 646:2).

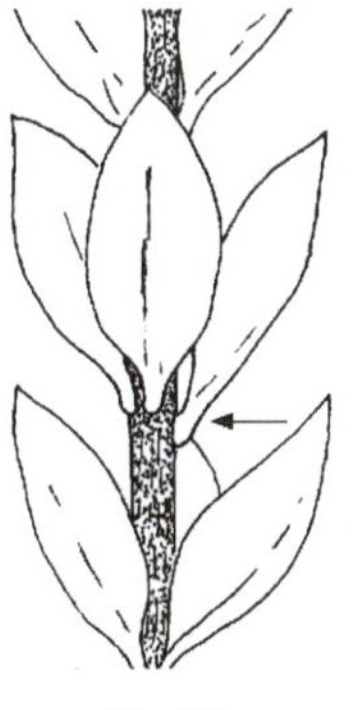

Fig. 24:
If the third leaf emerges on a lower level than the other two, this is not considered "braided" (see sec. 646:2).

6. *Sukkah* 32b.

7. In the original, *hadas shoteh* (cf. *Rashi* on *Bamidbar* 5:12, citing *Sotah* 3a).

ז רב יהודה שם בגמרא. טור ושו"ע שם. ח תוס' שם ד"ה תלתא. רא"ש פ"ג סי' ח. טור ולבוש ס"ג. ט רמב"ם שם. ריטב"א שם ד"ה היכי. שו"ע ולבוש שם. י רש"י שם ד"ה תרי וחד. ריטב"א שם. לבוש שם. יא גמרא שם. רמב"ם ושו"ע שם. יב תמים דעים סי' רכז. רבנו ירוחם נתיב ח ח"ג (נט, א). מ"א ריש הסי'. יג רמ"א ס"ג. יד ב"י סימן תרמ"ט ד"ה וכל הפסולים. וראה חידושי צמח צדק פ"ג דסוכה (עב, ב). טו סכ"ג, וש"נ. טז ראב"ד בתמים דעים סי'

שֶׁכֻּלּוֹ "עָבֹת", דְּהַיְנוּ שֶׁכָּל הַקִּנִּים שֶׁל עָלִין הַיּוֹצְאִין בְּכָל אֹרֶךְ שִׁעוּרוֹ, שֶׁהוּא שְׁלֹשָׁה טְפָחִים[8] כְּמוֹ שֶׁיִּתְבָּאֵר בְּסִימָן תר"נ, יֵשׁ בְּכָל קֵן וָקֵן שְׁלֹשָׁה עָלִין. וּמִכָּל מָקוֹם, אִם אֵין כֻּלּוֹ עָבֹת, כֵּיוָן שֶׁרֻבּוֹ עָבֹת, דְּהַיְנוּ שֶׁרֹב קִנִּים שֶׁל עָלִין הַיּוֹצְאִין בְּתוֹךְ אֹרֶךְ שִׁעוּרוֹ שֶׁהוּא שְׁלֹשָׁה טְפָחִים יֵשׁ בְּכָל אֶחָד וְאֶחָד מֵהֶם שְׁלֹשָׁה עָלִין – הֲרֵי זֶה כָּשֵׁר, וּמֻתָּר לְבָרֵךְ עָלָיו לְכַתְּחִלָּה:[טז]

entirely braided; i.e., all the sets of leaves throughout the three handbreadths — which is its minimum measure,[8] as will be explained in sec. 650[:1] — emerge in threes from the same point. Nevertheless, if it is not entirely braided but mostly braided — i.e., most of the sets of leaves throughout its minimum measure, which is three handbreadths, emerge in threes from the same point — it is valid. Even as an initial preference, one may recite a blessing over such a twig.

ד וְאִם בַּתְּחִלָּה הָיָה כֻּלּוֹ אוֹ רֻבּוֹ "עָבֹת" וְאַחַר כָּךְ נָשְׁרוּ[יז] מִמֶּנּוּ עָלִין, אֲפִלּוּ נָשַׁר עָלֶה אֶחָד מִכָּל קֵן וָקֵן[יח] מִכָּל הַקִּנִּים שֶׁל עָלִין הַיּוֹצְאִין בְּכָל אֹרֶךְ שִׁעוּרוֹ, וַאֲפִלּוּ מִקְצָת הַקִּנִּים נָשְׁרוּ עֲלֵיהֶן לְגַמְרֵי וְלֹא נִשְׁתַּיֵּר בָּהֶן אֲפִלּוּ עָלֶה אֶחָד,[יט] הוֹאִיל וּבְרֹב הַקִּנִּים נִשְׁתַּיֵּר בְּכָל אֶחָד וְאֶחָד מֵהֶן רֹב שִׁעוּר "עָבֹת", דְּהַיְנוּ שֶׁבְּכָל אֶחָד וְאֶחָד מֵהֶן נִשְׁתַּיֵּר שְׁנֵי עָלִין שְׁלֵמִין שֶׁלֹּא נָשְׁרוּ[9] – הֲרֵי זֶה כָּשֵׁר:[כ,6]

4 If, at the outset, [a myrtle twig] was either entirely or mostly braided, and then some of its leaves fell off, it is valid[6] if the majority of the leaves necessary for it to be considered braided — i.e., two complete leaves — remain attached in the majority of the sets of leaves.[9] [This applies even] if one leaf from every set of leaves [along the three handbreadths] fell off, and even if some of the sets fell off entirely without leaving even one leaf.

ה הֲדַס הַמִּצְרִי, שֶׁיֵּשׁ בְּכָל קֵן וָקֵן הַיּוֹצֵא מִמֶּנּוּ שִׁבְעָה עָלִין וְנָשְׁרוּ מֵהֶן אַרְבָּעָה עָלִין מִכָּל קֵן וָקֵן – הֲרֵי זֶה כָּשֵׁר, אַף עַל פִּי

5 [A twig from] an Egyptian myrtle, which has seven leaves emerging in each set, is valid even if four leaves fell off from each set, because even though

8. These three handbreadths are measured from the top of the myrtle downward. *Rama* (sec. 646:5) holds that the three handbreadths need not be measured from the top. The Alter Rebbe does not state this explicitly — possibly because he rules in subsection 11 below that the presence of dried-out leaves at the top of a myrtle twig cannot be overlooked, and hence the leaves at the top, too, must be braided. See R. Moshe Wiener, *Arbaas HaMinim*, Vol. 1, p. 94.

9. Even though most of the leaves fell off, the myrtle twig can still be valid, provided most of the leaves from the majority of the sets remain.

רכח, ובהשגות פ"ז ה"ב. רא"ש פ"ג ס"י. טור ושו"ע ס"ה. וכדלעיל סי' תרמה ס"ט (לענין לולב, דסגי ברוב עלין כשרים). וראה שערים המצויינים בהלכה סי' קלו ס"ק יא. **יז** משנה לב, ב (נפרצו). לפירוש רש"י שם ד"ה נפרצו (נשרו). רא"ש שם פ"ג ס"י. וראה לקמן סי' תרמט סכ"ג (במוסגר), טעם הפסול משום שאין שמו עליו. **יח** גמרא שם (שפסול רק כשנשרו תרי), לפירוש הרא"ה, הובא בר"ן (טו, ב) ד"ה משכחת, ובריטב"א שם ד"ה אמר ר"פ. רא"ש שם וטור, לפירוש הב"ח ד"ה היו בו. ט"ז ס"ק ח. אליה רבה ס"ק ב. **יט** כדלעיל ס"ג, דסגי ברוב עלין שבאורך שיעור ג' טפחים. **כ** קרבן נתנאל שם אות ח (שפסול רק כשנשרו רוב עליו מרוב ארכו). וכדלעיל סי' תרמה ס"ט (לענין לולב) דסגי בתרי רובי להכשיר (רוב העלין ברוב ארכן). וראה ביאור הלכה ס"ה ד"ה ולעיכובא. ארבעת המינים (ויינר) ע' צו.

שֶׁרֹב עָלָיו נָשְׁרוּ, מִכָּל מָקוֹם הֲרֵי נִשְׁתַּיֵּר שִׁעוּר "עָבֹת" בְּכָל קֵן וָקֵן.[כא,10] אֲבָל אִם בְּרֹב הַקִּינִים שֶׁל עָלִין הַיּוֹצְאִין מִמֶּנּוּ נָשְׁרוּ חֲמִשָּׁה עָלִין מִכָּל אֶחָד וְאֶחָד מֵהֶן, אֲפִלּוּ אִם מִעוּט הַקִּינִים לֹא נָשַׁר מֵהֶן כְּלָל וְהֵן שְׁלֵמִים שִׁבְעָה עָלִין בְּכָל אֶחָד וְאֶחָד מֵהֶן, מִכָּל מָקוֹם כֵּיוָן שֶׁרֹב הַקִּינִים נָשְׁרוּ רֹב עֲלֵיהֶן, וְגַם לֹא נִשְׁתַּיֵּר בְּכָל אֶחָד וְאֶחָד מֵהֶן שִׁעוּר "עָבֹת" דְּהַיְנוּ שְׁלֹשָׁה עָלִין — הֲרֵי זֶה פָּסוּל:[כב]

most of the leaves have fallen, every set still has [three leaves, which is] the minimum number that constitutes a braid.[10] If five leaves fell off from most of the sets, [the twig] is invalid. [This applies] even if no leaves at all fell from the minority of the sets, and they are complete, each with seven leaves. [The twig is] nevertheless invalid, since the majority of the leaves fell from the majority of the sets, and they were left without the minimal three leaves that enable a set to be considered "braided."

ו וּבִמְדִינוֹת אֵלּוּ שֶׁאֵין הֲדַסִּים כְּשֵׁרִים מְצוּיִין — נוֹהֲגִין לְבָרֵךְ עַל הֲדַס שֶׁאֵין בּוֹ שְׁלֹשָׁה עָלִין בְּקָנֶה אֶחָד אֶלָּא הֵן גְּדֵלִים שְׁנַיִם עַל גַּבֵּי שְׁנַיִם.[כג] וְיֵשׁ שֶׁלִּמְּדוּ עֲלֵיהֶם זְכוּת,[כד] שֶׁלֹּא אָמְרוּ שֶׁכָּל הֲדַס שֶׁאֵין בּוֹ שְׁלֹשָׁה עָלִין בְּקֵן אֶחָד הֲרֵי זֶה "הֲדַס שׁוֹטֶה" אֶלָּא כְּשֶׁעָלָה הַשְּׁלִישִׁי:[כה,11]

6 In these countries where valid myrtles are not common, it is customary to [use and] recite the blessing over a twig that does not have three leaves growing in one row, but [has leaves that] grow in rows of two. Some [authorities] offer support for this practice, [stating] that the statement that a myrtle that does not have three leaves in a row is deviant applies only when the third leaf.... [The conclusion of this subsection is not extant.][11]

ז וַהֲדַסִּים הָאֵלּוּ כֵּיוָן שֶׁאֵין בָּהֶן רַק שְׁנֵי עָלִים בְּכָל קֵן, לְפִיכָךְ אִם בְּרֹב הַקִּינִים שֶׁל עָלִין הַיּוֹצְאִין בְּאֹרֶךְ שִׁעוּרוֹ שֶׁהוּא שְׁלֹשָׁה טְפָחִים נָשַׁר עָלֶה אֶחָד מִכָּל אֶחָד וְאֶחָד מֵהֶן — הֲרֵי זֶה פָּסוּל, שֶׁהֲרֵי בְּרֹב הַקִּינִים לֹא נִשְׁתַּיֵּר בְּכָל קֵן וָקֵן רֹב שִׁעוּרֵי

7 Since such myrtles have only two leaves in each row, if one of the leaves from each of the majority of the rows within three handbreadths, its minimum measure, falls off, [such a twig] is invalid. [The rationale is that] the majority of the number [of leaves] necessary for [the twig

10. *Sukkah* 33a.

11. The remainder of this subsection is not extant in the present work. It appears, however, that the Alter Rebbe is referring to the explanation of *Rama* 646:3 (quoting *Maharik,* Responsum 41), that a myrtle twig is considered deviant when its leaves grow in groups of three and one leaf emerges lower down and overlaps the two higher leaves. If the third leaf emerges above the other two and is overlapped by them, the twig is not considered deviant. Moreover, if the leaves grow in ordered patterns of two, they are not deviant; they follow a set pattern.

כא גמרא לג, א. טור ושו"ע ס"ד. **כב** ב"ח שם. ט"ז שם. **כג** תרומת הדשן ח"ב סי' רנט. רמ"א ס"ג. **כד** מהרי"ק שורש מא ענף ב. וראה רמ"א שם. **כה** חסר הסיום. במהרי"ק שם: שהעלה השלישי למטה מהשנים עולה ורוכב כו' הוא דמיקרי הדם שוטה אבל אם הוא למעלה מן השנים כמו שהוא באותו שאנו רגילין לקרוא לו הדם שוטה אפשר שהוא כשר לרש"י [ראה לעיל ס"ב]. וברמ"א שם: אינן נקראים הדם שוטה הואיל והם שנים על גב שנים. **כו** ב"ח ד"ה ומ"ש

"עָבֹת", דְּהַיְנוּ שְׁנֵי עָלִין.[כו,12] וְצָרִיךְ לִזָּהֵר מְאֹד בָּזֶה, דְּהַרְבֵּה פְּעָמִים נוֹשְׁרִים עָלִין הַרְבֵּה מֵהֲדַס וְאֵין מַשְׁגִּיחִין עַל זֶה:[כז]

to be considered] "braided," i.e., two leaves,[12] does not remain in the majority of rows. Much care must be taken in this regard, for many leaves often fall from myrtle twigs and people do not pay attention to this.

ח יָבְשׁוּ עָלָיו – פָּסוּל,[כח,6] לְפִי שֶׁאֵין זֶה הִדּוּר.[כט,13] אֲבָל אִם לֹא הִגִּיעוּ לִכְלַל הַיַּבְשׁוּת אַף עַל פִּי שֶׁכְּבָר כָּמְשׁוּ – כָּשֵׁר.[ל]

וְכַמָּה שִׁעוּר הַיַּבְשׁוּת[לא]? כְּשֶׁהֵן נִפְרָכִין בְּצִפֹּרֶן[לב] כְּשֶׁמְּמַשְׁמֵשׁ בָּהֶן[לג] וְגַם[לד] כָּלָה כָּל מַרְאֵה יַרְקוּת שֶׁבָּהֶן וְהִלְבִּינוּ פְּנֵיהֶם[14] – אָז הֵן נִקְרָאִים יְבֵשִׁים, שֶׁהֲרֵי אֲפִלּוּ אִם תַּשְׁרֶה אוֹתָן בְּמַיִם כַּמָּה יָמִים – לֹא יַחְזְרוּ לְמַרְאֵיהֶן, וַהֲרֵי הֵן כְּעֵץ יָבֵשׁ שֶׁאֲפִלּוּ אִם תַּשְׁרֶה אוֹתוֹ בְּמַיִם כַּמָּה יָמִים לֹא יָסוּר מֵעָלָיו שֵׁם הַיָּבֵשׁ. אֲבָל קֹדֶם שֶׁהִלְבִּינוּ פְּנֵיהֶם, אַף עַל פִּי שֶׁהֵן נִפְרָכִין בְּצִפֹּרֶן מֵחֲמַת יַבְשׁוּתָן, מִכָּל מָקוֹם אִם תַּשְׁרֶה אוֹתָן בְּמַיִם יוֹם אוֹ יוֹמַיִם – יַחְזְרוּ לִכְמוֹת שֶׁהָיוּ בְּמִשְׁמוּשָׁן וּבְמַרְאִיתָן:[לה]

8 If the leaves [of a myrtle twig] dried out, it is invalid,[6] because it is not considered "beautiful."[13] If the leaves have not dried out, even though they have already withered, they are valid.

What degree of dryness [disqualifies them]? They crumble when handled by one's fingernail and their green color has faded to the extent that they become white.[14] [At this stage] they are called "dried out," for even if they would be soaked in water for several days, they would not return to their [natural] appearance. They are like dried wood which will not lose the description of being "dried out" even if it is left to soak in water for several days. Before they become white, even if they will crumble from dryness when handled by a fingernail, [they are not considered as "dried out"], for if they are placed in water for a day or two, [their leaves] will regain their [natural] texture and appearance.

ט אִם יָבְשׁוּ רֹב עָלִין שֶׁל כָּל שְׁלֹשָׁה בַּדֵּי הֲדַס[15] וְנִשְׁתַּיְּרוּ בְּכָל בַּד וּבַד קֵן אֶחָד שֶׁיֵּשׁ בּוֹ שְׁלֹשָׁה עָלִין לַחִין – כָּשֵׁר.[לו,10] וְהוּא שֶׁקֵּן הַלַּח הַזֶּה הוּא עוֹמֵד בְּרֹאשׁ

9 [The following rules apply if] most of the leaves of all three[15] myrtle twigs dried out. If each twig still has three fresh leaves in one row, they are valid.[10] [This applies] provided the row [of] fresh [leaves] is positioned at the top of the twig, because

---

12. As evident from sec. 648:20, half and half is not acceptable; a majority is required.

13. *Sukkah* 29b, 31a.

14. If the leaves darken and become blackish, they are still acceptable (*Nitei Gavriel*, p. 31). If, however, they blacken entirely, *Nitei Gavriel* maintains that they are valid, but *Hadar Hu LeChol Chassidav* (i.e., R. Moshe Wiener, *Arbaas HaMinim*, Vol. 1) rules that they are invalid.

15. See sec. 651:1.

ואדוני אבי. קרבן נתנאל שם. אליה רבה ס"ק ב. **כז** ט"ז סוף ס"ק ב. **כח** משנה לב, ב. טור ושו"ע ס"ו. **כט** גמרא כט, ב. לא, א (לענין לולב, וכדלעיל סי' תרמה סט"ז). רש"י לג, א ד"ה ובראש (לענין הדס). ט"ז ס"ק י. **ל** ברייתא לא, סע"א. טור ושו"ע שם. וראה גם לקמן סי' תרמז ס"ו (בערבה). סי' תרמח ס"א (באתרוג). **לא** ראב"ד בתמים דעים סי' רלב. הובא ברא"ש רפ"ג. טור ושו"ע ס"ז. וראה לעיל סי' תרמה סט"ז וש"נ. **לב** משאת בנימין סי' יז. מ"א ס"ק ו. **לג** רש"י בכורות לז, א ד"ה נפרכת (לענין בכור). וראה גם לעיל סי' תרמה סט"ז (לענין לולב). **לד** משאת בנימין שם. מ"א שם. **לה** ראב"ד שם. רא"ש שם. טור ולבוש ס"ו. **לו** ברייתא לג, א. לפירוש רש"י שם ד"ה שלשה. דעה הא' בטור ושו"ע ס"ח. **לז** רב חסדא בגמרא שם. טור ושו"ע שם.

הַבַּד,[לז] לְפִי שֶׁרֹאשׁ הַבַּד הוּא עִקַּר מַרְאִית הַהֲדַס שֶׁהָאָדָם רוֹאֶה אוֹתוֹ בִּתְחִלַּת הַשְׁקָפָתוֹ,[לח] וְאִם הוּא יָבֵשׁ – הֲרֵי אֵין הַהֲדַס הָדָר כְּלָל,[לט] שֶׁעִקַּר הֲדָרוֹ תָּלוּי בְּרֹאשׁוֹ:

[this] is what counts most towards the myrtle's appearance, for a person sees it at first glance. If it is dried out, the myrtle is not considered "beautiful," for its "beauty" depends primarily on the top of the twig.

י וְאִם הַשְּׁלֹשָׁה עָלִין אֵלּוּ שֶׁבְּרֹאשׁ הַבַּדִּים אֵינָן לַחִים גְּמוּרִים אֶלָּא הֵן כְּמוּשִׁים, אַף עַל פִּי שֶׁאִם הָיוּ כָּל עֲלֵי הֲדַס כְּמוּשִׁים הֲרֵי הוּא כָּשֵׁר,[מ] מִכָּל מָקוֹם עַכְשָׁו שֶׁכֻּלָּן יְבֵשִׁים – אֵין הַכָּמוּשׁ מַצִּיל מִיַּד הַיָּבֵשׁ שֶׁלֹּא יִפָּסֵל, אֶלָּא הַלַּח הֶהָדָר הוּא שֶׁמַּצִּיל.[מא] וְיֵשׁ חוֹלְקִין[מב] עַל זֶה וְאוֹמְרִים, כֵּיוָן שֶׁכָּמוּשׁ כָּשֵׁר – הֲרֵי הוּא כְּלַח לְכָל דָּבָר, וּמַצִּיל מִיַּד הַיָּבֵשׁ שֶׁלֹּא יִפָּסֵל. וְיֵשׁ לִסְמֹךְ עַל דִּבְרֵיהֶם מִיּוֹם שֵׁנִי שֶׁל חַג וָאֵילָךְ[16] שֶׁאֵין חִיּוּב נְטִילַת לוּלָב בָּהֶן אֶלָּא מִדִּבְרֵי סוֹפְרִים:[מג,17]

10 [There are two views on the validity of the twigs] if these three leaves at the top of the twigs are not entirely fresh, but are withered. [Some authorities hold that] although if all the leaves of a myrtle twig were withered it would be valid, now that all the [other] leaves are dry, these withered leaves do not save the dry leaves from disqualifying [the twigs]. That is possible only when the leaves are fresh and "beautiful."

However, other authorities differ and maintain that since a withered leaf is valid, it is considered as [if it were] fresh in all respects. Hence it also saves the dry leaves from disqualifying [the twigs]. One may rely on their opinion from the second day of the festival onward,[16] when the obligation of taking the *lulav* is only Rabbinic in origin.[17]

יא אַף עַל פִּי שֶׁכָּל הַמִּינִים שֶׁל לוּלָב[מד,18] שֶׁנִּקְטְמוּ רָאשֵׁיהֶן פְּסוּלִין לְפִי שֶׁאֵין זֶה הִדּוּר, אֲבָל הֲדַס שֶׁנִּקְטַם רֹאשׁוֹ,[מה] אֲפִלּוּ נִקְטַם גּוּף הָעֵץ[מו] שֶׁל הֲדַס עִם עָלָיו – הֲרֵי זֶה כָּשֵׁר,[19] לְפִי שֶׁהַהֲדַס

11 With regard to all the [other] species of the *lulav*,[18] if their tips have been cut off they are invalid, because then they are not considered "beautiful." [An exception is made] with regard to the myrtle. If its top has been cut off, and even if the top of the twig itself and its leaves have been cut off, it is valid.[19] [The rationale is that] since the myrtle has many

---

16. A blessing may be recited in such circumstances. On the first day, by contrast, if there are no other myrtle twigs, one should use such a twig, but should not recite a blessing (see *Pri Megadim: Eshel Avraham* 246:9).

17. See ch. 645, footnote 35 above.

18. "The *lulav*" here signifies all of the Four Species. See end of sec. 651:17 below.

19. *Sukkah* 34b.

לח רא"ש פ"ג סי' י (לפי פירושו בהלכה זו). לבוש ס"ח. וכדלקמן סי' תרמח סכ"א (לענין חוטמו של אתרוג) וש"נ. לט רש"י שם ד"ה ובראש. ט"ז ס"ק י. מ כדלעיל ס"ח וש"נ. מא ראב"ד בתמים דעים סי' רלב). ר"ן (טו, ב) ד"ה ת"ר. דעה הא' בשו"ע ס"ט. מב טור בשם הרא"ש פ"ג סי' י. ריטב"א שם ד"ה ת"ר, בשם הרא"ה. דעה הב' בשו"ע שם. מג ועד"ז לעיל סי' תרמה ס"כ וש"נ. וראה לקמן סי' תרמט סכ"ד (דין הדסים יבשים בשעת הדחק). מד לענין לולב, לעיל סי' תרמה סי"ז. לענין ערבה, לקמן סי' תרמז ס"ד. ועי' לקמן סי' תרמח סי"ז, לענין אתרוג. מה ר"ט במשנה לד, ב וכר"י אמר שמואל בגמרא שם, לפי' הרי"ף (טו, ב). רמב"ם פ"ח ה"ה. רמב"ן (מלחמות שם, תשובות ופסקים להראב"ד סי' ז). רא"ש פ"ג סוף ס"י וסי"ד. טור. שו"ע ס"א וס"י דעה הא' (בסתם). דרכי משה ס"ק א, בשם המנהגים (ר"א טירנא) ריש מנהגי סוכות. מו רא"ש שם ס"ב. ר"ן (יד, א) ד"ה נקטם. רמ"א ס"י. מז רא"ש שם סי"ד בשם

כֵּיוָן שֶׁהוּא מְרֻבֶּה בְּעָלִין – הֲרֵי עָלָיו הַנִּשְׁאָרִין חוֹפִין אֶת מְקוֹם הַקְּטִימָה וְאֵין הַקְּטִימָה נִכֶּרֶת.[מז] וְיֵשׁ חוֹלְקִין[מח] עַל זֶה וְאוֹמְרִים, דְּאַף הֲדַס שֶׁנִּקְטַם רֹאשׁוֹ, דְּהַיְנוּ שֶׁנִּקְטַם רֹאשׁ הָעֵץ[מט] עַצְמוֹ שֶׁהֶעָלִין יוֹצְאִין מִמֶּנּוּ, כֵּיוָן שֶׁרֹאשׁוֹ אֵינוֹ מְהֻדָּר – הֲרֵי זֶה פָּסוּל. וּלְפִי דִבְרֵיהֶם[נ] אֲפִלּוּ אִם לֹא נִקְטַם רֹאשׁוֹ אֶלָּא שֶׁהַשְּׁלֹשָׁה עָלִין שֶׁבְּרֹאשׁוֹ הֵן יְבֵשִׁים, אַף עַל פִּי שֶׁשְּׁאָר כָּל עָלִין הֵן לַחִין וּמְהֻדָּרִין, מִכָּל מָקוֹם כֵּיוָן שֶׁהֶעָלִין שֶׁבְּרֹאשׁוֹ אֵינָן מְהֻדָּרִין – הֲרֵי זֶה פָּסוּל. וְיֵשׁ לְהַחְמִיר כְּדִבְרֵיהֶם בְּמָקוֹם שֶׁאֶפְשָׁר לִמְצֹא הֲדַס אַחֵר,[נא] אֲבָל אִם אִי אֶפְשָׁר לִמְצֹא אַחֵר – מֻתָּר לְבָרֵךְ עָלָיו[נב] וְלִסְמֹךְ עַל סְבָרָא הָרִאשׁוֹנָה:

leaves, the remaining leaves cover the place where the tip was cut off and the cut is not obvious.

Differing authorities maintain that even if the tip of the myrtle — i.e., the twig itself from which the leaves emerge — is cut off, the twig is invalid, because the tip is not considered "beautiful." According to their opinion, even if the tip is not cut off, but the three leaves at the top [of the twig] have dried out, it is invalid. Since the leaves at its tip are not "beautiful," [the fact that] all the other leaves are fresh and "beautiful" [is not significant].

Where possible, one should be stringent and follow the latter view in a place where it is possible to find other myrtle twigs. If it is impossible to find another, one may rely on the first opinion and recite a blessing over such a myrtle twig.

יב דֶּרֶךְ עֵץ הַהֲדַס לְגַדֵּל פְּרִי הַדּוֹמֶה לַעֲנָבִים,[נג] וְאִם יֵשׁ בְּאֹרֶךְ שִׁעוּר הַהֲדַס שֶׁהוּא שְׁלֹשָׁה טְפָחִים[נד] כָּל כָּךְ עֲנָבִים הַלָּלוּ יוֹתֵר מִמִּנְיַן הֶעָלִין הַגְּדֵלִין בְּאֹרֶךְ זֶה – הֲרֵי זֶה פָּסוּל[נה,2] אֲפִלּוּ מִיּוֹם שֵׁנִי וְאֵילָךְ;[נו] לְפִי שֶׁעֲנָבִים הַלָּלוּ דֶּרֶךְ מַרְאֵיהֶן לִהְיוֹת שָׁחֹר אוֹ אָדֹם[נז] וְהַהֲדַס מַרְאֵהוּ יָרֹק – וַהֲרֵי זֶה כִּמְנֻמָּר[נח,20] וְאֵין זֶה הִדּוּר.[נט] לְפִיכָךְ, אִם הָיָה מַרְאֵה הָעֲנָבִים הַלָּלוּ יָרֹק כְּמַרְאֵה

12 The myrtle tree produces fruit similar to grapes [or berries]. If there are more of these berries than leaves along the three handbreadths that constitute the minimum length of the myrtle twig, it is invalid.[2] This applies even from the second day and onward. [The rationale is that] these berries are usually black or red, while the myrtle twig is green. It will thus appear speckled,[20] and this is not considered "beautiful." Therefore if the color of the berries is green like the color of the

---

20. *Op. cit.*, 33b.

ה״ר ישעיה (פסקי רי״ד לד, ב). הובא בב״י סד״ה נקטם. וראה רמב״ן שם. הובא במגיד משנה שם ה״ו. לבוש ס״ט. מ״א ס״ק ז. ט״ז ס״ק א. **מח** ראב״ד (בהשגות פ״ח ה״ה, תמים דעים סי׳ רכח). בעל המאור שם. רא״ה במשנה שם. ריטב״א ור״ן במשנה שם ד״ה מתני׳. שו״ע שם דעה הב׳ (ויש פוסלים). **מט** ר״ן (יד, א) ד״ה נקטם (טו, ב) ד״ה מתני׳. רמ״א שם. ט״ז ס״ק א. וראה עד״ז לקמן סי׳ תרמז ס״ד. **נ** משא״כ לדברי המכשירים בנקטם ה״ה ביבש (וכפסק הטור ושו״ע שם בדעה הא׳) — ב״י ד״ה ומ״ש הלכך, בשם הר״ן (שם) סד״ה ת״ר (ושהטעם דפוסל — ביבש בראשו — הוא לשיטתו, בנקטם ראשו). וכ״ה בריטב״א ורא״ה (הפוסלים בנקטם, כנ״ל) לג, א ד״ה ת״ר. לבוש שם (בדעה הב׳). ועיין אליה רבה ס״ק ז, בדעת הראב״ד. **נא** מ״מ פ״ח ה״ה. רמ״א שם. לבוש שם. ט״ז ס״ק א,. וראה גם לקמן סי׳ תרנא ס״א (ומציין לכאן). **נב** יראים השלם סי׳ תכב. הובא במרדכי רמז תשמו. ב״ח ד״ה נקטם. מ״א סי׳ תרמה ס״ק ו. וראה לעיל שם סי״ז וש״נ. **נג** רש״י במשנה לב, ב ד״ה ענביו. **נד** כדלעיל ס״ג וש״נ. **נה** משנה שם. טור ושו״ע ס״ב. **נו** בדק הבית סוף הסי׳. מ״א ס״ק ד. וככל פסולי הדר שפסולין כל שבעה, כדלקמן סי׳ תרמט סי״ז. וראה שם סי״ט, לענין שעת הדחק. **נז** גמרא לג, ב. טור ושו״ע שם. **נח** גמרא שם. דין מנומר ראה לקמן סי׳ תרמח סכ״ו. **נט** רש״י שם ד״ה מנומר. יא, ב ד״ה עבר. לבוש ס״י. מ״א שם (אף כשהם במקום א׳).

הַהֲדַס — כָּשֵׁר אֲפִלּוּ בְּיוֹם רִאשׁוֹן, אַף עַל פִּי שֶׁהֵן מְרֻבִּין מֵעָלָיו:[ס]

myrtle [leaves], it is valid, even on the first day, despite the fact that there are more berries than leaves.

יג וַאֲפִלּוּ אִם הָיוּ אֲדֻמּוֹת אוֹ שְׁחוֹרוֹת וְהָיוּ מְרֻבּוֹת עַל הֶעָלִין וּמִעֵט אוֹתָם, דְּהַיְנוּ שֶׁלִּקֵּט וְהֵסִיר מִקְצָתָן מֵהַהֲדַס עַד שֶׁהָיוּ הֶעָלִין מְרֻבִּין עַל הָעֲנָבִין,[סא] בֵּין שֶׁמִּעֲטָן מֵעֶרֶב יוֹם טוֹב בֵּין שֶׁעָבַר וּמִעֲטָן בְּיוֹם טוֹב — הֲרֵי זֶה כָּשֵׁר,[סב, 21] וּמֻתָּר לְבָרֵךְ עָלָיו לְכַתְּחִלָּה.[סג, 22] אֲבָל לְכַתְּחִלָּה אָסוּר לְמַעֲטָן בְּיוֹם טוֹב,[סד, 23] אַף עַל פִּי שֶׁמֻּתָּר לִתְלֹשׁ פֵּרוֹת בְּשַׁבָּת מֵעָנָף הַתָּלוּשׁ מֵהָאִילָן מֵעֶרֶב שַׁבָּת כְּמוֹ שֶׁנִּתְבָּאֵר בְּסִימָן של"ו,[סה] מִכָּל מָקוֹם כֵּיוָן שֶׁעַל יְדֵי תְּלִישָׁה זוֹ מִתְכַּשֵּׁר הַהֲדַס לְמִצְוָתוֹ[סו] — הֲרֵי זֶה כִּמְתַקֵּן כְּלִי בְּיוֹם טוֹב.[סז, 20] וַאֲפִלּוּ אִם הוּא אֵינוֹ מִתְכַּוֵּן כְּלָל לְהַכְשִׁיר אֶת הַהֲדַס אֶלָּא כַּוָּנָתוֹ לֶאֱכֹל אֶת הָעֲנָבִים,[24] מִכָּל מָקוֹם הֲרֵי עַל כָּרְחוֹ מִתְכַּשֵּׁר הַהֲדַס וְנַעֲשֶׂה כְּלִי עַל יְדֵי תְּלִישָׁה זוֹ, וַהֲרֵי זֶה כְּעֵין פְּסִיק רֵישֵׁהּ וְלָא יָמוּת[סח, 25] שֶׁנִּתְבָּאֵר בְּסִימָן ש"כ,[סט] עַיֵּן שָׁם:

13 Even when the berries are red or black and there are more berries than leaves, [the twig] is valid if one removed some of them until there were more leaves than berries. [This applies] whether one removed them before the festival or one transgressed and removed them on the festival itself.[21] A blessing may be recited over such a myrtle twig [even] as an initial preference.[22]

Nevertheless, at the outset, it is forbidden to remove the berries on the festival.[23] On *Shabbos,* it is permitted to pick fruit from a branch that was severed from its tree before *Shabbos,* as stated in sec. 336[:14]. Nevertheless, [different laws apply in the present instance. The rationale is] that since, by removing these berries, the myrtle is made fit to be used for its *mitzvah,* doing so resembles putting a utensil in working order on the festival.[20] [Moreover,] even if one has no intention whatever to make the myrtle twig fit [for the *mitzvah*] but desires to eat the berries, [this is forbidden].[24] [The rationale is] that independent of his will, due to the plucking [of the berries], the myrtle is made valid and becomes [like] a utensil. Thus it resembles a situation described as *psik reisha velo yamus,*[25] as explained in sec. 320[:22-24].

21. I.e., even if one intentionally removed them, we do not say that the twig may not be used because the *mitzvah* was performed at the expense of a forbidden act.

22. See sec. 649:5.

23. Even if this will prevent one from fulfilling the *mitzvah* of *lulav;* see sec. 586:22.

24. If, however, there is no other myrtle twig available, a non-Jew may be instructed to remove the berries in order to eat them (R. Akiva Eiger).

25. The term *psik reisha velo yamus* is borrowed from *Shabbos* 75a: "If its head is cut off, will it not die?!"

One transgresses the prohibition of performing a forbidden labor on *Shabbos* only if it was performed intentionally. However, if one has no intent to perform a forbidden labor, but his action will unavoidably result in the performance of the forbidden labor, this

ס גמרא שם. טור ושו"ע שם. סא משנה לב, ב. טור ושו"ע שם. סב גמרא לג, ב. טור ושו"ע שם. סג ראה לקמן סי' תרמט ס"ה. לעיל סי' תנד סי"ב. סד משנה שם. טור ושו"ע שם. סה סעיף יד. סו רש"י ד"ה מתקן. סז גמרא שם (קא מתקן). רמב"ם פ"ח ה"ה, ושו"ע שם (כמתקן). וראה תוס' שבת קג, א סד"ה לא (דלא אסיר אלא מדרבנן). רבנו מנוח שם (משום שבות). לבוש שם (דמיא למלאכה). לעיל סי' שמ סי"ז (בסכין חייב). סי' תקיד קו"א ס"ק ד. סח גמרא

14 When does the above apply? When he needs this myrtle twig, because he does not have another one. If, however, he has another myrtle twig, and has no need at all for this one, he may pluck the berries from this twig in order to eat them on the festival.[20] Even though the myrtle twig thereby becomes valid and thus this activity resembles making a utensil, [it is permitted,] because he himself does not need this myrtle at all. Hence he did not put anything in working order [for himself].

יד בַּמֶּה דְּבָרִים אֲמוּרִים? כְּשֶׁהוּא צָרִיךְ לַהֲדַס הַזֶּה שֶׁאֵין לוֹ הֲדַס אַחֵר, אֲבָל אִם יֵשׁ לוֹ הֲדַס אַחֵר וְאֵינוֹ צָרִיךְ כְּלָל לַהֲדַס הַזֶּה – מֻתָּר לוֹ לִתְלֹשׁ הָעֲנָבִים כְּדֵי לְאָכְלָן בְּיוֹם טוֹב,[ע,20] וְאַף עַל פִּי שֶׁעַל יְדֵי זֶה מִתְכַּשֵּׁר הַהֲדַס וְנַעֲשֶׂה כְּלִי, מִכָּל מָקוֹם כֵּיוָן שֶׁהוּא בְּעַצְמוֹ אֵינוֹ צָרִיךְ לַהֲדַס הַזֶּה כְּלָל – הֲרֵי לֹא תִקֵּן כְּלוּם:[עא]

SECTION 647 Laws Relating to the Willow. (1–6)

סימן תרמז דִּינֵי עֲרָבָה וּבוֹ ו' סְעִיפִים:

1 "The willows of the brook" mentioned in the Torah[1] are a known species referred to by this name. This species of willow has the following distinguishing signs:

[i] Its stem is red.[2] Nevertheless, even while it is still green, one may fulfill his obligation with it, because ultimately it will turn red through exposure to the sun.

[ii] Its leaf is not round, but is extended like a stream.

[iii] The mouth of the leaf, i.e., its edge, is smooth, not serrated.[3] [See fig. 25 (p. 386).]

[iv] Most [trees of] this species grow near streams of water; hence the name — "willows of the brook." Nevertheless, even the minority [of the trees of this species] that grow in the deserts and on the mountains are also fit to be

א "עַרְבֵי נַחַל" הָאָמוּר בַּתּוֹרָה,[1] הוּא מִין יָדוּעַ הַנִּקְרָא כֵּן,[א] וְזֶה סִימָנוֹ: קָנֶה שֶׁלּוֹ הוּא אָדֹם,[ב,2] וַאֲפִלּוּ בְּעוֹדוֹ יָרֹק – אָדָם יוֹצֵא בּוֹ יְדֵי חוֹבָתוֹ,[ג] לְפִי שֶׁסּוֹפוֹ לִהְיוֹת אָדֹם כְּשֶׁתַּגִּיעַ עָלָיו הַחַמָּה,[ד] וְעָלֶה שֶׁלּוֹ אֵינוֹ עָגֹל אֶלָּא הוּא מָשׁוּךְ כְּנַחַל, וּפִיו שֶׁל הֶעָלֶה[ה] דְּהַיְנוּ חִדּוֹ הוּא חָלוּק וְאֵינוֹ עָשׂוּי פְּגִימוֹת.[ו,3] וְרֹב מִין זֶה הוּא גָּדֵל עַל נַחֲלֵי מַיִם, וּלְכָךְ נִקְרָא מִין זֶה "עַרְבֵי נַחַל", וַאֲפִלּוּ מִעוּטוֹ הַגָּדֵל בַּמִּדְבָּר וּבֶהָרִים – גַּם כֵּן הוּא

---

is considered as if he performed it intentionally. Similarly, in the case at hand, although this individual may have intended simply to eat the berries and not to make the myrtle fit for the *mitzvah*, his action will inevitably make the myrtle fit — and it is therefore considered as if he intentionally made it fit for the *mitzvah*.

SECTION 647

1. In the original, *arvei nachal* (*Vayikra* 23:40); popularly, *aravos*. See sec. 645:1 and footnote 1 of that section.

2. *Sukkah* 34a.

3. See subsections 2 and 3 below.

שם ורש"י ד"ה שלקטן. לבוש שם. מ"א ס"ק ב. סט סעיף כד. ע גמרא שם. מגיד משנה בדעת הרמב"ם שם. לבוש שם. ט"ז ס"ק ה. מ"א שם. עא רש"י שם ד"ה לא צריכא. תוס' שם סד"ה מודה (בשם רש"י), ובכתובות ו, א ד"ה האי (בתירוץ הב'). וראה עד"ז לעיל סי' שכח סל"ב.

סימן תרמז: א רמב"ם פ"ז ה"ג. טור ושו"ע ס"א. ב גמרא לד, א. רמב"ם שם. טור ושו"ע שם. ג ב"י ד"ה וערבי. רמ"א ס"א. ד ב"י שם. לבוש ס"א. ט"ז ס"ק א. ה גמרא שם. טור ושו"ע שם. ו רש"י שם ד"ה ופיה חלק. לבוש שם.

כָּשֵׁר[ז] לְמִצְוַת עֲרָבָה שֶׁבַּלּוּלָב, כֵּיוָן שֶׁיֵּשׁ בּוֹ כָּל סִימָנִים הַלָּלוּ:[ח]

used for the *mitzvah* of the willow [together with] the *lulav,* because they have all the above distinguishing characteristics.

ב וְיֵשׁ מִין עֲרָבָה שֶׁקָּנֶה שֶׁלּוֹ הוּא אָדֹם וְעָלֶה שֶׁלּוֹ מָשׁוּךְ כַּנַּחַל,[ט] אֶלָּא שֶׁפִּי הֶעָלֶה אֵינוֹ חָלָק וְגַם אֵינוֹ דּוֹמֶה לְמַסּוֹר (פֵּרוּשׁ מְגֵרָה[י] שֶׁפְּגִימוֹתֶיהָ גְּדוֹלוֹת קְצָת[יא]), אֶלָּא יֵשׁ בּוֹ תְּלָמִים קְטַנִּים עַד מְאֹד כְּמוֹ פִּי מַגָּל קָטָן – וְגַם זֶה כָּשֵׁר:[יב]

2 There is a species of willow whose stalk is red and whose leaf is extended like a stream, but its edge is not smooth. [However, the edge] does not resemble [the edge of] a saw (which has [relatively] large ridges). Instead, it has very small grooves like the cutting edge of a small sickle. This species is also valid.

ג אֲבָל יֵשׁ מִין אֶחָד דּוֹמֶה לַעֲרָבָה, אֲבָל קָנֶה שֶׁלּוֹ אֵינוֹ אָדֹם וְעָלֶה שֶׁלּוֹ עָגֹל וּפִי הֶעָלֶה הוּא דּוֹמֶה לְמַסּוֹר, וְזֶהוּ הַנִּקְרָא "צַפְצָפָה", וְהִיא פְּסוּלָה[יג,2] אֲפִלּוּ בִּשְׁעַת הַדְּחָק[4] כְּמוֹ שֶׁיִּתְבָּאֵר בְּסִימָן תרמ"ט.[יד] וְכָל דְּבָרִים אֵלּוּ הֵן הֲלָכָה לְמשֶׁה מִסִּינַי:[טו]

3 There is, however, a certain species that resembles a willow, but its stalk is not red. Its leaf is round and its edge is [jagged] like a saw. [This species is called a] *tzaftzafah.* [See fig. 26.] It is not acceptable [for the *mitzvah*][2] even in a pressing situation,[4] as will be explained in sec. 649[:23]. All of these matters are *halachos* transmitted to Moshe at Sinai.

ד עֲרָבָה שֶׁנִּקְטַם רֹאשָׁהּ,[טז] דְּהַיְנוּ שֶׁנִּקְטַם רֹאשׁ הָעֵץ עַצְמוֹ שֶׁהֶעָלִין גְּדֵלִין בּוֹ[יז] – פְּסוּלָה,[5] לְפִי שֶׁאֵין זֶה הִדּוּר.[יח] וּלְכָךְ צָרִיךְ לִזָּהֵר מְאֹד כְּשֶׁהַבַּדִּין שֶׁל עֲרָבָה אֲרֻכִּין

4 When the tip of the willow — i.e., the tip of the twig from which the leaves actually emerge — has been cut off, the twig is invalid,[5] because it is not considered "beautiful." [See fig. 27.] For this reason, when the willow twigs are longer [than one

Fig. 25: The leaves of the willow have smooth edges (see sec. 647:1).

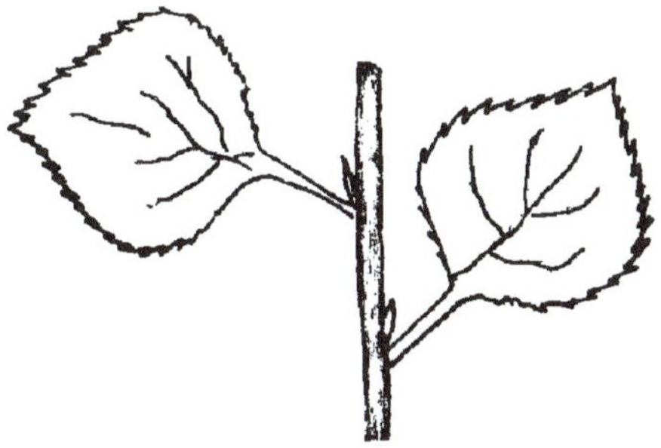

Fig. 26: The leaves of the *tzaftzafah* are conspicuously serrated, like a saw (see sec. 647:3).

---

4. Because it is not the species required by the Torah.

5. *Sukkah* 33b.

ז רמב"ם שם. רא"ש פ"ג סי"ג. טור ושו"ע שם. ח לבוש שם. ט טור. לבוש ס"א. ט"ז ס"ק ג. י רש"י שם ד"ה והתניא. יא מאירי שם ד"ה הצפצפה. רבנו מנוח על הרמב"ם פ"ז ה"ד. ב"י ד"ה וערבי. יב רמב"ם שם. שו"ע שם. יג גמרא שם. רמב"ם שם. טור ושו"ע שם. יד סכ"ג (אפי' בלא ברכה), וש"נ. טו רמב"ם שם. טז משנה לג, ב. מגיד משנה פ"ח ה"ו בדעת הרי"ף שם. רא"ש פ"ג סי"ג. טור ודעה הא' בשו"ע ס"ב. ב"ח ד"ה ומ"ש או שנקטם (דהכי נקטינן). וראה

יוֹתֵר מִדַּאי וְרוֹצֶה לְקַצְּצָן שֶׁלֹּא יְקַצְּצֵן בְּרֹאשָׁם, אֶלָּא לְמַטָּה בְּמָקוֹם שֶׁהֵן מִתְחַבְּרִים לְהֶעָנָף:

desires] and he wishes to trim them, he must be very careful not to trim them near the top, but at the bottom, where they were connected to the bough.

ה נָשְׁרוּ[יט] רֹב עָלֶיהָ – פְּסוּלָה. וְצָרִיךְ לִזָּהֵר מְאֹד בְּדָבָר זֶה, שֶׁלִּפְעָמִים נוֹשְׁרִים עַל יְדֵי תְּחִיבָתָן לְתוֹךְ הַלּוּלָב, וְגַם עַל יְדֵי נִעְנוּעַ.[כ] אֲבָל אִם לֹא נֶעֶקְרָה רַק מִקְצָת עָלֶיהָ – כְּשֵׁרָה.[כא, 5] וּמִכָּל מָקוֹם, לְכַתְּחִלָּה אֵין לִקַּח אוֹתָהּ אִם אֶפְשָׁר לוֹ בְּקַל לִמְצֹא אַחֶרֶת שְׁלֵמָה שֶׁלֹּא נָשְׁרוּ מֵעָלֶיהָ כְּלוּם, שֶׁהַשְּׁלֵמָה הִיא מִצְוָה מִן הַמֻּבְחָר:[כב]

5 If most of the leaves have fallen off, the willow twig is invalid. One must therefore be very careful, for often [the leaves] are stripped off when the willow twigs are pushed into [the binding of] the *lulav* or when [the Four Species] are shaken. If only some of the leaves have been detached, the willow twig is valid.[5] Nevertheless, at the outset, [such a willow twig] should not be used if one can readily find a perfect one, none of whose leaves have fallen off, for the optimal way to perform the *mitzvah* is to use a specimen that is intact.

ו יָבְשׁוּ[כג] רֹב עָלֶיהָ[כד] – פְּסוּלָה,[6] שֶׁאֵין זֶה הִדּוּר.[כה, 7] וְכַמָּה שִׁעוּר הַיַּבְשׁוּת? מִשֶּׁהִלְבִּינוּ פְּנֵיהֶם,[כו] אֲבָל אִם לֹא הִגִּיעוּ הֶעָלִין לְשִׁעוּר הַיַּבְשׁוּת אַף עַל פִּי שֶׁכְּבָר כָּמְשָׁה – הֲרֵי זוֹ כְּשֵׁרָה.[כז, 5]

6 If most of the leaves have dried out, the willow twig is invalid,[6] for it is not considered "beautiful."[7] What degree of dryness [disqualifies them]? Their surface becomes white. If the leaves have not dried out to this extent, then even if [the leaves] have withered, the twig is valid.[5]

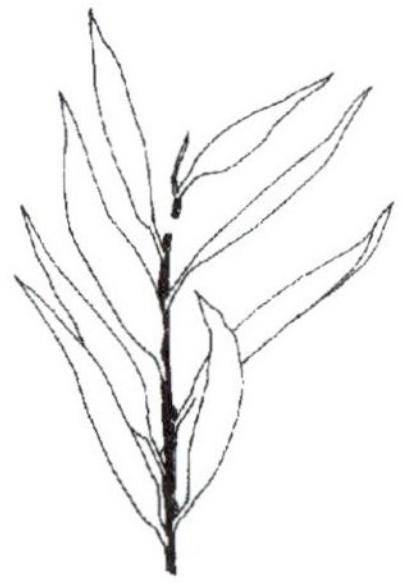

Fig. 27: This willow twig is now invalid (see sec. 647:4).

6. *Ibid.* Willow leaves that have blackened are not classified as "dried out" and thus are not invalidated thereby. However, like the berries of myrtle twigs, they can no longer be considered "beautiful" when they are discolored. See sec. 646:12; see also footnote 14 in that section.

7. *Sukkah* 31a.

לעיל סי׳ תרמו סי״א (הטעם לחלק בזה בין ערבה להדס). **יז** ראב״ד בתמים דעים סי׳ רלא. רא״ש שם ס״ב בשמו. מ״א ס״ק ב. וראה עד״ז לעיל סי׳ תרמו סי״א. **יח** ראב״ד ורא״ש שם. לבוש ס״ב. **יט** משנה שם (נפרצו), לפי׳ הרא״ש שם סי״ג. טור ושו״ע שם. וראה לקמן סי׳ תרמט סכ״ג (במוסגר), שטעם הפסול משום שאין שמו עליו. **כ** מ״א ס״ק א. אליה זוטא סי׳ תרנא ס״ק ו. **כא** משנה שם. טור ושו״ע שם. **כב** מ״א ס״ק ג. **כג** משנה שם. **כד** משמעות הטור והשו״ע שם. **כה** ברייתא לא, א. לבוש ס״ב. **כו** ראב״ד בתמים דעים סי׳ רלב. הובא ברא״ש רפ״ג. וראה לעיל סי׳ תרמה סט״ז וש״נ. **כז** משנה שם. טור ושו״ע שם. וראה גם לעיל סי׳ תרמז ס״ח (בהדס). לקמן סי׳ תרמח ס״א (באתרוג).

אִם נִדַּלְדְּלוּ רֹב הֶעָלִין[כח] וְנִתְּקוּ מִמְּקוֹם חִבּוּרָם בַּקָּנֶה, אַף עַל פִּי שֶׁלֹּא נָשְׁרוּ לְפִי שֶׁעֲדַיִן הֵם מְחֻבָּרִים קְצָת,[כט] וְכֵן אִם נִסְדְּקוּ רֹב הֶעָלִין וְנֶחְלְקוּ לִשְׁנַיִם בְּרֹב אֹרֶךְ הֶעָלֶה[ל] — הֲרֵי זֶה כְּאִלּוּ נָשְׁרוּ רֹב עָלֶיהָ וּפְסוּלָה:[לא,8]

The twig is invalid if most of its leaves are drooping and are dislodged from their point of connection to the stalk, even if they have not fallen off entirely, being still somewhat connected. [The twig is also invalid] if most of the leaves have cracked and are divided in two over most of the length of [each] leaf, for [in both of the above situations] it is considered as if most of the leaves have fallen off.[8]

סימן תרמח דְּבָרִים הַפְּסוּלִים בָּאֶתְרוֹג וּבוֹ ל״א סְעִיפִים:

SECTION 648 Factors that Disqualify an *Esrog*. (1–31)

א אֶתְרוֹג הַכָּמוּשׁ — כָּשֵׁר.[א,1] אֲבָל הַיָּבֵשׁ — פָּסוּל,[ב,2] שֶׁאֵין זֶה הָדוּר.[ג,3]

וְשִׁעוּר הַיַּבְשׁוּת, לִכְשֶׁתִּכְלֶה הַלֵּחָה וְאֵינוֹ מוֹצִיא שׁוּם לֵחָה[ד] (כִּי הַלֵּחָה לַפְּרִי כְּמוֹ הַדָּם לִבְשַׂר הַחַי;[ה] וְנֶאֱמַר[ו,4] ״לֹא הַמֵּתִים יְהַלְלוּ כו׳״);[5] שֶׁכָּל זְמַן שֶׁהוּא לַח — מוֹצִיא לֵחָה אוֹ מִדּוֹחַק הַסַּכִּין אוֹ מִסְּחִיטַת הַפְּרִי, אֲבָל לְאַחַר שֶׁיָּבַשׁ — לֹא יוֹצִיא שׁוּם לֵחָה.

אֶלָּא שֶׁהַבְּדִיקָה שֶׁלּוֹ קָשָׁה, לְפִי שֶׁאִי אֶפְשָׁר לְסָחֳטוֹ אוֹ לַחְתְּכוֹ שֶׁלֹּא יִפָּסֵל;[ז] אֲבָל אִם נִקַּב נֶקֶב שֶׁאֵין בּוֹ

1 An *esrog* that has withered is valid,[1] but one that has dried out is invalid[2] because it is not considered "beautiful."[3]

An *esrog* is defined as "dried out" when no moisture is left and it no longer discharges any moisture, (for moisture to a fruit is like blood to the flesh of a living creature, and it is written,[4] "The dead shall not praise You...").[5] As long as an *esrog* is fresh, it will discharge moisture, either by the pressure of a knife or when the fruit is squeezed. When it is dried out, it will not exude any moisture.

Checking [this factor] is difficult, because an *esrog* cannot be squeezed or cut without being disqualified. Nevertheless, if one punctures a hole that diminishes nothing from

---

8. See: sec. 645:9, 649:23.

SECTION 648

1. *Sukkah* 31a.

2. *op. cit.*, 34b.

3. This requirement appears in the verse, "And on the first day, you shall take for yourselves the fruit of a beautiful tree *(pri etz hadar)*, fronds of a date-palm, a branch of a braided tree, and willows of the brook" *(Vayikra 23:40)*. See *Sukkah* 31a.

4. *Tehillim* 115:17.

5. The implication is that an *esrog* which is dead — i.e., dried out like a creature without blood — cannot be used to praise G-d, to perform a *mitzvah*.

כח משנה שם (נפרצו), לפי' המגיד משנה פ"ח ה"ו, לדעת הרי"ף (טו, א) והרמב"ם פ"ח ה"ג (לענין לולב, וכדלעיל סי' תרמה ס"ו). רבנו מנוח שם. מ"א ס"ק ב. כט ראה ריטב"א כט, ב ד"ה נפרצו, ור"ן (יד, רע"ב), בדעת הרי"ף (הנ"ל). וראה לעיל סי' תרמה ס"ו, לענין לולב. ל מגיד משנה שם, לדעת הראב"ד בהשגות פ"ח ה"ג (לענין לולב). ריטב"א ור"ן שם. מ"א שם. לא ראה לעיל סי' תרמה ס"ט (לענין לולב, שנחלקו פסול מטעם הדר). לקמן סי' תרמט סכ"ג (במוסגר, שנשרו פסול מטעם שאין שמן עליהם).

סימן תרמח: א ברייתא לא, סע"א. רמב"ם פ"ח ה"א. מ"א ריש הסי', ממשמעות הפוסקים. וכדלעיל סי' תרמו ס"ח (בהדס). סי' תרמז ס"ו (בערבה). ב משנה לד, ב. טור ושו"ע ס"א. ג גמרא לא, א. לבוש ס"א. ד ראב"ד בתמים דעים סי' רלב, ע"פ הגמרא חולין מו, ב (לענין בשר). הובא ברא"ש פ"ג ס"כ. טור ושו"ע שם. ה ראב"ד שם. רא"ש וטור שם. לבוש ס"א. ו תהלים קטו, יז. ירושלמי פ"ג ה"א (לענין לולב). ראב"ד שם (לענין לולב הדס וערבה). הובא ברא"ש פ"ג ס"א. לבוש שם (לענין אתרוג). ז ראב"ד שם. רא"ש פ"ג ס"כ. טור. לבוש שם. ח כדלקמן ס"ג־ז. ט ראב"ד שם (לגירסת הב"י ד"ה ומ"ש יכול).

חֶסְרוֹן מִגּוּף הָאֶתְרוֹג – כָּשֵׁר אִם אֵינוֹ מְפֻלָּשׁ, דְּהַיְנוּ שֶׁאֵין הַנֶּקֶב מַגִּיעַ עַד חַדְרֵי הַזֶּרַע שֶׁבְּתוֹךְ הָאֶתְרוֹג,[ח,6] אִם כֵּן יָכוֹל לְבָדְקוֹ עַל יְדֵי שֶׁיַּעֲבִיר בּוֹ מַחַט עִם חוּט וְאִם יֵשׁ בּוֹ לֵחָה יִתְרָאֶה בַּחוּט,[ט] רַק שֶׁיִּזָּהֵר שֶׁלֹּא יַגִּיעַ הַמַּחַט עַד חַדְרֵי הַזֶּרַע,[7] וְגַם שֶׁלֹּא יַגִּיעַ לָעֵבֶר שֶׁכְּנֶגְדּוֹ[י,8] אֲפִלּוּ הוּא שֶׁלֹּא כְּנֶגֶד חַדְרֵי הַזֶּרַע,[יא] שֶׁלֹּא יַעֲשֶׂה נֶקֶב מְפֻלָּשׁ:

the body of the *esrog,* the *esrog* remains valid, provided it is not "perforated through and through," i.e., the perforation does not penetrate to the seed compartments of the *esrog.*[6] Thus one can check an *esrog* by puncturing it with a needle and thread. If it is [still] moist, this will be detectable on the thread. One must, however, take care that the needle does not reach the seed compartments[7] and also that it does not pass to the other side of the *esrog*[8] even if it did not reach the seed compartments, so that the *esrog* will not be perforated from side to side. [See fig. 28.]

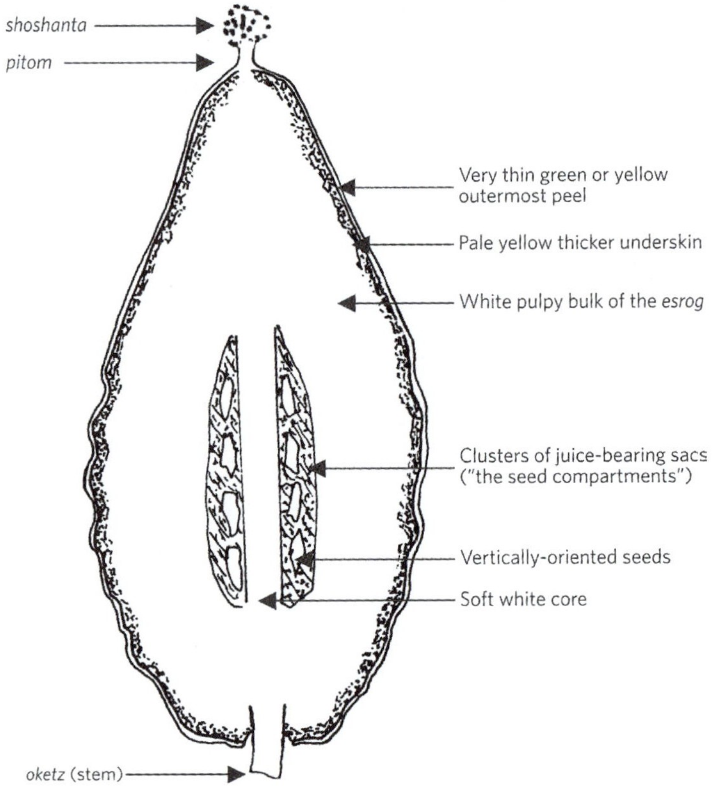

Fig. 28: The *esrog* in cross-section (see sec. 648:1).

6. See subsecs. 3-4.

7. See subsection 6.

8. See subsection 4. These specifications entail an obvious difficulty. Inserting an ordinary needle deep enough to enable the thread to enter the *esrog* will disqualify it. Among the solutions suggested is to use a needle whose eye is close to its point, but whose shaft continues above the eye.

ראʺש שם (לגירסת הגהות הבʺח שם). טור (לגירסת הבʺי שם). שוʺע שם. **י** רבנו ירוחם נתיב ח חʺג (נט, ב). בʺח דʺה ואם הוא. תויʺט במשנה הנʺל. פרישה אות א. מʺא סʺק א. **יא** ראה לקמן סʺד.

ב וּמִכָּל מָקוֹם אֵין חַיָּב כְּלָל לְבָדְקוֹ, אֶלָּא אִם כֵּן רוֹאִין אוֹתוֹ שֶׁהוּא כָּמוּשׁ.[יב] וְאֶתְרוֹג שֶׁבֵּרַךְ עָלָיו בְּשָׁנָה זוֹ – אֵין לְבָדְקוֹ כְּלָל בַּשָּׁנָה הָאַחֶרֶת, שֶׁבְּוַדַּאי יִמָּצֵא יָבֵשׁ:[יג,9]

2 There is, however, no obligation to check an *esrog* unless it is visibly withered. An *esrog* over which one recited a blessing during the previous year need not be checked, for it will certainly be found to be dried out.[9]

ג אֶתְרוֹג שֶׁנִּקַּב,[יד,10] אֲפִלּוּ אִם הַנֶּקֶב הוּא רָחָב אֶלָּא שֶׁאֵין בּוֹ חֶסְרוֹן מִגּוּף הָאֶתְרוֹג,[טו,11] כְּגוֹן שֶׁתָּחַב שָׁם יָתֵד עָב וְנִקַּב בְּעִנְיָן שֶׁלֹּא חָסַר כְּלוּם,[טז] אִם אֵין בְּאֹרֶךְ וְרֹחַב שֶׁל שֶׁטַח רֹחַב הַנֶּקֶב כְּאֹרֶךְ וְרֹחַב שֶׁל שֶׁטַח מַטְבֵּעַ הַנִּקְרָא אִסָּר – הֲרֵי זֶה כָּשֵׁר.[יז]

וְכֵיצַד מְשַׁעֲרִין? אִם הַנֶּקֶב הוּא עָגֹל – מַנִּיחַ הָאִסָּר עַל פִּי הַנֶּקֶב, וְאִם הַנֶּקֶב הוּא מְרֻבָּע אוֹ שֶׁהוּא אָרֹךְ וְקָצָר – רוֹאִין אוֹתוֹ כְּאִלּוּ הָיָה עָגֹל, דְּהַיְנוּ שֶׁהָיוּ עוֹשִׂין עֲגֻלָּה מִן אֹרֶךְ וְרֹחַב שֶׁל שֶׁטַח רֹחַב הַנֶּקֶב, וְאִם הָיָה גֹּדֶל שֶׁטַח הָעֲגֻלָּה הַזֹּאת פָּחוֹת מִגֹּדֶל שֶׁטַח הָאִסָּר – הֲרֵי זֶה כָּשֵׁר.[יח]

(וְעַיֵּן בְּיוֹרֶה דֵעָה סִימָן ל״ד[יט,12] הֵיכָן[כ] מְשַׁעֲרִין שִׁעוּר הָאִסָּר בַּזְּמַן הַזֶּה[13] שֶׁאֵין אָנוּ

3 [The following laws relate to] an *esrog* with a hole.[10] Even when the hole is wide, [but] if none of the substance of the *esrog*[11] is lacking — e.g., the *esrog* was pierced with a thick peg in a way that did not decrease its substance at all — it is valid. [This applies, provided] the length and width of the hole is less than the length and width of the coin called an *isar*.

How is this area measured? If the hole is round, the *isar* should be placed over the hole. If the hole is square or long and narrow, we consider it as if it were circular, i.e., we calculate the size of the circle that could be made from the area of the hole. If the size of this area is less than the size of an *isar*, the *esrog* is acceptable. (See *Yoreh Deah* 34[:2-3][12] [which explains] how the size of an *isar* is calculated today,[13] for [the size of] that coin is

---

9. Thus it is invalid *(Sukkah* 31b*)*. The question has been raised whether this restriction applies today, when new techniques of refrigeration or vacuum-packing can prolong a fruit's freshness. In his responsa, R. Moshe Feinstein notes that after defrosting, a frozen *esrog* will deteriorate within a few days. On that basis, he questions the acceptability of such an *esrog* even when outwardly it appears normal *(Igros Moshe, Orach Chayim,* Vol. 1, Responsum 185*)*.

10. *Sukkah* 34b. As will be explained, subsections 3-8 relate to a hole made after the *esrog* was picked.

11. The very thick peel of an *esrog* comprises a thin yellow or greenish outer rind that covers a large mass of white fiber. If this fiber is removed, the substance of the *esrog* is considered to have decreased. With regard to the removal of the outer rind, see subsection 15.

12. In the *Shulchan Aruch* of R. Yosef Caro. Sec. 34 of the Alter Rebbe's *Shulchan Aruch, Yoreh Deah,* is not extant.

13. The *isar* is a coin minted in *Eretz Yisrael* under Roman rule

יב מ״א ריש הסי׳ (בסופו). יג ברייתא לא, ב (אתרוג הישן פסול) כת״ק. תשובות מהרי״ל סי׳ ה. רמ״א ס״א (פסול). ב״ח שם (דלא מהני בדיקה). אליה רבה ס״ק ג. יד משנה לד, ב (ניקב וחסר פסול ניקב ולא חסר כשר). טור ושו״ע ס״ב. וטעם הפסול — לקמן סי״ד. טו רש״י לו, א ד״ה תני (שפסול כאיסר (ומפולש) הוא בנקב רחב ולא חסר). רמב״ם פ״ח ה״ז. רא״ש פ״ג סי״ח (ממשמעות הירושלמי פ״ג ה״ו). דעה הא׳ בטור ושו״ע ס״ב. ב״ח ד״ה ניקב (דהכי נקטינן). ודעה הב׳ — לקמן ס״ח. טז רש״י שם. טור ולבוש ס״ב. מ״א ס״ק ג. יז ברייתא שם. טור ושו״ע שם. יח מ״א שם, ע״פ המבואר ביו״ד סי׳ לד ס״ב

יוֹדְעִים אוֹתוֹ כְּלָל, עַיֵּן שָׁם):

not at all known to us.)

ד בַּמֶּה דְּבָרִים אֲמוּרִים? כְּשֶׁאֵין הַנֶּקֶב מְפֻלָּשׁ, אֲבָל אִם הַנֶּקֶב הוּא מְפֻלָּשׁ[כא] מֵעֵבֶר אֶל עֵבֶר שֶׁכְּנֶגְדּוֹ, אֲפִלּוּ לֹא הִגִּיעַ הַנֶּקֶב לְחַדְרֵי הַזֶּרַע שֶׁבְּתוֹךְ הָאֶתְרוֹג, כְּגוֹן שֶׁנִּקַּב בְּעֳבִי הַקְּלִפָּה הָעָבָה (הַמַּקֶּפֶת אֶת חַדְרֵי הַזֶּרַע) מִצַּד זֶה לְצַד זֶה שֶׁכְּנֶגְדּוֹ שֶׁלֹּא כְּנֶגֶד חַדְרֵי הַזֶּרַע,[כב] וַאֲפִלּוּ אֵין בְּרֹחַב הַנֶּקֶב אֶלָּא מַשֶּׁהוּ[כג] וְלֹא חָסַר כְּלוּם מִגּוּף הָאֶתְרוֹג[כד] — הֲרֵי זֶה פָּסוּל:[14]

4 When does the above apply? When the hole does not extend from side to side. If, however, it extends to the opposite side, then even if it does not reach the seed compartments within [the heart of] the *esrog* — e.g., it perforated the thick peel (which surrounds the seed compartments) from one side to another on a different plane than that of the seed compartments — the *esrog* is invalid.[14] [This applies] even if the diameter of the hole is miniscule and even if none of the substance of the *esrog* was lacking.

ה אֲבָל אִם אֵין הַנֶּקֶב מְפֻלָּשׁ מִצַּד זֶה לְצַד שֶׁכְּנֶגְדּוֹ, אֲפִלּוּ נִקַּב כְּנֶגֶד חַדְרֵי הַזֶּרַע, וּפִלּוּשׁ אֹרֶךְ הַנֶּקֶב עוֹבֵר כָּל חַדְרֵי הַזֶּרַע עַד סָמוּךְ לִקְצֵה הָאֶתְרוֹג שֶׁבַּצַּד שֶׁכְּנֶגְדּוֹ,[כה] וְכֵן אִם נִקַּב הָאֶתְרוֹג מִשְּׁנֵי צְדָדָיו עַד תּוֹךְ חַדְרֵי הַזֶּרַע,

5 If, however, the hole does not extend from one side to the other, then even if the hole is on the same plane as the seed compartments and extends through [them] until near the opposite surface of the *esrog*, [the *esrog* is valid].

Similarly, if the *esrog* was perforated from both sides, with the perforation [from either side] penetrating the seed compartments,

(hence its usual name: isar haltalki — "the Italian isar"). The *Talmud* mentions it in various halachic contexts *(Kiddushin* 2a, *Bava Metzia* 51b, *Mikvaos* 9:5, *et al.).* The *Shulchan Aruch (Yoreh Deah* 34:2*)* quotes *Rashba* as stating that in his times (13th cent.) the size of an *isar* was already not known. More recently, archeologists have discovered an *isar,* with the classical symbols of a lyre and a shepherd's crook that possibly represent David HaMelech. (See fig. 29.) Though archeological findings alone cannot be used to determine *halachah,* according to such findings R. Chaim Benish gives the diameter of an *isar* as 23 mm. (See his *Middos VeShiurei Torah* (Bnei Brak, 5747), p. 169.)

14. *Sukkah* 36a.

Fig. 29: Recently unearthed *isar*, showing King David's lyre and shepherd's crook (see sec. 648:3 and footnote 13).

(לענין גרגרת). אליה רבה ס"ק ד. **יט** סעיף ב. **כ** אוצ"ל: האיך. **כא** ברייתא לו, רע"א. טור ושו"ע שם. **כב** תוס' שם ד"ה אי (שלא כנגד אותם חדרים. וכדלקמן ס"ו לדעתם, שבניקב לחדרים פסול בכל אופן). רא"ש פ"ג סי' יח. מ"א ס"ק ב (שכ"ה לכולי עלמא). אליה רבה ס"ק ו. עטרת זקנים. **כג** ברייתא שם. טור ושו"ע שם. **כד** כדלעיל ס"ג וש"נ. **כה** הלכות גדולות הל' לולב (לה, א), לפירוש הראב"ד בתמים דעים סי' רל. רי"ף (דלקמן סי"ב), לפירוש הרא"ש פ"ג סי' יח. משמעות הרמב"ם פ"ח ה"ז (שפוסל רק במפולש), לפירוש הב"י ד"ה ומ"ש ואם ניקב. דעה הא' בשו"ע ס"ג.

וְחַדְרֵי הַזֶּרַע עַצְמָן נִשְׁאַר מֵהֶן קְצָת שָׁלֵם וְהַשָּׁלֵם הַזֶּה מַפְסִיק בֵּין הַנְּקָבִים שֶׁמִּשְּׁנֵי צְדָדָיו – כָּל זֶה אֵינוֹ נִקְרָא נֶקֶב מְפֻלָּשׁ:[כו,15]

then as long as part of the seed compartments themselves remains unimpaired and thus that intact part intercepts the holes on either side, the *esrog* is not considered as having been perforated from side to side.[15]

ו וְיֵשׁ חוֹלְקִין[כז] עַל זֶה וְאוֹמְרִים, דְּכָל שֶׁהִגִּיעַ הַנֶּקֶב עַד חַדְרֵי הַזֶּרַע אַף עַל פִּי שֶׁחַדְרֵי הַזֶּרַע וְצַד הַשֵּׁנִי שֶׁל הָאֶתְרוֹג נִשְׁאֲרוּ שְׁלֵמִים – הֲרֵי זֶה נִקְרָא נֶקֶב מְפֻלָּשׁ, לְפִי שֶׁהַקְּלִפָּה הָעָבָה הַמַּקֶּפֶת אֶת חַדְרֵי הַזֶּרַע אֵינָהּ נֶחְשֶׁבֶת עִם חַדְרֵי הַזֶּרַע לְדָבָר אֶחָד, אֶלָּא הִיא נֶחְשֶׁבֶת לְדָבָר בִּפְנֵי עַצְמוֹ לְעִנְיָן זֶה, וְכֵיוָן שֶׁנִּקְּבָה כֻּלָּהּ מִצַּד אֶחָד – הֲרֵי זֶה נֶקֶב מְפֻלָּשׁ.[כח]

וּלְעִנְיַן הֲלָכָה – יֵשׁ לְהַחְמִיר כַּסְּבָרָא הָאַחֲרוֹנָה.[כט] אֲבָל בִּשְׁעַת הַדְּחָק שֶׁאִי אֶפְשָׁר לִמְצֹא אֶתְרוֹג אַחֵר – יֵשׁ לִסְמֹךְ עַל סְבָרָא הָרִאשׁוֹנָה, וּמֻתָּר לְבָרֵךְ עַל אֶתְרוֹג זֶה:[ל,16]

6 Some authorities differ with the above and maintain that if the hole reaches the seed compartments it is considered as a perforation from side to side, even though the seed compartments and the other side of the *esrog* remain intact. [The rationale is that] the thick peel that surrounds the seed compartments is not considered as the same entity as the seed compartments, but in this context is considered as a separate entity. Thus if [the peel until the seed compartments] is perforated entirely on one side, it is considered as if the hole extends from one side to the other.

With regard to the *halachah,* one should be stringent and follow the latter view. Nevertheless, in a pressing situation, when it is impossible to find another *esrog,* one may rely on the first view and recite a blessing over such an *esrog.*[16]

ז וְכָל זֶה בְּנֶקֶב שֶׁאֵין בּוֹ חֶסְרוֹן מִגּוּף הָאֶתְרוֹג, אֲבָל אִם חָסֵר מִגּוּף הָאֶתְרוֹג אֲפִלּוּ מַשֶּׁהוּ[לא] – הֲרֵי זֶה פָּסוּל,[2] אַף עַל פִּי שֶׁאֵין הַנֶּקֶב מְפֻלָּשׁ וְאֵין בּוֹ כְּאִסָּר:

7 The above applies to a perforation that does not diminish the substance of the *esrog.* If, however, even if the smallest amount of its substance is lacking, the *esrog* is invalid,[2] even if the hole does not extend from side to side, and even if it is smaller than an *isar.*

ח וְיֵשׁ חוֹלְקִין[לב] עַל כָּל זֶה וְאוֹמְרִים, דְּנֶקֶב שֶׁאֵין בּוֹ חֶסְרוֹן מִגּוּף הָאֶתְרוֹג – אֵינוֹ פּוֹסֵל כְּלָל, וַאֲפִלּוּ הוּא

8 Other authorities differ with regard to all of the above and maintain that a perforation that does not decrease the substance of the *esrog* does not disqualify it at all, even

---

15. I.e., even though from the outside the *esrog* might appear to be perforated from side to side, it is valid.

16. See subsection 8 and also sec 645:17.

כו ראב״ד שם, בפירוש הירושלמי פ״ג ה״ו. הובא ברא״ש שם. כז תוס׳ לו, א ד״ה אי. רא״ש שם רס״י יח, ממשמעות הירושלמי הנ״ל (עכ״פ לדעת המחמירין שבסי״ב). ריטב״א שם ד״ה תני. ור״ן שם (יז, ב) ד״ה האי, בשם יש מחמירין, לפירוש הב״י ד״ה ומ״ש ואם ניקב, וט״ז ס״ק ו. טור ודעה הב׳ בשו״ע שם. כח ריטב״א ור״ן שם, לפירוש הב״י וט״ז שם. וראה לקמן סי״ב. כט ריטב״א שם (וראוי להחמיר). וראה לקמן סי״א (דהיינו דוקא בודאי הגיע לחדרי הזרע). חדושי צמח צדק סוכה פ״ג (עג, א) ד״ה בענין (להחמיר רק בחסרון משהו). ל כדלקמן ס״ח (במחלוקת הב׳ בדין ניקב). וראה עד״ז לעיל סי׳ תרמה סי״ז וש״נ. לא משנה לד, ב לפירוש הפוסקים דלעיל ס״ג. לב ראב״ד בתמים דעים סי׳ רל, ובהשגות פ״ח ה״ז. יראים השלם סי׳ תכב. טור בשם ה[ר]״ח

רָחָב הַרְבֵּה יוֹתֵר מִכְּאִסָּר, וַאֲפִלּוּ הוּא מְפֻלָּשׁ, וְלֹא חִלְּקוּ חֲכָמִים בֵּין מְפֻלָּשׁ לְשֶׁאֵינוֹ מְפֻלָּשׁ וּבֵין כְּאִסָּר לְפָחוֹת מִכְּאִסָּר אֶלָּא בְּנֶקֶב שֶׁיֵּשׁ בּוֹ חֶסְרוֹן מִגּוּף הָאֶתְרוֹג, שֶׁאִם יֵשׁ בְּרָחְבּוֹ כְּאִסָּר — פּוֹסֵל אַף עַל פִּי שֶׁאֵינוֹ מְפֻלָּשׁ, וְאִם אֵין בְּרָחְבּוֹ כְּאִסָּר — אֵינוֹ פּוֹסֵל אֶלָּא אִם כֵּן הוּא מְפֻלָּשׁ.[17] וְיֵשׁ לִסְמֹךְ עַל סְבָרָא זוֹ בִּשְׁעַת הַדְּחָק שֶׁאִי אֶפְשָׁר לִמְצֹא אֶתְרוֹג אַחֵר, וְאָז מֻתָּר לְבָרֵךְ עַל אֶתְרוֹג זֶה:[לג]

if the hole is much wider than an *isar,* and even if it extends from side to side. [They maintain that] our Sages did not make a distinction between a hole that extends from side to side and one that does not, or between a hole that is the size of an *isar* and one that is smaller, unless the hole decreases the substance of the *esrog.* [In such a situation,] they maintain that if the hole is as wide as an *isar,* the *esrog* is disqualified even if [the hole] does not extend from side to side, and if the hole is not as wide as an *isar,* it does not disqualify the *esrog* unless it extends from side to side.[17] In a pressing situation, when another *esrog* cannot be found, one may rely on the [more lenient] opinion and recite a blessing on such an *esrog.*

ט וְכָל זֶה בְּנֶקֶב שֶׁנַּעֲשָׂה בּוֹ לְאַחַר שֶׁנִּתְלַשׁ, אֲבָל נְקָבִים הַנַּעֲשִׂים בּוֹ כְּשֶׁהוּא מְחֻבָּר, כְּמוֹ שֶׁרְגִילוּת הוּא לְהֵעָשׂוֹת בּוֹ נְקָבִים עַל יְדֵי קוֹצִים שֶׁנּוֹפְלִים עָלָיו כְּשֶׁהוּא מְחֻבָּר — נוֹהֲגִין לְהַכְשִׁירוֹ אַף עַל פִּי שֶׁהֵן נְקָבִים שֶׁיֵּשׁ בָּהֶן חֶסְרוֹן, לְפִי שֶׁכָּל נֶקֶב שֶׁבָּאָה לוֹ בְּעוֹדוֹ גָּדֵל בָּאִילָן — חוֹזֵר לִבְרִיאוּתוֹ עַל יְדֵי שֶׁנִּקְרָם עָלָיו עוֹר מִלְמַעְלָה, כֵּיוָן שֶׁהוּא עֲדַיִן הוֹלֵךְ וְגָדֵל בְּאִילָנוֹ, וְאַף עַל פִּי שֶׁעַל גַּבֵּי עוֹר זֶה יֵשׁ גֻּמָּא וְחֶסְרוֹן בְּגוּף הָאֶתְרוֹג — אֵין בְּכָךְ כְּלוּם.[לד]

9 All of the above applies with regard to a perforation that occurred after the *esrog* was picked. When holes are made while the *esrog* is still on the tree, as commonly happens when thorns fall on it, it is customary to rule that it is valid, even when the holes decrease its substance. [The rationale is that] any perforation that occurs while the *esrog* is growing on the tree will be healed, for the rind will regenerate and cover it, since [the fruit] is continuing to grow on the tree. Though there will be a depression in the rind and some of the substance [of the *esrog*] will be lacking, this is not of consequence.

---

17. There are four situations in which these two views differ:

(a) When the perforation decreases the substance of the *esrog:* The first view disqualifies the *esrog,* whereas the second view considers the size of the hole or the extent of the penetration.

(b) When the hole is as wide as an *isar,* but the substance of the *esrog* is not decreased: The first view disqualifies the *esrog,* whereas the second view rules that it is valid.

(c) When a hole extends from side to side, but without decreasing the substance of the *esrog:* The first view disqualifies the *esrog,* whereas the second view rules that it is valid.

(d) According to the more stringent opinion (subsection 6), a hole that extends to the seed compartments is considered as if it had penetrated through the entire *esrog.* If none of the substance of the *esrog* is missing, the first opinion disqualifies the *esrog,* while according to the second opinion, it is acceptable.

וה"ר ישעיה שם. ריטב"א בגמרא שם ד"ה תני. ר"ן (יז, א) ד"ה מתני' עלתה. דעה הב' בשו"ע ס"ב. לג רמ"א ס"ב. ט"ז ס"ק ג. ועד"ז לעיל ס"ו. וראה שער הציון אות יא. לד תרומת הדשן סי' צט. רמ"א ס"ב. ט"ז ס"ק ד.

If, however, we see that the rind has not covered the perforation and that at that point the substance of the *esrog* is deficient, the *esrog* is invalid, even though a thorn perforated it while it was still attached to the tree.

אֲבָל אִם אָנוּ רוֹאִים שֶׁלֹּא נִקְרַם עָלָיו וְיֵשׁ בַּנֶּקֶב חֶסְרוֹן מִגּוּף הָאֶתְרוֹג – הֲרֵי זֶה פָּסוּל,[לה] אַף עַל פִּי שֶׁהַנֶּקֶב נַעֲשָׂה בּוֹ בְּעוֹדוֹ בָּאִילָן עַל יְדֵי קוֹץ:[לו]

10 When does the above apply? When it is clear and obvious that this depression indicates that the substance of the *esrog* has been diminished.[18] If, however, there is reason to suspect that its substance has not decreased, but rather the pressure of the thorn [merely] compressed the fiber of the *esrog* to the sides of the hole, the *esrog* may be deemed valid. For as long as we are not certain that the substance of the *esrog* has decreased, we may rely on the last view explained above[19] — that a perforation that does not extend from side to side and that is less than an *isar* in size does not disqualify the *esrog*, even though it decreases its substance.[20]

י בַּמֶּה דְּבָרִים אֲמוּרִים?[לז] כְּשֶׁנִּכָּר וְנִרְאֶה שֶׁיֵּשׁ בּוֹ בְּגֻמָּא זוֹ חֶסְרוֹן מִגּוּף בְּשַׂר הָאֶתְרוֹג,[לח, 18] אֲבָל אִם יֵשׁ לְהִסְתַּפֵּק שֶׁמָּא לֹא נֶחְסַר כְּלוּם מִגּוּף בְּשַׂר הָאֶתְרוֹג, אֶלָּא שֶׁעַל יְדֵי דֹּחַק הַקּוֹץ נִתְכַּוֵּץ בְּשַׂר הָאֶתְרוֹג לְצִדְדֵי הַנֶּקֶב – יֵשׁ לְהַכְשִׁיר, דְּכָל שֶׁאֵין בָּרוּר לָנוּ שֶׁיֵּשׁ חֶסְרוֹן מִגּוּף הָאֶתְרוֹג – יֵשׁ לִסְמֹךְ עַל סְבָרָא הָאַחֲרוֹנָה שֶׁבֵּאַרְנוּ[לט, 19] דְּכָל שֶׁאֵין הַנֶּקֶב מְפֻלָּשׁ וְאֵין בּוֹ כְּאִסָּר אַף עַל פִּי שֶׁיֵּשׁ בּוֹ חֶסְרוֹן אֵינוֹ פָּסוּל:[מ, 20]

11 Even if there is reason to suspect that the perforation reached the seed compartments, the *esrog* should be deemed valid. [The rationale is that] as long as we are not certain that the perforation reached the seed compartments, we may rely on the authorities[21] who hold that even a perforation that reached the seed compartments is not considered a perforation that extends from side to side.[20] Accordingly, [this factor] does not

יא וַאֲפִלּוּ אִם יֵשׁ לְהִסְתַּפֵּק שֶׁמָּא הִגִּיעַ פִּלּוּשׁ הַנֶּקֶב עַד חַדְרֵי הַזֶּרַע[מא] – יֵשׁ לְהַכְשִׁיר, שֶׁכָּל שֶׁאֵינוֹ בָּרוּר לָנוּ שֶׁהִגִּיעַ הַנֶּקֶב עַד חַדְרֵי הַזֶּרַע – יֵשׁ לִסְמֹךְ עַל דִּבְרֵי הָאוֹמְרִים[מב, 21] שֶׁאֲפִלּוּ אִם הִגִּיעַ הַנֶּקֶב לְחַדְרֵי הַזֶּרַע אֵינוֹ נִקְרָא נֶקֶב מְפֻלָּשׁ,[20] וְאֵינוֹ פּוֹסֵל

18. See subsections 3 and 6-8 above.

19. In subsection 8.

20. The Alter Rebbe's ruling follows the logic employed by the halachic convention of *sfeik sfeika*, i.e., one doubt superimposed on another. To begin with, it is possible that the substance of the *esrog* has not decreased. And even if it has decreased, the *halachah* possibly follows the authorities who maintain that such an *esrog* is disqualified only if it is perforated through and through. Because of the compound doubts involved, such an *esrog* is regarded as valid even in an ordinary situation — and obviously in an emergency, when no other *esrog* is available (see subsection 8 above).

21. See subsection 5.

לה ב"י ד"ה כתוב בתרומת, ממשמעות התרומת הדשן שם (דוקא בשעורו ובשרו קיים). דרכי משה ס"ק ב (שאין חוששין אלא אם כן רואים שאינו קיים). רמ"א וט"ז שם. לו ט"ז שם. אליה רבה ס"ק ה. לז זה שנתבאר לעיל ס"ו וס"ח שלכתחלה יש להחמיר כדעות הפוסלים. לח שלדעה הא' דלעיל ס"ג־ז הוא ודאי פסול. לט סעיף ח. מ ט"ז ס"ק ה, ממשמעות הרמ"א שם. אליה רבה שם. מא שאף אם לא נחסר כלום הוא פסול לדעה דלעיל ס"ו. מב לעיל ס"ה.

disqualify the *esrog* unless it decreases its substance.[22]

12 We have already explained that a decrease in the substance of the *esrog* disqualifies it, as described above.[23] When does the above apply? When the decrease [begins] from the outside, i.e., when the outer rind of the *esrog* is also perforated. [This refers to] the thin shell that surrounds the thick shell[24] which is called the fiber[25] of the *esrog* and which has a tart taste when eaten.

[Different rules apply] if the decrease [in the substance of the *esrog*] is only internal, i.e., all of the fibrous interior of the *esrog* has decomposed, but the outer rind and the seed compartments are still intact[26] and one can feel with his hand that they have not decomposed.[27] The Sages of the *Gemara*[14] were unsure whether this *esrog* should be likened to a lung, which is not disqualified by an internal decrease in its substance, such as when all its interior tissue has decomposed, but its external membranes and internal air passages remain intact. In such an instance, the ruling of *[Shulchan Aruch,] Yoreh Deah*, sec. 36,[28] is that [the animal] is kosher.[29]

אֶלָּא אִם כֵּן יֵשׁ בּוֹ חֶסְרוֹן:[מג,22]

יב כְּבָר בֵּאַרְנוּ שֶׁחֶסְרוֹן מִגּוּף הָאֶתְרוֹג פּוֹסֵל אֶת הָאֶתְרוֹג וְעַל דֶּרֶךְ שֶׁנִּתְבָּאֵר,[מד,23] בַּמֶּה דְּבָרִים אֲמוּרִים? כְּשֶׁהַחֶסְרוֹן הוּא מִבַּחוּץ, דְּהַיְנוּ שֶׁנִּקְּבָה גַּם הַקְּלִפָּה הַחִיצוֹנָה שֶׁל הָאֶתְרוֹג, דְּהַיְנוּ הַקְּלִפָּה הַדַּקָּה הַמַּקֶּפֶת אֶת הַקְּלִפָּה הֶעָבָה[מה,24] הַנִּקְרֵאת בְּשַׂר[25] הָאֶתְרוֹג,[מו] וְיֵשׁ בָּהּ טַעַם חֲרִיפוּת כְּשֶׁאוֹכְלִין אוֹתָהּ,[מז] אֲבָל אִם אֵין הַחֶסְרוֹן אֶלָּא בִּפְנִים, כְּגוֹן שֶׁנִּמּוֹחַ כָּל בְּשַׂר הָאֶתְרוֹג בִּפְנִים, וּקְלִפָּה הַחִיצוֹנָה קַיֶּמֶת וְגַם חַדְרֵי הַזֶּרַע קַיָּמִין,[מח,26] שֶׁמַּרְגִּישׁ בְּמִשְׁמוּשׁ הַיָּד שֶׁלֹּא נִמּוֹחוּ[מט,27] — דָּבָר זֶה נִסְתַּפֵּק לְחַכְמֵי הַגְּמָרָא[נ,14] אִם יֵשׁ לְדַמּוֹת אֶתְרוֹג לְרֵאָה שֶׁאֵינָהּ נִפְסֶלֶת מֵחֲמַת חֶסְרוֹן שֶׁמִּבִּפְנִים, כְּגוֹן שֶׁנִּמּוֹחַ כָּל בְּשָׂרָהּ מִבִּפְנִים וְעוֹרוֹתֶיהָ הַחִיצוֹנִים קַיָּמִין וְגַם סִמְפּוֹנוֹתֶיהָ שֶׁמִּבִּפְנִים הֵן קַיָּמִין שֶׁהִיא כְּשֵׁרָה[29] כְּמוֹ שֶׁיִּתְבָּאֵר בְּיוֹרֶה דֵעָה סִימָן ל"ו,[נא,28]

22. The *Tzemach Tzedek (Chiddushim Al HaShas*, p. 73a*)* states that even if the perforation definitely reaches the seed compartments, the *esrog* should not be disqualified unless in addition some of its substance is missing due to the perforation.

23. Subsection 7 above cites the view that a decrease in the substance of the *esrog* disqualifies it even when it is not perforated from side to side and even if the hole is smaller than an *isar.* Subsection 8 cites the view that a decrease in the substance of the *esrog* disqualifies it only if the perforation is larger than an *isar* or extends from side to side.

24. See subsections 15 and 31.

25. Lit., "flesh."

26. If the seed compartments, too, have decomposed, the *esrog* is invalid.

27. Today, this could be determined by ultrasound.

28. This section is not extant in the Alter Rebbe's *Shulchan Aruch.* See the *Shulchan Aruch* of R. Yosef Caro, sec. 36:7.

29. I.e., the above-described decomposition of tissue is not listed among the many disorders of the lungs that cause an animal to be considered as *treifah,* forbidden food. The question debated by the Sages was whether or not parallel principles apply to an *esrog*.

מג ט"ז שם. מד לדעה הא' דלעיל ס"ג־ז, אף באינו מפולש, ולדעה הב' דלעיל ס"ח, עכ"פ במפולש. מה כדלקמן סט"ו וסל"א וש"נ. מו ט"ז ס"ק ו. מז ריטב"א לד, ב ד"ה נקלף. ר"ן שם (יז, א) ד"ה מתני' עלתה. ט"ז ס"ק י. מח גמרא לו, א ורש"י ד"ה הכא וד"ה סרות. טור ושו"ע ס"ד. מט מ"א ס"ק ד. אליה רבה ס"ק ז. נ רבא שם. נא סימן זה בשוע"ר לא הגיע לידינו, וראה שו"ע שם ס"ז.

וְיֵשׁ פּוֹסְקִין[נב] סָפֵק זֶה לְהָקֵל, לְפִי שֶׁהֵן סוֹבְרִין שֶׁכָּל פְּסוּלִין אֵלּוּ (שֶׁאֵינָן מֵחֲמַת הַהִדּוּר כְּמוֹ שֶׁיִּתְבָּאֵר[נג,30]) — אֵין פְּסוּלָן מִן הַתּוֹרָה אֶלָּא מִדִּבְרֵי סוֹפְרִים,[31] וְכָל סְפֵק דִּבְרֵי סוֹפְרִים לְהָקֵל,[נד,32] וְיֵשׁ אוֹמְרִים[נה] שֶׁכָּל פְּסוּלִין אֵלּוּ הֵן מִן הַתּוֹרָה[נו] כְּמוֹ שֶׁיִּתְבָּאֵר,[נז,30] וּלְפִיכָךְ הוֹלְכִין בִּסְפֵק זֶה לְהַחְמִיר[נח,33] כְּכָל סְפֵק שֶׁל תּוֹרָה.[34] וְיֵשׁ לָחוּשׁ לַסְּבָרָא הָאַחֲרוֹנָה בִּמְקוֹם שֶׁאֶפְשָׁר:[נט,35]

Some authorities rule leniently on this uncertain situation. They argue that all these disqualifying factors (which do not depend on whether the *esrog* is "beautiful," as will be explained[30]) are not of Scriptural but of Rabbinic origin,[31] and whenever an uncertainty arises on a point of Rabbinic Law, we rule leniently.[32]

Other authorities maintain that all these disqualifying factors are of Scriptural origin, as will be explained.[30] Hence, [they argue,] this question should be viewed stringently,[33] as with all uncertainties that arise regarding Scriptural Law.[34]

Where possible, one should show concern for the latter view.[35]

יג אִם נִסְדַּק[ס,36] כֻּלּוֹ עַל פְּנֵי כָּל אָרְכּוֹ,[סא] אֲפִלּוּ לֹא נִסְדַּק אֶלָּא מִצַּד אֶחָד[סב] מֵרֹאשׁוֹ לְסוֹפוֹ, וְעֹמֶק הַסֶּדֶק מַגִּיעַ עַל פְּנֵי כָּל אָרְכּוֹ עַד רֹב עֳבִי שֶׁל קְלִפָּה הֶעָבָה — הֲרֵי זֶה פָּסוּל,[סג,2] אַף עַל פִּי שֶׁלֹּא חָסֵר כְּלוּם מִגּוּף הָאֶתְרוֹג.[סד] אֲבָל אִם נִשְׁתַּיֵּר בָּאֶתְרוֹג מַשֶּׁהוּ לְמַעְלָה וּמַשֶּׁהוּ לְמַטָּה,[סה,37] שֶׁלֹּא נִסְדַּק בָּעֹמֶק עַד

13 If an *esrog* is split[36] along [almost] its entire length, even if it is split only on one side from top to bottom, and the split along its entire length penetrates more than halfway into the thick peel, the *esrog* is invalid,[2] even though none of its substance is missing. If a minute part of the *esrog* near its tip and a minute part near its base remain[37] without a split that penetrates more than

---

30. Subsection 14.

31. Those authorities who hold that these disqualifying factors are of Rabbinic origin understand the interpretation of the prooftext at the end of subsection 14 to be merely an *asmachta* (lit., "a support"). I.e., the Sages ordained a law, and cited a Scriptural allusion that lends it support *(Aruch HaShulchan)*.

32. In the original, *lehakel*.

33. In the original, *lehachmir*.

34. Sec. 649:19 states that such an *esrog* is invalid only on the first day.

35. See subsection 15. The implication is that when no other *esrog* is available, a blessing may be recited over such an *esrog*.

36. This and the following subsection apply whether the split occurred before or after the *esrog* was picked, and whether it occurred naturally or was made with a knife *(Hadar Hu LeChol Chassidav)*.

37. I.e., this remnant is needed at both ends.

נב הלכות גדולות הל' לולב (לה, רע"א: מכפנים כשר). רי"ף (שלא הביא האיבעי), לפירוש הרא"ש פ"ג סי' יח. רמב"ם (שלא הביא האיבעי), לפירוש הב"י ד"ה ומ"ש ואם. דעה הא' בטור ושו"ע ס"ד. נג סעיף יד, וש"נ. נד רא"ש שם. נה משמעות הרא"ש שם (שתלוי בדעת הפוסלים לעיל ס"ו). ר"ן שם ד"ה תניא, בדעת הרי"ף. שלטי הגיבורים שם אות ה בשם ריא"ז. טור (יש מחמירין והכי מסתברא). דעה הב' בשו"ע שם. ב"ח ד"ה ומ"ש ויש שנקטינן לפסול. עטרת צבי ס"ק ה. נו ר"ן (יח, רע"א). טור (ראה ט"ז סי' תרמט ס"ק ג). נז סעיף יד. נח ראה לקמן סי' תרמט סי"ט, שאינו פסול אלא ביום הראשון. נט ראה עד"ז לקמן סט"ו. ס משנה לד, ב. טור ושו"ע ס"ה. סא רש"י לו, א ד"ה נסדק. תוס' שם ד"ה אי. רא"ש פ"ג סי"ח. טור ושו"ע שם. לבוש ס"ה. ט"ז ס"ק ט. מ"א ס"ק ו (אף כשנסדק משני צדדיו, כדלקמן בסוף הסעיף). סב מ"א ס"ק ה (ממשמעות הטור ושו"ע שם, דהכי קיי"ל). סג ריטב"א לד, ב ד"ה נסדק, ור"ן (יז, א) ד"ה מתני' עלתה, בשם ויש מחמירין. ט"ז שם (שאם נסדק כל העובי נפסל במשהו מטעם ניקב, לדעה דלעיל ס"ו). רמ"א ס"ה. סד טור ושו"ע שם (שאם נחסר נפסל במשהו מטעם ניקב, לדעה דלעיל ס"ז). סה טור ושו"ע שם (והיינו אפילו אם גם חלק מחוטמו נסדק. וכדלקמן סכ"א, שרק דבר הפוסל

רֹב עֳבִי הַקְּלִפָּה הֶעָבָה,[סו] אֲפִלּוּ נִסְדַּק מִשְּׁנֵי צְדָדָיו עַל פְּנֵי כָּל אָרְכּוֹ וְנִשְׁתַּיֵּר מִכָּל צַד מַשֶּׁהוּ לְמַעְלָה וּמַשֶּׁהוּ לְמַטָּה שֶׁלֹּא נִסְדַּק — כָּשֵׁר:[סז]

halfway into the thick peel, the *esrog* is valid. [This ruling applies] even if it is split on both sides along [almost] its entire length, but there remains a minute part near the tip and near the bottom on each side that is not split.

יד וְכֵן אִם נִסְדַּק עַל פְּנֵי הֶקֵּף רָחְבּוֹ, אֲפִלּוּ נִסְדַּק מִשְּׁנֵי צְדָדָיו זֶה כְּנֶגֶד זֶה, וְנִשְׁתַּיֵּר מַשֶּׁהוּ שָׁלֵם[38] לְמַעְלָה בֵּין שְׁנֵי הַסְּדָקִים שֶׁמִּשְּׁנֵי הַצְּדָדִין וּמַשֶּׁהוּ שָׁלֵם לְמַטָּה בֵּין שְׁנֵי הַסְּדָקִים שֶׁמִּשְּׁנֵי הַצְּדָדִים[39] — הֲרֵי זֶה כָּשֵׁר,[סח] אַף עַל פִּי שֶׁעֹמֶק הַסְּדָקִים מַגִּיעַ עַד רֹב עֳבִי שֶׁל קְלִפָּה הֶעָבָה.

וְכָל פְּסוּלִים אֵלּוּ דְּהַיְנוּ נִקַּב חָסֵר וְנִסְדַּק[40] — אֵינוֹ מֵחֲמַת שֶׁאֵינוֹ הָדוּר, אֶלָּא לְפִי שֶׁאֵינוֹ תָּם וְשָׁלֵם, וְהַתּוֹרָה אָמְרָה[41]

14 Similarly, if an *esrog* is split around its circumference, even if it is split on two opposite sides, the *esrog* is valid, as long as a minute part remains intact[38] on either side between [the ends of] the two splits.[39] [This applies] even if the splits penetrate more than halfway into the thick peel.

The reason that an *esrog* is disqualified by any of the above factors — by being perforated, by lacking part of its substance, or by being split[40] — is not its lack of "beauty." The reason for the disqualification is that such an *esrog* is not perfect and complete, whereas the Torah stated,[41]

---

38. *Hadar Hu LeChol Chassidav* notes that while subsection 13 required only that the split not penetrate more than halfway into the thick peel, subsection 14 requires in addition that part of the peel — i.e., even the outer skin — remain intact. That work explains that since the *pitom* and the stem of the *esrog* remain intact when the split runs lengthwise, they could enable the peel to regenerate itself. This would not be possible when the *esrog* is split around its circumference, unless the above-described two parts remained intact.

39. Lit., "if something remained intact above between the two splits and something remained intact below between the two splits."

This *esrog* should be pictured as lying on its side. Two splits encircle it like a belt, but at two points the "belt" is not continuous — at the side of the *esrog* that is now facing up, and at the side of the *esrog* that is now lying on the table. See fig. 30.

40. In the original: *nikav, chaser,* and *nisdak,* respectively.

41. *Vayikra* 23:40. This verse is translated in sec. 645:1.

Some authorities maintain that the above-described lack

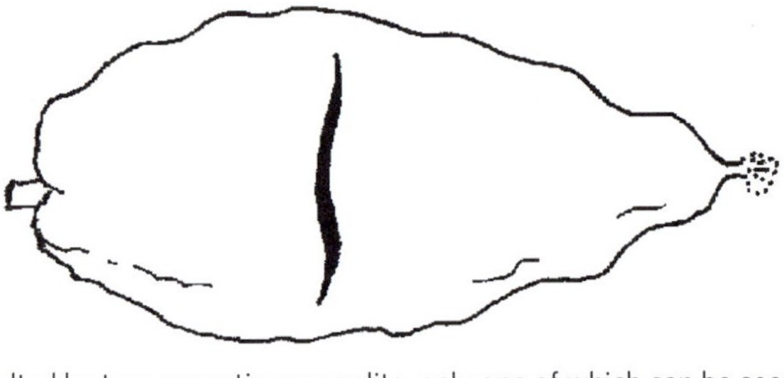

Fig. 30: *Esrog* belted by two uncontinuous splits, only one of which can be seen from this side (see sec. 648:14 and footnote 553).

משום הדר פוסל בחוטמו במשהו, וש"נ). **סו** רמ"א שם (שפחות מזה לא מיקרי נסדק). **סז** מ"א ס"ק ו (אף לדעת הר"ן שם). **סח** ר"ן (יז, א) ד"ה מתני' עלתה, לגירסת ופירוש המ"א ס"ק ו. אליה רבה ס"ק ח.

"וּלְקַחְתֶּם", וְדָרְשׁוּ חֲכָמִים:[סט] לְקִיחָה תַּמָּה וּשְׁלֵמָה:[ע, 42]

ולקחתם — "And you shall take." From this word the Sages learned that [what is taken] should be perfect and complete.[42]

טו אִם נִקְלַף[עא, 44] מִמֶּנּוּ הַקְּלִפָּה הַחִיצוֹנָה[עב] הַדַּקָּה[עג] הַמַּקֶּפֶת אֶת קְלִפָּה הָעָבָה,[עד, 43] אִם נִקְלַף כֻּלּוֹ — פָּסוּל,[עה, 14] שֶׁכֵּיוָן שֶׁכֻּלּוֹ נִקְלַף הוֹלֵךְ וּמִתְנַוְּנֶה וְאֵינוֹ הָדוּר,[עו] וְאִם נִשְׁתַּיֵּר מִמֶּנּוּ כָּל שֶׁהוּא שֶׁלֹּא נִקְלַף — כָּשֵׁר,[עז] שֶׁעַל יְדֵי אוֹתוֹ כָּל שֶׁהוּא הוּא חוֹזֵר לִבְרִיאוּתוֹ.[עח, 45] וְיֵשׁ אוֹמְרִים[עט] שֶׁאֵינוֹ כָּשֵׁר אֶלָּא אִם כֵּן נִשְׁתַּיֵּר מִמֶּנּוּ כְּסֶלַע[46] שֶׁלֹּא נִקְלַף. וְיֵשׁ לָחוּשׁ לְדִבְרֵיהֶם בְּמָקוֹם שֶׁאֶפְשָׁר:[פ, 47]

15 [The following rules apply] if the thin outer rind that surrounds the thick peel[43] has been stripped off.[44] If it has been stripped off entirely, the *esrog* is invalid,[14] because since the rind has been removed entirely, the *esrog* will progressively spoil; it is not considered "beautiful." If, however, there remains even the slightest amount of the rind that was not peeled off, the *esrog* is valid, for from that amount, [the entire rind] can be regenerated.[45]

Some authorities maintain that the *esrog* is invalid unless part of its rind the size of a *sela*[46] remains. Where possible, this view should be respected.[47]

טז בַּמֶּה דְּבָרִים אֲמוּרִים? כְּשֶׁמָּקוֹם הַנִּקְלָף הוּא שָׁוֶה בְּמַרְאִיתוֹ לְמַרְאֵה גּוֹן הָאֶתְרוֹג,[48] אֲבָל אִם הוּא

16 When does the above apply? When the place where the rind was stripped off remains the same color as the *esrog*.[48] If,

of perfection and completeness disqualifies an *esrog* according to Rabbinic Law alone (see subsection 12 above).

42. See sec. 645, footnote 19.

43. When part of the substance of the thick peel has also been removed, some authorities disqualify the *esrog;* see subsections 7 and 8.

44. *Sukkah, loc. cit.* As evident from subsection 16, we are not necessarily speaking of a situation in which the entire yellow rind was peeled off, leaving the white, fibrous peel exposed. (For in such a situation, the *esrog* is invalid if half the rind was removed when there was unnatural discoloration; see subsection 16.) Rather, this subsection also applies when the outer layer of the rind itself was skinned off, leaving its lower layer (see *Tzemach Tzedek, Orach Chayim,* Responsum 65).

These laws apply whether the *esrog* was peeled before or after it was picked, and whether it was peeled by man or lost its peel by natural causes *(Hadar Hu LeChol Chassidav).*

45. Were the *esrog* to be left on the tree *(Hadar Hu LeChol Chassidav).*

46. A coin of the Talmudic era whose circumference was approximately a handbreadth and whose diameter was hence approx. 2.66 cm., i.e., slightly more than an inch.

47. See subsection 12.

48. I.e., between the outer rind and the white fibrous peel.

סט גמרא לד, ב (לענין שד' המינים מעכבין זא"ז). וראה גם לעיל סי' תרמה ס"י (לענין לולב). **ע** רש"י לו, ב ד"ה ומשנינן (לענין חסר). תוס' לד, ב ד"ה שתהא. ר"ן (יח, רע"א). רבנו ירוחם נתיב ח ח"ג (נט, ד. לענין נסדק וניקב). וכ"ה לעיל סי"ב (במוסגר, לענין נימוח). וראה לקמן סי' תרמט סי"ז־ט, שמטעם זה (בלבד) פסול ביום הראשון בלבד. **עא** משנה לד, ב. טור ושו"ע ס"ו. **עב** רמב"ם פ"ח ה"ז. שו"ע ס"ו. **עג** ריטב"א לד, ב ד"ה נקלף. ר"ן שם (יז, א) ד"ה מתני' עלתה. הובא בב"י ד"ה ומ"ש רבנו. טור ולבוש שם. ט"ז ס"ק י. וראה לקמן סכ"ד, דהיינו שלא נחסר כלום מגוף האתרוג. **עד** כדלעיל סי"ב וש"נ. **עה** גמרא לו, רע"א לפירוש רבנו חננאל שם (הובא בתוס' שם ד"ה הא וברא"ש פ"ג סי' יז). רי"ף שם (יז, ב). רמב"ם שם. טור ושו"ע שם. **עו** לבוש שם. וראה חידושי צמח צדק (עב, א). **עז** רי"ף ורמב"ם שם. דעה הא' בשו"ע שם. **עח** לבוש שם. **עט** תוס' ורא"ש שם וטור בשם רבנו חננאל (כמו לענין טריפה בחולין נה, ב). דעה הב' בשו"ע שם. אליה רבה ס"ק יא. **פ** ראה עד"ז לעיל סי"ב. **פא** ראב"ד בתמים דעים סי' רל (בדברי עצמו, אפילו בנשתנה למראה הכשר). הובא ברא"ש פ"ג

מְשֻׁנֶּה בְּמַרְאִיתוֹ מִמַּרְאֵה הָאֶתְרוֹג[49] — אֵינוֹ כָּשֵׁר,[פא] אֶלָּא אִם כֵּן הַמָּקוֹם שֶׁנִּקְלַף הוּא מִעוּט הָאֶתְרוֹג, וְאֵינוֹ מְפֻזָּר בִּשְׁנַיִם וּשְׁלֹשָׁה מְקוֹמוֹת אֶלָּא כֻּלּוֹ עוֹמֵד בְּמָקוֹם אֶחָד,[50] וְאֵינוֹ עוֹמֵד בְּחָטְמוֹ שֶׁל הָאֶתְרוֹג אֶלָּא מֵחָטְמוֹ וּלְמַטָּה,[פב] כְּמוֹ שֶׁיִּתְבָּאֵר[פג] גַּבֵּי חֲזָזִית,[פד] עַיֵּן שָׁם הַטַּעַם לְכָל זֶה:[51]

however, its color is different from that of [the rind of][49] the *esrog*, it is invalid unless: [i] the peeled part [covers only] a minority of [the surface of] the *esrog;* [ii] it is not scattered in two or three places, but is located entirely in one place;[50] and [iii] it is not located near the tip of the *esrog,* but below it, as will be explained [in subsections 19-24] with regard to protrusions [that may erupt upon it]. Note the explanations provided there.[51]

יז יֵשׁ הַרְבֵּה אֶתְרוֹגִים שֶׁעַל רֹאשׁ הָאֶתְרוֹג גָּדֵל עֵץ אֶחָד שֶׁמִּקְצָתוֹ נִכְנָס לְתוֹךְ גּוּף הָאֶתְרוֹג וּמִקְצָתוֹ בּוֹלֵט לְמַעְלָה,[פה] וּבְמִקְצָת אֶתְרוֹגִים אֵין עֵץ זֶה נִכְנָס כְּלָל לְתוֹךְ אֶתְרוֹג אֶלָּא כֻּלּוֹ בּוֹלֵט לְמַעְלָה מֵרֹאשׁ הָאֶתְרוֹג,[פו] וְנִקְרָא "פִּטְמָא"[פז,52] אוֹ "דַּד",[פח,53] וְעַל עֵץ זֶה גָּדֵל כְּמִין פֶּרַח שׁוֹשָׁן, וְנִקְרָא "שׁוֹשַׁנְתָּא",[פט] וְהוּא (נֶחְשָׁב) מִגּוּף הָעֵץ הַנִּקְרָא "פִּטְמָא" אוֹ "דַּד",[צ] וְיֵשׁ הַרְבֵּה אֶתְרוֹגִים שֶׁאֵין לָהֶם כְּלָל פִּטְמָא זוֹ וְלֹא שׁוֹשַׁנְתָּא שֶׁעָלָיו[54] וְהֵן כְּשֵׁרִין,[צא]

17 Many *esrogim* have a woody projection growing from their tip whose [lower end] is embedded in the *esrog* and whose [upper end] juts out upward. In some *esrogim,* this projection is not embedded in the *esrog* at all, but its full length extends upwards from the tip of the *esrog.* [This projection] is called a *pitma*[52] or a *dad.*[53] On it grows a rose-like flower called a *shoshanta,* which is (considered) part of the woody projection that is called a *pitom* or a *dad.*

Many *esrogim* grow without this *pitom* and this flower at all.[54] They are valid,

---

49. The Sages differ as to whether the intent is that the color of this particular *esrog* is uniform (as appears to be the Alter Rebbe's intent; see subsection 21) or that the part from which the rind has been removed shares one of the common colors of *esrogim* even though it is different from the color of this particular *esrog* (*Tzemach Tzedek, Chiddushim Al HaShas,* p. 72c).

50. See subsection 26.

51. Some disqualifying factors invalidate an *esrog* only if they cover most of its surface. If, however, even the slightest amount of a disqualifying factor is found on the tip of the *esrog,* the *esrog* is invalid, because it is the tip that attracts most attention.

52. *Sukkah* 34b. Lit. (Aramaic), "pointy tip." (Since it is universally known today by its Hebrew name, the continuation of this text calls it a *pitom.*) *Sukkah* 35b also refers to it as a *buchna,* meaning "pestle," from its slight resemblance to a pestle positioned in a mortar.

53. This name, which generally means "nipple," is not commonly used.

54. Most Calabrian *esrogim* (see footnote 109 below) grow without a *pitom.*

סי׳ יז. טור. נחלת צבי ס״ק ו, ומ״א ס״ק ז, בדעת הרמב״ם ושו״ע שם. וראה לקמן סכ״ו (לענין מנומר). **פב** טור ולבוש ס״ו (שכל אלו פסולים אף בנשתנה למראה הכשר). **פג** סעיף יט־כג. וראה סכ״א, לענין נקלף מחוטמו ולמעלה במשהו. **פד** טור ומ״א ס״ק ז. **פה** תוס׳ לו, א דיבור הראשון, ורא״ש פ״ג סי׳ טז, בשם ר״ת. **פו** ט״ז סוף ס״ק יא. **פז** משנה לד, ב. **פח** רבנו חננאל לו, א. הובא בערוך ערך פטם הג׳. רי״ף יז, ב. תוס׳ ורא״ש שם. **פט** תוס׳ שם בשם הירושלמי פ״ג ה״ו. רי״ף שם. רמב״ם פ״ח ה״ז. שו״ע ס״ז. מ״א ס״ק ח. **צ** רי״ף שם, לפירוש הרמב״ן בהל׳ לולב (ענין נטילת פטמתו), והריטב״א לה, ב ד״ה ניטלה, והר״ן (יז, ב) ד״ה גמ׳ תאני. **צא** ראב״ד בתמים דעים רס״י רל. רא״ש פ״ג סט״ז. ב״י ד״ה ומ״ש להכשיר, בשם ארחות חיים בשם ה״ר שם טוב. טור ורמ״א ס״ז.

כֵּיוָן שֶׁכָּךְ הִיא בִּתְחִלַּת בְּרִיָּתָם וְזֶהוּ דֶּרֶךְ גִּדּוּלָן,[צב] וְנִכָּרִין הֵן אוֹתָן שֶׁכָּךְ הֵן מִתְּחִלַּת בְּרִיָּתָם כִּי יֵשׁ לָהֶן בִּמְקוֹם הַפִּטְמָא כְּמוֹ גֻּמָּא מִתְּחִלַּת בְּרִיאָתוֹ.[צג]

אֲבָל אֶתְרוֹג שֶׁהָיָה לוֹ פִּטְמָא וְנִטְּלָה פִּטְמָתוֹ,[צד] אֲפִלּוּ לֹא נִטַּל כָּל עֳבִי הַפִּטְמָא אֶלָּא מִקְצָת הָעֹבִי נִשְׁאַר מְחֻבָּר לָאֶתְרוֹג וּמִקְצָת הָעֹבִי נִטַּל לְגַמְרֵי מִן הָאֶתְרוֹג, בְּעִנְיָן שֶׁנִּשְׁאַר מַשֶּׁהוּ בָּאֶתְרוֹג מְגֻלֶּה[צה] בְּמָקוֹם שֶׁהָיָה מְכֻסֶּה בָּעֳבִי מִקְצָת הַפִּטְמָא שֶׁנִּטְּלָה — הֲרֵי זֶה פָּסוּל,[55] לְפִי שֶׁפִּטְמָא זוֹ נֶחְשֶׁבֶת מִגּוּף הָאֶתְרוֹג, וְכֵיוָן שֶׁהִיא חֲסֵרָה — הֲרֵי זֶה אֶתְרוֹג חָסֵר,[צו,56] אַף עַל פִּי שֶׁיֵּשׁ אוֹמְרִים שֶׁאֵין חֶסְרוֹן פּוֹסֵל אֶלָּא אִם כֵּן יֵשׁ בּוֹ כְּאִסָּר כְּמוֹ שֶׁנִּתְבָּאֵר,[צז,57] מִכָּל מָקוֹם כֵּיוָן שֶׁהַפִּטְמָא הִיא בְּגֹבַהּ הָאֶתְרוֹג עַל רֹאשׁוֹ וְהַחֶסְרוֹן נִכָּר בָּהּ יוֹתֵר, לְפִיכָךְ הֶחְמִירוּ בָּהּ שֶׁאֲפִלּוּ חֶסְרוֹן כָּל שֶׁהוּא שֶׁבָּהּ פּוֹסֵל,[צח] לְפִי שֶׁעִקַּר הִדּוּרוֹ שֶׁל אֶתְרוֹג תָּלוּי בְּרֹאשׁוֹ, שֶׁהָאָדָם רוֹאֶה אוֹתוֹ בִּתְחִלַּת הַשְׁקָפָתוֹ,[צט,58] וְאִם נֶחְסַר שָׁם כָּל שֶׁהוּא — אֵינוֹ הָדוּר.[ק,59]

אֲבָל אִם לֹא נִטַּל כְּלוּם מֵעֳבִי הַפִּטְמָא

because this is the way they were created and this is their natural pattern of growth. Those that naturally grow this way are readily identifiable, because in place of a *pitom*, they naturally grow with a small cavity there. If, however, an *esrog* had a *pitom* and it was removed, the *esrog* is invalid.[55] [This applies] even if the entire thickness of the *pitom* was not detached, but part of its thickness remained connected to the *esrog*, while part was detached, and thus a small portion of the *esrog* which was previously covered by part of the thickness of the *pitom* is [now] uncovered. [The reason for this disqualification is that] the *pitom* is considered part of the *esrog*. If it is lacking, the *esrog* is thus lacking [some of its substance].[56] As explained [above],[57] some authorities maintain that a decrease in the substance of an *esrog* does not disqualify it unless that decrease is the size of an *isar*. Nevertheless, since the *pitom* is on the tip of the *esrog* and its lack is more obvious, we are more stringent with regard to it. Even the slightest decrease in it disqualifies the *esrog* — because the beauty of an *esrog* primarily depends on its tip, for that is what one sees at first glance.[58] [Hence,] if even the slightest part is missing, the *esrog* is no [longer] considered "beautiful."[59]

If, however, nothing was removed from the width of the *pitom* at its point of

55. *Sukkah, loc. cit.*

56. See subsection 7.

57. Subsection 8.

58. See subsection 21.

59. The Alter Rebbe adds to this in sec. 649:17 that it is therefore invalid throughout all seven days of the festival.

צב שו"ת רדב"ז ח"ד סי' א'קפב. וראה חידושי צ"צ (עב, ב). צג שו"ת מבי"ט ח"ג סמ"ט. כנסת הגדולה הגה"ט. מ"א ס"ק י. וראה אג"ק ח"י ע' לה, שכ"ה גם אם דרך גדולן בלא פטמא ובלא גומא. צד משנה שם (פטמתו), לפירוש רש"י שם ד"ה נטלה, ובדף לה, ב ד"ה תני, בשם רבנו יעקב. ר"ח שם. רי"ף שם. רמב"ם שם. רא"ש שם. טור ושו"ע שם. צה ב"י ד"ה כתב הר"ן (לפסול לדעה זו כשניטלה מקצת הפיטמה), ולבוש ס"ח, לפירוש המ"א ס"ק ט (דהיינו שניטל עד האתרוג. וא"כ מ"ש הב"י ולבוש קצת היינו מקצת העובי). משמעות ט"ז שם (שחולק על הב"י ופוסל רק בניטל כולו, אפילו לא נעשה בזה גומא). צו רבנו ירוחם נתיב ח ח"ג (נט, ד). רבנו מנוח שם. רמ"א סי' תרמט ס"ה. מ"א ס"ק ט. וכדלקמן סי"ח לענין עוקץ, וש"נ. צז לעיל ס"ח. צח יראים השלם סי' תכב (רמב, ב), לדעת רבנו יעקב ב"ר יקר (דלקמן סי"ח, שמכשיר בניטל כל העוקץ). הגהות מיימוניות פ"ח אות מ. מרדכי סי' תשנב. מ"א סי' תרמט ס"ק יז. (ב"ח סי' תרמ"א). צט כדלקמן סכ"א וש"נ. ק לבוש ס"ז"ח. מ"א שם, ממשמעות המגיד משנה שם. וכדלקמן סכ"א, שכל הפוסל משום הדור פוסל על

בְּמָקוֹם שֶׁהִיא מְחֻבֶּרֶת לָאֶתְרוֹג,[60,קא] וַאֲפִלּוּ נִטְּלָה כָּל הַפִּטְמָא וְלֹא נִשְׁאַר מִמֶּנָּה רַק גֹּבַהּ מַשֶּׁהוּ,[קב] בְּעִנְיָן שֶׁמִּקְצָת רֹאשׁ הָאֶתְרוֹג הוּא מְכֻסֶּה בָּעֳבִי פִּטְמָא מַשֶּׁהוּ זוֹ שֶׁנִּשְׁתַּיֵּר כְּמוֹ שֶׁהָיָה מְכֻסֶּה בַּתְּחִלָּה[קג] כְּשֶׁהַפִּטְמָא הָיְתָה שְׁלֵמָה[61] – הֲרֵי זֶה כָּשֵׁר, דְּכֵיוָן שֶׁמִּקְצָת רֹאשׁ הָאֶתְרוֹג הוּא מְכֻסֶּה כְּמוֹ שֶׁהָיָה מִתְּחִלָּה – אֵין זֶה חֶסְרוֹן.[קד]

וְיֵשׁ חוֹלְקִין[קה] עַל זֶה וְאוֹמְרִים, דַּאֲפִלּוּ לֹא נִטְּלָה רַק הַשּׁוֹשַׁנְתָּא הָעֶלְיוֹנָה וְכָל הַפִּטְמָא קַיֶּמֶת – הֲרֵי זֶה פָּסוּל, שֶׁאֵינוֹ הִדּוּר, אֶלָּא אִם כֵּן הוּא שָׁלֵם לְגַמְרֵי בְּרֹאשׁוֹ. וְאַף עַל פִּי שֶׁאֵין הֲלָכָה כְּדִבְרֵיהֶם,[קו] מִכָּל מָקוֹם טוֹב לָחוּשׁ לְדִבְרֵיהֶם בְּמָקוֹם שֶׁאֶפְשָׁר,[קז] דְּהַיְנוּ שֶׁאִם יֵשׁ לְפָנָיו שְׁנֵי אֶתְרוֹגִים שָׁוִים בְּנוֹי וְהִדּוּר וּבְאֶחָד מֵהֶן נִטַּל הַשּׁוֹשַׁנְתָּא – אֲזַי יִקַּח אוֹתוֹ שֶׁיֵּשׁ בּוֹ הַשּׁוֹשַׁנְתָּא, אֲבָל אִם אוֹתוֹ שֶׁיֵּשׁ בּוֹ הַשּׁוֹשַׁנְתָּא אֵינוֹ מְהֻדָּר וּמְפֹאָר כָּל כָּךְ כְּמוֹ אוֹתוֹ שֶׁנִּטְּלָה מִמֶּנּוּ הַשּׁוֹשַׁנְתָּא – יִקַּח אֶת הַמְהֻדָּר וְאֶת הַמְפֹאָר יוֹתֵר אַף עַל פִּי שֶׁאֵין בּוֹ שׁוֹשַׁנְתָּא, שֶׁהָעִקָּר הוּא כַּסְּבָרָא הָרִאשׁוֹנָה:[קח]

יח נִטַּל הָעֹקֶץ, וְהוּא הָעֵץ שֶׁהָאֶתְרוֹג תָּלוּי בּוֹ בָּאִילָן – הֲרֵי זֶה פָּסוּל. וְהוּא שֶׁנִּטַּל הָעֹקֶץ מֵעִקָּרוֹ וְלֹא נִשְׁאַר

contact with the *esrog*,[60] the *esrog* is valid. [This applies] even if [almost] the entire *pitom* was removed and there remained merely a minimal projection. Since the extremity of the tip of the *esrog* is [still] covered — over the width of the *pitom* — by this remaining minimal projection as it was originally covered when the *pitom* was intact, the *esrog* is not disqualified][61] [The rationale:] Since the extremity of the tip of the *esrog* is covered as it was originally, the substance [of the *esrog*] is not considered to be lacking anything.

Some authorities differ and maintain that even if merely the top flower was removed and the entire *pitom* remains, the *esrog* is invalid, because an *esrog* is not considered "beautiful" unless its tip is utterly intact. Though the *halachah* does not follow their view, it is preferable to respect it where possible. Thus if one has the choice of two *esrogim* that are equally attractive and beautiful, but the flower of one has been removed, he should use the one that has a flower. If, however, the one that has the flower is not as beautiful and splendid as the one from which the flower was removed, one should use the beautiful and splendid one even though it lacks a flower, for primacy is given to the first view.

18 If the stem — i.e., the stalk by which the *esrog* hangs from the tree — is removed, the *esrog* is invalid. [This applies] only if the stem is removed entirely and no

60. I.e., the top of the *pitom* was clipped off, but its entire base remained.

61. As explained in subsection 18 with regard to the stem.

חוטמו במשהו. וראה לקמן סי' תרמט סי"ז (אין פיסולו מחמת חסרון בלבד אלא מחמת שאין זה הידור). **קא** רמב"ן שם בשם הרי"ץ גיאת (ע' קו). ריטב"א ור"ן שם. ארחות חיים הל' לולב סי' טז. ט"ז ס"ק יא. **קב** מ"א ס"ק ט. **קג** כדלקמן סי"ח לענין העוקץ. **קד** מ"א שם (דאין זה חסרון הניכר). **קה** רי"ף שם, לפירוש הרמב"ן והריטב"א והר"ן שם. רמ"א ס"ז (ויש מחמירין). **קו** שגם הרמב"ן והריטב"א והר"ן שפירשו כן ברי"ף, חלקו עליו בזה. ובב"י ד"ה והר"ן, פירש שגם הרי"ץ סובר כשאר הפוסקים בזה. ונתבאר בט"ז ס"ק יב. **קז** רמב"ן שם (כבר הורה זקן). דרכי משה ס"ק ג. רמ"א שם (בניטלה השושנתא). ב"ח סד"ה ניטלה (בניטלה גם חלק מהפטמא, שנקטינן לחומרא). אליה זוטא ס"ק ז. **קח** של"ה מס' סוכה (רמה, ב) ד"ה ארז"ל וד"ה כתב הב"י. ט"ז שם.

מִמֶּנּוּ כְּלוּם בָּאֶתְרוֹג, שֶׁאָז נִשְׁאַר מְקוֹמוֹ גֻּמָּא בָּאֶתְרוֹג, וַהֲרֵי זֶה אֶתְרוֹג חָסֵר,[קט, 62] אֲבָל אִם נִשְׁאַר מִמֶּנּוּ[קי] כָּל שֶׁהוּא[קיא] בָּאֶתְרוֹג, בְּעִנְיָן שֶׁנִּתְמַלֵּאת כָּל רֹחַב הַגֻּמָּא, דְּהַיְנוּ שֶׁלֹּא נִטַּל כְּלוּם מֵעֳבִי הָעֹקֶץ בְּמָקוֹם שֶׁהוּא מְמַלֵּא אֶת הַגֻּמָּא – הֲרֵי זֶה כָּשֵׁר,[2] שֶׁהֲרֵי גּוּף הָאֶתְרוֹג אֵינוֹ חָסֵר כְּלוּם.[קיב]

part of it remains in the *esrog*, so that the *esrog* is thus left with a cavity, and hence is now lacking part of its substance.[62] If, however, even the smallest part of the stem remained in the *esrog* so that the entire area of the cavity was filled, i.e., none of the thickness of the stem that fills the cavity has been removed, the *esrog* is valid,[2] for its substance lacks nothing.

וְיֵשׁ מַכְשִׁירִים[קיג] אֲפִלּוּ נִטַּל כָּל הָעֹקֶץ וְנִשְׁאַר מְקוֹמָהּ גֻּמָּא בָּאֶתְרוֹג שֶׁהָעֹקֶץ אֵינוֹ נֶחְשָׁב מִגּוּף הָאֶתְרוֹג, לְעִנְיָן שֶׁבְּחֶסְרוֹנוֹ יִפָּסֵל הָאֶתְרוֹג מִשּׁוּם אֶתְרוֹג חָסֵר. וְאַף עַל פִּי שֶׁאֵין הֲלָכָה כְּדִבְרֵיהֶם, מִכָּל מָקוֹם בִּשְׁעַת הַדְּחָק שֶׁאִי אֶפְשָׁר לִמְצֹא אֶתְרוֹג אַחֵר – יֵשׁ לִסְמֹךְ עַל דִּבְרֵיהֶם לְבָרֵךְ עַל אֶתְרוֹג זֶה,[קיד] שֶׁהֲרֵי יֵשׁ נוֹהֲגִין בִּשְׁעַת הַדְּחָק לְבָרֵךְ אֲפִלּוּ עַל הַפְּסוּלִין לְגַמְרֵי[קטו] כְּמוֹ שֶׁיִּתְבָּאֵר בְּסִימָן תרמ"ט,[קטז] עַיֵּן שָׁם הַטַּעַם:[63]

However, some authorities rule that an *esrog* is valid even though the entire stem has been removed, leaving a cavity. [They argue that] the stem is not considered as part of the substance of the *esrog* to the extent that its absence would disqualify the *esrog* on the grounds that it is now lacking part of its substance. Though the *halachah* does not follow their view, one may rely on it and use such an *esrog* in a pressing situation in which no other *esrog* is available. A blessing may be recited, for in a pressing situation, there are those who follow the practice of reciting the blessing even on specimens that are outright invalid, as explained in sec. 649[:22-23]. Note the rationale stated there.[63]

---

62. *Sukkah* 35b.

Subsections 7 and 8 presented two opinions as to whether an *esrog* is disqualified by a lack of substance of less than an *isar. Hadar Hu LeChol Chassidav* traces the positions of the various authorities on each of these laws, and concludes that the stricter position here is compatible with the more lenient position earlier; i.e., though a minimal lack of substance is acceptable, a missing stem is not, possibly because it is a distinct component of the *esrog.*

63. There the Alter Rebbe explains that the specimens that may be used in a pressing situation are not invalidated because they belong to a different species of plant, but because they are lacking (e.g.) in beauty or in completeness. In such cases, since the disqualifying factor is conspicuous, no one would mistakenly think that these specimens would be valid if superior ones were available. Hence the Sages felt no need for a stringent interpretation of the broad Scriptural requirements for beauty or completeness.

קט ברייתא דר' יצחק בן אלעזר לה, ב (בוכנתו) לפירוש רבנו חננאל שם. רי"ף (יז, ב). רמב"ם פ"ח ה"ז. מ"מ שם (שהוא כדעה דלעיל ס"ז, שחסר פסול במשהו). רא"ש פ"ג סי' טז. טור ושו"ע ס"ח. מ"א ס"ק יא (שפסול מטעם חסר). וראה גם לקמן סי' תרמט סי"ז וסי"ט. קי משנה לד, ב (ניטל עוקצו כשר), לפירוש ר"ח ורי"ף שם. ולפירוש רש"י לה, ב ד"ה תני בשם רבנו יצחק הלוי. קיא רי"ף שם. תוס'. רא"ש שם. טור ורמ"א שם. קיב ב"י סד"ה ניטלה. רמ"א שם. לבוש שם. ט"ז ס"ק יג. קיג רש"י שם בשם רבנו יעקב ב"ר יקר (שגם בוכנתו היא הפטמא שבראש האתרוג). ר"ת בתוס' שם ד"ה נטלה. הובא ברא"ש שם (שלהך פירושא אין פסול בזנב האתרוג). טור וט"ז ס"ק יא. קיד שו"ת חכם צבי סי' (קכ) [ט]. באר היטב ס"ק יד. וכדלעיל ס"ח (בחסר משהו ואינו מפולש). וראה עד"ז לעיל סי' תרמה סי"ז וש"נ. קטו חכם צבי שם. ועד"ז לקמן סוף ס"כ. סי' תרמט סי"ט. קטז סכ"ב־ג. קיז משנה לד, ב. טור ושו"ע ס"ט.

יט עָלְתָה עָלָיו חֲזָזִית[קיז, 64] (פֵּרוּשׁ[קיח] "אוֹ יַלֶּפֶת"[קיט] תַּרְגּוּמוֹ "אוֹ חֲזָזָן"), וְהוּא כְּמוֹ אֲבַעְבּוּעוֹת דַּקּוֹת,[קכ] וְיֵשׁ בּוֹ מַמָּשׁ שֶׁמְּקוֹמָן נִכָּר בְּמִשְׁמוּשׁ הַיָּד שֶׁהוּא גָּבוֹהַּ מִן הָאֶתְרוֹג,[קכא, 65] אִם הוּא בְּמָקוֹם אֶחָד[קכב] מֵהָאֶתְרוֹג בִּלְבַד – אֵינוֹ פָּסוּל אֶלָּא אִם כֵּן הוּא רֹב[קכג] שֶׁל כָּל[קכד] הָאֶתְרוֹג, אֲבָל אִם הוּא בִּשְׁנֵי מְקוֹמוֹת[קכה] וְיֵשׁ בֵּין שְׁנֵי הַמְּקוֹמוֹת מָקוֹם פָּנוּי (שֶׁאֵין בּוֹ חֲזָזִית) לְכָל הַפָּחוֹת כְּשִׁעוּר חֲזָזִית אַחַת, דְּהַיְנוּ שֶׁיָּכוֹל לִהְיוֹת בְּמָקוֹם זֶה טִפַּת חֲזָזִית מַשֶּׁהוּ (דְּהַיְנוּ שְׁתֵּי אֲבַעְבּוּעוֹת דַּקּוֹת, שֶׁפָּחוֹת מִכֵּן אֵין נִקְרָא חֲזָזִית כְּמוֹ שֶׁיִּתְבָּאֵר[קכו, 66]), וּמַרְאֵה אֶתְרוֹג מַשֶּׁהוּ כְּחוּט הַשַּׂעֲרָה מַפְסִיק בֵּין טִפָּה[67] זוֹ לְהַחֲזָזִית הַגָּדוֹל[קכז] שֶׁאֶצְלָהּ מִצַּד אֶחָד, וּמַרְאֵה אֶתְרוֹג מַשֶּׁהוּ כְּחוּט הַשַּׂעֲרָה מַפְסִיק בֵּין צַד הַשֵּׁנִי שֶׁל טִפָּה זוֹ לַחֲזָזִית הַגָּדוֹל שֶׁאֶצְלָהּ – הֲרֵי זֶה פָּסוּל,[קכח, 68] אֲפִלּוּ אִם כָּל הַחֲזָזִית בְּיַחַד אֵינוֹ אֶלָּא מִעוּט הָאֶתְרוֹג, שֶׁכֵּיוָן שֶׁיֵּשׁ בְּתוֹךְ הַחֲזָזִית מָקוֹם פָּנוּי מַרְאֵה אֶתְרוֹג – הֲרֵי זֶה כִּמְנֻמָּר[קכט, 69] וְאֵינוֹ הָדוּר:[קל]

19 The term *chazazis* ([in the Torah, the phrase][64] או ילפת is rendered by the Aramaic *Targum* as *o chazezan*) refers to an eruption like small boils whose substance is palpably raised from the surface of the esrog.[65] If the eruption covers only part of the esrog it does not disqualify it, provided it does not cover most of the surface of the entire esrog.

[More stringent rules apply, however, if the eruption] covers two areas [on the surface of the *esrog*] and between them there is [a miniscule] empty space (that does not have an eruption). [If this space] is large enough to contain an eruption — i.e., there could be a miniscule eruption in this place (i.e., two small boils, for anything less is not called an eruption, as will be explained[66]) leaving at least a hairsbreadth of space with the natural appearance of the *esrog* between this spot[67] and the large eruption on either side — the *esrog* is invalid.[68] This applies even if the entire area covered by the eruption totals less than half the surface of the *esrog*. [The rationale is] that since there is an empty space with the natural color of the *esrog* in the midst of the eruption, the *esrog* is blotchy[69] and is not considered "beautiful."

---

64. *Vayikra* 21:20.

65. The peel of a healthy *esrog* is naturally wrinkled. *Chazazis* is a decay of this outer rind that erupts in discolored protrusions filled with liquid (cf. *Tzemach Tzedek, Chiddushim* 72a). See *Sukkah* 34b, 35b.

The following laws apply, regardless of whether the eruption began before or after the *esrog* was picked from the tree.

66. Subsection 22.

67. Lit., "drop."

68. This follows the first opinion in subsection 20.

69. The intermingling of colors makes the *esrog* less desirable. See subsection 26.

קיח ערוך ערך חזז. מגיד משנה פ"ח ה"ז. באורי המלים בשו"ע שם. קיט ויקרא כא, כ. קכ רש"י שם ד"ה חזזית. רא"ש פ"ג סט"ו. טור ושו"ע סי"ג. וראה חידושי צמח צדק פ"ג דסוכה (עא, ד). קכא רא"ש שם. טור ושו"ע שם. וראה לקמן סכ"ג. קכב גמרא לה, ב. טור ושו"ע ס"ט. קכג משנה לד, ב. טור ושו"ע שם. קכד רא"ש שם (ולא רובו של צד אחד). מ"א ס"ק יב (ממשמעות השו"ע שם). קכה גמרא שם. טור ושו"ע שם. וראה חידושי צמח צדק שם (עג, א) שאפשר שזה אינו פסול אלא מדרבנן. קכו סעיף כב. קכז כדלקמן ס"כ (לדעה הא'), עד שיהיו ביחד כשיעור רוב היקפו כו'. קכח ט"ז ס"ק יד. אליה רבה ס"ק יח. קכט גמרא שם. לבוש ס"ט. ודין מנומר יתבאר לקמן סכ"ו. קל תוס' כט, ב ד"ה קפסיק (אף ברובו במקום א'). רא"ש שם. לבוש שם. מ"א סי' תרמט ס"ק כב. וכ"ה לקמן סכ"א. סי' תרמט סי"ז. וכדלעיל סי' תרמו סי"ב (בהדס), וש"נ.

כ בַּמֶּה דְּבָרִים אֲמוּרִים? כְּשֶׁיֵּשׁ מִתְּחִלַּת חֲזָזִית הָאַחַת עַד סוֹף חֲזָזִית הַשֵּׁנִית כְּשִׁעוּר רֹב הֶקֵּפוֹ שֶׁל הָאֶתְרוֹג,[קלא] כְּגוֹן שֶׁאִם הֵן עוֹמְדִין לְרֹחַב הָאֶתְרוֹג דְּהַיְנוּ סְבִיב הֶקֵּף עָבְיוֹ וּמִתְּחִלַּת הָאַחַת עַד סוֹף שֵׁנִית יֵשׁ רֹב הֶקֵּף עָבְיוֹ, וְכֵן אִם הֵן עוֹמְדִין לְאֹרֶךְ הָאֶתְרוֹג וּמִתְּחִלַּת הָאַחַת עַד סוֹף הַשֵּׁנִית יֵשׁ רֹב הֶקֵּף אֹרֶךְ הָאֶתְרוֹג, כְּגוֹן שֶׁחֲזָזִית אַחַת עוֹמֵד בְּצַד אֶחָד שֶׁל הָאֶתְרוֹג וַחֲזָזִית הַשֵּׁנִית נִמְשָׁךְ מְעַט עַל צַד הַשֵּׁנִי שֶׁל הָאֶתְרוֹג.[קלב]

אֲבָל אִם כָּל הַחֲזָזִית הוּא בְּצַד אֶחָד[קלג] שֶׁל הָאֶתְרוֹג, אַף עַל פִּי שֶׁיֵּשׁ מִתְּחִלַּת הָאַחַת עַד סוֹף הַשֵּׁנִית מֶחֱצָה[70] הֶקֵּף אֹרֶךְ הָאֶתְרוֹג, אוֹ מֶחֱצָה הֶקֵּף עָבְיוֹ, אוֹ אֲפִלּוּ מֶחֱצָה הֶקֵּף אָרְכּוֹ וּמֶחֱצָה הֶקֵּף עָבְיוֹ, כְּגוֹן שֶׁיֵּשׁ הַרְבֵּה חֲזָזִית קְצָת מֵהֶן נִמְשָׁכִים לְאֹרֶךְ הָאֶתְרוֹג עַד חֲצִי עָבְיוֹ וּקְצָת מֵהֶן נִמְשָׁכִים לְרֹחַב הָאֶתְרוֹג סְבִיב הֶקֵּף עָבְיוֹ עַד חֲצִי הַהֶקֵּף — הֲרֵי זֶה כָּשֵׁר.[קלד] וְיֵשׁ חוֹלְקִין[קלה] עַל זֶה וְאוֹמְרִים, דַּאֲפִלּוּ אֵין בּוֹ אֶלָּא שְׁתֵּי טִפּוֹת חֲזָזִית מַשֶּׁהוּ וּבֵין שְׁתֵּי טִפּוֹת אֵלּוּ אֵין מָקוֹם פָּנוּי שֶׁבּוֹ מַרְאֵה אֶתְרוֹג אֶלָּא כְּדֵי שִׁעוּר חֲזָזִית אַחַת

20 When does the above apply? When the surface covered from the beginning of one eruption until the end of the second eruption extends over most of the circumference of the *esrog*. For example, the eruptions were positioned along the width of the *esrog* — i.e., around its widest circumference — and the surface covered from the beginning of the first eruption until the end of the second eruption extends over most of the circumference of its width. Similarly, [the *esrog* is disqualified if] the eruptions were positioned along the length of the *esrog* and [the affected area] from the beginning of the first eruption until the end of the second eruption extends over the majority of the circumference of its length. This is the case, for example, when there is one eruption on one side of the *esrog* and the other eruption extends to the other side of the *esrog*.

If, by contrast, all of the eruptions are on one side, the *esrog* is valid. [This applies] even if [the area] from the beginning of the first eruption until the end of the second eruption [covers] half[70] of the circumference of the length of the *esrog*, half of the circumference of the width of the *esrog*, or even half of the circumference of [both] the length and the width of the *esrog*. [The *esrog* is thus valid if,] for example, there are many eruptions, some of them extending along its length and over as much as half its width, and others extending across its width around as much as half of the circumference.

Some authorities differ and maintain that even if an *esrog* has only two spots of an eruption of the smallest size and between these two spots there is an empty space with the ordinary color of the *esrog* no larger than the size

70. But not more than half.

קלא ראב״ד בתמים דעים סי׳ רלב (רובו של אתרוג). רא״ש פ״ג סי״ט. שו״ת הריב״ש סי׳ קלט. דעה הב׳ בטור ודעה הא׳ בשו״ע ס״י. מ״א ס״ק יג (רוב הקיפו). אליה רבה ס״ק ט. קלב מ״א שם (דאם נתפשט לצד השני הוי רוב הקיפו). קלג ראב״ד רא״ש וריב״ש שם. טור ושו״ע שם. קלד מ״א ס״ק טו (שהמחלוקת דלקמן לענין מחצה הוא רק ברובו ולא ברוב הקיפו). קלה הרי״ץ גיאת בהלכות לולב (עמ׳ קה). דעה הא׳ בטור ודעה הב׳ בשו״ע שם. וראה

– הֲרֵי זֶה כִּמְנֻמָּר וּפָסוּל. וְיֵשׁ לְהַחְמִיר כִּסְבָרָא הָאַחֲרוֹנָה. אֲבָל בִּשְׁעַת הַדְּחָק שֶׁאִי אֶפְשָׁר לִמְצֹא אֶתְרוֹג אַחֵר – יֵשׁ לִסְמֹךְ עַל סְבָרָא הָרִאשׁוֹנָה.[קלו]

וְאִם אֵין בּוֹ אֶלָּא חֲזָזִית אַחַת גָּדוֹל שֶׁנִּתְפַּשֵּׁט עַל פְּנֵי חֶצְיוֹ שֶׁל כָּל שֶׁטַח הָאֶתְרוֹג, דְּהַיְנוּ שֶׁכָּל מָקוֹם הַפָּנוּי שֶׁבּוֹ מַרְאֵה הָאֶתְרוֹג הוּא מֶחֱצָה עַל מֶחֱצָה עִם הַחֲזָזִית – פָּסוּל. וְכֵן כָּל דָּבָר הַפּוֹסֵל בָּרֹב בְּכָל אַרְבַּעַת הַמִּינִים, אִם הוּא מֶחֱצָה עַל מֶחֱצָה – פָּסוּל,[קלז] לְפִי שֶׁצָּרִיךְ לִהְיוֹת הָרֹב בְּהֶכְשֵׁר, וְאֵין מֶחֱצָה הַכָּשֵׁר נֶחְשָׁב כְּרֹב אֶלָּא לְעִנְיַן מְחִצּוֹת שֶׁל שַׁבָּת[קלח, 71] וְשֶׁל סֻכָּה[קלט, 72] וּלְעִנְיַן סְכַךְ הַסֻּכָּה,[קמ, 73] שֶׁבָּהֶן נֶאֶמְרָה הֲלָכָה לְמֹשֶׁה מִסִּינַי שֶׁהַמֶּחֱצָה הוּא כְּרֹב, אֲבָל בְּכָל הַתּוֹרָה[74] כֻּלָּהּ צָרִיךְ לִהְיוֹת הָרֹב בְּהֶכְשֵׁר.[קמא] וְיֵשׁ חוֹלְקִים[קמב] עַל זֶה וְאוֹמְרִים, דְּכָל שֶׁאֵין בַּפָּסוּל רֹב כְּנֶגֶד הַכָּשֵׁר – אֵינוֹ יָכוֹל לִפְסֹל, וַהֲרֵי הוּא

of an eruption, [the *esrog*] is considered as blotchy and invalid. One should be stringent and follow the latter view. Nevertheless, in a pressing situation in which no other *esrog* can be found, one may rely on the former view.

If an *esrog* has only one large eruption that has spread over half of its area, i.e., the part with the natural color and the eruption are of equal size, the *esrog* is invalid. Similarly, whenever there is a factor that would disqualify any one of the Four Species were it to cover most of it, it is disqualified if that factor covers half, for the majority must be valid.

The only situations in which a valid half is considered as a valid majority are the partitions [that enclose an area, allowing one to carry] on *Shabbos*,[71] the walls of a *sukkah*,[72] and the *s'chach* of a *sukkah*.[73] In these instances, there is a *halachah* communicated to Moshe at Sinai that [even] a [valid] half is considered equivalent to a [valid] majority. With regard to [the rest of] the Torah,[74] by contrast, a valid majority is required.

Some authorities differ with the above and maintain that whenever there are no more of the invalid materials than of the valid materials, they cannot disqualify the valid materials, and the invalid materials are

71. Sec. 362:18 of the present work states that if the open part of an enclosure is longer than the closed part, the enclosure is considered as if open entirely. If the two parts are equal in length, the enclosure is considered as complete and on *Shabbos* it is permitted to carry within the domain that it defines.

72. The relevant section (sec. 630) of the Alter Rebbe's *Shulchan Aruch* is not extant. *Magen Avraham* 630:6 speaks of a *sukkah*, one of whose [three required] sides is partly enclosed and partly not. If the length of the open space(s) exceeds that of the partitions (i.e., walls), the *sukkah* is invalid. Implied is that if the open space and the partitions are equal in length, the *sukkah* is valid.

73. Sec. 626:8 and sec. 631:10 in the present work speak of a *sukkah* that is partly covered with valid *s'chach* and partly with material that is invalid as *s'chach*, and these diverse materials are not mixed but are placed separately next to each other. Such a *sukkah* is valid even if there is no majority of valid *s'chach*; equal amounts suffice.

74. Lit., "the entire Torah."

חידושי צמח צדק (עג, א). קלו ראה עד"ז לעיל סי' תרמה סי"ז וש"נ. קלז ראב"ד שם. דעה הב' בטור ושו"ע סי"א. קלח כדלעיל סי' שסב סי"ח וש"נ. קלט שדינו כמחיצות שבת דפרוץ כעומד מותר, ראה שו"ע סי' תרל ס"ה ובמ"א שם ס"ק ו. קמ כדלעיל סי' תרכו ס"ח. סי' תרלא ס"י. קמא רשב"א פ"ב דחולין כט, א ד"ה אי. תוספות עירובין ט[ז], ע"ב ד"ה והלכתא, ובחולין שם ד"ה דכולי (לענין מחיצות). וראה פרישה אות ד. קמב טור בשם אחיו הרב רבנו יחיאל. דעה הא' בשו"ע שם.

כְּאִלּוּ לֹא הָיָה כָּאן פָּסוּל כְּלָל. וְאַף עַל פִּי שֶׁאֵין הֲלָכָה כְּדִבְרֵיהֶם,[קמג] מִכָּל מָקוֹם בִּשְׁעַת הַדְּחָק שֶׁאִי אֶפְשָׁר לִמְצֹא מִינִים אֲחֵרִים כְּשֵׁרִים — יֵשׁ לִסְמֹךְ עַל דִּבְרֵיהֶם לְבָרֵךְ עַל מִינִים אֵלּוּ, שֶׁהֲרֵי יֵשׁ נוֹהֲגִין בִּשְׁעַת הַדְּחָק לְבָרֵךְ אֲפִלּוּ עַל הַפְּסוּלִין לְגַמְרֵי[קמד] כְּמוֹ שֶׁיִּתְבָּאֵר בְּסִימָן תרמ"ט,[קמה] עַיֵּן שָׁם הַטַּעַם:[63]

considered as if they do not exist at all. Though the *halachah* does not follow this view, in a pressing situation where other valid specimens cannot be found, one may rely on their view, [use such specimens,] and recite a blessing over them. For in a pressing situation, as will be explained in sec. 649[:22-23], there are those who follow the practice of reciting a blessing even over specimens that are utterly invalid. Note the rationale stated there.[63]

כא כָּל דָּבָר הַפּוֹסֵל בָּאֶתְרוֹג מִשּׁוּם שֶׁאֵינוֹ הִדּוּר,[קמו] כְּגוֹן יָבֵשׁ[קמז, 75] אוֹ חֲזָזִית[קמח] אוֹ שִׁנּוּי מַרְאֵה הָאֶתְרוֹג,[קמט] דְּהַיְנוּ שֶׁנִּקְלַף מִקְצָת הָאֶתְרוֹג וְנִשְׁתַּנָּה מַרְאִיתוֹ מִמַּרְאֵה כָּל הָאֶתְרוֹג,[קנ, 76] אַף עַל פִּי שֶׁכָּל[77] אֵלּוּ אֵינָן פּוֹסְלִין אֶלָּא אִם כֵּן יֵשׁ בָּהֶן כְּשִׁעוּר שֶׁנִּתְפָּרֵשׁ בָּהֶן,[78] אֲבָל אִם הָיָה אֶחָד מֵהֶן עַל חָטְמוֹ[79] דְּהַיְנוּ מִמָּקוֹם שֶׁמְּשַׁפֵּעַ מִשָּׁם וְיוֹרֵד לְצַד רֹאשׁוֹ[קנא] וּמַתְחִיל מִשָּׁם לְהִתְקַצֵּר וּלְהִתְחַדֵּד[קנב, 80] כָּל מָקוֹם זֶה, אִם יֵשׁ בּוֹ אֶחָד מִכָּל אֵלּוּ הַדְּבָרִים הַפּוֹסְלִים מִשּׁוּם הִדּוּר אֲפִלּוּ אֵין בּוֹ אֶלָּא מַשֶּׁהוּ — הֲרֵי זֶה פָּסוּל,[81] לְפִי שֶׁעִקַּר הַהִדּוּר שֶׁל הָאֶתְרוֹג

21 [Various] factors disqualify an *esrog* because it is not "beautiful," e.g., it is dried out,[75] it has an eruption, or the appearance of the *esrog* has changed, meaning that part of its rind was removed and now looks different from the appearance of the *esrog* as a whole.[76] [Generally,][77] these factors do not disqualify an *esrog* unless they are of the size specified in each case.[78] [Different rules apply, however] if one [of these factors] is found on the tip of the *esrog*,[79] i.e., on the part that begins to become narrower and pointed and tapers down[80] towards its peak. If even the slightest trace of any of the factors that disqualify an *esrog* because it is not "beautiful" is found within this area, the *esrog* is invalid.[81] [The rationale is] that the beauty of an *esrog*

75. Apparently, the intent is not the factors mentioned in subsection 1, for that speaks about the inside of the *esrog* drying out. Here the Alter Rebbe appears to be speaking about a situation in which the outer rind of the *esrog* dries out and becomes discolored *(Hadar Hu LeChol Chassidav)*.

76. I.e., from the appearance of this particular *esrog*, although other *esrogim* may in fact have this color. See footnote 49 above.

77. Lit., "all."

78. I.e., an *esrog* could be partly affected and yet remain valid.

79. I.e., on any part of the cone that ends at the very tip.

80. I.e., if the *esrog* is laid on its side.

81. *Tzemach Tzedek, Orach Chayim,* Responsum 66, leaves room for debate as to whether this also applies to the *pitom.*

קמג ט"ז ס"ק טז. אליה רבה ס"ק כא. וראה גם לקמן סכ"ו. קמד עד"ז לעיל סי"ח וש"נ. קמה סכ"ב־ג. קמו רא"ש פ"ג ס"כ. רבנו ירוחם נתיב ח ח"ג (נט, א). דרכי משה ס"ק ה. ב"ח ד"ה ומ"ש ומחוטמו. מ"א ס"ק יז, ממשמעות השו"ע סי"ב. משא"כ בנסדק (שפסול מטעם חסר), כדלעיל סי"ג. וראה שו"ת צמח צדק או"ח סי' סו. קמז דלעיל ס"א (ולא נתפרש שם השיעור). הראב"ד בתמים דעים סי' רלב. רמב"ן בהל' לולב ד"ה ענין הפסולים. רא"ש שם. טור ושו"ע שם. קמח דלעיל סי"ט. גמרא לה, ב. טור ושו"ע שם, ובס"ט. קמט רא"ש פ"ג סי"ז. טור ושו"ע שם. קנ רא"ש שם. וכדלעיל סט"ז. וראה לקמן סכ"ו. קנא רא"ש פ"ג ס"כ. טור ושו"ע ס"ט וסי"ב. קנב שו"ע ס"ט. לבוש סי"ב. קנג רש"י שם ד"ה אפילו. לבוש שם. וראה גם לעיל סי"ז (לענין ניטלה פטמתו).

תָּלוּי בְּחָטְמוֹ שֶׁהוּא נִרְאֶה לָעֵינַיִם יוֹתֵר מִשְּׁאָר מְקוֹמוֹת, וּבוֹ אָדָם נוֹתֵן עֵינָיו[קנג] בִּתְחִלַּת הַשְׁקָפָתוֹ:

primarily depends on its tip, for this is more noticeable than the other parts of the *esrog* and it attracts one's attention at first glance.

כב מִכָּל מָקוֹם, אֲפִלּוּ בְּחָטְמוֹ אֵין הַחֲזָזִית פּוֹסֵל אֶלָּא אִם כֵּן יֵשׁ בּוֹ שְׁתֵּי אֲבַעְבּוּעוֹת, לֹא פָּחוֹת[קנד] (שֶׁפָּחוֹת מִכֵּן – אֵין נִקְרָא חֲזָזִית). וְהוּא שֶׁיִּהְיוּ נִרְאִין לָעַיִן כְּשֶׁאוֹחֲזוֹ בְּיָדוֹ, וְלֹא שֶׁיְּהֵא צָרִיךְ לְהָשִׂים עַיִן עִיּוּנוֹ עֲלֵיהֶם עַד שֶׁיִּרְאֵם.[קנה, 82] וְכֵן כָּל שִׁנּוּי מַרְאֶה אֵינוֹ פּוֹסֵל אֶלָּא אִם כֵּן נִרְאֶה לְרֹב בְּנֵי אָדָם בְּהַשְׁקָפָה רִאשׁוֹנָה:[קנו]

22 Nevertheless, even an eruption on the tip does not disqualify an *esrog* unless it comprises at least two boils. (Anything less is not considered an eruption.) [These boils] must be noticeable when one holds the *esrog* in hand without any need to focus one's attention until he sees them.[82] Similarly, none of the other factors [that could disqualify an *esrog* because of] a change in appearance disqualify it unless the factor is apparent to most people at first glance.

כג אֵין הַחֲזָזִית וְלֹא שִׁנּוּי מַרְאֶה[קנז, 83] פּוֹסְלִין אֶלָּא אִם כֵּן נוֹלְדוּ מֵעַצְמוּת הָאֶתְרוֹג. אֲבָל אִם מֵחֲמַת שֶׁעוֹקְצִים אוֹתוֹ קוֹצִים נַעֲשׂוּ בּוֹ מְקוֹמוֹת אֲדֻמִּים וַעֲקֻמִּים[84] – כָּשֵׁר.[קנח] וְכֵן אוֹתָן חֲזָזִית שֶׁקּוֹרִין בלא"ט מו"ל[85] – יֵשׁ לְהַכְשִׁיר,[קנט] אֲפִלּוּ יֵשׁ בָּהֶן מַמָּשׁוּת שֶׁמְּקוֹמָן נִכָּר בְּמִשּׁוּשׁ הַיָּד שֶׁהֵן גְּבוֹהִין מֵהָאֶתְרוֹג,[קס] לְפִי שֶׁהֵן נֶחְשָׁבִין גַּם כֵּן מַרְאֵה אֶתְרוֹג, מֵאַחַר שֶׁרְגִילוּת הוּא לִהְיוֹת כָּךְ הַרְבֵּה אֶתְרוֹגִים – אֵין זֶה שִׁנּוּי גָּדוֹל:[קסא, 86]

23 No eruption or [other] change in the appearance of an *esrog*[83] disqualifies it unless it comes about from the *esrog* itself. If it came about because thorns pricked it and therefore certain parts appear red or crooked,[84] the *esrog* is valid.

Similarly, the blotches that are called *blatt mol*[85] can be deemed valid even if they are substantial, i.e., one can feel that they project from the surface of the *esrog*, because such an appearance is considered ordinary. Since many *esrogim* have such [blotches], this is not considered a significant variation.[86]

---

82. I.e., an *esrog* is not disqualified by a factor that affects its beauty unless the blemish attracts immediate attention.

83. See subsections 21 and 26.

84. I.e., the leaves or branches caused the *esrog* to deviate from its natural pattern of growth.

85. This archaic Yiddish phrase means "blotches [caused by] leaves." In current Yiddish usage, these marks are called *bletlach* — lit., "leaves" (sing.: *blatt* or *bletl*).

86. Nevertheless, the initial preference is to choose an *esrog* that has no blotches or marks whatsoever.

Some authorities have questioned the validity of *esrogim* that became discolored by extensive use. Can such *esrogim* still be called "beautiful"?! The *Chasam Sofer* (gloss to *Sukkah* 36a) responds: Since this discoloration came about through the observance of the *mitzvah*, "this

סי' תרמה ס"י (לענין לולב, מטעם חסר). סי' תרמו ס"ט (לענין הדס). **קנד** שו"ת מבי"ט ח"ג סמ"ט. מ"א ס"ק ט"ז. וראה גם לעיל סי"ט (במוסגר: אבעבועות דקות). **קנה** שו"ת מבי"ט שם. מ"א שם. **קנו** שו"ת מבי"ט שם. מ"א ס"ק יח. **קנז** כדלעיל סכ"א, או כדלקמן סכ"ו. **קנח** שו"ת מבי"ט שם. מ"א ס"ק יט. **קנט** מהרי"ל הל' אתרוג (ע' שצט). תרומת הדשן סי' צט. רמ"א סי"ג. **קס** תרומת הדשן שם. מ"א ס"ק כ. והיינו אף שנתבאר לעיל סי"ט שחזזית היא דוקא כשניכר במישוש כו'. **קסא** תרומת הדשן שם. רמ"א שם, בשם ויש מי שכתב. וראה חידושי צמח צדק פ"ג דסוכה (עב, א־ב).

כד כָּל מָקוֹם[87] שֶׁנִּפְסַל הָאֶתְרוֹג מֵחֲמַת שִׁנּוּי מַרְאֶה[קסב] אוֹ מֵחֲמַת הַחֲזָזִית,[קסג] בֵּין שֶׁלֹּא הָיוּ אֶלָּא בְּמָקוֹם אֶחָד בִּלְבַד, בֵּין שֶׁהָיוּ בְּכַמָּה מְקוֹמוֹת,[קסד] וְקִלֵּף כָּל מְקוֹמוֹת הַפְּסוּלִין שֶׁבּוֹ וְחָזַר מַרְאֵיהֶן מַרְאֵה[קסה] כָּל הָאֶתְרוֹג, אִם נִזְהַר לְקַלְּפוֹ בְּעִנְיָן שֶׁלֹּא נֶחְסַר כְּלוּם מִגּוּף הָאֶתְרוֹג,[קסו] דְּהַיְנוּ שֶׁלֹּא קִלֵּף רַק קְלִפָּה הַחִיצוֹנָה הַדַּקָּה[קסז,88] — הֲרֵי זֶה כָּשֵׁר. וַאֲפִלּוּ לְכַתְּחִלָּה מֻתָּר לְהַכְשִׁירוֹ עַל יְדֵי כֵן.[קסח]

נָפְלוּ עָלָיו מַיִם בְּתָלוּשׁ וְתָפַח,[קסט] וְאֵין צָרִיךְ לוֹמַר[קע] אִם נִסְרַח[קעא] שֶׁיֵּשׁ לוֹ קְצָת רֵיחַ רַע[קעב] — פָּסוּל,[14] שֶׁאֵין זֶה הִדּוּר:[קעג]

24 Whenever[87] an *esrog* is disqualified because of a change in appearance or because of an eruption — whether the eruption is localized in one place or it is found in several places — and one cuts away the rind in all the invalid places, leaving the natural appearance of the *esrog*, it is valid. [One must, however,] be careful to cut away the rind in a manner that does not decrease the substance of the *esrog* itself, i.e., he cuts away only the thin, external rind.[88] [Indeed,] even at the outset, one may use such measures to make the *esrog* valid.

If water fell on an *esrog* after it was picked and it became bloated, it is invalid,[14] for this cannot be considered "beautiful." Needless to say, this applies if it became rotten, i.e., slightly malodorous.

כה אֶתְרוֹג הַמְבֻשָּׁל — פָּסוּל.[89] וְכֵן אִם הָיָה כָּבוּשׁ — פָּסוּל,[קעד] שֶׁהַכָּבוּשׁ כִּמְבֻשָּׁל.[קעה] וְאֵיזֶהוּ כָּבוּשׁ? כָּל שֶׁנִּשְׁרָה מֵעֵת לְעֵת[90] בְּמַיִם[91] אוֹ בִּשְׁאָר מַשְׁקִים[92] וּמֵי פֵרוֹת,[קעו] וַאֲפִלּוּ בִּדְבַשׁ שֶׁדַּרְכּוֹ לְהַעֲמִיד דָּבָר הַכָּבוּשׁ בְּתוֹכוֹ — אַף עַל פִּי כֵן נִפְסַל

25 A cooked *esrog* is invalid.[89] Similarly, a pickled *esrog* is invalid, for "pickling" is considered as cooking. What is meant by "pickled"? Anything that has been soaked for 24 hours[90] in water,[91] fruit juice, or other liquids.[92] Even if an *esrog* is soaked in honey, which tends to preserve substances that are soaked in it, it is

---

discoloration is its beauty."

In this spirit, the Rebbe was occasionally asked why he continued to use his *esrog* after it had been handled by the great numbers of chassidim to whom he had lent it for the fulfillment of the *mitzvah*. Citing the words of an unnamed Rebbe, the Rebbe would answer: "There can be no more beautiful *esrog* than one that thousands of Jews have used to fulfill the *mitzvah*." *(See Igros Kodesh,* Vol. 16, p. 38.*)*

87. Lit., "In every place." From these words, *Hadar Hu LeChol Chassidav* learns that the Alter Rebbe would accept an *esrog* as valid if a discoloration was cut away from its tip.

88. And leaves the remainder of the peel intact, including part of the yellow rind *(Tzemach Tzedek, Orach Chayim,* Responsum 65*)*.

89. *Loc. cit.*

90. In the original, *mei'eis le'eis* — lit., "from time to time."

91. An *esrog* should not be soaked for even less than 24 hours, for this will spoil it *(Pri Megadim: Eshel Avraham* 654:2*)*

92. This applies even if soaking it did not cause it to become inflated or spoiled, for such an *esrog* is disqualified regardless, as stated in subsection 24.

קסב כדלקמן סכ"ו. קסג רא"ש פ"ג ריש סי"ח. טור ושו"ע סי"ד. קסד רא"ש שם. קסה אולי צ"ל: למראה. וראה לעיל סט"ז. קסו רמ"א שם. וכדלעיל ס"ז שנחסר פסול במשהו. קסז כדלעיל סט"ו. קסח רא"ש שם (שיש לו תקנה ע"י קליפה). קסט טור ושו"ע סט"ו, מגמרא [ברייתא] לו, א (תפוח) ורש"י שם ד"ה לא (שנפלו גשמים בתלוש). קע ב"י ד"ה נפל. לבוש שם. קעא ברייתא שם. טור ושו"ע שם. קעב טור ולבוש שם. קעג אליה רבה ס"ק כו, בשם אמרכל. קעד גמרא [ברייתא] לו, א. טור ושו"ע סט"ו. קעה פסחים עו, א. שו"ע יו"ד סי' קה ס"א. קעו מ"א ס"ק כב, ע"פ מה דקיי"ל ביו"ד שם. וכדלעיל

disqualified as "pickled," if [it has been soaked] for 24 hours.

If it was soaked in strong vinegar that is very pungent, it is considered as cooked [and hence, disqualified. This applies] even if it was soaked in it very briefly, i.e., for as long as the vinegar takes to boil when placed on a fire, as stated in *Yoreh Deah*, sec. 105. Note the rationale explained there.[93]

הָאֶתְרוֹג מִשּׁוּם כָּבוּשׁ בְּמֵעֵת לְעֵת.[קעז] וְאִם כְּבָשׁוֹ בְּחֹמֶץ[קעח] חָזָק שֶׁהוּא חָרִיף מְאֹד,[קעט] אֲפִלּוּ לֹא שָׁהָה בְּתוֹכוֹ אֶלָּא שָׁעָה מוּעֶטֶת כְּדֵי שֶׁיִּתֵּן הַחֹמֶץ עַל הָאוּר וְיַרְתִּיחַ — הֲרֵי זֶה כִּמְבֻשָּׁל כְּמוֹ שֶׁיִּתְבָּאֵר בְּיוֹרֶה דֵעָה סִימָן ק"ה,[קפ] עַיֵּן שָׁם הַטַּעַם:[93]

26 An *esrog* that is not of uniform color[94] is not "beautiful" and therefore invalid.[14]

When is an *esrog* "not of uniform color"? When it has several colors that are not natural to the *esrog*,[95] such as black or white. [Moreover,] the *esrog* is considered "not of uniform color" and is disqualified even if one [such] color appears in two places, and even if they cover less than half of the *esrog*.

If the unacceptable color is found in one place, it does not disqualify the *esrog* unless it covers the majority or half of its surface, as stated above[96] regarding an eruption, for the laws governing a change in appearance are the same in every respect as those governing an eruption.

כו אֶתְרוֹג הַמְנֻמָּר[94] — פָּסוּל,[קפא] שֶׁאֵינוֹ הָדוּר.[קפב,14] אֵיזֶהוּ מְנֻמָּר? שֶׁיֵּשׁ בּוֹ כַּמָּה גְוָנִים[קפג] כְּגוֹן שָׁחֹר וְלָבָן שֶׁאֵינוֹ מִמַּרְאֵה הָאֶתְרוֹג.[קפד,95] וַאֲפִלּוּ גָּוֶן אֶחָד בִּשְׁנֵי מְקוֹמוֹת בָּאֶתְרוֹג[קפה] — הֲרֵי זֶה כִּמְנֻמָּר וּפָסוּל, אַף אִם אֵין בָּהֶם אֶלָּא מִעוּט הָאֶתְרוֹג. אֲבָל אִם גָּוֶן הַפָּסוּל הוּא בְּמָקוֹם אֶחָד בִּלְבַד — אֵינוֹ פּוֹסֵל אֶלָּא אִם כֵּן יֵשׁ בּוֹ רֹב הָאֶתְרוֹג[קפו] אוֹ חֶצְיוֹ, כְּמוֹ שֶׁנִּתְבָּאֵר[קפז,96] גַּבֵּי הַחֲזָזִית, שֶׁדִּין שִׁנּוּי מַרְאֶה — כְּדִין חֲזָזִית לְכָל דָּבָר:

27 If the appearance of an *esrog* is even slightly black,[97] it is invalid.

When does the above apply? When the *esrog* grows in those lands which produce

כז אֶתְרוֹג שֶׁמַּרְאֵהוּ שָׁחֹר אֲפִלּוּ מְעַט[97] — הֲרֵי זֶה פָּסוּל. בַּמֶּה דְּבָרִים אֲמוּרִים? בְּאֶתְרוֹג הַגָּדֵל בָּאֲרָצוֹת

---

93. This section in the Alter Rebbe's *Shulchan Aruch* is not extant. As explained by the commentaries on sec. 105:2 in the *Shulchan Aruch* of R. Yosef Caro, vinegar effects the same changes in this short time that water would effect over the longer time. See *Pesachim* 76b; see also sec. 447:29 in the present work.

94. In the original, *menumar* (from *namer* — tiger or leopard).

95. A combination of colors that are natural to the *esrog*, e.g., green and yellow, is acceptable (*Shaar HaTziyun* 648:62).

96. In subsections 19-20.

97. I.e., dark gray.

סי' תמז סכ"ז וש"נ. **קעז** ט"ז ס"ק יז. **קעח** רש"י שם ד"ה תניא. רבנו ירוחם נתיב ח ח"ג (נט, ג). טור ושו"ע סט"ו. **קעט** מ"א סי' (תעג) [תמז] ס"ק כח. וכדלעיל סי' תעג סכ"ט וש"נ. **קפ** סימן זה בשוע"ר לא הגיע לידינו, וראה שו"ע שם ס"א. ש"ך סק"ב. לעיל סי' תמז סכ"ט וש"נ. **קפא** גמרא [ברייתא] לו, א. טור ושו"ע סט"ו. **קפב** רש"י לג, רע"ב ד"ה מנומר. וכדלעיל סי"ט, וסי' תרמו סי"ב, וש"נ. **קפג** ריטב"א לה, ב ד"ה דה"ל כמנומר. **קפד** ראב"ד בתמים דעים סי' רל. ריטב"א שם. ר"ן (יז, ב) ד"ה אבל. וראה לעיל סט"ז (לענין נקלף). **קפה** ראה ארבעת המינים (ויינר) ע' רי. **קפו** רא"ש פ"ג סי' כב. טור ושו"ע סט"ז. **קפז** לעיל סי"ט־כ.

שֶׁהָאֶתְרוֹגִים הַגְּדֵלִין שָׁם הֵן יְרֻקִּים,[98] אֲבָל בִּמְקוֹמוֹת שֶׁהָאֶתְרוֹגִים הַגְּדֵלִין שָׁם הֵן שְׁחֹרִין מְעַט – כְּשֵׁרִים, שֶׁזֶּהוּ דֶּרֶךְ בְּרִיאָתָן וְגִדּוּלָן בְּאוֹתוֹ מָקוֹם, וְאֵין זֶה שִׁנּוּי כְּלָל. אֲבָל אֶתְרוֹג הַשָּׁחֹר בְּיוֹתֵר כְּשַׁחֲרוּת בְּנֵי אָדָם הַכּוּשִׁים – אֲפִלּוּ הַגָּדֵל בְּאֶרֶץ כּוּשׁ פָּסוּל,[קפח, 99] לְפִי שֶׁאֵין זֶה הִדּוּר כְּלָל:[קפט]

esrogim that are greenish yellow.[98] In the lands whose esrogim grow blackish, by contrast, this is acceptable, because it is the natural pattern of growth in such places and is not considered as a deviation at all. When, however, an esrog is very dark, like the skin color of Ethiopians, it is invalid[99] even if it grows in Ethiopia, for this is not considered "beautiful" at all.

כח הֶעָגֹל כְּכַדּוּר – פָּסוּל,[קצ, 14] שֶׁהֲרֵי אֵין עָלָיו צוּרַת אֶתְרוֹג כְּלָל.[קצא] וְכֵן מִטַּעַם זֶה[קצב] אִם גִּדְּלוֹ בִּדְפוּס[קצג] שֶׁעָשׂוּ לוֹ בְּעוֹדוֹ קָטָן וְנָתְנוּ בְּתוֹכוֹ כְּשֶׁהוּא עֲדַיִן מְחֻבָּר לָאִילָן וְגָדַל בְּתוֹכוֹ כְּמִדַּת הַדְּפוּס[קצד] וְכִתְמוּנָתוֹ[קצה] עַד שֶׁנִּשְׁתַּנָּה מִצּוּרַת הָאֶתְרוֹג וְנַעֲשָׂה כְּמִין בְּרִיָּה אַחֶרֶת[100] – פָּסוּל.[קצו] אֲבָל אִם נַעֲשָׂה כְּעֵין צוּרַת הָאֶתְרוֹג אַף עַל פִּי שֶׁאֵינוֹ דּוֹמֶה לוֹ מַמָּשׁ, כְּגוֹן שֶׁנַּעֲשׂוּ בוֹ כְּמִין קְרָשִׁים,[קצז] כְּעֵין גַּלְגַּל שֶׁל רֵחַיִם וְשֶׁל מַיִם[קצח, 101] – הֲרֵי זֶה כָּשֵׁר:

28 An esrog that is round like a ball is invalid,[14] because it is not shaped like an esrog at all. For the same reason, if an esrog was grown in a mold in which it was placed from the time that it was very small and still attached to the tree, and if it grows into the size and shape of the mold and is thus changed from its natural shape and now appears like a different created being,[100] it is invalid.

If, however, [the mold] gives it a shape similar to that of an esrog, then even though this is not entirely like its natural shape, e.g., it appears like beams resembling the millstone of a watermill,[101] it is valid.

98. In modern usage, the adjective *yarok* means nothing but green. In the varying contexts of Talmudic and Rabbinic usage, *yarok* can mean green, or yellow, or greenish yellow. Moreover, the same word signifies the color of the fluid exuded by the marine creature called *chilazon* that is used in the manufacture of *techeiles,* the *blue* coloring required for tzitzis *(Menachos* 44a on *Bamidbar* 15:38*).* And the color of *techeiles* in turn is described in one source as resembling the sea, grass, and the sky *(Talmud Yerushalmi, Berachos* 1:2*),* and in other sources is described as resembling the sea, the sky, and a sapphire *(Chullin* 89a, *et al.).*

This explains why — in subsection 30, for example — the Alter Rebbe not only writes *"yarok* like saffron," but for good measure adds the Yiddish word for yellow *(gehl).* Likewise, he not only writes *"yerukin* like the grass of the fields," but adds the Yiddish word for green *(grin).*

99. *Sukkah* 34b, 36a.

100. Or has any shape that is not natural to an *esrog.*

101. Translated according to *Rashi* on *Sukkah* 36b, and *Levush* 648:19. It appears that there is a slight printing error in the Hebrew text.

קפח משנה לד, ב וכאוקימתא דרבא לו, א — לפירוש הרי"ף שם יז, ב. רמב"ם פ"ח ה"ח. שו"ע סי"ז. אליה זוטא ס"ק יא (שכן עיקר). **קפט** לבוש שם.
קצ גמרא [ברייתא] לו, א ורש"י ד"ה ככדור. טור ושו"ע סי"ח. **קצא** לבוש סי"ח. **קצב** מגיד משנה פ"ח ה"ח (בישוב הרמב"ם שהשמיט דין הכדור).
קצג ברייתא שם. טור ושו"ע סי"ט. **קצד** רש"י ד"ה גידלו. לבוש סי"ט. **קצה** לבוש שם. **קצו** ברייתא שם. טור ושו"ע שם. **קצז** גמרא לו, ב. טור ושו"ע שם.
קצח רש"י שם ד"ה דעבידא. לבוש שם. ואוצ"ל: של מים. **קצט** גמרא לו, א וכת"ק. רמב"ם פ"ח ה"ח. שו"ת הרשב"א ח"א סי' תיא. דעה הא' בטור. שו"ע

כט הַתְּיוֹם,[קצט] דְּהַיְנוּ שֶׁגָּדְלוּ שְׁנַיִם דְּבוּקִים זֶה בָּזֶה[102] — כָּשֵׁר,[ר,14] שֶׁאֵין זֶה שִׁנּוּי כְּלָל, וְנוֹטֵל שְׁנֵיהֶן בְּיַחַד כְּשֶׁהֵן דְּבוּקִין[רא] וּמְבָרֵךְ.

אֵין שִׁעוּר לְגֹדֶל הָאֶתְרוֹג לְמַעְלָה,[רב,2] שֶׁאֲפִלּוּ הוּא גָּדוֹל כָּל כָּךְ עַד שֶׁנִּטָּל עַל הַכָּתֵף[רג,103] — הֲרֵי זֶה כָּשֵׁר. אֲבָל לְמַטָּה יֵשׁ לוֹ שִׁעוּר,[רד] שֶׁאִם הוּא פָּחוּת מִכַּבֵּיצָה — פָּסוּל,[רה] לְפִי שֶׁרֹב הָאֶתְרוֹגִים אֵין גִּדּוּלָן פָּחוּת מִכַּבֵּיצָה, וְזֶה שֶׁאֵין בּוֹ כְּבֵיצָה — הֲרֵי עֲדַיִן לֹא נִגְמַר פִּרְיוֹ, וְהַתּוֹרָה אָמְרָה,[104] "פְּרִי עֵץ" — שֶׁיְּהֵא פְּרִי גָּמוּר.[רו,105] וַאֲפִלּוּ אִם אֶתְרוֹג זֶה לֹא הָיָה גָּדֵל יוֹתֵר אַף אִם לֹא הָיוּ קוֹצְצִים אוֹתוֹ מִן הָאִילָן, מִכָּל מָקוֹם כֵּיוָן שֶׁבִּגְמַר גִּדּוּלוֹ אֵין בּוֹ כַּבֵּיצָה — אֵין זֶה פְּרִי חָשׁוּב.[רז] אֲבָל אִם יֵשׁ בּוֹ כַּבֵּיצָה — הֲרֵי הוּא כָּשֵׁר, אַף עַל פִּי שֶׁהוּא בֹּסֶר,[רח] דְּהַיְנוּ שֶׁלֹּא נִגְמַר גִּדּוּלוֹ שֶׁהָיָה גָּדוֹל יוֹתֵר אִם לֹא הָיוּ קוֹצְצִים אוֹתוֹ,[רט] מִכָּל מָקוֹם כֵּיוָן שֶׁיֵּשׁ הַרְבֵּה אֶתְרוֹגִים שֶׁאֵינָן גְּדֵלִין יוֹתֵר מִמֶּנּוּ — הֲרֵי זֶה פְּרִי חָשׁוּב, וְנִקְרָא גְּמַר פְּרִי:[רי]

29 Twin *esrogim* that grow coupled together[102] are acceptable,[14] for this is not considered a departure from the norm. One should take them both together in their bonded state and recite the blessing.

There is no upper limit to the size of an *esrog*.[2] It is valid even if it is so big that it must be carried on one's shoulder.[103] There is, however, a lower limit. An *esrog* smaller than the size of an egg is invalid, because most *esrogim* grow to no less than the size of an egg. Hence [the fact that] an *esrog* has not grown to that size shows that it is not fully grown — and the Torah's expression,[104] "The fruit of a… tree," implies a fruit that is complete.[105]

Even if a particular *esrog* would not grow bigger even if it had not been picked, since it is not the size of an egg when fully grown it is not considered a significant fruit. Conversely, if it is the size of an egg, it is valid even if it is unripe, i.e., not fully grown. [Though] it would have grown more if it had not been picked, since many *esrogim* do not grow to any larger than this one, it is considered a significant fruit and may be termed a fully-grown fruit.

ל בַּמֶּה דְּבָרִים אֲמוּרִים[ריא]? כְּשֶׁמַּרְאֵהוּ יָרֹק כְּעֵין כַּרְכֹּם[ריב,98] (שֶׁקּוֹרִין גע"ל[ריג]), כְּדֶרֶךְ כָּל הָאֶתְרוֹגִים שֶׁנִּגְמַר פִּרְיָם,

30 When does the above apply? When the color of [the *esrog*] is *yarok*, i.e., yellow like saffron,[98] as is the color of all the *esrogim* that have ripened. [It is] also [valid] even if it has not entirely become

---

102. I.e., their common base separates out into two heads, each topped by a *pitom*.

103. *Sukkah, loc. cit.*

104. *Vayikra* 23:40.

105. *Sukkah* 31b.

ס"כ. **ר** רש"י שם ד"ה התיום. רמב"ם וטור ושו"ע שם. **רא** ראה כפות תמרים שם ד"ה וי"א. **רב** משנה לד, ב כרבי יוסי. רי"ף שם (יח, א). רא"ש פ"ג סכ"ד. רמב"ם פ"ז ה"ח. טור ושו"ע סכ"ב. לבוש סכ"ב. וראה גם לקמן סי' תרנ ס"ב (לענין שאר המינים). **רג** גמרא [ברייתא] לו, ב ר"ן בגמרא שם ד"ה מתני' ובגדול. **רד** לשון הגמרא מנחות מב, א (לענין לולב). הובא ברי"ף (טו, סע"א). **רה** משנה שם כרבי יהודה. רי"ף ורא"ש שם. רמב"ם שם. טור ושו"ע שם. **רו** גמרא לא, ב (דלא גמר פירא). לבוש שם. **רז** תוס' לא, ב ד"ה שיעור. לבוש שם. וראה לקמן סי' תרמט סי"ח (שזהו שיעור אתרוג אף בנחסר), וש"נ. **רח** ברייתא לו, א כחכמים. רמב"ם פ"ח ה"ח. טור ושו"ע שם. **רט** תוס' שם. לבוש שם. **רי** תוס' שם. רא"ש שם. **ריא** משמעות מ"א ס"ק כד (שפסול ירוק ככרתי הוא רק בלא נגמר גידולו, וכדלקמן). **ריב** הנקרא זאפרי"ן, כדלעיל סי' תסז סכ"א. וראה שו"ע יו"ד סי' לח ס"א.

אוֹ אֲפִלּוּ שֶׁאֵין כֻּלּוֹ יָרֹק כְּכַרְכֹּם שֶׁבְּמִקְצָתוֹ הִתְחִיל לְהוֹרִיק כְּכַרְכֹּם,[ריד] שֶׁזֶּהוּ סִימָן שֶׁנִּגְמַר פִּרְיוֹ וְסוֹפוֹ לְהוֹרִיק כֻּלּוֹ בְּתָלוּשׁ כְּשֶׁיַּשְׁהוּ אוֹתוֹ זְמַן מְרֻבֶּה.[רטו] אֲבָל אֶתְרוֹגִים הַבָּאִים לְפָנֵינוּ כְּשֶׁהֵן עֲדַיִן יְרֻקִּין כְּעִשְׂבֵי הַשָּׂדֶה[2] (שֶׁקּוֹרִין גרי"ן)[רטז] — יֵשׁ לָחוּשׁ שֶׁמָּא עֲדַיִן לֹא נִגְמַר פִּרְיָם,[ריז, 106] וּלְכָךְ אֵין יְרֻקִּין כְּכַרְכֹּם. וּמִכָּל מָקוֹם, אִם הֵם גְּדוֹלִים הַרְבֵּה בְּעִנְיָן שֶׁיָּדוּעַ וּבָרוּר לָנוּ שֶׁנִּגְמַר פִּרְיָם וְסוֹפָן לְהוֹרִיק כְּכַרְכֹּם בְּתָלוּשׁ — מֻתָּר לִקַּח אוֹתָן וְלָצֵאת בָּהֶן יְדֵי חוֹבָה אֲפִלּוּ כְּשֶׁהֵן יְרֻקִּין.[ריח] וּמִכָּל מָקוֹם, כְּבָר נָהֲגוּ שֶׁלֹּא לִסְמֹךְ עַל בְּקִיאוּת זוֹ, וְאֵין לוֹקְחִין אֶלָּא אִם כֵּן הִתְחִילוּ לְהוֹרִיק קְצָת כְּעֵין כַּרְכֹּם:[ריט]

לא אֶתְרוֹג הַמֻּרְכָּב,[רכ, 107] דְּהַיְנוּ שֶׁהִרְכִּיבוּ עָנָף מֵאִילָן אַחֵר לְתוֹךְ אִילַן הָאֶתְרוֹג[רכא, 108] וְגָדַל מֵהֶן מִין הַדּוֹמֶה לָאֶתְרוֹג — פָּסוּל, שֶׁזֶּה אֵינוֹ אֶתְרוֹג כְּלָל אֶלָּא הוּא בְּרִיָּה בִּפְנֵי עַצְמָהּ. וְאַרְבָּעָה סִימָנִים יֵשׁ לְהַבְחִין בֵּין הָאֶתְרוֹג הַמֻּרְכָּב מִלִּימוֹנִ"י לָאֶתְרוֹג.[109] הָאֶחָד, כִּי הַמֻּרְכָּב הוּא חָלָק,

saffron colored, but part of it has begun to yellow, for that is a sign that the fruit is fully grown and ultimately, when left for a long time after being picked, it will become completely yellow.

When, however, *esrogim* are brought before us while they are still as green as the grass of the fields,[2] there is reason to suspect that they are not fully grown[106] and that this is why they are not yellow. Nevertheless, if they are so big that it is clear to us that they are fully grown and that they will ultimately become yellow after being picked, they may be used [to] fulfill one's obligation, even when they are still green. However, it has already become customary not to rely on this kind of expertise, and to [use] an *esrog* only if its color has started to turn yellowish.

31 An *esrog* produced by grafting[107] — i.e., a branch from a different tree was grafted onto an *esrog* tree[108] and the resultant fruit was a species that resembled an *esrog* — is invalid, for this is not an *esrog*, but a distinct species.

Four signs distinguish a lemon-grafted *esrog* from a genuine *esrog*:[109]

[i] a grafted *esrog* is smooth, whereas the entire surface of a genuine *esrog* is

106. *op. cit.,* 31a.

107. In the original, *esrog hamurkav.*

108. Or, more commonly, since the *esrog* tree is delicate and vulnerable, an *esrog* twig is grafted onto the hardier stock of a lemon tree.

109. The *Gemara* enumerates the anatomical characteristics that distinguish all the kosher species of birds. Nevertheless, no bird may be used for food unless there is a longstanding tradition attesting to the permissibility of the species to which it belongs. (See *Chullin* 59a-63b.) In the same way, the above four signs should not be relied upon to

ריג צהוב. וראה לקמן סי' קפח ס"ק ד. ריד מהרי"ל הל' אתרוג (ע' שצט). מ"א ס"ק כג. ט"ז סוף ס"ק יח. רטו מ"א שם. רטז משנה לד, ב (ככרתי) וכר' יהודה. רא"ש פ"ג סכ"א (דומה לעשבים). טור ושו"ע סכ"א. וראה חידושי צ"צ (עג, ב). ריז גמרא לא, ב. לבוש סכ"א. ריח תוס' לא, ב ד"ה הירוק (שכיון שחוזרים למראה אתרוגים ודאי נגמר פרים). רא"ש שם. רבנו ירוחם נתיב ח ח"ג (נט, ד). טור ושו"ע שם. לבוש סכ"א (שכשיודעים שיחזור למראה אתרוג כשר גם כשהוא בירקותו). מ"א וט"ז שם. מ"א ס"ק כד (שדוקא כשלא נגמר גידולו חיישינן בירוק ככרתי). ריט מ"א ס"ק כג, ע"פ המהרי"ל הנ"ל. אליה רבה ס"ק ל. וראה ספר המנהגים — חב"ד ע' 65: מראה האתרוג צ"ל געה"ל (כמראה שעוה). רכ תשובת הר"י פאדווא בשם אביו, בשו"ת רמ"א סי' קכו (שלא לצאת בהם אפילו ע"י הדחק). תשובת הרמ"א שם סי' קיז (לא נקרא אתרוג). מ"א ס"ק כג (דלא מקרי אתרוג כלל). ט"ז שם ס"ק ג. וראה גם לקמן סי' תרמט סכ"ג. וראה הר"י מפאדווא שם (שהיו מברכין על אתרוגים ממחוז פאליי, שהיא קלבריה. ראה קובץ יגדיל תורה נ.י. לא ע' שמ). ס' המנהגים —חב"ד (ע' 65, שכ"ה מנהג חב"ד). אוצר מנהגי חב"ד (תשרי ע' עדר־רפג). רכא ראה שו"ת צמח צדק או"ח סי' סד (שכ"ה גם כשהרכיב ענף מאילן אתרוג לתוך אילן אחר). יגדיל תורה

covered by slight protrusions;

[ii] the stem by which a grafted *esrog* hangs from the tree projects from the [convex] base of the fruit, whereas the stem of a genuine *esrog* is sunk [in the concave depression at its base];

[iii] [the fruit] inside a grafted *esrog* is larger and juicier, and its middle peel is not as extensive as the thick [white] peel [that characterizes] a [genuine] *esrog*, whose peel is very thick, and whose [fruit] inside is small and contains little juice;

[iv] the seeds of a genuine *esrog* stand upright, vertically, while those of a grafted *esrog* lie horizontally.

וּלְהָאֶתְרוֹג יֵשׁ בְּלִיטוֹת קְטַנּוֹת בְּכָל גּוּפוֹ וּקְצָת גֹּבַהּ לָהֶן. הַשֵּׁנִי, הַמֻּרְכָּב עָקְצוֹ שֶׁהוּא תָּלוּי בּוֹ בָּאִילָן הוּא בּוֹלֵט, וְעֹקֶץ הָאֶתְרוֹג שׁוֹקֵעַ. הַשְּׁלִישִׁי, כִּי תּוֹךְ שֶׁל הַמֻּרְכָּב דְּהַיְנוּ הַגּוּף הוּא רָחָב וּמֹהַל שֶׁלּוֹ רַב, וְהַקְּלִפָּה הַתִּיכוֹנָה דְּהַיְנוּ קְלִפָּה הֶעָבָה שֶׁבָּאֶתְרוֹג[רכב] הִיא אֵינָהּ עָבָה כָּל כָּךְ בְּמֻרְכָּב כְּמוֹ בָּאֶתְרוֹג, שֶׁהַקְּלִפָּה עָבָה מְאֹד וְתוֹךְ שֶׁלּוֹ קָצָר וְאֵין בּוֹ מֹהַל רַב.[רכג] הָרְבִיעִי, שֶׁבָּאֶתְרוֹג הַגַּרְעִינִין שֶׁבְּתוֹכוֹ זְקוּפִים לָאֹרֶךְ, וּבְמֻרְכָּב הַגַּרְעִינִין הֵן מֻשְׁכָּבִין לְרָחְבּוֹ:[רכד]

SECTION 649 Factors that Disqualify the Four Species. (1–24)

סימן תרמט דְּבָרִים הַפּוֹסְלִים בְּאַרְבַּעַת הַמִּינִים וּבוֹ כ"[ד] סְעִיפִים:

1 If any one of the four species was borrowed,[1] obtained by robbery,[2] or stolen,[3] whether from a Jew or from a non-Jew,[4] it is

א כָּל אַרְבַּעַת הַמִּינִים שֶׁהָיָה אֶחָד מֵהֶן שָׁאוּל בְּיָדוֹ[א,1] אוֹ גָּזוּל[ב,2] אוֹ

---

validate an *esrog* unless there is a longstanding tradition that the *esrogim* from a particular region are not hybrid. Only after such a tradition has been established can these four signs confirm that the *esrogim* coming from such a region are indeed valid. (See R. David Lavut in *Shaar HaKollel* 37:1, citing *Chasam Sofer, Orach Chayim,* Responsum 207.)

Accordingly, both these sources recommend the use of *esrogim* from Calabria in southern Italy. *Sefer HaMinhagim: The Book of Chabad-Lubavitch Customs,* p. 140, cites a tradition passed down by the Rebbes of *Chabad* in the name of the Alter Rebbe, that when G-d commanded Moshe concerning the Four Species, emissaries were seated on a cloud and dispatched to bring *esrogim* from Calabria.

Incidentally, Calabrian *esrogim* are also known as Yanover *esrogim,* because they used to reach Europe's Jewish communities via the northern Italian port town of Genova (Genoa).

SECTION 649

1. *Sukkah* 41b. I.e., a person borrowed one of the Four Species without specifying that he intended to use it for the *mitzvah.* If he did express his intent, it may be assumed that the owner gave it to him as a gift with the intent that it be returned. See the *Shulchan Aruch* of R. Yosef Caro 658:5; *Magen Avraham* 649:9; the present work, sec. 14:6 (Vol. 1, in this Bilingual Edition). Nevertheless, it is proper that the owner say explicitly that this is "a gift on condition that it is returned." (In the original, *matanah al-menas lehachzir;* see *Sefer HaMinhagim: The Book of Chabad-Lubavitch Customs,* p. 142.) Renting the Four Species is not acceptable *(Kaf HaChayim* 649:32).

2. *Sukkah* 29b, 32b, 33b, 34b.

(נ.י.) לא ע' שמא (שבזה אין הסימנים מועילים). לט ע' קיח. **רכב** ראה לעיל סי"ב וש"נ. **רכג** הר"י מפאדווא שם. מ"א שם. **רכד** עולת שבת ריש הסימן. מ"א שם.
סימן תרמט: א משנה וברייתא מא, ב. רמב"ם פ"ח ה"י. טור ושו"ע ס"ב וסי' תרנח ס"ג. ואם השאילו כדי לצאת בו, ראה לעיל סי' יד ס"ו (לענין ציצית). סי' תנד סי"ד (לענין מצה, כשהשאילו על מנת שיאכלנה ויחזיר מצה אחרת). דובר שלום ע' כה (דעת רבנו לענין ד' מינים). וראה ספר המנהגים — חב"ד ע' 66: כשנותנים הד' מינים לאחר לברך נכון לאמר בפירוש שהוא במתנה על מנת להחזיר, ובפרט ביום הראשון, והוא תועלת לנותן ולמקבל. **ב** משנה כט, ב (לולב). לב, ב (הדס). לג, ב (ערבה). לד, ב (אתרוג). רמב"ם פ"ח ה"א. טור ושו"ע ס"א.

גָּנוּב,[ג,3] בֵּין מִיִּשְׂרָאֵל בֵּין מִנָּכְרִי,[ד,4] אַף עַל פִּי שֶׁכְּבָר נִתְיָאֲשׁוּ הַבְּעָלִים מִמֶּנּוּ[ה,5] – הֲרֵי זֶה פָּסוּל בַּיּוֹם הָרִאשׁוֹן שֶׁל חַג מִן הַתּוֹרָה,[ו] שֶׁנֶּאֱמַר[ז,6] "וּלְקַחְתֶּם לָכֶם בַּיּוֹם הָרִאשׁוֹן וגו'", וְדָרְשׁוּ חֲכָמִים[ח,7] "לָכֶם" – "מִשֶּׁלָּכֶם", לְהוֹצִיא אֶת הַשָּׁאוּל וְאֶת הַגָּזוּל וְגָנוּב שֶׁאֵינוֹ שֶׁלּוֹ, שֶׁהֲרֵי חַיָּב לְהַחֲזִירוֹ לִבְעָלָיו וְאֵינוֹ יָכוֹל לִפְטֹר אֶת עַצְמוֹ בְּדָמִים:[ט,8]

invalid on the first day of the festival according to Scriptural Law. [This applies] even if the owners have already despaired of the object's return.[5] This is derived from the verse,[6] "And on the first day, you shall take for yourselves [the fruit of a beautiful tree, fronds of a date-palm, a branch of a braided tree, and willows of the brook]." The Sages[7] understand "for yourselves" (לכם) as implying "of your own" (משלכם), thereby excluding specimens that are borrowed, obtained by robbery, or stolen. They are not "one's own," for one is obligated to return them to their owner and cannot free oneself of liability by offering financial recompense.[8]

ב וּמִיּוֹם שֵׁנִי (דְּהַיְנוּ בְּאֶרֶץ יִשְׂרָאֵל, אֲבָל בְּחוּץ לָאָרֶץ – יִתְבָּאֵר לְקַמָּן[י,9]) וְאֵילָךְ שֶׁחִיּוּב נְטִילַת לוּלָב אֵינוֹ אֶלָּא מִדִּבְרֵי סוֹפְרִים[יא,10] – אָדָם יוֹצֵא יְדֵי חוֹבָתוֹ לְכַתְּחִלָּה בְּשָׁאוּל,[יב,11] דְּכֵיוָן שֶׁלֹּא תִּקְּנוּ אֶלָּא לְזֵכֶר לַמִּקְדָּשׁ[12] – לֹא הֶחְמִירוּ לִפְסֹל

2 From the second day [of the festival] onward (i.e., in *Eretz Yisrael;* [the laws that apply] in the Diaspora are explained below[9]), the obligation to take a *lulav* is only of Rabbinic authority.[10] Hence, one may fulfill his obligation with a borrowed *[lulav]* [even] as an initial preference.[11] For since [the Sages] instituted [this practice] only as a commemoration of [the observance of the *mitzvah* in] the *[Beis] HaMikdash,*[12] they were not stringent and did not disqualify a borrowed specimen.[13] The reason [for this leniency]

---

3. Strictly speaking, there is a halachic distinction between robbery *(gezeilah),* where an object is taken from its owner overtly and by force *(Rambam, Hilchos Geneivah* 1:3*),* and theft *(geneivah),* where the object is taken in stealth. In our context, the distinction is immaterial.

4. Stealing from a non-Jew violates a Scriptural prohibition *(Choshen Mishpat, Hilchos Gezeilah,* sec. 1, in the present work*).*

5. The owner's despair signifies that he is prepared to release it from his ownership (cf. *Bava Kama* 66a). Nevertheless, since it entered the thief's domain unlawfully, the thief is not able to take possession of it, but is obligated to return it.

6. *Vayikra* 23:40.

7. *Sukkah* 41b. Among the parallels in the present work are sec. 11:11, sec. 14:4, sec. 454:9, and sec. 636:3.

8. See subsection 5 below.

9. In subsection 21.

10. *Sukkah* 41a. See also ch. 645, footnote 35 above.

11. *Op cit.,* 41b. Nevertheless, *Pri Megadim: Mishbetzos Zahav* (649:7) advises prospective borrowers to bear in mind that not everyone would consent to having his *lulav* used by many people.

12. In the original, *zeicher laMikdash.*

ג רמב"ם שם. שו"ע שם. ד מ"א סי' תרלז ס"ק ג (אף לענין סוכה). עפ"י תשובת רבנו יואל, בראבי"ה סי' תרצ, ובשו"ת הרשב"א ח"א סי' תתנב (וכדלקמן ס"ח, דמיירי אף שנתייאשו הבעלים). רמ"א ס"א, לפירוש המ"א ס"ק ז. עולת שבת ס"ק א. ט"ז סי' תרסד ס"ק ו. וראה גם לעיל סי' תנד ס"י. סי' תרלז סי"א. חו"מ הל' גזילה ס"א. ה רמב"ם שם, לפי' הכסף משנה שם. טור ושו"ע שם. וכדלקמן ס"ח שיאוש בלבד אינו קונה, וש"נ. ו משנה מא, ב (ולא רק מטעם מצוה הבאה בעבירה, דלקמן ס"ד, שפסול מד"ס, כדלעיל סי' כה סל"ה). וראה תוס' ט, א ד"ה ההוא. ל, א ד"ה משום. ז ויקרא כג, מ. ח גמרא [ברייתא] שם. טור ושו"ע ס"א־ב. וראה עד"ז לעיל סי' יא סי"א. סי' יד ס"ד וסי"ד. סי' תנד ס"ט. ולענין סוכה ראה לעיל סי' תרלז ס"ג. ט כדלקמן ס"ה (שכשיכול לפטרו בדמים הוא כשלו לכל דבר), וש"נ. וכדלקמן הל' גזילה ס"ו (שאף אחר יאוש אינו יכול לפטרו בדמים), וש"נ. וכ"ה לעיל סי' תנד ס"ט־י וש"נ. וראה מ"מ וציונים. ולענין גזל הנכרי, ראה לעיל סי' תמ קו"א ס"ק יא. לקמן הל' גזילה סוף ס"ד וסוף סכ"ג. קו"א ס"ק ו. ולענין מצוה הבאה בעבירה, ראה לקמן ס"ד. י סעיף כא.

אֶת הַשָּׁאוּל,[יב] [13] כֵּיוָן שֶׁאֵין פְּסוּלוֹ בְּגוּפוֹ, שֶׁהֲרֵי הוּא מִין כָּשֵׁר, אֶלָּא שֶׁאֵינוֹ שֶׁלּוֹ:[יג]

is that there is nothing in the substance of such a specimen to disqualify it, for it belongs to a valid species. [The only difficulty is that] it does not belong to him.

ג וּמֻתָּר לִטֹּל לוּלָב שֶׁל חֲבֵרוֹ שֶׁלֹּא מִדַּעְתּוֹ וּלְבָרֵךְ עָלָיו בִּשְׁאָר הַיָּמִים חוּץ מִיּוֹם רִאשׁוֹן[יד] כְּמוֹ שֶׁיִּתְבָּאֵר בְּסִימָן תרנ"ח,[טו] [14] דִּמִּן הַסְּתָם לֹא יַקְפִּיד חֲבֵרוֹ עַל זֶה, שֶׁנּוֹחַ לוֹ לְאָדָם שֶׁתֵּעָשֶׂה מִצְוָה בְּמָמוֹנוֹ בְּדָבָר שֶׁאֵין בּוֹ חֶסְרוֹן כִּיס,[15] שֶׁהֲרֵי אֵין הַלּוּלָב מִתְקַלְקֵל בְּכָךְ.[טז] אֲבָל אָסוּר לְהוֹצִיא הַלּוּלָב מִמָּקוֹם שֶׁהִנִּיחוֹ בְּעָלָיו לְמָקוֹם אַחֵר כְּגוֹן מִבֵּיתוֹ לְבֵית הַכְּנֶסֶת,[יז] כְּמוֹ שֶׁנִּתְבָּאֵר בְּסִימָן י"ד,[יח] עַיֵּן שָׁם הַטַּעַם:[16]

3 On the other days of the festival, but not on the first day, it is permissible to take a friend's *lulav* without asking him, as will be explained in sec. 658.[14] A blessing may be recited. [The rationale is that] we assume that his friend will not object to this, for "a person is pleased to have a *mitzvah* performed with his property when he will not suffer a financial loss,"[15] for [his friend's use of the *lulav*] will not spoil it.

[Without permission,] however, it is forbidden to take the *lulav* from the place where its owner left it to another place, e.g., from his home to the synagogue, as is explained in sec. 14[:10,12]; note the reason explained there.[16]

ד אֲבָל הַגָּזוּל וְהַגָּנוּב[17] – אַף בִּשְׁאָר הַיָּמִים הוּא פָּסוּל,[יט] אַף עַל פִּי

4 By contrast, [a *lulav*] obtained by robbery or theft[17] is invalid even on the later days, and even if the owner despaired of its return.[11]

---

13. In the *Beis HaMikdash,* the *mitzvah* of *lulav* had the status of a Scriptural commandment for all seven days of the festival. It is written: "And on the first day, you shall take for yourselves the fruit of a beautiful tree, fronds of a date-palm, a branch of a braided tree, and willows of the brook, and you shall rejoice before the L-rd your G-d for seven days" *(Vayikra, loc. cit.).* Nevertheless, the command in that verse that "you shall take for yourselves" is stated only with regard to "the first day." Hence the *Rishonim* differ as to whether a borrowed *lulav* could be used in the *Beis HaMikdash* after the first day of the festival. The various views are enumerated in *Hadar Hu LeChol Chassidav.*

14. Sec. 658 of the Alter Rebbe's *Shulchan Aruch* is not extant. This concept can be derived from a comparison to the laws of *tzitzis;* see sec. 14:9, 11 in Vol. 1 of the present work.

15. This halachic presumption *(chazakah)* explains why a person who needs a *tallis,* for example, and cannot ask its owner for permission to use it because he is not present, is permitted to use it. This principle does not apply to the *mitzvah* of *lulav* on the first day of Sukkos. In order to fulfill the *mitzvah* on that day, one cannot simply take another's *lulav,* even if one intends to return it; he needs to have *acquired* it for that time (see sec. 14:8 in Vol. 1 of the present work).

16. Since the owner will presumably object to this, it is considered as if the *lulav* was taken without permission. This is tantamount to stealing, in which instance the borrower has not fulfilled his obligation.

17. As above, this applies whether the *lulav* was stolen from a Jew or a non-Jew.

יא משנה מא, א. טור ושו"ע סי' תרנח ס"א. **יב** משנה ובריייתא מא, ב. גמרא ל, א. טור ושו"ע ס"ב. רמ"א ס"ה. **יג** תוס' כט, ב ד"ה בעינן (תיקנו רק בעיקר הלקיחה). רא"ש פ"ג סי' ג. מ"א ס"ק כ (בגוף האתרוג). וראה גם לקמן סט"ז. **יד** תרומת הדשן סי' ק, ובח"ב סי' קנט. רמ"א ס"ה. **טו** סימן זה בשוע"ר לא הגיע לידינו, וראה שו"ע שם ס"ג־ד. ט"ז כאן ס"ק יא. לקמן סכ"א. וראה לעיל סי' יד סי"א (שבזה גם בטלית אין צריך לברך עליו). **טז** תרומת הדשן שם. ט"ז ס"ק ז. וראה גם לעיל שם ס"ט וש"נ. **יז** מ"א ס"ק טז. **יח** סעיף י. **יט** כר' יוחנן משום רשב"י כט, ב־ל, א. בה"ג הל' לולב (לד, ב). רמב"ן במלחמות (יד, ב), ורא"ש פ"ג ס"ג, ור"ן (יג, ב) ד"ה ולענין, בדעת הרי"ף. ראב"ד בהשגות פ"ח ה"ט. טור ורמ"א ס"ה (ושכן המנהג).

שֶׁכְּבָר נִתְיָאֲשׁוּ הַבְּעָלִים,[כ,11] לְפִי שֶׁהוּא מִצְוָה הַבָּאָה בַּעֲבֵרָה,[כא,18] כְּלוֹמַר כְּשֶׁהוּא מְקַיֵּם אֶת הַמִּצְוָה – הוּא מְקַיֵּם אוֹתָהּ בְּאִסּוּר גָּזֵל,[כב] שֶׁהֲרֵי אִם בָּאוּ הַבְּעָלִים לִתְבֹּעַ שֶׁלָּהֶם – חַיָּב לְהַחֲזִיר לָהֶם הַגְּזֵלָה בְּעֵינֶיהָ וְאֵינוֹ יָכוֹל לִפְטֹר אֶת עַצְמוֹ בְּדָמִים,[כג] וְנִמְצָא שֶׁהַגְּזֵלָה אֵינָהּ קְנוּיָה לוֹ כְּלָל וַעֲדַיִן הִיא שֶׁל הַנִּגְזָל, וְשֶׁלֹּא כְּדִין הוּא מִשְׁתַּמֵּשׁ בָּהּ:

[The rationale is that] this is "a *mitzvah* that comes about by means of a transgression,"[18] i.e., one performed the *mitzvah* by transgressing the prohibition against robbery. For if the owner came and demanded [the return of] his property, [the thief] would be obligated to return the stolen object intact; he could not free himself of liability by payment. Thus the stolen object has not been acquired by him at all. It still belongs to [its original owner] and [the thief] is using it unlawfully.

ה אֲבָל אִם כְּבָר קָנָה הַגַּזְלָן אֶת הַגְּזֵלָה עַל יְדֵי שִׁנּוּי,[כד,19] בֵּין שֶׁקְּנָאָהּ עַל יְדֵי שִׁנּוּי מַעֲשֶׂה[כה] בֵּין שֶׁקְּנָאָהּ עַל יְדֵי שִׁנּוּי הַשֵּׁם[כו] קֹדֶם שֶׁבָּא לְהִשְׁתַּמֵּשׁ בָּהּ לְשֵׁם מִצְוָה,[כז] כְּגוֹן שֶׁגָּזַל לוּלָב וְשִׁפָּהוּ[כח,20] – הֲרֵי זֶה כָּשֵׁר אֲפִלּוּ בַּיּוֹם הָרִאשׁוֹן,[כט] דְּכֵיוָן שֶׁאֲפִלּוּ אִם בָּא הַנִּגְזָל אֵינוֹ מְחֻיָּב לְהַחֲזִיר לוֹ הַגְּזֵלָה עַצְמָהּ אֶלָּא דָּמִים בִּלְבַד הוּא שֶׁחַיָּב לוֹ כְּמוֹ שֶׁכָּתוּב בְּחֹשֶׁן מִשְׁפָּט סִימָן שנ"ג[ל] –

5 [Different rules apply] if the robber already acquired the stolen article because it underwent a change.[19] Whether he acquired it because of a change that came about because of an action or whether he acquired it because of a change in its name that came about before he sought to use it for the *mitzvah*, e.g., he stole a *lulav* branch and planed it,[20] it is valid even on the first day of the festival.

[The rationale is that] even if the original owner would appear, [the thief] would not be obligated to return the stolen article itself, but only to make financial recompense, as stated in *Choshen Mishpat*, sec. 353. Thus

18. In the original, *mitzvah habaah baaveirah (Sukkah* 30a*)*.

19. *Sukkah* 30b. If a stolen article undergoes an irreversible change, the thief acquires it even if the original owner has not despaired of its return. (See the commentaries to the *Shulchan Aruch* of R. Yosef Caro, *Choshen Mishpat*, sec. 353:1.) If the owner has despaired of its return, the thief acquires it even if it undergoes a reversible change. If it does not undergo a change, he does not acquire it even if the owner despaired of its return, as stated above. See also *Hilchos Gezeilah*, sec. 6, 23, in the present work.

20. *Talmud Yerushalmi, Sukkah* 3:1. In order to bring about a change in ownership, an object must be transformed to the extent that its description is altered. In the instance at hand, the palm branch was called a palm branch — until it was whittled down, and from that moment was called a *lulav* *(Machtzis HaShekel* 649:1; *Hadar Hu LeChol Chassidav*, p. 240*)*.

כ גמרא שם. וכדלעיל ס"א (לענין אינו שלו). וכדלקמן ס"ח שיאוש בלבד אינו קונה, וש"נ. כא גמרא שם. לבוש ס"ב. ט"ז ס"ק ו. וכ"ה לעיל סי' כה סל"ה (בתפילין שאין צריך להיות שלו), וש"נ. ולענין ברכת הנהנין בעבירה, ראה לעיל סי' קצו ס"א (ב' דעות). כב תוס' שם ד"ה משום וד"ה הא. רא"ש פ"ג סט"ו. ר"ן שם. וראה גם לעיל סי' תנד סי"ב וש"נ. כג כדלעיל ס"א (לענין לכם), וש"נ. כד גמרא ל, ב (ולקניוהא בשינוי מעשה). כה כדלקמן הל' גזילה ס"ו וסכ"ג וש"נ. כו חושן משפט סי' שנ[ג] ס"א. כז תוס' ל, א ד"ה הא. ב"ק סז, א ד"ה אמר. ר"ן שם ד"ה ולענין. שו"ע ס"א. ט"ז ס"ק א. וראה גם לעיל סי' יא קו"א ס"ק ד. כח ירושלמי פ"ג ה"א. ר"ן שם. שו"ע שם. כט תוס' שם ד"ה הא (וקרינא ביה לכם משלכם). רמב"ן במלחמות (יד, ב). מ"א ס"ק א. וראה גם לעיל סי' יא סי"ב. סי' תנד ס"י. ל שם. לקמן שם. לא ירושלמי שם (דמים הוא חייב לו). ר"ן שם. וראה גם לעיל שם. לב תוס' שם, ע"פ ב"ק צד, א. רמב"ן שם. דרכי

נִמְצָא שֶׁהִיא קְנוּיָה לְגַמְרֵי לְהַגַּזְלָן, וַהֲרֵי הִיא כְּשֶׁלּוֹ מַמָּשׁ לְכָל דָּבָר.[לא]

וּמִכָּל מָקוֹם, כֵּיוָן שֶׁעַל יְדֵי עֲבֵרָה בָּאָה מִצְוָה זוֹ לְיָדוֹ – לֹא יְבָרֵךְ עָלֶיהָ[21] אֲפִלּוּ מִיּוֹם שֵׁנִי וְאֵילָךְ.[לב] וְאַף שֶׁיֵּשׁ חוֹלְקִים[לג,22] עַל זֶה – סָפֵק בְּרָכוֹת לְהָקֵל,[לד,23] דְּאֵין זֶה מְבָרֵךְ אֶלָּא מְנָאֵץ[לה,24] (שֶׁנִּרְאֶה כִּמְבָרֵךְ עַל עֲבֵרָה שֶׁנִּזְדַּמְּנָה לְיָדוֹ[לו]), אִם לוֹקְחוֹ לְצֹרֶךְ עַצְמוֹ לָצֵאת בּוֹ:[לז]

the object has become his property entirely. It is actually his in every respect.

Nevertheless, since [the thief] was enabled to perform this *mitzvah* through a transgression, he should not recite a blessing,[21] even from the second day onward. Although there are authorities who differ,[22] whenever there is a doubt whether a blessing is required, the lenient ruling prevails [and the blessing is not recited].[23] For when this individual takes [the stolen *lulav*] to fulfill his own obligation, he is not blessing G-d, but blaspheming [Him],[24] (since it appears that he is reciting a blessing over the transgression that presented itself to him).

ו וְכָל זֶה בְּגַנָּב וְגַזְלָן עַצְמוֹ, אֲבָל אִם מָכַר אוֹ נָתַן בְּמַתָּנָה גְּמוּרָה לְאָדָם אַחֵר,[25] אִם כְּבָר נִתְיָאֲשׁוּ הַבְּעָלִים קֹדֶם שֶׁמָּכַר וְנָתַן[לח,26] – הֲרֵי כְּבָר נִקְנֵית הַגְּזֵלָה לְהַלּוֹקֵחַ בְּיֵאוּשׁ בְּעָלִים וְשִׁנּוּי רְשׁוּת מֵהַגַּזְלָן לְהַלּוֹקֵחַ, שֶׁאַף אִם בָּא הַנִּגְזָל – אֵין הַלּוֹקֵחַ חַיָּב לְהַחֲזִיר לוֹ כְּלוּם,[לט] נִמְצָא שֶׁהִיא

6 The above applies with regard to the thief or robber himself. If, however, he sold or gave [the *lulav*] as an outright gift to another person[25] and the owner had despaired of its return before it was sold or given away,[26] the stolen article becomes acquired by the purchaser through the despair of the owner and the transfer of the article from the domain of the thief to that of the purchaser. For even if the original owner would appear, [the purchaser] is not obligated to return anything to him. Thus he has

---

21. Moreover, he should endeavor not to use such a *lulav*, for it is abominable in G-d's eyes (*Turei Zahav* 11:5). A blessing should not be recited even if the original owner despaired over its return and the *lulav* underwent an irreversible change. See sec. 11:12 in Vol. 1 of the present work.

22. And maintain that a blessing should be recited.

23. The last 20 English words translate the Hebrew phrase, *safek berachos — lehakel.*

24. *Bava Kama* 94a.

25. *Pri Megadim: Eshel Avraham* (649:1, based on *Shulchan Aruch, Choshen Mishpat* 361:7) states that inheriting a stolen *lulav* is not considered a change of domain, because the testator and the heir constitute one halachic continuum. By contrast, since a sale or a gift does effect a change of domain, one can infer that if a thief gives or sells a stolen *lulav* to a son who has attained majority, that son may use it to fulfill his obligation.

26. If the original owner despaired of its return after the purchaser acquired it, the purchaser is obligated to return it and may not use it to fulfill the *mitzvah*.

משה ס"ק ג, ממשמעות הר"ן שם. שו"ע שם. וראה לעיל סי' יא סי"ב דהיינו אף ביאוש עם שינוי (ח"י סי' תנד ס"ק ו). וראה לעיל סי' תנד ס"י דהיינו אפילו גזל מנכרי, ושלכתחלה אין לו לצאת ידי חובתו בו. **לג** רא"ש פ"ז דברכות ס"ב (שחייב לברך אלא שברכתו היא ניאוץ). שו"ת הרשב"א ח"א סי' תתקסח ד"ה ושינוי השם. **לד** ראה מ"א סי' תרלז סוף ס"ק ג, שלדעת האוסרים הוי ברכה לבטלה. **לה** ב"ק צד, א. וכדלעיל סי' יא סי"ב (ולא הביא דעת החולקים) וש"נ. וראה לעיל סי' קצו ס"ג (ב' דעות, לדעת האוסרים גם בברכת הנהנין). **לו** עד"ז לעיל סי' תנד ס"י. **לז** משא"כ אם נתנו לאחרים, וכדלעיל סי' תנד סוף ס"י (לענין מצה). וראה גם לקמן ס"ו (ביאוש ושינוי רשות) וס"ז (ביאוש בלא שינוי). **לח** וכ"ה לעיל סי' תנד סי"א (דוקא שהיאוש קודם שבא לרשותו). וראה לקמן הל' גזילה סי"א (שאף שעשה איסור בלקיחתו, כשיודע שהוא גזול, מותר ליהנות בו). **לט** אפילו דמיו. ראה רמ"א חו"מ סי' שנג ס"ג. סי' שנו ס"ג. סמ"ע שם ס"ק יג.

קְנוּיָה לוֹ לְגַמְרֵי, וַהֲרֵי הִיא כְּשֶׁלּוֹ מַמָּשׁ לְכָל דָּבָר,[מ, 27] וְיוֹצֵא בָּהּ יְדֵי חוֹבָתוֹ אַף בַּיּוֹם הָרִאשׁוֹן,[מא, 28] וּמֻתָּר לוֹ לְבָרֵךְ עָלֶיהָ,[מב, 29] שֶׁהֲרֵי לֹא עַל יְדֵי עֲבֵרָה בָּאָה מִצְוָה זוֹ לְיָדוֹ, שֶׁהֲרֵי הוּא לֹא גָּזַל (וְגַם קָנָה אוֹתָהּ אַחַר שֶׁנִּתְיָאֲשׁוּ הַבְּעָלִים מִמֶּנָּה).

אֲבָל אִם עֲדַיִן לֹא נִתְיָאֲשׁוּ הַבְּעָלִים מִמֶּנָּה — אֵין הַלּוֹקֵחַ יוֹצֵא בָּהּ יְדֵי חוֹבָתוֹ אַף בִּשְׁאָר הַיָּמִים,[30] לְפִי שֶׁהִיא מִצְוָה הַבָּאָה בַּעֲבֵרָה, שֶׁהֲרֵי שֶׁלֹּא כְּדִין מִשְׁתַּמֵּשׁ בָּהּ הַלּוֹקֵחַ, כֵּיוָן שֶׁעֲדַיִן הִיא בְּחֶזְקַת הַנִּגְזָל, שֶׁהֲרֵי עֲדַיִן לֹא נִתְיָאֵשׁ מִמֶּנָּה:[מג]

acquired [the *lulav*] entirely. It is his in every respect. Hence, he may use it to fulfill his obligation,[27] even on the first day,[28] and he may recite a blessing over it,[29] because the opportunity [to perform] this *mitzvah* did not come to him by means of a transgression, for he did not steal it. (Moreover, he acquired it after the owner despaired of its return.)

If, however, the [original] owner had not yet despaired of its return, the purchaser may not use it to fulfill his obligation, even on the remaining days [of the festival].[30] [The rationale is that] this would be "a *mitzvah* that comes about by means of a transgression" because [the purchaser] is using it unwarrantedly — for it is still considered as belonging to the original owner, since he did not despair of its return.

ז וְכָל זֶה כְּשֶׁמָּכַר אוֹ נָתַן בְּמַתָּנָה גְּמוּרָה, אֲבָל אִם הִשְׁאִילָהּ לְאַחֵר (אוֹ נְתָנָהּ לוֹ בְּמַתָּנָה עַל מְנָת לְהַחֲזִיר,[מד, 31] אַף עַל פִּי שֶׁכְּבָר נִתְיָאֲשׁוּ הַבְּעָלִים — אֵין הַשּׁוֹאֵל יוֹצֵא בָּהּ יְדֵי חוֹבָתוֹ בַּיּוֹם הָרִאשׁוֹן, שֶׁהֲרֵי אֵינָהּ קְנוּיָה לוֹ עַל יְדֵי יֵאוּשׁ וְשִׁנּוּי רְשׁוּת, וְאֵין זֶה

7 All of the above applies when [the thief] sold [the stolen *lulav*] or gave it as an outright gift. If, however, he lent it to another person (or gave it to him as a gift with the intent that it be returned,[31] the borrower cannot fulfill his obligation with it on the first day [of the festival], even if the original owner already despaired of its return. [The rationale is that] he did not acquire it through [the owner's] despair and the transfer [of the *lulav*] from one domain to another. For [the *lulav*]

---

27. In his *Mareh Mekomos VeTziyunim* to these laws, R. Mordechai Shmuel Ashkenazi maintains that this law applies even if the purchaser knew that the article was stolen when he purchased it. Although purchasing a stolen article from a thief violates the prohibition against placing a stumbling block before the [morally] blind, it does not violate the prohibition against theft. [See the present work, *Hilchos Geneivah* 9, 11.] Moreover, although it is forbidden to benefit from an object one knows is stolen, *mitzvos* were not given for our benefit. Hence it may be used to fulfill the *mitzvah*.

28. See *Sukkah* 30b.

29. In contrast to the thief himself, as stated in subsection 5 above.

30. When there is no requirement that the Four Species must be one's own.

31. See footnote 1 above.

מ ראה גם לעיל סי׳ יא סי״א וקו״א ס״ק ג. סי׳ כה סל״ו. סי׳ תנד סי״א. מא משמעות הגמרא (ל, ב). רמב״ן במלחמות (יד, ב) בשם בה״ג הל׳ לולב (לד, א). מ״א ס״ק ג (ובסוס״י תנד). עטרת זקנים ריש הסי׳. ונתבאר לעיל סי׳ יא קו״א ס״ק ג. וראה אמרי יעקב סי׳ ז ביאורים ד״ה ובמדינות. מב ב״י סוס״י כה, בשם ארחות חיים בשם בעל העיטור. לבוש שם סי״ב. וכדלעיל שם סל״ו. סי׳ קצו ס״ד. סי׳ תנד סי״א. וראה לעיל סי׳ תנד סי״א, שאם חזר ונתנו במתנה לגזלן גם הגזלן יכול לברך עליו. מג מ״א שם, ממשמעות הגמרא ובה״ג ורמב״ן שם. הובא בקו״א הנ״ל. מד שאין זה שינוי רשות (אף שנקראת מתנה, כדלקמן סכ״א). וראה מ״מ וציונים. פתחי חושן הל׳ גניבה פ״ב ס״ק מ״ו. אמרי יעקב שם ליקוטים ס״ק כ. מה ב״י ד״ה כתב בא״ח, בשם ארחות חיים הל׳ לולב סי׳ ט.

שִׁנּוּי רְשׁוּת (הַגַּזְלָן), כֵּיוָן שֶׁהוּא מְחֻיָּב לְהַחֲזִירָהּ לְהַגַּזְלָן,[32] אֲבָל בִּשְׁאָר הַיָּמִים יוֹצֵא בָּהּ יְדֵי חוֹבָתוֹ, וְאֵין כָּאן מִצְוָה הַבָּאָה בַּעֲבֵרָה,[מה,33] כֵּיוָן שֶׁכְּבָר נִתְיָאֲשׁוּ הַבְּעָלִים קֹדֶם שֶׁהִשְׁאִילָהּ לוֹ — נִמְצָא שֶׁאֵין עַל הַשּׁוֹאֵל שׁוּם עָוֹן[34] אֲשֶׁר חָטָא):[מו,35]

is not considered to have departed from (the thief's) domain since [the person desiring to perform the *mitzvah*] is obligated to return it to the thief.[32]

On the [later] days, by contrast, [another person] may fulfill his obligation [with such *lulav*]. It is not considered "a *mitzvah* that comes about by means of a transgression."[33] [The rationale is that] since the owner already despaired [of regaining the *lulav*] before it was lent to him, the borrower is not held liable for the violation[34] of any transgression.)[35]

ח יִשְׂרָאֵל הַלּוֹקֵחַ מִנָּכְרִי אֶחָד מִכָּל אַרְבָּעָה מִינִים שֶׁבְּלוּלָב הַגָּדֵל בְּקַרְקָעוֹ שֶׁל הַנָּכְרִי — לֹא יְקַצְּצֶנּוּ הַיִּשְׂרָאֵל בְּעַצְמוֹ מִקַּרְקָעוֹ שֶׁל הַנָּכְרִי,[מז,28] לְפִי שֶׁסְּתָם נָכְרִים הֵן גּוֹזְלִים שָׂדוֹת[מח] מִיִּשְׂרָאֵל[מט] אוֹ מִנָּכְרִי אַחֵר,[נ,36] וְקַרְקַע אֵינָהּ נִגְזֶלֶת,[נא] כְּלוֹמַר אֵין עָלֶיהָ תּוֹרַת גָּזֵל לִהְיוֹת עוֹמֶדֶת בְּחֶזְקַת הַגַּזְלָן וּבִרְשׁוּתוֹ לְכָל דָּבָר לְהִתְחַיֵּב בְּאַחֲרָיוּתָהּ,[נב,37] אֶלָּא לְעוֹלָם הִיא

8 [The following principle applies when] a Jew purchases any one of the Four Species of the *lulav* from a non-Jew who has this species growing on his land. The Jew should not pick it himself from the non-Jew's land.[28] The rationale is our operating presumption that non-Jews steal land from Jews or from other non-Jews.[36] Landed property can never be stolen — i.e., it never passes into the domain and ownership of the thief in every respect so that he becomes responsible for it.[37] Rather, it is always

32. And since the thief is obligated to return it to the original owner, it is not considered to have departed from the original owner's domain.

33. It appears that a blessing may also be recited, even (as above) if the borrower knew that the object was stolen. Since he is not aiding the thief at all, and is not even paying him for the stolen object, there is no reason to prevent him from using it for the *mitzvah*.

34. Cf. *Hoshea* 12:9. See *Hilchos Gezeilah*, sec. 10-12.

35. The parentheses, here and throughout, are part of the original text. In a letter that appears in *Igros Kodesh*, Vol. 2, p. 140, the Rebbe writes that parentheses in this work possibly indicate a matter that the Alter Rebbe desired to reconsider at a later date. (Cf. *She'eris Yehudah*, Responsum 363, and *Shaar HaKollel* 1:2.) *Kuntreis HaShulchan* enumerates nine distinct possible functions of parentheses in this work.

36. In the era of the *Talmud (Sukkah* 30a), the Jews lived among non-Jews who had little respect for property rights. This stringency may not apply in countries in which land ownership is registered by the government and where the rights of the individual are respected. See subsection 10 below.

37. *Bava Kama* 117b.

שו"ע ס"א (ויש מי שאומר). ומפרש רבנו דמיירי ביאוש בלא שינוי רשות (ליישב קושית המ"א ס"ק ג). וראה קו"א לעיל שם, שמביא פירוש המ"א (דמיירי קודם יאוש). **מו** ראה לקמן הל' גזילה ס"י"א (שאסור ליהנות ממנו אף אחרי יאוש). לקמן סי"ב (שמצות לאו ליהנות ניתנו). וראה מ"מ וציונים. **מז** גמרא ל, סע"א (לענין הדס). רמ"א ס"א (לענין ד' מינים). שו"ע סי' תרסד ס"י (לענין ערבה). וראה גם לעיל סי' תרלז סי"ב (לענין סכך). אלא יקצצנו הנכרי (גמרא שם. רמ"א שם). **מח** גמרא שם. **מט** רש"י שם ד"ה מאי טעמא. **נ** תשובת רבנו יואל, דלעיל ס"א וש"נ. רמ"א שם, לפירוש המ"א ס"ק ז. **נא** גמרא שם. רמ"א שם. וכדלעיל סי' תרלז ס"ד וש"נ. **נב** משנה ובריתא ב"ק קיז, ב. טור ושו"ע חו"מ סי' שעא ס"ב. וראה לעיל סי' תרלז ס"ד (שאם השביחה ברשות הגזלן).

בְּחֶזְקַת הַנִּגְזָל וּבִרְשׁוּתוֹ לְכָל דָּבָר,[נג] וְיִשְׂרָאֵל זֶה הַקּוֹצֵץ וְתוֹלֵשׁ מִקַּרְקַע זוֹ – הֲרֵי הוּא הַגּוֹזֵל מִבַּעַל הַקַּרְקַע מַה שֶּׁתּוֹלֵשׁ. וְאַף עַל פִּי שֶׁבַּעַל הַקַּרְקַע כְּבָר נִתְיָאֵשׁ מִמֶּנָּה, מִכָּל מָקוֹם יֵאוּשׁ בִּלְבַד בְּלֹא שִׁנּוּי רְשׁוּת – אֵינוֹ קוֹנֶה[נד], וַהֲרֵי הוּא גָּזֵל בְּיָדוֹ.[נה] אֲבָל אִם יִשְׂרָאֵל זֶה קוֹצֵץ כְּדֵי לִמְכֹּר אוֹ לִתֵּן לַאֲחֵרִים שֶׁיֵּצְאוּ בּוֹ יְדֵי חוֹבָתָן בֶּחָג – הֲרֵי זֶה מֻתָּר, שֶׁהֲרֵי יֵשׁ כָּאן גַּם שִׁנּוּי רְשׁוּת מֵהַגַּזְלָן, דְּהַיְנוּ יִשְׂרָאֵל זֶה הַקּוֹצֵץ לִרְשׁוּת הַלּוֹקֵחַ:[נו]

considered to be in the domain and the possession of the original owner in every respect. Thus when a Jew cuts or plucks [a specimen that is attached] to the ground, he is [at that time] stealing the severed [specimen] from the owner of the land. Though the [original] owner of the land already despaired of its return, despairing of an object's return without transferring ownership of the object does not enable it to be acquired. Hence, [though the severed specimen] is in [the Jew's] possession, it is considered a stolen article. If, however, the Jew severs the specimen to sell or to give to others so that they can fulfill their obligation on the festival, it is permitted, because [the stolen object, i.e., the specimen severed,] was transferred from the possession of the thief, i.e., the Jew who cuts it off, to the possession of the purchaser.

ט וְכָל זֶה לְכַתְּחִלָּה, אֲבָל בְּדִיעֲבַד שֶׁכְּבָר קָצַץ הַיִּשְׂרָאֵל – מֻתָּר הוּא בְּעַצְמוֹ גַּם כֵּן לְבָרֵךְ עָלָיו, כֵּיוָן שֶׁקָּצַץ בִּרְשׁוּת הַנָּכְרִי – אֵין אָנוּ חוֹשְׁשִׁין לְסָפֵק, שֶׁמָּא גְּזוּלָה הִיא בְּיָדוֹ מִיִּשְׂרָאֵל אוֹ מִנָּכְרִי אַחֵר:[נז,38]

9 The above applies as an initial preference. After the fact, if the Jew severed the specimen himself, he is permitted to [use it and] recite a blessing over it. Since he severed it with the permission of the non-Jew [in whose possession it is at present], we are not concerned with the possibility that the property was stolen from a Jew or from another non-Jew.[38]

י וְכֵן אִם נָכְרִי בַּעַל הַקַּרְקַע שֶׁנּוֹתֵן רְשׁוּת לְיִשְׂרָאֵל לִקְצֹץ הוּא מַחֲזִיק קַרְקַע זוֹ מִיַּד הַמֶּלֶךְ שֶׁנְּתָנָהּ לוֹ,[נח] אַף עַל פִּי שֶׁהַמֶּלֶךְ עַצְמוֹ[נט] כָּבַשׁ קַרְקַע זוֹ בְּמִלְחָמָה מִיַּד אַחֵר– אֵין זֶה גָּזֵל, שֶׁהַקַּרְקַע נִקְנֵית לְהַגַּזְלָן[39] בְּכִבּוּשׁ

10 Similarly, [specimens are valid when] the non-Jew owner of the land who allowed the Jew to sever them possesses the land by virtue of the authority of the king [of the country] who gave it to him. Even though the king himself conquered this land in war from others, this is not considered as robbery, for land that is acquired by a thief[39] through conquest

38. I.e., one should preferably show concern for this suspicion and have the non-Jew sever the specimens so that there is no question at all. After the fact, however, our concern is not strong enough to disqualify them.

39. This term — omitted in some printings of the Alter Rebbe's *Shulchan Aruch,* probably due to censorship — refers to a king who seizes conquered land unlawfully.

נג אף ביאוש עם שינוי רשות, כדלקמן הל' גזילה סי"א וש"נ. נד כדלקמן שם ס"ו וסי"א וש"נ. נה רש"י שם (והתולשו הוא גוזלו). רמ"א שם. וראה לעיל ס"ד (שאז יפסל אף בשאר הימים מטעם מצוה הבאה בעבירה). לקמן שם סי"א (ולענין מצוה שלא תהא באה בעבירה מחמירים אפילו בסתם כמ"ש בא"ח סי' תרמט). נו מ"א ס"ק ו. עטרת זקנים ריש הסי'. ט"ז סי' תרסד ס"ק ו. וראה לעיל סי' יא קו"א ס"ק ג. סי' תרלז סי"ב. נז מ"א ס"ק ה. חק יעקב סי' תנד ס"ק ו.

מִלְחָמָה קִנְיַן גָּמוּר,[ס] כְּמוֹ שֶׁלָּמְדוּ חֲכָמִים[סא] מִמִּדְרַשׁ הַפְּסוּקִים.[40]

וְכָל זֶה בְּחוּץ לָאָרֶץ, אֲבָל בְּאֶרֶץ יִשְׂרָאֵל שֶׁחַיֶּבֶת בִּתְרוּמוֹת וּמַעַשְׂרוֹת,[41] אִם קָצַץ יִשְׂרָאֵל בְּעַצְמוֹ אֶת הָאֶתְרוֹג – הֲרֵי נִתְחַיֵּב אֶתְרוֹג זֶה בִּתְרוּמוֹת וּמַעַשְׂרוֹת עַל יְדֵי קְצִיצָה שֶׁל הַיִּשְׂרָאֵל,[42] וְאִם נְטָלוֹ לְשֵׁם מִצְוָה קֹדֶם שֶׁהִפְרִישׁ עָלָיו תְּרוּמָה וּמַעֲשֵׂר מֵאֶתְרוֹג אַחֵר – לֹא יָצָא יְדֵי חוֹבָתוֹ, שֶׁהֲרֵי הוּא טֶבֶל,[סב,43] וְטֶבֶל פָּסוּל אֲפִלּוּ בִּשְׁאָר הַיָּמִים כְּמוֹ שֶׁיִּתְבָּאֵר:[סג,44]

in war is considered as a totally effective acquisition, as our Sages derived from the exegesis of verses.[40]

All of the above applies in the Diaspora. [Different laws apply] in *Eretz Yisrael,* where we are obligated [to separate] *terumah* and tithes from its [produce].[41] If a Jew picks an *esrog* himself, this fact obligates him to separate *terumah* and tithes from it.[42] If he would use it for the *mitzvah* before separating *terumah* and the tithes for it from another *esrog,* he would not fulfill his obligation. For the *esrog* is *tevel,*[43] and [hence] is invalid [for the *mitzvah*], even [after the first day of the festival], as will be explained.[44]

יא כָּל אַרְבַּעַת הַמִּינִים שֶׁהָיָה אֶחָד מֵהֶן שֶׁל אֲשֵׁרָה,[סד,45] אִם הִיא שֶׁל יִשְׂרָאֵל[סה,46] דְּהַיְנוּ שֶׁקָּנָה אוֹתָהּ יִשְׂרָאֵל מִיַּד

11 [The following laws apply if] any of the Four Species comes from an *asherah.*[45] If the *asherah* belongs to a Jew[46] — i.e., he bought it from those who

40. Sichon's conquest of the lands of Moab made them the property of his nation, the Amorites, and no longer of the Moabites *(Gittin* 38a*)*.

41. Even today, by Rabbinic ordinance, we are obligated to separate — from produce grown in *Eretz Yisrael* — *terumah* (the heave offering; see *Bamidbar* 15:19-21 and *Devarim* 18:4), *maaser* (the first tithe; see *Vayikra* 27:30), and either *maaser sheni* (the second tithe; see *Devarim* 12:17) or *maasar ani* (the tithe for the poor; see *op. cit.,* 14:28), depending on the position of the current year in the seven-year *Shemitah* cycle.

42. If the non-Jew picks the *esrog* and sells it to the Jew, there is no obligation to separate *terumah* and the tithes. If, however, the Jew purchases the *esrog* while it is on the tree, it is harvested while in his possession and he is obligated to separate the *terumah* and the tithes from it.

Even if the Jew does not intend to eat the *esrog* and desires merely to use it for the *mitzvah,* he is obligated to separate *terumah* and the tithes. This follows the ruling of R. Betzalel Ashkenazi (Responsum 2), as opposed to the position of *Maharashdam.*

43. I.e., produce grown in *Eretz Yisrael* that has not been tithed.

44. In subsection 15.

45. A tree that is worshiped (see *Devarim* 16:9). The disqualification of such species for use in this *mitzvah* is discussed in *Sukkah* 29a, 32b, 33b, and 34b. Subsection 14 below distinguishes between a tree that is actually worshiped and a tree planted in a garden before a false divinity.

46. *Sukkah* 31b.

וראה לקמן שם, שלענין איסור הנאה מגזל, אף לכתחלה אין חוששים. **נח** ט״ז סי׳ תרסד שם. **נט** ראה לקמן הל׳ הפקר ס״ג, דהיינו אפילו נכרי. **ס** מ״א ס״ק ה. וראה גם לקמן שם. לקו״ש חט״ו ע׳ 102. **סא** גמרא גיטין לח, א. לפירוש התוס׳ שם ד״ה אבל. וראה לקמן שם בקו״א ס״ק א. לקו״ש שם ובהערה 24. **סב** שו״ת הר״ר בצלאל אשכנזי סי׳ ב. כנסת הגדולה הגה״ט סי׳ תרמח. מ״א ס״ק ד. **סג** סעיף טו. **סד** משנה כט, ב (לולב). לב, ב (הדס). לג, ב (ערבה). לד, ב (אתרוג). טור ושו״ע ס״ג. ועי׳ סי׳ תקפו ס״ו שם נתבאר כ״ז (לענין שופר. וסיום הסעיף חסר שם). **סה** גמרא לא, ב (באשרה דמשה). תוס׳ שם ד״ה באשרה (בע״ז דישראל). טור ושו״ע שם.

עוֹבְדֶיהָ[סו, 47] — הֲרֵי זֶה פָּסוּל אֲפִלּוּ בִּשְׁאָר הַיָּמִים,[סז, 48] לְפִי שֶׁכָּל הַמִּינִים צָרִיךְ שֶׁיִּהְיוּ כְּשִׁעוּרָן הַמְפֹרָשׁ בָּהֶן[סח] (דְּהַיְנוּ שְׁלֹשָׁה טְפָחִים עַיֵּן סִימָן תר"נ[סט]), וַאֲשֵׁרָה שֶׁהִיא שֶׁל יִשְׂרָאֵל כֵּיוָן שֶׁאֵין בִּטּוּל[49] הַנָּכְרִים מוֹעִיל לָהּ לְהַתִּירָהּ בַּהֲנָאָה[ע] — הֲרֵי הִיא עוֹמֶדֶת לִשְׂרֵפָה, וְכָל הָעוֹמֵד לִשָּׂרֵף — הֲרֵי הוּא כְּשָׂרוּף,[עא] וְנִמְצָא שֶׁאֵין בּוֹ כַּשִּׁעוּר הַמְפֹרָשׁ בּוֹ:[עב, 50]

worship it[47] — it is invalid, even on the other days, [i.e. after the first day].[48] The rationale is that all the specimens must meet their respective minimum dimensions that are explicitly stated ([such as] three handbreadths [for the myrtle and willow twigs]; see sec. 650[:1]). If an *asherah* belongs to a Jew, there is no way that its [connection with idolatry] can be nullified[49] by a non-Jew and thus enable a Jew to derive benefit from it. Hence it is awaiting destruction by fire, and any object that is awaiting destruction by fire is considered as if already destroyed. Thus, it does not possess the minimum measure required of it.[50]

יב וְאִם הָאֲשֵׁרָה הִיא שֶׁל נָכְרִי — לְכַתְּחִלָּה לֹא יִקְצֹץ מִמֶּנָּה אֶחָד מִכָּל אַרְבַּעַת הַמִּינִים,[עג, 46] אֲפִלּוּ אִם כְּבָר בִּטְּלָהּ הַנָּכְרִי.[עד, 49] וַאֲפִלּוּ אִם אִילָן הַזֶּה נְטָעוּהוּ שֶׁלֹּא לְשֵׁם עֲבוֹדָה זָרָה וְאַחַר שֶׁגָּדַל עֲבָדוּהוּ בְּעִנְיָן שֶׁהוּא מֻתָּר בַּהֲנָאָה לְהֶדְיוֹט[51] אֲפִלּוּ בְּלֹא בִּטּוּל, שֶׁהַמְחֻבָּר[52] אֵינוֹ נֶאֱסָר[עה]

12 [Greater leniency is granted] if the *asherah* belongs to a non-Jew. As an initial preference, one should not cut off any of the Four Species from it[46] [to use for the *mitzvah*. This applies] even if the non-Jew has already nullified the tree's [connection with idolatry],[49] and even if the tree was not planted for idolatrous purposes, but was worshiped [only] after it grew. In such an instance, a private individual is permitted to benefit from it[51] even if it was not nullified [by a non-Jew], because an object that is connected to the earth[52] does not become forbidden.

47. Needless to say, this prohibition would apply if a Jew cultivated the tree and worshiped it himself.

48. See subsection 18.

49. A Jew may make use of an idol worshiped by non-Jews after an idolater has nullified it *(Rambam, Hilchos Avodas Kochavim* 8:8-10*)*. The idolater nullifies the object by doing something to it that indicates that he will never again revere it.

50. This doomed object will soon be nonexistent, and at that time will obviously not have the requisite minimal dimensions. Hence, it is considered to be lacking its minimal dimensions as of now (lit., "its measure is [already] crushed"; *Sukkah* 31b).

51. It may not be used in the *Beis HaMikdash*.

52. In the original, such an object is simply known as *mechubar* (lit., "connected").

סו תוס' שם, וביבמות קג, ב ד"ה סנדל. בעל המאור (יז, א). ריטב"א כט, ב ד"ה של אשרה. ר"ן (יד, א) ד"ה של אשרה. רבנו ירוחם נתיב ח ח"ג (נח, ב). מ"מ פ"ח ה"א. רמ"א ס"ג. וראה ב"ח יו"ד סי' קמו ד"ה ומ"ש ואפילו אליל, וש"ך שם ס"ק א (שאם זכה בה הישראל אין לו ביטול. דלא כט"ז שם ס"ק ג). לעיל סי' תלה קו"א סוף ס"ק ב, ושו"ת סוס"י יד (הוכחה מזה שיש בעלות באסורי הנאה). לעיל סי' תקפו ס"ו (כגון שהשתחווה לשופר). **סז** כדלקמן סי"ח וש"נ. **סח** רש"י שם ד"ה באשרה, ובחולין פט, ב ד"ה שיעורא (לענין לולב הדס וערבה). תוס' ל, א ד"ה משום (אף לענין אתרוג). רא"ש פ"ג סט"ו. לבוש ס"ג. **סט** ס"א (בהדס וערבה; ובלולב ד' טפחים). ובאתרוג כביצה, כדלקמן סי"ח. **ע** תוס' שם. ט"ז ס"ק ב. וכדלעיל שם (לענין ע"ז של ישראל). שו"ע יו"ד סי' קמו ס"ב (ע"ז של נכרי שזכה בה ישראל). **עא** ריטב"א שם, ע"פ מנחות קב, ב. רש"י שם. **עב** גמרא שם. לבוש שם. מ"א ס"ק יב. וראה גם לעיל שם. סי' שסג ס"י וסי"ח. קובץ ד"ת ה ע' סד. אהלי שם ב ע' קנז. **עג** רבא בגמרא לא, ב. טור ושו"ע ס"ג. **עד** בעל המאור (יז, א). רש"י שם ד"ה לא יטול (דמאים לגבוה), לפירוש ב"י ד"ה ובשל. רמ"א ס"ג (יוצא בדיעבד). לבוש ס"ד (לכתחלה אסורה). עטרת צבי ס"ק ה. וכ"ה לפירוש ר"ת בתוס' שם ד"ה באשרה. **עה** כרבנן בע"ז מח, א. שו"ע יו"ד סי' קמה ס"א וש"ך שם ס"ק ה. **עו** מ"א ס"ק יא, ממשמעות התוס' שם. רבנו ירוחם נתיב ח ח"ג (נח, ג). וראה לעיל סי'

– אַף עַל פִּי כֵן הוּא מָאוּס לְגָבוֹהַּ,[53] כֵּיוָן שֶׁנִּקְרָא עָלָיו שֵׁם עֲבוֹדָה זָרָה.[עו] אֲבָל בְּדִיעֲבַד שֶׁכְּבָר נָטַל אַרְבָּעָה מִינִים שֶׁל אֲשֵׁרָה זוֹ לְשֵׁם מִצְוָה – יָצָא יְדֵי חוֹבָתוֹ, וְאֵינוֹ צָרִיךְ לַחֲזוֹר וְלִטּוֹל.[עז,54]

וַאֲפִלּוּ אִם לֹא בִּטֵּל הַנָּכְרִי אֲשֵׁרָה זוֹ[עח] וַהֲרֵי הִיא אֲסוּרָה בַּהֲנָאָה,[עט] מִכָּל מָקוֹם כֵּיוָן שֶׁמּוֹעִיל לָהּ בִּטּוּל לְהַתִּירָהּ בַּהֲנָאָה – הֲרֵי אֵינָהּ עוֹמֶדֶת לִשְׂרֵפָה, שֶׁאֶפְשָׁר שֶׁיְּבַטְּלֶנּוּ נָכְרִי.[פ] וְאַף עַל פִּי שֶׁעַכְשָׁו עֲדַיִן הִיא אֲסוּרָה בַּהֲנָאָה – אֵין זוֹ חֲשׁוּבָה הֲנָאָה מַה שֶּׁיּוֹצֵא בָּהּ יְדֵי חוֹבָתוֹ, דְּמִצְוֹת לָאו לֵהָנוֹת נִתְּנוּ[פא] כְּמוֹ שֶׁנִּתְבָּאֵר בְּסִימָן תקפ"ו,[פב,55] עַיֵּן שָׁם:

Nevertheless, such an object is considered abominable for Divine service,[53] because it was once identified with idolatry.

After the fact, however, if one used any of the Four Species from such an *asherah* for the sake of the *mitzvah*, he has fulfilled his obligation and need not take [other specimens] again.[54] Moreover, even if a non-Jew did not nullify the *asherah* and thus it is forbidden to benefit from it, nevertheless, since such nullification would be effective in rendering it permissible, it is not [deemed to be] awaiting destruction by fire, because a non-Jew might nullify it. Though it is forbidden to benefit from it at the present time, the fact that it is used to fulfill one's obligation is not considered as deriving benefit. For "the *mitzvos* were not granted in order that one should derive pleasure [or: 'benefit'] from them," as explained in sec. 586;[55] note [the explanation] there. [Hence, in such a situation, a person is considered to have fulfilled his obligation.]

יג בַּמֶּה דְּבָרִים אֲמוּרִים?[56] כְּשֶׁלֹּא נִתְכַּוֵּן יִשְׂרָאֵל זֶה שֶׁקָּצַץ מִינִים אֵלּוּ מֵהָאֲשֵׁרָה לִזְכּוֹת בָּהֶן לְצֹרֶךְ עַצְמוֹ, אֶלָּא הָיָה בְּדַעְתּוֹ לְהַחֲזִירָן לְהַנָּכְרִי בַּעַל הָאֲשֵׁרָה בִּשְׁלֵמוּת, וְלֹא נְטָלָן לְשֵׁם מִצְוָה בַּיּוֹם הָרִאשׁוֹן שֶׁהֲרֵי הַשָּׁאוּל

13 When does the above apply?[56] When the Jew who cut the specimens from the *asherah* did not intend to acquire them for his personal needs but planned to return them intact to the non-Jew [who] owns it; nor did he use them for the *mitzvah* on the first day [of

53. In the original, *leGavoha* (lit., "for Above").

54. The Alter Rebbe does not state what should be done if a person has none of the species except this one. *Hadar Hu LeChol Chassidav* cites various views and concludes that this *lulav* should be taken, but that no blessing should be recited.

55. The reference appears to be to one of the missing subsections of sec. 586 in the present work. Apparently, the Alter Rebbe is referring here to the subject treated in the *Shulchan Aruch* of R. Yosef Caro 586:3 (cf. *Chullin* 89a). There the *Rama* states that if a non-Jew's *shofar* is forbidden because of a connection with idolatry, it must be nullified before being used for the *mitzvah*. *Magen Avraham* 586:6 differs and maintains that such a *shofar* may be used. *Turei Zahav* 586:4 notes that "the *mitzvos* were not granted in order that one should derive benefit [or: 'pleasure'] from them."

56. I.e., when can a Jew fulfill his obligation using species from an *asherah*?

יא סי"ג. ארבעת המינים (ויינר) ע' רנד ואילך. **עז** גמרא שם. טור ושו"ע שם. **עח** בעל המאור (שם). תוס' יבמות קג, ב ריש ד"ה סנדל. רא"ש ר"ה פ"ג ס"ט. **עט** מ"א ס"ק יג. וכדלקמן סט"ו שאתרוג של טבל וערלה פסול כל ז', מכל מקום כו'. **פ** תוס' יבמות שם. רא"ש שם. ב"ח ד"ה ובשל. **פא** רש"י שם ד"ה ואם נטל. ריטב"א לא, ב ד"ה והאמר. ר"ן (יד, א) ד"ה של אשרה. לבוש ס"ג. ב"ח שם. ט"ז ס"ק ג. **פב** סיום סעיף זה בשוע"ר לא הגיע לידינו. וראה ט"ז שם ס"ק ד. לעיל שם סעיף כד וש"נ.

פָּסוּל בּוֹ,[פג] אֶלָּא נִטָּלִן בִּשְׁאָר הַיָּמִים. אֲבָל אִם נִתְכַּוֵּן לִזְכּוֹת בָּהֶן לְגַמְרֵי שֶׁלֹּא לְהַחֲזִירָן לְהַנָּכְרִי – הֲרֵי מִיָּד בִּקְצִיצָה זוֹ זָכָה בָּהּ הַיִּשְׂרָאֵל[57] וְנַעֲשֵׂית עֲבוֹדָה זָרָה שֶׁל יִשְׂרָאֵל,[פד] וְאֵין בִּטּוּל הַנָּכְרִי מוֹעִיל לְהַתִּירָהּ בַּהֲנָאָה אִם לֹא בִּטְּלָהּ קֹדֶם קְצִיצָתוֹ, וַהֲרֵי הִיא עוֹמֶדֶת לִשְׂרֵפָה, לְפִיכָךְ אֲפִלּוּ בְּדִיעֲבַד לֹא יָצָא:[פה]

the festival], [when] borrowed [specimens] are invalid, but on the later days.

If, however, the Jew intended to fully acquire them and not to return them to the non-Jew, he acquired them as soon as he cut them off[57] and they become a false deity that belongs to a Jew. Thus the fact that a non-Jew might nullify [its connection with idolatry] will not be effective [in changing its status so that a Jew will be] permitted to benefit from it. Hence, it is considered to be awaiting destruction by fire, and even after the fact one cannot fulfill his obligation by using it, unless [the non-Jew] nullified [the tree's connection with idolatry] before [the Jew] cut off [the specimens].

יד וְכָל זֶה בִּימֵיהֶם שֶׁהַנָּכְרִים הָיוּ מִשְׁתַּחֲוִים לָאִילָן, אֲבָל בַּזְּמַן הַזֶּה שֶׁאֵין הַנָּכְרִים מִשְׁתַּחֲוִים לָאִילָן אֶלָּא (נוֹטְעִין אִילָן לִפְנֵי עֲבוֹדָה זָרָה[פו] אוֹ) שֶׁנּוֹטְעִים אִילָנוֹת בַּגַּן שֶׁל עֲבוֹדָה זָרָה וּדְמֵי פֵּרוֹת הָאִילָנוֹת הוּא לְכֹהֲנֵיהֶם[פז] – מֻתָּר לִקַּח מֵהֶן אַרְבָּעָה מִינִים שֶׁבַּלּוּלָב, וְעַל דֶּרֶךְ שֶׁנִּתְבָּאֵר בְּיוֹרֶה דֵעָה סִימָן קמ"ג[פח, 58] לְעִנְיַן הֲנָאַת הֶדְיוֹט, עַיֵּן שָׁם:

14 All of the above applied in the [Talmudic] era, when non-Jews would prostrate themselves before trees. Today, by contrast, the non-Jews do not prostrate themselves before trees, but rather (plant a tree in front of a false deity or) plant trees in a garden in the domain of a false deity and the proceeds from the fruit belong to the priests. [Today, therefore,] it is permitted to use such specimens for the Four Species of the *lulav,* according to the provisions noted in *Yoreh Deah,* sec. 143,[58] with regard to a private individual deriving benefit [from such trees]. Note [the explanation] there.

57. In his *Mareh Mekomos VeTziyunim,* R. Mordechai Shmuel Ashkenazi explains that generally, a person will pick fruit or cut off branches at a height of more than three handbreadths from the ground. Hence, as soon as he cuts off the species, he will acquire them through the *kinyan* of *hagbahah* ("lifting up").

Hadar Hu LeChol Chassidav notes that since stolen species are invalid, the above law is apparently speaking about a situation in which the non-Jew permitted the Jew to cut off the fruit or the branches. Nevertheless, such permission does not amount to nullifying their connection with idolatry.

58. This section of the Alter Rebbe's *Shulchan Aruch* is not extant. The *Shulchan Aruch* of R. Yosef Caro, *Yoreh Deah* 143:3, states that one may benefit from such trees, provided he does not pay the priests. The *Rama* rules more leniently — that as long as the trees are not growing directly in front of the false deity and the fee paid for the produce is not used for the false deity itself, but only for its priests, such benefit is permitted. The *Rama* and other commentaries *(Orach Chayim* 156:1) discuss whether or not Christianity is considered idolatry. All authorities agree that Moslem mosques are not considered idolatrous.

פג כדלעיל ס"א. פד כדלעיל סי"א וש"נ. פה תוס׳ לא, ב ד"ה באשרה. יבמות קג, ב ד"ה סנדל. בעל המאור (יז, א). ריטב"א כט, ב ד"ה של אשרה. ר"ן (יד, א) ד"ה של אשרה. רבנו ירוחם נתיב ח ח"ג (נח, ב). מ"מ פ"ח ה"א.טור ושו"ע ס"ג (שיצא רק מיום הראשון ואילך). רמ"א ס"ג (דוקא שלא נתכוין לזכות בו). פו רבנו ירוחם שם (נח, ג). רמ"א ס"ד. וראה ארבעת המינים (ויינר) ע׳ רס. פז רבנו ירוחם שם. ריטב"א שם. ארחות חיים הל׳ לולב סי׳ ח. שו"ע ס"ד. לבוש ס"ד. וראה נהר שלום ס"ק ד. פח סעיף ג, וברמ"א שם. פט תוס׳ לה, א ד"ה אתיא (דלא הוי לכם). ר"ן (יז, א) ד"ה של דמאי (ביום הראשון בלבד).

15 An *esrog* that is not fit to be eaten, such as when it is *tevel*[59] or *orlah,*[60] is invalid for all seven days [of the festival]. The Sages [derive this concept[61]] by expounding the phrase,[6] "You shall take for yourselves." They understand that phrase as implying [that any specimen used for the *mitzvah* must be] fit to be used in all the ways in which one would [ordinarily] benefit from it. Since the way one benefits from an *esrog* is by eating it, an *esrog* must be fit to be eaten.

[Leniency may be allowed with regard to] an *esrog* which is *orlah* that grew in the Diaspora. It may not be eaten,[62] but since some authorities[63] allow one to serve produce which is *orlah* that grew in the Diaspora to a friend who is not aware that it is *orlah,* [such an *esrog*] may be considered as "fit to be eaten." Though the *halachah* does not follow their view, as stated in *Yoreh Deah,* sec. 294,[64] one may rely on their opinion to deem such an *esrog* fit to be used for the *mitzvah.*

טו אֶתְרוֹג שֶׁאֵינוֹ רָאוּי לַאֲכִילָה, כְּגוֹן שֶׁהוּא שֶׁל טֶבֶל[פט,59] אוֹ שֶׁל עָרְלָה[צ,60] – פָּסוּל כָּל ז׳ יָמִים,[צא] שֶׁנֶּאֱמַר[6] "וּלְקַחְתֶּם לָכֶם", וְדָרְשׁוּ חֲכָמִים:[צב,61] הָרָאוּי לָכֶם לְכָל דַּרְכֵי הֲנָאָתוֹ, וְאֶתְרוֹג שֶׁדֶּרֶךְ הֲנָאָתוֹ הִיא הָאֲכִילָה – צָרִיךְ לִהְיוֹת רָאוּי לַאֲכִילָה.[צג]

וְאֶתְרוֹג שֶׁל עָרְלַת חוּץ לָאָרֶץ אַף עַל פִּי שֶׁאָסוּר בַּאֲכִילָה,[צד,62] מִכָּל מָקוֹם כֵּיוָן שֶׁיֵּשׁ[63] מַתִּירִין[צה] לְהַאֲכִיל עָרְלַת חוּץ לָאָרֶץ לַחֲבֵרוֹ שֶׁאֵינוֹ יוֹדֵעַ שֶׁזֶּה עָרְלָה, וְאִם כֵּן הֲרֵי הוּא רָאוּי לַאֲכִילָה,[צו] וְאַף עַל פִּי שֶׁאֵין הֲלָכָה כְּדִבְרֵיהֶם כְּמוֹ שֶׁיִּתְבָּאֵר בְּיוֹרֶה דֵעָה סִימָן רצ״ד,[צז,64] מִכָּל מָקוֹם יֵשׁ לִסְמֹךְ עַל דִּבְרֵיהֶם לְהַכְשִׁיר הָאֶתְרוֹג לַמִּצְוָה:[צח]

16 If a person takes a vow, forbidding himself to derive benefit from his own *lulav*

טז מִי שֶׁנָּדַר הֲנָאָה מִלּוּלָב שֶׁלּוֹ אוֹ

59. I.e., untithed. Such an *esrog* may, however, be made fit for the *mitzvah* by making these separations from other produce; see subsection 10 above and footnotes there.

60. I.e., fruit produced during the first three years of a tree's growth, which may not be eaten *(Vayikra* 19:23*)*. An *esrog* that is *orlah* may never be used for the *mitzvah* *(Sukkah* 34b*)*.

Though it is very unlikely for an *esrog* tree to produce fruit within three years, the laws of *orlah* also apply when a sapling is replanted *(Orlah* 1:3*)*, and this is commonly done.

61. *Sukkah* 35a.

62. *Orlah* 3:9.

63. *Shiltei Gibborim,* as cited by *Magen Avraham* 649:20, based on a *Rishon* known as *Riaz* (R. Yeshayahu ben Eliyahu di Trani).

64. This section of the present work is not extant. See the *Shulchan Aruch* of R. Yosef Caro, *Yoreh Deah* 294:8-9.

As a rule, whenever there is a doubt whether or not a Scriptural prohibition exists, we rule stringently. In the instance of *orlah,* however, the Oral Tradition specifies an exception, that fruit that grew in the Diaspora which is doubtfully *orlah* may be eaten. Now, if Shimon is unaware that this fruit is *orlah,* but Reuven is aware, may Reuven serve this fruit to Shimon? While some authorities did allow this, the prevailing ruling is that it is not allowed.

רמב"ם פ"ח ה"ב. רבנו מנוח שם (שאינו ראוי לאכילה), וה"ט (שפסול אף בשאר הימים). **צ** משנה לד, ב. רמב"ם שם. לבוש ס"ה. מ"א ס"ק כ. **צא** רמב"ם פ"ח ה"ט (אתרוג האסור באכילה). שו"ע ס"ה. **צב** גמרא לה, א. רש"י ותוס' ד"ה לפי. **צג** מ"א שם (כיון שאיסור אכילה הוא פסול בגוף האתרוג, פסול כל ז'). וראה חידושי צ"צ (עא, ד). אהלי שם ב ע' קנה. ז ע' נז. **צד** קדושין לח, ב. שו"ע יו"ד סי' רצד ס"ח. **צה** גמרא שם לט, א. לפירוש הב"י ביו"ד שם ד"ה ואיכא. **צו** שלטי הגבורים (יז, א) אות ב, בשם הריא"ז. כנסת הגדולה הגה"ט סוס"י תרמח. מ"א שם. אליה זוטא ס"ק ד. **צז** ב"י שם. ב"ח ביו"ד שם סד"ה ערלה. וראה שו"ע שם ס"ט ובנ"כ. **צח** מ"א שם.

מִלּוּלָב שֶׁל חֲבֵרוֹ — הֲרֵי לוּלָב זֶה פָּסוּל לוֹ בַּיּוֹם הָרִאשׁוֹן,[צט] שֶׁהֲרֵי אֵין לוּלָב זֶה רָאוּי לוֹ לִכְלוּם, כֵּיוָן שֶׁנָּדַר מִמֶּנּוּ הֲנָאָה, וְהַתּוֹרָה אָמְרָה "לָכֶם" — הָרָאוּי לָכֶם לְכָל דַּרְכֵי הֲנָאָתוֹ,[ק, 65] וּלְפִיכָךְ צָרִיךְ לִקַּח לוֹ לוּלָב אַחֵר לָצֵאת בּוֹ בַּיּוֹם הָרִאשׁוֹן,[66] אֲבָל בִּשְׁאָר הַיָּמִים כֵּיוָן שֶׁאֵין חִיּוּב נְטִילַת לוּלָב אֶלָּא זֵכֶר לַמִּקְדָּשׁ — לֹא הֶחְמִירוּ כָּל כָּךְ לְפָסְלוֹ בְּדָבָר שֶׁאֵין הַפְּסוּל בְּגוּפוֹ,[67] שֶׁהֲרֵי לוּלָב זֶה כָּשֵׁר הוּא בְּעַצְמוֹ, אֶלָּא שֶׁהוּא נָדַר מִמֶּנּוּ הֲנָאָה:[קא, 68]

or from the *lulav* of a friend, such a *lulav* is invalid for him on the first day. [The rationale is that] it is not fit for him for any use, since he has taken a vow forbidding himself to benefit from it — and the Torah stipulated that the *lulav* must be "for yourselves," i.e., fit to be used by you in all the ways in which you would benefit from it.[65] Therefore he must take for himself another *lulav* with which to fulfill his obligation on the first day.[66]

On the later days, by contrast, since we are obligated to take the *lulav* only to commemorate [the practice in] the *Beis HaMikdash*, the Sages were not stringent and did not disqualify [a *lulav*] when the disqualifying factor did not affect the substance of [the *lulav*].[67] For this *lulav* itself is valid; it is only that this individual has taken a vow not to derive benefit from it.[68]

יז אֲבָל שְׁאָר כָּל הַדְּבָרִים הַפְּסוּלִין בְּכָל אֶחָד מֵאַרְבָּעָה מִינִים שֶׁפְּסוּלָן הוּא מִגּוּפוֹ[קב] — פּוֹסֵל בֵּין בַּיּוֹם הָרִאשׁוֹן בֵּין בִּשְׁאָר הַיָּמִים, חוּץ מִפְּסוּל מֵחֲמַת חֶסְרוֹן[קג] כְּגוֹן נִקַּב נֶקֶב מְפֻלָּשׁ וְיֵשׁ בּוֹ חֶסְרוֹן מִגּוּף הָאֶתְרוֹג,[קד, 69] אוֹ שֶׁנִּטַּל עֻקְצוֹ וְנִשְׁאַר מְקוֹמוֹ גֻּמָּא,[קה, 70] אֲבָל נִטְּלָה פִּטְמָתוֹ אֵין פְּסוּלוֹ מֵחֲמַת חֶסְרוֹן בִּלְבַד אֶלָּא מֵחֲמַת שֶׁאֵין זֶה הָדוּר,[71] לְפִיכָךְ פָּסוּל כָּל שִׁבְעַת הַיָּמִים,[קו] כִּשְׁאָר כָּל פְּסוּלִים שֶׁמֵּחֲמַת הִדּוּר כְּגוֹן חֲזָזִית וְכַיּוֹצֵא בּוֹ[קז] שֶׁפּוֹסְלִין כָּל ז' יָמִים:[קח, 72]

17 By contrast, all the other disqualifying factors that affect the substance of any one of the Four Species invalidate it both on the first day and on the later days. The [only] exception is [an *esrog*] that was disqualified because its substance has been decreased; e.g., it was perforated from one side to the other and the substance of the *esrog* is lacking,[69] or its stem was removed, leaving a cavity.[70] If, however, the *pitom* has been removed, [the *esrog*] is disqualified not only because it is lacking in substance, but also because it is not "beautiful."[71] Hence, it is invalid throughout all seven days, as is the ruling with regard to all the factors that disqualify [an esrog] because it is not beautiful, such as an eruption.[72]

---

65. See subsection 15.

66. Alternatively, he may have his vow absolved (*Kaf HaChayim* 649:35).

67. As in subsection 2 above.

68. And using it to perform the *mitzvah* is not considered as deriving personal benefit, as in subsection 12 above.

69. See sec. 648:8.

70. See sec. 648:18.

71. See sec. 648:17.

72. See sec. 648:19-21.

צט שו"ת הרשב"א ח"א סי' תשמו"ז. ח"ד סי' רב. רמ"א ס"ב. ולענין אתרוג שנודר שלא יאכלנו, ראה לעיל סט"ו. פמ"ג א"א ס"ק י. **ק** כדלעיל סט"ו, לענין טבל וערלה (אלא ששם הוא פסול בגופו ופסול כל ז'). **קא** וראה לעיל סי"ב, שאף שאסור לו בהנאה אין זו חשובה הנאה. **קב** מ"א ס"ק כ. וראה גם ר"ן

יח וַאֲפִלּוּ חֶסְרוֹן אֵינוֹ כָּשֵׁר בִּשְׁאָר הַיָּמִים אֶלָּא אִם כֵּן נִשְׁתַּיֵּר בּוֹ שָׁלֵם כְּשִׁעוּר,[קט] דְּהַיְנוּ כַּבֵּיצָה בָּאֶתְרוֹג,[ק] אֲבָל אִם לֹא נִשְׁתַּיֵּר בּוֹ כַּבֵּיצָה – פָּסוּל.[73] וְכֵן הֲדַס וַעֲרָבָה שֶׁאֵין בָּהֶן כְּשִׁעוּר דְּהַיְנוּ שְׁלֹשָׁה טְפָחִים, וְלוּלָב שֶׁאֵין בּוֹ כְּשִׁעוּר דְּהַיְנוּ אַרְבָּעָה טְפָחִים[קיא] – פְּסוּלִין כָּל שִׁבְעַת הַיָּמִים:[קיב]

18 Even when [the difficulty is] a lack [in the substance of the *esrog*], the *esrog* is invalid on the remaining days unless its minimum measure — the size of an egg — remains intact. If [this] minimum measure does not remain [intact], it is invalid.[73] Similarly, a myrtle or willow twig that lack [their] minimum measure of three handbreadths, and a *lulav* that lacks [its] minimum measure of four handbreadths, are invalid for all seven days.

יט נִמְצֵאתָ לָמֵד, שֶׁכָּל הַפְּסוּלִין בָּרִאשׁוֹן מִן הַתּוֹרָה – פְּסוּלִין בִּשְׁאָר הַיָּמִים מִדִּבְרֵי סוֹפְרִים, חוּץ מִן עֲשָׂרָה דְּבָרִים וְאֵלּוּ הֵם:

א׳ הַשָּׁאוּל, בֵּין מִדַּעַת הַבְּעָלִים בֵּין שֶׁנָּטַל שֶׁלֹּא מִדַּעַת הַבְּעָלִים, אֲבָל לֹא נִתְכַּוֵּן לִגְזֹל.[קיג,74]

ב׳ הַנּוֹדֵר הֲנָאָה מִלּוּלָב וּמִינָיו.[קיד,75]

ג׳ לוּלָב שֶׁנִּסְדַּק בְּעִנְיָן שֶׁנִּפְסַל.

ד׳ נֶחְלְקָה עָלֶה הָעֶלְיוֹן הָאֶמְצָעִי (שֶׁשְּׁנֵי פְּסוּלִים אֵלּוּ הֵן מֵחֲמַת חֶסְרוֹן כְּמוֹ שֶׁנִּתְבָּאֵר בְּסִימָן תרמ״ה[קטו]).

ה׳ נִכְפְּפוּ רֹב רָאשֵׁי הֶעָלִין שֶׁבַּלּוּלָב.[קטז,76]

19 We can derive from the above that all the factors that disqualify an *esrog* according to Scriptural Law on the first day disqualify it according to Rabbinic Law on the later days, with the exception of ten factors. These cases are:

(i) a person who borrows [one or more of the species] with or without the knowledge of the owner, provided he does not have the intent of stealing it;[74]

(ii) a person who takes a vow not to benefit from a *lulav* or the other species;[75]

(iii) a *lulav* that is split to the extent that it is invalid;

(iv) a *lulav* that is disqualified because its middle, highest leaf is divided; (for the rationale for both of these disqualifying factors is that the substance [of the *lulav*] is considered to be lacking, as stated in sec. 645[:10, 12]);

(v) a *lulav* whose leaves are mostly bent at the top;[76]

---

73. See sec. 650:1.

74. See subsections 2-4 above.

75. See subsection 16 above.

76. See sec. 645:20.

(טו, א) ד״ה תניא. קג תוס׳ כט, ב ד״ה בעינן. רא״ש פ״ג ס״ג. טור ורמ״א ס״ה. קד שאז פסול לדברי הכל, כדלעיל סי׳ תרמח ס״ח. ואין פסולו מחמת הדור, אלא מטעם לקיחה תמה, כדלעיל שם סי״ד. קה רבנו ירוחם נתיב ח ח״ג (נט, ד). רמ״א שם (אף לענין נטלה פטמתו). מ״א ס״ק יז (רק לענין ניטל עוקצו). וכדלעיל שם סי״ח, שפסול מטעם חסר. קו מ״א ס״ק יז, ממשמעות הגהות מיימוניות פ״ח אות מ. וכדלעיל שם סי״ז. קז כדלעיל שם סי״ט־כא וש״נ. קח תוס׳ שם ד״ה קפסיק. רא״ש פ״ג סט״ו. ר״ן (יח, רע״א). רבנו ירוחם שם. רמ״א שם. מ״א ס״ק כב. קט תוס׳ מו, ב ד״ה אתרוג בשביעי. רא״ש פ״ג סי׳ כג. וראה לקמן ס״כ, דהיינו אף כשהנותר הוא מיעוט האתרוג. קי מ״א ס״ק כז. אליה רבה ס״ק יג. וראה לעיל סי׳ תרמח סכ״ט (ששיעור כביצה הוא שיהי׳ גמר פרי). תוס׳ ל, א ד״ה משום, ורא״ש פ״ג סי׳ טו (שמ״מ בעינן דמינכר לקיחתה). לעיל סי״א (שנפסל כשנחסר שיעורו). לקמן ס״כ. סכ״ג (אף בשעת הדחק). קיא כדלקמן סי׳ תרנ ס״א. קיב הראב״ד בהל׳ לולב (תשובות ופסקים ע׳ כז). ריטב״א כט, ב ד״ה לולב. ר״ן (יד, א) דיבור הראשון. מ״מ פ״ח ה״ט. טור ושו״ע ס״ה. וראה גם לעיל סי״א. לקמן סכ״ג. קיג כדלעיל ס״ב־ג. קיד כדלעיל סט״ז (לענין לולב). קטו ס״י (נחלק) וסי״ב (נסדק). קטז כדלעיל סי׳ תרמה ס״כ (אם אי אפשר לו למצוא בקל לולב אחר).

ו׳ הֲדַס שֶׁיָּבְשׁוּ עָלָיו וְנִשְׁאֲרוּ בּוֹ שְׁלֹשָׁה עָלִין כְּמוּשִׁין בְּרֹאשׁ הַבַּד.[קיז,77]

ז׳ אֶתְרוֹג שֶׁנִּקַּב, אֲפִלּוּ יֵשׁ בּוֹ חֶסְרוֹן, וַאֲפִלּוּ הַרְבֵּה יוֹתֵר מִכְּאִסָּר, וַאֲפִלּוּ הוּא מְפֻלָּשׁ.[קיח,78]

ח׳ נִמּוֹק כָּל בְּשָׂרוֹ מִבִּפְנִים.[קיט,79]

ט׳ נִסְדַּק בְּעִנְיָן שֶׁנִּפְסַל.[קכ,80]

י׳ נִטַּל עֻקְצוֹ.[קכא,78]

וְיֵשׁ מַכְשִׁירִין[קכב] בִּשְׁאָר הַיָּמִים אַף הַפָּסוּל מֵחֲמַת שֶׁאֵינוֹ הָדוּר, כְּגוֹן נִטְּלָה פִּטְמָתוֹ וַחֲזָזִית וְכַיּוֹצֵא בָּהֶם. וְיֵשׁ לִסְמֹךְ עַל דִּבְרֵיהֶם בִּשְׁעַת הַדְּחָק שֶׁאִי אֶפְשָׁר לִמְצֹא מִינִים אֲחֵרִים,[קכג] שֶׁהֲרֵי יֵשׁ נוֹהֲגִין לְבָרֵךְ בִּשְׁעַת הַדְּחָק עַל כָּל הַפְּסוּלִין אַף בְּיוֹם רִאשׁוֹן[קכד] כְּמוֹ שֶׁיִּתְבָּאֵר:[קכה,81]

(vi) a myrtle whose leaves became dried out and there remained three withered leaves at the top of the twig;[77]

(vii) an *esrog* that is perforated, even if its substance is lacking, and even if the hole is much larger than an *isar* and extends from side to side;[78]

(viii) an *esrog* whose fibrous substance has all decomposed from within;[79]

(ix) an *esrog* that is split in a manner that disqualifies it;[80]

(x) an *esrog* whose stem has been removed.[78]

Some authorities allow [an *esrog* or any other of the species] to be used on the later days if it is disqualified because it is not "beautiful," e.g., an *esrog* whose *pitom* has been removed, or one that has eruptions, and the like. One may rely on their opinion in a pressing situation when no other specimens can be found. For as will be explained,[81] there are those who follow the practice of reciting the blessing over specimens that have been disqualified for any reason, even on the first day.

כ אֶתְרוֹג שֶׁנִּקְּבוּהוּ עַכְבָּרִים, אַף עַל פִּי שֶׁהוּא כָּשֵׁר בִּשְׁאָר הַיָּמִים, שֶׁהֲרֵי הֶחָסֵר הוּא כָּשֵׁר בִּשְׁאָר הַיָּמִים מִיּוֹם שֵׁנִי וְאֵילָךְ,[קכו,82] מִכָּל מָקוֹם לְכַתְּחִלָּה[קכז] לֹא יִטְּלֶנּוּ אַף בִּשְׁאָר הַיָּמִים עַד שֶׁיָּסִיר נִקּוּר הָעַכְבָּרִים, מִשּׁוּם מִאוּס.[קכח,83]

20 If mice [have nibbled at] an *esrog*, creating holes, [there is a difficulty in using it,] even on the later days. It is valid, for an *esrog* whose substance is lacking is acceptable on the remaining days from the second day onward.[82] Nevertheless, as an initial preference, it should not be used even on [those] days until one removes [the part] that the mice nibbled at, because it is disgusting.[83]

77. See sec. 646:10.

78. See subsection 17 above.

79. See sec. 648:12.

80. See sec. 648:13-14.

81. In subsections 22-23 below.

82. *Sukkah* 36b.

83. In the spirit of the verse *(Malachi* 1:8*)*, "Present it, please, to your governor: would he be pleased with you?!"

קיז כדלעיל סי׳ תרמו ס״י. קיח כדלעיל סי״ז וש״נ. קיט כדלעיל סי׳ תרמח סי״ב (לדעת האוסרים מטעם חסר, שיש לחוש לה במקום שאפשר). קכ כדלעיל שם סי״ג־ד (שפסול מטעם חסר). קכא כדלעיל סי״ז וש״נ. קכב תוס׳ כט, ב ד״ה קפסיק, ורא״ש פ״ג סוף סט״ו, בדעת הירושלמי פ״ג ה״ו. הרי״ץ גיאת הל׳ לולב (ע׳ ק). רמב״ם פ״ח ה״ט (וכ״ד הראב״ד שם, בכל פסולי הדר חוץ מיבש). טור בשם בעל העיטור שם (פט, ב) ורבנו יונה. שו״ע ס״ה. קכג ראה ט״ז סוף ס״ק ט. אליה רבה ס״ק טו (אף בלא שעת הדחק). וראה משנה ברורה שעה״צ ס״ק נג. ראה עד״ז גם לעיל סי׳ תרמה סי״ז וש״נ. קכד עד״ז לעיל סי׳ תרמח סי״ח וש״נ. קכה לקמן סכ״ב־ג. קכו גמרא לו, ב וכלישנא בתרא. רבנו חננאל שם. רי״ף (יז, ב). רא״ש פ״ג סכ״ג. ב״י ד״ה ומ״ש רבינו הלכך, בדעת הרמב״ם פ״ח ה״ט. טור. קכז רמ״א ס״ה, לפירוש המ״א ס״ק יח. קכח כל בו סי׳ עב (מא, א). רמ״א שם. קכט ראבי״ה סי׳ תרצז. הגהות אשרי פ״ג סי׳

If, however, [an *esrog*] was disqualified because it was not "beautiful" — e.g., it was dried out or blotchy, which would invalidate it for all seven days — it cannot be made valid by cutting away the dried or blotchy parts, because their disqualification is inherent.

Even as an initial preference, from the second day of the festival onward, it is permissible to cut away part of the *esrog* and eat it and fulfill one's obligation with the remainder.[84] [This may be done] even if the remainder is less than half the *esrog*, as long as it is the size of an egg.[85]

When does [the leniency to partake of the esrog] apply? When one stipulated before *bein hashmashos*[86] of the first night of *Yom-Tov* that he was not foregoing the power and the right[87] to use the *esrog* throughout the time of *bein hashmashos* on the second night. Thus, during *bein hashmashos* of the first night — which is the beginning of the onset of the festival — this *esrog* did not become set aside for the fulfillment of the *mitzvah* of *esrog*. [This is possible, since] with regard to the remainder of the festival, he stipulated that he would have the power and the right [to use the *esrog*] at the onset of the remaining days of the festival, i.e., from *bein hashmashos* of the second day.

If, however, he did not explicitly stipulate that he was not distancing himself from [the *esrog*] during *bein hashmashos*, even though he stipulated that he would be permitted to

אֲבָל אִם הָיָה פְּסוּלוֹ מֵחֲמַת שֶׁאֵינוֹ הָדוּר, כְּגוֹן שֶׁהָיָה יָבֵשׁ אוֹ מְנֻמָּר שֶׁפָּסוּל כָּל שִׁבְעַת הַיָּמִים — אֵין מוֹעִיל לְהַכְשִׁירוֹ עַל יְדֵי שֶׁיַּחְתֹּךְ וְיָסִיר מְקוֹם הַיְבֵשׁוּת אוֹ מְקוֹם הַמְנֻמָּר, הוֹאִיל וּבָא מִכֹּחַ פָּסוּל.[קכט]

וַאֲפִלּוּ לְכַתְּחִלָּה מֻתָּר מִיּוֹם שֵׁנִי וְאֵילָךְ לַחְתֹּךְ מִן הָאֶתְרוֹג וְלֶאֱכֹל וְיוֹצֵא יְדֵי חוֹבָתוֹ בְּהַנּוֹתָר[קל, 84] אַף עַל פִּי שֶׁהוּא מִעוּט שֶׁל כָּל הָאֶתְרוֹג,[קלא] וּבִלְבַד שֶׁיִּהְיֶה בּוֹ כַּבֵּיצָה.[קלב, 85]

בַּמֶּה דְּבָרִים אֲמוּרִים? כְּשֶׁהִתְנָה עָלָיו[קלג] קֹדֶם בֵּין הַשְּׁמָשׁוֹת[86] שֶׁל לֵיל רִאשׁוֹן,[קלד] שֶׁאֵינוֹ בּוֹדֵל אֶת עַצְמוֹ מִלִּהְיוֹת כֹּחוֹ וּזְכוּתוֹ[87] בְּהָאֶתְרוֹג כָּל שֶׁהוּת בֵּין הַשְּׁמָשׁוֹת שֶׁל לֵיל שֵׁנִי,[קלה] דְּנִמְצָא אֶתְרוֹג זֶה לֹא הֻקְצָה בְּבֵין הַשְּׁמָשׁוֹת שֶׁל לֵיל רִאשׁוֹן[קלו] שֶׁהוּא תְּחִלַּת הַחַג לְמִצְוַת נְטִילַת אֶתְרוֹג, שֶׁהֲרֵי לִשְׁאָר יְמֵי הַחַג הִתְנָה עָלָיו שֶׁיְּהֵא כֹּחוֹ וּזְכוּתוֹ בּוֹ בִּתְחִלַּת כְּנִיסַת שְׁאָר יְמֵי הַחַג דְּהַיְנוּ בֵּין הַשְּׁמָשׁוֹת שֶׁל לֵיל שֵׁנִי.

אֲבָל אִם לֹא אָמַר בְּפֵרוּשׁ שֶׁאֵינוֹ בּוֹדֵל אֶת עַצְמוֹ מִמֶּנּוּ כָּל שֶׁהוּת בֵּין הַשְּׁמָשׁוֹת, אַף עַל פִּי שֶׁהִתְנָה עָלָיו שֶׁיְּהֵא

84. *Sukkah* 36b relates that R. Chanina once did this.

85. The minimum size of an *esrog* (sec. 648:29).

86. The twilight period between sunset and the appearance of the stars.

87. Lit., "that he was not separating himself from having the power and the right...."

כג. רמ"א שם. וראה לעיל סי' תרמח סכ"ד. קל ר' חנינא לו, ב. טור ורמ"א שם. קלא דרכי משה ס"ק ו, ממשמעות תרומת הדשן שם. מ"א ס"ק כז, ושכן גם דעת הטור. אליה רבה ס"ק יג. קלב מ"א שם. וכדלעיל סי"ח וש"נ. קלג תוס' מו, ב ד"ה אתרוג. רמ"א שם. קלד לבוש ס"ה. וראה גם לעיל סי' תרלח ס"ז (לענין נוי סוכה) וש"נ. קלה משא"כ בליל הראשון אתקצאי ליום ראשון בעל כרחו, כדלקמן בסוף הסעיף. קלו משא"כ אם הפריש אתרוג ליום ב' מותר לאכול ממנו בלא תנאי (מ"א ס"ק יט). וא"כ כל התנאי הוא שמליל ראשון לא יוקצה עבור ליל שני ואילך (לבוש שם).

מֻתָּר לְהִסְתַּפֵּק מִמֶּנּוּ[קלז] מִיּוֹם שֵׁנִי וְאֵילָךְ — אָסוּר לְהִסְתַּפֵּק מִמֶּנּוּ מִיּוֹם שֵׁנִי וְאֵילָךְ, דְּכֵיוָן שֶׁבְּבֵין הַשְּׁמָשׁוֹת שֶׁל לֵיל רִאשׁוֹן שֶׁהוּא תְּחִלַּת כְּנִיסַת הֶחָג הָיָה מֻקְצֶה וְעוֹמֵד לְמִצְוַת נְטִילַת אֶתְרוֹג שֶׁל כָּל שִׁבְעַת יְמֵי הֶחָג שֶׁהָיָה אָסוּר לוֹ לְהִסְתַּפֵּק מִמֶּנּוּ כָּל שְׁהוּת בֵּין הַשְּׁמָשׁוֹת שֶׁל לֵיל רִאשׁוֹן, שֶׁהֲרֵי הוּא כֻּלּוֹ מֻקְצֶה לְמִצְוָתוֹ לָצֵאת בּוֹ לְמָחָר בְּיוֹם רִאשׁוֹן שֶׁהֶחָסֵר פָּסוּל בּוֹ,[קלח] וְכֵיוָן שֶׁבֵּין הַשְּׁמָשׁוֹת שֶׁהוּא תְּחִלַּת כְּנִיסַת הֶחָג כָּל הָאֶתְרוֹג הוּא מֻקְצֶה[88] וְאָסוּר לְהִסְתַּפֵּק מִמֶּנּוּ אֲפִלּוּ מַשֶּׁהוּ — הֲרֵי כֻּלּוֹ הֻקְצָה וְנֶאֱסַר לְכָל שִׁבְעַת יְמֵי הֶחָג, שֶׁכָּל שִׁבְעַת הַיָּמִים הֵן כְּיוֹם אֶחָד אָרֹךְ לְעִנְיָן זֶה[קלט] מִן הַסְּתָם, אֶלָּא אִם כֵּן הִתְנָה בְּפֵרוּשׁ עַל שְׁאָר הַיָּמִים וְעַל דֶּרֶךְ שֶׁנִּתְבָּאֵר:

make [personal] use of it from the second day onward, he is forbidden to partake of it from the second day onward. [The rationale is that] during *bein hashmashos* of the first night, which is the beginning of the onset of the festival, [the *esrog*] was set aside and designated for use in the *mitzvah* of the *esrog* throughout the seven days of the festival.

[To explain:] During *bein hashmashos* of the first night he was forbidden to partake of the *esrog,* because it was set aside — to be used the next day in fulfillment of the *mitzvah* — in its entirety, for on the first day an *esrog* that is lacking substance is invalid. During *bein hashmashos,* which is the beginning of the onset of the festival, the entire *esrog* is thus *muktzeh,*[88] and it is forbidden to partake of even the slightest part of it. Hence it is now set aside and forbidden in its entirety throughout the seven days of the festival, for the ordinary rule is that all seven days are like one long day in this regard, unless one made an explicit stipulation regarding the other days, as explained above.

כא כָּל הַפְּסוּלִין בְּיוֹם רִאשׁוֹן וּכְשֵׁרִים מִיּוֹם שֵׁנִי וְאֵילָךְ — הַיְנוּ בְּאֶרֶץ יִשְׂרָאֵל שֶׁיּוֹם שֵׁנִי הוּא חֹל הַמּוֹעֵד. וּבְחוּץ לָאָרֶץ שֶׁעוֹשִׂין יוֹם טוֹב שְׁנֵי יָמִים[קמ] — יֵשׁ אוֹמְרִים[קמא] שֶׁכָּל הַפְּסוּלִין הַנּוֹהֲגִין בָּרִאשׁוֹן מִן הַתּוֹרָה נוֹהֲגִין בְּיוֹם טוֹב שֵׁנִי מִדִּבְרֵי סוֹפְרִים, דְּכֵיוָן שֶׁתִּקְּנוּ יוֹם טוֹב שֵׁנִי[89] מִפְּנֵי הַסָּפֵק

21 Whenever [we speak of] a factor disqualifying [one of the species] on the first day, but [not] from the second day onward, this relates to *Eretz Yisrael,* where the second day is *Chol HaMoed.* In the Diaspora, by contrast, where the first two days are [fully] celebrated as *Yom-Tov,* some authorities maintain that all the factors that disqualify [any of the species] on the first day according to Scriptural Law also disqualify it on the second by Rabbinic decree. [They argue that] since the Sages ordained the observance of the second day of *Yom-Tov*[89] because of the doubt that it

88. I.e., set aside.

89. The additional day is known as *Yom-Tov Sheini shel Galuyos* (lit., "the second festival of the exiles").

קלז כדלעיל שם ס"ח (לענין נוי סוכה). קלח וא"כ על כרחו הוא צריך להיות מובדל מהן בבה"ש. וכדלעיל שם סי"ב (לענין סכך ודפנות הסוכה). קלט כדלעיל שם ס"ט (לענין סוכה). אלא שבסוכה אינו מועיל תנאי ובאתרוג מועיל התנאי (ביצה ל, סע"ב. ורש"י שם ד"ה ומאי שנא). קמ כדלעיל סי' תצ ס"א וש"נ. קמא הראב"ד בתמים דעים סי' רכז. המנהיג ריש הל' לולב, וראבי"ה סי' תרנב, בשם ר"ת. רא"ש פ"ג סוף ס"ג. טור. דרכי משה ס"ק ז, בשם

שֶׁמָּא הוּא יוֹם טוֹב רִאשׁוֹן אִם כֵּן צָרִיךְ לִנְהֹג בּוֹ מֵחֲמַת הַסָּפֵק כָּל הַחֻמְרוֹת שֶׁל יוֹם טוֹב הָרִאשׁוֹן.[קמב, 90]

וְיֵשׁ אוֹמְרִים[קמג] כֵּיוָן שֶׁאָנוּ בְּקִיאִים בִּקְבִיעוּת הַחֹדֶשׁ[91] וְיוֹדְעִין אָנוּ שֶׁהַשֵּׁנִי הוּא חֹל,[92] וְאֵין אָנוּ נוֹהֲגִין בּוֹ קֹדֶשׁ אֶלָּא שֶׁלֹּא לְזַלְזֵל בְּמִנְהַג אֲבוֹתֵינוּ[קמד] שֶׁהָיוּ בִּזְמַן שֶׁמְּקַדְּשִׁין עַל פִּי הָרְאִיָּה,[93] שֶׁאָז לֹא הָיָה הַדָּבָר תָּלוּי בִּידִיעַת חֶשְׁבּוֹן קְבִיעוּת הֶחֳדָשִׁים, וְאֵין אָנוּ מְצֻוִּים אֶלָּא שֶׁלֹּא לְזַלְזֵל בְּעִקַּר קְדֻשַּׁת הַיּוֹם, וּלְפִיכָךְ אָנוּ מְקַדְּשִׁין עַל הַכּוֹס וּמְבָרְכִין זְמַן בְּיוֹם טוֹב שֵׁנִי כְּמוֹ בְּיוֹם טוֹב הָרִאשׁוֹן,[קמה] אֲבָל דְּבָרִים שֶׁאֵינָן מֵעִקַּר קְדֻשַּׁת הַיּוֹם אֶלָּא שֶׁהֵן מִצְוֹת הַנּוֹהֲגוֹת בְּאוֹתוֹ הַיּוֹם בִּלְבַד, כְּגוֹן כָּל הַפְּסוּלִין בְּיוֹם טוֹב הָרִאשׁוֹן בִּלְבַד, וְאַף אִם לֹא תִּהְיֶינָה מִצְוֹת הַלָּלוּ נוֹהֲגוֹת בְּיוֹם טוֹב שֵׁנִי אֵין כָּאן זִלְזוּל לְיוֹם טוֹב הַשֵּׁנִי כְּלָל, כֵּיוָן שֶׁאֵין הַמִּצְוֹת תְּלוּיוֹת בְּעִקָּר קְדֻשַּׁת הַיּוֹם כְּלָל, שֶׁהֲרֵי מִצְוַת נְטִילַת לוּלָב לֹא תָּלָה הַכָּתוּב חִיּוּבוֹ מֵחֲמַת שֶׁהוּא

might be the first day, all the stringencies of the first day must be observed because of this doubt.[90]

Other authorities, however, maintain that [these stringencies need not be observed. Their rationale is that] we know which day is to be established as Rosh Chodesh,[91] and we know that the second day is an ordinary weekday.[92] We treat it as a holy day only in order that we should not demean the custom of our forefathers, who would sanctify the months based on the sighting [of the new moon],[93] for in that era the matter did not depend on a knowledge of the calculations used in determining the months. We are commanded only not to demean the essence of the sanctity of the day, which is why we recite *Kiddush* over a cup [of wine] and recite the blessing *Shehecheyanu* on the second day of the festival just as on the first day. Nevertheless, [these latter authorities argue, this should not affect] matters that are not associated with the essence of the sanctity of the day, but are *mitzvos* that are observed on that [first] day alone, such as all the factors that disqualify [any of the Four Species] on the first day alone. If [the stringencies associated with this *mitzvah*] would not be observed on the second day, this would not be considered as demeaning the second day of the festival, for these *mitzvos* are not dependent on the essence of the sanctity of the day at all. [The rationale is that] the Torah did not make the *mitzvah* of taking the *lulav* dependent on the

90. Taking the *lulav* on the second day is certainly a Rabbinic ordinance. Nevertheless, it can be explained that our Sages ordained that in the Diaspora, the *lulav* should be taken on the second day of *Yom-Tov* — as opposed to the days of *Chol HaMoed* — with all the stringencies required on the first day (*Turei Zahav* 649:11).

91. For we operate according to a fixed calendar.

92. More specifically, a day of *Chol HaMoed.*

93. This entire subject is clarified in the text and footnotes of sec. 600:1 above.

המנהגים (טירנא) ריש מנהגי סוכות (ע' קכא). דעה הא' בלבוש סס"ה. **קמב** ריטב"א כט, ב ד"ה לולב (בבאור דעה זו). **קמג** רמב"ם פ"ח ה"ט, לפירוש המ"מ שם. דעה הב' בריטב"א שם, ובר"ן (יד, א) סוף דיבור הראשון. דרכי משה שם, בשם תרומת הדשן סי' צה, והר"א מפראג. **קמד** כדלעיל סי' תר ס"א (לקיים מנהג אבותיהם), וש"נ. **קמה** כדלעיל סי' תצ ס"א. וראה לעיל סי' תעה ס"ל (דאין לחלק בחיוב מצה בין ליל יו"ט שני לראשון). סי' תפט סכ"ט (איסור חדש בי"ז, כאבותינו). סי' תקפו סכ"א (שופר הפסול בראשון, פסול גם ביו"ט שני. וראה מ"א סוס"י תקפו).

יוֹם טוֹב אֶלָּא מֵחֲמַת שֶׁהוּא יוֹם הָרִאשׁוֹן, שֶׁנֶּאֱמַר[6] "וּלְקַחְתֶּם לָכֶם בַּיּוֹם הָרִאשׁוֹן".[קמו]

וּלְעִנְיַן הֲלָכָה – סְפֵק בְּרָכוֹת לְהָקֵל,[23] לְפִיכָךְ כָּל הַפְּסוּלִין בָּרִאשׁוֹן – נְטָלִין בְּיוֹם טוֹב שֵׁנִי שֶׁל גָּלֻיּוֹת בְּלֹא בְּרָכָה.[קמז, 94] וּמִכָּל מָקוֹם, אִם אֶפְשָׁר יִקַּח מֵחֲבֵרוֹ לוּלָב וּמִינָיו כְּשֵׁרִים בְּמַתָּנָה עַל מְנָת לְהַחֲזִיר[קמח] (כְּדֵי לָחוּשׁ לַסְּבָרָא הָרִאשׁוֹנָה דְּשָׁאוּל פָּסוּל בְּיוֹם טוֹב שֵׁנִי) וִיבָרֵךְ עָלָיו,[קמט] וְאַחַר כָּךְ יִטֹּל אֶת שֶׁלּוֹ[קנ] (וְיֹאמַר בּוֹ הַלֵּל עִם הַצִּבּוּר[קנא]):

כב כָּל אַרְבָּעָה מִינִים הַפְּסוּלִין וּפְסוּלָן נִכָּר בְּגוּפָן,[קנב] כְּגוֹן שֶׁפְּסוּלִין מֵחֲמַת חֶסְרוֹן אוֹ מֵחֲמַת הִדּוּר, אִם הוּא שְׁעַת הַדְּחָק שֶׁאִי אֶפְשָׁר לִמְצֹא מִינִין אֲחֵרִים כְּשֵׁרִים – מֻתָּר לְבָרֵךְ עַל מִינִים הַפְּסוּלִים אֵלּוּ[קנג] אֲפִלּוּ בַּיּוֹם הָרִאשׁוֹן,[קנד] לְפִי שֶׁכָּל פְּסוּלִים אֵלּוּ לֹא נִתְפָּרְשׁוּ הֵיטֵב

fact that [the first day] is celebrated as a festival, but on the fact that it is the first [of the seven days of the festival], as it is written,[6] "And on the first day, you shall take for yourselves...."

With regard to the *halachah,* [we follow the principle that] whenever there is a doubt whether a blessing is required, the lenient ruling prevails [and the blessing is not recited].[23] Therefore, [if] on the second day of *Yom-Tov* [that is celebrated] in the Diaspora one has [Four Species] with factors that would disqualify them on the first day [of *Yom-Tov*], they should be taken without a blessing.[94]

Nevertheless, if possible, one should take a valid set of the *lulav* and the other species that belong to a friend [and these should be given to him] as a gift with the intent that it be returned, (out of deference to the first opinion which maintains that a borrowed *lulav* is invalid on the second day of *Yom-Tov*). One should recite the blessing over [the borrowed] *lulav* and then take his own (while reciting *Hallel* together with the congregation).

22 In a pressing situation, in which one cannot find valid specimens, one may recite a blessing over invalid specimens of these Four Species when the disqualifying factor in any of them is physically apparent, e.g., they are invalid because their substance is lacking or because they are not "beautiful." [This applies] even on the first day.

[The rationale is that] these disqualifying factors were not fully specified in the Torah. For

94. The rationale is that, according to the first opinion, such specimens are invalid and the blessing would have been recited in vain.

However, *Pri Megadim: Mishbetzos Zahav* (649:10) asks: In a pressing situation, as stated in subsection 22 below, even on the first day one may use and recite a blessing over specimens that are invalid. What then is the difference between the first day and the second?

In resolution, that source continues: On the first day, one must seek out specimens of the Four Species that are valid according to all the specifications. On the second day, it is [minimally] sufficient to use specimens that would be disqualified on the first day and not to recite a blessing.

קמו ריטב"א ור"ן שם (בביאור דעה זו). קמז מסקנת הר"ן שם. שו"ע סס"ה. קמח דמועיל אף ביום הראשון, כמבואר בשו"ע סי' תרנח ס"ד. קמט רמ"א שם, כפירוש הט"ז ס"ק יא. קנ דרכי משה שם. מ"א ס"ק כג. קנא ראה לעיל סי' תפח ס"ג. קנב טור (מחמת מום). ב"י ד"ה ונראה שדייק. ולבוש ס"ו. מ"א ס"ק כד. וראה סכ"ג (בדעה הב': מחמת מום). קנג תוס' לא, סע"א ד"ה לא. רא"ש פ"ג סי"ד, בשם הר"י והרי"ד. שלטי הגבורים (יד, א) אות ג בשם ריא"ז. טור ודעה הב' בלבוש שם. קנד מ"מ פ"ח ה"א בשם הגאונים. כל בו הל' לולב סי' עב (מא, א), בשם הר"ם. קנה רא"ש שם. וראה גם ר"ן (יג, ב) ד"ה

בַּכָּתוּב, אַף עַל פִּי שֶׁכָּתוּב בַּתּוֹרָה "הָדָר", מִכָּל מָקוֹם לֹא פֵּרֵשׁ הַכָּתוּב מַהוּ הָדָר וּמַהוּ אֵינוֹ הָדָר, אֶלָּא כָּל פְּסוּלִין אֵלּוּ מְסָרָן הַכָּתוּב לַחֲכָמִים,[קנה] וְהֵם אָמְרוּ שֶׁלֹּא בִּשְׁעַת הַדְּחָק אֲפִלּוּ בְּדִיעֲבַד לֹא יָצָא, כְּדֵי שֶׁיִּהְיוּ יִשְׂרָאֵל זְהִירִים בְּמִצְווֹת וְיַחַזְרוּ אַחַר מִינִים הַכְּשֵׁרִים, אֲבָל בִּשְׁעַת הַדְּחָק כֵּיוָן שֶׁאִי אֶפְשָׁר בְּעִנְיָן אַחֵר – מְבָרְכִין עַל אֵלּוּ הַפְּסוּלִין,[קנו] שֶׁלֹּא תִשְׁתַּכַּח תּוֹרַת אֶתְרוֹג[95] מִיִּשְׂרָאֵל:[קנז, 96]

although, [for example,] the Torah describes [the tree of an *esrog* as] "beautiful," it does not specify what is considered "beautiful" and what is not. Instead, the Torah left the definition of these disqualifying factors to the Sages. They determined that when the situation is not pressing, one cannot fulfill his obligation [using such specimens] even after the fact — so that the Jewish people would be careful in their observance of the *mitzvos* and seek out valid specimens of the Four Species. In a pressing situation, since there is no alternative, a blessing may be recited on such invalid specimens, so that the concept of *esrog*[95] should not be forgotten by the Jewish people.[96]

כג אֲבָל כָּל הַפְּסוּלִין מֵחֲמַת שֶׁאֵינָן מִינָן כְּלָל, כְּגוֹן הֲדַס שׁוֹטֶה[97] וְהַצַּפְצָפָה[קנח, 98] וְאֶתְרוֹג הַמֻּרְכָּב[קנט, 99] (אוֹ מֵחֲמַת שֶׁאֵין שְׁמָן עֲלֵיהֶם כְּגוֹן נָשְׁרוּ רֹב עָלִין[קס, 100]), אוֹ מֵחֲמַת שֶׁהֵן חֲסֵרִין הַשִּׁעוּר,[קסא] דְּהַיְנוּ אֶתְרוֹג פָּחוּת מִכַּבֵּיצָה,[101] וְלוּלָב פָּחוּת מֵאַרְבָּעָה טְפָחִים וַהֲדַס וַעֲרָבָה פָּחוּת מִשְּׁלֹשָׁה טְפָחִים,[קסב, 102] אוֹ מֵחֲמַת מִצְוָה הַבָּאָה בַּעֲבֵרָה,[קסג, 103]

23 [Different rules apply with regard to] all the specimens that are disqualified because of [any of the following reasons]:

they are not of the species required, e.g., a deviant myrtle[97] or a *tzaftzafah*[98] or an *esrog* produced by grafting;[99]

(they are no longer called by their name, e.g., [a twig of myrtle or willow] that has lost most of its leaves;)[100]

they lack the minimum size required, i.e., an *esrog* smaller than an egg,[101] a *lulav* less than four handbreadths [long], or a myrtle or a willow twig that is less than three handbreadths [long];[102]

the *mitzvah* comes about through a transgression;[103]

---

95. I.e., of the Four Species.

96. I.e., "beautiful" is a relative term, and in a pressing situation even problematic specimens may be considered "beautiful." See *Sukkah* 31b.

97. See sec. 646:2.

98. Instead of the required species *(aravah);* see sec. 647:3.

99. See sec. 648:31.

100. See sec. 646:4, sec. 647:5. Similar laws apply with regard to a *lulav.*

101. See sec. 648:29.

102. See sec. 650:1.

103. Subsection 4 above states that a stolen *lulav* is invalid. In contrast to the authorities who maintain that from the second day onward — when there is no obligation to use one's own species — one may use a stolen *lulav* without reciting

ומיהו (לענין פסול הדר בכל ז'). **קנו** רא"ש שם. **קנז** ראה גמרא לא, ב. וכדלקמן סכ"ג לדעה הב' (שנוטלים בלא ברכה). **קנח** ריטב"א לא, ב ד"ה אמרו לו (שכשאין שמו עליו לא התירו בשעת הדחק). כט, ב ד"ה לולב (שפסול מטעם אין שמו עליו). ב"י שם, ממשמעות הטור ורבנו ירוחם נתיב ח ח"ג (נט, א). וראה גם לעיל סי' תרמו ס"ב. סי' תרמז ס"ג. **קנט** שגם זה אינו מינו — כדלעיל סי' תרמח סל"א. וראה תשובת מהר"י פאדווא (שמצויין לעיל שם: אפי' בשעת הדחק). **קס** ריטב"א כט, ב שם (שפסול מטעם אין שמו עליו). **קסא** ריטב"א שם. **קסב** כדלעיל סי"ח וש"נ. **קסג** ריטב"א לא, ב שם. דרכי משה ס"ק ד, בשם המנהגים (טירנא) ריש מנהגי סוכות (ע' קכב). מ"א ס"ק כד.

אוֹ מֵחֲמַת עֲבוֹדָה זָרָה,[קסד,104] אוֹ מֵחֲמַת שֶׁאֵין הָאֶתְרוֹג רָאוּי לַאֲכִילָה[קסה,105] — כָּל אֵלּוּ אֵין נוֹטְלִין בִּשְׁעַת הַדְּחָק אֲפִלּוּ בְּלֹא בְרָכָה,[106] גְּזֵרָה שֶׁמָּא יִטְעוּ וְיֹאמְרוּ שֶׁגַּם מִינִים אֵלּוּ כְּשֵׁרִים הֵן וּלְכָךְ הֵן נוֹטְלִין [וְיִטְעוּ לְהַכְשִׁירָן] אַף שֶׁלֹּא בִּשְׁעַת הַדְּחָק.[קסו] אֲבָל כְּשֶׁהַפְּסוּל הוּא מֵחֲמַת מוּם שֶׁיֵּשׁ בּוֹ חֶסְרוֹן בְּגוּפוֹ אוֹ שֶׁאֵינוֹ הָדָר – הַכֹּל רוֹאִים אֶת הַמּוּם, שֶׁהֶהָדוּר וְהַחֶסְרוֹן הוּא דָּבָר נִרְאֶה לָעֵינַיִם, וְהַכֹּל יוֹדְעִים שֶׁאֵין מַכְשִׁירִין אוֹתָם אֶלָּא לְפִי שֶׁהִיא שְׁעַת הַדְּחָק, שֶׁהֲרֵי בִּשְׁאָר כָּל הַשָּׁנִים מַחֲזִירִין אַחַר שְׁלֵמִים וַהֲדוּרִים.[קסז]

the specimens had been associated with idolatrous worship;[104]

the *esrog* is not fit to be eaten.[105]

None of the above should be taken, even in a pressing situation, and even if no blessing is recited.[106] This safeguard was ordained for fear that people might mistakenly think that such specimens, too, are valid and are being used for that reason. They might [then] mistakenly consider them valid even in a situation which is not pressing.

When, by contrast, [one of the Four Species is] disqualified because it is lacking in substance or is not "beautiful," everyone can see the blemish; the lack of beauty or of substance is overtly apparent. Everyone realizes that they are being considered acceptable only because of a pressing situation, as [indicated by the fact that] in other years people seek out specimens that are complete and "beautiful."

וְיֵשׁ חוֹלְקִין[קסח] עַל כָּל זֶה וְאוֹמְרִים, דְּאַף הַפְּסוּלִין מֵחֲמַת מוּם – אֵין מְבָרְכִין עֲלֵיהֶם לְעֵת הַדְּחָק, אֶלָּא נוֹטְלִין אוֹתָן בְּלֹא בְרָכָה לְזִכָּרוֹן בְּעָלְמָא, שֶׁלֹּא תִשְׁתַּכַּח תּוֹרַת אֶתְרוֹג.[107]

Some authorities differ with this approach entirely. Even in a pressing situation, they maintain that a blessing should not be recited even over specimens whose disqualification is a [visible] blemish. Instead, [they argue,] one should use them without reciting a blessing, merely as a remembrance, so that the concept of *esrog* should not be forgotten.[107]

וְיֵשׁ מְקוֹמוֹת[קסט] שֶׁנּוֹהֲגִין כִּסְבָרָא הָרִאשׁוֹנָה. וּבְאֵלּוּ הַמְּדִינוֹת[108] נוֹהֲגִין בְּכָל הַפְּסוּלִין כִּסְבָרָא הָאַחֲרוֹנָה, חוּץ

In certain places, it is customary to follow the first [and more lenient] view. In these countries[108] we follow the latter view with regard to all

---

the blessing, the Alter Rebbe rules that such a *lulav* may never be used. For a parallel situation regarding *tefillin,* see sec. 25:35.

104. See subsections 11-14 above.

105. See subsection 15 above.

106. I.e., to take specimens that are disqualified for these reasons — in commemoration of the *mitzvah* — is not merely undesirable, but forbidden.

107. I.e., according to this view, taking the invalid specimens in hand is not a *mitzvah,* but a commemorative act. In that vein, the *Mishnah Berurah* 649:53 states that if a person possesses only two or three of the Four Species, he should hold them — without reciting a blessing — during the recitation of *Hallel.*

108. I.e., in the Ashkenazic communities of Eastern Europe.

קסד דלעיל סי"א־ג, שפסול מטעם שאין בו כשיעור. קסה דלעיל סט"ו. קסו כמו בפריש ורמון שבגמרא לא, ב. לבוש שם. ב"ח ד"ה כתב. מ"א שם. קסז לבוש שם. קסח הראב"ד בהשגות פ"ח ה"א, ובתמים דעים סי' רלג (אחר חזרה. ראה תשובות ופסקים ע' כו וע' כח). הובא ברא"ש שם ובטור. מסקנת הב"י ד"ה ולענין מעשה. שו"ע ס"ו. דעה הא' בלבוש ס"ו. קסט שו"ת רדב"ז ח"ד סי' אלף קפב. הובא במ"א ס"ק כה. וראה גם לעיל סי' תרמה סי"ז. סי'

the disqualifying factors, except for a dried-out *lulav* and myrtle twigs. For if one would not be able to recite a blessing over [such species] in a pressing situation, a blessing would never be recited over the *mitzvah* of *lulav*, since fresh *lulavim* and myrtle twigs are not commonly found in these countries.

מִן לוּלָב וַהֲדַס הַיְבֵשִׁים[קע] שֶׁאִם לֹא הָיוּ מְבָרְכִין עֲלֵיהֶם בִּשְׁעַת הַדְּחָק – עַל הָרֹב לֹא הָיוּ מְבָרְכִין כְּלָל עַל מִצְוַת לוּלָב, שֶׁאֵין לוּלָבִין לַחִין וְאֵין הֲדַסִּים לַחִים מְצוּיִים בִּמְדִינוֹת אֵלּוּ:[קעא]

24 It is customary in these countries to recite a blessing over dried-out *lulavim* and myrtle twigs even when there are other fresh ones available in the town. The rationale for this custom is that even those that are called fresh are not entirely fresh, but are merely somewhat moist. Thus those that are called fresh are very similar to those that are dried out. By contrast, wherever there are specimens that are actually fresh,[109] one should not recite a blessing on dried-out specimens, even if they are not entirely dried out but are somewhat moist.

If one transgressed and recited a blessing on such specimens, it could be argued that one must recite a blessing again over fresh ones. After all, [the Sages] granted license to recite a blessing over dried-out species only in a pressing situation, and when the situation is not pressing, one cannot fulfill his obligation [with dried-out specimens] even after the fact. Here, since the blessing could have been recited over fresh specimens, this individual did not fulfill his obligation when he used dried-out ones. Nevertheless, since the dried-out specimens were not entirely dried out, it may be said that he fulfilled his obligation after the fact. Therefore, he should use the fresh specimens without reciting a blessing. If, by contrast, one recited a blessing over specimens that are entirely dried-out in a

כד וְנוֹהֲגִין בִּמְדִינוֹת אֵלּוּ לְבָרֵךְ עַל לוּלָב וַהֲדַס יְבֵשִׁים אַף בְּמָקוֹם שֶׁיֵּשׁ אֲחֵרִים לַחִים בָּעִיר.[קעב] וְטַעַם הַמִּנְהָג הוּא, מִשּׁוּם שֶׁגַּם הַלַּחִים אֵינָן לַחִים גְּמוּרִים, רַק שֶׁיֵּשׁ בָּהֶם מְעוּט לַחוּת, וְאִם כֵּן הַלַּחִין וְהַיְבֵשִׁין הֵן דּוֹמִין כִּמְעַט זֶה לָזֶה. אֲבָל בְּמָקוֹם שֶׁיֵּשׁ לַחִין גְּמוּרִין[109] – אֵין לְבָרֵךְ עַל הַיְבֵשִׁין, אֲפִלּוּ אֵינָן יְבֵשִׁין גְּמוּרִים רַק יֵשׁ בָּהֶם מְעוּט לַחוּת. וְאִם עָבַר וּבֵרַךְ עֲלֵיהֶם – יֵשׁ לְהִסְתַּפֵּק וְלוֹמַר דְּצָרִיךְ לַחֲזֹר וּלְבָרֵךְ עַל הַלַּחִין, שֶׁהֲרֵי לֹא הִתִּירוּ לְבָרֵךְ עַל הַיָּבֵשׁ אֶלָּא בִּשְׁעַת הַדְּחָק אֲבָל שֶׁלֹּא בִּשְׁעַת הַדְּחָק אֲפִלּוּ בְּדִיעֲבַד לֹא יָצָא, וְכָאן שֶׁהָיָה אֶפְשָׁר לְבָרֵךְ עַל הַלַּחִין אִם כֵּן לֹא יָצָא יְדֵי חוֹבָתוֹ בִּיבֵשִׁים, וּמִכָּל מָקוֹם כֵּיוָן שֶׁהַיְבֵשִׁים אֵינָן יְבֵשִׁים גְּמוּרִים – אֶפְשָׁר לוֹמַר דְּיָצָא בְּדִיעֲבַד, וְלָכֵן יִטֹּל אֶת הַלַּחִין בְּלֹא בְּרָכָה.[קעג] אֲבָל אִם בֵּרֵךְ עַל הַיְבֵשִׁים גְּמוּרִים

---

109. Wherever today's advances in travel and communications make fresh specimens obtainable, dried-out ones are invalid.

תרמח סי"ח וש"נ. **קע** יראים השלם סי' תכב (רמד, א: בלולב). הובא במרדכי סי' תשנ (לולב והדס). הגהות מיימוניות פ"ח אות ד (הדס). רמ"א ס"ו (אף בהדס). **קעא** ראה שו"ת משאת בנימין סי' יז. רמ"א סי' תרמה ס"ה. לעיל סי' תרמה סט"ז. **קעב** אגור סי' א'ז (לענין לולב). רמ"א ס"ו. **קעג** משאת בנימין סי' יז. מ"א ס"ק כו. אליה זוטא ס"ק ט.

בִּמְקוֹם שֶׁיֵּשׁ לַחִין גְּמוּרִין — לֹא יָצָא יְדֵי חוֹבָתוֹ, וְצָרִיךְ לַחֲזֹר וּלְבָרֵךְ עַל הַלַּחִין:[קעד]

place in which fresh specimens are available, he did not fulfill his obligation and he must recite a second blessing over the fresh species.

סימן תרנ שִׁעוּר הֲדַס וַעֲרָבָה וּבוֹ ב׳ סְעִיפִים:

SECTION 650 The Required Measure of the Myrtle and Willow Twigs. (1–2)

א שִׁעוּר אֹרֶךְ בַּדֵּי הֲדַס וַעֲרָבָה — אֵין פָּחוֹת מִשְּׁלשָׁה טְפָחִים[א,1] שֶׁהֵם י״ב גּוּדָלִין,[ב,2] וְשִׁדְרוֹ[3] שֶׁל הַלּוּלָב — אֵין פָּחוֹת מֵאַרְבָּעָה טְפָחִים, כְּדֵי שֶׁיִּהְיֶה שִׁדְרוֹ שֶׁל לוּלָב יוֹצֵא לְמַעְלָה מֵהַהֲדַס וַעֲרָבָה טֶפַח כְּדֵי נִעְנוּעַ,[ג] שֶׁטֶּפַח זֶה הַיּוֹצֵא לְמַעְלָה מֵהָאֲגֻדָּה[4] (פֵּרוּשׁ שְׁלשָׁה מִינִים אֵלּוּ בְּיַחַד נִקְרָא אֲגֻדָּה[ד,5]) הוּא הַמְנַעֲנֵעַ,[ה] וְטֶפַח זֶה צָרִיךְ שֶׁיְּהֵא מֵהַשִּׁדְרָה עַצְמָהּ, לְבַד מִן הֶעָלִין הָאֲרֻכִּים הַיּוֹצְאִים לְמַעְלָה לְאַחַר שֶׁכָּלְתָה הַשִּׁדְרָה.[ו]

וְיֵשׁ אוֹמְרִים[ז] שֶׁטְּפָחִים אֵלּוּ הֵן קְטַנִּים שֶׁאֵין בְּכָל טֶפַח רַק שְׁלשָׁה גּוּדָלִין וּשְׁלִישׁ,[6] וְנִמְצָא שֶׁשְּׁלשָׁה טְפָחִים אֵין בָּהֶם רַק עֲשָׂרָה גּוּדָלִין, וְהַלּוּלָב י״ג גּוּדָלִין וּשְׁלִישׁ.[ח] וְיֵשׁ לִסְמֹךְ עַל דִּבְרֵיהֶם

1 The minimum length that is required for the myrtle and willow twigs is three handbreadths,[1] i.e., 12 thumbbreadths.[2] The *shidrah* (the spine)[3] of the *lulav* may not be shorter than four handbreadths, so that the spine will extend [at least] a handbreadth above the myrtle and willow twigs, enabling [the *lulav*] to be shaken, for what is shaken is this handbreadth that extends beyond the bound set.[4] (The three species together are called "the bound set."[5]) This handbreadth must be part of the actual spine, without including the long leaves that continue upward beyond the spine.

Some authorities maintain that [it is sufficient that] these handbreadths be small, three-and-a-third thumbbreadths each.[6] Thus [the length of the myrtle and willow twigs] need not be more than ten thumbbreadths, and [the minimum length of] the *lulav*, thirteen-and-a-third thumbbreadths. This view may be

---

1. In the original, *tefachim;* see *Sukkah* 32b.

2. A thumbbreadth *(gudal;* often: *agudal)* is 2.04 cm. (R. Avraham Chayim Naeh, *Shiurei Torah,* p. 276). Thus the required length of each twig, not counting the length of the leaves that extend beyond the end of the stem, is at least 24.5 cm. (approx. 9½ inches).

3. The smooth central shaft is so called, for just as one's ribs fan out from either side of the spine, the leaves of the *lulav* branch out from either side of the *shidrah*.

4. *Sukkah* 29b.

5. In the original, *agudah*.

6. If a cubit of five handbreadths is divided by six, each *tefach* comes to 5/6 of a regular *tefach*. See *Sukkah* 32b and *Rashi* there.

קעד מ״א שם, ממשמעות המשאת בנימין שם.

סימן תרנ: א ברייתא וגמרא לב, ב. שו״ע ס״א. ב ת״ק בברייתא שם. משמעות הרי״ף (טו, א), והרמב״ם פ״ז ה״ח (מגיד משנה שם). דרכי משה ס״ק א, בשם המנהגים (טירנא) ריש מנהגי סוכות (ע׳ קכא). דעה הג׳ בשו״ע שם. רמ״א ס״א (שכן נוהגין לכתחלה). ולענין שיעור הגודל, ראה לעיל סי׳ יא ס״ו. ג משנה כט, ב. לפירוש רבי יוחנן בגמרא שם. רא״ש פ״ג סי׳ ז. רמב״ם שם. שו״ע שם. ד ראה יגדיל תורה (נ.י.) נ ע׳ נב. ה רש״י שם ד״ה אימא. ו רש״י שם ד״ה שדרו, בדעת רבי יוחנן שם. רמב״ם שם. טור ולבוש ס״א. ז ר׳ טרפון בברייתא שם, כפירוש רבין בגמרא שם, וכשמואל שפסק כר׳ טרפון. הרי״ץ גיאת הל׳ לולב (עמ׳ צו). השגות הראב״ד שם. רא״ש פ״ג ס״ז. טור ודעה הא׳ בשו״ע שם. ח הרי״ץ גיאת שם (שגם הטפח הרביעי של הלולב הוא קטן). רש״י שם ד״ה

בִּשְׁעַת הַדְּחָק.[ט] וְכֵן בְּדִיעֲבַד שֶׁכְּבָר בֵּרַךְ עַל אֲגֻדָּה שֶׁאֵין בָּהּ רַק כְּשִׁעוּר זֶה – יָצָא, וְאֵין צָרִיךְ לַחֲזֹר וּלְבָרֵךְ, אֶלָּא יִטֹּל מִינִים כְּשֵׁרִים בְּלֹא בְּרָכָה:[7]

relied upon in a pressing situation. Similarly after the event, if one already recited the blessing on a bound set [of the three species] that is only of the above length, he has discharged his obligation, and is not required to recite a blessing again. He should, however, take in hand valid [twigs of the desired length, though] without reciting a blessing.[7]

ב לְמַעְלָה – אֵין לָהֶם שִׁעוּר, שֶׁאִם רוֹצֶה לְהוֹסִיף עַל שִׁעוּרָן – הָרְשׁוּת בְּיָדוֹ לְהוֹסִיף כַּמָּה שֶׁיִּרְצֶה,[י] וּבִלְבַד שֶׁיְּהֵא שִׁדְרוֹ שֶׁל לוּלָב יוֹצֵא לְמַעְלָה מֵהָאֲגֻדָּה טֶפַח כְּדֵי נִעְנוּעוֹ:[יא,8]

2 There is no upper limit to the length [of the myrtle and willow twigs]. One may add beyond their minimum length as much as he desires, provided that the spine of the *lulav* continues upward [at least] a handbreadth beyond the bound set [of the three species], to enable [the *lulav*] to be shaken.[8]

7. I.e., he should perform the act that fulfills the *mitzvah* again, to make certain that he has fulfilled his obligation. The blessing is not repeated, however, because if he fulfilled his obligation the first time, the present blessing would be recited in vain.

8. As mentioned in subsection 1 above, the actual spine of the *lulav*, and not merely its upper leaves, must continue a handbreadth higher than the myrtle and willow twigs. Hence, if one uses very long twigs that reach up close to the upper extremity of the spine of the *lulav*, their lower ends must be trimmed. (See fig. 31.)

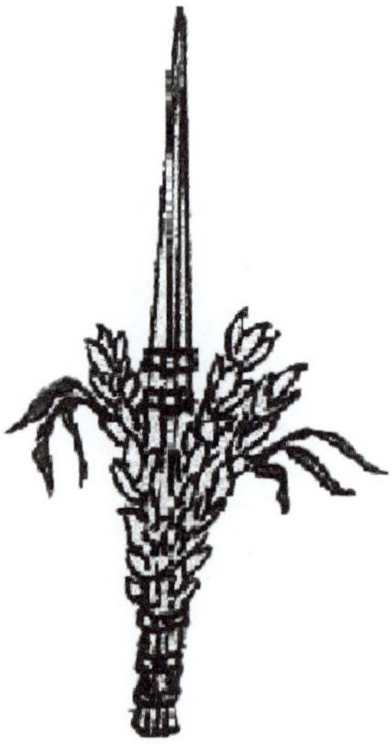

Fig. 31: The lower ends of the myrtle and willow twigs have been clipped to size (see sec. 650:2).

אמה. תוס' ד"ה צא. ריטב"א שם ד"ה גופא, ור"ן (טו, א) ד"ה מיהו, בשם רבנו יונה. טור ודעה הא' בשו"ע שם. **ט** רמ"א שם (שרק לכתחלה נוהגין כדעה הא'). וראה לעיל סי' תרמט סכ"ג, שאם הם פחותים מכשיעור, אין ניטלין אף בשעת הדחק אפילו בלא ברכה. **י** רי"ף שם, מגמרא מנחות מב, א. רא"ש שם. רמב"ם שם. טור ושו"ע ס"ב. וראה גם לעיל סי' תרמח סכ"ט (לענין אתרוג). **יא** רי"ץ גיאת הל' לולב (עמ' צז). ריטב"א שם ד"ה ור"י. ר"ן שם ד"ה אמר. שו"ע שם (ויש מי שאומר). לבוש ס"ב. וראה גם לקמן סי' תרנא סי"א.

סימן תרנא דִּין נְטִילַת לוּלָב וּבִרְכָתוֹ וּבוֹ י"ז סְעִיפִים:

א מִצְוַת[א] אַרְבָּעָה מִינִים הַלָּלוּ הוּא, שֶׁיִּטֹּל כָּל אֶחָד וְאֶחָד מִיִּשְׂרָאֵל[ב,1] אֶתְרוֹג אֶחָד בְּיָדוֹ אַחַת וּבְיָדוֹ הַשֵּׁנִית[ג] יִטֹּל לוּלָב אֶחָד וּשְׁנֵי בַּדֵּי עֲרָבָה וּשְׁלֹשָׁה בַּדֵּי הֲדַס.[ד,2]

וּבִשְׁעַת הַדְּחָק[ה] שֶׁאִי אֶפְשָׁר לִמְצֹא שְׁלֹשָׁה בַּדֵּי הֲדַס – יוֹצֵא יְדֵי חוֹבָתוֹ בְּבַד אֶחָד,[ו,3] אֲפִלּוּ נִקְטַם רֹאשׁוֹ[ז] (עַיֵּן סִימָן תרמ"ו[ח]).

SECTION 651 Law[s] Relating to the Taking of the *Lulav* and the Blessing Recited. (1–17)

1 The *mitzvah* involving these Four Species is for every Jew[1] to take an *esrog* in one hand, and in his other hand to take one *lulav,* two willow twigs, and three myrtle twigs.[2] In a pressing situation, when it is impossible to find three myrtle twigs, one may fulfill his obligation with one [myrtle] twig,[3] even if its tip has been snipped off. (See sec. 646[:11].)

---

1. *Sukkah* 41b.

2. See sec. 645:1.

Unless one takes all Four Species, no *mitzvah* has been fulfilled *(Menachos* 3:6*).* Indeed, in a classic homily that likens the Four Species to four kinds of Jews, the willow represents those individuals who are distinguished neither for their study of the Torah nor for their observance of the commandments. Yet the *mitzvah* that also includes the prestigious *lulav* and *esrog* and *hadassim* cannot be observed unless they join forces with the humble willow *(Perishah, Orach Chayim* 619:1*).*

For further manifestations of this concept see also sec. 619:1, in the context of the laws of Yom Kippur, in the present Bilingual Edition.

More than three myrtle twigs may be taken. See the *Shulchan Aruch* of R. Yosef Caro, sec. 651:15. Though that source concludes with the recommendation that one should not take more than three myrtle twigs, this practice was in fact widespread among Kabbalists and chassidim. Indeed, this was the practice of the Rebbes of *Chabad* and of some individuals who were meticulous in their observance of the *mitzvos.* In 5748 (1987) the Rebbe recommended that all chassidim should take at least three additional myrtle twigs.

3. *Sukkah* 34b explains the derivation of this leniency as follows: One *esrog* is taken because the verse *(Vayikra* 23:40*)* speaks of "the fruit of a beautiful tree," implying one fruit. In the phrase that means "fronds of a date-palm," the word כפת *(kapos)* is written without the penultimate letter *vav* that normally indicates its plural form. This implies that only one *lulav* is required. "Willows of the brook" *(arvei nachal)* is written in the plural; hence two twigs are taken. And in the same verse, the Hebrew phrase that means "and a branch of a braided tree" is expressed in three words (וענף עץ עבת), suggesting that three myrtle twigs should be taken. Nevertheless, since this requirement is not explicit, but rather derived through Rabbinic exegesis, it can be bypassed in a pressing situation *(Levush* 651:1*).*

Divrei Nechemiah (sec. 651, gloss 2) writes that the same law applies to the willow: if one used a single twig, he has fulfilled the *mitzvah.* However, the wording here appears to indicate that the leniency applies only to the myrtle, and even in a pressing situation, two willow twigs are required. The rationale for the distinction is that the plural wording in the phrase that refers to the willows implies that the obligation to use two willow twigs is of Scriptural origin *(Hadar Hu LeChol Chassidav).*

א לכללות סימן זה — ראה דברי נחמיה או"ח עד, ב ואילך. **ב** ברייתא מא, ב. תוס' כט, ב ד"ה בעינן. רא"ש פ"ג ס"ג. טור ושו"ע ס"א. וראה דברי נחמיה שם ס"א וקו"א ס"ק א. וראה לעיל סי' רצו קו"א ס"ק ג, שאף שנשים פטורות יכולות לברך (כל ז' ימי החג). **ג** גמרא לד, ב (שלא יהא אתרוג עמהם באגודה, כדלקמן בהמשך הסעיף). לז, ב (לולב בימין ואתרוג בשמאל, כדלקמן סי"ג). לפירוש המ"א ס"ק ו. **ד** משנה לד, ב כרבי ישמעאל. רמב"ם פ"ז ה"ז. מגיד משנה שם בשם כל הגאונים. טור ושו"ע שם. **ה** רמ"א ס"א (שבשעת הדחק סגי בחד דלא קטום). מ"א ס"ק א (שבשעת הדחק אפילו בחד קטום). וראה דברי נחמיה שם ס"ב וקו"א ס"ק ג. **ו** רמב"ן בהל' לולב סוף ענין הדס קטום, כרבי עקיבא שם. ריטב"א מט, ב סד"ה מ"ט. ארחות חיים הל' לולב סי' יב. רמ"א שם. ולענין ערבה ראה דברי נחמיה שם קו"א סק"ב. **ז** רמב"ן שם. מ"א שם. **ח** סעיף יא (דין הדס שנקטם ראשו). **ט** מאירי לז, ב סד"ה הדס במחובר, בשם חכמי לוניל. ארחות חיים

If one took these three species together with the *esrog* in the same hand, he has not fulfilled his obligation, because after [the verse in question[4]] speaks of "the fruit of a beautiful tree," it proceeds to speak of "fronds of a date-palm," but without including the prefix *vav;* i.e., כַּפֹּת *(kapos* — "fronds"*)* instead of וְכַפֹּת *(vechapos* — "and fronds"*).* [This implies a lack of conjunction.] In contrast, when the myrtle and willow twigs are added to the list, that prefix appears. From this one can infer that the *esrog* must be alone, not bound together with the *lulav* and the other species — [unlike] the myrtle and willow twigs, which the verse introduces by the prefix of a *vav*, implying that they should be joined to the previous subject, [namely, the *lulav*]. For this reason, they may be bound together with it. (Indeed, this is the optimum manner of performing the *mitzvah,* as will be explained.[5])

Some authorities differ with [the above conclusion] and maintain that the Torah only excluded the actual binding of the *esrog* together with the *lulav* and the other species in one bound set. As long as they are not actually tied together in one bound set, there is no objection to holding them [together] in one hand and [by doing so] one has fulfilled the *mitzvah* according to Scriptural Law.

With regard to the *halachah,* since a Scriptural *mitzvah* is involved, one should be stringent. [Even] if one recited the blessing and then held the two in one hand, one should take them again in separate hands. A second blessing should not, however, be recited, for whenever there is a doubt whether a blessing is required, the lenient ruling prevails [and the blessing is not recited],[6] since it is possible that he fulfilled his obligation with the first blessing.

וְאִם נָטַל שְׁלֹשָׁה מִינִים אֵלּוּ עִם הָאֶתְרוֹג בְּיָדוֹ הָאַחַת – לֹא יָצָא יְדֵי חוֹבָתוֹ,[ט] שֶׁהֲרֵי אַחֲרֵי שֶׁנֶּאֱמַר[4] "פְּרִי עֵץ הָדָר" נֶאֱמַר "כַּפֹּת תְּמָרִים" בְּלֹא וא"ו, כְּלוֹמַר שֶׁלֹּא נֶאֱמַר "וְכַפֹּת" כְּמוֹ שֶׁנֶּאֱמַר "וַעֲנַף וגו' וְעַרְבֵי וגו'", מִכָּאן אַתָּה לָמֵד שֶׁהָאֶתְרוֹג הוּא צָרִיךְ לִהְיוֹת בִּפְנֵי עַצְמוֹ, וְלֹא יִהְיֶה בַּאֲגֻדָּה אַחַת עִם הַלּוּלָב עִם מִינָיו כְּמוֹ הַהֲדַס וַעֲרָבָה שֶׁנִּכְתַּב בָּהֶן וא"ו הַמּוֹסִיף עַל עִנְיָן רִאשׁוֹן, וּלְכָךְ מֻתָּר לְאָגְדָן עִם הַלּוּלָב[י] (וְאַדְּרַבָּה מִצְוָה מִן הַמֻּבְחָר הוּא לְאָגְדָן כְּמוֹ שֶׁיִּתְבָּאֵר[יא,5]).

וְיֵשׁ חוֹלְקִין[יב] עַל זֶה וְאוֹמְרִים, שֶׁלֹּא מִעֵט הַכָּתוּב אֶלָּא שֶׁלֹּא יְהֵא הָאֶתְרוֹג נֶאֱגָד עִם הַלּוּלָב וּמִינָיו בַּאֲגֻדָּה אַחַת מַמָּשׁ, אֲבָל כָּל שֶׁאֵינוֹ אוֹגְדוֹ מַמָּשׁ בַּאֲגֻדָּה אַחַת אַף עַל פִּי שֶׁנּוֹטְלָן בְּיָדוֹ אַחַת – אֵין בְּכָךְ כְּלוּם, וְיוֹצֵא יְדֵי חוֹבָתוֹ מִן הַתּוֹרָה.

וּלְעִנְיַן הֲלָכָה – יֵשׁ לְהַחְמִיר בְּשֶׁל תּוֹרָה, וְאִם בֵּרַךְ וְנָטַל שְׁנֵיהֶם בְּיָדוֹ אַחַת – יַחֲזֹר וְיִטְּלֵם בִּשְׁתֵּי יָדָיו בְּלֹא בְּרָכָה,[יג] דִּסְפֵק בְּרָכוֹת לְהָקֵל,[6] וְשֶׁמָּא יָצָא בַּבְּרָכָה הָרִאשׁוֹנָה:

4. *Vayikra, loc. cit.*

5. In subsection 2.

6. Since binding the *lulav* and its associated species is part of the fulfillment of the *mitzvah,* it should initially not be done by a non-Jew, a woman, nor a child, because they are not obligated to fulfill the *mitzvah* of the *lulav (Magen Avraham* 649:8; *Pri Megadim: Eshel Avraham* 649:8*).* Nevertheless,

שם סי' יט, וכל בו הל' לולב סי' עא (לט, ב), בשם רבנו שלמיה. ב"י ד"ה וכתב עוד. לבוש ס"ב, בשם יש מי שאומרים. מ"א ס"ק י. וראה גם לקמן סט"ו. **י** גמרא לד, ב ורש"י ד"ה יכול. **יא** בסעיף הבא. **יב** ט"ז ס"ק י"ד. אליה רבה ס"ק י בשם אמרכל בשם רבנו ברוך. וראה דברי נחמיה שם סי"ד. **יג** ראה לקמן סי"ג, וש"נ.

ב וּמִצְוָה[יד] מִן הַמֻּבְחָר[טו] לֶאֱגֹד הַלּוּלָב עִם הַהֲדַס וַעֲרָבָה בַּאֲגֻדָּה אַחַת[7] מִשּׁוּם נוֹי,[טז] שֶׁנֶּאֱמַר[יז,8] "זֶה אֵלִי וְאַנְוֵהוּ" — הִתְנָאֵה לְפָנָיו בְּמִצְוֹת:[יח,9]

2 The choicest way of performing the *mitzvah* is to tie the *lulav* together with the myrtle and willow twigs in one bound set,[7] to make them beautiful, for it is written,[8] "This is my G-d and I will glorify Him." [And the Sages interpret this to mean:] "[Perform] the *mitzvos* before Him in a beautiful manner."[9]

ג וּמֻתָּר לְאָגְדוֹ אֲפִלּוּ בְּחוּט וּבִמְשִׁיחָה,[יט] אַף עַל פִּי שֶׁחוּט הָאוֹגֵד הוּא מִין אַחֵר וְאֵינוֹ מִמִּינִים שֶׁבַּלּוּלָב,[10] וַהֲרֵי יֵשׁ כָּאן בְּיָדוֹ חֲמִשָּׁה מִינִים — אַף עַל פִּי כֵן אֵינוֹ עוֹבֵר מִשּׁוּם "בַּל תּוֹסִיף",[11] כֵּיוָן שֶׁהָאִגּוּד אֵינוֹ מֵעִקַּר הַמִּצְוָה[כ] אֶלָּא הוּא הִדּוּר לַמִּצְוָה,[כא] וְלֹא הִזְהִירָה תּוֹרָה אֶלָּא שֶׁלֹּא לְהוֹסִיף בְּעִקַּר הַמִּצְוָה:[כב]

3 One may bind [the three species] together even with a thread or cord, even though it comes from a different species, not from one of the species used for the *lulav*.[10] Though one will then be holding five species in his hand, he is not considered to have transgressed the commandment against adding [to the *mitzvos*].[11] [The rationale is] that the binding is not an essential element of the *mitzvah;* it only beautifies the *mitzvah.* And the Torah only forbade making additions to the essential elements of the *mitzvah.*

ד וּמֻתָּר לֶאֱחֹז אֶת הַלּוּלָב בְּיָדוֹ בַּמָּקוֹם הָאָגוּד בְּשָׁעָה שֶׁאוֹחֲזוֹ לָצֵאת בּוֹ יְדֵי חוֹבָתוֹ, וְאַף עַל פִּי

4 [Even if the three species are held together by a binder of a different substance,] it is permitted to clasp [that part of] the *lulav* when holding it to fulfill the *mitzvah*. Though the

---

though women are exempt from this *mitzvah* because it is a positive obligation that is linked to a particular time *(mitzvas aseh shehazman grama),* a woman who does undertake it has of course fulfilled a *mitzvah.* Indeed, nowadays it is standard practice for women to fulfill this *mitzvah* every day of Sukkos. (See: Commentaries to the *Shulchan Aruch* of R. Yosef Caro, sec. 658:9; and sec. 17:1 and 17:3 in Vol. 1 of the present Bilingual Edition, and footnotes there.)

7. *Shmos* 15:2.

8. *Shabbos* 133b. The examples cited there by the Sages include the *mitzvos* of *sukkah, lulav, shofar* and *tzitzis,* and the script, writing materials and silk wrappings of a Torah scroll. The Rebbe understands this charge to be a Scriptural obligation, not merely a Rabbinic injunction associated with a verse *(Likkutei Sichos,* Vol. 11, p. 241*).*

9. *Sukkah* 36b. Nevertheless, those who are punctilious in their observance of the *mitzvos* bind the *lulav* only with one of its species *(Maharil).* This is the common custom.

10. One of the 613 *mitzvos* (commonly known as *bal tosif* — "not to add") is the prohibition against making additions to any of the *mitzvos.* For example, one may not add a fifth compartment to the head-*tefillin* or place five *tzitzis* on a garment. See: *Sefer HaMitzvos* (negative commandment 313); *Sefer HaChinuch (mitzvah* 454*);* the *Shulchan Aruch* of R. Yosef Caro, sec. 651:14-15.

11. I.e., it is not a *chatzitzah (Sukkah* 37a*).*

יד גמרא [ברייתא] לג, א. וכת"ק באידך ברייתא שם (שאין אגד מעכב). טור ושו"ע ס"א. טו רמב"ם פ"ז ה"ו. טז טור ושו"ע שם. יז שמות טו, ב. גמרא שם. רש"י שם ע"ב ד"ה ופליג. טור ולבוש ס"א. יח גמרא יא, ב. רש"י לג, א ד"ה ואנוהו. טור ולבוש שם. וראה לעיל סי' כד ס"ג (טלית נאה, ציצית נאה, מצות בהידור). לקו"ש חי"א ע' 241 (מהלשון נראה שהוא מן התורה). יט משנה לו, ב כרבי מאיר. רמב"ם פ"ז הי"ב. טור ושו"ע ס"א. כ גמרא שם (שרק הסוברים לולב צריך אגד עובר על בל תוסיף). רש"י שם לז, א ד"ה במינו. רא"ש פ"ג סי' כד. לבוש ס"א. מ"א ס"ק כז. כא כדלעיל ס"ב. כב ראה לעיל סי' לד ס"ד. כג גמרא לז,

binder intervenes between one's hand and the *lulav* with its species, this is of no consequence, because the binder [merely] glorifies and beautifies the *mitzvah*. And whenever something serves to enhance [the *mitzvah*], it is not considered an intervening substance.[12] It is considered subordinate to the *lulav* and its species and thus it is considered as if it were actually part of the *lulav* and its species.

שֶׁהָאָגוּד חוֹצֵץ בֵּין יָדוֹ לַלּוּלָב וּמִינָיו – אֵין בְּכָךְ כְּלוּם, כֵּיוָן שֶׁהָאָגוּד הוּא לְנוֹי וּלְהִדּוּר מִצְוָה, וְכָל שֶׁהוּא לְנוֹי – אֵינוֹ חוֹצֵץ,[כג,12] מִפְּנֵי שֶׁהוּא בָּטֵל לְגַבֵּי הַלּוּלָב וּמִינָיו, וּכְאִלּוּ הוּא מִגּוּף הַלּוּלָב וּמִינָיו:[כד]

5 Even if some of the leaves of the *lulav*, myrtle, or willow fell off and remained [lodged] within the binder and thus intervene between [one's] hand and the *lulav*, this is of no consequence.[13] [The rationale is that] the intervening substance comes from the same species as those used with the *lulav*, and[14] a substance of one type is never considered as an intervention relative to a substance of the same type.[15]

If, however, a substance that does not come from these species intervened between them and [one's] hand while one was taking hold of the *lulav*, he has not fulfilled his obligation by taking the *lulav*.[16] For this reason, one must be very careful to [first] remove the cord that is usually tied around myrtle twigs when they are brought from a distant place.

The myrtle twigs may be bound together with *lulav* leaves or thin willow twigs.[17] Since the substance used as a binder is one of the species [of the *lulav*], it is not considered an intervention.

ה וַאֲפִלּוּ אִם נָשְׁרוּ מֵעֲלֵי הַלּוּלָב אוֹ מֵעֲלֵי הַהֲדַס וַעֲרָבָה וְנִשְׁאֲרוּ הֶעָלִין בְּתוֹךְ הָאָגוּד, בְּעִנְיָן שֶׁעָלִין הַלָּלוּ חוֹצְצִין וּמַפְסִיקִין[כה] בֵּין יָדוֹ לַלּוּלָב[כו] – אֵין בְּכָךְ כְּלוּם,[13] כֵּיוָן שֶׁדָּבָר הַחוֹצֵץ הוּא מִמִּינִים שֶׁבַּלּוּלָב,[14] וּמִין בְּמִינוֹ – אֵינוֹ חוֹצֵץ.[כז,15] אֲבָל אִם דָּבָר שֶׁאֵינוֹ מִמִּינִים הַלָּלוּ מַפְסִיק בֵּינֵיהֶם לְיָדוֹ[כח] בִּשְׁעַת נְטִילָה – לֹא יָצָא יְדֵי חוֹבָתוֹ בִּנְטִילָה זוֹ,[16] לְכָךְ צָרִיךְ לִזָּהֵר מְאֹד לְהָסִיר הַחוּט שֶׁרָגִיל לִהְיוֹת כָּרוּךְ סְבִיב הַהֲדַס כְּשֶׁמְּבִיאִין אוֹתָן מִמֶּרְחַקִּים:[כט]

אֲבָל מֻתָּר לִכְרֹךְ הַהֲדַס בַּעֲלֵי הַלּוּלָב[ל] אוֹ בַּעֲצֵי עֲרָבָה דַּקִּים,[לא,17] כֵּיוָן שֶׁהַכֶּרֶךְ הוּא מִמִּינִים שֶׁבַּלּוּלָב – אֵינוֹ חוֹצֵץ:

12. *op. cit.*, 37b.

13. Likewise, it appears that the bast of a palm tree can also be used as a binder *(Sukkah* 36b*)*.

14. The 19 English words to follow translate the four words in the original, *min bemino eino chotzetz*.

15. The *lulav* must be taken again, and a blessing recited.

16. This refers to an instance in which the additional cord does not facilitate the observance of the *mitzvah*. When a cord is used to bind the three species together, it may even be from another species, as stated in subsection 4 above.

17. This is usually a superfluous leaf stripped from the base of the *lulav*. According to Lubavitch practice, every individual binds his own *lulav* in the *sukkah* on the day preceding the onset of *Yom-Tov (Sefer HaMinhagim: The Book of Chabad-Lubavitch Customs,* p. 141*)*.

א כרבא. טור ולבוש ס"א. מ"א ס"ק ב. כד ר"ן (יח, א) ד"ה לא לינקוט. לבוש ס"ז. כה גמרא לז, ב כרבא. טור ושו"ע ס"א. כו לבוש ס"א. כז גמרא שם. טור ורמ"א ס"א. כח ולענין בין מין למין, ראה דברי נחמיה שם קו"א ס"ק ד. ובסידור (דיני הלולב): לולב והדס וערבה יהיו קשורים ואגודים יחד ולא יהיה חוט או משיחה חוצץ ביניהם, וש"נ. כט מנהגים (קלויזנר) סי' מה. מהרי"ל הל' לולב (ע' שצב). רמ"א שם. ל מ"א ס"ק ב. לא ראה לבוש שם (סביב הג' מינים יחד).

ו יֵשׁ נוֹהֲגִים[לב] לַעֲשׂוֹת הָאֶגֶד בְּדֶרֶךְ זֶה, שֶׁכּוֹרְכִין[18] סְבִיבוֹת שְׁלֹשָׁה מִינִים אֵלּוּ עַד שֶׁיִּהְיוּ מְהֻדָּקִין הֵיטֵב, וְתוֹחֲבִין רָאשֵׁי הַכֶּרֶךְ לְתוֹךְ עִגּוּל הַכָּרוּךְ סְבִיב שְׁלֹשָׁה מִינִים אֵלּוּ. וְיֵשׁ מַחְמִירִים[לג] וְקוֹשְׁרִים שְׁנֵי רָאשֵׁי הַכֶּרֶךְ בִּשְׁנֵי קְשָׁרִים זֶה עַל גַּבֵּי זֶה, וּבְיוֹם טוֹב[לד] שֶׁאִי אֶפְשָׁר לְקָשְׁרָן בְּעִנְיָן זֶה,[13] שֶׁהֲרֵי הוּא קֶשֶׁר שֶׁל קְיָמָא[19] שֶׁאֵינוֹ חוֹשֵׁשׁ לְהַתִּירוֹ עוֹלָמִית[לה] — אוֹגְדִין אוֹתוֹ בַּעֲנִיבָה,[לו] דְּהַיְנוּ שֶׁעוֹשִׂין שְׁתֵּי עֲנִיבוֹת זוֹ עַל גַּבֵּי זוֹ (אֲבָל אָסוּר לַעֲשׂוֹת עֲנִיבָה עַל גַּבֵּי קֶשֶׁר, כֵּיוָן שֶׁאֵינוֹ חוֹשֵׁשׁ לְהַתִּירוֹ עוֹלָמִית עַיֵּן סִימָן (שמ"א) [שי"ז[לז]]), אוֹ שֶׁתּוֹחֲבִין רָאשֵׁי הַכֶּרֶךְ לְתוֹךְ עִגּוּל הַכֶּרֶךְ[לח] כְּמוֹ שֶׁנִּתְבָּאֵר:

6 There are those who follow the custom of binding [the *lulav*] in the following manner: They wind a binder[18] around these three species until they are held tightly together, and insert the tip of the binder into the ring that now encircles the three species. There are those who are stringent and tie both ends of the binder with two knots, one on top of the other.

On *Yom-Tov,* when this cannot be done[13] — for this would constitute a permanent knot[19] that one never intends to untie — [the *lulav* and its two species] should be bound together with a slipknot; i.e., two loops are made, one on top of the other. (It is, however, forbidden to make a loop over a knot, since one never intends to untie it; see sec. 317[:3].) Alternatively, the tip of the binder should be tucked into the [newly-made] ring, as explained above.

ז יֵשׁ נוֹהֲגִין[לט] לְהַגְבִּיהַּ הַהֲדַס בְּתוֹךְ הָאִגּוּד לְמַעְלָה מִן הָעֲרָבָה מְעַט, מִטַּעַם הַיָּדוּעַ לָהֶם:[20]

7 There are those whose custom is to raise the myrtle twigs slightly above the willow twigs in the binding, for an esoteric reason.[20]

ח יֵשׁ נוֹהֲגִין[מ] לֶאֱגֹד הַהֲדַס מִימִינוֹ שֶׁל הַלּוּלָב וְהָעֲרָבָה בִּשְׂמֹאלוֹ וְהַלּוּלָב בְּאֶמְצַע:

8 Some are accustomed to bind the myrtle twigs on the right side of the *lulav* and the willow twigs on the left side, with the *lulav* in the center.

---

18. In the original, *kesher shel kayama.* Tying a permanent knot is one of the labors forbidden on *Shabbos* and *Yom-Tov.*

19. Lit., "for a reason known to them."

One should try to make the *aravos* inconspicuous *(Sefer HaMinhagim: The Book of Chabad-Lubavitch Customs, loc. cit.).* The *Levush* writes (sec. 651:1) that the *hadassim* should be more visible because they appear earlier in the verse *(Vayikra* 23:40*).*

The Lubavitch custom is to bind the myrtle and willow twigs directly onto the *lulav* as they are, not encased in the slim, cylindrical containers woven of soft lulav-leaves, that are known by their Yiddish name as *keishiklach* (lit., "little baskets").

20. If — as is the Lubavitch custom — one includes additional myrtle twigs, they too are distributed according to the pattern to be described. See footnote 2 above.

לב מרדכי רמז תשמח, בשם ראבי"ה סי' תרסו (קשר א' וכריכה). דרכי משה ס"ק א (שכן נוהגין אף בחול). רמ"א ס"א (כריכה ותחיבה), כפירוש המ"א ס"ק ג (דהיינו אף בחול). לבוש ס"א. וראה דברי נחמיה שם ס"ה וקו"א ס"ק ד. לג רש"י שם ד"ה ופליג. רי"ף (טז, א). רא"ש פ"ג סי"ב (ראה הגהות אשרי שם). מרדכי שם בשם היראים (השלם) סי' תכב. טור ושו"ע ס"א. לד ברייתא שם (הותר אגדו ביו"ט). טור ושו"ע שם (אם לא אגדו מבע"י או שהותר ביו"ט). וראה ס' המנהגים — חב"ד ע' 65: מהדרין לאגוד הלולב בסוכה ובערב יו"ט. לה ברייתא ורש"י שם ד"ה הותר. לבוש שם. וכדלעיל סי' שיז ס"א וס"ג. לו גמרא שם. רי"ף ורא"ש שם. שו"ע שם. לז סעיף ג וש"נ. וראה לקו"ש חי"ד ע' 16 הערה 30. שלחן המלך ח"ב ע' רסב־ד. לח ברייתא ורש"י שם. רי"ף

9 Others follow the custom of binding the three myrtle twigs[21] as follows: one on the right of the *lulav,* i.e., to one's right,[22] one to his left, and one in the center, inclined towards the right.[23] One of the willow twigs is placed to one's right, and the other, to one's left.

10 It is advisable to position the myrtle and willow twigs deep in the binding of the *lulav* — i.e., they should be bound to the base of the *lulav* — so that when one takes the *lulav* in hand to fulfill the *mitzvah,* the myrtle and willow twigs will also be in his hands.[24]

(If one did not position [these twigs] near the base, and held the *lulav* alone, with the myrtle and willow twigs bound to it higher up, this is permitted. The fact that he does not hold [them] in his hand is of no consequence, for taking hold of one object by taking hold of another object [to which it is attached] is [still] considered "taking," as will be explained.[25])

11 It is customary to make three bindings on the *lulav* [to recall] the three

ט וְיֵשׁ נוֹהֲגִין[מא] לֶאֱגֹד שְׁלֹשָׁה הֲדַסִּים[21] אֶחָד מִימִין הַלּוּלָב דְּהַיְנוּ מִימִין הָאָדָם[מב,22] וְאֶחָד מִשְּׂמֹאלוֹ וְאֶחָד בָּאֶמְצַע נוֹטֶה לְצַד יָמִין,[23] וּשְׁתֵּי הָעֲרָבוֹת אֶחָד בִּימִינוֹ וְאֶחָד בִּשְׂמֹאלוֹ:

י וְטוֹב לְהַשְׁפִּיל הַהֲדַס וַעֲרָבָה תּוֹךְ אֶגֶד הַלּוּלָב, דְּהַיְנוּ שֶׁיֶּאֱגֹד אוֹתָם בְּתַחְתִּית הַלּוּלָב, בְּעִנְיָן שֶׁכְּשֶׁיִּטֹּל הַלּוּלָב בְּיָדוֹ לְשֵׁם מִצְוָה יִהְיוּ בְּיָדָיו גַּם כֵּן הַהֲדַס וַעֲרָבָה[מג,24] (וְאִם לֹא הִשְׁפִּיל וְנָטַל הַלּוּלָב לְבַדּוֹ בְּיָדוֹ וְהַהֲדַס וַעֲרָבָה אֲגוּדִין בּוֹ לְמַעְלָה – הֲרֵי זֶה מֻתָּר, אַף עַל פִּי שֶׁאֵינוֹ נוֹטֵל הַהֲדַס וְהָעֲרָבָה בְּיָדוֹ – אֵין בְּכָךְ כְּלוּם, דִּלְקִיחָה עַל יְדֵי דָּבָר אַחֵר – שְׁמָהּ לְקִיחָה כְּמוֹ שֶׁיִּתְבָּאֵר[מד,25]):

יא נוֹהֲגִין לַעֲשׂוֹת בַּלּוּלָב שָׁלֹשׁ אֲגֻדּוֹת כְּנֶגֶד שְׁלֹשָׁה אָבוֹת,[מה]

---

21. As one faces the spine of the *lulav.*

22. This is the Lubavitch custom. From a spiritual perspective, this distribution may be viewed in the Kabbalistic terms of the *AriZal* as follows: The right and left *hadassim* correspond respectively to the Divine attributes of *Chessed* and *Gevurah;* the middle one corresponds to *Tiferes,* which is why it inclines to the right. The right and left *aravos* correspond respectively to the Divine attributes of *Netzach* and *Hod.*

23. The base of these twigs is commonly on the same level as the base of the *lulav.*

24. This section is incomplete in the present work. See the *Shulchan Aruch* of R. Yosef Caro, sec. 651:7.

25. The Lubavitch custom is to make five bindings in all. Three rings, preferably within the space of a *tefach* (approx. 8 cm.), tie the myrtle and willow twigs to the base of the *lulav.* In addition, two rings are bound around the *lulav* itself. They are higher up, but should preferably be hidden — even the higher one — by the upper ends of the myrtle and willow twigs *(Sefer HaMinhagim: The Book of Chabad-Lubavitch Customs, loc. cit.).* On the morning of Hoshana Rabbah, before the recitation of *Hallel,* the two upper rings are removed *(op. cit.,* p. 146*).*

ורא"ש שם. טור ולבוש שם. **לט** שו"ת מהר"י ווייל סי' קצא. רמ"א ס"א. סדור האריז"ל. וראה ספר המנהגים — חב"ד ע' 66: משתדלים שהערבות לא יראו כל כך. **מ** דרשות הר"י אבן שועיב דרשה ליום א' דסוכות. מטה משה שם. של"ה מסכת סוכה, נר מצוה (רמה, ב) ד"ה מטה משה. מ"א ס"ק ד. ט"ז סוף סי' תרנ. **מא** האר"י בפרי עץ חיים שער כט ספ"א. מ"א שם. משנת חסידים מס' ימי מצוה וסוכה ספ"ד. סדור האריז"ל. וכ"ה בסדור (דיני הלולב). **מב** כי שדרת הלולב כנגד פניו (ראה סדור שם, וש"נ). **מג** מהרי"ל הל' לולב (ע' שצב, בשינויי נוסחאות). רמ"א ס"א. **מד** סיום הסי' בשוע"ר לא הגיע לידינו. וראה שו"ע ס"ז. דברי נחמיה שם סי"ב. **מה** מרדכי רמז תשמט. מהרי"ל הל' לולב (ע' שצב). רמ"א ס"א.

דְּהַיְנוּ שֶׁמִּלְּבַד הָאֶגֶד שֶׁאוֹגֵד שְׁלֹשָׁה מִינִים אֵלּוּ בְּיַחַד עוֹשִׂין בַּלּוּלָב עַצְמוֹ עוֹד שְׁתֵּי אֲגֻדּוֹת לֶאֱגֹד הֶעָלִין בַּשִּׁדְרָה.[מו, 26] וְצָרִיךְ לִזָּהֵר מְאֹד שֶׁיְּהֵא שִׁדְרוֹ שֶׁל לוּלָב יוֹצֵא לְמַעְלָה מֵאֶגֶד הָעֶלְיוֹן טֶפַח כְּדֵי נִעְנוּעַ,[מז] כְּמוֹ שֶׁנִּתְבָּאֵר בְּסִימָן תר"נ:[מח]

Patriarchs; i.e., in addition to the binding that holds the three species together, two additional bindings are made [above it] on the *lulav* itself, to bind the leaves to the spine.[26]

One must be very careful that the spine of the *lulav* extends [at least] a handbreadth above the upper binder so that it can be shaken, as explained in sec. 650[:2].

יב כָּל אַרְבָּעָה מִינִים הַלָּלוּ צָרִיךְ לִטְלָן דֶּרֶךְ גְּדִילָתָן,[מט, 27] דְּהַיְנוּ שֶׁיְּהֵא רָאשֵׁיהֶם לְמַעְלָה וְעִקְּרֵיהֶם לְמַטָּה.[נ] וְאִם הֲפָכָן בְּשָׁעָה שֶׁנְּטָלָן — לֹא יָצָא יְדֵי חוֹבָתוֹ בִּנְטִילָה זוֹ.[נא, 28] וְהָאֶתְרוֹג אַף עַל פִּי שֶׁהוּא תָּלוּי בָּאִילָן עֻקְצוֹ לְמַעְלָה, מִכָּל מָקוֹם דֶּרֶךְ גְּדִילָתוֹ נִקְרָא עֻקְצוֹ לְמַטָּה,[נב, 29] וְצָרִיךְ לִזָּהֵר מְאֹד בַּהֲדַס שֶׁבָּא מִמֶּרְחַקִּים לְהַתִּיר אֲגֻדָּתוֹ וְלִרְאוֹת אִם מֻנָּח כְּתִקּוּנוֹ, דִּלְפְעָמִים נוֹתְנִים רֹאשׁוֹ שֶׁל בַּד זֶה בְּצַד עִקָּרוֹ שֶׁל בַּד זֶה, וְגַם לִפְעָמִים כּוֹפְפִין רָאשֵׁי הַבַּדִּין:[נג]

12 All these Four Species must be taken in the manner in which they grow naturally,[27] i.e., with their tips pointing up and their stems below. If one turned them upside down while taking them, he did not fulfill the *mitzvah*.[28] As to the *esrog*, even though as it hangs from the tree its stem is above [and its *pitom* hangs down], when the stem is [now] below, this is considered its natural pattern of growth.[29]

Great care must be taken with regard to myrtle twigs that are brought from distant places. As they are untied, one must check that they are [standing upright], because sometimes they [are packed with] the tip of one next to the stem of another, and sometimes the tips of the twigs are bent over.

יג צָרִיךְ לִטֹּל הַלּוּלָב וּמִינָיו בְּיָדוֹ הַיְמָנִית וְאֶתְרוֹג בְּיָדוֹ הַשְּׂמָאלִית,[נד, 13] לְפִי שֶׁהַלּוּלָב יֵשׁ בּוֹ שָׁלֹשׁ מִצְוֹת, דְּהַיְנוּ לוּלָב הֲדַס וַעֲרָבָה, וְהָאֶתְרוֹג הוּא מִצְוָה אַחַת.[נה]

13 The *lulav* and its [two attached] species should be held in one's right hand and the *esrog* in one's left,[13] because the *lulav* has three [components of the] *mitzvah* and the *esrog*, only one.

---

26. *Sukkah* 45b.

27. *op. cit.,* 42b.

28. Because the stem is considered the base from which it grows.

29. As opposed to a situation in which one holds the *lulav* to transport it, for example.

מו ט"ז ס"ק א. וראה דברי נחמיה שם ס"ו וקו"א ס"ק ה. ובספר המנהגים — חב"ד ע' 66: על הלולב עצמו עושים שתי כריכות . . . נוסף על שתי כריכות הנ"ל — אוגד הלולב וההדסים והערבות ביחד ע"י שלש כריכות, שלוש כריכות אלו הן במשך טפח אחד. נמצא סך הכל חמש כריכות (ביאורו בלקו"ש ח"ד ע' 1368). ושם ע' 68: בהושענא רבה קודם הלל מסירים שתי הכריכות אשר על הלולב ואין נשארים אלא ג' הכריכות המאגדים את הלולב ההדסים וערבות ביחד (ראה טור ושו"ע סי' תרסד ס"א). וראה אוצר מנהגי חב"ד ע' רפז. **מז** ט"ז שם (שיוכל לכסכם). פרי מגדים משב"ז ס"ק א (יוצא לולב טפח). ובספר המנהגים — חב"ד שם: משתדלים ששתי הכריכות תהיינה מכוסות בההדסים וערבות. גם כריכה העליונה, מקצתה עכ"פ. וראה יגדיל תורה (נ.י.) נ ע' נ. **מח** סעיף ב. **מט** גמרא מה, ב. רמב"ם פ"ז ה"ו וה"ט. לבוש ס"ה. ט"ז ס"ק ב. **נ** רש"י שם ד"ה דרך. טור ושו"ע ס"ב. **נא** גמרא מב, א. לפירוש רש"י שם ד"ה ה"ג הא מדאגבהיה. לבוש שם. ט"ז שם. **נב** מ"א ס"ק ז, בשם הרי"ץ גיאת הל' לולב (ע' קיא). אליה רבה ס"ק יד, בשם המנהיג הל' אתרוג סי' כה. **נג** מהרי"ל הל' לולב (ע' שצב). הובא בדרכי משה ס"ק א. אליה זוטא ס"ק ג. **נד** גמרא לז, ב. טור ושו"ע ס"ב. וכ"ה בסידור. **נה** גמרא שם. לבוש ס"ב. ט"ז

וְאִם הָפַךְ — יָצָא יְדֵי חוֹבָתוֹ,[נו] וּמִכָּל מָקוֹם טוֹב לַחֲזֹר וְלִטֹּל כְּדִינוֹ בְּלֹא בְרָכָה.[נז]

אֲפִלּוּ אִם כְּבָר יָצָא יְדֵי חוֹבַת נְטִילָה וְרוֹצֶה לַחֲזֹר וְלִטְּלוֹ לְשֵׁם מִצְוָה,[30] כְּגוֹן בִּשְׁעַת אֲמִירַת "הוֹשַׁעְנוֹת" — צָרִיךְ לִטֹּל הַלּוּלָב בְּיָמִין וְהָאֶתְרוֹג בִּשְׂמֹאל:[נח, 31]

If one reversed this order, he has fulfilled his obligation. Nevertheless, it is proper to take the species anew in the manner mandated, without reciting a blessing.

Even if one already fulfilled his obligation to take the *lulav,* but seeks to take it again for the sake of the *mitzvah,*[30] e.g., as is done when reciting the hymns of *Hoshaanos,* the *lulav* should [likewise] be held in one's right hand, and the *esrog* in one's left.[31]

יד אִטֵּר יָד — נוֹטֵל הַלּוּלָב בִּימִינוֹ שֶׁהוּא שְׂמֹאל שֶׁל כָּל אָדָם וְהָאֶתְרוֹג בִּשְׂמֹאלוֹ שֶׁהוּא יָמִין שֶׁל כָּל אָדָם.[נט] אֲבָל מִי שֶׁהוּא שׁוֹלֵט בִּשְׁתֵּי יָדָיו — נוֹטֵל הַלּוּלָב בִּימִינוֹ וְהָאֶתְרוֹג בִּשְׂמֹאלוֹ כְּכָל אָדָם:[ס]

14 A lefthanded person should take the *lulav* in the hand which is his "right" and which others call left, and he should take the *esrog* in the hand which is his "left" and which others call right. If he is ambidextrous, he should take the *lulav* is his right hand and the *esrog* in his left, as others do.

טו מִי שֶׁנִּקְטְעָה יָדוֹ הַיְמָנִית — יִטֹּל הַלּוּלָב בִּזְרוֹעוֹ[סא] הַיְמָנִית,[סב] שֶׁהֲרֵי לֹא נֶאֱמַר בַּתּוֹרָה "וּלְקַחְתֶּם בַּיָּד", וּלְקִיחָה בַּזְּרוֹעַ — שְׁמָהּ לְקִיחָה.[סג] וְאִם אִי אֶפְשָׁר לִטֹּל הַלּוּלָב בִּזְרוֹעוֹ הַיְמָנִית — יִטֹּל הַלּוּלָב בְּיָדוֹ הַשְּׂמָאלִית שֶׁהִיא חֲשׁוּבָה לוֹ כְּיָמִין וְאֶתְרוֹג בִּזְרוֹעוֹ הַשְּׂמָאלִית,[סד] אֲבָל לֹא יִטֹּל שְׁנֵיהֶם בְּיָדוֹ אַחַת בְּבַת אַחַת כְּמוֹ שֶׁנִּתְבָּאֵר.[סה] וְאִם אִי אֶפְשָׁר לוֹ לִטֹּל הָאֶתְרוֹג בִּזְרוֹעוֹ הַשְּׂמָאלִית —

15 If one's right hand has been amputated, he should take the *lulav* with [the stump of] his right arm. The Torah did not say, "And you shall take with your hand," [but simply "And you shall take"]. And taking with one's arm is considered "taking."

If it is impossible for him to take the *lulav* with his right forearm, he should take it with his left hand, since for him it is [now] considered as his right hand, and he should take the *esrog* with his left forearm. He should not take them both together in one hand, as explained [in subsection 1 above]. If he cannot take the *esrog* with his left forearm, he should

30. In practice, one also has to hold a *Siddur* at the same time. Small *Hoshaanos* booklets have been published to make this easier.

31. The relevant section in the Alter Rebbe's *Shulchan Aruch* is not extant. See the *Shulchan Aruch* of R. Yosef Caro, sec. 651:12.

ס"ק ב. מ"א ס"ק ו. **נו** תשובת רבנו יואל, בראבי"ה הל' לולב סי' תרצד, ובשו"ת הרשב"א ח"א סי' אלף קכ. כל בו סי' עב (לט, רע"ג). רמ"א ס"ג, לפירוש המ"א ס"ק ט. ט"ז ס"ק ד. **נז** מ"א שם (לחוש לדעת ר"ח מב, א דלא יצא). **נח** מ"א ס"ק ו. **נט** תשובת רבנו יואל שם ושם. רא"ש פ"ג סכ"ה. רבנו ירוחם נתיב ח ח"ד (ס, ב). אגודה סוף סוכה סי' מז. מהרי"ל הל' לולב (ע' שצג). ב"ח ד"ה ויטול, בשם רש"ל (בהגהות הטור). רמ"א ס"ג. ט"ז ס"ק ג. **ס** כל בו סי' עב (לט, ג). רמ"א שם. **סא** רוקח הל' סוכות סי' רכ (ע' קכ ד"ה גידם). שו"ע ס"ד, לפירוש המ"א ס"ק י. **סב** משמעות כל בו סי' עב (לט, ב), לפירוש אליה רבה ס"ק יג. וראה שו"ת צמח צדק או"ח סי' ה ס"ח (אלמא ס"ל דע"י שנקטעה ידו הימנית לא מיחשב איטר). **סג** כל בו שם (לט, ב). מ"א שם. אליה רבה שם. **סד** מ"א שם. אליה רבה שם. וראה צמח צדק שם: אין ר"ל שהיא ימינו באמת כמו באיטר . . . אלא ר"ל דחשובה לו כימין אע"פ שאינה ימין ממש והוי נטילה חשובה. **סה** לעיל ס"א.

יִטֹּל הַלּוּלָב וְהָאֶתְרוֹג בְּיָדוֹ הַשְּׂמָאלִית בָּזֶה אַחַר זֶה[סו] כְּמוֹ שֶׁיִּתְבָּאֵר:[סז, 32]

take the *lulav* and then the *esrog* in his left hand, one after the other, as will be explained.[32]

טז וְכֵן מִי שֶׁנִּקְטְעָה יָדוֹ הַשְּׂמָאלִית – יִטֹּל הָאֶתְרוֹג בִּזְרוֹעוֹ הַשְּׂמָאלִית.[סח] וְאִם אִי אֶפְשָׁר – יִטֹּל בִּזְרוֹעוֹ הַיְמָנִית. וְאִם גַּם זֶה אִי אֶפְשָׁר – יִטֹּל שְׁנֵיהֶם בְּיָדוֹ הַיְמָנִית בָּזֶה אַחַר זֶה:

16 Similarly, if a person's left hand was amputated, he should take the *esrog* with his left forearm. If that is impossible, he should take it with his right forearm. If that, too, is impossible, he should take them both in his right hand, one after the other.

יז כָּל הַמִּצְוֹת מְבָרְכִין עֲלֵיהֶם עוֹבֵר לַעֲשִׂיָּתָן,[סט, 33] דְּהַיְנוּ סָמוּךְ וְקֹדֶם לִתְחִלַּת עֲשִׂיָּתָן,[ע] כְּמוֹ שֶׁנִּתְבָּאֵר בְּסִימָן כ"ה.[עא]

וּמַה הוּא מְבָרֵךְ עַל מִצְוַת נְטִילַת אַרְבָּעָה מִינִים אֵלּוּ? "אֲשֶׁר קִדְּשָׁנוּ בְּמִצְוֹתָיו וְצִוָּנוּ עַל נְטִילַת לוּלָב",[עב, 34] לְפִי שֶׁהַלּוּלָב גָּבוֹהַּ מִכֻּלָּן[עג] – חָשׁוּב הוּא, וְנִקְרֵאת כָּל הָאֲגֻדָּה עַל שְׁמוֹ:[עד, 13]

17 The blessing for the *mitzvos* should always be recited immediately before one begins their observance,[33] as stated in sec. 25[:17].

What blessing should be recited over taking these Four Species? "[Blessed are You...] Who has sanctified us with His commandments and commanded us concerning the taking of the *lulav*."[34] Because the *lulav* is taller than the other species, it is accorded status, and all the species together carry its name.[13]

תַּם וְנִשְׁלָם[עה] שֶׁבַח לָאֵל בּוֹרֵא עוֹלָם[35]

Complete and consummate, with praise to G-d, Creator of the World[35]

---

32. In the original, *over laasiyasan* (see *Sukkah* 39a).

33. *Sukkah* 46a. The wording of this blessing does not mention the other three species by name.

34. The original publishers placed this codicil here, because this point marks the end of the surviving manuscript of *Orach Chayim*, the first of the four parts of the Alter Rebbe's *Shulchan Aruch*. In fact, however, this point corresponds to the middle of one of the sections in the parent *Shulchan Aruch* of R. Yosef Caro. That work continues with several further sections on Sukkos, followed by the laws relating to Chanukah and Purim.

סו משמעות מ"א שם. סז לא הגיע לידינו. וראה שו"ע (הב"י) סי"ב. סח משמעות כל בו סי' עב (לט, ב), לפירוש אליה רבה ס"ק יג. סט גמרא לט, א. טור ושו"ע ס"ה. ע ראה תוס' שם ד"ה עובר. רא"ש פ"ג סל"ג. טור ושו"ע שם. לבוש ס"ה. מ"א ס"ק יא (לאחר נטילת הלולב קודם נטילת האתרוג). וכ"ה בסדור. עא סעיף יז (לענין תפילין, אחר ההנחה קודם הקשירה). עב ברייתא מו, א. טור ושו"ע שם. וכ"ה בסדור. וראה לעיל סי' תלב ס"ד. עג גמרא לז, ב. לבוש ס"ב. עד רש"י שם ד"ה הואיל (ונקרא האגד על שמו). מכתם שם (ונקראת כל האגודה על שמו, והרי הוא כאילו מברכין בפירוש על כל אחד ואחד בשמו). וכ"ה בכל בו סי' עב (לט, סע"ב). וראה גם רש"י לא, א ד"ה אין. עה סיום הסי' לא הגיע לידינו (וכן שאר הסי' עד סוף חלק או"ח סי' תרצז). וראה סידור (דיני הלולב. סדר הושענות. סדר הקפות בשמחת תורה. דיני חנוכה. סדר קריאת המגילה). השלמות דברי נחמיה או"ח עד, ב ואילך (סי' תרנא. עתר).

— ADDENDUM —

Summaries of Selected Sections of the Laws of Sukkah

SUMMARIES OF SELECTED SECTIONS OF THE LAWS OF SUKKAH

As noted in the Publisher's Foreword, the following summaries do not pretend to embrace all the practical directives that must be mastered if one is to rest assured that his *sukkah* is in fact kosher.

Summary of Section 626

(a) *S'chach* must be put in place for the purpose of shade. If it is put in place for other reasons, e.g., to create a dwelling or a storehouse, it is invalid (subsection 1).

(b) The *s'chach* must be positioned under the open sky, not under an invalid covering such as a tree or overhanging balcony. If it is placed under an invalid covering, the shade from the invalid covering disqualifies the shade produced by the *s'chach* directly beneath it (subsection 2).

(c) A *sukkah* is invalid if its *s'chach* casts a shadow over less than half of its floor area (subsection 3).

(d) If valid *s'chach* is mixed with invalid material, there are situations in which it would be considered acceptable. However, there are many factors involved. Hence if a person finds it necessary to construct a *sukkah* in such a manner, he should consult a competent Rabbinic authority with regard to the particulars.

(e) There is a general principle that applies with regard to *s'chach*. The Torah states, "Make the Sukkos festival for yourself." Implied is that the *s'chach* of a *sukkah* must be *made*. We may not use something that was initially invalid for *s'chach*, but which later became suitable as a matter of course, for the initial act of making, which was invalid, is not considered "making" at all (subsection 16).

(f) It is permitted to make a *sukkah* in a house below a roof from which the shingles were removed with the intent of making a *sukkah*, even if the wood or the beams on which the shingles had been resting remain. Indeed, the beams themselves can be considered as part of the *s'chach*. The reason that this is not considered as a contradiction to the above principle is that one performed an action and removed the shingles with the intent of making a *sukkah* for shade. Hence it is considered as if he performed an action with regard to the wood or the beams themselves and prepared them for the sake of the *sukkah* (subsection 17).

(g) If, however, a building was initially constructed with beams that were fixed in place as part of the structure, but they were never covered with roofing material, they are invalid for use as *s'chach*, and indeed can disqualify valid *s'chach* (subsection 12).

(h) If *s'chach* is disqualified by an external factor – e.g., one constructed his *sukkah* under the roof of a house and, after placing *s'chach* upon it as required by law, removed the roof of the house that was above the *sukkah* – it is valid, even though no action was taken with the *s'chach* itself to make it valid (subsection 17).

(i) When one is making a *sukkah* under a hinged roof that can be opened and closed at will, he must be careful to put the *s'chach* in place while the roof is open. Since it is already on hinges, opening it is not considered as an act of sufficient importance to validate *s'chach* placed upon it previously (subsection 19).

(j) Such a retractable roof fits the halachic definition of an entrance and may be closed and opened on *Shabbos* and the festivals. Doing so does not involve the forbidden labors of destroying or building (subsection 20).

(k) When the retractable roof is closed, one must be careful not to sit under it with the intent of fulfilling the *mitzvah* of the *sukkah,* for at that time the *sukkah* is not valid and one does not fulfill his obligation by dwelling in it (subsection 21).

Summary of Section 627

(a) One is required to dwell directly under the *s'chach,* with no other shelter *(ohel)* intervening. The term *ohel* is used only for a structure that is at least ten handbreadths above the ground. Even if it has no walls, it is placed in that category and it is forbidden to dwell under it (subsection 1).

(b) Any roof that is a handbreadth wide and ten handbreadths above the ground is defined as an *ohel* (subsection 2).

(c) Stringency is sometimes required even when a canopy within a *sukkah* does not have a roof that is a handbreadth wide; for example, a canopy that hangs down from its horizontal beam, and within three handbreadths of that beam it spreads out on either side, creating a horizontal span of a handbreadth. The rationale is that any space of less than three handbreadths is governed by the principle of *lavud,* so that the entire space is considered as if on the same level (subsection 3).

(d) Decorative objects may be hung in a *sukkah,* whether on the walls or under the *s'chach,* even though they are invalid as *s'chach.* Even a four-handbreadth piece of such fabric does not disqualify the *sukkah.* It is even permitted to sit directly below such decorative hangings, because they are subordinate to the *s'chach,* provided they are within four handbreadths of it. If they are lower than four handbreadths from the *s'chach,* they are not considered as subordinate to it and they disqualify the *sukkah,* as is the case with other materials that are invalid as *s'chach* (subsection 4).

The above leniencies do not apply if an object is hung under the *s'chach* for purposes other than decorating the *sukkah* (subsection 6).

(e) Material that is invalid as *s'chach* does not disqualify a *sukkah* unless it measures four handbreadths or more (subsection 4).

Summary of Section 628

(a) When one valid and sturdy *sukkah* is constructed on top of another, the lower *sukkah* is invalid by Scriptural decree. If the upper *sukkah* is either structurally or halachically unacceptable, the lower *sukkah* may be used if it is valid (subsection 1).

(b) Invalid material disqualifies the valid *s'chach* below it only when the invalid material is inherently unsatisfactory; e.g., it is still connected to the ground or it is susceptible to contracting ritual impurity. When, however, the *s'chach* is inherently valid but is invalidated by an external factor – for example, by being situated more than 20 cubits above ground level – it does not disqualify the valid *s'chach* below it, for it is inherently suitable for use as *s'chach* for the lower *sukkah* (subsection 2).

(c) A *sukkah* that cannot withstand ordinary land winds is invalid. This applies even when there is no wind at all. If the *sukkah* can withstand the winds common on land, it is valid even if it cannot withstand the winds common at sea (subsection 4).

(d) A *sukkah* on a camel or on top of a tree is valid. One may not, however, climb up to it on *Shabbos* or on a festival, when it is forbidden to make use of any living creature or of any plant connected to the ground. We do not override even a *shvus* – which was ordained by the Sages – in order to enable the observance of the *mitzvah* of *sukkah* (subsection 5).

(e) For several reasons, it is undesirable that the base of the *sukkah* be positioned on the ground, with its *s'chach* resting on a nearby tree (subsection 6-7).

(f) The supports for the *s'chach* of a *sukkah* must be stationary, unless the entire *sukkah* is built on a movable base, such as on a camel, a ship, or a wagon (subsection 4, 8).

(g) It is forbidden to make use of the appendages of a tree on *Shabbos* or on a festival (subsection 6). Hence one may not climb up to a *sukkah* using a ladder supported by a tree even if there is no problem in using the tree itself (subsection 9).

Summary of Section 629

(a) To be valid for use as *s'chach,* a substance must:
- (i) have grown from the ground;
- (ii) be presently detached from the ground; and
- (iii) not be susceptible to ritual impurity.

This excludes all kinds of foods, utensils, animal substances and metals (subsection 1).

(b) Anything that was susceptible to ritual impurity even briefly may not be used for *s'chach*, even though later its status changed and it was no longer susceptible to ritual impurity. This category includes:

(i) broken utensils, when the pieces are not large enough to be susceptible to ritual impurity;
(ii) pieces of cloth that are so tattered that less than three fingerbreadths by three fingerbreadths remains;
(iii) the detached handle of a utensil (subsection 2).

(c) Any article that serves as a receptacle is considered a utensil and hence is unfit for use as *s'chach* (subsection 3-4).

(d) Natural fibers that have been processed to be used as fabric are invalid for use as *s'chach* (subsection 5).

(e) Mats that were made to sit on or to lie on are invalid for use as *s'chach.* Those made for shade are acceptable (subsection 7).

(f) An object that is susceptible to ritual impurity, such as a chair or a bench, should preferably not be used to hold the *s'chach* in place or to support it (subsection 11). After the fact, if one already supported the *s'chach* itself with something that is susceptible to ritual impurity, one may sit under it and discharge one's obligation thereby (subsection 13).

(g) The *s'chach* may be placed on beams or pegs which are placed on an object that is susceptible to ritual impurity. It is of no consequence that the object that supports the *s'chach* or holds it in place is supported by something that is invalid as *s'chach* (subsection 12).

(h) All accessories to food – such as the straw of ears of grain, the twigs to which grapes are attached, and the branches to which dates are attached – are susceptible to ritual impurity. However, this applies only up to a certain length (subsection 15).

(i) As mentioned at the outset, fruit and vegetables are not valid for use as *s'chach.* Moreover, they and their accessories can disqualify valid *s'chach.* Nevertheless, if branches with fruit were cut down for the express purpose of being used as *s'chach,* the accessories are not disqualified as *s'chach* (subsection 16).

(j) Leaves that will dry, wither, and fall from a branch within seven days are considered from the outset as if they have already fallen, even though they have not yet dried. Hence, three handbreadths of such a covering, even if they are at the side of a *sukkah,* disqualifies the *sukkah* as empty space would (subsection 19).

(k) Anything that is still growing in the ground may not be used as *s'chach* because it does not resemble "the remnants of the threshing floor and the winepress," which have been detached from the ground (subsection 20).

(l) Moreover, if one covered a *sukkah* with branches that were connected to the ground and then detached them, the *s'chach* is invalid. This is derived from the verse, "Make the Sukkos festival...." Implied is that one must *make* the *sukkah,* and not use something which was already made in an unacceptable manner. One may rectify this disqualifying factor by picking up the *s'chach* and putting it down again after it was detached from the ground (subsection 20).

(m) The Sages forbade using the following materials as *s'chach* as an initial preference:

(i) grasses with an unpleasant smell, which are invalid even though they are not edible and are not susceptible to ritual impurity;

(ii) certain kinds of brambles whose leaves fall even when there is no wind.

The rationale is that they may cause people to leave the *sukkah.* Nevertheless, if one transgressed and used them as *s'chach,* the *sukkah* is valid (subsection 21).

(n) The Sages decreed that bundles of straw or bundles of wood may not be used for *s'chach* while they are bound together (subsection 22). If one transgressed and used a bundle as *s'chach,* he may untie it and thus render the *s'chach* valid, provided the bundle was placed there for the purpose of shade. This leniency is granted because bundles are deemed invalid only by Rabbinic ordinance, as explained above (subsection 28).

(o) The Talmudic Sages decreed that boards that are four handbreadths wide or more may not be used as *s'chach,* because the ceilings of most homes were once made of such boards (subsection 29). Even if the boards are laid on their sides and the sides are less than four handbreadths wide, the boards should not be used as *s'chach* (subsection 30).

(p) More recently, however, homes are sometimes roofed by boards that are less than three handbreadths wide. The medieval halachic authorities known as *Rishonim* therefore extended the above prohibition and ruled that a *sukkah* should be disqualified even if boards less than three handbreadths wide are used as *s'chach* (subsection 32).

(q) In a pressing situation, where there are no alternative materials for *s'chach,* one may use boards even if they are more than four handbreadths wide (subsection 33).

Summary of Section 631

(a) The shaded area of a *sukkah* floor must exceed the area exposed to sunlight (subsecs. 1-3). If a *sukkah* is constructed in this manner, one may even dwell in the part of a *sukkah* in which the sunlight exceeds the shade, for this area is *batel* – insignificant and therefore nullified – *vis-à-vis* the majority of *s'chach,* under which the shade exceeds the sunlit area.

Nevertheless, if the minority of *s'chach,* under which the sunlit area exceeds the shade, is as large as seven handbreadths by seven handbreadths, it is considered significant and one cannot fulfill one's obligation by dwelling under it (subsection 4).

(b) When *s'chach* is so thick that it prevents rain from entering, it is invalid, because the shelter then resembles a house (subsection 5).

(c) If the *s'chach* was disordered, i.e., parts of it were on a higher level than others, the *sukkah* is valid, because the two levels of *s'chach* together are considered as a single covering of *s'chach.* If, however, the two levels are separated by three handbreadths or more, they do not combine and are not considered as a covering of *s'chach* at all (subsecs. 6-7).

(d) Moreover, if the width of the higher level of *s'chach* meets at least the minimum requirement to be called a roof, a handbreadth by a handbreadth, and it is positioned exactly over a corresponding open space on the lower level, the *sukkah* is valid, even though there are more than three handbreadths between the two. We consider the *s'chach* on the higher level as if it had descended downward and was positioned in the empty space under it.

The above applies provided the area of the empty space is at least the same as the area of the upper level of *s'chach.* If it was less than it, or if the higher level of *s'chach* was not positioned exactly over the empty space below it, but instead, were it to be lowered, part of it would touch the lower level of *s'chach,* the higher level is not considered as if it had come down to the lower level (subsection 7).

(e) When canes of *s'chach* project outward behind the *sukkah* and two of the walls extend together with them, it is considered as if a new and valid *sukkah* was constructed, provided the following conditions are met:

- (i) these canes extend over the minimum area of a *sukkah,* which is seven handbreadths square;
- (ii) the shaded area on the floor under them exceeds the sunlit area; and
- (iii) there are now three walls – the middle wall and the two long walls that extend together with the canes.

This is true even though the middle wall was not constructed with this intent, but to serve the main *sukkah* (subsection 8).

(f) A similar law applies if a *sukkah* does not have a wall on its fourth side and the canes project outward on this open side. If the canes covering this addition extend over the minimum dimensions of a *sukkah,* this additional area is also considered as part of the *sukkah* and one may sit there even though it has only one wall (subsection 9).

(g) Four handbreadths of invalid covering in one place in a large *sukkah,* or three handbreadths of such covering in a small *sukkah* (i.e., one that is only seven handbreadths square), is considered as a separate area and can disqualify the entire *sukkah* in certain situations (subsection 10).

(h) When a *sukkah* is covered partly with valid *s'chach* and partly with materials that are invalid as *s'chach,* it is acceptable even if the valid *s'chach* is somewhat sparse, provided the length and the width of the area covered by valid *s'chach* are equivalent to the length and width of the area covered by invalid *s'chach.* One must, however, place a little additional valid *s'chach* to overlap the invalid *s'chach* (subsection 11).

(i) When a structure is roofed with boards, the boards are unacceptable for use as *s'chach* regardless of their size, because they were put in place to create a dwelling, not for shade alone. To make such a structure acceptable as a *sukkah,* every alternate board must be removed and valid *s'chach* must be put in its place (subsection 12).

Summary of Section 637

(a) A person who did not build a *sukkah* before the festival, whether unintentionally or intentionally, should build one during *Chol HaMoed* (subsection 1).

(b) It is permitted to leave one *sukkah* and dwell in another. There is no requirement to dwell in the same *sukkah* for all seven days (subsection 2).

(c) The Torah states, "Make the Sukkos festival for yourself," implying that the *sukkah* must be "your own" and not your friend's. One may, however, fulfill his obligation with a borrowed *sukkah.* Since he enters it with permission, it is considered as his (subsection 3).

(d) Although a *sukkah* must be one's own, a stolen *sukkah* is acceptable after the event in certain circumstances (subsections 4-9). Initially, however, one should not use a *sukkah* constructed on another's property. If one did, no blessing should be recited when such a *sukkah* is used (subsection 11).

(e) One should initially not build his *sukkah* on another's land without his consent, for the owner could possibly object to having a dwelling erected on his property in such a way (subsection 10).

(f) Similarly, a *sukkah* should preferably not be constructed on land belonging to people at large, such as a public place or thoroughfare (subsection 11).

Summary of Section 638

(a) It is forbidden to derive benefit from the *s'chach* of a *sukkah.* Since it is used for a *mitzvah,* holiness rests upon it. This prohibition applies throughout the entire festival and applies even if the *sukkah* collapses (subsection 1).

(b) According to Rabbinic decree, this prohibition also applies to the walls of the *sukkah* (subsection 2). Thus it is forbidden to take a sliver of wood from the walls or *s'chach* for use as a toothpick or the like. It is, however, permitted to use and derive benefit from the walls in a manner that does not deprive them of the holiness of the *sukkah*. Thus one may place or hang objects on them, or smell them if they are made of fragrant wood (subsection 5).

(c) Similarly, it is forbidden to make use of the decorations of the *sukkah* throughout the festival. This prohibition leads to a further restriction: It is forbidden to move them on *Shabbos* or *Yom-Tov*, even to protect them from rain or thieves (subsection 6).

(d) One may, however, avert the latter restriction by stating in advance that he intends to make use of the decorations in the course of the festival. For that stipulation to be effective, he must say, "I will not refrain from making use of them throughout the time of *bein hashmashos* on all the eight days of the festival." Thus, at the time the holiness of the *sukkah* would rest upon them – *bein hashmashos*, the twilight time with which the *Yom-Tov* begins – this holiness will not rest upon them at all and they are never considered as having been set aside for the *mitzvah* (subsection 7). If one does not use this exact wording, it is possible that the holiness of the *mitzvah* will rest on the decorations, despite his stipulation (subsection 8).

(e) According to one authority, when valuable objects are used as decorations for a *sukkah*, it is considered as if an appropriate stipulation has been made concerning them, for this is one's presumed intent. Nevertheless, an explicit stipulation should be made (subsection 11).

(f) The leniency effected by such a stipulation applies only to the decorations, but not to the *s'chach* or the walls (subsection 12).

(g) All of the above restrictions apply only after one has actually made use of the *sukkah* for the *mitzvah*. If one has not done so, even if he intended to do so and designated the walls and the *s'chach* for this purpose, they may still be used for mundane purposes (subsection 15).

(h) After the festival the *s'chach* may be used for mundane purposes, though not in a manner that would be disrespectful to the *mitzvah* (subsection 17).

INDEX

T

לזכרון עולם בהיכל ה'

לעילוי נשמת

הרה"ח הוו"ח אי"א בעל מדות טובות

רודף צדקה וחסד

ר' שלום

ב"ר יואל ע"ה

נפטר יו"ד שבט, ה'תשל"א

ורעיתו אשת חבר

האשה החשובה הצנועה והחסודה

מרת **צפורה**

בת ר' אברהם ע"ה

נפטרה ליל שמיני עצרת, ה'תש"ע

לפידות

ת. נ. צ. ב. ה.

נדפס על ידי חתנם ובתם

הרה"ת ר' **משה אהרן צבי** וזוגתו מרת **העניא רבקה רות** שיחיו **ווייס**

שלוחי כ"ק אדמו"ר זי"ע, בשערמאן אוקס, קאליפורניא

לזכרון עולם בהיכל ה'

לטובת ולעילוי נשמת חמי היקר, מופלג בתורה, וביראה טהורה, מתנהג בדכי החסידות,
זכה להעמיד אלפי תלמידים ולחנכם בדרך התורה והיראה, אשר נודע בהתקשרותו
אמיתי לנשיא דורנו כ"ק אדמו"ר מליובאוויטש זצוקללה"ה נבג"מ זי"ע

הרה"ת **ר' בן ציון ישראל מאיר**

בן הרה"ח וכו' ר' מנחם מאניש זצ"ל

שיינברגר

נכד של הצדיקים הקדושים והטהורים וכו'
מיקירא דירושלים עיה"ק תובב"א
הרה"ג ר' **יוסף חיים זאנענפעלד** זצוק"ל
רב ואב"ד דירושלים עיה"ק תובב"א
והרה"ג ר' **עקיבא יוסף שלעזינגער** זצוק"ל
בעמח"ס לב עברי

נלב"ע במיטב שנותיו ביום ט' כסלו ה' תשמ"ח

ת. נ. צ. ב. ה.

ולזכות
האשה החשובה הצנועה והחסודה
תלחט"א
מרת **צפורה פייגא**
בת הינדא בלומא
לודמיר

נדפס על ידי חתנם ובתם
הרה"ת ר' **יונה מרדכי** וזוגתו מרת **הדסה עלקא** שיחיו **ווייס**

הוצאת ספרים
קרני הוד תורה
ליובאוויטש

ISBN 978-0-8266-0870-3
9 780826 608703